CW00348052

ISBN 978-0-332-29519-0
PIBN 10468745

ACTS

AND

RESOLVES

PASSED BY THE

General Court of Massachusetts

IN THE YEAR

1943

TOGETHER WITH

TABLES SHOWING CHANGES IN THE STATUTES, ETC.

PUBLISHED BY THE
SECRETARY OF THE COMMONWEALTH

BOSTON
WRIGHT & POTTER PRINTING COMPANY
1943

REPL.

ACTS AND RESOLVES

OF

MASSACHUSETTS

1943

☞ The General Court, which was chosen November 3, 1942, assembled on Wednesday, the sixth day of January, 1943, for its biennial session.

The oaths of office were taken and subscribed by His Excellency LEVERETT SALTONSTALL and His Honor HORACE T. CAHILL on Thursday, the seventh day of January, in the presence of the two Houses assembled in convention.

ACTS.

AN ACT RELATIVE TO THE PLACING ON THE BALLOT OF CERTAIN DESCRIPTIVE WORDS AGAINST THE NAMES OF CERTAIN CANDIDATES FOR ELECTION AS TOWN MEETING MEMBERS UNDER THE PROVISIONS OF THE SO CALLED STANDARD FORM OF REPRESENTATIVE TOWN MEETING GOVERNMENT. *Chap.* 1

Be it enacted by the Senate and House of Representatives in General Court assembled, and by the authority of the same, as follows:

G. L. (Ter. Ed.), 43A, § 6, amended

Nominations, method of, etc.

SECTION 1. Chapter forty-three A of the General Laws is hereby amended by striking out section six, as appearing in the Tercentenary Edition, and inserting in place thereof the following: — *Section 6.* Nomination of candidates for town meeting members to be elected under this chapter shall be made by nomination papers, which shall bear no political designation, shall be signed by not less than ten voters of the precinct in which the candidate resides, and shall be filed with the town clerk at least ten days before the election; provided, that any town meeting member, including any town meeting member in office under the provisions of a special statute under which such town is operating immediately prior to the taking effect therein of the standard form of representative town meeting government provided by this chapter, may become a candidate for re-election by giving written notice thereof to the town clerk at least thirty days before the election. If a town meeting member is a candidate for re-election, the words "Candidate for Re-election" shall be printed against his name as it appears on the ballot for the election of town officers. No nomination papers shall be valid in respect to any candidate whose written acceptance is not thereon or attached thereto when filed.

Effective date.

SECTION 2. This act shall take effect upon its passage.

Approved January 22, 1943.

AN ACT AUTHORIZING THE PLACING OF THE OFFICE OF CHIEF OF POLICE OF THE TOWN OF MILLBURY UNDER THE CIVIL SERVICE LAWS. *Chap.* 2

Be it enacted, etc., as follows:

SECTION 1. The office of chief of police of the town of Millbury shall, upon the effective date of this act, become subject to the civil service laws and rules and regulations relating to police officers in towns, and the tenure of office of any incumbent thereof shall be unlimited, subject, however, to said laws, but the person holding said office on said effective date shall continue to serve therein only until the expiration of his term of office unless prior thereto he passes a non-competitive qualifying examination to which he shall be subjected by the division of civil service.

SECTION 2. This act shall be submitted for acceptance to the voters of said town at the annual town meeting in the current year in the form of the following question, which shall be placed upon the official ballot to be used for the election of town officers at said meeting: "Shall an act passed by the General Court in the year nineteen hundred and forty-three, entitled 'An Act authorizing the placing of the Office of Chief of Police of the Town of Millbury under the Civil Service Laws', be accepted?" If a majority of the votes in answer to said question is in the affirmative, then this act shall thereupon take full effect, but not otherwise. *Approved January 28, 1943.*

Chap. 3 AN ACT MAKING THE EFFECTIVE PERIODS OF CERTAIN EMERGENCY ACTS PROVIDING FOR THE SAFETY OF THE COMMONWEALTH CO-TERMINOUS.

Emergency preamble.

Whereas, The deferred operation of this act would tend to defeat its purpose, which is the continuing in effect without interruption of certain provisions of law providing for the safety of the commonwealth, therefore it is hereby declared to be an emergency law, necessary for the immediate preservation of the public safety.

Be it enacted, etc., as follows:

Chapter seven hundred and nineteen of the acts of nineteen hundred and forty-one is hereby amended by striking out section eleven and inserting in place thereof the following section: — *Section 11.* This act shall be in effect during the continuance of the existing state of war between the United States and any foreign country; provided, that this act shall cease to be in effect upon the earlier adoption by both branches of the general court of a joint resolution stating that it is no longer necessary for the public good and safety.
Approved January 28, 1943.

Chap. 4 AN ACT AUTHORIZING THE TOWN OF WATERTOWN TO ESTABLISH A PURCHASING DEPARTMENT.

Be it enacted, etc., as follows:

SECTION 1. The town of Watertown may establish a purchasing department, to consist of a purchasing agent and such assistants as the selectmen may determine. The agent and assistants shall be appointed by the selectmen subject to the provisions of chapter thirty-one of the General Laws. The purchasing agent shall purchase all supplies for the town and for every department thereof except in case of emergency. All contracts for purchases exceeding one hundred dollars in amount shall be based upon competition. A record shall be kept by the department of prices paid for the supplies and shall be open to the inspection of any citizen.

SECTION 2. This act shall take effect upon its acceptance by a majority of the town meeting members of the town of Watertown present and voting thereon at a meeting legally called for the purpose. *Approved February 2, 1943.*

AN ACT RELATIVE TO THE ESTABLISHMENT BY COUNTIES, CITIES, TOWNS AND DISTRICTS OF POST-WAR REHABILITATION FUNDS, TO THE VALIDATION OF CERTAIN ACTION TAKEN BY CITIES, TOWNS AND DISTRICTS IN PURCHASING BONDS THEREFOR, TO THE EXPENDITURE OF CERTAIN GRANTS OR ALLOCATIONS TO DISTRICTS FOR CIVILIAN DEFENSE PURPOSES AND TO THE MAKING OF CONTRACTS BY COUNTIES AND DISTRICTS WITH THE UNITED STATES FOR THE TEMPORARY USE AND OCCUPATION OF COUNTY OR DISTRICT PROPERTY. *Chap.* 5

Emergency preamble.

Whereas, The deferred operation of this act would tend to defeat its purpose, which in part is to empower the counties, cities, towns and districts of the commonwealth to take without delay in the existing emergency of war the action provided for therein, therefore it is hereby declared to be an emergency law, necessary for the immediate preservation of the public safety and convenience.

Be it enacted, etc., as follows:

SECTION 1. During the continuance of the existing state of war between the United States and any foreign country, any city, town or district may appropriate money for the purchase of defense bonds, war bonds or other bonds issued by the federal government, or other bonds which are legal investments for savings banks; provided, that the aggregate amount of such bonds held at any time under authority of this act shall not exceed five per cent of the assessed valuation of real estate and tangible personal property therein in the year nineteen hundred and forty-two. The aggregate amount purchased and invested under authority of this act and all interest earned thereon shall be set up as a separate fund in the custody of the treasurer of such city, town or district, who is hereby authorized, in case any bond held in the fund matures or is called, to reinvest, with the approval of the mayor, selectmen, prudential committee or commissioners, as the case may be, in other bonds authorized by this act to be purchased. No bonds held under this act may be sold prior to the termination of the existing state of war.

The proceeds from the sale of any such bonds shall be used only for purposes for which the city, town or district may borrow money for a period of not less than ten years in accordance with sections seven and eight of chapter forty-four of the General Laws; provided, that such proceeds may, in each instance with the approval of the board established under section one of chapter forty-nine of the acts of nineteen hundred and thirty-three, be appropriated and used in whole or in part for other purposes.

Said board in giving its approval shall give especial consideration to necessities then existing in such city, town or district involving rehabilitation following the war or due to unemployment conditions or otherwise.

The members of the board aforesaid, when acting under this section, shall receive from the commonwealth compensation to the same extent as provided for services under chapter three hundred and sixty-six of the acts of nineteen hundred and thirty-three, as amended.

SECTION 2. During the continuance of the existing state of war between the United States and any foreign country, any county may purchase bonds referred to in section one to the extent that money may be provided therefor by appropriation by the general court. The aggregate amount so invested and all interest earned thereon shall be set up as a separate fund in the custody of the treasurer of such county, who is hereby authorized, in case any bond held in the fund matures or is called, to reinvest, with the approval of the county commissioners, the proceeds so received in other bonds authorized by this act to be purchased. No bonds held under this act may be sold prior to the termination of the existing state of war.

The proceeds from the sale of any such bonds shall be used only for purposes authorized by the general court.

SECTION 3. During the continuance of the existing state of war between the United States and any foreign country, all funds granted or allocated by the federal government or by the commonwealth to a city, town or district for civilian defense purposes may be expended without appropriation in accordance with the terms of said grants or allocations.

SECTION 4. Counties, cities, towns and districts are hereby authorized, during the continuance of the existing state of war between the United States and any foreign country, to enter into contracts for the use and occupation by the United States of any properties, real or personal, owned or held by them.

SECTION 5. Any action taken by a city, town or district in nineteen hundred and forty-two, or in nineteen hundred and forty-three prior to the effective date of this act, in voting an emergency appropriation for purchasing bonds referred to in section one of this act shall have the same effect and validity as if this act had been in effect at the time of said vote.

SECTION 6. Chapter four of the acts of nineteen hundred and forty-two, except sections three and six, is hereby repealed, and bonds purchased under section one of said chapter four shall, for the purposes of this act, be deemed to have been purchased hereunder and shall be held subject to the provisions hereof. *Approved February 2, 1943.*

AN ACT AUTHORIZING THE SELECTMEN OF THE TOWN OF LEXINGTON TO APPOINT A BOARD OF PUBLIC WELFARE. *Chap.* 6

Be it enacted, etc., as follows:

SECTION 1. There shall be in the town of Lexington a board of public welfare, consisting of five members appointed annually by the selectmen of said town, which shall have all the powers and duties now or from time to time vested by general law in boards of public welfare; and upon the initial organization of the board of public welfare appointed under authority of this act, the board of selectmen, acting as the board of public works as provided by chapter one of the acts of nineteen hundred and twenty-two, shall cease to exercise the powers and duties of a board of public welfare.

SECTION 2. This act shall take full effect upon its acceptance by the town of Lexington at any town meeting held prior to January first, nineteen hundred and forty-five.

Approved February 2, 1943.

AN ACT ESTABLISHING IN THE TOWN OF READING REPRESENTATIVE TOWN GOVERNMENT BY LIMITED TOWN MEETINGS. *Chap.* 7

Be it enacted, etc., as follows:

SECTION 1. There is hereby established in the town of Reading the form of representative town government by limited town meetings hereinafter set forth.

SECTION 2. Upon the acceptance of this act by the town of Reading, as hereinafter provided, the selectmen shall forthwith divide the territory thereof into not less than four nor more than eight voting precincts, each of which shall be plainly designated and shall contain not less than four hundred registered voters. The precincts shall be so established as to consist of compact and contiguous territory to be bounded, as far as possible, by the center line of known streets and ways or by other well-defined limits. Their boundaries shall be reviewed, and, if need be, wholly or partly revised, by the selectmen in December, once in five years, or in December of any year when so directed by a vote of a representative town meeting held not later than November twentieth of that year. The foregoing provisions of this section shall not authorize any action contrary to the provisions of section nine A of chapter fifty-four of the General Laws.

The selectmen shall, within ten days after any establishment or revision of the precincts, file a report of their doings with the town clerk, the registrars of voters and the assessors, with a map or maps or description of the precincts and the names and residences of the registered voters therein. The selectmen shall also cause to be posted in the town hall a map or maps or description of the precincts as established or revised from time to time, with the names and residences of the registered voters therein; and they shall also cause to be posted in at least one public place in each precinct a map or description of that precinct, with the names and residences of the registered voters therein. The division of the town into voting precincts and any revision of such precincts shall take effect upon the date of the filing of the report thereof by the selectmen with the town clerk. Whenever the precincts are established or revised, the town clerk shall forthwith give written notice thereof to the state secretary, stating the number and designation of the precincts. Meetings of the registered voters of the several precincts for elections, for primaries, and for voting upon any question to be submitted to all the registered voters of the town, shall be held on the same day and at the same hour and at such place or places within the town as the selectmen shall in the warrant for such meeting direct. The provisions of chapters fifty to fifty-six, inclusive, of the General Laws relating to precinct voting at elections, so far as the same are not inconsistent with this act, shall apply to all elections and primaries in the town upon the establishment of voting precincts as hereinbefore provided.

SECTION 3. Other than the officers designated in the by-laws of the town as town meeting members at large, the representative town meeting membership shall in each precinct consist of the largest number divisible by three which will admit of a representation thereof in the approximate proportion which the number of registered voters therein bears to the total number of registered voters in the town, and which will cause the total elected membership to be as nearly one hundred and eighty as may be.

The registered voters in every precinct shall, at the first annual town election held after the establishment of such precinct, and the registered voters of any precinct affected by any revision of precincts at the first annual town election following such revision, conformably to the laws relative to elections not inconsistent with this act, elect by ballot the number of registered voters in the precinct, other than the officers designated in the by-laws as town meeting members at large, provided for in the first sentence of this section, to be town meeting members of the town. The first third, in the order of votes received, of members so elected shall serve three years, the second third in such order shall serve two years, and the remaining third in such order shall serve one year, from the day of the annual town meeting; in case of a tie vote affecting the division into thirds, as aforesaid, the members elected from the precinct shall by ballot determine the same; and thereafter, except as is otherwise provided herein, at each annual town election the registered voters of each precinct shall, in like manner, elect, for the term of three years, one third of the number of elected town meeting members to which such precinct is entitled, and shall at such election fill for the unexpired term or terms any vacancy or vacancies then existing in the number of elected town meeting members in such precinct.

The terms of office of all elected town meeting members from every precinct revised as aforesaid shall cease upon the election as hereinbefore provided of their successors. The town clerk shall, after every election of town meeting members, forthwith notify each such member by mail of his election.

SECTION 4. Any representative town meeting held under the provisions of this act, except as otherwise provided herein, shall be limited to the town meeting members elected under section three, together with such town meeting members at large as may be provided for by the by-laws of the town, and authority to adopt such by-laws is hereby conferred.

The town clerk shall notify the town meeting members of the time and place at which representative town meetings are to be held, the notices to be sent by mail at least seven days before the meeting. The town meeting members, as aforesaid, shall be the judges of the election and qualifications of the members. A majority of the town meeting members shall constitute a quorum for doing business; but a less number may organize temporarily and may adjourn from time to time, but no town meeting shall adjourn over the date of an election of town meeting members. All town meetings shall be public. The town meeting members as such shall receive no compensation. Subject to such conditions as may be determined from time to time by the members of the representative town meeting, any registered voter of the town who is not a town meeting member may speak at any representative town meeting, but shall not vote. A town meeting member may resign by filing a written resignation with the town clerk, and such resignation shall take effect on the date of such filing. A town meeting member who removes from the town shall cease to be a town meeting member, and a town meeting member who removes from the precinct from which he was elected to another precinct may serve only until the next annual town meeting.

SECTION 5. Nomination of candidates for town meeting members to be elected under this act shall be made by nomination papers, which shall bear no political designation, shall be signed by not less than ten voters of the precinct in which the candidate resides, and shall be filed with the town clerk at least ten days before the election; provided, that any town meeting member may become a candidate for re-election by giving written notice thereof to the town clerk at least thirty days before the election. No nomination papers shall be valid in respect to any candidate whose written acceptance is not thereon or attached thereto when filed.

SECTION 6. The articles in the warrant for every town meeting, so far as they relate to the election of the moderator, town officers and town meeting members, and, as herein provided, to referenda, and all matters to be acted upon and determined by ballot, shall be so acted upon and determined by the registered voters of the town in their respective precincts. All other articles in the warrant for any town meeting shall be acted upon and determined exclusively by town meeting members at a meeting to be held at such time and place as shall be set forth by the selectmen in the warrant for the meeting, subject to the referendum provided for by section nine.

SECTION 7. A moderator shall be elected by ballot at each annual town meeting, and shall serve as moderator of all town meetings, except as otherwise provided by law, until a successor is elected and qualified. Nominations for and election of a moderator shall be as in the case of other elective town officers, and any vacancy in the office may be filled by the town meeting members at a meeting held for that purpose. If a moderator is absent, a moderator pro tempore may be elected by the town meeting members.

SECTION 8. Any vacancy in the full number of town meeting members from any precinct, whether arising from a failure of the registered voters thereof to elect, or from any other cause, may be filled, until the next annual election, by the remaining members of the precinct from among the registered voters thereof. Upon petition therefor, signed by not less than ten town meeting members from the precinct, notice of any vacancy shall promptly be given by the town clerk to the remaining members from the precinct in which the vacancy or vacancies exist, and he shall call a special meeting of such members for the purpose of filling such vacancy or vacancies. He shall cause to be mailed to every such member, not less than five days before the time set for the meeting, a notice specifying the object, time and place of the meeting. At the said meeting a majority of the members from such precinct shall constitute a quorum, and they shall elect from their own number a chairman and a clerk. The choice to fill any vacancy shall be by ballot, and a majority of the votes cast shall be required for a choice. The chairman and clerk shall count the ballots and shall make a certificate of the choice and forthwith file the same with the town clerk, together with a written acceptance by the member or members so chosen, who shall thereupon be deemed elected and qualified as a town meeting member or members, subject to the right of all the town meeting members to judge of the election and qualifications of the members as set forth in section four.

SECTION 9. A vote passed by any representative town meeting authorizing the expenditure of twenty thousand dollars or more as a special appropriation, or establishing a new board or office or abolishing an old board or office or merging two or more boards or offices, or fixing the term of office of town officers, where such term is optional, or increasing or reducing the number of members of a board, or adopting a new by-law, or amending an existing by-law, shall not be operative until after the expiration of five days, exclusive of Sundays and holidays, from the dissolution of the meeting. If, within said five days, a petition, signed by not less than three per cent of the registered voters of the town, containing their names and addresses as they appear on the list of registered voters, is filed with the selectmen asking that the question or questions involved in such a vote be submitted to the registered voters of the town at large, then the selectmen, after the expiration of five days, shall forthwith call a special meeting for the sole purpose of presenting to the registered voters at large the question or questions so involved. The polls shall be opened at two o'clock in the afternoon and shall be closed not earlier than eight o'clock in the evening, and all votes upon any questions so submitted shall be taken by ballot, and the check list shall be used, in the several precinct meetings in the same manner as in the election of town officers. The questions so submitted shall be determined by a majority vote of the registered voters of the town voting thereon, but no action of the representative town meeting shall be reversed unless at least twenty per cent of the total number of registered voters shall vote for such reversal. Each question so submitted shall be in the form of the following question, which shall be placed upon the official ballot: — "Shall the town vote to approve the action of the representative town meeting whereby it was voted (brief description of the substance of the vote)?" If such a petition is not filed within said period of five days, the vote of the representative town meeting shall become operative and effective upon the expiration of said period.

SECTION 10. The town, after the acceptance of this act, shall have the capacity to act through and to be bound by its town meeting members, who shall, when convened from time to time as herein provided, constitute representative town meetings; and the representative town meetings shall exercise exclusively, so far as will conform to the provisions of this act, all powers vested in the municipal corporation. Action in conformity with all provisions of law now or hereafter applicable to the transaction of town affairs in town meetings, shall, when taken by any representative town meeting in accordance with the provisions of this act, have the same force and effect as if such action had been taken in a town meeting open to all the voters of the town as organized and conducted before the establishment in said town of representative town meeting government.

SECTION 11. This act shall not abridge the right of the inhabitants of the town to hold general meetings, as secured to them by the constitution of this commonwealth; nor shall this act confer upon any representative town meeting in the town the power finally to commit the town to any measure affecting its municipal existence or substantially changing its form of government without action thereon by the voters of the town at large, using the ballot and the check list therefor.

SECTION 12. This act shall be submitted to the registered voters of the town of Reading for acceptance at the annual town meeting in the year nineteen hundred and forty-three. The vote shall be taken by ballot in accordance with the provisions of the General Laws, so far as the same shall be applicable, in answer to the question which shall be placed upon the official ballot to be used for the election of town officers: "Shall an act passed by the general court in the year nineteen hundred and forty-three, entitled 'An Act establishing in the town of Reading representative town government by limited town meetings', be accepted by this town?" If accepted by a majority of the voters voting thereon, this act shall thereupon take effect for all purposes incidental to the next annual town election in said town, and shall take full effect beginning with said election.

SECTION 13. If this act is rejected by the registered voters of the town of Reading when first submitted to said voters under section twelve, it may again be submitted for acceptance in like manner from time to time to such voters at any annual town meeting within five years thereafter, and, if accepted by a majority of the voters voting thereon at such an election, shall thereupon take effect for all purposes incidental to the next annual town election in said town, and shall take full effect beginning with said election.

SECTION 14. Chapter two hundred and seventy-six of the acts of nineteen hundred and ten, as amended by chapter three hundred and fifty-nine of the acts of nineteen hundred and twelve, shall, on and after the date of the first annual election held in said town under this act, have no force or effect. *Approved February 2, 1943.*

Chap. 8 AN ACT CHANGING THE TIME OF HOLDING THE ANNUAL TOWN MEETING AND TOWN ELECTION OF THE TOWN OF STOUGHTON.

Be it enacted, etc., as follows:

SECTION 1. Chapter four hundred of the acts of nineteen hundred and twenty-one is hereby amended by striking out section one and inserting in place thereof the following: — *Section 1.* The annual town meeting of the town of Stoughton shall be held on the first Monday in March at eight o'clock in the evening, and all matters to be considered at the annual town meeting shall be considered at such meeting, except that the annual town election for the purpose of electing, by official ballot, town officers and voting on any question required by law to be placed upon the official ballot, shall take place at an adjournment of such meeting to be held on the third Monday in March.

SECTION 2. This act shall take effect on the first day of January in the year nineteen hundred and forty-four.

Approved February 4, 1943.

AN ACT CHANGING THE NAME OF OHEBEI SHALOM TO TEMPLE OHABEI SHALOM AND AUTHORIZING SAID CORPORATION TO HOLD ADDITIONAL REAL AND PERSONAL PROPERTY. *Chap.* 9

Be it enacted, etc., as follows:

SECTION 1. The name of the corporation incorporated by chapter one hundred and seventy-nine of the acts of eighteen hundred and forty-five, entitled "An Act to Incorporate Ohebei Shalom", and referred to in certain subsequent legislative acts as "Ohabei Shalom", is hereby changed to Temple Ohabei Shalom.

SECTION 2. Said corporation may hold real and personal property to the same amount and subject to the same conditions as a corporation to which section nine of chapter one hundred and eighty of the General Laws is applicable.

SECTION 3. This act shall not take effect until it shall have been accepted by a vote of two thirds of all members present and voting at an annual or special meeting of the corporation, and notice of such change of name shall have been published in a newspaper published in Suffolk county, and a copy of such vote and such notice, certified by the secretary of the corporation, shall have been filed with the state secretary. *Approved February 9, 1943.*

AN ACT RELATIVE TO CERTAIN LINES, POLES AND OTHER EQUIPMENT OF THE ELECTRIC LIGHT DEPARTMENT OF THE TOWN OF NORTH ATTLEBOROUGH, AND OF CERTAIN TELEPHONE AND TELEGRAPH COMPANIES IN SAID TOWN. *Chap.* 10

Be it enacted, etc., as follows:

SECTION 1. All lines for the transmission of electricity for light, heat or power heretofore acquired or constructed by the electric light department of the town of North Attleborough, and all lines for the transmission of intelligence by electricity heretofore acquired or constructed by the New England Telephone and Telegraph Company and any other telephone or telegraph company in said town, upon, along, over or under the public ways and places of said town, and the poles, piers, abutments, conduits and other fixtures necessary to sustain or protect the wires of said lines, and in actual use on the effective date of this act, are hereby made lawful notwithstanding the lack of any valid locations therefor or any informality in the proceedings relative to their location and erection; provided, that the validation aforesaid shall not be effective as to the lines, structures or fixtures aforesaid of such department or any such company in said town unless such department or company shall, not later than December thirty-first, nineteen hundred and forty-four, file with the clerk of said town a map or maps showing the location and nature of the said lines, structures and fixtures in said town; such map or maps so filed to be recorded and kept with the records of original locations for poles and wires in said town.

SECTION 2. This act shall take effect upon its passage.

Approved February 12, 1943.

Chap. 11 AN ACT RELATIVE TO CERTAIN LINES, POLES AND OTHER EQUIPMENT OF THE NEW ENGLAND TELEPHONE AND TELEGRAPH COMPANY, THE AMERICAN TELEPHONE AND TELEGRAPH COMPANY AND THE BROCKTON EDISON COMPANY IN THE CITY OF BROCKTON.

Be it enacted, etc., as follows:

SECTION 1. All lines for the transmission of intelligence by electricity heretofore acquired or constructed by the New England Telephone and Telegraph Company and the American Telephone and Telegraph Company in the city of Brockton, and all lines for the transmission of electricity for light, heat or power heretofore acquired or constructed by the Brockton Edison Company in said city, upon, along, over or under the public ways and places of said city, and the poles, piers, abutments, conduits and other fixtures necessary to sustain or protect the wires of said lines, actually in place on the effective date of this act, are hereby made lawful notwithstanding the lack of any valid locations therefor or any informality in the proceedings relative to their location and erection; provided, that the validation aforesaid shall not be effective as to the lines, structures or fixtures aforesaid of said companies in said city unless said companies shall, not later than December thirty-first, nineteen hundred and forty-four, file with the clerk of said city a map or maps showing the location and nature of said pole lines, structures and fixtures in said city, and file with the city engineer of said city a map or maps showing the location and nature of said underground conduits in said city; such map or maps so filed to be recorded and kept with the records of original locations for poles, wires and underground conduits in said city.

SECTION 2. This act shall take effect upon its passage.

Approved February 12, 1943.

AN ACT RELATIVE TO THE REIMBURSEMENT BY THE COMMONWEALTH OF CITIES AND TOWNS FOR CERTAIN SCHOOL SALARIES. *Chap.* 12

Be it enacted, etc., as follows:

Section two of chapter seventy of the General Laws is hereby amended by striking out paragraph (3), as appearing in section five of chapter one hundred and twenty-seven of the acts of nineteen hundred and thirty-two, and inserting in place thereof the following paragraph: — G. L. (Ter. Ed.), 70, § 2, etc., amended.

(3) One hundred dollars for every person so employed and not included in paragraphs (1) or (2) who received as salary not less than eight hundred and fifty dollars. Reimbursement of teachers, etc.

Approved February 12, 1943.

AN ACT RELATIVE TO THE CARE AND CUSTODY OF CERTAIN ILLEGITIMATE CHILDREN. *Chap.* 13

Be it enacted, etc., as follows:

Section fourteen of chapter two hundred and seventy-three of the General Laws, as appearing in the Tercentenary Edition, is hereby amended by adding at the end the following sentence: — Nothing herein shall give any court authority to order such child to the care or custody of any public department or institution. G. L. (Ter. Ed.), 273, § 14, amended. Custody of child. Limitation on courts.

Approved February 12, 1943.

AN ACT FURTHER DEFINING THE PHRASE "ASSURED MINIMUM" UNDER THE LAW PROVIDING FOR PAYMENTS TO CITIES AND TOWNS FROM THE MASSACHUSETTS SCHOOL FUND, SO CALLED. *Chap.* 14

Be it enacted, etc., as follows:

Section eleven of chapter seventy of the General Laws is hereby amended by striking out the paragraph contained in the sixth to the ninth lines, inclusive, as appearing in the Tercentenary Edition, and inserting in place thereof the following paragraph: — G. L. (Ter. Ed.), 70, § 11, amended.

"Assured minimum" shall mean the amount by which the sum of the following items for the last preceding town fiscal year exceeded the amount received by the town during said year under Part I and for the tuition of non-resident pupils and the tuition and transportation of state wards: "Assured minimum", definition of.

Approved February 12, 1943.

Chap. 15 AN ACT TO AUTHORIZE THE PLACING OF ALL POSITIONS IN THE LABOR SERVICE OF THE HIGHWAY, WATER, PARK AND SEWER DEPARTMENTS OF THE TOWN OF LONGMEADOW UNDER THE CIVIL SERVICE LAWS.

Be it enacted, etc., as follows:

SECTION 1. All positions in the labor service of the highway, water, park and sewer departments of the town of Longmeadow shall, upon the effective date of this act, become subject to the civil service laws and rules and regulations relating to the labor service in towns, and the tenure of office of persons in the labor service of said departments of said town shall be unlimited, subject, however, to said laws; but the persons in such service on said effective date may continue to serve as such.

SECTION 2. This act shall be submitted for acceptance to the voters of said town at the annual town meeting or a special town meeting in the current year, or at any subsequent annual town meeting, in the form of the following question which shall be placed, in case of an annual town meeting, upon the official ballot to be used for the election of town officers, or, in case of a special town meeting, upon the ballot to be used at said meeting: "Shall an act passed by the General Court in the year nineteen hundred and forty-three, entitled, 'An Act to authorize the placing of all positions in the labor service of the highway, water, park and sewer departments of the town of Longmeadow under the civil service laws', be accepted?" If a majority of the votes in answer to said question is in the affirmative, then this act shall thereupon take full effect, but not otherwise.

Approved February 12, 1943.

Chap. 16 AN ACT MAKING CERTAIN DENTAL DISPENSARIES OR CLINICS SUBJECT TO CERTAIN PROVISIONS OF LAW REGULATING DISPENSARIES AND EXEMPTING FROM SAID PROVISIONS CLINICS CONDUCTED BY CERTAIN LICENSED HOSPITALS.

Be it enacted, etc., as follows:

G. L. (Ter. Ed.), 111, § 51, amended.

"Dispensary", definition of.

SECTION 1. Chapter one hundred and eleven of the General Laws is hereby amended by striking out section fifty-one, as appearing in the Tercentenary Edition, and inserting in place thereof the following: — *Section 51.* In sections fifty-two to fifty-six, inclusive, "dispensary" shall mean any place or establishment, not conducted for profit, where medical, surgical or dental advice or treatment, medicine or medical or dental apparatus, is furnished to persons not residing therein; or any place or establishment, whether conducted for charitable purposes or for profit, advertised, announced, conducted or maintained under the name "dispensary" or "clinic", or other designation of like import; except that it shall not include a clinic conducted by a hospital, which is licensed under section seventy-one, as an integral part of such hospital.

SECTION 2. Section fifty-three of said chapter one hundred and eleven, as so appearing, is hereby amended by inserting after the word "medicine" in the fourth line the words: — and for all schools of dentistry, — so as to read as follows: — *Section 53.* Any person desiring to conduct a dispensary shall apply in writing to the department for a license. The application shall be in such form as the department shall prescribe, and shall be uniform for all schools of medicine and for all schools of dentistry. There shall be attached thereto a statement of the applicant on oath, containing such information as may be required by the department. If in its judgment the statement filed and other evidence submitted in relation to the application indicate that the operation of the proposed dispensary will be for the public benefit, a license, in such form as it shall prescribe, shall be issued to the applicant. Licenses shall expire at the end of the year in which they are issued, but may be renewed annually on application as above provided. No license shall be transferred except with the approval of the department. For the issue or renewal of each license a fee of five dollars shall be charged, except to incorporated charitable organizations which conduct dispensaries without charge and which report, as required by law, to the department of public welfare.

G. L. (Ter. Ed.), 111, § 53, amended.

Licensing of dispensaries.

SECTION 3. Section fifty-four of said chapter one hundred and eleven, as so appearing, is hereby amended by inserting after the word "medicine" in the fourth line the words: — or school of dentistry, — so as to read as follows: — *Section 54.* The council shall make rules and regulations, and may revise or change them, in accordance with which dispensaries shall be licensed and conducted, but no such rule or regulation shall specify any particular school of medicine or school of dentistry in accordance with which a dispensary shall be conducted.

G. L. (Ter. Ed.), 111, § 54, amended.

Rules and regulations.

Approved February 12, 1943.

AN ACT EXEMPTING CITIES AND TOWNS OF THE COMMONWEALTH FROM THE LAW REQUIRING THE FILING OF A BOND BY THE PLAINTIFF IN ACTIONS COMMENCED BY TRUSTEE PROCESS.

Chap. 17

Be it enacted, etc., as follows:

SECTION 1. Section one of chapter two hundred and forty-six of the General Laws, as amended by section one of chapter three hundred and three of the acts of nineteen hundred and thirty-eight, is hereby further amended by striking out, in the fourteenth line, the words "in such action" and inserting in place thereof the words: —, if other than a city or town of the commonwealth named therein, — so as to read as follows: — *Section 1.* All per-

G. L. (Ter. Ed.), 246, § 1, etc., amended.

Actions which may be commenced by trustee process.

sonal actions, except tort for malicious prosecution, for slander or libel, or for assault and battery, and except replevin, may be commenced by trustee process, and any person may be summoned as trustee of the defendant therein; but, except in the case of a writ which contains a statement that the action is upon a judgment or in contract for personal services or for goods sold and delivered or for money due under a contract in writing or in tort to recover damages on account of the operation of a motor vehicle not registered in the commonwealth, no writ the ad damnum of which is in excess of one thousand dollars shall be served upon any alleged trustee unless there shall have been filed by the plaintiff, if other than a city or town of the commonwealth named therein, in the court wherein such action is commenced a bond with a surety company authorized to do business in the commonwealth as surety, or with sureties approved by a justice, associate justice or special justice of such court, said bond to be in a penal sum not less than ten per cent of the ad damnum of the writ and not less than two hundred and fifty dollars and to be conditioned upon payment to the defendant, if the plaintiff fails to recover or if such action is discontinued, of all costs which may be awarded to the defendant and all damages which he may sustain by reason of such attachment, but not exceeding the penal sum of the bond, nor unless there shall have been endorsed on the writ by the justice, associate justice or special justice who approved said bond, or by the clerk of such court, the fact that the bond required by this section has been filed in such court. An individual who is not an inhabitant of the commonwealth, or a foreign corporation or association, shall not be so summoned unless he or it has a usual place of business in the commonwealth. The amount paid by the plaintiff to a surety company for becoming surety on such a bond shall be taxed in his costs if he prevails in the action.

Effective date.

SECTION 2. This act shall take effect on June first, nineteen hundred and forty-three.

Approved February 12, 1943.

Chap. 18 AN ACT ELIMINATING THE REQUIREMENT THAT NOTICES OF THE EXCISE ASSESSED ON MOTOR VEHICLES AND TRAILERS SHALL CONTAIN A COPY OF THE LAW PROVIDING FOR THE SUSPENSION OF CERTIFICATES OF REGISTRATION IN CASES OF NON-PAYMENT OF SUCH EXCISE.

Be it enacted, etc., as follows:

G. L. (Ter. Ed.), 60A, § 2A, etc., amended.

Section two A of chapter sixty A of the General Laws, inserted by section one of chapter four hundred and ninety-two of the acts of nineteen hundred and thirty-eight, is hereby amended by striking out the last sentence.

Approved February 12, 1943.

AN ACT RELATIVE TO THE PENALTY FOR ESCAPES OR ATTEMPTED ESCAPES FROM THE REFORMATORY FOR WOMEN. *Chap.* 19

Be it enacted, etc., as follows:

SECTION 1. Section sixteen of chapter two hundred and sixty-eight of the General Laws, as most recently amended by section twenty-eight of chapter three hundred and forty-four of the acts of nineteen hundred and forty-one, is hereby further amended by inserting after the word "institution" in the second line, as appearing in chapter three hundred and forty-four of the acts of nineteen hundred and thirty-four, the words: — other than the reformatory for women, — so as to read as follows: — *Section 16.* A prisoner who escapes or attempts to escape from any penal institution other than the reformatory for women, or from land appurtenant thereto, or from the custody of any officer thereof or while being conveyed to or from any such institution, may be pursued and recaptured and shall be punished by imprisonment in the state prison for not more than ten years or by imprisonment in a jail or house of correction for not more than two and one half years.

G. L. (Ter. Ed.), 268, § 16, etc., amended.

Escape or attempted escape from penal institution.

Penalty.

SECTION 2. Said chapter two hundred and sixty-eight is hereby further amended by inserting after section sixteen, as amended, the following section: — *Section 16A.* A prisoner who escapes or attempts to escape from the reformatory for women, or from land appurtenant thereto, or from the custody of any officer thereof, or while being conveyed to or from said reformatory, may be pursued and recaptured and shall be punished by imprisonment in said reformatory for a term not exceeding two years. Such sentence shall begin upon the expiration of the sentence which said prisoner was serving at the time of escape or attempted escape. *Approved February 12, 1943.*

G. L. (Ter. Ed.), 268, new § 16A, added.

Escape, etc., from reformatory for women.

Penalty.

AN ACT AUTHORIZING THE TOWN OF LEXINGTON TO REVOKE ITS ACCEPTANCE OF THE TENEMENT HOUSE LAW, SO CALLED. *Chap.* 20

Be it enacted, etc., as follows:

There may be submitted at any town meeting in the town of Lexington, called for the purpose within three years from the effective date of this act, the question of the revocation of its acceptance of chapter six hundred and thirty-five of the acts of nineteen hundred and twelve, being an act relative to tenement houses in towns, and if a majority of the town meeting members of said town voting thereon vote in favor of such revocation, then the provisions of chapter one hundred and forty-five of the General Laws shall not apply in said town. Nothing herein contained shall prevent said town from again accepting the provisions of said chapter one hundred and forty-five after the revocation of its acceptance thereof. *Approved February 12, 1943.*

Chap. 21 AN ACT FURTHER REGULATING THE FORMS OF REPORTS REQUIRED TO BE FILED WITH THE COMMISSIONER OF BANKS BY SAVINGS BANKS AND TRUST COMPANIES.

Be it enacted, etc., as follows:

G. L. (Ter. Ed.), 168, § 26, etc., amended.

SECTION 1. Chapter one hundred and sixty-eight of the General Laws is hereby amended by striking out section twenty-six, as amended by section nine of chapter three hundred and thirty-four of the acts of nineteen hundred and thirty-three, and inserting in place thereof the following: — *Section 26.* The treasurer of such corporation shall, annually within twenty days after the last business day of October, make a report to the commissioner in such form as he may prescribe, showing accurately the condition of such corporation at the close of business on that day, and containing such other information as the commissioner may require. The president, or in his absence from the commonwealth, or disability, a vice president, the treasurer, or in his absence from the commonwealth, or disability, an assistant treasurer, and a majority of the auditing committee shall certify on oath that such reports are correct according to their best knowledge and belief.

Annual report to commissioner, contents of.

G. L. (Ter. Ed.), 172, § 26, etc., amended.

SECTION 2. Chapter one hundred and seventy-two of the General Laws is hereby amended by striking out section twenty-six, as most recently amended by section sixteen of chapter three hundred and forty-nine of the acts of nineteen hundred and thirty-four, and inserting in place thereof the following: — *Section 26.* Such corporation shall at such times as the commissioner orders, but not exceeding five times within any calendar year, and within ten days after a day designated in the order, make a return to the commissioner, signed and sworn to by its president, secretary and treasurer and not less than four of its board of directors, showing accurately the condition of such corporation at the close of business on the day designated, and containing such other information as the commissioner orders. Such return shall be in the form of a trial balance of its books and shall specify the different kinds of its liabilities and assets, with the amount of each kind, and the amount of securities pledged to secure deposits as provided in sections thirty-one, fifty-four and sixty-two in accordance with a blank form furnished by the commissioner and shall be published by and at the expense of such corporation in a newspaper of the city or town where such corporation is located, at such times and in such manner as may be directed by the commissioner.

Returns to commissioner of banks

Publication.

Approved February 16, 1943.

AN ACT RELATIVE TO THE LOSS OF INVESTMENT CERTIFICATES OR PASS BOOKS ISSUED BY BANKING COMPANIES, AND OF PASS BOOKS AND CERTAIN CERTIFICATES ISSUED BY BANKS WHICH SUBSEQUENTLY MERGED WITH OTHER BANKS. *Chap.* 22

Be it enacted, etc., as follows:

G. L. (Ter. Ed.), 167, § 20, etc., amended.

Section twenty of chapter one hundred and sixty-seven of the General Laws, as amended by chapter one hundred and ninety of the acts of nineteen hundred and thirty-three, is hereby further amended by inserting after the word "bank", the second time it occurs in the second line, the words: — , a company subject to chapter one hundred and seventy-two A, — and by striking out the last sentence and inserting in place thereof the following: — The provisions of this section shall apply to trust company certificates of deposit, to matured and paid-up share certificates of co-operative banks, to investment certificates of companies subject to chapter one hundred and seventy-two A and to pass books and certificates hereinabove referred to issued by a bank which subsequently merged in, consolidated with or transferred its deposit liabilities to another bank, — so as to read as follows: — *Section 20.* When a pass book issued by a savings bank, a co-operative bank, a company subject to chapter one hundred and seventy-two A or the savings department of a trust company has been lost, stolen or destroyed, the person in whose name it was issued or his legal representative, may make written application to such bank, for payment of the amount of the deposit represented by said book or for the issuance of a duplicate book therefor. Thereupon with the written consent of the bank, he may give, or authorize the bank at his expense to give, public notice of such application by advertising the same at least once a week for three successive weeks in a newspaper published in or nearest to the town where such bank is situated. If such book shall not be presented to said bank within thirty days after the date of the first advertisement, as aforesaid, the bank shall, upon proof that such notice has been given, pay the amount due on said book or issue a duplicate book therefor; and upon such payment or delivery of a new book, all liability of the bank on account of the original book shall cease. The provisions of this section shall apply to trust company certificates of deposit, to matured and paid-up share certificates of co-operative banks, to investment certificates of companies subject to chapter one hundred and seventy-two A and to pass books and certificates hereinabove referred to issued by a bank which subsequently merged in, consolidated with or transferred its deposit liabilities to another bank.

Advertising lost pass books, etc.

Approved February 16, 1943.

Chap. 23 AN ACT TO AUTHORIZE THE PLACING OF THE OFFICE OF CHIEF OF POLICE OF THE TOWN OF ASHLAND UNDER THE CIVIL SERVICE LAWS.

Be it enacted, etc., as follows:

SECTION 1. The office of chief of police of the town of Ashland shall, upon the effective date of this act, become subject to the civil service laws and rules and regulations relating to police officers in towns, and the tenure of office of any incumbent thereof shall be unlimited, subject, however, to said laws, but the person holding said office on said effective date shall continue to serve therein only until the expiration of his term of office unless prior thereto he passes a non-competitive qualifying examination to which he shall be subjected by the division of civil service.

SECTION 2. This act shall be submitted to the voters of said town at the next annual town meeting in the form of the following question, which shall be placed upon the official ballot to be used for the election of town officers at said meeting: "Shall an act passed by the General Court in the year nineteen hundred and forty-three, entitled 'An Act to authorize the placing of the office of chief of police of the town of Ashland under the civil service laws', be accepted?" If a majority of the votes in answer to said question is in the affirmative, then this act shall thereupon take full effect, but not otherwise.

Approved February 18, 1943.

Chap. 24 AN ACT MAKING TEMPORARY PROVISION RELATIVE TO THE FILING OF ANNUAL STATEMENTS OF INSURANCE COMPANIES AND SCHEDULES ACCOMPANYING THE SAME.

Emergency preamble.

Whereas, The deferred operation of this act would tend in part to defeat its purpose, which is to permit the commissioner of insurance to exercise, during the current and certain subsequent years, the authority thereby given to him, therefore it is hereby declared to be an emergency law, necessary for the immediate preservation of the public convenience.

Be it enacted, etc., as follows:

SECTION 1. During the continuance of the existing state of war between the United States and any foreign country, but not later than June first, nineteen hundred and forty-five, the commissioner of insurance is hereby authorized to extend the time for the filing of schedules accompanying annual statements of insurance companies transacting business in the commonwealth for not more than sixty days beyond March first.

SECTION 2. During the continuance of the existing state of war between the United States and any foreign country, but not later than June first, nineteen hundred and forty-five, the commissioner of insurance is hereby authorized to exempt insurance companies transacting business in the commonwealth from filing such parts of their annual statements as in his judgment may be temporarily discontinued.

Approved February 18, 1943.

AN ACT PROVIDING FOR THE HOLDING OF BIENNIAL MUNICIPAL ELECTIONS IN THE CITY OF CHICOPEE IN ODD-NUMBERED YEARS AND ESTABLISHING THE DATE OF SAID ELECTIONS. *Chap.* 25

Be it enacted, etc., as follows:

SECTION 1. Beginning with the year nineteen hundred and forty-three, municipal elections in the city of Chicopee for the choice of mayor, members of the board of aldermen, city clerk, city treasurer and members of the school committee shall be held biennially on the first Tuesday after the first Monday of November in every odd-numbered year.

SECTION 2. At the biennial municipal election to be held in said city in the year nineteen hundred and forty-three, the city clerk shall be elected for the term of four years, and at the biennial municipal election to be held in every fourth year thereafter the city clerk shall be elected for the term of four years.

SECTION 3. The terms of office of the aldermen at large elected in the year nineteen hundred and forty-two shall continue until the qualification of their respective successors who shall be elected at the biennial municipal election to be held in the year nineteen hundred and forty-five. At the biennial municipal election to be held in the year nineteen hundred and forty-three, five aldermen at large and one alderman from each ward shall be elected for terms of two years each. At the biennial municipal election to be held in the year nineteen hundred and forty-five, and at each biennial municipal election held thereafter, all aldermen shall be elected for terms of two years each.

SECTION 4. At the biennial municipal election to be held in the year nineteen hundred and forty-five, the city treasurer shall be elected to hold office for the term of four years, and at the biennial municipal election to be held in every fourth year thereafter the city treasurer shall be elected for the term of four years.

SECTION 5. At the biennial municipal election to be held in the year nineteen hundred and forty-three, a member at large of the school committee shall be elected for a term of four years. The term of office of the member at large of the school committee elected in the year nineteen hundred and forty-one shall continue until the qualification of his successor who shall be elected at the biennial municipal election in the year nineteen hundred and forty-five. The terms of office of the members of the school committee from wards five, six and seven elected in the year nineteen hundred and forty-two, and of the members of the school committee from wards one and two elected in the year nineteen hundred and forty-one, shall continue until the qualification of their respective successors who shall be elected at the biennial municipal election in the year nineteen hundred and forty-five. At the biennial municipal election to be held in the year nineteen hundred and forty-three the members of the school committee from wards three, four, eight and nine shall be elected for terms of two years each. At each biennial municipal election, beginning with the year nineteen hundred and forty-five, all members of the school committee to be elected thereat from wards shall be elected for terms of two years each, and any member at large of the school committee to be elected thereat shall be elected for a term of four years.

SECTION 6. Except when voting to fill a vacancy caused by death, resignation or otherwise, at the biennial municipal election to be held in the year nineteen hundred and forty-five, and at all biennial municipal elections held thereafter, no voter shall vote for more than six of the persons who are candidates for election as members at large of the board of aldermen; and the ten candidates for such office receiving the largest number of votes shall be declared to be elected. Nothing in this section shall prevent a person voting to fill a vacancy or vacancies in the office of alderman at large at any such election, in addition to voting for the six candidates above referred to.

SECTION 7. Except for the purpose of filling a vacancy, at the biennial municipal election to be held in the year nineteen hundred and forty-three and in every fourth year thereafter no city treasurer shall be elected, and at the biennial municipal election to be held in the year nineteen hundred and forty-five and in every fourth year thereafter no city clerk shall be elected.

SECTION 8. So much of chapter two hundred and thirty-nine of the acts of eighteen hundred and ninety-seven, and acts in addition to and amendment thereof, as is inconsistent with any provision of this act is hereby repealed.

SECTION 9. This act shall take effect upon its passage.

Approved February 18, 1943.

Chap. 26 AN ACT SUSPENDING THE OPERATION OF CERTAIN PROVISIONS OF LAW RELATIVE TO THE REMOVAL OF OVERHEAD WIRES IN THE CITY OF BOSTON.

Be it enacted, etc., as follows:

SECTION 1. The duty placed upon the fire commissioner of the city of Boston by section one of chapter one hundred and one of the acts of nineteen hundred and thirty-one, as amended by section one of chapter one hundred and ten of the acts of nineteen hundred and thirty-six and by section one of chapter one hundred and ten of the acts of nineteen hundred and forty-one, to prescribe in said city, in the month of January of each year, to and including the year nineteen hundred and forty-six, not more than four miles of streets in said city in any one year, from which poles shall be removed and the wires buried underground, is hereby suspended. Said suspension shall be effective for the year nineteen hundred and forty-three, and for each year thereafter during any part of which the present state of war continues, but shall not affect prescriptions already made by said fire commissioner for years prior to the year nineteen hundred and forty-three, nor shall it affect the power of said commissioner to enforce any such prior prescription.

Section 2. This act shall take effect upon its passage.

Approved February 18, 1943.

An Act authorizing savings banks and trust companies having savings departments to make minimum interest or discount charges in the case of certain loans to their depositors. *Chap.* 27

Be it enacted, etc., as follows:

Section 1. Section fifty-one A of chapter one hundred and sixty-eight of the General Laws, as amended by section twenty of chapter three hundred and thirty-four of the acts of nineteen hundred and thirty-three, is hereby further amended by inserting after the word "corporation" in the tenth and eleventh lines the words: — ; provided, that a minimum of fifty cents may be charged or collected as such interest or discount in the case of any such loan, — so as to read as follows: — *Section 51A.* Such corporation shall, upon application by a depositor or by either of two joint depositors under section fourteen of chapter one hundred and sixty-seven, make a loan to him, secured by his deposit book up to the amount of said deposit account, for a time not extending beyond the end of the dividend period in which the loan was made. Said corporation may charge the depositor interest for, or may collect discount in advance upon, the loan at a rate not exceeding one per cent more than the combined rates of the next preceding dividend distribution of such corporation; provided, that a minimum of fifty cents may be charged or collected as such interest or discount in the case of any such loan. The corporation shall keep posted in its banking room a notice containing the substance of this section and section fifty-one in such form as the commissioner may prescribe.

G. L. (Ter. Ed.), 168, § 51A, etc., amended.

Loans to depositors.

Section 2. Chapter one hundred and seventy-two of the General Laws is hereby amended by striking out section sixty-six A, as appearing in the Tercentenary Edition, and inserting in place thereof the following: — *Section 66A.* Such a corporation shall, on application of a depositor, or of either of two joint depositors under section fourteen of

G. L. (Ter. Ed.), 172, § 66A, amended.

Loans to depositors.

chapter one hundred and sixty-seven, in said savings department, make a loan to him, secured by his deposit book, to an amount not exceeding ninety per cent of the amount of deposits shown therein, for a period not extending beyond the date when the next dividend of the savings department of said corporation shall be payable. The said corporation may charge the depositor interest for the loan at a rate not exceeding one half of one per cent more than the next previous regular dividend declared and paid by the savings department of such corporation; provided, that a minimum of fifty cents may be charged or collected as such interest in the case of any such loan.

The corporation shall keep posted conspicuously in the banking rooms of its savings department a notice containing the substance of this section and of section sixty-six in such form as the commissioner may prescribe.

Approved February 18, 1943.

Chap. 28 AN ACT ESTABLISHING THE NUMBER OF ELECTED TOWN MEETING MEMBERS IN THE TOWN OF WEYMOUTH AND AUTHORIZING SUCH MEMBERS TO BECOME CANDIDATES FOR RE-ELECTION BY GIVING WRITTEN NOTICE THEREOF TO THE TOWN CLERK.

Be it enacted, etc., as follows:

SECTION 1. Chapter sixty-one of the acts of nineteen hundred and twenty-one is hereby amended by striking out section two and inserting in place thereof the following: — *Section 2.* Other than the officers designated in section three as town meeting members at large, the representative town meeting membership shall in each precinct consist of the largest number divisible by three which will admit of a representation thereof in the approximate proportion which the number of registered voters therein bears to the total number of registered voters in the town, and which will cause the total elected membership to be as nearly two hundred and forty as may be.

The registered voters in every precinct, at the annual town election to be held in the year nineteen hundred and forty-four, and the registered voters of any precinct affected by any revision of precincts, at the first annual town election following such revision, shall, conformably to the laws relative to elections not inconsistent with this act, elect by ballot the number of registered voters in the precinct, other than the officers designated in section three as town meeting members at large, provided for in the first sentence of this section, to be town meeting members of the town. The first third, in the order of votes received, of members so elected shall serve three years, the second third in such order shall serve two years, and the remaining third in such order shall serve one year, from the day of the annual town meeting; in case of a tie vote affecting the division into thirds, as aforesaid, the members elected from the precinct shall by ballot determine the same; and thereafter, except as is otherwise provided herein, at each annual town election the registered voters of each precinct shall, in like manner, elect, for the term of three years, one third of the number of elected town meeting members to which such precinct is entitled, and shall at such election fill for the unexpired term or terms any vacancy or vacancies then existing in the number of elected town meeting members in such precinct.

The terms of office of all elected town meeting members from every precinct revised as aforesaid shall cease upon the election as hereinbefore provided of their successors. The town clerk shall, after every election of town meeting members, forthwith notify each such member by mail of his election.

SECTION 2. Section four of said chapter sixty-one is hereby amended by inserting after the word "election" in the sixth line the following: — ; provided, that any town meeting member may become a candidate for re-election by giving written notice thereof to the town clerk at least thirty days before the election, — so as to read as follows: — *Section 4.* Nomination of candidates for town meeting members to be elected under this act shall be made by nomination papers, which shall bear no political designation, and signed by not less than ten voters of the precinct in which the candidate resides, and filed with the town clerk at least ten days before the election; provided, that any town meeting member may become a candidate for re-election by giving written notice thereof to the town clerk at least thirty days before the election. No nomination papers shall be valid in respect to any candidate whose written acceptance is not thereon or attached thereto.

SECTION 3. This act shall take effect for the purposes of the annual election in the town of Weymouth to be held in the year nineteen hundred and forty-four, at which election all elected town meeting members provided for under section one shall be elected, and upon their qualification the terms of office of all elected town meeting members then in office shall cease, and for all other purposes this act shall take effect upon the date of such election.

Approved February 18, 1943.

AN ACT AUTHORIZING CERTAIN OFFICIALS OF THE LAND COURT TO PERFORM THE OFFICIAL DUTIES OF THE RECORDER THEREOF IN CERTAIN CASES. *Chap.* 29

Be it enacted, etc., as follows:

Chapter one hundred and eighty-five of the General Laws is hereby amended by striking out section twelve, as amended by chapter twenty-seven of the acts of nineteen hundred and forty-one, and inserting in place thereof the following section: — *Section 12.* The judge of the land

G. L. (Ter. Ed.), 185, § 12, etc., amended.

Examiners of title.

Chief examiner to act as deputy recorder, when.

court may appoint one or more examiners of title who shall be attorneys at law and he may also appoint a chief title examiner who shall perform all the duties of an examiner of title and such other duties in connection with the work of the court as the judge or associate judge may assign. Such chief title examiner shall also in case of the absence, sickness or disability of the recorder or if a vacancy exists in the office of recorder, perform, under the title of deputy recorder, all of the official duties of the recorder. In case of the absence, sickness or disability of both the recorder and the chief title examiner, or of the recorder alone if a vacancy exists in the position of chief title examiner, or of the chief title examiner alone if a vacancy exists in the office of recorder, any deputy recorder appointed under section six, who is designated for the purpose by the judge by a writing filed in the recorder's office, shall perform all of the official duties of the recorder. *Approved February 18, 1943.*

Chap. 30 AN ACT RELATIVE TO THE VERIFICATION BY BANKS OF THE DEPOSIT BOOKS OF THEIR DEPOSITORS OR SHAREHOLDERS DURING THE PRESENT WAR AND FOR A CERTAIN PERIOD AFTER THE TERMINATION THEREOF.

Emergency preamble.

Whereas, The deferred operation of this act would tend to defeat its purpose, which in part is to give the supervisory authority greater discretion as to the manner and extent of verification of deposit or pass books by thrift institutions so that the confidence of the public in such institutions may be maintained and preserved, therefore it is hereby declared to be an emergency law, necessary for the immediate preservation of the public convenience.

Be it enacted, etc., as follows:

SECTION 1. The provisions of any law which authorize a bank, as defined in section one of chapter one hundred and sixty-seven of the General Laws, as amended, to verify the deposit or pass books of its depositors or shareholders, are hereby suspended and shall have no force or effect during the effective period of this act. During said period any such bank, when so directed by the commissioner of banks, shall call in the deposit or pass books of its depositors or shareholders and said books shall be verified in the manner and to the extent prescribed by said commissioner.

SECTION 2. This act shall be in effect during the continuance of the existing state of war between the United States and any foreign country, and for six months after the termination of all existing states of war.

Approved February 19, 1943.

AN ACT RELATIVE TO THE OFFENSE OF FRAUDULENTLY PROCURING FOOD, ENTERTAINMENT OR ACCOMMODATION FROM HOTELS, INNS, COMMON VICTUALLERS, LODGING HOUSES OR BOARDING HOUSES. *Chap.* 31

Be it enacted, etc., as follows:

G. L. (Ter. Ed.), 140, § 12, etc., amended.

Chapter one hundred and forty of the General Laws is hereby amended by striking out section twelve, as most recently amended by chapter ninety-two of the acts of nineteen hundred and thirty-three, and inserting in place thereof the following: — *Section 12.* Whoever puts up at a hotel, inn, lodging house or boarding house and, without having an express agreement for credit, procures food, entertainment or accommodation without paying therefor, and with intent to cheat or defraud the owner or keeper thereof; or, with such intent, obtains credit at a hotel, inn, lodging house or boarding house for such food, entertainment or accommodation by means of any false show of baggage or effects brought thereto; or, with such intent, removes or causes to be removed any baggage or effects from a hotel, inn, lodging house or boarding house while a lien exists thereon for the proper charges due from him for fare and board furnished therein, shall be punished by a fine of not more than two hundred dollars or by imprisonment for not more than one year; and whoever, without having an express agreement for credit, procures food or beverage from a common victualler without paying therefor and with intent to cheat or defraud shall be punished by a fine of not more than fifty dollars or by imprisonment for not more than three months. The words "lodging house", as used herein, shall mean a lodging house as defined in section twenty-two.

Penalty for procuring food, accommodation, etc., or removing baggage from inn or lodging house with intent to defraud

Presumptive evidence of intent.

Proof that such food, entertainment, accommodation or beverage, or credit for the same, was obtained by a false show of baggage or effects, or that such baggage or effects were removed from any such place by any person while such a lien existed thereon without an express agreement permitting such removal, or, if there was not an express agreement for credit, that payment for such food, entertainment, accommodation or beverage was refused upon demand, shall be presumptive evidence of the intent to cheat or defraud referred to herein.

Approved February 19, 1943.

Chap. 32 AN ACT AUTHORIZING THE CONSTRUCTION AND MAINTENANCE OF A BRIDGE WITHOUT A DRAW ACROSS A PORTION OF THE MERRIMACK RIVER IN THE CITY OF HAVERHILL.

Be it enacted, etc., as follows:

SECTION 1. Charles E. Hubbard and Norman P. Cotton, both of the city of Haverhill, are hereby authorized to construct and maintain a bridge, without a draw, across the Merrimack river between land owned by said persons on Porter's island and on the Bradford shore in said city. The construction and maintenance of said bridge shall be subject to chapter ninety-one of the General Laws.

SECTION 2. This act shall take effect upon its passage.

Approved February 19, 1943.

Chap. 33 AN ACT PROVIDING THAT CERTAIN RAILROAD CORPORATIONS MAY ACQUIRE, HOLD, SELL AND GUARANTEE THE BONDS OR NOTES OF CERTAIN OTHER RAILROAD CORPORATIONS.

Emergency preamble.

Whereas, Conditions now exist which may make it necessary that certain railroad corporations be empowered forthwith to exercise powers set forth in this act, therefore it is hereby declared to be an emergency law, necessary for the immediate preservation of the public convenience.

Be it enacted, etc., as follows:

G. L. (Ter. Ed.), 160, § 68, amended.

Connecting roads may guarantee each other's bonds.

Chapter one hundred and sixty of the General Laws is hereby amended by striking out section sixty-eight, as appearing in the Tercentenary Edition, and inserting in place thereof the following section: — *Section 68.* A corporation owning a railroad connecting with another railroad, both of which are wholly constructed, or a corporation owning a railroad leasing, operating or controlling another railroad, may acquire, hold, sell and, upon such terms and to such an extent as may be authorized by a vote at a meeting called therefor, may guarantee the bonds or notes of such other railroad, whether such other railroad is located within or without this commonwealth; provided, that such bonds or notes are issued in conformity with law.

Approved February 23, 1943.

Chap. 34 AN ACT AUTHORIZING THE CITY OF GLOUCESTER TO USE A CERTAIN PORTION OF A PUBLIC LANDING IN SAID CITY AS A PUBLIC WAY.

Be it enacted, etc., as follows:

The city of Gloucester may lay out as a public way that portion or part of the Town Landing, so called, located near the southerly end of Washington street in said city, which has been used as a public way for many years without a formal layout and without authority for a changed public use from that of a town or city landing. Said part or portion is particularly bounded and described as follows: — A parcel of land bounded on the east by land of the Socony Vacuum Oil Company, Inc. and by the westerly terminus of Rogers street, a public way, a distance of about one hundred twenty-seven feet; on the south by remaining land of Town Landing No. 7, so called, a distance of about eighty-five feet; on the southwest by land of St. Peter's Club, Inc., a distance of about thirteen feet; and on the northwest by the south-easterly side line of Commercial street, a public way, a distance of about one hundred eighteen and six-tenths feet; and is shown more particularly on a plan thereof drawn by Robert C. Hennessy, city engineer.

Approved February 23, 1943.

AN ACT AMENDING THE LAW RELATIVE TO THE MILITIA. *Chap.* 35

Whereas, The deferred operation of this act would tend to defeat so much of its purpose as, in view of doubts which have arisen as to the status of the Massachusetts state guard, is to immediately ratify and confirm the raising, organizing and maintaining thereof and all acts done by, or by direction of, the commander-in-chief in connection therewith; therefore it is hereby declared to be an emergency law, necessary for the immediate preservation of the public safety and convenience. Emergency preamble.

Be it enacted, etc., as follows:

SECTION 1. Chapter thirty-three of the General Laws is hereby amended by striking out section one, as appearing in section one of chapter four hundred and twenty-five of the acts of nineteen hundred and thirty-nine, and inserting in place thereof the following section: — *Section 1.* The following words used in this chapter shall have the following meanings, unless a different meaning is clearly apparent from the language or context, or unless such construction is inconsistent with the manifest intention of the legislature: G. L. (Ter. Ed.), 33, § 1, etc., amended. Definitions.

1. "Military forces of the commonwealth" shall include the organized militia, as defined in section six, and members of the unorganized militia when drafted or accepted as volunteers under sections four and five.

2. "Soldier" or "enlisted man", a member, other than a commissioned officer or a warrant officer, of the military forces of the commonwealth.

3. "Officer", a commissioned officer or a warrant officer in the military forces of the commonwealth.

4. "Company" shall include battery, troop, naval division, and such other units as may be determined by the commander-in-chief to come under such designation.

SECTION 2. Section six of said chapter thirty-three, as so appearing, is hereby amended by striking out paragraph (*a*) and inserting in place thereof the following paragraph: — G. L. (Ter. Ed.), 33, § 6, etc., amended.

Organization of militia.

(a) The active or organized militia shall be composed of volunteers, and shall comprise the aides-de-camp of the commander-in-chief, the state staff and detachment, the land forces as defined in section sixty-six, and the naval forces.

G. L. (Ter. Ed.), 33, § 24, etc., amended.

Civil and criminal liability.

SECTION 3. Said chapter thirty-three is hereby further amended by striking out section twenty-four, as so appearing, and inserting in place thereof the following section: — *Section 24.* No officer or soldier shall be liable, either civilly or criminally, for any damage to property or injury to any person, including death resulting therefrom, caused by him or by his order, while performing any military duty lawfully ordered under any provision of this chapter, unless the act or order causing such damage or injury was manifestly beyond the scope of the authority of such officer or soldier.

G. L. (Ter. Ed.), 33, § 55, etc., amended.

Compensation for injuries, etc., when on duty.

SECTION 4. Said chapter thirty-three is hereby further amended by striking out section fifty-five, as so appearing, and inserting in place thereof the following section: — *Section 55.* An officer or soldier who shall, while performing any military duty lawfully ordered under any provision of this chapter, receive any injury by reason of such duty or who shall without fault or neglect on his part be wounded or disabled, or contract any sickness or disease, while performing any such lawfully ordered military duty, incapacitating him from pursuing his usual business or occupation, shall, during the period of such incapacity, receive compensation to be fixed by a board, appointed as hereinafter provided, to inquire into his claim, not exceeding in amount the special duty pay plus ration allowance provided for by this chapter and actual necessary expenses for care and medical attendance. In case of death resulting from such injury, sickness or disease, compensation shall be paid to the decedent's dependents, as determined in accordance with section thirty-two and clause (3) of section one, both of chapter one hundred and fifty-two, in the amounts provided by, and otherwise subject to, section thirty-one of said chapter; provided, that compensation to such dependents other than widows and children shall be based on the special duty pay plus ration allowance hereinbefore mentioned, and that, for the purposes hereof, said board shall exercise all the powers given by said provisions of chapter one hundred and fifty-two to the department of industrial accidents. All claims arising under this section shall be inquired into by a board of three officers, at least one of whom shall be a medical officer, appointed by the commander-in-chief. The board shall have the same power to take evidence, administer oaths, issue subpoenas and compel witnesses to attend and testify and produce books and papers, and to punish their failure to do so, as is possessed by a general court-martial. The findings of the board shall be subject to the approval of the commander-in-chief. The amount so found due and so approved shall be a charge against the commonwealth, and paid in the same manner as other military accounts.

SECTION 5. Said chapter thirty-three is hereby further amended by striking out section fifty-six, as so appearing, and inserting in place thereof the following section: — *Section 56.* Whoever wilfully deprives an officer or soldier of his employment, or denies him employment, or prevents his being employed by another, or obstructs or annoys him or his employer in respect of his trade, business or employment, because of his connection with the military forces of the commonwealth or because of his necessary absence from business in performance of his duty as such, and whoever dissuades any person from enlisting in the said military forces by threat of injury to him in respect of his employment, trade or business, or of other injury, if he shall so enlist, shall be punished by a fine of not more than five hundred dollars, or by imprisonment for not more than six months, or both.

G. L. (Ter. Ed.), 33, § 56, etc., amended.

Deprivation, etc., of employment. Penalty.

SECTION 6. Said chapter thirty-three is hereby further amended by striking out section sixty-six, as so appearing, and inserting in place thereof the following section: — *Section 66.* The land forces shall consist of the active national guard, the inactive national guard, retired officers, and such other units, officers and soldiers as the commander-in-chief, subject to federal authority, may from time to time prescribe, and, whenever so authorized by federal law, a state guard or similar military organization composed as prescribed by the commander-in-chief.

G. L. (Ter. Ed.), 33, § 66, etc., amended.

Composition of land forces.

SECTION 7. Said chapter thirty-three is hereby further amended by inserting after section sixty-eight, as so appearing, the following new section: — *Section 68A.* The state guard shall consist of such organizations and units as the commander-in-chief may from time to time prescribe or authorize to be formed, shall be composed of volunteers of eighteen years of age or older, but without specific maximum age limit, and shall be organized and maintained in accordance with pertinent federal law. While so organized and maintained the state guard and the officers and soldiers thereof shall have the benefit of and be subject to all provisions of law applicable to the organized militia and not inconsistent with this section.

G. L. (Ter. Ed.), 33, new § 68A, added.

Composition of state guard.

SECTION 8. The raising, organizing and maintaining of the Massachusetts state guard now in existence, and all acts done and orders made by, or by direction of, the commander-in-chief in connection therewith, are hereby expressly ratified and confirmed.

Ratification of prior acts.

Approved February 24, 1943.

Chap. 36 AN ACT RELATIVE TO THE IMPOSITION OF AN EXCISE ON ALCOHOLIC BEVERAGES.

Be it enacted, etc., as follows:

G. L. (Ter. Ed.), 138, § 21, etc., amended.

Section twenty-one of chapter one hundred and thirty-eight of the General Laws, as most recently amended by section two of chapter six hundred and thirty-seven of the acts of nineteen hundred and forty-one, is hereby further amended by striking out the paragraph inserted as the sixth paragraph by section one of chapter three hundred and sixty-seven of the acts of nineteen hundred and thirty-nine and inserting in place thereof the following paragraph: —

Excise.

For each proof gallon, or fractional part thereof, of all other alcoholic beverages containing more than fifty per cent of alcohol by volume at sixty degrees Fahrenheit or alcohol, at the rate of forty cents per proof gallon. The words "proof gallon", when used in this section with reference to an alcoholic beverage, shall be held to be a gallon of the alcoholic beverage which contains one half its volume of alcohol of a specific gravity of seven thousand nine hundred and thirty-nine ten thousandths (.7939) at sixty degrees Fahrenheit. Every person subject to this section shall keep a true and accurate account of all alcoholic beverages or alcohol sold by him other than malt beverages imported into the commonwealth by him, and a like account of all malt beverages imported into the commonwealth by him, and shall make a return thereof to the commissioner of corporations and taxation, hereinafter called the commissioner, within ten days after the last day of each month, covering such sales and importations by him during such month, and shall at the time of such return make payment to the commissioner of the amount due under this section for such sales and importations in such month. The commissioner shall assess on the basis of any available information any deficiency in the amount so payable which remains unpaid and shall notify the person so assessed who may within thirty days of the date of the notice make application for abatement thereof. Such assessment may be made at any time within two years after the making of the earliest sale, or importation, as the case may be, included in such assessment. If the commissioner shall determine that a deficiency so assessed should be abated or, upon application filed within six months of the making of the return that an overpayment has been made, he shall certify the amount of such abatement or overpayment to the state treasurer, who shall repay the amount so certified if paid, without further appropriation therefor. The commissioner is hereby authorized to prescribe rules and regulations governing the method of keeping accounts, making returns and paying the excise provided for in this section. Such rules and regulations shall provide for the waiver of payment of the excise in respect to any alcoholic beverages or alcohol if it appears that an excise has already been paid under the provisions of this section in respect thereto; provided, however, that alcoholic beverages or alcohol manufactured within or imported into the commonwealth and exported therefrom shall be exempt from such excise. Alcohol for the purposes of this section shall mean alcohol otherwise subject to any provision of this chapter but shall not include alcohol sold for scientific, chemical, mechanical, manufacturing, industrial, culinary, pharmaceutical or medical purposes in containers greater in capacity than one wine gallon. The taxes imposed by this section shall also be applicable to sales of alcoholic beverages, upon which an excise has not already been paid under the provisions of this section, made by a railroad or car corporation or the owner or operator of any vessel or shipping company licensed to sell alcoholic beverages under the provisions of section thirteen. *Approved February 25, 1943.*

AN ACT MAKING MINOR AND CORRECTIVE CHANGES IN THE LAWS RELATING TO COLLECTION OF LOCAL TAXES. *Chap.* 37

Be it enacted, etc., as follows:

SECTION 1. Section one of chapter sixty of the General Laws, as amended by section one of chapter one hundred and sixty-four of the acts of nineteen hundred and thirty-three, is hereby further amended by striking out the word ", summons" each time it occurs therein, so that the last two paragraphs, as appearing in the Tercentenary Edition, will read as follows: — G. L. (Ter. Ed.), 60, § 1, etc., amended.

"Service", as applied to any notice, demand or other paper, shall, except as otherwise provided in section sixteen, mean delivering it or a copy to the person for whom it is intended, or leaving it or a copy at his last and usual place of abode or of business, or sending it or a copy by mail postpaid addressed to him at his last and usual place of abode or of business or, if such notice or other paper relates to taxes on land, posting it or a copy conspicuously in some convenient and public place and sending a copy by mail postpaid addressed to the person for whom it is intended at the town where such land lies. Such service shall be sufficient whether made by the then collector of taxes or by any predecessor. Term "service" defined.

The affidavit of the collector, deputy collector, sheriff, deputy sheriff or constable serving the notice, demand or other paper of the manner of service shall be kept on file in the office of the collector, and shall be prima facie evidence that the same was so served.

SECTION 2. Section three of said chapter sixty, as most recently amended by section two of chapter two hundred and fifty-eight of the acts of nineteen hundred and forty-one, is hereby further amended by striking out the last sentence and inserting in place thereof the following sentence: — The tax notice and bill shall state that all payments shall G. L. (Ter. Ed.), 60, § 3, etc., amended.

be to or to the order of the city, town or district and not to or to the order of any officer, board or commission, — so as to read as follows: — *Section 3.* The collector shall forthwith, after receiving a tax list and warrant, send notice to each person assessed, resident or non-resident, of the amount of his tax; if mailed, it shall be postpaid and directed to the town where the assessed person resided on January first of the year in which the tax was assessed, and, if he resides in a city, it shall, if possible, be directed to the street and number of his residence. Notices of poll taxes shall be sent not later than June fourteenth of the year in which the tax is assessed. An omission to send a notice under this section shall not affect the validity either of a tax or of the proceedings for its collection. All tax bills or notices issued pursuant to this section shall be dated January first of the year to which the tax relates. The tax notice and bill shall state that all payments shall be to or to the order of the city, town or district and not to or to the order of any officer, board or commission. *Approved February 25, 1943.*

Tax bills, notices, duties of collector.

Chap. 38 AN ACT TO CLARIFY THE LAW RELATIVE TO THE POWER OF A BUSINESS CORPORATION TO MORTGAGE OR PLEDGE ITS PROPERTY AND ASSETS.

Be it enacted, etc., as follows:

G. L. (Ter. Ed.), 156, § 42, amended.

SECTION 1. Section forty-two of chapter one hundred and fifty-six of the General Laws, as appearing in the Tercentenary Edition, is hereby amended by inserting after the word "sale" in the ninth line the following: — , mortgage, pledge, — so as to read as follows: — *Section 42.* Every corporation may, at a meeting duly called for the purpose, by vote of two thirds of each class of stock outstanding and entitled to vote, or by a larger vote if the agreement of association or act of incorporation so requires, change its corporate name, the nature of its business, the classes of its capital stock subsequently to be issued and their preferences and voting power, or make any other lawful amendment or alteration in its agreement of association or articles of organization, or in the corresponding provisions of its act of incorporation, or authorize the sale, mortgage, pledge, lease or exchange of all its property and assets, including its good will, upon such terms and conditions as it deems expedient.

Amendments requiring two thirds or larger vote.

G. L. (Ter. Ed.), 156, § 46, amended.

Term "sell" limited.

SECTION 2. Section forty-six of said chapter one hundred and fifty-six, as so appearing, is hereby amended by adding at the end the following sentence: — The word "sell" as used in this section shall not include mortgage or pledge.

Approved February 25, 1943.

AN ACT MAKING PROVISION FOR THE PAYMENT OF COUNTY DEBT AND INTEREST IN CERTAIN CASES. *Chap.* 39

Be it enacted, etc., as follows:

Section thirty of chapter thirty-five of the General Laws, as amended by section three of chapter five hundred and one of the acts of nineteen hundred and thirty-nine, is hereby further amended by adding at the end the following sentence: — Notwithstanding the foregoing, the county commissioners shall also levy in any year as a county tax a sum sufficient to meet the debt and interest maturing in that year, if no other provision therefor has been made.

G. L. (Ter. Ed.), 35, § 30, etc., amended.

Amount of county tax.

Approved February 25, 1943.

AN ACT EXEMPTING THE COMMONWEALTH AND ITS POLITICAL SUBDIVISIONS AND CERTAIN NON-PROFIT LIBRARIES FROM THE FAIR TRADE LAW, SO CALLED, IN RESPECT TO PRICES OF BOOKS OR OTHER READING MATERIAL. *Chap.* 40

Be it enacted, etc., as follows:

Chapter ninety-three of the General Laws is hereby amended by striking out section fourteen C, inserted by chapter three hundred and ninety-eight of the acts of nineteen hundred and thirty-seven, and inserting in place thereof the following section: — *Section 14C.* Sections fourteen A and fourteen B shall not apply to any contract or agreement between producers or between wholesalers or between retailers as to sale or resale prices, nor shall they apply to prices at which books or other printed matter or material to be read, may be sold or offered for sale to the commonwealth or any department, board or commission thereof, or to any of its political subdivisions, or to any free public library or endowed library, or to any college, university or school library, or to any non-profit organization administering a collection of books for non-profit purposes, located in this commonwealth. *Approved February 26, 1943.*

G. L. (Ter. Ed.), 93, § 14C, etc., amended.

Application of sections 14A and 14B limited.

AN ACT RELATIVE TO REPORTS OF TREATMENT OF CERTAIN WOUNDS. *Chap.* 41

Be it enacted, etc., as follows:

Section twelve A of chapter one hundred and twelve of the General Laws, as appearing in the Tercentenary Edition, is hereby amended by inserting after the word "pistol" in the third line the words: — , BB gun, or other air rifle, — so that the first sentence will read as follows: — Every physician attending or treating a case of bullet wound, gunshot wound, powder burn or any other injury arising from or caused by the discharge of a gun, pistol, BB gun, or other air rifle or other firearm, or, whenever any such case is treated

G. L. (Ter. Ed.), 112, § 12A, amended.

Reports of treatment of certain wounds caused by BB guns, etc.

in a hospital, sanitarium or other institution, the manager, superintendent or other person in charge thereof, shall report such case at once to the commissioner of public safety and to the police authorities of the town where such physician, hospital, sanitarium or institution is located.

Approved February 26, 1943.

Chap. 42 AN ACT AUTHORIZING THE TRUSTEES OF THE BRISTOL COUNTY AGRICULTURAL SCHOOL TO PAY TRANSPORTATION COSTS OF CERTAIN PUPILS ATTENDING SAID SCHOOL.

Be it enacted, etc., as follows:

G. L. (Ter. Ed.), 74, § 31A, etc., amended.

Section thirty-one A of chapter seventy-four of the General Laws, inserted by chapter sixty-five of the acts of nineteen hundred and thirty-four, is hereby amended by inserting after the word "school" in the second line the words: — and of the Bristol county agricultural school, — and by inserting after the word "Essex" in the fifth line the words: — , or in the county of Bristol, as the case may be, — so as to read as follows: — *Section 31A.* The trustees of the Essex county agricultural school and of the Bristol county agricultural school may, if in their judgment the circumstances warrant, and it is not otherwise provided for, pay, in whole or part, the costs of transporting any pupil who resides in a town in the county of Essex, or in the county of Bristol, as the case may be, between the town and the school, and such expenditure shall be deemed to be a proper maintenance item.

Payment of transportation costs of certain pupils in Bristol and Essex counties.

Approved February 26, 1943.

Chap. 43 AN ACT RELATIVE TO THE POWERS AND DUTIES OF THE STATE BALLOT LAW COMMISSION.

Be it enacted, etc., as follows:

G. L. (Ter. Ed.), 6, § 32, etc., amended.

Section thirty-two of chapter six of the General Laws, as most recently amended by section one of chapter four hundred and seventy-three of the acts of nineteen hundred and thirty-eight, is hereby further amended by striking out the second paragraph and inserting in place thereof the following paragraph: —

Powers and duties of state ballot law commission.

The commission shall render a decision on any matter referred to it, pertaining to certificates of nomination or nomination papers for any presidential or biennial state primaries or any biennial state election or to withdrawals of nomination therefor, not later than fourteen days after the last day fixed for filing objections to such certificates or papers or for filing such withdrawals, as the case may be, under chapter fifty-three. The commission shall render a decision on any matter referred to it, pertaining to certificates of nomination or nomination papers for any special state primary or special state election or to withdrawals of nomination therefor, not later than four days after the last day fixed for filing objections to such certificates or papers or for filing such withdrawals, as the case may be, under chapter fifty-three. In the event that said commission fails to render its decision within the time herein required on any matter so referred, the state secretary shall, notwithstanding such failure, proceed forthwith to cause to be printed the ballots for such primaries or elections.

Approved February 26, 1943.

AN ACT AUTHORIZING CITIES, TOWNS AND DISTRICTS TO BORROW ON ACCOUNT OF PUBLIC WELFARE, SOLDIERS' BENEFITS, FEDERAL EMERGENCY UNEMPLOYMENT RELIEF PROJECTS, AND THE DISTRIBUTION OF SURPLUS COMMODITIES. *Chap.* 44

Whereas, It is necessary, in order to comply with the laws relative to the preparation and adoption of budgets, that the provisions of this act shall become effective immediately, and as the deferred operation of this act would tend to defeat such purpose, therefore this act is hereby declared to be an emergency law, necessary for the immediate preservation of the public convenience. Emergency preamble.

Be it enacted, etc., as follows:

SECTION 1. Subject to the provisions of this act, any city, town or district, by a two thirds vote as defined in section one of chapter forty-four of the General Laws, and with the approval of the mayor, selectmen or prudential committee or commissioners, as the case may be, and of the board established under section one of chapter forty-nine of the acts of nineteen hundred and thirty-three, may borrow, in each of the years nineteen hundred and forty-three and nineteen hundred and forty-four, inside its limit of indebtedness as prescribed by section ten of said chapter forty-four, for use only for meeting appropriations made or to be made for public welfare, including in such term old age assistance and aid to dependent children, for soldiers' benefits, for any federal emergency unemployment relief projects, exclusive of public works administration projects or substitutes therefor, and for distribution of surplus commodities in cooperation with the federal government, to an amount not more than one half of one per cent of the average of the assessors' valuations of its taxable property for the three preceding years, such valuations to be reduced and otherwise determined as provided in said section ten of said chapter forty-four, and may issue bonds or notes therefor, which shall bear on their face the words (name of city, town or district) Municipal Relief Loan, Act of 1943. Each authorized issue shall constitute a separate loan, and such loans shall be paid in not more than ten years from their dates, as said board shall fix, and, except as herein provided, shall be subject to said chapter forty-four, exclusive of the limitation contained in the first paragraph of section seven thereof.

Loans may be issued hereunder in the year nineteen hundred and forty-three or nineteen hundred and forty-four, as the case may be, only by a city, town or district which in such year has appropriated to be raised by taxation or appropriated from available funds for the purposes enumerated in the preceding paragraph, an amount not less than the aggregate of its expenditures made in the year preceding the year of issue for old age assistance and aid to dependent children to be met otherwise than from the proceeds of federal grants and of its expenditures made in said preceding year for soldiers' benefits, together with an amount equal to not less than seventy per cent of its expenditures made in said preceding year for all public welfare purposes other than old age assistance, aid to dependent children and soldiers' benefits and other than federal emergency unemployment relief projects, all as determined by said board.

If a loan under authority of this act has been approved by said board during the year nineteen hundred and forty-three or nineteen hundred and forty-four for a city, town or district, the amount of any appropriation voted by such city, town or district for said year for public welfare, including in such term old age assistance and aid to dependent children, and soldiers' benefits, shall not be reduced during said year by appropriation, transfer or otherwise, except with the written approval of the board. Whenever used in this section, the words "soldiers' benefits" shall include state aid, military aid, soldiers' burials, soldiers' relief and war allowances.

Section 2. The members of the board aforesaid, when acting under this act, shall receive from the commonwealth compensation to the same extent as provided for services under chapter three hundred and sixty-six of the acts of nineteen hundred and thirty-three, as amended.

Section 3. A loan order voted in any city under authority of this act shall be deemed to be an emergency order and as such may be passed in such manner as is provided for emergency orders or ordinances in its charter and shall be in full force and effect immediately upon final favorable action thereon by its city council or chief executive, as the case may be, or upon the expiration of any period specified by such charter for the approval or disapproval of such orders by its chief executive in any case where he fails to approve or disapprove such an order within such period, notwithstanding any provision of general or special law or ordinance to the contrary; provided, that in the city of Boston such loan orders may be passed in the manner provided in its charter for loan orders for temporary loans in anticipation of taxes.

Section 4. In any city a loan order under authority of this act may be passed by vote of two thirds of all of the members of the city council, or of each branch thereof where there are two branches, exclusive of those members who are in the military or naval forces of the United States and are not present at the meeting at which any such vote is taken at the time of the vote, notwithstanding any provision of law to the contrary. *Approved March 1, 1943.*

AN ACT MAKING CERTAIN CHANGES IN THE ADMINISTRATION OF THE INCOME TAX LAW, SO-CALLED. *Chap.* 45

Be it enacted, etc., as follows:

SECTION 1. Chapter sixty-two of the General Laws is hereby amended by striking out section three, as appearing in the Tercentenary Edition, and inserting in place thereof the following section: — *Section 3.* The deduction to be allowed under section two shall be determined in the following manner:

G. L. (Ter. Ed.), 62, § 3, amended.

Determination of interest deduction, filing of return, etc

A taxpayer claiming the benefit thereof shall file with the commissioner a return, in such form as the commissioner prescribes, of his entire income from all sources, together with such other information as said commissioner deems necessary for the determination of the amount of this deduction. The commissioner may, in lieu of such return, accept a sworn duplicate of the annual return of income made under the federal income tax law. He may also, in any case where he deems it necessary, require the taxpayer to file such a sworn duplicate.

From said return and information the commissioner shall determine the amount of interest paid during the year by the taxpayer on debts of class (*a*) or (*b*) enumerated in said section, for which deduction is authorized by said section two, which interest, for the purposes of this section, shall be called the net interest. He shall also determine the total net income of the taxpayer, exclusive of income taxable under section five, as such total net income would be if no deduction were made for interest paid during the year. The taxpayer may deduct from his income taxable under section one an amount of interest paid by him during the year which shall bear the same proportion to the net interest paid as his income taxable under section one bears to his total net income as above determined.

Determinations to be made from return, etc.

SECTION 2. Said chapter sixty-two is hereby further amended by striking out section twenty-four, as so appearing, and inserting in place thereof the following section: — *Section 24.* Returns under sections twenty-two and twenty-three shall be accompanied by a written declaration that they are made under the penalties of perjury, and shall be filed with the commissioner, shall be made in such form as the commissioner prescribes, and shall contain such further information as he deems pertinent. Except as otherwise provided in this chapter, the return shall be made on or before March first in each year and shall relate to the income received during the year ending on December thirty-first preceding.

G. L. (Ter. Ed.), 62, § 24, amended.

Returns to be on oath.

Place and date of filing

Period included.

G. L. (Ter. Ed.), 62, § 31, amended.

Writ of mandamus to compel filing return.

SECTION 3. Said chapter sixty-two is hereby further amended by striking out section thirty-one, as so appearing, and inserting in place thereof the following section: — *Section 31.* If any person fails to file, on or before May first of any year, a return required by this chapter, any justice of the supreme judicial or the superior court, on petition of the commissioner or of any ten taxable inhabitants of the commonwealth, shall issue a writ of mandamus requiring such person to file the return. The order of notice on the petition shall be returnable not later than ten days after the filing thereof. The petition shall be heard and determined on the return day or on such day thereafter as the court shall fix, having regard to the speediest possible determination of the cause consistent with the rights of the parties. The judgment shall include costs in favor of the prevailing party. All writs and processes may be issued from the clerk's office in any county, and, except as aforesaid, shall be returnable as the court orders.

G. L. (Ter. Ed.), 62, § 33, amended.

Employers, etc., required to file certain returns, etc.

SECTION 4. Section thirty-three of said chapter sixty-two is hereby amended by striking out the first paragraph, as so appearing, and inserting in place thereof the following paragraph: — Every employer, being an inhabitant of the commonwealth or doing business therein, shall file annually with the commissioner a return in such form as he shall from time to time prescribe, giving the names and addresses of all employees residing in the commonwealth to whom said employer has paid wages, salary or other compensation in excess of the sum of two thousand dollars during the preceding calendar year, and give the amount paid to each.

G. L. (Ter. Ed.), 62, § 56, amended.

Penalty for fraudulent return, etc.

SECTION 5. Said chapter sixty-two is hereby further amended by striking out section fifty-six, as so appearing, and inserting in place thereof the following section: — *Section 56.* Whoever files a fraudulent return, and whoever, having failed to file a return or having filed an incorrect or insufficient return without reasonable excuse fails to file a return within twenty days after receiving notice from the commissioner of his delinquency, shall be punished by a fine of not less than one hundred nor more than ten thousand dollars, or by imprisonment for not more than one year, or both, and shall forfeit his right to hold public office anywhere within the commonwealth for such period, not exceeding five years, as the court determines. Any person filing a fraudulent return of interest deduction under section three, or giving fraudulent information under said section or section four to the commissioner relative to any deduction given by section two, shall be punished as provided in this section. *Approved March 2, 1943.*

An Act relative to recording the treatment of infants at birth. *Chap.* 46

Be it enacted, etc., as follows:

G. L. (Ter. Ed.), 111, § 109A, etc., amended.

Section one hundred and nine A of chapter one hundred and eleven of the General Laws, inserted by chapter one hundred and fifteen of the acts of nineteen hundred and thirty-six, is hereby amended by adding at the end of the first sentence the following: — , and he shall record on the birth certificate the use of such prophylactic, — so as to read as follows: — *Section 109A.* The physician, or hospital medical officer registered under section nine of chapter one hundred and twelve, if any, personally attending the birth of a child shall treat his eyes within two hours after birth with a prophylactic remedy furnished or approved by the department, and he shall record on the birth certificate the use of such prophylactic. Whoever violates this section shall be punished by a fine of not more than one hundred dollars.

Eyes of infants to be treated.

Approved March 2, 1943.

An Act relative to certain lines, poles and other equipment of the Taunton municipal lighting plant of the city of Taunton and of the New England Telephone and Telegraph Company and the American Telephone and Telegraph Company in said city. *Chap.* 47

Be it enacted, etc., as follows:

Section 1. All lines for the transmission of steam and for the transmission of electricity for light, heat or power heretofore acquired or constructed by the municipal lighting plant of the city of Taunton, and all lines for the transmission of intelligence by electricity heretofore acquired or constructed by the New England Telephone and Telegraph Company and the American Telephone and Telegraph Company in said city, upon, along, over or under the public ways and places of said city, and the poles, piers, abutments, conduits and other fixtures necessary to sustain or protect the wires of said lines and actually in place on the effective date of this act, are hereby made lawful notwithstanding the lack of any valid locations therefor or any informality in the proceedings relative to their location and erection; provided, that the validation aforesaid shall not be effective as to the lines, structures or fixtures aforesaid of said municipal lighting plant or of said companies in said city unless said municipal lighting plant or said companies shall, not later than December thirty-first, nineteen hundred and forty-four, file with the clerk of said city a map or maps showing the location and nature of said lines, structures and fixtures in said city, such a map or maps so filed to be recorded and kept with the records of original locations for poles and wires in said city.

Section 2. This act shall take effect upon its passage.

Approved March 3, 1943.

Chap. 48 AN ACT RELATIVE TO CERTAIN LINES, POLES AND OTHER EQUIPMENT OF THE ELECTRIC LIGHT DEPARTMENT OF THE TOWN OF NORWOOD, OF THE NEW ENGLAND TELEPHONE AND TELEGRAPH COMPANY AND THE AMERICAN TELEPHONE AND TELEGRAPH COMPANY IN SAID TOWN.

Be it enacted, etc., as follows:

SECTION 1. All lines for the transmission of electricity for light, heat or power heretofore acquired or constructed by the electric light department of the town of Norwood, and all lines for the transmission of intelligence by electricity heretofore acquired or constructed by the New England Telephone and Telegraph Company and the American Telephone and Telegraph Company in said town, upon, along, over or under the public ways and places of said town, and the poles, piers, abutments, conduits, buried cables and other fixtures necessary to sustain or protect the wires of said lines, and actually in place on the effective date of this act, are hereby made lawful notwithstanding the lack of any valid locations therefor or any informality in the proceedings relative to their location and erection; provided, that the validation aforesaid shall not be effective as to the lines, structures or fixtures aforesaid of such department or companies in said town unless said department or companies shall, not later than December thirty-first, nineteen hundred and forty-three, file with the clerk of said town a map or maps showing the location and nature of the said lines, structures and fixtures in said town; such map or maps so filed to be recorded and kept with the records of original locations for poles and wires in said town.

SECTION 2. This act shall take effect upon its passage.

Approved March 3, 1943.

Chap. 49 AN ACT RELATIVE TO FILLING VACANCIES IN THE OFFICE OF SENATOR IN CONGRESS.

Be it enacted, etc., as follows:

G. L. (Ter. Ed.), 54, § 139, amended.

Section one hundred and thirty-nine of chapter fifty-four of the General Laws, as appearing in the Tercentenary Edition, is hereby amended by striking out, in the fourth line, the word "sixty" and inserting in place thereof the word: — seventy, — so as to read as follows: — *Section 139.* Upon failure to choose a senator in congress or upon a vacancy in said office, the vacancy shall be filled for the unexpired term at the following biennial state election provided said vacancy occurs not less than seventy days prior to the date of the primaries for nominating candidates to be voted for at such election, otherwise at the biennial state election next following. Pending such election the governor shall make a temporary appointment to fill the vacancy, and the person so appointed shall serve until the election and qualification of the person duly elected to fill such vacancy.

Failure to elect, or vacancy; senator in congress.

Approved March 3, 1943.

AN ACT RELATIVE TO THE NOMINATION OF CANDIDATES FOR OFFICES TO BE FILLED AT SPECIAL STATE ELECTIONS. *Chap.* 50

Be it enacted, etc., as follows:

Section six of chapter fifty-three of the General Laws, as most recently amended by chapter two hundred and sixty-six of the acts of nineteen hundred and forty-one, is hereby further amended by striking out, in the second line, the word "biennial", — so as to read as follows: — *Section 6.* Nominations of candidates for any offices to be filled at a state election may be made by nomination papers, stating the facts required by section eight and signed in the aggregate by not less than such number of voters as will equal three per cent of the entire vote cast for governor at the preceding biennial state election in the commonwealth at large or in the electoral district or division for which the officers are to be elected. Nominations of candidates for offices to be filled at a city or town election, except where city charters or general or special laws provide otherwise, may be made by like nomination papers, signed in the aggregate by not less than such number of voters as will equal one per cent of the entire vote cast for governor at the preceding biennial state election in the electoral district or division for which the officers are to be elected, but in no event by less than twenty voters in the case of an office to be filled at a town election. At a first election to be held in a newly established ward, the number of voters upon a nomination paper of a candidate who is to be voted for only in such ward need not exceed fifty; and at a first election in a town the number for the nomination of a candidate who is to be voted for only in such town need not exceed twenty. *Approved March 3, 1943.*

G. L. (Ter. Ed.), 53, § 6, etc., amended.

Number of signatures on nomination papers.

AN ACT RELATIVE TO OBJECTIONS TO INITIATIVE AND REFERENDUM PETITIONS. *Chap.* 51

Be it enacted, etc., as follows:

Section twenty-two A of chapter fifty-three of the General Laws, as most recently amended by chapter one hundred and ninety-two of the acts of nineteen hundred and thirty-eight, is hereby further amended by striking out the last sentence and inserting in place thereof the following sentence: — The state secretary shall refer the same to the state ballot law commission, which shall investigate the same, and for such purpose may exercise all the powers conferred upon it relative to objections to nominations for state offices, and if it shall appear to said commission that the objections have been sustained it shall forthwith reject the petition as not in conformity with the constitution and shall notify the state secretary of its action, — so as to read as follows: — *Section 22A.* The provisions of law relative to the signing of nomination papers of candidates

G. L. (Ter. Ed.), 53, § 22A, etc., amended.

Objections to signatures to

initiative, etc., petitions.

for state office, and to the identification and certification of names thereon and submission to the registrars therefor, shall apply, so far as apt, to the signing of initiative and referendum petitions and to the identification and certification of names thereon, and, except as otherwise provided, to the time of their submission to the registrars. Registrars shall receipt in writing for each initiative or referendum petition submitted to and received by them, and shall deliver such petitions only on receiving written receipts therefor. Objections that signatures appearing on an initiative or referendum petition have been forged or placed thereon by fraud and that in consequence thereof the petition has not been signed by a sufficient number of qualified voters actually supporting such petition, as required by the constitution, may be filed with the state secretary not later than the sixtieth day prior to the election at which the measure therein proposed or the law which is the subject of the petition is to be submitted to the voters, except that, if a referendum petition is lawfully filed after the sixty-third day prior to said election, such objections may be filed not later than seventy-two week day hours succeeding five o'clock of the day on which such petition is so filed. The state secretary shall refer the same to the state ballot law commission, which shall investigate the same, and for such purpose may exercise all the powers conferred upon it relative to objections to nominations for state offices, and if it shall appear to said commission that the objections have been sustained it shall forthwith reject the petition as not in conformity with the constitution and shall notify the state secretary of its action.

Approved March 3, 1943.

Chap. 52 AN ACT RELATIVE TO CONDITIONAL SALES OF SEATS FOR THEATRES, HALLS, PARKS AND PLACES OF PUBLIC ASSEMBLY.

Be it enacted, etc., as follows:

G. L. (Ter. Ed.), 184, § 13, etc., amended.

SECTION 1. Section thirteen of chapter one hundred and eighty-four of the General Laws, as most recently amended by section one of chapter two hundred and forty-five of the acts of nineteen hundred and thirty-seven, is hereby further amended by inserting after the word "machinery" in the fourth and fifth lines the words: — , seats for theatres, halls, parks and places of public assembly, — so that the first paragraph will read as follows: —

Conditional sales of fixtures, etc., notice, contents, recording.

No conditional sale of heating apparatus, plumbing goods, ranges, buildings of wood or metal construction of the class commonly known as portable or sectional buildings, elevator apparatus or machinery, seats for theatres, halls, parks and places of public assembly, or other articles of personal property, which are afterward wrought into or attached to real estate, whether they are fixtures at common law or not, shall be valid as against any mortgagee, purchaser or grantee of such real estate, unless not later than ten days after the delivery thereon of such personal property a notice such as is herein prescribed is recorded in the registry of deeds for the county or district where the real estate lies. The notice shall be signed by the vendor or a person claiming under him and shall contain the names of the contracting parties, the name of the record owner of the real estate at the time of recording the notice, the fact that it is agreed that title to such personal property shall remain in the vendor until the purchase price is paid, the terms of payment, including the date on which the final payment will become due, and the amount of such purchase price remaining unpaid, and descriptions, sufficiently accurate for identification, of such real estate and the personal property delivered or to be delivered thereon. If the sale is of several articles for a lump sum greater than the value of the personal property delivered or to be delivered on the real estate, the notice shall also state such lump sum and such value.

SECTION 2. This act shall apply only in case of conditional sales made after June first in the current year. **Effective date.**

Approved March 3, 1943.

AN ACT RELATIVE TO THE PRINTING ON THE BALLOT AT STATE PRIMARIES OF THE NAMES OF CANDIDATES FOR NOMINATION FOR CERTAIN OFFICES BY A POLITICAL PARTY. *Chap.* 53

Be it enacted, etc., as follows:

Section forty-eight of chapter fifty-three of the General Laws, as most recently amended by chapter six hundred and seventy-five of the acts of nineteen hundred and forty-one, is hereby further amended by striking out the words "where such person resides", wherever such words appear therein, and inserting in place thereof, in each instance, the words: — wherein such person is a registered voter, — so as to read as follows: — *Section 48.* All nomination papers of candidates to be voted for at state primaries shall be filed with the state secretary on or before the seventh Tuesday preceding the day of the primaries; except in the case of primaries before special elections, when nomination papers shall be filed on or before the second Tuesday preceding the day of the primaries. **G. L. (Ter. Ed.), 53, § 48, etc., amended.** **Last day for filing nomination papers.**

There shall not be printed on the ballot at a state primary the name of any person as a candidate for nomination for any office to be filled by all the voters of the commonwealth, or for councillor or representative in congress, unless a certificate from the registrars of voters of the city or town wherein such person is a registered voter that he is enrolled as a member of the political party whose nomination he seeks is filed with the state secretary on or before the last day herein provided for filing nomination papers. Said registrars shall issue such a certificate forthwith upon request of any such candidate so enrolled or of his authorized representative. **Nomination papers for state wide offices.**

Nomination papers for county commissioners and members of general court.

There shall not be printed on the ballot at a state primary the name of any person as a candidate for nomination for the office of county commissioner or senator or representative to the general court unless a certificate from the registrars of voters of the city or town wherein such person is a registered voter stating that he is enrolled as a member of a political party, giving the name of the party, or stating that he is not enrolled in any political party, as the case may be, is filed with the state secretary on or before the last day herein provided for the filing of nomination papers. Said registrars shall forthwith issue such a certificate upon request of any such candidate or of his authorized representative. Against the name of any such candidate on the ballot shall be printed the name of the party of which he is an enrolled member or, if he is not enrolled in any party, the word "unenrolled". *Approved March 3, 1943.*

Chap. 54 AN ACT PROVIDING FOR THE COLLECTION BY THE COMMISSIONER OF INSURANCE OF CHARGES AND FEES FOR THE VALUATION OF CERTAIN ANNUITY CONTRACTS AND FOR CERTAIN CERTIFICATES OF VALUATION.

Be it enacted, etc., as follows:

G. L. (Ter. Ed.), 175, § 14, etc., amended.

SECTION 1. Section fourteen of chapter one hundred and seventy-five of the General Laws, as most recently amended by chapter six hundred and ninety-three of the acts of nineteen hundred and forty-one, is hereby further amended by inserting after the paragraph contained in the fourteenth line the following paragraph: —

Collection of charges, etc.

For the valuation of each outstanding annuity contract of a domestic company, four cents;

G. L. (Ter. Ed.), 175, § 14, etc., further amended.

SECTION 2. Said section fourteen of said chapter one hundred and seventy-five, as so amended, is hereby further amended by striking out the paragraph contained in the sixty-third to the sixty-fifth lines, inclusive, and inserting in place thereof the following paragraph: —

Collection of charges, etc.

For each certificate of the valuation of life policies or annuity contracts, or both, of any company and for each certificate of the examination, condition or qualification of a company, two dollars; *Approved March 3, 1943.*

Chap. 55 AN ACT AMENDING THE LAW RELATIVE TO CERTAIN PURCHASES OF PROPERTY IN LIMITED AMOUNTS BY ELECTRIC COMPANIES.

Be it enacted, etc., as follows:

G. L. (Ter. Ed.), 164, § 97, amended.

Section ninety-seven of chapter one hundred and sixty-four of the General Laws, as appearing in the Tercentenary Edition, is hereby amended by striking out, in the first and second lines and in the ninth and tenth lines, the words "the four following sections" and inserting in place thereof, in each instance, the words: — sections ninety-eight to one hundred and one, inclusive, — and by inserting after the word "sale" in the sixteenth line the words: — of any property exceeding thirty-five thousand dollars in value, — so as to read as follows: — *Section 97.* An electric company may, subject to sections ninety-eight to one hundred and one, inclusive, from time to time purchase or acquire any or all of the property of any domestic or foreign corporation or association owning or operating a water storage reservoir or hydro-electric plant with which the lines of the said first mentioned electric company are actually connected, or owning and operating lines for the transmission of electricity within or without the commonwealth with which the lines of said first named electric company are actually connected; and any such domestic or foreign corporation or association may, subject to sections ninety-eight to one hundred and one, inclusive, the charter thereof and the laws of the state under which such corporation or association, if a foreign corporation or association, is organized, so far as applicable, sell any or all of its property to said first mentioned electric company, or consolidate or merge with said first mentioned electric company, or merge and consolidate its capital stock and property with said first mentioned electric company; but no such purchase and sale of any property exceeding thirty-five thousand dollars in value or merger and consolidation shall be valid or binding until the same and the terms thereof shall have been approved, at meetings called therefor, by vote of at least two thirds in interest of the stockholders of each of the contracting parties, and until the department, after notice and a public hearing, shall have approved the same and the terms thereof as consistent with the public interest; provided, that such electric company shall not exercise in this commonwealth any powers, rights, locations, licenses or privileges or any franchise so acquired which cannot be lawfully exercised by electric companies under this chapter. *Approved March 3, 1943.*

Consolidation of electric and hydro-electric companies.

Chap. 56

An Act further providing for the prevention of Bang's disease.

Be it enacted, etc., as follows:

G. L. (Ter. Ed.), 129, § 36B, etc., amended.

Chapter one hundred and twenty-nine of the General Laws is hereby amended by striking out section thirty-six B, inserted by chapter three hundred and fourteen of the acts of nineteen hundred and thirty-eight, and inserting in place thereof the following section: — *Section 36B.* For the purpose of preventing Bang's disease, the director or his agent may vaccinate cattle with the approval of the owner thereof. Said director may, with the approval of the governor and council, make such rules and regulations as may be necessary to carry out the purposes of this section.

Prevention of Bang's disease.

Approved March 3, 1943.

Chap. 57 AN ACT CONCERNING THE JUDICIAL DETERMINATION OF RIGHTS TO FORECLOSE MORTGAGES IN WHICH SOLDIERS AND SAILORS MAY BE INTERESTED BY ENTRY AND POSSESSION, BY EXERCISE OF POWERS OF SALE, OR OTHERWISE AS PROVIDED BY LAW, OR TO MAKE ANY SEIZURE OF PROPERTY THEREUNDER.

Emergency preamble.

Whereas, An act of congress, known as the soldiers' and sailors' civil relief act of nineteen hundred and forty, was amended in nineteen hundred and forty-two and affects the rights and relations existing between mortgagees and mortgagors and others interested in property subject to mortgage who are in the military service of the United States and its allies; and

Whereas, This act is enacted to adjust to the aforesaid act of congress, as amended in nineteen hundred and forty-two, the procedure provided by chapter twenty-five of the acts of nineteen hundred and forty-one to meet the requirements of the soldiers' and sailors' civil relief act of nineteen hundred and forty, as amended, for the protection of persons in the military service; and

Whereas, The adjusted procedure aforesaid should immediately be available for such mortgagees, mortgagors and others so that all future foreclosures of mortgages in which they are interested may be conducted in accordance with the soldiers' and sailors' civil relief acts above referred to, therefore this act is hereby declared to be an emergency law, necessary for the immediate preservation of the public convenience.

Be it enacted, etc., as follows:

SECTION 1. In any proceeding in equity for authority to foreclose a mortgage, which for the purposes of this act shall be construed to include a trust deed, or other security in the nature of a mortgage, covering real or personal property, or both, by entry and possession, by exercise of a power of sale contained therein, or otherwise as provided by law, or to make any seizure of property thereunder, brought because of an Act of Congress known as the Soldiers' and Sailors' Civil Relief Act of 1940, as amended, or any amendments thereto hereafter enacted, notice may be issued in substantially the following form by the court in which such proceeding is pending, returnable on any convenient date, irrespective of the return days otherwise prescribed by law or rule, and requiring all appearances and answers to be filed on or before the return day: —

Commonwealth of Massachusetts

....Court

.................................., ss. In Equity

To (insert the names of all defendants named in the bill) *and to all whom it may concern:*

.... claiming to be the holder of a mortgage — trust deed — security in the nature of a mortgage (strike out the descriptive words which are inapplicable) covering ....property (insert nature of property, whether real or personal) situated in (insert location of property, including name of city or town and, if stated in the mortgage or in the bill, the street and number) given by (insert names of parties, date and reference to record), has filed with said court a bill in equity for authority to foreclose said mortgage — trust deed — security in the nature of a mortgage — in the manner following: (insert contemplated method of foreclosure, whether by entry and possession, exercise of a power of sale, or otherwise) — to seize certain real — personal — property (strike out descriptive word which is inapplicable) covered by said mortgage — trust deed — security in the nature of a mortgage.

If you are entitled to the benefits of the Soldiers' and Sailors' Civil Relief Act of 1940 as amended, and you object to such foreclosure or seizure, you or your attorney should file a written appearance and answer in said court at.................. on or before....................(Return Day), or you may be forever barred from claiming that such foreclosure or seizure is invalid under said act.

Witness..............................Esquire, Judge of said Court, this..............................day of.....................19.....

The publication of a copy of said notice once not less than twenty-one days before the return day in a newspaper designated by the court, and the mailing of a copy thereof by registered mail not less than fourteen days before the return day to each defendant named in the bill, shall be sufficient service of said notice, unless the court otherwise orders, provided however that prior to the return day fixed in said notice a copy thereof shall be recorded in each registry of deeds and city or town clerk's office in which such mortgage is recorded.

Section 2. An entry and possession taken for the purpose of foreclosure, or a foreclosure effected by exercise of a power of sale or by any other method, or a seizure of property, done pursuant to authority granted in such proceedings, may be approved by the court but not until after the expiration of the period for appeal from the order authorizing the same. There shall be no appeal from or review of such approval.

The period of thirty days within which a copy of the notice

of sale and an affidavit are required to be recorded by section fifteen of chapter two hundred and forty-four of the General Laws, and the period of thirty days within which the memorandum or certificate of entry is required to be recorded by section two of said chapter two hundred and forty-four shall, in case such a proceeding has been had, be computed from the time the court approves the sale, or entry, rather than from the time of the sale, or entry, as provided in said sections.

A copy of the order authorizing foreclosure by entry, or by sale, or otherwise as provided by law, or a copy of the order authorizing the seizure of property, and the approval thereof, may be recorded in the registry of deeds and city or town clerk's office in which such mortgage is recorded, and if so recorded shall be conclusive evidence of compliance with the provisions of said Soldiers' and Sailors' Civil Relief Act of 1940, and any amendments thereto, in so far as the court has power to determine the same, as against all persons, except that such copy shall not be conclusive evidence of such compliance against persons whose interests appeared of record prior to the recording of the notice of said proceeding unless they were named as defendants or had notice of said proceeding.

SECTION 3. In proceedings under section one hereof where a mortgage includes land, the land court shall have jurisdiction as to said mortgage even though it may include personal property and shall have jurisdiction as to any additional or supplementary mortgage securing the same obligation although such mortgages include personal property.

SECTION 4. Chapter twenty-five of the acts of nineteen hundred and forty-one is hereby repealed, but the repeal thereof shall not be construed to affect any proceedings which shall have been brought heretofore under said chapter twenty-five. *Approved March 4, 1943.*

Chap. 58 AN ACT AUTHORIZING COUNTIES, CITIES, TOWNS AND DISTRICTS TO CO-OPERATE WITH THE FEDERAL GOVERNMENT IN RELATION TO DEFENSE PUBLIC WORKS.

Emergency preamble.

Whereas, In the existing state of war between the United States and certain foreign countries it is imperative that the political subdivisions of the commonwealth be authorized immediately to co-operate with the federal government in the national defense and the deferred operation of this act would in part tend to defeat its purpose, which is to grant such authority to such political subdivisions, therefore it is hereby declared to be an emergency law, necessary for the immediate preservation of the public safety and convenience.

Be it enacted, etc., as follows:

Section nine of chapter four hundred and four of the acts of nineteen hundred and thirty-five, added by chapter four hundred and fourteen of the acts of nineteen hundred and thirty-six, and as most recently amended by section one of chapter six hundred and thirty-nine of the acts of nineteen hundred and forty-one, is hereby further amended by striking out all after the word "forty-one" in the eleventh line and inserting in place thereof the following: — , nineteen hundred and forty-two, nineteen hundred and forty-three, nineteen hundred and forty-four, and nineteen hundred and forty-five, authorizing grants or loans of federal money for public works projects or defense public works, — so as to read as follows: — *Section 9.* Wherever, in Part I of chapter three hundred and sixty-six of the acts of nineteen hundred and thirty-three, and acts in amendment thereof and in addition thereto, reference is made to the National Industrial Recovery Act or any title or part thereof, or to the Emergency Relief Appropriation Act of 1935, such reference shall be deemed and held to refer also to all acts and joint resolutions of Congress enacted during nineteen hundred and thirty-six, nineteen hundred and thirty-seven, nineteen hundred and thirty-eight, nineteen hundred and thirty-nine, nineteen hundred and forty, nineteen hundred and forty-one, nineteen hundred and forty-two, nineteen hundred and forty-three, nineteen hundred and forty-four, and nineteen hundred and forty-five, authorizing grants or loans of federal money for public works projects or defense public works. *Approved March 4, 1943.*

AN ACT AUTHORIZING THE CITY OF HAVERHILL TO INVEST CERTAIN FUNDS IN BONDS ISSUED BY THE FEDERAL GOVERNMENT. *Chap.* 59

Be it enacted, etc., as follows:

The city of Haverhill is hereby authorized to invest in bonds of the United States government the sum of fourteen thousand dollars, being the unexpended balance in its treasury of a loan obtained by said city under authority of clause five of section eight of chapter forty-four of the General Laws; provided, that as soon as it shall be possible for the city to obtain the necessary materials to carry on the purposes for which the loan was obtained, following the termination of the existing state of war with any foreign country, said city shall dispose of such bonds and use the proceeds thereof, together with any income received from the bonds, for the purposes specified by the vote authorizing the loan. Bonds purchased under this act shall be in the custody of the city treasurer, and in case any bond so purchased matures or is called, the proceeds may be reinvested by the treasurer, with the approval of the mayor, in other bonds the purchase of which is authorized by this act.

Approved March 4, 1943.

Chap. 60 AN ACT RELATIVE TO THE RENEWAL OF CERTAIN TEMPORARY REVENUE LOANS BY CITIES, TOWNS AND DISTRICTS.

Be it enacted, etc., as follows:

Chapter twelve of the acts of nineteen hundred and thirty-five, as most recently amended by chapter one hundred and thirty-four of the acts of nineteen hundred and forty-one, is hereby further amended by striking out, in the seventh, eighth and ninth lines, the words "nineteen hundred and forty, nineteen hundred and forty-one or nineteen hundred and forty-two" and inserting in place thereof the words: — nineteen hundred and forty-two, nineteen hundred and forty-three or nineteen hundred and forty-four, — so as to read as follows: — Any city, town or district, with the approval of the board specified in clause nine of section eight of chapter forty-four of the General Laws, may extend, for a period or periods not exceeding in the aggregate six months beyond the maximum term provided by law for an original revenue loan, any loan issued in anticipation of the revenue of the year nineteen hundred and forty-two, nineteen hundred and forty-three or nineteen hundred and forty-four, and the approval as aforesaid of any such extension shall authorize the issue of renewal notes for the period or periods so approved, notwithstanding the provisions of said chapter forty-four. During the time that any such revenue loan, extended as aforesaid, remains outstanding, none of the receipts from the collection of taxes assessed by such city, town or district for the year against the revenue of which such loan was issued or for prior years shall be appropriated for any purpose without the approval of the board.

Approved March 4, 1943.

Chap. 61 AN ACT RELATIVE TO BORROWING AND EXPENDITURES BY DISTRICTS PRIOR TO THE ANNUAL APPROPRIATIONS.

Be it enacted, etc., as follows:

G. L. (Ter. Ed.), 44, new § 5B, added.

Districts may borrow in anticipation of revenue.

SECTION 1. Chapter forty-four of the General Laws is hereby amended by inserting after section five A, as amended, the following section: — *Section 5B.* To provide the necessary funds to meet liabilities authorized by section thirteen A, the district treasurer, with the approval of a majority of the prudential committee or commissioners, as the case may be, may borrow on notes of the district, during any one month between the end of the fiscal year and the time of making the next annual appropriations, a sum not exceeding one twelfth of the aggregate amount that might have been borrowed during the preceding fiscal year in anticipation of revenue. The amount so borrowed shall be deemed a part of the amount which may be borrowed under section four. Said notes shall be subject to certification in accordance with law by the director, and shall not be renewed or paid by the issue of new notes except as provided in section seventeen.

SECTION 2. Said chapter forty-four is hereby further amended by inserting after section thirteen, as appearing in the Tercentenary Edition, the following section: — *Section 13A.* In districts, during the interval between the end of the fiscal year and the time of making the next annual appropriations, district officers authorized to make expenditures may incur liabilities in carrying on the several departments intrusted to them, and payments therefor shall be made from the district treasury from any available funds therein, and the same shall be charged against the next annual appropriation; provided, that the liabilities incurred during said interval do not exceed in any month the sums spent for similar purposes during any one month of the preceding fiscal year; but all interest and debt falling due in the said interval shall be paid. *Approved March 4, 1943.*

G. L. (Ter. Ed.), 44, new § 13A, added.

Districts may incur liabilities, when.

AN ACT TO AMEND AND CLARIFY THE LAW RELATIVE TO BUDGETS IN CITIES.

Chap. 62

Be it enacted, etc., as follows:

Chapter forty-four of the General Laws is hereby amended by striking out section thirty-three A, as appearing in the Tercentenary Edition, and inserting in place thereof the two following sections: — *Section 33A.* The annual budget shall include sums sufficient to pay the salaries of officers and employees fixed by law or by ordinance, but no new position shall be created or increase in rate made by ordinance, vote or appointment during the financial year subsequent to the submission of the annual budget unless provision therefor has been made by means of a supplemental appropriation.

G. L. (Ter. Ed.), 44, § 33A, stricken out, and new §§ 33A and 33B, inserted.

Budget to include provision for salaries, etc.

Section 33B. On recommendation of the mayor, the city council may, by majority vote, transfer any amount appropriated in the then current year for the use of any department to another appropriation for the same department, but no transfer shall be made of any amount appropriated in the then current year for the use of any department to the appropriation for any other department except by a two thirds vote of the city council on recommendation of the mayor and with the written approval of the amount of such transfer by the department having control of the appropriation from which the transfer is proposed to be made.

Transfer from one appropriation to another.

Approved March 5, 1943.

Chap. 63 AN ACT RELATIVE TO APPROPRIATIONS FOR SCHOOL PURPOSES IN THE CITY OF LYNN DURING THE EXISTENCE OF THE PRESENT NATIONAL EMERGENCY AND FOR A CERTAIN PERIOD THEREAFTER.

Be it enacted, etc., as follows:

SECTION 1. Notwithstanding any provisions to the contrary contained in section one of chapter one hundred and seventy-eight of the acts of nineteen hundred and nine, as amended, the school committee of the city of Lynn, subject otherwise to the provisions of said section one, may increase appropriations for the purposes therein referred to for any financial year, including the current year, to an amount not exceeding the sum of one million, seven hundred thousand dollars instead of the maximum amount stated in said section.

SECTION 2. This act shall take effect upon its passage and shall be in full force and effect only during the continuance of the existing state of war between the United States and any foreign country and one year after the termination of such states of war. *Approved March 8, 1943.*

Chap. 64 AN ACT RELATIVE TO THE USE OF CERTAIN INFORMATION IN THE FILES OF THE BOARD OF PROBATION.

Be it enacted, etc., as follows:

G. L. (Ter. Ed.), 276, § 100, amended.

Section one hundred of chapter two hundred and seventy-six of the General Laws, as appearing in the Tercentenary Edition, is hereby amended by striking out the sentence contained in the eighteenth to the twentieth lines, inclusive, and inserting in place thereof the following sentence: — The information so obtained and recorded shall not be regarded as public records and shall not be open for public inspection but shall be accessible to the justices and probation officers of the courts, to the police commissioner for the city of Boston, to all chiefs of police and city marshals, and to such departments of the federal, state and local governments and such educational and charitable corporations and institutions as the board may from time to time determine, — so as to read as follows: — *Section 100.* Every probation officer, or the chief or senior probation officer of a court having more than one probation officer, shall transmit to the board of probation, in such form and at such times as it shall require, detailed reports regarding the work of probation in the court, and trial justices shall transmit to the board reports of cases coming before them in such form and at such times as the board may require, and the commissioner of correction, the penal institutions commissioner of Boston and the county commissioners of counties other than Suffolk shall transmit to the board, as aforesaid, detailed and complete records relative to all paroles and permits to be at

Detailed reports regarding probation work, etc.

Record.

Accessibility of information.

liberty granted or issued by them, respectively, to the revoking of the same and to the length of time served on each sentence to imprisonment by each prisoner so released specifying the institution where each such sentence was served; and under the direction of the board a record shall be kept of all such cases as the board may require for the information of the justices and probation officers. Police officials shall co-operate with the board and the probation officers in obtaining and reporting information concerning persons on probation. The information so obtained and recorded shall not be regarded as public records and shall not be open for public inspection but shall be accessible to the justices and probation officers of the courts, to the police commissioner for the city of Boston, to all chiefs of police and city marshals, and to such departments of the federal, state and local governments and such educational and charitable corporations and institutions as the board may from time to time determine. The commissioner of correction and the department of public welfare shall at all times give to the board and the probation officers such information as may be obtained from the records concerning prisoners under sentence or who have been released.

Approved March 8, 1943.

AN ACT FURTHER REGULATING THE METHOD OF PAYMENT OF COMPENSATION OR SALARIES OF CERTAIN COUNTY OFFICERS. *Chap. 65*

Be it enacted, etc., as follows:

Section eleven of chapter thirty-five of the General Laws, as appearing in the Tercentenary Edition, is hereby amended by inserting after the word "of", the first time said word appears in the third line, the word: — elected, — and by striking out, in said third line, the words "established by law", — so as to read as follows: — *Section 11.* No payments, except payments of expenses in criminal prosecutions, of expenses of the courts, of the compensation or salaries of elected county officers, of outstanding notes or bonds and of interest thereon, shall be made by a treasurer except upon orders drawn and signed by a majority of the county commissioners, certified by their clerk and accompanied, except in Suffolk county, by the original bills, vouchers or evidences of county indebtedness for which payment is ordered, stating in detail the items and confirming the account. Said clerk shall not certify such orders until he has recorded them in the records of the commissioners.

G. L. (Ter. Ed.), 35, § 11, amended.

Not to pay out certain money without order from commissioners.

Approved March 8, 1943.

Chap. 66 AN ACT AUTHORIZING THE CITY OF LYNN TO SELL CERTAIN UNUSED PLAYGROUND LAND.

Be it enacted, etc., as follows:

SECTION 1. The city of Lynn, by its proper authorities, may improve, lay out and sell any part or parts or the whole of the unused portion of Magnolia Avenue playground, so called, in said city; provided, that the board of park commissioners of said city shall, by vote at a regular meeting of said board, assent to such sale. Said unused portion lies on the southerly side of Broadway and is bounded westerly by Broadway two hundred and ninety-nine and twenty-nine one-hundredths feet; northerly by other land of the city of Lynn one hundred and one and thirty-two one-hundredths feet; easterly by other land of said city three hundred and ten and seventy-five one-hundredths feet; northeasterly by other land of said city forty-three and sixty-five one-hundredths feet; southeasterly by land of W. A. Keith forty-nine and seventy-five one-hundredths feet; southwesterly by land of J. H. Samuels eighty-three and twenty-five one-hundredths feet; westerly by land of E. H. Harnois thirty-seven and thirty-four one-hundredths feet; and southerly by land of said E. H. Harnois forty feet.

Said above-described parcel contains thirty-three thousand, eight hundred and sixty-five square feet of land, more or less.

SECTION 2. This act shall take full effect upon its acceptance during the current year by vote of the city council of said city, subject to the provisions of its charter.

Approved March 8, 1943.

Chap. 67 AN ACT AUTHORIZING THE CITY OF LYNN TO SELL A CERTAIN PORTION OF SLUICE POND, SO CALLED, IN SAID CITY.

Be it enacted, etc., as follows:

SECTION 1. The city of Lynn, by its proper authorities, may sell, transfer and convey to Edith M. Harnois six hundred and forty-four square feet, more or less, of land, comprising a portion of Sluice pond, so called, in said city, heretofore acquired by said city for park purposes by a taking by its city council. Said land is bounded northerly by the shores of Sluice pond and land of Edith M. Harnois a distance of eighty-four feet; easterly by Sluice pond a distance of thirty-seven feet; and southerly by Sluice pond a distance of sixty-five and twenty-seven one-hundredths feet.

SECTION 2. This act shall take full effect upon its acceptance during the current year by vote of the city council of said city, subject to the provisions of its charter.

Approved March 8, 1943.

AN ACT MAKING APPROPRIATIONS FOR THE MAINTENANCE OF DEPARTMENTS, BOARDS, COMMISSIONS, INSTITUTIONS AND CERTAIN ACTIVITIES OF THE COMMONWEALTH, FOR INTEREST, SINKING FUND AND SERIAL BOND REQUIREMENTS, AND FOR CERTAIN PERMANENT IMPROVEMENTS. *Chap.* 68

Be it enacted, etc., as follows:

SECTION 1. To provide for the maintenance of the several departments, boards, commissions and institutions, of sundry other services, and for certain permanent improvements, and to meet certain requirements of law, the sums set forth in section two, for the several purposes and subject to the conditions specified in said section two, are hereby appropriated from the general fund or revenue of the commonwealth, subject to the provisions of law regulating the disbursement of public funds and the approval thereof, for the period beginning December first, nineteen hundred and forty-two, and ending June thirtieth, nineteen hundred and forty-three, or for such other period as may be specified, this act being enacted in advance of final action on the general appropriation bill for the next fiscal biennium, pursuant to a message of the governor dated January eleventh of the current year.

SECTION 2.

Item	*Service of the Legislative Department.*	
0101-01	For the compensation of senators	$102,500 00
0101-02	For the compensation for travel of senators .	5,817 00
0101-03	For the compensation of representatives .	602,500 00
0101-04	For the compensation for travel of representatives	36,708 00
0101-05	For the salaries of the clerk of the senate and the clerk of the house of representatives . .	7,000 00
0101-06	For the salaries of the assistant clerk of the senate and the assistant clerk of the house of representatives	4,958 34
0101-07	For such additional clerical assistance to, and with the approval of, the clerk of the senate, as may be necessary for the proper despatch of public business, including not more than one permanent position	1,633 34
0101-08	For such additional clerical assistance to, and with the approval of, the clerk of the house of representatives, as may be necessary for the proper despatch of public business, including not more than three permanent positions .	4,725 00
0101-09	For the salary of the sergeant-at-arms . .	2,333 40
0101-10	For clerical and other assistance employed by the sergeant-at-arms, including not more than four permanent positions . . .	3,879 20
0101-11	For the compensation for travel of doorkeepers, assistant doorkeepers, general court officers, pages and other employees of the sergeant-at-arms, authorized by law to receive the same	5,000 00
0101-12	For the salaries of the doorkeepers of the senate and house of representatives, with the approval of the sergeant-at-arms, including not more than two permanent positions .	3,208 40

Item		
0101-13	For the salaries of assistant doorkeepers to the senate and house of representatives and of general court officers, with the approval of the sergeant-at-arms, including not more than twenty permanent positions	$28,351 40
0101-14	For compensation of the pages of the senate and house of representatives, with the approval of the sergeant-at-arms, including not more than twenty permanent positions	9,800 00
0101-15	For the salaries of clerks employed in the legislative document room, including not more than two permanent positions	3,937 60
0101-17	For the salaries of the chaplains of the senate and house of representatives, including not more than two permanent positions	1,500 00
0101-18	For personal services of the counsel to the senate and assistants, including not more than four permanent positions	12,980 00
0101-19	For personal services of the counsel to the house of representatives and assistants, including not more than seven permanent positions	19,580 00
0101-20	For clerical and other assistance of the senate committee on rules, including not more than one permanent position	3,112 50
0101-21	For clerical and other assistance of the house committee on rules, including not more than one permanent position	3,395 00
0102-01	For traveling and such other expenses of the committees of the present general court as may be authorized by order of either branch of the general court	4,000 00
0102-02	For printing, binding and paper ordered by the senate and house of representatives, or by concurrent order of the two branches, with the approval of the clerks of the respective branches	75,000 00
0102-03	For printing the manual of the general court, with the approval of the clerks of the two branches	5,100 00
0102-04	For expenses in connection with the publication of the bulletin of committee hearings and of the daily list, with the approval of the joint committee on rules, including not more than one permanent position	17,487 50
0102-05	For stationery for the senate, purchased by and with the approval of the clerk	400 00
0102-06	For office and other expenses of the committee on rules on the part of the senate	100 00
0102-07	For office expenses of the counsel to the senate	150 00
0102-08	For stationery for the house of representatives, purchased by and with the approval of the clerk	800 00
0102-09	For office and other expenses of the committee on rules on the part of the house	175 00
0102-10	For office expenses, including travel, of the counsel to the house of representatives	175 00
0102-11	For contingent expenses of the senate and house of representatives, and necessary expenses in and about the state house, with the approval of the sergeant-at-arms	7,000 00
0102-12	For telephone service	4,500 00
0102-13	For the purchase of outline sketches of members of the senate and house of representatives	1,850 00

Item		
0102-16	For the consolidation and arrangement of certain laws, including work, under the direction of the senate and house counsel, with the approval of the president of the senate and the speaker of the house of representatives, upon certain indexes and relating to recess committee investigations	$500 00
	For expenses in connection with the proceedings for the acceptance by the commonwealth of the gift of murals for the chamber of the house of representatives (under chapter fifty-one of the resolves of nineteen hundred and forty-one), the sum of three hundred eleven dollars and ninety cents, to be paid out of the unexpended balance of the appropriation made by item 0102-21 of chapter six hundred and eighty-three of the acts of nineteen hundred and forty-one.	
	Total	$980,156 68

Service of Legislative Investigations.

0227	For an investigation of the laws relating to primaries and elections, for the publication of certain reports, and related matters, as authorized by chapter seventy-four of the resolves of nineteen hundred and forty-one and by a joint order of the present general court, to be in addition to any amount heretofore appropriated for the purpose	$1,000 00

Service of the Judicial Department.

	Supreme Judicial Court, as follows:	
0301-01	For the salaries of the chief justice and of the six associate justices	$57,750 14
0301-02	For traveling allowances and expenses	220 63
0301-03	For the salary of the clerk for the commonwealth	3,791 69
0301-04	For clerical assistance to the clerk	916 65
0301-05	For law clerks, stenographers and other clerical assistance for the justices	13,728 52
0301-06	For office supplies, services and equipment	2,255 25
0301-07	For the salaries of the officers and messengers	1,816 13
0301-08	For the commonwealth's part of the salary of the clerk for the county of Suffolk	875 00
	Total	$81,354 01
	Reporter of Decisions:	
0301-11	For the salary of the reporter of decisions	$3,500 00
0301-12	For clerk hire and office supplies, services and equipment, including not more than four permanent positions	6,900 73
	Total	$10,400 73
	Superior Court, as follows:	
0302-01	For the salaries of the chief justice and of the thirty-one associate justices	$223,154 75
0302-02	For traveling allowances and expenses	5,024 22

Item		
0302-03	For the salary of the assistant clerk, Suffolk county	$583 31
0302-04	For clerical work, inspection of records and doings of persons authorized to admit to bail, for an executive clerk to the chief justice, and for certain other expenses incident to the work of the court	7,626 38
	Total	$236,388 66
	Justices of District Courts:	
0302-11	For compensation of justices of district courts while sitting in the superior court . .	$9,464 00
0302-12	For expenses of justices of district courts while sitting in the superior court . . .	849 95
0302-13	For reimbursing certain counties for compensation of certain special justices for services in holding sessions of district courts in place of the justice, while sitting in the superior court	831 93
	Total	$11,145 88
	Judicial Council:	
0303-01	For expenses of the judicial council, as authorized by section thirty-four C of chapter two hundred and twenty-one of the General Laws	$1,038 53
0303-02	For compensation of the secretary of the judicial council, as authorized by said section thirty-four C	2,041 69
	Total	$3,080 22
	Administrative Committee of the District Courts:	
0304-01	For compensation and expenses of the administrative committee of district courts . .	$1,622 80
	Probate and Insolvency Courts, as follows:	
0305-01	For the salaries of judges of probate of the several counties, including not more than twenty permanent positions	$92,458 17
0305-02	For the compensation of judges of probate when acting for other judges of probate .	5,855 00
0305-03	For expenses of judges of probate when acting for other judges of probate . . .	5 52
0305-04	For the salaries of registers of the several counties, including not more than fourteen permanent positions	36,925 00
0305-05	For the salaries of assistant registers, including not more than twenty-two permanent positions	45,860 00
0305-06	For reimbursing officials for premiums paid for procuring sureties on their bonds, as provided by law	155 00
	Total	$181,258 69
	For clerical assistance to Registers of the several counties, as follows:	
0306-01	Barnstable, including not more than two permanent positions	$1,509 15
0306-02	Berkshire, including not more than four permanent positions	3,341 70

Item		
0306–03	Bristol, including not more than ten permanent positions	$8,565 76
0306–04	Dukes County, including not more than one permanent position	319 96
0306–05	Essex, including not more than fourteen permanent positions	12,285 75
0306–06	Franklin, including not more than one permanent position	797 50
0306–07	Hampden, including not more than nine permanent positions	8,572 40
0306–08	Hampshire, including not more than two permanent positions	1,719 15
0306–09	Middlesex, including not more than thirty-four permanent positions	30,125 98
0306–10	Norfolk, including not more than thirteen permanent positions	10,839 14
0306–11	Plymouth, including not more than four permanent positions	3,174 16
0306–12	Suffolk, including not more than forty-four permanent positions	35,968 17
0306–13	Worcester, including not more than twelve permanent positions	10,063 65
0306–14	For clerical assistance to the register of probate and insolvency of Nantucket county	84 00
	Total	$127,366 47

Administrative Committee of Probate Courts:

0307–01	For expenses of the administrative committee of probate courts	$85 68

Service of the Land Court.

0308–01	For the salaries of the judge, associate judges, the recorder and court officer, including not more than five permanent positions	$22,644 02
0308–02	For engineering, clerical and other personal services, including not more than twenty-two permanent positions	33,234 48
0308–03	For personal services in the examination of titles, for publishing and serving citations and other services, traveling expenses, supplies and office equipment, and for the preparation of sectional plans showing registered land	12,888 70
	Total	$68,767 20

Pensions for Certain Retired Justices.

0309–01	For pensions of retired justices of the supreme judicial court and of the superior court, and judges of the probate courts and the land court	$26,980 85

Service of the District Attorneys.

District Attorneys, as follows:

0310–01	For the salaries of the district attorney and assistants for the Suffolk district, including not more than fourteen permanent positions	$38,291 68
0310–02	For the salaries of the district attorney and assistants for the northern district, including not more than seven permanent positions	16,333 28

Item		
0310-03	For the salaries of the district attorney and assistants for the eastern district, including not more than five permanent positions .	$10,216 68
0310-04	For the salaries of the district attorney, deputy district attorney and assistants for the southeastern district, including not more than five permanent positions	11,200 00
0310-05	For the salaries of the district attorney and assistants for the southern district, including not more than four permanent positions .	8,808 31
0310-06	For the salaries of the district attorney and assistants for the middle district, including not more than four permanent positions .	8,783 31
0310-07	For the salaries of the district attorney and assistants for the western district, including not more than three permanent positions .	6,141 69
0310-08	For the salary of the district attorney for the northwestern district	2,333 31
0310-09	For traveling expenses necessarily incurred by the district attorneys, except in the Suffolk district, including expenses incurred in previous years	2,904 54
	Total	$105,012 80

Service of the Board of Probation.

0311-01	For personal services of the commissioner, clerks and stenographers, including not more than forty-three permanent positions . .	$38,528 01
0311-02	For services other than personal, traveling expenses, rent, office supplies and equipment	9,525 64
	Total	$48,053 65

Service of the Board of Bar Examiners.

0312-01	For personal services of the members of the board, including not more than five permanent positions	$5,400 00
0312-02	For other services, including not more than one permanent position, traveling expenses, office supplies and equipment . . .	3,605 23
	Totals	$9,005 23

Service of the Executive Department.

0401-01	For the salary of the governor	$5,833 31
0401-02	For the salary of the lieutenant governor .	2,333 38
0401-03	For the salaries of the eight councillors . .	4,667 04
0401-04	For the salaries of officers and employees of the department, including not more than seventeen permanent positions	23,483 78
0401-05	For certain personal services for the lieutenant governor and council, including not more than three permanent positions . . .	3,444 96
0401-21	For travel and expenses of the lieutenant governor and council from and to their homes .	1,637 56
0401-22	For postage, printing, office and other contingent expenses, including travel, of the governor	4,557 11

Item		
0401-23	For postage, printing, stationery, traveling and contingent expenses of the governor and council	$850 26
0401-26	For certain maintenance expenses of the governor's automobile	310 19
0401-28	For expenses incurred in the arrest of fugitives from justice	2,500 00
0401-35	For payment of temporary emergency expenses which may arise by reason of the exigencies of the existing state of war and for transfers to meet unforeseen deficiencies in existing appropriations, with the approval of the governor and council	50,000 00
	Requests for payments and transfers from this item shall be referred to the commission on administration and finance, which, after investigation of the need for such expenditure, shall forthwith submit to the governor its written recommendation of the amount of funds required, together with pertinent facts relative thereto.	
	Total	$99,617 59

Service of the Adjutant General.

0402-01	For the salary of the adjutant general . .	$3,500 00
0402-02	For personal services of office assistants, including services for the preparation of records of Massachusetts soldiers and sailors, and including not more than eighteen permanent positions	23,605 00
0402-03	For services other than personal, and for necessary office supplies and expenses .	3,400 00
0402-04	For expenses not otherwise provided for in connection with military matters and accounts	5,200 00
	Total	$35,705 00

Service of the Organized Militia.

0403-01	For allowances to companies and other administrative units, to be expended under the direction of the adjutant general	$65,500 00
0403-03	For certain allowances for officers of the organized militia, as authorized by paragraph (*c*) of section one hundred and twenty of chapter thirty-three of the General Laws . . .	42,000 00
0403-05	For expenses of military training and instruction, including organization, administration and elements of military art, use of chemical gas, rifle practice, and pay and expenses of certain camps of instruction	63,000 00
0403-07	For transportation of officers and non-commissioned officers for attendance at military meetings	1,800 00
0403-08	For transportation to and from regimental and battalion drills	500 00
0403-10	(This item combined with item 0403-05.)	
0403-13	For compensation and expenses for special and miscellaneous duty	12,500 00

Item		
0403-14	For compensation for accidents and injuries sustained in the performance of military duty	$2,100 00
0403-15	To cover certain small claims for damages to private property arising from military maneuvers	200 00
0403-17	For services and expenses of the military reservation located in Barnstable county, including compensation of one commissioner	1,700 00
0403-18	For premiums on bonds for officers . .	2,255 00
0403-21	For expenses of operation of the second division of the state guard	2,950 00
0403-23	For personal services necessary for the operation of the commonwealth depot and motor repair park, including not more than eighteen permanent positions	14,920 00
	Total	$209,425 00

Service of the State Quartermaster.

0405-01	For personal services of the state quartermaster, superintendent of arsenal and certain other employees of the state quartermaster, including not more than eight permanent positions	$10,250 00
0405-02	For the salaries of armorers and assistant armorers of armories of the first class, superintendent of armories, and other employees, including not more than eighty-three permanent positions	89,700 00
0406-01	For certain incidental military expenses of the quartermaster's department . .	25 00
0406-02	For office and general supplies and equipment	5,900 00
0406-04	For the maintenance of armories of the first class, including the purchase of certain furniture	85,000 00
0406-06	For expense of maintaining and operating the Camp Curtis Guild rifle range, including not more than five permanent positions . .	5,350 00
	Total	$196,225 00

Service of the State Surgeon.

0407-01	For personal services of the state surgeon, and regular assistants, including not more than three permanent positions	$3,234 00
0407-02	For services other than personal, and for necessary medical and office supplies and equipment	995 00
0407-03	For the examination of recruits . . .	600 00
	Total	$4,829 00

Service of the State Judge Advocate.

0408-01	For compensation of the state judge advocate	$125 00

Service of the Commission on Administration and Finance.

0415-01	For personal services of the commissioners, including not more than four permanent positions	$15,458 33

Item		
0415-02	For personal services of the bureau of the comptroller, including not more than eighty-six permanent positions	$84,082 19
0415-03	For personal services of the bureau of the purchasing agent, including not more than forty-one permanent positions	45,018 16
0415-04	For other personal services of the commission, including not more than thirty-three permanent positions	37,899 19
0415-05	For other expenses incidental to the duties of the commission	25,479 76
0415-10	For telephone service in the state house and expenses in connection therewith	18,089 20
	Central Mailing Room:	
0415-12	For personal services of the central mailing room, including not more than eight permanent positions	6,626 85
	Total	$232,653 68
	Purchase of Paper:	
0415-11	For the purchase of paper used in the execution of the contracts for state printing, other than legislative, with the approval of the commission on administration and finance	$15,877 13
	Special:	
0415-25	For a general supply account for the purchasing bureau, as provided by section fifty-one of chapter thirty of the General Laws, to be expended with the approval of the commission on administration and finance, and to be in addition to any amount heretofore appropriated for the purpose, and any amounts heretofore expended for this purpose during the current fiscal period from funds available under chapter eighteen of the acts of the special session of nineteen hundred and forty-two are to be transferred to said funds from this appropriation	$20,000 00

Service of the State Superintendent of Buildings.

Item		
0416-01	For personal services of the superintendent and office assistants, including not more than five permanent positions	$7,225 12
0416-02	For personal services of engineers, assistant engineers, firemen and helpers in the engineer's department, including not more than forty-four permanent positions	41,477 37
0416-03	For personal services of capitol police, including not more than twenty-six permanent positions	27,307 77
0416-04	For personal services of janitors, including not more than twenty-one permanent positions	16,778 82
0416-05	For other personal services incidental to the care and maintenance of the state house and of the Ford building, so-called, including not more than eighty permanent positions	57,717 13
	Total	$150,506 21
	Other Annual Expenses:	
0416-11	For contingent, office and other expenses of the superintendent	$154 79

Item		
0416-13	For services, supplies and equipment necessary to furnish heat, light and power . .	$30,108 99
0416-14	For other services, supplies and equipment necessary for the maintenance and care of the state house and grounds, including repairs of furniture and equipment	21,112 04
	Special:	
0416-26	For the purchase by the state superintendent of buildings of certain property situated on Hingham street in the city of Cambridge, with the approval of the commission on administration and finance	4,500 00
	Total	$55,875 82

Service of the Alcoholic Beverages Control Commission.

	The following items shall be payable from fees collected under section twenty-seven of chapter one hundred and thirty-eight of the General Laws:	
0417-01	For personal services, including not more than forty-eight permanent positions . . .	$68,960 41
0417-02	For services other than personal, including rent of offices, travel, and office and incidental expenses	13,856 81
	Total	$82,817 22

Service of the State Racing Commission.

	The following items shall be payable from fees collected under chapter one hundred and twenty-eight A of the General Laws, as amended:	
0418-01	For personal services, including not more than eight permanent positions	$29,363 56
0418-02	For other administrative expenses, including rent of offices, travel, and office and incidental expenses	2,747 00
	Total	$32,110 56

Service of the State Planning Board.

0419-01	For personal services of secretary, chief engineer, and other assistants, including not more than fourteen permanent positions	$23,238 08
0419-02	For services other than personal, including rent of offices, travel, and office supplies and equipment	3,935 03
	Total	$27,173 11

Service of the State Library.

0423-01	For personal services of the librarian . .	$3,325 00
0423-02	For personal services of the regular library assistants, temporary clerical assistance, and for services for cataloguing, including not more than twenty-three permanent positions	24,918 85
0423-03	For services other than personal, office supplies and equipment, and incidental traveling expenses	1,400 86

Item		
0423-04	For books and other publications and things needed for the library, and the necessary binding and rebinding incidental thereto .	$4,498 84
	Total	$34,143 55

Service of the Art Commission.

0424-01	For expenses of the commission . . .	$46 77

Service of the Soldiers' Home in Massachusetts.

0430-00	For the maintenance of the Soldiers' Home in Massachusetts, with the approval of the trustees thereof, including not more than one hundred and ninety-five permanent positions, to be in addition to certain receipts from the United States government; provided, that this appropriation be reduced by any amount by which the receipts from the United States government may exceed forty-three thousand four hundred dollars; and, provided further, that if such receipts from the United States government are less than forty-three thousand four hundred dollars, this appropriation be increased by an amount equal to the difference between said amount and the amount actually received, and such increase shall be taken from item 0401-35	$201,030 31

Service of the Commissioner of State Aid and Pensions.

0440-01	For personal services of the commissioner and deputies, including not more than three permanent positions	$7,198 33
0440-02	For personal services of agents, clerks, stenographers and other assistants, including not more than nineteen permanent positions .	15,886 42
0440-03	For services other than personal, traveling expenses of the commissioner and his employees, and necessary office supplies and equipment .	2,892 15
	Total	$25,976 90

For Expenses on Account of Wars.

0441-02	For certain care of veterans of the civil war, their wives and widows, as authorized by section twenty-five of chapter one hundred and fifteen of the General Laws, as appearing in the Tercentenary Edition thereof .	$9,834 78
0441-10	For expenses in connection with the national convention of the United Spanish War Veterans, if held in the city of Boston in the year nineteen hundred and forty-three, as authorized by chapter eighty-seven of the resolves of nineteen hundred and forty-one; provided, that these funds shall not be available until May fifteenth, nineteen hundred and forty-three	10,000 00
	Total	$19,834 78

Service of the Massachusetts Aeronautics Commission.

Item		
0442-01	For personal services of employees, including not more than three permanent positions .	$4,857 39
0442-02	For administrative expenses, including consultants' services, office rent and other incidental expenses	3,086 51
	Total	$7,943 90

For the Maintenance of the Mount Greylock War Memorial.

0443-01	For expenses of maintenance of the Mount Greylock War Memorial, as authorized by section forty-seven of chapter six of the General Laws	$345 90

For the Maintenance of Old State House.

0444-01	For the contribution of the commonwealth toward the maintenance of the old provincial state house	$750 00

Service of the Massachusetts Committee on Public Safety.

0450-01	For personal and other expenses of the Massachusetts committee on public safety. No part of the appropriations herein authorized shall be available for the salaries of positions on a permanent basis. Persons employed by said committee shall not be subject to the civil service laws or the rules and regulations made thereunder, but their employment and salary rates shall be subject to the rules and regulations of the division of personnel and standardization. Further activities of the committee shall terminate whenever, in the opinion of the governor, its continuation is no longer required in the best interests of the commonwealth. Expenditures under this item shall be subject to the approval of a majority of the members of the executive committee of said committee on public safety. Any amounts heretofore expended for this purpose during the current fiscal period from funds available under chapter eighteen of the acts of the special session of nineteen hundred and forty-two are to be transferred to said funds from this appropriation . . .	$290,347 16

Service of the Secretary of the Commonwealth.

0501-01	For the salary of the secretary	$4,083 33
0501-02	For the salaries of officers and employees holding positions established by law, and other personal services, including not more than sixty-six permanent positions	69,827 47
0501-03	For services other than personal, traveling expenses, office supplies and equipment, for the arrangement and preservation of state records and papers, including traveling expenses of the supervisor of public records	14,500 00
0501-04	For postage and expressage on public documents, and for mailing copies of bills and resolves to certain state, city and town officials	807 36

Item		
0501-05	For printing registration books, blanks and indexes	$1,181 72
0501-06	For the preparation of certain indexes of births, marriages and deaths	1,280 00
0501-08	For the purchase of ink for public records of the commonwealth	419 15
	Total	$92,099 03
	Special:	
0502-01	For the purchase of certain supplies and equipment, and for other things necessary in connection with the reproduction of the manuscript collection designated "Massachusetts Archives"	$500 00
	For printing laws, etc.:	
0503-01	For printing and distributing the pamphlet edition and for printing and binding the blue book edition of the acts and resolves of the present year	$16,000 00
0503-02	For the printing of reports of decisions of the supreme judicial court	8,170 80
0503-03	For printing and binding public documents	805 91
	Total	$24,976 71
	For matters relating to elections:	
0504-01	For personal and other services in preparing for primary elections, including not more than one permanent position, and for the expenses of preparing, printing and distributing ballots for primary and other elections	$4,100 00
0504-02	For the printing of blanks for town officers, election laws and blanks and instructions on all matters relating to elections	250 00
0504-03	For furnishing cities and towns with ballot boxes, and for repairs to the same; for the purchase of apparatus to be used at polling places in the canvass and counting of votes; and for providing certain registration facilities	213 40
	Total	$4,563 40
	Commission on Interstate Co-operation:	
0506-01	For personal and other services of the commission, including travel and other expenses, as authorized by sections twenty-one to twenty-five, inclusive, of chapter nine of the General Laws, including not more than two permanent positions	$5,935 25
	Service of the Treasurer and Receiver-General.	
0601-01	For the salary of the treasurer and receiver-general	$3,500 00
0601-02	For salaries of officers and employees holding positions established by law and additional clerical and other assistance, including not more than thirty-seven permanent positions	41,661 25

Item		
0601-03	For services other than personal, traveling expenses, office supplies and equipment . .	$9,520 31
	Total	$54,681 56
	Commissioners on Firemen's Relief:	
0602-01	For relief disbursed, with the approval of the commissioners on firemen's relief . .	$6,432 50
0602-02	For expenses of administration by the commissioners on firemen's relief . . .	112 48
	Total	$6,544 98
	Payments to Soldiers:	
0603-01	For making payments to soldiers in recognition of service during the world war and the Spanish war, as provided by law . .	$344 69
	State Board of Retirement:	
0604-01	For personal services in the administrative office of the state board of retirement, including not more than eleven permanent positions	$9,955 00
0604-02	For services other than personal, office supplies and equipment	3,400 00
0604-03	For requirements of annuity funds and pensions for employees retired from the state service under authority of law, to be in addition to the amounts appropriated in item 2970-01 .	253,816 20
	Total	$267,171 20

Service of the Emergency Finance Board.

0605-01	For administrative expenses of the emergency finance board, including not more than eight permanent positions	$6,592 32

Service of the State Emergency Public Works Commission.

0606-01	For expenses of the board appointed to formulate projects or perform any act necessary to enable the commonwealth to receive certain benefits provided by any acts or joint resolutions of congress authorizing grants of federal money for public projects, including not more than eight permanent positions .	$5,118 58

Service of the Auditor of the Commonwealth.

0701-01	For the salary of the auditor . . .	$3,500 00
0701-02	For personal services of deputies and other assistants, including not more than twenty-three permanent positions . . .	44,053 52
0701-03	For services other than personal, traveling expenses, office supplies and equipment .	2,386 00
	Total	$49,939 52

Service of the Attorney General's Department.

0801-01	For the salary of the attorney general . .	$4,666 67
0801-02	For the compensation of assistants in his office, and for such other legal and personal services as may be required, including not more than thirty-six permanent positions . . .	67,776 41

Item		
0801-03	For services other than personal, traveling expenses, office supplies and equipment . .	$3,832 68
0802-01	For the settlement of certain claims, as provided by law, on account of damages by cars owned by the commonwealth and operated by state employees	6,521 10
0802-02	For the settlement of certain small claims, as authorized by section three A of chapter twelve of the General Laws . . .	351 33
	Total	$83,148 19

Service of the Department of Agriculture.

0901-01	For the salary of the commissioner. . . .	$2,906 00
0901-02	For personal services of clerks and stenographers, including not more than seventeen permanent positions	15,603 24
0901-03	For traveling expenses of the commissioner .	187 80
0901-04	For services other than personal, office supplies and equipment, and printing and furnishing trespass posters	2,557 05
0901-11	For compensation and expenses of members of the advisory board	71 79
0901-21	For services and expenses of apiary inspection, including not more than one permanent position	214 76
	Total	$21,540 64
	Division of Dairying and Animal Husbandry:	
0905-01	For personal services, including not more than five permanent positions	$8,351 82
0905-02	For other expenses, including the enforcement of the dairy laws of the commonwealth .	2,795 38
0905-03	For administering the law relative to the inspection of barns and dairies by the department of agriculture, including not more than eight permanent positions	12,950 44
	Total	$24,097 64
	Milk Control Board:	
0906-01	For personal services of members of the board and their employees, including not more than fifty-three permanent positions . . .	$60,772 02
0906-02	For other administrative expenses of the board, including office expenses, rent, travel, and special services	25,664 73
0906-03	For expenses in connection with certain activities conducted in co-operation with the federal government, as authorized by section twenty-three of chapter ninety-four A of the General Laws	2,969 42
	Total	$89,406 17
	Division of Livestock Disease Control:	
0907-01	For the salary of the director	$2,333 33
0907-02	For personal services of clerks and stenographers, including not more than eighteen permanent positions	14,041 39
0907-03	For services other than personal, traveling expenses of the director, office supplies and equipment, and rent	4,336 07

Item		
0907-04	For personal services of veterinarians and agents engaged in the work of extermination of contagious diseases among domestic animals, including not more than fifteen full-time permanent positions and not more than fifty-seven permanent intermittent positions	$31,621 78
0907-05	For traveling expenses of veterinarians and agents	4,679 06
0907-06	For reimbursement of owners of horses killed during the current fiscal period and previous years, travel, when allowed, of inspectors of animals, incidental expenses of killing and burial, quarantine and emergency services, and for laboratory and veterinary supplies and equipment	852 26
0907-07	For reimbursement of owners of tubercular cattle killed, as authorized by section twelve A of chapter one hundred and twenty-nine of the General Laws, and in accordance with certain provisions of law and agreements made under authority of section thirty-three of said chapter one hundred and twenty-nine, during the period December first, nineteen hundred and forty-two to June thirtieth, nineteen hundred and forty-three, inclusive, and for the previous year	17,491 89
	Total	$75,355 78
	Reimbursement of towns for inspectors of animals:	
0907-08	For the reimbursement of certain towns for compensation paid to inspectors of animals	$4,393 92
	Division of Markets:	
0908-01	For personal services, including not more than twelve permanent positions	$15,824 31
0908-02	For other expenses	3,452 86
0908-03	For the cost of work of inspecting certain orchards within the commonwealth to provide for effective apple pest control . .	72 32
	Total	$19,349 49
	Division of Plant Pest Control and Fairs:	
0909-01	For personal services, including not more than four permanent positions	$5,349 47
0909-02	For travel and other expenses	1,326 44
0909-11	For work in protecting the pine trees of the commonwealth from white pine blister rust, and for payments of claims on account of currant and gooseberry bushes destroyed in the work of suppressing white pine blister rust	579 19
0909-12	For quarantine and other expenses in connection with the work of suppression of the European corn borer, so called, to be in addition to any amount heretofore appropriated for the purpose	1,611 14
0909-21	For state prizes and agricultural exhibits including allotment of funds for the 4-H club activities	2,218 46
	Total	$11,084 70

Item		
	State Reclamation Board:	
0910-01	For expenses of the board, including not more than five permanent positions	$4,322 59
	Service of the Department of Conservation.	
	Administration:	
1001-01	For the salary of the commissioner	$3,500 00
1001-02	For traveling expenses of the commissioner	240 00
1001-03	For services other than personal, including printing, supplies and equipment, and rent	3,472 89
1001-04	For clerical and other assistance to the commissioner, including not more than twelve permanent positions	17,522 38
	Total	$24,735 27
	Division of Forestry:	
1002-01	For personal services of office assistants, including not more than four permanent positions	$3,709 15
1002-02	For services other than personal, traveling expenses, necessary office supplies and equipment, and rent	1,221 70
1002-11	For aiding towns in the purchase of equipment for extinguishing forest fires and for making protective belts or zones as a defence against forest fires for the current fiscal period and for previous years	736 91
1002-12	For personal services of the state fire warden and his assistants, and for other services, including traveling expenses of the state fire warden and his assistants, necessary supplies and equipment and materials used in new construction in the forest fire prevention service, including not more than twelve permanent positions	43,387 31
1002-14	For the expenses of forest fire patrol, as authorized by section twenty-eight A of chapter forty-eight of the General Laws	1,497 05
1002-21	For the development of state forests, including not more than twenty-one permanent positions, and including salaries and expenses of foresters and the cost of maintenance of such nurseries as may be necessary for the growing of seedlings for the planting of state forests, as authorized by sections one, six, nine and thirty to thirty-six, inclusive, of chapter one hundred and thirty-two of the General Laws, to be in addition to any amount heretofore appropriated for this purpose	70,856 06
1002-31	For the suppression of the gypsy and brown tail moths, including not more than eight permanent positions, and for expenses incidental thereto, to be in addition to any amount heretofore appropriated for the purpose	21,602 80
	Total	$143,010 98
	Division of Fisheries and Game:	
1004-01	For the salary of the director	$2,916 62
1004-02	For personal services of office assistants, including not more than ten permanent positions	10,612 60

Item		
1004-03	For services other than personal, traveling expenses and necessary office supplies and equipment, and rent	$2,848 02
	Enforcement of laws:	
1004-11	For personal services of conservation officers, including not more than thirty-seven permanent positions	29,600 00
1004-12	For traveling expenses of conservation officers, and for other expenses necessary for the enforcement of the laws	9,667 81
	Biological work:	
1004-21	For personal services to carry on biological work, including not more than two permanent positions	3,258 41
1004-22	For traveling and other expenses of the biologist and his assistants	300 27
	Propagation of game birds, etc.:	
1004-31	For personal services of employees at game farms and fish hatcheries, including not more than twenty-four permanent positions .	25,600 00
1004-32	For other maintenance expenses of game farms and fish hatcheries, and for the propagation of game birds and animals and food fish .	31,000 00
	Damages by wild deer and wild moose:	
1004-35	For the payment of damages caused by wild deer and wild moose, for the current fiscal period and for previous years, as provided by law	1,844 43
	Supervision of public fishing and hunting grounds:	
1004-41	For personal services	1,677 06
1004-42	For other expenses	310 45
1004-45	For expenses of providing for the establishment and maintenance of public fishing grounds	950 15
1004-46	For the cost of construction and improvement of certain fishways	804 95
	Special:	
1004-47	For consultants and other personal services, and for expenses, in connection with a biological survey of the streams and waters of the commonwealth, to be made under the direction of the commissioner of conservation, and to be in addition to any amount heretofore appropriated for the purpose . .	3,000 00
	Total	$124,390 77
	Division of Wild Life Research and Management:	
1004-51	For personal services, including not more than three permanent positions	$3,734 15
1004-52	For other expenses	503 24
	Total	$4,237 39
	Division of Marine Fisheries:	
1004-70	For the salary of the director	$2,916 62

Item		
1004–71	For personal services, including not more than six permanent positions; provided, that this appropriation shall not be used for the payment of salaries of food inspectors regulating the sale and cold storage of fresh food fish .	$6,121 87
1004–72	For services other than personal, traveling expenses, necessary office supplies and equipment, and rent	1,940 58
	Enforcement of shellfish and other marine fishery laws:	
1004–81	For personal services for the administration and enforcement of laws relative to shellfish and other marine fisheries, and for regulating the sale and cold storage of fresh food fish, including not more than sixteen permanent positions of which not more than five shall be food inspectors regulating the sale and cold storage of fresh food fish	25,170 42
1004–82	For other expenses of the administration and enforcement of laws relative to shellfish and other marine fisheries and for regulating the sale and cold storage of fresh food fish . .	5,391 59
1004–83	For expenses of purchasing lobsters, subject to the conditions imposed by section forty-three of chapter one hundred and thirty of the General Laws; provided, that the price paid for such lobsters shall not exceed the prevailing wholesale price for such lobsters in the district where purchased	154 50
1004–84	For the cost of assisting coastal cities and towns in the propagation of food fish and the suppression of enemies thereof, as authorized by section twenty of chapter one hundred and thirty of the General Laws . . .	4,050 66
1004–90	For services and expenses of the Atlantic States Marine Fisheries Commission, as authorized by chapter four hundred and eighty-nine of the acts of nineteen hundred and forty-one .	1,450 00
	Total	$47,196 24
	Bounty on seals:	
1004–91	For bounties on seals	$121 00

Service of the Department of Banking and Insurance.

	Division of Banks:	
1101–01	For the salary of the commissioner . . .	$3,500 00
1101–02	For services of deputy, directors, examiners and assistants, clerks, stenographers and experts, including not more than one hundred and thirty-six permanent positions	196,129 98
1101–03	For services other than personal, traveling expenses, office supplies and equipment . .	32,354 61
	Total	$231,984 59
	Supervisor of Loan Agencies:	
1102–01	For personal services of supervisor and assistants, including not more than seven permanent positions	$8,202 00
1102–02	For services other than personal, office supplies and equipment	645 63
	Total	$8,847 63

Item		
	Division of Insurance:	
1103-01	For the salary of the commissioner	$3,500 00
1103-02	For other personal services of the division, including expenses of the board of appeal and certain other costs of supervising motor vehicle liability insurance, and including not more than one hundred and fifty-eight permanent positions, partly chargeable to item 2970-02	160,193 18
1103-03	For other services, including traveling expenses, necessary office supplies and equipment and rent of offices	34,255 02
	Total	$197,948 20
	Board of Appeal on Fire Insurance Rates:	
1104-01	For expenses of the board	$20 00
	Division of Savings Bank Life Insurance:	
1105-01	For personal services of officers and employees, including not more than twenty-nine permanent positions	$28,058 42
1105-02	For services other than personal, traveling expenses, rent and equipment . . .	6,937 53
	Total	$34,995 95

Service of the Department of Corporations and Taxation.

Item		
	Corporations and Tax Divisions:	
1201-01	For the salary of the commissioner	$4,375 00
1201-02	For the salaries of certain positions filled by the commissioner, with the approval of the governor and council, and for additional clerical and other assistance, including not more than one hundred and twenty-six permanent positions, partly chargeable to item 2970-03; and it is hereby further provided that the sum of twenty-nine thousand dollars, which represents the estimated cost of collection of alcoholic beverages taxes, so-called, and which is hereby included in this appropriation shall be transferred to the General Fund from fees collected under section twenty-seven of chapter one hundred and thirty-eight of the General Laws, as amended	120,894 63
1201-03	For other services, necessary office supplies and equipment, travel, and for printing publications and valuation books	23,917 31
	Total	$149,186 94
	Administration of cigarette taxes:	
1201-11	For personal services for the administration of certain laws levying the cigarette taxes, so called, including not more than thirty-six permanent positions	$32,856 44
1201-12	For expenses other than personal services for the administration of certain laws levying the cigarette taxes, so called	7,505 89
	Total	$40,362 33

Item		
	The following two items shall be payable from amounts collected under chapter sixty-four B of the General Laws:	
	Excise upon charges for meals:	
1201-21	For personal services of the director, assistant director, and other necessary employees for the administration of an excise on meals, including not more than thirty-two permanent positions	$31,557 06
1201-22	For expenses other than personal services for the administration of an excise on meals, as provided by chapter sixty-four B of the General Laws	12,665 90
	Total	$44,222 96
	Income Tax Division (the two following appropriations are to be made from the receipts from the income tax):	
1202-01	For personal services of the director, assistant director, assessors, deputy assessors, clerks, stenographers and other necessary assistants, including not more than two hundred and sixty-three permanent positions	$306,129 59
1202-02	For services other than personal, and for traveling expenses, office supplies and equipment, and rent	75,004 65
	Total	$381,134 24
	Division of Accounts:	
1203-01	For personal services, including not more than one hundred and nine permanent positions partly chargeable to item 1203-11	$54,342 51
1203-02	For other expenses	3,585 34
1203-11	For services and expenses of auditing and installing systems of municipal accounts, the cost of which is to be assessed upon the municipalities for which the work is done	123,982 71
1203-12	For the expenses of certain books, forms and other material, which may be sold to cities and towns requiring the same for maintaining their system of accounts	13,525 58
1203-21	For the administrative expenses of the county personnel board, including not more than five permanent positions	4,458 51
	Total	$199,894 65
	Appellate Tax Board:	
1204-01	For personal services of the members of the board and employees, including not more than twenty-five permanent positions	$52,081 94
1204-02	For services other than personal, traveling expenses, office supplies and equipment, and rent	16,239 89
	Total	$68,321 83

Service of the Department of Education.

1301-01	For the salary of the commissioner	$5,250 00
1301-02	For personal services of officers, agents, clerks, stenographers and other assistants, including not more than forty-six permanent positions, but not including those employed in university extension work	74,486 47

Item		
1301-03	For traveling expenses of members of the advisory board and of agents and employees when required to travel in discharge of their duties	$1,941 24
1301-04	For services other than personal, necessary office supplies, and for printing bulletins as provided by law	6,057 69
1301-06	For printing school registers and other school blanks for cities and towns	250 08
1301-07	For expenses of holding teachers' institutes	634 58
1301-08	For aid to certain pupils in state teachers' colleges, under the direction of the department of education	2,000 00
1301-09	For assistance to children of certain war veterans, for the current fiscal period and for previous years, as authorized by chapter two hundred and sixty-three of the acts of nineteen hundred and thirty, as amended	10,039 28
1301-10	For the maintenance and operation of the state building on Newbury street, Boston, including not more than four permanent positions	9,364 85
	Total	$110,024 19
	Specials:	
1301-25	For sponsorship of certain Works Projects Administration or other federal projects	$2,054 08
	Division of Vocational Education:	
1301-30	For aid to certain persons receiving instruction in the courses for vocational rehabilitation, as authorized by section twenty-two B of chapter seventy-four of the General Laws	$1,608 70
1301-31	For the training of teachers for vocational schools, to comply with the requirement of federal authorities under the provisions of the Smith-Hughes act, so called, including not more than twenty permanent positions	17,693 20
1301-32	For the expenses of promotion of vocational rehabilitation in co-operation with the federal government, including not more than fifteen permanent positions	34,114 28
	Total	$53,416 18
	Education of deaf and blind pupils:	
1301-41	For the education of deaf and blind pupils of the commonwealth, as provided by section twenty-six of chapter sixty-nine of the General Laws	$254,180 26
	Reimbursement and aid:	
1301-52	For the reimbursement of certain towns for the payment of tuition of pupils attending high schools outside the towns in which they reside, as provided by law	$1,514 45
	University Extension Courses:	
1301-61	For personal services, including not more than forty-four permanent positions	$93,731 77
1301-62	For other expenses	17,489 51
	Total	$111,221 28

Item		
	English-speaking Classes for Adults:	
1301–64	For personal services of administration, including not more than four permanent positions .	$6,843 32
1301–65	For other expenses of administration . .	1,083 48
	Total	$7,926 80
	Division of Immigration and Americanization:	
1302–01	For personal services, including not more than nineteen permanent positions . . .	$21,688 78
1302–02	For other expenses	3,537 11
	Total	$25,225 89
	Division of Public Libraries:	
1303–01	For personal services of regular agents and office assistants, including not more than five permanent positions	$9,829 75
1303–02	For other services, traveling expenses, necessary office supplies and expenses incidental to the aiding of public libraries . . .	6,464 19
	Total	$16,293 94
	Division of the Blind:	
1304–01	For general administration, furnishing information, industrial and educational aid, and for carrying out certain provisions of the laws establishing said division, including not more than twenty-two permanent positions . .	$29,946 45
1304–03	For the maintenance of local shops, including not more than nine permanent positions .	35,349 71
1304–04	For maintenance of Woolson House industries, so called, to be expended under the authority of said division, including not more than four permanent positions	36,960 02
1304–05	For the maintenance of certain industries for men, to be expended under the authority of said division, including not more than six permanent positions	89,203 02
1304–06	For instruction of the adult blind in their homes, including not more than fourteen permanent positions	12,279 18
1304–08	For aiding the adult blind, subject to the conditions provided by law	95,589 00
1304–10	For expenses of administering and operating the services of piano tuning and mattress renovating under section twenty-five of chapter sixty-nine of the General Laws . . .	10,018 98
	Total	$309,346 36
	Teachers' Retirement Board:	
1305–01	For personal services of employees, including not more than nine permanent positions .	$9,986 59
1305–02	For services other than personal, traveling expenses, office supplies and equipment, and rent.	3,218 11
1305–03	For payment of pensions to retired teachers .	792,348 71
	Total	$805,553 41

Item		
	Massachusetts Maritime Academy:	
1306–01	For personal services of the secretary and office assistants, including not more than two permanent positions	$2,383 94
1306–02	For services other than regular clerical services, rent, office supplies and equipment	1,021 86
1306–10	For the maintenance of the academy and ship, including not more than thirty-one permanent positions	52,399 18
	Total	$55,804 98

	For the maintenance of the state teachers' colleges, and the boarding halls attached thereto, with the approval of the commissioner of education, as follows:	
1307–00	State teachers' college at Bridgewater, including not more than sixty permanent positions	$90,577 48
1307–21	State teachers' college at Bridgewater, boarding hall, including not more than thirty permanent positions	35,698 63
1308–00	State teachers' college at Fitchburg, including not more than fifty-eight permanent positions	105,947 96
1308–21	State teachers' college at Fitchburg, boarding hall, including not more than nine permanent positions	19,341 38
1309–00	State teachers' college at Framingham, including not more than sixty-one permanent positions	95,797 83
1309–21	State teachers' college at Framingham, boarding hall, including not more than twenty-five permanent positions	33,916 80
1310–00	State teachers' college at Hyannis, including not more than twenty-nine permanent positions	40,385 32
1310–21	State teachers' college at Hyannis, boarding hall, including not more than five permanent positions	7,734 78
1311–00	State teachers' college at Lowell, including not more than forty permanent positions	45,439 81
1312–00	State teachers' college at North Adams, including not more than twenty-nine permanent positions	38,679 09
1312–21	State teachers' college at North Adams, boarding hall, including not more than six permanent positions	5,984 87
1313–00	State teachers' college at Salem, including not more than fifty-one permanent positions	73,583 17
1314–00	State teachers' college at Westfield, including not more than thirty-five permanent positions	41,782 10
1314–21	State teachers' college at Westfield, boarding hall, including not more than one permanent position	1,009 98
1314–32	State teachers' college at Westfield, personal services and expenses of boarding hall for army signal corps trainees; and any amounts heretofore expended for this purpose during the current fiscal period from funds available under chapter eighteen of the acts of the special session of nineteen hundred and forty-two are to be transferred to said funds from this appropriation	44,000 00
1315–00	State teachers' college at Worcester, including not more than forty-four permanent positions	52,850 78

Item		
1321-00	Massachusetts School of Art, including not more than thirty-six permanent positions	$64,096 40
	Total	$796,826 38
	Textile Schools:	
1331-00	For the maintenance of the Bradford Durfee textile school of Fall River, with the approval of the commissioner of education and the trustees, including not more than twenty-three permanent positions	$38,498 51
1332-00	For the maintenance of the Lowell textile institute, with the approval of the commissioner of education and the trustees, including not more than sixty-one permanent positions	106,338 31
1333-00	For the maintenance of the New Bedford textile school, with the approval of the commissioner of education and the trustees, including not more than twenty-four permanent positions	38,599 99
	Total	$183,436 81
	Massachusetts State College:	
1341-00	For maintenance and current expenses of the Massachusetts state college, with the approval of the trustees, including not more than four hundred and eighty-one permanent positions	$669,050 04
1341-77	For personal services for the maintenance of the boarding hall, including not more than thirty-five permanent positions	22,616 73
1341-78	For other expenses of the maintenance of the boarding hall	41,024 98
1341-79	The amounts appropriated in items 1341-00, 1341-77 and 1341-78 are hereby made available for necessary expenditures in connection with the establishment and maintenance of the proposed fighter command training school at the Massachusetts state college, and the sum of one hundred thousand dollars is hereby appropriated and made available for transfer, with the approval of the commission on administration and finance, to accounts in said items where the amounts otherwise available are insufficient for meeting additional expenses made necessary by the establishment and maintenance of said school	100,000 00
1341-82	For aid to certain students, with the approval of the trustees	2,079 15
1341-83	For the cost of field and laboratory work in connection with the Dutch elm disease and other shade tree diseases and insects	2,788 92
1341-93	For payment of annual charges for sewage service by the town of Amherst	2,000 00
1341-97	For expenses of research work in connection with the cultivation of beach plums, as authorized by chapter five hundred and thirty-four of the acts of nineteen hundred and forty-one	95 79
	Total	$839,655 61

Service of the Department of Civil Service and Registration.

Item		
	Division of Civil Service:	
1402-01	For the salary of the director and for the compensation of members of the commission .	$8,081 67
1402-02	For other personal services of the division, including not more than one hundred and five permanent positions	102,246 45
1402-03	For other services, office supplies and equipment necessary for the administration of the civil service law	18,243 10
	Total	$128,571 22
	Division of Registration:	
1403-01	For the salary of the director	$1,433 35
1403-02	For clerical and certain other personal services of the division, including not more than thirty-six permanent positions	39,516 76
1403-03	For services of the division other than personal, office supplies and equipment, except as otherwise provided	9,507 57
	Total	$50,457 68
	Board of Registration in Medicine:	
1404-01	For personal services of the members of the board, including not more than seven permanent positions	$3,675 00
1404-03	For traveling expenses	300 00
	Total	$3,975 00
	Board of Dental Examiners:	
1405-01	For personal services of the members of the board, including not more than five permanent positions	$2,216 66
1405-02	For traveling expenses	248 40
	Total	$2,465 06
	Board of Registration in Chiropody:	
1406-01	For personal services of members of the board, including not more than five permanent positions	$525 00
1406-02	For traveling expenses	155 96
	Total	$680 96
	Board of Registration in Pharmacy:	
1407-01	For personal services of the members of the board, including not more than five permanent positions	$2,508 36
1407-02	For personal services of agents and investigators, including not more than four permanent positions	4,853 35
1407-03	For traveling expenses	1,244 17
	Total	$8,605 88
	Board of Registration in Nursing:	
1408-01	For personal services of the members of the board, and of the appointive members of the approving authority, including not more than ten permanent positions	$1,987 09
1408-02	For traveling expenses	600 00
	Total	$2,587 09

Item		
	Board of Registration in Embalming and Funeral Directing:	
1409-01	For personal services of members of the board, including not more than three permanent positions	$875 01
1409-02	For traveling expenses	1,015 63
	Total	$1,890 64
	Board of Registration in Optometry:	
1410-01	For personal services of members of the board, including not more than five permanent positions	$1,108 30
1410-02	For traveling expenses	134 72
	Total	$1,243 02
	Board of Registration in Veterinary Medicine:	
1411-02	For other services, traveling expenses, office supplies and equipment	$26 95
	Board of Registration of Professional Engineers and of Land Surveyors:	
1412-01	For personal services and other expenses, including travel	$1,500 00
	Board of Registration of Architects:	
1413-01	For personal services and other expenses, including travel	$1,204 94
	Board of Registration of Public Accountants:	
1414-01	For personal services of members of the board, including not more than five permanent positions	$393 82
1414-02	For expenses of examinations, including the preparation and marking of papers, and for other expenses	923 74
	Total	$1,317 56
	State Examiners of Electricians:	
1416-01	For personal services of members of the board, including not more than two permanent positions	$583 24
1416-02	For traveling expenses	2,026 00
	Total	$2,609 24
	State Examiners of Plumbers:	
1417-01	For personal services of members of the board, including not more than three permanent positions	$641 62
1417-02	For traveling expenses	765 43
	Total	$1,407 05
	Board of Registration of Barbers:	
1420-01	For personal services of members of the board and assistants, including not more than eight permanent positions	$9,949 96
1420-02	For travel and other necessary expenses, including rent	3,007 39
	Total	$12,957 35

Item		
	Board of Registration of Hairdressers:	
1421-01	For personal services of members of the board and assistants, including not more than eighteen permanent positions	$17,971 55
1421-02	For travel and other necessary expenses, including rent	5,156 20
	Total	$23,127 75

Service of the Department of Industrial Accidents.

Item		
1501-01	For personal services of members of the board, including not more than seven permanent positions	$23,291 62
1501-02	For personal services of secretaries, inspectors, clerks and office assistants, including not more than eighty-seven permanent positions	91,006 08
1501-03	For traveling expenses	3,385 70
1501-04	For other services, necessary office supplies and equipment	6,812 48
1501-05	For expenses of impartial examinations, and for expenses of industrial disease referees, as authorized by section nine B of chapter one hundred and fifty-two of the General Laws	12,638 50
	Total	$137,134 38

Service of the Department of Labor and Industries.

Item		
1601-01	For the salaries of the commissioner, assistant and associate commissioners, including not more than five permanent positions	$13,708 32
1601-02	For clerical and other assistance to the commissioner, including not more than four permanent positions	3,550 46
1601-11	For personal services for the inspectional services, including not more than sixty-six permanent positions, and for traveling expenses of the commissioner, assistant commissioner, associate commissioners and inspectors of labor, and for services other than personal, rent of district offices, and office supplies and equipment for the inspectional service	99,461 23
1601-31	For personal services for the division of occupational hygiene, including not more than five permanent positions	7,809 16
1601-32	For services other than personal, traveling expenses, office and laboratory supplies and equipment, and rent, for the division of occupational hygiene	2,822 66
1601-41	For personal services for the statistical service, including not more than thirty-five permanent positions, and for services other than personal, printing report and publications, traveling expenses and office supplies and equipment for the statistical service	42,503 77
1601-51	For personal services for the division on necessaries of life, including not more than five permanent positions	6,271 60
1601-52	For services other than personal, traveling expenses, office supplies and equipment for the division on necessaries of life	688 43

Item		
1601-53	For personal services in administering sections two hundred and ninety-five A to two hundred and ninety-five O, inclusive, of chapter ninety-four of the General Laws, relating to the advertising and sale of motor fuel at retail, including not more than twelve permanent positions	$12,299 88
1601-54	For other expenses in administering said sections two hundred and ninety-five A to two hundred and ninety-five O, inclusive	3,083 30
1601-61	For clerical and other assistance for the board of conciliation and arbitration, including not more than seven permanent positions	14,526 60
1601-62	For other services, printing, traveling expenses and office supplies and equipment for the board of conciliation and arbitration	2,709 58
1601-71	For personal services of investigators, clerks and stenographers for the minimum wage service, including not more than eighteen permanent positions	16,701 18
1601-72	For services other than personal, printing, traveling expenses and office supplies and equipment for minimum wage service	1,525 91
1601-73	For compensation and expenses of wage boards	862 16
1601-81	For personal services for the division of standards, including not more than sixteen permanent positions	17,816 31
1601-82	For other services, printing, traveling expenses and office supplies and equipment for the division of standards	5,423 41
	Total	$251,763 96

Massachusetts Development and Industrial Commission:

Item		
1603-01	For personal services of employees, including not more than five permanent positions	$7,995 60
1603-02	For administrative expenses, including office rent and other incidental expenses, and for the promotion and development of the industrial, agricultural and recreational resources of the commonwealth	7,513 46
	Total	$15,509 06

Labor Relations Commission:

Item		
1604-01	For personal services of the commissioners and employees, including not more than twenty permanent positions	$31,539 71
1604-02	For administrative expenses, including office rent	3,628 65
	Total	$35,168 36

Division of Apprentice Training:

Item		
1605-01	For personal services of the members of the apprenticeship council, the director of apprenticeship, and clerical and other assistants, as authorized by sections eleven E to eleven L, inclusive, of chapter twenty-three of the General Laws, including not more than eight permanent positions	$1,600 00

Item		
1605-02	For other expenses, including travel, as authorized by sections eleven E to eleven L, inclusive, of chapter twenty-three of the General Laws	$769 49
	Total	$2,369 49

Service of the Department of Mental Health.

1701-01	For the salary of the commissioner	$5,833 32
1701-02	For personal services of officers and employees, including not more than eighty permanent positions	98,453 09
1701-03	For transportation and medical examination of state charges under its charge	813 10
1701-04	For other services, traveling expenses, office supplies and equipment, and rent	20,675 52
1701-11	For the support of state charges in the Hospital Cottages for Children	12,015 71
	Total	$137,790 74

Division of Mental Hygiene:

1702-00	For expenses, including not more than sixty-two permanent positions, of investigating the nature, causes and results of mental diseases and defects and the publication of the results thereof, and of what further preventive or other measures might be taken and what further expenditures for investigation might be made which would give promise of decreasing the number of persons afflicted with mental diseases or defects	$65,167 11
1702-21	For the cost of boarding certain feeble-minded persons in private homes	2,088 01
	Total	$67,255 12

For the maintenance of the following institutions under the control of the Department of Mental Health:

1710-00	Boston psychopathic hospital, including not more than one hundred and fifty-six permanent positions	$155,301 16
1711-00	Boston state hospital, including not more than seven hundred and thirty-two permanent positions	658,074 32
1712-00	Danvers state hospital, including not more than five hundred and fifty-six permanent positions	613,275 26
1713-00	Foxborough state hospital, including not more than three hundred and thirty-six permanent positions	354,515 49
1714-00	Gardner state hospital, including not more than three hundred and thirty-seven permanent positions	406,832 14
1715-00	Grafton state hospital, including not more than four hundred and sixty-four permanent positions	472,652 51
1716-00	Medfield state hospital, including not more than four hundred and eighty permanent positions	476,202 26
1717-00	Metropolitan state hospital, including not more than four hundred and sixteen permanent positions	468,876 16

Item		
1718-00	Northampton state hospital, including not more than four hundred and eighty-one permanent positions	$483,663 45
1719-00	Taunton state hospital, including not more than four hundred and seventy-two permanent positions	443,024 20
1720-00	Westborough state hospital, including not more than four hundred and twenty-five permanent positions	443,782 90
1721-00	Worcester state hospital, including not more than six hundred and thirty-four permanent positions	666,761 44
1722-00	Monson state hospital, including not more than four hundred and fifteen permanent positions	440,731 95
1722-26	For certain improvements and additions to the water supply system at the Monson state hospital, to be in addition to any amount heretofore appropriated for the purpose	7,000 00
1723-00	Belchertown state school, including not more than three hundred and two permanent positions	340,123 16
1724-00	Walter E. Fernald state school, including not more than four hundred and sixty-seven permanent positions	488,938 60
1725-00	Wrentham state school, including not more than four hundred and eight permanent positions	463,456 89
	Total	$7,383,211 89

Service of the Department of Correction.

1801-01	For the salary of the commissioner	$3,500 00
1801-02	For personal services of deputies, agents, clerks and stenographers, including not more than twenty-two permanent positions	27,386 45
1801-03	For services other than personal, necessary office supplies and equipment	2,585 42
1801-04	For traveling expenses of officers and employees of the department, when required to travel in the discharge of their duties	353 96
1801-05	For the removal of prisoners, to and from state institutions	4,268 90
1801-06	For assistance to discharged prisoners	343 10
1801-07	For the expense of the service of the central index	500 00
	Total	$38,937 83

Division of Classification of Prisoners:

1801-08	For expenses of the division hereby authorized, including not more than eight permanent positions; provided, that the persons employed hereunder shall not be subject to civil service laws or the rules and regulations made thereunder	$13,336 39

Parole Board:

1801-21	For personal services of members of the parole board and advisory board of pardons, agents, clerical and other employees, including not more than forty permanent positions	$55,088 00
1801-22	For services other than personal, including necessary office supplies and equipment	2,161 04

Item		
1801-23	For traveling expenses of officers and employees of the parole board when required to travel in the discharge of their duties . . .	$6,912 43
	Total	$64,161 47
	For the maintenance of the following institutions under the control of the Department of Correction:	
1802-00	State farm, including not more than three hundred and seventy-eight permanent positions	$550,870 84
1803-00	State prison, including not more than one hundred and forty permanent positions . .	284,073 16
1805-00	Massachusetts reformatory, including not more than one hundred and sixty-three permanent positions	326,247 94
1806-00	Reformatory for women, including not more than one hundred and three permanent positions	156,270 71
1807-00	State prison colony, including not more than one hundred and seventy-five permanent positions	299,228 57
	Total	$1,616,691 22

Service of the Department of Public Welfare.

Item		
	Administration:	
1901-01	For the salary of the commissioner	$4,083 33
1901-02	For personal services of officers and employees, including not more than thirty-one permanent positions	34,086 47
1901-03	For services other than personal, traveling expenses, including expenses of auxiliary visitors, office supplies and expenses	1,731 39
	Total	$39,901 19
	State Board of Housing:	
1902-01	For personal services, including not more than nine permanent positions	$10,982 49
1902-02	For expenses, as authorized by section eighteen of chapter eighteen of the General Laws .	2,829 64
	Total	$13,812 13
	Division of Aid and Relief:	
1904-01	For personal services of officers and employees, including not more than one hundred and thirty-nine permanent positions	$139,644 47
1904-02	For services other than personal, including traveling expenses and office supplies and equipment	11,234 26
	Total	$150,878 73
	Division of Child Guardianship:	
1906-01	For personal services of officers and employees, including not more than one hundred and thirty-six permanent positions	$147,382 50
1906-02	For services other than personal, office supplies and equipment	3,767 78

Item		
1906-03	For the care and maintenance of children, including not more than two permanent positions	$797,968 91
	Total	$949,119 19
	The following items are for reimbursement of cities and towns, and are to be in addition to any unexpended balances of appropriations heretofore made for the purpose:	
1907-05	For the payment of suitable aid to certain dependent children	$1,900,000 00
1907-07	For the burial by cities and towns of indigent persons who have no legal settlement . .	16,509 85
1907-08	For expenses in connection with smallpox and other diseases dangerous to the public health	124,430 50
1907-09	For the support of sick indigent persons who have no legal settlement	279,646 45
1907-10	For temporary aid given to indigent persons with no legal settlement, and to shipwrecked seamen by cities and towns, and for the transportation of indigent persons under the charge of the department	3,000,000 00
	Total	$5,320,586 80
	Division of Juvenile Training, Trustees of Massachusetts Training Schools:	
1908-01	For services of the secretary and certain other persons employed in the executive office, including not more than nine permanent positions	$9,487 15
1908-02	For services other than personal, traveling and other expenses of the members of the board and employees, office supplies and equipment	904 49
	Boys' Parole:	
1908-11	For personal services of agents in the division for boys paroled and boarded in families, including not more than twenty-two permanent positions	28,706 05
1908-12	For services other than personal, including traveling expenses of the agents and boys, and necessary office supplies and equipment	9,112 57
1908-13	For board, clothing, medical and other expenses incidental to the care of boys	7,392 44
	Girls' Parole:	
1908-31	For personal services of agents in the division for girls paroled from the industrial school for girls, including not more than eighteen permanent positions	20,237 72
1908-32	For traveling expenses of said agents for girls paroled, for board, medical and other care of girls, and for services other than personal, office supplies and equipment	7,909 86
	Total	$83,750 28
	For the maintenance of the institutions under the control of the trustees of the Massachusetts training schools, with the approval of said trustees, as follows:	
1915-00	Industrial school for boys, including not more than one hundred permanent positions .	$114,199 21

Item		
1916-00	Industrial school for girls, including not more than eighty-nine permanent positions . .	$96,634 03
1917-00	Lyman school for boys, including not more than one hundred and thirty-eight permanent positions	181,875 32
	Massachusetts Hospital School:	
1918-00	For the maintenance of the Massachusetts hospital school, including not more than one hundred and fifty-two permanent positions, to be expended with the approval of the trustees thereof.	143,183 58
	Tewksbury State Hospital and Infirmary:	
1919-00	For the maintenance of the Tewksbury state hospital and infirmary, including not more than six hundred and eighty-five permanent positions, to be expended with the approval of the trustees thereof	769,071 47
	Total	$1,304,963 61

Service of the Department of Public Health.

Item		
	Administration:	
2001-01	For the salary of the commissioner. . . .	$4,375 00
2001-02	For personal services of the health council and office assistants, including not more than twenty-three permanent positions . .	14,226 33
2001-03	For services other than personal, traveling expenses, office supplies and equipment . .	5,009 66
	Service of Adult Hygiene (cancer):	
2003-01	For personal services of the division, including not more than twenty-two permanent positions	22,814 97
2003-02	For other expenses of the division, including cancer clinics	19,860 21
	Service of Child and Maternal Hygiene:	
2004-01	For personal services of the director and assistants, including not more than thirty-one permanent positions	35,302 63
2004-02	For services other than personal, traveling expenses, office supplies and equipment .	7,462 23
	Division of Communicable Diseases:	
2005-01	For personal services of the director, district health officers and their assistants, epidemiologists, bacteriologists and assistants in the diagnostic laboratory, including not more than thirty permanent positions	43,434 61
2005-02	For services other than personal, traveling expenses, laboratory, office and other necessary supplies, including the purchase of animals and equipment, and rent of certain offices .	5,879 50
	Venereal Diseases:	
2006-01	For personal services for the control of venereal diseases, including not more than eight permanent positions	7,865 01
2006-02	For services other than personal, traveling expenses, office supplies and equipment, to be in addition to any amount heretofore appropriated for the purpose . . .	149,225 93

Item		
	Wassermann Laboratory:	
2007-01	For personal services of the Wassermann laboratory, including not more than fifteen permanent positions	$11,332 73
2007-02	For expenses of the Wassermann laboratory	3,575 68
	Antitoxin and Vaccine Laboratories:	
2007-07	For personal services in the investigation and production of antitoxin and vaccine lymph and other specific material for protective inoculation and diagnosis of treatment, including not more than forty-seven permanent positions	42,737 40
2007-08	For other services, supplies, materials and equipment necessary for the production of antitoxin and other materials as enumerated above, and for rent	13,987 12
	Inspection of Food and Drugs:	
2012-01	For personal services of the director, analysts, inspectors and other assistants, including not more than thirty permanent positions	37,492 82
2012-02	For other services, including traveling expenses, supplies, materials and equipment	5,143 74
	Shellfish Enforcement Law:	
2013-01	For personal services for administering the law relative to shellfish, including not more than one permanent position	1,101 67
2013-02	For other expenses for administering the law relative to shellfish	195 36
	Water Supply and Disposal of Sewage:	
2015-01	For personal services of directors, engineers, chemists, clerks and other assistants in the division of engineering and the division of laboratories, including not more than fifty permanent positions	67,652 23
2015-02	For other services, including traveling expenses, supplies, materials and equipment, for the division of engineering and the division of laboratories	8,039 44
	Total	$506,714 27

Item		
	Division of Tuberculosis:	
2020-01	For personal services of the director, stenographers, clerks and other assistants, including not more than nineteen permanent positions	$26,037 50
2020-02	For services other than personal, traveling expenses and office supplies and equipment	1,141 54
2020-03	For expenses of hospitalization of certain patients suffering from chronic rheumatism, as authorized by section one hundred and sixteen A of chapter one hundred and eleven of the General Laws, to be in addition to any amount heretofore appropriated for the purpose	17,510 05
2020-21	For personal services for certain children's clinics for tuberculosis, including not more than seventeen permanent positions	21,916 54
2020-22	For other services for certain children's clinics for tuberculosis	7,456 61
	Total	$74,062 24

Item		
	For the maintenance of the sanatoria, as follows:	
2022–00	Lakeville state sanatorium, including not more than two hundred and twenty-five permanent positions	$202,914 11
2023–00	North Reading state sanatorium, including not more than one hundred and eighty-five permanent positions	158,238 34
2024–00	Rutland state sanatorium, including not more than two hundred and thirty-five permanent positions	226,040 85
2025–00	Westfield state sanatorium, including not more than two hundred and ninety-one permanent positions	265,484 04
2025–22	For the purchase and installation of certain coal burning equipment in the power plant at the Westfield state sanatorium . .	36,000 00
	Pondville Hospital:	
2031–00	For maintenance of the Pondville hospital, including care of radium, and including not more than two hundred and thirty-six permanent positions	209,804 03
	Total	$1,098,481 37

Service of the Department of Public Safety.

Item		
	Administration:	
2101–01	For the salary of the commissioner. . . .	$3,500 00
2101–02	For personal services of clerks and stenographers, including not more than sixty-seven permanent positions	60,576 47
2101–03	For contingent expenses, rent of district offices, supplies and equipment, and all other things necessary for the investigation of fires and motion picture licenses, as required by law, and for expenses of administering the law regulating the sale and resale of tickets to theatres and other places of public amusement by the department of public safety .	26,577 16
	Total	$90,653 63
	Division of State Police:	
2102–01	For the salaries of officers and detectives, including not more than three hundred and eighteen permanent positions partly chargeable to item 2970–04, and for the salary of one permanent state police crime prevention and juvenile delinquency investigator . .	$125,639 00
2102–02	For personal services of civilian employees, including not more than one hundred and six permanent positions	74,559 50
2102–03	For other necessary expenses of the uniformed division, including traveling expenses of detectives, to be in addition to the amounts appropriated in item 2970–05	105,000 00
2102–04	For expert assistance to the commissioner and for maintenance of laboratories, including not more than four permanent positions .	6,742 62
	Total	$311,941 12

Item		
	Fire Prevention Service:	
2103-01	For the salary of the state fire marshal	$2,333 33
2103-02	For personal services of fire and other inspectors, including not more than nineteen permanent positions	24,004 98
2103-03	For other services, office rent and necessary office supplies and equipment	1,467 35
2103-04	For traveling expenses of fire and other inspectors	4,376 23
	Total	$32,181 89
	Division of Inspection:	
2104-01	For the salary of the chief of inspections	$2,333 33
2104-02	For services, supplies and equipment necessary for investigations and inspections by the division	339 57
2104-11	For the salaries of officers for the building inspection service, including not more than twenty-one permanent positions	28,954 27
2104-12	For traveling expenses of officers for the building inspection service	5,746 56
2104-21	For the salaries of officers for the boiler inspection service, including not more than twenty-six permanent positions	38,587 06
2104-22	For traveling expenses of officers for the boiler inspection service	4,780 08
	Total	$80,740 87
	Board of Boiler Rules:	
2104-31	For personal services of members of the board, including not more than four permanent positions	$583 32
2104-32	For services other than personal and the necessary traveling expenses of the board	63 40
	Total	$646 72
	State Boxing Commission:	
2105-01	For compensation and clerical assistance for the state boxing commission, including not more than five permanent positions	$5,829 87
2105-02	For other expenses of the commission	3,485 46
	Total	$9,315 33
	Service of the Department of Public Works.	
2201-01	For administering the law relative to advertising signs near highways, including not more than six permanent positions	$10,264 03
	Functions of the department relating to waterways and public lands:	
2202-01	For personal services of the director, chief engineer and assistants, including not more than seventy-six permanent positions	36,188 98
2202-02	For services other than personal, including printing pamphlet of laws, and for necessary office and engineering supplies and equipment	911 33

Item		
2202-03	For the care and maintenance of the province lands and of the lands acquired and structures erected by the Provincetown tercentenary commission, including not more than five permanent positions	$4,238 52
2202-06	For the maintenance and repair of certain property in the town of Plymouth	2,047 92
2202-07	For the operation and maintenance of the New Bedford state pier, including not more than three permanent positions	4,838 60
2202-08	For the operation and maintenance of the Cape Cod Canal pier, including not more than one permanent position	2,219 94
2202-09	For the maintenance of structures, and for repairing damages along the coast line or river banks of the commonwealth, and for the removal of wrecks and other obstructions from tide waters and great ponds	3,840 77
2202-13	For expenses of surveying certain town boundaries, by the department of public works	40 77
	Total	$64,590 86

Service of the Department of Public Utilities.

2301-01	For personal services of the commissioners, including not more than five permanent positions	$20,844 44
2301-02	For personal services of secretaries, employees of the accounting division, engineering division, and rate and tariff division, including not more than sixteen permanent positions	29,955 10
2301-03	For personal services of the inspection division, including not more than twenty permanent positions	30,817 57
2301-04	For personal services of clerks, messengers and office assistants, including not more than ten permanent positions	9,974 80
2301-05	For personal services of the telephone and telegraph division, including not more than seven permanent positions	11,318 32
2301-06	For traveling expenses of the commissioners and employees	1,221 35
2301-07	For other services, necessary office supplies and equipment	4,561 40
2301-08	For stenographic reports of evidence at inquests held in cases of death by accident on or about railroads	32 50
	Total	$108,725 48

Special Investigations:

The unexpended balance of the appropriations made by Item 2301-09 of chapter four hundred and nineteen of the acts of nineteen hundred and forty-one, as amended by chapter six hundred and eighty-three of the acts of said year, is hereby reappropriated.

Investigation of Gas and Electric Light Meters:

2302-01	For personal services of the division of inspection of gas and gas meters, including not more than twelve permanent positions	$13,995 03

Item		
2302–02	For expenses of the division of inspection of gas and gas meters, including traveling and other necessary expenses of inspection . . .	$1,611 32
2302–03	For the examination and tests of electric meters	34 42
	Total	$15,640 77
	Commercial Motor Vehicle Division:	
2304–01	For personal services of the director and assistants, including not more than thirty-two permanent positions	$17,636 29
2304–02	For other services, necessary office supplies and equipment, and for rent	5,984 47
	Total	$23,620 76
	Sale of Securities:	
2308–01	For personal services in administering the law relative to the sale of securities, including not more than twelve permanent positions .	$14,089 57
2308–02	For expenses other than personal in administering the law relative to the sale of securities	843 61
	Total	$14,933 18

Interest on the Public Debt.

2410–00	For the payment of interest on the direct debt of the commonwealth, to be in addition to the amounts appropriated in item 2951–00 .	$62,208 50

Requirements for Extinguishing the State Debt.

2420–00	For sinking fund requirements and for certain serial bonds maturing	$85,000 00

Unclassified Accounts and Claims.

2805–01	For the payment of certain annuities and pensions of soldiers and others under the provisions of certain acts and resolves . .	$4,952 36
2805–02	For payment of any claims, as authorized by section eighty-nine of chapter thirty-two of the General Laws, for allowances to the families of members of the department of public safety doing police duty killed or fatally injured in the discharge of their duties . .	6,748 77
2811–01	For the compensation of veterans of the civil war formerly in the service of the commonwealth, now retired	577 50
2811–02	For the compensation of veterans who may be retired by the governor under the provisions of sections fifty-six to fifty-nine, inclusive, of chapter thirty-two of the General Laws .	83,626 32
2811–03	For the compensation of certain prison officers and instructors formerly in the service of the commonwealth, now retired . . .	34,423 13
2811–04	For the compensation of state police officers formerly in the service of the commonwealth, now retired	4,983 16
2811–05	For the compensation of certain women formerly employed in cleaning the state house, now retired	234 92

Item		
2820–02	For small items of expenditure for which no appropriations have been made, and for cases in which appropriations have been exhausted or have reverted to the treasury in previous years	$500 00
2820–04	For the compensation of certain public employees for injuries sustained in the course of their employment, as provided by section sixty-nine of chapter one hundred and fifty-two of the General Laws, for the current fiscal period and for previous years, to be in addition to the amount appropriated by item 2970–07	25,000 00
	Total	$161,046 16

THE FOLLOWING APPROPRIATIONS ARE MADE FROM THE HIGHWAY FUND:

Service of the Department of Public Works.

Administration:

2921–01	For the salaries of the commissioner and the associate commissioners, including not more than three permanent positions, partly chargeable to item 3131–01 . . .	$8,531 25
2921–02	For personal services of clerks and assistants to the commissioner, including not more than four permanent positions, partly chargeable to item 3131–02	3,510 00
2921–03	For traveling expenses of the commissioners, to be in addition to the amounts appropriated in item 3131–03	575 00
2921–04	For telephone service in the public works building, including not more than six permanent positions, partly chargeable to item 3131–04	9,313 00
	Total	$21,929 25

Public Works Building:

2922–01	For personal services for the maintenance and operation of the public works building, including not more than sixty-three permanent positions	$53,150 00
2922–02	For the salaries of guards for the public works building, including expense of uniforms, and including not more than seventeen permanent positions	19,250 00
2922–03	For other expenses for the maintenance and operation of the public works building .	24,600 00
	Total	$97,000 00

Functions of the department relating to highways:

The following items are for expenses for the current fiscal period, and for previous years:

2900–01	For personal services and expenses of the department secretary, department business agent, and for vacation, sick leave, and other compensated absence in the highway division	$207,000 00

Item		
2900-02	For personal services and expenses of administrative and engineering services performed in connection with all highway activities; for payment of damages caused by defects in state highways, with the approval of the attorney general	$904,000 00
2900-04	For the maintenance and repair of state highways and bridges, control of snow and ice on state highways and town roads, and for the maintenance of traffic signs and signals .	1,958,000 00
2900-09	For the construction and reconstruction of state highways by state forces	20,000 00
2900-10	For projects for the construction of state highways and grade crossing elimination for which there are agreements for reimbursement from the federal government, and for land damages, the sum of two million one hundred thousand dollars is hereby appropriated, including an estimated receipt from the federal government of one million one hundred thousand dollars. It is provided further that all sums received from the federal government as reimbursement for expenditures previously made shall be credited to the Highway Fund	2,100,000 00
2900-17	For maintenance project payments for the construction and repair of town and county ways	331,000 00
2900-18	For aiding towns in the repair and improvement of public ways	1,145,125 00
	Special:	
2900-50 } 2900-55 }	There is hereby established a Public Works Stores and Equipment account to finance the operation and maintenance of equipment, acquisition of stores, materials, stock manufacturing and nursery operation. The comptroller is hereby authorized to certify for payment liabilities incurred for this purpose not in excess of an amount to be charged to the appropriations listed above. It is further provided that the expenses for capital outlay during the current fiscal period shall not exceed thirty-six thousand dollars. This fund shall be operated subject to such rules and regulations as may be established by the commission on administration and finance.	
	Total	$6,665,125 00

In addition to the amounts hereby appropriated for functions of the department relating to highways, the following transfers are made to the following accounts from the unexpended balances on November thirtieth, nineteen hundred and forty-two, in items 2923-12, 2923-20, 2923-30, 2923-40, and 2923-71, contained in the several appropriation acts passed in the year nineteen hundred and forty-one, said transfers to cover expenses for the current fiscal period, and for previous years:

2900-01	Administration	$195 30
2900-02	Highways, engineering and administration, general overhead	67,673 85
2900-04	Maintenance and operation of highways . .	94,057 37

Item		
2900-10	State highway construction	$568,840 03
2900-11	Primary road construction, non-federal aid	1,026 00
2900-17	Construction and repair of town and county ways, maintenance projects	236,136 78
2900-18	Repair and improvement of public ways	405,065 97
2900-50	Stores and equipment operation	103,767 19
2900-55	Capital outlay	11,470 80
	Total	$1,488,233 29
	Registration of Motor Vehicles:	
2924-01	For personal services, including not more than six hundred and fifty-seven permanent positions	$629,000 00
2924-02	For services other than personal, including traveling expenses, purchase of necessary supplies and materials, including cartage and storage of the same, and for work incidental to the registration and licensing of owners and operators of motor vehicles	190,000 00
2924-03	For printing and other expenses necessary in connection with publicity for certain safety work	150 00
	Total	$819,150 00

Interest on the Public Debt.

2951-00	For the payment of interest on the direct debt of the commonwealth, to be in addition to the amounts appropriated in item 2410-00	$78,111 25

Requirements for Extinguishing the State Debt.

2952-00	For sinking fund requirements and for certain serial bonds maturing during the current fiscal period, to be in addition to the amounts appropriated in item 2420-00	$749,562 50

Service of the Treasurer and Receiver-General.

	State Board of Retirement:	
2970-01	For requirements of annuity funds and pensions for employees retired from the state service under authority of law, to be in addition to the amounts appropriated in item 0604-03	$21,000 00

Service of the Department of Banking and Insurance.

	Division of Insurance:	
2970-02	For other personal services of the division, including expenses of the board of appeal and certain other costs of supervising motor vehicle liability insurance, to be in addition to the amounts appropriated in item 1103-02	$40,833 00

Service of the Department of Corporations and Taxation.

	Corporations and Tax Divisions:	
2970-03	To cover the estimated cost of collection of the gasoline tax, so-called, to be in addition to the amounts appropriated in item 1201-02	$29,167 00

Service of the Department of Public Safety.

Item		
	Division of State Police:	
2970-04	For the salaries of officers and detectives, to be in addition to the amounts appropriated in item 2102-01	$187,500 00
2970-05	For other necessary expenses of the uniformed division, including traveling expenses of detectives, to be in addition to the amounts appropriated in item 2102-03	105,000 00
	Total	$292,500 00

Unclassified Accounts and Claims.

2970-07	For the compensation of certain public employees for injuries sustained in the course of their employment, as provided by section sixty-nine of chapter one hundred and fifty-two of the General Laws, to be in addition to any amounts heretofore appropriated for the purpose, and in addition to the amounts appropriated by item 2820-04	$32,500 00

THE FOLLOWING APPROPRIATIONS ARE MADE FROM THE PORT OF BOSTON FUND:

Service of the Department of Public Works.

	Administration:	
3131-01	For the salaries of the commissioner and the associate commissioners, to be in addition to the amounts appropriated in item 2921-01	$2,843 75
3131-02	For personal services of clerks and assistants to the commissioner, to be in addition to the amounts appropriated in item 2921-02	1,170 00
3131-03	For traveling expenses of the commissioners, to be in addition to the amounts appropriated in item 2921-03	191 66
3131-04	For telephone service in the public works building, to be in addition to the amounts appropriated in item 2921-04	3,104 33
	Total	$7,309 74
	Functions of the department relating to Port of Boston:	
3132-02	For the supervision and operation of commonwealth pier five, including not more than thirty-five permanent positions, and for the repair and replacement of equipment and other property	$45,389 98
3132-12	For the maintenance and improvement of commonwealth property under the control of the department in connection with its functions relating to waterways and public lands	55,999 25
3132-14	For personal services and other expenses of the cost of operating the Commonwealth Airport, so-called	23,078 89
	Special:	
3132-21	For the purchase of certain snow removal equipment for the commonwealth airport, so-called	19,000 00
	Total	$143,468 12

The Following Appropriations are Payable from Fees Collected under Section 27 of Chapter 138 of the General Laws, as amended:

Service of Old Age Assistance Administration.

Item		
3621	For personal services required for the administration of old age assistance provided by chapter one hundred and eighteen A of the General Laws, including not more than fifty-five permanent positions	$48,356 00
3622	For other expenses, including rent, travel, office supplies and other necessary expenses, required for the administration of old age assistance provided by said chapter one hundred and eighteen A	7,200 00
	Total	$55,556 00

The Following Appropriation is Payable from the Mosquito Control Fund:

State Reclamation Board.

3901	For the maintenance and construction of drainage ditches, as authorized by chapter three hundred and seventy-nine of the acts of nineteen hundred and thirty, as amended by section one of chapter two hundred and fifty of the acts of nineteen hundred and thirty-five, to be assessed upon certain towns as required by law and to be in addition to any amount heretofore appropriated for the purpose	$16,573 87

The Following Appropriations are Payable from the Parks and Salisbury Beach Reservation Fund:

Division of Parks and Recreation.

4011	For personal services for certain administrative purposes and for certain consulting services, including not more than six permanent positions	$12,186 67
4012	For travel and other administrative expenses, including supplies for reservation improvements	2,230 63
4013	For the development of recreational opportunities in state forests, including personal services and other expenses	6,386 00
4021	For the maintenance of the Standish monument reservation	551 87
	Salisbury Beach Reservation:	
4031	For the maintenance of Salisbury beach reservation, including not more than one permanent position	1,802 57
	Total	$23,157 74

The Following Appropriations are Payable from the Smoke Inspection Fund:

Division of Smoke Inspection.

4311	For personal services, including not more than fourteen permanent positions	$18,984 20
4312	For other services, travel, and necessary office supplies and equipment	1,514 23
	Total	$20,498 43

THE FOLLOWING APPROPRIATIONS ARE PAYABLE FROM THE PRISON INDUSTRIES FUND:

Item		
	The following amounts appropriated in Items 4411, 4511, 4611 and 4711 include, in each instance, partial compensation of not more than seven additional permanent employees in industries at the State Prison:	
4411	For salaries of persons employed in industries at the Massachusetts Reformatory, including not more than twenty-six permanent positions	$34,864 63
4511	For salaries of persons employed in industries at the Reformatory for Women, including not more than thirteen permanent positions	16,685 45
4611	For salaries of persons employed in industries at the State Prison, including not more than thirty-seven permanent positions . .	51,955 77
4711	For salaries of persons employed in industries at the State Prison Colony, including not more than sixteen permanent positions .	24,227 05
	Total, Prison Industries Fund . . .	$127,732 90

General Fund	$30,370,769 47
Highway Fund	8,846,878 00
Port of Boston Fund	150,777 86
Old Age Assistance Fund, administration	55,556 00
Special Assessment Funds . . .	60,230 04
Prison Industries Fund . . .	127,732 90

SECTION 3. No payment shall be made or obligation incurred under authority of any special appropriation made by this act for construction of public buildings or other improvements at state institutions until plans and specifications have been approved by the governor, unless otherwise provided by such rules and regulations as the governor may make.

SECTION 4. No person shall be reimbursed by the commonwealth for any expense incurred for a mid-day meal while traveling within the commonwealth at the expense thereof, nor shall any person be so reimbursed for the amount of any expense incurred for a breakfast while so traveling which is in excess of seventy-five cents or for the amount of any expense incurred for an evening meal while so traveling which is in excess of one dollar and twenty-five cents. Nothing herein contained shall apply to state employees who receive as part of their compensation a non-cash allowance in the form of full or complete boarding and housing or to members of legislative committees or special commissions. No passenger automobile the price whereof, delivered, exceeds one thousand dollars shall be paid for out of funds appropriated by this act, except upon the written order of the commission on administration and finance. Nothing herein contained shall be construed as preventing a department from approving allowances for meals, not exceeding two dollars and fifty cents in any one day, for its employees stationed beyond commuting distance from their homes for a period of more than twenty-four hours or for its employees when engaged on special emergency duty.

SECTION 5. The allowance to state employees for expenses incurred by them in the operation of motor vehicles owned by them and used in the performance of their official duties shall not exceed four and one half cents a mile.

SECTION 6. The budget commissioner is hereby directed to send a copy of sections three, four and five of this act to each departmental, divisional and institutional head immediately following the passage of this act.

SECTION 7. All money paid into the treasury of the commonwealth from federal subventions and grants may be expended without specific appropriation, if such expenditures are otherwise in accordance with law.

SECTION 8. This act shall take effect upon its passage.

Approved March 8, 1943.

Chap. 69 AN ACT MAKING TEMPORARY PROVISION RELATIVE TO THE FILING OF ANNUAL STATEMENTS OF INSURANCE COMPANIES, OR OF SCHEDULES ACCOMPANYING SUCH STATEMENTS.

Emergency preamble.

Whereas, The deferred operation of this act would tend to defeat its purpose, which in part is to permit the commissioner of insurance to exercise, on or before March first of the current year, the authority thereby given to him, therefore it is hereby declared to be an emergency law, necessary for the immediate preservation of the public convenience.

Be it enacted, etc., as follows:

SECTION 1. During the continuance of the existing state of war between the United States and any foreign country but not later than June first, nineteen hundred and forty-five, the commissioner of insurance is hereby authorized to extend in any year the time for the filing of annual statements of insurance companies transacting business in the commonwealth, or of schedules accompanying such statements, for not more than sixty days beyond March first in said year.

SECTION 2. Section one of chapter twenty-four of the acts of nineteen hundred and forty-three is hereby repealed.

SECTION 3. This act shall be effective as of March first in the current year. *Approved March 9, 1943.*

AN ACT AUTHORIZING THE PLACING OF THE OFFICE OF CHIEF OF POLICE OF THE TOWN OF DOUGLAS UNDER THE CIVIL SERVICE LAWS. *Chap.* 70

Be it enacted, etc., as follows:

SECTION 1. The office of chief of police of the town of Douglas shall, upon the effective date of this act, become subject to the civil service laws and rules and regulations relating to police officers in towns, and the tenure of office of any incumbent thereof shall be unlimited, subject, however, to said laws, but the person holding said office on said effective date shall continue to serve therein only until the expiration of his term of office unless prior thereto he passes a non-competitive qualifying examination to which he shall be subjected by the division of civil service.

SECTION 2. This act shall be submitted for acceptance to the voters of said town at a special town meeting to be held in the current year in the form of the following question, which shall be placed upon a ballot to be used at said meeting: — "Shall an act passed by the General Court in the year nineteen hundred and forty-three, entitled 'An Act authorizing the placing of the Office of Chief of Police of the Town of Douglas under the Civil Service Laws', be accepted?" If a majority of the votes in answer to said question is in the affirmative, this act shall thereupon take full effect, but not otherwise. *Approved March 10, 1943.*

AN ACT RELATIVE TO THE CONTROL OF FLAX POND IN THE CITY OF LYNN. *Chap.* 71

Be it enacted, etc., as follows:

SECTION 1. The city of Lynn, through its board of park commissioners, may from time to time make rules and regulations as to the erection, maintenance and control of all public bath houses on the shores of Flax pond in said city.

SECTION 2. The board of park commissioners of said city may from time to time make rules and regulations governing fishing, boating, bathing, skating and other recreational activities in or on Flax pond in said city. Such rules and regulations relative to fishing shall be subject to the approval of the division of fisheries and game of the department of conservation, and such other rules and regulations shall be subject to the approval of the department of public works, and in either case when so approved shall have the force of law.

SECTION 3. Any police officer of said city may patrol any part of the waters of said pond and shall have authority to arrest any person violating any law of the commonwealth in, on or adjacent to the waters of said pond or violating any rule or regulation established under this act.

SECTION 4. The violation of any rule or regulation

established under this act shall be punished by a fine of not more than twenty dollars.

SECTION 5. Nothing in this act shall be construed to abridge the powers and duties of said department of public works under chapter ninety-one of the General Laws.

SECTION 6. This act shall take full effect upon its acceptance, during the current year, by vote of the city council of said city, subject to the provisions of its charter, but not otherwise. *Approved March 11, 1943.*

Chap. 72 AN ACT PROVIDING FURTHER FOR LEGITIMATION OF ILLEGITIMATE CHILDREN AND FOR CORRECTION OF THEIR BIRTH RECORDS.

Be it enacted, etc., as follows:

G. L. (Ter. Ed.), 190, § 7, amended.

SECTION 1. Section seven of chapter one hundred and ninety of the General Laws, as appearing in the Tercentenary Edition, is hereby amended by inserting after the word "child" in the second line the words: — or has been adjudged his father under chapter two hundred and seventy-three, — so as to read as follows: — *Section 7.* An illegitimate child whose parents have intermarried and whose father has acknowledged him as his child or has been adjudged his father under chapter two hundred and seventy-three shall be deemed legitimate and shall be entitled to take the name of his parents to the same extent as if born in lawful wedlock.

When illegitimate child to be deemed legitimate.

G. L. (Ter. Ed.), 46, § 13, etc., amended.

SECTION 2. Section thirteen of chapter forty-six of the General Laws is hereby amended by striking out the second paragraph, as appearing in chapter sixty-three of the acts of nineteen hundred and thirty-eight, and inserting in place thereof the following paragraph: —

Correction of certain birth records.

If a person shall have acquired the status of a legitimate child by the intermarriage of his parents and the acknowledgment of his father or an adjudication of paternity under chapter two hundred and seventy-three, as provided in section seven of chapter one hundred and ninety, the record of his birth shall be amended or supplemented as hereinafter provided so as to read, in all respects, as if such person had been reported for record as born to such parents in lawful wedlock. For such purpose, the town clerk, if satisfied as to the identity of the persons and the facts, shall receive an affidavit setting forth the material facts, executed by the parents, or by either if the other is dead, or shall receive such an affidavit executed by the mother alone in the case of a child who has acquired the status of a legitimate child by the intermarriage of his parents and an adjudication of paternity as aforesaid, or shall receive, if both parents are dead, affidavits of the fact of such intermarriage, and of the acknowledgment of the father or of an adjudication of paternity as aforesaid, and of the death of each parent, executed by credible persons having knowledge of such facts, together with evidence substantiating such facts beyond all reasonable doubt, which affidavits and evidence shall have been submitted by the town clerk to a judge of probate or to a justice of a district court and shall have been approved by such judge or justice. Each such affidavit executed by the parent or parents shall be accompanied by a certified copy of the record of such intermarriage, if not recorded in the records in the custody of such clerk; and such affidavits executed by credible persons as aforesaid shall be accompanied by a certified copy of the record of such intermarriage and of the death of each parent, if not recorded in such records. Each affidavit of the fact of an adjudication of paternity as aforesaid shall be accompanied by a certified copy of such adjudication.

Approved March 11, 1943.

An Act relative to the control of Lake Massapoag in the town of Sharon. *Chap.* 73

Be it enacted, etc., as follows:

Section 1. The town of Sharon, through its board of selectmen, may from time to time make rules and regulations as to the erection, maintenance and control of all public bath houses on the shores of Lake Massapoag in said town.

Section 2. Said town, through its board of selectmen, may from time to time make rules and regulations governing fishing, boating, bathing, skating and other recreational activities in or on Lake Massapoag in said town. Such rules and regulations relative to fishing shall be subject to the approval of the division of fisheries and game of the department of conservation, and such other rules and regulations shall be subject to the approval of the department of public works, and, in either case, when so approved shall have the force of law.

Section 3. Any police officer of said town may patrol any part of the waters of said lake and shall have authority to arrest any person violating any law of the commonwealth in, on or adjacent to the waters of said lake or violating any rule or regulation established under this act.

Section 4. The violation of any rule or regulation established under this act shall be punished by a fine of not more than twenty dollars.

Section 5. Nothing in this act shall be construed to abridge the powers and duties of said department of public works under chapter ninety-one of the General Laws.

Approved March 11, 1943.

Chap. 74 AN ACT PROVIDING A PENALTY FOR THE ALTERATION, DEFACEMENT, MUTILATION, DESTRUCTION OR CONCEALMENT OF ANY RECORD OF A FRATERNAL BENEFIT SOCIETY.

Be it enacted, etc., as follows:

G. L. (Ter. Ed.), 176, new § 32A, added.

Fraudulent alteration, etc., of record.

Penalty.

Chapter one hundred and seventy-six of the General Laws is hereby amended by inserting after section thirty-two, as appearing in the Tercentenary Edition, the following section: — *Section 32A.* Whoever with fraudulent intent alters, defaces, mutilates, destroys or conceals any record of any fraternal benefit society made by or in the custody of the secretary thereof shall be punished by a fine of not more than one thousand dollars or by imprisonment for not more than one year, or both.

Approved March 11, 1943.

Chap. 75 AN ACT TO AUTHORIZE CITIES, TOWNS AND DISTRICTS TO MAKE CERTAIN EMERGENCY APPROPRIATIONS DURING THE EXISTING STATE OF WAR BETWEEN THE UNITED STATES AND ANY FOREIGN COUNTRY.

Emergency preamble.

Whereas, The present national emergency requires that cities, towns, and districts be given certain emergency powers not now contained in the General Laws, and the purpose of this act is to give such powers to cities, towns, and districts forthwith, therefore this act is hereby declared to be an emergency law, necessary for the immediate preservation of the public health, safety and convenience.

Be it enacted, etc., as follows:

SECTION 1. Any city, town or district is hereby authorized, during the existing state of war between the United States and any foreign country, to raise and appropriate such sums of money as it may deem necessary for the preservation of health and protection of persons and property; to purchase equipment, uniforms and supplies for auxiliary fire and police departments, air-raid wardens, first aid rescue squads, and other essential units of defense; to provide for the training of its citizens in first aid and other matters essential to civilian defense; and for the purpose of conserving the food supply, to do such things as it may deem necessary to assist in the raising and distribution of food products; and to provide for such other means as may be necessary during such existing state of war for the protection of the people and property in such city, town or district. If a city or town, acting under the authority herein granted, shall plough or harrow or furnish other aid in the cultivation of private land situated in such city or town upon application of the owner of such land and for his benefit, the cost of such work shall be paid by the owner and bills shall be rendered to the owner therefor, and if not paid on or before the first day of April of any year, the amount so due and unpaid may be assessed on the land upon which the work was done, and shall be a lien on the said land enforceable in the same manner and with the same effect as is provided in the case of assessments for the suppression of the gypsy and brown tail moth.

SECTION 2. For the purpose of meeting expenditures herein authorized, a city, town or district may raise such sums as may be necessary by taxation, or may borrow from time to time, and may issue bonds or notes therefor, which shall bear on their face the words, (city, town, or district) Defense Loan, Act of 1943. Each authorized issue shall constitute a separate loan, and such loans shall be paid in not more than five years from their dates. Indebtedness incurred under this act shall be in excess of the statutory limit, but shall, except as provided herein, be subject to chapter forty-four of the General Laws, exclusive of the limitation contained in the first paragraph of section seven thereof.

SECTION 3. No loan shall be made by a city, town or district under authority of this act without the approval of the board established under section one of chapter forty-nine of the acts of nineteen hundred and thirty-three. Notwithstanding any provision of general or special law, ordinance or by-law to the contrary, a loan order voted in any city under authority of this act shall be deemed to be an emergency order and as such may be passed in such manner as is provided for emergency orders or ordinances in its charter and shall be in full force and effect immediately upon final favorable action thereon by its city council or chief executive, as the case may be, or upon the expiration of any period specified by such charter for the approval or disapproval of such orders by its chief executive in any case where he fails to approve or disapprove such an order within such period, and a loan order voted in any town or district under said authority shall be in full force and effect immediately upon final favorable action thereon by the inhabitants of the town or district or the town meeting members, as the case may be; provided, that in the city of Boston such loan orders may be passed in the manner provided in its charter for loan orders for temporary loans in anticipation of taxes. In any city a loan order under authority of this act may be passed by vote of two thirds of all of the members of the city council, or of each branch thereof where there are two branches, exclusive of those members who are in the military or naval forces of the United States and are not present at the meeting at which any such vote is taken at the time of the vote, notwithstanding any provision of law to the contrary.

SECTION 4. Sections one to three, inclusive, of this act shall become inoperative on July first, nineteen hundred and forty-five, but this section shall not affect any bonds or notes issued under this act prior to said date.

SECTION 5. Chapter four hundred and eighty-seven of the acts of nineteen hundred and forty-one is hereby repealed, but the repeal thereof shall not affect any bonds or notes issued under said chapter.

Approved March 11, 1943.

Chap. 76 AN ACT AUTHORIZING THE TOWN OF FRANKLIN TO INVEST IN FEDERAL GOVERNMENT BONDS CERTAIN MONEYS RECEIVED FROM THE SALE OF REAL ESTATE.

Be it enacted, etc., as follows:

SECTION 1. Notwithstanding section sixty-three of chapter forty-four of the General Laws, the town of Franklin, under and subject to section one of chapter five of the acts of nineteen hundred and forty-three, may invest in defense bonds, war bonds or other bonds issued by the federal government a sum not exceeding nineteen thousand, one hundred and eighty-four dollars and twenty-four cents now in the town treasury, said sum having been received from the sale of real estate.

SECTION 2. This act shall take effect upon its passage.

Approved March 12, 1943.

Chap. 77 AN ACT AUTHORIZING THE SALE OF CHECKS BY CO-OPERATIVE BANKS.

Be it enacted, etc., as follows:

G. L. (Ter. Ed.), 170, new § 43A, added.

Chapter one hundred and seventy of the General Laws is hereby amended by inserting after section forty-three, as appearing in chapter one hundred and forty-four of the acts of nineteen hundred and thirty-three, the following section,

Sale of checks by co-operative banks.

under the caption *Negotiable Checks,*: — *Section 43A.* Any co-operative bank may, under regulations made by the commissioner, sell negotiable checks drawn by or on it and payable by or through a trust company or a national banking association. *Approved March 12, 1943.*

Chap. 78 AN ACT RELATIVE TO THE INCLUSION OF THE MARKET DEPARTMENT OF THE CITY OF BOSTON IN THE PUBLIC BUILDINGS DEPARTMENT OF SAID CITY.

Be it enacted, etc., as follows:

SECTION 1. The market department of the city of Boston is hereby merged with, and shall hereafter constitute the division of markets of, the public buildings department of said city.

SECTION 2. The title of the superintendent of markets of the city of Boston shall hereafter be the director of markets of the city of Boston.

SECTION 3. The office of director of markets established by this act shall, upon the effective date of this act, become subject to the civil service laws and rules and regulations, and the tenure of office of any incumbent thereof shall be unlimited, subject, however, to said laws, but the person holding the office of superintendent of markets of the city of Boston immediately prior to said effective date shall be subjected by the division of civil service to a non-competitive qualifying examination for the office of director of markets established by this act, and if he passes said examination he shall be certified for said office and shall be deemed to be permanently appointed thereto without being required to serve any probationary period.

SECTION 4. This act shall take full effect upon its acceptance during the current year by vote of the city council of the city of Boston, approved by the mayor.

Approved March 12, 1943.

AN ACT TO REGULATE THE FORM OF NOTICES OF DECISIONS OF ASSESSORS WITH RESPECT TO APPLICATIONS FOR ABATEMENT. *Chap.* 79

Be it enacted, etc., as follows:

Section sixty-three of chapter fifty-nine of the General Laws, as appearing in the Tercentenary Edition, is hereby amended by adding at the end the following sentence: — Said notice shall state that appeal from such decision may be taken as provided in sections sixty-four to sixty-five B, inclusive, — so as to read as follows: — *Section 63.* Assessors shall, within ten days after their decision on an application for an abatement, give written notice thereof to the applicant. Said notice shall state that appeal from such decision may be taken as provided in sections sixty-four to sixty-five B, inclusive. *Approved March 12, 1943.*

G. L. (Ter. Ed.), 59, § 63, amended.

Notice of assessors' decision.

AN ACT RELATIVE TO EMERGENCY LOANS BY COUNTIES. *Chap.* 80

Be it enacted, etc., as follows:

Chapter thirty-five of the General Laws is hereby amended by striking out section thirty-six A, as amended by section five of chapter five hundred and one of the acts of nineteen hundred and thirty-nine, and inserting in place thereof the following: — *Section 36A.* For the purpose of providing funds for any county for any emergency purpose approved by a board composed of the attorney general, the state treasurer and the director of accounts, hereinafter referred to as said board, such county may borrow money in such amount and for such period not exceeding two years as may be determined by said board, and may issue a note or notes therefor, signed by the county treasurer and countersigned by a majority of the county commissioners, which may be sold at such interest or discount as the county commissioners deem proper, any discount to be treated as interest paid in advance. All applications for approval by said board shall

G. L. (Ter. Ed.), 35, § 36A, etc., amended.

Emergency loans by counties.

be submitted by the county commissioners, but if any such application is made for funds for use for a purpose connected with a county institution in charge of trustees or with a reservation, supported in whole or in part by county funds, in charge of a special board or commission, such application shall not be approved by said board unless it is supported by a written request for such funds from said trustees or said special board or commission, as the case may be. The proceeds of any borrowing hereunder shall be expended by the county commissioners for the purpose for which made; except that, if such a borrowing is made for use for a purpose connected with a county institution in charge of trustees or with a reservation, supported in whole or in part by county funds, in charge of a special board or commission, the proceeds thereof shall be expended for the purpose for which made by said trustees or said special board or commission, as the case may be.

Approved March 15, 1943.

Chap. 81 AN ACT INCREASING THE AMOUNT WHICH CO-OPERATIVE BANKS MAY HOLD IN THEIR GUARANTY FUNDS AND SURPLUS ACCOUNTS.

Be it enacted, etc., as follows:

G. L. (Ter. Ed.), 170, § 46, etc., amended.

Amounts credited to surplus accounts, etc.

Chapter one hundred and seventy of the General Laws is hereby amended by striking out section forty-six, as appearing in chapter one hundred and forty-four of the acts of nineteen hundred and thirty-three, and inserting in place thereof the following section: — *Section 46.* At each distribution of profits not more than one per cent of the net profits accrued since the last preceding adjustment shall be credited to the surplus account, unless there shall have been reserved and credited to the guaranty fund the maximum per cent of the net profits under section forty-five. Any such corporation may hold in its surplus account such sum as the board of directors may, from time to time, deem wise; but whenever the guaranty fund and surplus account together exceed fifteen and one fourth per cent of its total liabilities, the board of directors shall declare an extra dividend, provided such dividend does not reduce the guaranty fund and surplus account together to less than fifteen per cent of the total liabilities. *Approved March 15, 1943.*

Chap. 82 AN ACT RELATIVE TO THE REIMBURSEMENT OF COUNTIES BY TOWNS FOR THE SUPPORT OF HABITUAL TRUANTS, ABSENTEES OR SCHOOL OFFENDERS COMMITTED TO A COUNTY TRAINING SCHOOL.

Be it enacted, etc., as follows:

G. L. (Ter. Ed.), 77, § 1, etc., amended.

Section one of chapter seventy-seven of the General Laws, as amended by section one of chapter two hundred and ninety-five of the acts of nineteen hundred and thirty-three, is hereby further amended by striking out, in the twentieth and twenty-first lines, the words "maintaining it" and inserting in place thereof the words: — from which he is committed, — so as to read as follows: — *Section 1.* The county commissioners of each county, except Barnstable, Berkshire, Bristol, Franklin, Hampshire, Dukes, Nantucket, Norfolk, Plymouth and Suffolk, shall maintain either separately or jointly with the commissioners of other counties as hereinafter provided, in a suitable place, remote from a penal institution, a school for the instruction and training of children committed thereto as habitual truants, absentees or school offenders. The commissioners of Barnstable, Berkshire, Bristol, Franklin, Hampshire, Dukes, Nantucket, Norfolk and Plymouth counties shall assign a training school established by law as the place for the instruction and training of children so committed within their respective counties, and shall pay for their support in said school such reasonable sum as the commissioners having control of said school may fix. Commitments from Boston, Chelsea, Revere and Winthrop shall be to the training school for Middlesex county. The town from which an habitual truant, absentee or school offender is committed to a county training school shall pay to the county from which he is committed two dollars a week toward his support, and reports of the condition and progress of its pupils in said school shall be sent each month to the superintendent of schools of such town; but Boston, Chelsea, Revere and Winthrop shall pay to Middlesex county, for the support of each child committed to the training school of said county, two dollars and fifty cents a week, and an additional sum for each child sufficient to cover the actual cost of maintenance. *Approved March 15, 1943.*

Certain counties to maintain training schools

Commitments from and payments by other counties.

Chap. 83

An Act repealing the provisions of law which authorize the appointment of an agent to examine and prosecute accounts and claims of the commonwealth against the United States, and transferring the duties of said officer to the attorney general.

Be it enacted, etc., as follows:

Section 1. Section three of chapter twelve of the General Laws, as amended by section two of chapter one hundred and eighty of the acts of nineteen hundred and thirty-two, is hereby further amended by inserting after the word "tribunal" in the seventh line, as appearing in the Tercentenary Edition, the words: —, including the prosecution of claims of the commonwealth against the United States, — so as to read as follows: — *Section 3.* The attorney general shall appear for the commonwealth and for state departments, officers and commissions in all suits and other civil proceedings in which the commonwealth is a party or interested, or in which the official acts

G. L. (Ter. Ed.), 12, § 3, etc., amended.

Attorney general to appear for commonwealth, when.

and doings of said departments, officers and commissions are called in question, in all the courts of the commonwealth, except upon criminal recognizances and bail bonds, and in such suits and proceedings before any other tribunal, including the prosecution of claims of the commonwealth against the United States, when requested by the governor or by the general court or either branch thereof. All such suits and proceedings shall be prosecuted or defended by him or under his direction. Writs, summonses or other processes served upon such officers shall be forthwith transmitted by them to him. All legal services required by such departments, officers, commissions and commissioners of pilots for district one in matters relating to their official duties shall, except as otherwise provided, be rendered by the attorney general or under his direction.

G. L. (Ter. Ed.), 29, § 62, repealed.

SECTION 2. Section sixty-two of chapter twenty-nine of the General Laws, as appearing in the Tercentenary Edition, is hereby repealed. *Approved March 15, 1943.*

Chap. 84 AN ACT AUTHORIZING WATER COMMISSIONERS AND OTHERS TO ENTER PREMISES WITHIN THE WATER SHED OF CERTAIN SOURCES OF WATER SUPPLY.

Be it enacted, etc., as follows:

G. L. (Ter. Ed.), 111, new § 173B, added.

Right to enter certain premises.

Chapter one hundred and eleven of the General Laws is hereby amended by inserting after section one hundred and seventy-three A, inserted by chapter two hundred and ninety-three of the acts of nineteen hundred and thirty-eight, the following section: — *Section 173B.* Any water board or board of water commissioners of a city, town or water district and any executive officer or agent of any such board or of a public institution or water company furnishing water for domestic purposes, and any police officer employed by such a water board, board of water commissioners, public institution or water company, may enter any premises except dwelling houses within the water shed of the source of water supply of such city, town, district, institution or company to ascertain whether the provisions of this chapter relative to water supply and the rules and regulations adopted under section one hundred and sixty are being obeyed. *Approved March 15, 1943.*

Chap. 85 AN ACT AUTHORIZING THE GRANTING OF LICENSES TO NON-RESIDENTS TO ACT AS INSURANCE AGENTS OF INSURANCE COMPANIES, AND LIMITING THE POWERS OF SUCH AGENTS ACTING FOR FOREIGN INSURANCE COMPANIES.

Be it enacted, etc., as follows:

G. L. (Ter. Ed.), 175, § 163, etc., amended.

Section one hundred and sixty-three of chapter one hundred and seventy-five of the General Laws is hereby amended by striking out the second paragraph, inserted by chapter five hundred and two of the acts of nineteen hundred and forty-one, and inserting in its place the following paragraph: —

Nothing in this chapter shall be construed to prohibit the issue of a license under this section as an insurance agent of a foreign company authorized to transact business in the commonwealth to a person resident in any other state of the United States granting similar licenses to residents of this commonwealth. A non-resident licensed as an insurance agent of such a company shall transact business in the commonwealth only through the lawfully constituted and licensed resident agents of such company in the commonwealth. Nothing in this chapter shall be construed to prohibit the issuance of a license under this section as an insurance agent of a domestic company to a person resident in any other state of the United States. Licenses of non-resident agents.

Approved March 15, 1943.

An Act authorizing certain limited fraternal benefit societies to pay increased benefits in certain cases. *Chap.* 86

Be it enacted, etc., as follows:

Section forty-six of chapter one hundred and seventy-six of the General Laws is hereby amended by adding at the end of the paragraph inserted therein by chapter two hundred and seventy-four of the acts of nineteen hundred and forty-one the following sentence: — A society to which the membership and funds of another society shall have been transferred as aforesaid may continue to transact business subject to this section, but may have a special class of members consisting of those persons who held membership in each of said societies immediately prior to the transfer, which members shall be entitled to dual benefits and shall pay dual membership dues and assessments. Said class of membership shall not be expanded or replaced and shall not in any event receive disability benefits of more than twenty dollars per week and death benefits of more than four hundred dollars. Benefits not exceeding said amounts may be paid notwithstanding any other provisions of law to the contrary. G. L. (Ter. Ed.), 176, § 46, etc., amended. Special membership.

Approved March 15, 1943.

An Act authorizing the trial in the Boston juvenile court of certain proceedings against parents. *Chap.* 87

Be it enacted, etc., as follows:

Section 1. Chapter two hundred and seventy-three of the General Laws is hereby amended by striking out section two, as amended by chapter two hundred and twenty-four of the acts of nineteen hundred and thirty-three, and inserting in place thereof the following section: — *Section 2.* Proceedings under section one shall be begun, if in the su- G. L. (Ter. Ed.), 273, § 2, etc., amended. Jurisdiction, etc., of certain proceedings against parents.

perior court, in the county in which is situated the place where the husband and wife last lived together or where the husband or wife or parent of the child is living, and, if begun in a district court or before a trial justice, in the court or before the trial justice having such place within its or his judicial district; provided, that such a proceeding for an offence committed within the territorial limits prescribed for the criminal jurisdiction of the municipal court of the city of Boston, if founded upon the same allegations as a proceeding under sections forty-two to forty-seven, inclusive, of chapter one hundred and nineteen, may be brought, heard and disposed of in the Boston juvenile court. Such a proceeding for an offence committed within the territorial limits prescribed for the criminal jurisdiction of any court other than the municipal court of the city of Boston, if founded upon the same allegations as a proceeding under said sections forty-two to forty-seven, inclusive, of said chapter one hundred and nineteen, may be heard and disposed of in the juvenile session of the court. Any parent placed on probation in such a proceeding in the Boston juvenile court shall at the request of the justice thereof be supervised by the probation officers of the municipal court of the city of Boston.

Effective date.

SECTION 2. This act shall take effect on July first in the current year. *Approved March 15, 1943.*

Chap. 88 AN ACT RELATIVE TO THE OFFICE OF MAYOR IN THE CITY OF LOWELL AND THE ADMINISTRATION OF THE AFFAIRS OF SAID CITY.

Be it enacted, etc., as follows:

SECTION 1. Notwithstanding any provisions of general law, of any special act relating to the city of Lowell or of any ordinance of said city, the president of the city council of said city in office on the effective date of this act, hereafter in this act called the president, or his successor in said office in the event of his death or resignation from said city council, hereafter in this act called his successor, shall exclusively, during the period beginning with said effective date and ending on the first Monday in January, nineteen hundred and forty-four, possess all the rights and powers, perform all the duties and be subject to all of the obligations of mayor of said city, subject, however, to the following provisions: —

(*a*) The terms of all persons appointed or reappointed, temporarily or otherwise, by the president or his successor, during the period covered by this act shall expire on said first Monday in January, nineteen hundred and forty-four, but such appointees shall continue to hold office until the qualification of their respective successors.

(*b*) The president or his successor, while exercising the rights and powers and performing the duties of mayor under any provision of this act, shall be entitled to compensation from January first, nineteen hundred and forty-three, payable in equal monthly instalments, at the rate of forty-four hundred dollars per annum, but shall not, during said period, be entitled to any compensation as a member of the city council.

(*c*) Nothing in this act shall be deemed to derogate from the powers and duties of the president or his successor in his capacity as president and a member of said city council or affect his tenure as such president or member.

(*d*) In case the president or his successor, for a continuous period of thirty days, shall be unable, because of disability or absence from the city, to exercise the powers and duties conferred upon him by this act, said city council shall thereupon elect a temporary president of said council to exercise and perform the powers, rights, duties and obligations conferred and imposed upon the president or his successor by this act, only in matters not admitting of delay, until such time as said president or his successor resumes the functions and duties of his office.

(*e*) During such period, prior to the election of a temporary president as provided in paragraph (*d*), as the president or his successor, because of disability or absence from said city, is unable to exercise the powers or perform the duties conferred upon him by this act, the city auditor is hereby authorized to approve warrants for payments from the city treasury and the city treasurer is hereby authorized to pay warrants so approved.

(*f*) During the period covered by this act, no permanent appointment, and no provisional or temporary appointment except to fill a vacancy until the said first Monday in January, nineteen hundred and forty-four, shall be made to any office or position within the classified civil service of said city, except with the approval of the director of civil service in the department of civil service and registration.

(*g*) During the period covered by this act no additional appointment, and no promotion or increase in salary except regular step-rate increases, shall be made in any appointive office, position or employment in the service of said city.

Section 2. No special election for a mayor shall be held in said city during the current year under the provisions of section twenty-six of chapter forty-three of the General Laws, as amended.

Section 3. During the period covered by this act, no loan shall be made by said city under any special act authorizing it to borrow money, or under the general authority granted by chapter forty-four of the General Laws, as amended, other than loans issued under section four of said chapter, as amended, without the approval of the emergency finance board established under section one of chapter forty-nine of the acts of nineteen hundred and thirty-three, as amended. The members of said board, when acting under this act, shall receive from the commonwealth compensation to the same extent as provided for services under chapter three hundred and sixty-six of the acts of nineteen hundred and thirty-three, as amended.

SECTION 4. The action of the president of the city council of said city in submitting the annual budget of said city to the city council thereof on February sixteenth in the current year shall have the same force and effect as if the provisions of this act had been in effect at the time said action was taken.

SECTION 5. This act shall take effect upon its passage.

Approved March 16, 1943.

Chap. 89 AN ACT RELATIVE TO THE REGISTRATION OF THE BLIND.

Be it enacted, etc., as follows:

G. L. (Ter. Ed.), 69, § 19, amended.

SECTION 1. Section nineteen of chapter sixty-nine of the General Laws, as appearing in the Tercentenary Edition, is hereby amended by striking out the second sentence and inserting in place thereof the following sentence: — The city clerk of each city and the selectmen of each town shall aid him by furnishing the names and addresses of all known blind persons residing within such city or town, — so as to read as follows: — *Section 19.* He shall maintain a register of the blind in the commonwealth, which shall describe their condition, cause of blindness and capacity for education and industrial training. The city clerk of each city and the selectmen of each town shall aid him by furnishing the names and addresses of all known blind persons residing within such city or town. The department of public welfare and boards of public welfare shall aid the director by reporting whenever outdoor or indoor aid is granted to families in which there is a blind member, and the director shall report in turn to the said department and the said board any activity on his part in relation to blind persons who or whose families are known to be receiving or to have received public outdoor or indoor aid.

Register of the blind.

Reports to department of public welfare.

G. L. (Ter. Ed.), 69, new § 19A, added.

Diagnosis of blindness, report of, etc.

SECTION 2. Said chapter sixty-nine is hereby further amended by inserting after said section nineteen the following section: — *Section 19A.* Whenever, upon examination at a clinic, hospital or other institution, or elsewhere, by a physician or optometrist, the visual acuity of any person is found to be with correction 20/200 or less in the better eye, or the peripheral field of his vision to have contracted to the ten degree radius or less regardless of visual acuity, the superintendent of such institution, or the physician, optometrist or other person who conducted or was in charge of the examination if it took place elsewhere than in such an institution, shall within thirty days report to the director the result of the examination and that blindness of the person examined has been established.

Approved March 17, 1943.

AN ACT RELATIVE TO THE OPEN SEASON ON OPOSSUMS OR RACCOONS. *Chap. 90*

Be it enacted, etc., as follows:

Section sixty-eight of chapter one hundred and thirty-one of the General Laws, as appearing in section two of chapter five hundred and ninety-nine of the acts of nineteen hundred and forty-one, is hereby amended by striking out, in the eighth line, the word "first" and inserting in place thereof the word: — tenth, — so that the first paragraph will read as follows: — Except as otherwise provided in this chapter, no person shall hunt or trap, or have in possession the living or dead bodies of, minks, otters, muskrats, opossums or raccoons; provided, that such mammals, other than opossums or raccoons, may be taken by hunting or trapping between November first and the following March first, both dates inclusive, and that opossums or raccoons may be taken with the aid or by the use of dogs or guns between October tenth and the following January first, both dates inclusive, and by trapping between November first and the following January first, both dates inclusive. No person shall remove or attempt to remove a raccoon from any hole in the ground, stone wall, from within any ledge, or from under any stone or from any hole in any log or tree. Not more than two raccoons shall be taken during any period from sunset of one day to sunset of the following day by any one person, or three raccoons by two or more persons hunting in one party, and not more than ten raccoons shall be taken by any person in any open season. *Approved March 17, 1943.*

G. L. (Ter. Ed.), 131, § 68, etc., amended.

Hunting, etc., of mink and other mammals, regulated.

AN ACT PROVIDING THAT CERTAIN PROCEEDINGS IN PROBATE COURTS BE ENTITLED PETITIONS FOR DISCOVERY. *Chap. 91*

Be it enacted, etc., as follows:

Section forty-four of chapter two hundred and fifteen of the General Laws, as amended by section one of chapter three hundred and twenty-three of the acts of nineteen hundred and forty-one, is hereby further amended by adding at the end the following sentence: — A proceeding hereunder shall be entitled "petition for discovery", — so as to read as follows: — *Section 44.* Upon complaint to a probate court by a person interested in the estate of a deceased person against a person suspected of having fraudulently received, concealed, embezzled or conveyed away any property, real or personal, of the deceased, the court may cite such suspected person, although he is executor or administrator, to appear and be examined on oath upon the matter of the complaint. If the person so cited refuses to appear and submit to examination, or to answer such interrogatories as may be lawfully propounded to him, the court may commit him to jail until he submits to the order

G. L (Ter. Ed), 215, § 44, etc., amended.

Petitions for discovery in probate proceedings.

of the court. The examination shall be had and recorded in such manner as the court shall direct, and the final record shall be signed by the party examined. A proceeding hereunder shall be entitled "petition for discovery".

Approved March 18, 1943.

Chap. 92 AN ACT AMENDING THE CHARTER OF THE CITY OF WORCESTER RELATIVE TO THE TIME OF ORGANIZATION OF THE CITY GOVERNMENT.

Be it enacted, etc., as follows:

Chapter four hundred and forty-four of the acts of eighteen hundred and ninety-three is hereby amended by striking out section ten, as affected by chapter two hundred and eighty-two of the acts of nineteen hundred and twenty-six, and inserting in place thereof the following section: — *Section 10.* The mayor elect and members elect of the city council shall be sworn to the faithful performance of their respective duties; and for that purpose shall meet on the first Monday in January following their election, or on the following day whenever said first Monday in January falls upon a holiday, at ten o'clock in the morning or at such other hour as may be set by the mayor and city council at least fourteen days before said first Monday in January, when such oath may be administered to the mayor elect by any judge of any court of record in the commonwealth or by any justice of the peace, and to the members elect of the city council by the mayor or by any justice of the peace. A certificate that such oath has been taken shall be entered in the journals of the board of aldermen and of the common council by their respective clerks. If the mayor elect or any one or more of the members elect of the city council shall not be present on the first Monday in January, or on the following day whenever said first Monday in January falls upon a holiday, to take the oath required of them, or if any of them shall be elected subsequent to the first Monday in January, or to the following day whenever said first Monday in January falls upon a holiday, the oath may be administered to the mayor or aldermen at any meeting of the board of aldermen thereafter, and to the common councilmen at any meeting of the common council thereafter, before entering upon office. A certificate that such oath has been taken shall, in case of the mayor, be entered in the journal of both branches of the city council, in the case of a member of the board of aldermen, be entered in the journal of said board, and in the case of a member of the common council, be entered in the journal of the common council, at the meeting at which such oath was administered. *Approved March 18, 1943.*

AN ACT RELATIVE TO THE UNAUTHORIZED HOLDING OR HARBORING OF DOGS OF OTHERS. *Chap.* 93

Be it enacted, etc., as follows:

G L (Ter Ed.), 140, § 175, etc., amended.

Chapter one hundred and forty of the General Laws is hereby amended by striking out section one hundred and seventy-five, as most recently amended by section thirty-three of chapter three hundred and twenty of the acts of nineteen hundred and thirty-four, and inserting in place thereof the following section: — *Section 175.* Whoever wrongfully kills, maims, entices or carries away a dog shall be liable in tort to its owner for its value. Whoever, without the authorization of the owner or keeper, removes from a dog of another its license tag, collar or harness, or holds or harbors a dog of another for more than forty-eight hours after it comes into his possession, without taking it to a police station or dog officer in the town where it came into his possession or reporting such holding or harboring to the officer in charge of a police station in such town or to a dog officer therein and informing such police officer or dog officer of the place where it came into his possession and giving his own name and address and as full a description as possible of the dog, or whoever shall cause a dog to wear an imitation or counterfeit of the official tag prescribed by section one hundred and thirty-seven, shall be punished by a fine of not more than one hundred dollars. *Approved March 18, 1943.*

Liability for killing, etc., a licensed dog.

AN ACT PROVIDING FOR PAYMENTS AT INTERVALS OF NOT MORE THAN THREE MONTHS ON CERTAIN SAVINGS BANK MORTGAGE LOANS, AND FOR DELAYED ORIGINAL PAYMENTS ON CERTAIN SAVINGS BANK CONSTRUCTION MORTGAGE LOANS. *Chap.* 94

Be it enacted, etc., as follows:

G. L. (Ter. Ed.), 168, § 54, etc., amended.

SECTION 1. Clause First of section fifty-four of chapter one hundred and sixty-eight of the General Laws, as most recently amended by chapter one hundred and eighty of the acts of nineteen hundred and thirty-seven, is hereby further amended by striking out subdivision (*d*), as appearing therein, and inserting in place thereof the following subdivision: —

Limitation on mortgage loans not exceeding sixty per cent of value of premises.

(*d*) A loan secured by a first mortgage of real estate located in the commonwealth, except real estate referred to in subsection (*b*) hereof, not exceeding sixty per cent of the value of the premises to be mortgaged, may be made for a period of not less than three nor more than twenty years from the date of the note, provided that the terms of such note shall require payments on the loan to be made in periodic installments, at intervals not exceeding three months, such payments to commence not later than three months after the date of the note, except that in the case of a construction loan under this subsection, such payments may commence not later than six months after the date of the note; and such payments on any loan referred to in this subsection shall be in amounts aggregating annually not less than two per cent of the original amount of the loan.

G. L. (Ter. Ed.), 168, § 54, etc., further amended.

SECTION 2. Said clause First is hereby further amended by striking out subdivision (*e*), as so appearing, and inserting in place thereof the following: —

Limitation on mortgage loans not exceeding seventy per cent of value of premises.

(*e*) A loan secured by a first mortgage of real estate located in the commonwealth, except real estate referred to in subsection (*b*) hereof, not exceeding seventy per cent of the value of the premises to be mortgaged, may be made for a period of not less than three nor more than twenty years from the date of the note, provided that the terms of the note shall require payments on the loan to be made in periodic installments, at intervals not exceeding three months, such payments to commence not later than three months after the date of the note, except that in the case of a construction loan under this subsection, such payments may commence not later than six months after the date of the note; and such payments on any loan referred to in this subsection shall be in amounts aggregating annually not less than three per cent of the original amount of the loan. No loan under this subsection shall be made for a sum in excess of twenty-five thousand dollars. *Approved March 18, 1943.*

Chap. 95 AN ACT ESTABLISHING THE TIME WITHIN WHICH PETITIONS FOR THE ASSESSMENT OF DAMAGES TO PROPERTY TAKEN BY EMINENT DOMAIN MAY BE BROUGHT IN CERTAIN CASES.

Be it enacted, etc., as follows:

G. L. (Ter. Ed.), 79, § 16, etc., amended.

Time for filing petition.

Chapter seventy-nine of the General Laws is hereby amended by striking out section sixteen, as most recently amended by chapter one hundred and eighty-five of the acts of nineteen hundred and thirty-eight, and inserting in place thereof the following section: — *Section 16.* A petition for the assessment of damages under section fourteen may be filed within one year after the right to such damages has vested; but any person, including every mortgagee of record, whose property has been taken or injured, and who has not received notice under section eight or otherwise of the proceedings whereby he is entitled to damages at least sixty days before the expiration of such year, may file such petition within six months after the taking possession of his property or the receipt by him of actual notice of the taking, whichever first occurs, or, if his property has not been taken, within six months after he first suffers actual injury in his property.

Approved March 19, 1943.

AN ACT AUTHORIZING THE TOWN OF DEDHAM TO PAY A CERTAIN SUM OF MONEY TO THOMAS T. DOGGETT, SENIOR, OF SAID DEDHAM. *Chap.* 96

Be it enacted, etc., as follows:

The town of Dedham is hereby authorized to pay during the current year, in accordance with a vote of the town meeting of said town on March thirtieth, nineteen hundred and forty-two, to Thomas T. Doggett, Senior, of said town the sum of one thousand four hundred and seven dollars and eighty-five cents to reimburse said Doggett for money expended for counsel fees and costs in the case of Doggett *vs.* Hooper, any statute or by-law to the contrary notwithstanding. *Approved March 24, 1943.*

AN ACT RELATIVE TO PAYMENT FOR MEDICAL, HOSPITAL AND OTHER SERVICES RENDERED ON ACCOUNT OF DEPENDENT CHILDREN AND THEIR PARENTS. *Chap.* 97

Emergency preamble.

Whereas, The result of the deferred operation of this act would be that the payment of reimbursement to certain cities and towns for money expended for aid to dependent children would be further postponed until after the expiration of the period of deferment, therefore this act is hereby declared to be an emergency law, necessary for the immediate preservation of the public convenience.

Be it enacted, etc., as follows:

G. L. (Ter. Ed.), 118, § 2, etc., amended.

Section two of chapter one hundred and eighteen of the General Laws, as most recently amended by section one of chapter five hundred and ninety-three of the acts of nineteen hundred and forty-one, is hereby further amended by inserting after the second sentence the two following sentences: — In the event of the commitment of any such parent to an institution as an insane person, expenses for medical, hospital and other services rendered on account of such parent or any dependent child in his or her care or custody, including expenses of the funeral of any such dependent child who may have died, which remain unpaid at the time of such commitment may be paid by the town directly to the person furnishing such services, subject to any rule or regulation of the department relative to reimbursement under this chapter. In the event of the death of any such parent, expenses for medical, hospital and other services rendered on account of such parent or any dependent child in his or her care or custody, including expenses of the funeral of any such dependent child who may have died, which remain unpaid at the time of the death of such parent, and also expenses of the funeral of such parent, may be paid by the town directly to the person furnishing such services, subject to any rule or regulation of the department relative to reimbursement under this chapter, — so as to

Duties of boards of public welfare.

read as follows: — *Section 2.* In every town the board of public welfare, subject to the supervision of the department and in compliance with the rules and regulations adopted by the department pursuant to the provisions of this chapter, shall aid every parent in properly bringing up, in his or her own home, each dependent child if such parent is fit to bring up such child, but no aid shall be granted under this chapter for or on account of any child unless (1) such child has resided in the commonwealth one year immediately preceding the application for such aid, or (2) such child was born within the commonwealth within one year immediately preceding such application, if its mother has resided in the commonwealth for one year immediately preceding the birth. The aid furnished shall be sufficient to enable such parent to bring up such child or children properly in his or her own home. In the event of the commitment of any such parent to an institution as an insane person, expenses for medical, hospital and other services rendered on account of such parent or any dependent child in his or her care or custody, including expenses of the funeral of any such dependent child who may have died, which remain unpaid at the time of such commitment may be paid by the town directly to the person furnishing such services, subject to any rule or regulation of the department relative to reimbursement under this chapter. In the event of the death of any such parent, expenses for medical, hospital and other services rendered on account of such parent or any dependent child in his or her care or custody, including expenses of the funeral of any such dependent child who may have died, which remain unpaid at the time of the death of such parent, and also expenses of the funeral of such parent, may be paid by the town directly to the person furnishing such services, subject to any rule or regulation of the department relative to reimbursement under this chapter. Nothing in this chapter shall be construed as authorizing any public official, agent or representative, in carrying out any provision of this chapter, to take charge of any child over the objection of either the father or the mother of such child, or of the person standing in loco parentis to such child, except pursuant to a proper court order.

Approved March 24, 1943.

Chap. 98 AN ACT FURTHER EXTENDING THE PERIOD OF PUBLIC CONTROL AND MANAGEMENT OF THE EASTERN MASSACHUSETTS STREET RAILWAY COMPANY.

Be it enacted, etc., as follows:

SECTION 1. Upon the termination on the fifteenth day of January, nineteen hundred and forty-four, of the five year period of the management and control by trustees of the Eastern Massachusetts Street Railway Company, hereinafter called the company, under the provisions of chapter one hundred and seventy-three of the acts of nineteen hundred and thirty-eight, the public management and control of the company by trustees shall be extended, subject to the provisions of this act, for a period of five years from said date. The company may, subject to the provisions of this act, exercise all the powers and privileges of a street railway company organized under general laws, so far as the same are applicable, and, subject to the approval of the department of public utilities, hereinafter referred to as the department, any powers or privileges granted by any special acts applicable to the company, until the general court shall otherwise provide, and shall be subject to all the duties, restrictions and liabilities imposed upon street railway companies, except as otherwise provided herein.

SECTION 2. The governor, with the advice and consent of the council, shall appoint two persons who with a representative appointed by the board of directors of the company from among their own number shall act as trustees of the company, with the powers, duties and responsibilities hereinafter set forth, for terms of five years from the fifteenth day of January, nineteen hundred and forty-four. If upon said date trustees have not been appointed and confirmed as aforesaid and organized, the trustees who shall hold office on the fourteenth day of January, nineteen hundred and forty-four under the provisions of chapter one hundred and seventy-three of the acts of nineteen hundred and thirty-eight, shall be trustees under the provisions of this act until trustees shall have been appointed, confirmed and organized under the provisions hereof. Upon such appointment, confirmation and organization, the provisions of chapter two hundred and ninety-eight of the acts of nineteen hundred and twenty-eight and of chapter one hundred and seventy-three of the acts of nineteen hundred and thirty-eight shall terminate, but such termination shall not affect the validity of any acts done or action taken theretofore under the authority of either of said acts.

SECTION 3. The trustees appointed or existing under the provisions of this act shall on said fifteenth day of January, nineteen hundred and forty-four, assume the management and control of the company and, subject to the provisions of this act, shall continue to exercise said management and control during said period of five years. The governor shall fill for the unexpired term any vacancy among the trustees appointed by the governor, and may remove any such trustee, in either case with the advice and consent of the council. The directors may at any time remove the trustee appointed by them and appoint a new trustee. Each trustee shall receive from the company an annual salary of six thousand, two hundred and fifty dollars. Section three of chapter twelve of the General Laws shall not apply to said trustees.

SECTION 4. For the purpose of refunding any maturing obligations of the company secured by mortgage or other liens underlying the general mortgage bonds of the company or of leased lines within the commonwealth or of making additions to or improvements on the property of the company or of such leased lines or for any other lawful purpose, the trustees may cause the company to issue stocks, bonds or other evidences of indebtedness in accordance with the provisions of general laws or of any special law applicable thereto. Equipment notes under conditional bill of sale or lease, payable serially in not more than fifteen years, may be authorized and issued without reference to the amount of capital stock outstanding. Nothing contained in this act shall authorize the trustees to issue any shares of capital stock or any bonds, notes or other evidences of indebtedness payable at periods of more than one year after the date thereof, without the approval of the department in accordance with any provisions of law applicable thereto.

SECTION 5. The trustees shall manage and operate the company for the extended period specified in section one, and for the purposes of this act shall, except as is otherwise provided herein, have and may exercise all the rights and powers of the company and its directors and upon its behalf shall receive and disburse its income and funds. They shall have the right to appoint and remove at their discretion the president, treasurer and clerk of the company and all other officers of the company except the board of directors. They shall have the right to regulate and fix rates and fares, including the issue, granting and withdrawal of transfers and the imposition of charges therefor, and shall determine the character and extent of the service and the facilities to be furnished, and in these respects their authority shall be exclusive and shall not be subject to the approval, control or discretion of any other state department, board or commission except as provided in this act, and except as to joint rates and fares or service with connecting companies other than the Boston Elevated Railway Company. The trustees may make changes in service or facilities without a prior public hearing, but upon complaint in writing relative to the character or extent of the service or facilities furnished, signed by the mayor of any city or the selectmen of any town in which the company operates, or by not less than twenty patrons of the company, the trustees shall give a public hearing, if requested so to do, shall fully investigate the matters complained of and shall take such action within their powers as the facts seem to justify, stating their reasons therefor. Any such hearing may be conducted by a single trustee. In the management and operation of the company and of the properties owned, leased, or operated by it, as authorized by this act, the trustees and their agents, servants and employees shall be deemed to be acting as agents of the company and the company shall be liable for their acts and negligence to the same extent as if they were in the immediate employ of the company, but said trustees shall not be liable personally for their acts except for malfeasance in office.

The trustees shall elect a chairman. A majority of the trustees shall constitute a quorum for the transaction of business.

SECTION 6. No contracts or arrangements for the construction, acquisition, rental or operation of any additional lines of street railway or bus service or for the abandonment or extension of existing lines or bus service or any portion thereof, shall be entered into without the consent of the directors of the company unless, after such consent has been refused, the department shall determine after a public hearing that public necessity and convenience require such construction, acquisition, abandonment or extension and that the same will not impair the return on outstanding stock, bonds or other evidences of indebtedness contemplated by the provisions of this act; and in case of such determination the directors shall have a right of appeal to the supreme judicial court and if the court shall decide that the said return would be so impaired, the contemplated action shall not be taken. No contract for the sale or lease of the existing lines or any portion thereof shall be entered into without the consent of the directors of the company.

SECTION 7. The trustees shall have authority to make contracts in the name and on behalf of the company, and to issue stocks, bonds and other evidences of indebtedness of the company. The stockholders of the company shall elect annually a board of directors who shall represent the stockholders and shall exercise, during the period of control by trustees, all the corporate powers not conferred by the provisions of this act upon the trustees, and thereafter shall have and exercise, until the general court shall otherwise provide, all of such powers hereby conferred upon the trustees and not inconsistent with the general laws.

The company and the stockholders and directors thereof shall be deemed to have assented to and authorized all issues of stock, bonds and other evidences of indebtedness which the trustees may find it necessary or advisable to issue, as authorized in this act, during the period of public operation or which may be required to carry out the obligations of said company as authorized herein.

The trustees shall allow to the board of directors each year such sums as may be reasonable to provide for the maintenance of the corporate organization of the company and the performance by the company and directors of necessary duties.

SECTION 8. The trustees shall from time to time, so far as is practicable, fix such rates and fares as in their judgment will produce sufficient income to meet the cost of the service, which shall include proper maintenance and all other operating expenses, taxes, rentals, interest on bonds and other interest payments and stated dividends on the preferred stock and six per cent on the common capital stock of the company, such allowances for depreciation of property and for obsolescence and rehabilitation and for losses in respect to property sold, destroyed or abandoned, as they may deem adequate, or as may be required by the department, and all other expenditures and charges which under the laws of the commonwealth now or hereafter in effect may properly be chargeable against income or surplus. The trustees shall cause the income applicable to interest and dividends to be distributed among the security and stockholders as their interest may appear.

SECTION 9. The trustees may from time to time after notice and a hearing revise any fare districts or divide the lines of the company into different fare districts, but they shall at all times make such allocation of the items entering into the cost of service as will in their judgment fairly distribute the aggregate of the same upon and among said districts, so as to avoid, so far as is consistent with the public interest and reasonably practicable, the inclusion of such items in the computation of the cost of service in any fare district as may properly be laid upon territory outside of such district.

Any city or town by majority vote of the voters voting thereon may, from time to time, during the period of the management and control of trustees, for the purpose of obtaining a lower schedule of fares or of avoiding a reduction or discontinuance of service, enter into an agreement or agreements with the trustees to pay any part or all of any excess of the cost of the service, as defined in section eight, on the lines of the company operating within such city or town, above the amount of the receipts of such lines arising from the schedule or schedules of rates and fares in effect thereon during the period covered by any such agreement; provided, that such contribution of a city or town shall not in any one year exceed the sum of two dollars per one thousand dollars of the preceding year's assessed valuation of such city or town; and provided, also, that any city or town contributing as aforesaid shall have a right of appeal from the decision of the trustees to the department on any question relating to the character or extent of the service rendered or facilities furnished in that city or town. If part only of the cities and towns in any fare district contribute to the cost of service under the above provisions, the trustees may make such adjustments in fares as in their judgment will be equitable. Such vote in cities shall be taken at the regular or biennial municipal election, and in towns at any town meeting called for the purpose. In either case the vote shall be taken by ballot and the question shall be submitted in such form as the city council or the selectmen may determine; provided, however, that if any city desires to enter into a temporary agreement with the trustees at any time more than sixty days prior to its next regular or biennial municipal election, it may do so by a majority vote, as defined in section one of chapter forty-four of the General Laws, and may bind said city to such agreement until said election, when the question shall be submitted to the voters in the manner provided herein.

SECTION 10. The company shall be and hereby is authorized to sell and dispose of to any person, firm or corporation, including municipal corporations, electricity for light or power to the extent that the same shall not be required for the proper operation of its street railway systems, at such rates and upon such terms and conditions as it may from time to time fix and determine, subject to the approval of the department, which shall first determine that public necessity and convenience require the same.

The company, for the purpose of constructing, using and maintaining transmission lines for the purchase, sale or disposal of electricity for light and power purposes only, shall have the same rights as electric companies under section seventy-two of chapter one hundred and sixty-four of the General Laws to take land for such purposes, and in respect to any such taking shall be subject to the provisions of said section.

SECTION 11. After the expiration of the five year period of management and operation by trustees as herein provided the company shall have all the powers and privileges and be subject to all the liabilities and restrictions of a street railway company organized under general laws now or hereafter in force, and, with the consent of the department, may exercise any additional powers and privileges conferred by special acts applicable to the company until the general court shall otherwise provide.

SECTION 12. The supreme judicial court shall have jurisdiction in equity to review and alter, modify, amend or enforce rulings or orders of the trustees to the same extent that such jurisdiction is given to said court over rulings and orders of the department by any existing law.

SECTION 13. Nothing in this act contained shall prevent the commonwealth from taking the whole or any part of the property of the company under the power of eminent domain.

SECTION 14. This act shall take effect upon its acceptance by the company given by a vote of the holders of not less than a majority of all the stock of the company at a meeting held for the purpose, a copy of which vote, certified by the clerk of the company, shall be filed with the state secretary; provided, however, that this act shall become void unless such a certified copy of said vote of acceptance shall so be filed on or before November first, nineteen hundred and forty-three.

Approved March 25, 1943.

Chap. 99 AN ACT TO ENABLE CITIES AND TOWNS TO APPROPRIATE MONEY FOR THE ERECTION OF MONUMENTS OR MEMORIALS FOR COMMEMORATING THE SERVICES AND SACRIFICES OF PERSONS IN THE MILITARY OR NAVAL FORCES OF THE UNITED STATES IN THE PRESENT WAR.

Be it enacted, etc., as follows:

G. L. (Ter. Ed.), 40, § 5, etc., amended.

Clause (12) of section five of chapter forty of the General Laws, as most recently amended by section two of chapter two hundred and seventeen of the acts of nineteen hundred and forty-one, is hereby further amended by striking out, in the sixth and seventh lines, the words "the World war" and inserting in place thereof the following: — World war I or in World war II, — so as to read as follows: —

Appropriations for care of certain graves.

(12) For erecting headstones or other monuments at the graves of persons who served in the war of the revolution, the war of eighteen hundred and twelve, the Seminole war, the Mexican war, the war of the rebellion or the Indian wars or who served in the military or naval service of the United States in the Spanish American war or in World war I or in World war II, or who served in the military service of the commonwealth in time of war; for acquiring land by purchase or by eminent domain under chapter seventy-nine, purchasing, erecting, equipping or dedicating buildings, or constructing or dedicating other suitable memorials, for the purpose of properly commemorating the services and sacrifices of persons who served as aforesaid; for the decoration of the graves, monuments or other memorials of soldiers, sailors and marines who served in the army, navy or marine corps of the United States in time of war or insurrection and the proper observance of Memorial Day and other patriotic holidays under the auspices of the following: — local posts of the Grand Army of the Republic, United Spanish War Veterans, The American Legion, Veterans of Foreign Wars of the United States and Jewish War Veterans of the United States, local chapters of the Disabled American Veterans of the World War, local units of the Massachusetts State Guard Veterans, Kearsarge Association of Naval Veterans, Inc., local garrisons of the Army and Navy Union of the United States of America, local chapters of the Massachusetts Society of the Sons of the American Revolution, local detachments of the Marine Corps League, local clubs of the Yankee Division Veterans Association, local camps or other duly organized units of the Sons of Union Veterans of the Civil War or local tents of The Daughters of Union Veterans of the Civil War, and The Society of the War of 1812 in the Commonwealth of Massachusetts (Incorporated); or for keeping in repair graves, monuments or other memorials erected to the memory of such persons or of the firemen and policemen of the town who died from injuries received in the performance of their duties in the fire or police service or for decorating the graves of such firemen

and policemen or for other memorial observances in their honor. Money appropriated in honor of such firemen may be paid over to, and expended for such purposes by, any veteran firemen's association or similar organization.

Approved March 25, 1943.

AN ACT PERMITTING THE SALE OF HEADS, HIDES AND HOOFS OF DEER IN CERTAIN CASES. *Chap.* 100

Be it enacted, etc., as follows:

Chapter one hundred and thirty-one of the General Laws is hereby amended by striking out section one hundred and one, as appearing in section two of chapter five hundred and ninety-nine of the acts of nineteen hundred and forty-one, and inserting in place thereof the following section: — *Section 101.* No person, except as provided in this chapter, shall buy, sell, barter, exchange, or in any way deal in or trade with respect to, the dead or living bodies of birds or mammals, or parts thereof, protected by the law in this commonwealth, whenever and wherever taken or killed, but a person who has lawfully killed a deer and has reported such killing under section seventy-nine or eighty may sell the head and hide thereof to any person licensed as a fur buyer under section one hundred and three or licensed as a taxidermist under section one hundred and four, and may sell the hoofs thereof, if the shinbones are attached thereto, to any person. Whoever violates any provision of this section shall be punished by a fine of not less than fifty nor more than one hundred dollars or by imprisonment for not more than thirty days, or both. *Approved March 25, 1943.*

G. L. (Ter. Ed.), 131, § 101, etc., amended.

Buying, selling, etc., of dead birds and mammals, regulated.

Penalty.

AN ACT AUTHORIZING THE ADMINISTRATIVE COMMITTEE OF THE DISTRICT COURTS, OTHER THAN THE MUNICIPAL COURT OF THE CITY OF BOSTON, TO PROHIBIT THE PRACTICE OF MOTOR VEHICLE TORT CASES, SO CALLED, BY JUSTICES OF CERTAIN DISTRICT COURTS. *Chap.* 101

Be it enacted, etc., as follows:

Section forty-three A of chapter two hundred and eighteen of the General Laws, as most recently amended by section one of chapter six hundred and eighty-two of the acts of nineteen hundred and forty-one, is hereby further amended by adding at the end of the first paragraph the following sentence: — The committee shall have power to prohibit the practice of motor vehicle tort cases, so called, by the justices of the district courts, other than the municipal court of the city of Boston, — so that said first paragraph will read as follows: — There shall be an administrative committee of the district courts, other than the municipal court of the city of Boston, which shall consist of five justices of such district courts, appointed by the chief justice of the supreme judicial court, each for a period not exceeding two years as

G. L. (Ter. Ed.), 218, § 43A, etc., amended.

Administrative committee of district courts.

Appointment of members.

said chief justice may determine. Any such justice may be reappointed. The committee shall be authorized to visit any district court, other than the municipal court of the city of Boston, or any trial justice, as a committee or by subcommittee, to require uniform practices, to prescribe forms of blanks and records, and to superintend the keeping of records by clerks and by trial justices. The committee shall have general superintendence of all the district courts, other than the municipal court of the city of Boston, and their clerks and other officers; but, except as otherwise provided by law, shall have no power to appoint any such officers. The committee may regulate the assignment of special justices in such district courts, determine the number of simultaneous sessions which may be held by any such district court, the sittings of special justices, and, subject to the provisions of section fifteen, shall determine the times for holding criminal and civil sessions. Without limiting the generality of the foregoing, the committee shall require records to be kept which shall be available to the general court and which shall show the hours of opening and adjourning of court and any simultaneous session thereof on each day, the names of the justices and special justices holding court or a simultaneous session thereof, and any other information which may generally assist in the determination of the nature and volume of, and the time required to complete, all work done by any of such district courts. The committee shall have power to prohibit the practice of motor vehicle tort cases, so called, by the justices of the district courts, other than the municipal court of the city of Boston. *Approved March 25, 1943.*

Duties of, etc.

---

*Chap.*102 AN ACT FURTHER REGULATING THE SALARIES OF THE COUNTY COMMISSIONERS OF BARNSTABLE COUNTY.

Be it enacted, etc., as follows:

G. L. (Ter. Ed.), 34, § 5, amended.

SECTION 1. Section five of chapter thirty-four of the General Laws, as appearing in the Tercentenary Edition, is hereby amended by striking out the schedule appearing therein and inserting in place thereof the following schedule: —

Salaries of county commissioners.

Dukes County	$400
Franklin, Hampshire	1,500
Barnstable, Berkshire, Plymouth	2,100
Norfolk, Hampden, Bristol	3,000
Worcester, Essex	3,600
Middlesex	4,200

Effective date

SECTION 2. This act shall take effect as of January first in the current year. *Approved March 25, 1943.*

AN ACT RELATIVE TO THE DISPOSAL OF SLASH OR BRUSH FOLLOWING WOOD OR LUMBER OPERATIONS. *Chap.* 103

Be it enacted, etc., as follows:

SECTION 1. Chapter forty-eight of the General Laws is hereby amended by striking out section sixteen, as appearing in the Tercentenary Edition, and inserting in place thereof the following section: — *Section 16.* Every owner, lessee, tenant or occupant of lands or of any rights or interests therein, except electric, telephone and telegraph companies, who cuts or permits the cutting of brush, wood or timber on lands which border upon woodland of another, or upon a highway or railroad location, shall dispose of the slash caused by such cutting in such a manner that the same will not remain on the ground within forty feet of any woodland of another, or of any highway or railroad location.

G. L. (Ter. Ed.), 48, § 16, amended.

Disposal of slash and brush.

SECTION 2. Said chapter forty-eight is hereby further amended by striking out section eighteen, as so appearing, and inserting in place thereof the following section: — *Section 18.* Electric, telephone and telegraph companies which, at the time of erecting their transmission lines, cut or cause to be cut brush, wood or timber on land which borders upon woodland of another, or upon a highway or railroad location, shall dispose of the slash caused by such cutting in such a manner that the same will not remain on the ground within forty feet of any woodland of another, or of any highway or railroad location; such companies which after the erection of their lines trim or cut brush, wood or timber which has grown up since the line was erected, and which borders upon woodland of another, or upon a highway or railroad location, shall, upon the request of the forester, and within a time limit set by him, dispose of the slash of second or subsequent cuttings if the same in his opinion constitutes a menace to adjoining property.

G. L. (Ter. Ed.), 48, § 18, amended.

Electric, etc., companies to clear land of slash.

Approved March 25, 1943.

AN ACT PROVIDING THAT THE DOORKEEPER OF EACH BRANCH OF THE GENERAL COURT SHALL HAVE THE TITLE OF ASSISTANT SERGEANT-AT-ARMS. *Chap.* 104

Be it enacted, etc., as follows:

Section eighteen of chapter three of the General Laws, as amended by section one of chapter four hundred and thirty-three of the acts of nineteen hundred and forty-one, is hereby further amended by inserting after the word "branch" in the first line the words: — , each with the title of assistant sergeant-at-arms and, — so as to read as follows: — *Section 18.* There shall be a doorkeeper for each branch, each with the title of assistant sergeant-at-arms and each at a salary of twenty-seven hundred and fifty dollars, and such assistant doorkeepers as it may direct,

G. L. (Ter. Ed.), 3, § 18, etc., amended.

Employees of sergeant-at-arms. Salaries.

each at a salary of twenty-two hundred dollars; a porter in the lobby of the house of representatives at a salary of sixteen hundred and fifty dollars; general court officers, each at a salary of two thousand dollars; pages whose compensation shall be seven hundred dollars each for the regular session and a sum not exceeding three dollars for each day's service after such session; a clerk to take charge of the legislative document room at a salary of twenty-seven hundred and fifty dollars, an assistant clerk of said room at a salary of twenty-one hundred dollars, and such assistants therein as may be necessary, for whose fitness and good conduct the sergeant-at-arms shall be responsible.

Approved March 25, 1943.

Chap. 105 AN ACT RELATIVE TO THE ADMISSIBILITY OF DECLARATIONS OF DECEASED PERSONS IN CERTAIN CIVIL JUDICIAL PROCEEDINGS.

Be it enacted, etc., as follows:

G. L. (Ter. Ed.), 233, § 65, etc., amended.

SECTION 1. Section sixty-five of chapter two hundred and thirty-three of the General Laws, as amended by section one of chapter three hundred and sixty-three of the acts of nineteen hundred and forty-one, is hereby further amended by inserting after the word "action", in the sixth line, the words: — or other civil judicial proceeding, — so as to read as follows: — *Section 65.* A declaration of a deceased person shall not be inadmissible in evidence as hearsay or as private conversation between husband and wife, as the case may be, if the court finds that it was made in good faith before the commencement of the action or other civil judicial proceeding and upon the personal knowledge of the declarant.

Declarations of deceased persons.

Effective date.

SECTION 2. This act shall take effect on October first in the current year. *Approved March 25, 1943.*

Chap. 106 AN ACT REVIVING J. PUCCIA & CO. INC.

Emergency preamble.

Whereas, The deferred operation of this act would tend to defeat its purpose, therefore it is hereby declared to be an emergency law, necessary for the immediate preservation of the public convenience.

Be it enacted, etc., as follows:

J. Puccia & Co. Inc., a corporation dissolved by section one of chapter eight of the acts of nineteen hundred and thirty-five, is hereby revived with the same powers, duties and obligations as if said chapter had not been passed.

Approved March 25, 1943.

AN ACT PROVIDING FOR THE PARTIAL DISCHARGE OF A COLLECTOR OF TAXES FROM LIABILITY ON HIS BOND UNDER CERTAIN CIRCUMSTANCES. *Chap.*107

Be it enacted, etc., as follows:

G. L. (Ter. Ed.), 60, § 95, etc., amended.

Discharge of collector from liability on bond, when.

Section ninety-five of chapter sixty of the General Laws, as most recently amended by section six of chapter three hundred and eighty of the acts of nineteen hundred and forty-one, is hereby further amended by adding at the end the following sentence: — A collector shall be discharged from liability upon his bond for failure to collect taxes outstanding for more than two years to the extent that the commissioner shall certify that such taxes are presently uncollectible because of judicial order or decree or because of similar reason and that such taxes are outstanding without fault of such collector. *Approved March 25, 1943.*

AN ACT RELATIVE TO THE REGISTRATION AS VOTERS OF PERSONS CLAIMING TO BE CITIZENS. *Chap.*108

Be it enacted, etc., as follows:

G. L. (Ter. Ed.), 51, § 45, amended.

Registration of naturalized citizens.

Chapter fifty-one of the General Laws is hereby amended by striking out section forty-five, as appearing in the Tercentenary Edition, and inserting in place thereof the following section: — *Section 45.* If an applicant for registration claims to be a naturalized citizen or to derive citizenship through the naturalization or citizenship of another, the registrars shall require him to produce for inspection the papers of naturalization, certificate of citizenship made under federal authority or any other papers upon which he relies and shall, if satisfied that the applicant is a citizen, make upon such papers a memorandum of the date of such inspection. If such papers have once been examined and record thereof made in the general register, the registrars need not again require their production.

Approved March 25, 1943.

AN ACT RELATIVE TO THE REGISTRATION OF VOTERS PRIOR TO PRELIMINARY ELECTIONS IN CERTAIN CITIES. *Chap.*109

Be it enacted, etc., as follows:

G. L. (Ter. Ed.), 51, § 27, etc., amended.

Sessions before primaries.

SECTION 1. Section twenty-seven of chapter fifty-one of the General Laws, as most recently amended by section three of chapter four hundred and seventy-three of the acts of nineteen hundred and thirty-eight, is hereby further amended by adding at the end the following sentence: — The provisions of this section applicable in the case of a city primary shall apply also in the case of a preliminary election held in any city under chapter forty-three, or under any special law except where it is otherwise provided, — so as to read as follows: — *Section 27.* They shall hold at least one session at some suitable place in every city or town on or before the last day for registration preceding the biennial state primary and the presidential primary, and on or before the Wednesday next but one preceding a city or town primary, except a primary preceding a special city or town election. The provisions of this section applicable in the case of a city primary shall apply also in the case of a preliminary election held in any city under chapter forty-three, or under any special law except where it is otherwise provided.

G. L. (Ter. Ed.), 51, § 29A, amended.

SECTION 2. Section twenty-nine A of said chapter fifty-one, as appearing in the Tercentenary Edition, is hereby amended by adding at the end the following sentence: — The provisions of this section applicable in the case of a special city primary shall apply also in the case of a special preliminary election held in any city under chapter forty-three, or under any special law except where it is otherwise provided, — so as to read as follows: — *Section 29A.* They shall, in some suitable place in every city or town wherein there is to be a special state, city or town primary, hold a session on the fourth day preceding such primary. Registration shall cease at ten o'clock in the evening of the day on which such a session is held. The provisions of this section applicable in the case of a special city primary shall apply also in the case of a special preliminary election held in any city under chapter forty-three, or under any special law except where it is otherwise provided.

Sessions prior to special primaries.

Approved March 25, 1943.

---

*Chap.*110 AN ACT MAKING CERTAIN CORRECTIVE CHANGES IN THE BANKING LAWS.

Be it enacted, etc., as follows:

G. L. (Ter. Ed.), 167, § 18, amended.

SECTION 1. Section eighteen of chapter one hundred and sixty-seven of the General Laws, as appearing in the Tercentenary Edition, is hereby amended by striking out, in the third and fourth lines, the words "the preceding section" and inserting in place thereof the words: — section sixty-seven of chapter one hundred and seventy-two or in section forty-seven of chapter one hundred and sixty-eight, — so as to read as follows: — *Section 18.* An officer, agent, clerk or servant of a trust company or savings bank who pays or authorizes the payment of any dividend or interest unless the same has been earned and collected as provided in section sixty-seven of chapter one hundred and seventy-two or in section forty-seven of chapter one hundred and sixty-eight shall be punished by a fine of not more than one thousand dollars or by imprisonment for not more than six months.

Payment of unearned dividends prohibited.

Penalty.

G. L. (Ter. Ed.), 167, § 46, amended.

SECTION 2. Section forty-six of said chapter one hundred and sixty-seven, as so appearing, is hereby amended by striking out, in the sixth line, the word "seventy-two" and inserting in place thereof the following: — seventy-two A, — so as to read as follows: — *Section 46.* In addition to the duties imposed by law upon the treasurer of a bank, or the officer or employee thereof charged with the duties and functions usually performed by the treasurer, he shall also be responsible for the performance of all acts and duties required of such corporation by the provisions of chapters one hundred and sixty-seven to one hundred and seventy-two A, inclusive, except in so far as such performance has been expressly imposed on some other officer or employee of such bank by its regulations or by-laws or by provision of law.

General duties of treasurer, etc.

SECTION 3. Section forty-seven of said chapter one hundred and sixty-seven, as so appearing, is hereby amended by striking out, in the fourth line, the word "seventy-two" and inserting in place thereof the following: — seventy-two A, — and by striking out, in the eleventh and twelfth lines, the words "the preceding section" and inserting in place thereof the words: — section forty-six, — so as to read as follows: — *Section 47.* Any officer, director, trustee, agent or employee of any bank, who knowingly and wilfully does any act forbidden to him or to such bank by any provision of chapters one hundred and sixty-seven to one hundred and seventy-two A, inclusive, or who knowingly and wilfully aids or abets the doing of any act so forbidden to such bank or to any other officer, director, trustee, agent or employee thereof, or who knowingly and wilfully fails to do any act required of him by any such provision, or who knowingly and wilfully fails to do any act which is required of such bank by any such provision the performance of which is imposed on him by the by-laws or regulations of the bank or by law or the responsibility for the non-performance of which is placed upon him by section forty-six, shall, if no other penalty against him in his aforesaid capacity is specifically provided, be punished by a fine of not more than one thousand dollars or by imprisonment for not more than one year, or both.

G. L. (Ter Ed.), 167, § 47, amended

General penalty.

SECTION 4. Paragraph (2) of subdivision (*e*) of clause Ninth of section fifty-four of chapter one hundred and sixty-eight of the General Laws, as appearing in section twenty-six of chapter three hundred and thirty-four of the acts of nineteen hundred and thirty-three, is hereby amended by striking out, in the second line, the word ", Fourth", — so as to read as follows: — (2) Bonds or notes authorized for investment by clause Second, Third, Fifth, Sixth, Sixth A, or Seventeenth at no more than ninety per cent of the market value thereof, at any time while such note is held by such corporation; or

G. L. (Ter. Ed.), 168, § 54, etc., amended.

Investments authorized.

SECTION 5. Paragraph (4) of said subdivision (*e*), as appearing in the Tercentenary Edition, is hereby repealed.

G. L. (Ter Ed.), 168, § 54, etc, repealed

SECTION 6. Paragraph (5) of said subdivision (*e*), as appearing in section twenty-six of chapter three hundred and thirty-four of the acts of nineteen hundred and thirty-three, is hereby amended by striking out, in the first line, the words "Such other" and inserting in place thereof the word: —

G. L. (Ter. Ed.), 168, § 54, etc., amended.

Investments regulated.

Other, — so as to read as follows: — (5) Other bonds, notes or shares of corporations or associations at no more than eighty per cent of the market value thereof, at any time while such note is held by such corporation; provided, that, if the commissioner shall disapprove any such bonds, notes or shares, he may make such written recommendations to the board of investment of such corporation as the case may require, and may in his discretion include in his annual report a statement of the facts in each case in which such board of investment has not complied with his recommendations in a manner satisfactory to him; or

G. L. (Ter. Ed.), 172, § 69, amended.

SECTION 7. Section sixty-nine of chapter one hundred and seventy-two of the General Laws, as appearing in the Tercentenary Edition, is hereby amended by striking out, in the first and second lines, the words "seventeen of chapter one hundred and", — so as to read as follows: — *Section 69.* Except as otherwise provided by section sixty-seven, no such corporation shall allow interest on any savings deposit from a date prior to that on which the deposit is made, nor shall a deposit which is withdrawn between its dividend days be entitled to interest after the prior dividend day except with the written permission of, and under regulations prescribed by, the commissioner.

Allowance of interest regulated.

G. L. (Ter. Ed.), 172, § 18, etc., amended.

SECTION 8. Section eighteen of said chapter one hundred and seventy-two, as most recently amended by chapter eighteen of the acts of nineteen hundred and thirty-five, is hereby further amended by striking out the second paragraph, and inserting in place thereof the following: —

Trust companies, payment of stock dividends.

In case dividends on the preferred stock are to be cumulative, no dividends shall be declared or paid on common stock until all such cumulative dividends shall have been paid in full and all requirements of any retirement fund shall have been met; and if such corporation is placed in voluntary liquidation, or a conservator is appointed therefor, or possession of its property and business has been taken by the commissioner, no payment shall be made to the holders of the common stock until the holders of the preferred stock shall have been paid in full such amount as may, with the approval of the commissioner, be provided in the articles of organization or amendments thereof, not in excess of the purchase price or other consideration received by the corporation for such preferred stock, plus all accumulated unpaid dividends. *Approved March 25, 1943.*

---

*Chap.*111 AN ACT RELATIVE TO THE LICENSING OF DOGS AND KENNELS.

Be it enacted, etc., as follows:

G. L. (Ter. Ed.), 140, § 136A, etc., amended.

SECTION 1. Section one hundred and thirty-six A of chapter one hundred and forty of the General Laws, inserted by section one of chapter three hundred and twenty of the acts of nineteen hundred and thirty-four, is hereby amended by striking out the definition of "Kennel" and inserting in place thereof the two following definitions: —

"Kennel", one pack or collection of dogs on a single premises, whether maintained for breeding, boarding, sale, training, hunting or other purposes and including any shop where dogs are on sale, and also including every pack or collection of more than three dogs three months old or over owned or kept by a person on a single premises irrespective of the purpose for which they are maintained. Definitions.

"License period", the time between April first and the following March thirty-first, both dates inclusive.

SECTION 2. Said chapter one hundred and forty is hereby further amended by striking out section one hundred and thirty-seven, as most recently amended by section two of said chapter three hundred and twenty, and inserting in place thereof the following section: — *Section 137.* A person who at the commencement of a license period is, or who during any license period becomes, the owner or keeper of a dog three months old or over which is not duly licensed, and the owner or keeper of a dog when it becomes three months old during a license period, shall cause it to be registered, numbered, described and licensed until the end of such license period, and the owner or keeper of a dog so registered, numbered, described and licensed during any license period, in order to own or keep such dog after the beginning of the succeeding license period, shall, before the beginning thereof, cause it to be registered, numbered, described and licensed for such period; provided, that the foregoing provisions shall not apply where it is otherwise provided by law nor shall they apply to a person having a kennel license. The registering, numbering, describing and licensing of a dog, if kept in Boston shall be in the office of the police commissioner or if kept in any other town in the office of the clerk thereof. G. L. (Ter. Ed.), 140, § 137, etc., amended. Licenses.

The license shall be in a form prescribed by the director, upon a blank to be furnished, except in the county of Suffolk, by the county in which the town is located, and shall be subject to the condition expressed therein that the dog which is the subject of the license shall be controlled and restrained from killing, chasing or harassing live stock or fowls. The owner or keeper of a licensed dog shall cause it to wear around its neck or body a collar or harness of leather or other suitable material, to which shall be securely attached a tag in a form prescribed by the director, and upon which shall appear the license number, the name of the town issuing such license and the year of issue. Such tags shall be furnished in the same manner as the license blanks, and if any such tag shall be lost the owner or keeper of such dog shall forthwith secure a substitute tag from the town clerk or, in Boston, from the police commissioner, at a cost of ten cents which, if received by a town clerk, shall be retained by him unless otherwise provided by law. Collars.

SECTION 3. Section one hundred and thirty-seven A of said chapter one hundred and forty, as amended by chapter ninety-five of the acts of nineteen hundred and thirty-seven, G. L. (Ter. Ed.), 140, § 137A, etc., amended.

is hereby further amended by striking out the first paragraph, as appearing in section three of said chapter three hundred and twenty, and inserting in place thereof the following paragraph: —

Licensing of kennels.

Every person maintaining a kennel shall have a kennel license. Any owner or keeper of less than four dogs three months old or over who does not maintain a kennel may elect to secure a kennel license in lieu of licensing such dogs under section one hundred and thirty-seven, and during such time as he does not license such dogs thereunder shall have a kennel license and shall be subject to this section and to sections one hundred and thirty-seven B and one hundred and thirty-seven C and to so much of section one hundred and forty-one as relates to violations of this section, section one hundred and thirty-seven B or section one hundred and thirty-seven C to the same extent as though he were maintaining a kennel. Kennel licenses under this section shall be issued by the police commissioner of the city of Boston if the dogs are to be kept under such license in said city or by the clerk of any other town if to be so kept in said town.

Such license shall be in a form prescribed by the director, upon a blank to be furnished, except in the county of Suffolk, by the county in which the town is located. Such license shall be in lieu of any other license for any dog while kept at such kennel during any portion of the period for which such kennel license is issued. The holder of a license for a kennel shall cause each dog kept therein to wear, while it is at large, a collar or harness of leather or other suitable material, to which shall be securely attached a tag upon which shall appear the number of such kennel license, the name of the town issuing such license and the year of issue. Such tags shall be in a form prescribed by the director, and shall be furnished to such owner or keeper by the clerk of the town in which such kennel is licensed, or, if licensed in Boston, by the police commissioner, in quantities not less than the number of dogs kept in such kennel. The fee for each license for a kennel shall be ten dollars if not more than four dogs are kept in said kennel, twenty-five dollars if more than four but not more than ten dogs are kept therein and fifty dollars if more than ten dogs are kept therein; provided, that, for the purpose of determining the amount of such fee for any kennel, dogs under the age of six months shall not be counted in the number of dogs kept therein. The name and address of the owner of each dog kept in any kennel, if other than the person maintaining the kennel, shall be kept on file thereat and available to inspection by the county commissioners and by any dog officer, conservation officer, deputy conservation officer, fish and game warden or police officer.

The clerk of any town, or in Boston the police commissioner, shall upon application issue without charge a kennel license to any domestic charitable corporation incorporated exclusively for the purpose of protecting animals from cruelty, neglect or abuse and for the relief of suffering among animals.

SECTION 4. Said chapter one hundred and forty is hereby further amended by striking out section one hundred and thirty-eight, as most recently amended by chapter ninety-two of the acts of nineteen hundred and thirty-eight, and inserting in place thereof the following section: — *Section 138.* A person who during any license period becomes the owner or keeper of a dog which is duly licensed in the town where it is to be kept shall forthwith give notice in writing to the clerk of such town, or if kept in Boston to the police commissioner, that he has become such owner or keeper and said clerk or police commissioner, as the case may be, shall change the record of such license to show the name and address of the new owner or keeper. Any person bringing or causing to be brought from another state or country any dog licensed under the laws thereof which is three months old or over or will be three months old before the expiration of thirty days therefrom shall, on or before the expiration of thirty days following the arrival of such dog within the commonwealth, cause such dog to be registered, numbered, described and licensed for the remainder of the then current license period. *Approved March 25, 1943.*

G. L. (Ter. Ed.), 140, § 138, etc., amended.

Licensing of dogs, etc.

AN ACT PROVIDING FOR THE HOLDING OF BIENNIAL MUNICIPAL ELECTIONS IN THE CITY OF BEVERLY IN ODD-NUMBERED YEARS AND ESTABLISHING THE DATE OF SAID ELECTIONS.

Chap. 112

Be it enacted, etc., as follows:

SECTION 1. Beginning with the year nineteen hundred and forty-five, biennial municipal elections in the city of Beverly for the choice of mayor, members of the board of aldermen and members of the school committee shall be held on the second Tuesday of November in every odd-numbered year.

SECTION 2. No biennial municipal election shall be held in said city in the year nineteen hundred and forty-four.

SECTION 3. The terms of office of the mayor and of the members of the board of aldermen elected in said city in the year nineteen hundred and forty-two shall continue until the qualification of their successors who shall be elected at the biennial municipal election to be held in the year nineteen hundred and forty-five. The terms of office of the members of the school committee elected in said city in the year nineteen hundred and forty shall continue until the qualification of their successors who shall be elected at the biennial municipal election to be held in the year nineteen hundred and forty-five. The terms of office of the members of the school committee elected in said city in the year nineteen hundred and forty-two shall continue until the qualification of their successors who shall be elected at the biennial municipal election to be held in the year nineteen hundred and forty-seven.

SECTION 4. Such provisions of chapter five hundred and forty-two of the acts of nineteen hundred and ten, and acts in amendment thereof or in addition thereto, as are inconsistent with this act are hereby repealed.

SECTION 5. This act shall be submitted to the registered voters of the city of Beverly at the biennial state election in the year nineteen hundred and forty-four in the form of the following question which shall be placed upon the official ballot to be used in said city at said election: — "Shall an act passed by the general court in the year nineteen hundred and forty-three, entitled 'An Act providing for the holding of biennial municipal elections in the city of Beverly in odd-numbered years and establishing the date of said elections', be accepted?" If a majority of the voters voting thereon vote in the affirmative in answer to said question, then this act shall thereupon take full effect in said city, but not otherwise. *Approved March 25, 1943.*

---

*Chap.*113 AN ACT AUTHORIZING THE COMMISSIONER OF CORRECTION TO REMOVE ANY PRISONER FROM THE STATE PRISON TO THE MASSACHUSETTS REFORMATORY.

Be it enacted, etc., as follows:

G. L. (Ter. Ed.), 127, § 97, amended.

Removal from state prison to reformatory.

Return.

Chapter one hundred and twenty-seven of the General Laws is hereby amended by striking out section ninety-seven, as appearing in the Tercentenary Edition, and inserting in place thereof the following section: — *Section 97.* The commissioner may remove to the Massachusetts reformatory any prisoner held in the state prison who, in his judgment, may properly be so removed, and may at any time return such prisoner to the state prison. Prisoners so removed shall be subject to the terms of their original sentences and to the provisions of law governing parole from the state prison. *Approved March 26, 1943.*

---

*Chap.*114 AN ACT AUTHORIZING THE TOWN OF CHATHAM TO ERECT A WHARF, BULKHEAD AND FISH PACKING HOUSE ON CERTAIN PROPERTY IN SAID TOWN.

Be it enacted, etc., as follows:

SECTION 1. The town of Chatham is hereby authorized to erect a wharf, bulkhead and fish packing house on a town landing between Shore road and the waters of Pleasant bay, better known as Aunt Lydia's cove, and to be known as Chatham Town Wharf, and said town may maintain and operate such property as a wharf, bulkhead and fish packing house and public landing. The erection and maintenance of said structures shall be subject to the provisions of chapter ninety-one of the General Laws, so far as applicable.

SECTION 2. The powers conferred by this act may be exercised by the selectmen of said town, who shall also have power to make rules and regulations governing the use of said wharf, bulkhead and fish packing house, subject, however, to such rules and regulations as the town may from time to time fix by vote.

SECTION 3. For the purpose of erecting said wharf, bulkhead and fish packing house, said town may borrow from time to time such sums as may be necessary, not exceeding, in the aggregate, ten thousand dollars, and may issue bonds or notes therefor, which shall bear on their face the words Chatham Wharf Loan, Act of 1943. Each authorized issue shall constitute a separate loan, and such loans shall be paid in not more than ten years from their date. Indebtedness incurred under this act shall be within the statutory limit, but shall, except as provided herein, be subject to chapter forty-four of the General Laws, exclusive of the limitation contained in the first paragraph of section seven thereof.

SECTION 4. This act shall be submitted to the voters of the town of Chatham at any time within five years after its passage at an annual meeting of the inhabitants of the town and it shall take full effect only upon its acceptance by a majority of the voters present and voting thereon.

Approved March 26, 1943.

AN ACT AUTHORIZING THE CITY OF SPRINGFIELD TO SELL OR OTHERWISE DISPOSE OF CERTAIN LAND SITUATED IN SAID CITY AND NOW HELD OR USED BY SAID CITY FOR PUBLIC PARK PURPOSES. *Chap.* 115

Be it enacted, etc., as follows:

The city of Springfield, by its board of park commissioners, may, by sale, exchange or otherwise, transfer and dispose of certain real property situated in said city and held or used by it for public park purposes, said property being bounded and described as follows: — Beginning at a stone bound at the intersection of the northeasterly line of Edgemont street with the southeasterly line of Roosevelt avenue and running thence north 45° 42′ 30″ east by said line of Roosevelt avenue one hundred and four and ninety-four one-hundredths (104.94) feet to an iron pin, thence south 26° 38′ 40″ east by land of said city fifty-two and thirty-eight one-hundredths (52.38) feet to an iron pin at land now or formerly of one Fillion, thence south 74° 58′ 40″ west by said last named land one hundred and two and nine one-hundredths (102.09) feet to the stone bound at the point of beginning, being a triangular parcel of land containing two thousand, six hundred and nineteen (2,619) square feet more or less.

Approved March 26, 1943.

Chap.116 AN ACT AUTHORIZING THE CITY OF SPRINGFIELD TO USE FOR PUBLIC PLAYGROUND AND RECREATION CENTER PURPOSES CERTAIN LAND SITUATED IN SAID CITY AND NOW HELD OR USED BY SAID CITY FOR PARK PURPOSES.

Be it enacted, etc., as follows:

The city of Springfield, by its board of park commissioners, may use for the purposes of a public playground or recreation center certain real property situated in said city and held or used by it for park purposes as a part of Blunt park, so called, said property being bounded and described as follows: — Beginning at a point on the south side of Bay road twelve hundred and one and 30/100 (1,201.30) feet west of the southwest corner of Roosevelt avenue and Bay road, and running thence along the land now or formerly of Patrick Fitzgerald south 3° 02′ 45″ west five hundred and eighty-one and 50/100 (581.50) feet to a stone bound; running thence along said last-named land south 86° 56′ 16″ east twelve hundred and sixty-eight and 13/100 (1,268.13) feet to Roosevelt avenue; running thence along the westerly edge of said Roosevelt avenue three thousand, two hundred and ninety-three and 84/100 (3,293.84) feet; running thence along the land now or formerly of trustees of Reed Realty Trust north 42° 18′ 49″ west three hundred and fifty-four and 52/100 (354.52) feet to a stone bound; running thence along said last-named land north 74° 42′ 15″ west ten hundred and thirteen and 18/100 (1,013.18) feet; running thence along said last-named land south 75° 52′ 03″ west five hundred and fifty and 61/100 (550.61) feet to a stone bound; running thence along the land now or formerly of the city of Springfield, Ewing S. Cook, Stoddard Motor Car Company and Patrick and Julia Wallace north 19° 06′ 20″ east six hundred and fifty-four and 65/100 (654.65) feet to a stone bound; running thence along the land now or formerly of Stoddard Motor Car Company, city of Springfield and Josephine S. Smith, Inc. north 9° 17′ 40″ west two hundred and sixty-four (264) feet to a stone bound; running thence along land now or formerly of Josephine S. Smith, Inc., Richard C. Larson, Rosaire J. Couture, city of Springfield, Mathilda Anderson and Emma M. Werson north 24° 17′ 40″ west seven hundred and forty-seven and 64/100 (747.64) feet to a stone bound in the south line of Bay road; running thence along the southerly side of Bay road twenty-five hundred and seventy-one and 01/100 (2,571.01) feet to the place of beginning, and may conduct and promote recreation, play, sport and physical education for which admission may be charged on such land and in the buildings thereon, and may construct buildings on this land owned by it, and may provide equipment for such purposes. The powers and authority conferred by section fourteen of chapter forty-five of the General Laws are hereby granted to the city of Springfield and its board of park commissioners or to such other board, commission or committee as the city council may determine, for the purposes of using said above described property for a public playground or recreation center.

Approved March 26, 1943.

AN ACT PERMITTING RECIPIENTS OF AID TO DEPENDENT CHILDREN, SO CALLED, TO LEAVE THE COMMONWEALTH WITHOUT SUSPENSION OF SUCH AID. *Chap.*117

Be it enacted, etc., as follows:

G. L. (Ter. Ed.), 118, new § 4A, added.

Chapter one hundred and eighteen of the General Laws is hereby amended by inserting after section four, as appearing in section one of chapter four hundred and thirteen of the acts of nineteen hundred and thirty-six, the following section: — *Section 4A.* Any parent receiving aid under this chapter, or any child for whose bringing up such aid is furnished, may be absent from the commonwealth on visit without having such aid suspended. Such parent, before his departure or the departure of the child from the commonwealth and following return thereto, shall notify the board of public welfare of the town granting such aid. The department may provide by rules or regulations for the continuation of such aid during such period as it may deem proper with respect to cases where the suspension of such aid because of absence from the commonwealth would result in undue hardship or be inconsistent with the purposes of this chapter. *Approved March 26, 1943.*

Parents receiving aid may be absent from commonwealth.

AN ACT FURTHER REGULATING INVESTMENTS OF CREDIT UNIONS. *Chap.*118

Be it enacted, etc., as follows:

G. L. (Ter. Ed.), 171, § 21, etc., amended.

Chapter one hundred and seventy-one of the General Laws is hereby amended by striking out section twenty-one, as most recently amended by chapter two hundred and twenty-eight of the acts of nineteen hundred and thirty-seven, and inserting in place thereof the following section: — *Section 21.* The capital, deposits and surplus of a credit union shall be invested in loans to members, with approval of the credit committee, as provided in section twenty-two, and also when so required herein, of the board of directors; and any capital, deposits or surplus funds in excess of the amount for which loans shall be approved by the credit committee and the board of directors, may be deposited in savings banks or trust companies incorporated under the laws of this commonwealth, or in national banks located therein, or invested in any bonds, notes, bankers' acceptances or bank stocks which are at the time of their purchase legal investments for savings banks in this commonwealth, or, to the extent authorized by section three of chapter two hundred and sixteen of the acts of nineteen hundred and thirty-two, in the shares of Central Credit Union Fund,

Investment of funds regulated.

Inc., or in the shares of co-operative banks incorporated in this commonwealth, but not more than three per cent of the assets of a credit union shall be invested in bank stocks at any one time. At least five per cent of the total assets of a credit union shall be carried as cash on hand or as balances due from banks and trust companies, or invested in the bonds or notes of the United States, or of any state, or subdivision thereof, which are legal investments for savings banks as above provided, or in the shares of Central Credit Union Fund, Inc.; provided, that such bonds, notes or shares are the absolute property and under the control of such credit union. Whenever the aforesaid ratio falls below five per cent, no further loans shall be made until the ratio as herein provided has been re-established. Investments, other than personal loans, shall be made only with the approval of the board of directors.

Approved March 26, 1943.

Chap. 119 AN ACT REDUCING THE RATE OF INTEREST ON CERTAIN SEWER ASSESSMENTS IN THE TOWN OF DANVERS.

Be it enacted, etc., as follows:

Section seven of chapter two hundred and twenty-nine of the Special Acts of nineteen hundred and sixteen, as amended by section three of chapter three hundred and twenty-eight of the acts of nineteen hundred and thirty-seven, is hereby further amended by striking out, in the thirty-eighth and in the forty-sixth lines, the word "six" and inserting in place thereof, in each instance, the word: — four, — so as to read as follows: — *Section 7.* The town shall by vote determine what proportion of the cost of said system or systems of sewerage and sewage disposal the town shall pay: *provided,* that it shall pay not less than one third or more than one half of the whole cost. In providing for the payment of the remaining portion of the cost of said system or systems the town may avail itself of any or all of the methods permitted by general laws, and at the same meeting at which it determines the proportion of the cost which is to be borne by the town, it may by vote determine by which of such methods the remaining portion of said cost shall be provided for. In case it determines that such remaining portion of said cost shall be provided for wholly or in part by assessments upon the owners of estates situated within the territory embraced by said system or systems and benefited thereby, then said owners shall be assessed by said board of commissioners their proportional parts, respectively, of such portion of said cost as said town shall have determined is to be provided for by assessment, but no estate shall be deemed to be benefited until a sewer is constructed into which it can be drained. For the purpose of fixing the amounts of such assessments the said board shall determine the value of the special benefit to each of said estates, respectively, from the said system or systems of sewers, taking into account all the circumstances of the case; and the proportionate part to be paid by the owners of said estates, respectively, shall be based upon the amount of the special benefit to each estate, determined as aforesaid, and in no case shall exceed such special benefit. When the sewerage system is available to an abutter on a street in which a lateral sewer has been laid, the water and sewer commissioners shall notify said abutter in writing to that effect and of the total amount of the assessment levied against his estate; and the board shall apportion such assessment into ten equal parts or assessments and shall certify such apportionment to the assessors of the town, and one of said parts or instalments, with interest from the date of the apportionment at four per cent per annum, shall be added by the assessors to the annual tax on such estate for each year next ensuing, until all the said parts have so been added, unless sooner paid as hereinafter provided, and *provided, further*, that nothing herein contained shall be construed to prevent the payment at any time in one payment, notwithstanding its prior apportionment, of any balance of said assessments then remaining unpaid, but interest on such balance at the rate of four per cent per annum shall be paid to the date of such payment, and thereupon the collector of taxes of said town shall receive the same and shall certify such payment or payments to the assessors, who shall preserve a record thereof. In case of corner lots abutting on more than one sewered street the same area shall not be assessed more than once. *Approved March 26, 1943.*

AN ACT AUTHORIZING THE REMOVAL AND HOSPITALIZATION OF PRISONERS HELD FOR SENTENCE OR TRIAL FOR A CAPITAL CRIME. *Chap.* 120

Be it enacted, etc., as follows:

Chapter one hundred and twenty-seven of the General Laws is hereby amended by striking out section one hundred and seventeen, as amended by section one of chapter five hundred and ten of the acts of nineteen hundred and forty-one, and inserting in place thereof the following section: — G. L. (Ter. Ed.), 127, § 117, etc., amended.

Section 117. Whenever the physician of any prison, or of any institution under the control of the department of correction at which a department for defective delinquents is maintained under section one hundred and seventeen of chapter one hundred and twenty-three, certifies that a person held in such prison for trial or sentence, or a person under commitment to such a department, as the case may be, requires medical treatment which cannot safely or properly be given in such prison or institution, as the case may be, the commissioner may temporarily place such person in any hospital, except in the case of a person held in such prison for trial or sentence for a capital crime, in which case the commissioner may temporarily place such person in the hospital at the state prison colony. *Approved March 26, 1943.* Hospitalization of prisoners.

*Chap.*121 AN ACT RELATIVE TO THE VOLUNTARY LIQUIDATION OF BANKING COMPANIES.

Be it enacted, etc., as follows:

G. L. (Ter. Ed.), 167, § 22, amended.

Section twenty-two of chapter one hundred and sixty-seven of the General Laws, as appearing in the Tercentenary Edition, is hereby amended by striking out, in the seventeenth line, the words "or trust company" and inserting in place thereof the words: — , trust company or company subject to chapter one hundred and seventy-two A, — and by inserting after the word "company" in the twentieth line the words: — or a company subject to chapter one hundred and seventy-two A, — so that the second paragraph will read as follows: —

Voluntary liquidation.

Subject to the written approval of the commissioner, any co-operative bank, trust company or company subject to chapter one hundred and seventy-two A may be dissolved and liquidate its affairs if authorized by a vote passed, at a meeting specially called to consider the subject, by at least two thirds of the shareholders in a co-operative bank or by stockholders of a trust company or a company subject to chapter one hundred and seventy-two A representing at least two thirds of its outstanding capital stock. A committee of three shareholders or stockholders shall thereupon be elected, and, under such regulations as may be prescribed by the commissioner, shall liquidate the assets, and after satisfying all debts of the corporation shall distribute the remaining proceeds among those entitled thereto in proportion to their respective interests therein. *Approved March 29, 1943.*

---

*Chap.*122 AN ACT POSTPONING THE TERMINATION OF THE DIVISION OF LIQUIDATIONS AND REGULATING THE DISPOSITION OF THE ASSETS OF CERTAIN CLOSED BANKING INSTITUTIONS.

Emergency preamble.

Whereas, The provisions of law sought to be extended by this act would, but for this act, shortly cease to be effective, but the circumstances and conditions which made advisable their enactment still continue and it is accordingly desirable that said provisions continue in effect without interruption; therefore this act is hereby declared to be an emergency law, necessary for the immediate preservation of the public convenience.

Be it enacted, etc., as follows:

SECTION 1. Section four of chapter five hundred and fifteen of the acts of nineteen hundred and thirty-nine, as amended by section two of chapter one hundred and forty-three of the acts of nineteen hundred and forty-one, is hereby further amended by striking out, in the fourth line, the word "April" and inserting in place thereof the word: — September, — so as to read as follows: — *Section 4.* This act shall take effect on September first, nineteen hundred and thirty-nine, and shall become inoperative on September first, nineteen hundred and forty-three.

Section 2. Any and all funds and property of any institution under the administration of the director of liquidations under chapter five hundred and fifteen of the acts of nineteen hundred and thirty-nine, which remain in the possession of said director at midnight on August thirty-first, nineteen hundred and forty-three shall thereupon be vested in the commissioner of banks, without action on the part of any person; provided, however, that upon the filing at any time prior thereto by said director, with the approval of said commissioner, in the office of the clerk of the supreme judicial court for Suffolk county of a certificate transferring to the possession of said commissioner any and all funds and property of such an institution which remain in the possession of said director, whether or not the liquidation thereof has then been completed, such funds and property shall be vested in said commissioner. Upon the vesting in said commissioner hereunder of the funds and property of any institution, said commissioner, in addition to all other powers vested in him by statute or otherwise, shall have and shall exercise all the powers, duties and functions theretofore had by said director by virtue of statute or otherwise in relation to the conservation and liquidation of such institution, its funds and property.

Section 3. Section three of chapter five hundred and fifteen of the acts of nineteen hundred and thirty-nine is hereby repealed. *Approved March 30, 1943.*

---

*Chap.*123

An Act authorizing the city of Salem to convey certain property held for park purposes by said city.

Be it enacted, etc., as follows:

Section 1. The city of Salem is hereby authorized to convey to Walter Opolski such portion of the property located at the corner of Orchard and Franklin streets in said city and held by it for park purposes as may be determined by the park commissioners of said city.

Section 2. This act shall take effect upon its passage.

Approved March 30, 1943.

---

*Chap.*124

An Act relative to non-partisan municipal elections in the city of Somerville.

Be it enacted, etc., as follows:

Section 1. The first paragraph of section three of chapter two hundred and eighty-one of the acts of nineteen hundred and thirty-two, as most recently amended by section one of chapter two hundred and eleven of the acts of nineteen hundred and thirty-seven, is hereby further amended by striking out, in the tenth line, the word "seventh" and inserting in place thereof the word: — eighth, — so as to read as follows: — Any person who is qualified to vote at any regular or special election for a candidate for any elective municipal office in said city, and who is a candidate for nomination thereto, shall be entitled to have his name as such candidate printed on the official ballot to be used at a preliminary election for nomination therefor; provided, that if he is a candidate to be voted for in a single ward he is a registered voter in the ward wherein he is a candidate; and provided, further, that on or before five o'clock in the afternoon of the eighth Tuesday preceding such regular or special municipal election there shall be submitted to the board of election commissioners, hereinafter called the board, a nomination paper prepared and issued by the board, wherein the candidate sets forth in writing his candidacy, and wherein the petition is signed by voters of the city qualified to vote for a candidate for said office to the number of at least two hundred and fifty for the office of mayor, one hundred and fifty for the office of alderman at large and one hundred for the office of ward alderman and of member of the school committee, whose signatures are certified as hereinafter provided.

SECTION 2. Section four of said chapter two hundred and eighty-one, as amended by section two of said chapter two hundred and eleven, is hereby further amended by striking out, in the tenth line, the word "sixth" and inserting in place thereof the word: — seventh, — so as to read as follows: — *Section 4.* After any such nomination paper has been submitted to the board, it shall certify thereon the number of signatures which are the names of registered voters in said city qualified to sign the same. All such papers found not to contain a number of names so certified equivalent to the number required to make a nomination shall be invalid, and such papers shall be preserved by the board for one year. The board shall complete their certification on or before five o'clock in the afternoon of the seventh Tuesday preceding such regular or special municipal election, and the board, or some member thereof, shall file in their office on or before five o'clock in the afternoon of the next day all papers not found to be invalid as aforesaid.

Approved March 30, 1943.

Chap. 125 AN ACT AUTHORIZING CERTAIN CITIES, TOWNS AND DISTRICTS, THROUGH THEIR WATER DEPARTMENTS, AND CERTAIN WATER COMPANIES, TO AID SIMILAR MUNICIPAL AND OTHER CORPORATIONS RELATIVE TO THEIR WATER SUPPLY.

Be it enacted, etc., as follows:

G. L. (Ter. Ed.), 40, new section 39H, added.

Aid by one water department to another.

Chapter forty of the General Laws is hereby amended by inserting after section thirty-nine G, inserted by section three of chapter one hundred and seventy-two of the acts of nineteen hundred and thirty-eight, the following section: — *Section 39H.* A city, town or district through its water department, if any, if thereunto authorized by ordinance or by-law, or by by-law or by vote of its governing body if a district, or a water company, as defined in section one of chapter one hundred and sixty-five, may go to aid any other city, town or district or any other water company, as so defined, in repairing and maintaining the physical properties of its water supply system. Any such ordinance, by-law or vote may authorize the head of the water department to extend such aid, subject to such conditions and restrictions as may be prescribed therein. Members of water departments of cities, towns and districts while in the performance of their duties in extending such aid shall have the same immunities and privileges as if performing the same work in their respective cities, towns and districts. Any city, town, district or water company aided under this section shall compensate any city, town, district or water company rendering aid as aforesaid, for such aid and for the whole or any part of any damage to its property sustained in the course of rendering such aid.

Approved March 30, 1943.

AN ACT FURTHER EXTENDING THE TERM DURING WHICH BANKING INSTITUTIONS AND INSURANCE COMPANIES MAY MAKE LOANS INSURED BY THE FEDERAL HOUSING ADMINISTRATOR AND FURTHER AUTHORIZING CERTAIN LOANS SO INSURED. *Chap.* 126

Emergency preamble.

Whereas, The provisions of law sought to be extended by this act would, but for this act, shortly cease to be effective, but the circumstances and conditions which made advisable their enactment still continue and it is accordingly desirable that said provisions continue in effect without interruption; therefore this act is hereby declared to be an emergency law, necessary for the immediate preservation of the public convenience.

Be it enacted, etc., as follows:

SECTION 1. The first paragraph of section one of chapter one hundred and sixty-two of the acts of nineteen hundred and thirty-five, as most recently amended by chapter two hundred and sixty of the acts of nineteen hundred and forty-one, is hereby further amended by striking out, in the tenth line, the word "forty-three" and inserting in place thereof the word: — forty-five, — so as to read as follows: — Subject to such regulations as the commissioner of banks deems to be necessary or advisable in respect to trust companies, savings banks, co-operative banks or credit unions, and to such regulations as the commissioner of insurance deems to be necessary or advisable in respect to insurance companies, any trust company, savings bank, co-operative bank, credit union or insurance company doing business in this commonwealth is authorized for a period ending July first, nineteen hundred and forty-five:

SECTION 2. Subdivision (*b*) of said section one, as most

recently amended by chapter two hundred and forty of the acts of nineteen hundred and thirty-seven, is hereby further amended by inserting after the word "make" in the first line, the words: — and acquire, — so as to read as follows: —

(*b*) To make and acquire such loans secured by mortgages on real property in this commonwealth as the federal housing administrator insures and to obtain such insurance.

SECTION 3. Said section one, as amended, is hereby further amended by inserting after subdivision (*b*), as appearing in section one of said chapter two hundred and forty, the following subdivision: —

(*bb*) To collect and apply payments due upon and otherwise to service any mortgage loan originated by it and insured by the federal housing administrator and with respect to such mortgage loan to make agreements with any mortgagees approved by the federal housing administrator to collect and apply payments due upon and otherwise to service any such mortgage loan. *Approved March 31, 1943.*

---

*Chap.*127 AN ACT TEMPORARILY AMENDING THE LAWS RELATIVE TO THE STAMPING AS CORRECT OF CERTAIN GAS METERS.

Emergency preamble.

Whereas, The War Production Board of the United States has adopted an order, entitled section 1001.3, Supplementary Order M–43–b, effective February fifteenth, nineteen hundred and forty-three, relative to the use of tin in gas meters, which provides in substance that tin-bearing solder or other tin-bearing material shall not be used in the adjustment, internal repair or resealing of any tin-cased gas meter having a rated capacity of less than three hundred cubic feet per hour, unless such meter is found not to be accurate within an accuracy range of plus or minus four per cent when tested by standard meter prover tests or has not been previously repaired internally for twelve years or more; and

Whereas, Section one hundred and three of chapter one hundred and sixty-four of the General Laws prohibits the stamping as correct of gas meters not accurate within a range of plus or minus two per cent; and

Whereas, No suitable substitute for tin in the adjustment, internal repair or resealing of gas meters has been found, and it is necessary in connection with the war effort of the United States that tin be conserved in accordance with said order of the War Production Board, and in order to accomplish this result it is necessary that said section one hundred and three be harmonized with said order in certain respects without delay; and

Whereas, Because of the conflicting provisions of said order and said section, a large number of gas meters may be kept unnecessarily out of service.

Now, therefore, This act, designed to harmonize said section with said order, is hereby declared to be an emergency law, necessary for the immediate preservation of the public safety and convenience.

Be it enacted, etc., as follows:

SECTION 1. Notwithstanding any provision to the contrary in section one hundred and three of chapter one hundred and sixty-four of the General Laws, during the effective period of this act a meter having a rated capacity of less than three hundred cubic feet per hour in the adjustment, internal repair or resealing of which tin-bearing solder or other tin-bearing material must be used, may be stamped correct as provided in said section one hundred and three if it varies not more than four per cent from the standard measure, except in the case of a meter that has not been internally repaired for a period of twelve years or more.

SECTION 2. This act shall remain in effect only while there is in force an order of the War Production Board of the United States or any successor of said board, containing the provisions of paragraph (*b*) of the order of said board issued January twenty-sixth, nineteen hundred and forty-three, entitled section 1001.3, Supplementary Order M-43-b, or any like provisions. *Approved March 31, 1943.*

AN ACT AUTHORIZING REGISTERS OF DEEDS TO DESTROY CERTAIN ORIGINAL PAPERS FILED IN THEIR OFFICES. *Chap.* 128

Be it enacted, etc., as follows:

G. L. (Ter. Ed.), 66, § 8, amended.

Section eight of chapter sixty-six of the General Laws, as appearing in the Tercentenary Edition, is hereby amended by adding at the end the following sentence: — Notwithstanding the foregoing, the register of deeds in any county may, without such written approval, destroy any papers pertaining to attachments or to the dissolution or discharge thereof in the files of his office following the expiration of twenty years after the latest original entry therein or thereon, unless otherwise specifically provided by law, — so as to read as follows: — *Section 8.* Every original paper belonging to the files of the commonwealth, or of any county, city or town, bearing date earlier than the year eighteen hundred, every book of registry or record, every town warrant, every deed to the commonwealth or to any county, city or town, every report of an agent, officer or committee relative to bridges, public ways, sewers or other state, county or municipal interests or matters not required to be recorded in a book, and not so recorded, shall be preserved and safely kept, and every other paper belonging to such files shall be kept for seven years after the latest original entry therein or thereon, unless otherwise provided by law; and no such paper shall be destroyed without the written approval of the supervisor of records. Notwithstanding the foregoing, the register of deeds in any county may, without such written approval, destroy any papers pertaining to attachments or to the dissolution or discharge thereof in the files of his office following the expiration of twenty years after the latest original entry therein or thereon, unless otherwise specifically provided by law. *Approved March 31, 1943.*

Preservation of certain books, papers and records.

Chap. 129 AN ACT RELATIVE TO POLLING HOURS AT REGULAR, PRELIMINARY AND SPECIAL CITY ELECTIONS IN THE CITY OF PEABODY.

Be it enacted, etc., as follows:

The hours during which the polls at every regular, preliminary and special city election in the city of Peabody shall be open shall be fixed by the city council of said city in accordance with the provisions of general law relating to polling hours at city elections, notwithstanding any provision of chapter three hundred of the Special Acts of nineteen hundred and sixteen or any act in amendment thereof or in addition thereto. *Approved March 31, 1943.*

Chap. 130 AN ACT FURTHER REGULATING THE INCORPORATION OF PROPRIETORS OF WHARVES, REAL ESTATE LYING IN COMMON, AND GENERAL FIELDS, AND THE ORGANIZATION OF CEMETERY AND CERTAIN OTHER CORPORATIONS.

Be it enacted, etc., as follows:

G. L. (Ter. Ed.), 179, § 3, amended.

SECTION 1. Chapter one hundred and seventy-nine of the General Laws is hereby amended by striking out section three, as appearing in the Tercentenary Edition, and inserting in place thereof the following section: — *Section 3.* At such meeting, by vote of a majority in number and interest of all of the proprietors, they may organize themselves as a corporation under this chapter; and they may thereupon choose a clerk, treasurer, collector and such committees and other officers as they deem necessary for the management of their affairs, and may agree upon and direct the manner of calling future meetings. Each officer chosen shall hold his office until his successor is qualified. The clerk, treasurer and collector shall forthwith make, sign and swear to a certificate setting forth the name of the corporation, its purpose, the town and county where it is located, the date of the meeting for organization and any adjournments thereof, and any other facts of importance contained in the proceedings of organization. The certificate and the record of the meeting, including any by-laws, shall be submitted to the commissioner of corporations and taxation, who shall examine them and who may require such amendments thereof or such additional information as he deems necessary. If he finds that the provisions of law relative to the organization of the corporation have been complied with, he shall endorse his approval on the certificate. The certificate shall, upon payment of a fee of five dollars, be filed in the office of the state secretary; otherwise, the organization shall be void.

Organization by proprietors of wharves, etc.

Scope of act.

SECTION 2. This act shall not affect the validity of any corporation heretofore organized and subject to said section three of chapter one hundred and seventy-nine of the General Laws as in force prior to the effective date of this act.

Approved March 31, 1943.

AN ACT PROVIDING THAT PERSONS HELD IN JAIL FOR TRIAL MAY BE REMOVED IN CERTAIN CASES TO A JAIL IN ANOTHER COUNTY. *Chap.* 131

Be it enacted, etc., as follows:

G. L. (Ter. Ed.), 276, new § 52A, added.

Removal of persons from one jail to another.

Chapter two hundred and seventy-six of the General Laws is hereby amended by inserting after section fifty-two, as appearing in the Tercentenary Edition, the following section: — *Section 52A.* Persons held in jail for trial may, with the approval of the district attorney, be removed by the commissioner of correction to a jail in another county, and said commissioner shall, at the request of the district attorney, cause them to be returned to the jail whence they were removed. The proceedings for such removal shall be the same as for the removal of prisoners from one jail or house of correction to another. The cost of support of a person so removed and of both removals shall be paid by the county whence he is originally removed.

Approved March 31, 1943.

AN ACT INCLUDING TASHMOO POND IN THE TOWN OF TISBURY WITHIN THE MEANING OF THE TERM "COASTAL WATERS" AS USED IN THE LAWS RELATING TO MARINE FISH AND FISHERIES. *Chap.* 132

Be it enacted, etc., as follows:

SECTION 1. The body of water located in the town of Tisbury, and known as Tashmoo pond is hereby declared to be coastal waters within the meaning of the term "coastal waters", as defined by section one of chapter one hundred and thirty of the General Laws, as appearing in section one of chapter five hundred and ninety-eight of the acts of nineteen hundred and forty-one.

SECTION 2. This act shall take effect upon its passage.

Approved March 31, 1943.

AN ACT AUTHORIZING THE TOWN OF BERNARDSTON TO PAY A SUM OF MONEY TO ARTHUR R. MAGOON. *Chap.* 133

Be it enacted, etc., as follows:

SECTION 1. For the purpose of discharging its moral obligation and promoting the public good, the town of Bernardston may pay to Arthur R. Magoon of said town the sum of three hundred dollars to reimburse him for expenses of doctors, nurses and other expenses incurred on account of the burning of his daughter, Rebecca Jane Magoon, while in the chemical laboratory of the public schools of said town, and her death resulting therefrom.

SECTION 2. Said sum may be paid from the appropriation made for said purpose by said town at its annual meeting in the year nineteen hundred and forty-two, and the action of said town in making said appropriation is hereby ratified and confirmed and shall have the same force and effect as if section one of this act had been in effect prior to the taking of said action.

SECTION 3. This act shall take effect upon its passage.

Approved April 1, 1943.

---

*Chap.*134 AN ACT AUTHORIZING THE TOWN OF NORFOLK OR ANY WATER SUPPLY DISTRICT THEREIN TO PURCHASE WATER FROM THE COMMONWEALTH.

Be it enacted, etc., as follows:

SECTION 1. Subject to the approval of the governor and council, the town of Norfolk, or any water supply district duly established therein, may obtain from the commonwealth, through an arrangement with the department of correction, water from the works of the state prison colony, and may obtain from the commonwealth, through an arrangement with the department of public health, water from the works of the Pondville hospital. In carrying out any such plan of supplying water to said town or district which is approved by the governor and council, the commissioner of correction or the commissioner of public health, or each of said commissioners, as the case may be, may, in his discretion, arrange for the delivery of, and deliver, water from the works under his control into the pipes of said town or district, from such places and on such conditions and terms as such commissioner and the water commissioners of said town or district may mutually agree upon. If either of such commissioners and said water commissioners are unable so to agree, the water from the works under the control of such commissioner shall be pumped and delivered from such places and upon such conditions and terms as shall be approved and authorized by the governor and council.

SECTION 2. This act shall take effect upon its passage.

Approved April 1, 1943.

---

*Chap.*135 AN ACT AUTHORIZING AN INCREASE OF THE SALARY OF THE MAYOR OF THE CITY OF GLOUCESTER.

Be it enacted, etc., as follows:

SECTION 1. Section nineteen of chapter six hundred and eleven of the acts of nineteen hundred and eight is hereby amended by striking out, in the seventh and eighth lines, the words "eighteen hundred" and inserting in place thereof the words: — three thousand, — so as to read as follows: — *Section 19.* For the municipal year nineteen hundred and nine and until otherwise ordered by the municipal council, the annual salary of the mayor shall be twelve hundred dollars and the salary of each alderman shall be one thousand dollars. These salaries may be changed by any municipal council, to take effect in the next municipal year thereafter, but the amounts shall not exceed three thousand dollars for the salary of the mayor nor fifteen hundred dollars for the salary of each alderman.

SECTION 2. This act shall be submitted for acceptance to the registered voters of the city of Gloucester at its regular city election in the current year in the form of the following question which shall be placed upon the official ballot to be used at said election: — "Shall an act passed by the general court in the year nineteen hundred and forty-three, entitled 'An Act authorizing an increase of the salary of the mayor of the city of Gloucester', be accepted?" If a majority of the votes in answer to said question is in the affirmative, then this act shall thereupon take full effect, but not otherwise. *Approved April 1, 1943.*

AN ACT PROVIDING FOR THE CLASSIFICATION BY THE COUNTY PERSONNEL BOARD OF THE OFFICES OF CLERKS AND ASSISTANT CLERKS OF THE CENTRAL DISTRICT COURT OF WORCESTER. *Chap.*136

Be it enacted, etc., as follows:

SECTION 1. Section forty-nine of chapter thirty-five of the General Laws, as most recently amended by section one of chapter four hundred and forty-seven of the acts of nineteen hundred and forty-one, is hereby further amended by inserting after the word "Suffolk" in the ninth line the words: — and of the central district court of Worcester, — so as to read as follows: — *Section 49.* Every office and position whereof the salary is wholly payable from the treasury of one or more counties, or from funds administered by and through county officials, except the offices of county commissioners, justices and special justices of the district courts, the messenger of the superior court in the county of Suffolk, clerks and assistant clerks of the district courts other than the clerks and assistant clerks of district courts in the county of Suffolk and of the central district court of Worcester, trial justices, other offices and positions filled by appointment of the governor with the advice and consent of the council, court officers appointed in Suffolk county under section seventy of chapter two hundred and twenty-one, and probation officers, but including the officer described in the first sentence of section seventy-six of said chapter two hundred and twenty-one, shall be classified by the board in the manner provided by sections forty-eight to fifty-six, inclusive, and every such office and position, now existing or hereafter established, shall be allocated by the board to its proper place in such classification. Offices and positions in the service of any department, board, school or hospital principally supported by the funds of the county or counties, or in the service of a hospital district established

G. L. (Ter. Ed.), 35, § 49, etc., amended.

Classification of certain county officers.

under sections seventy-eight to ninety-one, inclusive, of chapter one hundred and eleven, shall likewise be subject to classification as aforesaid. The word "salary", as used in this section, shall include compensation, however payable; but nothing in sections forty-eight to fifty-six, inclusive, and nothing done under authority thereof, shall prevent any person from continuing to receive from a county such compensation as is fixed under authority of other provisions of law or as is expressly established by law.

G. L. (Ter. Ed.), 218, § 79, etc., amended.

SECTION 2. Section seventy-nine of chapter two hundred and eighteen of the General Laws, as most recently amended by section two of said chapter four hundred and forty-seven, is hereby further amended by inserting after the word "county" in the second line the words: — and the central district court of Worcester, — so as to read as follows: — *Section 79.* In courts other than the courts in Suffolk county and the central district court of Worcester in which the salaries of justices are fixed by section seventy-eight, the salaries of clerks shall be equal to seventy-five per cent of the salaries established for the justices of their respective courts; and the salaries of assistant clerks, other than second, third and fourth assistant clerks, shall be equal to seventy-five per cent, and the salaries of second assistant clerks shall be equal to sixty per cent, and the salaries of third assistant clerks shall be equal to forty-five per cent, of the salaries of the clerks of their respective courts. The salary of the fourth assistant clerk of the municipal court of the Roxbury district shall be forty-five per cent of the salary of the clerk of said court.

Classified. salaries.

Same subject.

SECTION 3. The salaries of the several clerks and assistant clerks of the central district court of Worcester in office upon the effective date of the classification of their offices under authority of this act shall not be diminished by reason of such classification, and such salaries shall not be altered until the effective date of such classification.

Approved April 1, 1943.

---

*Chap.*137 AN ACT RELATIVE TO THE MEMBERSHIP OF THE CORPORATION CALLED TRUSTEES OF CLARK UNIVERSITY.

Whereas, The deferred operation of this act would prevent the election of alumni members of the corporation for the academic year nineteen hundred and forty-three to nineteen hundred and forty-four, as provided therein, therefore this act is hereby declared to be an emergency law, necessary for the immediate preservation of the public convenience.

Be it enacted, etc., as follows:

SECTION 1. Chapter one hundred and thirty-three of the acts of eighteen hundred and eighty-seven is hereby amended by striking out section four and inserting in place thereof the following section: — *Section 4.* (*a*) The number of members of the corporation shall be thirteen, nine of whom shall be life members, and four, to be known as alumni members, shall be elected by and from the members of the Clark University Alumni Association in the manner herein provided. Four alumni members shall be elected in the year nineteen hundred and forty-three, one to serve for one year, one for two years, one for three years and one for four years, from July first following their election. As the terms of the alumni members elected hereunder expire, their successors shall be elected by and from the members of said alumni association for the term of four years from July first following their election. One of said members shall always be a person who has held a degree from a graduate department of Clark University for ten years and the other three shall be persons who have held a degree from any department of said university for ten years. No alumni trustee shall be eligible for re-election within one year after the expiration of his term of office.

(*b*) In the year nineteen hundred and forty-three and each year thereafter, prior to April fifteenth, three candidates for each office of alumni member to be filled shall be nominated by the alumni council of Clark University, with the approval in each case of a majority of the members of the corporation. A printed ballot shall be prepared for the purpose by the secretary of said alumni association which shall contain, in alphabetical order, the names of persons nominated as aforesaid, and shall state as to each the year of his class at Clark University, the degrees received therefrom, and his residence and occupation. The ballots shall be mailed to all members of said association entitled to vote, not later than May first of such year, and each such member of the alumni association may vote for one of the three candidates for each office to be filled. All persons who have held for three years a degree from Clark University conferred in regular course, and all persons who have received from said university an honorary degree and no others, shall be entitled to vote. The ballot, when marked, shall be signed by the voter and shall be returned to the executive committee of said alumni association, on or before May fifteenth of such year. The candidate for alumni member receiving the highest number of votes for the office to which he is nominated shall be declared elected thereto.

(*c*) In the event that a vacancy occurs in the number of life members it shall be filled by vote of a majority of the remaining life members at a meeting duly called for the purpose; and in the event of a vacancy in the number of alumni members it shall be filled at the next annual election for the unexpired term of his predecessor in the manner hereinbefore set forth.

(*d*) When any member of the corporation, whether a life member or an alumni member, shall, in the judgment of the remaining members of the corporation, become incapable of discharging the duties of his office by reason of infirmity or otherwise, or shall neglect or refuse to perform such duties, he may be removed by the remaining members of the corporation.

SECTION 2. The members of the corporation called Trustees of Clark University in office on the effective date of this act shall retain their respective offices subject, however, to the provisions of this act.

Approved April 1, 1943.

---

*Chap.*138 AN ACT RELATIVE TO POLLING HOURS AT PRELIMINARY ELECTIONS IN THE CITY OF HAVERHILL.

Be it enacted, etc., as follows:

Section five of chapter five hundred and seventy-four of the acts of nineteen hundred and eight is hereby amended by striking out, in the twelfth, thirteenth and fourteenth lines, the words "At every preliminary election for nominations the polls shall be opened at six o'clock in the forenoon and kept open until four o'clock in the afternoon and, except" and inserting in place thereof the word: — Except.

Approved April 1, 1943.

---

*Chap.*139 AN ACT PROVIDING FOR THE HOLDING OF BIENNIAL MUNICIPAL ELECTIONS IN THE CITY OF HAVERHILL IN ODD NUMBERED YEARS BEGINNING IN NINETEEN HUNDRED AND FORTY-SEVEN.

Be it enacted, etc., as follows:

SECTION 1. Beginning with the year nineteen hundred and forty-seven, municipal elections in the city of Haverhill for the choice of mayor, aldermen and members of the school committee shall be held biennially on the Tuesday next following the first Monday of December in each odd numbered year.

SECTION 2. At the biennial municipal election to be held in said city in the year nineteen hundred and forty-seven, and at every biennial municipal election thereafter, a mayor, four aldermen and four members of the school committee shall be elected to serve for terms of two years each from the first Monday in January following their election and until the qualification of their respective successors. The mayor, the aldermen and the members of the school committee elected at the annual city election in the year nineteen hundred and forty-four shall serve for terms of three years each and until the qualifications of their respective successors, who shall be elected at the biennial municipal election in the year nineteen hundred and forty-seven. There shall be no city election in said city in the year nineteen hundred and forty-six.

SECTION 3. Such provisions of chapter sixty-one of the acts of eighteen hundred and sixty-nine and of chapter five hundred and seventy-four of the acts of nineteen hundred and eight, and acts in amendment thereof and in addition thereto, as are inconsistent with any provisions of this act are hereby repealed.

SECTION 4. This act shall be submitted to the voters of the city of Haverhill at the annual city election in the current year in the form of the following question which shall be placed upon the official ballot to be used in said city at said election: — "Shall an act passed by the General Court in the year nineteen hundred and forty-three, entitled 'An Act providing for the holding of biennial municipal elections in the city of Haverhill in odd numbered years beginning in nineteen hundred and forty-seven', be accepted?" If a majority of the voters voting thereon vote in the affirmative in answer to said question, then this act shall thereupon take full effect in said city; otherwise it shall be of no effect.

Approved April 1, 1943.

AN ACT EXTENDING FURTHER THE DURATION OF A LAW PROVIDING FOR THE TRIAL OR DISPOSITION OF CERTAIN CRIMINAL CASES BY DISTRICT COURT JUDGES SITTING IN THE SUPERIOR COURT. *Chap.*140

Be it enacted, etc., as follows:

Chapter four hundred and sixty-nine of the acts of nineteen hundred and twenty-three, as most recently amended by chapter five hundred and seventy-six of the acts of nineteen hundred and forty-one, is hereby further amended by striking out section five and inserting in place thereof the following section: — *Section 5.* This act shall not be operative after December thirty-first, nineteen hundred and forty-five.

Approved April 1, 1943.

AN ACT PROVIDING A PENALTY FOR THE IMPROPER OPERATION OF TRACKLESS TROLLEY VEHICLES, SO CALLED. *Chap.*141

Be it enacted, etc., as follows:

G. L. (Ter. Ed.), 163, new § 13, added.

Improper operation. Penalty.

Chapter one hundred and sixty-three of the General Laws, as amended, is hereby further amended by adding at the end the following section: — *Section 13.* Whoever upon any way or in any place to which the public has a right of access operates a trackless trolley vehicle while under the influence of intoxicating liquor, or operates such a vehicle recklessly, or operates such a vehicle negligently so that the lives or safety of the public are endangered, shall be punished by a fine of not less than twenty dollars nor more than two hundred dollars or by imprisonment for not less than two weeks nor more than two years, or both.

Approved April 1, 1943.

Chap.142 AN ACT RELATIVE TO CERTAIN SHARES OF CO-OPERATIVE BANKS OWNED BY PERSONS ENGAGED IN THE MILITARY OR NAVAL SERVICE OF THE UNITED STATES, OR BY THEIR DEPENDENTS.

Be it enacted, etc., as follows:

G.L. (Ter. Ed.), 170, § 17A, etc., amended.

Temporary suspension of payments by soldiers and sailors authorized.

Chapter one hundred and seventy of the General Laws is hereby amended by striking out section seventeen A, inserted by chapter one hundred and sixteen of the acts of nineteen hundred and forty-one, and inserting in place thereof the following section: — *Section 17A.* For the accommodation of any owner of serial shares not pledged for a real estate loan who is actually engaged in the military or naval service of the United States, or who is the wife or a dependent member of the family of a person so engaged, the directors, at the request of such shareholder, may cause such shares to be cancelled, whereupon there shall be transferred to a military share account as a credit of such shareholder the full value of such shares, less all monthly installments of interest and fines in arrears and less the amount of the unpaid balance of any share loan at that time secured by the shares so cancelled. So long as such credit remains in such military share account, no further monthly payments of any amount on account of such shares shall be required, nor shall any fines be imposed, but payments and withdrawals may be made on any such account at the option of the shareholder. At each regular distribution date there shall be credited to every such account a dividend at the rate declared upon serial shares, computed without regard to fractions of a dollar; provided, that amounts withdrawn between distribution dates shall not participate in the next distribution, but amounts deposited shall participate in profits from and after the bank day next following the deposit. Deferment of payments as aforesaid shall extend for the duration of such military or naval service and six months thereafter and at the termination of such period of deferment the shareholder shall be required by the directors to reinvest such portion of the accumulation as he may elect in serial shares and withdraw that portion not so reinvested. Upon failure of the shareholder to do so, the accumulated balance shall be transferred to the suspended share account and thereafter shall cease to participate in any profits.

Approved April 2, 1943.

Chap.143 AN ACT RELATIVE TO THE EXAMINATION OF THE MASSACHUSETTS HOSPITAL LIFE INSURANCE COMPANY BY THE COMMISSIONER OF BANKS.

Be it enacted, etc., as follows:

SECTION 1. Chapter eighty-two of the acts of eighteen hundred and eighty-one is hereby amended by striking out section three and inserting in place thereof the following section: — *Section 3.* The commissioner of banks shall inspect, examine and inquire into the business of said corporation, shall have access to the vaults, books and papers thereof, and shall have such supervision of its affairs as he would have if it were the trust department of a trust company; and said corporation shall make such returns and annual reports to said commissioner as he may require.

SECTION 2. This act shall take full effect upon its acceptance by the Massachusetts Hospital Life Insurance Company. *Approved April 2, 1943.*

AN ACT FURTHER REGULATING SUPPRESSION OF THE EUROPEAN CORN BORER. *Chap.* 144

Be it enacted, etc., as follows:

G. L. (Ter. Ed.), 128, § 31A, amended.

Suppression of European corn borer.

Chapter one hundred and twenty-eight of the General Laws is hereby amended by striking out section thirty-one A, as appearing in the Tercentenary Edition, and inserting in place thereof the following section: — *Section 31A.* In any town or part thereof in which an order issued under section thirty-one in connection with the suppression of the European corn borer shall be in effect, every person in possession of land on which corn of any kind has been grown shall, except as hereinafter provided, not later than December first of the year of its growth, plow or cause to be plowed the field in which it was grown, so as to bury the stubble to a depth of at least six inches, or pull up said stubble or cause it to be pulled up and destroy it, or cause it to be destroyed, by burning, and every person having in his possession corn stalks shall, not later than April tenth of the year following that of their growth, completely dispose of such corn stalks by using them as fodder or by burning them. Whenever it shall be determined by the director that such plowing or burning would be detrimental to soil conservation or to the production of food or feed crops, he may issue an order or permit which shall authorize postponement of such plowing or burning, or shall authorize replanting without plowing, under such conditions not inconsistent with the purpose of this section as he may specify. Such an order or permit may be issued to apply to an individual field, to a farm, or to a geographical or political unit. Whoever violates any provision of this section or any order or permit issued hereunder shall be punished by a fine of not less than twenty-five nor more than five hundred dollars.

Penalty.

Approved April 2, 1943.

Chap.145 AN ACT PROVIDING FOR A WEEKLY RETURN DAY IN THE SUPERIOR COURT FOR THE ENTRY OF APPEALS IN CRIMINAL CASES AND FOR SUITS ON RECOGNIZANCES AND BONDS GIVEN IN SUCH CASES.

Be it enacted, etc., as follows:

G. L. (Ter. Ed.), 212, § 22, etc., amended.

SECTION 1. Section twenty-two of chapter two hundred and twelve of the General Laws, as amended by chapter two hundred and eighty-seven of the acts of nineteen hundred and thirty-four, is hereby further amended by striking out, in the first and second lines, the words "The first Monday of every month" and inserting in place thereof the words: — Every Monday, — and by striking out, in the fourteenth line, the words "said first" and inserting in place thereof the word: — any, — so as to read as follows: — *Section 22.* Every Monday shall be a return day for the entry of appeals in criminal cases from district courts and trial justices and of suits upon recognizances and bonds in such cases. Such appeals shall be entered on the return day next after the appeal is taken. Such suits may be made returnable at the election of the district attorney at any such return day within three months after the date of the writ. Trials by jury of such suits shall take place at criminal sittings; and, for the purpose of docketing and recording such suits, they shall be deemed to be criminal cases, provided that the provisions of chapter two hundred and twenty-seven shall be applicable thereto as in other civil cases except that no bond shall be required as provided in section nine thereof. If any Monday is a legal holiday, such entry shall be made on the day following.

Return day in criminal cases.

Effective date.

SECTION 2. This act shall take effect on September first in the current year. *Approved April 2, 1943.*

Chap.146 AN ACT TO UNITE THE BEACON UNIVERSALIST PARISH AND THE CHURCH AFFILIATED THEREWITH WITH FIRST UNIVERSALIST SOCIETY IN WALTHAM AND FOR OTHER PURPOSES.

Be it enacted, etc., as follows:

SECTION 1. The voluntary religious association, commonly known as Beacon Universalist Church, of Brookline, affiliated with Beacon Universalist Parish, incorporated as Fifth Universalist Society in the city of Boston by an act approved March sixteenth, eighteen hundred and thirty-eight, the corporate name having been changed to Shawmut Universalist Society by an act approved February twenty-seventh, eighteen hundred and sixty-three, the corporate name having been again changed to Beacon Universalist Parish by an act approved March seventh, nineteen hundred and five, also situated in said Brookline, upon the acceptance of this act by a two thirds vote of its members present and voting at a meeting called for the purpose and by the recording in the registry of deeds for the county of Norfolk of a certificate of said vote, duly made and sworn to by the clerk of said meeting, shall be a corporation by the name of Beacon Universalist Church, with all the rights, powers, franchises and privileges which the said voluntary religious association has heretofore acquired, or enjoyed by statute, vote, gift, grant, usage, prescription or otherwise, and subject to all the duties and liabilities to which the said voluntary religious association has heretofore been subject, and also, except as may be provided otherwise in this act, with all the rights, powers and privileges, and subject to all the duties and liabilities, of religious corporations instituted under the general laws of the commonwealth; and upon the acceptance of this act as aforesaid, all members of the said voluntary religious association shall be members of the said new corporation, Beacon Universalist Church.

SECTION 2. All property, both real and personal, and all property rights, now held or owned by the said voluntary religious association, or by its deacons or other officers in trust for the said voluntary religious association or for other charitable purposes administered in connection with it or otherwise, shall be vested, upon the acceptance of this act as aforesaid, in the corporation created by section one of this act, and thereafter shall be held in fee simple by the said corporation upon the same uses and trusts upon which the same are now held and upon no other, and the said deacons, and any other officers of the said voluntary religious association who hold real or personal estate in trust as aforesaid under the general laws of this commonwealth, are hereby authorized, at any time after the acceptance of this act as aforesaid, subject to the same uses and trusts as when held by them, to convey such property, real and personal, to the corporation created by section one of this act.

SECTION 3. The corporation created by section one of this act is hereby authorized to take and hold for religious, benevolent and charitable purposes gifts, grants, bequests, devises of real and personal property to the amount permitted by section nine of chapter one hundred and eighty of the General Laws, with full power to sell and convey, free of trust, any part or the whole of its said property, real or personal, for purposes of investment and reinvestment, and for the improvement, alteration or relocation of any of its buildings, and upon any such sale the proceeds thereof shall be held upon the same uses and trusts upon which the property thus sold was held, and the purchaser shall not be responsible for the application of the purchase money. At any time after the acceptance of this act as aforesaid, the said corporation may convey any or all of its property, both real and personal, subject, nevertheless, as to any property held by it in trust, to the same trusts and uses as when held by it, in trust, either for its own benefit or for the general purposes of the grantee next hereinafter named, to the First Universalist Society in Waltham, incorporated by an act approved

March twenty-second, eighteen hundred and thirty-nine, and to its successors, if, and in such manner as, the said corporation, the Beacon Universalist Church, by a two thirds vote of its members present and voting, at a meeting called for the purpose, shall vote to make such a conveyance; and upon the acceptance of the said conveyance by the First Universalist Society in Waltham by a two thirds vote of its members present and voting at a meeting duly called for the purpose, and upon the recording in the registries of deeds for the counties of Norfolk and Middlesex of the said deeds and other instruments of transfer, together with certificates, duly made and sworn to by the clerks of the said meetings, respectively, of the said votes authorizing said conveyance and the acceptance thereof, the members of the corporation created by section one of this act shall become members of First Universalist Society in Waltham, with all the rights of any members thereof, and the corporate existence of the said corporation created by section one of this act shall cease and determine.

SECTION 4. At any time after the acceptance of this act by said Beacon Universalist Parish in the same manner as is prescribed for its acceptance by Beacon Universalist Church in section one, the said Beacon Universalist Parish may, by a two thirds vote of its members present and voting at a meeting called for the purpose, authorize one or more persons in its name and on its behalf to execute, acknowledge and deliver proper deeds and other instruments, conveying in fee simple all of its property, both real and personal, to First Universalist Society in Waltham, and upon the acceptance of the said conveyance by the First Universalist Society in Waltham by a two thirds vote of its members present and voting at a meeting duly called for the purpose, and upon the recording in the registries of deeds for the counties of Norfolk and Middlesex of the said deeds and other instruments of transfer, together with certificates, duly made and sworn to by the clerks of the said meetings, respectively, of the said votes authorizing the said conveyance and the acceptance thereof, the members of the said corporation, Beacon Universalist Parish, shall become members of First Universalist Society in Waltham, with all the rights of any members thereof, and the corporate existence of the said corporation, the Beacon Universalist Parish, shall cease and determine.

SECTION 5. When and if each one of the said two corporations, Beacon Universalist Church and Beacon Universalist Parish, shall, as above provided, convey all its real and personal property to First Universalist Society in Waltham, and shall cause to be recorded in the registries of deeds for the counties of Norfolk and Middlesex the deeds making such conveyance, and the certificates duly made and sworn to, as aforesaid, of the votes authorizing said conveyance and the acceptance thereof as herein provided, thereupon all property, both real and personal, held by or for the said corporation so conveying, in trust or otherwise, shall be held by First Universalist Society in Waltham, upon the same uses and trusts upon which said property was held previous to such conveying and recording, and all property, rights, powers, franchises and privileges which the said corporation so conveying may then possess or enjoy by statute, vote, gift, grant, usage, prescription or otherwise, shall thereupon be vested in First Universalist Society in Waltham; and all debts and other obligations of the said corporation so conveying, so far as the same shall be valid, including any obligation arising from any defect in the performance of the act of transfer, authorized as aforesaid, shall be assumed, paid and discharged by First Universalist Society in Waltham.

SECTION 6. In case of doubt as to the manner in which any property, held in trust or otherwise, conveyed to or vested in First Universalist Society in Waltham, under the provisions of this act, or the income thereof, should be held, administered or applied by the said corporation, the matter may be determined by the supreme judicial court upon the application of any person interested or of the attorney general; and until said court shall otherwise order, such property and the income thereof shall be held, administered and applied by the said corporation in accordance with the terms of the original trusts or as nearly in accordance therewith as is possible.

SECTION 7. The property conveyed to, or vested in, First Universalist Society in Waltham, under the provisions of this act, excepting only such property as prior to such conveyance or vesting may have been held for specific and limited charitable uses and trusts, shall not, after such conveyance and vesting, be applied or apportioned with reference to the source or the religious body aforesaid from which it was derived under the provisions of this act, but shall be administered and applied by First Universalist Society in Waltham, for its general church and charitable purposes and as a single consolidated property and fund.

SECTION 8. Any person aggrieved by any provision of this act may, at any time within six months after the recording of such of the various deeds or other instruments in this act provided for, as is alleged to be the cause of such injury, apply by petition to the supreme judicial court, to have his damages determined by a jury therein, or by or under the direction of said court; and damages so awarded, with the costs of suit allowed by statute in civil cases, attending such award, shall be paid by First Universalist Society in Waltham.

SECTION 9. The records, books of account and other papers of Beacon Universalist Church at the time of its merger in the corporation First Universalist Society in Waltham, and of Beacon Universalist Parish when it is so merged, shall thereupon become, and thereafter be, the property of said corporation First Universalist Society in Waltham.

SECTION 10. The first meeting of the corporation created by section one of this act shall be held within thirty days after the acceptance of this act as provided in section one hereof, and shall be warned by a notice in writing signed by one or more members of the said corporation, stating the object, time and place of the meeting, posted on the outer door of the meetinghouse of the said Beacon Universalist Parish, at least fourteen days before the meeting. At such meeting the said corporation created by section one of this act shall elect a moderator, a treasurer and a clerk, who shall be sworn, and such other officers, and shall adopt such other provisions, not inconsistent with this act or with the general laws of this commonwealth regarding religious corporations, as the said corporation may determine.

SECTION 11. All gifts, grants, bequests and devises made or accruing to, or for the benefit of, the said Beacon Universalist Parish, or of the church, or any of its officers, affiliated with it, after the merger in First Universalist Society in Waltham of the body, or its officers aforesaid, receiving such gift, grant, devise or bequest, shall vest in First Universalist Society in Waltham.

SECTION 11A. Whatever authority is granted by this act is hereby declared to be limited to such authority as the general court may constitutionally grant, without prejudice to any proceeding that may be instituted in any court of competent jurisdiction to effect the purposes of this act.

SECTION 12. This act shall take effect upon its passage.

Approved April 5, 1943.

---

*Chap.*147 AN ACT IN AID OF THE CONSTRUCTION AND ENFORCEMENT OF THE STATE MILK CONTROL LAW, SO CALLED.

Be it enacted, etc., as follows:

G. L. (Ter. Ed.), 94A, new § 22A, added.

Liability for acts of officers, etc.

Chapter ninety-four A of the General Laws, as appearing in section two of chapter six hundred and ninety-one of the acts of nineteen hundred and forty-one, is hereby amended by inserting after section twenty-two, under the heading "CONSTRUCTION", the following section: — *Section 22A.* When construing and enforcing the provisions of this chapter, the act, omission or failure of any officer, agent or other person acting for or employed by any individual, corporation, company, society or association within the scope of his employment or office, shall in each case be also deemed to be the act, omission or failure of such individual, corporation, company, society or association, as well as that of the officer, agent or other person acting for or employed by him or it.

Approved April 5, 1943.

AN ACT TO REMOVE THE LIMITATION ON THE AMOUNT WHICH A HOUSING AUTHORITY MAY AGREE TO PAY TO A CITY OR TOWN IN LIEU OF TAXES. *Chap.* 148

Be it enacted, etc., as follows:

G. L. (Ter. Ed.), 121, § 26W, etc., amended.

Section twenty-six W of chapter one hundred and twenty-one of the General Laws, as inserted by section one of chapter four hundred and eighty-four of the acts of nineteen hundred and thirty-eight, is hereby amended by striking out, in the eleventh and twelfth lines, the words ", or agree with such housing authority upon the amount of," and by inserting after the word "project" in the twenty-first line the following sentence: — Such a city or town may however agree with such a housing authority upon the payments to be made to the city or town as herein provided or such housing authority may make and such city or town may accept such payments, the amount of which shall not in either case be subject to the foregoing limitation, — so as to read as follows: — *Section 26W.* The real estate and tangible personal property of a housing authority held in connection with a project financed in whole or in part by the federal government under the United States Housing Act of 1937 shall be deemed to be public property used for essential public and governmental purposes and shall be exempt from taxation and from betterments and special assessments, provided, that in lieu of such taxes, betterments and special assessments, a city or town in which a housing authority holds real estate used or to be used in connection with such a project may determine a sum to be paid to the city or town annually in any year or period of years such sum to be in any year not in excess of the amount that would be levied at the current tax rate upon the average of the assessed value of such real estate, including buildings and other structures, for the three years preceding the acquisition thereof, the valuation of each year being reduced by all abatements thereon, as compensation for improvements, services and facilities, other than gas, water and electricity, furnished by such city or town for the benefit of such project. Such a city or town may however agree with such a housing authority upon the payments to be made to the city or town as herein provided or such housing authority may make and such city or town may accept such payments, the amount of which shall not in either case be subject to the foregoing limitation. The last paragraph of section six and all of section seven of chapter fifty-nine shall, so far as apt, be applicable to payments under this section.

Property acquired by housing authority to be public property.

Approved April 5, 1943.

Chap.149 AN ACT RELATIVE TO THE TAKING OF LOBSTERS AND EDIBLE CRABS FROM THE COASTAL WATERS OF ESSEX COUNTY.

Be it enacted, etc., as follows:

G. L. (Ter. Ed.), 130, § 37, etc., amended.

Section thirty-seven of chapter one hundred and thirty of the General Laws, as appearing in section one of chapter five hundred and ninety-eight of the acts of nineteen hundred and forty-one, is hereby amended by striking out, in the tenth line, the word "county" and inserting in place thereof the words: — and Essex counties, — so that the paragraph contained in the tenth and eleventh lines will read as follows: —

Buoying of lobster, etc., pots.

In Dukes and Essex counties no such pot, trap or other contrivance shall be buoyed otherwise than separately and plainly. *Approved April 5, 1943.*

Chap.150 AN ACT RELATIVE TO LIENS FOR SEWER ASSESSMENTS IN THE TOWN OF MILFORD.

Be it enacted, etc., as follows:

Chapter two hundred and sixty-one of the acts of nineteen hundred and eight is hereby amended by striking out section four and inserting in place thereof the following section: — *Section 4.* Every assessment made under this act shall, for two years after the certification thereof to the collector of taxes, as hereinbefore provided, constitute a lien on the land affected thereby and, except as hereinafter provided, the lien shall continue until the recorded alienation of the estate.

If no apportionment is made and within said two years the estate shall have been alienated and the instrument alienating the same shall have been recorded, the lien shall terminate at the expiration of said two years.

In case of apportionment the lien shall terminate at the expiration of two years from the date when the last portion or instalment becomes payable, if within said two years the estate shall have been alienated and the instrument alienating the same shall have been recorded, otherwise the lien shall continue until a recorded alienation of the estate.

Notwithstanding the foregoing, in any case where the amount or validity of the assessment is drawn in question by any suit or proceeding the lien shall continue for one year after final determination of such suit or proceeding.

Approved April 5, 1943.

Chap.151 AN ACT PROVIDING FOR THE ESTABLISHMENT OF A RIGHT OF WAY FOR PUBLIC ACCESS TO LITTLE HERRING POND IN THE TOWN OF PLYMOUTH.

Be it enacted, etc., as follows:

SECTION 1. The county commissioners of Plymouth county are hereby authorized to lay out a right of way in the town of Plymouth from the public road at the northerly end of Great Herring pond for public access to Little Herring pond, in accordance with plans to be approved by the department of public works and showing the location and dimensions of said right of way. Said right of way shall be a roadway forty feet wide along the westerly side of Little Herring pond to the shore in the vicinity of Duck cove, so called, with a suitable recreation area on the shore of the pond as a public landing. If it is necessary to acquire land for the purpose of laying out said right of way the commissioners shall at the time said right of way is laid out take such land by eminent domain under chapter seventy-nine of the General Laws. Any person sustaining damages in his property by the laying out of said right of way, or by specific repairs or improvements thereon, shall be entitled to recover the same under said chapter seventy-nine; provided, that the right to damages, if any, shall vest upon the recording of an order of taking by the commissioners, and that no entry or possession for the purpose of constructing a public way on land so taken shall be required for the purpose of validating such taking or for the payment of damages by reason thereof.

SECTION 2. The selectmen of the town of Plymouth from time to time may make specific repairs on or improve such way to such extent as they may deem necessary, but neither the county of Plymouth or any municipality therein shall be required to keep said right of way in repair, nor shall it be liable for injury sustained by persons travelling thereon; provided, that sufficient notice to warn the public is posted where such way enters upon or unites with an existing public way.

SECTION 3. All expenses incurred by the commissioners in connection with said right of way shall be borne by the county of Plymouth, or by such municipalities therein, and in such proportion as the commissioners may determine.

SECTION 4. Said right of way shall not be discontinued or abandoned without authority therefor from the general court.

SECTION 5. Nothing in this act shall be so construed as to limit the powers of the department of public health, or of any local board of health, under the General Laws or any special law. *Approved April 5, 1943.*

AN ACT AUTHORIZING RELEASES AND DISCLAIMERS OF POWERS OF APPOINTMENT AND PROVIDING FOR THE METHODS OF RELEASING AND DISCLAIMING THE SAME. *Chap.*152

Emergency preamble.

Whereas, By the provisions of the Revenue Act of 1942 as enacted and amended by the Congress of the United States of America certain powers of appointment must be released prior to July first, nineteen hundred and forty-three, in order to prevent application thereto of certain amendments to the Internal Revenue Code of the United States of America effected by said Revenue Act of 1942, under which the release of any such power will be subject to gift tax and in the event of the death of the donee of any such power the property then subject thereto will be included in his gross estate in the computation of the estate tax payable by reason of his death, and the deferred operation of this act would result in completely denying or substantially impairing the benefits of this act to donees desiring to release such powers; therefore this act is hereby declared to be an emergency law, necessary for the immediate preservation of the public convenience.

Be it enacted, etc., as follows:

G. L. (Ter. Ed.), 204, new §§ 27–36, added.

Release of power of appointment, etc.

Chapter two hundred and four of the General Laws, as amended, is hereby further amended by adding at the end the following ten new sections: — *Section 27.* A power of appointment, whether or not coupled with an interest, and whether or not existing at the time this section takes effect, and whether the power is held by the donee in an individual or in a fiduciary capacity, may be released, wholly or partially, by the donee thereof, unless otherwise expressly provided in the instrument creating the power. As used in sections twenty-seven to thirty-five, inclusive, the term power of appointment includes all powers which are in substance and effect powers of appointment regardless of the language used in creating them and whether they are: (*a*) general, special, or otherwise; (*b*) in gross, appendant, simply collateral, in trust, or otherwise; (*c*) exercisable by will, deed, deed or will, or instrument amending a trust, or otherwise; (*d*) exercisable presently or in the future.

Methods of release of power of appointment.

Section 28. A power releasable according to section twenty-seven, or under common law, may be released, wholly or partially, by the delivery of a written release executed by the donee of the power for consideration or under seal to any person who could be adversely affected by the exercise of the power, or to any person who alone or with another or others holds in trust property subject to the power, or, in the case of a power created by will, by the filing of such release in the registry of probate in the county in which such will was proved or allowed. No release of a power of appointment shall be valid as to land in the commonwealth subject to such power, except as against the releasor and persons having actual notice of the release, unless (*a*) in case of a power created by will or other written instrument, the release is acknowledged in the manner required in the case of deeds of land to entitle them to be recorded and is recorded in the registry of deeds for the county or district in which the land lies or, in the case of registered land, is filed and registered in the office of the assistant recorder for the registry district where the land lies or (*b*) in case of a power created by will, the release is filed in the registry of probate in the county in which such will was proved or allowed.

Effect and scope of release.

Section 29. A release executed by the donee of a power releasable according to section twenty-seven, or under common law, and delivered or filed in accordance with the first sentence of section twenty-eight, shall, subject to the second sentence of section twenty-eight, be effective to release the power to the extent in such release provided, whether it in substance provides for the release of all right of the donee to exercise the power, or for the release of all right of the donee to exercise the power otherwise than in respect of a part, therein defined, of the property subject to the power, or for the release of all right of the donee to exercise the power otherwise than to or for the benefit of, in trust for, or in favor of a person or persons or class or classes of persons, therein specified, or an object or objects or class or classes of objects, therein defined.

Section 30. If a power of appointment releasable according to section twenty-seven, or under common law, is or may be exercisable by two or more persons in conjunction with one another or successively, a release or disclaimer of the power, in whole or in part, executed, and delivered or filed, in accordance with the first sentence of section twenty-eight, by any one of the donees of the power, shall, subject to the second sentence of section twenty-eight, be effective to release or disclaim, to the extent therein provided, all right of such person to exercise or to participate in the exercise of the power, but, unless the instrument creating the power otherwise provides, shall not prevent or limit the exercise or participation in the exercise thereof by the other donee or donees thereof.

Release of one of two or more donees of a power, effect of.

Section 31. The word "release", as used in sections twenty-eight to thirty, inclusive, shall include (1) an instrument wherein the person who executes it in substance states that he wholly releases, or agrees in no respect to exercise or participate in the exercise of, a power of appointment, and (2) an instrument wherein the person who executes it in substance states that he releases all right to exercise or participate in the exercise of a power of appointment otherwise than within limits therein defined or agrees not to exercise or participate in the exercise of a power of appointment otherwise than within limits therein defined.

Word "release" defined.

Section 32. Release of a power of appointment otherwise releasable shall not be prevented merely by provisions in restraint of alienation or anticipation contained in the instrument creating the power.

Restraints on alienation, etc., not to prevent release.

Section 33. Sections twenty-seven to thirty-two, inclusive, shall so far as possible be deemed to be declaratory of the common law of this commonwealth. Said sections shall be liberally construed so as to effectuate the intent that all powers of appointment whatsoever shall be releasable unless otherwise expressly provided in the instrument creating the power.

Construction of act.

Section 34. A donee of a power of appointment may disclaim the same at any time, wholly or in part, in the same manner and to the same extent as he might release it.

Disclaimer by donee.

Section 35. Nothing in sections twenty-seven to thirty-

Previous sections limited.

four, inclusive, shall prevent the release in any lawful manner of any releasable power of appointment or the disclaimer in any lawful manner of any power of appointment.

Severability of sections. Constitutionality.

Section 36. If any of the provisions in sections twenty-seven to thirty-five, inclusive, shall be held invalid or unconstitutional in relation to any of the applications thereof, such invalidity or unconstitutionality shall not affect other applications thereof, or other provisions in said sections; and to these ends the provisions in said sections are declared to be severable. *Approved April 7, 1943.*

Chap. 153 AN ACT AUTHORIZING ASSOCIATE MEDICAL EXAMINERS IN BARNSTABLE COUNTY TO PERFORM THE DUTIES OF MEDICAL EXAMINER THEREOF IN CERTAIN CASES.

Be it enacted, etc., as follows:

G. L. (Ter. Ed.), 38, new § 2A, added.

SECTION 1. Chapter thirty-eight of the General Laws is hereby amended by inserting after section two, as appearing in the Tercentenary Edition, the following section: —

Duties of associate examiner, Barnstable county.

Section 2A. An associate medical examiner appointed in and for a medical examiner district of Barnstable county may perform the duties of medical examiner in any other such district of such county where there is no associate medical examiner, in case of the absence or inability to act of the medical examiner of such other district.

Effective date.

SECTION 2. This act shall take effect upon its passage. *Approved April 7, 1943.*

Chap. 154 AN ACT REQUIRING WRITTEN NOTICE OF THE INTENDED SALE OF CERTAIN ARTICLES DEPOSITED IN PAWN AND NOT REDEEMED.

Be it enacted, etc., as follows:

G. L. (Ter. Ed.), 140, § 71, amended.

Pawnbrokers to retain articles four months, etc.

Chapter one hundred and forty of the General Laws is hereby amended by striking out section seventy-one, as appearing in the Tercentenary Edition, and inserting in place thereof the following section: — *Section 71.* Articles deposited in pawn with a licensed pawnbroker shall, unless redeemed, be retained by him on the premises occupied by him for his business for at least four months after the date of deposit, if not of a perishable nature; and, if perishable, for at least one month after said date.

Exception.

After the expiration of the applicable period of time, he may sell the articles by public auction, apply the proceeds thereof in satisfaction of the debt or demand and the expense of the notice and sale, and pay any surplus to the person entitled thereto on demand;

Written notice.

provided, that no such sale of any article which is not of a perishable nature shall be made unless not less than ten days prior to the sale a written notice of the intended sale shall have been sent by registered mail to the person entitled to the payment of any surplus as aforesaid, addressed to his residence, as appearing in the records of such pawnbroker. No article taken in pawn by such pawnbroker exceeding twenty-five dollars in value shall be disposed of otherwise than as above provided, any agreement or contract between the parties thereto to the contrary notwithstanding. Articles of personal apparel shall not be deemed to be of a perishable nature within the meaning of this section. *Approved April 7, 1943.*

AN ACT PROVIDING FOR THE FILING IN CASES OF ADOPTION AND CHANGE OF NAME OF COPIES OF RECORDS OF BIRTH AND OF PREVIOUS DECREES OF ADOPTION AND CHANGE OF NAME. *Chap.*155

Be it enacted, etc., as follows:

SECTION 1. Section six of chapter two hundred and ten of the General Laws, as appearing in the Tercentenary Edition, is hereby amended by adding at the end the following paragraph: — G. L. (Ter. Ed.), 210, § 6, amended.

No decree shall be made under this section until there has been filed in the court a copy of the birth record of the person sought to be adopted and, in case such person has been previously adopted, either a copy of the record of his birth amended to conform to the previous decree of adoption or a copy of such decree; provided, that the filing of any such copy may be dispensed with if the judge is satisfied that it cannot be obtained. Decree of adoption, birth certificate to be filed.

SECTION 2. Section thirteen of said chapter two hundred and ten, as so appearing, is hereby amended by adding at the end the following paragraph: — G. L. (Ter. Ed.), 210, § 13, amended.

No decree shall be entered, however, until there has been filed in the court a copy of the birth record of the person whose name is sought to be changed and, in case such person's name has previously been changed by court decree, either a copy of the record of his birth amended to conform to the previous decree changing his name or a copy of such decree; provided, that the filing of any such copy may be dispensed with if the judge is satisfied that it cannot be obtained. *Approved April 7, 1943.* Decree of change of name, birth certificate to be filed.

AN ACT AUTHORIZING THE CITY COUNCIL OF THE CITY OF FITCHBURG TO APPROPRIATE MONEY FOR THE PAYMENT OF CERTAIN UNPAID BILLS OF SAID CITY INCURRED IN THE YEAR NINETEEN HUNDRED AND FORTY-ONE, AND AUTHORIZING SAID CITY TO PAY SUCH BILLS. *Chap.*156

Be it enacted, etc., as follows:

SECTION 1. The city council of the city of Fitchburg is hereby authorized to appropriate money for the payment of, and after such appropriation the treasurer of said city is hereby authorized to pay, such of the unpaid bills incurred during the year nineteen hundred and forty-one by said city, the total of such bills being two thousand and eighty-two dollars and ninety cents, as set forth in the list on file in the office of the director of accounts in the department of corporations and taxation, as are legally unenforceable against said city, either by reason of their being incurred in excess of available appropriations or by reason of the failure of said city to comply with the provisions of its charter, and as are certified for payment by the heads of the departments wherein the bills were contracted; provided, that the money so appropriated to pay such bills shall be raised by taxation in said city in the current year.

SECTION 2. No bill shall be approved by the city auditor of said city for payment or paid by the treasurer thereof under authority of this act unless and until certificates have been signed and filed with said city auditor, stating under the penalties of perjury that the goods, materials or services for which bills have been submitted were ordered by an official or an employee of said city, and that such goods and materials were delivered and actually received by said city or that such services were rendered to said city, or both.

SECTION 3. Any person who knowingly files a certificate required by section two which is false and who thereby receives payment for goods, materials or services which were not received by or rendered to said city shall be punished by imprisonment for not more than one year or by a fine of not more than three hundred dollars, or both.

SECTION 4. This act shall take effect upon its passage.

Approved April 12, 1943.

---

*Chap.*157 AN ACT TEMPORARILY AUTHORIZING CITIES AND TOWNS TO CONTRIBUTE TOWARD THE COST OF MOTOR BUS SERVICE THEREIN.

Emergency preamble.

Whereas, The result of the deferred operation of this act would be that during the period of deferment certain cities and towns would not be afforded relief from transportation problems due to existing war conditions, therefore this act is hereby declared to be an emergency law, necessary for the immediate preservation of the public convenience.

Be it enacted, etc., as follows:

During the continuance of the present emergency due to the existing state of war, any city or town may from time to time, for the purpose of providing transportation facilities or avoiding a reduction or discontinuance of transportation facilities, enter into agreements with any person lawfully authorized to operate any motor bus on any public way therein for the carrying of passengers for hire, to contribute to the cost of the service; provided, that no contribution under any such agreement shall in any year exceed the sum of one dollar for each one thousand dollars of the assessed valuation of such city or town of the year preceding the date of such agreement, except that, with the approval of the department of public utilities, a sum not to exceed two dollars on the valuation as provided herein may be contributed. Said department shall, upon application of a city or town, determine any question relating to the character or extent of the service rendered or facilities furnished in pursuance of said agreement in the event of any difference arising between the persons authorized as aforesaid and said city or town in relation thereto.

Approved April 12, 1943.

AN ACT RELATIVE TO CONTRIBUTIONS BY CERTAIN SMALL TOWNS IN ORDER TO OBTAIN IN THE CURRENT YEAR STATE AID FOR THE REPAIR AND IMPROVEMENT OF PUBLIC WAYS THEREIN. *Chap.158*

Emergency preamble.

Whereas, The deferred operation of this act would delay the proper determination of tax rates in certain towns in the current year and would impose an unnecessary financial burden on such towns, therefore it is hereby declared to be an emergency law, necessary for the immediate preservation of the public convenience.

Be it enacted, etc., as follows:

The amount of money which any town eligible for state aid under section twenty-six of chapter eighty-one of the General Laws is required to contribute or make available in order to be entitled to such aid in the current year shall be five sixths of the amount fixed for such town under said section. The assessors of any such town appropriating in the current year for the purpose aforesaid a sum in excess of five sixths of the amount so fixed for such town may, in determining the tax rate for the current year, use an amount equal to such excess as an estimated receipt to meet appropriations made for highway purposes.

Approved April 12, 1943.

AN ACT PROVIDING FOR PAYMENT BY THE COUNTIES OF DUKES AND NANTUCKET OF TRAVELING EXPENSES OF THE SHERIFFS THEREOF INCURRED IN THE TRANSPORTATION OF PRISONERS. *Chap.159*

Be it enacted, etc., as follows:

G. L. (Ter. Ed.), 37, § 21, amended.

SECTION 1. Chapter thirty-seven of the General Laws is hereby amended by striking out section twenty-one, as appearing in the Tercentenary Edition, and inserting in place thereof the following section: — *Section 21.* The sheriff of Dukes county and the sheriff of Nantucket county shall each be entitled to receive from the county his actual traveling expenses incurred in the transportation of prisoners to and from jails and other penal institutions; and the sheriff of each other county, except Suffolk, shall be entitled to receive from the county his actual traveling expenses incurred in the performance of his official duties.

Traveling expense of sheriffs.

SECTION 2. This act shall take effect upon its passage. Effective date.

Approved April 12, 1943.

Chap. 160 AN ACT RELATIVE TO THE ACKNOWLEDGMENT OF WRITTEN INSTRUMENTS BY PERSONS SERVING IN OR WITH THE ARMED FORCES OF THE UNITED STATES.

Emergency preamble.

Whereas, The deferred operation of this act would tend to defeat its purpose, which is in part to provide immediately an opportunity for persons serving in and with the armed forces of the United States in various parts of the world to make valid acknowledgments of written instruments before certain officers of the United States in such forces, therefore it is hereby declared to be an emergency law, necessary for the immediate preservation of the public convenience.

Be it enacted, etc., as follows:

SECTION 1. During the existing state of war between the United States and any foreign country, any person serving in or with the armed forces of the United States may acknowledge any instrument, in the manner and form required by the laws of this commonwealth, before any commissioned officer in the active service of the armed forces of the United States with the rank of second lieutenant or higher in the army or marine corps, or ensign or higher in the navy or United States coast guard, wherever such person serving is located. No such instrument shall be rendered invalid by the failure to state therein the place of execution or acknowledgment.

No authentication of the officer's certificate of acknowledgment shall be required but the officer taking the acknowledgment shall indorse thereon or attach thereto a certificate substantially in the following form: —

On this the day of , 19 , before me, , the undersigned officer, personally appeared known to me (or satisfactorily proven) to be serving in or with the armed forces of the United States and to be the person whose name is subscribed to the within instrument and acknowledged that he executed the same for the purposes therein contained. And the undersigned does further certify that he is at the date of this certificate a commissioned officer of the rank stated below and is in the active service of the armed forces of the United States.

Signature of Officer.

Rank of Officer and Command to which attached.

Instruments so acknowledged outside of the commonwealth, if otherwise in accordance with law, shall be received and may be used in evidence, or for any other purpose, in the same manner as if taken before a commissioner of the commonwealth appointed to take depositions in other states.

SECTION 2. So much of sections sixteen to eighteen, inclusive, of chapter seven hundred and eight of the acts of nineteen hundred and forty-one as is inconsistent herewith is hereby repealed. Any instrument executed or acknowledged under said sections, if otherwise executed or acknowledged in conformity with law, shall be valid notwithstanding the omission therefrom of a statement of the place of execution or acknowledgment.

Approved April 12, 1943.

AN ACT RELATIVE TO THE CONTENTS OF PAY ROLLS, BILLS AND ACCOUNTS FOR SALARY OR COMPENSATION OF PERSONS IN THE SERVICE OR EMPLOYMENT OF THE CITY OF BOSTON. *Chap.*161

Be it enacted, etc., as follows:

SECTION 1. Chapter two hundred and ten of the acts of nineteen hundred and eight is hereby amended by striking out section two and inserting in place thereof the following section: — *Section 2.* Every such pay roll, bill or account, before the certificate of the civil service commission or its authorized agent is affixed thereto, shall be sworn to by the head of the department, or by the person who is immediately responsible for the appointment, employment, promotion or transfer, of the persons named therein, and shall contain, in addition to such other information as the civil service commission or its authorized agent may require, the following information: — First, full name of each employee; second, title of office or position in which actually employed; third, salary, wages or other compensation; fourth, dates of employment.

SECTION 2. This act shall take effect upon its passage.

Approved April 12, 1943.

AN ACT SUSPENDING FOR THE DURATION OF THE PRESENT WAR CERTAIN RESTRICTIONS ON THE GRANTING OF NEW LICENSES WITHIN THE CITY OF REVERE FOR THE TRANSPORTATION OF PASSENGERS BY MOTOR VEHICLE FOR HIRE. *Chap.*162

Be it enacted, etc., as follows:

SECTION 1. So much of the provisions of section four of chapter two hundred and ninety-nine of the acts of nineteen hundred and thirty-two as provides that no new license or licenses within the cities of Chelsea and Revere for the operation of motor vehicles under the provisions of chapter one hundred and fifty-nine A of the General Laws shall be valid unless and until the department of public utilities issues a certificate that the granting of such license or licenses will not injuriously affect the revenue of the Boston Elevated Railway Company shall not, during the continuance of the existing state of war between the United States and any foreign country, be operative with respect to those sections of the city of Revere lying north of Revere street, commonly known as the Oak Island and Point of Pines sections of said city.

SECTION 2. This act shall take effect upon its passage.

Approved April 12, 1943.

*Chap.*163 AN ACT EXTENDING THE TIME FOR THE ACQUISITION BY THE CITY OF BOSTON OF THE PROPERTY OF THE DEDHAM AND HYDE PARK GAS AND ELECTRIC LIGHT COMPANY LOCATED WITHIN SAID CITY AND THE LEASE THEREOF TO THE BOSTON CONSOLIDATED GAS COMPANY.

Be it enacted, etc., as follows:

Section one of chapter three hundred and sixty-nine of the acts of nineteen hundred and forty-one is hereby amended by striking out, in the fifth line, the word "forty-three" and inserting in place thereof the word: — forty-five, — so as to read as follows: — *Section 1.* The city of Boston, hereinafter referred to as the city, acting through its public works department, and without other authority than that contained in this act, may at any time before January first, nineteen hundred and forty-five, purchase or take by eminent domain the property of the Dedham and Hyde Park Gas and Electric Light Company located within said city. *Approved April 12, 1943.*

---

*Chap.*164 AN ACT RELATIVE TO THE ENFORCEMENT OF THE STATE MILK CONTROL LAW, SO CALLED.

Be it enacted, etc., as follows:

G. L. (Ter. Ed.), 94A, § 22, amended.

Chapter ninety-four A of the General Laws, inserted by section two of chapter six hundred and ninety-one of the acts of nineteen hundred and forty-one, is hereby amended by striking out section twenty-two and inserting in place thereof the following section: — *Section 22.* Whoever violates any provision of this chapter or of any effective rule, regulation or order of the board made under this chapter or adopted by the former milk control board under any similar provision of earlier law, except as herein otherwise expressly provided, shall be punished by a fine of not more than one hundred dollars or by imprisonment for not more than one year, or both, and such fine may be imposed for each day during which such violation shall continue. A violation of any provision of this chapter or of any effective rule, regulation or order so made or adopted may be reported by any person to the director, who shall investigate such complaint and may institute such action at law or in equity in any court of competent jurisdiction as may be necessary to enforce compliance with any provision of this chapter or of any effective rule, regulation or order so made or adopted, and, in addition to any other remedy, may seek relief by injunction, if in the opinion of the board it is necessary to protect the public interest, without being compelled to allege or prove that an adequate remedy at law does not exist. *Approved April 12, 1943.*

Penalties.

AN ACT DEFERRING THE TAKING EFFECT OF CERTAIN PROVISIONS OF LAW RELATIVE TO THE EDUCATIONAL QUALIFICATIONS OF APPLICANTS FOR REGISTRATION AS PHARMACISTS. *Chap.*165

Be it enacted, etc., as follows:

Chapter fifty-two of the acts of nineteen hundred and forty-one is hereby amended by striking out section two and inserting in place thereof the following section: — *Section 2.* This act shall take effect on January first, nineteen hundred and forty-eight. *Approved April 12, 1943.*

AN ACT RELATIVE TO APPLICATIONS FOR ABATEMENT OF LOCAL TAXES IN CERTAIN CASES WHERE TAX BILLS ARE SENT OUT LATE. *Chap.*166

Be it enacted, etc., as follows:

SECTION 1. Section fifty-nine of chapter fifty-nine of the General Laws, as most recently amended by section one of chapter two hundred and fifty of the acts of nineteen hundred and thirty-nine, is hereby further amended by striking out the first sentence and inserting in place thereof the following sentence: — A person aggrieved by the tax assessed upon him may, except as hereinafter otherwise provided, on or before October first of the year to which the tax relates or, if the tax is other than a poll tax and the bill or notice was first sent after September first of such year, on or before the thirtieth day after the date on which the bill or notice was so sent, apply in writing to the assessors, on a form approved by the commissioner, for an abatement thereof, and if they find him taxed at more than his just proportion, or upon an assessment of any of his property in excess of its fair cash value, they shall make a reasonable abatement; provided, that a person aggrieved by a tax assessed upon him under section seventy-five or reassessed upon him under section seventy-seven may apply for such abatement at any time within six months after notice of such assessment or reassessment is sent to him. G. L. (Ter. Ed.), 59, § 59, etc., amended. Abatements

SECTION 2. Section three of chapter sixty of the General Laws, as most recently amended by section two of chapter thirty-seven of the acts of the current year, is hereby further amended by inserting after the third sentence the following sentence: — An affidavit of the collector or deputy collector sending a tax bill or notice as to the time of sending shall be prima facie evidence that the same was sent at such time. G. L. (Ter. Ed.), 60, § 3, etc., amended. Affidavit by collector, etc.

SECTION 3. Said chapter sixty is hereby further amended by striking out section three A, as amended by chapter one hundred and fifty-six of the acts of nineteen hundred and thirty-six, and inserting in place thereof the following section: — *Section 3A.* Every tax bill or notice shall be in a form approved by the commissioner and shall state G. L. (Ter. Ed.), 60, § 3A, etc., amended. Tax bill, form of.

that applications for abatement or exemptions, on forms so approved, must be filed with the assessors, in case of original assessments, on or before October first of the year to which the tax relates or, if the tax is other than a poll tax and the bill or notice is first sent after September first of such year, on or before the thirtieth day after the date on which the bill or notice is so sent or, in case of an assessment under section seventy-five of chapter fifty-nine or a reassessment under section seventy-seven of said chapter, within six months after the sending of the bill or notice.

Approved April 12, 1943.

---

*Chap.*167 AN ACT AUTHORIZING THE REGISTRATION OF CERTAIN PERSONS AS ARCHITECTS WITHOUT TAKING A WRITTEN EXAMINATION.

Be it enacted, etc., as follows:

G. L. (Ter. Ed.), 112, § 60C, etc., amended.

Section sixty C of chapter one hundred and twelve of the General Laws, inserted by section two of chapter six hundred and ninety-six of the acts of nineteen hundred and forty-one, is hereby amended by striking out clause (*c*), as appearing in the nineteenth to twenty-second lines, inclusive, and

Exemptions.

inserting in place thereof the following clause: — (*c*) any person who has lawfully practiced architecture within the commonwealth or any person who has lawfully practiced architecture outside the commonwealth for a period of at least ten years. *Approved April 12, 1943.*

---

*Chap.*168 AN ACT RELATIVE TO THE MARRIAGE OF A PARTY FROM WHOM A DIVORCE HAS BEEN GRANTED IN CASE OF THE DEATH OF THE OTHER PARTY.

Be it enacted, etc., as follows:

G. L. (Ter. Ed.), 208, § 24, amended.

SECTION 1. Section twenty-four of chapter two hundred and eight of the General Laws, as appearing in the Tercentenary Edition, is hereby amended by adding at the end the following: — if the other party is living, — so as to read as

Remarriage of divorced parties.

follows: — *Section 24.* After a decree of divorce has become absolute, either party may marry again as if the other were dead, except that the party from whom the divorce was granted shall not marry within two years after the decree has become absolute if the other party is living.

G. L. (Ter. Ed.), 207, § 21, amended.

SECTION 2. Section twenty-one of chapter two hundred and seven of the General Laws, as so appearing, is hereby amended by adding at the end the following paragraph: —

Death certificate to accompany notice, when.

A party from whom a divorce has been granted and who files a notice of intention to marry within two years after the decree of divorce has become absolute shall, if the party to whom the divorce was granted has died, also file with such notice of intention a certified copy of the certificate of such death. *Approved April 12, 1943.*

AN ACT RELATIVE TO THE INSPECTION AND DISCLOSURE OF RECORDS CONCERNING OLD AGE ASSISTANCE, AID TO DEPENDENT CHILDREN AND AID TO THE BLIND. *Chap.*169

Be it enacted, etc., as follows:

Chapter sixty-six of the General Laws is hereby amended by striking out section seventeen A, inserted by section one of chapter six hundred and thirty of the acts of nineteen hundred and forty-one, and inserting in place thereof the following section: — *Section 17A.* The records of the department of public welfare and of the several city and town welfare departments and bureaus of old age assistance relative to old age assistance and to aid to dependent children, and the records of the department of education relative to aid to the blind, shall be public records; provided, that they shall be open to inspection only by public officials, which term shall include members of the general court and representatives of the federal government, for purposes directly connected with the administration of such public assistance, or with the prosecution of war, and provided, further, that information relative to the record of an applicant for public assistance or a recipient thereof may be disclosed to him or his duly authorized agent.

G. L. (Ter. Ed.), 66, § 17A, etc., amended.

Inspection of certain records restricted.

Approved April 12, 1943.

AN ACT TEMPORARILY INCREASING THE SALARIES OF OFFICERS AND EMPLOYEES IN THE SERVICE OF THE COMMONWEALTH. *Chap.*170

Whereas, The deferred operation of this act would tend to defeat its purpose, which is to provide without delay additional income for officers and employees of the commonwealth in view of the increase in the cost of living due to the existence of the present state of war, therefore it is hereby declared to be an emergency law, necessary for the immediate preservation of the public convenience.

Emergency preamble.

Be it enacted, etc., as follows:

SECTION 1. The salary of each person in the service of the commonwealth and paid from the treasury thereof is hereby increased by an amount equal to fifteen per cent thereof; provided, that such increase shall not for full-time service be less than two hundred and forty dollars per annum nor more than three hundred and sixty dollars per annum; and provided, further, that said minimum or said maximum, in the case of any such person serving on a part-time basis, shall be adjusted by the division of personnel and standardization to an amount which bears the same ratio to said minimum or maximum as his service bears to full-time service and, in the case of any such person paid in part by the commonwealth, shall be adjusted to an amount which bears the same ratio to said minimum or maximum as the amount of salary paid by the commonwealth bears to his total salary. Said increase of salary shall be effective only for the period beginning July first, nineteen hundred and forty-three, and ending June thirtieth, nineteen hundred and forty-five. The temporary salary increase granted hereunder in the case of any person whose basic salary is changed during said period by promotion, step rate increase, transfer or otherwise shall be based on his basic salary as so changed.

SECTION 2. Every officer and employee entering the service of the commonwealth during said period shall be entitled to receive the compensation of his office or position as increased by this act.

SECTION 3. The word "salary" as used in this act shall include maintenance allowances the value of which is fixed in the manner provided by the rules and regulations established under the provisions of sections forty-five to fifty of chapter thirty of the General Laws. The word "salary" as so used shall also include compensation payable through the state treasury from moneys paid into the state treasury by the federal government. The word "employee", as so used, in addition to its usual meaning shall also include any blind person receiving wages from the division of the blind.

SECTION 4. The division of personnel and standardization of the commission on administration and finance is hereby directed to revise the schedules of standard rates of salaries incorporated in the rules and regulations governing the classification of personal services as prepared by said division and approved by the governor and council, to conform to section one.

SECTION 5. Said division and the comptroller are hereby directed to administer this act. Nothing in this act shall be construed to limit the respective powers of said division or said comptroller as now defined by law.

SECTION 6. No increase in salary made by this act shall, for any purpose of chapter thirty-two of the General Laws, be deemed or construed to be a portion of the regular compensation of any officer or employee now or hereafter in the service of the commonwealth.

SECTION 7. Notwithstanding the foregoing provisions of this act, the temporary salary increase to which a member of the general court shall be entitled hereunder shall be limited to three hundred and sixty dollars, which shall be payable in one sum on July first in the year nineteen hundred and forty-three. *Approved April 13, 1943.*

AN ACT MAKING AN APPROPRIATION FOR SERVICES AND EXPENSES IN CONNECTION WITH A PROGRAM OF INCREASED FOOD PRODUCTION AT VARIOUS INSTITUTIONS OF THE COMMONWEALTH. *Chap.*171

Be it enacted, etc., as follows:

SECTION 1. The sum of fifty thousand dollars, for expenditure for personal and other services and expenses in connection with a program of increased food production at the various institutions of the commonwealth, is hereby appropriated from the general fund or revenue of the commonwealth, subject to the provisions of law regulating the disbursement of funds and the approval thereof, in advance of final action on the general appropriation bill for the next fiscal biennium, pursuant to a message of the governor dated April sixth, nineteen hundred and forty-three. The amount herein appropriated is hereby made available for transfer, with the approval of the commission on administration and finance, to accounts in other appropriation items for the services of the various institutions of the commonwealth where the amounts otherwise available for carrying out said program at such institutions are insufficient.

SECTION 2. This act shall take effect upon its passage.

Approved April 13, 1943.

AN ACT INCLUDING MEMBERS OF CERTAIN WOMEN'S AUXILIARY MILITARY AND NAVAL UNITS WITHIN THE OPERATION OF AN ACT TO MEET CERTAIN CONTINGENCIES ARISING IN CONNECTION WITH THE SERVICE OF PUBLIC OFFICERS AND EMPLOYEES AND CERTAIN OTHER PERSONS IN THE MILITARY OR NAVAL FORCES OF THE UNITED STATES DURING THE EXISTENCE OF THE PRESENT STATE OF WAR. *Chap.*172

Emergency preamble.

Whereas, The deferred operation of this act would in part tend to defeat its purpose, which, in view of the large number of residents of this commonwealth now serving as members of certain women's auxiliary military and naval units, is to make immediately available to such persons the benefits conferred on persons in the military or naval service of the United States by the act of which this is an amendment, therefore this act is hereby declared to be an emergency law, necessary for the immediate preservation of the public convenience.

Be it enacted, etc., as follows:

Section one of chapter seven hundred and eight of the acts of nineteen hundred and forty-one is hereby amended by adding at the end the following sentence: — The phrase "serving in the military or naval forces of the United States", the phrase "service in the military or naval forces of the United States" and the phrase "military or naval service", as used in this act, shall be taken to include service other than in a civilian capacity as a member of any corps or unit established under the laws of the United States for the purpose of enabling women to serve with, or as auxiliary to, the armed forces of the United States.

Approved April 14, 1943.

Chap.173 AN ACT REVIVING BROWN REFLECTOR (INC.) FOR THE PURPOSE OF COLLECTING MONEY DUE IT.

Emergency preamble.

Whereas, The deferred operation of this act would tend to defeat its purpose, which in part is to immediately revive the corporation therein referred to, therefore it is hereby declared to be an emergency law, necessary for the immediate preservation of the public convenience.

Be it enacted, etc., as follows:

Brown Reflector (Inc.), a corporation dissolved by section one of chapter one hundred and eighty-seven of the acts of nineteen hundred and thirty-four, is hereby revived and continued for a period of two years from the effective date of this act for the purpose of collecting money due it and distributing the proceeds among those entitled thereto; provided, that the foregoing provisions of this act shall not take effect until there shall have been filed in the office of the commissioner of corporations and taxation an agreement, in form approved by the attorney general, for the payment in full of all excise taxes owed to the commonwealth by said corporation prior to its dissolution and subsequently abated as uncollectible, with interest thereon to the date of payment. *Approved April 14, 1943.*

Chap.174 AN ACT AUTHORIZING THE TOWN OF DENNIS TO RECEIVE AND ADMINISTER THE PROPERTY OF THE WEST DENNIS CEMETERY CORPORATION IN SAID TOWN.

Be it enacted, etc., as follows:

SECTION 1. The West Dennis Cemetery Corporation, a corporation duly incorporated by law and situated in the town of Dennis, hereinafter called the corporation, may, by deed duly executed, convey and transfer to said town, and said town is hereby authorized and empowered to receive, and thereafter to hold and maintain, but for cemetery purposes only, and subject to all rights heretofore existing in any burial lots, the real and personal property of the corporation not subject to any trust, and thereupon, and upon the transfer of the trust funds as hereinafter provided, the corporation shall be dissolved; and the cemetery of the corporation shall be and become a public burial place, ground or cemetery.

SECTION 2. In so far as authorized by a decree of a court of competent jurisdiction and in compliance with the terms and conditions of such decree, said town may receive from the corporation a conveyance and transfer of, and administer, all funds or other property held by the corporation in trust for the perpetual care of the lots in its cemetery and for other purposes, and also any property devised or bequeathed to the corporation under the will of any person living at the time of said transfer or conveyance or under the will of any deceased person not then probated. Interest and dividends accruing on funds deposited in trust with any savings bank, under authority of section thirty-seven or thirty-eight of chapter one hundred and sixty-eight of the General Laws, or with any other banking institution, for the benefit of the corporation, or of any lots in its cemetery, may, after such conveyance, be paid by such bank or institution to the treasurer of said town; and upon such payment said treasurer, under the direction of the cemetery commissioners, shall use the same for the purposes of said trusts.

SECTION 3. All real and personal property, and property rights, acquired by said town from the corporation under authority of section one shall be held and managed by said town in the same manner in which cities and towns are authorized by law to hold and manage property for cemetery purposes; provided, that all rights which any persons have acquired in the cemetery of the corporation, or any lots therein, shall remain in force to the same extent as if this act had not been passed and such transfer had not occurred. The records of the corporation shall be delivered to the clerk of said town, and such clerk may certify copies thereof.

SECTION 4. This act shall take full effect upon its acceptance by a majority of the registered voters of the town of Dennis voting thereon at a special town meeting of said town to be held in the current year, but not otherwise.

Approved April 14, 1943.

Chap. 175

AN ACT PROVIDING THAT CERTAIN AGE REQUIREMENTS SHALL NOT APPLY IN THE CASE OF ENLISTMENTS OF WOMEN AS OFFICERS OF THE DIVISION OF STATE POLICE.

Be it enacted, etc., as follows:

G. L. (Ter. Ed.), 22, § 9A, etc., amended.

Section nine A of chapter twenty-two of the General Laws, as amended by section four of chapter five hundred and three of the acts of nineteen hundred and thirty-nine, is hereby further amended by striking out the sentence inserted by said section four and inserting in place thereof the following sentence: — No person over thirty years of age shall be enlisted for the first time as an officer of the division of state police, except that said age qualification shall not apply in the case of the enlistment of any woman as such an officer. *Approved April 14, 1943.*

Enlistment age.

*Chap.*176 AN ACT RELATIVE TO THE CORPORATE POWERS OF THE DEDHAM TEMPORARY HOME FOR WOMEN AND CHILDREN.

Be it enacted, etc., as follows:

SECTION 1. Section two of chapter eighty-nine of the acts of nineteen hundred and ten is hereby amended by striking out, in the second line, the words "care for" and inserting in place thereof the words: — provide convalescent care for men, — so as to read as follows: — *Section 2.* The said corporation is hereby authorized to receive and provide convalescent care for men, women and children under such terms and conditions as it may from time to time determine, and to use for these purposes all the real and personal property which it now holds or which it may hereafter hold; and it is authorized to take and hold for the above purposes real and personal property, not exceeding in value one hundred and fifty thousand dollars.

SECTION 2. This act shall take full effect upon its acceptance, at a meeting duly called for the purpose, by the members of said corporation entitled to vote and the filing with the state secretary of a certificate of such acceptance, but not otherwise. *Approved April 14, 1943.*

---

*Chap.*177 AN ACT FURTHER REGULATING THE RIGHT OF CITIES AND TOWNS TO APPROPRIATE MONEY FOR PROVIDING PROPER FACILITIES FOR PUBLIC ENTERTAINMENT.

Emergency preamble.

Whereas, Certain cities and towns are desirous of immediately making appropriations of public funds to be expended for the public recognition and entertainment of their citizens now being inducted into the armed forces of the United States and the deferred operation of this act, which authorizes such appropriations, would in part defeat its purpose, therefore this act is hereby declared to be an emergency law, necessary for the immediate preservation of the public convenience.

Be it enacted, etc., as follows:

G. L. (Ter. Ed.), 40, § 5, etc., amended.

SECTION 1. Section five of chapter forty of the General Laws, as amended, is hereby further amended by striking out clause (37), as appearing in the Tercentenary Edition, and inserting in place thereof the following clause: —

Appropriations for public entertainments.

(37) For providing proper facilities for public entertainment in connection with the holding of conventions in the town, for paying expenses incidental to such entertainment, and for the entertainment of distinguished guests, a sum not exceeding, in any one year, one one-hundredth of one per cent of the assessed valuation of the preceding year, but in no event more than seventy-five thousand dollars.

Entertainment of persons inducted in armed forces.

SECTION 2. During the continuance of the existing state of war between the United States and any foreign country, a city or town may appropriate money for the purpose of providing for the entertainment of persons inducted into the armed forces of the United States, a sum not exceeding, in any one year, one two-hundredth of one per cent of the assessed valuation of the preceding year, but in no event more than ten thousand dollars. Any appropriation under this section shall be in addition to any appropriation for the purpose aforesaid authorized by any other provision of law. *Approved April 14, 1943.*

AN ACT AUTHORIZING THE LICENSING AUTHORITIES OF THE CITY OF HOLYOKE TO GRANT A LICENSE TO ZENAIDE JUBINVILLE TO CONDUCT A PACKAGE STORE. *Chap.* 178

Be it enacted, etc., as follows:

SECTION 1. The licensing authorities of the city of Holyoke may, upon proper application and the payment of the required fee, grant a license to conduct a package store to Zenaide Jubinville of said city, it having been adjudged by a decree of the superior court for the county of Hampden, entered after rescript from the supreme judicial court, that said Zenaide Jubinville was the owner of the assets of a package store business formerly conducted in said city under a license granted to Antonio Jubinville and Marie Jubinville, and ordering said Antonio Jubinville and Marie Jubinville to surrender to the licensing authorities for cancellation the license held by them. Such license may be granted notwithstanding that the granting thereof will cause the number of such licenses which may be granted in said city under section fifteen of chapter one hundred and thirty-eight of the General Laws, as set forth in section seventeen of said chapter one hundred and thirty-eight, to be exceeded. The granting of such license shall in no way affect the validity of any other package store license in said city. Said licensing authorities may renew such license upon application therefor as provided in section sixteen A of said chapter one hundred and thirty-eight.

SECTION 2. This act shall take effect upon its passage. *Approved April 15, 1943.*

AN ACT RELATIVE TO INTEREST, CHARGES AND FEES TO BE COLLECTED WITH DELINQUENT TAXES. *Chap.* 179

Be it enacted, etc., as follows:

G. L. (Ter. Ed.), 60, § 15, etc., amended.

Chapter sixty of the General Laws is hereby amended by striking out section fifteen, as most recently amended by section one of chapter two hundred and fifty-two of the acts of nineteen hundred and thirty-five, and inserting in place thereof the following section: — *Section 15.* Except as provided in section fifteen A, the following interest, charges and fees, and no other, when accrued, shall severally be added to the amount of the tax and collected as a part thereof: —

Interest, charges, etc., in collection of delinquent taxes.

1. For interest, as provided by law;
2. For each written demand provided for by law, thirty-five cents;
3. For preparing advertisement of sale or taking, fifty cents for each parcel of real estate included in the advertisement;
4. For advertisement of sale or taking in newspaper, the cost thereof;
5. For posting notices of sale or taking, fifty cents for each parcel of real estate included in the notice;
6. For affidavit, twenty-five cents for each parcel of land included therein;
7. For recording affidavit, one dollar for each parcel of land included therein;
8. For preparing deed or instrument of taking, two dollars;
9. For the issuance and delivery of a warrant to an officer, fifty cents;
10. For notice to the delinquent that warrant has been issued, one dollar;
11. For exhibiting a warrant or delivering a copy thereof to the delinquent or his representative or leaving it at his last and usual place of abode or of business, before and without distraint or arrest, two dollars;
12. For distraining goods of the delinquent, two dollars and the necessary cost thereof;
13. For the custody and safekeeping of the distrained goods of the delinquent, not more than three dollars for each day of not more than eight hours for the keeper while he is in charge, and one dollar a day for the officer, for a period not exceeding seven days, together with the expense of packing, storage, labor and towing or teaming, and other necessary expenses;
14. For selling goods distrained, the cost thereof;
15. For arresting the body, two dollars, and a sum, not exceeding five dollars, for travel, at the rate of eight cents per mile, from the office of the collector to the place where the arrest is made;
16. For custody of the body arrested, if payment of the delinquent tax is not made forthwith, three dollars, and in addition thereto travel at the rate of eight cents per mile from the place of arrest to the jail or, if payment is made before commitment to jail, for the distance from the place where the arrest is made to the place where payment is made;
17. For service of demand and notice under section fifty-three, if served in the manner required by law for the service of subpoenas on witnesses in civil cases, fifty cents and travel at the rate of eight cents per mile from the office of the collector to the place where service is made, but in no event more than five dollars.

The collector shall account to the town treasurer for all interest, charges and fees collected by him; but the town shall reimburse or credit him for all expenses incurred by him hereunder, including all lawful charges and fees paid or credited by him for collecting taxes.

Approved April 15, 1943.

An Act reviving the corporation known as the Mixer Brothers Company. *Chap.*180

Be it enacted, etc., as follows:

The Mixer Brothers Company, a corporation dissolved by section one of chapter two hundred and thirty-nine of the acts of the year nineteen hundred and thirty-seven, is hereby revived and continued with the same powers, duties and obligations as if said chapter had not been passed; provided, that the foregoing provisions of this act shall not take effect until there shall have been filed in the office of the commissioner of corporations and taxation an agreement satisfactory to said commissioner and to the mayor of the city of Boston, in form approved by the attorney general, for the payment in full of all taxes owed to the commonwealth and to said city by said corporation prior to its dissolution, whether or not subsequently abated as uncollectible, together with interest thereon to the date of payment.

Approved April 15, 1943.

An Act further regulating medical services rendered under the workmen's compensation law. *Chap.*181

Be it enacted, etc., as follows:

G. L. (Ter. Ed.), 152, § 30, etc., amended.

Chapter one hundred and fifty-two of the General Laws is hereby amended by striking out section thirty, as amended by chapter one hundred and sixty-four of the acts of nineteen hundred and thirty-six, and inserting in place thereof the following section: — *Section 30.* During the first two weeks after the injury, and, in unusual cases or cases requiring specialized or surgical treatment, in the discretion of the department, for a longer period, the insurer shall furnish adequate and reasonable medical and hospital services, and medicines if needed, together with the expenses necessarily incidental to such services. The employee may select a physician other than the one provided by the insurer; and in case he shall be treated by a physician of his own selection, or where in case of emergency or for other justifiable cause a physician other than the one provided by the insurer is called in to treat the injured employee, the reasonable cost of the physician's services shall be paid by the insurer, subject to the approval of the department. Such approval shall be granted only if the department finds that the employee was so treated by such physician or that there was such emergency or justifiable cause, and in all cases that the services were adequate and reasonable and the charges reasonable. In any case where the department is

Payments for medical services under compensation law.

of opinion that the fitting of the employee with an artificial eye or limb, or other mechanical appliance, will promote his restoration to or continue him in industry, it may order that he be provided with such an artificial eye, limb or appliance, at the expense of the insurer

Approved April 15, 1943.

---

*Chap.*182 AN ACT RELATIVE TO THE FILLING OF VACANCIES IN THE BOARD OF ALDERMEN OF THE CITY OF NEWTON.

Be it enacted, etc., as follows:

SECTION 1. Any vacancy in the board of aldermen of the city of Newton shall be filled for the unexpired term by the remaining members of the board.

SECTION 2. So much of chapter two hundred and eighty-three of the acts of eighteen hundred and ninety-seven, and acts in amendment thereof and in addition thereto, as is inconsistent with this act is hereby repealed.

SECTION 3. This act shall be submitted for acceptance to the registered voters of the city of Newton at the biennial municipal election to be held in said city in the current year, in the form of the following question which shall be placed upon the official ballot to be used at said election: "Shall an act of the general court passed in the year nineteen hundred and forty-three, entitled 'An Act relative to the Filling of Vacancies in the Board of Aldermen of the City of Newton', be accepted?" If a majority of the votes in answer to said question is in the affirmative, then this act shall thereupon take full effect, but not otherwise.

Approved April 15, 1943.

---

*Chap.*183 AN ACT RELATING TO THE COMPUTATION OF RESERVES REQUIRED OF INSURANCE COMPANIES WITH RESPECT TO CERTAIN POLICIES OF LIABILITY INSURANCE.

Be it enacted, etc., as follows:

G. L. (Ter. Ed.), 175, § 12, amended.

SECTION 1. Section twelve of chapter one hundred and seventy-five of the General Laws, as appearing in the Tercentenary Edition, is hereby amended by striking out all before the word "policies" in the twentieth line and inserting in place thereof the following: — Except as otherwise provided in section twelve A, the commissioner shall each year compute the reserve required of liability companies for outstanding losses under insurance against loss or damage from accident to or injuries suffered by an employee or other person, for which the insured is liable, as follows: —

Computation of reserves of liability companies.

1. For all liability suits being defended under policies written:

(*a*) Ten years or more prior to the date of determination, one thousand five hundred dollars for each suit.

(*b*) Five or more but less than ten years prior to the date of determination, one thousand dollars for each suit.

(c) Three or more but less than five years prior to the date of determination, eight hundred and fifty dollars for each suit.

2. For all liability policies written during the three years immediately preceding the date of determination, such reserves shall be the sum of the reserves for each such year, which shall be sixty per cent of the earned premiums on liability policies written during such year less all loss and loss expense payments made under such policies written in such year. In any event the reserves for each of such three years shall be not less than the aggregate of the estimated unpaid losses and loss expenses for claims incurred under such policies written in the corresponding year computed on an individual case basis.

2A. For all liability policies written more than three years prior to the date of determination the total loss and loss expense reserves shall be not less than the aggregate of the estimated unpaid losses and loss expenses for claims incurred under such policies computed on an individual case basis.

G. L. (Ter. Ed.), 175, new § 12A, added.

SECTION 2. Said chapter one hundred and seventy-five is hereby further amended by inserting after section twelve, as amended, the following section: — *Section 12A.* Whenever a domestic liability company authorized to transact business in the commonwealth, conducting an intrastate business only, so elects by the filing of a writing with the commissioner, he shall, instead of proceeding under section twelve, compute the reserve required of it for outstanding losses under insurance against loss or damage from accident to or injuries suffered by an employee or other person for which the insured is liable, under the earlier provisions of section twelve as appearing in the Tercentenary Edition.

Reserves of companies doing intrastate business only.

Approved April 16, 1943.

AN ACT PROVIDING THAT CERTAIN MEMBERS OF THE PERMANENT POLICE FORCE OF THE CITY OF SPRINGFIELD SHALL RECEIVE CREDIT FOR THEIR SERVICE IN THE REGULAR POLICE FORCE OF THE PARK DEPARTMENT OF SAID CITY.

*Chap.*184

Be it enacted, etc., as follows:

The members of the permanent police force of the city of Springfield who were formerly members of the regular police force of the park department of said city and who upon their transfer from said department became members of said permanent police force shall, as a part of their creditable service under section eighty-three of chapter thirty-two of the General Laws, receive credit for the period of their service in the regular police force of said park department and of any prior service in said permanent police force in the same manner and to the same extent as if their entire police service had been rendered as members of said permanent police force. *Approved April 16, 1943.*

Chap.185 AN ACT MAKING CHANGES IN THE LAWS RELATIVE TO DEFECTIVE DELINQUENTS.

Be it enacted, etc., as follows:

G. L. (Ter. Ed.), 123, § 113, etc., amended.

SECTION 1. Chapter one hundred and twenty-three of the General Laws is hereby amended by striking out section one hundred and thirteen, as amended by section twelve of chapter one hundred and ninety-four of the acts of nineteen hundred and forty-one, and inserting in place thereof the following section: — *Section 113.* At any time prior to the final disposition of a case in which the court might commit an offender to the state prison, the reformatory for women, any jail or house of correction, the Massachusetts reformatory, the state farm, the industrial school for boys, the industrial school for girls, the Lyman school, any county training school, or to the custody of the department of public welfare, for any offense not punishable by death or imprisonment for life, a district attorney, probation officer, or officer of the department of correction, public welfare or mental health may file in court an application for the commitment of the defendant in such a case to a department for defective delinquents established under sections one hundred and seventeen and one hundred and twenty-four, or to a department for the care and treatment of drug addicts, established under authority of said sections. On the filing of such an application the court may continue the original case from time to time to await disposition thereof. On the filing of an application for the commitment to a department for defective delinquents the court shall give notice to the department of mental health and said department shall cause such person to be examined by two experts in insanity with a view to determining whether or not he is mentally defective, and shall file a written report with the clerk of the court in which the case is pending and the report shall be accessible to the court, the probation officer, the district attorney and to the defendant and his attorney. If, on a hearing on an application for commitment as a defective delinquent, the defendant is found to be mentally defective, and the court, after examination into his record, character and personality, finds that he has shown himself to be an habitual delinquent or shows tendencies toward becoming such and that such delinquency is or may become a menace to the public, and that he is not a proper subject for a school for the feeble minded or for commitment as an insane person, the court shall make and record a finding to the effect that the defendant is a defective delinquent and may commit him to such a department for defective delinquents according to his age and sex, as hereinafter provided. If, on a hearing on an application for commitment as a drug addict, it appears that the defendant is addicted to the intemperate

Commitment to department for defective delinquents or for drug addicts.

use of stimulants or narcotics, the court may commit him to a department for the care and treatment of drug addicts.

SECTION 2. Said chapter one hundred and twenty-three is hereby further amended by striking out section one hundred and fourteen, as appearing in the Tercentenary Edition, and inserting in place thereof the following section: — *Section 114.* If an offender while under commitment to any of the institutions named in section one hundred and thirteen, to the state prison colony or to the custody of the department of public welfare, persistently violates the regulations of the institution or department in whose custody he is, or conducts himself so indecently or immorally, or otherwise so grossly misbehaves as to render himself an unfit subject for retention in said institution or by said department, and it appears that such offender is mentally defective or addicted to the intemperate use of stimulants or narcotics, and is not a proper subject for a school for the feeble minded, a physician in attendance at such institution or a physician employed by said department shall make a report thereof to the officer in charge of said institution or to the director of child guardianship, who shall transmit the same to one of the judges mentioned in section fifty. If it appears to said judge that such offender may be mentally defective the judge shall give notice to the department of mental health and said department shall cause the offender to be examined by two experts in insanity with a view to determining whether or not the offender is mentally defective and shall cause a written report to be made to said judge. The judge shall make inquiry into the facts and, if satisfied that the offender is mentally defective or so addicted, and not a proper subject for a school for the feeble minded, shall order his removal to a department for defective delinquents, or to a department for the care and treatment of drug addicts, as the case may be, according to his age and sex as hereinafter provided.

G. L. (Ter. Ed.), 123, § 114, amended.

Removal from institution because of violation of regulations.

SECTION 3. Said chapter one hundred and twenty-three is hereby further amended by striking out section one hundred and fifteen, as so appearing, and inserting in place thereof the following section: — *Section 115.* No person shall be committed to a department for defective delinquents under section one hundred and thirteen or one hundred and fourteen or be removed thereto under section one hundred and sixteen unless the report of the department of mental health required under said section contains a certificate by the two experts in insanity who examined him that such person is mentally defective. No person shall be committed to a department for the care and treatment of drug addicts under section one hundred and thirteen or one hundred and fourteen unless there has been filed with the judge a certificate by two physicians qualified as provided in section fifty-three that such person is addicted to the intemperate use of stimulants or narcotics. The fees of the

G. L. (Ter. Ed.), 123, § 115, amended.

Physicians' certificates to be filed in certain cases.

Fees.

experts or physicians issuing such certificates or issuing certificates under section one hundred and seventeen A shall be of the amount and paid in the manner provided for like service in sections three to one hundred and twelve, inclusive.

G. L. (Ter. Ed.), 123, § 116, amended.

SECTION 4. Said chapter one hundred and twenty-three is hereby further amended by striking out section one hundred and sixteen, as so appearing, and inserting in place thereof the following section: — *Section 116.* If an inmate of a school for the feeble minded persistently violates the regulations of the school, or conducts himself so indecently or immorally, or so grossly misbehaves as to render himself an unfit subject for retention therein, the officer in charge shall make a report thereof to one of the judges mentioned in section fifty. The judge shall give notice to the department of mental health and said department shall cause the offender to be examined by two experts in insanity with a view to determining whether or not the offender is an improper subject to be retained in a school for the feeble minded and should be committed as a defective delinquent and said department shall cause a written report to be made to said judge. The judge shall make inquiry into the facts and, if satisfied that such inmate is not a fit subject for retention in the school, shall order his removal to a department for defective delinquents, according to his age and sex as hereinafter provided.

Removal from school for feeble minded for violation of regulations, etc.

G. L. (Ter. Ed.), 123, § 117A, etc., amended.

SECTION 5. Said chapter one hundred and twenty-three is hereby further amended by striking out section one hundred and seventeen A, inserted by chapter thirty-two of the acts of nineteen hundred and thirty-six, and inserting in place thereof the following section: — *Section 117A.* When, in the opinion of the commissioner of correction and the superintendent of an institution wherein a department for defective delinquents has been established, or, in case of such a department established at the state farm, the medical director appointed under section forty-eight of chapter one hundred and twenty five, the mental condition of a person removed from any institution referred to in section one hundred and thirteen, one hundred and fourteen or one hundred and sixteen, is such that he should be returned to the institution from which he was removed, notice shall be given to the department of mental health and said department shall cause the person to be examined by two experts in insanity with a view to determining whether or not his mental condition is such that he should be returned. If upon examination by such experts a person committed as a defective delinquent is found to be in such mental condition that he should be returned to the institution from which he was removed, they shall so certify upon the order of commitment, and notice, accompanied by a written statement regarding the mental condition of such person, shall be given to the officer in charge of the institution from which he was removed who shall thereupon cause

Return of certain persons to penal institutions.

such person to be returned to such institution. A person so returned to a penal institution shall remain there pursuant to the original sentence, computing the time of his confinement in said department as part of the term of his imprisonment under such sentence.

SECTION 6. Said chapter one hundred and twenty-three is hereby further amended by striking out section one hundred and eighteen, as amended by section two of chapter two hundred and fifty-four of the acts of nineteen hundred and thirty-eight, and inserting in place thereof the following section: — *Section 118.* The parole board in the department of correction may parole inmates of the departments for defective delinquents or drug addicts on such conditions as it deems best, and may, at any time during the parole period, recall to the institution any inmate paroled. Said board shall not entertain a petition for parole of a person confined in any department for defective delinquents or for drug addicts, unless and until said person is recommended by the superintendent and physician of the institution at which the department is established, or if established at the state farm, by the superintendent and medical director thereof, for consideration for parole by the parole board. In all other respects the parole of defective delinquents may be regulated by rules of the parole board.

G. L. (Ter. Ed.), 123, § 118, etc., amended.

Parole of defective delinquents.

Approved April 16, 1943.

AN ACT AUTHORIZING THE ISSUE OF CERTAIN POLICIES OF LIFE OR ENDOWMENT INSURANCE WITHOUT MEDICAL EXAMINATION.

Chap. 186

Whereas, Owing to the scarcity of registered medical practitioners in the present emergency, the deferred operation of this act would result in postponing the issue of life insurance policies to persons who have immediate need thereof, therefore this act is hereby declared to be an emergency law, necessary for the immediate preservation of the public convenience.

Emergency preamble.

Be it enacted, etc., as follows:

Chapter one hundred and seventy-five of the General Laws is hereby amended by striking out section one hundred and twenty-three, as appearing in the Tercentenary Edition, and inserting in place thereof the following section: — *Section 123.* No life company shall issue any policy of life or endowment insurance in this commonwealth except upon a written application therefor signed or assented to in writing by the person to be insured, provided, that such a company may issue a policy on the life of a minor under the age of fifteen on an application signed by the parent, guardian or other person having legal custody of such minor.

G. L. (Ter. Ed.), 175, § 123, amended.

Medical examination, when required.

No such company shall issue any such policy for more than five thousand dollars unless the company has within one year prior thereto made or caused to be made a medical examination of the proposed insured by a registered medical practitioner.

This section shall not apply to contracts based upon the continuance of life, such as annuity or pure endowment contracts, whether or not they embody an agreement to refund, upon the death of the holder, to his estate or to a specified payee, any sum not exceeding the premiums paid thereon with compound interest, nor shall it apply to contracts of group life insurance.

Penalty. Any company violating this section, or any officer, agent or other person soliciting or effecting, or attempting to effect, a contract of insurance contrary to the provisions hereof, shall be punished by a fine of not more than one hundred dollars. *Approved April 16, 1943.*

---

*Chap.*187 AN ACT AUTHORIZING THE GENERAL ELECTRIC MUTUAL BENEFIT ASSOCIATION TO PAY FURTHER BENEFITS TO MEMBERS AND THEIR DEPENDENT WIVES AND CHILDREN.

Be it enacted, etc., as follows:

SECTION 1. Chapter one hundred and fifty-one of the acts of nineteen hundred and twenty is hereby amended by striking out section three, inserted by chapter one hundred and twenty-six of the acts of nineteen hundred and twenty-eight and as amended by section two of chapter one hundred and twenty-six of the acts of nineteen hundred and thirty-nine, and inserting in place thereof the following section: — *Section 3.* In addition to the relief and benefits provided for by sections two and four and subject to such conditions and limitations as may be fixed by the by-laws, said association may pay for the hospital care of a disabled member requiring and receiving such care not more than four dollars for each day that such member is in a hospital, but not exceeding one hundred and twenty-four dollars in any twelve consecutive months, and also may pay for any operating room, anesthesia, X-ray or therapeutics furnished for any such member not more than fifteen dollars in any twelve consecutive months.

SECTION 2. Said chapter one hundred and fifty-one is hereby further amended by adding at the end the following section: — *Section 4.* In addition to the relief and benefits provided for by sections two and three and subject to such conditions and limitations as may be fixed by the by-laws, said association may pay for hospital care of a disabled dependent wife or children of a member participating in a hospitalization plan for wives and children requiring and receiving such care, in the case of such a dependent under twelve years of age three dollars for each day, or in the case of any other such dependent four dollars for each day, that such dependent is in a hospital, not exceeding one hundred and twenty-four dollars in the aggregate for all such dependents in any twelve consecutive months, and also may pay for any operating room, anesthesia, X-ray or therapeutics furnished for a dependent wife or child of any such member not more than fifteen dollars for any one dependent in any twelve consecutive months.

Persons falling within the following descriptions shall be considered dependents for the purpose of participating in any such plan: —

(*a*) Wife of member;

(*b*) Any child born as the issue of the member participating in such plan, or as the issue of the wife of such member, or any legally adopted child of said parents or either of them; provided, that such child is legally dependent upon such parent or parents for maintenance and support, is unmarried and not employed and is more than three months of age but less than eighteen years of age.

Approved April 16, 1943.

---

*Chap.*188

AN ACT RELATIVE TO TAKING FOR NONPAYMENT OF TAXES LANDS SUBJECT TO TAX TITLES HELD BY MUNICIPALITIES WHEN THE ASSESSMENT UNIT IS CHANGED.

Be it enacted, etc., as follows:

G. L. (Ter. Ed.), 60, new § 61A, added.

Tax lien on land, etc., subject to prior tax title.

Chapter sixty of the General Laws is hereby amended by inserting after section sixty-one, as amended, the following section: — *Section 61A.* Anything contained in section sixty-one to the contrary notwithstanding, if a tax is a lien on land only part of which is subject to a tax title or tax titles held by the town or part of which is subject to a tax title held by the town and the remainder of which is subject to another tax title or tax titles held by the town, the tax shall not be certified as provided in section sixty-one; but the collector shall take the land for the nonpayment of the tax as if no part of such land were subject to a tax title held by the town, except that the notice prior to the taking and the instrument of taking shall, after describing the land, state: — "A portion or all of this land is subject to a tax title or tax titles held by the Town [or City] of ". The tax title account set up for the tax title resulting from such a taking and the tax title account set up for the prior tax title or tax titles shall be cross-referenced by the treasurer; and no tax title the account for which is so cross-referenced shall be assigned by the town.

Approved April 16, 1943.

Chap.189 AN ACT RELATIVE TO CERTAIN APPLICATIONS FOR ACCIDENTAL DISABILITY AND ACCIDENTAL DEATH BENEFITS UNDER THE LAWS RELATIVE TO CERTAIN RETIREMENT SYSTEMS ON ACCOUNT OF THE INJURY OR DEATH OF A MEMBER THEREOF WHO HAS RECEIVED COMPENSATION UNDER THE WORKMEN'S COMPENSATION LAW, WHERE NOTICE OF THE INJURY WAS NOT GIVEN SEASONABLY TO THE RETIREMENT BOARD OF SUCH SYSTEM.

Be it enacted, etc., as follows:

G. L. (Ter. Ed.), 32, § 37E, etc., amended.

Application for retirement, etc., filed more than two years after injury.

Section thirty-seven E of chapter thirty-two of the General Laws, as amended, is hereby further amended by adding at the end the following paragraph: —

(5) An application for the retirement of a member of a retirement system subject to this chapter on account of an injury which occurred more than two years prior to such application and was not reported in writing to the retirement board of such system within ninety days after its occurrence, or an application for an accidental death benefit on account of the death of a member of such a system resulting from an injury which occurred more than two years before such death and was not reported in writing to the retirement board of such system within ninety days after its occurrence, may be received and acted upon subject to the provisions of this chapter applicable in such a case, if such member has previously received compensation on account of such injury under any provision of chapter one hundred and fifty-two. *Approved April 16, 1943.*

Chap.190 AN ACT RELATIVE TO THE ADMISSIBILITY IN EVIDENCE OF UNATTESTED COPIES OF RULES AND REGULATIONS OF PUBLIC BODIES AND OF MUNICIPAL ORDINANCES AND BY-LAWS.

Be it enacted, etc., as follows:

G. L. (Ter. Ed.), 233, § 75, amended.

Certain rules and regulations as evidence, certification of.

SECTION 1. Section seventy-five of chapter two hundred and thirty-three of the General Laws, as appearing in the Tercentenary Edition, is hereby amended by adding at the end the following sentence: — Printed copies of rules and regulations purporting to be issued by authority of any department, commission, board or officer of the commonwealth or of any city or town having authority to adopt them, or printed copies of any city ordinances or town by-laws, shall be admitted without certification or attestation, but, if their genuineness is questioned, the court may require such certification or attestation thereof as it deems necessary.

Effective date.

SECTION 2. This act shall take effect on September first in the current year. *Approved April 16, 1943.*

AN ACT MAKING CERTAIN CHANGES IN EXISTING LAWS AFFECTING THE EXAMINATION AND AUDIT OF CO-OPERATIVE BANKS. *Chap.*191

Whereas, The recent change in the fiscal year of the commonwealth has made unworkable certain provisions of law relative to the assessment and collection of a certain portion of the cost of examinations and audits of co-operative banks, and the deferred operation of this act would tend to defeat its purpose which in part is to make immediately effective the amendments of existing law therein contained, therefore it is hereby declared to be an emergency law, necessary for the immediate preservation of the public convenience. Emergency preamble.

Be it enacted, etc., as follows:

Chapter one hundred and seventy of the General Laws is hereby amended by striking out section fifty-four, as appearing in chapter one hundred and forty-four of the acts of nineteen hundred and thirty-three, and inserting in place thereof the following section: — *Section 54.* To defray the expenses of the examination and audit provided for by section fifty-three, every such corporation so examined and audited shall, upon notice from the commissioner, pay to him as a fee therefor the actual cost of such examination and audit, including that portion of the overhead expense of the division of banks and loan agencies which shall be determined by the commissioner to be attributable to the supervision of such corporation; provided that such fee shall not exceed twenty cents per one thousand dollars of assets as shown by the statement of condition of such corporation on the date of such examination and audit. For the purpose of this section, traveling and hotel expense shall be included in the overhead expense of the aforesaid division. G. L. (Ter. Ed.), 170, § 54, etc., amended. Fees for examination and audit.

Approved April 20, 1943.

AN ACT PROVIDING FOR TEMPORARY CHANGES IN CERTAIN LAWS REGULATING THE ESTABLISHMENT OF BRANCHES AND MERGERS OF TRUST COMPANIES. *Chap.*192

Whereas, Unusual and extraordinary circumstances caused by the existing war emergency make it desirable that trust companies be permitted in certain instances to establish branch offices, or to merge and continue offices of the merging banks as branch offices, and in order that the public interest and necessity may better be served, this act is hereby declared to be an emergency law, necessary for the immediate preservation of the public convenience. Emergency preamble.

Be it enacted, etc., as follows:

SECTION 1. Sections forty-five and forty-six of chapter one hundred and seventy-two of the General Laws, as most recently amended by sections three and four, respectively, of chapter two hundred and forty-four of the acts of nine- G. L. (Ter. Ed.), 172, §§ 45 and 46, etc., suspended for duration of war, etc.

teen hundred and thirty-nine, are hereby suspended for the duration of the existing state of war between the United States and certain foreign countries, and for two years thereafter.

Maintenance of branch offices regulated.

SECTION 2. During the period of such suspension, no trust company shall maintain a branch office except as provided in this act or in section forty-seven of said chapter one hundred and seventy-two of the General Laws, but nothing herein shall affect the maintenance of branch offices lawfully established prior to the effective date hereof.

Same subject.

SECTION 3. During said period, any trust company may, with the approval of the board of bank incorporation, establish and operate one or more branch offices in the town where its main office is located, or in any other town within the same county having no commercial banking facilities or having facilities which, in the opinion of said board, are inadequate for the public convenience.

Acquisition of branch offices by purchase of assets, etc.

SECTION 4. During said period, any office or offices of a trust company the business of which has been taken over under section forty-four or section forty-four A of said chapter one hundred and seventy-two of the General Laws by a trust company whose main office is located in the same county, or any office or offices of a national banking association the whole or a substantial part of the assets of which has been purchased or otherwise acquired by a trust company so located, may, with the approval of the commissioner of banks, be maintained as a branch office or offices of such corporation. *Approved April 20, 1943.*

---

*Chap.*193 AN ACT MAKING PERMANENT CERTAIN EMERGENCY PROVISIONS RELATIVE TO RESERVE FUNDS OF TRUST COMPANIES.

Be it enacted, etc., as follows:

G. L. (Ter. Ed.), 172, § 75, etc., amended.

Section seventy-five of chapter one hundred and seventy-two of the General Laws, as amended by section twenty-nine of chapter three hundred and forty-nine of the acts of nineteen hundred and thirty-four, is hereby further amended by striking out the last sentence and inserting in place thereof the following sentence: — Notwithstanding the provisions of this section and of sections seventy-three and seventy-four, the commissioner may by regulation increase or decrease from time to time, in his discretion, the reserve balances required to be maintained against either demand or time deposits. *Approved April 20, 1943.*

Reserve balances against demand or time deposits.

---

*Chap.*194 AN ACT EXTENDING THE BENEFITS OF VETERANS' PREFERENCE, SO CALLED, UNDER THE CIVIL SERVICE LAWS.

Be it enacted, etc., as follows:

G. L. (Ter. Ed.), 31, § 21, etc., amended.

Section twenty-one of chapter thirty-one of the General Laws, as most recently amended by section twenty-eight of chapter two hundred and thirty-eight of the acts of nineteen hundred and thirty-nine, is hereby further amended by inserting after the word "decoration" in the seventeenth line, as appearing in chapter one hundred and thirty-seven of the acts of nineteen hundred and thirty-three, the words: — , or (3) any person who has served in time of war or insurrection in any corps or unit of the United States established for the purpose of enabling women to serve with, or as auxiliary to, the armed forces of the United States, and whose last discharge or release from active duty in such corps or unit was an honorable one, regardless of any prior discharge or release therefrom, — so as to read as follows: — *Section 21:* The word "veteran", as used in this chapter, shall mean (1) any person who has served in the army, navy or marine corps of the United States in time of war or insurrection and whose last discharge or release from active duty therein was an honorable one, regardless of any prior discharge or release therefrom, or (2) any person who has distinguished himself by gallant or heroic conduct while serving in the army, navy or marine corps of the United States and has received a decoration designated as the congressional medal of honor from the president of the United States or the secretary of war, or from a person designated by the president or the said secretary to act as the personal representative of the president or said secretary for the presentation of such decoration, and is recorded in the files of the war department or the navy department of the United States as having received such decoration, or (3) any person who has served in time of war or insurrection in any corps or unit of the United States established for the purpose of enabling women to serve with, or as auxiliary to, the armed forces of the United States, and whose last discharge or release from active duty in such corps or unit was an honorable one, regardless of any prior discharge or release therefrom; provided, that the person claiming to be a veteran under this section was a citizen of the commonwealth at the time of his induction into such service or has resided in the commonwealth for five consecutive years next prior to the date of filing application with the director under this chapter; and provided, further, that any such person who at the time of entering said service had declared his intention to become a subject or citizen of the United States and withdrew such intention under the provisions of the act of congress approved July ninth, nineteen hundred and eighteen, and any person designated as a conscientious objector upon his discharge, shall not be deemed a "veteran" within the meaning of this chapter.

Veterans' preference under civil service law.

"Veteran" defined.

Approved April 20, 1943.

*Chap.*195 AN ACT TEMPORARILY AUTHORIZING THE CITY OF BROCKTON TO MAINTAIN CERTAIN ABANDONED SCHOOL PROPERTY AS A MILITARY AND NAVAL SERVICE CENTER IN SAID CITY.

Be it enacted, etc., as follows:

SECTION 1. The city of Brockton is hereby authorized to maintain as a military and naval service center, during the existence of the present war and for six months after the termination thereof, the so-called Center School property located on White avenue in said city. Such service center shall be under the control of a board of five trustees who shall be appointed by the mayor of said city.

SECTION 2. This act shall take effect upon its passage.

Approved April 22, 1943.

---

*Chap.*196 AN ACT RELATIVE TO THE NAMING OF THIRD PERSONS IN DIVORCE PROCEEDINGS.

Be it enacted, etc., as follows:

G. L. (Ter. Ed.), 208, §§ 9, 10 and 11, amended.

SECTION 1. Chapter two hundred and eight of the General Laws is hereby amended by striking out sections nine, ten and eleven, as appearing in the Tercentenary Edition, and inserting in place thereof the following sections: — *Section 9.* A person named as co-respondent in an amended libel, cross libel or answer, or any person whose name has been inserted in the pleadings by amendment in accordance with section ten, may appear and contest the charge of adultery or defend himself against any other allegations therein made against him.

Co-respondent, etc., may contest.

Co-respondent not to be named, except, etc.

Section 10. In a libel or cross libel for divorce, in an answer thereto or in a bill of particulars or specifications filed in a divorce case, if any specific criminal act with a third person is alleged therein, or if any allegations are made therein which would be derogatory to the character or reputation of a third person if named therein, the pleadings shall not contain the name of such third person. The party making such allegations may at any time after filing the pleadings or other papers containing the same, upon an ex parte hearing before a justice or judge of the court in which the proceedings are pending, obtain permission to amend such pleadings or other papers by inserting the name of the person concerning whom the allegations are made, if the justice or judge finds probable cause has been shown that such allegations are true, and thereupon the pleadings or other papers may be amended accordingly and notice of said amendment shall be sent to all parties interested.

Evidence not to be reported.

Section 11. The evidence produced at such ex parte hearing shall not be reported or made a part of the record in the case and the motion for said amendment shall not be read in open court during the proceedings, but the clerk of the court or the register of probate shall make an entry in the docket of "Motion to insert name of third person allowed", or "Motion to insert name of third person denied", as the case may be. If the amendment is allowed upon affidavits, they shall be retained in the court and placed in the custody of the clerk or register, and shall be open for the purposes of inspection, and taking copies thereof, to counsel of record, the parties or the third person named in the amendment.

SECTION 2. This act shall take effect on September first in the current year. *Approved April 22, 1943.* Effective date.

AN ACT RELATIVE TO THE MEMBERSHIP OF THE BOARD OF TRUSTEES OF THE PUBLIC HOSPITAL IN THE CITY OF PEABODY. *Chap.*197

Be it enacted, etc., as follows:

SECTION 1. The board of trustees of the public hospital in the city of Peabody, established and maintained under authority of chapter two hundred and forty-one of the acts of nineteen hundred and thirty-one, shall consist of the mayor of said city, who shall be chairman, and four persons who shall be appointed by the mayor, subject to confirmation by the city council.

SECTION 2. In the initial appointments of the appointive members of said board, one shall be appointed to serve for four years, one to serve for three years, one to serve for two years and one to serve for one year. Thereafter, as the term of an appointive member expires his successor shall be appointed to serve for four years. Whenever any vacancy shall occur in the number of appointive members by death, resignation or otherwise, such vacancy shall be filled in the manner aforesaid for the remainder of the unexpired term.

SECTION 3. This act shall be submitted for acceptance to the registered voters of the city of Peabody at a special city election, which shall be held in said city during the current year, in the form of the following question which shall be placed upon the official ballot to be used at said election: "Shall an act of the general court passed in the year nineteen hundred and forty-three, entitled 'An Act relative to the Membership of the Board of Trustees of the Public Hospital in the City of Peabody', be accepted?" If a majority of the votes in answer to said question is in the affirmative, then this act shall thereupon take full effect, but not otherwise. *Approved April 22, 1943.*

AN ACT AUTHORIZING THE CITY OF BEVERLY TO COMPENSATE THE MEMBERS OF ITS BOARD OF ALDERMEN. *Chap.*198

Be it enacted, etc., as follows:

SECTION 1. Section thirteen of chapter five hundred and forty-two of the acts of nineteen hundred and ten is hereby amended by striking out the second sentence and inserting in place thereof the following sentence: — Its members shall receive in full compensation for their services as members of the board of aldermen, or of any committee thereof, such salary as may be established by ordinance, but not exceeding three hundred dollars per annum for each member, — so as to read as follows: — *Section 13.* The board of aldermen shall, so far as is consistent with this act, have and exercise all the legislative power of towns and of the inhabitants thereof, and shall have and exercise all the powers now vested by law in the city of Beverly and in the inhabitants thereof as a municipal corporation, and shall have all the powers and be subject to all the liabilities of city councils and of either branch thereof, and it may by ordinance prescribe the manner in which such powers shall be exercised. Its members shall receive in full compensation for their services as members of the board of aldermen, or of any committee thereof, such salary as may be established by ordinance, but not exceeding three hundred dollars per annum for each member. Sessions of the board whether as a board of aldermen or as a committee of the whole shall be open to the public, and a journal of its proceedings shall be kept, which journal shall be subject to public inspection. The vote of the board upon any question shall be taken by roll call when the same is requested by at least three members. Nothing herein shall prevent the board, by special vote, from holding private sittings for the consideration of nominations by the mayor.

SECTION 2. This act shall be submitted for acceptance to the registered voters of the city of Beverly at the next biennial city election in the form of the following question which shall be placed upon the official ballot to be used at said election: — "Shall an act passed by the general court in the year nineteen hundred and forty-three, entitled 'An act authorizing the city of Beverly to compensate the members of its board of aldermen', be accepted?" If a majority of the votes cast on said question is in the affirmative, this act shall take full effect on January first in the year nineteen hundred and forty-five, otherwise it shall have no effect.

Approved April 22, 1943.

---

*Chap.*199 AN ACT RELATIVE TO WITHHOLDING PAYMENT OF MONEY PAYABLE TO PERSONS OWING TAXES, ASSESSMENTS, RATES OR OTHER MUNICIPAL CHARGES.

Be it enacted, etc., as follows:

G. L. (Ter. Ed.), 60, § 93, amended.

Chapter sixty of the General Laws is hereby amended by striking out section ninety-three, as appearing in the Tercentenary Edition, and inserting in place thereof the following section: — *Section 93.* The treasurer or other disbursing officer of any town may, and if so requested by the collector shall, withhold payment of any money payable to any person from whom there are then due taxes, assessments, rates or other charges committed to such collector, which

Money payable by city or town to person owing taxes to be withheld, etc.

are wholly or partly unpaid, whether or not secured by a tax title held by the town, to an amount not exceeding the total of the unpaid taxes, assessments, rates and other charges, with interest and costs. The sum withheld shall be paid or credited to the collector, who shall, if required, give a written receipt therefor. The person taxed or charged may in such case have the same remedy as if he had paid such taxes, assessments, rates or other charges after a levy upon his goods. The collector's rights under this section shall not be affected by any assignment or trustee process.

Approved April 22, 1943.

AN ACT EXTENDING THE TIME FOR COMPLETING CERTAIN IMPROVEMENTS AND CONSTRUCTION ON PARK LAND IN THE CITY OF BOSTON KNOWN AS THE CHARLESBANK, TO BE PAID FOR OUT OF THE GEORGE ROBERT WHITE FUND. *Chap.*200

Be it enacted, etc., as follows:

Section one of chapter five hundred and eighty-five of the acts of nineteen hundred and forty-one is hereby amended by striking out, in the twenty-first line, the word "two" and inserting in place thereof the word: — four, — so as to read as follows: — *Section 1.* The park department of the city of Boston is hereby authorized to transfer to the care, custody and control of the trustees under the fourteenth clause of the will of George Robert White so much of the park land situate in Boston, and lying between the Longfellow bridge, the Charles river basin, the Charles river dam, and Charles street, and known as the Charlesbank, as said park department and said trustees shall agree upon, for the purposes of improving the bathing beach now located at said Charlesbank and of constructing on said park land a recreation center, including facilities for indoor and outdoor exercise, rest and recreation throughout the year, said improvement and said construction to be in accordance with plans approved by said park department; upon the express condition, however, that, upon the completion of said improvement and of said construction, the care, custody and control of said land, together with all erections thereon, shall revert without further act to said park department, to be held by said park department in furtherance of the provisions of the will of said George Robert White. Said transfer shall also be upon the further express condition that if, within four years from the date of such transfer, such improvement and construction at or on said park land shall not have been completed, then the care, custody and control of said park land shall thereupon revert without further act to said park department.

Approved April 22, 1943.

*Chap.*201 AN ACT AUTHORIZING THE RESIGNATION OF FIDUCIARIES BY THEIR GUARDIANS, CONSERVATORS OR COMMITTEES, OR OTHER LIKE OFFICERS, ACTING ON THEIR BEHALF.

Be it enacted, etc., as follows:

G. L. (Ter. Ed.), 203, § 13, amended.

Resignation of trustee.

SECTION 1. Chapter two hundred and three of the General Laws is hereby amended by striking out section thirteen, as appearing in the Tercentenary Edition, and inserting in place thereof the following section: — *Section 13.* A trustee may resign his trust if the court authorized to appoint the trustee finds it proper to allow such resignation.

G. L. (Ter. Ed.), 204, new § 37, added.

Resignation by guardian on behalf of ward, etc.

SECTION 2. Chapter two hundred and four of the General Laws is hereby amended by adding after section thirty-six, added by chapter one hundred and fifty-two of the acts of the current year, the following section: — *Section 37.* If an executor, administrator, guardian, conservator, trustee, receiver, commissioner, or other fiduciary officer, appointed by any court is the ward of a guardian, conservator or committee, or other like officer, appointed by any court in this commonwealth, or by any court at the place of his domicile, to have charge of his property or his person, such guardian, conservator or committee, or other like officer, may, on behalf of the ward, resign the trust or other office held by the ward if the court which appointed the ward finds it proper to allow such resignation, and the court may accept such resignation without notice to the ward. In the case of a fiduciary under a written instrument who was not appointed by a court, his guardian, conservator or committee, if one has been appointed, may, on behalf of the ward, resign with the approval in writing of the persons authorized by the instrument to appoint a new trustee in case of a vacancy if the instrument contains such a provision, and, if not, then with the approval of a court having jurisdiction to appoint a new trustee in case of vacancy.

Effective date.

SECTION 3. This act shall take effect on September first in the current year. *Approved April 22, 1943.*

---

*Chap.*202 AN ACT AUTHORIZING THE CITY OF WOBURN TO MAKE TEMPORARY INCREASES OF THE SALARIES AND WAGES OF CERTAIN OFFICERS AND EMPLOYEES OF SAID CITY.

Be it enacted, etc., as follows:

SECTION 1. The city council of the city of Woburn, with the approval of the mayor, may annually, during the continuance of the existing state of war between the United States of America and any foreign country, vote temporary increases in the salaries and wages of officials and employees of said city whose salaries or wages have been fixed by ordinance; provided, that such temporary increases shall be effective for a period of not more than one year following such vote and approval; and provided, further, that an appropriation has been made to cover the same prior to the fixing of the tax rate for the then current municipal year.

SECTION 2. This act shall take effect upon its passage.

Approved April 26, 1943.

AN ACT RELATIVE TO SIDEWALK ASSESSMENTS IN THE CITY OF BOSTON. *Chap.*203

Be it enacted, etc., as follows:

SECTION 1. Chapter four hundred and thirty-seven of the acts of eighteen hundred and ninety-three is hereby amended by striking out section one, as most recently amended by section one of chapter one hundred and ninety-six of the Special Acts of nineteen hundred and seventeen, and inserting in place thereof the following section: — *Section 1.* The city council of the city of Boston, with the approval of the mayor, may order the grading and construction of sidewalks, or the completion of any partly constructed sidewalk in any street of said city, as public convenience may require, with or without edgestones as the council shall deem expedient, and may order that the same be covered with brick, stone, concrete, artificial stone, gravel or other appropriate material. Within six months after the completion of such sidewalk, provided that entry for the purpose of constructing, grading or completing the sidewalk shall be made within two years after the date of the approval by the mayor of the order therefor, the board of street commissioners of said city shall assess upon each abutter on such sidewalk a just proportion, not exceeding one half, of the expense of the sidewalk. All assessments so made shall constitute a lien upon the abutting land from and after the date of entry to construct, grade or complete the sidewalk under order of the city council, but no lien or incumbrance shall be created by the passage of the order by the city council. The provisions of chapter eighty of the General Laws, and acts in amendment or revision thereof, relative to the apportionment, division, reassessment, abatement and collection of assessments, and to interest, shall apply to assessments made hereunder. The said sidewalks when constructed with edgestones and covered with brick, stone, concrete or artificial stone shall afterward be maintained at the expense of the city. When any such sidewalk shall permanently be constructed with edgestones and covered with brick, stone, concrete or artificial stone as aforesaid, there shall be deducted from the assessment therefor any sum previously assessed upon the abutting premises and paid to the city for the expense of the construction of the same in any other manner than with edgestones and brick, stone, concrete or artificial stone as aforesaid, and such deduction shall be made pro rata, and in just proportions, from the assessments upon different abutters who are owners of the land in respect to which such former assessment was paid.

SECTION 2. If at any time the commissioner of corporations and taxation of the commonwealth is of the opinion that the whole or any part of an assessment made under section one of chapter four hundred and thirty-seven of the acts of eighteen hundred and ninety-three, or acts in addition thereto or in amendment thereof, should be abated, he may in writing authorize such assessment or part thereof, provided that it remains unpaid, to be abated by the board of street commissioners of the city of Boston, which board may thereupon abate such assessment or part thereof, as the case may be.

SECTION 3. The board of street commissioners may, within six months after the date when this act takes full effect, make assessments for sidewalks completed prior to such effective date if assessments were not made therefor before such effective date.

SECTION 4. This act shall take full effect upon its acceptance by vote of the city council, with the approval of the mayor, of said city of Boston, but not otherwise.

Approved April 26, 1943.

---

*Chap.*204 AN ACT RELATIVE TO RETIREMENT ALLOWANCES FOR POLICEMEN AND FIREMEN RETIRED FOR ACCIDENTAL DISABILITY UNDER THE BOSTON RETIREMENT ACT, SO CALLED.

Be it enacted, etc., as follows:

SECTION 1. Clause (*c*) of section fourteen of chapter five hundred and twenty-one of the acts of nineteen hundred and twenty-two is hereby amended by adding at the end the following: — ; provided, that if the employee was a member of the fire fighting force of the fire department or a patrolman in the police department, the amount of such additional pension shall, together with the annuity and pension, be equal to three fourths of the highest annual compensation payable to such employees holding positions in the same grade and classification occupied by him at the time of the accident, — so as to read as follows: —

(*c*) An additional pension of such an amount as will, together with the annuity and pension, be equal to three fourths of the annual compensation received by him during the year immediately preceding the date of the accident; provided, that if the employee was a member of the fire fighting force of the fire department or a patrolman in the police department, the amount of such additional pension shall, together with the annuity and pension, be equal to three fourths of the highest annual compensation payable to such employees holding positions in the same grade and classification occupied by him at the time of the accident.

SECTION 2. This act shall apply to the retirement allowances of firemen and policemen retired for accidental disability under the provisions of said chapter five hundred and twenty-one, as amended, prior to the effective date of this act as well as to those retired therefor after said effective date.

Section 3. This act shall take full effect upon its acceptance by vote of the city council of the city of Boston, approved by the mayor, but not otherwise.

Approved April 26, 1943.

An Act relative to the number, qualifications and election of the members and officers of the trustees of the Methodist religious society in Boston. Chap.205

Be it enacted, etc., as follows:

Section 1. The Trustees of the Methodist Religious Society in Boston, a corporation incorporated by chapter seventy of the acts of eighteen hundred and eight, passed March third, eighteen hundred and nine, shall, in the manner provided by the discipline and usages of the Methodist Church as from time to time in full force and effect, determine the number and qualifications of its members, the number thereof necessary for a quorum, the method of electing its members and officers and of filling vacancies in their number and the terms of office of its members and officers.

Section 2. So much of said chapter seventy, and of any act in amendment or in addition thereto, as is inconsistent with the provisions of this act is hereby repealed.

Section 3. This act shall take full effect upon its acceptance by vote of the members of said corporation entitled to vote, and the filing with the state secretary of a certified copy of said vote, but not otherwise.

Approved April 26, 1943.

An Act authorizing Patrick J. Boyle, an employee of the city of Lawrence, to become a member of the contributory retirement system of said city, and making him eligible for certain retirement benefits thereunder. Chap.206

Be it enacted, etc., as follows:

Section 1. Patrick J. Boyle, employed as a laborer by the city of Lawrence since May, nineteen hundred and five, except from March, nineteen hundred and sixteen to June, nineteen hundred and seventeen and from March, nineteen hundred and thirty-six to April, nineteen hundred and thirty-nine, may become a member of the contributory retirement system of said city, notwithstanding any provision of law governing said retirement system that makes him ineligible for membership therein. Upon becoming such member, he shall be entitled to all the rights and privileges of members of said system which he would have enjoyed if he had become a member of the system on April tenth, nineteen hundred and thirty-nine, the date of his last re-entry into the service of said city; provided, that he first deposits in the annuity fund of said system such amount as the board of retirement under said system may determine in order to establish an account for him in said annuity fund in an amount equal to that which it would be if he had been a member of said system since said April tenth, nineteen hundred and thirty-nine.

SECTION 2. This act shall take full effect upon its acceptance by vote of the city council of said city, subject to the provisions of its charter, but not otherwise.

Approved April 26, 1943.

---

*Chap.*207 AN ACT AUTHORIZING DOMESTIC LIFE INSURANCE COMPANIES TO PURCHASE AND HOLD AND TO IMPROVE REAL ESTATE BY CONSTRUCTING LOW RENTAL HOUSING PROJECTS THEREON, AND TO OPERATE AND MAINTAIN SUCH PROJECTS.

Be it enacted, etc., as follows:

G. L. (Ter. Ed.), 175, new § 66A, added.

Life companies may invest in housing projects, etc.

SECTION 1. Chapter one hundred and seventy-five of the General Laws is hereby amended by inserting after section sixty-six, as appearing in the Tercentenary Edition, the following section: — *Section 66A.* Any domestic life company, with the prior written approval of the commissioner, may purchase and hold without any limitation of time land in any city, town or other municipality, having a population according to the last preceding federal census of not less than one hundred thousand persons, in any state of the United States in which it is authorized to transact business, and on such land, or on any other land owned by it in such city, town or municipality, may erect and thereafter hold, as aforesaid, and maintain, repair, alter, demolish, reconstruct, manage or sell, convey or mortgage, in whole or in part, apartment or tenement buildings designed for occupancy by more than fifty families or any other dwelling houses or buildings, not including hotels, but including such buildings or accommodations for retail stores, shops, offices and other community services as the company may deem proper and suitable for the convenience of the tenants and occupants of such buildings or houses, and may collect and receive rent or income from any such buildings or houses. No land shall be purchased or improved under this section if the cost of such land, or the cost of the improvements thereon, or both, as the case may be, plus the total amount of real estate then held by the company, exceeds twenty per centum of its invested assets including cash in banks.

G. L. (Ter. Ed.), 175, § 64, etc., amended.

SECTION 2. Section sixty-four of said chapter one hundred and seventy-five, as most recently amended by chapter five hundred and forty-eight of the acts of nineteen hundred and forty-one, is hereby further amended by striking out the third paragraph, as appearing in the Tercentenary

Edition, and inserting in place thereof the following paragraph: —

No domestic company hereafter acquiring title to real estate under the conditions of any mortgage owned by it, or by purchase or set-off on execution upon judgment for debts due it previously contracted in the course of its business, or by other process in settlement for debts, shall hold it, except as provided in section sixty-six A, for a longer period than five years without the written permission of the commissioner. Except as authorized by section sixty-six A, no such company shall invest in real estate except to the extent that may be necessary for its convenient accommodation in the transaction of its business but not to exceed ten per centum of its invested assets, including cash in banks, as shown by its last annual statement to the commissioner. Investments, deposits, sales and loans.

SECTION 3. Section eleven of said chapter one hundred and seventy-five is hereby amended by striking out the first paragraph, as most recently amended by section one of chapter ninety-two of the acts of nineteen hundred and thirty-four, and inserting in place thereof the following paragraph: — Beside the reserve provided for in sections nine and ten he shall, except as provided in section twelve, charge to each company as a liability all unpaid losses and claims for losses, and all other debts and liabilities, including in the case of a stock company its capital stock and including, in the case of a mutual company with a guaranty capital or guaranty fund, such guaranty capital or guaranty fund. He shall allow to the credit of a company in the account of its financial condition only such assets as are available for the payment of losses in this commonwealth, including all assets deposited with officers of other states or countries for the security of the policyholders of such company; but no holding or parcel of real estate described in section sixty-six A shall be allowed as an asset unless the average net rental value of the apartment, tenement or other dwelling house erected thereon, as estimated at the commencement of its construction, is sixteen dollars or less per room per month; and no holding or parcel of real estate shall be given a higher value than would be adequate to yield at three per cent annual interest the average amount of its net rental for three years next preceding, except that if a company shows to his satisfaction that the actual value of any of its real estate is greater than the value so ascertained, then the actual value of the said real estate as determined by the commissioner shall be allowed. The commissioner may, in his discretion, require any company to furnish such information as may be needed to substantiate the values above prescribed. G. L. (Ter. Ed.), 175, § 11, etc., amended. Computation of assets and liabilities.

SECTION 4. This act shall not take effect until the termination of the existing states of war between the United States and certain foreign countries. Effective date.

Approved April 26, 1943.

Chap.208 AN ACT FURTHER REGULATING INVESTMENT OF CAPITAL, SURPLUS, CERTIFICATE FUNDS AND INCOME OF BANKING COMPANIES.

Be it enacted, etc., as follows:

G. L. (Ter. Ed.), 172A, § 7, etc., amended.

Section seven of chapter one hundred and seventy-two A of the General Laws, as appearing in section four of chapter four hundred and fifty-two of the acts of nineteen hundred and thirty-five, is hereby amended by striking out clause Second and inserting in place thereof the following clause: —

Investment of funds, etc., regulated.

Second. In any securities authorized as investments for savings banks by clauses Second to Seventh, inclusive, of section fifty-four of chapter one hundred and sixty-eight; provided, that not more than twenty per cent of its certificate funds shall be invested by any such corporation in the classes of securities referred to in sub-divisions (*c*) to (*i*), inclusive, of said clause Second and in said clauses Third to Seventh, inclusive, of said section fifty-four.

Approved April 26, 1943.

Chap.209 AN ACT RELATIVE TO THE POSTING OR MAILING OF MAPS OR DESCRIPTIONS OF NEW VOTING PRECINCTS IN CITIES AND CERTAIN TOWNS AND OF PRINTED DESCRIPTIONS OF POLLING PLACES THEREIN.

Be it enacted, etc., as follows:

G. L. (Ter. Ed.), 54, § 5, amended.

Map or description of new precincts to be published and posted, etc.

SECTION 1. Chapter fifty-four of the General Laws is hereby amended by striking out section five, as appearing in the Tercentenary Edition, and inserting in place thereof the following section: — *Section 5.* When a ward has been divided into new voting precincts, or the voting precincts thereof have been changed, the aldermen shall forthwith cause a map or description of the division to be published, in which the new precincts shall be designated by numbers or letters and shall be defined clearly and, so far as possible, by known boundaries; and they shall cause copies thereof to be furnished to the registrars of voters, to the assessors, and to the election officers of each precinct so established. The aldermen shall cause copies thereof to be posted in such public places in each precinct of a ward so divided as they may determine or shall give notice by mail to each registered voter affected by such change of voting precinct.

G. L. (Ter. Ed.), 54, § 24, amended.

Polling places, designation of, notice, etc.

SECTION 2. Section twenty-four of said chapter fifty-four, as so appearing, is hereby amended by striking out the last sentence and inserting in place thereof the two following sentences: — When the polling places have been designated in the city of Boston, the board of election commissioners of said city may post in such places as it may determine a printed description of the polling places designated and may give further notice thereof; and when the polling places have been designated in any other city or in any town, the aldermen of such city in at least five public places in each precinct thereof, and the selectmen of such town in at least three public places in each precinct thereof, shall forthwith post a printed description of the polling places designated and may give further notice thereof. When a polling place in a voting precinct is changed from one location to another, the board of election commissioners in the city of Boston, the aldermen in any other city or the selectmen in any town shall cause printed descriptions of such polling place to be posted in such public places in such precinct as they determine or shall give notice by mail to each registered voter therein.

Approved April 26, 1943.

AN ACT RELATIVE TO PAYMENTS TO THE GENERAL INSURANCE GUARANTY FUND. *Chap.*210

Be it enacted, etc., as follows:

SECTION 1. Section eighteen of chapter one hundred and seventy-eight of the General Laws, as appearing in the Tercentenary Edition, is hereby amended by striking out, in the twelfth, thirteenth and fourteenth lines, the words ", with interest compounded semi-annually at the rate of five per cent per annum out of the surplus funds of said insurance department as soon and so far as an adequate surplus exists" and inserting in place thereof the words: — out of the surplus funds of its insurance department, at such times and in such amounts and with such interest, not exceeding five per cent per annum compounded semi-annually, as the General Insurance Guaranty Fund shall direct, — so as to read as follows: — *Section 18.* Every savings and insurance bank shall, on the third Wednesday of each month, pay to the General Insurance Guaranty Fund an amount equal to four per cent of all amounts paid to it as premiums on policies or in the purchase of annuities during the preceding month. Said sums shall be held as a guaranty for all obligations on policies or annuity contracts of the insurance departments of all savings and insurance banks; and so much thereof shall be paid over to any bank, to be applied in the payment of losses or satisfaction of other obligations on said policies or annuity contracts, as may be required to prevent or to make good an impairment of its insurance reserve. Any amount so paid to any bank shall be charged to its account, and be repaid out of the surplus funds of its insurance department, at such times and in such amounts and with such interest, not exceeding five per cent per annum compounded semi-annually, as the General Insurance Guaranty Fund shall direct. The amounts so advanced by the General Insurance Guaranty Fund to any bank shall be repaid only as above provided, and shall not be deemed a liability in determining the solvency of its insurance department.

G. L. (Ter. Ed.), 178, § 18, amended.

Payment of percentage of premiums to General Insurance Guaranty Fund as guaranty.

Disposition.

G. L. (Ter. Ed), 178, new § 18A, added.

Limitation on payments to General Insurance Guaranty Fund.

SECTION 2. Said chapter one hundred and seventy-eight is hereby further amended by inserting after section eighteen, as so appearing, the following section: — *Section 18A.* Every savings and insurance bank shall upon request by the General Insurance Guaranty Fund, pay to it forthwith such sums as may be so requested, provided that the sums so requested to be paid hereunder to the General Insurance Guaranty Fund by any savings and insurance bank shall not exceed, in the aggregate, six per cent of all amounts paid to it as premiums on insurance policies during the fiscal year next preceding the latest request made as aforesaid. The sums so paid to the General Insurance Guaranty Fund shall be held by it as a guaranty for all obligations on policies or annuity contracts of the insurance departments of all savings and insurance banks and be paid out by it in accordance with the provisions of section eighteen. Payments under this section shall be in addition to payments under said section eighteen. *Approved April 26, 1943.*

---

*Chap.*211 AN ACT RELATIVE TO WAR ALLOWANCES, STATE AND MILITARY AID AND SOLDIERS' RELIEF FOR CERTAIN RESIDENTS OF THE COMMONWEALTH WHO ARE IN THE MILITARY OR NAVAL SERVICE OF THE UNITED STATES, OR HAVE BEEN HONORABLY DISCHARGED THEREFROM, AND THEIR DEPENDENTS.

Emergency preamble.

Whereas, The deferred operation of this act would tend to defeat its purpose, which is to provide immediate financial assistance to certain soldiers, sailors and marines who are in the service of the United States, or have been honorably discharged therefrom, and to their dependent relatives, therefore it is hereby declared to be an emergency law, necessary for the immediate preservation of the public convenience.

Be it enacted, etc., as follows:

SECTION 1. Section one of chapter eleven of the acts of nineteen hundred and forty-two is hereby amended by inserting after the word "service" in the sixteenth and in the twenty-ninth lines, in each instance, the words: — to the credit of the commonwealth, — and by inserting after the word "sister" in the twenty-second line the words: — under eighteen years of age, — so as to read as follows: — *Section 1.* Any city or town, acting by the officers authorized by law to furnish state and military aid, may, during the continuance of the existing state of war between the United States and any foreign country and for six months thereafter, provide a war allowance for the dependent relatives of any soldier or sailor, which terms, for the purposes of this act, are hereby defined as in section one of chapter one hundred and fifteen of the General Laws, in the military or naval service of the United States during said state of war which, for the purposes of this act, shall be deemed to have begun on September sixteenth, nineteen hundred and forty; provided, that on said September sixteenth or, if after said date said soldier or sailor entered said service or was recalled thereto or was continued therein after the expiration of a prior enlistment, at the time of his entry into or recall to or continuance in said service to the credit of the commonwealth, said soldier or sailor was a resident of this commonwealth and had been a resident thereof for not less than one year. The dependent relatives of such a soldier or sailor who are eligible to receive such aid shall be the wife, children under eighteen years of age, or any child dependent by reason of physical or mental incapacity, or a brother or sister under eighteen years of age, or a dependent parent, or any person who stood in the relationship of a parent to such soldier or sailor for five years prior to said September sixteenth or, if after said date said soldier or sailor entered said service or was recalled thereto or was continued therein after the expiration of a prior enlistment, for five years prior to his entry into, recall to or continuance in said service to the credit of the commonwealth. The allowance authorized by this section shall cease on the termination of the service by death or discharge.

SECTION 2. Said chapter eleven is hereby further amended by striking out section two and inserting in place thereof the following section: — *Section 2.* Any person in the military or naval service of the United States, whose dependents are entitled to war allowance under section one, and who is honorably discharged from said service, shall be eligible to receive state or military aid and soldiers' relief under the provisions of said chapter one hundred and fifteen relating to world war service, so far as applicable. If any such person shall die in said service during said state of war, or shall die after an honorable discharge from said service, a needy parent, his mother, if a widow, his widow and his children, up to the age of eighteen, or any child dependent by reason of physical or mental incapacity, provided that the children were in being prior to his discharge, or prior to the termination of said state of war, or any person who stood to him in the relationship of a parent for five years prior to said September sixteenth or, if after said date said soldier or sailor entered said service or was recalled thereto or was continued therein after the expiration of a prior enlistment, for five years prior to his entry into, recall to or continuance in said service to the credit of the commonwealth, shall be entitled to the benefit of state aid and soldiers' relief in accordance with the provisions of said chapter one hundred and fifteen relating to world war service, so far as applicable.

Approved April 28, 1943.

*Chap.*212 AN ACT RELATIVE TO THE USE OF SILVERSHELL BEACH, SO CALLED, BY THE TOWN OF MARION.

Be it enacted, etc., as follows:

The town of Marion is hereby authorized to discontinue the use of Silvershell beach, so called, as a public bathing beach, and thereafter to use said beach for such municipal purposes as it may from time to time determine, and said town may restrict the use of the same to its inhabitants and its seasonal and temporary residents, and may adopt by-laws, not repugnant to law, relative to the use, care, regulation and control of the same for such purposes.

Approved April 28, 1943.

---

*Chap.*213 AN ACT PROVIDING FOR THE INVESTMENT OF CERTAIN FUNDS OF THE COMMONWEALTH IN THE CURRENT ISSUE OF UNITED STATES WAR BONDS, COMMONLY CALLED THE SECOND WAR LOAN BONDS.

Emergency preamble.

Whereas, The investment of certain funds of the commonwealth in the current issue of United States war bonds authorized by this act cannot be made unless its provisions become effective at once, therefore this act is hereby declared to be an emergency law, necessary for the immediate preservation of the public convenience.

Be it enacted, etc., as follows:

SECTION 1. The state treasurer may invest in the current issue of United States war bonds, commonly called the Second War Loan Bonds, such amount of the cash in the treasury of the commonwealth, not exceeding six million dollars, as he may, with the approval of the governor, determine, and bonds so purchased shall be held in a separate fund in his custody.

SECTION 2. Said state treasurer, in investing the funds of the state retirement system and of the teachers' retirement system under existing provisions of law, may purchase, at cost plus accrued interest, bonds held by him under section one, and bonds purchased under this section shall be transferred by him to the particular retirement system fund that was used for such purchases. The proceeds from sales of bonds made under this section shall be paid into the treasury of the commonwealth. *Approved April 29, 1943.*

---

*Chap.*214 AN ACT AUTHORIZING CERTAIN STATE, COUNTY AND MUNICIPAL OFFICERS, DURING THE EXISTING STATE OF WAR, TO EXCHANGE, LOAN OR SELL PUBLICLY OWNED PERSONAL PROPERTY FOR USE BY THE UNITED STATES GOVERNMENT IN THE PROSECUTION OF THE WAR.

Emergency preamble.

Whereas, The deferred operation of this act would tend to defeat its purpose, which is in part to authorize certain state, county and municipal officers to take without delay in the existing state of war any action provided for therein, therefore, it is hereby declared to be an emergency law, necessary for the immediate preservation of the public safety and convenience.

Be it enacted, etc., as follows:

The state purchasing agent subject to the approval of the commission on administration and finance, the county commissioners of a county, the mayor of a city subject to the approval of the city council, or the selectmen of a town may, during the existing state of war between the United States and any foreign country, exchange, or loan or sell for a fair consideration, personal property owned by the commonwealth, county, city or town, as the case may be, to the federal government or to any person or corporation designated by any agency of the federal government, provided that the federal government gives written assurance that the property is to be used by the United States in the prosecution of the war. *Approved April 29, 1943.*

---

*Chap.*215

AN ACT PERTAINING TO THE INVESTMENTS OF DEPOSITS AND THE INCOME DERIVED THEREFROM OF SAVINGS BANKS.

Emergency preamble.

Whereas, The provisions of this act impose upon the commissioner of banks certain duties which must be performed not later than July first each year, and the deferred operation would prevent him from performing said duties in the current year, therefore it is hereby declared to be an emergency law, necessary for the immediate preservation of the public convenience.

Be it enacted, etc., as follows:

G. L (Ter. Ed.), 168, § 54, etc., amended.

SECTION 1. Section fifty-four of chapter one hundred and sixty-eight of the General Laws is hereby amended by striking out subdivisions (*h*), (*i*) and (*j*) of clause Second, as appearing in section one of chapter four hundred and thirteen of the acts of nineteen hundred and forty-one, and inserting in place thereof the two following subsections: —

Investments authorized for savings banks.

(*h*) In the legally issued or assumed bonds, notes, or other interest bearing obligations of any city of any state of the United States, other than Maine, New Hampshire, Vermont, Massachusetts, Rhode Island, Connecticut or New York, which was incorporated as such at least ten years prior to the date of such investment and which has not less than thirty thousand nor more than one hundred thousand inhabitants, as established in the manner provided in subdivision (*f*), and whose net indebtedness does not exceed six per cent of the last preceding assessed valuation of the taxable real property therein; provided, that such obligations: —

(1) Mature not later than fifteen years from the date of investment; or

(2) Mature later than fifteen years, but not later than

forty years, from the date of investment and that the amount of the particular issue remaining unpaid is payable in serial installments annually in such manner that the amount of principal payable in any one year shall not be less than the amount of principal payable in any subsequent year; provided, that in the case of a new issue no installment need mature prior to two years from the date of issue.

(*i*) In the legally issued or assumed bonds, notes or other interest bearing obligations of any city of any state of the United States, other than Maine, New Hampshire, Vermont, Massachusetts, Rhode Island, Connecticut or New York, which was incorporated as such at least ten years prior to the date of such investment and which has more than one hundred thousand inhabitants, as established in the manner set forth in subdivision (*f*), and whose net indebtedness does not exceed eight per cent of the last preceding assessed valuation of the taxable real property therein; provided, that such obligations: —

(1) Mature not later than fifteen years from the date of investment; or

(2) Mature later than fifteen years, but not later than forty years, from the date of investment, and that the amount of the particular issue remaining unpaid is payable in serial payments annually in such manner that the amount of principal payable in any one year shall not be less than the amount of principal payable in any subsequent year; provided, that in the case of a new issue no installment need mature prior to two years from the date of issue.

G. L. (Ter. Ed.), 168, § 54, etc., further amended.

SECTION 2. Said section fifty-four is hereby further amended by striking out subdivision (3) of clause Third, as so appearing, and inserting in place thereof the following subdivision: —

Requirement for investment in railroad bonds.

(3) That in six of the seven years immediately preceding the date of such investment, and in the year immediately preceding the date of such investment, the railroad corporation which operates the railroad or railroad equipment upon which such obligations are secured shall have earned its fixed charges in full.

G. L. (Ter. Ed.), 168, § 54, etc., further amended.

SECTION 3. Said section fifty-four is hereby further amended by striking out subdivision (*d*) of the last paragraph of clause Third, as so appearing, and inserting in place thereof the following subdivision: —

When obligation deemed a first mortgage.

(*d*) Obligations shall be deemed to be secured by first mortgage or first mortgage lien if they are secured by such a lien on not less than sixty-six and two thirds per cent of all the railroad on which they are a lien.

G. L. (Ter. Ed.), 168, § 54, etc., further amended.

SECTION 4. Said section fifty-four is hereby further amended by inserting after clause Third, as so appearing, the following clause: —

Investment in obligations of railroads incorporated in other states, etc.

Third A. In obligations of any railroad corporation incorporated under the laws of the United States or of any state thereof, which is doing business principally within the United States; provided: —

(1) That the railroad corporation which operates the railroad or railroad equipment upon which such obligations are secured shall have been reorganized under the provisions of section seventy-seven of the federal bankruptcy act within six years prior to the date of investment, which reorganization shall have been finally consummated and made effective;

(2) That the railroad corporation which operates the railroad or railroad equipment upon which such obligations are secured shall own or operate under lease not less than one thousand miles of standard gauge railroad, exclusive of sidings;

(3) That the railroad corporation, or its predecessor or predecessors if a new corporation has been formed, which operates the railroad or railroad equipment upon which such obligations are secured shall:

(*a*) Have had at least four hundred million dollars gross railway operating revenues in the ten years preceding the date of investment;

(*b*) Have had net railway operating income, as shown in reports prescribed by the Interstate Commerce Commission, which in the year preceding the date of investment shall have been, and in the ten years preceding the date of investment shall have averaged, an amount which is at least equal to twice the annual fixed charges, as hereafter defined, of such reorganized railroad corporation and which shall exceed such annual fixed charges by an amount equal to at least eight per cent of the gross railway operating revenues of the year immediately preceding the date of investment and of the average gross railway operating revenues of the ten years immediately preceding the date of investment;

(4) That the railroad corporation which operates the railroad or railroad equipment upon which such obligations are secured shall not be in default, since completion of the reorganization, in the payment of principal or interest of any of its obligations or of rental for leased lines or terminal facilities;

(5) That such obligations contain an unconditional promise to pay the interest thereon regularly and the principal at a specified date and that they are secured by: —

(*a*) A first lien, lease, or conditional sale of railroad equipment in accordance with the provisions of subdivision (*d*) of paragraph (5) of clause Third; or

(*b*) A direct or collateral first mortgage lien on railroad owned and operated by a railroad corporation which meets the requirements of paragraphs (1), (2), (3) and (4) of this clause; or

(*c*) The irrevocable pledge of bonds, notes or other evidences of indebtedness which would be legal investments for savings banks if held directly, and the principal amount of bonds, notes or other evidences of indebtedness so pledged is at least equal to the principal amount of such obligations outstanding; or

(*d*) A direct or collateral first mortgage lien on a railroad owned by a corporation which leases said railroad to a railroad corporation which meets the requirements of paragraphs (1), (2), (3) and (4) of this clause, under a lease which extends at least three years beyond the maturity of such obligations and which provides for unconditional payment of interest on all funded indebtedness and for the payment or refunding of such obligations at maturity.

As used in this clause, the following terms shall have the following meanings unless the context otherwise clearly requires: —

(*a*) "Gross railway operating revenues" shall mean the total revenues received from railway operations, as shown in reports prescribed by the Interstate Commerce Commission.

(*b*) "Net railway operating income" shall be the amount so shown in reports prescribed by the Interstate Commerce Commission except that such amount shall be adjusted to include any amount deducted for federal income taxes in arriving at said net railway operating income.

(*c*) "Fixed charges" shall be the sum of the annual fixed interest on all indebtedness of the corporation outstanding at the date of investment plus the annual rental for lines operated under lease at the date of investment plus any amount of interest or rental which in the future shall or may become fixed for the remaining life of the obligation or lease at a presently determinable rate as the result of operation of provisions contained in the agreements, indentures or leases covering such payments, but interest which becomes a fixed obligation only if earned, or only upon maturity of the bonds, or only in event of issuance of additional bonds in connection with future financing, shall not be regarded as a fixed charge.

(*d*) Other terms shall have the meanings provided in clause Third.

The limitations to the amounts to be invested in railroad obligations provided in clause Third shall limit, by inclusion, amounts invested under the provisions of this clause.

G. L. (Ter. Ed.), 168, § 54, etc., further amended.

SECTION 5. Said section fifty-four is hereby further amended by striking out, in the fourth and in the twenty-eighth lines of subdivision (6) of clause Third, as so appearing, the words "five of the six" and inserting in place thereof, in each instance, the words: — six of the seven, — so that the first paragraph of said subdivision (6) will read as follows: — That unless the railroad corporation which operates the railroad or railroad equipment upon which such obligations are secured shall have earned its fixed charges at least one and one half times in six of the seven years immediately preceding the date of such investment, and in the year immediately preceding the date of such investment, such obligations shall be (*a*) equipment obligations as described in subdivision (5) (*d*), or (*b*) shall be secured by a first mortgage which is prior in lien to a junior mortgage or mortgages which secure at least one and one half

Investment in railroad bonds regulated.

times as much funded debt as is secured by all the first mortgages which are prior in lien to such junior mortgages, or (*c*) shall be secured by a first mortgage on a railroad which is operated under lease by a railroad corporation which meets the requirements of subdivisions (1), (2) and (3), which lease extends at least three years beyond the maturity of any such obligation, and provides for the payment or refunding thereof and for the unconditional payment of a rental equal to at least two and one half times the annual interest charge on all the first mortgage bonds of such lessor corporation; and no bonds shall be made eligible by provision (*b*) or (*c*) of this subdivision unless they are secured by a direct or collateral first lien on at least one third of the mileage owned, including all mileage owned beneficially, by the obligor and on at least five hundred miles of railroad, except that if the railroad corporation which operates the railroad upon which such bonds are secured shall have earned its fixed charges at least one and one quarter times in six of the seven years immediately preceding the date of such investment, and in the year immediately preceding the date of such investment, then such first mortgage need not be a lien on one third of the mileage owned directly and beneficially by the obligor but shall be a first lien on not less than one hundred miles of railroad, and the amount of debt secured by junior mortgages need not exceed, but shall be at least equal to, the amount of debt secured by first mortgages prior thereto.

SECTION 6. Said section fifty-four is hereby further amended by striking out clause Seventh, as so appearing, and inserting in place thereof the following clause: — G. L. (Ter. Ed.), 168, § 54, etc., further amended.

Seventh. In the common stock, provided there is no preferred stock outstanding, of a trust company incorporated under the laws of and doing business within this commonwealth, or in the common stock, provided there is no preferred stock outstanding, of a national banking association doing business within this commonwealth, which, in each of the five years immediately preceding the date of investment, has paid dividends in cash of not less than four per cent on its common stock without having reduced the aggregate par value thereof within such five-year period, and which, at the date of investment, has surplus at least equal to fifty per cent of its capital stock; provided, that: Investment in bank, etc., stock.

(*a*) No savings bank shall invest additional funds in stocks of such companies or associations if the cost thereof added to the amount already invested in such stocks shall exceed two thirds of the combined guaranty fund and profit and loss accounts of such bank;

(*b*) No savings bank shall invest additional funds in the stock of any one such company or association if the cost thereof added to the amount already invested in such stock shall exceed one fifteenth of the combined guaranty fund and profit and loss accounts of such bank;

(*c*) No savings bank shall purchase or accept as collateral for loans additional stock of any such company or association if the result of such purchase or acceptance would be to make its total holdings of such stock by way of investment and as collateral exceed fifteen per cent of the outstanding stock of such company, or association.

Nothing in this clause shall invalidate any holding of stock or stocks legally acquired before May first, nineteen hundred and forty-three.

A savings bank may deposit not more than two and one half per cent of its deposits in any national banking association doing business within this commonwealth or in any trust company incorporated under the laws of and doing business within this commonwealth; but such deposit shall not exceed twenty-five per cent of the capital stock and surplus fund of such association or trust company.

G. L. (Ter. Ed.), 168, § 54, etc., further amended.

SECTION 7. Said section fifty-four is hereby further amended by striking out paragraph (2) of subdivision (*e*) of clause Ninth, as most recently amended by section four of chapter one hundred and ten of the acts of nineteen hundred and forty-three, and inserting in place thereof the following paragraph: —

Notes secured by collateral.

(2) Bonds or notes authorized for investment by clause Second, Third, Third A, Fifth, Fifth A, Fifth B, Sixth or Sixth A or under subdivision (*c*) of clause Fifteenth, at no more than ninety per cent of the market value thereof at any time while such note is held by such corporation; or

G. L. (Ter. Ed.), 168, § 54, etc., further amended.

SECTION 8. Said section fifty-four is hereby further amended by striking out paragraph (3) of subdivision (*e*) of clause Ninth, as most recently amended by section twenty-six of chapter three hundred and thirty-four of the acts of nineteen hundred and thirty-three, and inserting in place thereof the following paragraph: —

Deposit books, etc., as collateral.

(3) Deposit books of depositors, or of one of two joint depositors, in savings banks and in savings departments of trust companies incorporated under the laws of and doing business within this commonwealth, and savings account books of depositors in national banking associations doing business within this commonwealth, up to the amount of said deposit accounts, and unpledged shares of co-operative banks incorporated in this commonwealth at not more than ninety per cent of their withdrawal value; or

G. L. (Ter. Ed.), 168, § 54, etc., further amended.

SECTION 9. Said section fifty-four is hereby further amended by striking out clause Twelfth, as most recently amended by section two of chapter two hundred and seventy-four of the acts of nineteen hundred and thirty-seven, and inserting in place thereof the following clause: —

Real estate acquired by foreclosure.

Twelfth. Such corporation may hold for a period of five years real estate acquired by the foreclosure of a mortgage owned by it, or by purchase at sales made under the provisions of such mortgages or upon judgments for debts due to it, or in settlements effected to secure such debts. Such corporation may sell, convey, or lease the real estate acquired by it, and notwithstanding the provisions of clause First may take a mortgage thereon from the purchaser to secure the whole or a part of the purchase price. The commissioner may, on petition of the board of investment of such corporation, and for cause, grant additional time for the holding of such real estate or of the securities mentioned in clause Thirteenth.

SECTION 10. Said section fifty-four is hereby further amended by striking out subdivision (*a*) of clause Fifteenth, as most recently amended by section nine of chapter four hundred and thirteen of the acts of nineteen hundred and forty-one, and inserting in place thereof the following subdivision: — G. L (Ter. Ed.), 168, § 54, etc., further amended.

(*a*) Annually, not later than July first, the commissioner shall prepare a list of all bonds, notes, and interest bearing obligations which are then legal investments under any provision of clauses Second, Third, Third A, Fifth, Fifth A, Fifth B, Sixth, Sixth A, paragraph (1) of subdivision (*c*) of clause Ninth, and subdivision (*c*) of clause Fifteenth. Said list shall at all times be open to public inspection and a copy thereof shall be sent to every savings bank and to every trust company having a savings department. In the preparation of any list hereunder which the commissioner is required to prepare or furnish, he may employ such expert assistance as he deems proper or may rely upon information contained in publications which he deems authoritative in reference to such matters; and he shall be in no way held responsible or liable for the omission from such list of the name of any state or political subdivision thereof, or corporation, the bonds, notes or other interest bearing obligations of which conform to this section, or of any bonds, notes or other interest bearing obligations which so conform, nor shall he be held responsible or liable for the inclusion in such list of any such names or bonds, notes or other interest bearing obligations which do not so conform. List of bonds and notes to be prepared.

SECTION 11. Said section fifty-four is hereby further amended by striking out clause Seventeenth, as appearing in the Tercentenary Edition, and inserting in place thereof the following clause: — G L. (Ter. Ed), 168, § 54, etc., further amended.

Seventeenth. This section shall not render illegal the investment in any mortgages of real estate held by such corporation on June eighth, nineteen hundred and eight. Effect of act limited.

SECTION 12. This act shall take effect on May first in the current year. *Approved April 30, 1943.* Effective date.

AN ACT RELATIVE TO THE STOCKING AND RESTOCKING OF CERTAIN INLAND WATERS IN DUKES AND NANTUCKET COUNTIES WITH FISH. *Chap.*216

Be it enacted, etc., as follows:

SECTION 1. Section fourteen of chapter one hundred and thirty-one of the General Laws, as appearing in section two of chapter five hundred and ninety-nine of the acts of nineteen hundred and forty-one, is hereby amended by G. L. (Ter Ed.), 131, § 14, etc., amended.

striking out, in the sixty-fifth and sixty-sixth lines, the words ", except in Dukes and Nantucket counties,", — so that the paragraph contained in the sixty-fifth to the seventy-third lines, inclusive, will read as follows: —

Duties and powers of director.

Cause any great pond to be stocked or restocked with such fish as he judges best suited to the waters thereof, and in every such instance he may prescribe and enforce such reasonable regulations relative to fishing in the pond or its tributaries, or both, with such penalties, not exceeding twenty dollars for each offence, as he deems for the public interest, but this paragraph shall not apply to ponds used as sources of public water supply;

G. L. (Ter. Ed.), 131, § 14, etc., further amended.

SECTION 2. Said section fourteen, as so appearing, is hereby amended by striking out, in the seventy-fourth line, the words "Except in Dukes and Nantucket counties, cause" and inserting in place thereof the word: — Cause, — so that the paragraph contained in the seventy-fourth to the eighty-sixth lines, inclusive, will read as follows: —

Same subject.

Cause any natural or artificial pond, other than a great pond, or any brook or stream, to be stocked or restocked with such fish as he judges best suited to the waters thereof; provided, that in respect to privately owned ponds such stocking shall only be with the written consent of the owner or lessee thereof, and shall not prevent such owner or lessee from drawing down or making such use of said waters for commercial or other purposes as appear to him to be advisable; and provided, further, that such stocking shall not prohibit such owner or lessee from excluding the public from such waters if and when this action appears to him necessary for the proper control and utilization thereof;

Effective date.

SECTION 3. This act shall take effect upon its passage.

Approved April 30, 1943.

---

*Chap.*217 AN ACT AUTHORIZING THE PLACING OF THE OFFICE OF CHIEF OF POLICE OF THE TOWN OF MANSFIELD UNDER THE CIVIL SERVICE LAWS.

Be it enacted, etc., as follows:

SECTION 1. The office of chief of police of the town of Mansfield shall, upon the effective date of this act, become subject to the civil service laws and rules and regulations relating to police officers in towns, and the tenure of office of any incumbent thereof shall be unlimited, subject, however, to said laws. The person holding said office on said effective date shall be subjected to a non-competitive qualifying examination by the division of civil service. If he passes said examination, he shall be certified for said office and shall be deemed to be permanently appointed thereto without being required to serve any probationary period. If he does not pass said examination, he may continue to serve in said office, but shall not be subject to said civil service laws.

SECTION 2. So much of paragraph (*i*) of section twenty

of chapter five hundred and eighty-six of the acts of nineteen hundred and twenty as is inconsistent with the provisions of this act is hereby repealed.

SECTION 3. This act shall be submitted for acceptance to the registered voters of said town at an annual or special meeting. The vote shall be taken by ballot, in answer to the following question, which shall be placed, in case of a special meeting, upon a ballot to be provided and used at said meeting, or, in case of an annual meeting, upon the official ballot to be used for the election of town officers: — "Shall an act passed by the general court in the year nineteen hundred and forty-three, entitled 'An Act authorizing the placing of the Office of Chief of Police of the Town of Mansfield under the Civil Service Laws', be accepted?" If a majority of the votes in answer to said question is in the affirmative, then this act shall thereupon take full effect, but not otherwise. *Approved April 30, 1943.*

AN ACT AUTHORIZING THE TRUSTEES OF THE PUBLIC LIBRARY OF THE CITY OF BOSTON TO PETITION IN EQUITY FOR AUTHORITY TO INVEST AND APPROPRIATE FUNDS AND PROPERTY HELD BY THEM IN ACCORDANCE WITH SUCH FINAL DECREE AS THE COURT SHALL MAKE, AND TO AUTHORIZE SAID TRUSTEES TO INVEST AND APPROPRIATE IN ACCORDANCE WITH THE COURT'S FINAL DECREE. *Chap.*218

Be it enacted, etc., as follows:

Section two of chapter one hundred and fourteen of the acts of eighteen hundred and seventy-eight, as amended by chapter one hundred and sixteen of the Special Acts of nineteen hundred and nineteen and by chapter fifty of the acts of nineteen hundred and thirty-one, is hereby further amended by adding at the end the following sentence: — But nothing herein contained shall restrict said corporation from bringing a petition in equity in the probate court or the supreme judicial court to be permitted to invest or appropriate the principal or income of funds or property held by said corporation in such manner as said court may by final decree authorize; and said corporation is hereby authorized to invest and appropriate in accordance with such decree, — so as to read as follows: — *Section 2.* Said corporation shall have authority to take and hold real and personal estate to an amount not exceeding twenty million dollars, which may be given, granted, bequeathed or devised to it, and accepted by the trustees for the benefit of the public library of the city of Boston or any branch library, or any purpose connected therewith. Money received by it shall be invested by the treasurer of the city of Boston under the direction of said corporation; and all securities belonging to said corporation shall be placed in the custody of said treasurer: *provided, always,* that both the principal and income thereof shall be invested and appropriated according to the terms of the donation, devise or bequest. But nothing herein contained shall restrict said corporation from bringing a petition in equity in the probate court or the supreme judicial court to be permitted to invest or appropriate the principal or income of funds or property held by said corporation in such manner as said court may by final decree authorize; and said corporation is hereby authorized to invest and appropriate in accordance with such decree.

Approved April 30, 1943.

---

*Chap.*219 AN ACT AMENDING THE LAW RELATIVE TO THE CO-OPERATIVE CENTRAL BANK.

Be it enacted, etc., as follows:

SECTION 1. Chapter forty-five of the acts of nineteen hundred and thirty-two is hereby amended by striking out section two and inserting in place thereof the following section: — *Section 2.* There shall be a board of twelve directors of the central bank, who shall be elected by the member banks in the manner hereinafter provided and shall be divided into three equal groups. Of the directors first elected hereunder, one group shall be elected and hold office until the annual meeting to be held in nineteen hundred and thirty-two, one group shall be elected and hold office until the annual meeting to be held in nineteen hundred and thirty-three, and one group shall be elected and hold office until the annual meeting to be held in nineteen hundred and thirty-four; and their successors, except in case of vacancies, shall be elected for terms of three years. Directors so elected to fill vacancies shall be elected for the unexpired terms. All directors shall be sworn and hold office until their successors are qualified. If a person elected does not, within thirty days thereafter, take the oath, his office shall thereupon become vacant. The directors shall fill any vacancies on the board until the next annual meeting. At all meetings of the directors seven members shall constitute a quorum, but a lesser number may adjourn from time to time. The board of directors shall from time to time adopt such rules and regulations as they may deem necessary to effect the purposes of this act. The central bank, by a vote of two thirds of the delegates of the member banks present and voting, may from time to time adopt such by-laws and amendments thereto as may be necessary to effect such purposes. Such by-laws and any amendments thereto shall not become effective until they shall have been approved by the commissioner of banks, hereinafter called the commissioner.

In the election of directors, and in voting on any other matter legally to come before a meeting, each member bank, by a delegate authorized by its board of directors, shall have one vote; provided, that such delegate shall not vote on behalf of more than one member bank. A majority of the votes so cast shall elect directors.

SECTION 2. Section five of said chapter forty-five is hereby amended by adding at the end the two following paragraphs: —

The clerk of the central bank shall call a special meeting of such bank if requested in writing so to do by twenty or more member banks. The request of each of such banks shall be signed by a duly authorized officer thereof, shall state the proposed purposes and proposed time and place of the meeting, and shall be given to said clerk at least forty-five days before the proposed time of the meeting. The call for such meeting shall state the time, place, and purpose or purposes thereof and shall be mailed to each member bank at its place of business at least thirty days before the date of the meeting. If any of the purposes of the meeting is to adopt an amendment to the by-laws such request and the call for the meeting shall contain notice of the proposed amendment and a copy thereof. Notwithstanding the foregoing, special meetings may be called by the clerk at the request of the directors if and as provided by the by-laws of the central bank.

If requests from twenty or more member banks for the adoption of an amendment to the by-laws at an annual meeting, containing a copy of the proposed amendment, are presented to said clerk on or before July fifteenth preceding such meeting, the call for such meeting shall include notice of such proposed amendment and a copy thereof.

SECTION 3. Said chapter forty-five is hereby further amended by striking out section eight and inserting in place thereof the following section: — *Section 8.* Dividends may be declared from the earnings of the central bank after the payment of all expenses and shall be distributed to member banks semi-annually, equally and ratably as determined by the board of directors of the central bank.

A surplus account may be accumulated and dividends declared therefrom in the discretion of the directors.

SECTION 4. All provisions of the by-laws of The Co-operative Central Bank in effect on the effective date of this act shall continue in force until annulled or amended in accordance with this act. *Approved April 30, 1943.*

AN ACT RELATIVE TO THE CIVIL SERVICE STATUS OF CERTAIN AGENTS OF THE BOARD OF REGISTRATION IN PHARMACY. *Chap.220*

Be it enacted, etc., as follows:

Joseph G. Turcotte and John V. O'Brien, agents of the board of registration in pharmacy appointed under section twenty-five of chapter thirteen of the General Laws, as amended, may, upon passing a qualifying examination to which they shall be subjected by the division of civil service, continue to serve in their respective positions and their tenure of office shall be unlimited, subject, however, to the civil service laws. *Approved April 30, 1943.*

Chap.221 AN ACT TO INCORPORATE GREATER BOSTON CHARITABLE TRUST, INC.

Be it enacted, etc., as follows:

SECTION 1. Charles Francis Adams, Robert P. Barry, Henry R. Guild, Maynard Hutchinson, Jacob J. Kaplan, Michael T. Kelleher, Charles F. Mills, Spencer B. Montgomery, Charles M. Rogerson, John O. Stubbs, and Raymond S. Wilkins, their associates and successors, who shall be appointed or elected as hereinafter described, are hereby made a corporation by the name of Greater Boston Charitable Trust, Inc., with all the powers and privileges set forth in all general laws now or hereinafter in force relating to charitable corporations, so far as the same are applicable.

SECTION 2. The said Greater Boston Charitable Trust, Inc., may establish one or more common trust funds for the purpose of furnishing investments to itself and to any organization which is a member of or eligible to membership in Greater Boston Community Fund, a Massachusetts charitable corporation, and the said Greater Boston Charitable Trust, Inc., or any such organization may, either as fiduciary or otherwise, invest any part or all of any of the funds which it holds for investment in interests in such common trust fund or funds; provided, that in the case of funds held as fiduciary such investment would not be inconsistent with the terms and conditions upon which such funds are held.

SECTION 3. The said Greater Boston Charitable Trust, Inc., shall have power to acquire, receive, hold in trust or otherwise, and manage all property in any amount necessary or proper for any of the objects of the said corporation, and to sell, convey, mortgage, or otherwise dispose of any property held by it.

SECTION 4. The persons named in the first section of this act shall be and hereby are constituted the first members of said corporation, and they shall hold office and have power to fill vacancies in their number until their successors shall be appointed or elected and qualified, under the by-laws to be adopted as hereinafter prescribed.

SECTION 5. Without restricting any power to make by-laws enjoyed by the said corporation under general laws, it is hereby empowered to prescribe by its by-laws the number of its members and the manner in which its membership shall be constituted and, in particular, to provide by its by-laws that persons holding designated offices in other organizations or having other specified qualifications shall become members automatically.

Approved April 30, 1943.

Chap.222

AN ACT PROVIDING IN THE EXISTING WAR EMERGENCY FOR THE PAROLE OF CERTAIN PRISONERS SENTENCED TO THE STATE PRISON.

Emergency preamble.

Whereas, The deferred operation of this act would tend to defeat its purpose which is to assist in the successful prosecution of the war, therefore it is hereby declared to be an emergency law, necessary for the immediate preservation of the public convenience.

Be it enacted, etc., as follows:

SECTION 1. If it appears to the parole board to be in the public interest and to aid in the successful prosecution of the existing state of war between the United States and certain foreign countries, said board may grant to a prisoner, other than a prisoner serving a life sentence, in the state prison or a prisoner transferred therefrom to the Massachusetts reformatory or the state prison colony who has served two and one half years of his sentence, a special permit to be at liberty during the remainder of his term of sentence, upon such terms and conditions as said board shall prescribe. A prisoner held upon two or more sentences, except those to be served concurrently, may be eligible for release under this section when he has served two and one half years of his aggregate sentences.

SECTION 2. This act shall be effective only during the continuance of the existing state of war between the United States and any foreign country.

Approved April 30, 1943.

Chap.223

AN ACT PENALIZING THE LIBEL OF GROUPS OF PERSONS BECAUSE OF RACE, COLOR OR RELIGION.

Be it enacted, etc., as follows:

G. L. (Ter. Ed.), 272, new § 98C, added.

Chapter two hundred and seventy-two of the General Laws is hereby amended by inserting after section ninety-eight B, inserted by chapter one hundred and seventy of the acts of nineteen hundred and forty-one, the following section: — *Section 98C.* Whoever publishes any false written or printed material with intent to maliciously promote hatred of any group of persons in the commonwealth because of race, color or religion shall be guilty of libel and shall be punished by a fine of not more than one thousand dollars or by imprisonment for not more than one year, or both. The defendant may prove in defense that the publication was privileged or was not malicious. Prosecutions under this section shall be instituted only by the attorney general or by the district attorney for the district in which the alleged libel was published. *Approved April 30, 1943.*

Libel of persons because of race, color, etc.

Penalty.

*Chap.*224 AN ACT TEMPORARILY INCREASING THE SALARIES OF OFFICERS AND EMPLOYEES IN THE SERVICE OF CERTAIN COUNTIES.

Emergency preamble.

Whereas, The deferred operation of this act would tend to defeat its purpose, which is to provide without delay additional income for officers and employees of certain counties in view of the increase in the cost of living due to the existence of the present state of war, therefore it is hereby declared to be an emergency law, necessary for the immediate preservation of the public convenience.

Be it enacted, etc., as follows:

SECTION 1. The salary of each person in the service of any county, except those referred to in section two, is hereby increased by an amount equal to fifteen per cent thereof; provided, that such increase shall not for full time service be less than at the rate of two hundred and forty dollars per annum nor more than at the rate of three hundred and sixty dollars per annum; and provided, further, that said minimum or said maximum, in the case of any such person serving on a part-time basis, shall be adjusted by the county personnel board to an amount which bears the same ratio to said minimum or maximum as his service bears to full time service.

SECTION 2. The salary of a justice, special justice, clerk, assistant clerk, probation officer or court officer of a district court, a probation officer of the superior court, a deputy sheriff acting as court officer, a trial justice, or a county commissioner, is hereby increased by an amount equal to fifteen per cent thereof but not more than three hundred and sixty dollars per annum.

SECTION 3. The increase of salary provided by this act shall be effective only for the period beginning July first, nineteen hundred and forty-three, and ending June thirtieth, nineteen hundred and forty-five. The temporary salary increase granted hereunder in the case of any person whose basic salary is changed during said period by promotion, step rate increase, transfer or otherwise shall subsequent to such salary change be based on his basic salary as so changed.

SECTION 4. Every officer and employee entering the service of any county during said period shall be entitled to receive the compensation of his office or position as increased by this act.

SECTION 5. The word "salary" as used in this act shall include maintenance allowances, the value of which is fixed in the manner provided by the rules and regulations established under the provisions of sections forty-eight to fifty-six, inclusive, of chapter thirty-five of the General Laws.

SECTION 6. The county personnel board is hereby directed to revise its schedules of rates and ranges to conform to the pertinent provisions of sections one and two.

SECTION 7. Said board shall administer so much of this

act as affects the salary of any person whose office or position is subject to any provision of sections forty-eight to fifty-six, inclusive, of chapter thirty-five of the General Laws, and the director of accounts shall administer so much thereof as affects the salary of any person whose office or position is not subject to said sections; provided, that nothing in this act shall be construed to limit the respective powers of said board and said director as now defined by law.

SECTION 8. No increase in salary made by this act shall, for any purpose of chapter thirty-two of the General Laws, be deemed or construed to be a portion of the regular compensation of any officer or employee now or hereafter in the service of any county.

SECTION 9. This act shall not apply to officers or employees of the county of Suffolk. *Approved May 3, 1943.*

Chap.225

AN ACT PROVIDING THAT CITIES AND TOWNS MAY APPROPRIATE MONEY FOR THE REMOVAL OF SNOW AND ICE FROM PRIVATE WAYS THEREIN OPEN TO PUBLIC USE, IF THE VOTERS THEREOF SO VOTE.

Be it enacted, etc., as follows:

G. L. (Ter. Ed.), 40, new §§ 6C and 6D, added.

Removal of snow and ice from private ways.

Appropriations for.

Chapter forty of the General Laws is hereby amended by inserting after section six B, as appearing in the Tercentenary Edition, the two following sections: — *Section 6C.* A city or town which accepts this section in the manner provided in section six D may appropriate money for the removal of snow and ice from such private ways within its limits and open to the public use as may be designated by the city council or selectmen; provided, that, for the purposes of section twenty-five of chapter eighty-four, the removal of snow or ice from such a way shall not constitute a repair of a way.

Submission to voters.

Section 6D. Section six C shall be submitted for acceptance to the registered voters of a city at a regular city election if the city council thereof so votes, and of a town at an annual town election upon petition of two hundred registered voters or of twenty per cent of the total number of registered voters, substantially in the form of the following question, which shall be placed on the official ballot used for the election of officers at such city or town election:

Shall the city (or town) vote to accept the provisions of section six C of chapter forty of the General Laws, which authorize cities and towns to appropriate money for the removal of snow and ice from private ways therein open to public use?

YES.	
NO.	

If a majority of the votes in answer to said question is in the affirmative, then said section shall thereupon take full effect in such city or town, but not otherwise.

Approved May 3, 1943.

Chap.226 AN ACT RELATING TO THE COMPENSATION OF LIFE INSURANCE AGENTS.

Be it enacted, etc., as follows:

G. L. (Ter. Ed.), 175, § 164A, etc., amended.

Chapter one hundred and seventy-five of the General Laws is hereby amended by striking out section one hundred and sixty-four A, inserted by chapter two hundred and twenty-five of the acts of nineteen hundred and thirty-eight, and inserting in place thereof the following section: — *Section 164A.* If a policy of industrial life insurance upon which premiums have been paid for three years or more lapses for non-payment of a premium and is surrendered to the company for a cash surrender value or continues in force as paid-up or extended term insurance, the company shall not charge any of its agents with a decrease for or on account of the premium on said policy nor make any deduction from his commission or salary for or on account of the lapse of said policy.

Decrease of commissions of agents prohibited in certain cases.

Nothing in this section shall prohibit a life company from contracting to pay any of its agents additional compensation for the conservation of insurance, based upon the relation of the lapse rate of premiums on one or more classes of industrial life insurance policies or combined industrial and monthly premium debit insurance policies under his supervision to the lapse rate of premiums on insurance policies of the same class or classes in the entire company; nor shall anything in this section prohibit a company, which has contracted to pay its agents in this commonwealth such additional compensation for the conservation of insurance, from also contracting with any such agent that he shall not be paid first-year commissions on any new policy issued on an application procured by him on the life of a person or a dependent sharing the home with such person who has terminated a policy issued by the company on his life or that of such a dependent not more than three months before, or who terminates such a policy within three months after, application for such new policy is made.

Approved May 3, 1943

Chap.227 AN ACT RELATIVE TO THE COMPUTATION OF THE RESERVE LIABILITY OF LIFE INSURANCE COMPANIES AND TO THE NON-FORFEITURE BENEFITS UNDER LIFE INSURANCE POLICIES.

Be it enacted, etc., as follows:

G. L. (Ter. Ed.), 175, § 9, etc., amended.

SECTION 1. Chapter one hundred and seventy-five of the General Laws is hereby amended by striking out section nine, as most recently amended by sections one and two of chapter three hundred and twenty-six of the acts of nineteen hundred and forty-one, and inserting in place thereof the following section: — *Section 9.* 1. The commissioner shall each year compute the reserve liability or net value

Computation of reserves of life companies.

on December thirty-first of the preceding year of every life company authorized to transact business in the commonwealth with respect to the policies or contracts hereinafter described in this subdivision and issued by such company prior to January first, nineteen hundred and forty-eight, in accordance with the following rules:

Acceptance of certificates of valuation of foreign companies.

First, The net value of all outstanding policies of life insurance issued before January first, nineteen hundred and one, shall be computed upon the basis of the "Combined Experience" or "Actuaries' Table" of mortality, with interest at four per cent per annum.

Second, The net value of all outstanding policies of life insurance issued after December thirty-first, nineteen hundred, shall be computed upon the basis of the "American Experience Table" of mortality, with interest at three and one half per cent per annum; but any life company may at any time elect to have the net value of such policies computed with interest at three per cent or two and one half per cent, and thereupon the net value of said policies shall be computed upon the basis of the "American Experience Table" of mortality, with interest at three per cent or two and one half per cent per annum, as the case may be, and any life company receiving premiums by weekly payments may elect to have the net value of such weekly payment business or any portion thereof computed upon any table showing a higher rate of mortality approved by the commissioner.

Third, The net value of all outstanding total and permanent disability provisions incorporated in, or supplementary to, policies or contracts shall be computed on the basis of "Hunter's Disability Table", or any similar table approved by the commissioner, with interest not exceeding three and one half per cent per annum; provided, that in no case shall said net value be less than one half of the net annual premium computed on such table for the disability benefit. The commissioner may accept a certificate of valuation from the company for the reserve liability with respect to its total and permanent disability provisions if he is satisfied by the use of general averages and percentages that such reserve has been computed in accordance with the foregoing rule.

Fourth, The net value of all outstanding annuity contracts and of all contracts issued as pure endowments shall be computed on the basis of "McClintock's Tables of Mortality among Annuitants" or on such higher table as the commissioner may prescribe, with interest at not more than four per cent per annum; provided, that annuities issued prior to January first, nineteen hundred and seven, and annuities deferred ten or more years and written in connection with life, endowment or term insurance shall be valued on the same mortality table from which the consideration or premiums were computed.

Fifth, The net value of all outstanding group life policies

written as yearly renewable term insurance shall be computed on a basis not lower than the "American Men Mortality Table", with interest at not more than three and one half per cent per annum.

The net value of any class or classes of policies or contracts described in this subdivision may be computed, at the option of the company, on any basis which produces aggregate reserves for such class or classes greater than those computed in accordance with the foregoing rules.

2. The commissioner shall each year compute the reserve liability or net value on December thirty-first of the preceding year of every life company authorized to transact business in the commonwealth with respect to the policies or contracts hereinafter described in this subdivision and issued by such company on and after January first, nineteen hundred and forty-eight, so that such reserve liability shall be at least equal to the amount computed in accordance with the minimum standard prescribed in this subdivision.

The minimum standard of valuation shall be the Commissioners Reserve Valuation Method, as defined in subdivision 3, interest at three and one half per cent per annum, and the tables of mortality hereinafter specified.

First, The "Commissioners 1941 Standard Ordinary Mortality Table" shall be used for all outstanding ordinary policies of life insurance issued on the standard basis, excluding any total and permanent disability and accidental death benefits.

Second, The "1941 Standard Industrial Mortality Table" shall be used for all outstanding industrial life insurance policies issued on the standard basis, excluding any total and permanent disability and accidental death benefits.

Third, The "1937 Standard Annuity Mortality Table" shall be used for all outstanding annuity contracts and for all contracts issued as pure endowments, excluding any total and permanent disability benefits.

Fourth, The "Class (3) Disability Table (1926)" shall be used for all outstanding total and permanent disability provisions incorporated in, or supplementary to, ordinary policies or contracts, which table, for active lives, shall be combined with a mortality table permitted for computing the reserves for life insurance policies. The commissioner may accept a certificate of valuation from a company for the reserve liability with respect to its total and permanent disability provisions if he is satisfied by the use of general averages and percentages that such reserve has been computed in accordance with this subdivision.

Fifth, The "Inter-Company Double Indemnity Mortality Table" shall be used for all outstanding accidental death benefit provisions incorporated in, or supplementary to, all policies, which table shall be combined with a mortality table permitted for computing the reserves for life insurance policies. The commissioner may accept a certificate of valuation from a company for the reserve liability with respect to such provisions, as provided in paragraph Fourth.

Sixth, Such tables as the commissioner shall approve shall be used for all outstanding group life policies, policies of life insurance issued on the substandard basis and any kind of insurance, annuity, or pure endowment benefits for the valuation of which specific provision is not made in this subdivision.

3. The net value of the life insurance and endowment benefits of policies, referred to in subdivision 2, providing for a uniform amount of insurance and requiring the payment of uniform premiums shall be the excess, if any, of the present value, at the date of valuation, of such future guaranteed benefits provided for by such policies, over the then present value of any future modified net premiums therefor. The modified net premiums for any such policy shall be such uniform percentage of the respective contract premiums for such benefits that the present value, at the date of issue of the policy, of all such modified net premiums shall be equal to the sum of the then present value of such benefits provided for by the policy and the excess of (*a*) a net level annual premium equal to the present value, at the date of issue, of such benefits provided for after the first policy year, divided by the present value, at the date of issue, of an annuity of one per annum payable on the first and each subsequent anniversary of such policy on which a premium falls due; provided, that such net level annual premium shall not exceed the net level annual premium on the nineteen year premium whole life plan for insurance of the same amount at an age one year higher than the age at issue of such policy, over (*b*) a net one year term premium for such benefits provided for in the first policy year.

The net value of (*a*) policies of life insurance providing for a varying amount of insurance or requiring the payment of varying premiums, (*b*) annuity and pure endowment contracts, (*c*) provisions for total and permanent disability or for accidental death benefits in, or supplementary to, all policies and contracts, and (*d*) provisions for any other insurance benefits shall be computed by a method consistent with the principles of the first paragraph of this subdivision 3.

The method of valuation set forth in this subdivision shall be known as the Commissioners Reserve Valuation Method.

4. The aggregate net value of all life insurance policies, excluding total and permanent disability and accidental death benefits, described in subdivision 2, shall in no case be less than the aggregate net value computed in accordance with the Commissioners Reserve Valuation Method, as defined in subdivision 3, and the mortality table or tables and the rate or rates of interest used in computing the nonforfeiture benefits under such policies.

The net value of any class or classes of policies or contracts described in subdivision 2, as established by the commissioner, may be computed, at the option of the company, on any basis which produces aggregate reserves for such class or classes greater than those computed according to the minimum standard prescribed by subdivision 2; provided, that the rate or rates of interest used shall not be higher than the corresponding rate or rates used in computing any nonforfeiture benefits thereunder; and provided, further, that the net value of life insurance policies issued on the participating basis shall not be computed with a rate of interest lower than that used in computing the nonforfeiture benefits thereunder except with the approval of the commissioner, with whom the company shall file, when the said rates differ by more than one half of one per cent, a plan providing for such equitable increases, if any, in the nonforfeiture benefits in such policies as the commissioner shall approve.

Any company which at any time shall have adopted any standard of valuation with respect to any class or classes of policies or contracts described in subdivision 2 and producing therefor greater aggregate reserves than those computed according to the minimum standard provided for in said subdivision, may adopt, with the approval of the commissioner, any lower standard of valuation for such policies not lower than the aforesaid minimum standard.

5. The commissioner, in every case in which the gross premium charged on any life policy or annuity or pure endowment contract, described in this section, is less than the net premium therefor according to the mortality table, the rate of interest, and the method used in computing the net value thereof, shall compute a deficiency reserve on such policy or contract in addition to any other reserve computed in accordance with this section. Such deficiency reserve shall be the present value, computed according to said basis, of an annuity of the difference between such net premium and the said gross premium, running for the remainder of the premium-paying period of such policy or contract.

6. When the commissioner is satisfied that the risks which a company has assumed under policies or contracts referred to in subdivision 1 cannot be properly measured by the mortality tables specified in said subdivision, he may compute such additional reserve as in his judgment is warranted by the extra hazard assumed, and he may further in his discretion prescribe such table or tables of mortality as he may deem necessary properly to measure such additional risks with interest at not greater than three and one half per cent per annum, for the computation of the net value of any special class or classes of risks.

7. The commissioner in computing the reserve liability under this section may use group methods and approximate averages for fractions of a year, or other reasonable approximations.

8. The aggregate net value computed in accordance with the requirements of this section shall be deemed the reserve liability of the company, to provide for which it shall hold funds of an amount equal thereto above all its other liabilities.

9. The commissioner may, in place of the computation of the reserve liability of a foreign life company required by this section, accept the certificate of valuation of the official having supervision over insurance companies in the state or other jurisdiction where the company is incorporated; provided, that such valuation is made in accordance with the requirements of this section or produces an aggregate net value at least as great as if made in accordance therewith; and provided, further, that such official is authorized to accept a similar certificate of the reserve liability of a domestic life company issued by the commissioner.

10. The commissioner shall issue, upon payment of the fee prescribed by section fourteen, a certificate in such form as he may prescribe, setting forth the amount of the reserve liability of a company computed by him, and specifying the mortality table or tables, the rate or rates of interest, and the methods, whether the net level premium or other method, used in the computation of said amount.

11. All policies of life insurance issued before July first, eighteen hundred and ninety-nine, by corporations formerly transacting a life insurance business on the assessment plan under chapter four hundred and twenty-one of the acts of eighteen hundred and ninety and acts in amendment thereof, and now having authority to do business in the commonwealth under this chapter, which policies are in force on December thirty-first of any year, and which contain a provision for a payment other than the premium stipulated therein, and under which the duration of the premium payment is the same as the duration of the contract, except in endowment policies, shall be valued and shall have a reserve maintained thereon on the basis of renewable term insurance as fixed by attained age in accordance with this chapter. To the reserve liability determined as above the commissioner shall add the determinate contract reserve under any other policies issued by said corporations before said July first and remaining in force on December thirty-first of any year, and in the absence of such contract reserve shall value them as contracts providing similar benefits are to be valued under this chapter. But under no policy shall a greater aggregate reserve liability be charged than is otherwise required by this section. All policies of life insurance issued by any such corporation subsequent to July first, eighteen hundred and ninety-nine, including those which contain a provision for a payment other than the premiums specified therein, shall be valued and a reserve maintained thereon according to this section; but all such policies issued by said corporations prior to January first, nineteen hundred and six, shall be valued taking the first year as one year term insurance.

G. L. (Ter. Ed.), 175, § 14, etc., amended.

SECTION 2. Section fourteen of said chapter one hundred and seventy-five, as most recently amended by chapter fifty-four of the acts of nineteen hundred and forty-three, is hereby further amended by striking out the seventeenth paragraph and inserting in place thereof the following: —

Charges and fees.

For each certificate of the valuation of life policies or annuity contracts, or both, of any life company issued under section nine and for each certificate of the examination, condition or qualification of a company, two dollars.

G. L. (Ter. Ed.), 175, § 144, etc., amended.

SECTION 3. Said chapter one hundred and seventy-five is hereby further amended by striking out section one hundred and forty-four, as most recently amended by section one of chapter two hundred and nine of the acts of nineteen hundred and thirty-eight, and inserting in place thereof the following section: — *Section 144.* 1. In the event of default in the payment of any premium on any policy of life insurance issued or delivered in the commonwealth by any life company, the holder thereof may elect by a writing filed with the company at its home office within sixty days after the due date of the defaulted premium and prior to the death of the insured, to (*a*) surrender the policy and receive its value in cash, provided that, except as provided in section one hundred and forty-six, premiums have been paid for at least three full years, or (*b*) take a specified paid-up nonforfeiture benefit effective from the due date of the premium in default.

Cash surrender value of certain policies upon default in payment of premiums, etc.

The policy shall provide that a specified paid-up nonforfeiture benefit shall become effective as specified in the policy unless the holder thereof elects another available option prior to the death of the insured and not later than sixty days after the due date of the premium in default.

2. Any cash surrender value available under the policy in the case of a default in the payment of a premium due on any anniversary of the policy shall be an amount not less than the excess, if any, of the present value on such anniversary of the future guaranteed benefits which would have been payable if there had been no default, including any existing paid-up additions, over the sum of (*a*) the then present value of the adjusted premiums, as defined in subdivision 5, corresponding to the premiums which would have fallen due on and after such anniversary, and (*b*) the amount of any existing indebtedness to the company on the policy or secured thereby.

3. Any paid-up nonforfeiture benefit available under the policy upon default in the payment of a premium due on any policy anniversary shall be such that its present value as of such anniversary shall be at least equal to the cash surrender value then provided for by the policy or, if none is provided for, that cash surrender value which would have been required by this section in the absence of the provision therein that premiums shall have been paid for at least a specified period.

4. Any cash surrender value or other nonforfeiture benefit

available upon default in the payment of a premium due at any time other than on an anniversary of the policy shall be consistent with the values prescribed in, and subject to the provisions of, subdivision 2, with allowance for the lapse of time and the payment of fractional premiums beyond the last preceding anniversary.

The cash surrender value of any paid-up additions, other than paid-up term additions, shall be not less than the dividends used to purchase them.

Any paid-up nonforfeiture benefit under any policy on which the premiums, except as provided in section one hundred and forty-six, were paid for at least three full years, and every policy which by its terms has become fully paid-up, shall have a cash surrender value payable upon written application and surrender of the policy to the company at its home office within thirty days after any anniversary of the policy. Any cash surrender value available under any paid-up insurance or under any paid-up nonforfeiture benefit, whether or not such cash surrender value is required by this paragraph, shall be an amount not less than the present value on said anniversary of the future guaranteed benefits provided for by the policy, including any paid-up additions thereto, less any indebtedness to the company on the policy or secured thereby.

5. The term "adjusted premiums," as used in this section, shall mean such uniform percentage of the respective premiums specified in the policy for each policy year that the present value, at the date of issue of the policy, of all such adjusted premiums shall be equal to the sum of (1) the then present value of the future guaranteed benefits provided for by the policy; (2) two per cent of the amount of insurance, if the insurance be uniform in amount, or of the equivalent uniform amount, as hereinafter defined, if the amount of insurance varies with duration of the policy; (3) forty per cent of the adjusted premium for the first policy year; (4) twenty-five per cent of either the adjusted premium for the first policy year or the adjusted premium for a whole life policy of the same uniform or equivalent uniform amount with uniform premiums for the whole of life issued at the same age for the same amount of insurance, whichever is less; provided, that in applying the percentages specified in (3) and (4) above, no adjusted premium shall be deemed to exceed four per cent of the amount of insurance or level amount equivalent thereto. The adjusted premiums shall be computed on an annual basis. The date of issue of a policy for the purpose of this section shall be the date as of which the rated age of the insured is determined.

The term "equivalent uniform amount," as used in this section, shall be deemed to be the level amount of insurance provided by an otherwise similar policy, containing the same endowment benefit or benefits, if any, issued at the same age and for the same term, the amount of which does not vary with duration and the benefits under which have the same present value at the inception of the insurance as the benefits under the policy.

6. All adjusted premiums and present values referred to in this section, except as provided in section one hundred and forty-six, shall be computed on the basis of the "Commissioners 1941 Standard Ordinary Mortality Table", and the rate of interest, not exceeding three and one half per cent per annum, specified in the policy for the computation of the cash surrender values and other nonforfeiture benefits; provided, that in computing the present value of any extended term insurance with accompanying pure endowment, if any, the rates of mortality assumed may be not more than one hundred and thirty per cent of the rates according to the applicable table of mortality; and provided, further, that in the case of any policy issued on a substandard basis, any such adjusted premiums and present values may be computed on such other table of mortality as the company may specify with the approval of the commissioner.

All values referred to in this section may be computed on the assumption that any death benefit is payable at the end of the policy year in which death occurs.

7. Any additional benefits payable (*a*) under accidental death or total and permanent disability benefit provisions incorporated in, or supplementary to, a policy of life insurance, or (*b*) as reversionary annuity or deferred reversionary annuity benefits under any policy of life insurance, or (*c*) as decreasing term insurance benefits provided by a rider or a supplemental policy provision, to which provision this section would not apply if it were evidenced by a separate policy, and (*d*) any other benefits additional to life insurance or endowment benefits, and premiums for any such additional benefits, hereinbefore described, shall be disregarded in computing adjusted premiums and cash surrender values and other nonforfeiture benefits under this section, and no such additional benefit shall be required to be granted in connection with any nonforfeiture benefits.

8. Except as provided in subdivision 9, this section shall not apply to contracts of reinsurance, policies of group life insurance, or annuity or pure endowment contracts of any kind with or without return of premiums or premiums and interest, whether simple or compound, or to survivorship annuity contracts; nor shall this section apply to any term policy of uniform amount, or any renewal thereof, of fifteen years or less expiring before age sixty-six for which uniform premiums are payable during its entire term, nor to any term policy providing for a decreasing amount of insurance on which each adjusted premium, computed as provided in this section, is less than the adjusted premium, so computed, on such fifteen year term policy issued at the same age and for the same initial amount of insurance.

9. Every deferred annuity contract, other than a single premium contract, issued and delivered in the commonwealth by a domestic life company, shall provide that, in

the event of the nonpayment of any premium after three full years' premiums have been paid, the annuity shall, without any further act or stipulation, be converted into a paid-up annuity for such proportion of the original annuity as the number of completed years' premiums paid bears to the total number of premiums required under the contract.

10. Nothing in this section shall be construed to prohibit the inclusion of a provision in a policy that any cash surrender value shall be payable with the written assent of the person to whom the policy is payable.

G. L. (Ter. Ed.), 175, § 146, amended.

SECTION 4. Said chapter one hundred and seventy-five is hereby further amended by striking out section one hundred and forty-six, as appearing in the Tercentenary Edition, and inserting in place thereof the following section: — *Section 146*. The provisions of section one hundred and forty-four shall, except as hereinafter provided, apply to any policy of industrial life insurance issued or delivered in the commonwealth by any life company.

Cash surrender value of industrial life policies, etc.

The provisions of said section one hundred and forty-four relative to cash surrender values shall be applicable to industrial life insurance policies only after the premiums thereon have been paid for five full years.

All adjusted premiums for and the present values of any such policy issued on a standard basis shall be computed on the basis of the "1941 Standard Industrial Mortality Table."

G. L. (Ter. Ed.), 175, § 126, amended.

SECTION 5. Section one hundred and twenty-six of said chapter one hundred and seventy-five, as so appearing, is hereby amended by striking out, in the tenth line, the words "the preceding section" and inserting in place thereof the words: — section one hundred and twenty-five, — and by striking out, in the twelfth line, the word "forty-eight," and inserting in place thereof the word: — forty-six, — so as to read as follows: — *Section 126*. Every policy of life or endowment insurance made payable to or for the benefit of a married woman, or after its issue assigned, transferred or in any way made payable to a married woman, or to any person in trust for her or for her benefit, whether procured by herself, her husband or by any other person, and whether the assignment or transfer is made by her husband or by any other person, and whether or not the right to change the named beneficiary is reserved by or permitted to the person effecting such insurance, shall enure to her separate use and benefit, and to that of her children, subject to the provisions of section one hundred and twenty-five relative to premiums paid in fraud of creditors and to sections one hundred and forty-four to one hundred and forty-six, inclusive. No court, and no trustee or assignee for the benefit of creditors, shall elect for the person effecting such insurance to exercise such right to change the named beneficiary.

Policy payable to married woman enures to her benefit.

G. L. (Ter. Ed.), 175, § 132, etc., amended.

SECTION 6. Section one hundred and thirty-two of said chapter one hundred and seventy-five, as amended by section one of chapter one hundred and one of the acts of nineteen hundred and thirty-three, is hereby further amended by striking out in the thirteenth and fourteenth lines of the first paragraph the words "policies of industrial insurance, on which the premiums are payable monthly or oftener" and inserting in place thereof the words: — as hereinafter provided, — so that said first paragraph will read as follows: —

Approval of form of life, annuity, etc., policies.

No policy of life or endowment insurance and no annuity, survivorship annuity or pure endowment contract shall be issued or delivered in the commonwealth until a copy of the form thereof has been on file for thirty days with the commissioner, unless before the expiration of said thirty days he shall have approved the form of the policy or contract in writing; nor if the commissioner notifies the company in writing, within said thirty days, that in his opinion the form of the policy or contract does not comply with the laws of the commonwealth, specifying his reasons therefor, provided that such action of the commissioner shall be subject to review by the supreme judicial court; nor shall any such policy or contract, except as hereinafter provided, and except annuity or pure endowment contracts, whether or not they embody an agreement to refund to the estate of the holder upon his death or to a specified payee any sum not exceeding the premiums paid thereon with compound interest, and except survivorship annuity contracts, be so issued or delivered unless it contains in substance the following:, — and by adding at the end the four following paragraphs: —

None of the foregoing provisions, except provisions numbered 6, 8 and 9, shall be required to be contained in industrial life insurance policies, but such portions of said provisions numbered 8 and 9 as relate to loans and loan values shall not be required to be contained therein.

Any of the foregoing provisions or portions thereof not applicable to single premium or non-participating or term policies shall to that extent not be incorporated therein.

This section shall not apply to policies of group life insurance issued or delivered in the commonwealth after June thirtieth, nineteen hundred and eighteen.

A policy shall be deemed to contain any such provision in substance when in the opinion of the commissioner the provision is stated in terms more favorable to the insured or his beneficiary than are herein set forth.

G. L. (Ter. Ed.), 175, § 132, etc., further amended.

SECTION 7. Said section one hundred and thirty-two, as amended by section one of said chapter one hundred and one of the acts of nineteen hundred and thirty-three, is hereby further amended by striking out provisions numbered 6, 7, 8 and 9 and inserting in place thereof the following provisions: —

Contents and approval of certain policies

6. A provision specifying the nonforfeiture benefits to which the holder of the policy is entitled under section one hundred and forty-four, together with a provision stating the mortality table and interest rate used in computing said benefits, the manner in which the said benefits are altered by the existence of any paid-up additions to the

policy or any indebtedness to the company on the policy or secured thereby, and the method used in computing such of said benefits as are not shown in the table required by provision eight. 7. A provision that the holder of the policy shall be entitled to a loan thereon from the company, as provided in and subject to the provisions of section one hundred and forty-two. 8. A table showing in figures the loan values, if any, and the amounts of the cash surrender values and the paid-up nonforfeiture benefits, if any, available under the policy on each anniversary thereof during the first twenty years of the policy. 9. A provision that the company may defer the granting of any loan other than to pay premiums on policies in the company, and the payment of any cash surrender value, for six months from the date of the written application, in the case of a loan, and from the date of the written election thereof with surrender of the policy, in the case of a cash surrender value.

SECTION 8. Said chapter one hundred and seventy-five is hereby further amended by striking out section one hundred and forty-two, as appearing in the Tercentenary Edition, and inserting in place thereof the following section: — *Section 142.* After premiums have been paid for at least three full years on any policy of life insurance issued or delivered in the commonwealth by any life company, the holder thereof, upon written application therefor to the company at its home office and upon an assignment of the policy to the company, in a form satisfactory to it, shall be entitled to a loan from the company of a sum not exceeding its loan value, on the sole security of the policy, with interest at a rate not exceeding six per cent per annum compounded annually or, at the option of the company, compounded semiannually. The loan value shall be an amount which, together with interest as aforesaid to the end of the current policy year, shall equal the cash surrender value available at the end of the said policy year under the policy, including the cash surrender value of any existing paid-up additions thereto, if the policy is then free from indebtedness. The company shall deduct from such loan value any existing indebtedness, including accrued interest thereon, and may also deduct any unpaid portion of the premium for the then current policy year. Failure to repay any loan under the policy or to pay interest thereon shall not avoid the policy until the total indebtedness, including accrued interest thereon, is equal to or exceeds the loan value, nor until thirty days after notice has been mailed by the company to the last known address of the holder. The affidavit of any officer, clerk or agent of the company or of any one authorized to mail such notice, that the notice required by this section has been duly mailed by the company, shall be prima facie evidence that such notice was duly given. Nothing in this section shall require any company to make a loan upon any policy for less than twenty-five dollars.

G. L. (Ter. Ed.), 175, § 142, amended.

Loans on policies.

This section shall not apply to term policies, nor to those in force as extended term insurance, nor to industrial life insurance policies.

G. L. (Ter. Ed.), 175, § 143, amended.

SECTION 9. Section one hundred and forty-three of said chapter one hundred and seventy-five is hereby further amended by striking out section one hundred and forty-three, as so appearing, and inserting in place thereof the following section: — *Section 143.* All policies of life insurance and deferred annuity contracts shall be subject to the laws limiting forfeiture applicable and in force at the date of their issue.

Policies subject to laws limiting forfeiture, etc.

G. L. (Ter. Ed.), 175, §§ 147, 147A and 147B, repealed.

SECTION 10. Section one hundred and forty-seven of said chapter one hundred and seventy-five, as amended, section one hundred and forty-seven A of said chapter one hundred and seventy-five, as appearing in the Tercentenary Edition, and section one hundred and forty-seven B of said chapter one hundred and seventy-five, inserted by chapter two hundred and thirty-two of the acts of nineteen hundred and thirty-five, are hereby repealed.

G. L. (Ter. Ed.), 175, § 1, etc., amended.

SECTION 11. Section one of said chapter one hundred and seventy-five, as amended, is hereby further amended by inserting after the paragraph defining "Foreign company" the following paragraph:—

"Industrial life insurance policy" defined.

"Industrial life insurance policy" or "policy of industrial life insurance", a policy of life insurance (*a*) the premiums on which are payable weekly, or (*b*) the premiums on which are payable monthly or oftener, but less often than weekly, and the face amount of insurance of which is less than one thousand dollars and on the face of which the words "industrial policy" are plainly printed.

G. L. (Ter. Ed.), 175, § 140, etc., amended.

SECTION 12. Section one hundred and forty of said chapter one hundred and seventy-five, as amended by section two of chapter one hundred and one of the acts of nineteen hundred and thirty-three, is hereby further amended by striking out the second paragraph and inserting in place thereof the following paragraph: —

Annual dividends, etc.

On industrial life insurance policies the annual surplus distribution shall begin not later than the end of the fifth policy year, and be applied to the payment of any premiums, or at the option of the holder of the policy be made in cash, but such distribution shall not be made contingent upon the payment of future premiums.

Effective date and application of act.

SECTION 13. The provisions of this act shall become fully effective on January first, nineteen hundred and forty-eight, and all policies of life insurance and all annuity and pure endowment contracts issued or delivered in the commonwealth on and after said date by any life insurance company authorized to transact business therein shall conform and be subject to said provisions.

Anything in this act to the contrary notwithstanding, any such life insurance company may file with the commissioner of insurance a written notice of its election to comply with the provisions of this act on and after a date specified in such notice occurring before January first, nineteen hundred and forty-eight, and upon such specified date the provisions of this act shall become operative with respect to the policies and contracts issued on or after such specified date by such company. The reserve liability of such company with respect to all policies and contracts issued by it on and after such specified date shall be computed by said commissioner in accordance with and subject to the provisions of section nine of chapter one hundred and seventy-five of the General Laws, as amended by section one of this act, which are applicable to the computation of the reserve liability with respect to policies and contracts issued on and after January first, nineteen hundred and forty-eight.

Anything in this act to the contrary notwithstanding, all policies of life insurance and all annuity and pure endowment contracts issued or delivered in the commonwealth by any life insurance company prior to the date specified in such a notice, if one is filed by it, otherwise prior to January first, nineteen hundred and forty-eight, shall conform and be subject to all applicable provisions of said chapter one hundred and seventy-five, as in force immediately prior to the effective date of this act.

This section shall not apply to savings and insurance banks, as defined in section one of chapter one hundred and seventy-eight of the General Laws, nor to policies or contracts issued by them, nor shall the words "life insurance company" as used in this section be taken to include any such bank.

Section 14. Sections one to twelve, inclusive, of this act shall not apply to savings and insurance banks, as defined in section one of chapter one hundred and seventy-eight of the General Laws, nor to policies or contracts issued by them, unless and until the General Insurance Guaranty Fund, a body corporate existing under chapter twenty-six of the General Laws, shall have filed with the commissioner of insurance a written notice of its election that such banks shall comply with said sections on and after a specified date, and, if such written notice is so filed, then upon such specified date the provisions of said sections shall become operative with respect to such banks and the policies and contracts thereafter issued by them, notwithstanding said chapter one hundred and seventy-eight. Anything in this act to the contrary notwithstanding, all policies of life insurance and all annuity and pure endowment contracts issued by such banks, except those issued after the date specified in such a notice if one is so filed, shall conform to and be subject to all the provisions of said chapter one hundred and seventy-eight and, so far as made applicable by said chapter, to the provisions of chapter one hundred and seventy-five of the General Laws, as in force immediately prior to the effective date of this act. *Approved May 5, 1943.*

Exceptions, etc.

Chap.228 AN ACT MAKING CERTIFICATES OF COPIES OF RECORDS IN THE OFFICE OF THE STATE SECRETARY RELATING TO BIRTHS, MARRIAGES AND DEATHS ADMISSIBLE IN EVIDENCE.

Be it enacted, etc., as follows:

G. L. (Ter. Ed.), 46, § 19, amended.

SECTION 1. Chapter forty-six of the General Laws is hereby amended by striking out section nineteen, as appearing in the Tercentenary Edition, and inserting in place thereof the following section: — *Section 19.* The record of the town clerk relative to a birth, marriage or death shall be prima facie evidence of the facts recorded. A certificate of such a record, signed by the town clerk or assistant clerk, or a certificate of the copy of the record relative to a birth, marriage or death required to be kept in the state secretary's office, signed by said state secretary or one of his deputies, shall be admissible as evidence of such record.

Clerk's and state secretary's record to be prima facie evidence.

Effective date.

SECTION 2. This act shall take effect on October first in the current year. *Approved May 5, 1943.*

Chap.229 AN ACT RELATIVE TO THE TIME FOR FILING CERTAIN NOMINATION STATEMENTS, PETITIONS OR OTHER PAPERS BY CANDIDATES TO BE VOTED FOR AT PRELIMINARY ELECTIONS IN CITIES, AND RELATIVE TO THE CERTIFICATION OF THE NAMES OF THE SIGNERS OF SUCH PETITIONS OR OTHER PAPERS.

Be it enacted, etc., as follows:

G. L. (Ter. Ed.), 43, § 44C, etc., amended.

SECTION 1. The first paragraph of section forty-four C of chapter forty-three of the General Laws, as most recently amended by chapter one hundred and forty-seven of the acts of nineteen hundred and thirty-seven, is hereby further amended by striking out, in the sixth and seventh lines, the words "at least twenty days prior to such preliminary election" and inserting in place thereof the words: — within the time prescribed by section ten of chapter fifty-three in the case of preliminary elections in cities, — so as to read as follows: — Any person who is qualified to vote for a candidate for any elective municipal office and who is a candidate for nomination thereto, shall be entitled to have his name as such candidate printed on the official ballot to be used at a preliminary election; provided, that within the time prescribed by section ten of chapter fifty-three in the case of preliminary elections in cities he shall file with the city clerk a statement in writing of his candidacy, and with it the petition of at least fifty voters, qualified to vote for a candidate for the said office. Said statement and petition shall be in substantially the following form: —

Candidates for nomination, eligibility.

Statement and petition.

G. L. (Ter. Ed.), 53, new § 7A, added.

SECTION 2. Chapter fifty-three of the General Laws is hereby amended by inserting after section seven, as amended, the following section: — *Section 7A.* Except where otherwise provided by law, every nomination petition

Candidates for nomination for city office, etc.

or other like paper of a candidate for a city office in a city wherein preliminary elections for the nomination of candidates for such office are held shall be submitted, on or before five o'clock in the afternoon of the seventh day preceding the day on which it must be filed, to the registrars of the city. In each case the registrars shall check each name to be certified by them on the nomination petition or other like paper and shall forthwith certify thereon the number of signatures so checked which are names of voters both in the city and in the district for which the nomination is made, and only names so checked shall be deemed to be names of qualified voters for the purposes of nomination. The registrars need not certify a greater number of names than are required to make a nomination, increased by one fifth thereof. Names not certified in the first instance shall not thereafter be certified on the same nomination petitions or other like papers.

G. L. (Ter Ed.), 53, § 10, etc., amended.

Section 3. The second paragraph of section ten of said chapter fifty-three, as most recently amended by section four of chapter four hundred and seventy-two of the acts of nineteen hundred and forty-one, is hereby further amended by adding at the end the following sentence: — In any city where preliminary elections for the nomination of candidates for a city office are held, nomination petitions or other like papers required to be filed by such candidates shall be filed on or before the twenty-first day preceding the day of the preliminary election, notwithstanding any contrary provision in any special law, — so as to read as follows: —

Time for filing certificates of nomination and nomination papers.

In any city which does not accept section one hundred and three A of chapter fifty-four, certificates of nomination for city offices and nomination papers shall be filed on or before the twenty-first day preceding the day of the election, except as otherwise provided in any special law affecting such city. In any city, except Boston, which accepts said section one hundred and three A, certificates of nomination and nomination papers for any regular city election shall be filed on or before the twenty-eighth day preceding such city election. In any such city, except Boston, the time for presenting nomination papers for certification to the registrars of voters, and for certifying the same, shall be governed by section seven of this chapter, notwithstanding any contrary provision in any special law. In any city where primaries are held, under authority of general or special law, for the nomination of candidates for city offices, certificates of nomination and nomination papers shall be filed not later than the last day fixed for the filing of nomination papers for such primaries. In any city where preliminary elections for the nomination of candidates for a city office are held, nomination petitions or other like papers required to be filed by such candidates shall be filed on or before the twenty-first day preceding the day of the preliminary election, notwithstanding any contrary provision in any special law. *Approved May 5, 1943.*

Chap.230 AN ACT RELATIVE TO THE APPOINTMENT OF ELECTION OFFICERS IN CITIES.

Be it enacted, etc., as follows:

G. L. (Ter. Ed.), 54, § 11B, etc., amended.

List of persons desiring appointment to be furnished.

Chapter fifty-four of the General Laws is hereby amended by striking out section eleven B, inserted by section two of chapter four hundred and thirty-two of the acts of nineteen hundred and forty-one, and inserting in place thereof the following section: — *Section 11B.* The chairman of the city committee of each political party entitled to representation in the appointment of election officers may, not later than June first in each year, file with the registrars lists of enrolled members of such party who desire appointment as election officers as submitted to him by the several ward committees. Upon the filing of such lists the registrars shall forthwith proceed to the consideration thereof and shall, on or before June thirtieth, submit to the mayor or other appointing authority the names of persons whose names appear on the lists, who in their opinion are qualified to act as election officers. The lists submitted by the several ward committees shall contain not more than eight names for each office to be filled. Supplemental lists for any election district as submitted by the several ward committees therein may be filed by the said chairman at any time before the appointments for such district are made, for the purpose of filling vacancies which may occur in the original lists. No person shall be appointed as an election officer until he is found qualified to act as such as herein provided. Appointments shall be made from the original list before any names are taken from any supplemental list.

If, upon the expiration of fifteen days after notice given in writing prior to June fifteenth in any year by the mayor or other appointing authority to the chairman of any political committee by whom lists are to be filed hereunder, such chairman shall not have filed original or supplemental lists, the mayor or other appointing authority may appoint as election officers enrolled members of the party who, in the opinion of the mayor or other appointing authority, are qualified to act as such.

The registrars may, if they deem it necessary, conduct examinations of persons whose names appear on the lists filed hereunder. Five days' notice shall be given of any such examination. The chairman of each city committee may appear and be heard either in person or by counsel, during the conduct of such examinations.

Approved May 5, 1943.

AN ACT SUBJECTING TO THE CIVIL SERVICE LAWS THE OFFICES AND POSITIONS OF THE MUNICIPAL EMPLOYMENT BUREAU OF THE CITY OF BOSTON. *Chap.231*

Be it enacted, etc., as follows:

SECTION 1. The offices and positions of the municipal employment bureau of the city of Boston shall, upon the effective date of this act, become subject to the civil service laws and the rules and regulations thereunder, and the terms of office of any incumbents of said offices and positions shall be unlimited, subject to said laws. The persons holding said offices and positions on said effective date shall be subjected to a non-competitive qualifying examination by the division of civil service, and those passing said examination shall be certified for their respective offices and positions and shall be deemed to be permanently appointed thereto without being required to serve any probationary period.

SECTION 2. This act shall take effect upon its passage.

Approved May 5, 1943.

AN ACT TO PERMIT THE ADMISSION IN EVIDENCE OF DECLARATIONS OF DECEASED PERSONS MADE AFTER THE COMMENCEMENT OF ACTIONS AND OTHER CIVIL JUDICIAL PROCEEDINGS. *Chap.232*

Be it enacted, etc., as follows:

G. L. (Ter. Ed.), 233, § 65, etc., amended.

SECTION 1. Chapter two hundred and thirty-three of the General Laws is hereby amended by striking out section sixty-five, as amended by section one of chapter one hundred and five of the acts of the current year, and inserting in place thereof the following section: — *Section 65.* In any action or other civil judicial proceeding, a declaration of a deceased person shall not be inadmissible in evidence as hearsay or as private conversation between husband and wife, as the case may be, if the court finds that it was made in good faith and upon the personal knowledge of the declarant.

Declaration of deceased person.

SECTION 2. This act shall take effect on October first in the current year. *Approved May 5, 1943.*

Effective date.

AN ACT RELATIVE TO THE ADMISSIBILITY IN EVIDENCE OF COPIES OF HOSPITAL RECORDS. *Chap.233*

Be it enacted, etc., as follows:

G. L. (Ter. Ed.), 233, § 79, etc., amended.

SECTION 1. Section seventy-nine of chapter two hundred and thirty-three of the General Laws, as amended by section two of chapter three hundred and eighty-nine of the acts of nineteen hundred and forty-one, is hereby further amended by inserting after the word "cases" in the fifth line the words: — and the court may, in its discretion, admit copies of such records, if certified by the persons in custody thereof to be true and complete, — so as to read as follows: — *Section 79.* Records kept by hospitals under section seventy of

Admissibility of hospital records.

chapter one hundred and eleven shall be admissible as evidence in the courts of the commonwealth so far as such records relate to the treatment and medical history of such cases and the court may, in its discretion, admit copies of such records, if certified by the persons in custody thereof to be true and complete; but nothing therein contained shall be admissible as evidence which has reference to the question of liability. Copies of photographic or micro-photographic records so kept by hospitals, when duly certified by the person in charge of the hospital, shall be admitted in evidence equally with the original photographs or micro-photographs.

Effective date.

SECTION 2. This act shall take effect on October first in the current year. *Approved May 5, 1943.*

---

*Chap.*234 AN ACT TO PROVIDE RELIEF AGAINST EXCESSIVE ATTACHMENTS.

Be it enacted, etc., as follows:

G. L. (Ter. Ed.), 223, new § 42A, added.

SECTION 1. Chapter two hundred and twenty-three of the General Laws is hereby amended by inserting after section forty-two, as amended, the following section: — *Section 42A.* In an action or suit for an amount which is liquidated or ascertainable by calculation, no attachment by trustee process or otherwise shall be made for a larger sum than the amount of the claim and such additional amount as is reasonably necessary to include interest thereon and costs likely to be taxed in the action.

Amount of attachment by trustee process limited.

G. L. (Ter. Ed.), 223, § 114, etc., amended.

SECTION 2. Said chapter two hundred and twenty-three is hereby further amended by striking out section one hundred and fourteen, as amended by section one of chapter three hundred and twenty-five of the acts of nineteen hundred and thirty-eight, and inserting in place thereof the following section: — *Section 114.* If an excessive or unreasonable attachment, by trustee process or otherwise, is made on mesne process, the defendant or person whose property has been attached may apply in writing, in any county, to a justice of the court to which such process is returnable, for a reduction of the amount of the attachment or for its discharge; and such justice shall order a notice to the plaintiff, or, if the plaintiff is a non-resident, to his attorney, which shall be returnable before himself or any other justice of the same court as speedily as circumstances permit. If, upon a summary hearing of the parties, it is found that the action is one to recover for an amount which is liquidated or ascertainable by calculation, and the attachment is for a larger sum than the amount of the claim and such additional amount as is reasonably necessary to include interest thereon and costs likely to be taxed in the action, or if it appears that the amount of the claim is unliquidated and unascertainable by calculation and that the amount of the attachment is excessive or unreasonable, the court shall reduce or dissolve

Excessive attachment, how reduced or discharged.

the attachment or order a part of the goods, estates, effects or credits to be released.

SECTION 3. This act shall take effect on October first in the current year. *Approved May 5, 1943.*

Effective date.

Chap.235

AN ACT FURTHER REGULATING THE CONVERSION OF CO-OPERATIVE BANKS INTO FEDERAL SAVINGS AND LOAN ASSOCIATIONS.

Emergency preamble.

Whereas, Under the present law relative to conversion of a co-operative bank into a federal savings and loan association such a bank may so convert upon vote of a majority of its shareholders and the best interests of the banking structure of the commonwealth requires that the law be so changed as to make such conversion less easy to accomplish and thereby to prevent impairment of the safety of co-operative bank shares, and the deferred operation of this act would in part defeat its purpose, which is to make immediately effective such change in the law relative to conversions, therefore it is hereby declared to be an emergency law, necessary for the immediate preservation of the public convenience.

Be it enacted, etc., as follows:

G. L. (Ter. Ed.), 170, § 50A, etc., amended.

SECTION 1. The first paragraph of section fifty A of chapter one hundred and seventy of the General Laws, as amended by section two of chapter one hundred and sixty-two of the acts of nineteen hundred and thirty-eight, is hereby further amended by striking out, in the fourth line, the words "a majority", and inserting in place thereof the words: — two thirds, — so as to read as follows: — Any corporation may convert itself into a federal savings and loan association, or other federal agency of a like nature, if authorized by a vote of at least two thirds of all the shareholders of such corporation, entitled to vote, voting in person or by proxy at a meeting especially called to consider the subject. Notice of such special meeting, containing a statement of the time, place and the purpose for which such meeting is called, shall be sent by the clerk of the corporation to each shareholder thereof by mail, postage prepaid, at least thirty days before the date of the meeting. Notice of the meeting shall also be advertised three times in one or more newspapers published in the city or town in which the main office of the corporation is situated, and if there be no such newspaper, then in a newspaper published in the county where the town is situated, the last publication to be at least one day before the meeting.

Conversion into federal savings and loan associations, procedure.

Operation of act deferred.

SECTION 2. The privilege of conversion permitted by said section fifty A shall not be exercised by any co-operative bank during the period of two years immediately following the effective date of this act.

Approved May 6, 1943.

Chap.236 AN ACT RELATIVE TO THE METHOD OF COMPUTATION OF PAYMENTS TO THE FUNDS OF ANY COUNTY RETIREMENT SYSTEM BY CERTAIN SMALL TOWNS WHOSE EMPLOYEES ARE MEMBERS OF SAID SYSTEM.

Emergency preamble.

Whereas, The result of the deferred operation of this act would be to continue, during the period of deferment, an improper method of allocating to certain towns the costs of maintenance of certain retirement systems; therefore it is hereby declared to be an emergency law, necessary for the immediate preservation of the public convenience.

Be it enacted, etc., as follows:

G. L. (Ter. Ed.), 32, § 31I, etc., amended.

SECTION 1. Section thirty-one I of chapter thirty-two of the General Laws, as amended, is hereby further amended by striking out paragraph (4) (*b*), as appearing in chapter three hundred and seventy-seven of the acts of nineteen hundred and forty-one, and inserting in place thereof the following paragraph: —

Certification to selectmen by county retirement board.

(*b*) On or before the fifteenth day of January in each year the county retirement board shall certify to the selectmen of any town whose employees are members of the county retirement system, as hereinbefore provided, the amount payable to the several funds of the retirement system of the county on account of such members, as actuarially computed, and the town shall pay to the several funds the amounts so payable. Should any such town fail to include the amounts so certified in the town appropriation the assessors shall nevertheless include said amounts in the tax levy.

Computation of amounts payable.

SECTION 2. All amounts payable by any town to the funds of the retirement system of any county under paragraph (4) (*b*) of section thirty-one I of chapter thirty-two of the General Laws during the current year shall be computed in the manner provided by paragraph (4) (*b*), as amended by section one of this act. *Approved May 6, 1943.*

Chap.237 AN ACT PROVIDING FOR NOTICE TO THE COMMISSIONER OF BANKS OF CERTAIN TRANSFERS OF STOCK OF TRUST COMPANIES.

Be it enacted, etc., as follows:

G. L. (Ter. Ed.), 172, new § 19A, added.

Transfer of stock, notice of.

Chapter one hundred and seventy-two of the General Laws is hereby amended by inserting after section nineteen, as amended, the following section: — *Section 19A.* The registrar, transfer agent or other officer or agent of any such corporation having charge of its stockholders' records or ledger shall, within ten days after recording thereon any transfer of stock of the corporation which makes the transferee the owner of record of ten per cent or more of the outstanding stock with voting power, report such transfer to the commissioner. Whoever violates this section shall be punished by a fine of not more than five hundred dollars or by imprisonment for not more than six months, or both.

Approved May 6, 1943.

AN ACT FURTHER REGULATING THE ADMISSION OF CERTAIN FOREIGN FRATERNAL BENEFIT SOCIETIES TO TRANSACT BUSINESS WITHIN THE COMMONWEALTH. *Chap.238*

Be it enacted, etc., as follows:

SECTION 1. Chapter one hundred and seventy-six of the General Laws is hereby amended by inserting after section forty-two, as amended, the following new section: — *Section 42A.* A foreign society, if formed under the laws of any government or state other than the United States or one of the United States, shall not be admitted and authorized to transact business in the commonwealth until, besides complying with the conditions of sections forty-one and forty-two, it has satisfied the commissioner that it has made a deposit, as hereinafter provided, with the state treasurer or with the proper board or officer of some other state of the United States or with trustees who are citizens or corporations of the United States and approved by the commissioner, appointed under a deed of trust executed in a form approved by the attorney general and the commissioner and who have filed with the commissioner a bond, in a form approved by the attorney general and the commissioner, with a surety company authorized to transact business in the commonwealth as surety, and in such sum as the commissioner may require, conditioned upon the faithful performance of their duties, and running to the commissioner or his successor for the benefit of all the members, certificate holders and creditors within the United States of such society. Such deposit shall be held in exclusive trust for the benefit and security of all the members, certificate holders and creditors in the United States of such society, and shall be in an amount not less than the reserves with respect to all its outstanding certificates of membership held by residents of the United States and may be made in the securities and subject to the limitations specified in sections sixty-three and sixty-six of chapter one hundred and seventy-five, or in cash or such other securities as the commissioner may approve. If made with the state treasurer, such deposit shall not be returned to the society until it has ceased to transact business in the commonwealth, nor until the commissioner is satisfied that the society is under no obligation to members, certificate holders or other persons in this commonwealth or in any other state of the United States for whose benefit such deposit was made, nor until he has given his written consent to such return; provided, that the commissioner may, in any case, authorize in writing the return to the society of any excess of any such deposit over the amount required by this sec-

G. L. (Ter. Ed.), 176, new § 42A, added.

Foreign societies to furnish bond, etc.

tion if he is satisfied that such return will not be prejudicial to the interests of its members, certificate holders or creditors.

G. L. (Ter. Ed.), 175, § 185, etc., amended.

SECTION 2. Chapter one hundred and seventy-five of the General Laws is hereby amended by striking out section one hundred and eighty-five, as most recently amended by section two of chapter six hundred and fifty-four of the acts of nineteen hundred and forty-one, and inserting in its place the following section: — *Section 185.* The state treasurer in his official capacity shall take and hold in trust deposits made by any domestic company for the purpose of complying with the laws of this commonwealth or of any other state or country to enable such company to do business in such state or country, and also in like manner take and hold any deposit made by a foreign company or foreign fraternal benefit society under any law of this commonwealth; provided, that bonds need not be accepted by the treasurer unless in registered form and of denominations satisfactory to him. The company or society making such deposit shall be entitled to the income thereof, and may from time to time, with the consent of the treasurer, when not forbidden by the law under which the deposit is made, change in whole or in part the securities composing the deposit for other approved securities of equal par value.

Certain deposits to be held in trust.

The state treasurer may, upon written request of any domestic company, return to it the whole or any portion of any deposit held by him on behalf of such company, if he is satisfied that the deposit or the portion thereof requested to be returned is subject to no liability and is no longer required to be held by any provision of law of this commonwealth or of any such other state or country or for the purpose of the original deposit. He shall return to any foreign company or foreign fraternal benefit society the whole or any portion of any deposit held by him on behalf of such company or such society, upon the written order of the commissioner.

A company or society which has made such deposit, or its trustees or resident manager in the United States, or the commissioner, or any creditor of such company or society may at any time bring, in the supreme judicial court for the county of Suffolk, a suit in equity against the commonwealth and other parties properly joined therein to enforce, administer or terminate the trust created by such deposit. The process in such suit shall be served on the state treasurer, who shall appear and answer on behalf of the commonwealth and perform such orders and decrees as the court may make thereon.

G. L. (Ter. Ed.), 176, § 5, etc., amended.

SECTION 3. Section five of said chapter one hundred and seventy-six, as most recently amended by section two of chapter fourteen of the acts of nineteen hundred and thirty-four, is hereby further amended by striking out, in the fourth line, the word "and" the last time it occurs therein and inserting in place thereof a comma, — and by inserting before the word "of" in the sixth line the words: — and one hundred and eighty-five. *Approved May 6, 1943.*

AN ACT PENALIZING THE IMPORTING, PRINTING, PUBLISHING, SALE OR DISTRIBUTION OF OBSCENE PHONOGRAPHIC RECORDS. *Chap.*239

Be it enacted, etc., as follows:

G. L. (Ter. Ed.), 272, § 28, etc., amended.

Section twenty-eight of chapter two hundred and seventy-two of the General Laws, as amended by chapter two hundred and thirty-one of the acts of nineteen hundred and thirty-four, is hereby further amended by inserting in the second and in the ninth lines, after the word "paper", in each instance, the words: —, phonographic record, — so as to read as follows: — *Section 28.* Whoever imports, prints, publishes, sells or distributes a book, pamphlet, ballad, printed paper, phonographic record or other thing which is obscene, indecent or impure, or manifestly tends to corrupt the morals of youth, or an obscene, indecent or impure print, picture, figure, image or description, manifestly tending to corrupt the morals of youth, or introduces into a family, school or place of education, or buys, procures, receives or has in his possession any such book, pamphlet, ballad, printed paper, phonographic record, obscene, indecent or impure print, picture, figure, image or other thing, either for the purpose of sale, exhibition, loan or circulation or with intent to introduce the same into a family, school or place of education, shall, for a first offence, be punished by imprisonment for not more than two years or by a fine of not less than one hundred nor more than one thousand dollars, or both, and for a subsequent offence by imprisonment for not less than six months nor more than two and one half years or by a fine of not less than two hundred nor more than two thousand dollars, or both.

Penalty for sale or distribution of obscene literature, etc.

Approved May 6, 1943.

AN ACT RELATIVE TO THE FURNISHING OF BALLOT BOXES TO CITIES AND TOWNS FOR ELECTION PURPOSES. *Chap.*240

Be it enacted, etc., as follows:

G. L. (Ter. Ed.), 54, § 26, etc., amended.

Section twenty-six of chapter fifty-four of the General Laws, as amended by section one of chapter two hundred and eighty-one of the acts of nineteen hundred and thirty-eight, is hereby further amended by striking out the last sentence, — so as to read as follows: — *Section 26.* The state secretary shall, at the expense of the commonwealth, provide every city and town for use at every polling place therein with a state ballot box and counting apparatus approved by the board of voting machine examiners as provided in section thirty-two. *Approved May 6, 1943.*

State ballot boxes and counting apparatus to be provided, when.

THE COMMONWEALTH OF MASSACHUSETTS,
EXECUTIVE DEPARTMENT, STATE HOUSE,
BOSTON, June 15, 1943.

Honorable FREDERIC W. COOK, *Secretary of the Commonwealth, State House, Boston.*

SIR: — I, Leverett Saltonstall, by virtue of and in accordance with the provisions of the Forty-eighth Amendment to the Constitution, "The Referendum II, Emergency Measures", do declare that in my opinion, the immediate preservation of the public peace, health, safety, or convenience requires that the law passed on the sixth day of May in the year nineteen hundred and forty-three entitled, "An Act relative to the furnishing of ballot boxes to cities and towns for election purposes" should take effect forthwith, that it is an emergency law and that the facts constituting the emergency are as follows:

Because it is necessary to provide ballot boxes for certain new voting precincts in which elections will be held in 1943 and war priority regulations make it difficult and slow to obtain the necessary metals for their construction.

Very truly yours,
LEVERETT SALTONSTALL,
Governor of the Commonwealth.

OFFICE OF THE SECRETARY, BOSTON, June 15, 1943.

I hereby certify that the accompanying statement was filed in this office by His Excellency the Governor of the Commonwealth of Massachusetts at twelve o'clock and two minutes, P.M., on the above date, and in accordance with Article Forty-eight of the Amendments to the Constitution said chapter takes effect forthwith, being chapter two hundred and forty of the acts of nineteen hundred and forty-three.

F. W. COOK,
Secretary of the Commonwealth.

---

*Chap.*241 AN ACT RELATING TO THE QUALITY OF COAL SOLD OR OFFERED FOR SALE IN THE COMMONWEALTH.

Emergency preamble.

Whereas, Because the serious shortage of fuel oil and the necessary conversion to the use of coal by persons using oil for heating purposes may result in an immediate shortage of coal and the sale of inferior grades of coal in the commonwealth, therefore this act is hereby declared to be an emergency law, necessary for the immediate preservation of the public safety and convenience.

Be it enacted, etc., as follows:

G. L. (Ter. Ed.), 94, § 248, etc., amended.

SECTION 1. Chapter ninety-four of the General Laws is hereby amended by striking out section two hundred and forty-eight, as most recently amended by section fourteen of chapter two hundred and sixty-one of the acts of nineteen hundred and thirty-nine, and inserting in place thereof the following section: — *Section 248.* Whoever violates any provision of sections two hundred and forty to two hundred and forty-seven, inclusive, if no other penalty is provided therein, or of a rule or regulation made under section two hundred and thirty-nine A, or fails to comply with any request for information or direction made under authority of sections two hundred and forty, two hundred and forty-one, two hundred and forty-four to two hundred and forty-six, inclusive, or gives a false answer to any such request, shall be punished by a fine of not more than fifty dollars; and whoever is guilty of fraud or deceit as to the weighing, selling or delivering of coke, charcoal or coal, or whoever, by himself, or by his servant, agent or employee, sells or delivers or attempts to sell or deliver coal which is short in weight or which contains an unreasonable amount of shale, slate, rock or other foreign substance or which produces an excessive amount of non-combustible residue, including ash, shall be punished by a fine of not more than one thousand dollars or by imprisonment for not more than one year, or both. The director of standards and necessaries of life and local sealers of weights and measures shall cause sections two hundred and forty to two hundred and forty-nine, inclusive, and rules and regulations made under section two hundred and thirty-nine A, to be enforced.

Penalty for certain offences.

SECTION 2. Said chapter ninety-four is hereby further amended by striking out section two hundred and forty-nine E, as appearing in the Tercentenary Edition, and inserting in place thereof the following section: — *Section 249E.* Whoever, by himself, or by his servant, agent or employee, in placing or packing coal in any basket, bag, sack or other receptacle, places or causes to be placed therein any foreign substance, or sells, or exposes or offers for sale, or has in his custody or possession with intent to sell, coal placed or packed in a basket, bag, sack or other receptacle containing an unreasonable amount of any foreign substance or producing an excessive amount of non-combustible residue, including ash, shall be punished by a fine of not more than one thousand dollars or by imprisonment for not more than one year, or both.

G. L. (Ter. Ed.), 94, § 249E, amended.

Placing, etc., of foreign substances in coal.

Penalty.

SECTION 3. Said chapter ninety-four is hereby further amended by inserting after section two hundred and forty-nine E, as so appearing, the following section: — *Section 249E½.* It shall be presumed in a prosecution under section two hundred and forty-eight or section two hundred and forty-nine E that the non-combustible residue, including ash, is excessive if a test, as determined by the current standard method of tests for sampling and analysis for coal and coke as published by the American Society for Testing Materials and designated as D 271, with the year of publication, produces non-combustible residue, including ash, in excess of the following percentages:

G. L. (Ter. Ed.), 94, new § 249E½, added.

Percentage of non-combustible residue in coal regulated.

Trade Term.	Maximum Non-Combustible Residue, including Ash (Dry Basis) (Per Cent).
Broken	12.5
Egg	12.5
Stove	13.5
Chestnut	14.0
Pea	15.5

G. L. (Ter. Ed.), 94, § 249F, etc., amended.

SECTION 4. Section two hundred and forty-nine F of said chapter ninety-four, as amended by section seventeen of chapter two hundred and sixty-one of the acts of nineteen hundred and thirty-nine, is hereby further amended by striking out in the fourth line the words "the five preceding sections", — and inserting in place thereof the words: — sections two hundred and forty-nine A to two hundred and forty-nine E½, inclusive, — so as to read as follows: — *Section 249F.* The department of public health, local boards of health, the director of standards and necessaries of life and local sealers of weights and measures shall cause sections two hundred and forty-nine A to two hundred and forty-nine E½, inclusive, to be enforced.

Enforcement of act.

Approved May 6, 1943.

---

*Chap.*242 AN ACT VALIDATING CERTAIN ACTION TAKEN BY THE TOWN OF MARSHFIELD IN RESPECT TO PROVIDING ADEQUATE TRANSPORTATION SERVICE THEREIN.

Be it enacted, etc., as follows:

SECTION 1. The action of the inhabitants of the town of Marshfield, at a special town meeting held on June thirteenth, nineteen hundred and forty-two, in voting to pay from surplus the sum of fifteen hundred dollars to provide adequate transportation service, by bus or otherwise, for the town and to avoid a reduction or discontinuance of such service, and in voting to authorize the selectmen to enter into agreements with transportation companies for said purpose, is hereby ratified and confirmed to the extent that such action was taken without authority of law.

SECTION 2. This act shall take effect upon its passage.

Approved May 6, 1943.

---

*Chap.*243 AN ACT RELATIVE TO THE PENSIONING OF LABORERS, FOREMEN, MECHANICS, CRAFTSMEN AND CHAUFFEURS IN THE EMPLOY OF THE CITY OF LOWELL.

Be it enacted, etc., as follows:

SECTION 1. Section one of chapter sixty-one of the acts of nineteen hundred and thirty, as amended by section one of chapter four hundred and thirty-two of the acts of nineteen hundred and thirty-five, is hereby further amended by striking out, in the thirteenth line, as appearing in said section one of said chapter sixty-one, the words "annual compensation paid him as a laborer" and inserting in place thereof the words: — highest compensation paid since May first, nineteen hundred and thirty-one, for the grade held by him, — so as to read as follows: — *Section 1.* Any laborer in the employ of the city of Lowell who has reached the age of sixty and has been in such employ for a period of not less than twenty-five years and has become physically or mentally incapacitated for labor, and any laborer in the employ of said city who has been in such employ for a period of not less than fifteen years and has become physically or mentally incapacitated for labor by reason of any injury received in the performance of his duties for said city, may, at his request and with the approval of the mayor and city council, be retired from service; and if so retired he shall receive from said city for the remainder of his life an annual pension equal to one half the highest compensation paid since May first, nineteen hundred and thirty-one, for the grade held by him at the time of his retirement. Any laborer in the employ of said city who has reached the age of sixty-five and has been in such employ for a period of not less than twenty-five years, including the time when incapacitated by reason of sickness, not exceeding two years in the aggregate, as certified by a physician in regular standing, shall be retired from service, and shall receive from said city an annual pension computed in the manner hereinbefore set forth. The word "laborer", as used in this section shall include foremen, mechanics, craftsmen and chauffeurs.

SECTION 2. This act shall take effect upon its passage.

Approved May 6, 1943.

AN ACT RELATIVE TO THE DETENTION, COMMITMENT AND CARE OF CHILDREN BETWEEN SEVEN AND SEVENTEEN YEARS OF AGE IN LOCKUPS, POLICE STATIONS, HOUSES OF DETENTION, JAILS AND HOUSES OF CORRECTION, PENDING ARRAIGNMENT, EXAMINATION OR TRIAL BY THE COURTS. *Chap.244*

Whereas, The deferred operation of this act would result in unnecessary delay in checking the present prevalence of juvenile delinquency, largely due to existing war time conditions, therefore it is hereby declared to be an emergency law, necessary for the immediate preservation of the public health, safety and convenience. Emergency preamble.

Be it enacted, etc., as follows:

SECTION 1. Chapter one hundred and nineteen of the General Laws is hereby amended by striking out section fifty-six, as appearing in the Tercentenary Edition, and inserting in place thereof the following section: — *Section 56.* Hearings upon cases arising under sections fifty-two to sixty-three, inclusive, may be adjourned from time to time. A child adjudged a wayward child or delinquent child may appeal to the superior court upon adjudication, and also may appeal to said court at the time of the order of com- G. L. (Ter. Ed.), 119, § 56, amended. Hearings. Appeals, etc.

mitment or sentence, and such child shall, at the time of such adjudication and also at the time of such order of commitment or sentence, be notified of his right to appeal. If such child appeals to the superior court at either of said times, said court shall thereupon have jurisdiction of such case, and such case shall forthwith be entered in said court. The appeal, if taken, shall be tried and determined in like manner as appeals in criminal cases, except that the trial of said appeals in the superior court shall not be in conjunction with the other business of that court, but shall be held in a session set apart and devoted for the time being exclusively to the trial of juvenile cases. This shall be known as the juvenile session of the superior court, and shall have a separate trial list and docket. All appealed juvenile cases in the superior court shall be transferred to this list, and shall be tried, unless otherwise disposed of by direct order of the court. In any appealed case the superior court, before passing sentence or before ordering other disposition, shall be supplied with a report of any investigation thereon made by the probation officer of the court from which the appeal was taken. Section thirty-five of chapter two hundred and seventy-six and section eighteen of chapter two hundred and seventy-eight, relative to recognizances in cases continued or appealed, shall apply to cases arising under sections fifty-two to sixty-three, inclusive.

G. L. (Ter. Ed.), 119, §§ 66–69, etc., amended.

Detention of children in lockups, etc., regulated.

SECTION 2. Said chapter one hundred and nineteen is hereby further amended by striking out sections sixty-six to sixty-nine, inclusive, as amended, and inserting in place thereof the four following sections: — *Section 66.* Except as otherwise provided in section sixty-seven, and in section twelve of chapter one hundred and twenty, no child under seventeen years of age shall be detained by the police in a lockup, police station or house of detention pending arraignment, examination or trial by the court. Except as otherwise provided in section sixty-eight, no child under seventeen years of age except when charged with an offense punishable by death or life imprisonment shall be committed by the court to a jail or house of correction or to the state farm, pending further examination or trial by the court or pending any continuance of his case or pending the prosecution of an appeal to the superior court or upon adjudication as a delinquent child.

Proceedings to avoid incarceration of children, etc.

Section 67. Whenever a child between seven and seventeen years of age is arrested with or without a warrant, as provided by law, the officer in charge of the place of custody to which the child has been taken shall immediately notify the probation officer of the district court within whose judicial district such child was arrested and at least one of the child's parents, or, if there is no parent, the guardian or person with whom it is stated that such child resides, and shall inquire into the case. Pending such notice and inquiry, such child shall be detained. Upon the acceptance by the officer in charge of said place of custody of the written promise by said parent, guardian or any other reputable person to be responsible for the presence of such child in court at the time and place when such child is to appear or upon the receipt by such officer in charge from said probation officer of a written request for the release of such child to him, such child shall be released to said person giving such promise or to said probation officer making such request; provided, that if the arresting officer requests in writing that a boy between twelve and seventeen years of age or a girl between fourteen and seventeen years of age be detained, or if the court or trial justice issuing a warrant for the arrest of a boy between twelve and seventeen years of age or a girl between fourteen and seventeen years of age directs in the warrant that such child shall be held in safe keeping pending his appearance in court, such child shall be detained in a police station or house of detention pending his appearance in court; and provided, further, that nothing contained in this section shall prevent the admitting of such child to bail in accordance with law. Said probation officer shall notify such child of the time and place of the hearing of his case.

Care of children held for examination or trial.

Section 68. A child between seven and fourteen years of age held by the court for further examination, trial or continuance, or to prosecute an appeal to the superior court, if unable to furnish bail shall be committed by the court to the care of the department or of a probation officer who shall provide for his safe keeping and for his appearance at such examination or trial, or at the prosecution of his appeal.

A child between fourteen and seventeen years of age so held by the court if unable to furnish bail shall be so committed to the department with its consent or to a probation officer, unless the court on immediate inquiry shall be of opinion that such child should be committed to jail, in which case said child may be committed to jail.

The department shall be allowed such sums as may be necessary to provide additional special foster homes, special supervisors and transportation facilities for the care, maintenance and safe keeping of such children between fourteen and seventeen years of age who may be committed by the court to the department under this section; provided, that no more than five such children shall be detained in any such foster home at any one time.

A child between seven and seventeen years of age so committed by the court to jail or to the department to await further examination or trial by the Boston juvenile court or a district court shall be returned thereto within fifteen days after the date of the order of such commitment, and final disposition of the case shall thereupon be made by adjudication or otherwise; unless, in the opinion of the court, the interests of the child and the public otherwise require.

Any child committed to jail under this section shall, while so confined, be kept in a place separate and apart from all other persons committed thereto who are seventeen years of age or over, and shall not at any time be permitted to associate or communicate with any other such persons committed as aforesaid, except when attending religious exercises or receiving medical attention or treatment.

The provisions of section twenty-four of chapter two hundred and twelve relative to the precedence of cases of persons actually confined in prison and awaiting trial shall apply to children held in jail under this section to prosecute appeals to the superior court.

Said probation officer shall have all the authority, rights and powers in relation to a child committed to his care under this section, and in relation to a child released to him as provided in section sixty-seven, which he would have if he were surety on the recognizance of such child.

Superintendent of schools to furnish information, etc.

Section 69. The superintendent of the public schools in any town, any teacher therein, and any person in charge of a private school, or any teacher therein, shall furnish to any court from time to time any information and reports requested by any justice thereof relating to the attendance, conduct and standing of any pupil enrolled in such school, if said pupil is at the time awaiting examination or trial by the court or is under the supervision of the court.

G. L. (Ter. Ed.), 212, § 22, etc., amended.

Application of section limited.

SECTION 3. Section twenty-two of chapter two hundred and twelve of the General Laws, as most recently amended by section one of chapter one hundred and forty-five of the acts of the current year, is hereby further amended by adding at the end the following sentence: — This section shall not apply to appeals arising under sections fifty-two to sixty-three, inclusive, of chapter one hundred and nineteen.

G. L. (Ter. Ed.), 212, § 24, amended.

Precedence of certain prosecutions.

SECTION 4. Section twenty-four of said chapter two hundred and twelve, as appearing in the Tercentenary Edition, is hereby amended by inserting after the word "chapters" in the second line the words: — one hundred and nineteen, — so as to read as follows: — *Section 24.* At a sitting of the court at which criminal business may be transacted, cases arising under chapters one hundred and nineteen, two hundred and forty-eight, one hundred and thirty-eight, one hundred and thirty-nine and two hundred and seventy-three shall have precedence in the order in which said chapters are herein named, next after the cases of persons who are actually confined in prison and awaiting trial; provided, that the court, on motion of the district attorney, may order that the trial of any specified case of crime shall take precedence over all other cases. *Approved May 6, 1943.*

AN ACT RELATIVE TO CERTAIN LINES, POLES AND OTHER EQUIPMENT OF THE MUNICIPAL LIGHTING PLANT OF THE CITY OF PEABODY, THE NEW ENGLAND TELEPHONE AND TELEGRAPH COMPANY AND THE AMERICAN TELEPHONE AND TELEGRAPH COMPANY IN SAID CITY. *Chap.245*

Be it enacted, etc., as follows:

SECTION 1. All lines for the transmission of steam and for the transmission of electricity for light, heat or power heretofore acquired or constructed by the municipal lighting plant of the city of Peabody, and all lines for the transmission of intelligence by electricity heretofore acquired or constructed by the New England Telephone and Telegraph Company and the American Telephone and Telegraph Company in said city, upon, along, over or under the public ways and places of said city, and the poles, piers, abutments, conduits and other fixtures necessary to sustain or protect the wires of said lines and actually in place on the effective date of this act, are hereby made lawful notwithstanding the lack of any valid locations therefor or any informality in the proceedings relative to their location and erection; provided, that the validation aforesaid shall not be effective as to the lines, structures or fixtures aforesaid of said municipal lighting plant or of said companies in said city unless said municipal lighting plant or said companies, as the case may be, shall, not later than December thirty-first, nineteen hundred and forty-four, file with the clerk of said city a map or maps showing the location and nature of said lines, structures, and fixtures in said city, such map or maps so filed to be recorded and kept with the records of original locations for poles and wires in said city.

SECTION 2. This act shall take effect upon its passage.

Approved May 6, 1943.

AN ACT TO PLACE CERTAIN CHILD WELFARE SERVICES EMPLOYEES UNDER THE CIVIL SERVICE. *Chap.246*

Be it enacted, etc., as follows:

SECTION 1. Section four of chapter thirty-one of the General Laws, as most recently amended by section two of chapter six hundred and eighty-six of the acts of nineteen hundred and forty-one, is hereby further amended by adding at the end the following paragraph: — G. L. (Ter. Ed.), 31, § 4, etc., amended.

Social workers and clerical employees in towns, whose salary and expenses are paid in whole or in part by United States grant through the child welfare services program, so called, under the department of public welfare. Employees paid by United States grant, etc.

SECTION 2. The incumbents, on the effective date of this act, of positions under child welfare services, so called, numbering not more than three, covering the towns of Southbridge, Sturbridge, Charlton, Webster, Sutton, Douglas, Operation of act regulated.

Oxford and Dudley, may continue to serve as such, subject to passing a qualifying civil service examination, and their tenure of office shall be unlimited, subject, however, to the civil service laws. *Approved May 6, 1943.*

---

*Chap.*247 AN ACT IMPOSING CERTAIN RESTRICTIONS ON THE ISSUE OF NON-ASSESSABLE POLICIES, SO CALLED, BY MUTUAL INSURANCE COMPANIES.

Emergency preamble.

Whereas, The purpose of this act is immediately to forbid the issuance of certain policies by certain mutual insurance companies doing business within the commonwealth, and the deferred operation of this act would to that extent tend to defeat its purpose; therefore, it is hereby declared to be an emergency law necessary for the immediate preservation of the public convenience.

Be it enacted, etc., as follows:

G. L. (Ter. Ed.), 175, § 85A, etc., amended.

SECTION 1. Section eighty-five A of chapter one hundred and seventy-five of the General Laws, inserted by section one of chapter seven hundred and sixteen of the acts of nineteen hundred and forty-one and as affected by chapter seven hundred and twenty-three of the acts of the same year, is hereby amended by adding at the end the following sentence: — This section shall not apply to any company unless such company or its predecessor or predecessors, if any, prior to merger or consolidation shall have been actively engaged in the insurance business in one or more states of the United States continuously for ten or more years.

Application of section limited.

G. L. (Ter. Ed.), 175, § 93F, etc., amended.

SECTION 2. Section ninety-three F of said chapter one hundred and seventy-five, inserted by section three of said chapter seven hundred and sixteen and as so affected, is hereby amended by adding at the end the following sentence: — This section shall not apply to any company unless such company or its predecessor or predecessors, if any, prior to merger or consolidation shall have been actively engaged in the insurance business in one or more states of the United States continuously for ten or more years.

Application of section limited.

G. L. (Ter. Ed.), 175, § 152A, etc., amended.

SECTION 3. Section one hundred and fifty-two A of said chapter one hundred and seventy-five, inserted by section four of said chapter seven hundred and sixteen and as so affected, is hereby amended by adding at the end the following sentence: — This section shall not apply to any company unless such company or its predecessor or predecessors, if any, prior to merger or consolidation shall have been actively engaged in the insurance business in one or more states of the United States continuously for ten or more years.

Application of section limited.

1941, 716, § 6, stricken out, effect of.

SECTION 4. Said chapter seven hundred and sixteen of the acts of nineteen hundred and forty-one is hereby amended by striking out section six, inserted by chapter seven hundred and twenty-three of the acts of the same year, but such action shall not affect the validity of any policy lawfully issued under authority of said section six prior to the effective date of this act. *Approved May 7, 1943.*

AN ACT MAKING THE ENTRY FEE FOR APPEALS TRANSFERRED TO THE APPELLATE TAX BOARD FROM COUNTY COMMISSIONERS THE SAME AS FOR APPEALS DIRECTLY TO SAID BOARD. *Chap.*248

Emergency preamble.

Whereas, The deferred operation of this act would result in the loss during the period of deferment of revenue which is much needed in the present emergency, therefore it is hereby declared to be an emergency law, necessary for the immediate preservation of the public convenience.

Be it enacted, etc., as follows:

G. L. (Ter. Ed.), 59, § 64, etc., amended.

The second paragraph of section sixty-four of chapter fifty-nine of the General Laws, as most recently amended by section two of chapter three hundred and sixty-six of the acts of nineteen hundred and thirty-nine, is hereby further amended by inserting after the second sentence the following sentence: — Upon the transfer of such complaint to said board the clerk of said board shall send notice by registered mail to the complainant that such complaint has been transferred, and the complainant shall, within ten days after receiving such notice, pay to said board the entry fee as required by section seven of said chapter fifty-eight A, — so as to read as follows: —

Election by town to have appeal heard by board.

Upon the filing of a complaint under this section the clerk of the county commissioners or of the board authorized to hear and determine the same shall forthwith transmit a certified copy of such complaint to the assessors and the assessors or the city solicitor or town counsel may within thirty days after receipt of said copy give written notice to said clerk and to the complainant that the town elects to have the same heard and determined by the appellate tax board. Thereupon, the clerk of the county commissioners or of the board authorized to hear and determine such complaints shall forward all papers with respect to such complaint then in the file of the county commissioners or other such board to the clerk of the appellate tax board and proceedings with respect to such complaint shall thenceforth be continued as provided in chapter fifty-eight A. Upon the transfer of such complaint to said board the clerk of said board shall send notice by registered mail to the complainant that such complaint has been transferred, and the complainant shall, within ten days after receiving such notice, pay to said board the entry fee as required by section seven of said chapter fifty-eight A. If upon hearing it appears that the complainant has complied with all applicable provisions of law and the appellate tax board finds that the complainant is duly entitled to an abatement, it may grant him such reasonable abatement as justice may require, and shall enter an order directing the treasurer of the town to refund said amount, if the tax sought to be abated has been paid, together with all charges and interest at four per cent on the amount of the abatement from the date of the payment of the tax. The board may make such order with respect to the payment of costs as justice may require.

Approved May 7, 1943.

---

*Chap.*249 AN ACT TO PROVIDE FOR THE ESTABLISHMENT OF A CONTRIBUTORY SAVINGS BANKS EMPLOYEES RETIREMENT ASSOCIATION.

Be it enacted, etc., as follows:

G. L. (Ter. Ed.), 168, new §§ 58-60, added.

Chapter one hundred and sixty-eight of the General Laws is hereby amended by adding after section fifty-seven, inserted by section twenty-eight of chapter three hundred and thirty-four of the acts of nineteen hundred and thirty-three, the three following sections: — *Section 58.* Fifteen or more savings banks may form the Savings Banks Employees Retirement Association, in this section and in sections fifty-nine and sixty called the association, for the purpose of providing pensions for eligible employees of the participating banks who retire on account of age or disability.

Formation of Savings Banks Employees Retirement Association authorized.

Contributions, pensions, etc.

All savings banks established under the laws of the commonwealth, the Savings Banks Association of Massachusetts, the Mutual Savings Central Fund, Inc., and the Savings Bank Life Insurance Council, and such of their respective employees as may be provided by the by-laws of the association shall be eligible for membership in the association. For the purposes of this section and sections fifty-nine and sixty a reference to "bank" or "banks" shall, unless the context otherwise requires, mean and include any or all of the organizations named in this paragraph, and a reference to "trustees" of a bank shall also, unless the context otherwise requires, mean and include the governing body of each of such organizations.

Eligible employees may contribute a portion of their salaries or wages, to be deducted by the employing banks and paid to the association. A participating bank may contribute to the funds of the association to the extent determined by its trustees, but its contributions for future service, as defined in the by-laws, on account of any employee shall not exceed such employee's contributions or five per cent of his wages or salary, whichever is less. A participating bank may also contribute for past service, as defined in the by-laws, amounts necessary to provide eligible employees with an annuity to begin at age sixty-five or later, such annuity not to exceed one per cent of the average salary for the five years preceding the date such bank joins the association for each year, but not exceeding thirty-five years, of continuous employment between age thirty and the date of such joining.

In the event that any employee who has been continuously in the employ of such a bank for ten years or more becomes incapacitated for further service by reason of physical or mental disability before age sixty-five, the employing bank may pay him a pension in an amount not to exceed one per cent of the average salary for the five years preceding the date of retirement for each year, not exceeding thirty-five years, of continuous service. Any pension paid on account of disability may be discontinued at any time by the trustees of the employing bank, and shall be discontinued when any such pensioner substantially recovers his earning capacity.

The funds contributed by participating banks and member employees shall be held or used by the trustees of the association for the purchase of annuities or payment of pensions to eligible employees upon their retirement from service, for the payments to beneficiaries or representatives of any member employee of the participating bank dying before reaching the age of retirement, and for the payment to any such employee retiring from service before becoming entitled to a pension or annuity. Expenses necessary for the administration of the association shall be paid by participating banks, on a proportionate basis as provided in the by-laws.

No annuity or pension provided by contributions from a participating bank for the benefit of any employee shall exceed two thousand, five hundred dollars yearly, or one half of the average salary of the employee for the five years preceding the date of retirement, whichever is less.

By-laws, approval by commissioner.

Section 59. The by-laws of the association shall be approved by the commissioner and shall prescribe the manner in which, and the officers and agents by whom, the association may be conducted and the manner in which its funds may be invested and paid out. Such association shall be formed when its by-laws have been approved and agreed to by a majority of the trustees of each of fifteen or more savings banks, and have been approved by the commissioner. Such association shall annually, on or before December first, report to the commissioner such statements of its membership and financial transactions for the year ending on the preceding October thirty-first as the commissioner may consider necessary to show its business and standing. The commissioner may verify such statement by an examination of the books and papers of the association.

The association shall not be subject to chapter thirty-two or chapter one hundred and seventy-five or to such other provisions of law as relate to insurance companies or other retirement associations.

Property, funds, exempt from taxation, etc.

Section 60. The property of the association, the portion of the wages or salary of any employee deducted or to be deducted under sections fifty-eight and fifty-nine, the right of an employee to an annuity or pension, and all his rights in the funds of the association, shall be exempt from taxation and from the operation of any law relating to insolvency, and shall not be attached or taken on execution or other process to satisfy any debt or liability of the association, a participating bank, or any employee member of the association. No assignment of any right in or to said funds or of any pension or annuity payable under section fifty-eight shall be valid. *Approved May 7, 1943.*

---

*Chap.*250 AN ACT REGULATING THE PUNISHMENT FOR ROBBERY IN CERTAIN CASES.

Be it enacted, etc., as follows:

G. L. (Ter. Ed.), 265, § 17, amended.

SECTION 1. Chapter two hundred and sixty-five of the General Laws is hereby amended by striking out section seventeen, as appearing in the Tercentenary Edition, and inserting in place thereof the following section: — *Section 17.* Whoever, being armed with a dangerous weapon, assaults another and robs, steals or takes from his person money or other property which may be the subject of larceny shall be punished by imprisonment in the state prison for life or for any term of years.

Punishment for robbery in certain cases.

Effective date and application of act.

SECTION 2. This act shall take effect on October first in the current year and shall apply in the case of crimes committed on or after said date; but the provisions of said section seventeen, as in effect immediately preceding said date, shall continue to apply in the case of crimes committed prior thereto. *Approved May 7, 1943.*

---

*Chap.*251 AN ACT RELATIVE TO THE RECORDING OF A CERTIFICATE OF ENTRY OR TAKING POSSESSION IN CERTAIN EMINENT DOMAIN CASES AND TO THE GIVING OF NOTICE OF SUCH ENTRY OR TAKING POSSESSION.

Be it enacted, etc., as follows:

G. L. (Ter. Ed.), 79, § 3, etc., amended.

SECTION 1. Section three of chapter seventy-nine of the General Laws, as amended by section six of chapter one hundred and seventy-two of the acts of nineteen hundred and thirty-eight, is hereby further amended by adding at the end of the first paragraph the two following sentences: — If, within two years after the date of an order of taking for any such way, drain or ditch, entry is made or possession taken thereunder for the purpose of constructing the same, the board of officers by whom the taking is made shall cause to be recorded in the registry of deeds of every county or district in which the property taken or any of it lies, a certificate of such entry or taking possession stating the date thereof and containing a reference to the record of the copy of the order of taking sufficient to identify it, signed by said board or certified by its secretary or clerk or, in case of a taking by or on behalf of a city by a board of officers having no secretary or clerk, certified by the city clerk. Failure to record any such certificate shall not affect the validity of the taking.

Entry, recording of, etc.

G. L. (Ter. Ed.), 79, § 8, etc., amended.

SECTION 2. Section eight of said chapter seventy-nine, as amended by section one of chapter one hundred and eighty-seven of the acts of nineteen hundred and thirty-six, is hereby further amended by inserting after the second sentence the following sentence: — If, within two years after the date of an order of taking for a highway or town way or for a ditch or drain for draining the same, entry is made or possession taken thereunder for the purpose of constructing the same, such notice of taking shall also state the date of such entry or taking possession. Contents of notice.

SECTION 3. Section sixteen of said chapter seventy-nine, as most recently amended by chapter ninety-five of the acts of the current year, is hereby further amended by adding at the end the following paragraph: — G. L. (Ter. Ed.), 79, § 16, etc., amended.

And, without limiting the foregoing provisions of this section, if within two years after the date of an order of taking for a highway or town way or for a ditch or drain for draining the same, entry is made or possession taken thereunder for the purpose of constructing the same, a petition for the assessment of damages may be filed at any time prior to the expiration of six months after the recording under section three of a certificate of such entry or taking possession. Petition for assessment of damages.

SECTION 4. This act shall take effect on September first of the current year, but shall apply only in the case of takings where the order of taking is made on or after said date. Effective date.

Approved May 7, 1943.

AN ACT RELATIVE TO THE TIME WITHIN WHICH CERTAIN BETTERMENT AND OTHER ASSESSMENTS SHALL BE PAID AND TO THE CONTINUANCE OF LIENS CREATED IN CONNECTION THEREWITH. *Chap.252*

Be it enacted, etc., as follows:

SECTION 1. Chapter eighty of the General Laws is hereby amended by striking out section twelve, as appearing in the Tercentenary Edition, and inserting in place thereof the following section: — *Section 12.* Assessments made under this chapter shall constitute a lien upon the land assessed. The lien shall take effect upon the recording of the order stating that betterments are to be assessed for the improvement. Except as otherwise provided, such lien shall terminate at the expiration of two years from October first in the year in which the assessment is first placed on the annual tax bill under section thirteen or, if an assessment has been apportioned, from October first in the year in which the last portion is so placed upon the annual tax bill, whichever is later, if in the meantime in either case the estate has been alienated and the instrument alienating the same has been recorded. If there is no recorded alienation within such period, the lien shall continue until there is a recorded alienation. If the validity of an assessment made under this chapter is called in question in any legal proceeding to which the board which made the assessment or the body politic for the benefit of which it was made is a party, instituted prior to the expiration of the lien therefor, the G. L. (Ter. Ed.), 80, § 12, amended. Assessments as liens. Effective date and duration of lien.

lien shall continue until one year after the validity of the assessment is finally determined, even though an alienation be recorded in the meantime; and, if while a lien established by this section is in force, the owner of the real estate on which it attaches is adjudicated bankrupt, the lien shall continue for six months after final termination of the bankruptcy proceedings, subject, however, to any lawful action under any paramount authority conferred by the bankruptcy laws of the United States. If the time for payment of an assessment is extended under section thirteen A, the lien herein provided shall continue until the expiration of two years from the date when the assessment is required to be paid under the extension granted under said section.

G. L. (Ter. Ed.), 80, new § 13A, added.

Assessment for betterment, payment deferred, when.

SECTION 2. Said chapter eighty is hereby further amended by inserting after section thirteen, as amended, the following section: — *Section 13A.* The board making the order for the assessment of any betterment upon land which is not built upon may extend the time of payment of the assessment until it is built upon or for a fixed time; but interest at the rate of four per cent per annum shall be paid annually upon the assessment from the time it was made, and the assessment shall be paid within three months after such land is built upon or at the expiration of such fixed time.

G. L. (Ter. Ed.), 83, new § 29, added.

Liens created by special act. Termination of, etc.

SECTION 3. Chapter eighty-three of the General Laws, as appearing in the Tercentenary Edition, is hereby amended by adding at the end the following section: — *Section 29.* Notwithstanding any provision in any special act to the contrary, any lien for sewer, drain or sidewalk assessments or for betterment assessments of any other nature created pursuant to the provisions of any special act shall continue in effect until the land subject to the lien has been alienated and the instrument alienating the same has been recorded and for such longer period as any special act may provide.

G. L. (Ter. Ed.), 83, § 19, amended.

Extension of time of payment.

SECTION 4. Said chapter eighty-three is hereby further amended by striking out section nineteen, as so appearing, and inserting in place thereof the following section: — *Section 19.* The aldermen of a city or the sewer commissioners, selectmen or road commissioners of a town may extend the time for the payment of such assessments upon land which is not built upon until it is built upon or for a fixed time; but interest at the rate of four per cent per annum shall be paid annually upon the assessment from the time it was made, and the assessment shall be paid within three months after such land is built upon or at the expiration of such fixed time.

G. L. (Ter. Ed.), 83, § 27, amended.

Recording of statement.

SECTION 5. Section twenty-seven of said chapter eighty-three, as appearing in the Tercentenary Edition, is hereby amended by striking out the last sentence and inserting in place thereof the following sentence: — All assessments made or charges imposed under this chapter upon land which abuts upon any such way in which such sewer, drain or sidewalk is located shall constitute a lien upon such land from the time such statement is recorded and all charges authorized by section sixteen shall from the time of assessment constitute a lien upon the land connected with the common sewer. Liens under this section shall continue for the same period and under the same conditions as a lien established under chapter eighty.

SECTION 6. The rate of interest established by section four of this act, amending section nineteen of chapter eighty-three of the General Laws, shall apply to assessments the time for payment of which is extended under said section nineteen on or after the effective date of this act; and the rate of interest set forth in said section nineteen as in effect immediately prior to the effective date of this act shall continue to apply to assessments the payment of which was extended under said section nineteen prior to such effective date. *Approved May 7, 1943.* Effective dates.

AN ACT TO PROVIDE FOR THE PROPER IDENTIFICATION AT THE POLLS OF REGISTERED VOTERS IN THE ARMED SERVICES DURING THE PRESENT WAR, AND TO RESTORE TO THE VOTING LISTS THE NAMES OF SUCH PERSONS STRICKEN THEREFROM AFTER ENTERING SUCH SERVICE. *Chap.253*

Be it enacted, etc., as follows:

SECTION 1. Notwithstanding any contrary provisions of general or special law, listing boards and registrars of voters shall list all persons who were registered voters in their respective cities and towns at the time of their entry into the armed services of the United States and whom they believe to be still living. If the name of any such voter has been removed from the list he, or any registered voter in his behalf, may file a written petition asking that the name be restored to the list of registered voters, and stating that at the time of his entry into such service he was a registered voter in the city or town. If such petition is filed prior to December first in any year, it shall be filed with the election commissioner or commissioners if there is such a board, or, if there is none, with the registrars of voters. If filed on or after December first in any year it shall be filed with the listing board or the registrars of voters, as the case may be. Upon the filing of such petition the board or officers above mentioned shall investigate its subject matter and if it appears that the name of such person is not on the lists of persons twenty years of age or older they shall restore the name to the list. If the listing of persons twenty years of age or older has been completed in any city or town such investigation shall be conducted by the election commission, election commissioners or the registrars of voters, as the case may be, and if the statements contained in any such petition are found to the satisfaction of said board or officers to be true, and to establish the fact that that person is in the armed services of the United States and was a registered voter at the time of entering such service his name shall be restored to the list and entered in the annual register of voters. Upon the entering of such name in the annual register and the subsequent printing of all voting lists while such person remains in the armed services of the United States there shall be printed on such lists of voters after the name thereof in every instance the letter "S" or some other appropriate identifying mark establishing the fact that such person is in such armed services.

SECTION 2. This act shall be operative during the existence of the present war between the United States and any foreign country and for six months after the termination thereof. *Approved May 7, 1943.*

---

*Chap.*254 AN ACT TO EXTEND THE PROVISIONS OF THE CONTRIBUTORY RETIREMENT SYSTEM IN THE CITY OF SALEM TO EMPLOYEES OF THE SALEM AND BEVERLY WATER SUPPLY BOARD.

Be it enacted, etc., as follows:

SECTION 1. On July first, nineteen hundred and forty-three, employees of the Salem and Beverly water supply board may become members of the contributory retirement system of the city of Salem. Said employees shall have all the rights and obligations provided under sections twenty-six to thirty-one H, inclusive, of chapter thirty-two of the General Laws, as appearing in section one of chapter three hundred and eighteen of the acts of nineteen hundred and thirty-six and as subsequently amended, which they would have had if said retirement system of said city of Salem had become operative on said date.

SECTION 2. The retirement board of the city of Salem shall, on or before the fifteenth day of January in the year nineteen hundred and forty-four, certify to the Salem and Beverly water supply board the amounts payable by it to the various funds of the contributory retirement system of said city on account of the employees of said water supply board for the period beginning on the first day of July, nineteen hundred and forty-three, and ending on the thirty-first day of December, nineteen hundred and forty-four, and thereafter shall, on or before the fifteenth day of January in each year, so certify amounts so payable for the year beginning on the first day of January in said year. The sums so certified shall be paid to the funds of said system in the same manner as provided by section three of chapter seven hundred of the acts of nineteen hundred and thirteen for the payment of other expenses of said water supply board.

SECTION 3. This act shall take effect upon its passage.

Approved May 10, 1943.

---

*Chap.*255 AN ACT TO ABROGATE THE MINIMUM WAGE COMPACT, SO CALLED.

Whereas, The general court, by chapter three hundred and eighty-three of the acts of nineteen hundred and thirty-four did approve and ratify a compact "for establishing uniform standards for conditions of employment, particularly with regard to the minimum wage, in states ratifying the same," said compact being usually known as the Minimum Wage Compact, which was formulated by commissioners and delegates from seven states at Concord, New Hampshire, on the twenty-ninth day of May, nineteen hundred and thirty-four; and

Whereas, The said compact was subsequently ratified in the year nineteen hundred and thirty-five by the state of New Hampshire and in the year nineteen hundred and thirty-six by the state of Rhode Island, and the consent of the congress of the United States was given thereto by public resolution fifty-eight of the seventy-fifth congress, which was approved by the president of the United States on the twelfth day of August, nineteen hundred and thirty-seven; and

Whereas, The field of operation of the said compact was fully occupied by federal legislation known as the Federal Fair Labor Standards Act or the Federal Wage and Hour Law, soon after the consent of the congress to said compact was given, and said federal legislation and the administration thereof, supported by decisions of the supreme court of the United States and of inferior federal courts, has made said compact inoperative and of no effect; and

Whereas, The governor of the state of New Hampshire has given notice to the governor of this commonwealth and the governor of the state of Rhode Island, under date of the twenty-eighth day of July, nineteen hundred and forty-one, that New Hampshire desires to withdraw from said compact; and

Whereas, The commissions established by this commonwealth and the state of Rhode Island have agreed that the compact should be abrogated, and the governor of this commonwealth, under date of December thirty-first, nineteen hundred and forty-two, has notified the governors of New Hampshire and Rhode Island of the desire of this commonwealth to withdraw from said compact; and

Whereas, It is desirable that said compact be abrogated at an early date, and it appears that this can be done by agreement of all three states parties thereto without delaying until the expiration of the two-year period of notice specified in said compact; and

Whereas, The deferred operation of this act beyond the effective date specified herein would tend to defeat its purpose, therefore it is hereby declared to be an emergency law, necessary for the immediate preservation of the public convenience; Now therefore,

Be it enacted, etc., as follows:

SECTION 1. The compact heretofore described, entitled "Compact for establishing Uniform Standards for Conditions of Employment, particularly with Regard to the Minimum Wage, in States ratifying the Same," usually known as the Minimum Wage Compact, whereof a copy is on file in the office of the state secretary, is hereby abrogated on the part of the commonwealth of Massachusetts.

SECTION 2. Section twenty-five of chapter nine of the General Laws, inserted by section one of chapter four hundred and four of the acts of nineteen hundred and thirty-seven, is hereby repealed.

SECTION 3. This act shall take effect, conformably to the constitution, if and when legislation to abrogate said compact, substantially similar to this act, becomes effective in both the states of New Hampshire and Rhode Island or in one of said states, if in the meantime the other has withdrawn from said compact. The state secretary, forthwith upon the effective date of this act, shall send a certified copy thereof to the governor of each of said states.

Approved May 10, 1943.

---

*Chap.*256 AN ACT AUTHORIZING THE BOSTON SCHOOL COMMITTEE TO PROVIDE FREE LUNCHES FOR CERTAIN UNDERNOURISHED AND NEEDY PUPILS.

Be it enacted, etc., as follows:

The school committee of the city of Boston is hereby authorized to provide free lunches for undernourished and needy children attending its public schools.

Approved May 10, 1943.

---

*Chap.*257 AN ACT ESTABLISHING THE SALARY OF THE PRESENT THIRD ASSISTANT CLERK OF THE DISTRICT COURT OF EAST NORFOLK.

Be it enacted, etc., as follows:

SECTION 1. Any provision of general law to the contrary notwithstanding, the salary of the present third assistant clerk of the district court of East Norfolk shall be equal to sixty per cent of the salary of the clerk of said court.

SECTION 2. This act shall take full effect upon its acceptance by the county commissioners of Norfolk county, but not otherwise. *Approved May 10, 1943.*

---

*Chap.*258 AN ACT ESTABLISHING THE SALARIES OF THE MAYOR AND CITY COUNCILLORS OF THE CITY OF LYNN.

Be it enacted, etc., as follows:

SECTION 1. Chapter three hundred and forty of the Special Acts of nineteen hundred and seventeen is hereby amended by striking out section seventeen, as amended by section one of chapter one hundred and twenty-seven of the acts of nineteen hundred and twenty-four, and inserting in place thereof the following section: — *Section 17.* The mayor shall receive in full compensation for all services to the city a salary of six thousand dollars a year. The council may, by yea and nay vote, establish a salary for its members, not exceeding one thousand dollars a year, which shall not be increased or diminished to take effect during the current municipal year.

SECTION 2. This act shall be submitted to the registered voters of the city of Lynn at the municipal election in said city to be held in the current year, in the form of the following question, which shall be placed upon the official ballot to be used at said election: — "Shall an act passed by the general court in the year nineteen hundred and forty-three, entitled 'An Act establishing the salaries of the mayor and city councillors of the city of Lynn', be accepted?" If a majority of the votes in answer to said question is in the affirmative, then this act shall thereupon take full effect, but not otherwise. *Approved May 10, 1943.*

AN ACT PROVIDING A PENALTY FOR THE CRIMES OF ASSAULT AND ASSAULT AND BATTERY. *Chap.259*

Be it enacted, etc., as follows:

SECTION 1. Chapter two hundred and sixty-five of the General Laws is hereby amended by inserting after section thirteen, as appearing in the Tercentenary Edition, the following section: — *Section 13A.* Whoever commits an assault or an assault and battery upon another shall be punished by imprisonment for not more than two and one half years in a house of correction or by a fine of not more than five hundred dollars.

G. L. (Ter. Ed.), 265, new § 13A, added.

Penalty for assault and battery, etc.

SECTION 2. . This act shall take effect on October first in the current year. *Approved May 10, 1943.*

Effective date.

AN ACT CHANGING THE METHOD OF FIXING THE COMPENSATION OF THE CLERKS AND ASSISTANT CLERKS OF THE SENATE AND HOUSE OF REPRESENTATIVES. *Chap.260*

Whereas, The deferred operation of this act would tend to defeat its purpose, which is to establish, at once, a more equitable method of fixing the salaries of the clerks and assistant clerks of the senate and house of representatives, and it is desirable to effect such change as early as possible during the present session of the general court, therefore this act is hereby declared to be an emergency law necessary for the immediate preservation of the public convenience.

Emergency preamble.

Be it enacted, etc., as follows:

SECTION 1. Chapter three of the General Laws is hereby amended by striking out section twelve, as amended by section one of chapter three hundred and sixty of the acts of nineteen hundred and thirty-seven, and inserting in place thereof the following section: — *Section 12.* The clerk of the senate and the clerk of the house of representatives shall each receive such salary as may be established by the com-

G. L. (Ter. Ed.), 3, § 12, etc., amended.

Salary of clerks.

Tenure of office.

mittee on rules of the senate or the committee on rules of the house of representatives, as the case may be, and each shall hold office until his successor is qualified. Salaries established under this section shall be for the period of two years commencing January first of the year in which established.

G. L. (Ter. Ed.), 3, § 13, etc., amended.

SECTION 2. Said chapter three is hereby further amended by striking out section thirteen, as most recently amended by chapter two hundred and thirty of the acts of nineteen hundred and forty-one, and inserting in place thereof the following section: — *Section 13.* The clerks of the senate and house of representatives, subject to the approval of the senate and house, respectively, may each appoint an assistant clerk who, in the absence of the clerk, shall perform his duties unless a temporary clerk is chosen, and who shall receive such salary as may be established by the committee on rules of the senate or the committee on rules of the house, as the case may be. Salaries established for said assistant clerks under this section shall be for the period of two years commencing January first of the year in which established. Each clerk may remove the assistant clerk appointed by him. Each clerk may also employ such clerical assistance as may be necessary, and may expend therefor such amounts as are appropriated.

Appointment, salaries, tenure of office of assistant clerks.

Clerical assistance.

Effective date.

SECTION 3. This act shall become operative when sufficient appropriations therefor have been made, and then as of January first of the current year.

Approved May 11, 1943.

---

*Chap.*261 AN ACT CLARIFYING THE LIMITS ON THE TOTAL LIABILITIES OF ANY ONE BORROWER TO A TRUST COMPANY IN ITS COMMERCIAL AND SAVINGS DEPARTMENTS.

Be it enacted, etc., as follows:

G. L. (Ter. Ed.), 172, new § 40A, added.

Liabilities of any one borrower limited.

Chapter one hundred and seventy-two of the General Laws is hereby amended by inserting after section forty, as amended, the following section: — *Section 40A.* The total liabilities of a person, including in the liabilities of a firm the liabilities of its several members, to the commercial department of a trust company, and to the savings department thereof for loans upon personal security, shall not exceed, in the aggregate, the limit upon the liabilities of one borrower to a trust company provided by section forty, or the maximum limit upon the liabilities of one borrower to the savings department thereof provided by clause Ninth of section fifty-four of chapter one hundred and sixty-eight, whichever limit is the larger; provided, that neither of said limitations shall apply to so much of any such loan as is unconditionally guaranteed as to the payment of principal and interest by the United States.

Approved May 11, 1943.

AN ACT FURTHER REGULATING ALLOWANCES IN THE MILITARY DIVISION OF THE EXECUTIVE DEPARTMENT. *Chap.* 262

Whereas, It is urgently necessary that, in the present national emergency, the amount of allowances to officers and enlisted personnel of the Massachusetts State Guard be clarified and determined, and the deferred operation of this act would tend to defeat such purpose; therefore it is hereby declared to be an emergency law, necessary for the immediate preservation of the public convenience. Emergency preamble.

Be it enacted, etc., as follows:

SECTION 1. Section one hundred and twenty-six of chapter thirty-three of the General Laws, as appearing in section one of chapter four hundred and twenty-five of the acts of nineteen hundred and thirty-nine, is hereby amended by inserting at the end the following sentence: — This section and sections one hundred and twenty-three to one hundred and twenty-five, inclusive, shall apply only to the Massachusetts national guard while not in federal service, but not to the Massachusetts state guard or to any other similar military organization. G. L. (Ter. Ed.), 33, § 126, etc., amended. Application of section limited.

SECTION 2. Said chapter thirty-three, as so appearing, is hereby further amended by inserting after said section one hundred and twenty-six, as amended by section one of this act, the two following sections: — *Section 126A.* There shall annually be allowed and paid to the Massachusetts state guard, or to any similar military organization, while legally in existence, under such regulations as may be promulgated by the commander-in-chief, for postage, printing, stationery, care of property, equipment, repair and alteration of uniforms, military expense, including clerical assistance: to division headquarters, seventeen hundred and fifty dollars; to each brigade headquarters, one hundred and fifty dollars; to each regimental headquarters, seven hundred and fifty dollars, and twenty-five dollars for every company in the regiment; to each region headquarters, five hundred dollars, and twenty-five dollars for each security company in the region; to each separate battalion or squadron and to each other organization designated by the commander-in-chief, one hundred and fifty dollars, and twenty-five dollars for each company therein; and to each company, four hundred dollars; to separate detachments and sections such proportionate amounts as may be approved by the commander-in-chief. G. L. (Ter. Ed.), 33, new §§ 126A and 126B, added. Allowances payable to state guard.

Section 126B. Allowances referred to in sections one hundred and twenty-three to one hundred and twenty-six A, inclusive, shall be paid quarterly in substantially equal installments; provided, that no such allowance may be anticipated, and that no obligation involving future or unpaid installments of any such allowances may be incurred, by Allowances to be paid quarterly.

any person or military unit subject to any provision of said sections.

Effective date.

Section 3. This act shall take effect as of December first, nineteen hundred and forty-two.

Approved May 13, 1943.

Chap.263 An Act authorizing the town of Scituate to acquire additional water supply.

Be it enacted, etc., as follows:

Section 1. For the purposes set forth in chapter three hundred and ninety-one of the acts of eighteen hundred and ninety-three, the town of Scituate, acting by and through its board of water commissioners, may purchase water from the town of Hanover, authority to sell being hereby granted, and may construct, lay, repair and maintain aqueducts, conduits, pipes and other works under or over any lands, water courses, public or other ways, and along any such way, in the town of Norwell in such manner as not unnecessarily to obstruct the same; and for the purpose of constructing, laying, repairing and maintaining apparatus and laying and repairing such conduits, pipes and other works, and for all other proper purposes of this act, the town of Scituate may enter upon and dig up or raise and embank any such lands, highways or other ways in such manner as to cause the least hindrance to public travel thereon; provided, that the town of Scituate shall restore to the satisfaction of the board of selectmen of the town of Norwell any ways so dug up; and provided, further, that all things done upon any way in the town of Norwell shall be done to the satisfaction of its board of selectmen. The town of Scituate shall pay all damages sustained by any person in consequence of any negligent act upon the part of said town, its agents or employees under this act.

Section 2. The town of Norwell and any person or corporation injured in his or its property by any action of the town of Scituate or its board of water commissioners taken under authority of this act may recover damages from said town of Scituate under chapter seventy-nine of the General Laws.

Section 3. If the town of Scituate shall construct and lay aqueducts, conduits or pipes in said town of Norwell as herein authorized, said town of Scituate shall furnish water for the extinguishment of fires to said town of Norwell and water for domestic and other purposes to such inhabitants of said town of Norwell as reside in the vicinity of the pipe lines of said town of Scituate, constructed and maintained under this act, at such rates and under such terms as the parties may mutually agree. In case of failure to agree as to the price for water furnished, or the manner or location of construction, the department of public utilities, upon petition of either town or of any aggrieved inhabitant of said town of Norwell, shall determine the price and the manner and location of construction and such determination shall be final.

SECTION 4. The towns of Scituate, Norwell and Hanover, or any two of them, each town acting through its board of water commissioners, or its board of selectmen if there is no board of water commissioners, may enter into agreements for the purchase or sale of, and purchase or sell, at such rates and under such terms as may be mutually agreed upon, water for the extinguishment of fires and for domestic and other purposes in such average annual amounts and from such sources in any of said towns so entering into agreement as may first be approved by the state department of public health and may enter into agreements for the laying of mains and construction of other works in any of said towns necessary for carrying out the purposes of this section.

SECTION 5. This act shall take effect upon its passage.

Approved May 13, 1943.

AN ACT GIVING PREFERENCE TO CERTAIN FORMER EMPLOYEES IN THE LABOR SERVICE OF THE CITY OF CAMBRIDGE FOR RE-EMPLOYMENT THEREIN. *Chap.264*

Be it enacted, etc., as follows:

Patsy Zuffreo, Leonardo Guida, Robert J. Adams, John Dussault, John C. Rooney, Frederick T. Igo, Edward P. Finnegan, John F. Carmichael, Charles M. Scully, Thomas E. Sheahan, Joseph Maccini and Louis Frongello, and any other former employees in the labor service of the city of Cambridge, who were removed therefrom by order of the division of civil service by reason of the fact that certain classification requirements under the civil service law were not complied with, shall, if duly registered as applicants for employment in the labor service of said city, be given preference for re-employment therein. The basis of such re-employment shall be the order of appointment to said labor service, or, if not ascertainable, the order of the respective registrations of said persons as applicants for employment in said labor service. *Approved May 13, 1943.*

AN ACT PROVIDING FOR THE ISSUANCE OF FISHING LICENSES WITHOUT CHARGE TO CERTAIN RECIPIENTS OF OLD AGE ASSISTANCE, SO CALLED. *Chap.265*

Be it enacted, etc., as follows:

Clause (1) of section eight of chapter one hundred and thirty-one of the General Laws, as appearing in section two of chapter five hundred and ninety-nine of the acts of nineteen hundred and forty-one, is hereby amended by striking out the last paragraph and inserting in place thereof the following paragraph: — G. L. (Ter. Ed.), 131, § 8, etc., amended.

No fee shall be charged for any license issued under this Fishing licenses for recipients of old age assistance.

clause to a person over the age of seventy or for a fishing license issued thereunder to a person seventy years of age or under who is a recipient of old age assistance granted under chapter one hundred and eighteen A.

Approved May 13, 1943.

---

*Chap.*266 AN ACT TO PROVIDE FOR FILING REPORTS OF LOCAL PLANNING BOARDS WITH THE STATE PLANNING BOARD INSTEAD OF WITH THE DEPARTMENT OF PUBLIC WELFARE.

Be it enacted, etc., as follows:

G. L. (Ter. Ed.), 41, § 71, amended.

Section seventy-one of chapter forty-one of the General Laws, as appearing in the Tercentenary Edition, is hereby amended by striking out, in the fifth line, the words "department of public welfare" and inserting in place thereof the words: — state planning board, — so as to read as follows: — *Section 71.* Every planning board shall make a report annually to the city council or to the annual town meeting, giving information regarding the condition of the town and any plans or proposals for its development and estimates of the cost thereof. Every such planning board shall file with the state planning board a copy of each report made by it.

Annual reports of planning boards.

Approved May 13, 1943.

---

*Chap.*267 AN ACT REPEALING THE PROVISIONS OF LAW AUTHORIZING THE LICENSING AND CONDUCTING OF THE GAME COMMONLY CALLED BEANO.

Be it enacted, etc., as follows:

G. L. (Ter. Ed.), 271, § 22A, etc., amended.

Chapter two hundred and seventy-one of the General Laws is hereby amended by striking out section twenty-two A, as most recently amended by chapters two hundred and twenty-two and two hundred and eighty-three of the acts of nineteen hundred and thirty-six, and inserting in place thereof the following section: — *Section 22A.* Nothing in this chapter shall authorize the prosecution, arrest or conviction of any person for conducting or promoting, or for allowing to be conducted or promoted, a game of cards commonly called whist or bridge, in connection with which prizes are offered to be won by chance; provided, that the entire proceeds of the charges for admission to such game are donated solely to charitable, civic, educational, fraternal or religious purposes.

Charity whists, permitted when.

Approved May 14, 1943.

THE COMMONWEALTH OF MASSACHUSETTS,
EXECUTIVE DEPARTMENT, STATE HOUSE,
BOSTON, June 15, 1943.

Honorable FREDERIC W. COOK, *Secretary of the Commonwealth, State House. Boston.*

SIR: — I, Leverett Saltonstall, by virtue of and in accordance with the provisions of the Forty-eighth Amendment to the Constitution, "The Referendum II, Emergency Measures", do declare that in my opinion, the immediate preservation of the public peace, health, safety or convenience requires that the law passed on the fourteenth day of May in the year nineteen hundred and forty-three, entitled "An Act repealing the provisions of law authorizing the licensing and conducting of the game commonly called Beano" should take effect forthwith and that it is an emergency law and that the facts constituting the emergency are as follows:

Because the manner in which the games of Beano have been and are conducted in many parts of the Commonwealth has been and is detrimental to the public welfare, and the Legislature, comprising the representatives of all the people, thoroughly debated all aspects of this subject and decided, as a matter of public policy and public protection, the law should be repealed. Any further delay in making this act effective will only delay the protection which it is designed to afford.

Very truly yours,
LEVERETT SALTONSTALL,
Governor of the Commonwealth.

OFFICE OF THE SECRETARY, BOSTON, June 15, 1943.

I hereby certify that the accompanying statement was filed in this office by His Excellency the Governor of the Commonwealth of Massachusetts at twelve o'clock and fifty-five minutes, P.M., on the above date, and in accordance with Article Forty-eight of the Amendments to the Constitution said chapter takes effect forthwith, being chapter two hundred and sixty-seven of the acts of nineteen hundred and forty-three.

F. W. COOK,
Secretary of the Commonwealth.

AN ACT RELATIVE TO THE HOURS DURING WHICH HORSE RACES ON WHICH THE PARI-MUTUEL SYSTEM OF WAGERING IS PERMITTED MAY BE CONDUCTED DURING THE PRESENT WAR. *Chap.*268

Whereas, The deferred operation of this act would delay the application of its provisions to horse racing meetings during the current year, therefore it is hereby declared to be an emergency law, necessary for the immediate preservation of the public convenience. Emergency preamble.

Be it enacted, etc., as follows:

During the existing war between the United States and any foreign country, the state racing commission may permit horse races at any horse racing meeting held under a license issued by it to be conducted until seven-fifteen o'clock, post meridian, notwithstanding the provisions of chapter one hundred and twenty-eight A of the General Laws which prohibit such races from being conducted later than seven o'clock, post meridian. *Approved May 14, 1943.*

Chap.269 AN ACT RELATIVE TO PUBLIC HEARINGS ON APPLICATIONS FOR LICENSES TO CONDUCT HORSE AND DOG RACING MEETINGS.

Emergency preamble.

Whereas, The deferred operation of this act would delay the application of its provisions to horse and dog racing meetings during the current year, therefore it is hereby declared to be an emergency law, necessary for the immediate preservation of the public convenience.

Be it enacted, etc., as follows:

G. L. (Ter. Ed.), 128A, § 3, etc., amended.

Public hearings on applications for licenses.

Section three of chapter one hundred and twenty-eight A of the General Laws is hereby amended by striking out the first paragraph, as amended by section two of chapter four hundred and fifty-four of the acts of nineteen hundred and thirty-five, and inserting in place thereof the following paragraph: — If any application for a license, filed as provided by section two, shall be in accordance with the provisions of this chapter, the commission, after reasonable notice and a public hearing in the city or town wherein the license is to be exercised, may issue a license to the applicant to conduct a racing meeting, in accordance with the provisions of this chapter, at the race track specified in such application; provided, that if the commission has already taken action on an application for any calendar year, after such notice and public hearing, no other public hearing need be granted on any other application from the same applicant relating to the same premises filed prior to the expiration of said year; and provided, further, that on an application for a license to conduct a horse or dog racing meeting in connection with a state or county fair no hearing need be held unless a request signed by at least one per cent of the registered voters of the city or town in which the track is located is filed with the commission at least thirty days prior to the first day on which the racing meeting requested is proposed to be held.

Approved May 14, 1943.

Chap.270 AN ACT FURTHER EXTENDING THE TIME DURING WHICH THERE SHALL BE COLLECTED AN ADDITIONAL TAX ON SALES OF GASOLINE AND CERTAIN OTHER MOTOR VEHICLE FUEL.

Emergency preamble.

Whereas, The provisions of law referred to in this act will shortly cease to be effective, but the circumstances and conditions which made advisable their enactment still continue and accordingly this act should take effect before such provisions cease to be effective, therefore it is hereby declared to be an emergency law, necessary for the immediate preservation of the public convenience.

Be it enacted, etc., as follows:

Chapter two hundred and forty-eight of the acts of nineteen hundred and thirty-two, as most recently amended by chapter three hundred and thirty of the acts of nineteen hundred and forty-one, is hereby further amended by striking out, in the fifth line, the word "forty-three" and inserting in place thereof the word: — forty-six, — so as to read as follows: — The time during which the additional excise tax of one cent is imposed on each gallon of fuel, as defined in section one of chapter sixty-four A of the General Laws, sold in the commonwealth, is hereby extended to and including the thirtieth day of June, nineteen hundred and forty-six, and the provisions of section four of chapter one hundred and twenty-two of the acts of nineteen hundred and thirty-one shall apply to the tax so imposed during such extended period. *Approved May 14, 1943.*

AN ACT AUTHORIZING THE CITY OF BOSTON TO PAY CERTAIN UNPAID BILLS. *Chap.271*

Be it enacted, etc., as follows:

SECTION 1. The city of Boston is hereby authorized to expend a sum of money not to exceed three thousand one hundred and sixty-four dollars and sixty-four cents to pay such unpaid bills incurred in the year nineteen hundred and thirty-nine by the public welfare department of said city with Nutter's System, Inc. as are now on file in the city auditor's office, such bills being legally unenforceable against said city by reason of an error in the contract executed to cover the services rendered by said company.

SECTION 2. No bills shall be approved by the city auditor of said city for payment under authority of this act unless and until certificates have been signed and filed with said auditor stating, under the penalties of perjury, that the services for which bills have been submitted were ordered by an official or an employee of said city and that such services were rendered to said city. Payment of said bills shall be charged to the encumbered balance set aside or reserved by the city auditor at the time orders were originally issued to Nutter's System, Inc. for the performance of the services represented by the bills.

SECTION 3. This act shall take effect upon its passage.

Approved May 14, 1943.

AN ACT REMOVING THE STATUTORY LIMITATION ON THE AMOUNT OF THE SALARY OF THE COMMISSIONER OF PUBLIC WORKS OF THE CITY OF WORCESTER. *Chap.272*

Be it enacted, etc., as follows:

Section one of chapter two hundred and ten of the acts of nineteen hundred and thirty-nine is hereby amended by striking out the last sentence. *Approved May 14, 1943.*

Chap.273 AN ACT AMENDING THE PROVISIONS OF THE CORRUPT PRACTICES LAW RELATIVE TO THE ACTIVITIES OF CERTAIN CORPORATIONS WHEN AFFECTED BY INITIATIVE PETITIONS.

Be it enacted, etc., as follows:

G. L. (Ter. Ed.), 55, § 7, etc., amended.

Political contributions by certain corporations regulated.

SECTION 1. Chapter fifty-five of the General Laws is hereby amended by striking out section seven, as amended by chapter seventy-five of the acts of nineteen hundred and thirty-eight, and inserting in place thereof the following section: — *Section 7.* No corporation carrying on the business of a bank, trust, surety, indemnity, safe deposit, insurance, railroad, street railway, telegraph, telephone, gas, electric light, heat, power, canal, aqueduct, or water company, no company having the right to take land by eminent domain or to exercise franchises in public ways, granted by the commonwealth or by any county, city or town, no trustee or trustees owning or holding the majority of the stock of such a corporation, no business corporation incorporated under the laws of or doing business in the commonwealth and no officer or agent acting in behalf of any corporation mentioned in this section, shall directly or indirectly give, pay, expend or contribute, or promise to give, pay, expend or contribute, any money or other valuable thing for the purpose of aiding, promoting or preventing the nomination or election of any person to public office, or aiding, promoting or antagonizing the interests of any political party, or influencing or affecting the vote on any question submitted to the voters, other than one materially affecting any of the property, business or assets of the corporation. No person or persons, no political committee, and no person acting under the authority of a political committee, or in its behalf, shall solicit or receive from such corporation or such holders of stock any gift, payment, expenditure, contribution or promise to give, pay, expend or contribute for any such purpose.

G. L. (Ter. Ed.), 55, new § 17A, added.

Statement of contributions to be filed.

SECTION 2. Said chapter fifty-five is hereby further amended by inserting after section seventeen, as amended, the following section: — *Section 17A.* The treasurer of any corporation mentioned in section seven which has given, paid, expended or contributed, or promised to give, pay, expend or contribute, any money or other valuable thing in order to influence or affect the vote on any question submitted to the voters which materially affects any of the property, business or assets of the corporation, shall, within thirty days after the election at which the question was submitted to the voters, file a statement with the state secretary setting forth the amount of every gift, payment, expenditure or contribution or promise to give, pay, expend or contribute, together with the date, purpose, and name and last known address of the person to whom it was made.

Approved May 14, 1943.

AN ACT PROVIDING FOR ONE DAY OFF IN EVERY SIX DAYS FOR POLICE OFFICERS IN THE CITY OF BOSTON. *Chap.274*

Be it enacted, etc., as follows:

SECTION 1. Members of the police department of the city of Boston shall be excused from duty for one day out of every six without loss of pay. The time and manner of excusing members of said police department from duty shall be determined by the police commissioner for said city. A member so excused shall be exempt from duty and from attendance at a police station or other place, but otherwise shall be subject to all laws, rules and regulations relating to members of said department. Said police commissioner, in case of any public emergency, or of any unusual demand for the services of the police in said city, may prevent any member of said department from taking the day off at the time when he is entitled thereto, or at the time assigned therefor; provided, that such day off shall be granted to him as soon thereafter as is practicable. In no case shall the number of such days off be less than sixty in each year and they shall be in addition to any annual vacation now or hereafter allowed to members of said department, and such annual vacation shall not be diminished on account thereof.

SECTION 2. This act shall take full effect upon its acceptance by vote of the city council of said city, subject to the provisions of its charter; provided, that no such acceptance shall take place prior to the expiration of ninety days after the termination of the existing states of war between the United States and any foreign country has been officially proclaimed. *Approved May 14, 1943.*

AN ACT TO MAKE UNIFORM THE PERIOD OF TIME OF LIABILITY OF THE COMMONWEALTH IN CONNECTION WITH NOTICES OF THE GIVING OF PUBLIC ASSISTANCE BY CITIES AND TOWNS. *Chap.275*

Be it enacted, etc., as follows:

G. L. (Ter. Ed.), 111, § 116, amended.

SECTION 1. Section one hundred and sixteen of chapter one hundred and eleven of the General Laws, as appearing in the Tercentenary Edition, is hereby amended by striking out, in the twenty-ninth line, the word "five" and inserting in place thereof the word: — ten, — so that the sentence appearing in the twenty-fourth to the thirty-second lines will read as follows: — In any case liable to be maintained by the commonwealth when public aid has been rendered to such sick person, a written notice shall be sent to the department of public welfare, containing such information as will show that the person named therein is a proper charge to the commonwealth, and reimbursement shall be made for reasonable expenses incurred within ten days next before such notice is mailed, and thereafter until such sick person

Payment of certain expenses regulated.

is removed under section twelve of chapter one hundred and twenty-one, or is able to be so removed without endangering his or the public health.

G. L. (Ter. Ed.), 122, § 18, etc., amended.

Section 2. Section eighteen of chapter one hundred and twenty-two of the General Laws, as most recently amended by chapter four hundred and twelve of the acts of nineteen hundred and forty-one, is hereby further amended by striking out, in the second line, the word "five" and inserting in place thereof the word: — ten, — so that the first sentence will read as follows: — Reasonable expenses incurred by a town under section seventeen within ten days next before notice has been given as therein required and also after the giving of such notice and until said sick person is able to be removed to said hospital and infirmary shall be reimbursed by the commonwealth.

Towns reimbursed, when.

Approved May 14, 1943.

---

*Chap.*276 An Act increasing the minimum and maximum amounts of weekly compensation to be paid for total and permanent disability under the workmen's compensation law.

Be it enacted, etc., as follows:

G. L. (Ter. Ed.), 152, § 34A, etc., amended.

Section thirty-four A of chapter one hundred and fifty-two of the General Laws, inserted by chapter three hundred and sixty-four of the acts of nineteen hundred and thirty-five, is hereby amended by striking out, in the fifteenth line, the word "eighteen" and inserting in place thereof the word: — twenty, — and by striking out, in the sixteenth and eighteenth lines, the word "nine", and inserting in place thereof in each instance the word: — eleven, — so as to read as follows: — *Section 34A.* At any time before or after an injured employee has received the maximum compensation to which he is or may be entitled under sections thirty-four and thirty-five, or either of them, such employee and the insurer may agree, or, on application for a hearing by either party, a member or, on review, the board may find, that the disability suffered by the injured employee is total and permanent. After such an agreement or finding, during the continuance of such total and permanent disability, the insurer shall make or continue to make payments to the injured employee under section thirty-four so long as compensation is payable under said section, and thereafter during such continuance shall pay to the injured employee a weekly compensation equal to one half his average weekly wages, but not more than twenty dollars a week nor less than eleven dollars a week, except that the weekly compensation of the injured employee shall be equal to his average weekly wages in case such wages are less than eleven dollars; but in no case shall such compensation be less than seven dollars a week where the normal working hours of the injured employee were fifteen hours or more a week. In any hearing or investigation under this chapter,

Payments for total disability regulated.

loss of both hands, or both feet, or both legs, or both eyes, or injury to the skull resulting in incurable imbecility or insanity, or injury to the spine resulting in permanent and complete paralysis of both legs or both arms shall, in the absence of conclusive proof to the contrary, constitute permanent total disability. In all other cases permanent total disability shall be determined in accordance with the facts, and proof thereof shall be by weight of the evidence. If an employee who has been agreed or found to be totally and permanently disabled earns wages at any time thereafter, payments of compensation may be suspended in the manner provided by section twenty-nine. If such wages are earned before the injured employee has received the maximum compensation to which he is or may be entitled as aforesaid, such employee, during the period of suspension, may, if otherwise entitled thereto, receive payments under section thirty-five; but if such wages are earned after he has received such maximum, no payments shall be made during such period. *Approved May 14, 1943.*

AN ACT RELATIVE TO APPROPRIATIONS FOR SCHOOL PURPOSES IN THE CITY OF CAMBRIDGE. *Chap.277*

Be it enacted, etc., as follows:

SECTION 1. Chapter one hundred and eighty-two of the acts of nineteen hundred and thirty-eight is hereby repealed.

SECTION 2. This act shall take effect on November first in the current year and shall not affect any appropriation for school purposes in the city of Cambridge made prior to its effective date. *Approved May 14, 1943.*

AN ACT RELATIVE TO THE FURNISHING AND USE OF MOTOR VEHICLE NUMBER PLATES DURING THE EXISTING STATE OF WAR AND FOR A CERTAIN PERIOD OF TIME THEREAFTER. *Chap.278*

Be it enacted, etc., as follows:

SECTION 1. If, during the continuance of the existing state of war between the United States and any foreign country and the six months next following the termination of said states of war, the registrar of motor vehicles determines that a sufficient supply of steel or other suitable material is not available for compliance with the provisions of chapter ninety of the General Laws which require that two number plates furnished by him be displayed on motor vehicles operated in or upon any way in this commonwealth, said registrar may, in the case of such class or classes of motor vehicles as he may determine, furnish one such number plate instead of two, and the display of said number plate at the rear of any motor vehicle for which such plate is furnished shall be lawful notwithstanding the requirements of said chapter ninety pertaining to number plates.

SECTION 2. During the effective period of section one of this act, no fee shall be charged by said registrar for any additional number plate furnished by him to replace a plate which has been mutilated or is illegible.

Approved May 14, 1943.

---

*Chap.*279 AN ACT TO EXEMPT FROM TAXATION THE REAL ESTATE IN BOSTON OF THE ISABELLA STEWART GARDNER MUSEUM, INCORPORATED, TRUSTEE UNDER THE WILL OF ISABELLA STEWART GARDNER.

Be it enacted, etc., as follows:

The real estate, hereinafter described, located in the city of Boston and held by The Isabella Stewart Gardner Museum, Incorporated as trustee under the will of Isabella Stewart Gardner, shall be exempt from taxation beginning January first, nineteen hundred and forty-three, and continuing so long as the museum, known as the Isabella Stewart Gardner Museum, is operated by said corporation for the education and enjoyment of the public. Said real estate includes the building housing said museum and is bounded northwesterly by Worthington street; northeasterly by the Fenway; southeasterly by Evans Way; southwesterly by land now or formerly of Carol H. Powers et al one hundred and twenty-one hundredths feet; and northwesterly thirty-two and sixty-nine hundredths feet and southwesterly eighty-four and eighty-nine hundredths feet by land now or formerly of Harold J. Coolidge et al, Trustees; containing about sixty-six thousand, seven hundred and ninety-four square feet.

Approved May 14, 1943.

---

*Chap.*280 AN ACT PROVIDING FOR PAYMENTS TO CERTAIN MUNICIPAL EMPLOYEES IN LIEU OF VACATIONS IN CERTAIN CASES.

Be it enacted, etc., as follows:

G. L. (Ter. Ed.), 41, § 111, etc., amended.

Payments in lieu of vacations.

Section one hundred and eleven of chapter forty-one of the General Laws, as most recently amended by chapter three hundred and sixty-eight of the acts of nineteen hundred and forty-one, is hereby further amended by striking out the fourth sentence and inserting in place thereof the following two sentences: — Any such person who has actually worked for such a city or town for thirty-two weeks in the aggregate during the preceding calendar year and whose employment is terminated without his having been granted the vacation based thereon to which he would otherwise be entitled under this section shall be paid an amount equal to two weeks' wages at the rate at which he was entitled to be compensated for the two weeks immediately preceding the termination of his employment; and in such case the official head of the department in which he was last employed shall enter such amount on the departmental pay roll. Any official of a city or town whose duty it is to grant a vacation as provided by this section who wilfully refuses to grant the same or to make such entry on the departmental pay roll shall be punished by a fine of not more than one hundred dollars. *Approved May 14, 1943.*

AN ACT RELATIVE TO THE PROVIDING OF BALLOTS AND BALLOT LABELS AT ELECTIONS. *Chap.281*

Be it enacted, etc., as follows:

SECTION 1. Section forty-five of chapter fifty-four of the General Laws, as appearing in the Tercentenary Edition, is hereby amended by striking out the first sentence and inserting in place thereof the following sentence: — One set of ballots, not less than one for each registered voter, shall be provided for each polling place at which an election for state, city or town officers is to be held. G. L. (Ter. Ed.), 54, § 45, amended. Ballots to be provided.

SECTION 2. Said section forty-five, as so appearing, is hereby further amended by adding at the end the following paragraph: — G. L. (Ter. Ed.), 54, § 45, amended.

Where voting machines are used the state secretary or the city and town clerk, as the case may be, shall provide not less than three sets of ballot labels for each such machine used. Official ballots shall also be furnished in accordance with section thirty-five A. *Approved May 14, 1943.* Ballot labels for voting machines.

AN ACT ESTABLISHING A MINIMUM ENTRY FEE IN CERTAIN APPEALS TO THE APPELLATE TAX BOARD FROM TAXES ON CERTAIN TANGIBLE PERSONAL PROPERTY. *Chap.282*

Be it enacted, etc., as follows:

Section seven A of chapter fifty-eight A of the General Laws, as amended, is hereby further amended by striking out the third sentence, as appearing in chapter three hundred and eighty-four of the acts of nineteen hundred and thirty-eight, and inserting in place thereof the following sentence: — An appellant desiring to be heard under the informal procedure shall pay to the clerk the entry fee provided in section seven, except that the minimum entry fee shall be two dollars if the assessed valuation of the property on which the tax appealed from was assessed does not exceed twenty thousand dollars and such property is occupied in whole or in part by the appellant as his dwelling, or if the assessed valuation of the property on which the tax appealed from was assessed does not exceed five thousand dollars and such property is within the class of tangible personal property described in clause Twentieth of section five of chapter fifty-nine, and shall file a written waiver of the right of appeal to the supreme judicial court, except upon questions of law raised by the pleadings or by an agreed statement of facts or shown by the report of the G. L. (Ter. Ed.), 58A, § 7A, etc., amended. Informal procedure. Entry fee.

board, an election of the informal procedure and a written statement of the facts in the case and of the amount claimed in abatement together with such additional information as the clerk may require. *Approved May 14, 1943.*

Chap.283 AN ACT PROVIDING FOR THE REINSTATEMENT OF RICHARD A. LINEHAN IN THE SERVICE OF THE CITY OF LAWRENCE FOR THE PURPOSE OF RETIREMENT.

Be it enacted, etc., as follows:

SECTION 1. Richard A. Linehan, who was employed in the water department of the city of Lawrence from February, nineteen hundred and seven to September, nineteen hundred and thirty-eight, except for a period beginning in February, nineteen hundred and thirty-seven and ending in June, nineteen hundred and thirty-eight, may be reinstated by said city in the service of said department for the purpose of being retired as hereinafter provided. Upon such reinstatement said Linehan may become a member of the contributory retirement system of said city, notwithstanding any provision of law governing said retirement system that makes him ineligible for membership therein. Upon becoming such member, he shall be entitled to all the rights and privileges of members of said system which he would have enjoyed if he had become a member of the system on June sixth, nineteen hundred and thirty-eight, the date of his re-entry into the service of said city; provided, that he first deposits in the annuity fund of said system such amount as the board of retirement of said system may determine in order to establish an account for him in said annuity fund in an amount equal to that which it would be if he had been a member of said system since said June sixth, nineteen hundred and thirty-eight.

SECTION 2. This act shall take full effect upon its acceptance by vote of the city council of said city, subject to the provisions of its charter, but not otherwise.

Approved May 14, 1943.

Chap.284 AN ACT AUTHORIZING THE SUSPENSION AND REMOVAL OF CITY AND TOWN COLLECTORS AND THE APPOINTMENT OF TEMPORARY COLLECTORS UNDER CERTAIN CIRCUMSTANCES.

Be it enacted, etc., as follows:

G. L. (Ter. Ed.), 41, new § 39B, added.

Chapter forty-one of the General Laws is hereby amended by inserting after section thirty-nine A, inserted by chapter eighty-nine of the acts of nineteen hundred and thirty-nine, the following section: — *Section 39B.* If, in the opinion of the commissioner of corporations and taxation, hereinafter referred to as the commissioner, the safety of any city or town funds may be jeopardized by the continuation in office of a city or town collector or a treasurer acting as such col-

Removal of collectors by commissioner.

lector, the commissioner may petition the superior court for the removal of such officer. Pending a hearing upon the petition, any justice of such court, if in his judgment the public good so requires, may, after a hearing, summary or otherwise, as he determines, suspend the authority of such officer to act until final action upon the petition is taken. In case of such suspension, the commissioner shall notify the selectmen of such town or the mayor of such city and the officer so suspended shall be deemed to be unable to perform his duties because of disability within the meaning of section forty or section sixty-one A.

The petition of the commissioner may be heard by a justice of the superior court sitting in any county after such notice to the commissioner and to the officer as the court deems necessary. The court shall hear the parties and their witnesses and the decision of the court shall be final and conclusive. Proceedings under this section shall be advanced for speedy hearing, upon the request of either party. If, after hearing, the court shall be of the opinion that the public good so requires, the court shall by decree remove the officer. Otherwise, the court shall dismiss the petition and, if the authority of the officer to act has been suspended, shall restore such authority.

The word "collector" as used in this section shall include a collector of taxes. *Approved May 14, 1943.*

AN ACT RELATIVE TO THE TAXATION OF INCOMES AND OF CERTAIN BUSINESS AND MANUFACTURING CORPORATIONS. *Chap.285*

Be it enacted, etc., as follows:

SECTION 1. Chapter three hundred and seven of the acts of nineteen hundred and thirty-three is hereby amended by striking out section nine, as most recently amended by section one of chapter three hundred and thirty-one of the acts of nineteen hundred and forty-one, and inserting in place thereof the following section: — *Section 9.* Income received by any inhabitant of the commonwealth during the years nineteen hundred and thirty-three, nineteen hundred and thirty-four and nineteen hundred and thirty-five from dividends on shares in all corporations, joint stock companies and banking associations, organized under the laws of this commonwealth or under the laws of any state or nation, except co-operative banks, building and loan associations and credit unions chartered by the commonwealth, and except savings and loan associations under the supervision of the commissioner of banks, and income received by any inhabitant of the commonwealth during the years nineteen hundred and thirty-six, nineteen hundred and thirty-seven, nineteen hundred and thirty-eight, nineteen hundred and thirty-nine, nineteen hundred and forty, nineteen hundred and forty-one, nineteen hundred and forty-two, nineteen hundred and forty-three, nineteen hundred and forty-four and nineteen hundred and forty-five from such dividends, other than stock dividends paid in new stock of the company issuing the same, shall be taxed at the rate of six per cent per annum. Inhabitant of the commonwealth shall include (*a*) estates and fiduciaries specified in sections nine, ten, thirteen and fourteen of chapter sixty-two of the General Laws, (*b*) partnerships specified in section seventeen of said chapter sixty-two, and (*c*) partnerships, associations or trusts, the beneficial interest in which is represented by transferable shares, specified in paragraphs entitled First, Second and Third of subsection (*c*) of section one of said chapter sixty-two. Except as otherwise provided in this section, the provisions of said chapter sixty-two shall apply to the taxation of income received by any such inhabitant during said years. Subsection (*b*) of section one of said chapter sixty-two shall not apply to income received during said years.

SECTION 2. Said chapter three hundred and seven is hereby further amended by striking out section nine A, as most recently amended by section two of said chapter three hundred and thirty-one, and inserting in place thereof the following section: — *Section 9A.* The credit for dividends paid to inhabitants of this commonwealth by foreign corporations provided by section forty-three of chapter sixty-three of the General Laws in determining the tax leviable on such corporations under paragraph (2) of section thirty-nine of said chapter sixty-three shall not be allowed to foreign corporations or to foreign manufacturing corporations in respect to dividends so paid in the years nineteen hundred and thirty-three, nineteen hundred and thirty-four, nineteen hundred and thirty-five, nineteen hundred and thirty-six, nineteen hundred and thirty-seven, nineteen hundred and thirty-eight, nineteen hundred and thirty-nine, nineteen hundred and forty, nineteen hundred and forty-one, nineteen hundred and forty-two, nineteen hundred and forty-three, nineteen hundred and forty-four and nineteen hundred and forty-five.

SECTION 3. Said chapter three hundred and seven is hereby further amended by striking out section ten, as most recently amended by section three of said chapter three hundred and thirty-one, and inserting in place thereof the following section: — *Section 10.* Every corporation organized under the laws of this commonwealth, and every corporation doing business therein, including every banking association organized under the laws of any state or nation, and every partnership, association or trust the beneficial interest in which is represented by transferable shares, doing business in the commonwealth unless the dividends paid on its shares are exempt from taxation under section one of said chapter sixty-two shall, in the years nineteen hundred and thirty-four, nineteen hundred and thirty-five, nineteen hundred and thirty-six, nineteen hundred and thirty-seven, nineteen hundred and thirty-eight, nineteen hundred and thirty-nine, nineteen hundred and forty, nineteen hundred and forty-one, nineteen hundred and forty-two, nineteen hundred and forty-three, nineteen hundred and forty-four, nineteen hundred and forty-five and nineteen hundred and forty-six, file with the commissioner of corporations and taxation, hereinafter called the commissioner, in such form as he shall prescribe, a complete list of the names and addresses of its shareholders as of record on December thirty-first next preceding, or on any other date satisfactory to the commissioner, or, in its discretion, of such shareholders as are residents of the commonwealth, together with the number and class of shares held by each shareholder, and the rate of dividends paid on each class of stock for said preceding year. The second paragraph of section thirty-three of said chapter sixty-two shall not apply to returns relative to shareholders receiving dividends in the years nineteen hundred and thirty-three, nineteen hundred and thirty-four, nineteen hundred and thirty-five, nineteen hundred and thirty-six, nineteen hundred and thirty-seven, nineteen hundred and thirty-eight, nineteen hundred and thirty-nine, nineteen hundred and forty, nineteen hundred and forty-one, nineteen hundred and forty-two, nineteen hundred and forty-three, nineteen hundred and forty-four and nineteen hundred and forty-five.

SECTION 4. Said chapter three hundred and seven is hereby further amended by striking out section eleven, as most recently amended by section four of said chapter three hundred and thirty-one, and inserting in place thereof the following section: — *Section 11.* The state treasurer shall, on or before November twentieth, in the years nineteen hundred and thirty-four, nineteen hundred and thirty-five, nineteen hundred and thirty-six, nineteen hundred and thirty-seven, nineteen hundred and thirty-eight, nineteen hundred and thirty-nine, nineteen hundred and forty, nineteen hundred and forty-one, nineteen hundred and forty-two, nineteen hundred and forty-three, nineteen hundred and forty-four, nineteen hundred and forty-five and nineteen hundred and forty-six, distribute to the several cities and towns, in proportion to the amounts of state tax imposed upon such cities and towns in said years, respectively, the proceeds of the taxes collected by the commonwealth under section nine of this act, after deducting a sum sufficient to reimburse the commonwealth for the expenses incurred in the collection and distribution of said taxes, and for such of said taxes as have been refunded under section twenty-seven of chapter fifty-eight of the General Laws, during said years, together with any interest or costs paid on account of refunds, which shall be retained by the commonwealth. Any amount payable to a city or town hereunder shall be included by the assessors thereof as an estimated receipt, and be deducted, in accordance with section twenty-three of chapter fifty-nine of the General Laws, from the amount required to be raised by taxation to meet appropriations made in such years for public welfare, soldiers' benefits and maturing debts, in that order.

SECTION 5. Section one of chapter three hundred and seventeen of the acts of nineteen hundred and thirty-four is hereby amended by striking out the first paragraph, as most recently amended by section five of said chapter three hundred and thirty-one, and inserting in place thereof the following paragraph: — During the years nineteen hundred and thirty-four, nineteen hundred and thirty-five, nineteen hundred and thirty-six, nineteen hundred and thirty-seven, nineteen hundred and thirty-eight, nineteen hundred and thirty-nine, nineteen hundred and forty, nineteen hundred and forty-one, nineteen hundred and forty-two, nineteen hundred and forty-three, nineteen hundred and forty-four, nineteen hundred and forty-five and nineteen hundred and forty-six, every corporation subject to section thirty-eight B of chapter sixty-three of the General Laws shall, except as provided in section fifty-six A of said chapter, as amended by section three hereof, pay annually a minimum excise of not less than the amount, if any, by which the sum of (1), (2), (3) and (4) following exceeds six per cent of the dividends paid by such corporation during the year corresponding to that in which the income is received: —

SECTION 6. Any reference in said chapter three hundred and seventeen or in section four of chapter three hundred and sixty-two of the acts of nineteen hundred and thirty-six to section nine of chapter three hundred and seven of the acts of nineteen hundred and thirty-three shall be taken to refer to said section, as most recently amended by section one of this act. *Approved May 14, 1943.*

---

*Chap.*286 AN ACT EXTENDING THE TIME FOR ACCEPTANCE OF AN ACT TO ESTABLISH IN THE TOWN OF NATICK REPRESENTATIVE TOWN GOVERNMENT BY LIMITED TOWN MEETINGS.

Be it enacted, etc., as follows:

Section thirteen of chapter two of the acts of nineteen hundred and thirty-eight is hereby amended by striking out, in the fifth line and in the sixth line, the word "five" and inserting in place thereof, in each instance, the word: — ten, — so as to read as follows: — *Section 13.* If this act is rejected by the registered voters of the town of Natick when first submitted to said voters under section twelve, it may again be submitted for acceptance in like manner from time to time to such voters at any annual or special town meeting within ten years thereafter, but not more than ten times in the aggregate, and, if accepted by a majority of the voters voting thereon at such an election, shall thereupon take effect for all purposes incidental to the next annual town election in said town, and shall take full effect beginning with said election. *Approved May 14, 1943.*

AN ACT AUTHORIZING CITIES AND TOWNS TO MAKE APPROPRIATIONS PRIOR TO JANUARY FIRST, NINETEEN HUNDRED AND FORTY-SIX FOR THE SUPPRESSION AND ERADICATION OF RAGWEED. *Chap.*287

Be it enacted, etc., as follows:

SECTION 1. Any city or town may appropriate money to acquire information regarding the growth of ragweed within its limits and to do such things as are considered necessary to suppress, eradicate and destroy ragweed. Appropriations voted for this purpose shall be expended under the direction of such department as may be designated by the town meeting in a town or the city council in a city.

SECTION 2. Duly authorized officials of any city or town in which an appropriation is voted under authority of this act, or their agents, representatives or employees, may enter upon land within the limits thereof to carry out the purposes for which such appropriation is voted.

SECTION 3. This act shall become inoperative on January first, nineteen hundred and forty-six.

Approved May 14, 1943.

AN ACT REGULATING THE CHARGES AND FEES TO BE COLLECTED BY THE COMMISSIONER OF INSURANCE FOR AUDITING FINANCIAL STATEMENTS OF CERTAIN FOREIGN INSURANCE COMPANIES IN CERTAIN CASES. *Chap.*288

Be it enacted, etc., as follows:

G. L. (Ter. Ed.), 175, § 14, etc., amended.

Section fourteen of chapter one hundred and seventy-five of the General Laws, as amended, is hereby further amended by striking out the paragraph contained in the twenty-second to the twenty-sixth lines, as appearing in chapter six hundred and ninety-three of the acts of nineteen hundred and forty-one, and inserting in place thereof the following: —

Collection of charges and fees.

For filing financial statement with the application for admission of a foreign company under section one hundred and fifty-one, and for the filing of each annual statement of a foreign company under section twenty-five, and for the auditing of each financial statement of an unadmitted foreign company filed for the purpose of qualifying as a reinsurer under clause (*b*) of section twenty, twenty dollars;

Approved May 14, 1943.

AN ACT RELATIVE TO THE VOTE REQUIRED FOR THE PASSAGE OF CERTAIN ORDERS BY THE CITY COUNCIL OF THE CITY OF BOSTON AND TO THE NUMBER OF MEMBERS THEREOF NECESSARY TO PROCEED WITH THE DRAWING OF JURORS, DURING THE PRESENT WAR. *Chap.*289

Be it enacted, etc., as follows:

SECTION 1. During the continuance of the existing state of war between the United States and any foreign country, the vote required for the passage of orders by the city council of the city of Boston under section two of chapter four hundred and eighty-six of the acts of nineteen hundred and nine, as amended, or under any other general or special law applicable to said city which requires a vote of two thirds of the members, shall be the vote of two thirds of the members of said city council exclusive of those members who are in the military or naval forces of the United States and are not present at the meeting at which any such vote is taken at the time of the vote.

SECTION 2. When jurors are to be drawn in the city of Boston during the continuance of the existing state of war between the United States and any foreign country, a majority of the members of the city council, exclusive of those members who are in the military or naval forces of the United States, shall be a sufficient number to proceed with such drawing in the manner prescribed by section eighteen of chapter two hundred and thirty-four of the General Laws.

SECTION 3. This act shall take full effect upon its acceptance by vote of the city council of said city, subject to the provisions of its charter, but not otherwise.

Approved May 14, 1943.

---

*Chap.*290 AN ACT RELATIVE TO CERTAIN INFORMATION TO BE FURNISHED TO VOTERS AT ELECTIONS WHERE VOTING MACHINES ARE USED.

Be it enacted, etc., as follows:

G. L. (Ter. Ed.), 54, § 48, amended.

Section forty-eight of chapter fifty-four of the General Laws, as appearing in the Tercentenary Edition, is hereby amended by adding after the second sentence the following sentence: — For each polling place where voting machines are used they shall also provide ten voting machine sample ballots which shall be facsimiles of the face of the voting machine as it will appear when set up for use, — so as to read as follows: — *Section 48.* The state secretary in state elections, city clerks in city elections, and town clerks in town elections at which official ballots are used, shall, for every such election, prepare and cause to be printed in large clear type cards containing full instructions to voters for obtaining ballots, marking them, obtaining assistance and new ballots in place of those accidentally spoiled; and on separate cards such abstracts of the laws imposing penalties upon voters as they shall deem proper. They shall also provide for each polling place ten or more specimen ballots which shall be facsimiles of the ballots provided for voting, but printed without the endorsements and on colored paper. For each polling place where voting machines are used they shall also provide ten voting machine sample ballots which shall be facsimiles of the face of the voting machine as it will appear when set up for use. The state secretary shall

Instructions to voters.

provide copies of any proposed amendment to the constitution, law or proposed law, submitted to the people, with a heading in large type, "Proposed Amendment to the Constitution", "Law Submitted upon Referendum after Passage", "Law Proposed by Initiative Petition", as the case may be. *Approved May 14, 1943.*

Copies of proposed amendments to constitution

AN ACT TO RESTRICT THE SALE, USE, AND THE KEEPING OR OFFERING FOR SALE OF FIREWORKS.

Chap. 291

Be it enacted, etc., as follows:

G. L. (Ter. Ed.), 148, § 39, amended.

Sale, etc., of fireworks regulated.

SECTION 1. Chapter one hundred and forty-eight of the General Laws is hereby amended by striking out section thirty-nine, as appearing in the Tercentenary Edition, and inserting in place thereof the following section: — *Section 39.* No person shall sell, or keep or offer for sale, or use, explode, or cause to explode, any combustible or explosive composition or substance, or any combination of such compositions or substances, or any other article, which was prepared for the purpose of producing a visible or audible effect by combustion, explosion, deflagration or detonation, including in the above terms blank cartridges or toy cannons in which explosives are used, the type of balloon which requires fire underneath to propel the same, firecrackers, torpedoes, sky-rockets, Roman candles, bombs, sparklers, rockets, wheels, colored fires, fountains, mines, serpents, or other fireworks of like construction or any fireworks containing any explosive or flammable compound, or any tablets or other device containing any explosive substance; provided, that the term "fireworks" as used herein shall not include toy pistols, toy canes, toy guns, or other devices in which paper caps containing twenty-five hundredths grains or less of explosive compound are used, if they are so constructed that the hand cannot come in contact with the cap when in place for the explosion, or toy pistol paper caps which contain less than twenty hundredths grains of explosive mixture, the sale and use of which shall be permitted at all times; and provided, further, that this section shall not apply (1) to the sale of any article herein named to be shipped directly out of the commonwealth, or (2) to the sale of any such article for the use of, and its use by, persons having obtained a permit for a supervised display of fireworks from the marshal or some officer designated by him therefor, under any provision of section thirty-nine A, or (3) to the sale of flares, lanterns or fireworks for the use of, and their use by, railroads, railways, boats, motor vehicles or other transportation agencies, or other activity, lawfully permitted or required to use any or all of such articles for signal purposes, illumination or otherwise, or (4) to the sale or use of blank cartridges for a duly licensed show or theatre or for signal or ceremonial purposes in athletics or sports, or (5) to experiments at a factory for explosives, or (6) to the sale of blank cartridges for the use of, or their use by, the militia or any organization of war veterans or other organizations authorized by law to parade in public a color guard armed with firearms, or (7) in teaching the use of firearms by experts, or (8) to the sale of shells for firearms, cartridges, gunpowder and explosives for the purpose of using, and their use, in or in connection with the hunting of game or in target practice with firearms.

G. L. (Ter. Ed.), 148, new § 39A, added.

Permits for displays of fireworks.

SECTION 2. Said chapter one hundred and forty-eight is hereby further amended by inserting after section thirty-nine, as amended, the following section: — *Section 39A.* The marshal shall make rules and regulations for the granting of permits for supervised displays of fireworks by municipalities, fair associations, amusement parks and other organizations or groups of individuals. Such rules and regulations shall provide in part that (*a*) every such display shall be handled by a competent operator to be approved by the chiefs of the police and fire departments, or officer or officers having similar powers and duties, of the municipality in which the display is to be held and shall be of such a character, and so located, discharged or fired as, in the opinion of the chief of the fire department or the officer or officers having similar powers and duties, after proper inspection, not to be hazardous to property or to endanger any person or persons, (*b*) application for permits shall be made in writing at least fifteen days in advance of the date of the display, and (*c*) no permit so granted shall be transferable.

G. L. (Ter. Ed.), 148, § 50, amended.

Search warrants for explosives illegally kept.

SECTION 3. Section fifty of said chapter one hundred and forty-eight, as so appearing, is hereby amended by inserting after the word "fluids" in the fifth line the words: — , or any of the articles named in section thirty-nine, — so as to read as follows: — *Section 50.* Upon complaint made to a court or justice authorized to issue warrants in criminal cases that the complainant has probable cause to suspect and does suspect that gunpowder, dynamite or any other explosives, crude petroleum or any of its products, or explosive or inflammable fluids, or any of the articles named in section thirty-nine, are kept or are to be found in any place contrary to this chapter or regulations made hereunder, such court or justice may issue a search warrant in conformity with chapter two hundred and seventy-six, so far as applicable, commanding the officer to whom the warrant is directed to enter any shop, building, manufactory, vehicle or vessel specified in the warrant, and there make diligent search for the articles specified in the warrant, and make return of his doings forthwith to the court or justice having jurisdiction thereof. Such warrants may be directed to an inspector or to the head of the fire department.

G. L. (Ter. Ed.), 148, § 53, repealed.

SECTION 4. Said chapter one hundred and forty-eight is hereby further amended by striking out section fifty-three, as so appearing. *Approved May 18, 1943.*

AN ACT RELATIVE TO ORDERS FOR PAYMENT BY JUDGMENT DEBTORS UNDER SUPPLEMENTARY PROCESS. *Chap.*292

Be it enacted, etc., as follows:

SECTION 1. Section sixteen of chapter two hundred and twenty-four of the General Laws, as appearing in the Tercentenary Edition, is hereby amended by striking out, in the twelfth, thirteenth and fourteenth lines, the words "a reasonable amount for the support of himself and family, which amount need not be stated" and inserting in place thereof the words: — an amount not less than twenty dollars each week for the support of himself and family if he be the head of a family, — so as to read as follows: — *Section 16.* If the court finds that the debtor has no property not exempt from being taken on execution, and is unable to pay the judgment, in full or by partial payments, or if the creditor fails to appear at the examination, personally or by attorney, the proceedings may be dismissed. If the court is satisfied that the debtor has property not exempt from being taken on execution, the court may order him to produce it, or so much thereof as may be sufficient to satisfy the judgment and costs of the proceedings, so that it may be taken on the execution; or may order him to execute, acknowledge if necessary, and deliver to the judgment creditor, or to a person in his behalf, a transfer, assignment or conveyance thereof; or if the debtor is able to pay the judgment in full or by partial payments the court may, after allowing the debtor out of his income an amount not less than twenty dollars each week for the support of himself and family if he be the head of a family, order the debtor to pay the judgment and costs of the proceedings in full or by partial payments from time to time; or the court may make an order combining any of the orders above mentioned. The court may prescribe the times, places, amounts of payments, forms of instruments and other details in making any of the orders above mentioned. The court may at any time renew, revise, modify, suspend or revoke any order made in any proceedings under the provisions of this chapter. Failure, without just excuse, to obey any lawful order of the court in supplementary proceedings shall constitute a contempt of court.

G. L. (Ter. Ed.), 224, § 16, amended.

Dismissal of proceedings, when.

Orders for payment, etc.

Failure to obey orders to constitute contempt of court.

SECTION 2. This act shall take effect on September first in the current year. *Approved May 18, 1943.*

Effective date.

AN ACT PROHIBITING EMPLOYEES OF HOSPITALS FROM NEGOTIATING FOR THE SETTLEMENT OF CERTAIN PERSONAL INJURY CLAIMS. *Chap.*293

Be it enacted, etc., as follows:

Section forty-four A of chapter two hundred and twenty-one of the General Laws, inserted by section two of chapter one hundred and ninety-seven of the acts of nineteen hun-

G. L. (Ter. Ed.), 221, § 44A, etc., amended.

dred and thirty-nine, is hereby amended by inserting after the word "institution" in the tenth line the following sentence: — No such person in the employ of any hospital shall negotiate or attempt to negotiate the settlement of any such claim, — so as to read as follows: — *Section 44A.* No person in the employ of, or in any capacity attached to or connected with, any hospital, infirmary or other institution, public or private, which receives patients for medical or surgical treatment, shall communicate, directly or indirectly, with any attorney at law, or any person representing such attorney, for the purpose of enabling such attorney, or any associate or employee of such attorney, to solicit employment to present a claim for damages or prosecute an action for the enforcement thereof, on behalf of any patient in any such institution. No such person in the employ of any hospital shall negotiate or attempt to negotiate the settlement of any such claim. A district court, upon complaint alleging violation of any provision of this section by any person employed by, or attached to, or connected with, any such hospital, infirmary or other institution situated within its judicial district, may issue an order of notice to the person complained of to show cause why he should not be ordered to desist and refrain from violation of any such provision on penalty of contempt. *Approved May 18, 1943.*

Hospital, etc., employees prohibited from assisting attorneys to secure employment in claim for damages.

---

*Chap.*294 AN ACT ESTABLISHING THE BASIS OF APPORTIONMENT OF STATE AND COUNTY TAXES.

Be it enacted, etc., as follows:

The amount of property and the proportion of every thousand dollars of state tax for each city and town in the several counties of the commonwealth, as contained in the following schedule, are hereby established, and shall constitute a basis of apportionment for state and county taxes for the years nineteen hundred and forty-four and nineteen hundred and forty-five, or until another is made and enacted by the general court, to wit:

BARNSTABLE COUNTY.

CITIES AND TOWNS.	Property.	Tax of $1,000.
Barnstable	$27,882,385	$4 11
Bourne	10,204,332	1 52
Brewster	2,245,971	34
Chatham	7,455,507	1 10
Dennis	4,704,024	71
Eastham	1,528,689	23
Falmouth	23,738,631	3 50
Harwich	7,745,170	1 15
Mashpee	1,008,934	15

BARNSTABLE COUNTY — CONCLUDED.

Cities and Towns.	Property.	Tax of $1,000.
Orleans	$4,579,546	$0 69
Provincetown	5,656,332	89
Sandwich	2,955,066	45
Truro	1,693,414	26
Wellfleet	2,180,873	33
Yarmouth	6,674,483	99
Totals	$110,253,357	$16 42

BERKSHIRE COUNTY.

Cities and Towns.	Property.	Tax of $1,000.
Adams	$11,690,534	$1 90
Alford	358,338	05
Becket	860,045	13
Cheshire	1,235,950	19
Clarksburg	946,151	14
Dalton	7,644,806	1 15
Egremont	1,064,148	16
Florida	1,530,580	23
Great Barrington	9,496,855	1 45
Hancock	509,884	08
Hinsdale	1,016,063	15
Lanesborough	1,530,142	23
Lee	5,602,589	85
Lenox	5,168,096	78
Monterey	923,528	14
Mount Washington	212,790	03
New Ashford	136,486	02
New Marlborough	1,559,241	24
North Adams	22,968,759	3 59
Otis	740,055	11
Peru	305,216	05
Pittsfield	66,625,332	10 23
Richmond	817,253	12
Sandisfield	748,222	11
Savoy	205,216	03
Sheffield	1,772,822	27
Stockbridge	4,926,999	75
Tyringham	512,397	08
Washington	230,216	03
West Stockbridge	1,553,162	23
Williamstown	7,650,974	1 16
Windsor	510,432	08
Totals	$161,053,281	$24 76

BRISTOL COUNTY.

Cities and Towns.	Property.	Tax of $1,000.
Acushnet	$3,562,975	$0 54
Attleboro	29,331,683	4 56
Berkley	982,261	15
Dartmouth	12,794,738	1 98
Dighton	3,649,206	55

BRISTOL COUNTY — Concluded.

Cities and Towns.	Property.	Tax of $1,000.
Easton	$5,573,399	$0 84
Fairhaven	12,097,287	1 83
Fall River	118,261,192	17 89
Freetown	1,539,671	23
Mansfield	8,380,034	1 30
New Bedford	123,466,066	18 67
North Attleborough	11,287,794	1 71
Norton	2,561,799	39
Raynham	2,015,791	30
Rehoboth	3,099,981	47
Seekonk	5,988,005	92
Somerset	14,343,310	2 17
Swansea	4,882,200	74
Taunton	38,439,784	5 81
Westport	5,882,349	91
Totals	$408,139,525	$61 96

DUKES COUNTY.

Cities and Towns.	Property.	Tax of $1,000.
Chilmark	$814,344	$0 12
Edgartown	5,058,103	75
Gay Head	173,912	03
Gosnold	1,322,169	20
Oak Bluffs	5,050,008	75
Tisbury	6,100,586	90
West Tisbury	783,404	12
Totals	$19,302,526	$2 87

ESSEX COUNTY.

Cities and Towns.	Property.	Tax of $1,000.
Amesbury	$8,791,107	$1 33
Andover	19,736,226	3 00
Beverly	41,747,108	6 29
Boxford	1,261,858	19
Danvers	14,479,191	2 22
Essex	1,616,490	24
Georgetown	2,042,763	31
Gloucester	38,763,610	5 86
Groveland	1,635,660	25
Hamilton	5,915,914	88
Haverhill	52,704,032	7 97
Ipswich	7,544,807	1 18
Lawrence	101,077,836	15 29
Lynn	143,715,272	21 78
Lynnfield	5,595,973	85
Manchester	10,244,261	1 55
Marblehead	23,619,687	3 56
Merrimac	2,102,794	32
Methuen	22,076,331	3 34
Middleton	2,312,860	35
Nahant	6,088,433	90

ESSEX COUNTY — Concluded.

Cities and Towns.	Property.	Tax of $1,000.
Newbury	$2,429,095	$0 37
Newburyport	13,181,239	1 99
North Andover	8,805,212	1 36
Peabody	25,186,090	3 95
Rockport	6,209,169	94
Rowley	1,732,617	26
Salem	60,383,956	9 17
Salisbury	3,215,223	49
Saugus	16,404,206	2 48
Swampscott	25,650,238	3 82
Topsfield	3,035,059	46
Wenham	4,177,516	63
West Newbury	1,535,026	23
Totals	$685,016,859	$103 81

FRANKLIN COUNTY.

Cities and Towns.	Property.	Tax of $1,000.
Ashfield	$1,335,958	$0 20
Bernardston	1,020,865	15
Buckland	3,091,131	47
Charlemont	975,909	15
Colrain	1,713,042	26
Conway	1,025,599	16
Deerfield	4,415,192	67
Erving	2,487,499	38
Gill	1,026,251	16
Greenfield	32,168,555	4 81
Hawley	255,910	04
Heath	409,337	06
Leverett	525,444	08
Leyden	331,520	05
Monroe	1,076,882	16
Montague	10,747,352	1 64
New Salem	357,824	05
Northfield	2,060,374	31
Orange	4,982,009	75
Rowe	713,828	11
Shelburne	3,591,141	54
Shutesbury	407,824	06
Sunderland	1,328,185	20
Warwick	368,037	06
Wendell	321,108	05
Whately	1,395,141	21
Totals	$78,131,917	$11 78

HAMPDEN COUNTY.

Cities and Towns.	Property.	Tax of $1,000.
Agawam	$9,923,593	$1 53
Blandford	918,256	14
Brimfield	1,116,072	17
Chester	1,430,975	22

HAMPDEN COUNTY — CONCLUDED.

CITIES AND TOWNS.	Property.	Tax of $1,000.
Chicopee	$42,317,076	$6 63
East Longmeadow	5,112,237	77
Granville	2,053,367	31
Hampden	1,026,578	16
Holland	239,094	04
Holyoke	86,598,821	13 14
Longmeadow	18,736,083	2 77
Ludlow	8,528,104	1 33
Monson	3,682,807	56
Montgomery	306,521	05
Palmer	8,490,658	1 36
Russell	4,509,907	68
Southwick	2,221,759	34
Springfield	276,365,523	41 45
Tolland	457,824	07
Wales	397,235	06
West Springfield	27,560,547	4 18
Westfield	22,273,243	3 47
Wilbraham	3,452,200	52
Totals	$527,718,480	$79 95

HAMPSHIRE COUNTY.

CITIES AND TOWNS.	Property.	Tax of $1,000.
Amherst	$10,700,944	$1 63
Belchertown	1,714,675	26
Chesterfield	612,749	09
Cummington	595,614	09
Easthampton	11,723,701	1 77
Goshen	409,530	06
Granby	1,029,989	16
Hadley	3,064,213	46
Hatfield	3,062,429	46
Huntington	1,145,940	17
Middlefield	356,520	05
Northampton	29,316,062	4 49
Pelham	715,009	11
Plainfield	356,520	05
South Hadley	9,643,976	1 47
Southampton	1,229,316	19
Ware	7,145,455	1 08
Westhampton	375,900	06
Williamsburg	1,498,287	23
Worthington	815,648	12
Totals	$85,512,477	$13 00

MIDDLESEX COUNTY.

CITIES AND TOWNS.	Property.	Tax of $1,000.
Acton	$4,346,064	$0 66
Arlington	60,335,449	9 12
Ashby	1,326,821	20
Ashland	2,975,082	45
Ayer	4,119,790	62

MIDDLESEX COUNTY — CONCLUDED.

CITIES AND TOWNS.	Property.	Tax of $1,000.
Bedford	$3,062,259	$0 46
Belmont	55,049,420	8 23
Billerica	9,618,284	1 45
Boxborough	407,824	06
Burlington	2,553,466	39
Cambridge	184,326,566	27 88
Carlisle	1,223,473	19
Chelmsford	8,258,498	1 25
Concord	13,028,069	1 97
Dracut	4,983,950	75
Dunstable	443,007	07
Everett	78,817,491	11 97
Framingham	37,599,843	5 68
Groton	4,938,974	75
Holliston	4,023,374	61
Hopkinton	3,606,425	55
Hudson	7,649,530	1 16
Lexington	25,329,895	3 76
Lincoln	4,576,960	69
Littleton	3,171,534	48
Lowell	102,599,923	15 93
Malden	76,576,832	11 58
Marlborough	16,934,978	2 56
Maynard	7,777,660	1 18
Medford	85,750,742	12 97
Melrose	41,656,140	6 31
Natick	21,609,664	3 28
Newton	174,560,417	25 86
North Reading	2,723,596	41
Pepperell	3,194,486	48
Reading	18,824,803	2 85
Sherborn	3,056,074	46
Shirley	2,520,169	38
Somerville	114,046,295	17 25
Stoneham	15,896,158	2 40
Stow	1,427,510	22
Sudbury	3,680,300	56
Tewksbury	4,904,601	74
Townsend	2,601,264	39
Tyngsborough	1,532,549	23
Wakefield	22,733,751	3 48
Waltham	57,897,104	8 79
Watertown	56,487,036	8 52
Wayland	6,081,269	92
Westford	4,748,684	72
Weston	11,660,508	1 75
Wilmington	4,596,499	70
Winchester	35,974,250	5 35
Woburn	22,849,849	3 46
Totals	$1,450,675,159	$219 13

NANTUCKET COUNTY.

Nantucket	$13,297,877	$1 96
Totals	$13,297,877	$1 96

NORFOLK COUNTY.

CITIES AND TOWNS.	Property.	Tax of $1,000.
Avon	$2,052,311	$0 31
Bellingham	2,905,503	44
Braintree	29,121,683	4 42
Brookline	154,794,783	23 41
Canton	9,513,406	1 44
Cohasset	10,639,718	1 57
Dedham	27,470,224	4 14
Dover	6,072,676	89
Foxborough	6,423,648	97
Franklin	9,632,033	1 46
Holbrook	3,726,548	56
Medfield	3,102,568	47
Medway	3,473,503	53
Millis	3,305,375	50
Milton	42,797,675	6 38
Needham	27,657,831	4 17
Norfolk	1,642,442	25
Norwood	28,751,416	4 35
Plainville	1,880,317	28
Quincy	135,062,673	20 30
Randolph	7,561,018	1 14
Sharon	6,330,738	96
Stoughton	9,627,181	1 46
Walpole	18,486,445	2 78
Wellesley	46,789,158	6 90
Westwood	7,965,223	1 20
Weymouth	54,413,987	8 14
Wrentham	4,235,315	64
Totals	$665,435,398	$100 06

PLYMOUTH COUNTY.

CITIES AND TOWNS.	Property.	Tax of $1,000.
Abington	$5,752,344	$0 87
Bridgewater	6,890,366	1 04
Brockton	75,206,798	11 37
Carver	2,986,113	45
Duxbury	8,105,098	1 20
East Bridgewater	5,124,595	78
Halifax	1,531,645	23
Hanover	4,795,233	73
Hanson	2,928,211	44
Hingham	17,766,188	2 67
Hull	17,175,545	2 51
Kingston	4,884,281	74
Lakeville	1,732,812	26
Marion	5,608,836	83
Marshfield	8,607,908	1 27
Mattapoisett	3,979,335	60
Middleborough	9,889,930	1 50
Norwell	2,550,942	39
Pembroke	2,886,302	44
Plymouth	24,697,763	3 73
Plympton	823,912	12
Rochester	1,556,403	24

PLYMOUTH COUNTY — CONCLUDED.

CITIES AND TOWNS.	Property.	Tax of $1,000.
Rockland	$9,241,262	$1 44
Scituate	13,720,531	2 04
Wareham	15,042,776	2 26
West Bridgewater	3,771,899	57
Whitman	8,766,894	1 33
Totals	$266,023,922	$40 05

SUFFOLK COUNTY.

CITIES AND TOWNS.	Property.	Tax of $1,000.
Boston	$1,389,431,556	$210 13
Chelsea	46,553,557	7 04
Revere	40,658,081	6 15
Winthrop	25,513,108	3 86
Totals	$1,502,156,302	$227 18

WORCESTER COUNTY.

CITIES AND TOWNS.	Property.	Tax of $1,000.
Ashburnham	$1,933,976	$0 29
Athol	13,820,783	2 16
Auburn	7,243,701	1 14
Barre	3,128,275	47
Berlin	1,246,603	19
Blackstone	2,578,010	39
Bolton	1,203,482	18
Boylston	1,022,169	15
Brookfield	1,511,367	23
Charlton	2,240,729	34
Clinton	12,183,206	1 84
Douglas	2,547,524	39
Dudley	4,064,697	61
East Brookfield	1,112,302	17
Fitchburg	54,276,243	8 21
Gardner	23,901,657	3 61
Grafton	4,937,387	75
Hardwick	1,740,708	26
Harvard	2,553,527	39
Holden	4,059,592	61
Hopedale	7,332,861	1 10
Hubbardston	866,953	13
Lancaster	2,569,650	39
Leicester	3,660,635	55
Leominster	27,247,450	4 12
Lunenburg	2,593,917	39
Mendon	1,563,996	24
Milford	16,695,755	2 53
Millbury	6,789,691	1 03
Millville	1,029,188	16
New Braintree	646,956	10
North Brookfield	2,872,368	43
Northborough	2,379,782	36
Northbridge	10,757,890	1 70

WORCESTER COUNTY — CONCLUDED.

CITIES AND TOWNS.	Property.	Tax of $1,000.
Oakham	$459,128	$0 07
Oxford	3,486,746	53
Paxton	1,122,169	17
Petersham	1,465,350	22
Phillipston	376,104	06
Princeton	1,327,715	20
Royalston	819,032	12
Rutland	1,531,297	23
Shrewsbury	10,437,045	1 61
Southborough	3,613,558	55
Southbridge	16,554,677	2 50
Spencer	4,995,075	76
Sterling	2,261,461	34
Sturbridge	2,132,639	32
Sutton	2,270,225	34
Templeton	3,466;381	52
Upton	1,642,252	25
Uxbridge	8,518,056	1 29
Warren	2,777,322	42
Webster	12,259,436	1 85
West Boylston	2,858,151	43
West Brookfield	1,562,606	24
Westborough	4,917,241	74
Westminster	2,041,729	31
Winchendon	5,789,451	88
Worcester	306,565,806	46 51
Totals	$639,563,682	$97 07

RECAPITULATION.

COUNTIES.	Property.	Tax of $1,000.
Barnstable	$110,253,357	$16 42
Berkshire	161,053,281	24 76
Bristol	408,139,525	61 96
Dukes	19,302,526	2 87
Essex	685,016,859	103 81
Franklin	78,131,917	11 78
Hampden	527,718,480	79 95
Hampshire	85,512,477	13 00
Middlesex	1,450,675,159	219 13
Nantucket	13,297,877	1 96
Norfolk	665,435,398	100 06
Plymouth	266,023,922	40 05
Suffolk	1,502,156,302	227 18
Worcester	639,563,682	97 07
Totals	$6,612,280,762	$1,000 00

Approved May 18, 1943.

AN ACT REGULATING THE ASSUMPTION OF NAMES BY CERTAIN CORPORATIONS. *Chap.*295

Be it enacted, etc., as follows:

Chapter one hundred and fifty-five of the General Laws is hereby amended by striking out section nine, as amended by section one of chapter three hundred and twenty-seven of the acts of nineteen hundred and thirty-eight, and inserting in place thereof the following section: — *Section 9.* A corporation organized under general laws may assume any name which, in the judgment of the commissioner, indicates that it is a corporation; but it shall not assume the name or trade name of another corporation established under the laws of the commonwealth, or of a corporation, firm, association or person carrying on business in the commonwealth, at the time of incorporation of the corporation so organized or within three years prior thereto, or assume a name so similar thereto as to be likely to be mistaken for it, except with the written consent of said existing corporation, firm or association or of such person previously filed with the commissioner; provided, that no business corporation, bank or insurance company shall have as a part of its corporate name the word "Commonwealth", "State" or "United States". The supreme judicial or superior court shall have jurisdiction in equity, upon the application of any person interested or affected, to enjoin such corporation from doing business under a name assumed in violation of any provision of this section, although its certificate or articles of organization may have been approved and a certificate of incorporation may have been issued to it.

G. L. (Ter. Ed.), 155, § 9, etc., amended.

Corporate name. Use of certain words prohibited.

If within thirty days of the date when the certificate or articles of organization of any corporation are filed in the office of the state secretary any other corporation or any firm, association or person carrying on business in the commonwealth at the time when such certificate or articles are so filed, or within three years prior thereto, shall protest in writing to the commissioner that the name assumed by the corporation the certificate or articles of organization of which have been so filed is the same as the name or trade name of the protesting corporation, firm, association or person or so similar thereto as to be likely to be mistaken for it, the commissioner shall, as soon as reasonably may be, hear the party protesting and the corporation which assumed the name, giving written notice of the hearing to each. If after hearing the commissioner shall be of the opinion that the assuming of the name violates any provision of this section he shall, as soon as reasonably may be, file with the state secretary a statement withdrawing his approval of said certificate or articles in so far as it or they relate to the name assumed by the corporation, such withdrawal to take effect sixty days from the date of filing. After the expiration of said period of sixty days the corporation shall have no right to use the name assumed and may be enjoined from doing business under such name by the supreme judicial or superior court upon application of the attorney general or any person interested or affected.

Approved May 18, 1943.

---

*Chap.*296 AN ACT RELATIVE TO JURISDICTION AND VENUE OF MOTOR VEHICLE TORT CASES, SO CALLED.

Be it enacted, etc., as follows:

G. L. (Ter. Ed.), 218, § 19, etc., amended.

SECTION 1. Section nineteen of chapter two hundred and eighteen of the General Laws, as amended by section one of chapter three hundred and eighty-seven of the acts of nineteen hundred and thirty-four, is hereby further amended by striking out, in the first and second lines, the words "Except as herein otherwise provided, district" and inserting in place thereof the word: — District, — and by striking out the last sentence, — so as to read as follows: — *Section 19.* District courts shall have original jurisdiction concurrent with the superior court of actions of contract, tort and replevin, and also of actions in summary process under chapter two hundred and thirty-nine and proceedings under section forty-one of chapter two hundred and thirty-one.

Civil jurisdiction of district courts.

G. L. (Ter. Ed.), 223, § 2, etc., amended.

SECTION 2. Section two of chapter two hundred and twenty-three of the General Laws, as amended, is hereby further amended by striking out the last sentence of the first paragraph and inserting in place thereof the following sentence: — An action of tort arising out of the ownership, operation, maintenance, control or use of a motor vehicle or trailer as defined in section one of chapter ninety may be brought in a district court within the judicial district of which one of the parties lives or in any district court the judicial district of which adjoins and is in the same county as the judicial district in which the defendant lives or has his usual place of business; provided, that if one of the parties to any such action lives in Suffolk county such action may be brought in the municipal court of the city of Boston.

Venue of actions arising from operation of motor vehicles.

G. L. (Ter. Ed.), 231, § 102A, etc., repealed.

SECTION 3. Section one hundred and two A of chapter two hundred and thirty-one of the General Laws, inserted by section three of said chapter three hundred and eighty-seven, and as amended, is hereby repealed.

G. L. (Ter. Ed.), 231, § 107, amended.

SECTION 4. Said chapter two hundred and thirty-one is hereby further amended by striking out section one hundred and seven, as appearing in the Tercentenary Edition, and inserting in place thereof the following section: — *Section 107.* No bond or deposit under section one hundred and four or one hundred and six shall be required of a county, city, town or other municipal corporation or of a party who has given bond according to law to dissolve an attachment or of a defendant in an action of tort arising out of the

Bond or deposit not required, when.

ownership, operation, maintenance, control or use, of a motor vehicle or trailer as defined in section one of chapter ninety if the payment of any judgment for costs which may be entered against him is secured, in whole or in part, by a motor vehicle liability bond or policy, or a deposit as provided in section thirty-four D of chapter ninety; and the court may in any case, for cause shown, after notice to adverse parties, order that no bond be given. Said district court may, upon cause shown and after notice to all adverse parties, permit such removal to the superior court, upon the terms above specified, at any time prior to final judgment.

SECTION 5. Section one hundred and forty-one of said chapter two hundred and thirty-one, as most recently amended by section four of said chapter three hundred and eighty-seven, is hereby further amended by striking out, in the eighteenth line, the words ", one hundred and two A", — so as to read as follows: — *Section 141.* Sections one, two, three, four, five, six, seven, ten, eleven, twelve, thirteen, thirteen A, fourteen, fifteen, sixteen, seventeen, eighteen, nineteen, twenty, twenty-one, twenty-two, twenty-three, twenty-five, twenty-six, twenty-seven, twenty-eight, twenty-nine, thirty, thirty-one, thirty-two, thirty-three, thirty-four, thirty-five, thirty-six, thirty-seven, thirty-eight, thirty-nine, forty, forty-one, forty-two, forty-three, forty-four, forty-five, forty-seven, forty-eight, forty-nine, fifty, fifty-one, fifty-two, fifty-three, fifty-four, fifty-six, fifty-seven, fifty-eight, fifty-eight A, fifty-nine B, sixty-one, sixty-two, sixty-three, sixty-four, sixty-five, sixty-six, sixty-seven, sixty-eight, sixty-nine, seventy, seventy-two, seventy-three, seventy-four, seventy-five, seventy-nine, eighty-five, eighty-five A, eighty-seven, eighty-eight, eighty-nine, ninety, ninety-one, ninety-two, ninety-three, ninety-four, ninety-five, ninety-seven, ninety-eight, ninety-nine, one hundred and one, one hundred and two, one hundred and three, one hundred and four, one hundred and five, one hundred and six, one hundred and seven, one hundred and eight, one hundred and nine, one hundred and ten, one hundred and twenty-four, one hundred and twenty-five, one hundred and twenty-six, one hundred and thirty-two, one hundred and thirty-three, one hundred and thirty-four, one hundred and thirty-five, one hundred and thirty-six, one hundred and thirty-seven, one hundred and thirty-eight, one hundred and thirty-nine, one hundred and forty, one hundred and forty A and one hundred and forty-seven shall apply to civil actions before district courts, and no other sections of this chapter shall so apply, except to the municipal court of the city of Boston under section one hundred and forty-three.

G. L. (Ter. Ed.), 231, § 141, etc., amended.

Sections applicable to civil actions before district courts.

SECTION 6. This act shall take effect on September first in the current year and shall apply only to actions commenced thereafter. *Approved May 18, 1943.*

Effective date.

Chap.297 AN ACT AUTHORIZING AN INCREASE IN THE SALARY OF THE MAYOR OF THE CITY OF LEOMINSTER.

Be it enacted, etc., as follows:

SECTION 1. Section twelve of chapter three hundred and thirty-eight of the Special Acts of nineteen hundred and fifteen is hereby amended by striking out, in the third line, the words "exceeding one" and inserting in place thereof the words: — more than four, — so as to read as follows: — *Section 12.* The mayor shall receive for his services such salary as the city council shall by ordinance determine, not more than four thousand dollars a year, and he shall receive no other compensation from the city. His salary shall not be increased or diminished during the term for which he is elected. The council may by a two thirds vote of all its members, taken by call of the yeas and nays, establish a salary for its members, not exceeding five hundred dollars each a year. Such salary may be reduced, but no increase therein shall be made to take effect during the year in which the increase is voted.

SECTION 2. This act shall be submitted for acceptance to the registered voters of the city of Leominster at its regular city election in the current year in the form of the following question which shall be placed upon the official ballot to be used at said election: — "Shall an act passed by the general court in the year nineteen hundred and forty-three, entitled 'An Act authorizing an increase in the salary of the mayor of the city of Leominster', be accepted?" If a majority of the votes in answer to said question is in the affirmative, then this act shall thereupon take full effect, but not otherwise. *Approved May 19, 1943.*

Chap.298 AN ACT REGULATING THE ATTACHMENT OF PERSONAL PROPERTY SOLD ON CONDITIONAL SALE AND MAKING A CERTAIN METHOD OF ATTACHMENT APPLICABLE IN THE CASE OF PERSONAL PROPERTY SUBJECT TO PLEDGE OR LIEN.

Be it enacted, etc., as follows:

G. L. (Ter. Ed.), 223, § 74, amended.

SECTION 1. Chapter two hundred and twenty-three of the General Laws is hereby amended by striking out section seventy-four, as appearing in the Tercentenary Edition, and inserting in place thereof the following section: — *Section 74.*

Attachment of mortgaged property.

Personal property of a debtor which is subject to a mortgage, pledge or lien, and of which he has the right of redemption, or personal property sold under a contract of conditional sale reserving title in the vendor, may be attached and held as if it were unencumbered, if the attaching creditor pays or tenders to the mortgagee, pledgee, lienor, conditional vendor, or his assigns, the amount for which the property is so liable within ten days after demand as hereinafter provided.

G. L. (Ter. Ed.), 223, § 75, amended.

SECTION 2. Said chapter two hundred and twenty-three is hereby further amended by striking out section seventy-five, as so appearing, and inserting in place thereof the following section: — *Section 75.* Within a reasonable time after such property has been attached, or, in the case of property subject to a recorded mortgage, within a reasonable time after written notice of the attachment, the mortgagee, pledgee, lienor or conditional vendor, or his assigns, may demand payment of the money for which the property is liable, giving a just and true account of the debt or demand for which the property is liable to him, showing clearly the balance thereof, whether then payable or payable thereafter, and accompanying it by a reference to the record of recording of a mortgage. Such demand shall be served, either in hand or by registered mail with a request for a return receipt, upon the attaching creditor, or his attorney, or the attaching officer. If the balance as stated in the account, whether then payable or not, is not paid, or tendered to the mortgagee, pledgee, lienor or conditional vendor, or his assigns, within ten days after such service, the attachment shall be dissolved and the attaching creditor shall be liable to him for any damage he has sustained by the attachment, and the property shall be restored to the person entitled thereto.

Mortgagee to state account.

SECTION 3. Said chapter two hundred and twenty-three is hereby further amended by striking out section seventy-six, as so appearing, and inserting in place thereof the following section: — *Section 76.* If the mortgagee, pledgee, lienor or conditional vendor, or his assigns, demands and receives more than the amount due to him, he shall be liable to the attaching creditor for money had and received for the excess, with interest thereon at the rate of twelve per cent a year.

G. L. (Ter. Ed.), 223, § 76, amended.

Penalty for excessive demand.

SECTION 4. Said chapter two hundred and twenty-three is hereby further amended by striking out section seventy-eight, as so appearing, and inserting in place thereof the following section: — *Section 78.* If the attaching creditor, after having redeemed the property, does not recover judgment, he may nevertheless hold the property until the debtor repays to him the amount or amounts which he paid for the redemption, or as much thereof as the debtor would have been obliged to pay to the mortgagee, pledgee, lienor or conditional vendor, or his assigns, or any of them, if the property had not been attached, with interest from the time when it was demanded of the debtor.

G. L. (Ter. Ed.), 223, § 78, amended.

Defendant to pay attaching plaintiff for redemption of mortgage.

SECTION 5. Said chapter two hundred and twenty-three is hereby further amended by striking out section seventy-nine, as so appearing, and inserting in place thereof the following section: — *Section 79.* Personal property upon which a mortgage or lien is claimed, or which is claimed to have been sold under a contract of conditional sale reserving title in the vendor, may be attached as if unencumbered; and the mortgagee, pledgee, lienor or conditional vendor, or his assigns, may be summoned in the same action in which the property is attached as the trustee of the mortgagor, pledgor, lienee or conditional vendee, or his assigns, to answer such

G. L. (Ter. Ed.), 223, § 79, amended

Attachment of mortgaged personalty in debtor's possession.

questions as may be put to him by the court or by its order relative to the consideration of the alleged mortgage, pledge, lien or contract of conditional sale, and the amount due thereon.

G. L. (Ter. Ed.), 223, § 80, amended.

Determination of amount due.

SECTION 6. Said chapter two hundred and twenty-three is hereby further amended by striking out section eighty, as so appearing, and inserting in place thereof the following section: — *Section 80.* If, upon such examination, or, upon the verdict of a jury as provided in section eighty-one, it appears that the mortgage, pledge, lien or contract of conditional sale is valid, the court, having first ascertained the amount justly due upon it, may direct the attaching creditor to pay the same to the mortgagee, pledgee, lienor or conditional vendor, or his assigns, within such time as it orders; and if he does not pay or tender the amount within the time prescribed the attachment shall be void and the property shall be restored.

G. L. (Ter. Ed.), 223, § 81, amended.

Determination of validity of mortgage.

SECTION 7. Said chapter two hundred and twenty-three is hereby further amended by striking out section eighty-one, as so appearing, and inserting in place thereof the following section: — *Section 81.* If the attaching creditor denies the validity of the mortgage, pledge, lien or contract of conditional sale, and moves that its validity be tried by jury, the court shall order such trial upon an issue which shall be framed under its direction. If, upon such examination or verdict, the mortgage, pledge, lien or contract of conditional sale is adjudged valid, the mortgagee, pledgee, lienor or conditional vendor, or his assigns, shall recover his costs.

G. L. (Ter. Ed.), 223 § 82, amended.

Creditor to retain amount paid by him, etc.

SECTION 8. Said chapter two hundred and twenty-three is hereby further amended by striking out section eighty-two, as so appearing, and inserting in place thereof the following section: — *Section 82.* When the creditor has paid to the mortgagee, pledgee, lienor or conditional vendor, or his assigns, the amount ordered by the court, he may retain out of the proceeds of the property attached, when sold, the amount so paid with interest, and the balance shall be applied to the payment of his debt.

G. L. (Ter. Ed.), 223, new § 83A, added.

Certain sections not to apply, when.

SECTION 9. Said chapter two hundred and twenty-three is hereby further amended by inserting after section eighty-three, as so appearing, the following section: — *Section 83A.* Sections seventy-four to eighty-three, inclusive, shall not apply to conditional sales notices of which are recordable under section thirteen of chapter one hundred and eighty-four.

Effective date.

SECTION 10. This act shall take effect on October first in the current year. *Approved May 19, 1943.*

AN ACT INCREASING THE MAXIMUM AMOUNT OF WEEKLY COMPENSATION TO BE PAID FOR PARTIAL INCAPACITY UNDER THE WORKMEN'S COMPENSATION LAW. *Chap.*299

Be it enacted, etc., as follows:

Section thirty-five of chapter one hundred and fifty-two of the General Laws, as appearing in the Tercentenary Edition, is hereby amended by striking out, in the fifth line, the word "eighteen" and inserting in place thereof the word: — twenty, — so as to read as follows: — *Section 35.* While the incapacity for work resulting from the injury is partial, the insurer shall pay the injured employee a weekly compensation equal to two thirds of the difference between his average weekly wages before the injury and the average weekly wages which he is able to earn thereafter, but not more than twenty dollars a week; and the amount of such compensation shall not be more than forty-five hundred dollars. *Approved May 19, 1943.*

G. L. (Ter. Ed.), 152, § 35, amended.

Partial incapacity. Amount of payments.

AN ACT RELATIVE TO CERTAIN LINES, POLES AND OTHER EQUIPMENT OF THE FITCHBURG GAS AND ELECTRIC LIGHT COMPANY, THE NEW ENGLAND TELEPHONE AND TELEGRAPH COMPANY AND THE AMERICAN TELEPHONE AND TELEGRAPH COMPANY IN THE CITY OF FITCHBURG. *Chap.*300

Be it enacted, etc., as follows:

SECTION 1. All lines for the transmission of electricity for light, heat or power heretofore acquired or constructed by the Fitchburg Gas and Electric Light Company in the city of Fitchburg, and all lines for the transmission of intelligence by electricity heretofore acquired or constructed by the New England Telephone and Telegraph Company and the American Telephone and Telegraph Company in said city, upon, along, under or over the public ways and places of said city, and the poles, piers, abutments, conduits and other fixtures necessary to sustain or protect the wires of said lines and actually in place on the effective date of this act, are hereby made lawful notwithstanding the lack of any valid locations therefor or any informality in the proceedings relative to their location and erection; provided, that the validation aforesaid shall not be effective as to the lines, structures or fixtures aforesaid of said companies in said city unless said companies shall, not later than December thirty-first, nineteen hundred and forty-four, file with the clerk of said city a map or maps showing the location and nature of said lines, structures, and fixtures in said city, such map or maps so filed to be recorded and kept with the records of original locations for poles and wires in said city.

SECTION 2. This act shall take full effect upon its acceptance by vote of the city council of said city, subject to the provisions of its charter, but not otherwise.

Approved May 19, 1943.

Chap.301 AN ACT RELATIVE TO PASTERS OR STICKERS FOR USE AT PRIMARIES.

Be it enacted, etc., as follows:

G. L. (Ter. Ed.), 53, new § 35A, added.

Size of pasters.

Chapter fifty-three of the General Laws is hereby amended by inserting after section thirty-five, as amended, the following section: — *Section 35A.* Pasters, commonly called stickers, to be used at primaries shall not be more than one half inch in width and four and one half inches in length and shall be subject to the same restrictions with respect to names and residences of candidates and the size of the type in which the names shall be printed as are imposed by sections forty-one and forty-four of chapter fifty-four with respect thereto in the case of election ballots.

Approved May 19, 1943.

Chap.302 AN ACT PROVIDING FOR THE PAYMENT OF WORKMEN'S COMPENSATION IN CERTAIN CASES OF HEAT EXHAUSTION.

Be it enacted, etc., as follows:

G. L. (Ter. Ed.), 152, § 26, etc., amended.

Payments.

Presumption of employment.

Extraterritoriality.

Chapter one hundred and fifty-two of the General Laws is hereby amended by striking out section twenty-six, as amended by section one of chapter three hundred and seventy of the acts of nineteen hundred and thirty-seven, and inserting in place thereof the following section: — *Section 26.* If an employee who has not given notice of his claim of common law rights of action, under section twenty-four, or who has given such notice and has waived the same, receives a personal injury arising out of and in the course of his employment, or arising out of an ordinary risk of the street while actually engaged, with his employer's authorization, in the business affairs or undertakings of his employer, and whether within or without the commonwealth, he shall be paid compensation by the insurer, as hereinafter provided, if his employer is an insured person at the time of the injury; provided, that as to an injury occurring without the commonwealth he has not given notice of his claim of rights of action under the laws of the jurisdiction wherein such injury occurs or has given such notice and has waived it. For the purposes of this section, any person while operating or using a motor or other vehicle, whether or not belonging to his employer, with his employer's general authorization or approval, in the performance of work in connection with the business affairs or undertakings of his employer, and whether within or without the commonwealth, and any person who, while engaged in the usual course of his trade, business, profession or occupation, is ordered by an insured person, or by a person exercising superintendence on behalf of such insured person, to perform work which is not in the usual course of such trade, business, profession or occupation, and, while so performing such work, receives a personal injury, shall be conclusively presumed to be an employee, and if an employee while acting in the course of his employment receives injury resulting from frost bite, heat exhaustion or sun stroke, without having voluntarily assumed increased peril not contemplated by his contract of employment, or is injured by reason of the physical activities of fellow employees in which he does not participate, whether or not such activities are associated with the employment, such injury shall be conclusively presumed to have arisen out of the employment. *Approved May 19, 1943.*

AN ACT RELATIVE TO THE TIME DURING WHICH CERTAIN BASEBALL GAMES MAY BE CONDUCTED ON THE LORD'S DAY DURING THE PRESENT WAR. *Chap.303*

Emergency preamble.

Whereas, The deferred operation of this act would, in part, tend to defeat its purpose, which is to make immediately possible, during the existing state of war, the conduct of certain games of baseball on the Lord's day after the terminal hour now fixed by law, therefore it is hereby declared to be an emergency law, necessary for the immediate preservation of the public convenience.

Be it enacted, etc., as follows:

During the continuance of the existing state of war between the United States and any foreign country, baseball games conducted on the Lord's day under authority of law may, when conducted as doubleheaders, so called, be continued beyond the hour of six thirty post meridian for the purpose of completing the second game of such doubleheader, so called; provided, that said second game is commenced before the hour of four thirty post meridian.

Approved May 19, 1943.

AN ACT SUBJECTING THE OFFICES OF COMMISSIONER OF SOLDIERS' RELIEF AND STATE AND MILITARY AID AND SUPERVISOR OF SOLDIERS' AND SAILORS' GRAVES IN THE CITY OF CHICOPEE TO THE CIVIL SERVICE LAWS. *Chap.304*

Be it enacted, etc., as follows:

SECTION 1. The offices of commissioner of soldiers' relief and state and military aid and supervisor of soldiers' and sailors' graves in the city of Chicopee shall, upon the effective date of this act, become subject to the civil service laws and rules and regulations, and the terms of the office of any incumbents thereof shall be unlimited, except that they may be removed in accordance with such laws and rules and regulations; but the persons holding said offices on said effective date may respectively continue therein by passing a qualifying civil service examination to which they shall be subjected by the division of civil service.

SECTION 2. This act shall be submitted for acceptance

to the qualified voters of the city of Chicopee at the biennial municipal election to be held in said city in the current year in the form of the following question, which shall be placed upon the official ballot to be used at said election: — "Shall an act passed by the general court in the current year, entitled 'An Act subjecting the offices of commissioner of soldiers' relief and state and military aid and supervisor of soldiers' and sailors' graves in the city of Chicopee to the civil service laws', be accepted?" If a majority of the votes cast on said question is in the affirmative, this act shall thereupon take full effect, but not otherwise.

Approved May 20, 1943.

---

*Chap.*305 AN ACT MAKING CLEAR THAT MARIHUANA OR MARIJUANA IS SUBJECT TO CERTAIN LAWS RELATING TO NARCOTIC DRUGS.

Be it enacted, etc., as follows:

G. L. (Ter. Ed.), 94, § 197, etc., amended.

SECTION 1. The paragraph of section one hundred and ninety-seven of chapter ninety-four of the General Laws defining "Narcotic drug", as amended by section one of chapter four hundred and twelve of the acts of nineteen hundred and thirty-five, is hereby further amended by inserting after the word "cannabis" in the seventh and eighth lines the following: — (sometimes called marihuana or marijuana), — so as to read as follows: — "Narcotic drug", coca leaves, cocaine, alpha or beta eucaine, or any synthetic substitute for them or any salts, compound or derivative thereof except decocainized coca leaves and preparations thereof, opium, morphine, heroin, codeine, or any preparation thereof or any salt, compound or derivative of the same; and, subject to section two hundred and six, cannabis (sometimes called marihuana or marijuana), including (*a*) the dried flowering or fruiting tops of the pistillate plant cannabis sativa L., from which the resin has not been extracted, (*b*) the resin extracted from such tops, and (*c*) every compound, manufacture, salt, derivative, mixture, or preparation of such resin, or of such tops from which the resin has not been extracted.

"Narcotic drug" defined.

G. L. (Ter. Ed.), 94, § 197, amended.

SECTION 2. Said section one hundred and ninety-seven is hereby further amended by striking out the fourth paragraph, as appearing in the Tercentenary Edition, and inserting in place thereof the following paragraph: —

Certain terms to include synthetics, etc.

"Opium", "morphine", "heroin", "codeine", "cocaine", and "cannabis" (sometimes called marihuana or marijuana), as used in statutes or in complaints or indictments include any synthetic substitute for such drugs or any salts, compounds, derivatives or preparations thereof, except decocainized coca leaves and preparations thereof.

Approved May 20, 1943.

AN ACT AUTHORIZING THE COMMISSIONER OF LABOR AND INDUSTRIES TO SUSPEND UNTIL APRIL FIRST, NINETEEN HUNDRED AND FORTY-FIVE, THE SIX O'CLOCK LAW, SO CALLED, RELATING TO THE HOURS OF EMPLOYMENT OF WOMEN IN THE TEXTILE INDUSTRY. *Chap.* 306

Whereas, Provisions of law similar to those set forth in this act have recently ceased to be effective, but the circumstances and conditions which made advisable their enactment still continue, and it is accordingly desirable that said provisions be made effective at once so that the period of interruption in the effectiveness thereof will be as short as possible, therefore it is hereby declared to be an emergency law, necessary for the immediate preservation of the public convenience. Emergency preamble.

Be it enacted, etc., as follows:

Section one of chapter three hundred and forty-seven of the acts of nineteen hundred and thirty-three, as most recently amended by chapter one hundred and fifty-four of the acts of nineteen hundred and forty-one, is hereby further amended by striking out, in the fifth line, the word "forty-three" and inserting in place thereof the word: — forty-five, — so as to read as follows: — *Section 1.* The commissioner of labor and industries is hereby authorized, in conformity with Article XX of Part the First of the Constitution of the Commonwealth, to suspend, until April first, nineteen hundred and forty-five, subject to such restrictions and conditions as the said commissioner may prescribe, so much of section fifty-nine of chapter one hundred and forty-nine of the General Laws, as amended, as prohibits the employment of women in the manufacture of textile goods after six o'clock in the evening; and, during the time of such suspension, those parts of said section fifty-nine which are so suspended shall be inoperative and of no effect.

Approved May 24, 1943.

AN ACT RELATIVE TO CERTAIN LIMITATIONS ON THE INVESTMENTS OF TRUST COMPANIES IN THEIR COMMERCIAL DEPARTMENTS. *Chap.* 307

Be it enacted, etc., as follows:

The limitations upon the liability of one borrower to a corporation subject to chapter one hundred and seventy-two of the General Laws prescribed by section forty or section forty A of said chapter shall not apply to any loan or loans made prior to July first, nineteen hundred and forty-five, to the extent that they are secured or covered by guaranties, or by commitments or agreements to take over or to purchase the same, made by the United States, the war department, the navy department, or the maritime commission thereof, or by any federal reserve bank or the Reconstruction Finance Corporation; provided, that such guaranties, agreements or commitments are subject to no condition beyond the control of the corporation making the loan, and must be performed by payment of cash or its equivalent within sixty days after demand; and provided, further, that for the performance of such guaranties, commitments or agreements the faith of the United States or of such federal reserve bank or of said Reconstruction Finance Corporation is pledged. *Approved May 24, 1943.*

---

*Chap.*308 AN ACT FURTHER REGULATING THE PERFORMANCE OF ELECTRICAL WORK.

Be it enacted, etc., as follows:

G. L. (Ter. Ed.), 141, § 1, amended.

Section one of chapter one hundred and forty-one of the General Laws, as appearing in the Tercentenary Edition, is hereby amended by striking out, in the fourth and fifth lines, the words: — , either as master electrician or as journeyman electrician, — so that the first paragraph will read as follows: — No person, firm or corporation shall enter into, engage in, or work at the business of installing wires, conduits, apparatus, fixtures or other appliances for carrying or using electricity for light, heat or power purposes, unless such person, firm or corporation shall have received a license and a certificate therefor, issued by the state examiners of electricians and in accordance with the provisions hereinafter set forth. *Approved May 24, 1943.*

Licensing of electricians.

---

*Chap.*309 AN ACT RELATIVE TO THE POWERS AND DUTIES OF CERTAIN FRATERNAL BENEFIT SOCIETIES.

Be it enacted, etc., as follows:

G. L. (Ter. Ed.), 176, § 11, amended.

SECTION 1. Section eleven of chapter one hundred and seventy-six of the General Laws, as appearing in the Tercentenary Edition, is hereby amended by inserting after the word "change" in the second line the words: — the location of its place of business to another location in the commonwealth, or change, — and by inserting after the word "change" in the eighth line the words: — in the location of its place of business or, — so as to read as follows: — *Section 11.* A domestic fraternal benefit corporation may, with the approval of the commissioner, change the location of its place of business to another location in the commonwealth, or change the purposes for which it was incorporated so as to permit it to transact any business authorized by this chapter. Upon such approval the presiding, financial and recording officers, and a majority of its other officers having the powers of directors, shall file in the office of the state secretary a certificate, with the approval of the commissioner endorsed thereon, setting forth the change in the location of its place of business or in the purposes of the corporation. The state secretary shall, upon receipt of five

Corporation may change location, purposes, etc.

dollars, cause such certificate to be filed in his office. Every domestic fraternal beneficiary corporation may exercise all the rights, powers and privileges conferred by this chapter, including the powers specified in section thirty-two, or its certificate of incorporation or charter, not inconsistent herewith, and shall be subject to this chapter, as if reincorporated hereunder.

G. L. (Ter. Ed.), 176, § 32, amended.

SECTION 2. Said chapter one hundred and seventy-six is hereby further amended by striking out section thirty-two, as so appearing, and inserting in place thereof the following section: — *Section 32.* Every society may, subject to this chapter, make a constitution and by-laws for its government, admission of members, management of its affairs, and the fixing and readjusting of the rates and contributions of its members from time to time, and may amend its constitution and by-laws, and it shall have such other powers as are necessary or incidental to carry into effect its objects and purposes. The constitution and by-laws may prescribe the officers and elected members of standing committees, who may be ex officiis directors or other officers corresponding thereto, and may, with the approval of the commissioner, provide for a system of absent voting, other than proxy voting, under which absent members entitled to vote may vote in the election of the officers and directors or similar governing body; provided, that the commissioner shall not approve any provision for such a system of absent voting unless the society submitting such provision for approval satisfies the commissioner that absent voting is necessary in order to have an adequate representation of the membership of the society at its elections.

Constitution and by-laws

G. L. (Ter. Ed.), 176, § 45, etc., amended.

SECTION 3. Section forty-five of said chapter one hundred and seventy-six, as amended, is hereby further amended by inserting after the first paragraph the following paragraph: —

Corporation may furnish physician and nurses.

Any corporation subject to this section may furnish physicians and nurses for its members and their families, or pay for the services of physicians or nurses engaged by its members for the care of themselves or their families; provided, that the expense incurred hereunder by any such corporation in any year shall not exceed five thousand dollars in the aggregate, and shall not exceed one hundred dollars in the case of any member thereof and his family.

Approved May 24, 1943.

AN ACT RELATIVE TO THE USE OF VOTING MACHINES AT PRIMARIES AND ELECTIONS. *Chap.*310

Be it enacted, etc., as follows:

G. L. (Ter. Ed.), 54, § 30, amended.

SECTION 1. Section thirty of chapter fifty-four of the General Laws, as appearing in the Tercentenary Edition, is hereby amended by inserting after the word "envelopes" in the fourth line the words: — or other containers, — so

Precinct seals, use, custody, etc.

as to read as follows: — *Section 30.* The clerk of every city and of every town divided into voting precincts shall furnish to the clerk of each voting precinct a seal of suitable device, with a designation thereon of such precinct; and such seal shall be used in sealing all envelopes or other containers required by law to be used at elections. The clerk of the precinct shall retain custody of the seal, and shall, at the end of his term of office, deliver it, with the records of the precinct and other official documents in his custody, to the city or town clerk.

G. L. (Ter. Ed.), 54, new § 30A, added.

Custodian of voting machines, duties of.

SECTION 2. Said chapter fifty-four is hereby further amended by inserting after section thirty, as so appearing, the following section: — *Section 30A.* Notwithstanding any contrary provision of section thirteen, where voting machines are used one or more of the election officers shall be designated by the city or town clerk as custodian of voting machines to assist him in the preparation and upkeep thereof, and in the performance of his duties may enter within the guard rail in any polling place. He shall perform such duties under the supervision of the city or town clerk as the board, body or official charged with the conduct of the elections may require, or the board of voting machine examiners may by regulation prescribe, but shall perform no other duties in connection with the conduct of the election. Each election officer shall be instructed in the use of the machines by a custodian acting under the direction of the city or town clerk. For the purpose of giving such instructions the city or town clerk shall call such meeting or meetings of the election officers as may be necessary. The city or town clerk shall keep on file in his office a record of the names of the precinct election officers who have received instructions and are properly qualified to perform the duties.

G. L. (Ter. Ed.), 54, § 31, amended.

SECTION 3. Section thirty-one of said chapter fifty-four, as so appearing, is hereby amended by inserting at the end the following: —

Installation of voting machines.

Where voting machines are used the city or town clerk on or before the day of election and before the hour fixed for the opening of the polls shall provide for the installation of the machines in the polling places. He shall send to the election officers before the polls are opened on election days blank forms and other necessary supplies, including voters' authority certificates, not less than one for each registered voter, in a form approved by the state secretary substantially as follows:

City (or Town) of..

Ward and Precinct (or Precinct)................................

Date...

Voting Authority No..

This certificate must be handed to the election officer in charge of the voting machines in order to vote.

Each voter's certificate shall be so prepared as to be capable of being inserted by the election officer after receiving it from the voter in a suitable container to be furnished by the board or officer responsible for the conduct of the election.

G. L. (Ter. Ed.), 54, new §§ 33A–33D, added.

SECTION 4. Said chapter fifty-four is hereby further amended by inserting after section thirty-three, as so appearing, the four following sections: — *Section 33A*. Voting machines shall be provided with convenient spaces, which shall be specified and described on the cards of instructions, where the name of a person may be written in or a paster or sticker affixed by a voter who desires to vote for a person whose name does not appear on the voting machine. They shall be suitably lighted so that the voter will be able to easily read the titles of the offices, the names of the candidates and the questions submitted to the voters. The machines shall be equipped with proper devices or locks to prevent any operation of the machine before or after the voting, and with the following counters or indicators: — A "Public Counter", which shall mean the counter or other device that registers each time the machine is operated during the election and shows the number of persons who have voted thereon, a "Protective Counter", which shall mean the device or counter which registers the grand total of times that the machine has been operated, a "Candidate Counter", which shall mean the counters on which are registered numerically the votes cast for candidates, a "Question Counter", which shall mean the counters upon which are registered numerically the votes cast on questions submitted to the voters, and the "Vote Indicators", which shall mean the pointers or other devices upon which are registered the votes for candidates or on questions submitted to voters. All voting machines used in primary elections shall be so equipped that the election officers can adjust the machines to prevent voters from voting for candidates of any party in which they are not enrolled.

Equipment of voting machines.

Counters, etc.

Section 33B. During the period the polls are open for voting, the exterior of the voting machine shall remain in plain view of the election officers. If so requested, an election officer shall instruct voters outside the guard rail in the manner of operating the machine. When the name of a voter has been checked on the voting list and he is found qualified to vote, he shall be given a voter's authority certificate and admitted within the guard rail. Before entering a machine, the voter shall hand his voter's authority certificate to the officer in charge of the machine, who shall deposit it in the receptacle provided therefor and shall then release the machine to permit the voter to close the curtain and cast his ballot. Except as otherwise provided in section seventy-nine, during the voting no officer shall be, nor permit any other person to be, in any position to see or learn how any voter is voting or has voted. The election officer attending the machine shall from time to time inspect the face of the machine to see that neither the ballot labels nor the voting indicators have been tampered with or injured. During the election the doors of the counter compartment

Method of operating voting machines, etc.

Instructions

shall not be unlocked or opened. If through mechanical failure a machine ceases to function, it shall be inspected and put in working order, if possible, by the custodian of voting machines, designated under section thirty A, in the presence of two election officers of different political parties, who shall make and sign a statement setting forth the cause of the failure of the machine to properly operate and such statement shall be filed with the election returns. If the machine cannot be put in working order, it shall be placed out of service for that election and a statement that the machine is out of order shall be signed by the election officers and filed with the election returns.

Instructions to voter after inclosure in booth.

Section 33C. If any voter, after he has inclosed himself in the voting machine booth, shall ask for further instructions concerning the manner of operating the machine, two election officers of different political parties shall give him such instructions. No officer or person instructing him shall in any manner request or seek to persuade or induce any such voter to vote for any candidate or candidates, or for or against any question submitted to the voters. After giving such instructions, and before such voter shall have registered his vote, the officers or persons instructing him shall retire, and such voter shall then register his vote as he may desire. No voter after registering his vote and emerging from the machine booth shall be permitted to re-enter it.

Voting for persons whose names are not on ballot labels.

Section 33D. Every vote cast for any person whose name does not appear on the ballot labels of the machine as a nominated candidate for office shall be written or affixed or enclosed on or in the appropriate place on the machine provided for that purpose, or it shall not be counted.

G. L. (Ter. Ed.), 54, § 35, amended.

Exhibition of voting machines.

SECTION 5. Said chapter fifty-four is hereby further amended by striking out section thirty-five, as so appearing, and inserting in place thereof the following section: — *Section 35.* The body, board or official charged with the conduct of elections shall cause to be done all things necessary to properly carry on primaries and elections where voting machines are used. Before every primary and election they shall cause to be placed on public exhibition one or more machines for the instruction of voters. Such machines shall be equipped with ballot labels as nearly as practicable like those to be used on the machine at the primary or election, as to titles of offices, names of candidates and forms of questions. On the day of the election they shall provide at each polling place a mechanical model of the voting machine, which shall be placed outside the guard rail and shall be suitable for the instruction of the voters and illustrating the manner of voting. Before the opening of the polls they shall cause each machine to be prepared for use and delivered at the polling place. On the day of the election the keys to each voting machine shall be delivered by the city or town clerk to the election officers a reasonable time before the opening of the polls in a separate sealed envelope on which shall be

Delivery at polling places

Examination of.

written the number and location of the election precinct or polling place, the number of the voting machine, the number of the seal with which it is sealed and the number registered on the protective counter as reported by the city or town clerk. No such envelope shall be opened until at least one of the election officers from each of two political parties are present at the polling place and have examined the envelope to see that it has not been opened. Before opening such an envelope, all election officers present shall examine the seal on the machine to see that it is intact, and they shall compare the numbers on the envelope with the numbers registered on the protective counter and on the seal on the machine to see whether or not they agree. If they do not agree, the machine shall not be opened until the city or town clerk shall have been notified and personally or by the custodian designated under section thirty A shall have examined such machine and certified that it is properly prepared and arranged for the election. If the numbers agree, the election officers shall open the doors of the counter compartment of the machine. All the election officers present shall examine the counter compartment of every machine to see whether or not it registers zero. After such examination the doors of each counter compartment shall be closed and locked and not again opened until the polls are closed. If any counter shall be found not to be set at zero, the number and letter of such counter, together with the number registered thereon, shall be stated in a writing signed by the election officers and posted on the wall of the polling place, and a duplicate of such writing shall be filed with the election returns. At the close of the polls such number shall be subtracted from the number then found registered on the counter. Each machine shall remain locked and sealed against voting until the time set for opening the polls. It shall be then unlocked for voting and the seal removed.

G. L. (Ter. Ed.), 54, § 35B, etc., amended.

SECTION 6. Section thirty-five B of said chapter fifty-four, inserted by section three of chapter two hundred and eighty-one of the acts of nineteen hundred and thirty-eight, and as most recently amended by sections six and seven of chapter five hundred and eleven of the acts of nineteen hundred and forty-one, is hereby further amended by striking out the second paragraph and inserting in place thereof the following paragraph: —

Procedure as to voting machines after closing of polls.

After the closing of the polls, where voting machines are used, the warden, or an election officer, in the presence of an election officer of a different political party, and subject to verification by any or all election officers present, shall, in the order of the offices as arranged on the voting machine, read and announce in distinct tones the result as shown by the counters. He shall, in the same manner, read and announce the vote on each constitutional amendment or other question as shown by the same machine. As each vote is read and announced, it shall be recorded on the total sheets, and, when completed, the record thereof shall be compared with the numbers on the counters of the machine. The votes written in, or voted by pasters or stickers, for persons not named on the ballot labels of the machine shall then be announced and recorded. The result shall, in like manner, be read, compared and announced, one at a time, from each machine in the polling place until all the votes on the counters have been read, compared and announced, after which the total vote shall be tabulated and entered in the official returns. After the vote is tabulated, the election officers shall lock and seal each machine, and enclose and seal the keys in an envelope on which shall be written the number, if any, and the location of the election precinct or polling place, the number of the machine, the number on the seal and the number registered on the counters. In tabulating the votes, total sheets shall be used upon which shall be set down the total number of votes cast for each candidate and the total number of yes and no votes cast on each question as recorded by the voting machines. The totals on ballots cast by challenged voters and on absent voter ballots shall be recorded separately or on separate total sheets and added to the total vote cast by the use of voting machines for each candidate and each question. The total sheets shall be sealed up in envelopes and transmitted to the city or town clerk with the ballots, keys, voting lists and records of the election officers.

Approved May 24, 1943.

---

*Chap.*311 AN ACT RELATIVE TO THE VENUE OF THE CRIME OF BUYING, RECEIVING OR AIDING IN THE CONCEALMENT OF STOLEN OR EMBEZZLED PROPERTY.

Be it enacted, etc., as follows:

G. L. (Ter. Ed.), 277, new § 58A, added.

SECTION 1. Chapter two hundred and seventy-seven of the General Laws is hereby amended by inserting after section fifty-eight, as appearing in the Tercentenary Edition, the following section: — *Section 58A.* The crime of buying, receiving or aiding in the concealment of stolen or embezzled property, as defined in section sixty of chapter two hundred and sixty-six, may be prosecuted and punished in the same jurisdiction in which the larceny or embezzlement of any property involved in the crime may be prosecuted and punished.

Venue for crime of receiving, etc., stolen or embezzled property.

Effective date.

SECTION 2. This act shall take effect on October first in the current year. *Approved May 24, 1943.*

---

*Chap.*312 AN ACT REVISING THE PENALTY FOR CERTAIN VIOLATIONS AND FALSE STATEMENTS UNDER THE LAW RELATING TO MARRIAGE.

Be it enacted, etc., as follows:

G. L. (Ter. Ed.), 207, § 52, amended.

SECTION 1. Chapter two hundred and seven of the General Laws is hereby amended by striking out section fifty-two, as appearing in the Tercentenary Edition, and inserting in place thereof the following section: — *Section 52.* Whoever violates any provision of section twenty, and whoever falsely swears or affirms in making any statement required under section twenty, shall be punished by a fine of not more than one hundred dollars. Penalty.

SECTION 2. This act shall take effect on October first in the current year and shall apply in the case of crimes committed on or after said date; but the provisions of said section fifty-two, as in effect immediately preceding said date, shall continue to apply in the case of crimes committed prior thereto. *Approved May 24, 1943.* Effective date.

AN ACT RELATIVE TO THE PUBLICATION AND DISTRIBUTION OF BOOKS CONTAINING PORTRAITS AND BIOGRAPHICAL SKETCHES OF MEMBERS OF THE GENERAL COURT AND OTHER STATE OFFICERS, AND OTHER MATTERS OF PUBLIC INTEREST. *Chap.*313

Be it enacted, etc., as follows:

Chapter five of the General Laws is hereby amended by striking out section eighteen, as amended by section one of chapter two hundred and twenty-six of the acts of nineteen hundred and thirty-five, and inserting in place thereof the following section: — *Section 18.* The clerks of the two branches shall, in every odd-numbered year, prepare a book containing portraits and biographical sketches of members of the general court and other state officers, lists of committees and such other information as may be deemed pertinent, of which not more than four hundred copies shall be printed under the direction of said clerks, for the use of the general court. The clerks shall furnish one such copy to each member of the general court and shall distribute the other copies as the committees on rules of the senate and house of representatives may direct. G. L. (Ter. Ed.), 5, § 18, etc., amended. Preparation and distribution of books containing portraits of members of general court, etc.

In addition to the copies of such book printed under authority of the foregoing provisions of this section, there shall be printed such additional copies thereof as said clerks may from time to time determine. Such additional copies shall be delivered to the state secretary, who shall place the same on public sale at a price not less than the cost thereof, as determined by said committees on rules.

Approved May 24, 1943.

AN ACT RELATIVE TO THE SALARIES OF MEMBERS OF THE COUNCIL. *Chap.*314

Be it enacted, etc., as follows:

SECTION 1. Section three of chapter six of the General Laws, as appearing in the Tercentenary Edition, is hereby amended by striking out, in the first line, the word "one" and inserting in place thereof the word: — two, — so as to read as follows: — *Section 3.* Each member of the council shall receive a salary of two thousand dollars. G. L. (Ter. Ed.), 6, § 3, amended. Salaries of councillors.

Effective date.

SECTION 2. The salary established hereby shall be allowed from the time the members of the council elected at the biennial state election of nineteen hundred and forty-two took office. *Approved May 24, 1943.*

---

*Chap.*315 AN ACT RELATIVE TO THE SALARY OF THE COMMISSIONER OF BANKS.

Be it enacted, etc., as follows:

G. L. (Ter. Ed.), 26, § 2, amended.

Commissioner of banks.

Salary and bond.

Section two of chapter twenty-six of the General Laws, as appearing in the Tercentenary Edition, is hereby amended by striking out, in the fourth line, the words "six thousand" and inserting in place thereof the words: — seventy-five hundred, — so as to read as follows: — *Section 2.* Upon the expiration of the term of office of a commissioner of banks, his successor shall be appointed for three years by the governor, with the advice and consent of the council. The commissioner shall receive such salary, not exceeding seventy-five hundred dollars, as the governor and council determine. He shall not be an officer of or directly or indirectly interested in any national bank or in any bank, trust company, corporation, business or occupation that requires his official supervision, and he shall not engage in any other business. He shall give bond with sureties in the sum of twenty thousand dollars, to be approved by the state treasurer, for the faithful performance of his duties.

Approved May 24, 1943.

---

*Chap.*316 AN ACT RELATIVE TO THE SALARY OF THE COMMISSIONER OF CORPORATIONS AND TAXATION.

Be it enacted, etc., as follows:

G. L. (Ter. Ed.), 14, § 2, amended.

Commissioner of corporations and taxation.

Salary and bond.

Section two of chapter fourteen of the General Laws, as appearing in the Tercentenary Edition, is hereby amended by striking out, in the fourth line, the word "seventy-five" and inserting in place thereof the word: — eighty-five, — so as to read as follows: — *Section 2.* Upon the expiration of the term of office of a commissioner, his successor shall be appointed for three years by the governor, with the advice and consent of the council. The commissioner shall receive such salary, not exceeding eighty-five hundred dollars, as the governor and council determine and shall give to the state treasurer a bond for the faithful performance of his official duties in a penal sum and with sureties approved by the governor and council. *Approved May 24, 1943.*

---

*Chap.*317 AN ACT RELATIVE TO THE SALARY OF THE COMMISSIONER OF INSURANCE.

Be it enacted, etc., as follows:

G. L. (Ter. Ed.), 26, § 6, amended.

Section six of chapter twenty-six of the General Laws, as appearing in the Tercentenary Edition, is hereby amended by striking out, in the fourth line, the words "six thousand"

and inserting in place thereof the words: — seventy-five hundred, — so as to read as follows: — *Section 6.* Upon the expiration of the term of office of a commissioner of insurance, his successor shall be appointed for three years by the governor, with the advice and consent of the council. The commissioner shall receive such salary, not exceeding seventy-five hundred dollars, as the governor and council determine. He shall give bond with sureties in the sum of ten thousand dollars, to be approved by the state treasurer, for the faithful performance of his duties. *Approved May 24, 1943.*

Commissioner of insurance.

Salary and bond.

AN ACT RELATIVE TO CORRUPT PRACTICES. *Chap.318*

Be it enacted, etc., as follows:

SECTION 1. Chapter fifty-five of the General Laws is hereby amended by striking out section one, as appearing in the Tercentenary Edition, and inserting in place thereof the following section: —*Section 1.* Except as otherwise provided in this chapter, no person, in order to aid or promote his own nomination or election to public office, shall himself or through another person give, pay, expend or contribute any money or other thing of value, or promise so to do, in excess of the following amounts.

G. L. (Ter. Ed.), 55, § 1, amended.

Campaign expenses of candidates limited and defined.

	Primary.	Election.
United States Senator,	$5,000	$10,000
Governor,	5,000	10,000
Lieutenant Governor, State Secretary, State Treasurer, State Auditor, Attorney General,	3,000	6,000
Representative in Congress,	3,000	6,000
State Senator,	1,000	1,000
Representative in the General Court: — Each candidate may spend:		
In a district entitled to three representatives,	600	600
In a district entitled to two representatives,	500	500
In a district entitled to one representative,	400	400

A candidate for any other office may expend an amount not exceeding forty dollars for each one thousand, or major portion thereof, of the registered voters qualified to vote for candidates for the office in question at the next preceding election; but no such candidate shall expend more than fifteen hundred dollars for the expenses of a primary, nor more than three thousand dollars for the expenses of an election. Any candidate may, however, expend a sum not exceeding two hundred dollars for primary or election expenses. Contributions by a candidate to political committees shall be included in the foregoing sums.

The sums hereby authorized shall include all contributions from individuals, political committees or other sources to a candidate or person acting under his authority, and shall include every payment or promise of payment for any purpose, made directly or indirectly by, or for the benefit of, a candidate, except payments or promises of payments of expenses by a political committee as authorized by this chapter; and the gift, payment, contribution or promise of any money or thing of value in excess of those sums, by a candidate directly or indirectly, shall be deemed a corrupt practice.

G. L. (Ter. Ed.), 55, § 5, amended.

SECTION 2. Section five of said chapter fifty-five, as so appearing, is hereby amended by inserting after the word "publications" in the fourth line the words: — , radio broadcasts or other forms of publicity, — and by striking out the last paragraph and inserting in place thereof the following: — Such committee may contribute to other political committees and may contribute to the personal fund of a candidate. A political committee or a candidate may hire conveyances or workers at primaries or elections, but not more than two persons at each polling place shall be hired to represent the same political party, candidate or principle, — so as to read as follows: — *Section 5.* Political committees, duly organized, may receive, pay and expend money or other things of value for the following purposes, and no others: advertising, writing, printing and distributing circulars or other publications, radio broadcasts or other forms of publicity, hire and maintenance of political headquarters, and clerical hire incidental thereto, meetings, refreshments, not including intoxicating liquors, but including cigars and tobacco, decorations and music, postage, stationery, printing, expressage, traveling expenses, telephone, telegraph and messenger service, and the hire of conveyances and workers at polling places.

Payments by political committees restricted.

Such committee may contribute to other political committees and may contribute to the personal fund of a candidate. A political committee or a candidate may hire conveyances or workers at primaries or elections, but not more than two persons at each polling place shall be hired to represent the same political party, candidate or principle.

G. L. (Ter. Ed.), 55, § 6, amended.

SECTION 3. Section six of said chapter fifty-five, as so appearing, is hereby amended by inserting after the word "of" in the seventh line the second time it appears the words: — a candidate at a primary or election or, — and by striking out the third sentence and inserting in place thereof the following: — Any individual, not a candidate, may contribute to any political committee and to any candidate, except as provided in section one, a sum which shall not exceed one thousand dollars in any election and primary preliminary thereto, — so as to read as follows: — *Section 6.* No person or combination of persons shall in connection with any nomination or election receive money or its equivalent, expend or disburse or promise to expend or disburse the same, except as authorized by this chapter. A political committee or a person acting under the authority or on behalf of such a committee may receive money or its equivalent, or expend or disburse or promise to expend or

Receipts and disbursements regulated.

Certain services not prohibited.

disburse the same for the purpose of aiding or promoting the success or defeat of a candidate at a primary or election or a political party or principle in a public election or favoring or opposing the adoption or rejection of a question submitted to the voters, and for other purposes expressly authorized by this chapter subject, however, to the provisions thereof. Any individual, not a candidate, may contribute to any political committee and to any candidate, except as provided in section one, a sum which shall not exceed one thousand dollars in any election and primary preliminary thereto. This section shall not prohibit the rendering of services by speakers, publishers, editors, writers, checkers and watchers at the polls or by other persons for which no compensation is asked, given or promised, expressly or by implication; nor shall it prohibit the payment by themselves of such personal expenses as may be incidental to the rendering of such services; nor shall it prohibit the free use of property belonging to an individual and the exercise of ordinary hospitality for which no compensation is asked, given or promised, expressly or by implication.

G. L. (Ter. Ed.), 55, § 37, amended.

SECTION 4. Said chapter fifty-five is hereby further amended by striking out section thirty-seven, as so appearing, and inserting in place thereof the following: — *Section 37.* (*a*) If five or more voters have reasonable cause to believe that a corrupt practice, as defined in the preceding section, has been committed by any successful candidate, other than a candidate for the United States congress, or for the general court, for whom such voters had the right to vote, with reference to his election, or by any other person in his interest or behalf with reference thereto, such voters may apply to a justice of the superior court, sitting in equity within and for Suffolk county, for leave to bring an election petition against such candidate praying that the election of such candidate be declared void. Such application shall be subscribed and sworn to by the petitioners and it shall be heard ex parte by the justice of the superior court upon such evidence as he may require; and if the petitioners shall establish to his satisfaction that there is reasonable cause to believe that a corrupt practice has been committed with reference to the election of the candidate in question, which materially affected the results of the election, and that upon the evidence obtainable there is reasonable cause to believe that such violations may be proved, he shall make an order granting leave to the petitioners to bring an election petition against such candidate

Election petitions for corrupt practices.

Entry, notice, procedure, etc.

(*b*) After the entry of such order, and within two months after the election to which it relates, the election petition may be filed in the superior court within and for Suffolk county.

Notice of the petition shall be by writ of subpoena according to the usual course of proceedings in equity and shall be returnable fourteen days after the date on which the petition is filed.

A subpoena issued upon an election petition shall be served not less than seven days before the return day.

A defence to an election petition shall be by answer, filed within seven days after the return day, and no replication need be filed.

Election petitions shall be entered on the equity docket.

Must be heard by three justices, etc.

(*c*) Election petitions and all motions and other applications, whether interlocutory or final, and all hearings on the merits or upon the making, entering or modifying of decrees therein shall be heard and determined by three justices of the superior court who shall, immediately following the filing of an election petition, be assigned by the chief justice of said court for the hearing and determination of all matters arising under election petitions prior to the next state election. No reference to a master shall be had upon any matter arising under an election petition, except in matters of fact relating to financial statements and the examination of accounts and vouchers. All proceedings under election petitions shall have precedence over any case of a different nature pending in any court, and the justices of the superior court may from time to time make such rules regulating the practice and proceedings in matters of such election petitions, not inconsistent with this chapter, as they deem expedient. In the absence of any such rules, the practice and procedure in election petitions shall be governed by such laws or rules of court, not inconsistent with this chapter, as may from time to time be in force relating to the practice and proceedings in matters of equity.

Decision to be final.

(*d*) Upon an election petition the decision of the three justices of the superior court assigned as aforesaid, or of a majority of them, shall be final and conclusive upon all matters in controversy, whether interlocutory or final, and whether in matters of fact or matters of law. But the said justices, or a majority of them, may, after a finding of facts, either of their own motion or at the request of either party, report the case to the supreme judicial court for determination by the full court; and thereupon like proceedings shall be had as upon a report after a finding of facts by a justice of the superior court in equity proceedings.

Case may be reported.

Defences.

(*e*) If upon an election petition one or more violations of the preceding section are proved, it shall be a defence to the petition if the defendant establishes to the satisfaction of a majority of the justices hearing the same, with reference to all of said violations, the following:

As to every such violation, either that

(1) Such violation was not committed by the candidate or by any person with his knowledge and in his behalf, but was committed contrary to the orders and without the sanction or connivance of the candidate;

(2) The participation, if any, of the candidate in such violation, arose from inadvertence or from accidental miscalculation, or from some other reasonable cause of a like

nature, and in any case did not arise from any want of good faith;

(3) The candidate took all reasonable means for preventing the commission of violations of this chapter with reference to the election in question;

(4) The violation in question was of a trivial, unimportant and limited character;

(5) The violation in question did not materially affect the results of the election.

(*f*) The court may by an order make the final disposition of an election petition conditional upon the filing of a statement required by this chapter in a modified form, or within an extended time, and upon compliance with such other terms as the court may deem best calculated to carry into effect the objects hereof, and in such case the court shall require, within a time certain, further proof as to the compliance with the conditions of such order, whereupon a final decree shall be entered. Final decision may be conditional.

(*g*) If upon the hearing of an election petition a majority of the justices hearing the same shall find that in relation to the election of the candidate in question a corrupt practice, as defined in the preceding section, was committed, either by the defendant or by any person in his interest or behalf, a decree shall be entered subject to the limitations and conditions hereinbefore prescribed, declaring void the election of the defendant to the office in question, and ousting and excluding him from such office and declaring the office vacant. Decree upon finding of corrupt practice.

(*h*) No person called to testify upon an election petition shall be excused from testifying or producing any papers on the ground that his testimony may tend to criminate him or subject him to a penalty or forfeiture; but he shall not be prosecuted or subjected to any penalty or forfeiture except forfeiture of election to office, for or on account of any action, matter or thing concerning which he may so testify, except for perjury committed in such testimony. Immunity of witnesses.

(*i*) No decree entered upon an election petition shall be a bar to or affect in any way any criminal prosecution of any candidate or other person, or any inquest in accordance with sections thirty-nine to forty-five, inclusive. Decree no bar to criminal prosecution.

(*j*) A certified copy of any final decree entered upon an election petition, as provided by this chapter, shall forthwith be transmitted by the clerk to the state secretary; and any vacancy in any office created by any such decree shall be filled in the manner provided by law in case of the death of the incumbent, but in no case shall the candidate so excluded from the office be eligible therefor. Certified copy of decree to state secretary. Filling of vacancy.

(*k*) If upon the hearing of an election petition it shall appear to a majority of the justices hearing the same that with reference to the election in question there is a reasonable presumption that any violation of this chapter was committed, they shall cause notice of the facts to be given by the clerk of said court to the district attorney for the county Notice to district attorney, process, etc.

where the violation appears to have been committed, with a list of the witnesses to establish the violation, and any other information which they may consider proper; and thereupon the district attorney shall cause complaint therefor to be made before a court or magistrate having jurisdiction thereof, or shall present the evidence thereof to the grand jury. If it shall appear that a successful candidate for district attorney has been guilty of any such violation, a majority of said justices shall order the notice of the facts to be given to the attorney general, who shall designate a district attorney to make such complaint or presentment. A majority of said justices may issue process for the apprehension of any person so appearing to have committed a violation of this chapter, and may bind over, as in criminal prosecutions, such witnesses as they deem necessary to appear and testify at the court having jurisdiction of the crime.

G. L. (Ter. Ed.), 50, § 1, etc., amended.

SECTION 5. Section one of chapter fifty of the General Laws, as amended by sections one and two of chapter five hundred and eleven of the acts of nineteen hundred and forty-one, is hereby further amended by inserting after the word "defeat" in the sixtieth line, the words: — of a candidate at a primary or election or the success or defeat, — so that lines fifty-six to sixty-two, as appearing in the Tercentenary Edition, will read as follows: — "Political committee" shall apply only to a committee elected as provided in chapter fifty-two, except that in chapter fifty-five it shall also apply, subject to the exception contained in section thirty-eight thereof, to every other committee or combination of five or more voters of the commonwealth who shall aid or promote the success or defeat of a candidate at a primary or election or the success or defeat of a political party or principle in a public election or shall favor or oppose the adoption or rejection of a question submitted to the voters.

'Political committee' defined.

Approved May 24, 1943.

---

*Chap.*319 AN ACT RELATIVE TO THE PAYMENT OF UNEMPLOYMENT COMPENSATION BENEFITS TO PERSONS UPON TERMINATION OF SERVICE IN THE MILITARY OR NAVAL FORCES OF THE UNITED STATES.

Be it enacted, etc., as follows:

SECTION 1. Section one of chapter seven hundred and one of the acts of nineteen hundred and forty-one is hereby amended by striking out subsection (*c*) and inserting in place thereof the following subsection: —

(*c*) He has been paid wages of one hundred and fifty dollars or more in the base period effective at the time of his induction or enlistment combined with the quarters of the calendar year next succeeding such base period provided that such quarters have elapsed prior to his termination of active military or naval service, and is otherwise eligible for weekly benefits for unemployment under the provisions of the employment security law.

SECTION 2. Section two of said chapter seven hundred and one is hereby amended by striking out subsection (*a*) and inserting in place thereof the following subsection: —

(*a*) The aggregate amount of benefits payable to such person shall be the total amount of benefits not previously paid to him, based on wages paid in the base period effective at the time of his induction or enlistment combined with the quarters of the calendar year next succeeding such base period, provided that such quarters have elapsed prior to his termination of active military or naval service.

Approved May 24, 1943.

AN ACT RELATIVE TO THE SECURING OF INFORMATION CONCERNING PERSONS RESIDING AT INNS, LODGING HOUSES AND PUBLIC LODGING HOUSES. *Chap.*320

Be it enacted, etc., as follows:

SECTION 1. Chapter fifty-one of the General Laws is hereby amended by striking out sections ten A and ten B, inserted by section one of chapter three hundred and sixty-nine of the acts of nineteen hundred and thirty-nine, and inserting in place thereof the following section: — *Section 10A.* Every innholder licensed under any provision of chapter one hundred and forty, and every keeper of a lodging house or public lodging house licensed thereunder shall, on or before January fifth of each year, report in writing to the registrars of voters of the city or town wherein such inn, lodging house or public lodging house is located, under the penalties of perjury, the name of every person twenty years of age or older on January first of said year whose place of residence on said January first was at such inn, lodging house or public lodging house, together with the other information relative to each such person required to be secured by registrars under section four. The registrars of voters of every city and town shall, not later than the fifteenth day of December in each year, furnish to such innholder, keeper of a lodging house or keeper of a public lodging house suitable blank forms for the making of the reports required under this section. G. L. (Ter. Ed.), 51, §§ 10A and 10B, etc., amended. Statement relative to residents of inns, etc.

In preparing the lists required by section four, the registrars shall not include therein as residing at any licensed inn, lodging house or public lodging house the name of any person which has not been reported to them as provided by this section.

SECTION 2. The fourth sentence of section thirty-seven of said chapter fifty-one, as most recently amended by section two of said chapter three hundred and sixty-nine, is hereby further amended by striking out the words "or the name of a person who neglects to file the return required" and inserting in place thereof the words: — nor shall they enter in such register as residing at any licensed inn, lodging house or public lodging house the name of a person which has not been reported to them, — so as to read as follows: G. L. (Ter. Ed.), 51, § 37, etc., amended.

Entries in annual register.

— They shall make all inquiries and investigations necessary to identify such person, and they shall not enter in the annual register the name of a person objected to by any registrar, nor shall they enter in such register as residing at any licensed inn, lodging house or public lodging house the name of a person which has not been reported to them under section ten A, until such person has been duly notified and given an opportunity to be heard.

G. L. (Ter. Ed.), 51, § 41A, etc., amended.

Election commissioners to have similar duties as registrars.

SECTION 3. Said chapter fifty-one is hereby further amended by striking out section forty-one A, inserted by section one of chapter three hundred and twenty-eight of the acts of nineteen hundred and forty-one, and inserting in place thereof the following section: — *Section 41A.* The duties imposed by sections ten A and thirty-seven, respectively, upon registrars of voters shall be performed in Boston and in other cities not having registrars by the election commissioners or other persons or boards having the powers and duties of registrars, or similar powers and duties. The reports required by said section ten A shall in Boston and in such other cities be filed with said commissioners or other persons or boards.

G. L. (Ter. Ed.), 56, § 5, etc., amended.

Penalty.

SECTION 4. Section five of chapter fifty-six of the General Laws, as amended by section nineteen of chapter four hundred and forty of the acts of nineteen hundred and thirty-eight, is hereby further amended by adding at the end the following sentence: — Whoever, being a licensed innholder or keeper of a lodging house or public lodging house, fails in any respect to make the reports required by section ten A of chapter fifty-one in the detail and manner and within the time therein provided shall be punished by a fine of not less than ten nor more than fifty dollars.

Approved May 25, 1943.

---

*Chap.*321 AN ACT RELATIVE TO THE SALARIES OF THE ASSISTANT COMMISSIONER AND THE ASSOCIATE COMMISSIONERS OF THE DEPARTMENT OF LABOR AND INDUSTRIES.

Be it enacted, etc., as follows:

G. L. (Ter. Ed.), 23, § 2, amended.

Commissioner, etc., of labor and industries.

Salary.

Chapter twenty-three of the General Laws is hereby amended by striking out section two, as appearing in the Tercentenary Edition, and inserting in place thereof the following section: — *Section 2.* Upon the expiration of the term of office of a commissioner, an assistant commissioner or an associate commissioner, his successor shall be appointed for three years by the governor, with the advice and consent of the council. The commissioner shall receive such salary not exceeding seventy-five hundred dollars, and the assistant commissioner, and the associate commissioners such salaries, not exceeding five thousand dollars each, as the governor and council determine.

Approved May 25, 1943.

AN ACT PROHIBITING UNLAWFUL INJURY TO, INTERFERENCE WITH OR OPERATION OF MOTOR BUSES AND TRACKLESS TROLLEY VEHICLES AND TO PROHIBIT RIDING UPON THE REAR OR SIDE OF TRACKLESS TROLLEY VEHICLES. *Chap.*322

Be it enacted, etc., as follows:

SECTION 1. Section one hundred and three of chapter one hundred and fifty-nine of the General Laws, as most recently amended by chapter fifty-four of the acts of nineteen hundred and forty-one, is hereby further amended by striking out the words "or car" in the eighth line and inserting in place thereof the words: — , car, motor bus or trackless trolley vehicle, — and by inserting after the word "car" in the eleventh and in the twelfth lines, in each instance, the words: — , motor bus or trackless trolley vehicle, — so as to read as follows: — *Section 103.* Whoever unlawfully and intentionally injures, molests or destroys any signal of a railroad corporation or railway company, or any line, wire, post or other structure or mechanism used in connection with such signal, or prevents or in any way interferes with the proper working of such signal, or whoever unlawfully and intentionally injures, molests, meddles or tampers with or destroys a track, car, motor bus or trackless trolley vehicle or any part, appliance or appurtenance thereof, of a railroad corporation or railway company, or the mechanism or apparatus used in the operation of any such car, motor bus or trackless trolley vehicle, or whoever without right operates any such car, motor bus or trackless trolley vehicle or any mechanism or appliance thereof, shall be punished by a fine of not more than five hundred dollars or by imprisonment for not more than two years, or both.

G. L. (Ter. Ed.), 159, § 103, etc., amended.

Injury to railroad signals, etc.

SECTION 2. Chapter eighty-five of the General Laws is hereby amended by striking out section seventeen B, inserted by chapter forty-three of the acts of nineteen hundred and thirty-three, and inserting in place thereof the following section: — *Section 17B.* Whoever rides upon the rear or side of any street railway car, motor bus, or trackless trolley vehicle without the consent of the person in charge thereof shall be punished by a fine of not more than twenty dollars. *Approved May 25, 1943.*

G. L. (Ter. Ed.), 85, § 17B, etc., amended.

Riding upon rear of street railway cars, etc., when prohibited.

AN ACT AUTHORIZING THE CITY OF MEDFORD TO PAY A SUM OF MONEY TO MARTHA A. GAVEL IN COMPENSATION FOR DAMAGES SUSTAINED BY REASON OF A CERTAIN LAND TAKING BY SAID CITY. *Chap.*323

Be it enacted, etc., as follows:

SECTION 1. The city of Medford is hereby authorized to pay to Martha A. Gavel of said city a sum not exceeding nine hundred dollars in full compensation for damages sustained by her by reason of the taking by said city, for street construction purposes, of land owned by her.

SECTION 2. This act shall take effect upon its passage.

Approved May 25, 1943.

Chap.324 AN ACT AUTHORIZING THE CITY OF PEABODY TO APPROPRIATE MONEY FOR THE PAYMENT OF, AND TO PAY, CERTAIN UNPAID BILLS.

Be it enacted, etc., as follows:

SECTION 1. The city of Peabody is hereby authorized to appropriate money for the payment of, and after such appropriation the treasurer of said city is hereby authorized to pay, such of the unpaid bills incurred during the year nineteen hundred and forty-one by said city, the total of such bills being one thousand and fifty-seven dollars and sixty-eight cents, as set forth in the list on file in the office of the director of accounts in the department of corporations and taxation, as are legally unenforceable against said city, either by reason of their being incurred in excess of available appropriations or by reason of the failure of said city to comply with the provisions of its charter, and as are certified for payment by the heads of the departments wherein the bills were contracted; provided, that the money so appropriated to pay such bills shall be raised by taxation in said city in the current year.

SECTION 2. No bill shall be approved by the city auditor of said city for payment or paid by the treasurer thereof under authority of this act unless and until certificates have been signed and filed with said city auditor, stating under the penalties of perjury that the goods, materials or services for which bills have been submitted were ordered by an official or an employee of said city, and that such goods and materials were delivered and actually received by said city or that such services were rendered to said city, or both.

SECTION 3. Any person who knowingly files a certificate required by section two which is false and who thereby receives payment for goods, materials or services which were not received by or rendered to said city shall be punished by imprisonment for not more than one year or by a fine of not more than three hundred dollars, or both.

SECTION 4. This act shall take effect upon its passage.

Approved May 25, 1943.

Chap.325 AN ACT AUTHORIZING THE THREE RIVERS FIRE DISTRICT OF THE TOWN OF PALMER TO ESTABLISH A SYSTEM OF WATER SUPPLY.

Be it enacted, etc., as follows:

SECTION 1. The Three Rivers Fire District of the town of Palmer located within the following boundary lines, to wit: — beginning at a stone monument near the intersection of the road leading from Palmer to Three Rivers with the road leading from Palmer to Bondsville, said intersection being just southerly from a crossing at grade of said

Three Rivers road and the track of the Ware River railroad known as Burleigh's crossing; thence in a course south seventy-one and one half degrees (71½°) west to a stone monument on the town line between Palmer and Wilbraham, said monument being four hundred fifty (450) feet northerly measured along said town line, from a stone monument set to mark an angle in the town lines between Palmer and Monson; thence northerly on said town line between Palmer and Wilbraham to a stone monument set to mark a corner of the towns of Palmer, Wilbraham, Ludlow and Belchertown; thence easterly along the town line between Palmer and Belchertown to the Swift river, nearly opposite its junction with the Ware river; thence crossing said Swift river and following up the Ware river easterly to the southerly end of a bridge crossing said river, known as Dutton's bridge; thence southeasterly in a straight line to the center line of track of the Ware River railroad at a point where said center line crosses at grade the center line of the main road leading from Three Rivers to Thorndike; thence southerly along said center line of said Ware River railroad to its crossing at grade with the road leading from Palmer to Three Rivers; thence along said road southeasterly to the place of beginning, — may supply itself and its inhabitants with water for the extinguishment of fires and for domestic and other purposes, and is hereby empowered to establish fountains and hydrants and to relocate and discontinue the same, to regulate the use of such water and to fix and collect rates to be paid therefor, and to assess and raise taxes as provided herein for the payment of such services, and for defraying the necessary expenses of carrying on the business of said district, subject to all general laws now or hereinafter in force relating to water districts, water supply districts or fire districts supplying water to their inhabitants, except as otherwise provided herein. The district shall have power to prosecute and defend all actions relating to its property and affairs.

SECTION 2. For the purposes aforesaid, the district, acting by and through its board of water commissioners hereinafter provided for, may contract with any municipality, acting through its water department, or with any water company, or with any water district, for whatever water may be required, authority to furnish the same being hereby granted, and may take by eminent domain under chapter seventy-nine of the General Laws, or acquire by lease, purchase or otherwise, and hold, the waters, or any portion thereof, of any pond, spring or stream, or of any ground sources of supply by means of a driven, artesian or other well, within the town of Palmer not already appropriated for the purposes of a public supply, and the water and flowage rights connected with any such water sources; and for said purposes may take as aforesaid, or acquire by purchase or otherwise, and hold, all lands, rights of way and other easements necessary for collecting, storing, holding, purifying and preserving the purity of the water and for conveying the same to any part of said district; provided, that no source of water supply or lands necessary for preserving the quality of the water shall be so taken or used without first obtaining the advice and approval of the state department of public health, and that the location and arrangement of all dams, reservoirs, springs, wells, pumping, purification and filtration plants and such other works as may be necessary in carrying out the provisions of this act shall be subject to the approval of said department. The district may construct and maintain on lands acquired and held under this act proper dams, wells, springs, reservoirs, standpipes, tanks, pumping plants, buildings, fixtures and other structures, including also the establishment and maintenance of filter beds and purification works or systems, and may make excavations, procure and operate machinery and provide such other means and appliances, and do such other things as may be necessary for the establishment and maintenance of complete and effective waterworks; and for that purpose may construct pipe lines, wells and reservoirs and establish pumping works, and may construct, lay, acquire and maintain aqueducts, conduits, pipes and other works under or over any land, water courses, railroads, railways and public or other ways, and along such ways, in said town, in such manner as not unnecessarily to obstruct the same; and for the purposes of constructing, laying, maintaining, operating and repairing such aqueducts, conduits, pipes and other works, and for all proper purposes of this act, the district may dig up or raise and embank any such lands, highways or other ways in such manner as to cause the least hindrance to public travel on such ways; provided, that the manner in which all things are done upon any such way shall be subject to the direction of the selectmen of the town of Palmer. The district shall not enter upon, or construct or lay any conduit, pipe or other works within, the location of any railroad corporation except at such time and in such manner as it may agree upon with such corporation, or, in case of failure so to agree, as may be approved by the department of public utilities. The district may enter upon any lands for the purpose of making surveys, test wells or pits and borings, and may take or otherwise acquire the right to occupy temporarily any lands necessary for the construction of any work or for any other purpose authorized by this act.

SECTION 3. Any person sustaining damages in his property by any taking under this act or any other thing done under authority thereof may recover such damages from the district under said chapter seventy-nine; but the right to damages for the taking of any water, water right or water source, or for any injury thereto, shall not vest until water is actually withdrawn or diverted under authority of this act.

SECTION 4. Any land taken or acquired under this act shall be managed, improved and controlled by the board of water commissioners hereinafter provided for, in such manner as they shall deem for the best interest of the district. All authority vested in said board by this section shall be subject to section six.

SECTION 5. Whenever a tax is duly voted by the district for the purposes of this act, the clerk shall send a certified copy of the vote to the assessors of said town, who shall assess the same on property within the district in the same manner in all respects in which town taxes are required by law to be assessed; provided, that no estate shall be subject to any tax assessed on account of the system of water supply under this act if, in the judgment of the board of water commissioners hereinafter provided for, after a hearing, due notice whereof shall have been given, such estate is so situated that it can receive no aid in the extinguishment of fire from the said system of water supply, or if such estate is so situated that the buildings thereon, or the buildings that might be constructed thereon, could not be supplied with water from said system in any ordinary or reasonable manner; but all other estates in the district shall be deemed to be benefited and shall be subject to such tax. A certified list of the estates exempt from taxation under this section shall annually be sent by said board of water commissioners to said assessors, at the same time at which the clerk shall send a certified copy of the vote as aforesaid. The assessment shall be committed to the town collector, who shall collect said tax in the manner provided by law for the collection of town taxes, and shall deposit the proceeds thereof with the district treasurer for the use and benefit of the district. The district may collect interest on overdue taxes in the manner in which interest is authorized to be collected on town taxes.

SECTION 6. The district shall, after the acceptance of this act as hereinafter provided, elect by ballot, either at the same meeting at which this act shall have been accepted, or thereafter, at an annual or at a special meeting called for the purpose, three persons, inhabitants of and voters in said district, to hold office, one until the expiration of three years, one until the expiration of two years, and one until the expiration of one year, from the day of the next succeeding annual district meeting, to constitute a board of water commissioners; and at every annual district meeting following such next succeeding annual district meeting one such commissioner shall be elected by ballot for the term of three years. All the authority granted to said district by this act and not otherwise specifically provided for, shall be vested in said board of water commissioners, who shall be subject, however, to such instructions, rules and regulations as the district may by vote impose. No water commissioner shall serve as treasurer of the district during his term. The treasurer of the district shall give bond to the district, in such amount as may be approved by said water commissioners and the prudential committee of the district, and with a surety company authorized to transact business in the commonwealth as surety. A majority of the commissioners shall constitute a quorum for the transaction of business. Any vacancy occurring in said board from any cause may be filled for the remainder of the unexpired term by said district at any legal meeting called for the purpose. No money shall be drawn from the treasury of the district on account of its waterworks except upon the written order of said water commissioners or a majority of them.

SECTION 7. Said board of water commissioners shall fix just and equitable prices and rates for the use of water, and shall prescribe the time and manner of payment. The income of the waterworks shall be appropriated to defray all operating expenses, interest charges and payments on the principal as they shall accrue upon any bonds or notes issued under authority of this act. If there should be a net surplus remaining after providing for the aforesaid charges, it may be appropriated for such new construction as said water commissioners may recommend, and in case a surplus should remain after payment for such new construction the water rates shall be reduced proportionately. Said water commissioners shall annually, and as often as the district may require, render a report upon the condition of the works under their charge, and an account of their doings including receipts and expenditures.

SECTION 8. The district may adopt by-laws governing the conduct of its water department and may establish rules and regulations for the management of the same, not inconsistent with this act or any other provision of law, and may choose such other officers not provided for in this act as it may deem necessary or proper.

SECTION 9. The district may, by vote, in lieu of electing a board of water commissioners under this act, delegate to the prudential committee of the Three Rivers Fire District of the town of Palmer all the powers and duties of said board of water commissioners. In such event, the said prudential committee shall have all the powers and duties of the said board of water commissioners as given under this act.

SECTION 10. Nothing in this act shall authorize the district to supply water for the extinguishment of fires or for domestic or other purposes to the inhabitants of the area served on the effective date of this act by George B. Cheney or of the area served on said date by Palmer Industries, Inc., without first having acquired by purchase, or by eminent domain under chapter seventy-nine of the General Laws, as the occasion may arise, all of the properties of said George B. Cheney or said Palmer Industries, Inc., as the case may be, on said date appurtenant to the business of water supply and located within the area served by said George B. Cheney or said Palmer Industries, Inc., as the case may be. In case of dispute as to the area served by either said George B. Cheney or said Palmer Industries, Inc. on said date, the department of public utilities, upon application of the district or of said George B. Cheney or said Palmer Industries, Inc., as the case may be, shall determine such area and such determination shall be final.

Section 11. Whoever wilfully or wantonly corrupts, pollutes or diverts any water obtained or supplied under this act, or wilfully or wantonly injures any reservoir, well, standpipe, aqueduct, pipe or other property owned or used by the district for any of the purposes of this act, shall forfeit and pay to the district three times the amount of damages assessed therefor, to be recovered in an action of tort, and upon conviction of any of the above wilful or wanton acts shall be punished by a fine of not more than three hundred dollars or by imprisonment for not more than one year, or both.

Section 12. Upon a petition in writing addressed to said board of water commissioners requesting that certain real estate, accurately described therein, located in said town and abutting on said district and not otherwise served by a public water supply, be included within the limits thereof, and signed by the owners of such real estate or a major portion of such real estate, said water commissioners shall cause a duly warned meeting of the district to be called, at which meeting the voters may vote on the question of including said real estate within the district. If a majority of the voters present and voting thereon vote in the affirmative the district clerk shall within ten days file with the town clerk of said town and with the state secretary an attested copy of said petition and vote; and thereupon said real estate shall become and be part of the district and shall be holden under this act in the same manner and to the same extent as the real estate described in section one.

Section 13. The question of the acceptance of this act shall be submitted to the duly qualified voters of the district at any annual or special meeting called by the district in accordance with section sixty-six of chapter forty-eight of the General Laws and held within four years after the passage of this act, and if it is accepted by a majority of the voters present and voting thereon it shall thereupon take full effect. *Approved May 25, 1943.*

An Act placing certain positions in the health department of the city of Boston under the civil service laws. *Chap.*326

Be it enacted, etc., as follows:

The positions of dentists, dental hygienists and supply clerks in the health department of the city of Boston shall, upon the effective date of this act, become subject to the civil service laws and rules and regulations, and the tenure of office of any incumbent thereof shall be unlimited, subject, however, to said laws. The persons holding said positions on said effective date may continue to serve therein, but they shall not be subject to said civil service laws and rules and regulations unless and until they pass a qualifying examination to which they shall be subjected by the division of civil service. *Approved May 25, 1943.*

---

*Chap.*327 AN ACT RELATIVE TO THE USE OF LAKE COCHITUATE IN THE TOWNS OF NATICK, FRAMINGHAM AND WAYLAND FOR BATHING PURPOSES.

Be it enacted, etc., as follows:

SECTION 1. It shall be lawful for any inhabitant of the town of Natick, Framingham or Wayland to bathe in the waters of so much of Lake Cochituate as lies in any of said towns during such time as said waters are not used for water supply purposes of the metropolitan water district as authorized by law.

SECTION 2. This act shall not become effective until the termination of the existing states of war between the United States and any foreign country.

Approved May 25, 1943.

---

*Chap.*328 AN ACT REQUIRING THE SUPPLYING OF FOOD BY COMMON VICTUALLERS ON SUNDAYS IF THEY HOLD LICENSES TO SELL ALCOHOLIC BEVERAGES THEREON.

Be it enacted, etc., as follows:

G. L. (Ter. Ed.), 140, § 8, etc., amended.

Chapter one hundred and forty of the General Laws is hereby amended by striking out section eight, as most recently amended by section fourteen of chapter three hundred and sixty-eight of the acts of nineteen hundred and thirty-six, and inserting in place thereof the following section: — *Section 8.* A common victualler who, upon request, on any day but Sunday, or on any day if he holds a license to sell alcoholic beverages on Sundays, refuses to supply food to a stranger or traveler shall be punished by a fine of not more than fifty dollars; provided, that nothing in this chapter shall be construed to permit or require a common victualler, who holds a license to keep a tavern under chapter one hundred and thirty-eight, to admit a woman as a patron in such tavern.

Penalty for refusal to serve food to traveler.

Approved May 25, 1943.

---

*Chap.*329 AN ACT RELATIVE TO THE CONSTITUTION OF A QUORUM FOR THE TRANSACTION OF BUSINESS BY THE PROPRIETORS OF FOREST HILLS CEMETERY, AND RELATIVE TO THE INVESTMENT OF THE FUNDS OF SAID CORPORATION.

Be it enacted, etc., as follows:

SECTION 1. Section six of chapter fifty-seven of the acts of eighteen hundred and sixty-eight is hereby amended by striking out, in the ninth line, the word "persons" and inserting in place thereof the words: — members, either present in person or represented by proxy, — so as to read as follows: — *Section 6.* The annual meetings of said corporation shall be held on the fourth Monday of March in each year, at such place in the city of Boston as the trustees shall direct, and notices thereof, signed by the secretary, shall be published in two or more of the newspapers printed in Boston, at least seven days before the meeting; special meetings may be called by order of the trustees in the same manner. At all meetings of said corporation a quorum for business shall consist of not less than fifteen members, either present in person or represented by proxy, and any business may be transacted, of which notice shall be given in the advertisements for the meeting, and all questions shall be decided by a majority of the members present and represented, and voting either in person or by proxy.

SECTION 2. The trustees of The Proprietors of Forest Hills Cemetery are hereby authorized to invest any funds in their hands in any securities or investments in which, under the laws of the commonwealth, trustees appointed by courts of the commonwealth are now, or may hereafter be, authorized or permitted to invest.

SECTION 3. So much of said chapter fifty-seven of the acts of eighteen hundred and sixty-eight, or any act in amendment thereof or in addition thereto, as is inconsistent with the provisions of this act, is hereby repealed.

SECTION 4. Nothing in this act shall be deemed to affect the validity of any investment of funds made by said trustees prior to the effective date of this act.

Approved May 25, 1943.

AN ACT RELATIVE TO THE ADMISSION TO BAIL OF PERSONS CHARGED WITH CERTAIN SEX CRIMES, SO CALLED. *Chap.*330

Be it enacted, etc., as follows:

G. L. (Ter. Ed.), 276, § 57, etc., amended.

Section fifty-seven of chapter two hundred and seventy-six of the General Laws, as amended by section four of chapter two hundred and ninety-nine of the acts of nineteen hundred and thirty-nine, is hereby further amended by adding at the end of the second paragraph, as appearing in the Tercentenary Edition, the following sentence: — If it appears that any such prior criminal prosecution was for an offence committed in violation of any provision of sections twenty-two to twenty-four, inclusive, of chapter two hundred and sixty-five or section thirty-four or thirty-five of chapter two hundred and seventy-two the court shall, before the amount of bail is fixed, obtain from the department of mental health a report containing all information in its possession relative to the prisoner, particularly with respect to any mental disease or defect with which he may have been afflicted; and said department shall furnish any such report to the court promptly upon its request.

Bail of persons charged with sex crimes.

Approved May 25, 1943.

Chap.331 AN ACT RELATIVE TO THE ANALYSIS OF NARCOTIC DRUGS AND OTHER MATERIALS AND THE ADMISSIBILITY IN EVIDENCE OF CERTIFICATES OF ANALYSIS.

Be it enacted, etc., as follows:

G. L. (Ter. Ed.), 111, § 12, amended.

Analyses of poisons, drugs, etc.

SECTION 1. Chapter one hundred and eleven of the General Laws is hereby amended by striking out section twelve, as appearing in the Tercentenary Edition, and inserting in place thereof the following section: — *Section 12.* It shall make, free of charge, a chemical analysis of any narcotic drug, or any synthetic substitute for the same, or any preparation containing the same, or any salt or compound thereof, and of any poison, drug, medicine or chemical, when submitted to it by police authorities or by such incorporated charitable organizations in the commonwealth, as the department shall approve for this purpose; provided, that it is satisfied that the analysis is to be used for the enforcement of law.

G. L. (Ter. Ed.), 111, § 13, amended.

Analyses to be prima facie evidence.

SECTION 2. Section thirteen of said chapter one hundred and eleven, as so appearing, is hereby amended by striking out the last sentence and inserting in place thereof the following sentence: — When properly executed it shall be prima facie evidence of the composition and quality of the narcotic or other drug, poison, medicine or chemical analyzed, and the court shall take judicial notice of the signature of the analyst or assistant analyst, and of the fact that he is such.

Approved May 25, 1943.

Chap.332 AN ACT MAKING HORSES AND MULES SUBJECT TO THE LAW REGULATING THE SLAUGHTERING OF CERTAIN ANIMALS, AND FURTHER REGULATING THE INSPECTION AND STAMPING OR BRANDING OF CERTAIN ANIMALS SLAUGHTERED WITHOUT THE COMMONWEALTH.

Be it enacted, etc., as follows:

G. L. (Ter. Ed.), 94, § 118, amended.

Slaughter houses to be licensed.

SECTION 1. Section one hundred and eighteen of chapter ninety-four of the General Laws, as appearing in the Tercentenary Edition, is hereby amended by inserting after the word "cattle" in the fourth and in the thirteenth lines the following: — , horses, mules, — so as to read as follows: — *Section 118.* The proprietor of each slaughter house, canning, salting, smoking or rendering establishment, and of each establishment used for the manufacture of sausages or chopped meat of any kind, who is engaged in the slaughter of neat cattle, horses, mules, sheep or swine, the meat or product of which is to be sold or used for food, shall annually in April apply for a license to the aldermen of the city or to the selectmen or, in a town having a population of more than five thousand, to the board of health, if any, of the town where such slaughter house or establishment is located. The application shall be in writing signed and sworn to by one or more of the owners or persons carrying on such business, or, if a corporation, by some authorized officer thereof, shall state the name and address of all the owners or persons carrying on said business, the location of the slaughter house or establishment, the estimated number of neat cattle, horses, mules, sheep or swine to be slaughtered per week, the days of the week upon which they are to be slaughtered and the nature of the products thereof to be sold or used for food.

G. L. (Ter. Ed.), 94, § 119, amended.

SECTION 2. Section one hundred and nineteen of said chapter ninety-four, as so appearing, is hereby amended by inserting after the word "cattle" in the fourth line the following: — , horses, mules, — by striking out, in the fifth line, the words "the two following sections" and inserting in place thereof the words: — sections one hundred and twenty and one hundred and twenty A, — and by striking out, in the eleventh and in the fourteenth and fifteenth lines, the words "the preceding section" and inserting in place thereof, in each instance, the words: — section one hundred and eighteen, — so as to read as follows: — *Section 119.* The aldermen, selectmen, or such other officers as they shall designate, or, in a town having a population of more than five thousand, the board of health, if any, may annually issue licenses to carry on the business of slaughtering neat cattle, horses, mules, sheep or swine to applicants therefor. Except as provided in sections one hundred and twenty and one hundred and twenty A, the fee for each license shall be one dollar. The license shall name the persons licensed to conduct such business, and the building or establishment where it is to be carried on, and it shall continue in force until May first of the year next ensuing, unless sooner forfeited or rendered void. A record shall be kept by the board or officers authorized to issue such licenses of all applications for licenses under section one hundred and eighteen and of all licenses issued, which shall be evidence of the issue of any such license. Such board or officers shall annually, on or before June first, send to the department of public health a copy of each application made to them under section one hundred and eighteen and of their action thereon, together with a list of the names and addresses of all persons who, although engaged in the business named in said section on the preceding April thirtieth, failed to make application for a license.

Issue of licenses.

Fee.

Record.

G. L. (Ter. Ed.), 94, § 120, amended.

SECTION 3. Section one hundred and twenty of said chapter ninety-four, as so appearing, is hereby amended by inserting after the word "cattle" in the fourth line the following: — , horses, mules, — so as to read as follows: — *Section 120.* In towns having less than ten thousand inhabitants which accept this section or have accepted corresponding provisions of earlier laws at any annual town meeting, the annual license fee for carrying on the business of slaugh-

License fee for small towns.

tering neat cattle, horses, mules, sheep or swine shall be such sum not exceeding one hundred dollars as the selectmen fix.

G. L. (Ter. Ed.), 94, § 120A, amended.

SECTION 4. Section one hundred and twenty A of said chapter ninety-four, as so appearing, is hereby amended by inserting after the word "cattle" in the fourth line the following: — , horses, mules, — so as to read as follows: —

Additional fees in certain towns regulated.

Section 120A. A town which accepts this section may, in addition to the annual fee under section one hundred and nineteen or one hundred and twenty for a license to carry on the business of slaughtering neat cattle, horses, mules, sheep or swine, require the payment by the licensee of a further fee of not exceeding one dollar for each animal slaughtered under such license, but such further fee shall not be required for any animal slaughtered under federal inspection. Additional fees provided for under this section shall be paid to the town treasurer at such times and in such manner as the selectmen by vote determine. This section shall not apply to cities.

G. L. (Ter. Ed.), 94, § 123, etc., amended.

SECTION 5. Section one hundred and twenty-three of said chapter ninety-four, as amended by section fifteen of chapter one hundred and eighty of the acts of nineteen hundred and thirty-two, is hereby further amended by striking out, in the second line, the words "the preceding section" and inserting in place thereof the words: — section one hundred and twenty-two, — and inserting after the word "cattle" in the fourth line the following: — , horses, mules, — so as to read as follows: —

Inspectors, etc., to visit slaughter houses.

Section 123. Inspectors, officers, agents and assistants mentioned in section one hundred and twenty-two shall visit and keep under observation each place within their respective districts where neat cattle, horses, mules, sheep, swine or other animals intended for slaughter or for sale or use as food are delivered from transportation, and shall have at all times free access to each such place and to each railroad train or car or other vehicle in which such animals are transported, to prevent, detect and punish violations of section one hundred and thirty-eight.

G. L. (Ter. Ed.), 94, § 131, amended.

SECTION 6. Said chapter ninety-four is hereby further amended by striking out section one hundred and thirty-one, as appearing in the Tercentenary Edition, and inserting in place thereof the following section: —

Branding of carcasses slaughtered without the commonwealth.

Section 131. Carcasses of neat cattle, horses, mules, sheep or swine slaughtered without the commonwealth shall be deemed unfit for human food, and shall not be sold or offered for sale as such, unless they have been inspected at the time of slaughter by an inspector of the bureau of animal industry of the United States department of agriculture and have been stamped or branded by said inspector.

G. L. (Ter. Ed.), 94, § 133, amended.

SECTION 7. Section one hundred and thirty-three of said chapter ninety-four, as so appearing, is hereby amended by inserting after the word "cattle" in the sixth line the following: — , horses, mules, — so as to read as follows: —

Private slaughter houses.

Section 133. Sections one hundred and eighteen, one hundred and nineteen, one hundred and twenty-five to one hundred and twenty-seven, inclusive, one hundred and twenty-nine and one hundred and thirty, shall not apply to a person not engaged in the slaughtering business, who, upon his own premises and not in a slaughter house, slaughters his own neat cattle, horses, mules, sheep or swine, but the carcass of any such animal, intended for sale, shall be inspected, and, unless condemned, shall be stamped or branded under section one hundred and twenty-seven by an inspector at the time of slaughter.

G. L. (Ter. Ed.), 94, § 135, amended.

SECTION 8. Section one hundred and thirty-five of said chapter ninety-four, as so appearing, is hereby amended by inserting after the word "cattle" in the second, sixth and twelfth lines the following: — , horses, mules, — so as to read as follows: — *Section 135.* Whoever, being engaged in the business of slaughtering neat cattle, horses, mules, sheep or swine, without a license slaughters the same or knowingly authorizes or causes the same to be slaughtered with intent to sell the meat or product thereof for food, or, having such license, slaughters or knowingly authorizes or causes to be slaughtered any neat cattle, horses, mules, sheep or swine without causing the carcass thereof to be inspected as provided in section one hundred and twenty-six, or sells or authorizes or causes to be sold any carcass or the meat or product thereof knowing that such carcass has not been inspected according to sections one hundred and twenty-six and one hundred and thirty-three, or, except as provided in section one hundred and thirty-three, slaughters or knowingly authorizes or causes to be slaughtered any neat cattle, horses, mules, sheep or swine upon his own premises, being other than a slaughter house or establishment mentioned in section one hundred and eighteen, without causing the carcass of such animal to be inspected, or sells or authorizes or causes to be sold the carcass or any meat or product thereof of any such animal slaughtered upon his own premises, knowing that the same has not been inspected as provided in section one hundred and thirty-three, shall be punished by a fine of not more than five hundred dollars or by imprisonment for not more than two months, or both.

Penalty for slaughtering, etc., without license.

G. L. (Ter. Ed.), 111, § 151, amended.

SECTION 9. Section one hundred and fifty-one of chapter one hundred and eleven of the General Laws, as so appearing, is hereby amended by inserting after the word "cattle" in the second line the following: — , horses, mules, — so as to read as follows: — *Section 151.* No person shall occupy or use a building for carrying on the business of slaughtering cattle, horses, mules, sheep or other animals, or for a melting or rendering establishment, or for other noxious or offensive trade and occupation, or permit or allow said trade or occupation to be carried on upon premises owned or occupied by him, without first obtaining the written consent and permission of the mayor and city council, or of the selectmen, or, in any town having a population of more than five thousand, of the board of health, if any, of the town where the build-

Slaughter houses, etc., regulated.

Exceptions.

ing or premises are situated. This section shall not apply to any building or premises occupied or used for said trade or occupation on May eighth, eighteen hundred and seventy-one; but no person who used or occupied any building or premises on said date for said trades or occupations shall enlarge or extend the same without first obtaining the written consent and permission of the mayor and city council or the selectmen, or, in any town having a population of more than five thousand, of the board of health, if any.

G. L. (Ter. Ed.), 129, § 9, amended.

SECTION 10. Section nine of chapter one hundred and twenty-nine of the General Laws, as so appearing, is hereby amended by inserting after the word "cattle" in the second line the following: — , horses, mules, — so as to read as follows: — *Section 9.* The agents of the Massachusetts Society for the Prevention of Cruelty to Animals may visit all places at which neat cattle, horses, mules, sheep, swine or other animals are delivered for transportation or are slaughtered, for the purpose of preventing violations of any law and of detecting and punishing the same; with power to prosecute any such violation coming to their notice. Any person who prevents, obstructs or interferes with any such agent in the performance of such duties shall be punished by a fine of not more than one hundred dollars or by imprisonment for not more than two months, or both.

Agents of Massachusetts Society for the Prevention of Cruelty to Animals may visit slaughter houses.

Approved May 25, 1943.

---

*Chap.*333 AN ACT PROVIDING THAT RAILROAD AND TERMINAL CORPORATIONS SHALL PROVIDE REASONABLE LAVATORY AND SANITARY FACILITIES FOR THEIR EMPLOYEES.

Be it enacted, etc., as follows:

G. L. (Ter. Ed.), 160, new § 185A, added.

Chapter one hundred and sixty of the General Laws is hereby amended by inserting after section one hundred and eighty-five, as appearing in the Tercentenary Edition, the following section: — *Section 185A.* Every railroad and terminal corporation shall furnish, in its stations and other quarters provided for the use of its employees, adequate lavatory and sanitary facilities for their use, keep the same clean and free from unsanitary conditions and furnish adequate heat therefor when reasonably necessary. Whenever the department is of opinion, after a hearing had upon its own motion or upon complaint, that a violation of this section exists it shall thereupon order such changes as it deems necessary. *Approved May 26, 1943.*

Sanitary facilities for railroad employees.

---

*Chap.*334 AN ACT MAKING CERTAIN CORRECTIONAL CHANGES IN THE ELECTION LAWS PERTAINING TO NOMINATIONS OF CANDIDATES FOR PUBLIC OFFICE AND TO PRIMARIES AND CAUCUSES.

Be it enacted, etc., as follows:

G. L. (Ter. Ed.), 53, § 3, etc., amended.

SECTION 1. Chapter fifty-three of the General Laws is hereby amended by striking out section three, as most recently amended by section one of chapter forty-five of the acts of nineteen hundred and thirty-seven, and inserting in place thereof the following section: — *Section 3.* A person whose name is not printed on a state, city or town primary ballot as a candidate for an office, but who receives sufficient votes to nominate him therefor, shall file written acceptance of the nomination in the office of the state secretary within six days, or the city or town clerk within three days, as the case may be, succeeding five o'clock in the afternoon of the day of holding the primaries, otherwise his name shall not be printed on the ballot at the ensuing election.

Acceptance of nomination by candidate whose name was not printed on primary ballot.

SECTION 2. Said chapter fifty-three is hereby further amended by striking out section six, as most recently amended by chapter fifty of the acts of the current year, and inserting in place thereof the following section: — *Section 6.* Nominations of candidates for any offices to be filled at a state election may be made by nomination papers, stating the facts required by section eight and signed in the aggregate by not less than such number of voters as will equal three per cent of the entire vote cast for governor at the preceding biennial state election in the commonwealth at large or in the electoral district or division for which the officers are to be elected. In the case of offices to be filled by all the voters in the commonwealth, no more than one third of the required number of signatures shall be from any one county. Nominations of candidates for offices to be filled at a city or town election, except where city charters or general or special laws provide otherwise, may be made by like nomination papers, signed in the aggregate by not less than such number of voters as will equal one per cent of the entire vote cast for governor at the preceding biennial state election in the electoral district or division for which the officers are to be elected, but in no event by less than twenty voters in the case of an office to be filled at a town election. At a first election to be held in a newly established ward, the number of signatures of voters upon a nomination paper of a candidate who is to be voted for only in such ward shall be at least fifty.

G. L. (Ter. Ed.), 53, § 6, etc., amended.

Nomination papers, number of signatures.

SECTION 3. Said chapter fifty-three is hereby further amended by striking out the first and second sentences of section seven, as most recently amended by section five of chapter three hundred and forty-one of the acts of nineteen hundred and thirty-eight, and inserting in place thereof the two following sentences: — Every voter signing a nomination paper shall sign in person, with his name as registered, and shall state his residence on January first preceding, or his residence when registered if subsequent thereto, and the place where he is then living, with the street and number, if any; but any voter who is prevented by physical disability from writing may authorize some person to write his name and residence in his presence; and, except as provided in section three of chapter fifty-four A, every voter may sign as many nomination papers for each office as there are per-

G. L. (Ter. Ed.), 53, § 7, etc., amended.

Voter to sign nomination paper in person, etc.

sons to be elected thereto, and no more. Every nomination paper of a candidate for a state or a city or town office shall be submitted to the registrars of the city or town where the signers appear to be voters, on or before five o'clock in the afternoon of the seventh day preceding the day on which it must be filed with the state secretary or the city or town clerk.

G. L. (Ter. Ed.), 53, § 8, etc., amended.

SECTION 4. Said chapter fifty-three is hereby further amended by striking out section eight, as most recently amended by section six of chapter four hundred and seventy-three of the acts of nineteen hundred and thirty-eight, and inserting in place thereof the following: — *Section 8.* All certificates of nomination and nomination papers shall, in addition to the names of candidates, specify as to each, (1) his residence, with street and number, if any, (2) the office for which he is nominated, and (3), except as otherwise provided in this section and in city charters, the party or political principle, if any, which he represents, expressed in not more than three words. Certificates of nomination made by convention or caucus shall also state what provision, if any, was made for filling vacancies caused by the death, withdrawal or ineligibility of candidates. The surnames of the candidates for president and vice president of the United States shall be added to the party or political designation of the candidates for presidential electors. To the name of each candidate for alderman at large shall be added the number of the ward in which he resides. To the name of a candidate for a town office who is an elected incumbent thereof there may be added the words "Candidate for Re-election".

Certificates of nomination and nomination papers, contents, party designation.

If a candidate is nominated otherwise than by a political party, the name of a political party shall not be used in his political designation. Certificates of nomination and nomination papers for city or town offices need not include a designation of the party or principle which the candidate represents. Except as otherwise provided in section sixty, in the case of nomination papers of candidates for town offices no nomination paper shall contain the name of more than one candidate. Such nomination papers for town offices may contain the names of candidates for any or all of the offices to be filled at the town election, but the number of names of candidates on such paper for any one office shall not exceed the number to be elected thereto.

G. L. (Ter. Ed.), 53, § 10, etc., amended.

SECTION 5. The third paragraph of section ten of said chapter fifty-three, as most recently amended by section two of chapter seventy-seven of the acts of nineteen hundred and thirty-seven, is hereby further amended by striking out, in the second sentence of said third paragraph, the words "Thursday following the fourth Tuesday" and inserting in place thereof the words: — twenty-eighth day, — so that said third paragraph will read as follows: —

Time for filing certificates of nomination and nomination papers.

In any town which does not accept section one hundred and three A of chapter fifty-four, certificates of nomination for town offices shall be filed on or before the second Wednesday, and nomination papers on or before the second Thursday, preceding the day of the election; but if such Wednesday or Thursday falls on a legal holiday, the said certificates of nomination or nomination papers shall be filed on or before the succeeding day; but if a town election is held on a day of the week other than Monday, such certificates of nomination and nomination papers shall be filed, respectively, on or before the twelfth and eleventh days preceding the day of the election, except as otherwise provided in any special law affecting such town. In any town which accepts said section one hundred and three A, certificates of nomination and nomination papers for any regular town election shall be filed on or before the twenty-eighth day preceding such election, notwithstanding any special law affecting such town. In any such town the time for presenting nomination papers for certification to the registrars of voters, and for certifying the same, shall be governed by section seven of this chapter, notwithstanding any contrary provision in any special law.

SECTION 6. Section eleven of said chapter fifty-three, as most recently amended by section one of chapter two hundred and twelve of the acts of nineteen hundred and thirty-seven, is hereby further amended by inserting after the third sentence the following new sentence: — Objections filed with the city or town clerk shall forthwith be transmitted by him to the board authorized to hear such objections as provided under section twelve, — so as to read as follows: — *Section 11.* When certificates of nomination and nomination papers have been filed, and are in apparent conformity with law, they shall be valid unless written objections thereto are made. Such objections shall be filed as to state offices with the state secretary, and as to city or town offices with the city or town clerk, and in the case of state offices within the seventy-two week day hours, in the case of city offices, except where city charters provide otherwise, within the forty-eight week day hours, and in the case of town offices within the twenty-four week day hours, succeeding five o'clock in the afternoon of the last day fixed for filing the certificate of nomination or nomination papers to which objections are made. Objections so filed with the state secretary shall forthwith be transmitted by him to the state ballot law commission. Objections filed with the city or town clerk shall forthwith be transmitted by him to the board authorized to hear such objections as provided under section twelve. This section shall be in force in any city or town which accepts section one hundred and three A of chapter fifty-four, any special provision of law to the contrary notwithstanding.

G. L. (Ter. Ed.), 53, § 11 etc., amended

Objections to be in writing, time for filing.

SECTION 7. Section twelve of said chapter fifty-three, as most recently amended by chapter one hundred and sixty-six of the acts of nineteen hundred and thirty-nine, is hereby further amended by striking out, in the fifth line, the words ", the city clerk", — so that the first paragraph will read

G. L. (Ter. Ed.), 53, § 12, etc., amended.

Objections, by whom considered.

as follows: — Objections to nominations for state offices, and all other questions relating thereto, shall be considered by the state ballot law commission; to nominations for city offices, except in Boston, by the board of registrars and the city solicitor; and to nominations for town offices, by the board of registrars.

G. L. (Ter. Ed.), 53, § 14, amended.

SECTION 8. Section fourteen of said chapter fifty-three, as appearing in the Tercentenary Edition, is hereby amended by inserting after the third sentence the following sentence: — In cities and towns where candidates are nominated by nomination papers, such papers may contain the names of members of a committee of not more than five registered voters who may fill any vacancy caused by the death or physical disability of the candidate whose name appears upon such nomination paper.

Nomination to fill vacancy.

G. L. (Ter. Ed.), 53, § 15, amended.

SECTION 9. Section fifteen of said chapter fifty-three, as so appearing, is hereby amended by adding at the end the following sentence: — Such certificate shall be filed with the state secretary in the case of state elections and with the city or town clerk in city or town elections, — so as to read as follows: — *Section 15.* When a nomination is made to fill a vacancy caused by the death, withdrawal or ineligibility of a candidate, the certificate of nomination shall, in addition to the other facts required, state the name of the original nominee, the fact of his death, withdrawal or ineligibility, and the proceedings had for filling the vacancy; and the presiding officer and secretary of the convention or caucus, or the chairman and secretary of an authorized committee, shall sign and make oath to the truth of the certificate, and it shall be accompanied by the written acceptance of the candidate nominated. Such certificate shall be filed with the state secretary in the case of state elections and with the city or town clerk in city or town elections.

Certificate in case of nomination to fill vacancy, acceptance.

G. L. (Ter. Ed.), 53, § 17, amended.

SECTION 10. Section seventeen of said chapter fifty-three, as so appearing, is hereby amended by adding at the end the following sentence: — In cities blank forms for the nomination of candidates for city offices shall be provided by the city clerk, — so as to read as follows: — *Section 17.* The state secretary shall, upon application, provide blank forms for the nomination of candidates for all state offices; and he shall send blank forms for certificates of nomination for the office of representative in the general court to the clerk of each city and town for the use of any caucus or convention other than of political parties held therein for the nomination of candidates for that office. He shall likewise provide the clerks of towns wherein official ballots are used with blank forms for the nomination of candidates for town offices. In cities blank forms for the nomination of candidates for city offices shall be provided by the city clerk.

Blanks for nomination.

G. L. (Ter. Ed.), 53, § 20, amended.

SECTION 11. Said chapter fifty-three is hereby further amended by striking out section twenty, as so appearing, and inserting in place thereof the following section: — *Sec-*

tion 20. The provisions of law relative to the signing of nomination papers of candidates for state office, and to the identification and certification of names thereon and submission to the registrars therefor, shall apply, so far as apt, to applications submitted under section nineteen.

Applications, signing, certification, etc.

SECTION 12. Section twenty-six of said chapter fifty-three, as so appearing, is hereby amended by adding at the end the following sentence: — No such objection shall be considered by the boards provided for in section twelve, unless there is filed with such board a certificate of enrolment issued by the board of registrars of voters, or the clerk of the same, where the person filing the objections resides, stating that he is an enrolled voter of the party whose nomination is sought, — so as to read as follows: — *Section 26.* Section eleven shall apply to nomination papers of candidates to be voted for at primaries, except that the date from which the time for filing objections shall be computed shall be the last day for filing nomination papers for such primaries. No such objection shall be considered by the boards provided for in section twelve, unless there is filed with such board a certificate of enrolment issued by the board of registrars of voters, or the clerk of the same, where the person filing the objections resides, stating that he is an enrolled voter of the party whose nomination is sought.

G. L. (Ter. Ed.), 53, § 26, amended.

Nomination papers, validity.

Objections, time for filing.

SECTION 13. Section thirty-four of said chapter fifty-three, as most recently amended by chapter three hundred and fifty-two of the acts of nineteen hundred and forty-one, is hereby further amended by striking out, in the first line of the fifth paragraph, the word "No" and inserting in place thereof the words: — Except where vacancies caused by death, withdrawal or physical disability are filled, no, — so that said fifth paragraph will read as follows: —

G. L. (Ter. Ed.), 53, § 34, etc., amended.

Except where vacancies caused by death, withdrawal or physical disability are filled, no names shall be printed on a ballot other than those received on nomination papers. Immediately following the names of candidates on ballots at city and town primaries, blank spaces equal to the number of persons to be chosen shall be provided for the insertion of other names. Immediately following the names of candidates on ballots at state and presidential primaries, where there are fewer names than there are persons to be chosen, blank spaces shall be provided, equal in number to the deficiency, for the insertion of other names.

Ballots, blank spaces on, at primaries.

SECTION 14. Said chapter fifty-three is hereby further amended by striking out section thirty-seven, as appearing in the Tercentenary Edition, and inserting in place thereof the following section: — *Section 37.* The voting lists used at primaries shall contain the party enrolment of the voters whose names appear thereon established as provided in this and section thirty-eight. A voter desiring to vote in a primary shall give his name, and, if requested, his residence, to one of the ballot clerks, who shall distinctly announce

G. L. (Ter. Ed.), 53, § 37, amended.

Party enrolment at primaries.

Obtaining and depositing ballots, etc.

the same, and, if the party enrolment of such voter is shown on the voting list, the name of the party in which he is enrolled. If the party enrolment of the voter is not shown on the voting list he shall be asked by the ballot clerk with which political party he desires to be enrolled, and the ballot clerk, upon reply, shall distinctly announce the name of such political party and shall record the voter's selection upon the voting list. The ballot clerk shall then give the voter one ballot of the political party in which he is thus enrolled.

After marking his ballot the voter shall give his name, and, if requested, his residence, to the officer in charge of the voting list at the ballot box, who shall distinctly announce the same. If the party enrolment of the voter is shown on the voting list he shall also make announcement of such enrolment and the officer in charge of the ballot box shall, before the voter's ballot is deposited, ascertain that it is of the political party in which such voter is enrolled. If the enrolment of the voter is not shown on such voting list, the officer in charge of the ballot box shall announce the political party whose ballot the voter is about to deposit, and the officer in charge of the voting list shall repeat the same distinctly and record the same upon such voting list.

The voting lists used at primaries shall be returned to the city or town clerk to be retained in his custody as long as he retains the ballots cast, whereupon such voting lists shall be transmitted to the registrars of voters for preservation for five years, after the expiration of which they may be destroyed. Said officers shall, upon receiving a written request therefor, signed by a candidate at such primary, or by the chairman or other officer of any ward, town or city committee, furnish a certified copy of said requested list to said candidate, or to any ward, town or city committee. The party enrolment of each voter, if any, shall be recorded in the current annual register of voters, and whenever a voter shall establish, cancel or change his enrolment it shall likewise be so recorded. In preparing the current annual register of voters, the party enrolment, if any, of each voter included therein, as shown by the register of voters for the preceding year, shall be transferred thereto.

G. L. (Ter. Ed.), 53, § 38, etc., amended.

SECTION 15. Section thirty-eight of said chapter fifty-three, as most recently amended by chapter two hundred and ninety-nine of the acts of nineteen hundred and thirty-eight, is hereby further amended by striking out, in the sixteenth and seventeenth lines, the words "preserved as part of the records of such primary" and inserting in place thereof the following: — shall be attached to, and considered a part of the voting list and returned and preserved therewith, — so as to read as follows: — *Section 38.* No voter enrolled under this or the preceding section shall be allowed to receive the ballot of any political party except that with which he is so enrolled; but a voter may, except within a

Voter enrolled in one political party not to receive ballot of another party, except, etc.

period of thirty-one days prior to a primary, establish, change or cancel his enrolment by appearing in person before a member of the board of registrars of voters and requesting in writing to have his enrolment established with a party, changed to another party, or cancelled, and such enrolment, change or cancellation shall take effect at the expiration of thirty days thereafter. No voter enrolled as a member of one political party shall be allowed to receive the ballot of any other political party, upon a claim by him of erroneous enrolment, except upon a certificate of such error from the registrars, which shall be presented to the presiding officer of the primary and shall be attached to, and considered a part of the voting list and returned and preserved therewith; but the political party enrolment of a voter shall not preclude him from receiving at a city or town primary the ballot of any municipal party, though in no one primary shall he receive more than one party ballot.

SECTION 16. Said chapter fifty-three is hereby further amended by inserting after section forty, as amended, the following section: — *Section 40A.* Petitions for recounts of the ballots cast at a primary of a political party may be signed only by enrolled voters of such political party.

G. L. (Ter. Ed.), 53, new § 40A, added

Petitions for recounts, signing of.

SECTION 17. Section fifty-six of said chapter fifty-three, as appearing in the Tercentenary Edition, is hereby amended by adding at the end the following paragraph: — The provisions of law relative to the signing of nomination papers of candidates for state office, and to the identification and certification of names thereon and submission to the registrars therefor, shall apply, so far as apt, to the signing of petitions under this section and to the identification and certification of names thereon, — so as to read as follows: — *Section 56.* In any city or town which has adopted the provisions of law for nominating by primaries, the following question shall be put on the official ballot at any city election or annual town meeting on petition of five per cent of the voters registered at the time of the preceding city election or annual town meeting, filed with the city or town clerk on or before the last day for filing nomination papers: "Shall primaries for the nomination of candidates to be voted for at city (or town) elections continue to be held in this city (or town)?" In any city or town not nominating by primaries, where such nominations are permitted by law, the following question may, by similar petition, be put on the ballot at the next city election or annual town meeting: "Shall primaries for the nomination of candidates to be voted for at city (or town) elections be held in this city (or town)?" In accordance with the result of such vote, such primaries shall or shall not thereafter be held.

G. L. (Ter. Ed.), 53, § 56, amended.

Submission of question of holding primaries.

Notice of result to state secretary

Clerks of cities or towns which vote to hold primaries or to rescind such action shall forthwith notify the state secretary of such vote.

The provisions of law relative to the signing of nomination papers of candidates for state office, and to the identification and certification of names thereon and submission to the registrars therefor, shall apply, so far as apt, to the signing of petitions under this section and to the identification and certification of names thereon.

Approved May 26, 1943.

---

*Chap.*335 AN ACT RELATIVE TO THE CIVIL SERVICE STATUS OF CERTAIN EMPLOYEES OF THE DEPARTMENT OF PUBLIC SAFETY.

Emergency preamble.

Whereas, The uncertainty which exists in respect to the civil service status of the persons referred to in this act should be removed without delay, therefore it is hereby declared to be an emergency law, necessary for the immediate preservation of the public convenience.

Be it enacted, etc., as follows:

Any person holding a position in the classified civil service of the commonwealth and employed in the department of public safety on the effective date of this act who was originally appointed or was promoted thereto during the period when the present commissioner of public safety was designated to perform the duties of such commissioner, as provided by section six of chapter thirty of the General Laws, and was so acting, may, upon request of said commissioner and with the approval of the director of civil service, continue to serve on a permanent basis in the position and grade to which he was appointed or promoted as aforesaid, notwithstanding any contrary provision of said section six of said chapter thirty. *Approved May 26, 1943.*

---

*Chap.*336 AN ACT PROVIDING FOR A SECOND AND A THIRD ASSISTANT CLERK OF COURTS FOR THE COUNTY OF BRISTOL.

Be it enacted, etc., as follows:

G. L. (Ter. Ed.), 221, § 4, etc., amended.

SECTION 1. Section four of chapter two hundred and twenty-one of the General Laws, as most recently amended by section one of chapter one hundred and fifty-eight of the acts of nineteen hundred and thirty-seven, is hereby further amended by inserting after the word "assistant" in the seventh line the words: — , and a second assistant, — so as to read as follows: — *Section 4.* The justices of the supreme judicial court shall appoint for a term of three years from the date of their appointment, and may remove, assistant clerks of courts, as follows:

Assistant clerks of supreme judicial court.

For the county of —

Barnstable, an assistant;

Bristol, an assistant, and a second assistant;

Essex, an assistant, a second assistant, a third assistant, a fourth assistant and a fifth assistant;

Hampden, an assistant, a second assistant and, subject to the approval of the county commissioners, a third assistant;

Middlesex, an assistant, a second assistant, a third assistant, a fourth assistant and a fifth assistant;

Norfolk, an assistant;

Plymouth, an assistant;

Suffolk, an assistant of the supreme judicial court;

Worcester, an assistant, a second assistant, a third assistant and a fourth assistant.

Assistant clerks of courts except in Suffolk county shall act as assistant clerks of the supreme judicial court, the superior court and the county commissioners.

The fifth assistant clerk of courts for the county of Middlesex shall keep reasonable daily office hours, on days other than Sundays and holidays, at the office of the clerk of courts for said county in the county court house in the city of Lowell.

G. L. (Ter. Ed.), 221, § 5, etc., amended.

Section 2. Section five of said chapter two hundred and twenty-one, as most recently amended by chapter fifty-one of the acts of nineteen hundred and thirty-two, is hereby further amended by striking out, in the second line, the words "the preceding section" and inserting in place thereof the words: — section four, — and by inserting after the paragraph contained in the sixth line the following paragraph: — Bristol, subject to the approval of a justice of the superior court, a third assistant, — so as to read as follows: — *Section 5.* In addition to the assistant clerks provided for in section four, the clerks of the courts for the following counties may appoint assistant clerks, with the same powers and duties, as follows:

Same subject.

For the county of —

Bristol, subject to the approval of a justice of the superior court, a third assistant.

Norfolk, a second assistant, subject to removal by the court or by the clerk.

Middlesex, subject to approval of a justice of the supreme judicial or superior court, not more than three assistant clerks.

Suffolk, by the clerk of the superior court for criminal business, assistant clerks pro tempore or for the term of one year, subject to removal by the court or by the clerk; and by the clerk of the supreme judicial court for said county, a second assistant clerk, designated from his office force.

All other counties having no permanent second assistant clerks, assistant clerks pro tempore or for a term of one year, subject to removal by the court or by the clerk.

Assistants pro tempore or for the term of one year appointed under this section shall be paid by the county monthly.

Acceptance and effective date.

Section 3. This act shall take full effect upon its acceptance during the current year by the county commissioners of the county of Bristol, but not otherwise.

Approved May 26, 1943.

*Chap.*337 AN ACT FURTHER REGULATING PAYMENTS FROM THE FUNDS OF THE TEACHERS' RETIREMENT SYSTEM TO MEMBERS THEREOF WITHDRAWING FROM THE PUBLIC SCHOOL SERVICE.

Be it enacted, etc., as follows:

G. L. (Ter. Ed.), 32, § 11, etc., amended.

SECTION 1. Section eleven of chapter thirty-two of the General Laws, as amended by section two of chapter four hundred of the acts of nineteen hundred and thirty-six, is hereby further amended by striking out paragraph (1) and inserting in place thereof the following paragraph: —

Retiring allowances.

(1) Any member withdrawing from the public school service before becoming eligible for retirement, except for the purpose of accepting a position which under section thirty-seven D will require the transfer of his accumulated assessments with regular interest to another contributory retirement system, and any member retired as a veteran under any provision of sections fifty-six to sixty, inclusive, shall be entitled to receive from the annuity fund established by paragraph (2) of section nine all amounts contributed as assessments, together with regular interest thereon, either in one sum or, at the election of the board, in four quarterly payments. If a member dies before receiving all his quarterly payments the balance thereof shall be paid to his estate.

G. L. (Ter. Ed.), 32, § 11, par. (2), stricken out.

SECTION 2. Said section eleven of said chapter thirty-two, as so amended, is hereby further amended by striking out paragraph (2).

Application of act.

SECTION 3. Section one of this act shall apply to any member of the teachers' retirement association retired as a veteran prior to the effective date of this act under any provision of sections fifty-six to sixty, inclusive, of chapter thirty-two of the General Laws.

Approved May 26, 1943.

---

*Chap.*338 AN ACT RELATIVE TO COMPUTING THE CONTINUOUS SERVICE OF CERTAIN CALL FIREMEN, PART CALL FIREMEN OR SUBSTITUTE CALL FIREMEN SERVING IN THE MILITARY OR NAVAL FORCES OF THE UNITED STATES DURING THE PRESENT WAR.

Be it enacted, etc., as follows:

Section thirteen of chapter seven hundred and eight of the acts of nineteen hundred and forty-one is hereby amended by adding at the end the following paragraph: — In computing the period of five years of continuous service required by section thirty-six of chapter forty-eight of the General Laws as a prerequisite to the promotion of a call man, part call man or substitute call man to the permanent force of a fire department, the time such call man, part call man or substitute call man has served in such military or naval service or the merchant marine shall be counted, — so as to read as follows: — *Section 13.* In computing the period of five years of continuous service required under section forty-nine A of chapter thirty-one of the General Laws of an incumbent of a municipal office who has entered said military or naval service and returns to said office within one year after the termination of said service, the period between his entry into said service and his return to said office shall be counted.

In computing the period of five years of continuous service required by section thirty-six of chapter forty-eight of the General Laws as a prerequisite to the promotion of a call man, part call man or substitute call man to the permanent force of a fire department, the time such call man, part call man or substitute call man has served in such military or naval service or the merchant marine shall be counted.

Approved May 26, 1943.

AN ACT CORRECTING REFERENCES TO THE FEDERAL HOUSING ADMINISTRATOR IN CERTAIN GENERAL AND SPECIAL LAWS. *Chap.*339

Emergency preamble.

Whereas, The title of the federal official formerly known as federal housing administrator has been changed to federal housing commissioner and the deferred operation of this act would in part tend to defeat its purpose, which is to make immediately effective provisions of law recognizing such change of name, therefore this act is hereby declared to be an emergency law, necessary for the immediate preservation of the public convenience.

Be it enacted, etc., as follows:

Whenever in any general or special law reference is made to the federal housing administrator, such reference shall be deemed and held to refer to such administrator, to the federal housing commissioner, and to the successor or successors of either of said officers. *Approved May 27, 1943.*

AN ACT PROVIDING FOR THE REIMBURSEMENT OF THE TOWN OF BURLINGTON FOR CERTAIN MONEYS EXPENDED BY IT FOR WELFARE AID. *Chap.*340

Be it enacted, etc., as follows:

SECTION 1. For the purpose of reimbursing the town of Burlington for moneys expended by it from the twenty-ninth day of May, nineteen hundred and twenty-four, to the fourth day of August, nineteen hundred and thirty-six, both dates inclusive, for welfare aid, which sum was not repaid to said town by reason of the failure of the officials to make due application therefor, the state treasurer is hereby authorized and directed to pay out of the state treasury to said town, subject to appropriation and to the approval of the department of public welfare, the sum of five hundred and fourteen dollars and twenty-one cents.

SECTION 2. This act shall take effect upon its passage.

Approved May 27, 1943.

*Chap.*341 AN ACT PROVIDING FOR THE FORECLOSURE OF LIENS UPON MOTOR VEHICLES FOR THE USE OF THE UNITED STATES DURING THE PRESENT EMERGENCY.

Emergency preamble.

Whereas, The deferred operation of this act would tend to defeat its purpose that the metal content of certain motor vehicles should be available to the United States during the present state of war,

Therefore, It is declared to be an emergency law, necessary for the immediate preservation of the public convenience.

Be it enacted, etc., as follows:

SECTION 1. During the continuance of the existing state of war between the United States and any foreign country, the holder of a lien upon a motor vehicle described in section twenty-five of chapter two hundred and fifty-five of the General Laws, upon the written certificate of an official of an agency of the United States dealing with the collection of metals for war uses that the value of said motor vehicle is less than the amount of the charges of said lien holder against said motor vehicle, may sell such motor vehicle at public auction in the lien holder's garage, notice of the time and place of sale first being posted in a conspicuous place in the office of the garage for four weeks prior to the date of such sale, and published once in each of three successive weeks in a newspaper published in the city or town where the garage is situated, the first publication of such notice to be not less than twenty-one days before the date of sale. Such notice shall state the make, type of body, number of cylinders, presumed year of manufacture, engine number and serial number of such motor vehicle, if such numbers are known to or can be found by the lien holder. Such notice shall also state the amount of the indebtedness for which the lien is claimed, and shall contain an affidavit of the lien holder that the registered owner of the motor vehicle, if it is registered, or, if the motor vehicle is not registered, that the owner of the vehicle so far as he is known to the lien holder, is not in the military service of the United States or any of its allies. A copy of such notice shall be sent by registered mail addressed to the registered owner of the motor vehicle at the address furnished to the garage, or, if the motor vehicle is not registered, to the address of the owner, if his name and address are known or can be ascertained by the lien holder.

If, within five days after publication of the final notice, the registered owner, if the motor vehicle is registered, or a person claiming to be the owner, if it is not registered, shall notify the lien holder that he disputes the amount of the indebtedness claimed, the lien holder shall proceed no further, but may pursue his remedy under section twenty-six of chapter two hundred and fifty-five of the General

Laws. If the owner or person claiming to be such fails to establish his claim in any proceeding under this section he shall be assessed double costs in said proceedings, and the lien holder's expense for advertising.

The lien holder shall bid at such auction the full amount of his lien and the expense of advertising, and no more. If he becomes the purchaser at said auction, he shall deliver said motor vehicle to such officer or agency of the federal government as the official who gave him the original certificate shall direct, and shall accept such sum therefor as said official shall determine to be its fair scrap value, but in no case less than the expense of advertising, the cost of sale and an attorney's fee, if any is necessarily incurred.

SECTION 2. If some person other than the lien holder shall become the purchaser at said auction, or in case the lien holder, having become the purchaser, receives a sum from the government or government agency in excess of the amount of his bid, the surplus after reimbursement of the lien holder for the amount of the debt, and the expenses incurred in the publication and sale as above provided, shall be paid to the registered owner of the motor vehicle, if it is registered, or, if it is not registered, to the true owner if he can be ascertained. If the whereabouts of an owner cannot be ascertained, or if the motor vehicle is unregistered and the owner thereof cannot be ascertained, the lien holder shall be liable to pay to the owner such surplus at any time within one year from the date of the auction, or from the date of resale to the government or government agency if the lien holder purchased at the auction.

Approved May 27, 1943.

AN ACT RELATIVE TO THE RATIO BETWEEN THE PREFERRED AND COMMON CAPITAL STOCK OF STREET RAILWAY COMPANIES. ***Chap.342***

Be it enacted, etc., as follows:

Section thirty-five of chapter one hundred and sixty-one of the General Laws, as appearing in the Tercentenary Edition, is hereby amended by inserting after the word "stock" in the seventh line the words: — , except when such excess shall result from a reduction in the aggregate par value of its outstanding common stock made under either section twenty A or section twenty-seven, — so as to read as follows: — *Section 35.* Preferred stock issued under sections thirty-two to thirty-five, inclusive, shall have the same voting power as the common stock, except that, in any case, there may be such limitations of the voting power of said preferred stock as the department approves and finds consistent with public interest. The aggregate amount at par of preferred stock of all classes issued by a company shall at no time exceed twice the amount at par value of its outstanding common stock, except when such excess shall result from a

G. L. (Ter. Ed.), 161, § 35, amended.

Preferred stock, amount of. Voting powers, issue, etc.

reduction in the aggregate par value of its outstanding common stock made under either section twenty A or section twenty-seven, and no class of preferred stock shall be created which is not, in a manner approved by the department, made subordinate in respect to dividends or to participation in the proceeds of liquidation to the preferences of every previously created class of preferred stock. Upon any issue of preferred stock the new shares shall, unless the common stockholders with the approval of the department otherwise provide, first be offered to the common stockholders in the manner prescribed in sections fifty to fifty-two, inclusive, of chapter one hundred and fifty-nine, and any shares of the preferred stock not duly subscribed and paid for by the common stockholders or their assigns shall be offered in the same manner to the holders of preferred stock of the same class; and any of such preferred shares then remaining untaken, and all of the preferred shares if the common stockholders so determine and the department approves, may be sold in the manner provided by and subject to section fifty-one of chapter one hundred and fifty-nine. In case of any increase in the common stock of the company, holders of preferred stock shall be entitled to have offered to them shares of the new stock in the manner provided in sections fifty to fifty-two, inclusive, of chapter one hundred and fifty-nine, whenever the vote creating such preferred stock as approved by the department shall so provide. *Approved May 27, 1943.*

Chap. 343 AN ACT AMENDING THE PENALTY FOR BREAKING AND ENTERING IN THE NIGHT TIME A BUILDING, SHIP OR VESSEL.

Be it enacted, etc., as follows:

G. L. (Ter. Ed.), 266, § 16, amended.

SECTION 1. Chapter two hundred and sixty-six of the General Laws is hereby amended by striking out section sixteen, as appearing in the Tercentenary Edition, and inserting in place thereof the following section: — *Section 16.* Whoever, in the night time, breaks and enters a building, ship or vessel, with intent to commit a felony, shall be punished by imprisonment in the state prison for not more than twenty years or in a jail or house of correction for not more than two and one half years.

Breaking, in night time, building or ships.

Effective date.

SECTION 2. This act shall take effect on October first in the current year and shall apply in the case of crimes committed on or after said date; but the provisions of said section sixteen, as in effect immediately preceding said date, shall continue to apply in the case of crimes committed prior to said date. *Approved May 27, 1943.*

AN ACT RELATIVE TO THE PRINTING AND DISTRIBUTION OF CERTAIN REPORTS OF STATE DEPARTMENTS, OFFICERS AND COMMISSIONS, AND TO PURCHASES AND TRANSFERS OF SUPPLIES OF SUCH STATE AGENCIES. *Chap.*344

Be it enacted, etc., as follows:

SECTION 1. Chapter five of the General Laws is hereby amended by striking out section six, as most recently amended by section nine of chapter five hundred and eight of the acts of nineteen hundred and thirty-nine, and inserting in place thereof the following section: — *Section 6.* All reports required to be made by permanent state departments, officers and commissions may, subject to the approval of the commission on administration and finance and except as otherwise provided, be printed annually. The division of personnel and standardization shall designate the number of copies of each report to be printed. The department, officer or commission required to make an annual report may, with the approval of the commission on administration and finance, authorize the printing and distribution of such reports or parts thereof by outside agencies; provided, that any such publications shall not be offered for sale.

G. L. (Ter. Ed.), 5, § 6, etc., amended.

Publication of annual reports as public documents.

SECTION 2. Chapter seven of the General Laws is hereby amended by inserting after section twenty-five, as appearing in the Tercentenary Edition, the following section: — *Section 25A.* The state purchasing agent may provide for the transfer of supplies from one state agency to another when, in his opinion, such transfer is for the best interests of the commonwealth, and may provide for the making of suitable adjustments on the state comptroller's books on account of such transfer. He shall also have authority to approve the amount or quantities of all supplies and materials purchased by state agencies, notwithstanding that such agency has conformed to the regulations relative to such purchases and that an appropriation is available therefor. In case an application by a state agency is not approved by the state purchasing agent, such agency may appeal in writing to the commission, whose decision shall be final.

G. L. (Ter. Ed.), 7, new § 25A, added.

Transfer of supplies from one state agency to another.

Approved May 27, 1943.

AN ACT RELATIVE TO TRANSFERS OF FUNDS ON BOOKS OF CERTAIN STATE OFFICERS OR BOARDS. *Chap.*345

Be it enacted, etc., as follows:

Section twenty-nine of chapter twenty-nine of the General Laws, as amended by section fourteen of chapter five hundred and two of the acts of nineteen hundred and thirty-nine, is hereby further amended by striking out, in the seventh line, the word "comptroller" and inserting in place thereof the words: — budget commissioner, — so as to read as follows: — *Section 29.* No transfer of funds from one

G. L. (Ter. Ed.), 29, § 29, etc., amended.

Transfer of funds with

approval of commissioner.

item of account to another on the books of any officer or board having charge of any office, department, institution or undertaking receiving a periodic appropriation from the commonwealth, upon which items of account such periodic appropriation is based, shall be made without the written approval of the budget commissioner.

Approved May 27, 1943.

---

*Chap.*346 AN ACT RELATIVE TO BUDGET ESTIMATES OF THE DIVISION OF SAVINGS BANK LIFE INSURANCE.

Be it enacted, etc., as follows:

G. L. (Ter. Ed.), 26, § 10, amended.

Budget estimates, approval of.

Section ten of chapter twenty-six of the General Laws, as appearing in the Tercentenary Edition, is hereby amended by adding at the end the following sentence: — The budget estimates of the division required by section three of chapter twenty-nine shall be approved by the trustees.

Approved May 27, 1943.

---

*Chap.*347 AN ACT PROVIDING FOR THE TRANSFER TO THE GENERAL FUND OF CERTAIN SURPLUS INTEREST ACCRUING TO THE COMMONWEALTH UNDER PROVISIONS OF LAW AUTHORIZING MUNICIPALITIES TO BORROW FROM THE COMMONWEALTH AND ELSEWHERE ON ACCOUNT OF PUBLIC WELFARE.

Be it enacted, etc., as follows:

The state treasurer is hereby authorized and directed to transfer to the general fund the sum of thirty-six thousand, one hundred and sixty-five dollars and nine cents, being the excess of the amount of interest payments received by the commonwealth on account of bonds and notes issued by cities and towns under chapter three hundred and seven of the acts of nineteen hundred and thirty-three, as amended by chapter three hundred and thirty-five of the acts of nineteen hundred and thirty-four, over the amount of interest payments on money borrowed by the commonwealth for the purposes of said provisions. *Approved May 27, 1943.*

---

*Chap.*348 AN ACT RELATIVE TO EXTRAORDINARY EXPENSES OF THE GOVERNOR AND CERTAIN MILITARY EXPENSES.

Be it enacted, etc., as follows:

G. L. (Ter. Ed.), 6, § 8, etc., amended.

SECTION 1. Chapter six of the General Laws is hereby amended by striking out section eight, as amended by section one of chapter seven hundred and twenty-two of the acts of nineteen hundred and forty-one, and inserting in place thereof the following section: — *Section 8.* The governor may expend each year such sums as may be appropriated for the entertainment of the president of the United States and other distinguished guests while visiting or passing through the commonwealth.

Entertainment of distinguished guests, appropriation.

SECTION 2. Chapter thirty-three of the General Laws, as appearing in section one of chapter four hundred and twenty-five of the acts of nineteen hundred and thirty-nine, is hereby amended by inserting after section twenty-six the following section: — *Section 26A.* The governor may expend each year for carrying out the provisions of sections seventeen to twenty-six, inclusive, such sums as may be appropriated therefor. *Approved May 27, 1943.*

G. L. (Ter. Ed.), 33, new § 26A, added.

Expenditures and appropriations.

---

*Chap.*349

AN ACT TO PROVIDE THAT CERTAIN PERSONS AGAINST WHOM COMPLAINTS ARE MADE IN DISTRICT COURTS MAY BE GIVEN AN OPPORTUNITY TO BE HEARD BEFORE THE ISSUANCE OF PROCESS THEREON.

Be it enacted, etc., as follows:

SECTION 1. Chapter two hundred and eighteen of the General Laws is hereby amended by inserting after section thirty-five, as appearing in the Tercentenary Edition, the following section: — *Section 35A.* If a complaint is received by a district court, or by a justice or special justice thereof, or by a clerk, assistant clerk, temporary clerk or temporary assistant clerk thereof under section thirty-two, thirty-three or thirty-five, as the case may be, the person against whom such complaint is made, may, if not under arrest for the offence for which the complaint is made, upon request in writing, seasonably made, be given an opportunity to be heard personally or by counsel in opposition to the issuance of any process based on such complaint. Failure to permit such person to be present and heard as aforesaid shall not invalidate any process issued thereon.

G. L. (Ter. Ed.), 218, new § 35A, added.

Persons complained against may be heard, when.

SECTION 2. This act shall take effect on September first in the current year. *Approved May 27, 1943.*

Effective date.

---

*Chap.*350

AN ACT PROVIDING FOR THE JOINDER OF PARTIES IN ONE ACTION IN CERTAIN CASES.

Be it enacted, etc., as follows:

SECTION 1. Chapter two hundred and thirty-one of the General Laws is hereby amended by inserting after section four, as appearing in the Tercentenary Edition, the following section: — *Section 4A.* Two or more persons may join in one action as plaintiffs if they assert any right to recover jointly, severally, or in the alternative, in respect of or arising out of the same matter, transaction, occurrence, or series of matters, transactions or occurrences. Two or more persons may be joined in one action as defendants if there is asserted against them jointly, severally, or in the alternative, any right to recover in respect of or arising out of the same matter, transaction, occurrence, or series of matters, transactions or occurrences. A party need not be interested in obtaining or defending against all the recovery demanded. The claims of plaintiffs may be set forth in one

G. L. (Ter. Ed.), 231, new § 4A, added.

Joinder of parties in action arising out of same matter, etc.

count, or in several counts, as clarity in the statement and consideration of the action may require. Judgment may be given for one or more of the plaintiffs according to their respective rights and against one or more of the defendants according to their respective liabilities, and the court may issue one or more executions and make such order relative to costs as may be necessary and proper. Misjoinder of parties shall not be ground for the dismissal of the action. A plaintiff or defendant may be dropped by order of the court on motion of any party or of its own initiative at any stage of the action and on such terms as are just. Any claim against a party may be severed and proceeded with separately.

The provisions of this section shall be in addition to sections two, three and four and to clause Sixth of section seven.

G. L. (Ter. Ed.), 231, § 141, etc., amended.

SECTION 2. Section one hundred and forty-one of said chapter two hundred and thirty-one, as most recently amended by section five of chapter two hundred and ninety-six of the acts of the current year, is hereby further amended by inserting after the word "four", the first time such word occurs therein, the following: — , four A, — so as to read as follows: — *Section 141.* Sections one, two, three, four, four A, five, six, seven, ten, eleven, twelve, thirteen, thirteen A, fourteen, fifteen, sixteen, seventeen, eighteen, nineteen, twenty, twenty-one, twenty-two, twenty-three, twenty-five, twenty-six, twenty-seven, twenty-eight, twenty-nine, thirty, thirty-one, thirty-two, thirty-three, thirty-four, thirty-five, thirty-six, thirty-seven, thirty-eight, thirty-nine, forty, forty-one, forty-two, forty-three, forty-four, forty-five, forty-seven, forty-eight, forty-nine, fifty, fifty-one, fifty-two, fifty-three, fifty-four, fifty-six, fifty-seven, fifty-eight, fifty-eight A, fifty-nine B, sixty-one, sixty-two, sixty-three, sixty-four, sixty-five, sixty-six, sixty-seven, sixty-eight, sixty-nine, seventy, seventy-two, seventy-three, seventy-four, seventy-five, seventy-nine, eighty-five, eighty-five A, eighty-seven, eighty-eight, eighty-nine, ninety, ninety-one, ninety-two, ninety-three, ninety-four, ninety-five, ninety-seven, ninety-eight, ninety-nine, one hundred and one, one hundred and two, one hundred and three, one hundred and four, one hundred and five, one hundred and six, one hundred and seven, one hundred and eight, one hundred and nine, one hundred and ten, one hundred and twenty-four, one hundred and twenty-five, one hundred and twenty-six, one hundred and thirty-two, one hundred and thirty-three, one hundred and thirty-four, one hundred and thirty-five, one hundred and thirty-six, one hundred and thirty-seven, one hundred and thirty-eight, one hundred and thirty-nine, one hundred and forty, one hundred and forty A and one hundred and forty-seven shall apply to civil actions before district courts, and no other sections of this chapter shall so apply, except to the municipal court of the city of Boston under section one hundred and forty-three.

Sections applicable to actions before district courts.

Construction of act.

SECTION 3. Nothing in this act shall be held or construed

to affect any provision of sections one to fifteen, inclusive, of chapter two hundred and twenty-three of the General Laws or any other provision of general law relative to the venue of actions.

SECTION 4. This act shall take effect on September first of the current year. *Approved May 27, 1943.* Effective date.

Chap.351

AN ACT AUTHORIZING THE FIRE COMMISSIONER OF THE CITY OF BOSTON TO ISSUE PERMITS TO THE BOSTON SCHOOL COMMITTEE FOR THE KEEPING, STORAGE AND MAINTENANCE OF AUTOMOTIVE EQUIPMENT AND VOLATILE INFLAMMABLE FLUIDS ON THE PREMISES OF A SCHOOL IN CONNECTION WITH THE CONDUCT OF "SHOP COURSES", SO-CALLED.

Be it enacted, etc., as follows:

SECTION 1. The fire commissioner of the city of Boston, upon application by the school committee of said city, may issue a permit authorizing said school committee to keep, store and maintain on the premises of such school or schools as may be specified in such permit, motor vehicles, motors, engines and any automotive equipment for use in connection with "shop courses", so-called, conducted at such school or schools, and to keep, store and use such quantities of volatile inflammable liquids as are reasonably necessary to conduct said courses; provided, that no such permit shall be issued hereunder if, in the opinion of the fire commissioner, the keeping, storage or maintenance of such motor vehicles, motors, engines and automotive equipment and the keeping, storage or use of volatile inflammable liquids would constitute a fire or explosion hazard. Permits granted hereunder shall be in accordance with and subject to such terms and conditions as said fire commissioner may prescribe, and shall expire on the thirty-first day of August following the date of issue or on such other date as may be specified therein.

Any permit issued under the provisions of this act shall be in lieu of any other permit that may be required by the provisions of any law, ordinance, rule or regulation with respect to the keeping, storage or maintenance of motor vehicles, motors, engines or other automotive equipment or to the keeping, storage or use of volatile inflammable liquids, and no school building wherein motor vehicles are kept, stored or maintained as provided by this act shall be deemed to be a garage for the purposes of any law, ordinance, rule or regulation pertaining to garages in the city of Boston.

SECTION 2. This act shall take effect upon its passage.

Approved May 28, 1943.

Chap.352 AN ACT RELATIVE TO THE FILING IN THE CITY OF LOWELL BY CANDIDATES FOR ELECTION TO MUNICIPAL OFFICE THEREIN OF CERTAIN STATEMENTS AND PETITIONS.

Be it enacted, etc., as follows:

SECTION 1. Notwithstanding the provisions of section one hundred and ten of chapter forty-three of the General Laws limiting the period within which certain statements and petitions shall be filed with the city clerk of a city, in the city of Lowell during the current year and while such city remains under the provisions of Plan E, so called, such statements and petitions shall be so filed at least twenty-one week days prior to any regular municipal election in said city.

SECTION 2. This act shall take effect upon its passage.

Approved May 28, 1943.

Chap.353 AN ACT AUTHORIZING THE CITY OF SALEM TO APPROPRIATE MONEY FOR THE PAYMENT OF, AND TO PAY, CERTAIN UNPAID BILLS.

Be it enacted, etc., as follows:

SECTION 1. The city of Salem is hereby authorized to appropriate money for the payment of, and to pay, such of the unpaid bills incurred in the year nineteen hundred and forty-one, as shown by a list filed with the director of accounts in the department of corporations and taxation, as are legally unenforceable against said city by reason of its failure to comply with the provisions of its charter or by reason of the fact that no appropriation was available at the time of incurring such bills.

SECTION 2. No bill shall be paid under authority of this act unless and until a certificate has been signed and filed with the auditor of said city, stating under the penalties of perjury that the goods, materials or services for which such bill has been submitted were ordered by an official or employee of said city and that such goods and materials were delivered and actually received by said city or that such services were rendered to said city, or both, nor unless and until such bill has been approved by the board established by section one of chapter forty-nine of the acts of nineteen hundred and thirty-three.

SECTION 3. Any person who knowingly files a certificate required by section two which is false and who thereby receives payment for goods, materials or services which were not received by or rendered to said city shall be punished by imprisonment for not more than one year or by a fine of not more than three hundred dollars, or both.

SECTION 4. This act shall take effect upon its passage.

Approved May 28, 1943.

AN ACT TO EMPOWER THE CITY OF CAMBRIDGE TO PAY CERTAIN EXPENSES FROM THE APPROPRIATIONS OF THE SCHOOL COMMITTEE. *Chap.354*

Be it enacted, etc., as follows:

SECTION 1. The city of Cambridge is hereby authorized to pay from the appropriations made for the maintenance and expenses of the school department, for the fiscal year commencing January first, nineteen hundred and forty-three, such of the unpaid bills incurred during the years nineteen hundred and thirty-six to nineteen hundred and forty-one, inclusive, the total of such bills being three thousand, one hundred and seventy-five dollars, as set forth in a list on file in the office of the director of accounts in the department of corporations and taxation, as are legally unenforceable against said city, either by reason of their being incurred in excess of available appropriations or by reason of failure to present them for payment during the year in which they were incurred.

SECTION 2. No bill shall be approved by the city auditor of said city for payment or paid by the treasurer thereof under authority of this act unless and until certificates have been signed and filed with said city auditor, stating under the penalties of perjury that the goods, materials or services for which bills have been submitted were ordered by an official or an employee of said city, and that such goods and materials were delivered and actually received by said city or that such services were rendered to said city, or both.

SECTION 3. Any person who knowingly files a certificate required by section two which is false and who thereby receives payment for goods, materials or services which were not received by or rendered to said city shall be punished by imprisonment for not more than one year or by a fine of not more than three hundred dollars, or both.

SECTION 4. This act shall take effect upon its passage.

Approved May 28, 1943.

AN ACT FOR THE MORE EFFECTIVE REGULATION OF FIRES IN THE OPEN AIR IN BOSTON. *Chap.355*

Be it enacted, etc., as follows:

SECTION 1. No person shall set, maintain or increase a fire in the open air in the city of Boston without obtaining a permit from the fire commissioner as hereinafter provided. Permits for the setting and maintaining of fires in the open air in said city may be issued by the fire commissioner of said city for such periods of time, not exceeding one year from the date thereof, and subject to such reasonable conditions as said fire commissioner may establish by regulation. Any such permit may be revoked at any time by said fire commissioner. Violation of this section shall be punished by a fine of not more than one hundred dollars or by imprisonment for not more than one month, or both.

SECTION 2. Section thirteen of chapter forty-eight of the General Laws shall not apply to the city of Boston.

SECTION 3. This act shall take effect upon its passage.

Approved May 28, 1943.

---

*Chap.*356 AN ACT MAKING APPROPRIATION FOR THE TEACHERS' RETIREMENT BOARD IN THE DEPARTMENT OF EDUCATION.

Be it enacted, etc., as follows:

SECTION 1. The sum herein set forth, for the purposes herein specified, is hereby appropriated from the general fund or revenue of the commonwealth, subject to the provisions of law regulating the disbursement of public funds and the approval thereof, in advance of final action on the general appropriation bill for the next fiscal biennium, pursuant to a message of his excellency the governor of May twenty-fifth of the current year.

Item		
1305–03	For payment of pensions to retired teachers, to be in addition to any amount heretofore appropriated for the purpose	$105,000 00

SECTION 2. This act shall take effect upon its passage.

Approved May 28, 1943.

---

*Chap.*357 AN ACT FURTHER REGULATING THE LAWS RELATIVE TO SEARCH FOR AND SEIZURE OF CERTAIN NARCOTIC DRUGS.

Be it enacted, etc., as follows:

G. L. (Ter. Ed.), 94, § 214, etc., amended.

Section two hundred and fourteen of chapter ninety-four of the General Laws, as amended by section eight of chapter four hundred and twelve of the acts of nineteen hundred and thirty-five, is hereby further amended by striking out, in the sixth line, the word "hypnotic" and inserting in place thereof the word: — narcotic, — so as to read as follows: — *Section 214.* If a person makes complaint under oath to a district court, or to a trial justice or justice of the peace authorized to issue warrants in criminal cases, that he has reason to believe that opium, morphine, heroin, codeine, cannabis, peyote or any other narcotic drug, or any salt, compound or preparation of said substances, or any cocaine, alpha or beta eucaine, or any synthetic substitute for them, or any preparation containing the same, or any salts or compounds thereof, is kept or deposited by a person named therein in a store, shop, warehouse, building, vehicle, steamboat, vessel or any place whatever, such person being other than a licensee under sections one hundred and ninety-eight A and one hundred and ninety-eight B, registered pharmacist, registered physician, registered veterinarian, registered dentist, registered nurse, employee of

Issue of search warrants.

an incorporated hospital, or a common carrier or messenger when transporting any drug mentioned herein between parties hereinbefore mentioned, such court or justice, if it appears that there is probable cause to believe that said complaint is true, shall issue a search warrant to a sheriff, deputy sheriff, city marshal, chief of police, deputy marshal, police officer or constable, commanding him to search the premises where it is alleged that any of the above mentioned drugs is kept or deposited, and to seize and securely keep the same until final action, and to arrest the person in whose possession such drug is found, together with all persons present where such drug is found, and to return forthwith the warrant with his doings thereon, to a court or trial justice having jurisdiction in the town where said drug is alleged to be kept or deposited. Whoever is so present where any of the aforesaid drugs is found shall be punished by a fine of not more than one thousand dollars or by imprisonment in the house of correction for one year, or both. **Penalty for being present.**

Approved May 28, 1943.

AN ACT REVOKING THE POWER OF THE DIRECTOR OF THE DIVISION OF EMPLOYMENT SECURITY TO REMOVE CERTAIN EMPLOYEES FORMERLY TRANSFERRED TO SUCH DIVISION. *Chap.*358

Be it enacted, etc., as follows:

Section six of chapter twenty of the acts of nineteen hundred and thirty-nine is hereby amended by striking out all after the word "employment" in the nineteenth line, — so as to read as follows: — *Section 6.* The unemployment compensation commission existing on the effective date of this section is hereby abolished, and all books and papers of said commission shall upon said date be turned over to the director of the division of unemployment compensation appointed as provided in section one of this act. The state advisory council existing on said date is hereby abolished. All unexpended balances of moneys heretofore appropriated for said unemployment compensation commission shall be immediately available for expenditure by said division of unemployment compensation. Persons lawfully employed and serving under said unemployment compensation commission are hereby transferred to serve under said director without impairment of any rights to which they may be lawfully entitled; provided, that nothing herein shall be construed to validate or ratify the appointment or employment of any employee of said commission that may not have been made in compliance with any law, rule or regulation governing or regulating such appointment or employment.

Approved May 28, 1943.

Chap.359 AN ACT EXTENDING THE AUTHORITY OF THE INDUSTRIAL ACCIDENT BOARD IN OBTAINING DEPOSITIONS AND TESTIMONY OF PERSONS AND WITNESSES RESIDING WITHOUT THE COMMONWEALTH.

Be it enacted, etc., as follows:

G. L. (Ter. Ed.), 152, § 5, amended.

Section five of chapter one hundred and fifty-two of the General Laws, as appearing in the Tercentenary Edition, is hereby amended by adding at the end the following paragraph: —

Depositions of persons, etc., residing without the commonwealth.

In lieu of the foregoing procedure relative to depositions, the department or any member thereof may upon the filing of a written request of any party, together with interrogatories and cross-interrogatories, if any there be, with the department or member, request officers in other jurisdictions, having powers and duties similar to those of the department or members, to take depositions or testimony of persons or witnesses residing in such jurisdictions. Upon the return of any such deposition to the department it shall be opened by the secretary of the department, who shall endorse thereon the date when it was received. The department may allow a reasonable fee for stenographic services in connection with the taking of such depositions and the expenses thereof shall be assessed upon the parties requesting such depositions.

Approved May 28, 1943.

Chap.360 AN ACT RELATIVE TO RETRACTION AND DAMAGES IN LIBEL CASES AND TO DAMAGES IN SLANDER CASES.

Be it enacted, etc., as follows:

G. L. (Ter. Ed.), 231, § 93, amended.

Chapter two hundred and thirty-one of the General Laws is hereby amended by striking out section ninety-three, as appearing in the Tercentenary Edition, and inserting in place thereof the following section: — *Section 93.* Where the defendant in an action for libel, at any time after the publication of the libel hereinafter referred to, either before or after such action is brought, but before the answer is required to be filed therein, gives written notice to the plaintiff or to his attorney of his intention to publish a retraction of the libel, accompanied by a copy of the retraction which he intends to publish, and the retraction is published, he may prove such publication, and, if the plaintiff does not accept the offer of retraction, the defendant may prove such non-acceptance in mitigation of damages. If within a reasonable time after receiving notice in writing from the plaintiff that he claims to be libelled the defendant makes such offer and publishes a reasonable retraction, and such offer is not accepted, he may prove that the alleged libel was published in good faith and without actual malice, and, unless the proof is successfully rebutted, the plaintiff shall recover only for any actual damage sustained. In no action of slan-

Retraction of libel, publication of, etc.

der or libel shall exemplary or punitive damages be allowed, whether because of actual malice or want of good faith or for any other reason. Proof of actual malice shall not enhance the damages recoverable for injury to the plaintiff's reputation. *Approved May 28, 1943.*

AN ACT RELATIVE TO MITIGATION OF DAMAGES IN CASES OF CHAIN LIBEL, SO CALLED. *Chap.*361

Be it enacted, etc., as follows:

G. L. (Ter Ed.), 231, § 94, amended.

Section ninety-four of chapter two hundred and thirty-one of the General Laws, as appearing in the Tercentenary Edition, is hereby amended by striking out, in the second line, the words "has already" and inserting in place thereof the words: — already has brought action for or, — so as to read as follows: — *Section 94.* In an action for libel, the defendant may allege and prove in mitigation of damages that the plaintiff already has brought action for or recovered damages for, or has received or has agreed to receive compensation in respect of, substantially the same libel as that for which such action was brought. In an action for libel or slander, he may introduce in evidence, in mitigation of damages and in rebuttal of evidence of actual malice, acts of the plaintiff which create a reasonable suspicion that the matters charged against him by the defendant are true.

Evidence in mitigation of damages.

Approved May 28, 1943.

AN ACT AUTHORIZING THE ADJUTANT GENERAL TO ACCEPT FOR MILITARY PURPOSES, ON BEHALF OF THE COMMONWEALTH, GIFTS OF PERSONAL PROPERTY. *Chap.*362

Be it enacted, etc., as follows:

G. L. (Ter. Ed.), 33, new § 104A, added.

SECTION 1. Chapter thirty-three of the General Laws, as appearing in section one of chapter four hundred and twenty-five of the acts of nineteen hundred and thirty-nine, is hereby amended by inserting after section one hundred and four, as so appearing, the following section: — *Section 104A.* The adjutant general, with the approval of the governor and council, may accept on behalf of the commonwealth any gift or bequest of personal property to or for the use of the military forces of the commonwealth, and shall forthwith transfer any money or securities so received to the state treasurer who shall administer the same as provided in section seventeen A of chapter ten.

Gifts or bequests, acceptance of.

G. L. (Ter. Ed.), 10, new § 17A, added.

SECTION 2. Chapter ten of the General Laws is hereby amended by inserting after section seventeen, as amended by section one of chapter one hundred and ninety-four of the acts of nineteen hundred and forty-one, the following section: — *Section 17A.* The state treasurer shall receive all funds given to the commonwealth for the use of the military forces as provided in section one hundred and four A of chap-

To receive, etc., trust funds for military forces.

ter thirty-three. The said funds, if in cash, shall be invested safely by the state treasurer, or, if in securities, he may hold them in their original form or, upon the approval of the governor and council, sell them and reinvest the proceeds in securities which are legal investments for the commonwealth sinking funds. Upon the request of the adjutant general, approved by the governor and council, he shall expend such funds or any part thereof for the use of the military forces of the commonwealth. He shall be held responsible for the faithful management of said funds in the same manner as for other funds held by him in his official capacity.

Approved May 28, 1943.

---

*Chap.*363 AN ACT RELATIVE TO THE STATUS OF CERTAIN PERSONS IN THE EMPLOY OF THE DEPARTMENT OF LABOR AND INDUSTRIES.

Be it enacted, etc., as follows:

Persons who, on the effective date of this act, are in the employ of the division of industrial safety of the department of labor and industries as painters' experts to assist in conducting examinations of painters' riggers may, upon passing a non-competitive qualifying examination to which they shall be subjected by the division of civil service, continue to serve as such and their tenure of office shall be unlimited, subject, however, to the civil service laws.

Approved May 28, 1943.

---

*Chap.*364 AN ACT AUTHORIZING THE ESTABLISHMENT OF A PARK DEPARTMENT, TO BE IN CHARGE OF A PARK COMMISSIONER, IN THE CITY OF PITTSFIELD.

Be it enacted, etc., as follows:

SECTION 1. The city of Pittsfield may by ordinance establish a park department, to be under the charge of an official who shall be known as the park commissioner. The commissioner shall have entire charge of and full control over the maintenance and care of the public parks and playgrounds, including all buildings and trees thereon, located in said city, except playgrounds within the limits of school property, and may conduct and promote recreation, play, sports and physical education, for which admission may be charged. The commissioner shall be appointed biennially, beginning with the year nineteen hundred and forty-four, by the mayor, subject to confirmation by the city council in accordance with the provisions of its charter, and shall receive such compensation, if any, as the mayor and city council may determine.

SECTION 2. Except as otherwise provided by this act, all powers and duties relating to parks and playgrounds under chapter forty-five of the General Laws shall be exercised and performed in said city by the mayor and city council thereof.

SECTION 3. The employees in the park department of said city, as existing immediately prior to the establishment of the park department hereunder, shall be transferred to the park department established hereunder without impairment of their civil service status or retirement rights.

SECTION 4. So much of chapter two hundred and eighty of the acts of nineteen hundred and thirty-two, and acts in amendment thereof and in addition thereto, as is inconsistent with this act, is hereby repealed.

SECTION 5. This act shall be submitted for acceptance to the registered voters of said city at the biennial municipal election to be held in said city in the current year in the form of the following question, which shall be placed upon the official ballot to be used at said election: — "Shall an act passed by the general court in the year nineteen hundred and forty-three, entitled 'An Act authorizing the Establishment of a Park Department, to be in Charge of a Park Commissioner, in the City of Pittsfield', be accepted?" If a majority of the votes cast on said question is in the affirmative, this act shall take full effect on the first Monday of January in the year nineteen hundred and forty-four, but not otherwise. *Approved May 28, 1943.*

AN ACT RELATIVE TO THE PROOF OF MALICE IN ACTIONS OF LIBEL AND SLANDER. **Chap. 365**

Be it enacted, etc., as follows:

SECTION 1. Chapter two hundred and thirty-one of the General Laws is hereby amended by striking out section ninety-one, as appearing in the Tercentenary Edition, and inserting in place thereof the following: — *Section 91.* If the defendant in an action for slander or for publishing a libel justifies that the words spoken or published were true, such allegation, although not maintained by the evidence, shall not of itself be proof of the malice alleged in the declaration, nor shall statements of the defendant differing in import from those declared on be admissible to establish his malice unless such statements were published in pursuance of a general scheme to defame or otherwise injure the plaintiff. If the plaintiff proposes to introduce evidence of statements of the defendant other than those declared on, he shall give the defendant written notice of such intention, specifying the date and content of each such statement, at least fourteen days before trial begins, or earlier if the court so orders; and, if any such statement is introduced in evidence, the defendant shall be permitted to prove that it was true, or was privileged, or any other facts relating thereto which tend to negative malice.

G. L. (Ter. Ed.), 231, § 91, amended.

Justification in slander not proof of malice

Effective date.

SECTION 2. This act shall become operative on October first in the current year, but shall not apply to any action pending on said effective date. *Approved May 28, 1943.*

---

*Chap.*366 AN ACT RELATIVE TO THE PAYMENT OF ANNUITIES TO DEPENDENTS OF CERTAIN PUBLIC EMPLOYEES KILLED OR DYING FROM INJURIES RECEIVED OR HAZARDS UNDERGONE IN THE PERFORMANCE OF DUTY.

Be it enacted, etc., as follows:

G. L. (Ter. Ed.), 32, § 89, etc., amended.

Section eighty-nine of chapter thirty-two of the General Laws, as most recently amended by chapter three hundred and twenty-six of the acts of nineteen hundred and thirty-six, is hereby further amended by striking out, in the nineteenth line, the word "all" and inserting in place thereof the words: — a majority of the, — by striking out, in the forty-sixth line, the word "if" and inserting in place thereof the words: — , or to or for the benefit of an unmarried or widowed sister of the deceased with whom he was living at the time of his death, if such father, mother or sister was, — and by striking out, in the forty-eighth line, the word "remarry" and inserting in place thereof the following: — marry. The members of said board to be designated by the retiring authority and the commissioner of public health, as aforesaid, shall be so designated within thirty days after the filing of an application for an annuity hereunder, — so that the first paragraph will read as follows: — If a member of the police or fire force, or a forest warden, of a city or town, or a member of the department of public safety doing police duty, or an investigator or examiner of the registry of motor vehicles in the department of public works doing police duty, or an inspector of the department of labor and industries, or a prison officer or any technical employee of the department of public works or public health, of the metropolitan district commission, or of the division of metropolitan planning, included in class twenty-seven of rule four of the civil service rules, is killed, or dies from injuries received, or dies as a natural and proximate result of undergoing a hazard peculiar to his employment, while in the performance of his duty, and it shall be proved to the satisfaction of the appropriate public authority as hereinafter defined that such death was the natural and proximate result of an accident occurring, or of undergoing a hazard peculiar to his employment, while he was acting in the performance and within the scope of his duty, and a majority of the members of a board consisting of two physicians designated by the public authority hereinafter defined, and one physician to be designated by the commissioner of public health shall certify to the treasurer of the body politic and corporate by which the compensation of such deceased person was payable, that the death was the natural and proximate result of the said injury or hazard, there shall, except

Annuities to dependents of policemen or firemen killed, etc., in performance of duty.

as hereinafter provided, be paid out of the treasury of such body politic and corporate, to the following dependents of such deceased person the following annuities: To the widow, so long as she remains unmarried, an annuity not exceeding one thousand dollars a year, increased by not exceeding two hundred dollars for each child of such deceased person during such time as such child is under the age of eighteen or over said age and physically or mentally incapacitated from earning; and, if there is any such child and no widow or the widow later dies, such an annuity as would have been payable to the widow had there been one or had she lived, to or for the benefit of such child, or of such children in equal shares, during the time aforesaid; and, if there is any such child and the widow remarries, in lieu of the aforesaid annuity to her, an annuity not exceeding two hundred and sixty dollars to or for the benefit of each such child during the time aforesaid; and, if there is no widow and no such child, an annuity not exceeding one thousand dollars to or for the benefit of the father or mother of the deceased, or to or for the benefit of an unmarried or widowed sister of the deceased with whom he was living at the time of his death, if such father, mother or sister was dependent upon him for support at the time of his death, during such time as such beneficiary is unable to support himself or herself and does not marry. The members of said board to be designated by the retiring authority and the commissioner of public health, as aforesaid, shall be so designated within thirty days after the filing of an application for an annuity hereunder. The total amount of all such annuities shall not, except as hereinafter provided, exceed the annual rate of compensation received by such deceased person at the date of his death. If such deceased person was a reserve or special policeman or a reserve or call fireman of a city or town and, at the time he was killed or at the time he received the injuries or underwent the hazard resulting in his death, was performing duty to which he was assigned or called as such policeman or fireman and for the performance of which he was entitled to compensation from said city or town, the total amount of all such annuities shall not exceed the annual rate of compensation payable to a regular or permanent member of the police or fire force thereof, as the case may be, for the first year of service therein, and if there are no regular or permanent members of the police or fire force thereof, as the case may be, said total amount shall not exceed the sum of one thousand dollars. The amount of any such annuity shall from time to time be determined within the limits aforesaid by the appropriate public authority as hereinafter defined. *Approved May 28, 1943.*

Chap.367 AN ACT DECREASING THE AMOUNT TO BE PAID INTO THE TREASURY OF THE COMMONWEALTH IN CERTAIN CASES OF INDUSTRIAL ACCIDENTS RESULTING IN DEATH, AND PROVIDING FOR CERTAIN EXPENSES RELATIVE THERETO.

Be it enacted, etc., as follows:

G. L. (Ter. Ed.), 152, § 65 etc., amended.

Section sixty-five of chapter one hundred and fifty-two of the General Laws, as most recently amended by section three of chapter four hundred and sixty-five of the acts of nineteen hundred and thirty-nine, is hereby further amended by striking out, in the sixth line, the words "one thousand", and inserting in place thereof the words: — five hundred, — and by adding at the end the following new sentence: — The reasonable expense of prosecution, if any, by the attorney general, of claim for deposit under this section, shall, subject to the approval of the department, be payable out of the special fund established hereunder, — so as to read as follows: — *Section 65.* For every case of personal injury resulting in death covered by this chapter, except silicosis or other occupational pulmonary dust disease, when there are no dependents, the insurer shall pay into the treasury of the commonwealth five hundred dollars. Such payments shall constitute a special fund in the custody of the state treasurer, who shall make payments therefrom upon the written order of the department for the purposes set forth in section thirty-seven. The reasonable expense of prosecution, if any, by the attorney general, of claim for deposit under this section, shall, subject to the approval of the department, be payable out of the special fund established hereunder.

Special fund.

Approved May 28, 1943.

Chap.368 AN ACT INCREASING THE AMOUNT OF PAYMENTS TO CERTAIN DEPENDENTS OF EMPLOYEES KILLED IN INDUSTRIAL ACCIDENTS.

Be it enacted, etc., as follows:

G. L. (Ter. Ed.), 152, § 31, etc., amended.

The second paragraph of section thirty-one of chapter one hundred and fifty-two of the General Laws, as amended, is hereby further amended by striking out, in the first line, the word "ten" and inserting in place thereof the word: — twelve, — by striking out, in the sixth line, the word "twelve" and inserting in place thereof the word: — fifteen, — and by striking out, in the seventh line, the word "two" and inserting in place thereof the word: — three, — by striking out, in the twentieth line, the word "eighteen" and inserting in place thereof the word: — twenty-four, — and by striking out, in the twenty-second line, the word "three" and inserting in place thereof the word: — four, — so as to read as follows: —

Death payments.

To the widow, so long as she remains unmarried, twelve dollars a week if and so long as there is no child of the employee, who is under the age of eighteen, or over said age and physically or mentally incapacitated from earning; to or for the use of the widow and for the benefit of all children of the employee, fifteen dollars a week if and so long as there is one such child, and three dollars more a week for each such additional child; provided, that in case any such child is a child by a former wife, the death benefit shall be divided between the surviving wife and all living children of the deceased employee in equal shares, the surviving wife taking the same share as a child. If the widow dies, such amount or amounts as would have been payable to or for her own use and for the benefit of all children of the employee shall be paid in equal shares to all the surviving children of the employee. If the widow remarries, all payments under the foregoing provisions shali terminate and the insurer shall pay each week to each of the children of the employee, if and so long as there are more than five, his or her proportionate share of twenty-four dollars and shall pay each of such children, if and so long as there are five or less, four dollars a week. If there is no surviving wife or husband of the deceased employee, such amount or amounts as would have been payable under this section to or for the use of a widow and for the benefit of all such children of the employee, shall be paid in equal shares to all such surviving children of the employee. The total amount of payments and the period of payments in all cases under this section shall not be more than sixty-four hundred dollars nor continue for more than four hundred weeks, except that payment to or for the benefit of children of the deceased employee under the age of eighteen shall not be discontinued prior to the age of eighteen. When weekly payments have been made to an injured employee before his death, compensation under the foregoing provisions of this section shall begin from the date of the death of the employee, but shall not amount to a total of more than sixty-four hundred dollars, including such payments as were made to the injured employee before his death, and shall not continue for more than four hundred weeks, including weeks during which payments were made to the injured employee before his death, except as above provided in cases where children of the deceased employee continue to be under the age of eighteen. *Approved May 28, 1943.*

AN ACT RELATIVE TO THE TRIAL AND DISPOSITION OF CERTAIN ACTIONS AND PROCEEDINGS PENDING IN DIFFERENT COURTS. *Chap.*369

Be it enacted, etc., as follows:

SECTION 1. Chapter two hundred and twenty-three of the General Laws is hereby amended by striking out section two A, inserted by section one of chapter four hundred and eighty-three of the acts of nineteen hundred and thirty-five, G. L. (Ter. Ed.), 223, § 2A, stricken out, and new §§ 2A–2C, inserted.

and inserting in place thereof the three following sections: —

Consolidation of certain actions.

Section 2A. Whenever cross actions between the same parties or two or more actions, including for the purposes hereof other court proceedings, arising out of or connected with the same accident, event or transaction are pending in one or more district courts, the appellate division of any such district court may, upon motion of any party to any such action in such court, order the consolidation of such actions for the purpose of trial together in any district court to be designated in the order; provided, that if motions to consolidate the same actions are filed in more than one appellate division, such motions shall be referred to the appellate division in which the first motion is filed; and provided, further, that if all the principal parties to all such actions agree upon such consolidation for trial together in one district court they shall be consolidated and tried in such court. The party making such motion shall give notice thereof to the clerks of the district courts in which said actions are pending and to all parties to such actions, and thereafter none of said actions shall be placed on any trial list until after the disposition of said motion. This section shall apply only to actions as to which the time limit for removal to the superior court under section one hundred and four of chapter two hundred and thirty-one has expired.

Transfer of certain actions to superior court.

Section 2B. Whenever cross actions between the same parties or two or more actions, including for the purposes hereof other court proceedings, arising out of or connected with the same accident, event or transaction are pending, one or more in the superior court and also one or more in one or more district courts, the superior court, upon petition filed therein by any party to any of such actions, may order that the action or actions pending in the district court or courts, with all the papers relating thereto, be transferred to the superior court without the payment of any entry fee, or, with the consent of all principal parties to all such actions, may order that such actions be transferred without the payment of any entry fee to a designated district court in which any of such actions is pending.

Transfer of action, procedure.

Section 2C. Whenever any action or proceeding is transferred to another court under any provision of section two A or section two B, such action or proceeding shall thereafter proceed in the court to which it is thus transferred as though originally entered there.

Effective date.

SECTION 2. This act shall take effect on October first in the current year. *Approved May 28, 1943.*

AN ACT MAKING APPROPRIATIONS FOR THE MAINTENANCE OF DEPARTMENTS, BOARDS, COMMISSIONS, INSTITUTIONS AND CERTAIN ACTIVITIES OF THE COMMONWEALTH, FOR INTEREST, SINKING FUND AND SERIAL BOND REQUIREMENTS, AND FOR CERTAIN PERMANENT IMPROVEMENTS. *Chap.370*

Be it enacted, etc., as follows:

SECTION 1. To provide for the maintenance of the several departments, boards, commissions and institutions, of sundry other services, and for certain permanent improvements, and to meet certain requirements of law, the sums set forth in section two, for the several purposes and subject to the conditions specified in said section two, are hereby appropriated from the general fund or revenue of the commonwealth, unless some other source of revenue is expressed subject to the provisions of law regulating the disbursement of public funds and the approval thereof, for the fiscal year ending June thirtieth, nineteen hundred and forty-four, and for the fiscal year ending June thirtieth, nineteen hundred and forty-five, or for such other period as may be specified.

SECTION 2.

Item		Appropriation Fiscal Year 1944.	Appropriation Fiscal Year 1945.
	Service of the Legislative Department.		
0101-01	For the compensation of senators .	–	$102,500 00
0101-02	For expense allowance of senators for the year nineteen hundred and forty-four and for compensation for travel for the year nineteen hundred and forty-five .	$20,000 00	6,000 00
0101-03	For the compensation of representatives	–	602,500 00
0101-04	For expense allowance of representatives for the year nineteen hundred and forty-four and for compensation for travel for the year nineteen hundred and forty-five	120,000 00	37,000 00
0101-05	For the salaries of the clerk of the senate and the clerk of the house of representatives . . .	12,000 00	12,000 00
0101-06	For the salaries of the assistant clerk of the senate and the assistant clerk of the house of representatives	8,500 00	8,630 00
0101-07	For such additional clerical assistance to, and with the approval of, the clerk of the senate, as may be necessary for the proper despatch of public business, including not more than one permanent position	2,800 00	2,800 00

Item		Appropriation Fiscal Year 1944.	Appropriation Fiscal Year 1945.
0101-08	For such additional clerical assistance to, and with the approval of, the clerk of the house of representatives, as may be necessary for the proper despatch of public business, including not more than three permanent positions	$7,800 00	$8,100 00
0101-09	For the salary of the sergeant-at-arms	4,000 00	4,000 00
0101-10	For clerical and other assistance employed by the sergeant-at-arms, including not more than four permanent positions . .	6,510 00	6,630 00
0101-11	For the compensation for travel of doorkeepers, assistant doorkeepers, general court officers, pages and other employees of the sergeant-at-arms, authorized by law to receive the same . .	4,000 00	8,000 00
0101-12	For the salaries of the doorkeepers of the senate and house of representatives, with the approval of the sergeant-at-arms, including not more than two permanent positions	5,500 00	5,500 00
0101-13	For the salaries of assistant doorkeepers of the senate and house of representatives and of general court officers, with the approval of the sergeant-at-arms, including not more than twenty-two permanent positions . .	44,600 00	44,600 00
0101-14	For compensation of the pages of the senate and house of representatives, with the approval of the sergeant-at-arms, including not more than fourteen permanent positions	–	9,800 00
0101-15	For the salaries of clerks employed in the legislative document room, including not more than two permanent positions . .	4,850 00	6,250 00
0101-17	For the salaries of the chaplains of the senate and house of representatives, including not more than two permanent positions .	–	1,500 00
0101-18	For personal services of the counsel to the senate and assistants, including not more than four permanent positions . . .	22,000 00	23,000 00
0101-19	For personal services of the counsel to the house of representatives and assistants, including not more than seven permanent positions	31,600 00	34,400 00
0101-20	For clerical and other assistance of the senate committee on rules, including not more than one permanent position . . .	4,300 00	5,000 00
0101-21	For clerical and other assistance of the house committee on rules, including not more than four per-		

Item		Appropriation Fiscal Year 1944.	Appropriation Fiscal Year 1945.
	manent positions in the year nineteen hundred and forty-four and three permanent positions in the year nineteen hundred and forty-five	$8,390 00	$5,215 00
0101–22	For clerical and other assistance of the joint recess committee on ways and means	500 00	250 00
0102–01	For traveling and such other expenses of the committees of the present general court as may be authorized by order of either branch of the general court	400 00	4,000 00
0102–02	For printing, binding and paper ordered by the senate and house of representatives, or by concurrent order of the two branches, with the approval of the clerks of the respective branches	–	90,000 00
0102–03	For printing the manual of the general court, with the approval of the clerks of the two branches		5,100 00
0102–04	For expenses in connection with the publication of the bulletin of committee hearings and of the daily list, with the approval of the joint committee on rules, including not more than two permanent positions in the year nineteen hundred and forty-five	–	18,975 00
0102–05	For stationery for the senate, purchased by and with approval of the clerk	100 00	400 00
0102–06	For office and other expenses of the committee on rules on the part of the senate	100 00	200 00
0102–07	For office expenses of the counsel to the senate	100 00	300 00
0102–08	For stationery for the house of representatives, purchased by and with the approval of the clerk	350 00	800 00
0102–09	For office and other expenses of the committee on rules on the part of the house	200 00	300 00
0102–10	For office expenses, including travel, of the counsel to the house of representatives	300 00	300 00
0102–11	For contingent expenses of the senate and house of representatives, and necessary expenses in and about the state house, with the approval of the sergeant-at-arms	5,000 00	9,500 00
0102–12	For telephone service	1,500 00	10,000 00
0102–13	For biographical sketches of certain state and federal officials		1,700 00
0102–14	For the payment of witness fees to persons summoned to appear before committees of the general court, and for expenses incidental to summoning them, with the approval of the sergeant-at-arms		200 00

Item		Appropriation Fiscal Year 1944.	Appropriation Fiscal Year 1945.
0102-16	For the consolidation and arrangement of certain laws, including work, under the direction of the senate and house counsel, with the approval of the president of the senate and the speaker of the house of representatives, upon certain indexes and relating to recess committee investigations .	$2,000 00	$2,000 00
	Totals	$317,400 00	$1,077,450 00

Service of the Judicial Department.

Item		Appropriation Fiscal Year 1944.	Appropriation Fiscal Year 1945.
	Supreme Judicial Court, as follows:		
0301-01	For the salaries of the chief justice and of the six associate justices .	$99,000 00	$99,000 00
0301-02	For traveling allowances and expenses	1,500 00	1,500 00
0301-03	For the salary of the clerk for the commonwealth . . .	6,500 00	6,500 00
0301-04	For clerical assistance to the clerk	1,800 00	1,800 00
0301-05	For law clerks, stenographers and other clerical assistance for the justices	28,000 00	28,000 00
0301-06	For office supplies, services and equipment	5,500 00	5,500 00
0301-07	For the salaries of the officers and messengers	3,290 00	3,290 00
0301-08	For the commonwealth's part of the salary of the clerk for the county of Suffolk . . .	1,500 00	1,500 00
	Totals	$147,090 00	$147,090 00
	Reporter of Decisions:		
0301-11	For the salary of the reporter of decisions	$6,000 00	$6,000 00
0301-12	For clerk hire and office supplies, services and equipment, including not more than four permanent positions . . .	13,000 00	13,000 00
	Totals	$19,000 00	$19,000 00
	Superior Court, as follows:		
0302-01	For the salaries of the chief justice and of the thirty-one associate justices	$385,000 00	$385,000 00
0302-02	For traveling allowances and expenses	14,000 00	14,500 00
0302-03	For the salary of the assistant clerk, Suffolk county . . .	1,000 00	1,000 00
0302-04	For clerical work, inspection of records and doings of persons authorized to admit to bail, for an executive clerk to the chief justice, and for certain other expenses incident to the work of the court	13,300 00	13,550 00
	Totals	$413,300 00	$414,050 00

Item		Appropriation Fiscal Year 1944.	Appropriation Fiscal Year 1945.
	Justices of District Courts:		
0302-11	For compensation of justices of district courts while sitting in the superior court	$4,500 00	$5,000 00
0302-12	For expenses of justices of district courts while sitting in the superior court	650 00	650 00
0302-13	For reimbursing certain counties for compensation of certain special justices for services in holding sessions of district courts in place of the justice, while sitting in the superior court . .	1,000 00	1,000 00
	Totals	$6,150 00	$6,650 00
	Judicial Council:		
0303-01	For expenses of the judicial council, as authorized by section thirty-four C of chapter two hundred and twenty-one of the General Laws, to be in addition to any amount heretofore appropriated for the purpose	$1,800 00	$1,800 00
0303-02	For compensation of the secretary of the judicial council, as authorized by said section thirty-four C of said chapter two hundred and twenty-one . .	3,500 00	3,500 00
	Totals	$5,300 00	$5,300 00
	Administrative Committee of District Courts:		
0304-01	For compensation and expenses of the administrative committee of district courts	$4,500 00	$4,500 00
	Probate and Insolvency Courts, as follows:		
0305-01	For the salaries of judges of probate of the several counties, including not more than twenty permanent positions . .	$158,500 00	$158,500 00
0305-02	For the compensation of judges of probate when acting for other judges of probate	8,000 00	8,000 00
0305-03	For expenses of judges of probate when acting for other judges of probate	300 00	300 00
0305-04	For the salaries of registers of the several counties, including not more than fourteen permanent positions	63,900 00	63,900 00
0305-05	For the salaries of assistant registers, including not more than twenty-two permanent positions	79,380 00	80,100 00
0305-06	For reimbursing officials for premiums paid for procuring sureties on their bonds, as provided by existing laws	300 00	300 00
	Totals	$310,380 00	$311,100 00

Item		Appropriation Fiscal Year 1944.	Appropriation Fiscal Year 1945.
	For clerical assistance to Registers of the several counties, as follows:		
0306-01	Barnstable, including not more than two permanent positions .	$2,580 00	$2,700 00
0306-02	Berkshire, including not more than four permanent positions . .	5,280 00	5,400 00
0306-03	Bristol, including not more than ten permanent positions . .	14,730 00	15,030 00
0306-04	Dukes County, including not more than one permanent position	660 00	660 00
0306-05	Essex, including not more than fourteen permanent positions	20,040 00	20,820 00
0306-06	Franklin, including not more than one permanent position . .	2,160 00	2,160 00
0306-07	Hampden, including not more than nine permanent positions .	14,370 00	14,730 00
0306-08	Hampshire, including not more than two permanent positions .	3,030 00	3,090 00
0306-09	Middlesex, including not more than thirty-five permanent positions	49,590 00	50,670 00
0306-10	Norfolk, including not more than thirteen permanent positions .	18,000 00	18,300 00
0306-11	Plymouth, including not more than four permanent positions . .	5,220 00	5,340 00
0306-12	Suffolk, including not more than forty-five permanent positions .	61,600 00	62,800 00
0306-13	Worcester, including not more than twelve permanent positions .	16,860 00	17,040 00
0306-14	Nantucket	150 00	150 00
	Totals	$214,270 00	$218,890 00
	Administrative Committee of Probate Courts:		
0307-01	For expenses of the administrative committee of probate courts .	$100 00	$100 00
	Service of the Land Court.		
0308-01	For the salaries of the judge, associate judges, the recorder and court officer, including not more than five permanent positions .	$38,984 00	$38,984 00
0308-02	For engineering, clerical and other personal services, including not more than twenty-four permanent positions	58,740 00	59,480 00
0308-03	For personal services in the examination of titles, for publishing and serving citations and other services, traveling expenses, supplies and office equipment, and for the preparation of sectional plans showing registered land .	23,500 00	23,500 00
	Totals	$121,224 00	$121,964 00
	Pensions for Certain Retired Justices.		
0309-01	For pensions of retired justices of the supreme judicial court and of the superior court, and judges of the probate courts and the land court	$50,000 00	$50,000 00

Item		Appropriation Fiscal Year 1944.	Appropriation Fiscal Year 1945.
	Service of the District Attorneys.		
	District Attorneys, as follows:		
0310-01	For the salaries of the district attorney and assistants for the Suffolk district, including not more than fourteen permanent positions	$66,000 00	$66,000 00
0310-02	For the salaries of the district attorney and assistants for the northern district, including not more than seven permanent positions	28,000 00	28,000 00
0310-03	For the salaries of the district attorney and assistants for the eastern district, including not more than five permanent positions	17,400 00	17,400 00
0310-04	For the salaries of the district attorney, deputy district attorney and assistants for the southeastern district, including not more than five permanent positions	18,600 00	18,600 00
0310-05	For the salaries of the district attorney and assistants for the southern district, including not more than four permanent positions	15,100 00	15,100 00
0310-06	For the salaries of the district attorney and assistants for the middle district, including not more than four permanent positions	15,000 00	15,000 00
0310-07	For the salaries of the district attorney and assistants for the western district, including not more than three permanent positions	10,400 00	10,400 00
0310-08	For the salary of the district attorney for the northwestern district	4,000 00	4,000 00
0310-09	For traveling expenses necessarily incurred by the district attorneys, except in the Suffolk district, including expenses incurred in previous years	4,500 00	4,500 00
	Totals	$179,000 00	$179,000 00
	Service of the Board of Probation.		
0311-01	For personal services of the commissioner, clerks and stenographers, including not more than forty-three permanent positions	$70,020 00	$71,280 00
0311-02	For services other than personal, including printing the annual report, traveling expenses, rent, office supplies and equipment	6,500 00	6,500 00
	Totals	$76,520 00	$77,780 00

Item		Appropriation Fiscal Year 1944.	Appropriation Fiscal Year 1945.
	Service of the Board of Bar Examiners.		
0312-01	For personal services of the members of the board, including not more than five permanent positions	$12,500 00	$12,500 00
0312-02	For other services, including not more than one permanent position, and including printing the annual report, traveling expenses, office supplies and equipment	6,657 00	6,657 00
	Totals	$19,157 00	$19,157 00
	Suffolk County Court House.		
0318-01	For reimbursing the city of Boston for thirty per cent of the cost of maintenance of the Suffolk County Court House, as provided by and subject to the conditions of section six of chapter four hundred and seventy-four of the acts of the year nineteen hundred and thirty-five; provided, that this appropriation shall not be construed as fixing the specific amount for which the commonwealth shall be liable on account of said maintenance .	$100,000 00	$100,000 00
	Service of the Executive Department.		
0401-01	For the salary of the governor .	$10,000 00	$10,000 00
0401-02	For the salary of the lieutenant governor	4,000 00	4,000 00
0401-03	For the salaries of the eight councillors	8,000 00	8,000 00
0401-04	For the salaries of officers and employees of the department, including not more than seventeen permanent positions . .	41,190 00	41,190 00
0401-05	For certain personal services for the lieutenant governor and council, including not more than three permanent positions .	5,700 00	5,700 00
0401-21	For travel and expenses of the lieutenant governor and council from and to their homes . . .	3,000 00	3,000 00
0401-22	For postage, printing, office and other contingent expenses, including travel, of the governor .	11,000 00	11,000 00
0401-23	For postage, printing, stationery, traveling and contingent expenses of the governor and council	1,500 00	3,000 00
0401-24	For the cost of entertainment of distinguished visitors to the commonwealth and for the payment of other extraordinary expenses not otherwise provided for .	10,000 00	10,000 00

Item		Appropriation Fiscal Year 1944.	Appropriation Fiscal Year 1945.
0401-26	For certain maintenance expenses of the governor's automobile .	$1,000 00	$1,000 00
0401-31	For the purchase of portraits of former governors, as authorized by section nineteen of chapter eight of the General Laws .	–	3,000 00
0401-32	For restoring and protecting certain portraits of former governors, with the approval of the art commission . . .	500 00	–
	Totals	$95,890 00	$99,890 00

Service of the Adjutant General.

Item		Appropriation Fiscal Year 1944.	Appropriation Fiscal Year 1945.
0402-01	For the salary of the adjutant general	$6,000 00	$6,000 00
0402-02	For personal services of office assistants, including services for the preparation of records of Massachusetts soldiers and sailors, and including not more than eighteen permanent positions	37,260 00	37,740 00
0402-03	For services other than personal, and for necessary office supplies and expenses	9,500 00	9,500 00
0402-04	For expenses not otherwise provided for in connection with military matters and accounts .	6,000 00	6,000 00
	Totals	$58,760 00	$59,240 00

Service of the Organized Militia.

Item		Appropriation Fiscal Year 1944.	Appropriation Fiscal Year 1945.
0403-01	For allowances to companies and other administrative units, to be expended under the direction of the adjutant general . .	$122,000 00	$122,200 00
0403-03	For certain allowances for officers of the organized militia, as authorized by paragraph (c) of section one hundred and twenty of chapter thirty-three of the General Laws . . .	38,000 00	43,000 00
0403-05	For expenses of military training and instruction, including organization, administration and elements of military art, use of chemical gas, rifle practice, and pay and expenses of certain camps of instruction . .	125,000 00	125,000 00
0403-07	For transportation of officers and non-commissioned officers to and from military meetings and regimental and battalion drills .	3,000 00	3,000 00
0403-08	(This item combined with Item 0403-07.)		
0403-13	For compensation for special and miscellaneous duty . .	27,000 00	27,000 00
0403-14	For compensation for accidents and injuries sustained in the performance of military duty .	4,500 00	4,500 00

Item		Appropriation Fiscal Year 1944.	Appropriation Fiscal Year 1945.
0403-15	To cover certain small claims for damages to private property arising from military maneuvers	$500 00	$500 00
0403-17	For services and expenses of the military reservation located in Barnstable county, including compensation of one commissioner	3,000 00	3,000 00
0403-18	For premiums on bonds for officers	1,550 00	2,500 00
0403-21	For expenses of operation of the second division of the state guard	6,500 00	6,500 00
0403-23	For personal services necessary for the operation of the commonwealth depot and motor repair park, including not more than fourteen permanent positions	24,500 00	24,800 00
	Totals	$355,550 00	$362,000 00
	Specials:		
0404-31	The unexpended balance of the appropriation made by Item 0404-31 of chapter four hundred and nineteen of the acts of nineteen hundred and forty-one and of transfers made to this account during the fiscal year nineteen hundred and forty-two from chapter eighteen of the acts of the Special Session of nineteen hundred and forty-two is hereby reappropriated.		
0404-32	For certain expenses of maintaining regional posts of command of the state guard, including rent	$8,000 00	$8,000 00

Service of the State Quartermaster.

Item		Appropriation Fiscal Year 1944.	Appropriation Fiscal Year 1945.
0405-01	For personal services of the state quartermaster, superintendent of arsenal and certain other employees of the state quartermaster, including not more than eight permanent positions	$16,880 00	$17,200 00
0405-02	For the salaries of armorers and assistant armorers of armories of the first class, superintendent of armories, and other employees, including not more than eighty-two permanent positions	145,793 00	147,705 00
0406-01	For certain incidental military expenses of the quartermaster's department	25 00	25 00
0406-02	For office and general supplies and equipment	14,000 00	14,000 00
0406-03	For the care and maintenance of the state camp ground and buildings at Framingham	100 00	100 00
0406-04	For the maintenance of armories of the first class, including the purchase of certain furniture	180,000 00	175,000 00

Item		Appropriation Fiscal Year 1944.	Appropriation Fiscal Year 1945.
0406–05	For reimbursement for rent and maintenance of armories not of the first class	$16,900 00	$16,900 00
0406–06	For expense of maintaining and operating the Camp Curtis Guild rifle range, including not more than five permanent positions .	13,000 00	13,000 00
0406–07	For maintenance, other than personal services, of the commonwealth depot and motor repair park	500 00	500 00
	Totals	$387,198 00	$384,430 00

Service of the State Surgeon.

Item		1944	1945
0407–01	For personal services of the state surgeon, and regular assistants, including not more than three permanent positions . .	$5,340 00	$5,340 00
0407–02	For services other than personal, and for necessary medical and office supplies and equipment .	1,500 00	1,500 00
0407–03	For the examination of recruits .	5,000 00	5,000 00
	Totals	$11,840 00	$11,840 00

Service of the State Judge Advocate.

Item		1944	1945
0408–01	For compensation of the state judge advocate	$1,500 00	$1,500 00

Service of the Armory Commission.

Item		1944	1945
0409–01	For compensation of one member .	$200 00	$200 00
0409–02	For office, incidental and traveling expenses	100 00	100 00
	Totals	$300 00	$300 00

Service of Special Military Expenses.

Item		1944	1945
0411–01	For the expense of testimonials to soldiers and sailors of the world war, to be expended under the direction of the adjutant general	$25 00	$25 00

Service of the Commission on Administration and Finance.

Item		1944	1945
0415–01	For personal services of the commissioners, including not more than four permanent positions .	$26,500 00	$26,500 00
0415–02	For personal services of the bureau of the comptroller, including not more than eighty-five permanent positions	146,295 00	150,410 00
0415–03	For personal services of the bureau of the purchasing agent, including not more than forty-one permanent positions	77,040 00	78,360 00
0415–04	For other personal services of the commission, including not more than thirty-two permanent positions	73,340 00	74,700 00

Item		Appropriation Fiscal Year 1944.	Appropriation Fiscal Year 1945.
0415–05	For other expenses incidental to the duties of the commission .	$60,000 00	$60,000 00
	Totals	$383,175 00	$389,970 00
	Telephone service:		
0415–10	For telephone service in the state house and expenses in connection therewith . . .	$43,000 00	$44,500 00
	Purchase of paper:		
0415–11	For the purchase of paper used in the execution of the contracts for state printing, other than legislative, with the approval of the commission on administration and finance . . .	$25,000 00	$40,000 00
	Central mailing room:		
0415–12	For personal services of the central mailing room, including not more than eight permanent positions	$13,500 00	$14,160 00
	Service of the State Superintendent of Buildings.		
0416–01	For personal services of the superintendent and office assistants, including not more than five permanent positions . .	$12,480 00	$12,660 00
0416–02	For personal services of engineers, assistant engineers, firemen and helpers in the engineer's department, including not more than forty permanent positions .	71,580 00	73,200 00
0416–03	For personal services of capitol police, including not more than twenty-seven permanent positions	49,380 00	50,580 00
0416–04	For personal services of janitors, including not more than twenty-three permanent positions .	31,500 00	31,860 00
0416–05	For other personal services incidental to the care and maintenance of the state house and of the Ford building, so-called, including not more than seventy-eight permanent positions .	95,820 00	96,060 00
	Totals	$260,760 00	$264,360 00
	Other annual expenses:		
0416–11	For contingent, office and other expenses of the superintendent .	$325 00	$325 00
0416–13	For services, supplies and equipment necessary to furnish heat, light and power . . .	90,000 00	90,000 00
0416–14	For other services, supplies and equipment necessary for the maintenance and care of the state house and grounds and of the Ford building, so-called, including repairs of furniture and equipment	36,500 00	36,500 00
	Totals	$126,825 00	$126,825 00

Item		Appropriation Fiscal Year 1944.	Appropriation Fiscal Year 1945.
	Service of the Alcoholic Beverages Control Commission.		
	The following items shall be payable from fees collected under section twenty-seven of chapter one hundred and thirty-eight of the General Laws:		
0417–01	For personal services, including not more than forty-five permanent positions	$112,860 00	$112,980 00
0417–02	For services other than personal, including rent of offices, travel, and office and incidental expenses	26,000 00	26,000 00
	Totals	$138,860 00	$138,980 00
	Service of the State Racing Commission.		
	The following items shall be payable from fees collected under chapter one hundred and twenty-eight A of the General Laws:		
0418–01	For personal services, including not more than eight permanent positions	$69,000 00	$69,000 00
0418–02	For other administrative expenses, including rent of offices, travel, and office and incidental expenses	7,700 00	7,700 00
	Totals	$76,700 00	$76,700 00
	Service of the State Planning Board.		
0419–01	For personal services of secretary, chief engineer, and other assistants, including not more than thirteen permanent positions .	$42,380 00	$42,440 00
0419–02	For services other than personal, including rent of offices, travel, and office supplies and equipment	9,500 00	9,500 00
	Totals	$51,880 00	$51,940 00
	Service of the Commissioners on Uniform State Laws.		
0420–01	For expenses of the commissioners	$400 00	$400 00
	Service of the State Library.		
0423–01	For personal services of the librarian	$5,700 00	$5,700 00
0423–02	For personal services of the regular library assistants, temporary clerical assistance, and for services for cataloguing, including not more than twenty-two permanent positions . . .	41,460 00	41,580 00

Item		Appropriation Fiscal Year 1944.	Appropriation Fiscal Year 1945.
0423-03	For services other than personal, including printing the annual report, office supplies and equipment, and incidental traveling expenses	$4,500 00	$4,500 00
0423-04	For books and other publications and things needed for the library, and the necessary binding and rebinding incidental thereto .	8,500 00	8,500 00
	Totals	$60,160 00	$60,280 00

Service of the Art Commission.

Item		1944	1945
0424-01	For expenses of the commission .	$310 00	$60 00

Service of the Ballot Law Commission.

Item		1944	1945
0425-01	For compensation of the commissioners, including not more than three permanent positions .	$750 00	$750 00
0425-02	For expenses, including travel, supplies and equipment . .	250 00	250 00
	Totals	$1,000 00	$1,000 00

Service of the Soldiers' Home in Massachusetts.

Item		1944	1945
0430-00	For the maintenance of the Soldiers' Home in Massachusetts, with the approval of the trustees thereof, including not more than two hundred and thirteen permanent positions, to be in addition to certain receipts from the United States government; provided, that these appropriations be reduced by any amount by which the receipts from the United States government may exceed ninety thousand five hundred dollars in each of the years nineteen hundred and forty-four and nineteen hundred and forty-five; and, provided further, that if such receipts from the United States government are less than ninety thousand five hundred dollars, these appropriations be increased by an amount equal to the difference between said amount and the amount actually received, and such increases shall be taken from the War Emergency Fund	$332,920 00	$332,950 00

Service of the Commissioner of State Aid and Pensions.

Item		1944	1945
0440-01	For personal services of the commissioner and deputies, including not more than three permanent positions . . .	$12,390 00	$12,880 00

Item		Appropriation Fiscal Year 1944.	Appropriation Fiscal Year 1945.
0440–02	For personal services of agents, clerks, stenographers, and other assistants, including not more than twenty-six permanent positions	$40,780 00	$42,100 00
0440–03	For services other than personal, including printing the annual report, traveling expenses of the commissioner and his employees, and necessary office supplies and equipment . .	10,400 00	10,400 00
	Totals	$63,570 00	$65,380 00

For Expenses on Account of Wars.

Item		Appropriation Fiscal Year 1944.	Appropriation Fiscal Year 1945.
0441–01	For reimbursing cities and towns for money paid on account of state and military aid to Massachusetts soldiers and their families, to be paid on or before the fifteenth day of November in the years nineteen hundred and forty-three and nineteen hundred and forty-four, in accordance with the provisions of existing laws relative to state and military aid other than chapter eleven of the acts of the Special Session of nineteen hundred and forty-two	$349,652 78	$375,000 00
0441–02	For certain care of veterans of the civil war, their wives and widows, as authorized by section twenty-five of chapter one hundred and fifteen of the General Laws	20,000 00	18,000 00
0441–11	For reimbursing cities and towns for money paid on account of war allowance, state and military aid, and soldiers' relief to certain residents of the commonwealth and their dependents, as authorized by chapter eleven of the acts of the Special Session of nineteen hundred and forty-two	248,647 56	350,000 00
	Totals	$618,300 34	$743,000 00

Service of the Massachusetts Aeronautics Commission.

Item		Appropriation Fiscal Year 1944.	Appropriation Fiscal Year 1945.
0442–01	For personal services of employees, including not more than three permanent positions . . .	$2,400 00	$2,520 00
0442–02	For administrative expenses, including consultants' services, office rent and other incidental expenses	5,600 00	5,600 00
	Totals	$8,000 00	$8,120 00

Item		Appropriation Fiscal Year 1944.	Appropriation Fiscal Year 1945.
	For the Maintenance of the Mount Greylock War Memorial.		
0443-01	For expenses of maintenance of the Mount Greylock War Memorial, as authorized by section forty-seven of chapter six of the General Laws	$1,200 00	$1,200 00
	For the Maintenance of Old State House.		
0444-01	For the contribution of the commonwealth toward the maintenance of the old provincial state house	$1,500 00	$1,500 00
	Service of the Governor's Committee on Public Safety.		
0450-01	For personal and other expenses of the governor's committee on public safety. No part of the appropriations herein authorized shall be available for the salaries of positions on a permanent basis. Persons employed by said committee shall not be subject to the civil service laws or the rules and regulations made thereunder, but their employment and salary rates shall be subject to the rules and regulations of the division of personnel and standardization. Further activities of the committee shall cease within six months of the termination of the existing state of war between the United States and any foreign country or earlier if, in the opinion of the governor, its continuation is no longer required in the best interests of the commonwealth. Expenditures under this item shall be subject to the approval of a majority of the members of the executive committee of said committee on public safety .	$470,787 00	$470,287 00
	Service of the Industrial Committee for National Defense.		
0460-01	For personal services and for administrative expenses, including office rent and other incidental expenses. No part of the appropriation herein authorized shall be available for the salaries of positions on a permanent basis, and persons employed by said committee shall not be subject to the civil service laws or the rules and regulations made thereunder, but their employment and salary rates shall be subject to the rules and regulations of the division of personnel and stand-		

Item		Appropriation Fiscal Year 1944.	Appropriation Fiscal Year 1945.
	ardization. Further activities of the committee shall terminate whenever, in the opinion of the governor, its continuation is no longer required in the best interests of the commonwealth .	$13,000 00	$13,000 00
	Service of the Secretary of the Commonwealth.		
0501–01	For the salary of the secretary .	$7,000 00	$7,000 00
0501–02	For the salaries of officers and employees holding positions established by law, and other personal services, including not more than sixty-five permanent positions .	124,600 00	126,600 00
0501–03	For services other than personal, traveling expenses, office supplies and equipment, for the arrangement and preservation of state records and papers, including traveling expenses of the supervisor of public records .	19,000 00	19,000 00
0501–04	For postage and expressage on public documents, and for mailing copies of bills and resolves to certain state, city and town officials	2,000 00	2,000 00
0501–05	For printing registration books, blanks and indexes . . .	2,000 00	2,000 00
0501–06	For the preparation of certain indexes of births, marriages and deaths	6,000 00	6,000 00
0501–08	For the purchase of ink for public records of the commonwealth .	1,000 00	1,000 00
0501–09	For the purchase of copies of certain town records prior to eighteen hundred and fifty . .	1,800 00	4,000 00
0501–10	For expenses required in taking the decennial census . . .	–	10,000 00
	Totals	$163,400 00	$177,600 00
	Specials:		
0502–01	For the purchase of certain supplies and equipment, and for other things necessary in connection with the reproduction of the manuscript collection designated "Massachusetts Archives" .	$1,300 00	$1,300 00
0502–02	For the purchase and distribution of copies of certain journals of the house of representatives of Massachusetts Bay from seventeen hundred and fifteen to seventeen hundred and eighty, inclusive, as authorized by chapter four hundred and thirteen of the acts of nineteen hundred and twenty	750 00	750 00
0502–04	(Funds for this item in Governor's War Emergency Fund.)		
	Totals	$2,050 00	$2,050 00

Item		Appropriation Fiscal Year 1944.	Appropriation Fiscal Year 1945.
	For printing laws, etc.:		
0503-01	For printing and distributing the pamphlet edition and for printing and binding the blue book edition of the acts and resolves of the year nineteen hundred and forty-five . . .	–	$16,000 00
0503-02	For the printing of reports of decisions of the supreme judicial court	$24,510 00	24,510 00
0503-03	For printing and binding public documents	2,500 00	2,500 00
	Totals	$27,010 00	$43,010 00
	For matters relating to elections:		
0504-01	For personal and other services in preparing for primary elections, including not more than one permanent position, and for the expenses of preparing, printing and distributing ballots for primary and other elections . .	$90,000 00	$221,000 00
0504-02	For the printing of blanks for town officers, election laws and blanks and instructions on all matters relating to elections . .	6,300 00	3,000 00
0504-03	For furnishing cities and towns with ballot boxes, and for repairs to the same; for the purchase of apparatus to be used at polling places in the canvass and counting of votes; and for providing certain registration facilities	1,000 00	2,000 00
0504-04	For expenses of publication of lists of candidates and forms of questions before state elections .	–	18,500 00
0504-05	For services and expenses of the electoral college	–	500 00
0504-07	For expenses of compiling and publishing information to voters, as required by section fifty-three of chapter fifty-four of the General Laws	–	40,000 00
	Totals	$97,300 00	$285,000 00
	Medical Examiners' Fees:		
0505-01	For medical examiners' fees, as provided by law	$1,300 00	$1,300 00
	Commission on Interstate Co-operation:		
0506-01	For personal and other services of the commission, including travel and other expenses, as authorized by sections twenty-one to twenty-five, inclusive, of chapter nine of the General Laws, including not more than two permanent positions . .	$10,700 00	$10,950 00

Item		Appropriation Fiscal Year 1944.	Appropriation Fiscal Year 1945.
	Service of the Treasurer and Receiver-General.		
0601-01	For the salary of the treasurer and receiver-general	$6,000 00	$6,000 00
0601-02	For salaries of officers and employees holding positions established by law and additional clerical and other assistance, including not more than thirty-eight permanent positions . .	70,500 00	72,400 00
0601-03	For services other than personal, traveling expenses, office supplies and equipment . .	18,150 00	16,900 00
	Totals	$94,650 00	$95,300 00
	Commissioners on Firemen's Relief:		
0602-01	For relief disbursed, with the approval of the commissioners on firemen's relief, subject to the provisions of law	$15,000 00	$15,000 00
0602-02	For expenses of administration by the commissioners on firemen's relief	300 00	300 00
	Totals	$15,300 00	$15,300 00
	Payments to Soldiers:		
0603-01	For making payments to soldiers in recognition of service during the world war and the Spanish war, as provided by law . .	$1,000 00	$1,000 00
	State Board of Retirement:		
0604-01	For personal services in the administrative office of the state board of retirement, including not more than eleven permanent positions	$18,860 00	$19,460 00
0604-02	For services other than personal, printing the annual report, and for office supplies and equipment	1,385 00	1,600 00
0604-03	For requirements of annuity funds and pensions for employees retired from the state service under authority of law, to be in addition to the amounts appropriated in item 2970-01 . .	414,000 00	464,000 00
	Totals	$434,245 00	$485,060 00
	Service of the Emergency Finance Board.		
0605-01	For administrative expenses of the emergency finance board, including not more than eight permanent positions	$13,640 00	$13,820 00
	Service of the State Emergency Public Works Commission.		
0606-01	For expenses of the board appointed to formulate projects or perform any act necessary to enable the commonwealth to receive certain benefits provided		

Item		Appropriation Fiscal Year 1944.	Appropriation Fiscal Year 1945.
	by any acts or joint resolutions of congress authorizing grants of federal money for public projects, including not more than six permanent positions . .	$11,950 00	$12,000 00
	Service of the Auditor of the Commonwealth.		
0701–01	For the salary of the auditor .	$6,000 00	$6,000 00
0701–02	For personal services of deputies and other assistants, including not more than twenty-five permanent positions . . .	73,680 00	75,000 00
0701–03	For services other than personal, traveling expenses, office supplies and equipment . .	6,700 00	6,700 00
	Totals	$86,380 00	$87,700 00
	Service of the Attorney General's Department.		
0801–01	For the salary of the attorney general	$8,000 00	$8,000 00
0801–02	For the compensation of assistants in his office, and for such other legal and personal services as may be required, including not more than thirty-six permanent positions	118,660 00	118,900 00
0801–03	For services other than personal, traveling expenses, office supplies and equipment . .	11,000 00	11,000 00
0802–01	For the settlement of certain claims, as provided by law, on account of damages by cars owned by the commonwealth and operated by state employees	8,000 00	8,000 00
0802–02	For the settlement of certain small claims, as authorized by section three A of chapter twelve of the General Laws . . .	3,000 00	3,000 00
	Totals	$148,660 00	$148,900 00
	Specials:		
0803–04	For expenses incidental to special litigation to recover certain bank deposits, as authorized by section forty-one of chapter one hundred and sixty-eight of the General Laws, to be in addition to any amount heretofore appropriated for the purpose . .	$3,000 00	
0803–06	(This item omitted.)		
	Service of the Department of Agriculture.		
0901–01	For the salary of the commissioner	$6,000 00	$6,000 00
0901–02	For personal services of clerks and stenographers, including not more than seventeen permanent positions	26,300 00	26,520 00
0901–03	For traveling expenses of the commissioner	700 00	700 00

Item		Appropriation Fiscal Year 1944.	Appropriation Fiscal Year 1945.
0901-04	For services other than personal, printing the annual report, office supplies and equipment, and printing and furnishing trespass posters	$5,100 00	$5,100 00
0901-11	For compensation and expenses of members of the advisory board	500 00	500 00
0901-21	For services and expenses of apiary inspection, including not more than one permanent position .	1,900 00	1,900 00
	Totals	$40,500 00	$40,720 00
	Division of Dairying and Animal Husbandry:		
0905-01	For personal services, including not more than five permanent positions	$13,860 00	$13,860 00
0905-02	For other expenses, including the enforcement of the dairy laws of the commonwealth . . .	4,800 00	4,800 00
0905-03	For administering the law relative to the inspection of barns and dairies by the department of agriculture, including not more than ten permanent positions .	29,400 00	29,500 00
	Totals	$48,060 00	$48,160 00
	Milk Control Board:		
0906-01	For personal services of members of the board and their employees, including not more than fifty-three permanent positions .	$114,380 00	$117,680 00
0906-02	For other administrative expenses of the board, including office expenses, rent, travel and special services	53,500 00	53,500 00
0906-03	For expenses in connection with certain activities conducted in co-operation with the federal government, as authorized by section twenty-three of chapter ninety-four A of the General Laws	7,500 00	7,500 00
	Totals	$175,380 00	$178,680 00
	Division of Livestock Disease Control:		
0907-01	For the salary of the director .	$4,000 00	$4,000 00
0907-02	For personal services of clerks and stenographers, including not more than eighteen permanent positions	24,600 00	25,000 00
0907-03	For services other than personal, including printing the annual report, traveling expenses of the director, office supplies and equipment, and rent . .	8,100 00	8,100 00

Item		Appropriation Fiscal Year 1944.	Appropriation Fiscal Year 1945.
0907-04	For personal services of veterinarians and agents engaged in the work of extermination of contagious diseases among domestic animals, including not more than twelve full-time permanent positions and not more than one hundred and twenty-five permanent intermittent positions	$51,360 00	$52,360 00
0907-05	For traveling expenses of veterinarians and agents . . .	8,000 00	8,000 00
0907-06	For reimbursement of owners of horses killed during the fiscal years nineteen hundred and forty-four and nineteen hundred and forty-five and previous years, travel, when allowed, of inspectors of animals, incidental expenses of killing and burial, quarantine and emergency services, and for laboratory and veterinary supplies and equipment	3,560 00	3,560 00
0907-07	For reimbursement of owners of tubercular cattle killed, including the payment of two claims of the previous years amounting to nine hundred seventy-nine dollars and fifty-three cents, as authorized by section twelve A of chapter one hundred and twenty-nine of the General Laws, and in accordance with certain provisions of law and agreements made under authority of section thirty-three of said chapter one hundred and twenty-nine during the years nineteen hundred and forty-four and nineteen hundred and forty-five and the previous year, to be in addition to any amount heretofore appropriated for the purpose; and any unexpended balance remaining at the end of either of the years nineteen hundred and forty-four and nineteen hundred and forty-five may be used in the succeeding year .	30,000 00	30,000 00
	Totals	$129,620 00	$131,020 00
	Reimbursement of towns for inspectors of animals:		
0907-08	For the reimbursement of certain towns for compensation paid to inspectors of animals . .	$5,200 00	$5,200 00
	Division of Markets:		
0908-01	For personal services, including not more than twelve permanent positions	$23,250 00	$23,550 00
0908-02	For other expenses . . .	5,700 00	5,700 00

Item		Appropriation Fiscal Year 1944.	Appropriation Fiscal Year 1945.
0908-03	For the cost of work of inspecting certain orchards within the commonwealth to provide for effective apple pest control	$1,700 00	$1,700 00
	Totals	$30,650 00	$30,950 00
	Division of Plant Pest Control and Fairs:		
0909-01	For personal services, including not more than four permanent positions	$11,070 00	$11,070 00
0909-02	For travel and other expenses	4,900 00	4,900 00
0909-11	For work in protecting the pine trees of the commonwealth from white pine blister rust, and for payments of claims on account of currant and gooseberry bushes destroyed in the work of suppressing white pine blister rust	5,000 00	5,000 00
0909-12	For quarantine and other expenses in connection with the work of suppression of the European corn borer, so-called, to be in addition to any amount heretofore appropriated for the purpose	2,000 00	2,000 00
0909-13	For quarantine and other expenses in connection with the work of suppression of the Japanese beetle, so-called	2,750 00	2,750 00
0909-14	For personal services and expenses in connection with the work of suppression of the Dutch elm disease, so-called	4,000 00	4,000 00
0909-21	For state prizes and agricultural exhibits including allotment of funds for the 4-H club activities, to be in addition to any amount heretofore appropriated for this purpose, and any unexpended balance remaining at the end of either of the years nineteen hundred and forty-four and nineteen hundred and forty-five may be used in the succeeding year	11,000 00	11,000 00
	Totals	$40,720 00	$40,720 00
	State Reclamation Board:		
0910-01	For expenses of the board, including not more than four permanent positions	$8,600 00	$8,600 00

Service of the Department of Conservation.

Item		Appropriation Fiscal Year 1944.	Appropriation Fiscal Year 1945.
	Administration:		
1001-01	For the salary of the commissioner	$6,000 00	$6,000 00
1001-02	For traveling expenses of the commissioner	400 00	400 00
1001-03	For services other than personal, including printing, supplies and equipment, and rent	6,500 00	6,500 00

Item		Appropriation Fiscal Year 1944.	Appropriation Fiscal Year 1945.
1001-04	For clerical and other assistance to the commissioner, including not more than twelve permanent positions	$32,548 00	$33,028 00
	Totals	$45,448 00	$45,928 00
	Division of Forestry:		
1002-01	For personal services of office assistants, including not more than four permanent positions . .	$6,180 00	$6,240 00
1002-02	For services other than personal, including printing the annual report, and for traveling expenses, necessary office supplies and equipment, and rent . .	2,800 00	2,800 00
1002-11	For aiding towns in the purchase of equipment for extinguishing forest fires and for making protective belts or zones as a defence against forest fires, for the fiscal years nineteen hundred and forty-four and nineteen hundred and forty-five and for previous years	1,500 00	1,500 00
1002-12	For personal services of the state fire warden and his assistants, and for other services, including traveling expenses of the state fire warden and his assistants, necessary supplies and equipment and materials used in new construction in the forest fire prevention service, including not more than thirteen permanent positions . . .	77,600 00	77,600 00
1002-14	For the expenses of forest fire patrol, as authorized by section twenty-eight A of chapter forty-eight of the General Laws .	6,800 00	6,800 00
1002-15	For reimbursement to certain towns, as authorized by section twenty-four of said chapter forty-eight	200 00	200 00
1002-16	For reimbursement of certain towns for part of the cost of certain forest fire patrol, as authorized by chapter six hundred and eighty-eight of the acts of nineteen hundred and forty-one	2,000 00	–
1002-21	For the development of state forests, including not more than twenty permanent positions, and including salaries and expenses of foresters and the cost of maintenance of such nurseries as may be necessary for the growing of seedlings for the planting of state forests, as authorized by sections one, six, nine and thirty to thirty-six, inclusive, of chapter one hundred and thirty-two of the General		

Item		Appropriation Fiscal Year 1944.	Appropriation Fiscal Year 1945.
	Laws, to be in addition to any amount heretofore appropriated for this purpose, and any unexpended balance remaining at the end of either of the years nineteen hundred and forty-four and nineteen hundred and forty-five may be used in the succeeding year	$117,300 00	$118,700 00
1002-31	For the suppression of the gypsy and brown tail moths, including not more than seven permanent positions, and for expenses incidental thereto, to be in addition to any amount heretofore appropriated for the purpose, and any unexpended balance remaining at the end of either of the years nineteen hundred and forty-four and nineteen hundred and forty-five may be used in the succeeding year	31,000 00	31,500 00
	Totals	$245,380 00	$245,340 00
	Special:		
1002-54	For payment to the federal government of one half of the proceeds of the sale of certain forest products, as provided by chapter ninety-four of the acts of nineteen hundred and forty-one	$4,137 43	
	Division of Fisheries and Game:		
	The comptroller is authorized to establish on the books of the commonwealth an account to record the excess, if any, of the aggregate amount of money received by the division of fisheries and game and the division of wildlife research and management in the department of conservation, during the period beginning December first, nineteen hundred and forty-two, and ending June thirtieth, nineteen hundred and forty-five, from license fees, fines and other sources, over the aggregate amount expended by or on account of said divisions during the same period. The amount so recorded shall be available for appropriation for expenditure by or on account of the said divisions during the next fiscal biennium.		
1004-01	For the salary of the director .	$5,000 00	$5,000 00
1004-02	For personal services of office assistants, including not more than ten permanent positions . .	17,700 00	18,000 00
1004-03	For services other than personal, including printing the annual report, traveling expenses and nec-		

Item		Appropriation Fiscal Year 1944.	Appropriation Fiscal Year 1945.
	essary office supplies and equipment, and rent	$5,400 00	$5,400 00
	Enforcement of laws:		
1004-11	For personal services of conservation officers, including not more than thirty-seven permanent positions	69,660 00	68,640 00
1004-12	For traveling expenses of conservation officers, and for other expenses necessary for the enforcement of the laws . . .	25,000 00	25,000 00
	Biological work:		
1004-21	For personal services to carry on biological work, including not more than one permanent position	2,760 00	2,880 00
1004-22	For traveling and other expenses of the biologist and his assistants	660 00	660 00
	Propagation of game birds, etc.:		
1004-31	For personal services of employees at game farms and fish hatcheries, including not more than seventeen permanent positions .	47,000 00	47,720 00
1004-32	For other maintenance expenses of game farms and fish hatcheries, and for the propagation of game birds and animals and food fish .	55,000 00	55,000 00
	Damages by wild deer and wild moose:		
1004-35	For the payment of damages caused by wild deer and wild moose, for the years nineteen hundred and forty-four and nineteen hundred and forty-five and for previous years, as provided by law	4,000 00	4,000 00
	Supervision of public fishing and hunting grounds:		
1004-41	For personal services . . .	2,280 00	2,280 00
1004-42	For other expenses . . .	1,000 00	1,000 00
	Specials:		
1004-44	For the purchase of fish and game	10,000 00	10,000 00
1004-46	For the cost of construction and improvement of certain fishways	1,000 00	1,000 00
1004-47	For consultants and other personal services, and for expenses, in connection with a biological survey of the streams and waters of the commonwealth to be made under the direction of the commissioner of conservation . .	8,000 00	8,000 00
	Totals	$254,460 00	$254,580 00
	Division of Wild Life Research and Management:		
1004-51	For personal services, including not more than three permanent positions	$1,410 00	$1,410 00

Item		Appropriation Fiscal Year 1944.	Appropriation Fiscal Year 1945.
1004-52	For other expenses	$1,500 00	$1,500 00
1004-53	For expenses of establishing and conducting co-operative wild life restoration projects, as authorized by chapter three hundred and ninety-two of the acts of nineteen hundred and thirty-eight, and federal funds received as reimbursements under this item are to be credited to the General Fund as income of the division of fisheries and game .	24,000 00	25,000 00
	Totals	$26,910 00	$27,910 00
	Division of Marine Fisheries:		
1004-70	For the salary of the director .	$5,000 00	$5,000 00
1004-71	For personal services, including not more than six permanent positions	13,140 00	13,380 00
1004-72	For services other than personal, traveling expenses, necessary office supplies and equipment, and rent	6,000 00	5,900 00
	Enforcement of shellfish and other marine fishery laws:		
1004-81	For personal services for the administration and enforcement of laws relative to shellfish and other marine fisheries, and for regulating the sale and cold storage of fresh food fish, including not more than sixteen permanent positions . . .	42,786 00	42,885 00
1004-82	For other expenses of the administration and enforcement of laws relative to shellfish and other marine fisheries and for regulating the sale and cold stórage of fresh food fish	11,100 00	10,300 00
1004-83	For expenses of purchasing lobsters, subject to the conditions imposed by section forty-three of chapter one hundred and thirty of the General Laws; provided, that the price paid for such lobsters shall not exceed the prevailing wholesale price for such lobsters in the district where purchased . . .	500 00	500 00
1004-84	For the cost of assisting coastal cities and towns in the propagation of shellfish through the purchase of shellfish seed, as authorized by section twenty of chapter one hundred and thirty of the General Laws . .	10,000 00	10,000 00
1004-85	For reimbursement to coastal cities and towns of a part of the cost of work done by them in the suppression of enemies of shellfish, as authorized by section		

Item		Appropriation Fiscal Year 1944.	Appropriation Fiscal Year 1945.
	twenty of chapter one hundred and thirty of the General Laws .	$5,000 00	$5,000 00
	Totals	$93,526 00	$92,965 00
	Special:		
1004-90	For services and expenses of the Atlantic States Marine Fisheries Commission, as authorized by chapter four hundred and eighty-nine of the acts of nineteen hundred and forty-one .	$3,800 00	$3,800 00
	Bounty on seals:		
1004-91	For bounties on seals	$100 00	$100 00
	Service of the Department of Banking and Insurance.		
	Division of Banks:		
1101-01	For the salary of the commissioner	$6,000 00	$6,000 00
1101-02	For services of deputy, directors, examiners and assistants, clerks, stenographers and experts, including not more than one hundred and thirty-five permanent positions	340,000 00	342,000 00
1101-03	For services other than personal, printing the annual report, traveling expenses, office supplies and equipment	60,000 00	60,000 00
	Totals	$406,000 00	$408,000 00
	Supervisor of Loan Agencies:		
1102-01	For personal services of supervisor and assistants, including not more than seven permanent positions	$13,800 00	$13,920 00
1102-02	For services other than personal, printing the annual report, office supplies and equipment . .	1,300 00	1,300 00
	Totals	$15,100 00	$15,220 00
	Division of Insurance:		
1103-01	For the salary of the commissioner	$6,000 00	$6,000 00
1103-02	For other personal services of the division, including expenses of the board of appeal and certain other costs of supervising motor vehicle liability insurance, and including not more than one hundred and fifty-nine permanent positions, partly chargeable to item 2970-02	268,000 00	273,000 00
1103-03	For other services, including printing the annual report, traveling expenses, necessary office supplies and equipment and rent of offices	78,000 00	78,000 00
	Totals	$352,000 00	$357,000 00

Item		Appropriation Fiscal Year 1944.	Appropriation Fiscal Year 1945.
	Board of Appeal on Fire Insurance Rates:		
1104-01	For expenses of the board . .	$100 00	$100 00
	Division of Savings Bank Life Insurance:		
1105-01	For personal services of officers and employees, including not more than twenty-nine permanent positions	$50,845 00	$52,405 00
1105-02	For services other than personal, printing the annual report, traveling expenses, rent and equipment	16,300 00	16,500 00
	Totals	$67,145 00	$68,905 00

Service of the Department of Corporations and Taxation.

Item		Appropriation Fiscal Year 1944.	Appropriation Fiscal Year 1945.
	Corporations and Tax Divisions:		
1201-01	For the salary of the commissioner	$7,500 00	$7,500 00
1201-02	For the salaries of certain positions filled by the commissioner, with the approval of the governor and council, and for additional clerical and other assistance, including not more than one hundred and twenty-six permanent positions, partly chargeable to item 2970-03; and it is hereby further provided that the sum of fifty thousand dollars, which represents the estimated annual cost of collection of alcoholic beverages taxes, so-called, and which is hereby included in these appropriations for each of the years nineteen hundred and forty-four and nineteen hundred and forty-five, shall be transferred to the General Fund from fees collected under section twenty-seven of chapter one hundred and thirty-eight of the General Laws .	211,820 00	212,280 00
1201-03	For other services, necessary office supplies and equipment, travel, and for printing the annual report, other publications and valuation books	45,000 00	45,000 00
1201-04	(This item combined with item 1201-03.)		
	Totals	$264,320 00	$264,780 00
	Reimbursement for loss of taxes:		
1201-05	For reimbursing cities and towns for loss of taxes on land used for state institutions and certain other state activities, as certified by the commissioner of corporations and taxation for the calendar years nineteen hundred and forty-three and nineteen hundred and forty-four . .	$163,019 32	$165,000 00

Item		Appropriation Fiscal Year 1944.	Appropriation Fiscal Year 1945.
	Administration of cigarette taxes:		
1201-11	For personal services for the administration of certain laws levying the cigarette taxes, so-called, including not more than thirty-six permanent positions .	$62,460 00	$64,740 00
1201-12	For expenses other than personal services for the administration of certain laws levying the cigarette taxes, so-called . .	19,400 00	19,400 00
	Totals	$81,860 00	$84,140 00
	Excise upon charges for meals (the following two items shall be payable from amounts collected under chapter 64B of the General Laws):		
1201-21	For personal services of the director, assistant director, and other necessary employees for the administration of an excise on meals, including not more than thirty-two permanent positions .	$52,380 00	$54,660 00
1201-22	For expenses other than personal services for the administration of an excise on meals, as provided by chapter sixty-four B of the General Laws . .	13,300 00	13,300 00
	Totals	$65,680 00	$67,960 00
1201-28	(This item omitted.)		
	Income Tax Division (the three following appropriations are to be made from the receipts from the income tax):		
1202-01	For personal services of the director, assistant director, assessors, deputy assessors, clerks, stenographers and other necessary assistants, including not more than two hundred and sixty-three permanent positions . .	$517,820 00	$520,000 00
1202-02	For services other than personal, and for traveling expenses, office supplies and equipment, and rent.	175,000 00	175,000 00
1202-21	For expenses in connection with certain bonds filed in the state of Texas, and for legal fees in connection with certain suits to recover judgment against Edgar B. Davis in relation to an unpaid income tax, to be in addition to any amount heretofore appropriated for the purpose . .	35,551 34	25,551 34
	Totals	$728,371 34	$720,551 34

Item		Appropriation Fiscal Year 1944.	Appropriation Fiscal Year 1945.
	Division of Accounts:		
1203-01	For personal services, including not more than one hundred and ten permanent positions partly chargeable to item 1203-11 .	$105,000 00	$106,000 00
1203-02	For other expenses	10,800 00	10,000 00
1203-11	For services and expenses of auditing and installing systems of municipal accounts, the cost of which is to be assessed upon the municipalities for which the work is done	226,240 00	230,870 00
1203-12	For the expenses of certain books, forms and other material, which may be sold to cities and towns requiring the same for maintaining their system of accounts .	24,000 00	24,000 00
1203-21	For the administrative expenses of the county personnel board, including not more than five permanent positions . .	7,900 00	7,720 00
	Totals	$373,940 00	$378,590 00
	Appellate Tax Board:		
1204-01	For personal services of the members of the board and employees, including not more than twenty-five permanent positions . .	$86,540 00	$86,900 00
1204-02	For services other than personal, traveling expenses, office supplies and equipment, and rent .	24,500 00	24,500 00
	Totals	$111,040 00	$111,400 00

Service of the Department of Education.

Item		Appropriation Fiscal Year 1944.	Appropriation Fiscal Year 1945.
1301-01	For the salary of the commissioner	$9,000 00	$9,000 00
1301-02	For personal services of officers, agents, clerks, stenographers and other assistants, including not more than forty-nine permanent positions, but not including those employed in university extension work	131,000 00	132,000 00
1301-03	For traveling expenses of members of the advisory board and of agents and employees when required to travel in discharge of their duties	4,000 00	4,000 00
1301-04	For services other than personal, necessary office supplies, and for printing the annual report and bulletins as provided by law .	11,400 00	11,400 00
1301-05	For expenses incidental to furnishing school committees with rules for testing the sight and hearing of pupils	200 00	200 00
1301-06	For printing school registers and other school blanks for cities and towns	2,000 00	2,000 00
1301-07	For expenses of holding teachers' institutes	1,000 00	1,000 00

Item		Appropriation Fiscal Year 1944.	Appropriation Fiscal Year 1945.
1301-08	For aid to certain pupils in state teachers' colleges, under the direction of the department of education	$5,000 00	$5,000 00
1301-09	For assistance to children of certain war veterans, for the years nineteen hundred and forty-four and nineteen hundred and forty-five and for previous years, as authorized by chapter two hundred and sixty-three of the acts of nineteen hundred and thirty, as amended	10,000 00	10,000 00
1301-10	For the maintenance and operation of the state building on Newbury Street, Boston, including not more than four permanent positions	17,000 00	17,180 00
	Totals	$190,600 00	$191,780 00
	Specials:		
1301-11	(This item omitted.)		
1301-12	For the cost of interior painting and refinishing at the state building on Newbury Street, Boston, and the amount appropriated for the year nineteen hundred and forty-five is in addition to the amount appropriated for the year nineteen hundred and forty-four for the same purpose	$1,000 00	$1,000 00
1301-13	For certain repairs to the roof of the state building on Newbury Street, Boston, and the amount appropriated for the year nineteen hundred and forty-five is in addition to the amount appropriated for the year nineteen hundred and forty-four for the same purpose	1,000 00	1,000 00
1301-26	For the cost of preparation, printing and distribution of courses of study for elementary grades in certain subjects, including science	4,500 00	–
	Totals	$6,500 00	$2,000 00
	Division of Vocational Education:		
1301-30	For aid to certain persons receiving instruction in the courses for vocational rehabilitation, as authorized by section twenty-two B of chapter seventy-four of the General Laws	$2,500 00	$2,500 00
1301-31	For the training of teachers for vocational schools, to comply with the requirement of federal authorities under the provisions of the Smith-Hughes act,		

Item		Appropriation Fiscal Year 1944.	Appropriation Fiscal Year 1945.
	so called, including not more than twenty permanent positions	$29,775 00	$30,470 00
1301-32	For the expenses of promotion of vocational rehabilitation in co-operation with the federal government, including not more than sixteen permanent positions	41,000 00	41,000 00
	Totals	$73,275 00	$73,970 00
	Education of deaf and blind pupils:		
1301-41	For the education of deaf and blind pupils of the commonwealth, as provided by section twenty-six of chapter sixty-nine of the General Laws	$425,000 00	$425,000 00
	Reimbursement and aid:		
1301-51	For assisting small towns in providing themselves with school superintendents, as provided by law	$96,500 00	$96,500 00
1301-52	For the reimbursement of certain towns for the payment of tuition of pupils attending high schools outside the towns in which they reside, as provided by law	195,000 00	195,000 00
1301-53	For the reimbursement of certain towns for the transportation of pupils attending high schools outside the towns in which they reside, as provided by law	210,000 00	210,000 00
1301-54	For the reimbursement of certain cities and towns for a part of the expenses of maintaining agricultural and industrial vocational schools, as provided by law; provided, that a sum not exceeding fifty-six hundred seventeen dollars and thirty-nine cents may be paid in the year nineteen hundred and forty-four to the city of Revere as reimbursement on account of expenses of said city prior to the year nineteen hundred and forty-two	1,829,293 90	1,900,000 00
1301-55	For reimbursement of certain cities and towns for adult English-speaking classes	78,000 00	78,000 00
	Totals	$2,408,793 90	$2,479,500 00
	University Extension Courses:		
1301-61	For personal services, including not more than forty-three permanent positions	$150,640 00	$151,960 00
1301-62	For other expenses	28,500 00	28,500 00
	Totals	$179,140 00	$180,460 00

Item		Appropriation Fiscal Year 1944.	Appropriation Fiscal Year 1945.
	English-speaking Classes for Adults:		
1301-64	For personal services of administration, including not more than four permanent positions . .	$11,700 00	$11,760 00
1301-65	For other expenses of administration	2,000 00	2,000 00
	Totals	$13,700 00	$13,760 00
	Division of Immigration and Americanization:		
1302-01	For personal services, including not more than nineteen permanent positions	$36,780 00	$37,140 00
1302-02	For other expenses . . .	7,500 00	7,500 00
	Totals	$44,280 00	$44,640 00
	Division of Public Libraries:		
1303-01	For personal services of regular agents and other assistants, including not more than eight permanent positions	$17,240 00	$17,720 00
1303-02	For other services, including printing the annual report, traveling expenses, necessary office supplies and expenses incidental to the aiding of public libraries .	11,000 00	11,000 00
	Totals	$28,240 00	$28,720 00
	Division of the Blind:		
1304-01	For general administration, furnishing information, industrial and educational aid, and for carrying out certain provisions of the laws establishing said division, including not more than twenty-two permanent positions	$50,500 00	$51,500 00
1304-03	(See items 1304-11 and 1304-12.)		
1304-04	(See items 1304-13, 1304-14, and 1304-15.)		
1304-05	(See items 1304-16 and 1304-17.)		
1304-06	For instruction of the adult blind in their homes, including not more than fourteen permanent positions	19,500 00	19,500 00
1304-07	(See item 1304-27.)		
1304-08	For aiding the adult blind, subject to the conditions provided by law	200,000 00	200,000 00
1304-10	For expenses of administering and operating the services of piano tuning and mattress renovating under section twenty-five of chapter sixty-nine of the General Laws	20,000 00	20,000 00
1304-11	For personal services and other expenses in connection with the operation of local shops, including not more than nine permanent positions, but excluding the purchase of merchandise and payments to blind employees .	18,500 00	18,500 00

Item		Appropriation Fiscal Year 1944.	Appropriation Fiscal Year 1945.
1304-12	For the purchase of merchandise and payments to blind employees in connection with the operation of local shops	$52,500 00	$52,500 00
1304-13	For personal services and other expenses in connection with the operation of the Woolson House industries, including not more than two permanent positions, but excluding the purchase of merchandise and payments to blind persons	8,000 00	8,000 00
1304-14	For the purchase of merchandise and payments to blind employees in connection with the Woolson House industries . .	43,000 00	43,000 00
1304-15	For the operation of the salesroom and other expenses in connection with the sale of materials made by blind persons, including not more than two permanent positions	20,000 00	20,000 00
1304-16	For personal services and other expenses in connection with the operation of certain industries for men, including not more than five permanent positions, but excluding the purchase of merchandise and payments to blind persons	20,000 00	20,000 00
1304-17	For the purchase of merchandise and payments to blind employees in connection with certain industries for men . . .	143,000 00	143,000 00
	Reimbursement:		
1304-27	For expenses of providing sight-saving classes, with the approval of said division . . .	21,000 00	21,000 00
	Totals	$616,000 00	$617,000 00
	Teachers' Retirement Board:		
1305-01	For personal services of employees, including not more than nine permanent positions . .	$15,900 00	$16,100 00
1305-02	For services other than personal, including printing the annual report, traveling expenses, office supplies and equipment, and rent	6,000 00	5,400 00
1305-03	For payment of pensions to retired teachers	1,840,000 00	1,930,000 00
1305-05	For the reimbursement by the state treasurer of the surplus interest account of the teachers' retirement fund in each of the years nineteen hundred and forty-four and nineteen hundred and forty-five, the sum of one hundred thousand dollars on account of deficits in the annuity fund paid from surplus interest during the calendar years nineteen hundred		

Item		Appropriation Fiscal Year 1944.	Appropriation Fiscal Year 1945.
	and forty, nineteen hundred and forty-one and nineteen hundred and forty-two, and the teachers' retirement board is hereby authorized and directed to transfer from any surplus interest account to the annuity reserve fund an amount necessary to meet any deficiencies in the annuity reserve fund during the calendar years nineteen hundred and forty-three and nineteen hundred and forty-four, notwithstanding the provisions of paragraph two of section nine of chapter thirty-two of the General Laws .	$100,000 00	$100,000 00
1305-06	For the payment of retirement assessments of teachers formerly in military or naval service, as authorized by section nine of chapter seven hundred and eight of the acts of nineteen hundred and forty-one	59 83	100 00
	Reimbursement:		
1305-04	For reimbursement of certain cities and towns for pensions to retired teachers	381,049 83	400,000 00
	Totals	$2,343,009 66	$2.451,600 00
	Massachusetts Maritime Academy:		
1306-01	For personal services of the secretary and office assistants, including not more than three permanent positions . . .	$5,640 00	$6,000 00
1306-02	For services other than regular clerical services, including printing the annual report, rent, office supplies and equipment . .	2,400 00	2,400 00
1306-10	For the maintenance of the academy and ship, including not more than thirty-two permanent positions	94,820 00	99,520 00
	Totals	$102,860 00	$107,920 00
	For the maintenance of and for certain improvements at the following state teachers' colleges, and the boarding halls attached thereto, with the approval of the commissioner of education; provided, that, if in the opinion of said commissioner, the continued operation of any state teachers' college is impractical because of a decline in enrollment or other condition arising from the present war emergency, said commissioner, with the approval of the governor, may		

Item		Appropriation Fiscal Year 1944.	Appropriation Fiscal Year 1945.
	temporarily suspend operation of said college and make satisfactory provision elsewhere for the pupils of said college:		
1307-00	State teachers' college at Bridgewater, including not more than fifty-nine permanent positions .	$152,190 00	$152,350 00
1307-21	State teachers' college at Bridgewater, boarding hall, including not more than twenty-nine permanent positions	55,200 00	55,200 00
1308-00	State teachers' college at Fitchburg, including not more than fifty-seven permanent positions	177,980 00	178,670 00
1308-21	State teachers' college at Fitchburg, boarding hall, including not more than nine permanent positions	37,200 00	37,200 00
1308-32	For renovation of electric wiring in Palmer Hall at the state teachers' college at Fitchburg . .	3,500 00	
1308-33	For the cost of painting at the state teachers' college at Fitchburg .	5,000 00	
1309-00	State teachers' college at Framingham, including not more than sixty-one permanent positions .	164,964 00	163,374 00
1309-21	State teachers' college at Framingham, boarding hall, including not more than twenty-five permanent positions . . .	53,700 00	54,100 00
1309-31	For the cost of replacing certain floors in Horace Mann Hall at the state teachers' college at Framingham	750 00	
1309-32	(This item included under item 1309-00, Repairs and Renewals.)		
1310-00	State teachers' college at Hyannis, including not more than twenty-nine permanent positions .	64,138 00	65,328 00
1310-21	State teachers' college at Hyannis, boarding hall, including not more than three permanent positions .	10,000 00	10,000 00
1310-35	For the cost of relining certain boilers at the state teachers' college at Hyannis . . .	2,500 00	
1311-00	State teachers' college at Lowell, including not more than thirty-eight permanent positions .	79,018 00	77,650 00
1312-00	State teachers' college at North Adams, including not more than twenty-eight permanent positions	65,965 00	66,235 00
1312-21	State teachers' college at North Adams, boarding hall, including not more than four permanent positions	10,000 00	10,120 00
1313-00	State teachers' college at Salem, including not more than fifty-one permanent positions . .	126,800 00	126,920 00
1313-31	For the cost of replacing two flagpoles at the state teachers' college at Salem . . .	880 00	

Item		Appropriation Fiscal Year 1944.	Appropriation Fiscal Year 1945.
1313-32	(This item included under item 1313-00, Repairs and Renewals.)		
1314-00	State teachers' college at Westfield, including not more than thirty-four permanent positions	$64,525 00	$64,945 00
1314-21	State teachers' college at Westfield, boarding hall, including not more than one permanent position	1,650 00	1,650 00
1314-32	State teachers' college at Westfield, personal services and expenses of boarding hall for army signal corps trainees, to be in addition to any amount heretofore appropriated for the purpose	74,090 00	75,310 00
1315-00	State teachers' college at Worcester, including not more than forty-one permanent positions	90,810 00	92,050 00
1315-31	For the cost of certain exterior painting at the state teachers' college at Worcester . .	500 00	–
1321-00	Massachusetts School of Art, including not more than thirty-one permanent positions . .	78,950 00	79,340 00
	Totals	$1,320,310 00	$1,310,442 00
	Textile Schools:		
1331-00	For the maintenance of the Bradford Durfee textile school of Fall River, with the approval of the commissioner of education and the trustees, including not more than twenty-one permanent positions, and including the sum of ten thousand dollars which is to be assessed upon the city of Fall River as a part of the state tax for each of the calendar years nineteen hundred and forty-three and nineteen hundred and forty-four	$65,700 00	$66,200 00
1332-00	For the maintenance of the Lowell textile institute, with the approval of the commissioner of education and the trustees, including not more than sixty-one permanent positions, and including the sum of ten thousand dollars which is to be assessed upon the city of Lowell as a part of the state tax for each of the calendar years nineteen hundred and forty-three and nineteen hundred and forty-four . .	179,965 00	180,465 00
1333-00	For the maintenance of the New Bedford textile school, with the approval of the commissioner of education and the trustees, including not more than twenty-four permanent positions, and in-		

Item		Appropriation Fiscal Year 1944.	Appropriation Fiscal Year 1945.
	cluding the sum of ten thousand dollars which is to be assessed upon the city of New Bedford as a part of the state tax for each of the calendar years nineteen hundred and forty-three and nineteen hundred and forty-four	$65,375 00	$64,975 00
	Totals	$311,040 00	$311,640 00
	Massachusetts State College:		
1341-00	For maintenance and current expenses of the Massachusetts state college, with the approval of the trustees, including not more than four hundred and eighty-one permanent positions .	$1,165,871 00	$1,161,891 00
1341-01	For personal services and expenses of the summer session, and the amount hereby appropriated for the year nineteen hundred and forty-four is in addition to sums heretofore made available for this purpose	7,067 00	12,950 00
1341-77	For personal services for the maintenance of the boarding hall, including not more than thirty permanent positions . .	40,000 00	40,000 00
1341-78	For other expenses of the maintenance of the boarding hall .	75,000 00	75,000 00
1341-82	For aid to certain students, with the approval of the trustees .	5,000 00	5,000 00
1341-83	For the cost of field and laboratory work in connection with the Dutch elm disease and other shade tree diseases and insects .	5,000 0	5,000 00
1341-91	For repointing and repairing the exterior walls of South College administration building . .	5,000 00	
1341-92	For the annual cost of lease of dormitories, as authorized by chapter three hundred and eighty-eight of the acts of nineteen hundred and thirty-nine . .	30,000 00	30,000 00
1341-93	For payment of annual charges for sewage service by the town of Amherst	2,000 00	2,000 00
1341-98	For certain repairs to the power plant	2,000 00	-
	Totals	$1,336,938 00	$1,331,841 00

Service of the Department of Civil Service and Registration.

Item		Appropriation Fiscal Year 1944.	Appropriation Fiscal Year 1945.
	Division of Civil Service:		
1402-01	For the salary of the director and for the compensation of members of the commission . .	$12,500 00	$12,500 00
1402-02	For other personal services of the division, including not more than one hundred and ten permanent positions . . .	173,660 00	173,880 00

Item		Appropriation Fiscal Year 1944.	Appropriation Fiscal Year 1945.
1402-03	For other services and for printing the annual report, and for office supplies and equipment necessary for the administration of the civil service law	$37,100 00	$34,800 00
	Totals	$223,260 00	$221,180 00
	Division of Registration:		
1403-01	For the salary of the director	$2,400 00	$2,400 00
1403-02	For clerical and certain other personal services of the division, including not more than thirty-eight permanent positions	69,560 00	70,560 00
1403-03	For services of the division other than personal, printing the annual reports, office supplies and equipment, except as otherwise provided	18,000 00	18,200 00
	Totals	$89,960 00	$91,160 00
	Board of Registration in Medicine:		
1404-01	For personal services of the members of the board, including not more than seven permanent positions	$6,300 00	$6,300 00
1404-03	For traveling expenses	500 00	500 00
	Totals	$6,800 00	$6,800 00
	Board of Dental Examiners:		
1405-01	For personal services of the members of the board, including not more than five permanent positions	$3,800 00	$3,800 00
1405-02	For traveling expenses	700 00	700 00
1405-03	For travel and other expenses necessary in providing for the enforcement of law relative to the registration of dentists	100 00	100 00
	Totals	$4,600 00	$4,600 00
	Board of Registration in Chiropody:		
1406-01	For personal services of members of the board, including not more than five permanent positions	$900 00	$900 00
1406-02	For traveling expenses	300 00	300 00
	Totals	$1,200 00	$1,200 00
	Board of Registration in Pharmacy:		
1407-01	For personal services of the members of the board, including not more than five permanent positions	$4,300 00	$4,300 00
1407-02	For personal services of agents and investigators, including not more than four permanent positions	8,760 00	9,120 00
1407-03	For traveling expenses	3,500 00	3,500 00
	Totals	$16,560 00	$16,920 00

Item		Appropriation Fiscal Year 1944.	Appropriation Fiscal Year 1945.
	Board of Registration of Nurses:		
1408-01	For personal services of the members of the board, and of the appointive members of the approving authority, including not more than ten permanent positions	$3,570 00	$3,570 00
1408-02	For traveling expenses . .	700 00	700 00
	Totals	$4,270 00	$4,270 00
	Board of Registration in Embalming and Funeral Directing:		
1409-01	For personal services of members of the board, including not more than three permanent positions .	$1,500 00	$1,500 00
1409-02	For traveling expenses . .	2,000 00	2,000 00
1409-03	For the dissemination of useful knowledge among and for the benefit of licensed embalmers .	100 00	100 00
	Totals	$3,600 00	$3,600 00
	Board of Registration in Optometry:		
1410-01	For personal services of members of the board, including not more than five permanent positions .	$1,900 00	$1,900 00
1410-02	For traveling expenses . .	400 00	400 00
	Totals	$2,300 00	$2,300 00
	Board of Registration in Veterinary Medicine:		
1411-01	For personal services of members of the board, including not more than five permanent positions .	$600 00	$600 00
1411-02	For other services, printing the annual report, traveling expenses, office supplies and equipment .	275 00	275 00
	Totals	$875 00	$875 00
	Board of Registration of Professional Engineers and of Land Surveyors:		
1412-01	For personal services and other expenses, including travel . .	$2,100 00	$2,100 00
	Board of Registration of Architects:		
1413-01	For personal services of members of the board, including not more than five permanent positions .	$2,500 00	$2,500 00
1413-02	For travel and other necessary expenses	900 00	900 00
	Totals	$3,400 00	$3,400 00
	Board of Registration of Public Accountants:		
1414-01	For personal services of members of the board, including not more than five permanent positions .	$675 00	$675 00

Item		Appropriation Fiscal Year 1944.	Appropriation Fiscal Year 1945.
1414–02	For expenses of examinations, including the preparation and marking of papers, and for other expenses	$2,000 00	$2,000 00
	Totals	$2,675 00	$2,675 00
	State Examiners of Electricians:		
1416–01	For personal services of members of the board, including not more than two permanent positions	$1,000 00	$1,000 00
1416–02	For traveling expenses	4,000 00	4,000 00
	Totals	$5,000 00	$5,000 00
	State Examiners of Plumbers:		
1417–01	For personal services of members of the board, including not more than three permanent positions	$1,100 00	$1,100 00
1417–02	For traveling expenses	1,500 00	1,500 00
	Totals	$2,600 00	$2,600 00
	Board of Registration of Barbers:		
1420–01	For personal services of members of the board and assistants, including not more than eight permanent positions	$16,700 00	$16,700 00
1420–02	For travel and other necessary expenses, including rent	6,000 00	6,000 00
	Totals	$22,700 00	$22,700 00
	Board of Registration of Hairdressers:		
1421–01	For personal services of members of the board and assistants, including not more than eighteen permanent positions	$29,715 00	$30,075 00
1421–02	For travel and other necessary expenses, including rent	9,500 00	9,500 00
	Totals	$39,215 00	$39,575 00
	Service of the Department of Industrial Accidents.		
1501–01	For personal services of members of the board, including not more than seven permanent positions	$42,500 00	$42,500 00
1501–02	For personal services of secretaries, inspectors, clerks and office assistants, including not more than eighty-seven permanent positions	158,000 00	160,000 00
1501–03	For traveling expenses	6,300 00	6,300 00
1501–04	For other services, printing the annual report, necessary office supplies and equipment	14,100 00	14,100 00
1501–05	For expenses of impartial examinations, and for expenses of industrial disease referees, as authorized by section nine B of chapter one hundred and fifty-two of the General Laws	25,000 00	25,000 00
	Totals	$245,900 00	$247,900 00

Item		Appropriation Fiscal Year 1944.	Appropriation Fiscal Year 1945.
	Service of the Department of Labor and Industries.		
1601-01	For the salaries of the commissioner, assistant and associate commissioners, including not more than five permanent positions	$23,500 00	$23,500 00
1601-02	For clerical and other assistance to the commissioner, including not more than five permanent positions	6,360 00	6,480 00
1601-11	For personal services for the inspectional service, including not more than sixty-nine permanent positions, and for traveling expenses of the commissioner, assistant commissioner, associate commissioners and inspectors of labor, and for services other than personal, printing the annual report, rent of district offices, and office supplies and equipment for the inspectional service .	175,000 00	176,000 00
1601-31	For personal services for the division of occupational hygiene, including not more than six permanent positions	14,040 00	14,520 00
1601-32	For services other than personal, traveling expenses, office and laboratory supplies and equipment, and rent, for the division of occupational hygiene . .	5,000 00	5,000 00
1601-41	For personal services for the statistical service, including not more than thirty-five permanent positions, and for services other than personal, printing report and publications, traveling expenses and office supplies and equipment for the statistical service .	71,300 00	72,000 00
1601-51	For personal services for the division on necessaries of life, including not more than five permanent positions	10,620 00	10,620 00
1601-52	For services other than personal, traveling expenses, office supplies and equipment for the division on necessaries of life . .	1,200 00	1,200 00
1601-53	For personal services in administering sections two hundred and ninety-five A to two hundred and ninety-five O, inclusive, of chapter ninety-four of the General Laws, relating to the advertising and sale of motor fuel at retail, including not more than twelve permanent positions .	23,160 00	24,300 00
1601-54	For other expenses in administering said sections two hundred and ninety-five A to two hundred and ninety-five O, inclusive	7,500 00	7,500 00
1601-61	For clerical and other assistance for the board of conciliation and		

Item		Appropriation Fiscal Year 1944.	Appropriation Fiscal Year 1945.
	arbitration, including not more than seven permanent positions	$27,180 00	$27,180 00
1601-62	For other services, printing, traveling expenses and office supplies and equipment for the board of conciliation and arbitration .	4,500 00	4,500 00
1601-71	For personal services of investigators, clerks and stenographers for the minimum wage service, including not more than nineteen permanent positions .	32,520 00	33,720 00
1601-72	For services other than personal, printing, traveling expenses and office supplies and equipment for minimum wage service . .	3,250 00	3,250 00
1601-73	For compensation and expenses of wage boards	1,750 00	1,750 00
1601-81	For personal services for the division of standards, including not more than seventeen permanent positions	33,000 00	33,540 00
1601-82	For other services, printing, traveling expenses and office supplies and equipment for the division of standards	9,500 00	9,500 00
	Totals	$449,380 00	$454,560 00
	Massachusetts Development and Industrial Commission:		
1603-01	For personal services of employees, including not more than five permanent positions . . .	$13,520 00	$13,760 00
1603-02	For administrative expenses, including office rent and other incidental expenses, and for the promotion and development of the industrial, agricultural and recreational resources of the commonwealth . . .	18,900 00	18,800 00
	Totals	$32,420 00	$32,560 00
	Labor Relations Commission:		
1604-01	For personal services of the commissioners and employees, including not more than twenty permanent positions . . .	$54,350 00	$55,070 00
1604-02	For administrative expenses, including office rent . . .	7,220 00	7,220 00
	Totals	$61,570 00	$62,290 00
	Division of Apprentice Training:		
1605-01	For personal services of the members of the apprenticeship council and clerical and other assistants, as authorized by sections eleven E to eleven L, inclusive, of chapter twenty-three of the General Laws, including not more than eight permanent positions	$2,820 00	$2,940 00

Item		Appropriation Fiscal Year 1944.	Appropriation Fiscal Year 1945.
1605–02	For other expenses, including travel, as authorized by sections eleven E to eleven L, inclusive, of chapter twenty-three of the General Laws . . .	$1,150 00	$1,050 00
	Totals	$3,970 00	$3,990 00

Service of the Department of Mental Health.

Item		Appropriation Fiscal Year 1944.	Appropriation Fiscal Year 1945.
1701–01	For the salary of the commissioner	$10,000 00	$10,000 00
1701–02	For personal services of officers and employees, including not more than eighty-two permanent positions . . .	158,000 00	160,000 00
1701–03	For transportation and medical examination of state charges under its charge for the years nineteen hundred and forty-four and nineteen hundred and forty-five and for previous years .	3,500 00	3,500 00
1701–04	For other services, including printing the annual report, traveling expenses, office supplies and equipment, and rent . .	38,000 00	38,000 00
1701–11	For the support of state charges in the Hospital Cottages for Children	26,000 00	26,000 00
	Totals	$235,500 00	$237,500 00
	Division of Mental Hygiene:		
1702–00	For expenses, including not more than fifty-seven permanent positions, of investigating the nature, causes and results of mental diseases and defects and the publication of the results thereof, and of what further preventive or other measures might be taken and what further expenditures for investigation might be made which would give promise of decreasing the number of persons afflicted with mental diseases or defects	$117,560 00	$119,780 00
	Special:		
1702–21	For the cost of boarding certain feeble-minded persons in private homes	$5,000 00	$5,000 00

For the maintenance of and for certain improvements at the following institutions under the control of the Department of Mental Health; provided, that from the amounts herein appropriated for the year nineteen hundred and forty-four sums not exceeding three thousand one hundred and four dollars shall be paid to certain employees as compensation in lieu of vacations

Item		Appropriation Fiscal Year 1944.	Appropriation Fiscal Year 1945.
	which they did not receive in the year nineteen hundred and forty-two:		
1710–00	Boston psychopathic hospital, including not more than one hundred and fifty-six permanent positions	$261,985 00	$260,790 00
1711–00	Boston state hospital, including not more than seven hundred and thirty-two permanent positions	1,107,930 00	1,097,580 00
1711–26	For the cost of painting a certain iron fence at the Boston state hospital	6,800 00	
1712–00	Danvers state hospital, including not more than five hundred and fifty-seven permanent positions	1,010,640 00	1,006,250 00
1713–00	Foxborough state hospital, including not more than three hundred and forty-eight permanent positions	619,260 00	616,360 00
1713–25	For the cost of completing the installation of a certain hydrotherapeutic suite in E building at the Foxborough state hospital	800 00	
1714–00	Gardner state hospital, including not more than three hundred and thirty-seven permanent positions	639,721 00	638,228 00
1715–00	Grafton state hospital, including not more than four hundred and sixty-four permanent positions	752,050 00	747,060 00
1715–24	For the cost of replacing certain wooden floors in the Pines B building at the Grafton state hospital	2,500 00	
1715–27	The unexpended balance of the amount appropriated by item 1715–27 of chapter 419 of the acts of nineteen hundred and forty-one, for certain improvements to drainage of the sewer beds at the Grafton state hospital, is hereby reappropriated.		
1716–00	Medfield state hospital, including not more than four hundred and eighty permanent positions .	778,520 00	776,140 00
1716–22	For the purchase of beds for the Medfield state hospital, to be in addition to any amounts heretofore appropriated for the purpose	2,000 00	2,000 00
1716–28	For the cost of certain reconstruction work in connection with the bakery and kitchen elevators at Medfield state hospital .	6,000 00	
1717–00	Metropolitan state hospital, including not more than four hundred and seventeen permanent positions	786,855 00	784,640 00
1718–00	Northampton state hospital, including not more than four hundred and eighty-one permanent positions	796,692 00	796,860 00

Item		Appropriation Fiscal Year 1944.	Appropriation Fiscal Year 1945.
1719–00	Taunton state hospital, including not more than four hundred and seventy-three permanent positions	$750,855 00	$747,755 00
1720–00	Westborough state hospital, including not more than four hundred and twenty-four permanent positions . . .	743,665 00	739,485 00
1721–00	Worcester state hospital, including not more than six hundred and thirty-four permanent positions	1,111,610 00	1,106,835 00
1721–22	The unexpended balance of the appropriation made by item 1721–22 of chapter four hundred and nineteen of the acts of nineteen hundred and forty-one, for the purchase and installation of certain laundry machinery at the Worcester state hospital, is hereby reappropriated.		
1721–23	The unexpended balance of the appropriation made by item 1721–23 of chapter four hundred and nineteen of the acts of nineteen hundred and forty-one, for the purchase and installation of certain kitchen equipment at the Worcester state hospital, is hereby reappropriated.		
1721–27	For the purchase of beds for the Worcester state hospital . .	3,000 00	
1721–28	For the cost of certain painting at the main hospital of the Worcester state hospital, and the amount appropriated for the year nineteen hundred and forty-five is in addition to the amount appropriated for the year nineteen hundred and forty-four for the same purpose . . .	10,000 00	10,000 00
1721–29	For the cost of certain repairs to roofs at the Worcester State hospital	7,500 00	
1722–00	Monson state hospital, including not more than four hundred and nineteen permanent positions .	753,074 00	750,906 00
1723–00	Belchertown state school, including not more than three hundred and two permanent positions .	554,290 00	545,240 00
1724–00	Walter E. Fernald state school, including not more than four hundred and sixty-eight permanent positions	830,741 00	830,651 00
1725–00	Wrentham state school, including not more than four hundred and nine permanent positions .	701,300 00	700,300 00
	Totals . . .	$12,237,788 00	$12,157,080 00

Item		Appropriation Fiscal Year 1944.	Appropriation Fiscal Year 1945.
	Service of the Department of Correction.		
1801-01	For the salary of the commissioner	$6,000 00	$6,000 00
1801-02	For personal services of deputies, agents, clerks and stenographers, including not more than twenty-one permanent positions . .	41,760 00	42,120 00
1801-03	For services other than personal, necessary office supplies and equipment	4,800 00	4,800 00
1801-04	For traveling expenses of officers and employees of the department, when required to travel in the discharge of their duties .	1,000 00	1,000 00
1801-05	For the removal of prisoners, to and from state institutions .	7,000 00	7,000 00
1801-07	For the expense of the service of the central index	1,000 00	1,000 00
	Totals	$61,560 00	$61,920 00
	Division of Classification of Prisoners:		
1801-08	For expenses of the division hereby authorized, including not more than eight permanent positions; provided, that the persons employed hereunder shall not be subject to civil service laws or the rules and regulations made thereunder	$22,040 00	$22,460 00
	Parole Board:		
1801-21	For personal services of the parole board and advisory board of pardons, agents, clerical and other employees, including not more than forty-one permanent positions	$94,395 00	$95,175 00
1801-22	For services other than personal, including necessary office supplies and equipment . .	3,200 00	3,200 00
1801-23	For traveling expenses of officers and employees of the parole board when required to travel in the discharge of their duties .	10,000 00	10,000 00
1801-24	For assistance to discharged prisoners	600 00	600 00
	Totals	$108,195 00	$108,975 00
	For the maintenance of the following institutions under the control of the Department of Correction:		
1802-00	State farm, including not more than three hundred and eighty-one permanent positions . .	$922,405 00	$917,265 00
1803-00	State prison, including not more than one hundred and thirty-seven permanent positions .	472,550 00	471,550 00
1805-00	Massachusetts reformatory, including not more than one hundred and sixty-four permanent positions	564,015 00	560,900 00

Item		Appropriation Fiscal Year 1944.	Appropriation Fiscal Year 1945.
1806-00	Reformatory for women, including not more than one hundred and seven permanent positions .	$276,820 00	$274,220 00
1807-00	State prison colony, including not more than one hundred and seventy-five permanent positions	517,550 00	515,850 00
	Totals	$2,753,340 00	$2,739,785 00
	Service of the Department of Public Welfare.		
	Administration:		
1901-01	For the salary of the commissioner	$7,000 00	$7,000 00
1901-02	For personal services of officers and employees, including not more than thirty-one permanent positions	56,120 00	57,000 00
1901-03	For services other than personal, printing the annual report, traveling expenses, including expenses of auxiliary visitors, office supplies and expenses . .	4,000 00	4,000 00
	Totals	$67,120 00	$68,000 00
	Special:		
1901-22	(This item omitted.)		
	State Board of Housing:		
1902-01	For personal services, including not more than nine permanent positions	$19,040 00	$19,160 00
1902-02	For expenses, as authorized by section eighteen of chapter eighteen of the General Laws . .	5,000 00	5,000 00
	Totals	$24,040 00	$24,160 00
	Division of Aid and Relief:		
1904-01	For personal services of officers and employees, including not more than one hundred and thirty-two permanent positions .	$241,000 00	$243,000 00
1904-02	For services other than personal, including traveling expenses and office supplies and equipment .	19,000 00	19,000 00
	Totals	$260,000 00	$262,000 00
	Division of Child Guardianship:		
1906-01	For personal services of officers and employees, including not more than one hundred and thirty-seven permanent positions .	$260,000 00	$264,000 00
1906-02	For services other than personal, office supplies and equipment .	6,000 00	6,000 00
1906-03	For the care and maintenance of children, including not more than two permanent positions .	1,771,500 00	1,795,000 00
	Totals	$2,037,500 00	$2,065,000 00
	Tuition of children:		
1907-01	For tuition in the public schools, including transportation to and from school, of children boarded by the department, for the		

Item		Appropriation Fiscal Year 1944.	Appropriation Fiscal Year 1945.
	twelve months ending June thirtieth, nineteen hundred and forty-three, and June thirtieth, nineteen hundred and forty-four, respectively	$330,000 00	$330,000 00
	Instruction in public schools:		
1907-03	For reimbursement of cities and towns for tuition of children attending the public schools	$7,500 00	$7,500 00
	The following items are for reimbursement of cities and towns, and are to be in addition to any unexpended balances of appropriations heretofore made for the purpose:		
1907-05	For the payment of suitable aid to certain dependent children	$2,500,000 00	$2,400,000 00
1907-07	For the burial by cities and towns of indigent persons who have no legal settlement	25,000 00	25,000 00
1907-08	For expenses in connection with smallpox and other diseases dangerous to the public health	150,000 00	150,000 00
1907-09	For the support of sick indigent persons who have no legal settlement	–	300,000 00
1907-10	For temporary aid given to indigent persons with no legal settlement, and to shipwrecked seamen by cities and towns, and for the transportation of indigent persons under the charge of the department	1,750,000 00	1,500,000 00
	Totals	$4,425,000 00	$4,375,000 00
	Division of Juvenile Training, Trustees of Massachusetts Training Schools:		
1908-01	For services of the secretary and certain other persons employed in the executive office, including not more than nine permanent positions	$16,030 00	$16,390 00
1908-02	For services other than personal, including printing the annual report, traveling and other expenses of the members of the board and employees, office supplies and equipment	2,000 00	2,000 00
	Boys' Parole:		
1908-11	For personal services of agents in the division for boys paroled and boarded in families, including not more than twenty-two permanent positions	48,740 00	49,280 00
1908-12	For services other than personal, including traveling expenses of the agents and boys, and necessary office supplies and equipment	18,000 00	18,000 00

Item		Appropriation Fiscal Year 1944.	Appropriation Fiscal Year 1945.
1908-13	For board, clothing, medical and other expenses incidental to the care of boys	$20,000 00	$20,000 00
	Girls' Parole:		
1908-31	For personal services of agents in the division for girls paroled from the industrial school for girls, including not more than eighteen permanent positions .	35,230 00	35,670 00
1908-32	For traveling expenses of said agents for girls paroled, for board, medical and other care of girls, and for services other than personal, office supplies and equipment . . .	17,500 00	17,500 00
	Totals	$157,500 00	$158,840 00
	For the maintenance of and for certain improvements at the institutions under the control of the trustees of the Massachusetts training schools, with the approval of said trustees, as follows:		
1915-00	Industrial school for boys, including not more than one hundred and one permanent positions .	$199,400 00	$199,600 00
1915-22	For the purchase of certain land at the industrial school for boys	3,000 00	
1916-00	Industrial school for girls, including not more than ninety-one permanent positions .	171,250 00	171,250 00
1917-00	Lyman school for boys, including not more than one hundred and thirty-eight permanent positions	313,800 00	310,700 00
1917-24	For the cost of renovation and replacement of fire damage at Bowlder cottage at the Lyman school for boys . . .	6,000 00	–
	Totals	$693,450 00	$681,550 00
	Massachusetts Hospital School:		
1918-00	For the maintenance of the Massachusetts hospital school, including not more than one hundred and fifty-two permanent positions, to be expended with the approval of the trustees thereof .	$234,440 00	$233,940 00
	Tewksbury State Hospital and Infirmary:		
1919-00	For the maintenance of the Tewksbury state hospital and infirmary, including not more than six hundred and eighty-six permanent positions, to be expended with the approval of the trustees thereof . .	$1,215,100 00	$1,215,100 00

Item		Appropriation Fiscal Year 1944.	Appropriation Fiscal Year 1945.
	Service of the Department of Public Health.		
	Administration:		
2001-01	For the salary of the commissioner	$7,500 00	$7,500 00
2001-02	For personal services of the health council and office assistants, including not more than twenty-three permanent positions	30,970 00	31,280 00
2001-03	For services other than personal, including printing the annual report, traveling expenses, office supplies and equipment	11,100 00	8,100 00
	Service of Adult Hygiene (cancer):		
2003-01	For personal services of the division, including not more than nineteen permanent positions	38,880 00	40,140 00
2003-02	For other expenses of the division, including cancer clinics	42,800 00	42,800 00
	Service of Child and Maternal Hygiene:		
2004-01	For personal services of the director and assistants, including not more than thirty-one permanent positions	61,500 00	62,280 00
2004-02	For services other than personal, traveling expenses, office supplies and equipment	22,300 00	22,300 00
	Division of Communicable Diseases:		
2005-01	For personal services of the director, district health officers and their assistants, epidemiologists, bacteriologists and assistants in the diagnostic laboratory, including not more than thirty permanent positions	76,150 00	77,300 00
2005-02	For services other than personal, traveling expenses, laboratory, office and other necessary supplies, including the purchase of animals and equipment, and rent of certain offices	12,300 00	12,300 00
	Venereal Diseases:		
2006-01	For personal services for the control of venereal diseases, including not more than eight permanent positions	11,397 00	11,750 00
2006-02	For services other than personal, traveling expenses, office supplies and equipment, to be in addition to any amount heretofore appropriated for the purpose	239,000 00	239,000 00
	Wassermann Laboratory:		
2007-01	For personal services of the Wassermann laboratory, including not more than fifteen permanent positions	19,870 00	20,540 00
2007-02	For expenses of the Wassermann laboratory	6,500 00	6,500 00

Item		Appropriation Fiscal Year 1944.	Appropriation Fiscal Year 1945.
	Antitoxin and Vaccine Laboratories:		
2007-07	For personal services in the investigation and production of antitoxin and vaccine lymph and other specific material for protective inoculation and diagnosis of treatment, including not more than forty-seven permanent positions	$75,834 00	$77,625 00
2007-08	For other services, supplies, materials and equipment necessary for the production of antitoxin and other materials as enumerated above, and for rent . .	41,800 00	41,800 00
	Inspection of Food and Drugs:		
2012-01	For personal services of the director, analysts, inspectors and other assistants, including not more than thirty permanent positions	65,160 00	65,940 00
2012-02	For other services, including traveling expenses, supplies, materials and equipment . .	11,200 00	11,200 00
	Shellfish Enforcement Law:		
2013-01	For personal services for administering the law relative to shellfish, including not more than one permanent position . . .	2,040 00	2,160 00
2013-02	For other expenses for administering the law relative to shellfish .	500 00	500 00
	Water Supply and Disposal of Sewage:		
2015-01	For personal services of directors, engineers, chemists, clerks and other assistants in the division of engineering and the division of laboratories, including not more than fifty permanent positions	121,380 00	121,380 00
2015-02	For other services, including traveling expenses, supplies, materials and equipment, for the division of engineering and the division of laboratories . .	20,000 00	20,000 00
	Totals	$918,181 00	$922,395 00
	Division of Tuberculosis:		
2020-01	For personal services of the director, stenographers, clerks and other assistants, including not more than nineteen permanent positions	$43,920 00	$44,100 00
2020-02	For services other than personal, including printing the annual report, traveling expenses and office supplies and equipment .	2,800 00	2,800 00
2020-03	For expenses of hospitalization of certain patients suffering from		

Item		Appropriation Fiscal Year 1944.	Appropriation Fiscal Year 1945.
	chronic rheumatism, as authorized by section one hundred and sixteen A of chapter one hundred and eleven of the General Laws	$34,000 00	$34,000 00
2020-11	To cover the payment of certain subsidies for the maintenance of hospitals for tubercular patients	510,000 00	470,000 00
2020-21	For personal services for certain children's clinics for tuberculosis, including not more than seventeen permanent positions . .	37,980 00	38,280 00
2020-22	For other services for certain children's clinics for tuberculosis .	10,900 00	10,900 00
	Totals	$639,600 00	$600,080 00
	For the maintenance of and for certain improvements at the sanatoria, as follows:		
2022-00	Lakeville state sanatorium, including not more than two hundred and twenty-six permanent positions	$338,940 00	$337,090 00
2023-00	North Reading state sanatorium, including not more than one hundred and eighty-five permanent positions	248,470 00	247,450 00
2024-00	Rutland state sanatorium, including not more than two hundred and thirty-eight permanent positions	378,680 00	380,150 00
2024-21	For improvements in the sewage disposal system at the Rutland state sanatorium, to be in addition to any amount heretofore appropriated for the purpose .	1,000 00	
2025-00	Westfield state sanatorium, including not more than two hundred and ninety permanent positions	444,670 00	442,120 00
2025-22	For the purchase and installation of certain x-ray equipment at the Westfield state sanatorium	8,000 00	-
	Totals	$1,419,760 00	$1,406,810 00
	Pondville Hospital:		
2031-00	For maintenance of the Pondville hospital, including care of radium, and including not more than two hundred and thirty-four permanent positions . .	$331,500 00	$331,300 00
2031-24	For the purchase and installation of certain fire protection equipment, to be in addition to any amount heretofore appropriated for the purpose	2,160 00	
2031-26	For the purchase and installation of certain x-ray equipment .	8,500 00	-
	Totals	$342,160 00	$331,300 00

Item		Appropriation Fiscal Year 1944.	Appropriation Fiscal Year 1945.
	Service of the Department of Public Safety.		
	Administration:		
2101-01	For the salary of the commissioner	$6,000 00	$6,000 00
2101-02	For personal services of clerks and stenographers, including not more than seventy-one permanent positions	102,000 00	103,000 00
2101-03	For contingent expenses, including printing the annual report, rent of district offices, supplies and equipment, and all other things necessary for the investigation of fires and motion picture licenses, as required by law, and for expenses of administering the law regulating the sale and resale of tickets to theatres and other places of public amusement by the department of public safety . .	55,000 00	55,000 00
	Totals	$163,000 00	$164,000 00
	Division of State Police:		
2102-01	For the salaries of officers and detectives, including not more than two hundred and ninety-five permanent positions partly chargeable to item 2970-04, and for the salary of one permanent state police crime prevention and juvenile delinquency investigator	$200,000 00	$200,000 00
2102-02	For personal services of civilian employees, including not more than one hundred and twenty-nine permanent positions .	156,000 00	157,000 00
2102-03	For other necessary expenses of the uniformed division, to be in addition to the amounts appropriated in item 2970-05 . .	180,000 00	180,000 00
2102-04	For expert assistance to the commissioner and for maintenance of laboratories, including not more than five permanent positions	14,680 00	14,800 00
	Totals	$550,680 00	$551,800 00
	Fire Prevention Service:		
2103-01	For the salary of the state fire marshal	$4,000 00	$4,000 00
2103-02	For personal services of fire and other inspectors, including not more than eighteen permanent positions	50,640 00	51,040 00
2103-03	For other services, office rent and necessary office supplies and equipment	2,900 00	2,900 00
2103-04	For traveling expenses of fire and other inspectors . . .	10,000 00	10,000 00
	Totals	$67,540 00	$67,940 00

Item		Appropriation Fiscal Year 1944.	Appropriation Fiscal Year 1945.
	Division of Inspection:		
2104-01	For the salary of the chief of inspections	$4,000 00	$4,000 00
2104-02	For services, supplies and equipment necessary for investigations and inspections by the division .	500 00	500 00
2104-11	For the salaries of officers for the building inspection service, including not more than twenty-one permanent positions . .	58,180 00	61,520 00
2104-12	For traveling expenses of officers for the building inspection service	10,000 00	10,000 00
2104-21	For the salaries of officers for the boiler inspection service, including not more than twenty-six permanent positions . .	73,110 00	76,560 00
2104-22	For traveling expenses of officers for the boiler inspection service	10,000 00	10,000 00
	Totals	$155,790 00	$162,580 00
	Board of Boiler Rules:		
2104-31	For personal services of members of the board, including not more than four permanent positions .	$1,000 00	$1,000 00
2104-32	For services other than personal and the necessary traveling expenses of the board . .	600 00	500 00
	Totals	$1,600 00	$1,500 00
	State Boxing Commission:		
2105-01	For compensation and clerical assistance for the state boxing commission, including not more than five permanent positions .	$10,320 00	$10,380 00
2105-02	For other expenses of the commission	6,500 00	6,500 00
	Totals	$16,820 00	$16,880 00

Service of the Department of Public Works.

Item		Appropriation Fiscal Year 1944.	Appropriation Fiscal Year 1945.
2201-01	For administering the law relative to advertising signs near highways	$19,073 16	$19,067 92
	Functions of the department relating to waterways and public lands:		
2202-01	For personal services of the director, chief engineer and assistants, including not more than eighty permanent positions . .	$55,000 00	$55,000 00
2202-02	For services other than personal, including printing pamphlet of laws and the annual report, and for necessary office and engineering supplies and equipment .	1,600 00	1,600 00
2202-03	For the care and maintenance of the province lands and of the lands acquired and structures erected by the Provincetown		

Item		Appropriation Fiscal Year 1944.	Appropriation Fiscal Year 1945.
	tercentenary commission, including not more than five permanent positions . . .	$7,000 00	$7,000 00
2202-04	For the compensation of dumping inspectors	300 00	300 00
2202-06	For the maintenance and repair of certain property in the town of Plymouth, including not more than two permanent positions .	3,500 00	3,500 00
2202-07	For the operation and maintenance of the New Bedford state pier, including not more than seven permanent positions .	15,000 00	15,000 00
2202-08	(This item omitted.)		
2202-09	For the maintenance of structures, and for repairing damages along the coast line or river banks of the commonwealth, and for the removal of wrecks and other obstructions from tide waters and great ponds	15,000 00	15,000 00
2202-11	The unexpended balance of the appropriation made by item 2202-11 of chapter four hundred and nineteen of the acts of nineteen hundred and forty-one is hereby reappropriated.		
2202-12	For re-establishing and permanently marking certain triangulation points and stations, as required by order of the land court in accordance with section thirty-three of chapter ninety-one of the General Laws . .	800 00	800 00
2202-13	For expenses of surveying certain town boundaries, by the department of public works . .	300 00	300 00
	Totals	$98,500 00	$98,500 00

Service of the Department of Public Utilities.

Item		Appropriation Fiscal Year 1944.	Appropriation Fiscal Year 1945.
2301-01	For personal services of the commissioners, including not more than five permanent positions .	$36,000 00	$36,000 00
2301-02	For personal services of secretaries, employees of the accounting division, engineering division, and rate and tariff division, including not more than sixteen permanent positions . . .	52,920 00	53,520 00
2301-03	For personal services of the inspection division, including not more than twenty permanent positions	53,814 00	54,594 00
2301-04	For personal services of clerks, messengers and office assistants, including not more than ten permanent positions . . .	17,160 00	17,520 00
2301-05	For personal services of the telephone and telegraph division, including not more than seven permanent positions . . .	19,260 00	19,260 00

Item		Appropriation Fiscal Year 1944.	Appropriation Fiscal Year 1945.
2301-06	For traveling expenses of the commissioners and employees	$3,600 00	$3,600 00
2301-07	For other services, including printing the annual report and necessary office supplies and equipment	8,500 00	11,000 00
2301-08	For stenographic reports of evidence at inquests held in cases of death by accident on or about railroads, or caused by the operation of motor vehicles for the carriage of passengers for hire	300 00	300 00
	Totals	$191,554 00	$195,794 00
	Special Investigations:		
2301-09	For personal services and expenses of special investigations, including legal assistants and stenographic services as needed	$5,000 00	$5,000 00
2301-10	The unexpended balance of the amounts appropriated by item 2301-09 of chapter four hundred and nineteen of the acts of nineteen hundred and forty-one, as amended by chapter six hundred and eighty-three of the acts of said year, for an investigation of the New York, New Haven and Hartford Railroad Company, is hereby reappropriated.		
	Investigation of Gas and Electric Light Meters:		
2302-01	For personal services of the division of inspection of gas and gas meters, including not more than twelve permanent positions	$28,500 00	$29,100 00
2302-02	For expenses of the division of inspection of gas and gas meters, including traveling and other necessary expenses of inspection	2,500 00	2,500 00
2302-03	For the examination and tests of electric meters	50 00	50 00
	Totals	$31,050 00	$31,650 00
	Commercial Motor Vehicle Division:		
2304-01	For personal services of the director and assistants, including not more than eighteen permanent positions	$38,850 00	$39,450 00
2304-02	For other services, necessary office supplies and equipment, and for rent	17,000 00	17,000 00
	Totals	$55,850 00	$56,450 00
	Sale of Securities:		
2308-01	For personal services in administering the law relative to the sale of securities, including not more than ten permanent positions	$21,280 00	$21,520 00

Item		Appropriation Fiscal Year 1944.	Appropriation Fiscal Year 1945.
2308-02	For expenses other than personal in administering the law relative to the sale of securities .	$1,000 00	$1,000 00
	Totals	$22,280 00	$22,520 00
2320-01	The sum of twenty-five thousand dollars is hereby reappropriated from the unexpended balance of the appropriation authorized by chapter eighty-nine of the resolves of nineteen hundred and forty-one.		

Interest on the Public Debt.

Item		1944	1945
2410-00	For the payment of interest on the direct debt of the commonwealth, to be in addition to the amounts appropriated in item 2951-00	$112,844 50	$97,059 50

Requirements for Extinguishing the State Debt.

Item		1944	1945
2420-00	For sinking fund requirements and for certain serial bonds maturing during the years nineteen hundred and forty-four and nineteen hundred and forty-five, to be in addition to the amounts appropriated in item 2952-00 .	$1,638,500 00	$570,000 00

Bunker Hill Monument.

Item		1944	1945
2801-00	For the maintenance of Bunker Hill monument and the property adjacent, to be expended by the metropolitan district commission; provided, that from the amount herein appropriated for the year nineteen hundred and forty-four sums not exceeding six thousand dollars, in the aggregate, shall be available for expenditure prior to December first, nineteen hundred and forty-three, and sums not exceeding seven thousand dollars, in the aggregate, shall be available for expenditure during the period from December first, nineteen hundred and forty-three, through June thirtieth, nineteen hundred and forty-four; and provided, further, that not exceeding one thousand dollars shall be expended prior to December first, nineteen hundred and forty-three, for shrubbery purposes .	$12,712 00	$4,310 00

Item		Appropriation Fiscal Year 1944.	Appropriation Fiscal Year 1945.
	Unclassified Accounts and Claims.		
2805-01	For the payment of certain annuities and pensions of soldiers and others under the provisions of certain acts and resolves . .	$8,200 00	$8,200 00
2805-02	For payment of any claims, as authorized by section eighty-nine of chapter thirty-two of the General Laws, for allowances to the families of members of the department of public safety doing police duty killed or fatally injured in the discharge of their duties	12,500 00	13,300 00
2811-01	For the compensation of veterans of the civil war formerly in the service of the commonwealth, now retired	990 00	990 00
2811-02	For the compensation of veterans who may be retired by the governor under the provisions of sections fifty-six to fifty-nine, inclusive, of chapter thirty-two of the General Laws . .	195,000 00	220,000 00
2811-03	For the compensation of certain prison officers and instructors formerly in the service of the commonwealth, now retired .	62,000 00	63,000 00
2811-04	For the compensation of state police officers formerly in the service of the commonwealth, now retired	11,300 00	13,100 00
2811-05	For the compensation of certain women formerly employed in cleaning the state house, now retired	300 00	300 00
2820-02	For small items of expenditure for which no appropriations have been made, and for cases in which appropriations have been exhausted or have reverted to the treasury in previous years	1,000 00	1,000 00
2820-04	For the compensation of certain public employees for injuries sustained in the course of their employment, for the years nineteen hundred and forty-four and nineteen hundred and forty-five and for previous years, as provided by section sixty-nine of chapter one hundred and fifty-two of the General Laws, to be in addition to the amounts appropriated by item 2970-07 . .	45,000 00	45,000 00
2820-06	For reimbursement of persons for funds previously deposited in the treasury of the commonwealth and escheated to the commonwealth	5,000 00	5,000 00
	Totals	$341,290 00	$369,890 00

Item		Appropriation Fiscal Year 1944.	Appropriation Fiscal Year 1945.
THE FOLLOWING APPROPRIATIONS ARE MADE FROM THE HIGHWAY FUND:			
	Service of the Department of Public Works.		
	Administration:		
2921-01	For the salaries of the commissioner and the associate commissioners, including not more than three permanent positions, partly chargeable to item 3131-01 .	$14,625 00	$14,625 00
2921-02	For personal services of clerks and assistants to the commissioner, including not more than four permanent positions, partly chargeable to item 3131-02 .	5,745 00	5,790 00
2921-03	For traveling expenses of the commissioners, to be in addition to the amounts appropriated in item 3131-03	1,100 00	1,100 00
2921-04	For telephone service in the public works building, including not more than six permanent positions, partly chargeable to item 3131-04	19,500 00	19,500 00
	Totals	$40,970 00	$41,015 00
	Public Works Building:		
2922-01	For personal services for the maintenance and operation of the public works building, including not more than sixty-eight permanent positions . .	$85,000 00	$85,000 00
2922-02	For the salaries of guards for the public works building, including expense of uniforms, and including not more than seventeen permanent positions . .	31,920 00	31,920 00
2922-03	For other expenses for the maintenance and operation of the public works building . . .	51,000 00	51,000 00
	Totals	$167,920 00	$167,920 00
	Functions of the department relating to highways:		
2900-01	For personal services and expenses of the department secretary, department business agent, and for vacation, sick leave, and other compensated absence in the highway division	$435,530 06	$433,925 03
2900-02	For personal services and expenses of administrative and engineering services performed in connection with all highway activities; for payment of damages caused by defects in state highways, with the approval of the attorney general	1,576,196 34	1,558,159 35
2900-04	For the maintenance and repair of state highways and bridges, con-		

Item		Appropriation Fiscal Year 1944.	Appropriation Fiscal Year 1945.
	trol of snow and ice on state highways and town roads, and for the maintenance of traffic signs and signals	$2,833,968 64	$2,841,588 60
2900-09	For the construction and reconstruction of state highways by state forces	76,836 66	84,728 66
2900-10	For projects for the construction and reconstruction of state highways and grade crossing elimination for which there are agreements for reimbursement from the federal government and for land damages in connection with such projects, to be in addition to any amounts heretofore appropriated for these purposes .	3,825 00	3,825 00
2900-11	For projects for the construction and reconstruction of state highways without assistance from the federal government . .	33,920 00	14,300 00
2900-17	For maintenance project payments for the construction and repair of town and county ways . .	343,248 74	299,750 52
2900-18	For aiding towns in the repair and improvement of public ways .	1,145,125 00	1,145,125 00
	Specials:		
2900-50 2900-55	The existence of the Public Works Stores and Equipment account, established by items 2900-50 and 2900-55 of chapter sixty-eight of the acts of nineteen hundred and forty-three, is hereby continued for the years nineteen hundred and forty-four and nineteen hundred and forty-five under the terms and conditions as authorized in said chapter sixty-eight; provided, that the expenses for capital outlay from this account shall not exceed seventy-one thousand dollars in the year nineteen hundred and forty-four, and sixty-four thousand dollars in the year nineteen hundred and forty-five.		
2923-72	The unexpended balance of the appropriation made by item 2923-72 of chapter four hundred and nineteen of the acts of nineteen hundred and forty-one, as amended by chapter seven hundred and thirty of the acts of said year, is hereby reappropriated.		
	Totals	$6,448,650 44	$6,381,402 16
	Registration of Motor Vehicles:		
2924-01	For personal services, including not more than six hundred and seven permanent positions . .	$1,008,500 00	$1,015,500 00

Item		Appropriation Fiscal Year 1944.	Appropriation Fiscal Year 1945.
2924-02	For services other than personal, including traveling expenses, purchase of necessary supplies and materials, including cartage and storage of the same, and for work incidental to the registration and licensing of owners and operators of motor vehicles .	$260,000 00	$260,000 00
2924-03	For printing and other expenses necessary in connection with publicity for certain safety work	500 00	500 00
	Totals	$1,269,000 00	$1,276,000 00

Metropolitan District Commission.

Item		Appropriation Fiscal Year 1944.	Appropriation Fiscal Year 1945.
	The following items are to be paid with the approval of the metropolitan district commission:		
2931-00	For maintenance of boulevards and parkways, including installation of traffic lights, to be in addition to any amounts heretofore appropriated for the same purpose; provided, that from the amount herein appropriated for the year nineteen hundred and forty-four sums not exceeding three hundred fifty-eight thousand two hundred and ninety-five dollars, in the aggregate, shall be available for expenditure prior to December first, nineteen hundred and forty-three, and sums not exceeding five hundred thousand dollars, in the aggregate, shall be available for expenditure during the period from December first, nineteen hundred and forty-three through June thirtieth, nineteen hundred and forty-four	$854,795 00	$319,286 00
2932-00	For resurfacing of boulevards and parkways, to be in addition to any unexpended balance of the appropriation made for the purpose in the previous years . .	50,000 00	25,000 00
	Specials:		
2937-04	For the construction of a certain drain on the West Roxbury Parkway, so-called . . .	8,000 00	-
2937-05	For the cost of certain repairs for shore protection at Lynn shore and Quincy shore . . .	10,000 00	-
2937-06	For the construction of cement sidewalks on both sides of Neponset Valley Parkway from Wollcott Square, Readville, to Paul's Bridge, Milton . .	3,500 00	-
	Totals	$926,295 00	$344,286 00

Item		Appropriation Fiscal Year 1944.	Appropriation Fiscal Year 1945.
	Interest on the Public Debt.		
2951–00	For the payment of interest on the direct debt of the commonwealth, to be in addition to the amounts appropriated in item 2410–00 .	$85,540 00	$41,145 00
	Requirements for Extinguishing the State Debt.		
2952–00	For sinking fund requirements and for certain serial bonds maturing during the years nineteen hundred and forty-four and nineteen hundred and forty-five, to be in addition to the amounts appropriated in item 2420–00 . .	$4,238,573 00	$1,206,449 00
	Service of the Treasurer and Receiver-General.		
	State Board of Retirement:		
2970–01	For requirements of annuity funds and pensions for employees retired from the state service under authority of law, to be in addition to the amounts appropriated in item 0604–03 . .	$36,000 00	$36,000 00
	Service of the Department of Banking and Insurance.		
	Division of Insurance:		
2970–02	For other personal services of the division, including expenses of the board of appeal and certain other costs of supervising motor vehicle liability insurance, to be in addition to the amounts appropriated in item 1103–02 .	$70,000 00	$70,000 00
	Service of the Department of Corporations and Taxation.		
	Corporations and Tax Divisions:		
2970–03	To cover the estimated cost of collection of the gasoline tax, so-called, and to be in addition to the amounts appropriated in item 1201–02	$50,000 00	$50,000 00
	Service of the Department of Public Safety.		
	Division of State Police:		
2970–04	For the salaries of officers and detectives, to be in addition to the amounts appropriated in item 2102–01	$300,000 00	$300,000 00
2970–05	For other necessary expenses of the uniformed division, including traveling expenses of detectives, to be in addition to the amounts appropriated in item 2102–03	180,000 00	180,000 00
	Totals	$480,000 00	$480,000 00

Item		Appropriation Fiscal Year 1944.	Appropriation Fiscal Year 1945.
	Unclassified Accounts and Claims.		
2970–07	For the compensation of certain public employees for injuries sustained in the course of their employment, for the years nineteen hundred and forty-four and nineteen hundred and forty-five and for previous years, as provided by section sixty-nine of chapter one hundred and fifty-two of the General Laws, to be in addition to the amounts appropriated by item 2820–04	$55,000 00	$55,000 00

THE FOLLOWING APPROPRIATIONS ARE MADE FROM THE PORT OF BOSTON FUND:

Item		Appropriation Fiscal Year 1944.	Appropriation Fiscal Year 1945.
	Service of the Department of Public Works.		
	Administration:		
3131–01	For the salaries of the commissioner and the associate commissioners, to be in addition to the amounts appropriated in item 2921–01 .	$4,875 00	$4,875 00
3131–02	For personal services of clerks and assistants to the commissioner, to be in addition to the amounts appropriated in item 2921–02 .	1,915 00	1,930 00
3131–03	For traveling expenses of the commissioners, to be in addition to the amounts appropriated in item 2921–03	400 00	400 00
3131–04	For telephone service in the public works building, to be in addition to the amounts appropriated in item 2921–04	6,500 00	6,500 00
	Totals	$13,690 00	$13,705 00
	Functions of the department relating to Port of Boston:		
3132–02	For the supervision and operation of commonwealth pier five, including not more than forty permanent positions, and for the repair and replacement of equipment and other property . .	$80,000 00	$80,000 00
3132–04	For the construction of railroads and piers and for the development of certain land . .	2,000 00	2,000 00
3132–11	(This item omitted.)		
3132–12	For the maintenance and improvement of commonwealth property under the control of the department in connection with its functions relating to waterways and public lands	70,000 00	70,000 00
3132–14	For personal services and other expenses of the cost of operating the East Boston airport, so-called	43,000 00	43,000 00
	Totals	$195,000 00	$195,000 00

Item		Appropriation Fiscal Year 1944.	Appropriation Fiscal Year 1945.
	Boston Port Authority.		
3134–01	For reimbursement of the city of Boston for a part of the cost of the Boston Port Authority, as authorized by chapter four hundred and fifty-three of the acts of nineteen hundred and thirty-eight	$26,000 00	$26,000 00

THE FOLLOWING APPROPRIATIONS ARE PAYABLE FROM FEES COLLECTED UNDER SECTION 27 OF CHAPTER 138 OF THE GENERAL LAWS:

Item		Appropriation Fiscal Year 1944.	Appropriation Fiscal Year 1945.
	Service of Old Age Assistance Administration.		
3621	For personal services required for the administration of old age assistance provided by chapter one hundred and eighteen A of the General Laws, including not more than fifty-four permanent positions	$85,000 00	$86,000 00
3622	For other expenses, including rent, travel, office supplies and other necessary expenses, required for the administration of old age assistance provided by said chapter one hundred and eighteen A .	12,500 00	12,500 00
	Totals	$97,500 00	$98,500 00

THE FOLLOWING APPROPRIATION IS PAYABLE FROM THE MOSQUITO CONTROL FUND:

Item		Appropriation Fiscal Year 1944.	Appropriation Fiscal Year 1945.
	State Reclamation Board.		
3901	For the maintenance and construction of drainage ditches, as authorized by chapter three hundred and seventy-nine of the acts of nineteen hundred and thirty as amended by section one of chapter two hundred and fifty of the acts of nineteen hundred and thirty-five, except that the amount so assessed shall not exceed thirty-seven thousand one hundred eighty-four dollars and forty-eight cents in each of the calendar years nineteen hundred and forty-three and nineteen hundred and forty-four . . .	$37,184 48	$37,184 48

THE FOLLOWING APPROPRIATIONS ARE PAYABLE FROM THE PARKS AND SALISBURY BEACH RESERVATION FUND:

Item		Appropriation Fiscal Year 1944.	Appropriation Fiscal Year 1945.
	Division of Parks and Recreation.		
4011	For personal services for certain administrative purposes and for certain consulting services, including not more than six permanent positions	$22,780 00	$22,840 00

Item		Appropriation Fiscal Year 1944.	Appropriation Fiscal Year 1945.
4012	For travel and other administrative expenses, including supplies for reservation improvements	$5,500 00	$5,500 00
4013	For the development of recreational opportunities in state forests, including personal services and other expenses	27,300 00	27,300 00
4021	For the maintenance of the Standish monument reservation	2,000 00	2,000 00
	Salisbury Beach Reservation:		
4031	For the maintenance of Salisbury beach reservation, including not more than one permanent position	17,000 00	17,000 00
4037	(This item omitted.)		
	Totals	$74,580 00	$74,640 00

THE FOLLOWING APPROPRIATIONS ARE PAYABLE FROM THE SMOKE INSPECTION FUND:

Division of Smoke Inspection.

Item		Appropriation Fiscal Year 1944.	Appropriation Fiscal Year 1945.
4311	For personal services, including not more than thirteen permanent positions	$27,420 00	$27,540 00
4312	For other services, printing the annual report, travel, and necessary office supplies and equipment	2,800 00	2,600 00
	Totals	$30,220 00	$30,140 00

THE FOLLOWING APPROPRIATIONS ARE PAYABLE FROM THE PRISON INDUSTRIES FUND:

Item		Appropriation Fiscal Year 1944.	Appropriation Fiscal Year 1945.
	The following amounts appropriated in Items 4411, 4511, 4611 and 4711 include, in each instance, partial compensation of not more than seven additional permanent employees in industries at the State Prison:		
4411	For salaries of persons employed in industries at the Massachusetts Reformatory, including not more than twenty-six permanent positions	$55,000 00	$55,500 00
4511	For salaries of persons employed in industries at the Reformatory for Women, including not more than thirteen permanent positions	27,146 00	27,386 00
4611	For salaries of persons employed in industries at the State Prison, including not more than thirty-seven permanent positions	84,000 00	84,500 00
4711	For salaries of persons employed in industries at the State Prison Colony, including not more than sixteen permanent positions	43,146 00	44,766 00
	Totals	$209,292 00	$212,152 00

Item		Appropriation Fiscal Year 1943.	Appropriation Fiscal Year 1944.
	METROPOLITAN DISTRICT COMMISSION FUNDS.		
	The following appropriations are for the fiscal year ending November thirtieth, nineteen hundred and forty-three, and for the fiscal year ending November thirtieth, nineteen hundred and forty-four, or for such other period as may be specified, and are to be assessed upon the several districts in accordance with the methods fixed by law, unless otherwise provided, and to be expended under the direction and with the approval of the metropolitan district commission:		
8602-00	For maintenance of parks reservations, including the retirement of veterans under the provisions of the General Laws . .	$645,019 00	$631,765 00
8602-27	For the cost of suppressing gypsy moths, including certain equipment, to be assessed as part of the cost of maintenance of parks reservations, and the amount herein appropriated for the year nineteen hundred and forty-four is in addition to the amount appropriated for the year nineteen hundred and forty-three . .	5,000 00	5,000 00
8602-31	For the cost of certain research plans and studies regarding the Neponset river valley, to be assessed as part of the cost of maintenance of parks reservations	2,500 00	
8607-00	For maintenance of the Charles River basin, including retirement of veterans under the provisions of the General Laws .	165,797 00	154,203 00
8611-00	For maintenance of the Nantasket Beach reservation . . .	59,293 00	58,185 00
8611-22	For the cost of certain repairs for shore protection at the Nantasket Beach reservation, to be in addition to any amount heretofore appropriated for the purpose	5,000 00	
8802-00	For the maintenance and operation of a system of sewage disposal for the north metropolitan sewerage district, including retirement of veterans under the provisions of the General Laws .	465,305 00	459,080 00
8802-23	For the cost of building a certain roadway for the trucking of coal at the Deer Island pumping station, to be assessed as part of the cost of maintenance of the north metropolitan sewerage system	10,000 00	

Item		Appropriation Fiscal Year 1943	Appropriation Fiscal Year 1944
8807-00	For the maintenance and operation of a system of sewage disposal for the south metropolitan sewerage district, including retirement of veterans under the provisions of the General Laws .	$331,945 00	$324,905 00
8902-00	For the maintenance and operation of the metropolitan water system, including retirement of veterans under the provisions of the General Laws	1,071,815 00	1,050,093 00
8902-22	For emergency repairs to water mains, to be assessed as a part of the cost of maintenance of the metropolitan water system, and the amount herein appropriated for the year nineteen hundred and forty-four is in addition to the amount appropriated for the year nineteen hundred and forty-three	5,000 00	5,000 00
8902-24	For payment to the commissioners of Worcester county of certain assessments upon the former town of Dana, to be assessed as a part of the cost of maintenance of the metropolitan water system	745 48	327 00
8902-25	For personal services of metropolitan district police at the Quabbin reservoir, so-called, including not more than ten permanent positions, to be assessed as a part of the cost of maintenance of the metropolitan water system .	22,750 00	22,700 00
8902-27	For certain repairs to the building containing the chlorinating apparatus at Weston, to be assessed as a part of the cost of maintenance of the metropolitan water system	2,000 00	
8902-28	For personal services of metropolitan district police and other employees engaged in guarding locations on the metropolitan water system, to be assessed as a part of the cost of maintenance of the metropolitan water system; provided, that if the police at present assigned to this duty shall return to their former stations the cost of their salaries shall then be charged to the appropriate funds, as provided by law	276,300 00	271,474 00
8902-29	For other expenses of metropolitan district police and other employees engaged in guarding locations on the metropolitan water system, to be assessed as a part of the cost of maintenance of the metropolitan water system; provided, that if the police		

Item		Appropriation Fiscal Year 1943.	Appropriation Fiscal Year 1944.
	at present assigned to this duty shall return to their former stations the cost of their expenses shall then be charged to the appropriate funds, as provided by law	$13,600 00	$13,600 00
8902-32	(This item omitted.)		
8902-34	For the construction of additions and improvements to certain supply and distribution mains, as a part of the cost of maintenance of the metropolitan water system, to be in addition to any unexpended balance of an appropriation made for the purpose in the previous years . . .	161,000 00	176,000 00
8902-35	For maintenance expenses, including personal services, of property held and operated by the metropolitan water supply commission, to be assessed as a part of the cost of maintenance of the metropolitan water system .	133,000 00	143,000 00
	Totals	$3,376,069 48	$3,315,332 00

General Fund	$58,405,412 65	$56,570,821 76
Highway Fund	16,367,948 44	10,649,217 16
Port of Boston Fund	234,690 00	234,705 00
Old Age Assistance Fund, administration .	97,500 00	98,500 00
Special Assessment Funds . . .	141,984 48	141,964 48
Prison Industries Fund . . .	209,292 00	212,152 00
Metropolitan District Commission Funds .	3,676,069 48	3,615,332 00

SECTION 3. No payment shall be made or obligation incurred under authority of any special appropriation made by this act for construction of public buildings or other improvements at state institutions until plans and specifications have been approved by the governor, unless otherwise provided by such rules and regulations as the governor may make.

SECTION 4. No person shall be reimbursed by the commonwealth for any expense incurred for a mid-day meal while traveling within the commonwealth at the expense thereof. nor shall any person be so reimbursed for the amount of any expense incurred for a breakfast while so traveling which is in excess of seventy-five cents or for the amount of any expense incurred for an evening meal while so traveling which is in excess of one dollar and twenty-five cents. Nothing herein contained shall apply to state employees who receive as part of their compensation a non-cash allowance in the form of full or complete boarding and housing or to members of legislative committees or special commissions. No passenger automobile the price whereof, delivered, exceeds one thousand dollars shall be paid for out of funds appropriated by this act, except upon the written order of the commission on administration and finance.

Nothing herein contained shall be construed as preventing a department from approving allowances for meals, not exceeding two dollars and fifty cents in any one day, for its employees stationed beyond commuting distance from their homes for a period of more than twenty-four hours or for its employees when engaged on special emergency duty.

SECTION 5. The allowance to state employees for expenses incurred by them in the operation of motor vehicles owned by them and used in the performance of their official duties shall not exceed four and one half cents a mile.

SECTION 6. The budget commissioner is hereby directed to send a copy of sections three, four and five of this act to each departmental, divisional and institutional head immediately following the passage of this act.

SECTION 7. All money paid into the treasury of the commonwealth from federal subventions and grants may be expended without specific appropriation, if such expenditures are otherwise in accordance with law.

SECTION 8. The state treasurer is hereby authorized and directed to charge off from the accounts of deposits heretofore made with certain banks now closed the sum of three hundred thousand dollars in the year nineteen hundred and forty-four and the sum of three hundred thousand dollars in the year nineteen hundred and forty-five.

SECTION 9. To provide in part for meeting the cost of increasing the salaries of employees in the service of the commonwealth, as authorized by chapter one hundred and seventy of the acts of the current year, the sum of three million five hundred thousand dollars in the General Fund and the sum of five hundred thousand dollars in the Highway Fund are hereby appropriated in each of the years nineteen hundred and forty-four and nineteen hundred and forty-five, and the sum of three hundred thousand dollars in the Metropolitan District Funds for each of the years nineteen hundred and forty-three and nineteen hundred and forty-four. The governor, with the approval of the council, and upon recommendation of the commission on administration and finance, is hereby authorized to transfer the said sums to items of appropriation in section two of this act which are available in whole or in part for personal services. For the purpose aforesaid, the governor, with the approval of the council, and upon recommendation of the commission on administration and finance is hereby authorized to transfer between items of appropriation in section two of this act which are available in whole or in part for personal services.

SECTION 10. To provide for divers emergency expenditures which may be necessary to meet any emergency which may arise by reason of the exigencies of the existing state of war and to meet deficiencies in existing appropriations, there may be expended under the direction of the governor sums not exceeding seven million dollars in the aggregate, and for said purposes there is hereby appropriated from the

General Fund the sum of two million dollars and from the Highway Fund the sum of two million dollars which amounts shall be available for expenditure on and after July first in the current year, and said amounts, together with any unexpended balance remaining from the funds previously provided under chapter eighteen of the acts of nineteen hundred and forty-two, are to be credited on the books of the commonwealth to a fund to be known as the War Emergency Fund. All expenditures hereinbefore referred to shall be subject to the approval of the council. Requests for any such expenditures shall be referred by the governor to the commission on administration and finance, which, after investigation of the need of such expenditure, shall forthwith submit to the governor its written recommendation of the amount of funds required, together with pertinent facts relative thereto. All expenditures authorized under this section and the employment of persons whose positions have been created by reason of money made available by this section shall cease not later than thirty days after the governor, with the advice and consent of the council, shall have proclaimed that the existing emergency has ended, and no new obligations may be authorized after January third, nineteen hundred and forty-five.

SECTION 11. The governor, upon recommendation of the commission on administration and finance and with the approval of the council, may make allocations by transfer or otherwise from the unexpended balances of appropriations for the fiscal years ending June thirtieth, nineteen hundred and forty-four and June thirtieth, nineteen hundred and forty-five, respectively, contained in appropriation items of this act and of any subsequent appropriation act passed in the current year, for use for meeting in whole or in part the expenditures referred to in section ten and also for setting up such reserves as are deemed necessary to compensate for shrinkage in estimated revenue. In determining the items from which allocations are to be made, consideration shall be given to the necessity of the expenditures authorized by such items in relation to the defense of the commonwealth and its participation in the conduct of the war.

SECTION 12. This act shall take effect upon its passage.

Approved June 1, 1943.

---

*Chap.*371 AN ACT RELATIVE TO THE OFFICE OF CITY AUDITOR OF THE CITY OF LOWELL AND TO THE PRESENT INCUMBENT OF SAID OFFICE.

Be it enacted, etc., as follows:

SECTION 1. Notwithstanding the provisions of any general law or any special act relating to the city of Lowell, the office of city auditor of the city of Lowell, which was placed under the civil service laws by chapter one hundred and seventy-eight of the acts of nineteen hundred and thirty-eight, shall continue thereunder when plan E, so called, takes effect in said city, and thereafter, and the tenure of office of Daniel E. Martin, the present incumbent of said office, shall be unlimited, subject, however, to said laws, and said Daniel E. Martin may continue in said office without taking a civil service examination.

SECTION 2. This act shall take effect upon its passage.

Approved June 1, 1943.

AN ACT TEMPORARILY AUTHORIZING THE ISSUANCE AND USE BY CERTAIN INSURANCE COMPANIES OF RENEWAL CERTIFICATES, RENEWAL AGREEMENTS AND RENEWAL RECEIPTS. *Chap.*372

Whereas, Owing to the lack of manpower due to the emergency caused by the existing state of war, as well as the temporary shortage of material and resources caused thereby, it is necessary to conserve the material and resources, clerical and otherwise, of insurance companies authorized to transact business within the commonwealth, and the deferred operation of this act would in part tend to defeat its purpose, which is to make immediately available the relief offered by its terms, therefore this act is hereby declared to be an emergency law, necessary for the immediate preservation of the public convenience.

Be it enacted, etc., as follows:

SECTION 1. Any company, as such term is defined in chapter one hundred and seventy-five of the General Laws, may issue and use renewal certificates, renewal agreements and renewal receipts, or any of them, anything in chapter ninety, chapter one hundred and fifty-two and chapter one hundred and seventy-five of the General Laws to the contrary notwithstanding. The commissioner of insurance may require such a company to submit for his inspection forms of renewal certificates, renewal agreements and renewal receipts, or applications used in connection therewith, issued or used, or to be issued or used, by it in relation to policies subject to section one hundred and ninety-one of said chapter one hundred and seventy-five. All provisions of general law relative to the filing of policy forms with, and the approval of such forms by, said commissioner shall also apply to all renewal certificates, renewal agreements and renewal receipts issued or used in connection with such policy forms, and applications used in connection therewith.

SECTION 2. This act shall cease to be effective upon the termination of the existing state of war between the United States and any foreign country, or upon July first in the year nineteen hundred and forty-five, whichever is the earlier date.

Approved June 1, 1943.

*Chap.*373 AN ACT RELATIVE TO COURT PROCEEDINGS TO ENFORCE PAYMENTS OF CONTRIBUTIONS, INTEREST AND PENALTIES UNDER THE EMPLOYMENT SECURITY LAW.

Be it enacted, etc., as follows:

G. L. (Ter. Ed.), 151A, § 15, etc., amended.

Section fifteen of chapter one hundred and fifty-one A of the General Laws, as appearing in section one of chapter six hundred and eighty-five of the acts of nineteen hundred and forty-one, is hereby amended by striking out subsection (*c*) and inserting in place thereof the following subsection: —

Procedure for collection of interest or penalties.

(*c*) In any case based upon a return by an employer, in addition to any other remedy provided by law the director may file in a district court within the judicial district of which the employer hereinafter referred to lives or has a usual place of business a petition for entry of judgment against an employer in default in any payment of contributions, interest or penalties assessed in lieu thereof provided by this chapter. At least twenty days prior to filing such petition the director shall send by registered mail to such employer a written notice, addressed to him at his last known residence or place of business. Such notice shall state (*a*) the name and address of such employer, (*b*) the amount for which the director alleges he is in default in the payment of contributions, interest or penalties, as the case may be, and to what date, (*c*) the name and location of the district court in which said petition will be filed and the date, which shall be a regular return day of said court, (*d*) that the director has complied with all the provisions of this chapter in relation to the computation and levy of said contributions, interest or penalty, as the case may be, and (*e*) that judgment will be entered against such employer by said court for the total amount alleged in said notice, with interest, unless said employer within the time (which shall be specified in the notice) allowed in that court for filing an answer in an action of contract brings an assignment of error in said proceeding, stating specifically sufficient reasons why such judgment should not be entered, and requests the court to issue an order of notice to the director thereon. Such order of notice, with a copy of the assignment of error, shall be served upon the director by registered mail or by an officer qualified to serve civil process.

A general denial of the allegations of the director's petition shall not constitute a sufficient assignment of error for the issuance by the court of an order of notice thereon, and the employer shall not avail himself of any defense in matters of fact which he had adequate opportunity to present to the director. The director's petition, when filed in the district court, shall be accompanied by a copy of the notice mailed by the director to the employer and the registered mail return receipt received in reply thereto. If no sufficient assignment of error is brought by the employer within the time above specified, he shall be defaulted and judgment shall be entered against him for the amount alleged due in the petition, with interest from the date to which interest was computed in said petition, and execution issued therefor as in other civil cases. If a sufficient assignment of error is seasonably brought by the employer and an order of notice served thereon the case shall be ripe for hearing, and such employer desiring to place the case on the trial list shall do so within forty-five days thereof and shall give notice thereof by registered mail to all other parties entitled to be heard, and their attorneys, and shall also, at least fourteen days before the trial day, file with the clerk of such district court a request that the case be placed upon the trial list, together with a certificate of the service of such notice. Failure by the employer to request a hearing within said period of forty-five days shall be deemed a waiver thereof. A default shall thereupon be recorded and judgment shall be entered by the clerk under the general orders of the court as to judgments on default. At the hearing on the assignment of error the court shall inquire only whether the director acted within his jurisdiction and whether his action was founded on evidence and free from any error of law affecting substantial rights. If the court is in doubt as to whether the employer has received proper notice, it may order such further notice as it deems proper. If the defense raised by the employer is not meritorious, the court may impose additional costs against the employer. The petition and the assignment of error may, upon motion, be amended by leave of the court. *Approved June 1, 1943.*

AN ACT CHANGING THE PRACTICE WITH RESPECT TO PETITIONS FOR CERTIORARI AND FOR MANDAMUS. *Chap.374*

Be it enacted, etc., as follows:

SECTION 1. Section four of chapter two hundred and forty-nine of the General Laws, as appearing in the Tercentenary Edition, is hereby amended by inserting after the first sentence the following: — It shall be open to the petitioner to contend at the hearing upon the petition that the evidence which formed the basis of the action complained of or the basis of any specified finding or conclusion was as matter of law insufficient to warrant such action, finding or conclusion, — and by striking out, in the fifth line, the word "six" and inserting in place thereof the word: — two, — so as to read as follows: — *Section 4.* A petition for a writ of certiorari to correct errors in proceedings which are not according to the course of the common law may be presented to a justice of the supreme judicial court, and he may, after notice, hear and determine the same. It shall be open to the petitioner to contend at the hearing upon the petition that the evidence which formed the basis of the action complained of or the basis of any specified finding

G. L. (Ter. Ed.), 249, § 4, amended.

Petition for certiorari, writ, decree and costs.

or conclusion was as matter of law insufficient to warrant such action, finding or conclusion. The writ shall not be issued unless the petition therefor is presented within two years next after the proceedings complained of. It may be issued from the clerk's office in any county and shall be returnable as the court orders. The court at any time after the petition is presented may impose costs upon any party, may issue an injunction and may order the proceedings brought up; and, after they are brought up, may quash or affirm them, or may make such order, judgment or decree as law and justice may require.

G. L. (Ter. Ed.), 249, § 5, etc., amended.

SECTION 2. Section five of said chapter two hundred and forty-nine, as amended by chapter two hundred and two of the acts of nineteen hundred and thirty-eight, is hereby further amended by striking out the second sentence and inserting in place thereof the two following sentences: — Upon the return of the order of notice, the person required to appear shall file an answer showing cause why the writ should not issue, and the petitioner may demur thereto. Unless a demurrer is filed any affirmative allegation contained in the answer shall be considered to be denied by the petitioner without a replication, unless the court, upon motion by the respondent, requires him to reply thereto, and to state what part, if any, he admits or denies, — so as to read as follows: — *Section 5.* A petition for a writ of mandamus may be presented to a justice of the supreme judicial court, and he may, after notice, hear and determine the same. Upon the return of the order of notice, the person required to appear shall file an answer showing cause why the writ should not issue, and the petitioner may demur thereto. Unless a demurrer is filed any affirmative allegation contained in the answer shall be considered to be denied by the petitioner without a replication, unless the court, upon motion by the respondent, requires him to reply thereto, and to state what part, if any, he admits or denies. The court may require a third person who has or claims a right or interest in the subject matter to appear and answer and to stand as the real party. If the respondent is the holder of a public office and pending the determination of the cause he ceases to hold that office, the court in its discretion may, after notice, allow an amendment to substitute his successor in office as a party respondent. If the petitioner prevails, his damages shall be assessed and judgment shall be rendered therefor, with costs, and for a peremptory writ of mandamus; otherwise, the party answering shall recover costs of the petitioner. No action shall be maintained for a false answer. All writs and processes may be issued from the clerk's office in any county and shall be returnable as the court orders.

Writ of mandamus.

Notice, procedure, etc.

G. L. (Ter. Ed.), 213, § 3, amended.

SECTION 3. Section three of chapter two hundred and thirteen of the General Laws, as appearing in the Tercentenary Edition, is hereby amended by inserting after clause

"Tenth A" the following clause: — Tenth B, Specifying the means whereby at a hearing upon a petition for certiorari the evidence adduced before the respondent shall be exhibited to the court.

Rules as to certiorari.

SECTION 4. Said chapter two hundred and thirteen is hereby further amended by inserting after section one B, inserted by section one of chapter two hundred and fifty-seven of the acts of nineteen hundred and thirty-nine, the two following sections: — *Section 1C.* The supreme judicial or the superior court may, before final judgment, and upon terms, allow an amendment changing a petition for a writ of certiorari into a petition for a writ of mandamus, or a petition for a writ of mandamus into a petition for a writ of certiorari, if it is necessary to enable the plaintiff to sustain the proceeding for the cause for which it was intended to be brought. The court in which the amendment is allowed may retain jurisdiction of the cause as amended.

G. L. (Ter. Ed.), 213, new §§ 1C and 1D, added.

Amendment of petitions for certiorari or mandamus.

Section 1D. A person aggrieved by a final judgment rendered by a single justice of the supreme judicial court or by the superior court upon a petition for a writ of certiorari or a writ of mandamus may appeal therefrom to the full court of the supreme judicial court. Upon such appeal all questions, whether of fact, of law or of discretion, which were open at the hearing before the single justice or before the superior court, as the case may be, shall be open to the same extent as before such justice or court. The appeal shall be subject to the provisions of sections nineteen and twenty-two to twenty-eight, inclusive, of chapter two hundred and fourteen relative to appeals in equity suits, so far as applicable. *Approved June 1, 1943.*

Appeals in cases of certiorari or mandamus.

AN ACT PROVIDING FOR THE INCLUSION OF ACCIDENT BENEFITS IN CERTAIN LIABILITY INSURANCE POLICIES. *Chap.*375

Be it enacted, etc., as follows:

SECTION 1. Chapter one hundred and seventy-five of the General Laws is hereby amended by inserting after section one hundred and eleven B, as appearing in the Tercentenary Edition, the following section: — *Section 111C.* A policy of insurance issued under subdivision (*b*) of clause Sixth of section forty-seven affording insurance against legal liability for loss or damage on account of the bodily injury or death of any person may also insure, or an endorsement or rider may be attached thereto to insure, any person including the named insured under the policy in respect to medical, surgical, ambulance, hospital, professional nursing and funeral expenses on account of the bodily injury or death of any person including the named insured. The provisions of sections one hundred and eight and one hundred and nine shall not apply to any such policy or any endorsement or rider providing for any or all of the benefits permitted by this section.

G. L. (Ter. Ed.), 175, new § 111C, added.

Inclusion of medical, etc., expense in certain policies.

SECTION 2. Section one hundred and ninety-two of said

G. L. (Ter. Ed.), 175, § 192, amended.

chapter one hundred and seventy-five, as so appearing, is hereby amended by adding at the end the following sentence: — All such provisions of law shall also apply to all forms of riders or endorsements, designed to be attached to motor vehicle liability policies as defined in section thirty-four A of chapter ninety, providing for additional coverage permitted by section one hundred and eleven C.

Riders to certain policies.

Approved June 1, 1943.

---

*Chap.*376 AN ACT PLACING UNDER CIVIL SERVICE CERTAIN EMPLOYEES OF THE STATE FARM.

Be it enacted, etc., as follows:

All employees of the state farm on the effective date of this act, except those specifically exempted from civil service by section four of chapter thirty-one of the General Laws, who were employed on or after September fourth, nineteen hundred and forty-one and prior to November third in said year, and who at all times between the date of their employment and the effective date of this act have been employees of the state farm, may continue to serve in their respective positions without taking a civil service examination, and their tenure of office shall be unlimited, subject, however, to the civil service laws. *Approved June 1, 1943.*

---

*Chap.*377 AN ACT RELATIVE TO CERTAIN CRIMES AGAINST CHASTITY, MORALITY, DECENCY AND GOOD ORDER AND THE PUNISHMENT THEREFOR.

Be it enacted, etc., as follows:

G. L. (Ter. Ed.), 272, § 53, amended.

Idle and disorderly persons, etc.

Chapter two hundred and seventy-two of the General Laws is hereby amended by striking out section fifty-three, as appearing in the Tercentenary Edition, and inserting in place thereof the following section: — *Section 53.* Stubborn children, runaways, common drunkards, common night walkers, both male and female, common railers and brawlers, persons who with offensive and disorderly act or language accost or annoy persons of the opposite sex, lewd, wanton and lascivious persons in speech or behavior, idle and disorderly persons, disturbers of the peace, keepers of noisy and disorderly houses and persons guilty of indecent exposure may be punished by imprisonment in a jail or house of correction for not more than six months, or by imprisonment at the state farm, or by a fine of not more than two hundred dollars, or by both such fine and imprisonment. *Approved June 1, 1943.*

AN ACT REQUIRING THAT EMPLOYERS PAYING WAGES BY CHECK SHALL PROVIDE REASONABLE FACILITIES FOR THE CASHING OF THE SAME WITHOUT CHARGE. *Chap.*378

Be it enacted, etc., as follows:

Section one hundred and forty-eight of chapter one hundred and forty-nine of the General Laws, as most recently amended by chapter one hundred and sixty of the acts of nineteen hundred and thirty-six, is hereby further amended by inserting after the third paragraph the following paragraph: — G. L. (Ter. Ed.), 149, § 148, etc., amended.

Any employer paying wages to an employee by check or draft shall, unless facilities for the cashing of such check or draft at a bank or elsewhere without charge by deduction from the face amount thereof or otherwise are otherwise available, provide to such employee reasonable facilities therefor. *Approved June 1, 1943.* Payment of wages by check.

AN ACT PROVIDING THAT CERTAIN PERSONS RESIDING IN CERTAIN CHARITABLE INSTITUTIONS SHALL NOT GAIN OR LOSE A SETTLEMENT WHILE SO RESIDING. *Chap.*379

Be it enacted, etc., as follows:

Section two of chapter one hundred and sixteen of the General Laws, as amended by chapter two hundred and thirteen of the acts of nineteen hundred and thirty-three, is hereby further amended by adding at the end the following sentence: — No person residing in an incorporated charitable institution the personal property of which is exempt from taxation, other than an employee of such institution, shall gain or lose a settlement nor be in the process of gaining or losing a settlement while residing therein, — so as to read as follows: — *Section 2.* No person shall acquire a settlement, or be in the process of acquiring a settlement, while receiving public relief other than aid or relief received under chapter one hundred and fifteen, unless, within two years after receiving such relief, he tenders reimbursement of the cost thereof to the commonwealth or to the town furnishing it. No former patient of a state or county tuberculosis sanatorium or hospital, who is employed in such an institution, shall lose or gain a settlement or be in the process of losing or gaining a settlement while so employed. No person residing in an incorporated charitable institution the personal property of which is exempt from taxation, other than an employee of such institution, shall gain or lose a settlement nor be in the process of gaining or losing a settlement while residing therein. *Approved June 1, 1943.* G. L. (Ter. Ed.), 116, § 2, etc., amended. Settlement not acquired while receiving public relief, etc.

*Chap.*380 AN ACT SUBJECTING TO THE CIVIL SERVICE LAWS THE OFFICES AND POSITIONS OF THE AMERICANIZATION DEPARTMENT OF THE CITY OF BOSTON.

Be it enacted, etc., as follows:

The offices and positions of the Americanization department of the city of Boston shall, upon the effective date of this act, become subject to the civil service laws and rules and regulations, and the terms of office of any incumbents of said offices and positions shall be unlimited, subject to said laws. The persons holding said offices and positions on said effective date shall be subjected to a non-competitive qualifying examination by the division of civil service, and those passing said examination shall be certified for their respective offices and positions and shall be deemed to be permanently appointed thereto without being required to serve any probationary period. *Approved June 1, 1943.*

---

*Chap.*381 AN ACT RELATIVE TO THE MARKING OF COMFORTERS, QUILTS AND PUFFS CONSISTING IN WHOLE OR IN PART OF REPROCESSED MATERIAL.

Be it enacted, etc., as follows:

G. L. (Ter. Ed.), 94, §§ 270–277, inc., not applicable, when.

SECTION 1. The provisions of sections two hundred and seventy to two hundred and seventy-seven, inclusive, of chapter ninety-four of the General Laws shall apply with respect to comforters, quilts and puffs, except as otherwise provided in this act.

"Reprocessed material" defined.

SECTION 2. For the purposes of this act, "reprocessed material" shall mean any material which has formed a part or portion of another manufactured article, has never been used in any way by an ultimate consumer, and, except, in the case of down, feathers or kapok, has subsequently been made into a fibrous state, and "ultimate consumer" shall mean a person who acquires material otherwise than for the purpose of sale, barter or exchange.

Branding of goods made from reprocessed material.

SECTION 3. If any comforter, quilt or puff is composed in whole or in part of reprocessed material and is composed in no part of material which has been used in any way by an ultimate consumer, there shall be plainly marked upon each such article, or upon a tag sewed thereon or otherwise securely attached thereto, in addition to the statement of the kind of material used for filling and the name of the manufacturer or vendor as required by said section two hundred and seventy, the words "reprocessed material", and not the words "second hand", and if any such article is enclosed in a bag, box, crate or other receptacle, there shall be plainly marked upon such receptacle, or upon a tag securely attached thereto, a statement that the contents of the receptacle are so marked.

Expiration of act.

SECTION 4. This act shall be operative only until July first, nineteen hundred and forty-five.

Approved June 1, 1943.

Chap.382

AN ACT PROVIDING RELIEF TO CERTAIN INDUSTRIES AND ESTABLISHMENTS FROM CONDITIONS RESULTING FROM THE SHORTAGE OF MAN POWER DUE TO THE EXISTING WAR.

Emergency preamble.

Whereas, The deferred operation of this act would deprive certain industries and establishments of immediately necessary personnel, therefore this act is hereby declared to be an emergency law, necessary for the immediate preservation of the public safety and convenience.

Be it enacted, etc., as follows:

Commissioner may suspend certain provisions of law.

SECTION 1. The commissioner of labor and industries is hereby authorized, in conformity with Article XX of Part the First of the constitution of the commonwealth, to suspend the application or operation of any provision of chapter one hundred and forty-nine of the General Laws, or of any rule or regulation made thereunder, regulating, limiting or prohibiting the employment of women or minors, in such instances, and for such periods of time, as said commissioner deems such suspension necessary to supply any deficiency in man power due directly or indirectly to the existing state of war between the United States and certain foreign countries. Nothing in this act shall authorize the suspension of any such provision in any case where such suspension may be effected under other authority granted by the general court.

Expiration of act.

SECTION 2. This act shall be operative only during the continuance of the existing state of war between the United States and any foreign country. *Approved June 2, 1943.*

Chap.383

AN ACT PROVIDING THAT THE COMMISSIONER OF CORPORATIONS AND TAXATION SHALL FURNISH TO COUNTY LAW LIBRARIES A LIST OF CERTAIN CORPORATIONS DISSOLVED BY THE SUPREME JUDICIAL COURT.

Be it enacted, etc., as follows:

G. L. (Ter. Ed.), 155, § 50A, etc., amended.

Section fifty A of chapter one hundred and fifty-five of the General Laws, inserted by section one of chapter four hundred and fifty-six of the acts of nineteen hundred and thirty-nine, is hereby amended by adding at the end the following sentence: — The commissioner shall furnish to each county law library within the commonwealth, upon application therefor, a copy, mimeographed or otherwise prepared as he shall determine, of the list of the corporations dissolved as herein provided, — so as to read as follows: — *Section 50A.* If a corporation has failed to comply with the provisions of law requiring the filing of reports or returns with the commissioner or the state secretary for two consecutive years, or if the commissioner is satisfied that a corporation has become inactive and that its dissolution would be in the public interest, the commissioner may apply to the supreme judicial court for its dissolution, and the court, after notice by mail

Dissolution of corporations.

or otherwise as it may order, may decree such dissolution subject to the provisions of sections fifty-one, fifty-two and fifty-six. The commissioner may include as many corporations in a single application as he deems fit and the court may include in its decree any or all thereof. The commissioner shall furnish to each county law library within the commonwealth, upon application therefor, a copy, mimeographed or otherwise prepared as he shall determine, of the list of the corporations dissolved as herein provided.

Approved June 2, 1943.

---

*Chap.*384 AN ACT PROVIDING FOR THE EXAMINATION OF SCHOOL CHILDREN'S FEET.

Be it enacted, etc., as follows:

G. L. (Ter. Ed.), 71, § 57, amended.

Testing as to defective sight, etc.

Chapter seventy-one of the General Laws is hereby amended by striking out section fifty-seven, as appearing in the Tercentenary Edition, and inserting in place thereof the following section: — *Section 57.* The committee shall cause every child in the public schools to be separately and carefully tested and examined at least once in every school year to ascertain defects in sight or hearing, and other physical defects tending to prevent his receiving the full benefit of his school work, or requiring a modification of the same in order to prevent injury to the child or to secure the best educational results, and to ascertain defects of the feet which might unfavorably influence the child's health or physical efficiency, or both, during childhood, adolescence and adult years, and shall require a physical record of each child to be kept in such form as the department may prescribe. The tests of sight and hearing shall be made by the teachers, directions for which shall be prescribed by the department of public health, and the examinations of feet shall be made by the school physicians. *Approved June 2, 1943.*

---

*Chap.*385 AN ACT PENALIZING THE REQUIREMENT BY ANY LABOR UNION OR PERSON ACTING IN ITS BEHALF OF THE PAYMENT OF CERTAIN FEES AND ASSESSMENTS AS A CONDITION OF SECURING OR CONTINUING EMPLOYMENT.

Be it enacted, etc., as follows:

G. L. (Ter. Ed.), 149, new § 150B, added.

Fees payable to labor unions regulated.

Chapter one hundred and forty-nine of the General Laws is hereby amended by inserting after section one hundred and fifty A, inserted by chapter four hundred and three of the acts of nineteen hundred and thirty-eight, the following section: — *Section 150B.* No labor union, or person acting in its behalf, shall require any person, as a condition of securing or continuing employment, to pay any fee or assessment other than such initiation fees, dues and assessments as are, by the constitution and by-laws of such union, chargeable upon members thereof. Any union or person violating any provision of this section shall be punished by a fine of not less than one hundred dollars.

Approved June 2, 1943.

AN ACT RELATIVE TO THE FINANCIAL RELIEF OF THE TOWN OF MILLVILLE. *Chap.*386

Be it enacted, etc., as follows:

Section three of chapter five hundred and fourteen of the acts of nineteen hundred and thirty-nine is hereby amended by striking out, in the fourth line, the word "forty-four" and inserting in place thereof the word: — forty-three, — so as to read as follows: — *Section 3.* In the distribution of the proceeds of income taxes under the provisions of section eighteen of chapter fifty-eight of the General Laws in each of the years nineteen hundred and forty-one to nineteen hundred and forty-three, inclusive, there shall be distributed to said town, in addition to its normal share, the sum of thirty thousand dollars. *Approved June 2, 1943.*

AN ACT TEMPORARILY REDUCING THE AGE REQUIREMENTS FOR REGISTRATION AS NURSES AND FOR LICENSES AS ATTENDANTS. *Chap.*387

Emergency preamble.

Whereas, The acute shortage of registered nurses and licensed attendants in the commonwealth during the existing emergency makes it necessary that this act become effective without delay, therefore it is hereby declared to be an emergency law, necessary for the immediate preservation of the public health, safety and convenience.

Be it enacted, etc., as follows:

Age requirement for registration of nurses.

SECTION 1. Subject to the limitations contained in section two, the minimum age prescribed by section seventy-four of chapter one hundred and twelve of the General Laws for applicants for registration as nurses is hereby changed from twenty-one years to twenty years, and the minimum age prescribed by section seventy-four A of said chapter one hundred and twelve for applicants for licenses as attendants is hereby changed from twenty years to nineteen years.

Expiration of act.

SECTION 2. This act shall apply only to applicants for registration as nurses or for licenses as attendants during the existing war between the United States and certain foreign countries, and to applicants therefor after the termination of said war who shall have matriculated during said war in an approved school for nurses or an approved school for attendants, as the case may be.

Approved June 2, 1943.

AN ACT TEMPORARILY AUTHORIZING THE ISSUANCE TO PERSONS IN THE MILITARY OR NAVAL SERVICE OF THE UNITED STATES OF SPECIAL CERTIFICATES ENTITLING THEM TO HUNT AND FISH IN THIS COMMONWEALTH. *Chap.*388

Emergency preamble.

Whereas, The deferred operation of this act would tend in part to defeat its purpose, which is to grant to persons in the military or naval service of the United States during the present war certain privileges with respect to hunting and fishing in this commonwealth, therefore it is hereby declared to be an emergency law necessary for the immediate preservation of the public convenience.

Be it enacted, etc., as follows:

Persons in armed forces may hunt, etc., without license.

SECTION 1. A person in the military or naval service of the United States may hunt any bird or mammal within the commonwealth, or may fish in any of the inland waters of the commonwealth, if he holds a special certificate entitling him so to do, which certificate the director of the division of fisheries and game of the department of conservation and the clerk of any city or town are hereby authorized to issue, and the holder of such certificate shall have the same rights and privileges and be subject to the same duties as if he held a sporting license. Such certificate shall be in the form prescribed upon a blank furnished by said division of fisheries and game. In case of residents of the commonwealth no fee shall be charged for such certificate, and in case of non-residents a fee of two dollars shall be charged therefor.

Expiration of act.

SECTION 2. This act shall be in effect only during the continuance of the existing state of war between the United States and certain foreign countries.

Approved June 2, 1943.

---

*Chap.*389 AN ACT RELATING TO SALVAGE OPERATIONS OF TRUSTEES.

Be it enacted, etc., as follows:

G. L. (Ter. Ed.), 203, new §§ 24A and 24B, added.

SECTION 1. Chapter two hundred and three of the General Laws is hereby amended by inserting after section twenty-four, as appearing in the Tercentenary Edition, the two following sections, under the caption SALVAGE OPERATIONS OF TRUSTEES: — *Section 24A.* Unless otherwise expressly provided by the will or other instrument by which a trust is created, upon the sale of real estate acquired by a trustee under a will or other instrument as a result of a foreclosure or a deed in lieu of foreclosure of any mortgage held by the trust, for a consideration consisting in part or in whole of a note or other obligation secured by a mortgage thereon or on a part thereof, the cash proceeds of such sale, plus the net cash receipts of the trust from the property since default, shall first be applied to the payment of all reasonable expenses and charges involved in acquiring, managing, maintaining, caring for and selling the property. Any balance of cash remaining may in the discretion of the trustee forthwith be apportioned between income and principal as though such cash constituted the entire proceeds of the sale.

Disposition of cash proceeds from sale.

Apportionment of cash proceeds.

Section 24B. Cash payments, whether of principal or interest, on a note or other obligation of the type referred to in section twenty-four A, received subsequent to the time when such note or obligation was accepted as the, or part of the, consideration shall, if the total net cash receipts referred to in said section twenty-four A were insufficient to pay the expenses and charges therein referred to, be first applied in reduction of such expenses and charges until cancelled. Subject to such provision, all such receipts, whether of principal or interest, may in the discretion of the trustee be apportioned between capital and income at such times as the trustee deems advisable.

If any apportionment is made under said section twenty-four A, all subsequent apportionments between income and principal shall be made in the same ratio, unless subsequent conditions or other circumstances render a different ratio of apportionment more equitable. The trustee, after the expenses and charges referred to in said section twenty-four A have been paid, may treat as income all or any part of the interest received on such note. A trustee who makes, in good faith, an apportionment provided for in this section or said section twenty-four A shall not be charged with personal liability for such acts.

Nothing in this section or section twenty-four A shall prevent a trustee from seeking the instruction of the proper court if he deems it advisable. The term "mortgage" as used in said section twenty-four A shall include a mortgage participation or a mortgage certificate or any other form of interest in a single entire mortgage, but shall not include a mortgage participation or a mortgage certificate or any other form of interest in a group of mortgages.

SECTION 2. The various provisions of this act are hereby declared to be severable and if any such provision or its application to any person or circumstance shall be held to be invalid or unconstitutional such invalidity or unconstitutionality shall not affect the validity or constitutionality of any of the remaining provisions or application to persons or circumstances other than those as to which it is held invalid. Severability of act.

Approved June 2, 1943.

AN ACT RELATIVE TO ABSENT VOTING BY RESIDENTS OF MASSACHUSETTS SERVING IN THE ARMED FORCES OF THE UNITED STATES DURING THE PRESENT WAR AND TO THE QUALIFICATION OF SUCH RESIDENTS AS VOTERS AT CERTAIN ELECTIONS. *Chap.*390

Be it enacted, etc., as follows:

SECTION 1. Except as herein provided, words and terms used in this act shall be construed in accordance with the definitions set forth in chapter fifty of the General Laws. For the purpose of this act, the word "kindred" shall mean spouse, father, mother, sister or brother of the whole or half blood, son, daughter, adopting parent or adopted child, step parent or step child, uncle, aunt, niece or nephew.

SECTION 2. Notwithstanding any contrary provision of general or special law, any legal resident of the commonwealth while serving in the armed forces of the United States during the existing war between the United States and any foreign country and whose name is included in the current annual register of voters of any city or town therein, or who may be determined to be qualified as a voter thereof in accordance with section eight of this act, may be furnished with an official absent voting ballot, prepared in accordance with clause (*a*) of section eighty-seven of chapter fifty-four of the General Laws, for, and may vote by means of such ballot at, any regular biennial state election or at any regular annual or biennial city or town election at which absent voting is permitted, provided an application therefor is filed with the clerk of the city or town of which he is such legal resident and the same is certified by the registrars of voters thereof, in the manner hereinafter provided.

SECTION 3. Application for an official absent voting ballot to be furnished to such resident for any such election may be made to the clerk of the city or town in which such resident is registered as a voter, or in which he has been determined to be qualified to vote as provided in said section eight, by any registered voter of the commonwealth who is a kindred of such resident. The applicant shall state therein his name and that of the city or town in which he is registered as a voter, together with the street and number of his address, if any, the name of the resident in whose behalf the application is made, the place of his legal residence on January first of the current year, or on such subsequent date when he first became a legal resident of such city or town, and the address to which such ballot is to be mailed. The applicant shall also make a statement of his relationship to such resident, shall make oath to the truth of all statements in such application and shall sign the same.

SECTION 4. The state secretary, or the clerk of each city and town subject to this act, as the case may be, shall seasonably prepare, prior to each regular biennial state election or regular annual or biennial city or town election, in such quantities as he shall deem necessary, all of the papers prescribed by said section eighty-seven of said chapter fifty-four, as amended, with such changes therein as may be required to give effect thereto. On the envelopes prepared for returning the official absent voting ballots furnished to any person determined to be qualified to vote under said section eight, except as to his ability to sign his name and to read, there shall be provided a space for him to sign his name and there shall be printed five lines of the constitution of the commonwealth in English. There shall be included in the jurat to be executed by the officer in whose presence such person makes his affidavit a statement setting forth that the affiant has signed his name in the officer's presence, and has read the said five lines in such a manner as to show that he was neither prompted nor reciting from memory, or was prevented by a physical disability from doing either.

SECTION 5. When an application is made for an official absent voting ballot as provided in section three and the same is filed with the city or town clerk, it shall be transmitted by said clerk forthwith to the registrars of voters of such city or town and, if they are satisfied that the statements therein are true and that the person in whose behalf the application is made is a duly registered voter of such city or town or has been determined to be qualified to vote therein at such election as provided in said section eight, they shall so certify thereon and return such application to the city or town clerk. If the person in whose behalf such an application is made is a duly registered voter, the clerk shall cause to be placed upon the voting list to be used at the election, to vote at which such application is made, the letters SAV, in capitals, opposite the name of such voter. The said clerk shall then mail, postage prepaid, to such resident at the address designated in such application, such ballot together with all blank forms and envelopes required.

SECTION 6. Any such resident who has received an official absent voting ballot furnished in accordance with this act may vote by mailing the same to the clerk of the city or town where he resides. He shall mark such ballot in the presence of a commissioned officer in the armed forces, in a municipality or place other than the city or town in which it is determined that such voter is qualified to vote. Before marking his ballot he shall exhibit it to said officer, who shall satisfy himself that it is unmarked, but he shall not allow such officer to see how he marks it. Such officer shall hold no communication with such voter, nor he with such officer, as to how he votes. After marking his ballot he shall enclose it in the proper envelope provided for the purpose and shall execute in the presence of such officer the affidavit thereon. He shall then seal the envelope with the ballot therein and shall mail the same, postage prepaid, to the city or town clerk, on or before the day of the election in a municipality or place other than the city or town in which he has been determined to be qualified as a voter. The postmark, if legible, shall be evidence of the time and place of mailing.

SECTION 7. Except as otherwise provided in this act, the provisions of sections eighty-six to one hundred and three A of chapter fifty-four of the General Laws relating to absent voting, and of sections twenty-seven and thirty-four of chapter fifty-six of the General Laws prescribing penalties for violations of laws relating to absent voting, shall, where pertinent, apply to absent voting under this act.

The provisions of section ninety-five of said chapter fifty-four relating to the duties of election officers at polling places with respect to absent voting ballots shall apply to ballots cast under this act. In addition to the duties prescribed by said section ninety-five, the warden or his deputy shall, in comparing the statements appearing in the affidavits upon the envelopes in which such ballots are enclosed with the applications therefor, determine whether the statements appearing in such affidavits conform to those appearing in such applications, and whether the persons signing such affidavits have been determined to be qualified to vote at such election. All envelopes, opened and unopened, enclosing ballots returned by persons determined to be qualified to vote at such election in accordance with said section eight shall, instead of being retained and returned with the ballots cast, be enclosed and sealed in an envelope provided for the purpose of returning the same to the city or town clerk, and said clerk shall retain such envelope as long as he retains the ballots cast, after which he shall transmit the same to the registrars of voters who shall preserve such envelope for five years from the date of such election.

SECTION 8. Any legal resident of the commonwealth who is serving in the armed forces of the United States during the existing war between the United States and any foreign country and who has the qualifications for voting prescribed by the constitution of the commonwealth, but whose name is not included in the current annual register of the city or town of his legal residence, may be qualified for voting at any regular biennial state election or at any regular annual or biennial city or town election at which absent voting is permitted upon the personal application of a registered voter of the commonwealth of the kindred of such resident made to the registrars of voters of the city or town in which the right of such resident to vote may be claimed. Such application may be made not less than twenty days before the day of such election at any time during regular business hours or at sessions held for the purpose of registering voters for such election, and shall be upon a form prescribed by the state secretary. The person making such application shall state thereon his name, and that of the city or town in which he is registered as a voter, with the street and number of his address, if any; the name of the person in whose behalf the application is made, his place of legal residence when he entered the service, on January first of the preceding year, on January first of the current year or on such later date when he first became a legal resident of such city or town, and at the time of making such application, and the place and date of his birth, and shall make a declaration that such resident has legally resided in the commonwealth one year, and in the city or town in which his right to vote is claimed six months, next preceding the election at which such right is claimed. The applicant shall also make thereon a statement of his relationship to the resident in whose behalf such application is made, shall make oath to the truth of the statements therein and sign his name thereto.

If the resident in whose behalf such an application is made claims to be a naturalized citizen, or to derive United States citizenship through the naturalization or citizenship of some other person, the applicant shall produce for inspection papers of naturalization, certificate of citizenship made under federal authority, or any other papers upon which he relies to prove the citizenship of the resident, and, if the registrars are satisfied that the resident is a citizen, they shall make upon such papers a memorandum of the date of such inspection.

The registrars shall make and certify on the application made under this section a statement of their determination as to whether or not the resident in whose behalf the application is made appears to be entitled to be registered, except the ability to sign his name and to read in the manner prescribed by Article XX of the amendments to the constitution. In case it is determined that such resident is not entitled to be registered, the registrars shall give written notice thereof to the applicant and give him an opportunity to be heard.

If the registrars certify that the resident has the qualifications entitling him to registration, except that his ability to sign his name and to read as prescribed by Article XX of the amendments to the constitution has not been determined, he shall nevertheless be entitled to receive an official absent voting ballot and application therefor may be made in the manner provided in section three of this act. Before permitting him to mark his ballot the officer referred to in section six of this act shall require him to sign his name if he is physically able to do so, and to read in his presence and in such a manner as to show that he was neither prompted nor reciting from memory the five lines of the constitution printed on the return envelope as provided in section four of this act. If he is unable to do either, and is not prevented by physical disability from so doing, the officer shall so certify on said envelope, and shall not permit him to vote but shall return the envelope with the ballot enclosed and unmarked, and the ballot shall not be counted.

Applications for qualification of residents as voters under this section shall be preserved by the registrars for five years and the registrars shall cause a suitable index to be made containing the name of each person determined to be so qualified, his place of legal residence, with street and number of his address, if any, at the time of making such application, the name of the military or naval unit in which he is then serving and his rank, his place and date of birth and, if he is a naturalized citizen or has derived United States citizenship through the naturalization of some other person, the facts appearing in such application relating thereto. Such index shall be preserved as a public record, but shall not be deemed to be a part of the general register of voters.

Persons registered under this section shall be subject to the provisions of sections forty-eight and forty-nine of chapter fifty-one of the General Laws and, except as herein otherwise provided, to all of the provisions of said chapter fifty-one prescribing qualifications for voting. The provisions of sections two, three, six, seven, eight, nine, ten and eleven of chapter fifty-six of the General Laws prescribing penalties for offenses concerning the listing or registration of voters shall, so far as pertinent, apply to persons applying for registration under this section.

SECTION 9. The registrars of voters may cause an investigation of any application under this act to be made by a police officer who shall forthwith after such investigation report to them his findings with respect thereto, and for this purpose the board or officer in charge of the police force of each city or town shall give the registrars such assistance as they may require.

SECTION 10. The registrars of voters shall include in the voting lists prepared in accordance with section fifty-five of chapter fifty-one of the General Laws for use at each regular biennial state election and at each regular annual or biennial city or town election at which absent voting is permitted the names and residences on January first preceding, or subsequently, as the case may be, of all residents of their respective cities and towns who have been registered at any such election as provided in section eight of this act and shall cause to be placed opposite the name of each such resident the letters SAV, in capitals. They shall forthwith, following the twentieth day preceding any such election, give written notice to the state secretary, or the city or town clerk, as the case may be, of the number of residents who have been registered under this act in such city or town, and in each ward and precinct therein, and shall likewise furnish the said secretary with mailing lists of such residents before each such state election.

SECTION 11. The provisions of section forty-six of chapter fifty-one of the General Laws shall apply to all applications for registration under this act on behalf of persons who have all the qualifications of a voter, except that of age, and who will, on or before the day of the next regular biennial state election or next regular annual or biennial city or town election at which absent voting is permitted, as the case may be, attain the age of twenty-one years.

SECTION 12. The state secretary shall forthwith, after the effective date of this act, prepare in such quantities as he may deem necessary, the following papers:

(*a*) Blank forms for registration application worded substantially as follows:

I,...................., a duly registered voter of the city or
(Name of Applicant)
town of......................, residing at.................in
(Name of City or Town where Applicant is registered as a Voter) (Street and Number)
such city or town, do hereby make application for an official absent voting ballot for the.............to be held in...............,
(Name of Election) (Name of City or Town)
on...................., 19.., for....................., serv-
(Name of Person in Service)
ing in the....................with the rank of.........., and
(Name of Unit)

a duly qualified voter for such election at.......................in
(Street and Number)
the city or town of...................., and, as I believe, en-
(Name of City or Town)
titled to vote at said election in Ward..., Precinct...., in the city or town of...................., said ballot to be mailed to..... ....

I hereby further declare that I am the......................of
(Relationship)
the person in whose behalf this application is made.

Signature of applicant.................(Date)........, 19...

Personally appeared before me the above-named............. and made oath that the foregoing statements are true to the best of his knowledge and belief.

....
(Registrar of Voters)

....

(Not to be filled in by applicant)

We, the undersigned, a majority of the registrars of voters of ...., hereby certify that.................,
(Name of City or Town) (Name of Person in Service)
in whose behalf the foregoing application has been made, has been determined to be a duly qualified voter at the................. election to be held in Ward......, Precinct......, of the city or town of....................., and is entitled to vote therein at such election.

(Four blank lines for signatures of registrars)

(*b*) Blank forms of affidavit to be printed on envelope for enclosing official absent voting ballot furnished to person whose name is included in current annual register of voters and serving in the armed forces of the United States, worded substantially as follows:

I,...................., serving in the..............with the
(Name of Military or Naval Unit)
rank of......................., do hereby make oath that I am a registered voter in the city or town of...................., Massachusetts, at......................in Precinct..., Ward.....;
(Street and Number)
that the place where I now am is not the municipality in which I am registered as a voter; that I have carefully read the instructions forwarded to me with the ballot herein enclosed; and that I have marked and sealed the within ballot as stated hereon by the person taking my oath.

(Signature of voter)....................

Subscribed and sworn to before me this................day of ...., 19..; and I hereby certify that when I was alone with the affiant he showed me the ballot herein enclosed unmarked, and then in my presence marked the same without my seeing how he marked it, after which he sealed said ballot in this envelope. I had no communication with the affiant as to how he was to vote.

Name of Officer..................
(Seal, if any) Unit..............................
Military or Naval Rank...........

(c) Blank forms of affidavit to be printed on envelope for enclosing absent voting ballot furnished to resident determined to be qualified to vote as provided in section eight, worded substantially as follows:

I, ..., serving in the .... with the rank of ...., do hereby make oath that at the time I entered the military or naval service or on the first day of January I was a legal resident of .... at
(City or Town and State)

......................; that on the first day of January of this
(Street and Number)

year I was a legal resident of .... at ...., and
(City or Town and State) (Street and Number)

that I am now a legal resident of .... at ....;
(City or Town and State) (Street and Number)

that I was born on .... in ....; that
(Date of Birth) (City or Town and State or Country)

I am a citizen of the United States, and that I have been a legal resident of the commonwealth of Massachusetts one year and of the city or town of .... six months next preceding the election at which I claim this right to vote.

(The voter shall then sign his name and read the following aloud to the officer taking his oath.)

(Print five lines of the State Constitution here)

I do hereby further make oath that the place where I now am is not the municipality in which I claim this right to vote; that I have carefully read the instructions forwarded to me with the ballot enclosed, and that I have marked and sealed the within ballot as stated by the person taking my oath.

(Signature of voter) ....

Subscribed and sworn to before me by the above affiant this .... day of ...., 19..; and I hereby certify that such affiant has signed his name in my presence, or was prevented by physical incapacity from so doing, read aloud the five lines of the state constitution appearing hereon in such a manner as to show he was neither prompted nor reciting from memory, and that when I was alone with him, he showed me the ballot herein enclosed, unmarked, and then in my presence marked the same without my seeing how he marked it, after which he sealed the said ballot in this envelope. I had no communication with the affiant as to how he was to vote.

Name of Officer ....
(Seal, if any) Unit ....
Military or Naval Rank ....

(d) Blank forms of application for qualification of person in service as a voter as provided in this act, worded substantially as follows:

I, ..., a duly registered voter of the city or
(Name of Applicant)

town of ...., residing at .... hereby
(Name of City or Town where Applicant is registered as a Voter) (Street and Number)

make oath that .... is now serving in the ....
(Name of Person in Service) (Name of Unit)

of the United States ....; that on January first of

last year he was a legal resident of................at..........,
(City or Town and State) (Street and Number)
and, on January first of this year, of..........................at
(City or Town and State)
....................; that he is now a legal resident of........
(Street and Number) (City or Town and State)
............at......................; that he was born in....
(Street and Number)
.....................on......................; and that he
(City or Town and State or Country) (Date of Birth)
has legally resided in the commonwealth of Massachusetts for one year and in the city or town of.........................for six months next preceding the election at which his right to vote is now being claimed.

I hereby further declare that I am....................of the
(Degree of Relationship)
person herein named in whose behalf this application for qualification as a voter at said election is claimed.

(Signature of applicant).............(Date)........., 19...

Personally appeared before me the above-named............and made oath that the foregoing statements are true to the best of his knowledge and belief.

....
(Registrar of Voters)

(If the person in whose behalf the application is made is a naturalized citizen or has derived United States citizenship through the naturalization of another, the registrars shall record in the space below, from the papers presented by the applicant, the facts required to show the citizenship of the person in service.)

(Not to be filled in by applicant)

We, the undersigned, a majority of the registrars of voters of the....................of......................, acting under
(City or Town) (Name of City or Town)
authority of section.....of chapter.........of the Acts of 1943, do hereby determine that......................is (is not) quali-
(Name of Person in Service)
fied to vote at the.................to be held in Ward.........,
(Name of Election)
Precinct.........of the city or town of.....................on
..............., 19..

(Four blank lines for signatures of registrars)

(*e*) Blank forms of report of police investigation, worded substantially as follows:

This is to certify that, after investigation, I find that, on January first of this year,...................................was a
(Name of Person in whose Behalf Application for Qualification as Voter is made)
resident of......................, and that he is now a legal
(City or Town and State)
resident of.....................at................... This
(City or Town and State) (Street and Number)
information was furnished to me by..........................re-
(Name of Informant)
siding at....................................
(Place of Residence of Informant)

(Signed)........................
(Police Officer)

(*f*) Suitable forms of certificates of listing, notices of omitted, additional or corrected listings to assessors and collectors of taxes and notices to registrars of voters of other cities or towns.

Section 13. The registrars of voters in the preparation of their annual register shall remove therefrom the name of each person registered under the provisions of this act who does not re-register in person as a voter within six months of the time of his or her discharge from the armed forces of the United States or of the termination of the existing states of war between the United States and certain foreign countries.

Section 14. If any part of this act, or section thereof, shall be declared unconstitutional, the validity of the remaining parts thereof shall not be affected thereby.

Section 15. This act shall remain in force only during such period as the existing war between the United States and certain foreign countries shall continue and until a declaration of the termination thereof by the President of the United States. *Approved June 2, 1943.*

---

*Chap.*391 An Act relative to the disposition of receipts from the public golf course maintained by the city of Salem.

Be it enacted, etc., as follows:

Section 1. Notwithstanding any provision of law to the contrary, the board of park commissioners in the city of Salem shall deposit with the city treasurer all moneys received from the use of the public golf course maintained by said city and from the sale of supplies or other articles thereat. Such deposits shall be kept in a separate account to be known as the Fund Receipts from Golf Course. Expenditures shall, subject to appropriation, be made from said fund by said board of park commissioners for improving and maintaining the parks or playgrounds in said city.

Section 2. This act shall take effect upon its passage.

Approved June 2, 1943.

---

*Chap.*392 An Act authorizing appropriations for temporary increases in the salaries of certain officers and employees in the service of the city of Lowell.

Be it enacted, etc., as follows:

Section 1. Any provision of general law or of chapter eighty-eight of the acts of the current year, or of any other special act relating to the city of Lowell, to the contrary notwithstanding, the mayor of said city may recommend and the city council thereof may vote to appropriate additional sums of money for temporary increases of not more than ten per cent of the salaries and wages of each officer and employee, except officers and employees of the school department, in the service of said city. The increase in salaries provided for by this act shall be effective June first in the current year and shall continue in effect until the adoption of the annual budget for the year nineteen hundred and forty-four, and such increases shall not prevent an officer or employee from receiving during said period step rate increases to which he may be entitled.

SECTION 2. No increase in salary made by this act shall, for any purpose of chapter thirty-two of the General Laws or any other provision of law providing for pensions, annuities or retirement allowances for officers or employees of said city, be deemed or construed to be a portion of the regular compensation of any officer or employee now or formerly in the service of said city.

SECTION 3. No appropriation or transfer of funds voted for such increases shall be valid without the approval of the emergency finance board established under section one of chapter forty-nine of the acts of nineteen hundred and thirty-three, as amended.

SECTION 4. This act shall take effect upon its passage.

Approved June 2, 1943.

AN ACT TO PROVIDE FOR CERTAIN WORK AT THE GLOUCESTER FISH PIER, SO CALLED, IN THE CITY OF GLOUCESTER. *Chap.*393

Be it enacted, etc., as follows:

SECTION 1. The department of public works is hereby authorized and directed to expend such sum, not exceeding fifteen thousand dollars, as may hereafter be appropriated therefor, for work at the Gloucester fish pier, so called, as follows: — For filling said pier to grade and repairing the main sewer.

SECTION 2. This act shall take effect upon its passage.

Approved June 2, 1943.

AN ACT FURTHER REGULATING PAY AND ALLOWANCES OF OFFICERS, WARRANT OFFICERS AND SOLDIERS OF THE LAND FORCES OF THE COMMONWEALTH. *Chap.*394

Emergency preamble.

Whereas, The deferred operation of this act would tend, in part, to defeat its purpose, which is to provide immediately a more equitable system of pay and allowances for the land forces of the commonwealth; therefore it is hereby declared to be an emergency law, necessary for the immediate preservation of the public convenience.

Be it enacted, etc., as follows:

G. L. (Ter. Ed.), 33, § 114, etc., amended.

SECTION 1. Section one hundred and fourteen of chapter thirty-three of the General Laws, as appearing in section one of chapter four hundred and twenty-five of the acts of nineteen hundred and thirty-nine, is hereby amended by striking out paragraphs (*a*) and (*b*) and inserting in place thereof the following two paragraphs: —

Pay of officers and men.

(*a*) There shall be allowed and paid per diem to officers and warrant officers of the land forces, on rolls and accounts kept in such form as the commander-in-chief may prescribe, for the duty prescribed by sections seventeen, eighteen, nineteen or one hundred and five, the same per diem pay as would be received by them if they were in the military service of the United States, and for the duty prescribed by section eleven either pay of grade as specified above or special duty pay, as directed by the commander-in-chief.

(*b*) There shall be allowed and paid per diem to soldiers of the land forces, on rolls and accounts kept in such form as the commander-in-chief may prescribe, for the duty prescribed by sections seventeen, eighteen or nineteen, as follows: bandsmen, four dollars and fifty-five cents; cooks, three dollars and fifty-five cents, if it is certified and made to appear that in each case the duty of superintending and assisting in the preparation of the food of the company was actually performed by the cook in person during the tour of duty or day of duty for which he is returned for pay, otherwise, the pay of other enlisted men of like grade; and every other enlisted man the same per diem pay received by soldiers of like grade in the regular army; provided, that the per diem pay of soldiers of the land forces for the duty prescribed by section eleven shall be either pay of grade as specified above or special duty pay, as directed by the commander-in-chief.

G. L. (Ter. Ed.), 33, § 114, etc., amended.

SECTION 2. Paragraph (*d*) of said section one hundred and fourteen of said chapter thirty-three, as so appearing, is hereby amended by inserting after the word "diem" in the third line the words: — special duty pay as follows: —, — so as to read as follows: —

Same subject.

(*d*) For all other duty under orders of the commander-in-chief unless specially provided, or as a witness or defendant under summons, there shall be paid per diem special duty pay as follows: — to all officers above the rank of captain, four dollars; to every other commissioned officer, two dollars and fifty cents; to every member of a band, three dollars and fifty-five cents, and if with troops one dollar additional; and to every other enlisted man, one dollar and fifty-five cents, except where payment is made therefor from federal funds. *Approved June 2, 1943.*

---

*Chap.*395 AN ACT RELATIVE TO THE EXCISE ON CORPORATIONS INTERESTED IN SHIPS AND VESSELS.

Be it enacted, etc., as follows:

G. L. (Ter. Ed.), 63, § 45, etc., amended.

Section forty-five of chapter sixty-three of the General Laws, as most recently amended by section five of chapter four hundred and seventy-three of the acts of nineteen hundred and thirty-five, is hereby further amended by inserting after the word "inclusive" in the fourth line the following: — , or under section sixty-seven, — so as to read as follows: — *Section 45.* If the commissioner discovers from the verification of a return, or otherwise, that the full amount of any tax due under sections thirty to fifty-one, inclusive, or under section sixty-seven, has not been assessed, he may, at any time within two years after September first of the year in which such assessment should have been made, assess the same, with interest as provided in section forty-eight to the date when the additional tax so assessed is required to be paid hereunder, first giving notice to the corporation to be assessed of his intention; and a representative of the corporation shall thereupon have an opportunity, within ten days after such notification, to confer with the commissioner as to the proposed assessment. After the expiration of ten days from the notification the commissioner shall assess the amount of the tax remaining due the commonwealth with interest as aforesaid, and shall give notice to the corporation so assessed. Any tax so assessed shall be required to be paid to the commissioner fourteen days after the date of the notice. Assessment of additional tax.

Approved June 2, 1943.

AN ACT RELATIVE TO THE UNINCORPORATED ASSOCIATION KNOWN AS "RELIEF PLAN OF BETHLEHEM STEEL CORPORATION AND SUBSIDIARY COMPANIES". *Chap.*396

Be it enacted, etc., as follows:

SECTION 1. The persons who from time to time are or shall be members of the unincorporated association known as "Relief Plan of Bethlehem Steel Corporation and Subsidiary Companies", while acting as members of and on behalf of said unincorporated association, and said association, are hereby exempted from all provisions of general and special law, other than this act, relative to insurance and to fraternal benefit societies.

SECTION 2. Membership in said association shall consist only of employees of corporations ninety per cent or more of the outstanding capital stock of which is from time to time owned, directly or indirectly, by Bethlehem Steel Corporation.

SECTION 3. Said association may afford relief to its members, not exceeding twelve dollars a week or six hundred and twenty-four dollars in any period of twelve consecutive months, for disability caused by sickness or accident, and may pay death or funeral benefits not exceeding fifteen hundred dollars in any one case; but, except as aforesaid, shall not engage in the business of insurance.

Approved June 2, 1943.

*Chap.*397 AN ACT RELATIVE TO LIMITED ACCESS WAYS.

Be it enacted, etc., as follows:

G. L. (Ter. Ed.), 81, new § 7C, added.

Laying out of limited access ways.

Chapter eighty-one of the General Laws is hereby amended by inserting after section seven B, inserted by chapter five hundred and nineteen of the acts of nineteen hundred and forty-one, the following section: — *Section 7C.* If the department determines that public necessity and convenience require that a limited access way shall be laid out, it shall lay out such way in the same manner as state highways. A limited access way is hereby defined to be a highway over which the easement of access in favor of abutting land exists only at such points and in such manner as is designated in the order of laying out. All of the provisions of law in regard to the laying out, relocation, alteration or discontinuance of state highways and to damages therefor shall apply to limited access ways. If a limited access way is laid out in whole or in part in the location of an existing public way, the owners of land abutting upon such existing public way shall be entitled to recover damages under chapter seventy-nine for the taking of or injury to their easements of access to such public way. No highway, town way or private way shall be laid out by county commissioners, by the selectmen of a town or by the appropriate officer or board of a city which crosses, enters upon or unites with a limited access way, without the consent in writing of the department.

Approved June 2, 1943.

---

*Chap.*398 AN ACT RELATIVE TO PENSIONS OF SPECIAL JUSTICES OF DISTRICT COURTS.

Be it enacted, etc., as follows:

G. L. (Ter. Ed.), 32, § 65B, etc., amended.

Pensions for special justices of district courts.

Chapter thirty-two of the General Laws is hereby amended by striking out section sixty-five B, inserted by section one of chapter six hundred and eighty-nine of the acts of nineteen hundred and forty-one, and inserting in place thereof the following section: — *Section 65B.* A special justice of a district court, including the municipal court of the city of Boston, who shall be retired under Article LVIII of the amendments to the constitution, or a special justice thereof sixty-five years of age or over who shall resign his office, after in either case having served as a special justice for at least ten years, shall be entitled to receive a pension for life at an annual rate equal to three fourths of his average yearly earnings as special justice during the period of ten years next preceding such retirement or resignation or at an annual rate equal to three fourths of his average yearly earnings as special justice during the entire period of his service in said office, whichever is the higher rate, but not exceeding in any event an annual rate equal to three fourths of the annual rate of salary of the justice of his court or, in the case of the municipal court of the city of Boston, three fourths of the annual rate of salary of an associate justice of said court, payable from the same source and in the same manner as the salary of such justice or associate justice, as the case may be. *Approved June 2, 1943.*

AN ACT AUTHORIZING THE PLACING OF THE OFFICE OF CHIEF ENGINEER OF THE FIRE DEPARTMENT OF THE PALMER FIRE DISTRICT NUMBER ONE OF PALMER UNDER THE CIVIL SERVICE LAWS. *Chap.*399

Be it enacted, etc., as follows:

SECTION 1. The office of chief engineer of the fire department of the Palmer Fire District Number One of Palmer shall, upon the effective date of this act, become subject to the civil service laws and rules and regulations relating to permanent members of fire departments in towns, and the tenure of office of any incumbent of said office shall be unlimited, subject, however, to said laws, but the present incumbent of said office may continue to serve therein only until the expiration of his term of office unless prior thereto he passes a non-competitive qualifying examination to which he shall be subjected by the division of civil service. After this act takes full effect, any vacancy in said office shall be filled by appointment by the prudential committee of said district.

SECTION 2. This act shall take full effect upon its acceptance by a majority vote of the voters of the said Palmer Fire District Number One of Palmer present and voting thereon at a district meeting called for the purpose within three years after its passage, but not otherwise.

Approved June 2, 1943.

AN ACT INCREASING THE AMOUNTS OF CERTAIN DEATH BENEFITS UNDER THE WORKMEN'S COMPENSATION LAW. *Chap.*400

Be it enacted, etc., as follows:

Section thirty-one of chapter one hundred and fifty-two of the General Laws, as amended, is hereby further amended by striking out the last paragraph, as appearing in the Tercentenary Edition, and inserting in place thereof the following: — G. L. (Ter. Ed.), 152, § 31, etc., amended.

In all other cases of total dependency, the insurer shall pay the dependents of the employee wholly dependent upon his earnings for support at the time of the injury a weekly payment equal to two thirds of his average weekly wages, but not more than twelve dollars nor less than five dollars a week, for a period of five hundred weeks; but in no case shall the amount be more than four thousand dollars. If the employee leaves dependents only partially dependent upon his earnings for support at the time of his injury the insurer shall pay such dependents a weekly compensation equal to the same proportion of the weekly payments for the benefit Death payments, amount of.

of persons wholly dependent as the amount contributed by the employee to such partial dependents bears to the annual earnings of the deceased at the time of his injury. In the event of the parties agreeing or the department finding that a partial dependent is the next of kin of the deceased employee and has, during the year preceding the injury, received from such deceased employee contributions for his support independent of gifts and gratuities, such partial dependent shall be paid by the insurer a minimum weekly compensation of five dollars. When weekly payments have been made to an injured employee before his death, compensation under this paragraph to dependents shall begin from the date of the death of the employee, but shall not continue for more than five hundred weeks; but in no case of partial dependency shall the amount be more than four thousand dollars.

Approved June 2, 1943.

---

*Chap.*401 AN ACT PROVIDING FOR A REBATE OF MOTOR VEHICLE REGISTRATION FEES IN THE CASE OF REGISTRANTS WHO SURRENDER THEIR REGISTRATION CERTIFICATES AND NUMBER PLATES BECAUSE OF THEIR ENTRANCE INTO THE MILITARY OR NAVAL SERVICE OF THE UNITED STATES.

Be it enacted, etc., as follows:

SECTION 1. If, during the existing state of war between the United States and certain foreign countries, a person, because of his entry into the military or naval service of the United States, surrenders the certificate of registration and number plates of a motor vehicle or trailer registered in his name he shall be entitled to a rebate equal in amount to that proportion of the registration fee paid for a full year which the number of months in said year following the last day of the month in which such surrender of certificate of registration and number plates occurred bears to twelve; provided, that in case such surrender occurs prior to August first in any year no rebate hereunder shall be less in amount than the rebate provided by section two of chapter ninety of the General Laws. No such rebate shall be paid unless written application therefor is made by the owner of the vehicle, or by his mother or father, wife or husband, sister or brother, child eighteen years of age or over, or a person certified by the registrar of motor vehicles as having authority, express or implied, from the owner of such vehicle to make such application, nor unless the application is filed before the date of expiration of the registration of said vehicle. Except as otherwise provided herein, any such rebate shall be made subject to the provisions of said section two of said chapter ninety.

SECTION 2. This act shall apply to certificates of registration of motor vehicles and trailers surrendered since January first in the current year and prior to the effective date of this act as well as to those surrendered on or after said effective date. *Approved June 2, 1943.*

AN ACT PLACING THE LABOR SERVICE OF THE DEPARTMENT OF PUBLIC UTILITIES UNDER THE CIVIL SERVICE LAWS. *Chap.*402

Be it enacted, etc., as follows:

SECTION 1. Section four of chapter thirty-one of the General Laws, as amended, is hereby further amended by adding at the end the following paragraph: — G. L. (Ter. Ed.), 31, § 4, etc., amended.

The labor service of the state department of public utilities. Labor service of department of public utilities.

SECTION 2. Any person holding, on January first of the year nineteen hundred and forty-three, a position in the labor service of the department of public utilities and continuing to serve in a position in such labor service to and including the effective date of this act may continue to serve in such position after passing a non-competitive qualifying examination to which he shall be subjected by the division of civil service. Examinations. *Approved June 2, 1943.*

AN ACT EXTENDING THE ADVANTAGES OF FREE CORRESPONDENCE COURSES TO CERTAIN PRESENT AND FORMER TUBERCULAR PATIENTS OF MUNICIPAL HOSPITALS AND SANATORIA. *Chap.*403

Be it enacted, etc., as follows:

Chapter sixty-nine of the General Laws is hereby amended by striking out section seven, as most recently amended by chapter five hundred and sixty-one of the acts of nineteen hundred and forty-one, and inserting in place thereof the following section: — *Section 7.* The department may co-operate with existing institutions of learning in the establishment and conduct of university extension and correspondence courses; may supervise the administration of all such courses supported in whole or in part by the commonwealth; and also, where deemed advisable, may establish and conduct such courses for the benefit of residents of the commonwealth and, provided that the fees charged exceed the cost of service, may enroll in correspondence courses such non-residents as are approved by the department. The department may offer correspondence courses, free of charge, to inmates of county and state hospitals and sanatoria, municipal sanatoria and tuberculosis divisions and tuberculosis wards of municipal hospitals, county and state correctional institutions, the Tewksbury state hospital and infirmary, and federal hospitals situated within the commonwealth, and to veterans, as such term is defined in section twenty-one of chapter thirty-one, who come within the class referred to as disabled veterans in section twenty-three of said chapter thirty-one, and may permit university extension courses to be taken, free of charge, by such veterans, and also by blind persons who have resided in the commonwealth at least one year immediately prior to the taking of such courses. The department may also furnish correspond- G. L. (Ter. Ed.), 69, § 7, etc., amended. University extension and correspondence courses.

ence courses, free of charge, to former inmates of any of said county or state hospitals or sanatoria, municipal sanatoria and tuberculosis divisions and tuberculosis wards of municipal hospitals, for a period of one year immediately following their discharge therefrom; provided, that such courses shall be furnished only for the purpose of completing correspondence courses in which said former inmates had enrolled prior to their discharge. It may, in accordance with rules and regulations established by it, grant to students satisfactorily completing such courses suitable certificates.

Approved June 2, 1943.

---

*Chap.*404 An Act authorizing the establishment within the town of Weymouth of a hospital for the inhabitants of such town.

Be it enacted, etc., as follows:

Section 1. Mrs. Gertrude A. Cassese, Clement N. Curtis, Preston A. DePlacido, Allan C. Emery, John Gallant, Roger P. Loud, Mrs. Lucy P. Mahoney, Mrs. Emily L. McGovern, Honorable Kenneth L. Nash, Timothy G. Osborn, George E. Pruden, A. Wesley Sampson, Mrs. Marguerite W. Shaftoe, Russell A. Stiles and C. Parker Whittle, Jr., all of the town of Weymouth, and their successors who shall be residents of said town, are hereby made a corporation by the name of the Laban Pratt Hospital, for the sole purpose of establishing and maintaining a public hospital for the use of the inhabitants of said town and others who may be admitted thereto under the provisions of the will, and the codicil thereto, of Laban Pratt, late of Boston, deceased, and may require medical and surgical treatment.

Section 2. Said corporation shall have authority for the purpose aforesaid, and no other, to hold real and personal estate to the amount of one million dollars.

Section 3. The chairman of the board of selectmen, the town accountant and the town treasurer, severally for the time being, and their successors, shall be trustees, ex-officiis during the terms of their respective offices, and, together with the corporators above named, shall constitute the board of trustees, of whom the chairman of the board of selectmen shall be ex-officio chairman, and whose terms of office, except as above provided, shall be as follows: — The trustees shall in the year next following the acceptance of this act as hereinafter provided, elect five of their members whose terms of office are not fixed as above, who shall hold for the term of one year from the first day of the following February, and five of their own number who shall hold for the term of two years from said first day of the following February, and the remaining five shall be elected to hold for the term of three years from the said first day of the following February, and who shall severally hold for the terms for which they are elected and until their successors are chosen, and thereafter, as the terms of office of the members, other than the members ex-officiis, expire, the town shall annually, by ballot, elect such number of trustees, for the term of three years each, as are necessary to fill such vacancies. Six members of the board shall constitute a quorum, except in the election or removal of trustees when a majority of the board shall be required. Whenever a vacancy shall occur in the board of trustees by reason of the death, resignation or otherwise of the members so elected, the remaining trustees shall fill the vacancy for the unexpired term. No member of the board as such shall receive compensation for his services. The town of Weymouth is hereby authorized and empowered to place in trust in the hands of the trustees of said corporation all funds, gifts and bequests, which are or may be held by it for the purpose of establishing and maintaining said hospital, especially all sums it has or may from time to time receive from the trustees appointed under the will of the said Laban Pratt, deceased. And said corporation shall, upon the acceptance of this act as hereinafter provided, receive and hold all past and future bequests and gifts that may be made for the maintenance of said hospital, and the same shall be appropriated, held and used by said corporation for the sole use and purpose aforesaid as a trust in behalf of and for the inhabitants of said town, and to such other persons as may be permitted to enjoy the benefits of said hospital in pursuance of the provisions of said will and codicil. Said trustees shall render to the board of selectmen annually as of the first of January a report of their proceedings, with a statement of the condition of the hospital, the property and funds pertaining to the same, with an accurate account of all receipts and expenditures, together with such other information or suggestions they may deem desirable, which report shall be published by the board of selectmen in the annual town report. Said trustees shall in behalf of said town carefully and considerately carry into execution the generous plan of the testator as contemplated by the said will and codicil.

Section 4. The town treasurer of said town of Weymouth shall be the custodian of all funds and securities of the hospital, and shall, as directed by the trustees, invest and reinvest them, and make expenditures therefrom. The town treasurer shall furnish a bond satisfactory to the trustees for the faithful performance of his duties, and his books of account and vouchers shall at all times be open to the trustees, or any one of them.

Section 5. The trustees shall appoint a clerk whose duty it shall be to keep a full and fair record of the proceedings of the board, and to discharge such other duties as they shall from time to time prescribe. The compensation of the clerk shall be fixed by the trustees.

Section 6. The trustees shall have full power to elect such other officers as they may from time to time think necessary or expedient, and to determine and fix the tenure of their offices, to remove any trustee who shall be incapable through age, removal from the town, infirmity or otherwise for the discharge of his duties as said trustee, or who by unreasonable absence from the meetings of the board shall fail to discharge the duties of his office, and generally to do all acts and things necessary or expedient to be done for the purpose of carrying into full effect the provisions and purposes of this act.

SECTION 7. It shall be the duty of the trustees to safely and securely invest, or to hold invested, the trust funds derived under said will or otherwise, and they shall have regard at all times to all the provisions of said will affecting said trust and the desire of the testator as expressed therein.

SECTION 8. Nothing in this act contained shall be held to alter or impair any trust created by said will and codicil. The corporation hereby created, acting through its trustees and proper officers, shall be deemed the agent of said town of Weymouth for the proper execution of all trusts arising under the provisions of said will and codicil. Nothing in this act contained shall be construed as releasing said town of Weymouth from any obligation arising from the acceptance of said bequest under said will and codicil or from any condition made therein. Said Allan C. Emery is hereby authorized and empowered to prescribe the time and place for the holding of the first meeting of said trustees and to notify them thereof.

SECTION 9. This act shall take full effect upon its acceptance by a majority of the town meeting members of the town of Weymouth present and voting thereon at a meeting legally called for this purpose not later than five years after the date of the passage of this act, but not otherwise.

Approved June 2, 1943.

---

*Chap.*405 AN ACT RELATIVE TO THE FILING FEES TO BE PAID IN CONNECTION WITH THE CONSOLIDATION OF BUSINESS CORPORATIONS.

Be it enacted, etc., as follows:

G. L. (Ter. Ed.), 156, § 46B, etc., amended.

SECTION 1. Section forty-six B of chapter one hundred and fifty-six of the General Laws, as inserted by section two of chapter five hundred and fourteen of the acts of nineteen hundred and forty-one, is hereby amended by striking out the paragraph contained in the one hundred and second to the one hundred and eighth lines, inclusive, and inserting in place thereof the following paragraph: —

Filing fee.

The filing fee to be paid to the state secretary for any increase of capital stock, based upon the increase of the authorized capital stock of the consolidated corporation above the total aggregate capital stock theretofore authorized for the constituent corporations, shall be determined in the manner provided by section fifty-four, but in no event shall the fee for filing the articles of consolidation be less than fifty dollars.

SECTION 2. Section forty-six D of said chapter one hundred and fifty-six, as so inserted, is hereby amended by striking out the paragraph contained in the sixty-fourth to the seventy-third lines, inclusive, and inserting in place thereof the following paragraph: — G. L. (Ter. Ed.), 156, § 46D, etc., amended.

If the consolidated corporation is to be a domestic corporation the filing fee to be paid to the state secretary for any increase of capital stock, based upon the increase of the authorized capital stock of the consolidated corporation over the total aggregate capital previously authorized for the constituent domestic corporations, shall be determined in the manner provided by section fifty-four, but in no event shall the fee for filing the articles of consolidation be less than fifty dollars if the consolidated corporation is to be a domestic corporation nor less than one hundred dollars if the consolidated corporation is to be a foreign corporation. Filing fee.

Approved June 2, 1943.

AN ACT TO EXEMPT PERSONS IN THE MILITARY AND NAVAL SERVICE OF THE UNITED STATES FROM THE PAYMENT OF POLL TAXES. *Chap.* 406

Whereas, The deferred operation of this act would tend to defeat its purpose, which is to exempt immediately persons who served or are serving in the armed forces of the United States during the existing states of war between the United States and certain foreign countries from the payment of poll taxes and to provide for the reimbursement to such persons of such taxes which may already have been paid, therefore it is hereby declared to be an emergency law, necessary for the immediate preservation of the public convenience. Emergency preamble.

Be it enacted, etc., as follows:

SECTION 1. Inhabitants of the commonwealth liable to be assessed for a poll tax who were engaged in the military or naval service of the United States during the existing states of war between the United States and certain foreign countries before the effective date of this act, and those who, on or after said date, engage in said service, shall be assessed in accordance with law for poll taxes, but shall be exempt from the payment of all poll taxes assessed for the year nineteen hundred and forty-one and for any subsequent year during the continuance of said states of war. Suspension of poll tax for members of armed forces.

SECTION 2. All taxes heretofore collected which would be exempt from payment under section one shall, at the request of the person assessed, be refunded by the city or town receiving the same and charged to the overlay of the year in which the tax so exempted from payment was assessed. Refunds

Approved June 3, 1943.

Chap.407 AN ACT PROVIDING FOR THE EXTENSION OF THE TEMPORARY CIGARETTE TAX.

Emergency preamble.

Whereas, The deferred operation of this act would tend to defeat its purpose by depriving the commonwealth of necessary revenue, therefore it is hereby declared to be an emergency law, necessary for the immediate preservation of the public convenience.

Be it enacted, etc., as follows:

Section nineteen of chapter four hundred and seventeen of the acts of nineteen hundred and forty-one is hereby amended by striking out, in the fourth line, the word "forty-three" and inserting in place thereof the word: — forty-five, — so as to read as follows: — *Section 19.* Sections one to seventeen, inclusive, of this act shall become effective on July first of the current year and shall continue in effect until July first, nineteen hundred and forty-five; and this section and section eighteen of this act shall take effect upon its passage. *Approved June 3, 1943.*

Chap.408 AN ACT RELATIVE TO BIRTHS, DEATHS AND MARRIAGES TAKING PLACE ON FEDERAL RESERVATIONS.

Emergency preamble.

Whereas, The deferred operation of this act would delay the accomplishment of one of its principal purposes, which is to remove immediately certain impediments to the solemnization of marriages on federal reservations of persons in the armed forces and others, therefore this act is hereby declared to be an emergency law, necessary for the immediate preservation of the public convenience.

Be it enacted, etc., as follows:

Births and deaths on federal reservations.

SECTION 1. For the purposes of chapter forty-six of the General Laws, all births and deaths occurring on any federal reservation not a part of the commonwealth shall be deemed to take place in the city or town of which the place of birth or death formed a part immediately prior to its inclusion in such reservation.

Marriages solemnized on federal reservations, recording of.

SECTION 2. For the purpose of solemnizing marriages, any federal reservation not a part of the commonwealth shall be deemed to be a part thereof. If both parties to a marriage proposed to be solemnized on any federal reservation, whether or not it be a part of the commonwealth, dwell without the commonwealth, they may cause notice of their intention to be filed in the office of the clerk or registrar of any city or town contiguous to or partly contained in such reservation, and the provisions of chapters forty-six and two hundred and seven of the General Laws shall apply to the filing of such notice, the issuance of a certificate or license pursuant thereto and to the solemnization and recording of the marriage, in all respects as though such city or town were the place of such marriage.

SECTION 3. This act shall take effect as of October first, nineteen hundred and forty-two, and shall be effective only during the continuance of the existing states of war between the United States and any foreign country. Expiration of act.

Approved June 3, 1943.

AN ACT TO PROVIDE FOR THE ACQUIRING OF MOTOR VEHICLES OR FOR OBTAINING THE USE THEREOF BY THE MILITARY DIVISION OF THE EXECUTIVE DEPARTMENT AND FOR THE SETTLEMENT OF CERTAIN CLAIMS AGAINST THE COMMONWEALTH ARISING OUT OF THE OPERATION OF MOTOR VEHICLES. *Chap.*409

Whereas, In the existing state of war public safety and convenience require a just, adequate and prompt method of acquiring and of operating motor vehicles by the military forces of the commonwealth and of disposing of claims against the commonwealth caused by such operation, and the deferred operation of this act would tend to delay and in part to defeat that purpose, therefore it is hereby declared to be an emergency law, necessary for the immediate preservation of the public safety and convenience. Emergency preamble.

Be it enacted, etc., as follows:

SECTION 1. Chapter thirty-three of the General Laws is hereby amended by inserting after section fifty-five, as appearing in section one of chapter four hundred and twenty-five of the acts of nineteen hundred and thirty-nine, the six following sections: — *Section 55A.* In the event that an enemy which is at war with the United States shall commence or threaten operations to endanger the peace or safety of this commonwealth, or in the event of tumult, riot, mob or catastrophe within the purview of section eighteen or section nineteen, or in the event that any unit of the military forces of the commonwealth shall, by order of the commander-in-chief, be directed or authorized to participate in or engage in, any military training, exercise or duty in which the use of motor vehicles in excess of the number issued to such unit by the state quartermaster is authorized or directed in writing, the adjutant general, in the name and on behalf of the commonwealth, may, under orders issued by the commander-in-chief, accept the gift or loan of, or the grant of the temporary right to the use and control of, or may hire, or purchase such motor vehicle for military use. G. L. (Ter. Ed.), 33, new §§ 55A–55F, added. Acquisition of motor vehicles for military use.

Section 55B. Claims against the commonwealth for the destruction of or damage to any motor vehicle so given, loaned or hired, or for any damage to property or any injury (including death resulting therefrom) to any person caused by any motor vehicle during any such period of use, shall be referred to a board established under a second paragraph Claims for damages.

of section fifty-five C, and all pertinent provisions of said paragraph shall apply to the settlement of such claims. The commonwealth shall not be liable for the depreciation of any motor vehicle so acquired.

Compensation for personal injuries or death arising from use of borrowed or hired motor vehicles.

Section 55C. An officer, or soldier of the military forces of the commonwealth, a person not a member of the military forces of the commonwealth but who is the owner, or is employed by the owner, of a motor vehicle lawfully loaned to or hired by the commonwealth under section fifty-five A and whose services are loaned or given to the commonwealth for any purpose set forth in said section, or a person rendering assistance to any of the military forces of the commonwealth in connection with the use of a motor vehicle under any provision of said section fifty-five A by request or order of a responsible officer of said military forces, and who by reason of such voluntary action or employment or assistance and without fault or neglect on his part shall receive any injury, be disabled, or contract any sickness or disease, incapacitating him from pursuing his usual business or occupation shall, during the period of such incapacity, receive compensation to be fixed by a board appointed as herein provided to inquire into his claim, the amount of such compensation not to exceed, in the case of an officer or soldier, special duty pay plus ration allowance provided by this chapter or, in the case of a person not a member of the military forces of the commonwealth, three dollars per day and in addition, in each instance, actual necessary expenses for medical services and care, medicines and hospitalization.

In case of death resulting from such injury, sickness or disease, compensation shall be paid to the decedent's dependents as determined in accordance with section thirty-two and clause (3) of section one, both of chapter one hundred and fifty-two, in the amount provided by, and otherwise subject to, section thirty-one of said chapter; provided, that compensation to such dependents other than widows and children shall be based on the compensation provided in the preceding sentence and that, for the purposes thereof, said board shall exercise all the powers given by said chapter one hundred and fifty-two to the department of industrial accidents. All claims arising under this section and claims referred to in the first sentence of section fifty-five B shall be inquired into by a board of three officers, at least one of whom shall be a medical officer, appointed by the commander-in-chief. The board shall have the same power to take evidence, administer oaths, issue subpoenas and compel witnesses to attend and testify and produce books and papers, and to punish their failure to do so, as is possessed by a general court-martial. The findings of the board shall be subject to the approval of the commander-in-chief. The amount so found due and so approved shall be a charge against the commonwealth, and paid in the same manner as other military accounts.

Section 55D. If any person makes a claim against the commonwealth by giving a notice as authorized by section fifty-five F, he shall be deemed thereby to have waived any and all right or remedy against the commonwealth relative to the subject matter of such claim to which he would otherwise be entitled by law.

Person making claim waives other rights, etc.

Section 55E. Where the damage or injury for which compensation is claimed under section fifty-five B or section fifty-five C was caused under circumstances creating a legal liability in some person other than the commonwealth to pay damages in respect thereof, the commonwealth may enforce, in the name of the claimant or in its own name and for its own benefit, the liability of such other person. The sum recovered shall be for the benefit of the commonwealth unless such sum is greater than that paid by it to the claimant, in which case four fifths of the excess shall be paid to the claimant.

Liability of person other than commonwealth, enforcement of.

Section 55F. No person performing any services under section fifty-five C shall, by reason of such services, be deemed to be an employee of the commonwealth or, if not already an officer or soldier of the military forces of the commonwealth, to be such an officer or soldier, or to be entitled to receive any pension or retirement allowance from the commonwealth, or to have acquired any right, or to be entitled to receive any other benefit or compensation. Any person claiming the right to receive compensation from the commonwealth under any provision of said last mentioned section shall, within thirty days after receiving an injury, or contracting any sickness or disease, while performing services referred to therein, give to the adjutant general notice of his name and place of residence, and the time, place and cause of such injury, sickness or disease; provided, that such notice shall not be invalid or insufficient solely by reason of any inaccuracy in stating the name or place of residence of the person receiving the injury, or contracting sickness or disease, or the time, place or cause of the injury, sickness or disease, if it is shown that there was no intention to mislead and the adjutant general was not in fact misled thereby. Such notice shall be in writing, signed by the person claiming compensation or by someone in his behalf. If by reason of physical or mental incapacity it is impossible for such person to give notice within the time required, he may give it within thirty days after such incapacity has been removed, and if he dies within said thirty days his executor or administrator may give the notice within thirty days after his appointment. Any form of written communication signed by the person, or by someone in his behalf, or by his executor or administrator, or by someone in behalf of such executor or administrator, which contains the information that the person was so injured, or so contracted sickness or disease, giving the name and place of residence of such person and the time, place and cause of the injury, sickness or disease, shall be considered a sufficient notice.

Certain persons not to be deemed employees of commonwealth.

G. L. (Ter. Ed.), 90, new § 5A, added.

Plates for use on vehicles used by military forces.

SECTION 2. Chapter ninety of the General Laws is hereby amended by inserting after section five, as appearing in the Tercentenary Edition, the following section: — *Section 5A.* The adjutant general, in behalf of the military forces of the commonwealth, may make application, in such form and containing such information as the registrar of motor vehicles may determine, for a general distinguishing number or mark, and the registrar shall issue to him a certificate of registration. All motor vehicles under the control of the military forces of the commonwealth shall be regarded as registered under such general distinguishing number or mark, provided number plates furnished as hereinafter provided are properly displayed thereon.

The adjutant general shall provide for use on the vehicles aforesaid one pair of number plates for each vehicle, which shall contain the general distinguishing number or mark assigned by the registrar and be of such color and form as the registrar shall approve. When a pair of number plates is issued for use the adjutant general shall keep a record of the plates so issued and report said issuance to the registrar.

Whoever attaches a number plate or other distinctive mark as provided in this section to a motor vehicle or trailer without being authorized so to do shall be punished by a fine of not more than one hundred dollars.

Whoever upon any way of the commonwealth operates a motor vehicle to which number plates or marks of distinction, as provided in this section, have been attached without authority, or whoever without authority operates a motor vehicle to which such number plates or marks have been legally attached, shall be punished by a fine of not less than twenty-five nor more than fifty dollars.

G. L. (Ter. Ed.), 12, § 3B, etc., amended.

SECTION 3. Section three B of chapter twelve of the General Laws, as most recently amended by section one of chapter two hundred and ninety-one of the acts of nineteen hundred and thirty-four, is hereby further amended by inserting after the first paragraph the following paragraph:—

Members of military forces deemed employees of commonwealth, when.

For the purposes only of this section, an officer, or soldier of the military forces of the commonwealth, as defined in chapter thirty-three, shall while performing any lawfully ordered military duty be deemed to be an officer or employee of the commonwealth and a motor vehicle given to the commonwealth, loaned to it or hired or purchased by it under section fifty-five A of chapter thirty-three shall, while being used in the performance of any lawfully ordered military duty, be deemed to be a motor vehicle owned by the commonwealth.

G. L. (Ter. Ed.), 260, § 4, etc., amended.

SECTION 4. Section four of chapter two hundred and sixty of the General Laws, as most recently amended by section nine of chapter three hundred and eighty-five of the acts of nineteen hundred and thirty-seven, is hereby amended by adding at the end the following paragraph: —

To whom section applicable.

For the purposes only of this section, an officer or soldier of the military forces of the commonwealth, as defined in chapter thirty-three, shall while performing any lawfully ordered military duty be deemed to be an officer or employee of the commonwealth. *Approved June 3, 1943.*

Chap.410

AN ACT RELATIVE TO CONTRACTS OF CONDITIONAL SALE OF PERSONAL PROPERTY.

Be it enacted, etc., as follows:

G. L. (Ter. Ed.), 255, § 12, etc., amended.

SECTION 1. Chapter two hundred and fifty-five of the General Laws is hereby amended by striking out section twelve, as appearing in section one of chapter five hundred and nine of the acts of nineteen hundred and thirty-nine, and inserting in place thereof the following section: — *Section 12.* Each conditional sale which includes one or more articles of personal property shall be embodied in a single written contract, which contract shall contain the entire agreement between the parties. Said contract shall specifically set forth, captioned in print of not less than eight-point type in case a printed form is used, the following: — a description of the property to be sold to the vendee; the cash price thereof; the down payment; a description of property to be traded in, if any, and the trade-in allowance therefor; other credit allowances, if any; the difference between the cash price and the aggregate of down payment and allowances, if any; a description of each policy of insurance for which a charge is made by the vendor; the total amount of finance charges, which shall include the insurance premiums, if any; the "total time price"; the net balance due from the vendee; the number and amount of weekly, monthly or other instalment payments; a statement of delinquency charges, if any; a statement of prepayment allowances, if any; and, if any promissory note is to be executed in the transaction, a statement that a promissory note or notes, as the case may be, are being executed in connection with the contract. Where any insurance premium is part of the total time price or finance charge, the vendor or his assignee shall, within twenty days after execution of the contract, send or cause to be sent to the vendee a policy or policies or certificate of insurance clearly setting forth the exact nature of the insurance coverage. If such contract does not substantially contain the subject matter as herein set forth, the vendee shall have a valid defence against the recovery of all finance charges and fees, exclusive of insurance premiums, in any action or proceeding to enforce said contract.

Conditional sales contracts.

Effective date.

SECTION 2. This act shall become effective on January first, nineteen hundred and forty-four.

Approved June 3, 1943.

*Chap.*411 AN ACT MAKING CERTAIN CORRECTIONAL CHANGES IN THE LAWS PERTAINING TO THE CONDUCT OF ELECTIONS.

Be it enacted, etc., as follows:

G. L. (Ter. Ed.), 54, § 2, amended.

SECTION 1. Section two of chapter fifty-four of the General Laws, as appearing in the Tercentenary Edition, is hereby amended by striking out, in the tenth line, the word "July" and inserting in place thereof the word: — October, — and by adding at the end the following sentence: — Except as provided in section three, when new precincts are established, the new division shall take effect on the thirty-first day of December next following, — so as to read as follows: — *Section 2.* Each city shall be divided into convenient voting precincts, designated by numbers or letters and containing not more than two thousand voters. Every ward shall constitute a voting precinct by itself, or shall be divided into precincts containing as nearly as may be an equal number of voters, consisting of compact and contiguous territory entirely within the ward, and bounded, so far as possible, by the center line of known streets or ways or by other well defined limits. If a ward constituting one precinct contains more than two thousand voters, according to the registration at the preceding annual or biennial city election, the aldermen, on or before the first Monday of October, shall divide it into two or more voting precincts. They may so divide a ward or precinct containing less than two thousand voters. If in any year, according to such registration, a voting precinct contains more than two thousand voters, the aldermen shall in like manner either divide such precinct into two or more voting precincts or make a new division of the ward into voting precincts. Except as provided in section three, when new precincts are established, the new division shall take effect on the thirty-first day of December next following.

Voting precincts, division of cities and wards into.

G. L. (Ter. Ed.), 54, § 6, amended.

Voting precincts in towns.

SECTION 2. Said chapter fifty-four is hereby further amended by striking out section six, as so appearing, and inserting in place thereof the following section: — *Section 6.* A town may direct its selectmen to prepare a division of the town into convenient voting precincts. The selectmen shall, so far as possible, make the center line of streets or ways, or other well defined limits, the boundaries of the proposed precincts, and shall designate them by numbers or letters. They shall, within sixty days, file a report of their doings with the town clerk, with a map or description of the proposed precincts, and with a statement of the number of voters registered in each for the preceding state or town election. The report shall be presented by the town clerk at the next town meeting, but shall not be acted upon except at a meeting held at least seven days after the report has been filed. The division so reported may be amended at such meeting, and shall take effect on the thirty-first day of December following its adoption. If such report shall be rejected the town may at any time direct the selectmen to prepare a new division.

SECTION 3. Said chapter fifty-four is hereby further amended by striking out section seven, as so appearing, and inserting in place thereof the following section: — *Section 7.* Except in towns of twelve thousand inhabitants or over, a town may make any change in its voting precincts which the selectmen recommend in a statement giving the boundaries, the designations of the proposed precincts and the number of voters registered in each for the preceding state or town election, filed with the town clerk at least seven days before a town meeting; but no changes other than those so proposed by the selectmen shall be made at such meeting. Changes in voting precincts under this section shall take effect on the thirty-first day of December following such change.

G. L. (Ter. Ed.), 54, § 7, amended.

Changes in voting precincts in towns.

SECTION 4. Section thirteen of said chapter fifty-four, as amended by section three of chapter one hundred and fifty-eight of the acts of nineteen hundred and thirty-four, is hereby further amended by striking out the fourth sentence and inserting in place thereof the following sentence: — Every election officer shall hold office for one year, beginning with September first succeeding his appointment, and until his successor is qualified, or until his removal, except that election officers appointed to count and tabulate votes shall serve at such primaries or elections and at such times as shall be designated by the appointing authority, — so as to read as follows: — *Section 13.* Such election officers shall be enrolled voters so appointed as equally to represent the two leading political parties, except that, without disturbing the equal representation of such parties, not more than two of such election officers not representing either of them may be appointed. The warden shall be of a different political party from the clerk, and not more than one half of the inspectors shall be of the same political party. In each case the principal officer and his deputy shall be of the same political party. Every election officer shall hold office for one year, beginning with September first succeeding his appointment, and until his successor is qualified, or until his removal, except that election officers appointed to count and tabulate votes shall serve at such primaries or elections and at such times as shall be designated by the appointing authority. An election officer may be removed by the mayor, with the approval of the aldermen, or by the selectmen, after a hearing, upon written charge of incompetence or official misconduct preferred by the city or town clerk, or by not less than six voters of the ward, or, in a town, of the voting precinct where the officer is appointed to act.

G. L. (Ter. Ed.), 54, § 13, etc., amended.

Party representation of election officers, term of office, removal.

SECTION 5. Section fourteen of said chapter fifty-four, as appearing in the Tercentenary Edition, is hereby amended by striking out the last sentence and inserting in place thereof the following sentence: — Appointments to fill vacancies shall not be subject to confirmation by the aldermen,

G. L. (Ter. Ed.), 54, § 14, amended.

Filling of vacancies.

any provision of general or special law to the contrary notwithstanding, — so as to read as follows: — *Section 14.* If there is a vacancy in the number of the election officers, or if an election officer declines his appointment and gives notice thereof to the city or town clerk within ten days following the date of his appointment, the mayor or the selectmen shall, except as provided in section sixteen, fill the vacancy; and the appointment shall be so made as to preserve the equal representation of the two leading political parties. Appointments to fill vacancies shall not be subject to confirmation by the aldermen, any provision of general or special law to the contrary notwithstanding.

G. L. (Ter. Ed.), 54, new § 16A, added.

Filling of vacancies in cities or towns.

SECTION 6. Said chapter fifty-four is hereby further amended by inserting after section sixteen, as so appearing, the following section: — *Section 16A.* In any city or town divided into voting precincts which accepts this section, if the warden, clerk or inspector, or the deputy of any such officer, if any, is not present at the opening of the polls, the city or town clerk may appoint a person to fill such vacancy who shall be an enrolled voter of the same political party as the absent officer, if any competent person enrolled in such party is present and willing to serve.

G. L. (Ter. Ed.), 54, § 22, amended.

Compensation of election officers.

SECTION 7. Section twenty-two of said chapter fifty-four, as so appearing, is hereby amended by striking out, in the first and second lines, the words "for each day's actual service", — so as to read as follows: — *Section 22.* Election officers shall receive such compensation as the city council or the selectmen respectively may determine; but no deputy officer shall receive compensation except for attendance at the opening of the polls or for services in place of an absent officer.

G. L. (Ter. Ed.), 54, § 23, amended.

Supervisors of elections, petition for appointment, etc.

SECTION 8. Section twenty-three of said chapter fifty-four, as so appearing, is hereby amended by striking out the last sentence and inserting in place thereof the following sentence: — Supervisors shall receive such compensation as the city council or selectmen may determine, — so as to read as follows: — *Section 23.* Upon the written petition of ten qualified voters of a ward or of a town, presented at least twenty-one days before a state or city election therein, the governor, with the advice and consent of the council, shall appoint for such ward or town or for each voting precinct named in the petition, two voters of the city or town, who shall not be signers of the petition or members of any political committee or candidates for any office, to act as supervisors at such election. One supervisor shall be appointed from each of the two leading political parties. They shall be sworn by the city or town clerk or by an officer qualified to administer oaths. The supervisors shall attend the polling places for which they are appointed, may challenge persons offering to vote, and shall witness the conduct of the election and the counting of votes; but they shall not make any statement tending to reveal the state of the polls before the public declaration of the vote. They shall remain where the ballot boxes are kept after the polls are open and until the ballots are sealed for transmission to the officers entitled to receive them. Each supervisor may affix his signature, for the purpose of identification, to the copy of the record of votes cast, or attach thereto any statement touching the truth or fairness or conduct of the election. Supervisors shall receive such compensation as the city council or selectmen may determine.

SECTION 9. Said chapter fifty-four is hereby further amended by striking out section twenty-five, as so appearing, and inserting in place thereof the following section:— *Section 25.* The aldermen or selectmen shall cause each polling place in their respective cities and towns to be provided with a sufficient number of suitable marking shelves or compartments where voters may conveniently and secretly mark their ballots; and they shall cause a guard rail to be so placed that only persons inside thereof can approach within six feet of the ballot boxes or of the marking shelves or compartments, or of the voting machines if any are used. The ballot boxes, marking shelves or compartments and voting machines, if any are used, shall be in view of persons in the polling place outside the guard rail. The number of marking shelves or compartments shall be not less than one for every seventy-five voters at such polling place, and not less than five in any voting precinct of a city, and not less than three in any town or voting precinct thereof, except that, where voting machines are used, only one such marking shelf or compartment need be provided, which shall be for the use of challenged voters. Every marking shelf or compartment shall at all times be provided with proper supplies and conveniences for marking the ballots. Where voting machines are used, one voting machine shall be provided at each polling place for every four hundred voters, or the major part thereof, entitled to vote therein.

G. L. (Ter. Ed.), 54, § 25, amended.

Marking shelves and guard rails to be provided, etc.

SECTION 10. For the purpose of providing funds for the purchase or lease of voting machines, for use at primaries and elections in the city of Boston, on orders of the board consisting of the election commissioners and the mayor of said city, as authorized under section one of chapter forty-three of the General Acts of nineteen hundred and sixteen, the treasurer of said city, without further authority than that contained in this section, shall borrow from time to time, as ordered by said board, such sums as may be necessary, not exceeding, in the aggregate, one million dollars and may issue bonds or notes therefor, which shall bear on their face the words "City of Boston, Voting Machine Loan, Act of 1943". Each authorized issue shall constitute a separate loan, and such loans shall be payable in not more than ten years from their dates. Such indebtedness incurred under this act shall be in excess of the statutory limit, but shall, except as herein otherwise provided, be subject to all laws relative to the incurring of debt by said city.

Funds for purchasing, etc., voting machines in city of Boston.

G. L. (Ter. Ed.), 54, § 41, amended.

SECTION 11. Section forty-one of said chapter fifty-four is hereby amended by striking out the last paragraph, as appearing in the Tercentenary Edition, and inserting in place thereof the three following paragraphs: —

Designation of candidate receiving nomination of more than one party.

If a candidate shall receive the nomination of more than one party or more than one political designation for the same office, he may, by a writing delivered to the officer or board required by law to prepare the official ballot, direct in what order the several nominations or political designations shall be added to his name upon the official ballot, and such directions shall be followed by such officer or board.

For state elections, such direction shall be filed within six days next succeeding five o'clock in the afternoon of the day of the primary immediately preceding; for city and town elections, where nominations are made by primaries, within seventy-two hours next succeeding five o'clock in the afternoon of the day of the primary immediately preceding; and for all other elections, within seventy-two hours next succeeding the last time for filing nomination papers or certificates of nomination papers.

If, during said time, said candidate shall neglect to so direct, said officer or board shall add said nominations or political designations to the name of said candidate upon the official ballot in such order as said officer or board shall determine.

G. L. (Ter. Ed.), 54, § 42, etc., amended.

SECTION 12. Section forty-two of said chapter fifty-four, as most recently amended by chapter two hundred and ninety-two of the acts of nineteen hundred and forty-one, is hereby further amended by striking out the last sentence of the last paragraph, as appearing in section five of chapter one hundred and thirty-five of the acts of nineteen hundred and thirty-two, and inserting in place thereof the following sentence: — On the back and outside of each ballot when folded shall be printed the words "Official Ballot for", followed by the name of the city or town for which the ballot is prepared, together with the ward and precinct of the city or the precinct of the town, if any, the date of the election, and a facsimile of the signature of the officer who has caused the ballot to be prepared, — so that the last paragraph will read as follows: —

Ballots, contents, arrangement of names thereon, etc.

Ballots shall be so printed as to give to each voter an opportunity to designate by a cross (X), in a square at the right of the name and designation of each candidate, and at the right of each question, his choice of candidates and his answer to such question; and upon the ballots may be printed such directions as will aid the voter; for example, "vote for one", "vote for two", "yes", "no", and the like. On the back and outside of each ballot when folded shall be printed the words "Official Ballot for", followed by the name of the city or town for which the ballot is prepared, together with the ward and precinct of the city or the precinct of the town, if any, the date of the election, and a facsimile of the signature of the officer who has caused the ballot to be prepared.

SECTION 13. Section forty-four of said chapter fifty-four, as appearing in the Tercentenary Edition, is hereby amended by striking out the third sentence and inserting in place thereof the following sentence: — The names of all candidates shall be in capital letters not less than one eighth nor more than one quarter of an inch in height, — so as to read as follows: — *Section 44.* The official ballots shall, except as otherwise provided in this chapter, be of ordinary white printing paper, of two or more pages, and shall, before distribution, be so folded as to measure not less than four and one half nor more than five inches in width and not less than six nor more than thirteen and one half inches in length. The names of all candidates shall be printed in black ink in lines at a right angle with the length of the ballot. The names of all candidates shall be in capital letters not less than one eighth nor more than one quarter of an inch in height. The surnames and political designations of the candidates for president and vice president shall be in capital letters not less than three sixteenths of an inch in height.

G. L. (Ter. Ed.), 54, § 44, amended.

Official ballots, paper, size, form, type, etc.

SECTION 14. Section forty-nine of said chapter fifty-four, as so appearing, is hereby amended by striking out, in the second line, the word "registrars" and inserting in place thereof the words: — city or town clerk, — and by striking out the last sentence and inserting in place thereof the following sentence: — Upon the receipt thereof the city or town clerk shall conspicuously post in not less than three public places in each ward of a city, or in each town, or in towns divided into voting precincts in each precinct, the lists and copies aforesaid for such ward, town or precinct, — so as to read as follows: — *Section 49.* The state secretary, at least five days before state elections, shall transmit to the city or town clerk printed lists of the names, residences and designations of candidates to be voted for at each polling place, substantially in the form of the official ballot, and also printed copies of any proposed amendment to the constitution, law, or proposed law, to be submitted to the people. Upon the receipt thereof the city or town clerk shall conspicuously post in not less than three public places in each ward of a city, or in each town, or in towns divided into voting precincts in each precinct, the lists and copies aforesaid for such ward, town or precinct.

G. L. (Ter. Ed.), 54, § 49, amended.

Lists of candidates, etc., at state elections to be transmitted to registrars and posted.

SECTION 15. Section sixty-five of said chapter fifty-four, as amended by section one of chapter two hundred and eighty-nine of the acts of nineteen hundred and thirty-three, is hereby further amended by striking out, in the ninth and tenth lines, the words "and the cards of instruction", — so as to read as follows: — *Section 65.* At an election of state or city officers, and of town officers in towns where official ballots are used, the presiding election officer at each polling place shall, before the opening of the polls, post at least three cards of instruction, three cards containing abstracts of the laws imposing penalties upon voters, three copies of measures to be submitted to the people, if any, and at least five speci-

G. L. (Ter. Ed.), 54, § 65, etc., amended.

Posting instructions, etc. Pasters. Other posters or cards forbidden. Opening of ballots, etc.

men ballots within the polling place outside the guard rail, and a copy of each measure to be submitted to the people in each marking compartment; and no other poster, card, handbill, placard, picture or circular intended to influence the action of the voter shall be posted, exhibited, circulated or distributed in the polling place, in the building where the polling place is located, on the walls thereof, on the premises on which the building stands, on the sidewalk adjoining the premises where such election is being held, or within one hundred and fifty feet of the entrance to such polling place. Pasters, commonly called stickers, shall not be posted in the polling place, in the building where the polling place is located, on the walls thereof, on the premises on which the building stands, on the sidewalk adjoining the premises where such election is being held, or within one hundred and fifty feet of the entrance to such polling place, nor shall they be circulated or distributed in such polling place. Such pasters shall be subject to all the restrictions imposed by sections forty-one and forty-four as to names and residences of candidates and the size of the type in which the names shall be printed; but no political or other designation shall appear on such pasters, and no vote by paster shall be counted if such designation appears. The presiding election officer shall, at the opening of the polls, publicly open the packages containing the ballots and deliver them to the ballot clerks. All specimen ballots not posted shall be kept in the custody of the presiding officer until after the closing of the polls.

G. L. (Ter. Ed.), 54, § 70, amended.

SECTION 16. Said chapter fifty-four is hereby further amended by striking out section seventy, as appearing in the Tercentenary Edition, and inserting in place thereof the following section: — *Section 70.* No more than four voters, besides election officers and supervisors, and the city or town clerk, in excess of the number of marking compartments provided, shall be allowed at one time within the guard rail. Where voting machines are used, the number of voters allowed within the guard rail shall not be more than twice the number of voting machines provided. After the time fixed for closing the polls, no voters shall be admitted within the guard rail, except the election officers and supervisors, and except voters who are then in the polling place or in line at the door thereof. The presiding officer of the polling place shall provide or cause to be provided to each voter so outside the guard rail a card or slip bearing such voter's name, and the voter shall as soon as practicable present the same to one of the ballot clerks and shall then be permitted to vote if otherwise qualified. When the polls are closed, the presiding officer shall cause a police officer or other qualified person to be stationed at the end of the line of persons waiting to vote to see that no other persons vote than those who were in the polling place or in line at the door at the time fixed for closing the polls. After the last voter in line at the door has entered within the guard rail, the voters shall be allowed five minutes in which to cast their votes.

Number of voters allowed within guard rail.

SECTION 17. Said chapter fifty-four is hereby further amended by inserting after section seventy-one, as so appearing, the following section: — *Section 71A*. Election officers in cities and in towns divided into voting precincts shall perform their duties under the supervision of the city or town clerk.

G. L. (Ter. Ed.), 54, new § 71A, added.

Supervision of election officers in cities and towns.

SECTION 18. Section seventy-five of said chapter fifty-four, as so appearing, is hereby amended by striking out, in the second line, the word "sixty-two" and inserting in place thereof the word: — sixty-five, — so as to read as follows: — *Section 75*. Every election officer shall forthwith report every violation of any provision of sections sixty-five to eighty-five and one hundred and four to one hundred and thirty-seven, both inclusive, to the police officer or constable in attendance at the polling place, and such police officer or constable shall cause the offender to be prosecuted.

G. L. (Ter. Ed.), 54, § 75, amended.

Duties of officers when law is violated.

SECTION 19. Said chapter fifty-four is hereby further amended by striking out section seventy-six, as so appearing, and inserting in place thereof the following section: — *Section 76*. Each voter desiring to vote at a polling place shall give his name and, if requested, his residence to one of the officers at the entrance to the space within the guard rail, who shall thereupon distinctly announce the same. If such name is found upon the voting list, the election officer shall check and repeat the name and shall admit the voter to the space enclosed by the guard rail, and, in case official ballots are used, such voter shall be given one ballot. If not entitled to vote for all of the offices upon the ballot, the voter shall either receive a partial ballot or shall be permitted to vote only by the machine or machines upon which are designated the offices for which he is entitled to vote, as the case may be.

G. L. (Ter. Ed.), 54, § 76, amended.

Voting, giving name, delivery of ballot, etc.

SECTION 20. Said chapter fifty-four is hereby further amended by inserting after section seventy-six, as so appearing, the following section: — *Section 76A*. Every person upon applying to vote shall, when requested by any election officer, write his name in a book prepared for the purpose, unless the voter declares under oath to the presiding officer that by reason of blindness or other physical disability he is unable to write.

G. L. (Ter. Ed.), 54, new § 76A, added.

Voter may be requested to sign name.

SECTION 21. Section seventy-nine of said chapter fifty-four, as so appearing, is hereby amended by striking out, in the second and third lines, the words "that he had the right to vote on May first, eighteen hundred and fifty-seven, and cannot read, or", — so as to read as follows: — *Section 79*. A voter who declares on oath to the presiding officer that from blindness or other physical disability he is unable to prepare his ballot or register his vote upon a voting machine, shall be assisted in such marking or registering by any qualified voter whom he may designate.

G. L. (Ter. Ed.), 54, § 79, amended.

Assistance in marking ballot.

SECTION 22. Said chapter fifty-four is hereby further amended by striking out section one hundred and seven, as so appearing, and inserting in place thereof the following section: — *Section 107*. The presiding officer at every poll-

G. L. (Ter. Ed.), 54, § 107, amended.

Ballots, cast and not cast,

and voting lists, to be sealed up, etc.

ing place at elections of state and city officers and of town officers in towns where official ballots are used shall, after the record of the counting has been made, cause all ballots cast to be publicly enclosed in an envelope or container and sealed up with the seal provided therefor, and also with the private seal of any election officer who may desire to affix the same; and a majority of the election officers of the voting precinct or town shall endorse upon such envelope or container the polling place, the election and the date, and also a certificate that all the ballots cast by the voters of such precinct or town, and none other, are contained therein. He shall cause all ballots not cast to be enclosed in an envelope or container and sealed up as aforesaid, and shall certify on the envelope or container the contents thereof. Such presiding officer shall cause the voting lists to be enclosed in an envelope and sealed up as aforesaid, and a majority of the election officers shall certify thereon to the identity of the voting lists enclosed. He shall forthwith personally deliver to the city or town clerk or transmit to him, by the police officer or constable in attendance at the election, all the ballots cast, and not cast, the voting lists, the ballot box, ballot box seals and counting apparatus.

G. L. (Ter. Ed.), 54, § 109, amended.

SECTION 23. Section one hundred and nine of said chapter fifty-four, as so appearing, is hereby amended by striking out, in the second line, the word "envelope" and inserting in place thereof the words: — envelopes or containers, — so as to read as follows: — *Section 109.* City and town clerks shall retain in their custody the envelopes or containers containing the ballots cast, without examining them or permitting them to be examined by any person except as required by law, and upon the expiration of the period fixed for their preservation shall cause such ballots to be destroyed.

Custody and disposition of ballots and lists in cities and towns.

City and town clerks shall retain in their custody the voting lists and ballots not cast as long as they retain the ballots cast. They shall then transmit such voting lists to the registrars of voters, and shall destroy the ballots marked "Spoiled", without examining them or permitting them to be examined, and may make such disposition of the undistributed ballots as they may deem proper. Such voting lists shall be preserved by the registrars of voters for reference for five years after the expiration of which they may be destroyed.

G. L. (Ter. Ed.), 54, § 134, amended.

SECTION 24. Section one hundred and thirty-four of said chapter fifty-four, as so appearing, is hereby amended by inserting after the word "envelopes", wherever the word occurs, the words: — or containers, — so as to read as follows: — *Section 134.* If a person who has received votes for any office at an election shall, within thirty days thereafter, himself or by his agent serve upon a city or town clerk a written claim to such office or a declaration of an intention to contest the election of any other person, the clerk shall retain the envelopes or containers containing the ballots for

Contested election, ballots to be retained.

Power to recount, etc.

such office until such claim is withdrawn or the contest is determined. The envelopes or containers and ballots shall be subject to the order of the body to which such person claims to be elected, or of the officers required by law finally to examine the records and to issue certificates of election to such office, or of any court having jurisdiction thereof. Such body or officers may require the clerk to produce such envelopes or containers and ballots, and may recount the ballots and amend any record or copy thereof in relation to such office.

G. L. (Ter. Ed.), 54, § 135A, etc., amended.

SECTION 25. Section one hundred and thirty-five A of said chapter fifty-four, inserted by section five of chapter two hundred and eighty-one of the acts of nineteen hundred and thirty-eight, is hereby amended by inserting after the word "envelopes" in the fifteenth line the words: — or containers, — so as to read as follows: — *Section 135A.* The recount of any election in an election district where voting machines are used shall consist of the checking with the records and voting lists of the total sheets containing the results of the votes counted, including those cast by voting machines, by ballots of challenged voters and by absent voting ballots; also the rejection or counting of ballots cast by challenged voters and the counting of absent voting ballots cast, the determination of the questions raised by the petition for recount, the retabulation of the results, and the certification of the corrected results to the city or town clerk. Upon completion of such recount such records, total sheets, voting lists and ballots shall be returned to the city or town clerk, after being sealed up in their proper envelopes or containers, in the manner and with the certificate required by section one hundred and thirty-five.

Manner of conducting recount.

G. L. (Ter. Ed.), 56, § 22, etc., amended.

SECTION 26. Section twenty-two of chapter fifty-six of the General Laws, as amended by section eight of chapter three hundred and forty-one of the acts of nineteen hundred and thirty-eight, is hereby further amended by inserting after the word "envelopes" in the fourth line the words: — or containers, — so as to read as follows: — *Section 22.* A primary or election officer, or a director of the count or assistant appointed under section six of chapter fifty-four A, who wilfully or negligently violates any provision relating to the enclosing in envelopes or containers, sealing, endorsing and delivering or transmitting of ballots and voting lists, before or after the votes have been counted and recorded, shall be punished by imprisonment for not more than one year. *Approved June 3, 1943.*

Failure to comply with laws relating to disposition of ballots and lists.

*Chap.*412 AN ACT TEMPORARILY EXEMPTING FROM TAXATION CERTAIN REAL PROPERTY OF RESIDENTS OF THE COMMONWEALTH SERVING IN THE ARMED FORCES OF THE UNITED STATES, AND THEIR SPOUSES.

Be it enacted, etc., as follows:

Certain real estate of members of armed forces, etc., exempt from taxation. Duration of act.

SECTION 1. Real estate of a resident of the commonwealth serving in the armed forces of the United States during the existing state of war between the United States and any foreign country, or of the spouse of such resident, or of both if the real estate is owned by them as joint tenants, as tenants in common or tenants by the entirety, and the interest in such real estate which either or both may own in real estate owned by them or either of them with others, shall, in each year during any portion of which such resident is in such service, and for six months after the termination of such service, but in no event later than the year during which such existing states of war are terminated, be exempt from taxation under the provisions of chapter fifty-nine of the General Laws to the extent that the assessors shall find that the payment of the tax thereon by the resident, or by the spouse of such resident, would constitute a hardship, but in no event in excess of five thousand dollars in value in the aggregate; provided, that such real estate shall be occupied in whole or in part as a home by such resident; and provided, further, that such resident, or the spouse of such resident, or a person thereunto authorized by such resident or spouse, in a writing filed with the assessors prior to February first following the effective date of this act if such resident is then in such service or prior to February first of the year following the entry of such resident into such service, as the case may be, and also filed prior to February first in each subsequent year while such resident remains in such service, shall apply for exemption, stating under the penalties of perjury that such real estate is so occupied and that payment of the full amount of the tax imposed by said chapter fifty-nine would constitute a hardship to such resident or the spouse of such resident, as the case may be.

Effective date.

SECTION 2. This act shall take effect on January first, nineteen hundred and forty-four.

Approved June 3, 1943.

---

*Chap.*413 AN ACT FURTHER EXTENDING THE OPPORTUNITY TO CITIES AND TOWNS TO BORROW UNDER THE ACT CREATING THE EMERGENCY FINANCE BOARD.

Be it enacted, etc., as follows:

SECTION 1. Chapter forty-nine of the acts of nineteen hundred and thirty-three is hereby amended by striking out section two, as most recently amended by section one of chapter one hundred and twenty-nine of the acts of nineteen hundred and forty-one, and inserting in place thereof the following section: — *Section 2.* The treasurer of any city or town, if authorized by a two thirds vote, as defined by section one of chapter forty-four of the General Laws, and with the approval of the mayor or the selectmen, may, on behalf of such city or town, petition the board to approve of its borrowing money from the commonwealth for ordinary maintenance expenses and revenue loans, and the board may, if in its judgment the financial affairs of such city or town warrant, grant its approval to the borrowing as aforesaid of specified sums not at any time exceeding, in the aggregate, the total amount represented by tax titles taken or purchased by such city or town and held by it; provided, that such borrowing is made at any time or times prior to July first, nineteen hundred and forty-five. In case of such approval, the treasurer of such city or town shall, without further vote, issue notes, with interest at such rate as may be fixed by the treasurer with the approval of the board, in the amount approved by the board, for purposes of sale to the commonwealth only, and said notes, upon their tender to the state treasurer, shall forthwith be purchased by the commonwealth at the face value thereof. Such notes shall be payable in not more than one year, and may be renewed from time to time, if authorized by the board, but no renewal note shall be for a period of more than one year, and the maturity of any loan or renewal shall not be later than July first, nineteen hundred and forty-six. Such notes shall be general obligations of the city or town issuing the same, notwithstanding the foregoing provisions. Indebtedness incurred by a city or town under authority of this act shall be outside its limit of indebtedness as fixed by chapter forty-four of the General Laws. The excess, if any, of the amount of interest payments received by the commonwealth on account of notes issued by cities and towns hereunder over the cost to the commonwealth for interest on money borrowed under section five, expenses of the board, including compensation paid to its appointive members, and expenses of administration of the funds provided by sections three and five shall be distributed to such cities and towns in November, nineteen hundred and forty-nine, or earlier at the discretion of the board, in the proportion which the aggregate amounts payable by them on account of interest on such notes bear to the total amounts so payable by all cities and towns hereunder.

Section 2. Said chapter forty-nine is hereby further amended by striking out section five, as most recently amended by section two of chapter one hundred and twenty-nine of the acts of nineteen hundred and forty-one, and inserting in place thereof the following section: — *Section 5.* The state treasurer, with the approval of the governor and council, may borrow from time to time, on the credit of the commonwealth, such sums as may be necessary to provide funds for loans to municipalities as aforesaid, and may issue and renew notes of the commonwealth therefor, bearing interest payable at such times and at such rate as shall be fixed by the state treasurer, with the approval of the governor and council; provided, that the total indebtedness of the commonwealth under this section, outstanding at any one time, shall not exceed twenty-five million dollars. Such notes shall be issued for such maximum term of years as the governor may recommend to the general court in accordance with section three of Article LXII of the amendments to the constitution of the commonwealth, but such notes, whether original or renewal, shall be payable not later than November thirtieth, nineteen hundred and forty-nine. All notes issued under this section shall be signed by the state treasurer, approved by the governor and countersigned by the comptroller. *Approved June 3, 1943.*

---

*Chap.*414 AN ACT ESTABLISHING A BUDGET SYSTEM FOR COUNTY TUBERCULOSIS HOSPITALS.

Be it enacted, etc., as follows:

G. L. (Ter. Ed.), 111, § 85, amended.

SECTION 1. Section eighty-five of chapter one hundred and eleven of the General Laws, as appearing in the Tercentenary Edition, is hereby amended by striking out the first sentence and inserting in place thereof the following sentence: — The county commissioners of each county having a tuberculosis hospital shall provide for the care, maintenance and repair of said hospital, which shall, for the purposes of this section and section eighty-five A, include the care, maintenance and repair of any preventorium erected by said county in accordance with section eighty-five B and also the cost of its construction and original equipment except when the cost of its construction, original equipment, care, maintenance or repair is provided under said section eighty-five B to be paid from appropriations, and shall for said purposes include the establishment and maintenance of out-patient departments and the furnishing of supplementary diagnostic service under section eighty-five C; provided, that the expenditure of money for the purposes of this section shall be limited to such amounts as may be authorized by the general court.

Care, maintenance, etc., of tuberculosis hospitals.

G. L. (Ter. Ed.), 35, new § 28A, added.

SECTION 2. Chapter thirty-five of the General Laws is hereby amended by inserting after section twenty-eight, as amended, the following section: — *Section 28A.* The county commissioners of each county having a tuberculosis hospital established under sections seventy-eight to ninety, inclusive, of chapter one hundred and eleven shall, in each even numbered year, prepare estimates of receipts of said hospital and of the cost of its care, maintenance and repair for each of the two ensuing years in the form prescribed by the director of accounts and upon blanks furnished by him. The clerk of the commissioners shall record the foregoing in a book kept therefor and, on or before February fifteenth in the following

Preparation and submission of estimates of receipts and cost of tuberculosis hospitals.

year, shall send a copy thereof, attested by him and signed by the chairman, to said director, who shall analyze and classify said estimates and report the same to the general court not later than March first next following. The director, upon request of the mayor or selectmen of any city or town in the tuberculosis hospital district of any such county, shall send to him or them so much of said report as relates to such district. *Approved June 3, 1943.*

AN ACT RELATIVE TO PORTIONS OF THE BOUNDARY LINE BETWEEN THE CITIES OF FITCHBURG AND LEOMINSTER AND TO CERTAIN MATTERS INCIDENTAL TO THE RECENT EXCHANGES OF TERRITORY BETWEEN SAID CITIES. *Chap.*415

Be it enacted, etc., as follows:

SECTION 1. Chapter thirty-seven of the acts of nineteen hundred and forty-one is hereby amended by striking out sections one and two and inserting in place thereof the two following sections: — *Section 1.* The location of each angle point in the boundary described below is fixed by X and Y coordinates referred to the Massachusetts State Coordinate System, and is shown on a plan entitled "Plan of Land in Leominster to be Annexed to the City of Fitchburg", drawn on a scale of one inch = three hundred feet by the Fitchburg department of public works, said plan or copies thereof to be filed with the state secretary and the Worcester northern district registry of deeds and being hereby made a part of the description.

All that part of the city of Leominster, with the inhabitants and estates therein, within the area bounded and described as follows: — Beginning at a granite monument marked F–L–L, at a point formerly marked by a white oak tree, which marked the corner of Fitchburg, Leominster and Lunenburg prior to this annexation, and having the following coordinates: X = 528502.40, Y = 569580.94; thence by the former Lunenburg–Leominster Town Line, N 53° 14′ 23″ E 656.55 feet to a point which is the southeasterly corner of the Fitchburg Sewage Disposal Area; thence by land of the Boston and Maine Railroad S 66° 03′ 34″ E 1678.79 feet to a point in the southwesterly sideline of the Boston and Maine Railroad location, said point measuring 46.75 feet southwesterly from the baseline of location at a point of tangency in said location line; thence southeasterly on the arc of a circle having a radius of 3227.4 feet more or less curving to the right 493.9 feet more or less to a point of compound curvature, the chord of said arc bearing S 48° 18′ 09″ E, 493.55 feet; thence southeasterly on the arc of a circle having a radius of 3425.8 feet more or less, curving to the right 789.2 feet more or less to a point of compound curvature, the chord of said arc bearing S 37° 19′ 02″ E, 787.57 feet; thence southeasterly on the arc of a circle having a radius of 3497.4 feet more or less, curving to the right 459.6 feet more or less to a point of tangency, the chord of said arc bearing S 26° 56′ 58″ E, 459.26 feet; thence S 23° 10′ 12″ E, 1665.87 feet to a point of curve; thence southeasterly on the arc of a circle having a radius of 5621.5 feet more or less, curving to the left 271.1 feet more or less to a point of compound curvature, the chord of said arc bearing S 24° 32′ 49″ E, 271.01 feet; thence southeasterly on the arc of a circle having a radius of 4821.5 feet more or less, curving to the left 327.1 feet more or less to a point of tangency, the chord of said arc bearing S 27° 50′ 46″ E, 327.04 feet; thence S 29° 49′ 11″ E, 1152.45 feet to an angle — the seven last named courses lying on a line parallel to the baseline of location of the Boston and Maine Railroad and 46.75 feet distant southwesterly therefrom measured at right angles thereto; thence by land of Vincent D'Onfro, et ux, S 83° 41′ 56″ W, 572.79 feet to a point in the easterly sideline of Crawford Street; thence southeasterly on the arc of a circle having a radius of 800.00 feet curving to the left along the easterly sideline of said Crawford Street, 321.07 feet to a point of tangency, the chord of said arc bearing S 36° 21′ 05″ E, 318.92 feet; thence crossing said Crawford Street, S 7° 20′ 57″ W, 977.13 feet to an angle on the westerly bank of the Nashua River between the lands of the City of Fitchburg and the heirs of George Davey; thence by land of said heirs of George Davey S 2° 53′ 04″ W, 433.52 feet to an angle; thence still by land of said heirs of George Davey, N 75° 26′ 56″ W, 1248.23 feet to an angle; thence N 46° 26′ 44″ W, 1334.93 feet to a point which marks an angle in the boundary between land of the City of Fitchburg and land of the Standard Pyroxoloid Corporation; thence S 63° 56′ 05″ W, 775.97 feet to a concrete monument marking Traverse Station 18 AL of the Massachusetts Geodetic Survey, whose coordinates are: X = 529710.95, Y = 564032.20, and thence by the same bearing 3.99 feet to a point which lies 33.00 feet distant from the New York, New Haven and Hartford Railroad monumented baseline measured along a radial line; thence northwesterly on the arc of a circle having a radius of 2834.52 feet curving to the left along a line which lies concentric to the arc of said monumented baseline and 33.00 feet distant therefrom measured along a radial line, 894.53 feet to a point lying in the easterly sideline of location and 33.00 feet distant, measured on a radial line from a concrete bound which marks the point of tangency of said monumented baseline; the chord to said first named arc bearing N 28° 10′ 44″ W, 890.82 feet; thence N 6° 50′ 44″ E, 784.16 feet to an angle; thence N 32° 11′ 22″ W, 858.97 feet to a stone bound which marks the northeasterly sideline of Funston Street at Moore Street; thence by the same bearing 486.88 feet to the northwesterly terminus of said sideline of Funston Street; thence N 49° 13′ 22″ W, 1742.77 feet to a point which lies approximately on the boundary line between the Riverview Subdivision, so-called, and land of Paul Sandrowski; thence along the northeasterly sideline of Kenwood Avenue and crossing Battles

Street, N 55° 15′ 27″ W, 708.26 feet to a point on the Fitchburg–Leominster City Line as established by Legislative Act, February 24, 1925; thence along the aforesaid city line and crossing the Nashua River N 53° 07′ 38″ E, 2176.23 feet to the point of beginning, is hereby set off from the city of Leominster and annexed to the city of Fitchburg.

The annexation lines above described encompass an area of 476.32 acres.

Section 2. The location of each angle point in the boundary described below is fixed by X and Y coordinates referred to the Massachusetts State Coordinate System, and is shown on a plan entitled "Plan of land in Fitchburg to be annexed to the City of Leominster", drawn on a scale of one inch = three hundred feet by the Fitchburg department of public works, said plan or copies thereof to be filed with the state secretary and the Worcester northern district registry of deeds, and being hereby made a part of this description. The bearings and distances along the state highway conform to those given on two plans of said state highway drawn by the Massachusetts department of public works on a scale of one inch = forty feet and dated, respectively, July 14, 1937 and June 4, 1940; and these bearings must be decreased in azimuth four seconds to conform strictly to the Massachusetts State Coordinate System.

All that part of the city of Fitchburg, with the inhabitants and estates therein, within the area bounded and described as follows: — Beginning at a granite monument, designated F. L. W. in the Harbor and Land Commission Town Boundary Survey of 1909, which marks the corner of Fitchburg, Leominster and Westminster, and which has the following coordinates: X = 508831.83; Y = 562708.26; thence N 6° 18′ 56″ E, 1743.95 feet to an angle at a point in the southerly sideline of the State Highway location, said point measuring 100 feet southerly from station 149 + 09.40 on the State Highway baseline of location, measured at right angles thereto; thence N 82° 07′ 55″ E, 1168.37 feet to a point of curve; thence easterly on the arc of a circle having a radius of 1918.11 feet curving to the right 1035.07 feet to a point of tangency; thence S 66° 56′ 58″ E, 1422.77 feet to a point of curve; thence easterly on the arc of a circle having a radius of 2683.84 feet curving to the left 1605.63 feet to a point of tangency; thence N 78° 46′ 22″ E, 888.78 feet to a point of curve; thence easterly on the arc of a circle having a radius of 3082.50 feet curving to the right 957.38 feet to a point of tangency; thence S 83° 26′ 11″ E, 369.93 feet to a point of curve; thence easterly to northeasterly on the arc of a circle having a radius of 2099.97 feet curving to the left 2098.25 feet to a point of tangency; thence N 39° 18′ 53″ E, 1153.77 feet to a point of curve; thence northeasterly to southeasterly on the arc of a circle having a radius of 900.00 feet curving to the right 1037.47 feet to a point of tangency; thence S 74° 00′ 28″ E, 2169.69 feet to an angle; thence N 87° 30′ 44″ E, 902.64 feet to an angle at a point which lies on the

Fitchburg-Leominster City line as established by Legislative Act, February 24, 1925, and which measures 100.00 feet from Station 1 + 48.93 on the State Highway baseline of location measured at right angles thereto, said point having the following coordinates: X = 522796.44, Y = 565301.02; the twelve last named courses are intended substantially to be parallel to the State Highway baseline of location and 100 feet distant therefrom; thence along the Fitchburg-Leominster City Line as established by Legislative Act, February 24, 1925, S 53° 07′ 38″ W, 5268.26 feet to an angle at a granite monument marked F–L, which marks a city corner in the boundary line as described in said Legislative Act, said point having the following coordinates: X = 518581.97, Y = 562139.84; thence along the former Fitchburg–Leominster City Line as it existed prior to this annexation, N 86° 39′ 49″ W, 9766.69 feet to the place of beginning, is hereby set off from the city of Fitchburg and annexed to the city of Leominster.

The annexation lines above described encompass an area of 561.20 acres.

SECTION 2. Said chapter thirty-seven is hereby further amended by striking out section two C, inserted by section one of chapter six hundred and ninety-eight of the acts of nineteen hundred and forty-one, and inserting in place thereof the five following sections: — *Section 2C.* The inhabitants of the territory set off from the city of Leominster and annexed to the city of Fitchburg and of that set off from the city of Fitchburg and annexed to the city of Leominster by this act shall, if qualified to vote in such territory for state officers, be entitled to vote for all purposes in the city to which the territory of which they are inhabitants is annexed as aforesaid, any provision of general law to the contrary notwithstanding.

Section 2D. There shall be reserved to the city of Leominster easements for the purpose of the upkeep, maintenance and replacement of all water and sewer lines owned on the effective date of this act by the city of Leominster in the areas affected by this act, and there shall be reserved to the city of Fitchburg similar rights with respect to any such lines owned on such effective date by the city of Fitchburg in said areas. For said purposes, each of said cities shall have the right to enter upon and dig up private or other lands within said areas in such manner as not unnecessarily to obstruct the same and shall do such work in a reasonable and workmanlike manner.

Section 2E. Said cities of Leominster and Fitchburg are hereby authorized to contract with each other relative to the sale and purchase of water for water supply, either for themselves or for their inhabitants, within the areas affected by this act upon such terms and conditions as may be mutually agreed upon.

Section 2F. Tax assessments levied in the years nineteen hundred and forty-two and nineteen hundred and forty-three by the city of Fitchburg on property within the area annexed to the city of Leominster by this act, as amended, and those levied in said years by the city of Leominster on property within the area annexed to the city of Fitchburg by this act, as amended, shall, notwithstanding said annexations, be payable to and collected by the city which levied said assessments.

Section 2G. The city of Fitchburg is hereby authorized to appropriate and to pay to the city of Leominster the sum of two thousand dollars, which sum the city of Leominster is hereby authorized to receive. Upon the making of such payment, the city of Leominster shall transfer to the city of Fitchburg its rights to liens, other than water liens, so called, and tax titles and fees in the area annexed to the city of Fitchburg by this act, as amended, and the city of Leominster shall release the city of Fitchburg from all claims for municipal services rendered by the city of Leominster prior to the effective date of this section within the area annexed to the city of Leominster by this act, as amended.

SECTION 3. Nothing contained in chapter thirty-seven of the acts of nineteen hundred and forty-one, as amended by chapter six hundred and ninety-eight of the acts of nineteen hundred and forty-one and by this act, shall be deemed to affect any right, action or cause or right of action of any inhabitant of the territory which was formerly in Leominster, was set off and annexed to Fitchburg by section one of said chapter thirty-seven, and is reannexed to Leominster by said chapter thirty-seven as amended by this act; and the inhabitants of said territory above referred to and reannexed to and included in the city of Leominster by this act shall hereafter be inhabitants of said city of Leominster and shall enjoy all the rights and privileges and shall be subject to all the duties and liabilities of such inhabitants of said city of Leominster in the same manner and to the same extent as if said territory above referred to had never been set off and annexed to said city of Fitchburg, except as otherwise provided by this act.

SECTION 4. This act shall take full effect upon its acceptance by vote of the city council, with the approval of the mayor, of said city of Fitchburg and by vote of the city council, with the approval of the mayor, of said city of Leominster, but not otherwise. *Approved June 3, 1943.*

AN ACT AUTHORIZING THE DEPARTMENT OF PUBLIC WORKS TO LAY OUT AND ALTER WAYS OTHER THAN STATE HIGHWAYS, AND TO FACILITATE THE SECURING OF FEDERAL AID IN CONNECTION THEREWITH. *Chap.416*

Be it enacted, etc., as follows:

Chapter eighty-one of the General Laws is hereby amended by inserting after section twenty-nine, as appearing in the Tercentenary Edition, the following section: — *Section 29A.* G. L. (Ter. Ed.), 81, new § 29A, added

Laying out, etc., ways other than state highways.

The department may lay out or alter ways other than state highways in any city or town provided that federal aid may be secured toward the damages sustained, and provided that the mayor of the city or the board of selectmen of the town consents thereto. Land or rights in land may be acquired for this purpose by eminent domain under chapter seventy-nine by the department in behalf of the city or town in which the land lies. Any person whose property has been taken or injured by any action of said department under authority of this section may recover from the commonwealth under chapter seventy-nine such damages therefor as he may be entitled to. For this purpose the department may use any funds which may be available for the purpose of securing federal aid in the construction of highways, and may also use any money appropriated for a county, or by a city or town, toward the damages sustained, provided that the county commissioners, selectmen or mayor have agreed in writing to pay the money thus appropriated upon the order of the department. *Approved June 3, 1943.*

---

*Chap.*417 AN ACT RELATIVE TO RECOUNTS AT PRIMARIES AND ELECTIONS.

Be it enacted, etc., as follows:

G. L. (Ter. Ed.), 54, § 135, etc., amended.

Chapter fifty-four of the General Laws is hereby amended by striking out section one hundred and thirty-five, as most recently amended by chapter three hundred and fifty of the acts of nineteen hundred and forty-one, and inserting in place thereof the following section: — *Section 135.* If, on or before five o'clock in the afternoon on the third day following an election in a ward of a city or in a town, ten or more voters of such ward or town, except a town having more than twenty-five hundred voters and voting by precincts and except Boston, and in such a town voting by precincts ten or more voters of each precinct in which a recount is petitioned for and in Boston fifty or more voters of a ward, shall sign in person, adding thereto their respective residences on the preceding January first, and cause to be filed with the city or town clerk a statement, sworn to by one of the subscribers, that they have reason to believe and do believe that the records, or copies of records, made by the election officers of certain precincts in such ward or town, or, in case of a town not voting by precincts, by the election officers of such town, are erroneous, specifying wherein they deem such records or copies thereof to be in error, or that challenged votes were cast by persons not entitled to vote therein, and that they believe a recount of the ballots cast in such precincts or town will affect the election of one or more candidates voted for at such election, specifying the candidate or candidates, or will affect the decision of a question voted upon at such election, specifying the question, the city or town clerk shall forthwith transmit such statement and the envelopes or containers con-

Local or state-wide recount, how and by whom conducted, notice of result, amendment of record, etc

taining the ballots, sealed, to the registrars of voters, who shall first examine the statement and attach thereto a certificate of the number of names of subscribers which are names of registered voters in such ward or town and shall then, without unnecessary delay, but not before the last hour for filing requests for recounts as aforesaid, open the envelopes or containers, recount the ballots and determine the questions raised, and shall examine all ballots cast by or for challenged voters and reject any such ballot cast by or for a person found not to have been entitled to vote. They shall endorse on the back of every ballot so rejected the reason for such rejection and said statement shall be signed by a majority of said registrars. A member of the board of registrars shall endorse over his signature on the back of each protested ballot the block number of which it is a part and the office for which the vote is protested, together with the name of the candidate for whom the vote is counted. Upon a recount of votes for town officers in a town where the selectmen are members of the board of registrars of voters, the recount shall be made by the moderator, who shall have all the powers and perform all the duties conferred or imposed by this section upon registrars of voters.

Recounts where voting machines have been used

In cases of recounts at elections where voting machines have been used the city or town clerk shall transmit to the registrars the records of the election officers, the envelopes or containers containing the total sheets showing the votes recorded by the voting machines, cast by challenged voters and cast by absent voting ballots, respectively, and containing the ballots cast by challenged voters and the absent voting ballots cast.

State-wide recounts, petition for, etc

State-wide recounts in cases of offices to be filled or questions to be voted upon at the state election by all the voters of the commonwealth may be requested as provided in the foregoing provisions of this section so far as applicable, except that any petition therefor shall be on a form approved and furnished by the state secretary, shall be signed in the aggregate by at least one thousand voters, not less than two hundred and fifty to be from each of four different counties, and shall be submitted on or before five o'clock in the afternoon of the tenth day following such election to the registrars of voters of the city or town in which the signers appear to be voters, who shall forthwith certify thereon the number of signatures which are names of registered voters in said city or town, and except that such petitions for recount shall be filed with the state secretary on or before five o'clock in the afternoon of the fifteenth day following such election. He shall hold such petitions for recount until after the official tabulation of votes by the governor and council and if it then appears that the difference in the number of votes cast for the two leading candidates for the office, or in the number of affirmative and negative votes on a question, for which the recount is desired, is more than one per cent of the total number of votes cast for such office or on such question, the petitions for recount shall be void. If such difference in the votes so cast appears to be one per cent or less of the total votes cast for such office or on such question, he shall forthwith order the clerk of each city and town of the commonwealth to transmit forthwith, and said clerk shall so transmit, the envelopes or containers containing the ballots, sealed except in the case of those containing ballots which have already been recounted in respect to said office or question under authority of this section, to the registrars of the city or town who shall, without unnecessary delay, open the envelopes or containers, recount the ballots cast for said office or on said question and determine the questions raised. If a state-wide recount is petitioned for, all ballots cast at a state election shall be held, except as otherwise provided herein, by the city and town clerks until the expiration of sixty days after said election.

Candidates and persons representing petitioners, to be notified, etc.

The registrars shall, before proceeding to recount the ballots, give not less than three days' written notice to each candidate who appears to have been elected to the office in question and to each candidate for such office specified in any statement filed under authority of this section, or to such person as shall be designated by the petitioners for a recount of ballots cast upon questions submitted to the voters, of the time and place of making the recount, and each such candidate or person representing petitioners as aforesaid shall be allowed to be present and to witness such recount at each table where a recount of the ballots affecting such candidate is being held, accompanied by counsel, if he so desires. Each such candidate or person may also be represented by agents, appointed by him or his counsel in writing, sufficient in number to provide one such agent for each officer counting or checking such ballots; provided, that no such candidate or person may have more than one such agent, other than his counsel, witnessing the work of any one officer at any one time. Each such candidate, person, counsel and agent shall have the right to watch and inspect the ballots, tally sheets and all other papers used in the recount, and to watch every individual act performed in connection therewith. In the case of a recount of ballots cast for offices which are filled by all the voters of the commonwealth, such notice may be given to the duly organized state political committees. In the case of a recount of the ballots cast upon a question submitted to all the voters as aforesaid, one representative from any committee organized to favor or to oppose the question so submitted shall be permitted to be present and witness the recount.

Recounts to be upon questions designated in statements, etc.

All recounts shall be upon the questions designated in the statements or petitions filed, and no other count shall be made, or allowed to be made, or other information taken, or allowed to be taken, from the ballots on such recount, except that in the case of a recount of the ballots cast for an office, the votes cast for all of the candidates for such office, including blanks cast, shall be recounted.

Discontinuance of recount in city or town, how effected.

If, after a petition for a recount of the votes for an office in any ward, town or precinct of a town has been filed, all the candidates for such office shall file a written request with the city or town clerk that the recount petitioned for be discontinued the city or town clerk shall immediately order such recount discontinued whereupon such proceedings shall terminate.

Discontinuance of state-wide recount, how effected.

If, after a petition for state-wide recount for an office has been filed, the leading candidate, together with every other candidate whose votes therefor are not exceeded in number by the votes of the leading candidate by more than one per cent of the total number of votes cast for such office, shall file a written request with the state secretary that the recount petitioned for be discontinued, the state secretary shall immediately order such recount discontinued whereupon such proceedings shall terminate.

Record and notice of result.

The registrars shall, when the recount is complete, enclose all the ballots in their proper envelopes or containers, seal each envelope or container with a seal provided therefor, and certify upon each envelope or container that it has been opened and again sealed in conformity to law; and shall likewise make and sign a statement of their determination of the questions raised. They shall also enclose all protested ballots in a separate envelope, seal the envelope with a seal provided therefor and certify upon the envelope that it contains all ballots that have been protested. When ballots are summoned to court, only such ballots as have been duly recorded as protested at a recount shall be required to be produced except by express order of the court. The envelopes or containers, with such statement, shall be returned to the city or town clerk, who shall alter and amend, in accordance with such determination, such records as have been found to be erroneous; and the records so amended shall stand as the true records of the election. Copies of such amended records of votes cast at a state election shall be made and transmitted as required by law in the case of copies of original records; provided, that such copies of amended records shall in case of a state-wide recount be transmitted by the city or town clerk to the state secretary within four days of the completion of such recount. If, in case of a recount of votes for town officers, it shall appear that a person was elected other than the person declared to have been elected, the registrars of voters shall forthwith make and sign a certificate of such fact, stating therein the number of votes cast, as determined by the recount, for each candidate for the office the election to which is disputed, and shall file the same with the town clerk. The town clerk shall record the certificate and shall, within twenty-four hours after such filing, cause a copy of such certificate, attested by him, to be delivered to or left at the residence of the person so declared to have been elected, and to the person who by such certificate appears to be elected.

Clerical assistance.

Registrars of voters may employ such clerical assistance as they deem necessary to enable them to carry out this section and in the investigation of challenged votes may summon witnesses and administer oaths.

Approved June 3, 1943.

---

*Chap.*418 AN ACT AUTHORIZING THE SALE OF CERTAIN LAND HELD BY THE CITY OF CHICOPEE FOR PARK AND PLAYGROUND PURPOSES.

Be it enacted, etc., as follows:

The city of Chicopee, upon vote of the city council and with the approval of the mayor, may sell, by public or private sale, real estate located in said city and taken and acquired by it by eminent domain for park and playground purposes, which taking is recorded in Hampden county registry of deeds, March third, nineteen hundred and thirty-eight, Book 1634, page 371. Said property is more fully described as follows: — Tract on northerly side of Harrison avenue, as shown on plan of lots recorded in said registry of deeds in Book S, page 38. Beginning at a point in said northerly line of Harrison avenue, one hundred feet west of the westerly line of Wheatland avenue; thence west along the northerly line of Harrison avenue, three hundred and sixty-five feet more or less to the easterly line of property of Mary C. Swan; thence by said Swan property in a northerly direction to a point on the rear boundary line of present lots facing on Front street and now or formerly of one Harrison; thence along the southerly boundary of aforesaid lots three hundred and ten feet more or less to a point one hundred feet westerly from the westerly line of Wheatland avenue; thence southerly by an angle of ninety degrees one hundred and twenty-five feet to point of beginning: also certain other lots as shown on certain plans recorded in said registry of deeds as follows: — Lots number 161, 162, 163, 228 to 233, inclusive, 236, all as shown on plan recorded in Hampden county registry of deeds in book of plans A, page 42; Lots 350 to 356, inclusive, 362 to 365, inclusive, 335 to 342, inclusive, 394, 395, 400 to 404, inclusive, 413, 440 to 443, inclusive, 456, all as shown on plan of lots recorded in said registry of deeds in book of plans A, page 46; and Lots 527 to 535, inclusive, 540 to 544, inclusive, 549 to 561, inclusive, 571 to 580, inclusive, 605, 606, 607, 608, 616, 625 to 630, inclusive, all as shown on a plan recorded in said registry of deeds in book of plans S, page 38; subject to the rights of the owners of parcels shown on plan of lots recorded in said registry of deeds in book of plans A, page 42; book of plans A, page 46; book of plans 4, page 83; and book of plans S, page 38; to use certain streets and avenues as granted them by Edward

S. Bemis and Robert E. Bemis under deeds duly recorded in said registry of deeds, being as described in deed to city of Chicopee recorded in said registry of deeds, book 1635, page 331. *Approved June 3, 1943.*

Chap.419

AN ACT PROVIDING FOR SPECIAL FUNDS TO MEET THE LIABILITY OF THE COMMONWEALTH AND POLITICAL SUBDIVISIONS THEREOF TO PAY CONTRIBUTIONS TO CONTRIBUTORY RETIREMENT SYSTEMS ON ACCOUNT OF MEMBERS THEREOF IN THE MILITARY OR NAVAL SERVICE.

Be it enacted, etc., as follows:

Chapter seven hundred and eight of the acts of nineteen hundred and forty-one, as amended, is hereby further amended by inserting after section nine the following section: — *Section 9A.* In order to provide funds to carry out the provisions of section nine, there shall be appropriated biennially, in the case of the commonwealth and the several counties, except Suffolk and Nantucket, and annually, in the case of cities, towns and districts, sums equal to not less than one half the amount which would have been paid by members on military leave of absence referred to in said section nine had they remained in the service of the commonwealth or of a political subdivision thereof during the preceding budgetary period. Sums so appropriated by the commonwealth and the several political subdivisions thereof shall be paid into their respective retirement systems and shall be invested and reinvested by the retirement boards as a special fund to be used only for carrying out the purposes of said section nine. To cover accrued liability on account of said section nine for the period from January first, nineteen hundred and forty-one, to the effective date of this act, sufficient sums shall be appropriated, as soon as may be, in the case of the commonwealth and the several political subdivisions thereof, to the special funds hereinbefore provided for. *Approved June 3, 1943.*

Chap.420

AN ACT MAKING CERTAIN CHANGES IN THE LAW RELATING TO THE GASOLINE AND MOTOR VEHICLE FUEL TAX.

Be it enacted, etc., as follows:

G. L. (Ter. Ed.), 64A, § 3, amended.

SECTION 1. Section three of chapter sixty-four A of the General Laws, as appearing in the Tercentenary Edition, is hereby amended by striking out, in the thirteenth line, the words "one year" and inserting in place thereof: — two years, — so that the last sentence will read as follows: —

Records of sales, etc.

Said records and said written statements shall be in such form as the commissioner shall prescribe, and shall be preserved by said distributors and said purchasers, respectively, for a period of two years and shall be offered for inspection at any time upon oral or written demand by the commissioner or his duly authorized agents.

G. L. (Ter. Ed.), 64A, § 5, etc., amended.

SECTION 2. Said chapter sixty-four A is hereby further amended by striking out section five, as most recently amended by section thirty-two of chapter four hundred and fifty-one of the acts of nineteen hundred and thirty-nine, and inserting in place thereof the following section: — *Section 5.* If a distributor, having failed to file a return, or, having filed an incorrect or insufficient return, without reasonable excuse fails to file an original or corrected return, as the case may require, within twenty days after the giving of notice to him by the commissioner of his delinquency, the commissioner shall determine the amount due, at any time within two years after the making of the earliest sale included in such determination, and shall notify the distributor of such determination. The distributor shall forthwith after the giving of such notice pay to the commissioner the amount so determined to be due, with interest at six per cent from the last day of the month in which the return is required to be made pursuant to section four. Any distributor may within sixty days of the date of notice of such determination apply to the commissioner upon a form prescribed by him for an abatement, and may appeal to the appellate tax board from the decision of the commissioner on such application for an abatement within ten days of the date of notice of such decision, which notice the commissioner shall send by mail, postage prepaid, to the distributor forthwith upon making such decision. Any distributor who shall discover that any overpayment of an excise has been made by him under section four may within six months of the date of overpayment apply to the commissioner on a form prescribed by him for a refund and may appeal to the appellate tax board from the decision of the commissioner on such application for a refund within ten days of the date of notice of such decision, which notice the commissioner shall send by mail, postage prepaid, to the distributor forthwith upon making such decision.

Determination of excise upon failure to file returns.

G. L. (Ter. Ed.), 64A, § 7, amended.

SECTION 3. Said chapter sixty-four A is hereby further amended by striking out section seven, as appearing in the Tercentenary Edition, and inserting in place thereof the following section: — *Section 7.* Any person who shall buy any fuel, on which an excise has been paid or is chargeable under this chapter, and shall consume the same in any manner except in the operation of motor vehicles upon or over the highways of the commonwealth, shall be reimbursed the amount of said excise in the manner and subject to the conditions herein provided. All claims for reimbursement shall be made by affidavit in such form and containing such information as the commissioner shall prescribe, and shall be accompanied by original invoices or sales receipts, and shall be filed with the commissioner within ninety days from the date of purchase or invoice. The commissioner may require such further information as he shall deem necessary for the determination of such claims, and shall within thirty days after receipt trans-

Reimbursement of excise; sale free from, regulated.

mit all claims approved by him to the comptroller for certification; and the amount approved by the commissioner and certified as aforesaid shall be paid forthwith from the proceeds of the excise tax levied under this chapter, without specific appropriation.

G. L. (Ter. Ed.), 64A, § 10, etc., amended.

SECTION 4. Said chapter sixty-four A is further amended by striking out section ten, as amended by section thirty-three of chapter four hundred and fifty-one of the acts of nineteen hundred and thirty-nine, and inserting in place thereof the following section: — *Section 10.* Sums due to the commonwealth under this chapter as excise or as penalties or forfeitures may be recovered by the attorney general in an action brought in the name of the commissioner. The commissioner may suspend the license of a distributor for violation of any provision of this chapter, but the distributor may appeal from his decision within ten days thereafter to the appellate tax board, whose decision shall be final. The commissioner shall have the same powers and remedies with respect to the collection of said sums as he has with respect to the collection of income taxes under chapter sixty-two.

Recovery of excise, penalties, etc.

Suspension of distributor's license, etc

Approved June 3, 1943.

---

*Chap.*421

AN ACT RELATIVE TO THE RENEWAL OF CERTAIN LICENSES, PERMITS AND CERTIFICATES OF REGISTRATION HELD BY PERSONS SERVING IN THE MILITARY AND NAVAL FORCES OF THE UNITED STATES AND TO THE REMISSION OF CERTAIN FEES IN CONNECTION THEREWITH.

Be it enacted, etc., as follows:

Section twenty-three of chapter seven hundred and eight of the acts of nineteen hundred and forty-one is hereby amended by striking out, in the fifth line, the word "four" and inserting in place thereof the word: — six, — and by adding at the end thereof the following: — ; and provided, further, that no fee shall be charged or collected for the period between such expiration and such renewal, — so as to read as follows: — *Section 23.* Any license, permit or certificate of registration issued by any department, division, board, commission or officer of the commonwealth that expires while the holder thereof is serving in the military or naval service of the United States may be renewed within six months after the termination by such holder of such service, to the same extent as though the application for such renewal were made upon the expiration of such license, permit or certificate of registration; provided, that nothing in this section shall be construed to authorize such holder of a license, permit or certificate of registration to exercise any rights thereunder after its expiration and prior to its renewal as aforesaid; and provided, further, that no fee shall be charged or collected for the period between such expiration and such renewal. *Approved June 3, 1943.*

Chap. 422 AN ACT TEMPORARILY PROVIDING FOR THE TRANSFER TO AND FROM, AND THE MAINTENANCE IN, MUNICIPAL AND COUNTY INSTITUTIONS OF PATIENTS IN OR INMATES OF CERTAIN STATE INSTITUTIONS.

Emergency preamble.

Whereas, The deferred operation of this act would tend to defeat its purpose, which is, during the existing state of war and for six months thereafter, to provide for the transfer and relief of persons in certain state institutions, therefore it is hereby declared to be an emergency law, necessary for the convenience of the public health.

Be it enacted, etc., as follows:

SECTION 1. The commissioner of public health, the commissioner of public welfare and the commissioner of mental health may respectively transfer a patient in or an inmate of a state institution under his control, and the mayor of a city, the board of selectmen of a town or the county commissioners in charge of an institution may accept such patient or inmate for treatment and care therein. Any person so transferred may, within the effective period of this act, and forthwith upon the termination of such effective period shall, be transferred to a state institution under the control of the state department the commissioner of which made the original transfer under authority of this act. The expense of transfer and maintenance of such patient or inmate, when approved by the commissioner, shall be paid by the commonwealth, provided, that, if the amount to be paid cannot be agreed upon by the commissioner making the transfer and the mayor, the board of selectmen or the county commissioners, as the case may be, it may be determined by such commissioner, the mayor or board of selectmen or county commissioners, as the case may be, and the commission on administration and finance, sitting as a board for the purpose of such determination.

SECTION 2. This act shall be in full force and effect only during the continuance of the existing state of war between the United States and any foreign country, and for six months after the termination of all such existing states of war. *Approved June 4, 1943.*

Chap. 423 AN ACT EXTENDING THE TIME DURING WHICH THERE SHALL BE IMPOSED A TEMPORARY ADDITIONAL EXCISE WITH RESPECT TO THE SALE OF ALCOHOLIC BEVERAGES AND ALCOHOL.

Emergency preamble.

Whereas, The deferred operation of this act would tend to defeat its purpose by depriving the commonwealth of necessary revenue, therefore it is hereby declared to be an emergency law, necessary for the immediate preservation of the public convenience.

Be it enacted, etc., as follows:

Section one of chapter four hundred and thirty-four of the acts of nineteen hundred and thirty-nine is hereby amended by striking out the introductory paragraph, as amended by chapter three hundred and thirty-nine of the acts of nineteen hundred and forty-one, and inserting in place thereof the following paragraph: — There is hereby imposed an additional excise on the sale of alcoholic beverages and of alcohol during the period from September first, nineteen hundred and thirty-nine, to June thirtieth, nineteen hundred and forty-five, inclusive, as follows:

Approved June 4, 1943.

---

*Chap.*424

AN ACT RELATIVE TO THE ISSUANCE OF GROUP LIFE AND GENERAL OR BLANKET ACCIDENT AND HEALTH INSURANCE POLICIES COVERING MEMBERS OF CERTAIN ASSOCIATIONS OF PUBLIC EMPLOYEES AND AUTHORIZING PAY-ROLL DEDUCTIONS ON ACCOUNT OF SUCH POLICIES AND CERTAIN OTHER CONTRACTS FOR SUCH EMPLOYEES.

Be it enacted, etc., as follows:

G. L. (Ter. Ed.), 175, § 133, etc., amended.

SECTION 1. Clause (*b*) of section one hundred and thirty-three of chapter one hundred and seventy-five of the General Laws, as most recently amended by section two of chapter three hundred and sixty-two of the acts of nineteen hundred and thirty-eight, is hereby further amended by striking out, in the third and fourth lines, the words "or any association of state, county or municipal employees", — so as to read as follows: — or (*b*) the members of any trade union or other association of wage workers described in section twenty-nine, with or without medical examination, written under a policy issued to such union or association, the premium on which is to be paid by the union or association or by the union or association and the members thereof jointly, and insuring all of the members thereof for amounts of insurance based upon some plan which will preclude individual selection, and for the benefit of persons other than the union or association or any officers thereof, provided, that when the premium is to be paid by the union or association and its members jointly and the benefits of the policy are offered to all members, not less than seventy-five per cent of such members may be so insured, and provided further that any member or members insured under the policy may apply for amounts of insurance additional to those granted by said policy, in which case any percentage of the members may be insured for additional amounts if they pass satisfactory medical examinations.

Group insurance for members of trade unions, etc.

G. L. (Ter. Ed.), 175, § 133, etc., amended.

SECTION 2. Said section one hundred and thirty-three, as amended, is hereby further amended by adding at the end the following: — ; or (*d*) the members of any association of state, county or municipal employees, who are regularly

Group insurance for state,

county or municipal employees.

and permanently employed by the commonwealth, a county or a municipality and, if employed by the commonwealth or the city of Boston, are paid by a common paymaster and are eligible for membership in the retirement association for the employees of the commonwealth or of the city of Boston, or the members of any association of employees of two or more municipalities within one county who are regularly and permanently employed by one or more such municipalities, with or without medical examination, written under a policy issued to the association, the premium on which is to be paid by its members and insuring not less than fifty members and seventy-five per cent of all persons eligible for membership therein, for amounts of insurance based upon some plan which will preclude individual selection, and for the benefit of persons other than the association or any officers thereof; provided, that any member or members insured under such policy may apply for amounts of insurance additional to those granted by said policy, in which case any percentage of the members may be insured for additional amounts if they pass satisfactory medical examinations; and provided, further, that no person shall be eligible for coverage under such a policy as a member of more than one such association.

The term "common paymaster", as used in clause (*d*) of this section, shall mean any officer or employee of the commonwealth or the city of Boston or any board, department, or commission thereof, whose duties include the payment of salaries or wages to employees of the commonwealth, said city or any board, department or commission thereof.

G. L. (Ter. Ed.), 175, § 110, etc., amended.

SECTION 3. Said chapter one hundred and seventy-five is hereby further amended by striking out section one hundred and ten, as most recently amended by chapter one hundred and eighteen of the acts of nineteen hundred and forty-one, and inserting in place thereof the following section: — *Section 110.* Nothing in sections one hundred and eight and one hundred and nine shall be construed to apply to or affect or prohibit the issue of any general or blanket policy of insurance to (*a*) any employer, whether an individual, association, copartnership, or corporation, or (*b*) any municipal corporation or any department thereof not referred to in (*c*), or (*c*) any police or fire department, or (*d*) any college, school or other institution of learning, or to the head or principal thereof, or (*e*) any organization for health, recreational or military instruction or treatment, or (*f*) any underwriters' corps, salvage bureau or like organization, under which the officers, members or employees, or classes or departments thereof, or the students or patients thereof, as the case may be, are insured against loss or damage from disease or specified accidental bodily injuries or death caused by such injuries, contracted or sustained while exposed to the hazards of the occupation, the course of instruction or treatment, or otherwise, for a premium intended to cover the risks of all persons insured under such policy. A policy

Certain sections not applicable to certain policies of insurance.

on which the premiums are paid by the employer and the employees jointly, or by the employees, and the benefits of which are offered to all eligible employees, and insuring not less than seventy-five per cent of such employees, or the members of an association of such employees if the members so insured constitute not less than seventy-five per cent of all eligible employees, shall be deemed a general or blanket policy within the meaning of this section.

Nothing in sections one hundred and eight and one hundred and nine shall be construed to apply to or affect or prohibit the issue of any general or blanket policy of insurance to any association of state, county or municipal employees who are regularly and permanently employed by the commonwealth, a county or a municipality and, if employed by the commonwealth or the city of Boston are paid by a common paymaster, as defined in section one hundred and thirty-three, and are eligible for membership in the retirement association for the employees of the commonwealth or of the city of Boston, or to an association of employees of two or more municipalities within one county who are regularly and permanently employed by one or more such municipalities, insuring the members of the association against loss or damage from disease or specified accidental bodily injuries or death caused by such injuries, contracted or sustained while exposed to the hazards of their occupation, for a premium intended to cover the risks of all the persons insured under such policy. No person shall be eligible for coverage under such a policy as a member of more than one such association. A policy on which the premium is paid by the members of the association and the benefits of which are offered to all its members, and insuring not less than fifty members and seventy-five per cent of all persons eligible for membership in the association shall be deemed to be a general or blanket policy within the meaning of this section.

The provisions of section one hundred and thirty-eight A shall apply to deductions on pay-roll schedules from the salary of any state, county or municipal employee for the payment of premiums on a general or blanket policy issued to such an association of state, county or municipal employees.

Any blanket or general policy issued under this section to an employer or to an association of state, county or municipal employees may also insure the dependents of employees or members insured thereunder, in respect to medical, surgical and hospital expenses.

G. L. (Ter. Ed.), 175, new § 138A, added.

SECTION 4. Said chapter one hundred and seventy-five is hereby further amended by inserting after section one hundred and thirty-eight, as appearing in the Tercentenary Edition, the following section: — *Section 138A.* Deductions on pay-roll schedules may be made from the salary of any state, county or municipal employee of any amount which such employee may specify in writing to any state, county or mu-

Deduction from salaries of state, etc., employees for payment of premiums.

nicipal officer, or the head of the state, county, or municipal department, board or commission, by whom or which he is employed, for the payment of premiums on a group life policy issued under section one hundred and thirty-three to an association of state, county or municipal employees and insuring such employee as a member thereof. Any such authorization may be withdrawn by the employee by giving at least sixty days' notice in writing of such withdrawal to the state, county or municipal officer, or the head of the state, county or municipal department, board or commission, by whom or which he is then employed and by filing a copy thereof with the treasurer of the association.

The state treasurer, the common paymaster, as defined in said section one hundred and thirty-three, or the treasurer of the county or municipality by which such employee is employed, shall deduct from the salary of such employee such amount of insurance premiums as may be certified to him on the pay-roll, and transmit the sum so deducted to the treasurer of said association for transmittal to the company, including in such term a savings and insurance bank, which issued the policy; provided, that the state treasurer, the state comptroller or the county or municipal treasurer, as the case may be, is satisfied by such evidence as he may require that the treasurer of such association has given to said association a bond, in a form approved by the commissioner, for the faithful performance of his duties, in a sum and with such surety or sureties as are satisfactory to the state treasurer or comptroller or county or municipal treasurer.

G. L. (Ter. Ed.), 176A, new § 12, added.

SECTION 5. Chapter one hundred and seventy-six A of the General Laws, inserted by chapter four hundred and nine of the acts of nineteen hundred and thirty-six, is hereby amended by inserting after section eleven the following section: — *Section 12.* The pertinent provisions of section one hundred and thirty-eight A of chapter one hundred and seventy-five shall apply to deductions on pay-roll schedules from the salary of any state, county or municipal employee for the payment of the amount payable by such an employee under a contract issued to him as a subscriber by a non-profit hospital service corporation described in this chapter.

Certain provisions of law applicable in case of state, etc., employees.

G. L. (Ter. Ed.), 176B, new § 16A, added.

SECTION 6. Chapter one hundred and seventy-six B of the General Laws, inserted by chapter three hundred and six of the acts of nineteen hundred and forty-one, is hereby amended by inserting after section sixteen the following section: — *Section 16A.* The pertinent provisions of section one hundred and thirty-eight A of chapter one hundred and seventy-five shall apply to deductions on pay-roll schedules from the salary of any state, county or municipal employee for the payment of the amount payable by such an employee under a subscription certificate issued to him as a subscriber by a medical service corporation.

Certain provisions of law applicable in case of state, etc., employees

SECTION 7. Chapter one hundred and seventy-six C of the General Laws, inserted by chapter three hundred and thirty-four of the acts of nineteen hundred and forty-one, is hereby amended by inserting after section sixteen the following section: — *Section 16A*. The pertinent provisions of section one hundred and thirty-eight A of chapter one hundred and seventy-five shall apply to deductions on pay-roll schedules from the salary of any state, county or municipal employee for the payment of the amount payable by such an employee under a contract issued to him as a subscribing member by a medical service corporation.

G. L. (Ter. Ed.), 176C, new § 16A, added.

Certain provisions of law applicable in case of state, etc., employees.

Approved June 4, 1943.

AN ACT REGULATING THE AMOUNT OF ALLOWANCE FOR CERTAIN MEMBERS OF CERTAIN RETIREMENT SYSTEMS RETIRED FOR ORDINARY DISABILITY.

*Chap.*425

Be it enacted, etc., as follows:

SECTION 1. Section twenty-four of chapter thirty-two of the General Laws, as appearing in section one of chapter four hundred of the acts of nineteen hundred and thirty-six and as amended, is hereby further amended by inserting after subdivision (2) (*c*) the following subdivision: —

G. L. (Ter. Ed.), 32, § 24, etc., amended.

(3) In no case shall a member be retired under this section at such annual rate of pension as would, when added to his annuity, amount to a total retirement allowance of less than four hundred and eighty dollars or two thirds of his average annual compensation for the five years next preceding his retirement, whichever is the lesser.

Amount of allowance.

SECTION 2. Section thirty of said chapter thirty-two, as appearing in section one of chapter three hundred and eighteen of the acts of nineteen hundred and thirty-six and as amended, is hereby further amended by inserting after subdivision (2) (*c*) the following subdivision: —

G. L. (Ter. Ed.), 32, § 30, etc., amended.

(3) In no case shall a member be retired under this section at such annual rate of pension as would, when added to his annuity, amount to a total retirement allowance of less than four hundred and eighty dollars or two thirds of his average annual compensation for the five years next preceding his retirement, whichever is the lesser.

Amount of allowance.

Approved June 4, 1943.

AN ACT REGULATING THE PUBLICATION AND SALE OF REPRINTS OF VOLUMES OF THE MASSACHUSETTS REPORTS.

*Chap.*426

Be it enacted, etc., as follows:

Chapter nine of the General Laws is hereby amended by striking out section twenty, inserted by chapter four hundred and two of the acts of nineteen hundred and thirty-five, and inserting in place thereof the following section: — *Section 20.* There shall be in the department of the state secretary, but

G. L. (Ter. Ed.), 9, § 20, etc., amended.

Publication and sale of decisions of supreme judicial court.

not subject to his supervision or control except as herein provided, a board, consisting of the attorney general, the state secretary, the reporter of decisions of the supreme judicial court, and a member of the commission on administration and finance to be designated by its chairman, which board shall from time to time advertise for proposals for the execution of the printing and binding, and provide for the sale to the public at such price as said board may fix, of the reports of the decisions of the supreme judicial court, styled "Massachusetts Reports", and of reprints of volumes of "Massachusetts Reports" previously published. Any advertisement for proposals for the execution of the printing and binding of "Massachusetts Reports" shall call for proposals for the execution thereof during a term of one, two or three years from a date specified by said board in such advertisement. Said board shall take into consideration the circumstances and facilities of the several bidders for the above-mentioned work, as well as the terms offered; may reject any bids received; shall award the contract to such bidder as in its judgment the interests of the commonwealth may require; and shall execute the contract in the name and behalf of the commonwealth. Said board may from time to time negotiate for, and execute in the name and behalf of, the commonwealth a contract for the printing and sale to the public, during such period of time and at such price as said board may fix, of advance copies of opinions of said court filed with the reporter of decisions. Bonds or securities satisfactory to said board, in an amount not less than ten thousand dollars, shall be given to or deposited by each person to whom any contract is awarded under authority of this section, to secure faithful performance thereof.

Approved June 4, 1943.

Chap. 427 AN ACT PROVIDING THAT CERTAIN FEDERAL HIGHWAY GRANTS SHALL BE PAID INTO THE HIGHWAY FUND, AND FURTHER REGULATING THE PURPOSES FOR WHICH SAID FUND SHALL BE USED.

Be it enacted, etc., as follows:

G. L. (Ter. Ed.), 10, § 8, etc., amended.

SECTION 1. Chapter ten of the General Laws is hereby amended by striking out section eight, as amended by section one of chapter one hundred and eighty of the acts of nineteen hundred and thirty-two, and inserting in place thereof the following section: — *Section 8.* He shall receive from the United States all sums of money payable to the commonwealth under any act of congress for the construction of any highways therein. The sums so received shall be credited to the Highway Fund.

To receive money from the United States for highways.

G. L. (Ter. Ed.), 90, § 34, etc., amended.

SECTION 2. Chapter ninety of the General Laws is hereby amended by striking out section thirty-four, as amended, and inserting in place thereof the following section: — *Section 34.* The fees received under the preceding sections,

Disposition of fees.

Highway Fund.

together with all other fees received by the registrar or any other person under the laws of the commonwealth relating to the use and operation of motor vehicles and trailers, shall be paid by the registrar or by the person collecting the same into the treasury of the commonwealth, and said fees, together with all contributions and assessments paid into the state treasury by cities, towns or counties for maintaining, repairing, improving and constructing ways, whether before or after the work is completed, all refunds and rebates made on account of expenditures on ways by the department of public works, all receipts paid into the treasury of the commonwealth under the provisions of chapter sixty-four A, and all receipts received by the state treasurer under the provisions of section eight of chapter ten shall be credited on the books of the commonwealth to a fund to be known as the Highway Fund. Said Highway Fund, subject to appropriation, shall be used as follows:

(1) Such portion as is authorized shall be expended to carry out the provisions of law relative to the use and operation of motor vehicles and trailers and for expenses authorized to administer the law relative to the taxation of the sales of gasoline and certain other motor vehicle fuel;

(2) The balance then remaining shall be used —

(*a*) For expenditure, under the direction of said department, for maintaining, repairing, improving and constructing town and county highways together with any money which any town or county may appropriate for said purpose to be used on the same highways. The said ways shall remain town or county ways. In this subdivision the word "town" shall include city;

(*b*) For expenditure, under the direction of said department, for maintaining, repairing and improving state highways and bridges;

(*c*) For expenditure, under the direction of said department, in addition to federal aid payments received under section thirty of chapter eighty-one, for construction of state highways;

(*d*) For expenditure, under the direction of said department, for engineering services and expenses, for care, repair, storage, replacement and purchase of road building machinery and tools, for snow removal, for the erection and maintenance of direction signs and warning signs and for the care of shrubs and trees on state highways, and for expenses incidental to the foregoing or incidental to the purposes specified in subdivisions (*a*), (*b*) or (*c*) of this clause;

(*e*) To meet interest, sinking fund and serial payments on state highway and western Massachusetts highway and abolition of grade crossing bonds;

(*f*) To meet the commonwealth's share of the interest, sinking fund and serial payments on metropolitan parks loans, series two, and to pay such sums as the commonwealth may be required to pay out of receipts from motor vehicle fees for particular traffic routes now or hereafter authorized;

(*g*) For expenditure, under the direction of the metropolitan district commission, to meet the cost of maintenance of boulevards in the metropolitan parks district under section fifty-six of chapter ninety-two, and the commonwealth's share of the cost of construction of boulevards within said district now or hereafter authorized;

(*h*) For expenditure, under the direction of the department of public safety, for the maintenance, in part, of the division of state police;

(*i*) For expenditure, under the direction of the state auditor, for the maintenance, in part, of his department;

(*j*) For expenditure, under the direction of the state treasurer, for the maintenance, in part, of his department;

(*k*) For expenditure, under the direction of the commission on administration and finance, for the maintenance, in part, of said commission. *Approved June 4, 1943.*

---

*Chap.*428 AN ACT PROVIDING FOR THE SETTLEMENT OF DISPUTES RESPECTING THE DOMICILE OF DECEDENTS FOR DEATH TAX PURPOSES.

Emergency preamble.

Whereas, The settlement of certain disputes relating to taxes in a manner advantageous to the commonwealth may be delayed or defeated unless this act becomes immediately operative, therefore it is hereby declared to be an emergency law, necessary for the immediate preservation of the public convenience.

Be it enacted, etc., as follows:

G. L. (Ter. Ed.), new chapter 65B, added.

SECTION 1. The General Laws are hereby amended by inserting after chapter sixty-five A the following new chapter: —

CHAPTER 65B.

SETTLEMENT OF DISPUTES RESPECTING THE DOMICILE OF DECEDENTS FOR DEATH TAX PURPOSES.

Definitions.

Section 1. When used in this chapter the following terms shall have the following meanings:

(*a*) "Executor", any executor of the will or administrator of the estate of a decedent, except an ancillary administrator;

(*b*) "Taxing official", the commissioner of corporations and taxation in this commonwealth, and in any other reciprocal state the officer or body designated in the statute of such state substantially similar to this chapter;

(*c*) "Death tax", any tax levied by a state on account of the transfer or shifting of economic benefits in property at death, or in contemplation thereof, or intended to take effect in possession or enjoyment at or after death, whether denominated an "inheritance tax", "transfer tax", "succession tax", "estate tax", "death duty", "death dues", or otherwise;

(*d*) "Interested person", any person who may be entitled to receive, or who has received any property or interest which may be required to be considered in computing the death tax of any state involved.

Determination of domicile for death tax purposes.

Election, notice, etc.

Section 2. In any case in which this commonwealth and one or more other states each claims that it was the domicile of a decedent at the time of his death, and no judicial determination of domicile for death tax purposes has been made in any of such states, any executor, or the taxing official of any such state, may elect to invoke the provisions of this chapter. Such election shall be evidenced by the sending of a notice by registered mail, receipt requested, to the taxing officials of each such state and to each executor, ancillary administrator and interested person. Any executor may reject such election by sending a notice by registered mail, receipt requested, to the taxing officials involved and to all other executors within forty days after the receipt of such notice of election. If such election be rejected, no further proceedings shall be had under this chapter. If such election be not rejected, the dispute as to the death taxes shall be determined solely as hereinafter provided, and no other proceedings to determine or assess such death taxes shall thereafter be instituted in the courts of this commonwealth or otherwise.

Commissioner may agree with other taxing officials or with executors to accept certain sum in payment of death taxes.

Section 3. In any case in which an election is made as provided in section two and not rejected, the commissioner may enter into a written agreement with the other taxing officials involved and with the executors, to accept a certain sum in full payment of any death tax, together with interest and penalties, that may be due this commonwealth; provided, that said agreement also fixes the amount to be paid the other state or states. If an agreement cannot be reached and the arbitration proceeding specified in section four is commenced, and thereafter an agreement is arrived at, a written agreement may be entered into at any time before such proceeding is concluded, notwithstanding the commencement of such proceeding. Upon the filing of such agreement or duplicate thereof with the authority which would have jurisdiction to assess the death tax of this commonwealth if the decedent died domiciled in this commonwealth, an assessment shall be made as therein provided and such assessment, except as hereinafter provided, shall finally and conclusively fix and determine the amount of death tax due this commonwealth. In the event that the aggregate amount payable under such agreement to the states involved is less than the maximum credit allowable to the estate against the United States estate tax imposed with respect thereto, the executor forthwith shall also pay to the commissioner the same percentage of the difference between such aggregate amount and the amount of such credit, as the amount payable to the commissioner under the agreement bears to such aggregate amount.

Procedure when payment of certain sum

Section 4. If in any such case it shall appear that an agreement cannot be reached as provided in section three, or if one

cannot be agreed upon.

year shall have elapsed from the date of the election without such an agreement having been reached, the domicile of the decedent at the time of his death shall be determined solely for death tax purposes as follows:

(*a*) Where only this commonwealth and one other state are involved, the commissioner and the taxing official of such other state shall each appoint a member of a board of arbitration, and the members so appointed shall select the third member of the board. If this commonwealth and more than one other state are involved, the taxing officials thereof shall agree upon the authorities charged with the duty of administering death tax laws in three states not involved, each of which authorities shall appoint a member of the board. The members of the board shall elect one of their number as chairman.

(*b*) Such board shall hold hearings at such places as are deemed necessary, upon reasonable notice to the executors, ancillary administrators, all other interested persons, and the taxing officials of the states involved, all of whom shall be entitled to be heard.

(*c*) Such board shall have power to administer oaths, take testimony, subpoena and require the attendance of witnesses and the production of books, papers and documents and issue commissions to take testimony. Subpoenas may be issued by any member of the board. Failure to obey a subpoena may be punished by a judge or justice of any court of record in the same manner as if the subpoena had been issued by such judge or justice or by the court in which such judge or justice functions.

(*d*) Such board shall apply, whenever practicable, the rules of evidence which prevail in federal courts under the federal rules of civil procedure at the time of the hearing.

(*e*) Such board shall, by majority vote, determine the domicile of the decedent at the time of his death. Such determination shall be final and conclusive, and shall bind this commonwealth and all of its judicial and administrative officials on all questions concerning the domicile of the decedent for death tax purposes.

(*f*) The reasonable compensation and expenses of the members of the board and employees thereof shall be agreed upon among such members, the taxing officials of the states involved, and the executors. In the event an agreement cannot be reached, such compensation and expenses shall be determined by such taxing officials, and, if they cannot agree, by the appropriate probate court of the state determined to be the domicile. Such amount shall be borne by the estate and shall be deemed an administration expense.

(*g*) The determination of such board and the record of its proceeding shall be filed with the authority having jurisdiction to assess the death tax in the state determined to be the domicile of the decedent and with the authorities which would have had jurisdiction to assess the death tax in each of the other states involved if the decedent had been found to be domiciled therein.

Section 5. In any case where it is determined by the board of arbitration referred to in section four that the decedent died domiciled in this commonwealth, penalties and interest for nonpayment of the tax, between the date of the election and the final determination of the board, shall not exceed, in the aggregate, four per centum of the amount of the taxes per annum. Amount of interest limited

Section 6. The provisions of this chapter shall apply only to cases in which each of the states involved has in effect a law substantially similar to this chapter. Application of act

Section 7. If, in any case to which this chapter applies, the provisions of this chapter conflict with any other law of this commonwealth, this chapter shall control. Law applicable in case of conflict

SECTION 2. Section one of chapter fifty-eight of the General Laws, as amended, is hereby further amended by striking out the first sentence, as appearing in the Tercentenary Edition, and inserting in place thereof the following sentence: — The commissioner of corporations and taxation, in chapters fifty-eight to sixty-five B, inclusive, called the commissioner, may visit any town, inspect the work of its assessors and give them such information and require of them such action as will tend to produce uniformity throughout the commonwealth in valuation and assessments. G. L (Ter Ed.), 58, § 1, etc., amended. Powers and duties of commissioner

SECTION 3. This act shall apply to the settlement of disputes among states with respect to death taxes which come within its scope, without regard to whether the decedent died before or after the effective date hereof. Scope of act.

Approved June 4, 1943.

AN ACT RELATING TO THE ACQUISITION OF CERTAIN PROPERTY BY THE CITY OF BEVERLY FOR A PUBLIC PARK. *Chap.*429

Be it enacted, etc., as follows:

SECTION 1. The proceedings of the city council of the city of Beverly on April fifth, nineteen hundred and forty-three, authorizing an agreement with the Beverly Hospital Corporation, whereby the Beverly Hospital Corporation sells to the city for a public park the property commonly known as the Hunt property and the city gives therefor its note for fifty thousand dollars payable solely from whatever the city may receive under the will of David S. Lynch, if and when so received, the city meanwhile paying interest on the said fifty thousand dollars at the rate of two and one half per cent per annum, are hereby validated, and said city and said Beverly Hospital Corporation are hereby authorized to carry out the said agreement; provided, that if the receipts under said will are insufficient to pay said note in full, the city shall not be liable to make good any such deficiency.

SECTION 2. This act shall take effect upon its passage.

Approved June 4, 1943.

*Chap.*430 An Act relative to taxation of costs by the appellate tax board in certain appeals from local assessments.

Be it enacted, etc., as follows:

G. L. (Ter. Ed.), 58A, new § 12A, added. Taxation of costs in certain appeals.

Chapter fifty-eight A of the General Laws is hereby amended by inserting after section twelve, as amended, the following section: — *Section 12A.* If, at a hearing of an appeal relative to the assessed value of property brought within three years after a determination by the appellate tax board of the value thereof, it appears that the assessed value is greater than the value as so determined, the burden shall be upon the appellee to satisfy the board that the increased value was warranted and upon failure so to do the board may, in its discretion, tax as costs against the appellee, in addition to witness fees and expenses of service of process, the whole or any part of the reasonable expense of the taxpayer incurred in the preparation, entry and trial of his appeal. Should the board find that the increased value was warranted then it may tax such costs against the appellant. Such costs shall be certified and paid as provided in section twelve.

Approved June 4, 1943.

---

*Chap.*431 An Act to permit cities and towns to indemnify military substitutes serving in their fire forces or fire departments.

Be it enacted, etc., as follows:

Section 1. Members of the "fire force", as the term is used in chapter three hundred and twenty-four of the acts of nineteen hundred and thirty-three, and "fireman" or "member of the fire department" as used in section one hundred of chapter forty-one of the General Laws, shall include military substitutes serving in said forces or departments by appointment, transfer or promotion under authority of section two of chapter seven hundred and eight of the acts of nineteen hundred and forty-one. Cities, including Boston, and towns may indemnify such a member of the fire force, fireman or member of the fire department, his widow or next of kin, as the case may be, in the manner described in said chapter three hundred and twenty-four and said section one hundred of said chapter forty-one, irrespective of whether the expense or damage sustained by such member of the fire force, fireman or member of the fire department in the actual performance of his duty occurred prior to or on or after the effective date of this act.

Section 2. This act shall become operative in any city upon its acceptance by the mayor and city council, and in any town upon its acceptance by the town, and shall continue to be operative in such city or town until the termination of the present states of war between the United States and certain foreign countries and for six months thereafter.

Approved June 4, 1943.

AN ACT RELATIVE TO THE EXCESS OF THE DAMAGES RECOVERED FROM A PERSON LEGALLY LIABLE, OTHER THAN THE INSURED, ON ACCOUNT OF AN INJURY TO AN EMPLOYEE OVER THE COMPENSATION PAID UNDER THE WORKMEN'S COMPENSATION LAW ON ACCOUNT THEREOF. *Chap.*432

Be it enacted, etc., as follows:

Chapter one hundred and fifty-two of the General Laws is hereby amended by striking out section fifteen, as amended by chapter four hundred and one of the acts of nineteen hundred and thirty-nine, and inserting in place thereof the following section: — *Section 15.* Where the injury for which compensation is payable was caused under circumstances creating a legal liability in some person other than the insured to pay damages in respect thereof, the employee may at his option proceed either at law against that person to recover damages or against the insurer for compensation under this chapter, but, except as hereinafter provided, not against both. If compensation be paid under this chapter, the insurer may enforce, in the name of the employee or in its own name and for its own benefit, the liability of such other person, and if, in any case where the employee has claimed or received compensation within six months of the injury, the insurer does not proceed to enforce such liability within a period of nine months after said injury, the employee may so proceed. In either event the sum recovered shall be for the benefit of the insurer unless such sum is greater than that paid by it to the employee. If the insurer brings the action four fifths of the excess shall be paid to the employee, and if the employee brings the action he shall retain the entire excess. The party bringing the action shall be entitled to retain any costs recovered by him and any interest received in such action shall be apportioned between the insurer and the employee in proportion to the amounts received by them respectively under this section, exclusive of interest and costs. For the purposes of this section, "excess" shall mean the amount by which the total sum received in payment for the injury, exclusive of interest and costs, exceeds the compensation paid under this chapter. The insurer and the employee may share the expense of any attorney's fee in accordance with such agreement as they may make, provided that when the insurer brings the action no such agreement shall be valid if the employee would be required thereunder to bear a greater proportion of such expenses than the proportion that the part of the excess received hereunder by him bears to the total sum received hereunder by him and the insurer, exclusive of interest and costs. Except in the case of a settlement by agreement by the parties to, and during a trial of, such an action at law, no settlement by agreement shall be made with such other person without the approval of the industrial accident board after an opportunity has been afforded both the insurer and the employee to be heard on

G. L. (Ter. Ed.), 152, § 15, etc., amended.

Legal liability for injuries.

the merits of the settlement and on the amount, if any, to which the insurer is entitled out of such settlement by way of reimbursement, which amount shall be determined by said board at the time of such approval. In the case of a settlement by agreement by the parties to, and during a trial of, such an action at law the justice presiding at the trial shall have and exercise, relative to the approval of such settlement by agreement and to the protection of the rights and interests of the employee, all the powers hereinbefore granted to the industrial accident board. An employee shall not be held to have exercised his option under this section to proceed at law if, at any time prior to trial of an action at law brought by him against such other person, he shall after notice to the insurer discontinue such action, provided that upon payment of compensation following such discontinuance the insurer shall not have lost its right to enforce the liability of such other person as hereinbefore provided.

Approved June 4, 1943.

---

*Chap.*433 AN ACT PROVIDING FOR LOANS TO DISCHARGED PRISONERS.

Be it enacted, etc., as follows:

G. L. (Ter. Ed.), 127, § 160, etc., amended.

Chapter one hundred and twenty-seven of the General Laws is hereby amended by striking out section one hundred and sixty, as amended by section twenty-five of chapter three hundred and forty-four of the acts of nineteen hundred and forty-one, and inserting in place thereof the following section: — *Section 160.* The parole board may expend such sum as may be appropriated for the assistance of prisoners released from the state prison, the Massachusetts reformatory, the reformatory for women, the state farm, the state prison colony, or from any institution to which they were removed therefrom. Such assistance may be in the form of a loan on such conditions as the board may determine. Any loans paid back to the board may be expended by them for the same purpose without appropriation; provided, that at the end of each fiscal year any unexpended balance of an appropriation or loan so repaid shall revert to the treasury.

Expenditure of parole board.

Approved June 4, 1943.

---

*Chap.*434 AN ACT ESTABLISHING IN THE CITY OF BOSTON THE BOARD OF REAL ESTATE COMMISSIONERS, AND SETTING FORTH ITS POWERS AND DUTIES.

Be it enacted, etc., as follows:

SECTION 1. There shall be in the city of Boston hereinafter referred to as the city, a board, to be known as the board of real estate commissioners of the city of Boston, hereinafter referred to as the board, which shall consist of the city treasurer and the chairman of the city planning board, ex officiis, and three other persons to be appointed by the mayor as hereinafter provided. The initial appointments hereunder shall be made by the mayor within sixty days after the effective date of this act, and in making the same he shall appoint one appointive member for a term expiring on May first, nineteen hundred and forty-six, one for a term expiring on May first, nineteen hundred and forty-five, and one for a term expiring on May first, nineteen hundred and forty-four, and thereafter, as the term of office of an appointive member expires, his successor shall be appointed by the mayor for a term of three years. If the office of any of the appointive members becomes vacant, the vacancy or vacancies shall be filled for the unexpired term by the mayor. The mayor shall designate one of the appointive members as chairman. The chairman shall receive as compensation such sum, not exceeding five thousand dollars per annum, as may be fixed by the mayor. The other members shall serve without pay.

SECTION 2. The chairman, subject to the regulations of the board with respect to his procedure, shall have the care, custody, management and control of all property acquired by the city by foreclosure of tax titles or acquired under section eighty of chapter sixty of the General Laws, whether acquired before or after the effective date of this act.

SECTION 3. The chairman, subject to appropriation, may employ one or more assistants as may be necessary for the proper performance of his duties, and such assistants shall receive as compensation such amounts as may be approved by the mayor.

SECTION 4. The mayor shall appoint from the board a committee consisting of the chairman and two other members, to be known as the committee on foreclosed real estate. The chairman, acting on behalf of the city, may, subject to the restrictions hereinafter provided, let or lease real estate referred to in section two or any portion thereof, or interest therein. The chairman, acting on behalf of the city, subject to such restrictions, may also sell such real estate, or any portion thereof, or any interest therein, at public auction, first posting a notice thereof in two or more convenient and public places in the city at least fourteen days before such sale. A similar notice shall be sent by registered mail to the person who was the owner of record immediately prior to the acquisition by the city of absolute title to such property, at least fourteen days before the sale. Such notice shall contain a description of the property to be sold sufficient to identify it, and shall state the date, time and place appointed for the sale thereof and the terms and conditions of such sale. The chairman may reject any and all bids at such sale or any adjournment thereof if in his opinion no bid is made which approximates the fair value of the property, and he may adjourn the sale from time to time for such periods as he deems expedient, giving notice thereof at the time and place appointed for the sale or any adjournment thereof. Failure to post or send a notice as herein provided, or any insufficiency in the notice posted or sent, shall not invalidate the title to any property sold hereunder.

SECTION 5. No lease or sale made under section four shall be valid unless approved by a unanimous vote of the committee on foreclosed real estate, or by a vote, approved by the mayor, of a majority of the board. A certificate of the vote of the committee on foreclosed real estate, or of the vote of a majority of the board and the approval of the mayor, as the case may be, shall be made by the secretary of the board and attached to the lease or deed.

SECTION 6. The board shall elect a secretary, and may from time to time make such regulations with respect to its own procedure, and, with respect to the procedure of the chairman, in respect to the care, custody, management, control, sale or lease of any real estate, as it may deem advisable in the public interest. Such regulations shall not enlarge the powers given to the board or the chairman under this act, nor shall the validity of any sale or lease be affected by such regulation.

SECTION 7. The city treasurer of the city shall, in the name and on behalf of the city, execute and deliver any instrument necessary to convey any interest of the city under any provision of this act.

SECTION 8. This act shall apply to the city of Boston notwithstanding any provision of law, ordinance or by-law inconsistent herewith; provided, that, until the qualification of the appointive members of the board initially appointed under this act, chapter three hundred and fifty-eight of the acts of nineteen hundred and thirty-eight, as amended, shall continue to apply to the city. *Approved June 4, 1943.*

---

*Chap.*435 AN ACT VALIDATING CERTAIN ACTS AND PROCEEDINGS OF THE TOWN OF OXFORD AND OF ITS OFFICERS.

Be it enacted, etc., as follows:

SECTION 1. The by-laws of the town of Oxford adopted or amended at any town meeting of said town held on or before February seventh, nineteen hundred and thirty-eight, shall have the same force and validity as if the laws relative to the publishing thereof had been fully complied with by said town.

SECTION 2. The acts and proceedings of said town, at the several annual town meetings and elections held since January first, nineteen hundred and thirty-four, and at any adjournment of any such meeting or election, and all acts and proceedings of said town and of its officers done in pursuance thereof, are hereby confirmed and made valid to the same extent as if said meetings and elections had been called, held and conducted in strict compliance with law.

SECTION 3. This act shall take effect upon its passage.

Approved June 4, 1943.

AN ACT PERMITTING THE DEPARTMENT OF PUBLIC HEALTH TO ESTABLISH AND MAINTAIN CANCER CLINICS. *Chap.*436

Emergency preamble.

Whereas, The deferred operation of this act would delay the accomplishment of one of its principal purposes which is to remove doubt immediately as to the validity of certain payments claimed to have been made without authority of law, therefore this act is hereby declared to be an emergency law, necessary for the immediate preservation of the public convenience.

Be it enacted, etc., as follows:

G. L. (Ter. Ed.), 111, new § 57A, added.

SECTION 1. Chapter one hundred and eleven of the General Laws is hereby amended by inserting after section fifty-seven, as appearing in the Tercentenary Edition, the following section: — *Section 57A*. The department, with or without the cooperation of local boards of health, hospitals, dispensaries or other agencies, shall establish and maintain cancer clinics in such parts of the commonwealth as it may deem most advantageous to the public health, and may otherwise provide services and treatment for cancer, subject to such rules and regulations as the department may from time to time establish. For the purposes of this section, "providing treatment" shall include providing transportation, or the reasonable cost of such transportation, to and from the place where treatment is given whenever the patient is not able to pay for such transportation.

Establishment and maintenance of cancer clinics.

Validation of prior payments.

SECTION 2. All payments heretofore made by or on behalf of the commonwealth for cancer clinics under authority of section two of chapter three hundred and ninety-one of the acts of nineteen hundred and twenty-six are hereby validated to the same extent as if the provisions of section one had been in effect at the time of such payments.

Approved June 4, 1943.

AN ACT RELATIVE TO THE JURISDICTION OF THE SUPERIOR COURT OF CERTAIN MOTOR VEHICLE TORT CASES, SO CALLED, COMMENCED IN SAID COURT. *Chap.*437

Emergency preamble.

Whereas, In view of the fact that chapter two hundred and ninety-six of the acts of the current year, repealing the Fielding act, so called, does not become operative until September first in the current year and that the deferred operation of this act would in part tend to defeat its purpose, which is in part to make immediately possible the rectification of certain mistakes of law or fact resulting in erroneously bringing in the superior court certain motor vehicle tort cases, so called, therefore this act is hereby declared to be an emergency law, necessary for the immediate preservation of the public convenience.

Be it enacted, etc., as follows:

Nothing in section nineteen of chapter two hundred and eighteen of the General Laws shall prevent the superior court from having jurisdiction of any action of tort arising out of the operation of a motor vehicle which has been or prior to September first of the current year shall be commenced in such court. *Approved June 5, 1943.*

---

*Chap.*438 AN ACT SUBJECTING CERTAIN EMPLOYEES OF THE DEPARTMENT OF PUBLIC WORKS TO THE CIVIL SERVICE LAWS.

Emergency preamble.

Whereas, The civil service status of the persons referred to in this act should be established without delay in order that said persons may continue to serve in their respective positions without the existence of any doubt as to their status, therefore this act is hereby declared to be an emergency law, necessary for the immediate preservation of the public convenience.

Be it enacted, etc., as follows:

Any person who, on July first, nineteen hundred and forty-one, was in the employ of the state department of public works and was in the labor service of said department, and who, at all times between said July first and the effective date of this act was, and on said effective date is, in the employ of said department and holding a position classified within the official service under the civil service laws, shall be deemed to be permanently appointed to said position without serving any probationary period, and his tenure of office shall be unlimited subject, however, to the civil service laws, rules and regulations; provided, that he passes a qualifying examination to which he shall be subjected by the division of civil service. *Approved June 5, 1943.*

---

*Chap.*439 AN ACT TEMPORARILY AUTHORIZING FISHING WITHIN A PORTION OF THE COASTAL WATERS OF THE COMMONWEALTH ADJACENT TO THE TOWN OF PROVINCETOWN.

Emergency preamble.

Whereas, In view of the shortage of certain types of food in the present emergency, due to the existing state of war, it is necessary that certain provisions of law restricting fishing be temporarily suspended, and the deferred operation of this act would tend in part to defeat its purpose, which is to make immediately effective the suspension of such laws, therefore this act is hereby declared to be an emergency law, necessary for the immediate preservation of the public health and convenience.

Be it enacted, etc., as follows:

Any provision of general or special law to the contrary notwithstanding, during the existing state of war between the United States and any foreign country it shall be lawful for any inhabitant of the commonwealth to take fish by dragging or by otter trawling in such waters adjacent to Provincetown as lie within the area bounded by an imaginary line starting at Long Point light running due east to longitude seventy degrees, ten minutes, west; thence in a southerly direction along said line of longitude to where it first intersects the offshore territorial limits of the commonwealth; thence in a northwesterly direction along the line of the offshore territorial limits of the commonwealth to the intersection of an imaginary line running due west from Race Point light; thence along said imaginary line to Race Point light; thence along the shore line to said Long Point light; provided, that it shall not be lawful to fish within one half mile from mean low water mark.

Approved June 5, 1943.

AN ACT DEFINING THE AUTHORITY OF THE COMMISSION ON ADMINISTRATION AND FINANCE RELATIVE TO THE FURNISHING OF QUARTERS WITHIN AND WITHOUT THE STATE HOUSE FOR USE BY STATE AGENCIES. *Chap.* 440

Be it enacted, etc., as follows:

G. L. (Ter Ed.), 8, § 10, etc., amended.

SECTION 1. Section ten of chapter eight of the General Laws, as amended by section four of chapter two hundred and forty-nine of the acts of nineteen hundred and thirty-eight, is hereby further amended by inserting after the word "council" in the second line the words: — and with the approval of the commission on administration and finance, — so as to read as follows: — *Section 10.* He shall, under the supervision of the governor and council and with the approval of the commission on administration and finance, assign the rooms in the state house and rooms elsewhere used by the commonwealth, and may determine the occupancy thereof in such manner as the public service may require; provided, that the executive and administrative departments of the commonwealth shall be provided with suitable quarters which shall, so far as is expedient, be in the state house; and provided further, that this section shall not apply to rooms assigned to or used by either branch of the general court or any committees or officers thereof, except with the written consent of the presiding officer of the branch using such rooms, or to rooms assigned to or used by joint committees of the general court, except with the written consent of the presiding officers of both branches of the general court, nor shall it apply to the rooms used by the Grand Army of the Republic of the department of Massachusetts under section seventeen, except with the consent of the commander thereof. He shall during the sessions of the general court, upon application of the sergeant-at-arms, assign such rooms as may be required for the use of committees and other purposes.

Assignment of rooms in state house, etc.

G. L. (Ter. Ed.), 8, § 10A, etc., amended.

SECTION 2. Section ten A of said chapter eight, as most recently amended by chapter two hundred and sixty-seven of the acts of nineteen hundred and forty-one, is hereby further amended by inserting after the word "council" in the fourth line the words: — and of the commission on administration and finance, — so as to read as follows: —

Leasing of premises outside of state owned buildings.

Section 10A. The commonwealth, acting through the executive or administrative head of a state department, commission or board and with the approval of the superintendent and of the governor and council and of the commission on administration and finance, may lease for the use of such department, commission or board, for a term not exceeding five years, premises outside of the state house or other building owned by the commonwealth, if provision for rent of such premises for so much of the term of the lease as falls within the then current biennium, as defined in section one of chapter twenty-nine, has been made by appropriation. If the term of a lease under which premises are being used for the purposes of a particular activity by any such department, commission or board expires between the beginning of a biennium, as so defined, and the effective date of the general appropriation act for such biennium and no appropriation for rent for said premises has been made and if the general court has not provided otherwise, the commonwealth, acting through the executive or administrative head of such department, commission or board, and with like approval, may hire or lease for such purposes the same or different premises, for a term not exceeding five years, obligating the commonwealth to pay no greater aggregate amount of rent for any period than was paid for a corresponding period under the expiring lease. *Approved June 5, 1943.*

---

*Chap.*441 AN ACT RELATIVE TO THE PUBLICATION OF RULES AND REGULATIONS ADOPTED BY THE DEPARTMENT OF LABOR AND INDUSTRIES AND THE TAKING EFFECT THEREOF.

Be it enacted, etc., as follows:

G. L. (Ter. Ed.), 149, § 8, amended.

Section eight of chapter one hundred and forty-nine of the General Laws, as appearing in the Tercentenary Edition, is hereby amended by striking out the second sentence and inserting in place thereof the following sentence: — Such rules or regulations, when approved by the associate commissicners and the assistant commissioner, shall, subject to section thirty-seven of chapter thirty, take effect thirty days after such approval or at such later time as the associate commissioners and the assistant commissioner may fix, — so as to read as follows: —

Hearing on proposed rules. Publication and effective date of.

Section 8. Before adopting any rule or regulation under section six, a public hearing shall be given, and not less than ten days before the hearing a notice thereof shall be published in at least three newspapers, of which one shall be published in Boston. Such rules or regulations, when approved by the associate commissioners and the assistant commissioner, shall, subject to section thirty-seven of chapter thirty, take effect thirty days after such approval or at such later time as the associate commissioners and the assistant commissioner may fix. Before adopting any order a hearing shall be given thereon, of which a notice of not less than ten days shall be given to the persons affected thereby. *Approved June 5, 1943.*

AN ACT RELATIVE TO FURNISHING STATE AID IN THE YEARS NINETEEN HUNDRED AND FORTY-FOUR AND NINETEEN HUNDRED AND FORTY-FIVE TO CERTAIN SMALL TOWNS FOR THE REPAIR AND IMPROVEMENT OF PUBLIC WAYS THEREIN. *Chap.442*

Be it enacted, etc., as follows:

In each of the years nineteen hundred and forty-four and nineteen hundred and forty-five, any town eligible for state aid under section twenty-six of chapter eighty-one of the General Laws upon contributing or making available a proportionate part, not exceeding five-sixths, of the amount fixed for such town under said section, shall be entitled to receive the same proportionate part of the maximum amount of state aid authorized for such town under said section.

Approved June 5, 1943.

AN ACT MAKING CERTAIN PERSONS ELIGIBLE FOR ADMISSION TO AND TREATMENT AT THE SOLDIERS' HOME IN MASSACHUSETTS. *Chap.443*

Be it enacted, etc., as follows:

Eligibility for admission to Soldiers' Home.

Persons who were in the service of the United States in any branch of the military or naval forces thereof, who enlisted to the credit of this commonwealth, who were engaged in any campaign or expedition that has been recognized by the Congress of the United States, or in the Cuban Pacification campaign between October sixth, nineteen hundred and six and April first, nineteen hundred and nine, the Nicaraguan campaign between August twenty-eighth, nineteen hundred and twelve and October thirtieth, nineteen hundred and twenty-nine, the Vera Cruz expedition between April twenty-first, nineteen hundred and fourteen and November twenty-sixth, nineteen hundred and fourteen, the Dominican campaigns between May fifth, nineteen hundred and sixteen and September seventeenth, nineteen hundred and twenty-four, the Haiti campaign between July ninth, nineteen hundred and fifteen and October thirtieth, nineteen hundred and twenty-nine, or the China expeditionary service between October thirtieth, nineteen hundred and twenty-nine and June thirtieth, nineteen hundred and thirty, and who received an honorable discharge from such service, shall be eligible for admission to and treatment at the Soldiers' Home in Massachusetts to the same extent as veterans of the world war and of the Mexican border mobilization of the year nineteen hundred and sixteen.

Approved June 5, 1943.

Chap.444 An Act altering the disposition of proceeds of recovery in certain actions for death.

Be it enacted, etc., as follows:

G. L. (Ter. Ed.), 229, § 1, amended.

Section 1. Chapter two hundred and twenty-nine of the General Laws is hereby amended by striking out section one, as appearing in the Tercentenary Edition, and inserting in place thereof the following: — *Section 1.* If the life of a person is lost by reason of a defect or a want of repair of or a want of a sufficient railing in or upon a way, causeway or bridge, the county, city, town or person by law obliged to repair the same shall, if it or he had previous reasonable notice of the defect or want of repair or want of railing, be liable in damages not exceeding one thousand dollars, to be assessed with reference to the degree of culpability of the defendant and recovered in an action of tort commenced within one year after the injury causing the death by the executor or administrator of the deceased person, to the use of the following persons and in the following shares: —

Damages for death from a defective way, who may recover.

(1) If the deceased shall have been survived by a wife or husband and no children or issue surviving, then to the use of such surviving spouse.

(2) If the deceased shall have been survived by a wife or husband and by one child or by the issue of one deceased child, then one half to the use of such surviving spouse and one half to the use of such child or his issue by right of representation.

(3) If the deceased shall have been survived by a wife or husband and by more than one child surviving either in person or by issue, then one third to the use of such surviving spouse and two thirds to the use of such surviving children or their issue by right of representation.

(4) If there is no surviving wife or husband, then to the use of the next of kin.

G. L. (Ter. Ed.), 229, new §§ 6A and 6B, added.

Section 2. Said chapter two hundred and twenty-nine is hereby further amended by inserting after section six the two following sections: — *Section 6A.* All sums recovered under section one, two, three, four, five or five A shall, if and to the extent that the assets of the estate of the deceased shall be insufficient to satisfy the same, be subject to the charges of administration and funeral expenses of said estate, to all medical and hospital expenses necessitated by the injury which caused the death, and to reasonable attorneys' fees incurred in such recovery.

Sums recovered subject to certain charges.

Sums recovered, treated as new assets, when.

Section 6B. In the event that any sum recovered under section one, two, three, five, five A or six comes into the hands of the executor or administrator of the deceased after the expiration of one year from the time of his giving bond, such sum shall be treated as new assets of the estate of the deceased within the meaning of section eleven of chapter one hundred and ninety-seven. *Approved June 5, 1943.*

AN ACT DEFINING THE POWERS AND DUTIES OF THE MILK CONTROL BOARD IN CASE OF A FAILURE TO PAY THE OFFICIAL MINIMUM PRICE FOR THE SALE OR DELIVERY OF MILK. *Chap.*445

Be it enacted, etc., as follows:

G. L. (Ter. Ed.), 94A, new § 12A, added.

Chapter ninety-four A of the General Laws, inserted by section two of chapter six hundred and ninety-one of the acts of nineteen hundred and forty-one, is hereby amended by inserting after section twelve the following section: — *Section 12A*. If any producer is paid by a milk dealer less than the minimum price for the sale or delivery of milk, as fixed by official order or orders of the board, such producer may recover in a civil action against such milk dealer the full amount that would have been due him for such milk at the minimum price as so fixed, less the amount actually paid him for said milk, together with costs and such reasonable attorney's fees as may be allowed by the court, and any agreement between such producer and such milk dealer to sell or deliver milk for less than such minimum price shall be no defence to such action. At the written request of any such producer paid less than the minimum price for such sale or delivery of milk to which such producer is entitled under the provisions of the official order or orders of the board, the director may take an assignment of such claim in trust for the assigning producer and may bring an action to collect such claim, and such milk dealer shall be required to pay the costs and such reasonable attorney's fees as may be allowed by the court. The director shall not be required to pay any entry fee in connection with any such court action. *Approved June 5, 1943.*

Failure to pay official minimum price for milk.

Procedure, etc.

AN ACT PROVIDING FOR THE SANDING OF MALIBU BEACH, SO CALLED, IN THE DORCHESTER DISTRICT OF THE CITY OF BOSTON. *Chap.*446

Be it enacted, etc., as follows:

The metropolitan district commission is hereby authorized and directed to sand Malibu beach, so called, in the Dorchester district of the city of Boston. For said purposes said commission may expend such sum as may hereafter be appropriated therefor. *Approved June 5, 1943.*

AN ACT PROVIDING FOR AN ASSISTANT DIRECTOR IN THE DIVISION OF LIVESTOCK DISEASE CONTROL OF THE DEPARTMENT OF AGRICULTURE. *Chap.*447

Be it enacted, etc., as follows:

G. L. (Ter. Ed.), 20, § 4, etc., amended.

Section four of chapter twenty of the General Laws, as most recently amended by section fifteen of chapter five hundred and ninety-six of the acts of nineteen hundred and forty-one, is hereby further amended by inserting after the word "council" in the eleventh line the following: — There shall be in said division of livestock disease control an assistant director who shall be a veterinarian and who shall be appointed and may be removed by said director, with the approval of the governor and council. Said assistant director shall perform such duties as said director may prescribe, — so as to read as follows: — *Section 4.* The commissioner shall organize the department in divisions, including a division of dairying and animal husbandry, a division of plant pest control and fairs, a division of markets, a division of livestock disease control, and such other divisions as he may from time to time determine, and shall assign to said divisions their functions. The work of each division shall be in charge of a director. The director of the division of livestock disease control shall be known as the director of livestock disease control, and shall be appointed and may be removed by the governor, with the advice and consent of the council. There shall be in said division of livestock disease control an assistant director who shall be a veterinarian and who shall be appointed and may be removed by said director, with the approval of the governor and council. Said assistant director shall perform such duties as said director may prescribe. The commissioner shall appoint and may remove a director for each of the other divisions. The commissioner may also appoint, except as to the division of livestock disease control, such other assistants as the work of the department may require and may assign them to divisions, transfer and remove them.

Organization of department of agriculture.

Director of divisions, etc.

Approved June 5, 1943.

---

*Chap.*448 AN ACT AUTHORIZING THE TOWN OF WINTHROP TO ESTABLISH A BOARD OF PUBLIC WORKS EXERCISING THE POWERS OF CERTAIN OTHER BOARDS, DEPARTMENTS AND TOWN OFFICERS.

Be it enacted, etc., as follows:

SECTION 1. There shall be established in the town of Winthrop a board of public works, hereinafter called the board, to consist of three members. Upon the acceptance of this act the members of the board of water commissioners then in office shall forthwith be termed, constituted and serve as a board of public works and shall continue to so serve during their respective terms of office. Said commissioners shall have all the powers, duties and authority granted to a board of public works by this act, and any appropriations voted for street construction, general highways including tar, asphalt and oil, sidewalks maintenance and construction, driveways and removal of snow and ice, and for sewer maintenance and construction, parks and playgrounds, or balances of such appropriations remaining unexpended, may be expended under the direction of said commissioners, while acting as a board of public works. When the term of any member expires his successor shall be elected to serve for three years as a member of the board of public works. In all cases the members shall serve until their successors are qualified. The members of the board shall, forthwith after each annual town election, elect one of their members to act as chairman for the ensuing year. In case of a vacancy, the remaining members of the board, if they constitute a quorum, may fill such vacancy until the next annual town election, when a new member shall be elected to fill the unexpired term. No person shall serve on the board who holds another elective or appointive office in the town, except town meeting member.

SECTION 2. Upon the qualification of the initial members of the board, the board shall have all the powers, rights and duties now or from time to time vested by general or special law in the following boards, departments and officers in said town, to wit: water commissioners, park commissioners, highway department including the superintendent of streets, sidewalks and driveways, and superintendent of sewers, and such boards, departments and offices shall thereupon be abolished during such time as this act is in effect as to them, respectively. No contracts or liabilities in force on the date when this act becomes fully effective shall be affected by such abolition, but the board shall in all respects be the lawful successor of the boards, departments and offices so abolished.

SECTION 3. The board may appoint and fix the compensation of a superintendent of public works, who shall exercise and perform, under its supervision and direction, such powers, rights and duties, and shall hold office subject to the will of the board. He shall be specially fitted by education, training and experience to perform the duties of said office, and may or may not be a resident of the town. During his tenure he shall hold no elective or other appointive office, nor shall he be engaged in any other business or occupation. He shall give to the town a bond with a surety company authorized to transact business in the commonwealth as surety, for the faithful performance of his duties, in such sum and upon such conditions as the board may require, and shall, subject to the approval of the board, appoint such assistants, agents and employees as the exercise and performance of his powers, rights and duties may require. He shall keep full and complete records of the doings of his office and render to the board as often as it may require a full report of all operations under his control during the period reported upon; and annually, and from time to time as required by the board, he shall make a synopsis of such reports for publication. He shall keep the board fully advised as to the needs of the town within the scope of his duties, and shall annually furnish to the board, not less than ten days prior to the expiration of the fiscal year of said town, a carefully prepared and detailed estimate in writing of the appropriations required during the next succeeding fiscal year for the proper exercise and performance of all said powers, rights and duties. The board by a majority vote may at any time remove the superintendent for cause, after a hearing or an opportunity therefor; provided, that a written statement setting forth specific reasons for such removal is filed with the town clerk and a copy thereof delivered to or sent by registered mail to said superintendent at least five days before the date of said proposed hearing. The action of the board shall be final.

SECTION 4. The income of the water works shall be appropriated to defray all operating expenses, interest charges and payments on the principal as they accrue upon any bonds or notes issued for the purpose of extending, increasing or improving the water system. The metropolitan water assessments shall be paid from water revenue. If in any year there should be a net surplus remaining after providing for the aforesaid charges for that year, such surplus, or so much thereof as may be necessary to reimburse the town for moneys theretofore paid on account of its water department, shall be paid into the town treasury. If in any year there should be a net surplus remaining after providing for the aforesaid charges and assessments and for the payment of any such reimbursement, such surplus may be accumulated, and may be expended, after an appropriation has been duly voted for such new construction, as the board may determine upon; and in case a net surplus should remain after payment for such new construction the water rates shall be reduced proportionately.

SECTION 5. The town may rescind all or any part of the action taken by it in pursuance of this act by a majority vote of the legal voters of said town at any annual or special town meeting held after three years following the annual town election at which this act becomes fully effective and at least thirty days before the annual town election next to be held after such meeting, and thereupon said town shall, at said next annual town election, nominate and elect such officers as are necessary to exercise and perform such of the powers, rights and duties transferred to the board under section two as are affected by such later vote.

SECTION 6. This act shall be submitted for acceptance to the legal voters of said town at the annual town election in the year nineteen hundred and forty-four, in the form of the following question which shall be placed on the official ballot to be used for the election of town officers at said election: "Shall an act passed by the General Court in the year nineteen hundred and forty-three, entitled 'An Act authorizing the Town of Winthrop to establish a Board of Public Works exercising the powers of certain other Boards, Departments and Town Officers', be accepted?" If a majority of the votes cast in answer to such question is in the affirmative, this act shall become fully effective forthwith; otherwise it shall be of no effect. *Approved June 5, 1943.*

An Act authorizing the city of Somerville to pay certain unpaid bills of the year nineteen hundred and thirty-seven. Chap.449

Be it enacted, etc., as follows:

Section 1. The city of Somerville is hereby authorized to appropriate money for the payment of, and after such appropriation the treasurer of said city is hereby authorized to pay, certain unpaid bills against the city for board of patients at the Middlesex County Tuberculosis Hospital during the calendar year nineteen hundred and thirty-seven in the amount of two thousand, four hundred and eighty-five dollars and fifty cents, as set forth in a list on file in the office of the director of accounts in the department of corporations and taxation; provided, that the money so appropriated to pay such bills shall be raised by taxation in said city in the current year.

Section 2. No bill shall be approved by the city auditor of said city for payment or paid by the treasurer thereof under authority of this act unless and until certificates have been signed and filed with said city auditor, stating under the penalties of perjury that the services for which bills have been submitted were ordered by an official or an employee of said city, and unless and until certificates have been signed and filed under the penalties of perjury by the superintendent of the hospital that the services were rendered and payment not yet received.

Section 3. Any person who knowingly files a certificate required by section two which is false and who thereby receives payment for services which were not rendered to said city shall be punished by imprisonment for not more than one year or by a fine of not more than three hundred dollars, or both.

Section 4. This act shall take effect upon its passage.

Approved June 7, 1943.

An Act authorizing the town of Sudbury to receive and administer the property of the corporation called Mount Wadsworth Cemetery in said town, and validating certain actions of the town and of the corporation in connection therewith. Chap.450

Be it enacted, etc., as follows:

Section 1. Mount Wadsworth Cemetery, a corporation duly incorporated under the Public Statutes and situated in the town of Sudbury, hereinafter called the corporation, is hereby empowered and authorized to convey and transfer to said town, and said town is hereby authorized and empowered to receive, and thereafter to hold and maintain, but for cemetery purposes only, and subject to all rights heretofore existing in any burial lots, the real and personal property of the corporation not subject to any trust, and thereupon, and upon the transfer of the trust funds as hereinafter provided, the corporation shall be dissolved; and the cemetery of the corporation shall be and become a public burial place, ground or cemetery.

SECTION 2. In so far as authorized by a decree of a court of competent jurisdiction and in compliance with the terms and conditions of such decree, said town may receive from the corporation a conveyance and transfer of, and administer, all funds or other property held by the corporation in trust for the perpetual care of the lots in its cemetery and for other purposes, and also any property devised or bequeathed to the corporation under the will of any person living at the time of said transfer or conveyance or under the will of any deceased person not then probated. Interest and dividends accruing on funds deposited in trust with any savings bank, under authority of section thirty-seven or thirty-eight of chapter one hundred and sixty-eight of the General Laws, or with any other banking institution, for the benefit of the corporation, or of any lots in its cemetery, may, after such conveyance, be paid by such bank or institution to the treasurer of said town; and upon such payment said treasurer shall use the same for the purposes of said trusts.

SECTION 3. All real and personal property and property rights, acquired by said town from the corporation under authority of this act shall be held and managed by said town in the same manner in which cities and towns are authorized by law to hold and manage property for cemetery purposes; provided, that all rights which any persons have acquired in its cemetery or lots therein shall remain in force to the same extent as if this act had not been passed and such transfer had not occurred. The records of the corporation shall be delivered to the clerk of said town and such clerk may certify copies thereof.

SECTION 4. The action of the inhabitants of the town of Sudbury, at its annual town meeting in the year nineteen hundred and forty-one, in voting to accept a transfer of real and personal property of said cemetery, and all acts of the corporation purporting to assign, set over, grant or convey to said town the real or personal property, or both, of the corporation, together with any or all rights of the corporation thereto, in law or in equity, are hereby ratified and confirmed, and shall have the same effect and validity as if section one had been in effect prior to said vote.

SECTION 5. This act shall take full effect upon its acceptance by a majority of the registered voters of the town of Sudbury voting thereon at a regular or special town meeting of said town not later than the regular town meeting in the year nineteen hundred and forty-four, but not otherwise. *Approved June 7, 1943.*

AN ACT ESTABLISHING A BOARD OF RECREATION IN THE CITY OF BOSTON, AND SETTING FORTH ITS POWERS AND DUTIES. *Chap.*451

Be it enacted, etc., as follows:

SECTION 1. A board of recreation, hereinafter referred to as the board, is hereby established in the city of Boston. The board shall consist of seven members. The chairman of the board of park commissioners of said city shall be, ex officio, a member of the board. Two members shall be appointed by the school committee of said city and each member so appointed shall serve for a term expiring on December thirty-first of each even-numbered year. Four suitable persons shall be appointed by the mayor of said city in accordance with chapter four hundred and eighty-six of the acts of nineteen hundred and nine, as amended. Of the members initially appointed hereunder by the mayor, one shall serve for a term of one year, one for a term of two years, one for a term of three years and one for a term of four years. Upon the expiration of the term of office of a member appointed by the mayor, his successor shall be appointed by the mayor for a term of four years. Vacancies in the membership of the board shall be filled in the manner of original appointments.

SECTION 2. The members of the board shall serve without compensation, and shall annually elect a chairman from their own number to serve for one year or until his successor is elected. The board shall have power to adopt rules of procedure and prescribe regulations for the conduct of all business by employees within its jurisdiction. A majority of the membership of the board shall constitute a quorum.

SECTION 3. The board shall appoint a superintendent of recreation who shall devote his whole time to such duties as are imposed upon him by this act. The board may also appoint such assistants and other employees as it may deem necessary to accomplish the purposes of this act and as may be consistent with its appropriation. Said superintendent and all employees of the board shall be subject to chapter thirty-one of the General Laws and the rules and regulations made thereunder, except that the play instructors and supervisors may be appointed from the list of persons eligible to be appointed as school teachers for said city. Appropriations for the board shall be made therefor in the manner prescribed by law for city departments of said city.

SECTION 3A. The incumbent on the effective date of this act of the office of director of recreation of the park department of said city may be transferred to the office of superintendent of recreation established by section three.

SECTION 4. The board shall study the recreation needs of said city and shall formulate plans for adequately distributed, co-ordinated and diversified recreational services. Such plans, with recommendations of the board, shall be submitted to departments of said city empowered by law to provide recreational services. The board shall encourage the establishment of voluntary committees to advise and co-operate with the board with respect to the operation and supervision of neighborhood play areas. The board may submit recommendations to any licensing authority or authorities.

Section 5. The board may, from time to time, consult with the park department, school committee, police department, public buildings department, board of street commissioners and traffic commission of said city, and any other department thereof empowered under any general or special law or any ordinance to provide recreational services or having jurisdiction over premises and facilities which might be used for recreation, in relation to the recreational services or premises and facilities provided by said departments and in relation to plans for recreational services formulated by the board.

Section 6. The park department, school committee, police department, public buildings department, board of street commissioners and traffic commission of said city, and any other department thereof empowered under any general or special law or any ordinance to provide recreational services or having jurisdiction over premises and facilities which might be used for recreation, may, from time to time, delegate to the board, with the consent of the board, and under such terms, including provisions for the transfer of personnel, as may be agreed upon, the management of any such recreational services or make available to the board premises and facilities under their control.

Section 7. The board may provide and may conduct recreational activities and supervise recreational premises and facilities delegated or made available to it by other departments of said city under section six. The board may co-operate with and promote by advice, suggestion and otherwise, such voluntary or amateur organizations for recreation, entertainment or mutual improvement as shall meet its approval. The board may acquire and utilize recreational supplies and equipment and other supplies and equipment necessary for the conduct of its work.

Section 8. The board shall annually make a report of its activities during the preceding year to the mayor with such recommendations for the development of playgrounds and recreational facilities, including additions thereto, as it may deem advisable.

Section 9. This act shall take full effect on January first of the year next succeeding its acceptance by vote of the city council of said city, subject to the provisions of its charter.

Approved June 7, 1943.

AN ACT AUTHORIZING CERTAIN CITIES AND TOWNS TO INCREASE THE RETIREMENT ALLOWANCES OF CERTAIN FORMER EMPLOYEES THEREOF WHO WERE RETIRED ON ACCOUNT OF ACCIDENTAL DISABILITY. *Chap.*452

Be it enacted, etc., as follows:

SECTION 1. Chapter thirty-two of the General Laws is hereby amended by inserting after section ninety, as amended, the following section: — *Section 90A.* Any city or town which accepts the provisions of this section in the manner hereinafter provided may, in the case of a city by two thirds vote of the city council and with the approval of the mayor, or, in the case of a town, by two thirds vote at the annual town meeting, increase the retirement allowance of any former employee thereof who has been retired under any provision of this chapter or similar provision of earlier law on account of injuries sustained or of hazard undergone in the performance of his duty, to an amount not exceeding one half the rate of regular compensation payable to employees of such city or town holding similar positions, at the time of increasing such allowance, in the same grade or classification occupied by such former employee at the time of his retirement. G. L. (Ter. Ed.), 32, new § 90A, added. Increase of retirement allowances in certain cases.

SECTION 2. This act may be accepted by a town by two thirds vote at its annual town meeting, or by a city by two thirds vote of the city council with the approval of the mayor. Acceptance of act.

Approved June 7, 1943.

AN ACT TO MAKE CERTAIN CORRECTIONAL CHANGES IN THE LAWS RELATING TO ELECTIONS. *Chap.*453

Be it enacted, etc., as follows:

SECTION 1. Section fourteen of chapter thirty-nine of the General Laws, as appearing in the Tercentenary Edition, is hereby amended by striking out the first paragraph and inserting in place thereof the following paragraph: — At every town meeting when moderators are not elected for the term of one or three years, a moderator shall first be elected. The election of a moderator at a meeting for the choice of town officers shall be by ballot, and the voting list shall be used thereat. G. L. (Ter. Ed.), 39, § 14, amended. Election of moderator.

SECTION 2. Said section fourteen of said chapter thirty-nine, as so appearing, is hereby further amended by striking out, in the seventh line, the word "inhabitants" and inserting in place thereof the words: — registered voters, — so that the second paragraph will read as follows: — G. L. (Ter. Ed.), 39, § 14, amended.

Any town or fire, water, light or improvement district which has so voted or hereafter so votes may at any annual election of town or district officers elect from the registered voters thereof by ballot a moderator to preside at all town or district meetings. His term of office shall begin as soon as he Election of moderator by ballot.

is qualified, and shall continue until the next annual town or district meeting and until his successor is qualified. Any town or district which has elected a moderator for the term of one year shall thereafter elect a moderator at every annual election of town or district officers, unless the town or district votes to discontinue the electing of moderators for said term.

G. L. (Ter. Ed.), 41, § 1, etc., amended.

SECTION 3. Section one of chapter forty-one of the General Laws, as most recently amended by chapter one hundred and twenty-nine of the acts of nineteen hundred and thirty-nine, is hereby further amended by striking out the first paragraph, as appearing in the Tercentenary Edition, and inserting in place thereof the following paragraph: — Every town at its annual meeting shall in every year when the term of office of any incumbent expires, and except when other provision is made by law, choose by ballot from its registered voters the following town officers for the following terms of office:

Officers to be elected.

G. L. (Ter. Ed.), 43A, § 6, etc., amended.

SECTION 4. Chapter forty-three A of the General Laws is hereby amended by striking out section six, as amended by section one of chapter one of the acts of the current year, and inserting in place thereof the following section: — *Section 6.* Nomination of candidates for town meeting members to be elected under this chapter shall be made by nomination papers, which shall show clearly whether he has been a former town meeting member, and, if an elected incumbent of such office, that he is a candidate for re-election and shall bear no other political designation. Such papers shall be signed by not less than ten voters of the precinct in which the candidate resides, shall be filed with the town clerk at least ten days before the election or, in towns which have accepted section one hundred and three A of chapter fifty-four, within the time provided by section ten of chapter fifty-three. They shall be submitted to the registrars of voters and shall be certified in the manner provided in section seven of said chapter fifty-three; provided, that any town meeting member, including any town meeting member in office under the provisions of a special statute under which such town is operating immediately prior to the taking effect therein of the standard form of representative town meeting government provided by this chapter, may become a candidate for re-election by giving written notice thereof to the town clerk at least thirty days before the election. If a town meeting member is a candidate for re-election, the words "Candidate for Re-election" shall be printed against his name as it appears on the ballot for the election of town officers. No nomination papers shall be valid in respect to any candidate whose written acceptance is not thereon or attached thereto when filed.

Nomination of candidates for town meeting members.

G. L. (Ter. Ed.), 43A, § 8, amended.

SECTION 5. Section eight of said chapter forty-three A, as appearing in the Tercentenary Edition, is hereby amended by striking out the first sentence and inserting in place thereof the following sentence: — A moderator shall be elected by ballot at the annual town meeting when his term of office expires, for the term of one or three years, and shall serve as moderator of all town meetings, except as otherwise provided by law, until a successor is elected and qualified. Moderator; moderator pro tempore.

SECTION 6. Section one of chapter fifty of the General Laws, as amended, is hereby further amended by striking out the paragraph included in the nineteenth to the twenty-first lines, inclusive, as appearing in the Tercentenary Edition, and inserting in place thereof the following paragraph: — G. L. (Ter Ed.), 50, § 1, etc., amended.

"City election" shall apply to any election held in a city at which a city officer is to be chosen by the voters, whether for a full term or for the filling of a vacancy, or at which any question to be voted upon at a city election is to be submitted to the voters. "City election" defined.

SECTION 7. Said section one of said chapter fifty, as amended, is hereby further amended by striking out the paragraph included in the ninety-first and ninety-second lines, as so appearing, and inserting in place thereof the following paragraph: — G. L. (Ter. Ed.), 50, § 1, etc., amended.

"State officer" shall apply to, and include, any person to be nominated at a state primary or chosen at a state election and shall include United States senator and representative in Congress. "State officer" defined.

SECTION 8. Said section one of said chapter fifty, as so amended, is hereby further amended by inserting after the paragraph included in the ninety-third line, as so appearing, the following paragraph: — G. L. (Ter. Ed.), 50 § 1, etc., amended.

"Town officer" shall apply to and include town meeting members. "Town officer" defined.

SECTION 9. Section eight of said chapter fifty, as appearing in the Tercentenary Edition, is hereby amended by striking out, in the second line, the word "assessment", and inserting in place thereof the words: — listing of persons twenty years of age and over and to the, — so as to read as follows: — *Section 8.* In any criminal prosecution for the violation of any law relating to the listing of persons twenty years of age and over and to the qualification or registration of voters, to voting lists or ballots or matters pertaining thereto, or to primaries, caucuses or elections or matters pertaining thereto, the presumption shall be that every proceeding or official act was valid, regular and formal; but evidence may be introduced either to rebut or support the presumption. As to an alleged election or primary, the testimony of the city or town clerk, and as to an alleged caucus, the testimony of the presiding officer, secretary or clerk thereof, that such election, primary or caucus was held, shall be prima facie evidence that the same was regularly and duly held. G. L. (Ter. Ed.), 50, § 8, amended. Presumption of validity of registration, election, etc., in criminal cases.

SECTION 10. Section one of chapter fifty-one of the General Laws, as most recently amended by chapter two hundred and six of the acts of nineteen hundred and thirty-two, is hereby further amended by striking out, in the fifteenth G. L. (Ter. Ed.), 51, § 1, etc., amended.

and sixteenth lines, the words ", or who had the right to vote on May first, eighteen hundred and fifty-seven", — so that the first paragraph will read as follows: — Every citizen twenty-one years of age or older, not being a pauper or person under guardianship and not being temporarily or permanently disqualified by law because of corrupt practices in respect to elections, who can read the constitution of the commonwealth in English and write his name, and who has resided in the commonwealth one year and in the city or town where he claims a right to vote six months last preceding a state, city or town election, and who has complied with the requirements of this chapter, may have his name entered on the list of voters in such city or town, and may vote therein in any such election or, except in so far as restricted in any town in which a representative town meeting form of government has been established, in any meeting held for the transaction of town affairs. No other person shall have his name entered upon the list of voters or have the right to vote; except that no person who is prevented from reading or writing as aforesaid by a physical disability, shall, if otherwise qualified, be deprived of the right to vote by reason of not being able so to read or write; and no person who, having served in the army or navy of the United States in time of war, has been honorably discharged from such service, if otherwise qualified to vote, shall be disqualified therefrom on account of receiving or having received aid from any city or town, or because he is exempted by section five of chapter fifty-nine from the assessment of a poll tax; and no person otherwise qualified to vote for national or state officers shall, by reason of a change of residence within the commonwealth, be disqualified from voting for such officers in the city or town from which he has removed his residence until the expiration of six months from such removal. A married woman dwelling or having her home separate and apart from her husband shall for the purpose of voting and registration therefor be deemed to reside at the place where she dwells or has her home.

Qualifications of voters.

G. L. (Ter. Ed.), 51, § 3, etc., amended.

SECTION 11. Said chapter fifty-one is hereby further amended by striking out section three, as most recently amended by section four of chapter two hundred and fifty-four of the acts of nineteen hundred and thirty-three, and inserting in place thereof the following section: — *Section 3.* For all elections and primaries held prior to June first in any year, a person shall be registered and may vote in the ward or voting precinct where he resided on January first of the preceding year or, if he became a resident of the city or town after January first, in the ward or voting precinct where he first became a legal resident. For all elections and primaries held on or after June first a person shall be registered and may vote in the ward or voting precinct where he resided on January first preceding the election, or, if he became an inhabitant of such city or town after January first, in the

Place of registration and voting.

ward or voting precinct in which he first became a resident thereafter.

G. L. (Ter. Ed.), 51, new heading before § 4.

SECTION 12. Said chapter fifty-one is hereby further amended by striking out the heading before section four and inserting in place thereof the following heading: — LISTING OF PERSONS TWENTY YEARS OF AGE OR OVER.

G. L. (Ter. Ed.), 51, § 4, etc., amended.

SECTION 13. Section four of said chapter fifty-one, as most recently amended by section two of chapter four hundred and forty of the acts of nineteen hundred and thirty-eight, is hereby further amended by striking out, in the eighth line, the word "male", — by striking out all after the word "towns" in the tenth line down to and including the word "towns" in the thirteenth line, — and by striking out the last paragraph, — so as to read as follows: — *Section 4.* Except as otherwise provided by law, the registrars, assistant registrars, or one or more of them, shall annually in January or February, visit every building in their respective cities and towns, and, after diligent inquiry, shall make true lists containing, as nearly as they can ascertain, the name, age, occupation, nationality if not a citizen of the United States, and residence on January first in the preceding year and in the current year, of every person twenty years of age or older, residing in their respective cities and towns.

Registrars to make lists of persons twenty years of age or older.

Any inmate of the soldiers' home in Chelsea shall have the same right as any other resident of that city to be assessed and to vote therein.

G. L. (Ter. Ed.), 51, § 10, etc., repealed.

SECTION 14. Section ten of said chapter fifty-one, as amended by section eight of said chapter four hundred and forty, is hereby repealed.

G. L. (Ter. Ed.), 51, § 13, repealed.

SECTION 15. Section thirteen of said chapter fifty-one, as appearing in the Tercentenary Edition, is hereby repealed.

G. L. (Ter. Ed.), 51, § 14B, etc., amended.

SECTION 16. Section fourteen B of said chapter fifty-one, as amended by section twelve of chapter four hundred and forty of the acts of nineteen hundred and thirty-eight, is hereby further amended by striking out, in the third and fourth lines, the words "and of determining their liability to be assessed a poll tax", — so as to read as follows: — *Section 14B.* In cities and towns in which the duty of listing residents for the purposes of determining their right to vote is performed by officers other than registrars or assistant registrars, the provisions of this chapter relative to registrars and assistant registrars shall apply to such officers when performing like duties in such cities and towns, except as otherwise expressly provided in any special law or in this section. Where in any special law April first is stated as the date as of which the legal residence of any person shall be determined, such residence shall be determined as of January first instead of April first, and if any provision of this chapter contains a date for the performance of an official act by a board of registrars, registrar or assistant registrar, and by special law a different date is fixed for the performance of such act in any city or town by the same or any other board

Inconsistent provision of special laws superseded.

or officer, the earlier of such dates shall in such city or town prevail over the later date.

G. L. (Ter. Ed.), 51, § 20, amended.

Temporary vacancies.

SECTION 17. Said chapter fifty-one is hereby further amended by striking out section twenty, as appearing in the Tercentenary Edition, and inserting in place thereof the following section: — *Section 20.* If there is a vacancy in the board of registrars caused by death, resignation or retirement or if a member of the board of registrars is unable to perform the duties of his office, or is, at the time of any meeting of said board, absent from the city or town, the mayor or selectmen may, upon the request in writing of a majority of the remaining members of the board, appoint in writing some person to fill such vacancy temporarily, who is of the same political party as the member whose position he is appointed to fill. Such temporary registrar shall perform the duties and be subject to the requirements and penalties provided by law for a registrar of voters.

G. L. (Ter. Ed.), 51, § 22, etc., amended.

Assistant registrars in cities, appointment, etc.

SECTION 18. Said chapter fifty-one is hereby further amended by striking out section twenty-two, as amended by chapter two hundred and eighty of the acts of nineteen hundred and thirty-eight, and inserting in place thereof the following section: — *Section 22.* The registrars in cities and towns may appoint assistant registrars for the term of one year, beginning with April first, unless sooner removed by the registrars, and they shall, as nearly as may be, equally represent the different political parties. Assistant registrars shall be subject to the same obligations and penalties as registrars. Registrars may remove an assistant registrar, and may fill a vacancy for the remainder of the term. Registrars may also appoint temporary assistant registrars from time to time to assist in the listing of persons twenty years of age or over. Except in Boston, persons appointed to serve temporarily as assistant registrars, or as temporary assistant registrars, shall not be subject to chapter thirty-one.

G. L. (Ter. Ed.), 51, § 23, amended.

Registrars, oath of office, etc.

SECTION 19. Section twenty-three of said chapter fifty-one, as appearing in the Tercentenary Edition, is hereby amended by inserting after the word "names" in the fifth line the words: — listed or, — so as to read as follows: — *Section 23.* The registrars and assistant registrars shall, before entering upon their official duties, each take and subscribe an oath faithfully to perform the same. They shall receive such compensation for their services as the city council or selectmen may determine; but such compensation shall not be regulated by the number of names listed or registered by them, and a reduction of compensation shall apply only to registrars and assistant registrars appointed thereafter. The city council or selectmen shall provide them suitable rooms, and necessary assistance. The city or town clerk, when a member of the board of registrars, shall act as clerk thereof, shall keep a full and accurate record of its proceedings and shall cause such notices as the registrars may require to be properly given.

SECTION 20. Section twenty-six of said chapter fifty-one, as most recently amended by section two of chapter four hundred and seventy-three of the acts of nineteen hundred and thirty-eight, is hereby further amended by striking out, in the twelfth line, the words "the city election" and inserting in place thereof the words: — a city election, or a city primary or preliminary election, — so as to read as follows: — *Section 26.* The registrars, for the purpose of registering voters in the manner hereinafter provided, shall hold such day and such evening sessions as the town by by-law or the city by ordinance shall prescribe, and such other sessions as they deem necessary; but, except as provided in sections thirty-four and fifty, there shall be no registration of voters between ten o'clock in the evening on the twentieth day preceding, and the day following, the biennial state primary, the presidential primary and the biennial state election, nor in any city between ten o'clock in the evening on the twentieth day preceding and the day following a city election, or a city primary or preliminary election, nor in any town between ten o'clock in the evening on the Wednesday next but one preceding and the day following the annual town meeting. The time and place of registration shall be the same for male and female applicants.

G. L. (Ter. Ed.), 51, § 26, etc., amended.

Sessions of registrars.

SECTION 21. Said chapter fifty-one is hereby further amended by striking out section twenty-seven, as most recently amended by section one of chapter one hundred and nine of the acts of the current year, and inserting in place thereof the following section: — *Section 27.* They shall hold at least one session at some suitable place in every city or town on or before the last day for registration preceding the biennial state primary, the presidential primary and any city primary, and on or before the Wednesday next but one preceding a town primary, except a primary preceding a special town election. The provisions of this section applicable in the case of a city primary shall apply also in the case of a preliminary election held in any city under chapter forty-three, or under any special law except where it is otherwise provided.

G. L. (Ter. Ed.), 51, § 27, etc., amended.

Sessions before primaries.

SECTION 22. Section twenty-nine B of said chapter fifty-one, inserted by chapter one hundred and seventy-nine of the acts of nineteen hundred and thirty-eight, is hereby amended by adding at the end the words: —, unless the city council votes otherwise, — so as to read as follows: — *Section 29B.* In cities the registrars shall, within forty days before the biennial state election, but on or before the last day fixed for registration, hold one or more sessions in one or more suitable places in each ward of the city, unless the city council votes otherwise.

G. L. (Ter. Ed.), 51, § 29B, etc., amended.

Sessions of registrars in cities.

SECTION 23. Section thirty of said chapter fifty-one, as appearing in the Tercentenary Edition, is hereby amended by adding after the word "precinct" in the fifth line the words: — , unless the selectmen or town votes otherwise, —

G. L. (Ter. Ed.), 51, § 30, amended.

Sessions in towns.

so that the first sentence will read as follows: — In towns divided into voting precincts the registrars shall, within forty days before the biennial state election, and also within twenty days before the annual town meeting, but in each case on or before the last day fixed for registration, hold one or more sessions in each voting precinct, unless the selectmen or town votes otherwise.

G. L. (Ter. Ed.), 51, § 36, etc., amended.

SECTION 24. Section thirty-six of said chapter fifty-one, as most recently amended by section twelve of chapter two hundred and fifty-four of the acts of nineteen hundred and thirty-three, is hereby further amended by adding at the end the following paragraph: —

General register.

There shall be added in the above column designated "Remarks" such information pertaining to the status of a married woman and of a person claiming derivative citizenship as the registrars deem of value.

G. L. (Ter. Ed.), 51, § 37, etc., amended.

Annual register, entries, arrangement.

SECTION 25. Said chapter fifty-one is hereby further amended by striking out section thirty-seven, as amended, and inserting in place thereof the following section: — *Section 37.* The registrars, after April first, shall prepare an annual register containing the names of all qualified voters in their city or town for the current year, beginning with January first. Such names shall be arranged in alphabetical order, and, opposite to the name of each voter, shall be placed his residence on January first preceding or on any subsequent day when he became an inhabitant of the city or town. The registrars shall enter in the annual register every name contained in the lists prepared by them under section four, which they can identify as that of a person whose name was borne on the voting list of the city or town at the last preceding election or town meeting, giving the residence of each such person on January first, which, in the case of a person assessed a poll tax, shall be the place at which he was so assessed. They shall make all inquiries and investigations necessary to identify such person, and they shall not enter in the annual register the name of a person objected to by any registrar, nor shall they enter in such register as residing at any licensed inn, lodging house or public lodging house the name of a person which has not been reported to them under section ten A, until such person has been duly notified and given an opportunity to be heard. They shall forthwith enter in the annual register the name of every person whose qualifications as a voter have been determined by them in the current year and whose name has accordingly been entered in the general register. They shall, on or before the first Monday of June in each year, send notice in writing to each voter of the preceding year whose name has not been entered in the annual register of the current year that the name of such voter has not been so entered, such notice to be sent by first class mail enclosed in an envelope bearing the proper address to which the same may be returned in case of non-delivery, and the registrars shall prepare a list of the names of voters not so entered, which shall be open to public inspection in their principal office, or shall be posted by copy in the places where copies of voting lists are required to be posted under section fifty-seven of chapter fifty-one.

SECTION 26. Said chapter fifty-one is hereby further amended by striking out section thirty-eight, as appearing in the Tercentenary Edition, and inserting in place thereof the following section: — *Section 38.* The registrars shall, upon the personal application of a listed person for the correction of any error in their original lists, and whenever informed of any such error, make due investigation, and, upon proof thereof, correct the same on their books. When informed of the omission of the name of a person who is averred to have resided in the city or town on January first in the then current year and to have been listed there in the preceding year, they shall make due investigation, and, upon proof thereof, add the name to their books. They shall revise and correct the general register and the current annual register in accordance with any facts they may have presented to them. They shall strike therefrom the name of every deceased person which has been transmitted to them under section fourteen; but after the name of a voter has been placed upon the current annual register, they shall not change the place of residence as given thereon, nor, unless the voter has died or unless they have received notice under section nine from the registrars of another city or town that the voter has been listed therein, strike such name therefrom, until they have sent him a notice of their intention so to do, naming a certain date when he may be heard.

G. L. (Ter. Ed.), 51, § 38, amended.

Revision and correction of registers.

SECTION 27. Said chapter fifty-one is hereby further amended by striking out section forty-one, as so appearing, and inserting in place thereof the following: — *Section 41.* The registrars shall preserve all written applications, complaints, certificates and affidavits received by them, and all other documents in their custody relative to listing and registration, for two years after the dates thereof.

G. L. (Ter. Ed.), 51, § 41, amended.

Documents to be preserved.

SECTION 28. Section forty-four of said chapter fifty-one, as so appearing, is hereby amended by striking out, in the third and fourth lines, the words ", or unless he had the right to vote on May first, eighteen hundred and fifty-seven", — so as to read as follows: — *Section 44.* The registrars shall examine on oath an applicant for registration relative to his qualifications as a voter, and shall, unless he is prevented by physical disability, require him to write his name in the general register and to read in such manner as to show that he is neither prompted nor reciting from memory. Registrars shall be provided by the state secretary with a copy of the constitution of the commonwealth printed in English on uniform pasteboard slips, each containing five lines of said constitution printed in type of a size not less than twenty-four point, and with a box so constructed as to conceal them from view. The registrars shall place said slips in the box, and shall require each applicant to draw one of said slips

G. L. (Ter. Ed.), 51, § 44, amended.

Examination of applicants for registration. Oath. Reading slips, etc.

from the box and read aloud, in full view and hearing of the registrars, the five lines printed thereon. Each slip shall be returned to the box immediately after the test is finished, and the contents of the box shall be shaken up by a registrar before another drawing is made. No person failing to read the constitution as printed on the slip thus drawn shall be registered as a voter. The registrars shall keep said slips in said box at all times. The state secretary shall upon request provide new slips to replace those worn out or lost.

G. L. (Ter. Ed.), 51, § 55, etc., amended.

SECTION 29. Section fifty-five of said chapter fifty-one, as most recently amended by section four of chapter four hundred and seventy-three of the acts of nineteen hundred and thirty-eight, is hereby further amended by striking out the last sentence and inserting in place thereof the following sentence: — Notwithstanding the foregoing, the voting lists to be used at presidential primaries or any primary or election held prior to June first in any year may be that of the year preceding, revised as aforesaid, — so as to read as follows: — *Section 55.* Registrars shall, from the names entered in the annual register of voters, prepare voting lists for use at elections. In such voting lists they shall place the names of all voters entered on the annual register, and no others, and opposite to the name of each his residence on January first preceding or at the time of his becoming an inhabitant of such place after said day. They may enter the names of women voters in separate columns or lists. In cities, they shall prepare such voting lists by wards, and if a ward or a town is divided into voting precincts, they shall prepare the same by precincts, in alphabetical order, or by streets. Names shall be added thereto or taken therefrom as persons are found to be qualified or not qualified to vote. Notwithstanding the foregoing, the voting lists to be used at presidential primaries or any primary or election held prior to June first in any year may be that of the year preceding, revised as aforesaid.

Voting lists, contents, arrangement, etc.

G. L. (Ter. Ed.), 51, § 57, amended.

SECTION 30. Section fifty-seven of said chapter fifty-one, as appearing in the Tercentenary Edition, is hereby amended by striking out, in the sixth line, the words "precinct therein" and inserting in place thereof the words: — ward of a city and in each precinct of a town, — so as to read as follows: — *Section 57.* They shall, at least twenty days before the annual or biennial city or town election, and except in Boston, at least sixty days before the biennial state election, cause copies of the voting lists provided for in the two preceding sections to be posted in their principal office and in one or more other public places in the city or town, and in each ward of a city and in each precinct of a town. Upon application made by any state political committee organized in accordance with law, the clerk of the board of registrars shall furnish to it a copy of the voting list free of charge.

Posting of voting lists. Copies of lists, when furnished to state committees.

G. L. (Ter. Ed.), 51, § 62, amended.

SECTION 31. Section sixty-two of said chapter fifty-one, as so appearing, is hereby amended by striking out, in the eighth line, the words "held in a city", — so as to read as follows: — *Section 62.* When a caucus is called, the registrars, on the request of the chairman of the ward or town committee of the party whose caucus is to be held or of the person designated to call the caucus to order, shall furnish him for use in the caucus a certified copy of the last published voting list of the town, or of the ward of the city for which the caucus is to be held, adding thereto the names of voters registered since such publication. Said lists, if intended for use in the caucus of a political party, shall contain the party enrollment of voters whose names appear thereon established as provided in sections thirty-seven and thirty-eight of chapter fifty-three. Voting list for use at caucus.

SECTION 32. Said chapter fifty-one is hereby further amended by striking out section sixty-three, as so appearing, and inserting in place thereof the following section: — G. L. (Ter. Ed.), 51, § 63, amended. *Section 63.* After the biennial state election in nineteen hundred and forty-four, and in every tenth year thereafter for the purpose of furnishing the information necessary for a new division of a city into wards and voting precincts and of a town of twelve thousand inhabitants or over, which has been divided into voting precincts, into new voting precincts, the registrars shall deliver to the clerk of each city and of each such town, on or before the first Tuesday after the said election, a list of all voters therein who were registered for such election, which shall be so arranged as to show the number of voters residing in each ward or in each precinct, as the case may be, by streets. The registrars shall likewise in any other year, upon the request of the aldermen in cities or of the selectmen in such towns, furnish, for the purpose of dividing a ward into voting precincts or, unless otherwise prohibited by law, of dividing any such town into new voting precincts, a list of the voters of any ward in a city or of any precinct in such town, arranged as aforesaid. List of voters before a new division of a city into wards.

Approved June 7, 1943.

AN ACT CHANGING THE TIME OF HOLDING THE ANNUAL TOWN MEETING AND TOWN ELECTION OF THE TOWN OF HOPKINTON, AND PROVIDING FOR THE SUBMISSION OF CERTAIN VOTES FOR REFERENDUM IN SAID TOWN. *Chap.* 454

Be it enacted, etc., as follows:

SECTION 1. The annual town meeting of the town of Hopkinton shall be held on the first Monday in March, and all matters to be considered at the annual town meeting shall be considered at such meeting, except that the annual town election for the purpose of electing, by official ballot, town officers and voting on any question required by law to be placed upon the official ballot, shall take place at an adjournment of such meeting to be held on the third Monday in March.

SECTION 2. Any vote passed at any town meeting of said town shall not become operative until after the expiration of a period of five days, terminating at five o'clock P.M. on the fifth day, exclusive of Sundays and holidays, from the day of the dissolution of such meeting. If, within the period of the said five days, a petition is addressed to and filed with the selectmen, and is signed by not less than fifty voters of the town, containing their names and addresses as they appear on the list of registered voters, asking that the question or questions involved in such vote be submitted to the voters of the town, the selectmen shall then frame and present the question or questions involved in such vote at the next annual election of officers at which time the question or questions involved shall be voted upon by ballot, using the check list, and such question or questions shall be determined by a majority vote of the registered voters of the town voting thereon. If such a petition is not filed within said period of five days, the vote in the town meeting shall become operative and effective upon the expiration of said period.

SECTION 3. This act shall take effect upon its acceptance by a majority of the voters of said town at a town meeting held not later than the annual town meeting in the year nineteen hundred and forty-four.

Approved June 7, 1943.

---

*Chap.*455 AN ACT MAKING CERTAIN CHANGES IN THE LAWS RELATING TO STATE AID, MILITARY AID, SOLDIERS' RELIEF AND CERTAIN WAR ALLOWANCES.

Emergency preamble.

Whereas, The deferred operation of this act would tend to defeat its purpose, which is to provide immediate financial assistance to certain soldiers, sailors and marines in the service of the United States and to their dependent relatives, therefore it is hereby declared to be an emergency law, necessary for the immediate preservation of the public convenience.

Be it enacted, etc., as follows:

G. L. (Ter. Ed.), 6, § 22, etc., amended.

SECTION 1. Section twenty-two of chapter six of the General Laws, as amended by section one of chapter three hundred and forty-one of the acts of nineteen hundred and thirty-six, is hereby further amended by striking out, in the heading and in the third line, the word "state" and inserting in place thereof, in each instance, the word: — veterans, — so that the heading and section will read as follows: — COMMISSIONER OF VETERANS AID AND PENSIONS.

New heading.

Commissioner of veterans aid and pensions.

Section 22. There shall be an officer to be known as the commissioner of veterans aid and pensions, who shall be appointed by the governor, with the advice and consent of the council, for three years, at such salary, not exceeding fifty-five hundred dollars, as the governor and council shall determine. He shall devote his whole time to the duties of his office. He shall be state agent for the settlement of pension, bounty, back pay, compensation and other claims of citizens of the commonwealth against the government of the United States, or of any state thereof, on account of military or naval service, and he shall assist and advise war veterans, and their dependents, heirs or legal representatives, with respect to the filing, prosecution and settlement of such claims.

SECTION 2. Section twenty-four of said chapter six, as amended by section one of chapter five hundred and ninety-six of the acts of nineteen hundred and forty-one, is hereby further amended by striking out, in the third line, the word "state" and inserting in place thereof the word: — veterans, — so as to read as follows: — *Section 24.* The governor, with the advice and consent of the council, shall appoint a deputy and a second deputy commissioner of veterans aid and pensions for three years, who shall devote their whole time to the duties of their offices. They shall be subject to the direction and control of said commissioner. The deputy commissioner, or in case of a vacancy in his office or in his absence or disability the second deputy commissioner, shall perform the duties of said commissioner during his absence on account of disability or other cause.

G. L. (Ter. Ed.), 6, § 24, etc., amended.

Deputy commissioner, etc

SECTION 3. Section one of chapter one hundred and fifteen of the General Laws, as appearing in the Tercentenary Edition, is hereby amended by striking out, in the third line, the paragraph defining "Commissioner" and inserting in place thereof the following paragraph: —

G. L. (Ter. Ed.), 115, § 1, amended.

"Commissioner", commissioner of veterans aid and pensions.

"Commissioner" defined.

SECTION 4. Section two A of said chapter one hundred and fifteen, inserted by chapter one hundred and thirteen of the acts of nineteen hundred and thirty-two, is hereby amended by adding at the end the following paragraph: —

G. L. (Ter. Ed.), 115, § 2A, etc., amended

The employer of any applicant for aid or relief under this chapter who, upon like written request, unreasonably refuses to inform the commissioner of the amount of money paid by such employer to the applicant at any time during his employment by such employer or who wilfully renders false information in respect to such a request shall forfeit fifty dollars to the use of the commonwealth.

Employer to inform commissioner of amount paid applicant

SECTION 5. Section six of said chapter one hundred and fifteen, as appearing in the Tercentenary Edition, is hereby amended by striking out, in the forty-eighth, forty-ninth and fiftieth lines, the words "having been appointed or having enlisted in such service after February fifteenth, eighteen hundred and ninety-eight and prior to July fourth, nineteen hundred and two" and inserting in place thereof the words: — which for the purposes of this chapter shall be defined as having begun on February fifteenth, eighteen hundred and ninety-eight and having ended on July fourth, nineteen hundred and two, — and by striking out, in the fifty-third and fifty-fourth lines, the words "having been appointed or having enlisted in such service between said dates", — so that the fourth paragraph will read as follows: —

G. L (Ter. Ed.), 115, § 6, amended

Invalid pensioners of the United States who served in the army or navy of the United States to the credit of this commonwealth in or during the period of the war with Spain,

Spanish war service.

which for the purposes of this chapter shall be defined as having begun on February fifteenth, eighteen hundred and ninety-eight and having ended on July fourth, nineteen hundred and two; or who served in the regular army or navy of the United States during said war or in the army, navy or marine corps of the United States in or during the period of the Philippine Insurrection or the China Relief Expedition, while a citizen of this commonwealth, having a residence and actually residing therein;

G. L. (Ter. Ed.), 115, § 6, amended.

SECTION 6. Said section six of said chapter one hundred and fifteen, as so appearing, is hereby further amended by inserting after the word "war" in the sixty-seventh line the words: — to the credit of this commonwealth, — so that the sixth paragraph will read as follows: —

World war service.

Any soldier, sailor or nurse who served in the army or navy of the United States in the world war to the credit of this commonwealth, which for the purposes of this chapter shall be defined as having begun on February third, nineteen hundred and seventeen, and as having ended on November eleventh, nineteen hundred and eighteen; provided, that such soldier, sailor or nurse receives a pension or compensation from the United States for disability incurred in such service, and was mustered into such service while an inhabitant of a town in the commonwealth and actually residing therein.

G. L. (Ter. Ed.), 115, § 6, amended.

SECTION 7. Said section six of said chapter one hundred and fifteen, as so appearing, is hereby further amended by striking out, in the one hundred and twenty-sixth to the one hundred and twenty-ninth lines, the words "if such parents had been in receipt of state war allowance under chapter one hundred and eight of the General Acts of nineteen hundred and eighteen between February third, nineteen hundred and seventeen, and November eleventh, nineteen hundred and eighteen" and inserting in place thereof the words: — or after honorable discharge therefrom, — so that the sixteenth paragraph will read as follows: —

Fourth class qualifications.

Fathers or mothers, the fathers being alive, of soldiers or sailors who served in the world war, in the same manner and under the same limitations described herein for the service of said soldiers or sailors, and who died in such service, or after honorable discharge therefrom. No aid shall be granted to persons in this class unless in each case the aldermen, selectmen, or, in Boston, the soldiers' relief commissioner, are satisfied, on evidence first reported to the commissioner and satisfactory to him, that justice and necessity require a continuance of the aid to prevent actual suffering.

G. L. (Ter. Ed.), 115, § 9, amended.

SECTION 8. Section nine of said chapter one hundred and fifteen, as so appearing, is hereby amended by striking out all after the word "month" in the eighth line.

G. L. (Ter. Ed.), 115, § 10, amended.

SECTION 9. Section ten of said chapter one hundred and fifteen, as so appearing, is hereby amended by striking out, in the eighth line, the words "shall be poor and indigent", — and by inserting after the comma in the ninth line the words: — shall be, —, so that the second paragraph will read as follows: —

First Class, Each person of the first class shall have his settlement in the town aiding him; shall have served as a soldier, sailor or nurse in the manner and under the limitations prescribed in the first class of section six; shall have been honorably discharged or released from active duty in such United States service and from all appointments and enlistments therein; and, by reason of sickness or other physical disability, shall be in such need as would entitle him to relief under chapter one hundred and seventeen; shall not be, directly or indirectly, in receipt of any other state or military aid, or of any pension for services rendered or disabilities incurred either in the civil or Spanish wars, Indian wars or campaigns, the Philippine Insurrection, the China Relief Expedition, Mexican border service or world war service as defined in section six. The disability must have arisen from causes independent of his military or naval service aforesaid. First class qualifications

SECTION 10. Section nineteen of said chapter one hundred and fifteen, as most recently amended by section two of chapter three hundred and sixteen of the acts of nineteen hundred and thirty-eight, is hereby further amended by striking out, in the nineteenth line, the word "dependent" and inserting in place thereof the word: — needy, — so as to read as follows: — *Section 19.* The mayor of each city and the selectmen of each town or, in Boston, the soldiers' relief commissioner, shall designate a burial agent, who shall not be one of the board of public welfare or be employed by said board, and who shall, under regulations established by the commissioner, cause properly to be interred the body of any honorably discharged soldier or sailor who served in the army or navy of the United States during the war of the rebellion, or in the Indian campaigns if he died in receipt of a pension from the United States, or during the war between the United States and Spain or the Philippine Insurrection after February fourteenth, eighteen hundred and ninety-eight and prior to July fourth, nineteen hundred and two, or in the Mexican border service of nineteen hundred and sixteen and of nineteen hundred and seventeen, or in the world war; provided, that the soldier or sailor died in such service or after an honorable discharge therefrom or release from active duty therein; and shall also so inter the body of his wife, widow or needy father or mother, and the bodies of army nurses entitled to state aid under section six, if they die without sufficient means to defray funeral expenses, and the bodies of dependent children eighteen years of age or under, of such soldier or sailor, if such soldier or sailor and his wife, or his widow, be without sufficient means to defray funeral expenses; but no wife or widow of any soldier or sailor of the civil war shall be entitled to the benefits of this section unless she was married to him prior

G. L. (Ter. Ed.), 115, § 19, etc., amended.

Burial agents, designation of, powers and duties.

Burial of wives, etc., of soldiers regulated.

to June twenty-seventh, nineteen hundred and five, and no wife or widow of any soldier of the Indian campaigns unless she was married to him prior to March fourth, nineteen hundred and seventeen, and unless she was, if his widow, in receipt of a pension under the act of congress of March fourth, nineteen hundred and seventeen, and no wife or widow of any soldier or sailor of the Spanish war, or the Philippine Insurrection, unless she was married to him prior to September first, nineteen hundred and thirty; and no wife or widow of any soldier or sailor of the Mexican border service or of the world war unless she was married to him on or before January first, nineteen hundred and thirty-three. If an interment has taken place without the knowledge of the burial agent, application may be made to him within thirty days after the date of death, or after final interment if the soldier or sailor dies in the world war service; and if upon investigation he shall find that the deceased was within the provisions of this section and the rules of the commissioner, he may certify the same as provided in the following section.

G. L. (Ter. Ed.), 115, § 20, etc., amended.

SECTION 11. Said chapter one hundred and fifteen is hereby further amended by striking out section twenty, as most recently amended by section two of chapter three hundred and thirty-six of the acts of nineteen hundred and thirty-four, and inserting in place thereof the following section: — *Section 20.* The amount of the allowance for a burial as aforesaid, in the case of a soldier, sailor, wife, widow, needy father or mother or army nurse, shall not exceed one hundred dollars, and in the case of a dependent child, fifty dollars up to the age of thirteen, and one hundred dollars from the age of thirteen up to the age of eighteen; but if the total expense of the burial, by whomsoever incurred, in the case of a soldier, sailor, wife, widow, needy father or mother or army nurse, shall exceed two hundred and fifty dollars, or in the case of a child up to the age of thirteen, one hundred and fifty dollars, from the age of thirteen up to the age of eighteen two hundred and fifty dollars, no payment therefor shall be made by the commonwealth. The burial shall not be made in any cemetery or burial ground used exclusively for the burial of persons buried under the provisions of chapter one hundred and seventeen, or in any part of any cemetery or burial ground so used. Relatives of the deceased who are unable to bear the expense of burial may be allowed to conduct the funeral. The full amount so expended, the name of the deceased soldier or sailor, the regiment, company, station, organization or vessel in which he served, the date of death, place of interment, and in case of a wife or widow the name of the husband and date of marriage, and in the case of a dependent child the name of the father, and such other details as the commissioner may require, shall be certified on oath to him, in such manner as he may approve, by the burial agent and the treasurer of the town expending the amount, within three

Expense of burial limited. Conduct of funeral. Returns and reimbursement.

months after the burial; and the commissioner shall endorse upon the certificate his allowance of such amounts as he finds have been paid, and reported according to the foregoing provisions, and shall transmit the certificate to the comptroller. The amounts legally paid and so allowed, with no expense for disbursement, shall be reimbursed by the commonwealth to the several towns on or before November tenth in the year after the expenditures have been made.

SECTION 12. Section twenty-one of said chapter one hundred and fifteen, as appearing in the Tercentenary Edition, is hereby amended by striking out, in the second line, the word "indigent" and inserting in place thereof the word: — needy, — so as to read as follows: — *Section 21*. The provisions of the two preceding sections relative to burial of needy soldiers or sailors and their dependents and of section seventeen relative to soldiers' relief shall not apply to any person who at the time of entering the federal service during the world war was a subject or citizen of a neutral country who had filed his intention to become a citizen of the United States and who afterward withdrew such intention under the act of congress approved July ninth, nineteen hundred and eighteen, nor to any person designated upon his discharge as a conscientious objector.

G. L. (Ter. Ed.), 115, § 21, amended.

Application of §§ 17, 19 and 20 limited.

SECTION 13. Section one of chapter one hundred and sixteen of the General Laws, as so appearing, is hereby amended by striking out, in the thirty-third line, the word "the" the second time it occurs and inserting in place thereof the word: — any, — so that clause Fifth will read as follows: —

G. L. (Ter. Ed.), 116, § 1, amended.

Fifth, A person who enlisted and was mustered into the military or naval service of the United States, as a part of the quota of a town in the commonwealth under any call of the president of the United States during the war of the rebellion or any war between the United States and any foreign power, or who was assigned as a part of the quota thereof after having enlisted and been mustered into said service, and his wife or widow and minor children, shall be deemed thereby to have acquired a settlement in such town; and any person who would otherwise be entitled to a settlement under this clause, but who was not a part of the quota of any town, shall, if he served as a part of the quota of the commonwealth, be deemed to have acquired a settlement, for himself, his wife or widow and minor children, in the place where he actually resided at the time of his enlistment. Any person who was inducted into the military or naval forces of the United States under any federal selective service act, or who enlisted in said forces in time of war between the United States and any foreign power, whether he served as a part of the quota of the commonwealth or not, or who enlisted and served in said forces during the Philippine insurrection, and his wife or widow and minor children shall be deemed to have acquired a settlement in the place where he actually resided in this commonwealth at the time of his

Legal settlement of soldiers and sailors.

induction or enlistment. But these provisions shall not apply to any person who enlisted and received a bounty for such enlistment in more than one place unless the second enlistment was made after an honorable discharge from the first term of service, nor to any person who has been proved guilty of wilful desertion, or who left the service otherwise than by reason of disability or an honorable discharge.

G. L. (Ter. Ed.), 116, § 5, amended.

SECTION 14. Section five of said chapter one hundred and sixteen, as so appearing, is hereby amended by inserting after the word "remarries" in the twenty-first line the following: — , minor children, — so as to read as follows: —

Existing settlements; continuance and loss.

Section 5. Except as otherwise provided in this section, each settlement existing on August twelfth, nineteen hundred and eleven, shall continue in force until defeated under this chapter, but from and after said date failure for five consecutive years by a person, after reaching twenty-one years of age, to reside in a town where he had a settlement, shall defeat a settlement acquired under clause First of section one, or a settlement of a woman acquired under clause Second of said section one provided the settlement of her husband is defeated. The settlement of a minor acquired under either clause Third or Fourth of section one, except the settlement of a female minor who has married, shall be defeated with the settlement of the parents.

Time in certain institutions not counted.

The time during which a person shall be an inmate of any infirmary, jail, prison, or other public or state institution, within the commonwealth or in any manner under its care and direction, or that of an officer thereof, or of a soldiers' or sailors' home whether within or without the commonwealth, shall not be counted in computing the time either for acquiring or defeating a settlement, except as provided in section two. The settlement existing on August twelfth, nineteen hundred and sixteen, or any settlement subsequently acquired, of a person whose service in or with the army, navy or marine corps of the United States qualifies him to receive aid or relief under the provisions of chapter one hundred and fifteen, and the settlement of his wife, widow until she remarries, minor children, father or mother, qualified by his service to receive relief under said chapter one hundred and fifteen, shall not be defeated, except by failure to reside in the commonwealth for five consecutive years or by the acquisition of a new settlement.

"Commissioner of state aid and pensions" defined.

SECTION 15. When used in any statute, ordinance, by-law, rule or regulation the phrase "commissioner of state aid and pensions", or any words connoting the same, shall mean the commissioner of veterans aid and pensions.

Approved June 7, 1943.

AN ACT GRANTING THE CONSENT OF THE COMMONWEALTH TO THE ACQUISITION BY THE UNITED STATES OF AMERICA OF CERTAIN LANDS IN THE CITY OF CHELSEA FOR USE AS AN ANNEX TO THE UNITED STATES NAVY YARD, BOSTON, MASSACHUSETTS, AND GRANTING AND CEDING JURISDICTION OVER SUCH LANDS. *Chap.*456

Whereas, The deferred operation of this act would tend to defeat its purpose, which is to provide land for the immediate construction of an annex to the navy yard in Boston harbor for the purpose of national defense; therefore it is hereby declared to be an emergency law necessary for the immediate preservation of the public safety. Emergency preamble.

Be it enacted, etc., as follows:

SECTION 1. The consent of the commonwealth is hereby granted to the acquisition by the United States of America by purchase or condemnation for use as an annex to the United States Navy Yard, Boston, Massachusetts, of two certain adjoining tracts of land in the city of Chelsea which tracts were acquired by the United States of America under proceedings in the District Court of the United States for the District of Massachusetts miscellaneous civil cases numbers six four one two and six five three five. Said tract taken under miscellaneous civil case number six four one two formerly of Richard T. Green et al. as set forth on plan of land entitled "U. S. Navy Yard, Boston, Mass. Chelsea Annex No. 3. Plan showing Lands, Boundaries and Harbor Lines in the Vicinity of Chelsea Annex No. 3, Chelsea, Mass., Approved June 20, 1942, P. W. Drawing No. 623-9", and as more fully described as follows: —

Beginning at the most easterly corner of said tract at a point at the intersection of the southerly side line of Williams street with the westerly side line of Pearl street, thence running southwesterly along the westerly side line of said Pearl street and Meridian Street bridge 419.25 feet to a point at the intersection of the westerly side line of said Meridian Street bridge with the United States Pierhead line approved by the secretary of war June twentieth, eighteen hundred and ninety, said pierhead line coinciding with the Massachusetts Harbor line established by chapter three hundred and forty-four, acts of eighteen hundred and eighty-seven, thence running southwesterly, along said pierhead line 695 feet more or less to a point; thence running northeasterly 269.10 feet to a point on the sea wall, thence running northeasterly more easterly 188.09 feet to a point, the last two courses are a portion of the easterly limit of the tract taken under Miscellaneous Civil Case No. 6535 hereinafter described, thence running southeasterly 90 feet to a point in the center line of Winnisimmet street, thence running southwesterly along the center line of Winnisimmet street 4.6 feet to a point; thence running southeasterly 30 feet to a point in the east side line of Winnisimmet street, thence running northeasterly, along the east side line of Winnisimmet street, 260 feet to a point at the intersection of the east side line of Winnisimmet street with the south side line of Wharf street, thence running southeasterly along the south side line of Wharf street 60 feet to a point; thence running northeasterly across Wharf street 80.54 feet to a point, thence running northwesterly 60 feet to a point in the easterly side line of Winnisimmet street; thence running northeasterly along the easterly side line of Winnisimmet street 100.67 feet to a point; thence running southeasterly 90 feet to a point; thence running northeasterly 24.72 feet to a point, thence running southeasterly 50 feet to a point in the easterly side line of Division street, thence running northeasterly, along the easterly side line of Division street, 35.3 feet to a point, thence running southeasterly 45 feet to a point, thence running northeasterly 40.8 feet to a point in the southerly side line of Williams street; thence running southeasterly along the southerly side line of Williams street 82.8 feet to the point of beginning containing 5 acres more or less.

Said tract taken under miscellaneous civil case number six five three five formerly of Metropolitan Coal Co. et al. as set forth on plan of land entitled "U. S. Navy Yard, Boston, Mass. Chelsea Annex No. 3. Plan showing Lands, Boundaries and Harbor Lines in the Vicinity of Chelsea Annex No. 3, Chelsea, Mass., Approved June 20, 1942, P. W. Drawing No. 623–9", and as more fully described as follows: —

Beginning at the most northerly corner of said tract, at a point at the intersection of the southwesterly side line of Broadway with the southerly side line of Medford street, thence running south 50° 02′ 40″ east, along the southerly side line of Medford street 44.80 feet to a point, thence running south 39° 57′ 20″ west 25.45 feet to a point, thence running south 14° 29′ 20″ west 122.53 feet to a point, thence running south 49° 20′ 30″ east 210.17 feet to a point; thence running north 40° 51′ 50″ east 68.70 feet to a point, thence running south 50° 02′ 40″ east 121.20 feet to a point; thence running north 39° 57′ 20″ east 70.0 feet to a point in the southerly side line of Medford street; thence running south 50° 02′ 40″ east, along the southerly side line of Medford street, 24.30 feet to a point; thence running south 39° 57′ 20″ west 70.0 feet to a point, thence running south 50° 02′ 40″ east 91.80 feet to a point; thence running north 39° 57′ 20″ east, 46.75 feet to a point, thence running south 41° 04′ 00″ east, 121.50 feet to a point, thence running north 49° 00′ 00″ east, 40.0 feet to a point, thence running north 41° 04′ 00″ west, 2.60 feet to a point, thence running north 49° 00′ 00″ east, 141.74 feet to a point in the southerly side line of Ferry street, a private way, thence running south 41° 04′ 00″ east, along the southerly side line of Ferry street, 155.80 feet to a point at the intersection of the southerly side line of Ferry street and the westerly side line of Winnisimmet street, thence running south 48° 52′ 00″ west, along the westerly side line of Winnisimmet street, 70.0 feet to a point; thence running north 41° 04′ 00″ west 60.0 feet to a point, thence running south 48° 52′ 00″ west 188.09 feet to a point on the sea wall, thence south 38° 00′ 55″ west 269.10 feet to a point in the United States Pierhead line approved by the secretary of war June twentieth, eighteen hundred and ninety, said pierhead line coinciding with the Massachusetts Harbor line established by chapter three hundred and forty-four, acts of eighteen hundred and eighty-seven, the last two courses are a portion of the westerly limit of the tract taken under miscellaneous civil case number six four one two hereinbefore described, thence running south 83° 28′ 00″ west, along the said pierhead line, 503.77 feet to a point, thence running north 10° 44′ 20″ east 862.26 feet to a point in the southwesterly side line of Broadway, thence running north 82° 12′ 50″ east, along the southwesterly side line of Broadway 18.65 feet to the point of beginning containing 7.58 acres more or less.

SECTION 2. Jurisdiction over the above described lands is hereby granted and ceded to the United States of America, but upon the express condition that the commonwealth shall retain concurrent jurisdiction with the United States of America in and over said lands, in so far that all civil processes, and such criminal processes as may issue under the authority of the commonwealth against any person or persons charged with crimes committed without said lands and all processes for collection of taxes levied under authority of the laws of the commonwealth, including the service of warrants, may be executed thereon in the same manner as though this cession had not been granted; provided that the exclusive jurisdiction in and over such tracts shall revert to and revest in the commonwealth whenever such tracts shall cease to be used for the purpose set forth in section one.

SECTION 3. The United States of America is hereby authorized to fill said ceded areas and to place such structures in or over said areas as may be necessary for the purpose for which the same are granted, in accordance with plans to be filed with and approved by the state department of public works.

SECTION 4. This act shall take full effect upon the depositing in the office of the state secretary within one year after its effective date of a suitable plan of the tracts of land described in section one, but not otherwise.

Approved June 7, 1943.

Chap.457 AN ACT GRANTING THE CONSENT OF THE COMMONWEALTH TO THE ACQUISITION BY THE UNITED STATES OF AMERICA OF CERTAIN LAND IN THE CITY OF BOSTON FOR THE PURPOSE OF EXTENDING THE UNITED STATES NAVY YARD AT BOSTON AND GRANTING AND CEDING JURISDICTION OVER SUCH LAND.

Emergency preamble.

Whereas, The deferred operation of this act would tend to defeat its purpose, which is to provide land for the immediate extension of the United States Navy Yard in the city of Boston for the purpose of national defense; therefore it is hereby declared to be an emergency law, necessary for the immediate preservation of the public safety.

Be it enacted, etc., as follows:

SECTION 1. The consent of the commonwealth is hereby granted to the acquisition by the United States of America by purchase or condemnation for use as an extension of the United States Navy Yard at Boston of a certain parcel of land acquired by the United States of America in fee simple by declaration of taking filed May fifteenth, nineteen hundred and forty-two, in the case of the United States of America *v.* 16,703 square feet of land more or less in Suffolk county, Massachusetts, and A. George Goldberg, et al., Civil No. 6533, under authority of the act of Congress approved February sixth, nineteen hundred and forty-two (Public Law 438, 77th Congress), as more fully described as follows: —

A certain parcel of land with buildings thereon situated on the easterly side of Chelsea street and the northerly side of Henley street as shown on plan, T. B. Kenney, C. E., recorded with Suffolk Deeds, book 4809, page 461, in that part of Boston called Charlestown, bounded and described as follows: Northerly on Chelsea street 93.67 feet; easterly on the U. S. Navy Yard, 243.25 feet; southerly on Henley street (formerly Henley place) 99.67 feet; westerly by four lines as shown on said plan measuring respectively 51.50 feet, 21.67 feet, 50.58 feet and 66.96 feet and containing 16,703 square feet.

SECTION 2. Jurisdiction over the above described lands is hereby granted and ceded to the United States of America, but upon the express condition that the commonwealth shall retain concurrent jurisdiction with the United States of America in and over said lands, in so far that all civil processes, and such criminal processes as may issue under the authority of the commonwealth against any person or persons charged with crimes committed without said lands and all processes for collection of taxes levied under authority of the laws of the commonwealth, including the service of warrants, may be executed thereon in the same manner as though this cession had not been granted; provided, that the exclusive jurisdiction in and over such tracts shall revert to and revest in the commonwealth whenever such tracts shall cease to be used for the purpose set forth in section one.

SECTION 3. This act shall take full effect upon the depositing in the office of the state secretary within one year after its effective date of a suitable plan of the tracts of land described in section one, but not otherwise.

Approved June 7, 1943.

AN ACT GRANTING THE CONSENT OF THE COMMONWEALTH TO THE ACQUISITION BY THE UNITED STATES OF AMERICA OF CERTAIN LANDS IN THE CITY OF BOSTON FOR THE PURPOSE OF A COAST GUARD BASE IN BOSTON HARBOR, GRANTING TO THE UNITED STATES OF AMERICA THE RIGHT, TITLE AND INTEREST OF THE COMMONWEALTH IN AND TO CERTAIN LAND COVERED BY NAVIGABLE WATER ADJACENT THERETO, AND GRANTING AND CEDING JURISDICTION OVER SUCH LANDS. *Chap.*458

Whereas, The deferred operation of this act would tend to defeat its purpose, which is to provide land for the immediate construction of a coast guard base in Boston harbor for the purposes of national defense; therefore it is hereby declared to be an emergency law, necessary for the immediate preservation of the public safety. Emergency preamble.

Be it enacted, etc., as follows:

SECTION 1. The consent of the commonwealth is hereby granted to the acquisition by the United States of America by purchase or condemnation for use as a Coast Guard Base in Boston Harbor in the city of Boston of a certain tract of land situated in said city bounded and described as follows: —

Beginning at a point at the most southeasterly corner of said tract, said point being in the boundary line of the property of the Quincy Market Cold Storage and Warehouse Company at its intersection with the head of the dock between Battery and Constitution Wharves and distant 236 feet northeasterly from the northeasterly side line of Commercial street, thence N 41° 28′ 03″ W 233.24 feet to a point; thence N 65° 15′ 43″ W 99.91 feet to a point in the southeasterly side line of Hanover street; thence N 24° 44′ 17″ E 52.04 feet in the southeasterly side line of said Hanover street to a point; thence N 65° 52′ 43″ W 62.76 feet in the northerly end of said Hanover street to a point; thence S 24° 07′ 17″ W 307.15 feet in the northwesterly side line of Hanover street to a point at its intersection with the northeasterly side line of Commercial street; thence N 62° 43′ 43″ W 141.18 feet in the northeasterly side line of said Commercial street to a point; thence N 29° 16′ 37″ E 75.06 feet to a point; thence S 62° 43′ 03″ E 17.09 feet to a point; thence N 26° 38′ 47″ E 183.07 feet to a point; thence N 64° 44′ 03″ W 8.61 feet to a point; thence N 25° 19′ 07″ E 30.09 feet to a point; thence N 64° 15′ 13″ W 31.89 feet to a point; thence S 26° 34′ 27″ W 30.03 feet to a point; thence N 60° 59′ 03″

W 40.67 feet to a point; thence N 61° 26′ 53″ W 10.00 feet to a point; thence N 29° 16′ 27″ E 15.0 feet to a point; thence N 61° 29′ 33″ W 10.10 feet to a point; thence N 60° 42′ 23″ W 166.61 feet to a point in the southeasterly boundary line of property of the city of Boston, called North End park; thence N 31° 14′ 37″ E 472.43 feet in the said southeasterly boundary line of property of said city of Boston to a point; thence N 82° 00′ 17″ E 87.94 feet to a point; thence S 59° 17′ 53″ E 168.75 feet to a point; thence S 29° 32′ 57″ W 100.02 feet to a point; thence S 59° 17′ 53″ E 84.91 feet to a point; thence S 51° 14′ 33″ E 68.67 feet to a point; thence S 59° 19′ 23″ E 65.67 feet to a point; thence S 61° 52′ 23″ E 127.83 feet to a point; thence S 48° 58′ 33″ E 218.36 feet to a point; thence S 25° 10′ 03″ E 97.22 feet to a point; thence S 48° 31′ 57″ W 405.43 feet to the point of beginning, containing 400,957 square feet more or less.

SECTION 2. For the purpose of enabling the United States of America to extend the limits of the areas to be acquired for the Coast Guard Base described in section one the commonwealth, subject to the conditions hereinafter imposed, hereby grants and cedes to the United States of America any and all right, title and interest which the commonwealth may have in and to that portion of the areas described in section one which lies below low water line and further grants and cedes to the United States of America all right, title and interest of the commonwealth to certain lands covered by navigable waters outboard of said land described in section one and between said land and the pierhead and bulkhead line approved by the secretary of war April twenty-fourth, nineteen hundred and forty, and more particularly bounded and described as follows: —

Beginning at a point at the southeasterly corner of said lands said point being the northeasterly corner of the tract described in section one; thence N 25° 10′ 03″ W 97.22 feet to a point; thence N 48° 58′ 33″ W 218.36 feet to a point; thence N 61° 52′ 23″ W 127.83 feet to a point; thence N 59° 19′ 23″ W 65.67 feet to a point; thence N 51° 14′ 33″ W 68.67 feet to a point; thence N 59° 17′ 53″ W 84.91 feet to a point; thence N 29° 32′ 57″ E 100.02 feet to a point; thence N 59° 17′ 53″ W 168.75 feet to a point; thence S 82° 00′ 17″ W 87.94 feet to a point; thence N 31° 14′ 37″ E 5.3 feet more or less to a point in the United States Pierhead and Bulkhead line approved by the secretary of war April twenty-fourth, nineteen hundred and forty; thence N 81° 39′ 00″ E 160.33 feet more or less in said Pierhead and Bulkhead line to a point marked 0′; thence S 59° 34′ 35″ E 561.3 feet in said Pierhead and Bulkhead line to a point marked N′ thence S 20° 49′ 02″ E 280.85 feet more or less in said Pierhead and Bulkhead line to a point; thence S 48° 31′ 57″ W 80.7 feet more or less to the point of beginning, containing 104,930 square feet more or less.

The areas hereinbefore described are shown on a plan entitled "Constitution Wharf Boston — Mass. Detailed Property Limit Survey United States Coast Guard Engineering First Naval District — Boston, Mass. V. C. Gibson Lieut. Comdr. M. R. Daniels Captain in Coast Guard Eng. Office Scale 60′ = 1″ Jan. 7, 1943 Drawing No. 1644."

SECTION 3. Jurisdiction over the above described lands is hereby granted and ceded to the United States of America, but upon the express condition that the commonwealth shall retain concurrent jurisdiction with the United States of America in and over said lands, in so far that all civil processes, and such criminal processes as may issue under the authority of the commonwealth against any person or persons charged with crimes committed without said lands and all processes for collection of taxes levied under authority of the laws of the commonwealth, including the service of warrants, may be executed thereon in the same manner as though this cession had not been granted; provided, that the right, title and interest to and in the lands covered by navigable waters described in section two and the exclusive jurisdiction in and over the lands described in section one and section two shall revert to and revest in the commonwealth whenever such areas shall cease to be used for the purposes set forth in section one.

SECTION 4. The United States of America is hereby authorized to fill said ceded areas and to place such structures in or over said areas as may be necessary for the purpose for which the same are granted, in accordance with plans to be filed with and approved by the state department of public works.

SECTION 5. This act shall take full effect upon the depositing in the office of the state secretary within one year from its effective date of a suitable plan of the lands described in section one and section two, but not otherwise.

Approved June 7, 1943.

AN ACT RELATIVE TO THE REGISTRATION OF CERTAIN FOREIGN CORPORATIONS, AND TO THE TAXATION OF CERTAIN DOMESTIC AND FOREIGN BUSINESS AND MANUFACTURING CORPORATIONS. *Chap.*459

Be it enacted, etc., as follows:

SECTION 1. Section thirty of chapter sixty-three of the General Laws, as amended, is hereby further amended by striking out paragraph 2, as appearing in the Tercentenary Edition, and inserting in place thereof the following paragraph: — G. L. (Ter. Ed.), 63, § 30, etc., amended.

2. "Foreign corporations", every corporation, association or organization established, organized or chartered under laws other than those of the commonwealth, for purposes for which domestic corporations may be organized under chapter one hundred and fifty-six, which has a usual place of business in this commonwealth, or is engaged here, permanently or temporarily, in the construction, erection, alteration or repair "Foreign corporations" defined.

of a building, bridge, railroad, railway or structure of any kind, or in the construction or repair of roads, highways or waterways, or in any other activity requiring the performance of labor; provided, that said term shall not apply to such corporations, associations or organizations without capital stock as are subject to taxation under section eighteen of chapter one hundred and fifty-seven, or to foreign manufacturing corporations as defined in section forty-two B.

G. L. (Ter. Ed.), 63, § 30, etc., amended.

SECTION 2. Said section thirty, as amended, is hereby further amended by striking out the paragraph appearing in section three of chapter fifty-eight of the acts of nineteen hundred and thirty-three and inserting in place thereof the following paragraph: —

Value of corporate excess in certain cases, how determined.

If by reason of recent organization, or otherwise, the corporation is not required to make to the commissioner a return of net income for a taxable year, the value of the corporate excess or the value of such of the corporation's tangible property situated in the commonwealth as is not subject to local taxation nor taxable under section sixty-seven shall be determined as of the first day of April of the year in which the tax is to be assessed.

G. L. (Ter. Ed.), 63, § 30, etc , amended.

SECTION 3. Said section thirty, as amended, is hereby further amended by striking out the last paragraph, inserted by section one of chapter two hundred and thirty-seven of the acts of nineteen hundred and thirty-four, and inserting in place thereof the following paragraph: —

Date for determining value of corporate excess.

If by reason of recent organization, or otherwise, the corporation is not required to make to the commissioner a return of net income for a taxable year, the value of the corporate excess employed in this commonwealth or the value of such of the corporation's tangible property situated in the commonwealth as is not subject to local taxation nor taxable under section sixty-seven shall be determined as of the first day of April of the year in which the tax is to be assessed.

G. L. (Ter. Ed.), 181, § 3, amended.

Commissioner to be appointed attorney for service of process.

SECTION 4. Chapter one hundred and eighty-one of the General Laws is hereby amended by striking out section three, as appearing in the Tercentenary Edition, and inserting in place thereof the following section: — *Section 3.* Every foreign corporation, which has a usual place of business in this commonwealth, or owns real property therein without having such a usual place of business, or which is engaged therein, permanently or temporarily, and with or without a usual place of business therein, in the construction, erection, alteration or repair of a building, bridge, railroad, railway or structure of any kind, or in the construction or repair of roads, highways or waterways, or in any other activity requiring the performance of labor, shall, before doing business in this commonwealth, in writing appoint the commissioner and his successor in office to be its true and lawful attorney upon whom all lawful processes in any action or proceeding against it may be served, and in such writing shall agree that any lawful process against it which is served on said attorney shall be of the same legal force and validity as if served on the corporation, and that the authority shall continue in force so long as any liability remains outstanding against the corporation in this commonwealth. The power of attorney and a copy of the vote authorizing its execution, duly certified and authenticated, shall be filed in the office of the commissioner, and copies certified by him shall be sufficient evidence thereof. Service of such process shall be made by leaving a copy of the process with a fee of two dollars in the hands of the commissioner, or of his deputy or second deputy when acting under section six of chapter fourteen or in the office of the commissioner, and such service shall be sufficient service upon the corporation. *Approved June 7, 1943.*

AN ACT GRANTING THE CONSENT OF THE COMMONWEALTH TO THE ACQUISITION BY THE UNITED STATES OF AMERICA OVER CERTAIN LANDS FOR USE AS MILITARY RESERVATIONS AND GRANTING AND CEDING JURISDICTION OVER SUCH LANDS. *Chap.*460

Be it enacted, etc., as follows:

SECTION 1. Subject to the conditions hereinafter imposed the consent of the commonwealth is hereby granted to the acquisition by the United States of America of the following described parcels of land for use by the War Department as military reservations and to the acquisition on or before December thirty-first, nineteen hundred and forty-four, of such additional parcels of land as may be necessary for use in connection with such reservations.

1. All that certain piece or parcel of land, together with the improvements if any thereon, situated in the town of Fairhaven, county of Bristol and commonwealth of Massachusetts, located at the southerly end of a larger tract of land owned by the Fairhaven West Island Company and known as West Island, and bounded and described as follows: —

Beginning at a stake located at a new division line through the land of the said Fairhaven West Island Company, the co-ordinates of which stake referred to U. S. Engineer Department Station "West Island Army" (1934) as the zero of co-ordinates, are north 39.75 feet, west 30.32 feet; thence by the said new division line through the land of the said Fairhaven West Island Company south 52 degrees 40 minutes west about 676 feet to Buzzards bay; thence by the said Buzzards bay about 2,240 feet in a general southeasterly and northerly direction around the southerly tip of the said West Island to the new division line through the land of the Fairhaven West Island Company; thence by the said new division line south 52 degrees 40 minutes west about 738 feet to the stake at the point or place of beginning and containing 14.20 acres of land, more or less, being more particularly shown and described on the plan to be filed with the state secretary, as hereinafter provided, and being the same premises acquired by the United States by judgment dated

December twenty-second, nineteen hundred and forty-one, on the declaration of taking in the condemnation proceeding entitled United States of America *v.* 14.20 acres of land, more or less, situate in Bristol county, state of Massachusetts, and Fair Haven West Island Company (Misc. Civil No. 6451), filed December twenty-second, nineteen hundred and forty-one, in the District Court of the United States for the district of Massachusetts.

2. All that certain piece or parcel of land, consisting of two tracts, together with the improvements if any thereon, situated in the town of Gay Head, county of Dukes County, commonwealth of Massachusetts, being a portion of tracts formerly owned by the county of Dukes County and the town of Gay Head, bounded and described as follows:

Tract No. 1. Beginning at a point marked by a Massachusetts highway bound, the co-ordinates of which bound referred to U. S. Engineer Department Station Gay Head as the zero of co-ordinates, are south 199.8 feet and east 71.2 feet; thence by the westerly side of the Massachusetts state highway north 30 degrees 07 minutes 15 seconds east 296.3 feet to a corner; thence by other land belonging to the county of Dukes County north 34 degrees 07 minutes west 164.5 feet to a corner; thence by the common land belonging to the town of Gay Head south 30 degrees 27 minutes west 297 feet to a stone bound at a corner; thence by land belonging to the estate of E. D. Vanderhoop south 34 degrees 36 minutes east 165.8 feet to the Massachusetts highway bound at the point or place of beginning and containing 1.02 acres of land, more or less. Being a portion of a larger tract of land, all of which was formerly owned by the county of Dukes County.

Tract No. 2. Beginning at a stone bound located at the northwesterly corner of the land hereinbefore described as tract No. 1; thence by other common land belonging to the town of Gay Head north 34 degrees 36 minutes west 515 feet, more or less, to Vineyard sound; thence by the said Vineyard sound 276 feet, more or less, in a general northeasterly direction to a point; thence by other common land belonging to the town of Gay Head south 34 degrees 07 minutes east about 385 feet to a corner of land belonging to the county of Dukes County; thence by the said land belonging to the county of Dukes County south 30 degrees 27 minutes west 297 feet to the stone bound at the point or place of beginning and containing 2.8 acres of land, more or less. Being a portion of a larger tract of common land, all of which was formerly owned by the town of Gay Head, being more particularly shown and described on the plan to be filed with the state secretary, as hereinafter provided, and, being the same premises acquired by the United States by a declaration of taking dated February fourth, nineteen hundred and forty-two, in the condemnation proceeding entitled United States of America *v.* Certain lands situate in Dukes County, state of Massachusetts, and county of Dukes, *et al.* (Misc.

Civil No. 6470), filed February eleventh, nineteen hundred and forty-two, in the United States District Court in and for the district of Massachusetts.

3. A certain piece or parcel of land situated at Strawberry Point, town of Scituate, county of Plymouth, commonwealth of Massachusetts, bounded and described as follows:

Beginning at a point located at the northwesterly corner of said parcel thence south 77 degrees 17 minutes 52 seconds east 83.75 feet to a point; thence on a curve to the right having a radius of 176.77 feet 24.84 feet to a point at the northeasterly corner of said parcel; thence south 36 degrees 30 minutes west 342.12 feet to a point at the southeasterly corner of said parcel; thence north 53 degrees 30 minutes west 100 feet to a point at the southwesterly corner of said parcel; thence north 36 degrees 30 minutes east 299.92 feet to the point of beginning, and containing 0.74 of an acre of land, more or less, being more particularly shown and described on the plan to be filed with the state secretary, as hereinafter provided, and being the same premises acquired by the United States by a declaration of taking dated February twenty-eighth, nineteen hundred and forty, in the condemnation proceeding entitled United States of America *v.* 0.74 of an acre of land and rights of way situate in Plymouth county, commonwealth of Massachusetts, and The Glades Association, *et al.* (Misc. Civil No. 6237), filed on March fourteenth, nineteen hundred and forty, in the District Court of the United States in and for the district of Massachusetts.

4. All that certain piece or parcel of land, situated in the village of Brant Rock, town of Marshfield, county of Plymouth and commonwealth of Massachusetts, bounded and described as follows:

Beginning at an iron pipe driven in the ground marking the northwesterly corner of said tract, and the southwesterly corner of land of Julia A. Bates, said beginning point being located at the southeasterly corner of South street; thence by land of said Bates north 62 degrees 36 minutes 30 seconds east 164.45 feet to a chiselled cross on a concrete sea wall, said point bearing south 43 degrees 14 minutes 00 seconds east 56.28 feet from a U. S. C. & G. S. plug marked "Brant Rock Sea Wall Datum" set in said sea wall; thence along said sea wall south 2 degrees 05 minutes 30 seconds east 141.00 feet to a second chiselled cross on said sea wall, said cross marking the northeasterly corner of land of one Baldwin; thence by said Baldwin land south 77 degrees 00 minutes 00 seconds west 42.22 feet to a stake set in the ground, and south 13 degrees 22 minutes 30 seconds east 44 feet to a stake set in the ground at the northeasterly corner of a passageway, thence in the northwesterly boundary line of said passageway on the following courses and distances; south 71 degrees 01 minutes 30 seconds west 15.08 feet along a fence to an angle in said fence, south 58 degrees 56 minutes 30 seconds west 20.40 feet to a second angle in said fence, and south 67 degrees 23 minutes 24 seconds west 14.47 feet to a third angle in said fence; said point marking the southeasterly corner of land of one Goddard; thence by land of said Goddard north 16 degrees 12 minutes 00 seconds west 35.90 feet to a stake set in the ground, and south 73 degrees 30 minutes 15 seconds west 43.92 feet to a post, said post marking the southeasterly corner of land of one Freeman; thence by land of said Freeman north 16 degrees 23 minutes 15 seconds west 46.70 feet to a stake marking the northeasterly corner of said Freeman land and the southeasterly corner of land of one Nasser; thence by land of said Nasser north 8 degrees 00 minutes 45 seconds west 72.94 feet to the point of beginning. Containing 0.47 of an acre of land, more or less, being more particularly shown and described on the plan to be filed with the state secretary, as hereinafter provided, and being the same premises acquired by the United States by a declaration of taking dated January nineteenth, nineteen hundred and forty-two, in the condemnation proceeding entitled United States of America *v.* 0.47 of an acre of land, more or less, situate in Plymouth county, state of Massachusetts, and James F. Flynn, *et al.*, filed February seventh, nineteen hundred and forty-two, in the United States District Court in and for the district of Massachusetts.

5. All that certain piece or parcel of land, situated in the town of Manchester, county of Essex, Massachusetts, bounded and described as follows:

Beginning at a point on the boundary between the properties of Robert T. Paine, 2nd, and F. Goldthaite Sherrill 147.83 feet south 9 degrees 09 minutes east from a stone bound, marking respectively the northeast and northwest corners of said properties; thence along said boundary south 9 degrees 09 minutes east for a distance of 100 feet; thence south 80 degrees 51 minutes west for a distance of 100 feet to an iron pipe set in the ground; thence north 9 degrees 09 minutes west for a distance of 100 feet to a drill hole in ledge; thence north 80 degrees 51 minutes east for a distance of 100 feet to the point of beginning, containing ten thousand square feet or 0.23 of an acre of land, more or less, being more particularly shown and described on the plan to be filed with the state secretary, as hereinafter provided, and being a portion of the same premises acquired by the United States by a declaration of taking dated December twenty-sixth, nineteen hundred and forty-one, in the condemnation proceeding entitled United States of America *v.* 0.28 acre of land, more or less, situate in Essex county, state of Massachusetts, and Robert T. Paine, 2nd, *et al.* (Misc. Civil No. 6479), filed February fourth, nineteen hundred and forty-two, in the United States District Court in and for the district of Massachusetts.

6. All that certain piece or parcel of land consisting of two tracts situated in the town of Gosnold, county of Dukes County and commonwealth of Massachusetts, bounded and described as follows:

Tract No. 1. Beginning at the northwesterly corner of the said tract, the co-ordinates of which, referred to U. S. Engineer Department Station Cuttyhunk (1934) as the zero of co-ordinates are north 29.94 feet and west 125.28 feet; thence extending north 64 degrees 32 minutes 30 seconds east 216.32 feet through the land of the Arden Trust to the northeasterly corner; thence south 36 degrees 03 minutes 20 seconds east 145.66 feet through the land of the said Arden Trust to the southeasterly corner; thence south 64 degrees 48 minutes 40 seconds west 212.76 feet to the southwesterly corner; thence north 37 degrees 30 minutes 25 seconds west 145.37 feet to the place of beginning and containing 0.7 of an acre of land.

Tract No. 2. Beginning at the southeasterly corner of the said tract; thence south 50 degrees 00 minutes west 300.00 feet through the land of the said Arden Trust to the southwesterly corner; thence north 40 degrees 00 minutes west 544.8 feet to the northwesterly corner; thence north 50 degrees 00 minutes east 300.00 feet to the northeasterly corner; thence south 40 degrees 00 minutes east 544.8 feet to the place of beginning, and containing 3.75 acres of land.

Said tracts constituting a portion of a larger tract of land owned by the Arden Trust, being more particularly shown and described on the plan to be filed with the state secretary, as hereinafter provided, and being the same premises acquired by the United States by a declaration of taking dated January third, nineteen hundred and forty-two, in the condemnation proceeding entitled United States of America *v.* 4.45 acres of land, more or less, situate in Dukes County, state of Massachusetts, and the Arden Trust, Cornelius E. Wood, trustee, *et al.* (Misc. Civil No. 6467), filed January twelfth, nineteen hundred and forty-two, in the United States District Court in and for the district of Massachusetts.

SECTION 2. Jurisdiction over the above described lands is hereby granted and ceded to the United States of America, but upon the express condition that the commonwealth shall retain concurrent jurisdiction with the United States of America in and over said lands, in so far that all civil processes, and such criminal processes as may issue under the authority of the commonwealth against any person or persons charged with crimes committed without said lands and all processes for collection of taxes levied under authority of the laws of the commonwealth, including the service of warrants, may be executed thereon in the same manner as though this cession had not been granted; provided, that the jurisdiction in and over the lands above described shall revert to and revest in the commonwealth whenever such areas shall cease to be used for the purposes set forth in section one; and provided, further, that any jurisdiction over public rights in navigable waters is expressly excluded from this grant and chapter ninety-one of the General Laws shall apply to any encroachment, filling or structure placed in the tide waters of the commonwealth.

SECTION 3. This act shall take full effect as to each piece or parcel of land acquired under authority of section one upon the depositing in the office of the state secretary before December thirty-first, nineteen hundred and forty-four, of a suitable plan of said parcel, but not otherwise.

Approved June 7, 1943.

---

*Chap.*461 AN ACT AMENDING THE LAW RELATING TO THE CLASSIFICATION AND TAXATION OF FOREST LANDS AND FOREST PRODUCTS.

Be it enacted, etc., as follows:

G. L. (Ter. Ed.), 61, § 1, etc., amended.

SECTION 1. Section one of chapter sixty-one of the General Laws, as inserted by section one of chapter six hundred and fifty-two of the acts of nineteen hundred and forty-one, is hereby amended by striking out the first paragraph and inserting in place thereof the following paragraph: — Except as otherwise hereinafter provided, all forest land, not used for grazing and other purposes incompatible with forest production, having a value not in excess of twenty-five dollars per acre for land and growth thereon, shall be tentatively listed by the assessors as classified forest land; provided, that the owner, by written notification filed with the assessors within thirty days after he has been notified that the land has been listed as classified forest land as hereinafter provided, may elect not to have his land so classified, and in such event such land shall continue to be assessed under chapter fifty-nine and not under this chapter; and, except upon written request of the owner, such land shall not thereafter be listed as classified forest land until a new owner shall have taken title to it. Upon such request, or upon change of ownership, such land, if conforming to the requirements of this section, shall, in the year next subsequent to such election or such change of ownership, as the case may be, again be listed as classified forest land; provided, that, in the case of land the title to which is held by a new owner, such listing shall be subject to the right of the new owner, to elect, in the manner herein provided, not to have such land so classified. For the purposes of this section, the phrase "new owner" shall include a person taking land by inheritance or devise. If after such listing and notification by the assessors the owner does not exercise his right of election as herein provided, the land tentatively listed as classified forest land shall be deemed to be classified forest land as of January first in the year of classification and shall thereafter continue as such until withdrawn as provided in section six. Classified forest land shall be exempt from taxation under chapter fifty-nine but shall be subject to the taxes provided in section two of this chapter. Buildings and other structures, and the land on which they are erected and necessary for their use, shall be excluded from the classified forest land.

Classification of forest land.

Election.

Exception.

If a single parcel or tract of land consists in part of forest land and in part of other land, the portion consisting of forest land, if it comprises at least ten acres in area and otherwise conforms to the requirements of this section shall, upon election and on the conditions hereafter provided, be listed as classified forest land and the remainder of the tract shall be subject to taxation under chapter fifty-nine. Such election shall be filed in writing by the owner or owners of record in the month of January and shall contain a description of the forested area and of the unforested area sufficient for identification of each area.

G. L. (Ter. Ed.), 61, § 2, etc., amended.

SECTION 2. Section two of said chapter sixty-one, as so appearing, is hereby amended by striking out the second schedule and all preceding such schedule and inserting in place thereof the following: — The following terms shall have the following meanings when used in this chapter: "Forest products", wood, timber and all other tree or forest growth. "Stumpage value", value immediately prior to severance. "Cut", severed or taken from the soil.

Taxation of classified forest lands.

The owner of classified forest land shall pay a products tax of such percentage of the stumpage value of all forest products cut therefrom as is set forth in the following schedule; provided, that the owner may annually cut, free of tax, forest products from such land for his own use or for the use of a tenant of said land, not exceeding twenty-five dollars in stumpage value.

Schedule. Forest Products Cut from Land Classified:

	Per Cent.
In the year of classification	1
In the first year following such year	2
In the second year following such year	3
In the third year following such year	4
In the fourth year following such year	5
In the fifth year following such year and thereafter	6

Annual reports of timber cut, etc.

The owner shall annually before May first make a return, under the penalties of perjury, in such form as shall be approved by the commissioner, setting forth the amount of forest products cut from classified forest land during the then preceding year and such other information as may be required for assessment of the foregoing tax. On the basis of such return or any other available information the assessors shall assess such tax. The owner shall also pay annually a land tax upon an adjusted valuation as hereinafter provided at the rate determined for the taxation of property under chapter fifty-nine. The adjusted valuation of classified forest land shall be the percentage of the full value of the land, including the growth thereon, as of January first of each year, set forth in the following schedule; provided, that in no year shall such adjusted valuation be less than the lesser of (*a*) or (*b*) of this paragraph; and provided, further, that in the sixth year following the year of classification, and thereafter, the adjusted valuation shall be the lesser of said (*a*) or (*b*):

(*a*) Five dollars per acre.

(*b*) The full value of the land including the growth thereon.

Schedule.

	Per Cent.
In the year of classification and the first year following such year .	75
In the second and third years following the year of classification .	50
In the fourth and fifth years following the year of classification .	25

G. L. (Ter. Ed.), 61, § 6, etc., amended.

SECTION 3. Section six of said chapter sixty-one, as so appearing, is hereby amended by striking out in the third line the words "wood or timber" and inserting in place thereof: — forest products, — so that the first sentence of said section shall read as follows: — When in the judgment of the assessors classified forest land has become more valuable for other uses than the production of forest products, or when such land shall be used for purposes inconsistent with forest production, they shall on or before December first notify the owner of their intention to withdraw said land from the operation of this chapter on the following January first and shall give the owner an opportunity to be heard upon his written request made within ten days of the date of such notice.

Withdrawal of land from classification.

Land classified prior to act.

SECTION 4. Land heretofore classified as forest land under any provision of chapter sixty-one of the General Laws, as inserted by section one of chapter six hundred and fifty-two of the acts of nineteen hundred and forty-one, shall continue as classified forest land irrespective of its area, but shall otherwise be subject to the provisions of said chapter sixty-one as amended by this act.

Effective date.

SECTION 5. This act shall take effect on January first, nineteen hundred and forty-four.

Approved June 7, 1943.

---

*Chap.*462 AN ACT AMENDING CERTAIN PROVISIONS OF THE STANDARD FIRE INSURANCE POLICY.

Be it enacted, etc., as follows:

G. L. (Ter. Ed.), 175, § 99, etc., amended.

Section ninety-nine of chapter one hundred and seventy-five of the General Laws, as amended, is hereby further amended by striking out the paragraph of the standard form appearing in the fourteenth to the twenty-third lines, inclusive, of said form, and inserting in place thereof the following paragraph: —

Standard form of fire policy.

Said property is insured for the term of beginning on the day of , in the year nineteen hundred and , at noon, and continuing until the day of , in the year nineteen hundred and , at noon, against all loss or damage by FIRE originating from any cause, except that this company shall not be liable for loss by fire or other perils insured against in this policy caused directly or indirectly by: (*a*) enemy attack by armed forces, including action taken by military, naval or air forces in resisting an actual or an immediately impending enemy attack; (*b*) invasion; (*c*) insurrection; (*d*) rebellion; (*e*) revolution; (*f*) civil war; (*g*) usurped power; (*h*) order of any civil authority except acts of destruction at the time of and for the purpose of preventing the spread of fire, provided that such fire did not originate from any of the perils excluded by this policy; (*i*) neglect of the insured to use all reasonable means to save and preserve the property at and after a loss, or when the property is endangered by fire in neighboring premises; (*j*) nor shall this company be liable for loss by theft; the amount of said loss or damage to be estimated according to the actual value of the insured property at the time when such loss or damage happens, but not to include loss or damage caused by explosions of any kind unless fire ensues, and then to include that caused by fire only. *Approved June 7, 1943.*

AN ACT RELATIVE TO THE DISPOSITION BY COUNTIES OF REVENUE RECEIVED FROM FEDERAL WILDLIFE REFUGES SITUATED THEREIN. *Chap.* 463

Be it enacted, etc., as follows:

G. L. (Ter. Ed.), 131, new § 97A, added.

Chapter one hundred and thirty-one of the General Laws is hereby amended by inserting after section ninety-seven, as appearing in section two of chapter five hundred and ninety-nine of the acts of nineteen hundred and forty-one, the following section: — *Section 97A.* All moneys received by any county from the federal government by reason of the establishment and maintenance therein of federal wildlife refuges under said migratory bird conservation act, so called, shall be payable to the municipality or municipalities within which such refuge is situated. Within thirty days after the receipt by a county of such moneys from the federal government, the county treasurer thereof shall determine the proportion due each municipality in the county within which such a wildlife refuge is located and shall forthwith forward the proper proportion to the treasurer of each municipality affected. The division of revenue shall be in the proportion which the acreage of the federal refuge in a particular municipality bears to the total acreage of the federal refuges within the county. *Approved June 7, 1943.*

Disposition of moneys received from federal government.

AN ACT PROVIDING FOR THE APPOINTMENT OF A SECOND ASSISTANT REGISTER OF PROBATE FOR THE COUNTY OF BRISTOL. *Chap.* 464

Emergency preamble.

Whereas, The deferred operation of this act would in part defeat its purpose, which is to assist the probate court referred to by making possible the immediate appointment of an additional assistant register of probate therein, therefore this act is hereby declared to be an emergency law, necessary for the immediate preservation of the public convenience.

Be it enacted, etc., as follows:

G. L. (Ter. Ed.), 217, § 24, amended.

SECTION 1. Section twenty-four of chapter two hundred and seventeen of the General Laws, as appearing in the Tercentenary Edition, is hereby further amended by inserting after the word "of" the second time it appears in the first line, the word: — Bristol, — so as to read as follows: — *Section 24.* The judges of probate for the counties of Bristol, Essex, Norfolk, Hampden, Middlesex, Suffolk and Worcester may appoint a second assistant register for their respective counties, who shall hold office for three years unless sooner removed by the judge. They shall be subject to the laws relative to assistant registers.

Second assistant registers.

Effective date.

SECTION 2. This act shall take effect as of June first in the current year. *Approved June 7, 1943.*

---

*Chap.*465 AN ACT MAKING APPROPRIATIONS FOR THE MAINTENANCE OF CERTAIN COUNTIES, FOR INTEREST AND DEBT REQUIREMENTS, FOR CERTAIN PERMANENT IMPROVEMENTS, AND GRANTING A COUNTY TAX FOR SAID COUNTIES.

Emergency preamble.

Whereas, The deferred operation of this act would result in unnecessarily extending the period during which county expenditures would be made in anticipation of appropriation, therefore it is hereby declared to be an emergency law, necessary for the immediate preservation of the public convenience.

Be it enacted, etc., as follows:

SECTION 1. The following sums are hereby appropriated for the counties hereinafter specified for the years nineteen hundred and forty-three and nineteen hundred and forty-four. No direct drafts against the account known as the reserve fund shall be made, but transfers from this account to other accounts may be made to meet extraordinary or unforeseen expenditures upon the request of the county commissioners and with the approval of the director of accounts.

Barnstable County.

Item		Appropriation Fiscal Year 1943.	Appropriation Fiscal Year 1944.
1	For interest on county debt, a sum not exceeding	$1,962 50	$1,205 00
2	For reduction of county debt, a sum not exceeding	37,000 00	32,000 00
3	For salaries of county officers and assistants, a sum not exceeding	27,135 00	28,760 00
4	For clerical assistance in county offices, a sum not exceeding	15,214 50	15,920 00
5	For salaries and expenses of district courts, a sum not exceeding	25,505 00	26,200 00

Item		Appropriation Fiscal Year 1943.	Appropriation Fiscal Year 1944.
6	For salaries of jailers, masters and assistants, and support of prisoners in jails and houses of correction, a sum not exceeding	$44,060 00	$46,020 00
7	For criminal costs in superior court, a sum not exceeding	10,000 00	10,200 00
8	For civil expenses in supreme judicial, superior, probate and land courts, a sum not exceeding	7,200 00	7,400 00
10	For transportation and expenses of county and acting commissioners, a sum not exceeding	1,200 00	1,200 00
11	For medical examiners and commitments of insane, a sum not exceeding	1,500 00	1,500 00
12	For auditors, masters and referees, a sum not exceeding	2,000 00	2,000 00
14	For repairing, furnishing and improving county buildings, a sum not exceeding	14,380 00	6,340 00
15	For care, fuel, lights and supplies in county buildings, other than jails and houses of correction, a sum not exceeding	18,725 00	19,580 00
16	For highways, including state highways, bridges and land damages, a sum not exceeding	15,400 00	15,000 00
18	For law library, a sum not exceeding	945 00	930 00
19	For training school, a sum not exceeding	250 00	250 00
20	For county aid to agriculture, a sum not exceeding	17,280 00	18,350 00
21	For sanatorium, a sum not exceeding	99,800 00	103,225 00
22	For health service, a sum not exceeding	10,955 00	11,315 00
23	For state fire patrol, a sum not exceeding	1,500 00	1,500 00
25	For contributory retirement system, a sum not exceeding	11,880 00	12,094 00
25a	For contributory retirement audit, a sum not exceeding	87 60	
26	For miscellaneous and contingent expenses, including insurance, a sum not exceeding	4,385 00	2,435 00
27	For unpaid bills of previous years, a sum not exceeding	250 00	250 00
28	For police training school, a sum not exceeding	3,070 00	3,390 00
29	For police radio station, a sum not exceeding	8,025 00	8,665 00
30	For advertising the recreational advantages of the county, a sum not exceeding	–	1,000 00
31	For reserve fund, a sum not exceeding	10,000 00	10,000 00
33	For post-war rehabilitation fund, a sum not exceeding	7,000 00	7,000 00
	And the county commissioners of Barnstable county are hereby authorized to levy as the county tax of said county for the current year, in the manner provided by law, the following sum to be expended together with the cash balance on hand and the receipts from other sources, for the above purposes	$279,156 40	
	And the county commissioners of Barnstable county are hereby authorized to levy as the county tax of said county for the year nineteen hundred and forty-four, in the manner provided by law, such sum as is certified to said county commissioners on or before April first		

Item		Appropriation Fiscal Year 1943.	Appropriation Fiscal Year 1944.
	in said year by the director of accounts. In so certifying said director shall set forth, (1) the amount of the net unappropriated cash balance in the treasury of said county as of January first, nineteen hundred and forty-four, (2) the amount of the estimated receipts of said county for said year, and, (3) a sum, which shall constitute the county tax, and which shall be the difference between the sum of the two foregoing items and the total amount of the authorized expenditures hereinbefore appropriated.		
	Berkshire County.		
1	For interest on county debt, a sum not exceeding	$500 00	$500 00
3	For salaries of county officers and assistants, a sum not exceeding . . .	31,650 00	33,500 00
4	For clerical assistance in county offices, a sum not exceeding	14,970 00	15,840 00
5	For salaries and expenses of district courts, a sum not exceeding	50,478 00	52,632 00
6	For salaries of jailers, masters and assistants, and support of prisoners in jails and houses of correction, a sum not exceeding	38,725 00	39,690 00
7	For criminal costs in superior court, a sum not exceeding	8,714 00	8,900 00
8	For civil expenses in supreme judicial, superior, probate and land courts, a sum not exceeding	9,700 00	9,900 00
10	For transportation and expenses of county and acting commissioners, a sum not exceeding	900 00	700 00
11	For medical examiners and commitments of insane, a sum not exceeding . .	5,000 00	5,000 00
12	For auditors, masters and referees, a sum not exceeding	3,000 00	1,500 00
14	For repairing, furnishing and improving county buildings, a sum not exceeding	4,000 00	4,000 00
15	For care, fuel, lights and supplies in county buildings, other than jails and houses of correction, a sum not exceeding	18,960 00	18,200 00
16	For highways, including state highways, bridges and land damages, a sum not exceeding	20,350 00	20,050 00
17	For examinations of dams, a sum not exceeding	700 00	200 00
18	For law library, a sum not exceeding .	3,250 00	3,300 00
19	For training school, a sum not exceeding .	800 00	800 00
20	For county aid to agriculture, a sum not exceeding	16,275 00	16,900 00
21	For sanatorium, a sum not exceeding .	15,724 00	15,500 00
23	For Mount Greylock state reservation, a sum not exceeding	6,210 00	6,260 00
23a	For Mount Everett state reservation, a sum not exceeding	1,925 00	1,950 00
25	For contributory retirement system, a sum not exceeding	8,214 00	8,409 00

Item		Appropriation Fiscal Year 1943.	Appropriation Fiscal Year 1944.
25a	For contributory retirement audit, a sum not exceeding	$52 80	
26	For miscellaneous and contingent expenses including insurance, a sum not exceeding	6,200 00	$5,000 00
27	For unpaid bills of previous years, a sum not exceeding	500 00	500 00
28	For W. P. A. projects, a sum not exceeding	100 00	–
30	For advertising the recreational advantages of the county, a sum not exceeding	2,000 00	2,000 00
31	For reserve fund, a sum not exceeding .	5,000 00	5,000 00
	And the county commissioners of Berkshire county are hereby authorized to levy as the county tax of said county for the current year, in the manner provided by law, the following sum to be expended together with the cash balance on hand and the receipts from other sources, for the above purposes .	$205,142 47	
	And the county commissioners of Berkshire county are hereby authorized to levy as the county tax of said county for the year nineteen hundred and forty-four, in the manner provided by law, such sum as is certified to said county commissioners on or before April first in said year by the director of accounts. In so certifying said director shall set forth, (1) the amount of the net unappropriated cash balance in the treasury of said county as of January first, nineteen hundred and forty-four, (2) the amount of the estimated receipts of said county for said year, and, (3) a sum, which shall constitute the county tax, and which shall be the difference between the sum of the two foregoing items and the total amount of the authorized expenditures hereinbefore appropriated.		

Bristol County.

Item		Appropriation Fiscal Year 1943.	Appropriation Fiscal Year 1944.
1	For interest on county debt, a sum not exceeding	$3,000 00	$3,000 00
2	For reduction of county debt, a sum not exceeding	16,000 00	16,000 00
3	For salaries of county officers and assistants, a sum not exceeding	52,500 00	55,050 00
4	For clerical assistance in county offices, a sum not exceeding	62,600 00	69,100 00
5	For salaries and expenses of district courts, a sum not exceeding . .	136,800 00	143,600 00
6	For salaries of jailers, masters and assistants and support of prisoners in jails and houses of correction, a sum not exceeding	87,000 00	91,050 00
7	For criminal costs in superior court, a sum not exceeding	66,200 00	67,600 00
8	For civil expenses in supreme judicial, superior, probate and land courts, a sum not exceeding	40,800 00	41,900 00

Item		Appropriation Fiscal Year 1943.	Appropriation Fiscal Year 1944.
10	For transportation and expenses of county and acting commissioners, a sum not exceeding	$1,200 00	$1,200 00
11	For medical examiners and commitments of insane, a sum not exceeding . .	20,000 00	20,000 00
12	For auditors, masters and referees, a sum not exceeding	5,000 00	5,000 00
14	For repairing, furnishing and improving county buildings, a sum not exceeding	20,000 00	20,000 00
14a	For repairs and furnishings of jail and house of correction, a sum not exceeding	5,000 00	5,000 00
14b	For repairs and furnishings of Taunton court house building, a sum not exceeding	5,000 00	5,000 00
14c	For repairs and furnishings of New Bedford court house building, a sum not exceeding	5,000 00	5,000 00
15	For care, fuel, lights and supplies in county buildings, other than jails and houses of correction, a sum not exceeding	67,300 00	70,650 00
16	For highways, including state highways, bridges and land damages, a sum not exceeding	11,000 00	11,000 00
18	For law libraries, a sum not exceeding .	9,650 00	10,000 00
19	For training school, a sum not exceeding .	5,600 00	5,600 00
20	For agricultural school, a sum not exceeding	126,997 97	128,292 00
24	For non-contributory pensions, a sum not exceeding	9,000 00	9,000 00
25	For contributory retirement system, a sum not exceeding	21,730 00	22,245 00
25a	For contributory retirement audit, a sum not exceeding	696 93	
26	For miscellaneous and contingent expenses, including insurance, a sum not exceeding	7,000 00	7,000 00
27	For unpaid bills of previous years, a sum not exceeding	2,000 00	2,000 00
31	For reserve fund, a sum not exceeding .	10,000 00	10,000 00
33	For post-war rehabilitation fund, a sum not exceeding	25,000 00	25,000 00
	And the county commissioners of Bristol county are hereby authorized to levy as the county tax of said county for the current year, in the manner provided by law, the following sum to be expended together with the cash balance on hand and the receipts from other sources, for the above purposes . .	$615,019 34	

And the county commissioners of Bristol county are hereby authorized to levy as the county tax of said county for the year nineteen hundred and forty-four, in the manner provided by law, such sum as is certified to said county commissioners on or before April first in said year by the director of accounts. In so certifying said director shall set forth, (1) the amount of the net unappropriated cash balance in the treasury of said county as of January first, nineteen hundred and forty-four, (2) the

Item		Appropriation Fiscal Year 1943.	Appropriation Fiscal Year 1944.
	amount of the estimated receipts of said county for said year, and, (3) a sum, which shall constitute the county tax, and which shall be the difference between the sum of the two foregoing items and the total amount of the authorized expenditures hereinbefore appropriated.		

County of Dukes County.

Item		Appropriation Fiscal Year 1943.	Appropriation Fiscal Year 1944.
1	For interest on county debt, a sum not exceeding	$300 00	$300 00
2	For reduction of county debt, a sum not exceeding	5,000 00	–
3	For salaries of county officers and assistants, a sum not exceeding	7,000 00	7,400 00
4	For clerical assistance in county offices, a sum not exceeding	3,000 00	3,300 00
5	For salaries and expenses of district courts, a sum not exceeding	7,125 00	7,475 00
6	For salaries of jailers, masters and assistants, and support of prisoners in jails and houses of correction, a sum not exceeding	5,100 00	3,200 00
7	For criminal costs in superior court, a sum not exceeding	2,050 00	1,100 00
8	For civil expenses in supreme judicial, superior, probate and land courts, a sum not exceeding	1,000 00	1,000 00
10	For transportation and expenses of county and acting commissioners, a sum not exceeding	450 00	450 00
11	For medical examiners and commitments of insane, a sum not exceeding	400 00	400 00
12	For auditors, masters and referees, a sum not exceeding	100 00	100 00
14	For repairing, furnishing and improving county buildings, a sum not exceeding	3,000 00	1,200 00
15	For care, fuel, lights and supplies in county buildings, other than jails and houses of correction, a sum not exceeding	5,875 00	4,150 00
16	For highways, including state highways, bridges and land damages, a sum not exceeding	15,025 00	5,050 00
18	For law libraries, a sum not exceeding	300 00	300 00
20	For county aid to agriculture, a sum not exceeding	2,125 00	2,250 00
21	For sanatorium, a sum not exceeding	7,700 00	7,700 00
23	For Gay Head reservation, a sum not exceeding	1,900 00	1,500 00
25	For contributory retirement system, a sum not exceeding	1,000 00	1,000 00
25a	For contributory retirement audit, a sum not exceeding	40 42	
26	For miscellaneous and contingent expenses, including insurance, a sum not exceeding	1,700 00	1,600 00
27	For unpaid bills of previous years, a sum not exceeding	500 00	1,000 00
28	For civilian defense, a sum not exceeding	1,000 00	1,000 00
29	For Indian burial ground, a sum not exceeding	300 00	300 00

Item		Appropriation Fiscal Year 1943.	Appropriation Fiscal Year 1944.
30	For advertising the recreational advantages of the county, a sum not exceeding	$1,000 00	$1,000 00
31	For reserve fund, a sum not exceeding .	1,500 00	1,500 00
33	For post-war rehabilitation fund, a sum not exceeding	–	5,000 00
	And the county commissioners of Dukes County are hereby authorized to levy as the county tax of said county for the current year, in the manner provided by law, the following sum to be expended together with the cash balance on hand and the receipts from other sources, for the above purposes .	$57,790 79	–
	And the county commissioners of Dukes County are hereby authorized to levy as the county tax of said county for the year nineteen hundred and forty-four, in the manner provided by law, such sum as is certified to said county commissioners on or before April first in said year by the director of accounts. In so certifying said director shall set forth, (1) the amount of the net unappropriated cash balance in the treasury of said county as of January first, nineteen hundred and forty-four, (2) the amount of the estimated receipts of said county for said year, and, (3) a sum, which shall constitute the county tax, and which shall be the difference between the sum of the two foregoing items and the total amount of the authorized expenditures hereinbefore appropriated.		

Essex County.

Item		Appropriation Fiscal Year 1943.	Appropriation Fiscal Year 1944.
1	For interest on county debt, a sum not exceeding	$3,700 00	$3,700 00
2	For reduction of county debt, a sum not exceeding	58,000 00	52,000 00
3	For salaries of county officers and assistants, a sum not exceeding . . .	69,800 00	73,500 00
4	For clerical assistance in county offices, a sum not exceeding	145,265 00	157,860 00
5	For salaries and expenses of district courts, a sum not exceeding	223,000 00	233,450 00
6	For salaries of jailers, masters and assistants and support of prisoners in jails and houses of correction, a sum not exceeding	101,140 00	105,560 00
7	For criminal costs in superior court, a sum not exceeding	66,900 00	69,200 00
8	For civil expenses in supreme judicial, superior, probate and land courts, a sum not exceeding	77,300 00	79,100 00
9	For trial justices, a sum not exceeding .	5,300 00	5,600 00
10	For transportation and expenses of county and acting commissioners, a sum not exceeding	1,000 00	1,000 00
11	For medical examiners and commitments of insane, a sum not exceeding . .	16,000 00	16,000 00
12	For auditors, masters and referees, a sum not exceeding	7,500 00	7,500 00

Item		Appropriation Fiscal Year 1943.	Appropriation Fiscal Year 1944.
14	For repairing, furnishing and improving county buildings, a sum not exceeding	$21,350 00	$16,650 00
15	For care, fuel, lights and supplies in county buildings, other than jails and houses of correction, a sum not exceeding	90,300 00	93,700 00
16	For highways, including state highways, bridges and land damages, a sum not exceeding	153,700 00	160,250 00
18	For law libraries, a sum not exceeding .	12,800 00	13,150 00
19	For training school, a sum not exceeding	56,300 00	59,500 00
20	For agricultural school, a sum not exceeding	212,140 00	226,405 00
24	For non-contributory pensions, a sum not exceeding	4,375 00	4,375 00
25	For contributory retirement system, a sum not exceeding	37,997 00	40,007 00
25a	For contributory retirement audit, a sum not exceeding	970 79	
26	For miscellaneous and contingent expenses, including insurance, a sum not exceeding	12,500 00	12,500 00
27	For unpaid bills of previous years, a sum not exceeding	3,500 00	3,500 00
31	For a reserve fund, a sum not exceeding .	15,000 00	15,000 00
	And the county commissioners of Essex county are hereby authorized to levy as the county tax of said county for the current year, in the manner provided by law the following sum to be expended together with the cash balance on hand and the receipts from other sources, for the above purposes . .	$974,635 79	
	And the county commissioners of Essex county are hereby authorized to levy as the county tax of said county for the year nineteen hundred and forty-four, in the manner provided by law, such sum as is certified to said county commissioners on or before April first in said year by the director of accounts. In so certifying said director shall set forth, (1) the amount of the net unappropriated cash balance in the treasury of said county as of January first, nineteen hundred and forty-four, (2) the amount of the estimated receipts of said county for said year, and, (3) a sum, which shall constitute the county tax, and which shall be the difference between the sum of the two foregoing items and the total amount of the authorized expenditures hereinbefore appropriated.		

Franklin County.

Item		Appropriation Fiscal Year 1943.	Appropriation Fiscal Year 1944.
1	For interest on county debt, a sum not exceeding	$7,125 00	$6,387 50
2	For reduction of county debt, a sum not exceeding	20,000 00	15,000 00
3	For salaries of county officers and assistants, a sum not exceeding . . .	20,590 00	21,940 00

Item		Appropriation Fiscal Year 1943.	Appropriation Fiscal Year 1944.
4	For clerical assistance in county offices, a sum not exceeding	$9,100 00	$9,380 00
5	For salaries and expenses of district courts, a sum not exceeding	18,200 00	19,100 00
6	For salaries of jailers, masters and assistants and support of prisoners in jails and houses of correction, a sum not exceeding	20,400 00	21,300 00
7	For criminal costs in superior court, a sum not exceeding	8,200 00	8,300 00
8	For civil expenses in supreme judicial, superior, probate and land courts, a sum not exceeding	8,200 00	8,400 00
10	For transportation and expenses of county and acting commissioners, a sum not exceeding	400 00	400 00
11	For medical examiners and commitments of insane, a sum not exceeding	1,800 00	1,800 00
12	For auditors, masters and referees, a sum not exceeding	700 00	700 00
13	For building county buildings and purchase of land, a sum not exceeding	750 00	
14	For repairing, furnishing and improving county buildings, a sum not exceeding	2,500 00	2,000 00
15	For care, fuel, lights and supplies in county buildings, other than jails and houses of correction, a sum not exceeding	14,500 00	14,900 00
16	For highways, including state highways, bridges and land damages, a sum not exceeding	18,000 00	18,000 00
17	For examination of dams, a sum not exceeding	300 00	500 00
18	For law library, a sum not exceeding	3,075 00	3,100 00
19	For training school, a sum not exceeding	300 00	300 00
20	For county aid to agriculture, a sum not exceeding	13,745 00	14,645 00
21	For sanatorium (Hampshire county), a sum not exceeding	6,738 66	7,500 00
22	For Greenfield health camp (chapter 354, Acts of 1928), a sum not exceeding	2,000 00	2,000 00
23	For Mount Sugar Loaf state reservation, a sum not exceeding	1,200 00	1,200 00
24	For non-contributory pensions, a sum not exceeding	870 00	870 00
25	For contributory retirement system, a sum not exceeding	9,701 71	10,146 00
25a	For contributory retirement audit, a sum not exceeding	196 43	
26	For miscellaneous and contingent expenses, including insurance, a sum not exceeding	1,350 00	1,350 00
27	For unpaid bills of previous years, a sum not exceeding	500 00	500 00
30	For advertising the recreational advantages of the county, a sum not exceeding	500 00	500 00
31	For reserve fund, a sum not exceeding	5,000 00	5,000 00
33	For post-war rehabilitation fund, a sum not exceeding	25,000 00	25,000 00

And the county commissioners of Franklin county are hereby authorized to levy as the county tax of said county for

Item		Appropriation Fiscal Year 1943.	Appropriation Fiscal Year 1944.
	the current year, in the manner provided by law, the following sum to be expended together with the cash balance on hand and the receipts from other sources, for the above purposes .	$157,645 62	
	And the county commissioners of Franklin county are hereby authorized to levy as the county tax of said county for the year nineteen hundred and forty-four, in the manner provided by law, such sum as is certified to said county commissioners on or before April first in said year by the director of accounts. In so certifying said director shall set forth, (1) the amount of the net unappropriated cash balance in the treasury of said county as of January first, nineteen hundred and forty-four, (2) the amount of the estimated receipts of said county for said year, and, (3) a sum, which shall constitute the county tax, and which shall be the difference between the sum of the two foregoing items and the total amount of the authorized expenditures hereinbefore appropriated.		
	Hampden County.		
1	For interest on county debt, a sum not exceeding	$15,600 00	$10,700 00
2	For reduction of county debt, a sum not exceeding	121,000 00	121,000 00
3	For salaries of county officers and assistants, a sum not exceeding . .	52,200 00	55,400 00
4	For clerical assistance in county offices, a sum not exceeding	59,300 00	65,600 00
5	For salaries and expenses of district courts, a sum not exceeding . .	134,800 00	143,500 00
6	For salaries of jailers, masters and assistants and support of prisoners in jails and houses of correction, a sum not exceeding	91,200 00	97,400 00
7	For criminal costs in superior court, a sum not exceeding	28,500 00	28,900 00
8	For civil expenses in supreme judicial, superior, probate and land courts, a sum not exceeding	51,000 00	51,900 00
9	For trial justices, a sum not exceeding .	2,100 00	2,200 00
10	For transportation and expenses of county and acting commissioners, a sum not exceeding	750 00	750 00
11	For medical examiners and commitments of insane, a sum not exceeding . .	12,000 00	12,000 00
12	For auditors, masters and referees, a sum not exceeding	4,000 00	4,000 00
13	For building county buildings and purchase of land, a sum not exceeding .	2,000 00	–
14	For repairing, furnishing and improving county buildings, a sum not exceeding .	9,000 00	9,000 00
15	For care, fuel, lights and supplies in county buildings, other than jails and houses of correction, a sum not exceeding	62,500 00	65,900 00

Item		Appropriation Fiscal Year 1943.	Appropriation Fiscal Year 1944.
16	For highways, including state highways, bridges and land damages, a sum not exceeding	$22,200 00	$20,000 00
17	For examination of dams, a sum not exceeding	3,000 00	3,000 00
18	For law library, a sum not exceeding	10,800 00	11,300 00
19	For training school, a sum not exceeding	32,700 00	35,300 00
20	For county aid to agriculture, a sum not exceeding	41,200 00	45,700 00
22	For preventorium, a sum not exceeding	3,000 00	3,000 00
23	For Mount Tom state reservation, a sum not exceeding	13,212 14	13,912 14
24	For non-contributory pensions, a sum not exceeding	7,000 00	9,000 00
25	For contributory retirement system, a sum not exceeding	23,391 00	24,288 00
25a	For contributory retirement audit, a sum not exceeding	126 60	
26	For miscellaneous and contingent expenses, including insurance, a sum not exceeding	7,564 37	7,000 00
27	For unpaid bills of previous years, a sum not exceeding	1,000 00	1,000 00
30	For advertising the recreational advantages of the county, a sum not exceeding	500 00	500 00
31	For reserve fund, a sum not exceeding	12,000 00	12,000 00
33	For post-war rehabilitation fund, a sum not exceeding	25,000 00	25,000 00
	And the county commissioners of Hampden county are hereby authorized to levy as the county tax of said county for the current year, in the manner provided by law, the following sum to be expended together with the cash balance on hand and the receipts from other sources, for the above purposes	$695,171 50	

And the county commissioners of Hampden county are hereby authorized to levy as the county tax of said county for the year nineteen hundred and forty-four, in the manner provided by law, such sum as is certified to said county commissioners on or before April first in said year by the director of accounts. In so certifying said director shall set forth, (1) the amount of the net unappropriated cash balance in the treasury of said county as of January first, nineteen hundred and forty-four, (2) the amount of the estimated receipts of said county for said year, and, (3) a sum, which shall constitute the county tax, and which shall be the difference between the sum of the two foregoing items and the total amount of the authorized expenditures hereinbefore appropriated.

Hampshire County.

Item		Appropriation Fiscal Year 1943.	Appropriation Fiscal Year 1944.
1	For interest on county debt, a sum not exceeding	$500 00	$750 00
3	For salaries of county officers and assistants, a sum not exceeding	23,900 00	25,200 00

Item		Appropriation Fiscal Year 1943.	Appropriation Fiscal Year 1944.
4	For clerical assistance in county offices, a sum not exceeding	$12,500 00	$12,500 00
5	For salaries and expenses of district courts, a sum not exceeding	28,600 00	30,100 00
6	For salaries of jailers, masters and assistants and support of prisoners in jails and houses of correction, a sum not exceeding	32,500 00	34,000 00
7	For criminal costs in superior court, a sum not exceeding	21,500 00	12,900 00
8	For civil expenses in supreme judicial, superior, probate and land courts, a sum not exceeding	12,000 00	12,000 00
10	For transportation and expenses of county and acting commissioners, a sum not exceeding	600 00	400 00
11	For medical examiners and commitments of insane, a sum not exceeding	3,200 00	3,200 00
12	For auditors, masters and referees, a sum not exceeding	2,000 00	1,500 00
14	For repairing, furnishing and improving county buildings, a sum not exceeding	4,000 00	4,500 00
15	For care, fuel, lights and supplies in county buildings, other than jails and houses of correction, a sum not exceeding	15,900 00	16,800 00
16	For highways, including state highways, bridges and land damages, a sum not exceeding	25,600 00	31,200 00
17	For examination of dams, a sum not exceeding	250 00	400 00
18	For law libraries, a sum not exceeding	2,400 00	2,400 00
20	For county aid to agriculture, a sum not exceeding	17,900 00	19,300 00
21	For sanatorium, a sum not exceeding	34,000 00	38,300 00
22	For preventorium, a sum not exceeding	1,400 00	1,400 00
23	For state reservations, a sum not exceeding	2,450 00	2,550 00
24	For non-contributory pensions, a sum not exceeding	3,622 85	3,622 85
25	For contributory retirement system, a sum not exceeding	10,000 00	10,000 00
25a	For contributory retirement audit, a sum not exceeding	278 90	
26	For miscellaneous and contingent expenses, including insurance, a sum not exceeding	6,000 00	6,000 00
27	For unpaid bills of previous years, a sum not exceeding		100 00
30	For advertising the recreational advantages of the county, a sum not exceeding	500 00	500 00
31	For reserve fund, a sum not exceeding	7,500 00	7,500 00
33	For post-war rehabilitation fund, a sum not exceeding	10,000 00	10,000 00
	And the county commissioners of Hampshire county are hereby authorized to levy as the county tax of said county for the current year, in the manner provided by law, the following sum to be expended together with the cash balance on hand and the receipts from other sources, for the above purposes	$205,276 50	

Item		Appropriation Fiscal Year 1943.	Appropriation Fiscal Year 1944
	And the county commissioners of Hampshire county are hereby authorized to levy as the county tax of said county for the year nineteen hundred and forty-four, in the manner provided by law, such sum as is certified to said county commissioners on or before April first in said year by the director of accounts. In so certifying said director shall set forth, (1) the amount of the net unappropriated cash balance in the treasury of said county as of January first, nineteen hundred and forty-four, (2) the amount of the estimated receipts of said county for said year, and, (3) a sum, which shall constitute the county tax, and which shall be the difference between the sum of the two foregoing items and the total amount of the authorized expenditures hereinbefore appropriated.		
	Middlesex County.		
1	For interest on county debt, a sum not exceeding	$5,800 00	$10,000 00
2	For reduction of county debt, a sum not exceeding	59,000 00	25,000 00
3	For salaries of county officers and assistants, a sum not exceeding	88,100 00	91,600 00
4	For clerical assistance in county offices, a sum not exceeding	287,400 00	312,200 00
5	For salaries and expenses of district courts, a sum not exceeding	422,200 00	446,200 00
6	For salaries of jailers, masters and assistants and support of prisoners in jails and houses of correction, a sum not exceeding	265,020 00	279,790 00
7	For criminal costs in superior court, a sum not exceeding	184,800 00	189,500 00
8	For civil expenses in supreme judicial, superior, probate and land courts, a sum not exceeding	148,100 00	156,200 00
9	For trial justices, a sum not exceeding	1,250 00	1,300 00
10	For transportation and expenses of county and acting commissioners, a sum not exceeding	500 00	500 00
11	For medical examiners and commitments of insane, a sum not exceeding	32,000 00	32,000 00
12	For auditors, masters and referees, a sum not exceeding	20,000 00	20,000 00
13	For building county building and purchase of land, a sum not exceeding	600 00	–
14	For repairing, furnishing and improving county buildings, a sum not exceeding	92,000 00	50,000 00
15	For care, fuel, lights and supplies in county buildings, other than jails and houses of correction, a sum not exceeding	134,900 00	139,800 00
16	For highways, including state highways, bridges and land damages, a sum not exceeding	101,300 00	102,500 00
18	For law libraries, a sum not exceeding	13,400 00	13,800 00
19	For training school, a sum not exceeding	87,600 00	91,100 00

Item		Appropriation Fiscal Year 1943.	Appropriation Fiscal Year 1944.
20	For county aid to agriculture, a sum not exceeding	$46,500 00	$49,100 00
23	For Walden Pond state reservation, a sum not exceeding	16,500 00	16,900 00
24	For non-contributory pensions, a sum not exceeding	29,000 00	30,000 00
25	For contributory retirement system, a sum not exceeding	75,000 00	77,000 00
25a	For contributory retirement audit, a sum not exceeding	945 60	
26	For miscellaneous and contingent expenses, including insurance, a sum not exceeding	10,000 00	10,000 00
27	For unpaid bills of previous years, a sum not exceeding	3,000 00	3,000 00
31	For reserve fund, a sum not exceeding	15,000 00	20,000 00
33	For post-war rehabilitation fund, a sum not exceeding	25,000 00	25,000 00
	And the county commissioners of Middlesex county are hereby authorized to levy as the county tax of said county for the current year, in the manner provided by law the following sum to be expended together with the cash balance on hand and the receipts from other sources, for the above purposes	$1,618,560 19	
	And the county commissioners of Middlesex county are hereby authorized to levy as the county tax of said county for the year nineteen hundred and forty-four, in the manner provided by law, such sum as is certified to said county commissioners on or before April first in said year by the director of accounts. In so certifying said director shall set forth, (1) the amount of the net unappropriated cash balance in the treasury of said county as of January first, nineteen hundred and forty-four, (2) the amount of the estimated receipts of said county for said year, and, (3) a sum, which shall constitute the county tax, and which shall be the difference between the sum of the two foregoing items and the total amount of the authorized expenditures hereinbefore appropriated.		

Norfolk County.

Item		Appropriation Fiscal Year 1943.	Appropriation Fiscal Year 1944.
1	For interest on county debt, a sum not exceeding	$3,500 00	$5,900 00
2	For reduction of county debt, a sum not exceeding	75,000 00	75,000 00
3	For salaries of county officers and assistants, a sum not exceeding	41,000 00	44,100 00
4	For clerical assistance in county offices, a sum not exceeding	90,600 00	98,200 00
5	For salaries and expenses of district and municipal courts, a sum not exceeding	154,200 00	168,200 00
6	For salaries of jailers, masters and assistants and support of prisoners in jails and houses of correction, a sum not exceeding	63,500 00	69,700 00

Item		Appropriation Fiscal Year 1943.	Appropriation Fiscal Year 1944.
7	For criminal costs in superior court, a sum not exceeding	$53,100 00	$58,200 00
8	For civil expenses in supreme judicial, superior, probate and land courts, a sum not exceeding	44,800 00	40,500 00
10	For transportation and expenses of county and acting commissioners, a sum not exceeding	750 00	750 00
11	For medical examiners and commitments of insane, a sum not exceeding . .	12,000 00	12,000 00
12	For auditors, masters and referees, a sum not exceeding	7,000 00	7,000 00
14	For repairing, furnishing and improving county buildings, a sum not exceeding .	13,000 00	15,000 00
15	For care, fuel, lights and supplies in county buildings, other than jails and houses of correction, a sum not exceeding	95,700 00	102,900 00
16	For highways, including state highways, bridges and land damages, a sum not exceeding	51,000 00	53,700 00
18	For law library, a sum not exceeding .	2,400 00	2,500 00
19	For training school, a sum not exceeding .	5,000 00	6,000 00
20	For agricultural school, a sum not exceeding	114,755 00	123,165 00
24	For non-contributory pensions, a sum not exceeding	8,000 00	9,000 00
25	For contributory retirement system, a sum not exceeding	21,000 00	23,000 00
25a	For contributory retirement audit, a sum not exceeding	282 00	
26	For miscellaneous and contingent expenses, including insurance, a sum not exceeding	9,000 00	9,800 00
27	For unpaid bills of previous years, a sum not exceeding	4,000 00	3,000 00
31	For reserve fund, a sum not exceeding .	10,000 00	10,000 00
33	For post-war rehabilitation fund, a sum not exceeding	20,000 00	20,000 00
	And the county commissioners of Norfolk county are hereby authorized to levy as the county tax of said county for the current year, in the manner provided by law, the following sum to be expended together with the cash balance on hand and the receipts from other sources, for the above purposes . .	$661,894 30	

And the county commissioners of Norfolk county are hereby authorized to levy as the county tax of said county for the year nineteen hundred and forty-four, in the manner provided by law, such sum as is certified to said county commissioners on or before April first in said year by the director of accounts. In so certifying said director shall set forth, (1) the amount of the net unappropriated cash balance in the treasury of said county as of January first, nineteen hundred and forty-four, (2) the amount of the estimated receipts of said county for said year, and, (3) a sum, which shall constitute the county

Item		Appropriation Fiscal Year 1943.	Appropriation Fiscal Year 1944
	tax, and which shall be the difference between the sum of the two foregoing items and the total amount of the authorized expenditures hereinbefore appropriated.		
	Plymouth County.		
1	For interest on county debt, a sum not exceeding	$5,515 00	$4,900 00
2	For reduction of county debt, a sum not exceeding	24,000 00	23,000 00
3	For salaries of county officers and assistants, a sum not exceeding	33,200 00	34,400 00
4	For clerical assistance in county offices, a sum not exceeding	43,000 00	46,500 00
5	For salaries and expenses of district courts, a sum not exceeding . . .	76,800 00	81,200 00
6	For salaries of jailers, masters and assistants and support of prisoners in jails and houses of correction, a sum not exceeding	96,510 00	100,750 00
7	For criminal costs in superior court, a sum not exceeding	38,800 00	39,800 00
8	For civil expenses in supreme judicial, superior, probate and land courts, a sum not exceeding	26,500 00	27,000 00
10	For transportation and expenses of county and acting commissioners, a sum not exceeding	1,000 00	1,200 00
11	For medical examiners and commitments of insane, a sum not exceeding .	6,500 00	6,500 00
12	For auditors, masters and referees, a sum not exceeding	3,000 00	3,000 00
14	For repairing, furnishing and improving county buildings, a sum not exceeding	7,000 00	8,000 00
15	For care, fuel, lights and supplies in county buildings, other than jails and houses of correction, a sum not exceeding	34,750 00	33,700 00
16	For highways, including state highways, bridges and land damages, a sum not exceeding	48,400 00	48,000 00
17	For examination of dams, a sum not exceeding	1,000 00	1,000 00
18	For law library, a sum not exceeding .	3,600 00	3,700 00
19	For training school, a sum not exceeding	3,000 00	3,000 00
20	For county aid to agriculture, a sum not exceeding	23,700 00	24,900 00
24	For non-contributory pensions, a sum not exceeding	3,775 00	3,450 00
25	For contributory retirement system, a sum not exceeding	15,750 00	16,250 00
25a	For contributory retirement audit, a sum not exceeding	106 80	
26	For miscellaneous and contingent expenses, including insurance, a sum not exceeding	4,525 00	4,450 00
27	For unpaid bills of previous years, a sum not exceeding	2,500 00	2,500 00
31	For reserve fund, a sum not exceeding .	7,500 00	10,000 00
	And the county commissioners of Plymouth county are hereby authorized to levy as the county tax of said county		

Item		Appropriation Fiscal Year 1943.	Appropriation Fiscal Year 1944.
	for the current year, in the manner provided by law, the following sum to be expended together with the cash balance on hand and the receipts from other sources, for the above purposes .	$385,193 43	
	And the county commissioners of Plymouth county are hereby authorized to levy as the county tax of said county for the year nineteen hundred and forty-four, in the manner provided by law, such sum as is certified to said county commissioners on or before April first in said year by the director of accounts. In so certifying said director shall set forth, (1) the amount of the net unappropriated cash balance in the treasury of said county as of January first, nineteen hundred and forty-four, (2) the amount of the estimated receipts of said county for said year, and, (3) a sum, which shall constitute the county tax, and which shall be the difference between the sum of the two foregoing items and the total amount of the authorized expenditures hereinbefore appropriated.		
	Worcester County.		
1	For interest on county debt, a sum not exceeding	$2,000 00	$2,000 00
3	For salaries of county officers and assistants, a sum not exceeding	64,825 02	67,690 00
4	For clerical assistance in county offices, a sum not exceeding	98,729 62	106,335 00
5	For salaries and expenses of district courts, a sum not exceeding . .	193,733 46	200,230 00
6	For salaries of jailers, masters and assistants, and support of prisoners in jails and houses of correction, a sum not exceeding	118,648 92	122,800 00
7	For criminal costs in superior court, a sum not exceeding	72,324 95	74,300 00
8	For civil expenses in supreme judicial, superior, probate and land courts, a sum not exceeding	86,500 00	88,000 00
9	For trial justices, a sum not exceeding .	1,050 00	1,100 00
10	For transportation and expenses of county and acting commissioners, a sum not exceeding	2,000 00	2,000 00
11	For medical examiners and commitments of insane, a sum not exceeding . .	20,000 00	20,000 00
12	For auditors, masters and referees, a sum not exceeding	10,000 00	10,000 00
13	For building county buildings and purchase of land, a sum not exceeding .	–	40,000 00
14	For repairing, furnishing and improving county buildings, a sum not exceeding	28,200 00	77,700 00
15	For care, fuel, lights and supplies in county buildings, other than jails and houses of correction, a sum not exceeding	81,991 07	83,920 00

Item		Appropriation Fiscal Year 1943.	Appropriation Fiscal Year 1944.
16	For highways, including state highways, bridges and land damages, a sum not exceeding	$119,748 06	$121,500 00
18	For law libraries, a sum not exceeding .	14,846 25	15,140 00
19	For training school, a sum not exceeding	37,451 08	38,000 00
20	For county aid to agriculture, a sum not exceeding	42,308 20	43,800 00
22	For preventorium, a sum not exceeding .	3,000 00	3,000 00
23	For Mount Wachusett State reservation, a sum not exceeding	10,000 00	11,000 00
23a	For Purgatory Chasm State reservation, a sum not exceeding	4,857 94	5,200 00
24	For non-contributory pensions, a sum not exceeding	15,000 00	15,000 00
25	For contributory retirement system, a sum not exceeding	42,000 00	42,000 00
25a	For contributory retirement audit, a sum not exceeding	554 40	
26	For miscellaneous and contingent expenses, including insurance, a sum not exceeding	10,000 00	10,000 00
27	For unpaid bills of previous years, a sum not exceeding	10,000 00	10,000 00
31	For reserve fund, a sum not exceeding .	12,500 00	12,500 00
33	For post-war rehabilitation fund, a sum not exceeding	25,000 00	25,000 00
	And the county commissioners of Worcester county are hereby authorized to levy as the county tax of said county for the current year, in the manner provided by law, the following sum to be expended together with the cash balance on hand and the receipts from other sources, for the above purposes .	$838,598 97	
	And the county commissioners of Worcester county are hereby authorized to levy as the county tax of said county for the year nineteen hundred and forty-four, in the manner provided by law, such sum as is certified to said county commissioners on or before April first in said year by the director of accounts. In so certifying said director shall set forth, (1) the amount of the net unappropriated cash balance in the treasury of said county as of January first, nineteen hundred and forty-four, (2) the amount of the estimated receipts of said county for said year, and, (3) a sum, which shall constitute the county tax, and which shall be the difference between the sum of the two foregoing items and the total amount of the authorized expenditures hereinbefore appropriated.		

SECTION 2. No person, except as hereinafter provided, shall be reimbursed by any county, out of funds appropriated by this act, for any expense incurred for a mid-day meal while traveling within the commonwealth, nor shall any person be so reimbursed for the amount of any expense incurred for a breakfast while so traveling which is in excess of seventy-five

cents or for the amount of any expense incurred for an evening meal while so traveling which is in excess of one dollar and twenty-five cents; provided, that officers or employees who have charge of juries or who have the care and custody of prisoners, insane persons or other persons placed in their charge by a court or under legal proceedings for transfer to or from court to an institution or from institution to institution and persons certified by a district attorney as engaged in investigation shall be reimbursed for the expense of mid-day meals when necessarily engaged on such duty; and provided, further, that officers and employees in attendance at meetings and conferences called by or for any group or class on a state-wide basis shall be so reimbursed.

Nothing herein contained shall apply to county employees who receive as part of their compensation a non-cash allowance in the form of full or complete boarding and housing, nor be construed as preventing the payment of allowances for meals, not exceeding two dollars and fifty cents in any one day, for officers or employees stationed beyond commuting distance from their homes for a period of more than twenty-four hours.

SECTION 3. The allowance to county employees for expenses incurred by them in the operation of motor vehicles owned by them or by any member of their immediate families and used in the performance of their official duties shall not exceed four and one half cents per mile except in cases where a higher allowance is specifically provided by statute; provided, that in the case of insane commitments the justice of the court ordering the commitment may order a higher rate.

Approved June 7, 1943.

---

*Chap.*466 AN ACT PROVIDING FOR THE CONSTRUCTION BY THE METROPOLITAN DISTRICT COMMISSION OF A FENCE ALONG PORTIONS OF THE BANKS OF THE NEPONSET RIVER IN THE HYDE PARK AND MATTAPAN DISTRICTS OF THE CITY OF BOSTON.

Be it enacted, etc., as follows:

SECTION 1. For the purpose of protecting the lives of children in the area specified below and to prevent further loss of life, by drowning, among the children of the Hyde Park district of the city of Boston, the metropolitan district commission is hereby authorized and directed to erect a suitable protective fence along portions of the banks of the Neponset river in said district as follows: — On the westerly bank, from a point near the junction of Reservation road and Hyde Park avenue to the Dana avenue bridge; on the easterly bank, from a point opposite Foster street to the Dana avenue bridge; on the northerly bank, from the Dana avenue bridge to a point three hundred and sixty feet easterly therefrom; and on both banks, from the railroad trestle bridge opposite Walnut street to the Fairmount bridge. For said purposes said commission may expend such sums, not exceeding, in the aggregate, thirteen thousand dollars, as may hereafter be appropriated therefor.

SECTION 2. The metropolitan district commission is further authorized and directed to erect a suitable protective fence along portions of the banks of said river in the Mattapan district of the city of Boston as follows: — On the westerly bank, from a point near the junction of Riverside place and River street to a point approximately one thousand feet in a northerly direction above the junction of Fremont street and River street; and from a point three hundred feet south of Duxbury road to a point approximately opposite the junction of Cedar street and River street. For said purposes said commission may expend such sums, not exceeding, in the aggregate, five thousand dollars, as may hereafter be appropriated therefor. *Approved June 7, 1943.*

AN ACT RELATIVE TO THE WEEKLY PAYMENT OF COMMISSIONS DUE TO CERTAIN EMPLOYEES. *Chap.467*

Be it enacted, etc., as follows:

G. L. (Ter. Ed.), 149, § 148, etc., amended.

Section one hundred and forty-eight of chapter one hundred and forty-nine of the General Laws, as most recently amended by chapter three hundred and seventy-eight of the acts of the current year, is hereby further amended by inserting after the first paragraph, as appearing in chapter one hundred and sixty of the acts of nineteen hundred and thirty-six, the following paragraph: —

Section applicable to payment of commissions.

This section shall apply, so far as apt, to the payment of commissions when the amount of such commissions, less allowable or authorized deductions, has been definitely determined and has become due and payable to such employee, and commissions so determined and due such employees shall be subject to the provisions of section one hundred and fifty. *Approved June 7, 1943.*

AN ACT RELATIVE TO THE POWERS OF BOARDS OF HEALTH WITH RESPECT TO CERTAIN UNFIT DWELLINGS. *Chap.468*

Be it enacted, etc., as follows:

G. L. (Ter. Ed.), 111, § 128, amended.

Section one hundred and twenty-eight of chapter one hundred and eleven of the General Laws, as appearing in the Tercentenary Edition, is hereby amended by adding at the end the two following paragraphs: —

Housing standards. Finding of unfitness, etc.

Without limiting the foregoing, failure to conform with two or more of the following housing standards shall, in the case of a building or portion thereof which is leased and occupied as a dwelling place, be a sufficient reason for a finding of unfitness for human habitation and for proceedings in accordance with the preceding paragraph: — (1) that the building and premises appurtenant thereto shall be kept reasonably clean and free from rubbish; (2) that the floors, ceilings, walls, stairs and windows shall be kept in reasonably good repair and serviceable; (3) that the cellar, basement, floors, walls and ceilings shall be reasonably free from dampness; (4) that the water closets and drains for waste therefrom shall be maintained in good repair; (5) that the heat generating equipment shall be reasonably adequate and be maintained in a reasonably safe and serviceable condition.

Procedure. Equity jurisdiction.

Instead of proceeding under the first paragraph of this section, the board of health, if satisfied that such a building or portion thereof in its town is unfit for human habitation, as defined in this section, may issue a written notice to the owner of such building, as appearing in the current records of the assessors of such town, setting forth the particulars of such unfitness and requiring that the conditions be remedied. If the person so notified fails within a reasonable time to remedy the conditions thus set forth, the superior court, on a petition in equity brought by the board of health, shall have jurisdiction, by injunction or otherwise, to enforce the standards of this section and said requirements of the board of health. *Approved June 8, 1943.*

---

*Chap.*469 An Act including persons in the coast guard service of the United States within the veterans' preference provisions of the civil service law.

Be it enacted, etc., as follows:

G. L. (Ter. Ed.), 31, § 21, etc., amended.

Section twenty-one of chapter thirty-one of the General Laws, as most recently amended by chapter one hundred and ninety-four of the acts of the current year, is hereby further amended by inserting after the word "navy" in the third and eighth lines, in each instance, the words: — , coast guard, — so as to read as follows: — *Section 21.* The word "veteran", as used in this chapter, shall mean (1) any person who has served in the army, navy, coast guard or marine corps of the United States in time of war or insurrection and whose last discharge or release from active duty therein was an honorable one, regardless of any prior discharge or release therefrom, or (2) any person who has distinguished himself by gallant or heroic conduct while serving in the army, navy, coast guard or marine corps of the United States and has received a decoration designated as the congressional medal of honor from the president of the United States or the secretary of war, or from a person designated by the president or the said secretary to act as the personal representative of the president or said secretary for the presentation of such decoration, and is recorded in the files of the war department or the navy department of the United States as having received such decoration, or (3) any person who has served in time of war or insurrection in any corps or unit of the United States established for the purpose of enabling women to serve with, or as auxiliary to, the armed forces of the United States, and whose last discharge or release from active duty in such corps

"Veteran" defined.

or unit was an honorable one, regardless of any prior discharge or release therefrom; provided, that the person claiming to be a veteran under this section was a citizen of the commonwealth at the time of his induction into such service or has resided in the commonwealth for five consecutive years next prior to the date of filing application with the director under this chapter; and provided, further, that any such person who at the time of entering said service had declared his intention to become a subject or citizen of the United States and withdrew such intention under the provisions of the act of congress approved July ninth, nineteen hundred and eighteen, and any person designated as a conscientious objector upon his discharge, shall not be deemed a "veteran" within the meaning of this chapter; and provided, further, that no member of the United States coast guard auxiliary and no temporary member of the United States coast guard reserve shall be deemed a "veteran" within the meaning of this chapter.

Approved June 8, 1943.

AN ACT PERMITTING RECIPIENTS OF OLD AGE ASSISTANCE, SO CALLED, TO LEAVE THE COMMONWEALTH ON VISIT WITHOUT SUSPENSION OF SUCH ASSISTANCE. *Chap.470*

Be it enacted, etc., as follows:

Chapter one hundred and eighteen A of the General Laws is hereby amended by striking out section six A, inserted by chapter one hundred and sixty-five of the acts of nineteen hundred and thirty-seven, and as amended by section seven of chapter seven hundred and twenty-nine of the acts of nineteen hundred and forty-one, and inserting in place thereof the following section: — *Section 6A.* Any person receiving assistance under this chapter may be absent on visit from the commonwealth without having such assistance suspended. Such person, before departure from the commonwealth and following return thereto, shall notify the bureau of old age assistance of the town granting such assistance. The department may provide by rule or regulation for the continuation of such assistance during such period as it may deem proper with respect to cases where the suspension of such assistance because of absence from the commonwealth would result in undue hardship or be inconsistent with the provisions of this chapter. *Approved June 8, 1943.*

G. L. (Ter. Ed.), 118A, § 6A, etc., amended.

Absence from commonwealth without suspension of benefits.

AN ACT RELATIVE TO THE RATE OF INTEREST ON REFUNDS OF TAXES IMPOSED UPON TRANSFERS OF CERTAIN ESTATES. *Chap.471*

Be it enacted, etc., as follows:

Section six of chapter sixty-five A of the General Laws, as amended by section two of chapter four hundred and twenty of the acts of nineteen hundred and thirty-seven, is hereby

G. L. (Ter. Ed.), 65A, § 6, etc., amended.

further amended by striking out the last sentence and inserting in place thereof the following sentence: — Any excess tax received by the commonwealth shall be refunded within thirty days after the amount shall have been certified by the commissioner, with interest at four per cent from the date of payment, without appropriation.

Refund of excess tax.

Approved June 8, 1943.

---

*Chap.*472 AN ACT TO BRING CERTAIN PROVISIONS OF LAW RELATING TO THE TAXATION OF MORRIS PLAN BANKS INTO CONFORMITY.

Be it enacted, etc., as follows:

G. L. (Ter. Ed.), 63, § 1, etc., amended.

Section one of chapter sixty-three of the General Laws, as amended by section one of chapter three hundred and twenty-seven of the acts of nineteen hundred and thirty-three, is hereby further amended by striking out the paragraph defining "Bank" and inserting in place thereof the following paragraph: —

"Bank" defined.

"Bank", Any bank, banking association or trust company doing business within the commonwealth, whether of issue or not, existing by authority of the United States or of a foreign country, or of any law of the commonwealth not contained in chapters one hundred and sixty-eight to one hundred and seventy-one, inclusive, and chapters one hundred and seventy-three and one hundred and seventy-four, and any corporation authorized by section one of chapter one hundred and seventy-two A to do the business of a banking company. *Approved June 8, 1943.*

---

*Chap.*473 AN ACT RELATIVE TO THE HANDLING, TRANSPORTATION AND DELIVERY OF FISH AND PERISHABLE FOODSTUFFS AT WHOLESALE ON THE LORD'S DAY.

Emergency preamble.

Whereas, It is in the interest of the public that the handling, transportation and delivery of fish and perishable foodstuffs at wholesale be permitted on the Lord's day, especially during the existing state of war between the United States and certain foreign countries, and the deferred operation of this act would in part tend to defeat its purpose, which is to make immediately possible such handling, transportation and delivery on the Lord's day, therefore it is hereby declared to be an emergency law, necessary for the immediate preservation of the public convenience.

Be it enacted, etc., as follows:

G. L. (Ter. Ed.), 136, § 6, etc., amended.

Section six of chapter one hundred and thirty-six of the General Laws is hereby amended by striking out the fourth paragraph, as most recently amended by chapter one hundred and forty-three of the acts of nineteen hundred and thirty-eight, and inserting in place thereof the following paragraph: —

Sale of perishable foods, etc., on the Lord's day.

Nor shall it prohibit the preparation, printing and publication of newspapers, or the sale and delivery thereof; the wholesale or retail sale and delivery of milk, or the transportation thereof, or the delivery of frozen desserts or ice cream mix, or both, or the retail sale of ice or of fuel; the handling, transportation and delivery of fish and perishable foodstuffs at wholesale; the sale at wholesale of dressed poultry, and the transportation of such poultry so sold, on the Lord's day next preceding Thanksgiving day, and on the Lord's day next preceding Christmas day except when Christmas day occurs on Saturday, the Lord's day or Monday; the making of butter and cheese; the keeping open of public bathhouses; the making or selling by bakers or their employees, before ten o'clock in the forenoon and between the hours of four o'clock and half past six o'clock in the afternoon, of bread or other food usually dealt in by them; whenever Rosh Hashonah, or the Day of Atonement, begins on the Lord's day, the retail sale and delivery of fish, fruit and vegetables before twelve o'clock noon of that day; the selling or delivering of kosher meat by any person who, according to his religious belief, observes Saturday as the Lord's day by closing his place of business during the day until six o'clock in the afternoon, or the keeping open of his shop on the Lord's day for the sale of kosher meat between the hours of six o'clock and ten o'clock in the forenoon.

(This bill, returned by the governor to the Senate, the branch in which it originated, with his objections thereto, was passed by the Senate, June 4, 1943, and, in concurrence, by the House of Representatives, June 8, 1943, the objections of the governor notwithstanding, in the manner prescribed by the constitution; and thereby has "the force of a law".)

AN ACT TEMPORARILY PROVIDING FOR THE USE OF CERTAIN ROAD AND SNOW REMOVAL EQUIPMENT BY THE COMMONWEALTH AND THE VARIOUS SUBDIVISIONS THEREOF. *Chap.*474

Emergency preamble.

Whereas, Owing in part to conditions arising out of the present existing state of war, many of the ways of the commonwealth are falling into serious disrepair and the purpose of this act is in part to make immediately available for use by the commonwealth and its various political subdivisions machinery and apparatus adapted to road construction and repair and not now available for such use, therefore this act is hereby declared to be an emergency law, necessary for the immediate preservation of the public safety and convenience.

Be it enacted, etc., as follows:

SECTION 1. The county commissioners of any county, or any municipal board, department or officer, having possession and control of any vehicle, machinery or equipment adapted to the construction, maintenance, alteration or repair of public ways, or to the removal of snow therefrom, may, in the case of a city with the approval of the mayor or otherwise as provided by its charter, and in the case of a town with the approval of the selectmen, lease such vehicle, machinery or equipment to any department, board, commission or other agency of the commonwealth or to any political subdivision of the commonwealth, and any department, board, commission or other agency of the commonwealth having any such vehicle, machinery or equipment in its possession and control may allow the use of the same by any other department, board, commission or other agency of the commonwealth and may lease the same to any political subdivision of the commonwealth, in each instance upon such terms and conditions as may be mutually agreed upon.

Section 2. This act shall be in full force and effect only during the continuance of the existing state of war between the United States and certain foreign countries.

Approved June 9, 1943.

---

*Chap.*475 An Act authorizing the department of public health to approve the taking of water for public water supply purposes during the present emergency.

Emergency preamble.

Whereas, The deferred operation of this act would tend to defeat its purpose, which is to protect the public health during the existing state of war, therefore it is hereby declared to be an emergency law, necessary for the immediate preservation of the public health.

Be it enacted, etc., as follows:

Section 1. During the time this act is in effect, the authority to take by eminent domain under section forty of chapter forty of the General Laws, as amended by chapter three hundred and fourteen of the acts of nineteen hundred and thirty-three, either permanently or for a limited period of time, the right to draw water shall extend to streams, ponds or reservoirs or ground sources of supply, wherever located, if not already appropriated to uses of a municipality or other public water supply, and if such taking is first approved by the state department of public health, and water may be purchased under said section forty, and may be sold thereunder to any body politic or corporate desiring to purchase the same as aforesaid, for such period as said department may approve; but in case of any such taking or purchase for water supply purposes of a town or a water supply or fire and water district, the prior vote of the voters at a town meeting or a district meeting, as the case may be, shall be dispensed with, if said department determines that the emergency warrants such action, and such determination shall be conclusive evidence of the emergency. Nothing in this act shall affect the provisions of chapter seven hundred and twenty-seven of the acts of nineteen hundred and forty-one.

SECTION 2. This act shall be in effect only during the continuance of the existing states of war between the United States and any foreign country and one year thereafter.

Approved June 9, 1943.

AN ACT RELATIVE TO HOSPITAL AND MEDICAL EXPENSES IN CONNECTION WITH THE SUPPORT OF POOR PERSONS. *Chap.*476

Whereas, The deferred operation of this act would tend to defeat its purpose which is to provide immediately a more equitable reimbursement to cities and towns for sums paid by them to hospitals, therefore it is hereby declared to be an emergency law, necessary for the immediate preservation of the public health and convenience. Emergency preamble.

Be it enacted, etc., as follows:

Section eighteen of chapter one hundred and twenty-two of the General Laws, as most recently amended by section two of chapter two hundred and seventy-five of the acts of nineteen hundred and forty-three, is hereby further amended by striking out the fourth sentence, as appearing in chapter four hundred and twelve of the acts of the year nineteen hundred and forty-one, and inserting in place thereof the two following sentences: — Bills for such support shall not be allowed unless endorsed with the declaration that, after full investigation, no kindred able to pay the amount charged have been found, and that the amount has actually been paid from the town treasury, nor unless they are approved by the department or by a person designated by it. There shall be allowed for the support of a person in a hospital such amounts, not exceeding four dollars a day, as may be provided by rules and regulations made by the department, authority to make the same being hereby granted; provided, that expenses incurred by a town for tonsil and adenoid operations shall be reimbursed by the commonwealth to an amount not exceeding fifteen dollars in the case of any one such operation. *Approved June 9, 1943.*

G. L. (Ter Ed.), 122, § 18, etc., amended.

Reimbursement to cities and towns for care of certain indigent sick.

AN ACT GRANTING THE CONSENT OF THE COMMONWEALTH TO THE ACQUISITION BY THE UNITED STATES OF AMERICA OF CERTAIN PARCELS OF LAND IN THE CITY OF BOSTON AND IN THE TOWN OF HINGHAM TO FACILITATE THE WAR EFFORT OF THE UNITED STATES NAVY AND GRANTING AND CEDING JURISDICTION OVER SUCH PARCELS OF LAND. *Chap.*477

Whereas, The deferred operation of this act would tend to defeat its purpose, which is to provide land for the immediate use of the United States Navy for the purpose of national defense, therefore it is hereby declared to be an emergency law, necessary for the immediate preservation of the public safety. Emergency preamble.

Be it enacted, etc., as follows:

SECTION 1. Subject to the conditions hereinafter imposed the consent of the commonwealth is hereby granted to the acquisition by the United States of America by purchase or condemnation the following described parcels of land for use by the Navy Department in connection with the war effort and for the purposes hereinafter stated.

1. All that certain piece or parcel of land situated in that part of Boston called Charlestown, County of Suffolk, being more particularly shown and described on the plan to be filed with the secretary of state as hereinafter provided and being the same premises acquired by the United States under the authority of the Act of Congress approved January 29, 1942 (Public Law 420, 77th Congress) for the expansion of the Boston Navy Yard, in fee simple by a declaration of taking filed June 24, 1942 in the District Court of the United States for the District of Massachusetts in the case of the United States of America v. 0.193 of an acre of land more or less in Charlestown, Suffolk County, Massachusetts, City Associates Incorporated, et al., Civil No. 6551 and bounded and described as follows:

Beginning at the northeast corner of the intersection of Charles River Avenue and Water Street and following the easterly line of said Water Street a distance of 102.02 feet to the southwesterly line of Lot 122 on plan drawn by S. M. Felton, dated May 10, 1843, and recorded with Middlesex South District Office, Book of Plans, #1 Plan 39, and following the southeast boundary of said land a distance of 82.19 feet to the land of the Fitchburg Railroad Company; thence along the northwest line of said railroad a distance of 99.33 feet to the northeast side of Charles River Avenue; thence continuing along said Avenue a distance of 82.04 feet to the point of beginning, containing 0.193 of an acre of land, more or less.

2. All that certain piece or parcel of land situated in that part of Boston called South Boston, County of Suffolk being more particularly shown and described on the plan to be filed with the Secretary of State as hereinafter provided and being the same premises acquired by the United States of America under authority of the Act of Congress approved February 6, 1942 (Public Law 440, 77th Congress) for the expansion of the United States Naval Dry Dock at South Boston Massachusetts in fee simple by declaration of taking filed May 27, 1942 in the United States District Court for the District of Massachusetts in the case of the United States of America v. 17.29 acres of land more or less in South Boston Suffolk County Massachusetts and Jesse Tirrel Estate, et al., Civil No. 6537 and bounded and described as follows:

Beginning on the northerly side of East First Street 300 feet westerly of the westerly side of K Street; thence running S. 88° 41′ 10″ W., by said East First Street 349.10 feet; thence running N. 1° 13′ 50″ W., by the center of I Street as it extends northerly from East First Street 516 feet; thence running N. 32° 24′ 36″ E., 69.03 feet; thence running N. 4° 04′ 15″ E., 84 feet; thence running N. 82° 13′ 38″ E., 75 feet; thence running N. 42° 27′ 15″ E., 75.61 feet; thence running N. 11° 04′ 00″ E., 593.72 feet to the U. S. Pierhead and Bulkhead line; thence running N. 88° 41′ 10″ E. by the U. S. Pierhead and Bulkhead line 539.53 feet; thence running S. 11° 04′ 00″ W., 893.27 feet; thence running S. 1° 18′ 50″ E. by K Street 294.50 feet; thence running S. 88° 41′ 10″ W. by land now or formerly of the Linde Air Products Company 300 feet; thence running S. 1° 18′ 50″ E., by land of the Linde Air Products Company 133 feet to East First Street, the point of beginning, containing 17.29 acres, more or less.

3. All those ten pieces or parcels of land situated in that part of Boston called East Boston, County of Suffolk being more particularly shown and described on the plan or plans to be filed with the Secretary of State as hereinafter provided and being the same premises acquired by the United States under the authority of the Act of Congress approved August 21, 1941 (Public Law 241, 77th Congress) for the establishment of fuel storage facilities at Orient Heights East Boston Massachusetts in fee simple by a declaration of taking filed August 13, 1942 in the United States District Court for the District of Massachusetts in the case of the United States of America v. 60.325 acres of land more or less, Boston, Suffolk County, Massachusetts and Boston Port Development Company et al., Civil No. 6503 and bounded and described as follows:

Parcel "A". Commencing in the westerly side of the location of the Boston and Maine Railroad at a point eighty (80) feet from the southerly side line of Boardman Street extended, measured south 31° 32′ West along the said westerly side line of railroad location, thence running south 31° 32′ west by the said westerly side line of location of said Railroad thirteen hundred seventy-two and seventy-seven one hundredths (1372.77) feet to the former division between Noddles Island and Breeds Island; thence running south 58° 28′ east by said division and still by said Railroad location sixteen and twenty-five one hundredths (16.25) feet; thence running south 31° 32′ west, still by the westerly side of said Railroad location, eighteen hundred ninety-five and five tenths (1895.50) feet; thence running southwesterly, still by the westerly side of said Railroad location, by a curved line having a radius of seven thousand eighty and five tenths (7080.50) feet, about three hundred ten (310) feet to the location of the Boston and Albany Railroad; thence running northerly by the location of the said Boston and Albany Railroad by a curved line, having a radius of nine hundred forty-one and twenty-five one hundredths (941.25) feet about five hundred forty-three (543) feet; thence running north 33° 52′ 55″ east by land of the Commonwealth of Massachusetts, two hundred twenty-eight and seventy-three one hundredths (228.73) feet; thence running north 61° 02′ 30″ east, still by land of the Commonwealth of Massachusetts and by a right of way, one hundred thirty and fifty-five one hundredths (130.55) feet; thence running north 12° 35′ 30″ west, still by land of the Commonwealth of Massachusetts and the end of the right of way above referred to, fifteen and sixty-three one hundredths (15.63) feet; thence running north 61° 02′ 30″ east, still by land of the Commonwealth of Massachusetts thirty-three and eight tenths (33.80) feet; thence running north 12° 35′ 30″ west, still by land of the Commonwealth of Massachusetts about one hundred sixty (160) feet to the original low water line of Chelsea River; thence running northerly by Chelsea River by the original low water line about twenty-seven hundred fifty-five (2755) feet; thence running south 58° 28′ east by lands now or formerly of the Boston Port Development Company about five hundred twenty-five (525) feet to the point of beginning, said Parcel A extending from the Boston and Maine Railroad westerly to the original low water line of Chelsea River, including appurtenant riparian rights.

Parcel "B". Commencing in the easterly side of the location of the Boston and Maine Railroad at a point one hundred one and eleven one hundredths (101.11) feet from the southerly side line of Boardman Street, measured south 31° 32′ west along the said easterly side line of Railroad location; thence running south 45° 34′ 30″ east by land now or formerly of the Boston Port Development Company three hundred fourteen and thirty-two one hundredths (314.32) feet; thence running south 41° 26′ 17″ east by land now or formerly of Vecchio forty-five and two tenths (45.20) feet; thence running south 35° 38′ 04″ east, still by land of said Vecchio, thirty-three and four tenths (33.40) feet to the State Highway, called the McClellan Highway; thence running south 30° 57′ 51″ west by said State Highway eight hundred seventy-six and seven tenths (876.70) feet; thence running southwesterly by a curved line having a radius of nine hundred fifty (950) feet, and still by said State Highway, five hundred fifty-six and six tenths (556.60) feet; thence running south 64° 32′ west, still by said State Highway, one hundred fifty-one and sixty-two one hundredths (151.62) feet; thence running southwesterly by a curved line having a radius of ten hundred fifty (1050) feet, still by said State Highway, six hundred four and seventy-six one hundredths (604.76) feet to the easterly side of the location of the Boston and Maine Railroad, thence running north 31° 32′ east by the easterly side line of location of the said Railroad eight hundred sixty-six and one tenth (866.10) feet; thence running south 58° 28′ east by the former division between Noddles Island and Breeds Island, still by said Railroad location, sixteen and twenty-five one hundredths (16.25) feet; thence running north 31° 32′ east by the easterly side line of the said Railroad location thirteen hundred thirty-two and eighty-three one hundredths (1332.83) feet to the point of beginning.

Parcel "C". Commencing in the westerly side of Boardman Street at a stone monument at the point of curve of the State Highway line, thence running south 27° 17′ 09″ east by said Boardman Street forty-nine and Thirty-one one hundredths (49.31) feet; thence running south 32° 12′ 16″ east by said Boardman Street one Hundred sixty-one and thirty-two one hundredths (161.32) feet; thence running southeasterly, still by said Boardman Street, by a curved line having a radius of sixteen hundred twelve and eighty-eight one hundredths (1612.88) feet, two hundred twenty and sixty-two one hundredths (220.62) feet; thence running south 40° 02′ 31″ east, still by said Boardman Street, seventy-three and fifty-four one hundredths (73.54) feet; thence running south 42° 59′ 04″ east, still by said Boardman Street, four hundred thirty-eight and seven tenths (438.70) feet; thence running south 63° 19′ 56″ west by lands of the City of Boston two hundred forty-six and four tenths (246.40) feet; thence running south 54° 54′ 18″ west by land of the Boston Port Development Company fourteen hundred twenty-seven and three tenths (1427.30) feet; thence running north 73° 12′ 50″ west by lands of the Boston Port Development Company and of the Maverick Mills six hundred sixty-one and forty-three one hundredths (661.43) feet to the State Highway; thence running northeasterly by said State Highway by a curved line having a radius of nine hundred eleven and four one hundredths (911.04) feet; four hundred twenty and forty-five one hundredths (420.45) feet; thence running north 64° 32′ east by said State Highway one hundred sixty-four and ninety-nine one hundredths (164.99) feet; thence running northeasterly by said State Highway by a curved line having a radius of ten hundred fifty (1050) feet, six hundred fifteen and eighteen one hundredths (615.18) feet; thence running north 30° 57′ 51″ east by said State Highway eight hundred sixty-one and sixty-three one hundredths (861.63) feet to a stone bound near Boardman Street, thence running northeasterly, easterly and southeasterly by a curved line at the junction of the State Highway and Boardman Street having a radius of forty (40) feet, eighty-five (85) feet to a stone monument at Boardman Street at the point of beginning, excepting from the above description that portion thereof owned by Guiseppe Visconti hereinafter described as Parcel "I".

Parcel "D". Commencing in the westerly side of the location of the Boston and Maine Railroad at a stone monument eighty (80) feet from the southerly side line of Boardman Street extended, measured south 31° 32′ west along the said westerly side line of Railroad location, thence running north 58° 28′ west by land now or formerly of the Boston Port Development Company about five hundred twenty-five (525) feet to the original low water line of Chelsea River; thence running northerly by Chelsea River by the original low water line about four hundred seventy-five (475) feet; thence running northeasterly by a curved line having a radius of five hundred thirty-five (535) feet about two hundred seventy-three (273) feet by land and flats of the Tide Water Oil Company; thence running north 62° 51′ 28″ east by land and flats of the said Tide Water Oil Company nine hundred ninety-nine and thirty-five one hundredths (999.35) feet; thence running south 67° 54′ 39″ east by land and flats of the Commonwealth of Massachusetts one Hundred forty-seven and sixty-three one hundredths (147.63) feet to the location of the Boston and Maine Railroad; thence running south 31° 32′ 28″ west by the westerly side of the location of the Boston and Maine Railroad fifteen hundred forty-nine and twenty-three one hundredths (1549.23) feet to the point of beginning, said parcel "D" extending to the original low water line of Chelsea River, including appurtenant riparian rights of Parcel "D".

Parcel "E". Commencing in the westerly side of the State Highway at land of the Tide Water Oil Company, thence running south 30° 57′ 51″ west by the State Highway five hundred forty-one and nine one hundredths (541.09) feet to a stone monument at land of the Boston and Maine Railroad — Branch line; thence running north 79° 32′ 32″ west by said Railroad — branch line two and nineteen one hundredths (2.19) feet; thence running westerly and southwesterly by said Railroad — branch line by a curved line having a radius of six hundred sixty and seventy-seven one hundredths (660.77) feet five hundred seventeen and fifty-five one hundredths (517.55) feet to a stone monument in the easterly side of the location of the Boston and Maine Railroad; thence running north 31° 32′ 28″ east by the location of the said Boston and Maine Railroad eight hundred fifty-three and twenty-nine one hundredths (853.29) feet to a stone monument; thence running south 67° 50′ 22″ east by land of the Tide Water Oil Company eighty-one and fifty-nine one hundredths (81.59) feet to a stone monument; thence running south 59° 48′ 17″ east by land of the said Tide Water Oil Company one hundred fifty-seven and fifty-four one hundredths (157.54) feet to a stone monument; thence running south 67° 06′ 52″ east still by land of the Tide Water Oil Company one hundred twenty-five and eight tenths (125.80) feet to the State Highway at the point of beginning — said last three lines and courses being along the boundary line between the Cities of Boston and Revere.

Parcel "F". Commencing at a stone monument in the northeasterly side of Boardman Street at the westerly end of the curve at the junction of Boardman Street and the State Highway, thence running north 45° 34′ 30″ west three hundred thirty-seven and nine tenths (337.90) feet to the location of the Boston and Maine Railroad; thence running north 31° 32′ 28″ east by the easterly side of the location of the Boston and Maine Railroad four hundred ninety-nine and sixty-two one hundredths (499.62) feet to a stone monument; thence running northeasterly and easterly by the location of the Boston and Maine Railroad — branch line by a curved line having a radius of six hundred thirteen and seventy-seven one hundredths (613.77) feet six hundred ten and thirteen one hundredths (610.13) feet to a stone monument at the State Highway; thence running south 30° 57′ 51″ west by the State Highway; nine hundred ninety and forty-six one hundredths (990.46) feet to a stone monument; thence running southwesterly, westerly and northwesterly by a curved line at the junction of the State Highway and Boardman Street having a radius of forty (40) feet seventy-two and twenty-three one hundredths (72.23) feet to a stone monument at the point of beginning.

Parcel "G". Commencing in the southwesterly side of Boardman Street at the easterly side of the location of the Boston and Maine Railroad, thence running south 45° 34′ 30″ east three hundred thirty and seventy-two one hundredths (330.72) feet to a stone monument; thence running southeasterly by a curved line having a radius of seventy-four and two one hundredths (74.02) feet, still by said Boardman Street, seven and sixty-eight one hundredths (7.68) feet to land now or formerly of Vecchio; thence running south 45° 18′ 30″ west by land now or formerly of Vecchio ninety-eight and sixteen one hundredths (98.16) feet; thence running north 45° 34′ 30″ west by land now or formerly of the Boston Port Development Company three hundred fourteen and thirty-two one hundredths (314.32) feet to the location of the Boston and Maine Railroad; thence running north 31° 32′ east by the location of the Boston and Maine Railroad one hundred one and eleven one hundredths (101.11) feet to the point of beginning.

Parcel "I". Beginning at the westerly side of Boardman Street at a stone monument at the point of curve of the State Highway line; thence running south 27° 17′ 9″ east by said Boardman Street 49.31 feet; thence running south 32° 12′ 16″ east 56.79 feet; thence running south 62° 42′ 51″ west 104.85 feet; thence north 27° 17′ 9″ west 115.81 feet to a point in the easterly boundary line of the State Highway; thence north 30° 57′ 51″ east 45.81 feet to a stone monument; thence running northeasterly, easterly, and southeasterly by a curved line to the junction of the State Highway and Boardman Street, having a radius of 40 feet, 85 feet to a stone monument at Boardman Street, at the point of beginning.

Parcel "J". Beginning at the southerly side of Marginal Street at a point about opposite the easterly line of Jeffries Street at land now or formerly of the Union Welting Company, thence running south 71° 56′ 20″ east by Marginal Street two hundred and twenty-two one hundredths (200.22) feet; thence running south 4° 01′ 31″ west by land and flats now or formerly of the International Glue Company about three hundred forty-four and eleven hundredths (344.11) feet to the original low water line in Boston Harbor; thence running westerly by the original low water line in Boston Harbor about two hundred twenty-five (225) feet; thence running north 4° 01′ 31″ east about four hundred seventy-nine and ninety-nine one hundredths (479.99) feet to Marginal Street to the point of beginning, said parcel of land extending from Marginal Street to low water line in Boston Harbor and including all the appurtenant riparian rights.

Parcel "K". That portion of Boardman Street lying west of the west line of the State of Massachusetts Highway known as McClellan Highway and east of the east line of the Boston and Maine Railroad Company right of way.

4. All that certain piece or parcel of land situated in the town of Hingham, County of Plymouth, Commonwealth of Massachusetts being more particularly shown and described on the plan or plans to be filed with the Secretary of State as hereinafter provided and being the same premises acquired by the United States under the authority of the Act of Congress approved August 6, 1942 (Public Law 700, 77th Congress) for use in connection with the Naval Ammunition Depot at Hingham, Massachusetts, in fee simple by declaration of taking filed December 30, 1942 in the United States District Court for the District of Massachusetts in the case of the United States of America v. 9.85 acres of land more or less in Hingham, Plymouth County, Commonwealth of Massachusetts, Carrie A. Litchfield, et al., Misc. Civil No. 6616 and bounded and described as follows:

Beginning at a stone bound on the westerly side of Fort Hill Street, a corner of land of the United States Naval Ammunition Depot, Hingham, Massachusetts, thence along said westerly side of Fort Hill Street, S. 8° 44′ 20″ W., 221.56 feet to a stone bound; thence S. 4° 17′ 40″ W., 46.73 feet to a stone bound; thence S. 2° 31′ 20″ E., 33.19 feet to a stone bound; thence S. 4° 54′ 20″ W., 33.69 feet to a corner of land of Henry B. Backenstoss and Violet Pendleton; thence with the northerly line of said lands N. 86° 40′ 00″ W., 95 feet to a corner; thence with the westerly line of said lands S. 3° 56′ 15″ W., 105.70 feet to a corner; thence S. 13° 25′ 40″ W., 20 feet to a point, thence S. 70° 02′ 30″ E., 97.39 feet to a point on the westerly line of Fort Hill Street; thence with said westerly line of Fort Hill Street S. 13° 25′ 40″ W., 88.63 feet to a stone bound; thence southwesterly following the arc of a curve with a radius of 118.50 feet, a distance of 67.60 feet to a stone bound; thence S. 46° 06′ 40″ W., 81.63 feet to a stone bound; thence S. 49° 05′ 20″ W., 118.42 feet to a stone bound on the northerly line of the land of Ethel MacKiernan; thence along said line N. 67° 25′ 40″ W., 75.14 feet to a point; thence N. 81° 59′ 40″ W., 99.30 feet to a point; thence N. 88° 47′ 10″ W., 55.56 feet to a point; thence S. 76° 47′ 40″ W., with the North line of the lands of said Ethel MacKiernan and the lands of Mary G. and Francis J. Murray, 212.37 feet to a point on the boundary of the United States Naval Ammunition Depot, Hingham, Massachusetts; thence along the land of the United States Naval Ammunition Depot, N. 2° 52′ 25″ E., 744.97 feet to a stone bound, a corner of land of the United States Naval Ammunition Depot, Hingham, Massachusetts; thence N. 87° 47′ 22″ E. 222.30 feet to a point; thence S. 85° 56′ 05″ E., 70 feet to a point; thence S. 85° 23′ 56″ E., 32.32 feet to a point; thence N. 85° 54′ 54″ E., 157.08 feet to a point; thence N. 86° 17′ 58″ E., 168.42 feet to a stone bound, the first mentioned point and place of beginning; containing 9.85 acres, more or less.

5. All those certain three pieces or parcels of land situated in the town of Hingham, Plymouth County, Massachusetts, being more particularly shown and described on the plan to be filed with the Secretary of State as hereinafter provided and being the same premises acquired by the United States under authority of the Acts of Congress approved July 14, 1941 (Public Law 174, 77th Congress) and July 3, 1941 (Public Law 150, 77th Congress) for use in connection with the Naval Ammunition Depot at Hingham, Massachusetts, in fee simple by a declaration of taking filed February 3, 1942 in the United States District Court for the District of Massachusetts in the case of the United States of America v. 29.71 acres of land more or less in Hingham, Plymouth County, Massachusetts and Mary Lee Lincoln, et al., Misc. Civil No. 6478 and bounded and described as follows:

Parcel No. 1. Beginning at a point on the South side of Beal Street approximately 290 feet East of the centerline intersection of Beal Street and Lincoln Street, in the Town of Hingham; thence running North 81° 21′ 00″ East along Beal Street, a distance of 4.52 feet to the beginning of a curve of 400.10 feet radius; thence by said curve in a Southeasterly direction a distance of 271.15 feet; thence South 59° 49′ 11″ East a distance of 350.36; thence by land formerly of Seth Sprague and Robert H. Birchmore in a Southwesterly direction 339.50 feet; thence by land formerly of Seth Sprague and Robert H. Birchmore in a Northwesterly direction a distance of 52.69 feet; thence by land formerly of the Town of Hingham, North 60° 40′ 07″ West a distance of 478.58 feet; thence by land formerly of the Town of Hingham North 16° 37′ 03″ East a distance of 261.45 feet to the point of beginning; containing 4.35 acres of land, more or less.

Parcel No. 2. Beginning at a point on the Southwest side of Beal Street approximately 915 feet East of the centerline intersection of Beal Street and Lincoln Street in the Town of Hingham; thence along said Beal Street South 59° 52′ 34″ East a distance of 194.97 feet; thence South 58° 18′ 11″ East a distance of 6.15 feet; thence South 59° 11′ 12″ East a distance of 62.70 feet; thence South 59° 50′ 03″ East a distance of 146.47; thence South 60° 10′ 52″ East a distance of 89.86 feet; thence South 60° 02′ 26″ East a distance of 97.10 feet; thence in a Southeasterly direction by land formerly of the Town of Hingham a distance of 325.51 feet; thence in a Northwesterly direction by land formerly of Town of Hingham a distance of 351.15; thence in a Southwesterly direction by land formerly of the Town of Hingham a distance of 391.94 feet; thence in a Northwesterly direction by land formerly of Town of Hingham a distance of 324.91 feet; thence in a Northeasterly direction by land formerly of Town of Hingham a distance of 437.06 feet; thence in a Southeasterly direction by land formerly of Mary Lee Lincoln a distance of 52.69 feet; thence in a Northeasterly direction by land formerly of Mary Lee Lincoln a distance of 339.50 feet to the point of beginning; containing 7.77 acres of land, more or less.

Parcel No. 3. Beginning at a stone monument on the South side of Beal Street approximately 120 feet East of the centerline intersection of Beal Street and Lincoln Street, in the Town of Hingham; thence running North 81° 21′ 00″ East along Beal Street; a distance of 169.50 feet; thence by land formerly of Mary Lee Lincoln South 16° 37′ 03″ West a distance of 261.45 feet; thence by land formerly of Mary Lee Lincoln South 60° 40′ 07″ East a distance of 478.58 feet; thence by land formerly of Seth Sprague and Robert H. Birchmore in a Southwesterly direction 437.06 feet; thence by land formerly of Seth Sprague and Robert H. Birchmore in a Southeasterly direction 324.91 feet; thence by land formerly of Seth Sprague and Robert H. Birchmore in a Northeasterly direction a distance of 391.94 feet; thence by land formerly of Seth Sprague and Robert H. Birchmore in a Southeasterly direction a distance of 351.15 feet; thence by land formerly of Seth Sprague and Robert H. Birchmore in a Northeasterly direction a distance of 325.51 feet to a point on the Southwesterly side of Beal Street; thence by said Beal Street South 59° 52′ 50″ East a distance of 217.36 feet to a stone monument; thence from here on by land of the United States of America South 13° 32′ 17″ West a distance of 172.46 feet; thence South 13° 33′ 35″ West a distance of 170.27 feet; thence South 19° 37′ 26″ West a distance of 146.14 feet; thence South 20° 24′ 35″ West a distance of 240.01 feet; thence South 32° 07′ 12″ West a distance of 297.93 feet; thence South 32° 25′ 56″ West a distance of 214.54 feet; thence North 32° 18′ 58″ West a distance of 777.57 feet to a stone monument; thence North 49° 13′ 14″ West a distance of 364.33 feet; thence North 28° 39′ 36″ West a distance of 202.10 feet; thence North 28° 12′ 41″ East a distance of 122.35; thence North 60° 55′ West a distance of 321.72 feet to a stone monument; thence North 8° 11′ 00″ East a distance of 405.44 feet to a stone monument at the point of beginning; containing 17.59 acres of land, more or less.

SECTION 2. Jurisdiction over the above described lands is hereby granted and ceded to the United States of America, but upon the express condition that the commonwealth shall retain concurrent jurisdiction with the United States of America in and over said lands, in so far that all civil processes, and such criminal processes as may issue under the authority of the commonwealth against any person or persons charged with crimes committed without said lands and all processes for collection of taxes levied under authority of the laws of the commonwealth, including the service of warrants, may be executed thereon in the same manner as though this cession had not been granted; provided, that the jurisdiction in and over the lands above described shall revert to and revest in the commonwealth whenever such areas shall cease to be used for the purposes set forth in section one; and provided, further, that any jurisdiction over public rights in navigable waters is expressly excluded from this grant and chapter ninety-one of the General Laws, Tercentenary Edition, shall apply to any encroachment, filling or structure placed in the tide waters of the commonwealth.

SECTION 3. This act shall take full effect as to each piece or parcel of land acquired under authority of section one upon the depositing in the office of the state secretary before December thirty-first, nineteen hundred and forty-four, of a suitable plan of said parcel but not otherwise.

Approved June 9, 1943.

AN ACT RELATIVE TO LIENS FOR REAL ESTATE TAXES AND ASSESSMENTS. *Chap.*478

Be it enacted, etc., as follows:

G. L. (Ter. Ed.), 60, § 37, etc., amended.

SECTION 1. Chapter sixty of the General Laws is hereby amended by striking out section thirty-seven, as most recently amended by section one of chapter eighty-four of the acts of nineteen hundred and forty-one, and inserting in place thereof the following section: — *Section 37.* Taxes assessed upon land, including those assessed under sections twelve, thirteen and fourteen of chapter fifty-nine, shall with all incidental charges and fees be a lien thereon from January first in the year of assessment. Except as provided in section sixty-one, such lien shall terminate at the expiration of two years from October first in said year, if in the meantime the estate has been alienated and the instrument alienating the same has been recorded, otherwise it shall continue until a recorded alienation thereof; but if while such lien is in force a tax sale or taking has been made, and the deed or instrument of taking has been duly recorded within sixty days, but the sale or taking is invalid by reason of any error or irregularity in the proceedings subsequent to the assessment, the lien and also the lien or liens for any subsequent taxes or charges which have been added to the tax title account under authority of section sixty-one shall continue for ninety days after a surrender and discharge under section forty-six or a release, notice or disclaimer under sections eighty-two to eighty-four, inclusive, has been duly recorded, or for ninety days after the sale or taking has been finally adjudged invalid by a court of competent jurisdiction. If at any time while a lien established by this section is in force, a sale or taking cannot in the opinion of the collector be legally made because of any federal or state law or because of any injunction or other action of, or proceeding in, any federal or

Tax lien on real estate, levy by sale, validity of title.

state court or because of the action of any administrative body, the lien, if the statement provided for in section thirty-seven A is filed, shall continue as provided in said section thirty-seven A, subject, however, to any lawful action under any paramount authority conferred by the constitution or laws of the United States or the constitution of the commonwealth. Said taxes, if unpaid for fourteen days after demand therefor, may, with said charges and fees, be levied by sale or taking of the real estate, if the lien or liens thereon have not terminated. No tax title and no item included in a tax title account shall be held to be invalid by reason of any error or irregularity which is neither substantial nor misleading, whether such error or irregularity occurs in the proceedings of the collector or the assessors or in the proceedings of any other official or officials charged with duties in connection with the establishment of such tax title or the inclusion of such item in the tax title account.

G. L. (Ter. Ed.), 60, new § 37A, added.

Procedure when sale or taking cannot be effected.

SECTION 2. Said chapter sixty is hereby further amended by inserting after section thirty-seven, as amended, the following section: — *Section 37A.* If at any time while a lien established by section thirty-seven of this chapter or under chapter eighty or chapter eighty-three is in force, a sale or taking cannot in the opinion of the collector be legally made because of any federal or state law or because of any injunction or other action of, or proceeding in, any federal or state court or because of the action of any administrative body, the collector may file with the register of deeds for record or registration, as the case may be, a statement reciting that the statement is filed pursuant to this section to continue, until abatement or payment, the lien for a tax or assessment in an amount stated, which need not include accrued interest and costs, assessed for a year or on a date specified to a person or persons named upon an estate described. The statement shall also recite the reason why, in the opinion of the collector, a sale or taking cannot then be legally made; but any error or omission in the recitation of such reason shall not affect the validity of such statement. The register of deeds as such or as assistant recorder of the land court shall receive and record or register such statement upon the payment of a fee of one dollar which shall be paid by the town, but which shall not be added to or become part of the unpaid tax. The filing of such statement for record or registration shall operate to extend the time within which a sale or taking may lawfully be made by continuing until payment or abatement of the lien for such tax or assessment and all assessments or portions thereof, rates and charges of every nature which have been added to or become a part thereof; but the filing of such statement shall not discharge the collector from liability upon his bond for failure to collect such tax, assessment or portion thereof, rate or charge, and the collector shall proceed to sell or take the land within six months after he first gets notice that the disability has been removed. The collector at any time may, and upon the payment or abatement of the tax to which such statement relates shall, file a renunciation of all rights under such statement; and the provisions relative to the recordation of such statement shall apply to the recordation of such renunciation.

SECTION 3. Section twenty-three of said chapter sixty, as most recently amended by section one of chapter one hundred and ninety-seven of the acts of nineteen hundred and thirty-two, is hereby further amended by adding at the end the two following sentences: — A certificate issued on or after October first, nineteen hundred and forty-three, under this section may be filed for record or registration, as the case may be, within thirty days after its date, and if so filed shall operate to discharge the parcel of real estate specified from the liens for all taxes, assessments or portions thereof, rates and charges which do not appear by said certificate to constitute liens thereon, except the taxes, assessments or portions thereof, rates and charges which have accrued within the three years immediately preceding the date of the certificate, the taxes, assessments or portions thereof, rates and charges which are included in a tax title account, and the taxes, assessments or portions thereof, rates and charges concerning which a statement has been filed for record or registration under section thirty-seven A of this chapter or section forty-two B of chapter forty or any other provision of law; but a certificate issued under this section shall not affect the obligation of any person liable for the payment of any tax, assessment, rate or charge. The register of deeds as such or as assistant recorder of the land court shall receive and record or register such certificate upon the payment of a fee of one dollar.

G. L. (Ter. Ed.), 60, § 23, etc., amended.

Statement of liens, filing of.

SECTION 4. Chapter eighty of the General Laws is hereby amended by striking out section twelve, as most recently amended by section one of chapter two hundred and fifty-two of the acts of the current year, and inserting in place thereof the following section: — *Section 12.* Assessments made under this chapter shall constitute a lien upon the land assessed. The lien shall take effect upon the recording of the order stating that betterments are to be assessed for the improvement. Except as otherwise provided, such lien shall terminate at the expiration of two years from October first in the year in which the assessment is first placed on the annual tax bill under section thirteen or, if an assessment has been apportioned, from October first in the year in which the last portion is so placed upon the annual tax bill, whichever is later, if in the meantime in either case the estate has been alienated and the instrument alienating the same has been recorded. If there is no recorded alienation within such period, the lien shall continue until there is a recorded alienation. If the validity of an assessment made under this chapter is called in question in any legal proceeding to which the board which made the assessment or the body politic for the benefit of which it was made is a party, instituted prior to the expiration of the lien therefor, the lien shall continue

G. L. (Ter. Ed.), 80, § 12, etc., amended.

Betterment assessment as lien.

Effective date and duration.

until one year after the validity of the assessment is finally determined, even though an alienation be recorded in the meantime. If at any time while a lien established by this section is in force, a sale or taking cannot in the opinion of the collector be legally made because of any federal or state law or because of any injunction or other action of, or proceeding in, any federal or state court or because of the action of any administrative body, the lien shall, if the statement provided for in section thirty-seven A of chapter sixty is filed, continue as provided in said section thirty-seven A, subject, however, to any lawful action under any paramount authority conferred by the constitution or laws of the United States or the constitution of the commonwealth. If the time for payment of an assessment is extended under section thirteen A, the lien shall, if the statement provided for in section thirty-seven A of chapter sixty is filed, continue as provided in said section thirty-seven A.

Approved June 9, 1943.

---

*Chap.*479 AN ACT FURTHER REGULATING THE COMPENSATION OF MEMBERS OF THE STATE BALLOT LAW COMMISSION, AND THE EXPENDITURES THEREOF.

Be it enacted, etc., as follows:

G. L. (Ter. Ed.), 6, § 31, amended.

Chapter six of the General Laws is hereby amended by striking out section thirty-one, as appearing in the Tercentenary Edition, and inserting in place thereof the following section: — *Section 31.* The members of said commission shall each be paid such compensation for their services, not exceeding seven hundred and fifty dollars annually, as the governor and council may determine; and shall be allowed for expenses such sum, not exceeding one thousand dollars, as may be determined by the governor and council.

Compensation, state ballot law commission.

Approved June 9, 1943.

---

*Chap.*480 AN ACT EXEMPTING THE CHARITABLE TRUST KNOWN AS EDWARDS SCHOLARSHIP FUND FROM TAXATION UNDER THE PROVISIONS OF CHAPTER FIFTY-NINE AND CHAPTER SIXTY-TWO OF THE GENERAL LAWS.

Be it enacted, etc., as follows:

SECTION 1. The property and the income of Edwards Scholarship Fund, a charitable trust created under clause twenty-seventh of the will of Grace M. Edwards, late of Boston in the commonwealth, for the purpose of educating deserving and ambitious young men and women domiciled in the city of Boston, without discrimination as to race, sex or creed, shall be exempt from taxation under the provisions of chapter fifty-nine and chapter sixty-two of the General Laws so long as such property and income are employed for the aforesaid purpose. The trustees of such fund shall annually not later than sixty days after the end of the fiscal year of said trust file with the commissioner of corporations and taxation a copy of the trustees' annual account filed with the probate court for such fiscal year and such additional information as the commissioner may require.

SECTION 2. This act shall take effect as of January first, nineteen hundred and forty-three, and shall apply to income received during the year nineteen hundred and forty-two, and thereafter. *Approved June 9, 1943.*

AN ACT ESTABLISHING MUNICIPAL LIABILITY FOR RELIEF OF NEEDY PERSONS IN CERTAIN CASES. *Chap.*481

Be it enacted, etc., as follows:

G. L. (Ter. Ed.), 117, § 24, etc., amended.

Section twenty-four of chapter one hundred and seventeen of the General Laws, as amended by chapter one hundred and sixty-four of the acts of nineteen hundred and thirty-five, is hereby further amended by adding at the end the following sentence: — In case such relief is furnished to a person in a hospital, the town shall be liable for his support therein in a sum not exceeding the maximum amount then allowable to a town under section eighteen of chapter one hundred and twenty-two as reimbursement from the commonwealth for like support in a hospital. *Approved June 9, 1943.*

Liability of town for hospital care of needy.

AN ACT FURTHER EXTENDING TEMPORARY SURTAXES ON CERTAIN SUBJECTS OF EXISTING TAXATION. *Chap.*482

Be it enacted, etc., as follows:

SECTION 1. There is hereby imposed, in addition to the taxes levied under the provisions of chapter sixty-two of the General Laws, and all acts in amendment thereof and in addition thereto, taxes levied under the provisions of section nine of chapter three hundred and seven of the acts of nineteen hundred and thirty-three, as amended, and taxes levied under the provisions of sections thirty to sixty, inclusive, of chapter sixty-three of the General Laws, and all acts in amendment thereof and in addition thereto, an additional tax equal to ten per cent of the taxes assessed under the provisions of said sections, acts and chapters in or on account of each of the calendar years nineteen hundred and forty-four and nineteen hundred and forty-five, and nineteen hundred and forty-six, and all provisions of law relative to the assessment, payment, collection and abatement of the said taxes shall apply to the taxes imposed by this section.

A fiduciary shall be liable to pay a tax under this section upon income received and distributed by him prior to the effective date thereof only to the extent that such fiduciary shall, after said effective date, hold as such fiduciary funds of an estate or trust due to the beneficiary to whom said income was distributed.

SECTION 2. All property subject to a legacy and succession tax under the provisions of chapter sixty-five of the

General Laws, and of any further amendments thereof or additions thereto, shall be subject to an additional tax of ten per cent of all taxes imposed by said provisions with respect to property or interests therein passing or accruing upon the death of persons who die during the period beginning July first, nineteen hundred and forty-three, and ending June thirtieth, nineteen hundred and forty-six. All provisions of law relative to the determination, certification, payment, collection and abatement of such legacy and succession taxes shall apply to the additional tax imposed by this section.

SECTION 3. Surtaxes imposed hereby shall be in addition to surtaxes imposed by sections nine and nine A of chapter seven hundred and twenty-nine of the acts of nineteen hundred and forty-one. In the computation of surtaxes imposed hereby, the amount of surtaxes imposed by said sections shall be excluded.

SECTION 4. All taxes provided by this act shall be retained by the commonwealth. *Approved June 9, 1943.*

---

*Chap.*483 AN ACT RELATIVE TO THE DELIVERY TO VOTERS OF CIRCULARS AND OTHER PRINTED MATTER INTENDED TO INFLUENCE THEIR ACTION.

Be it enacted, etc., as follows:

G. L. (Ter. Ed.), 55, new § 34B, added.

Interference with distribution of circulars, etc., forbidden.

SECTION 1. Chapter fifty-five of the General Laws is hereby amended by inserting after section thirty-four A, as appearing in the Tercentenary Edition, the following section: — *Section 34B.* No person shall prevent, hinder or interfere with the lawful distribution of any circular, poster, card, handbill, placard, picture or other printed matter intended to influence the action of a voter, and no person shall, wilfully and with intent to injure the person in whose behalf such printed matter was distributed, remove such matter from any residential premises to which it was delivered.

G. L. (Ter. Ed.), 55, § 36, amended.

SECTION 2. Section thirty-six of said chapter fifty-five, as so appearing, is hereby amended by inserting after the paragraph contained in the tenth line the following paragraph: —

Corrupt practice.

Violation of any provision of section thirty-four B.

G. L. (Ter. Ed.), 56, new § 65A, added.

Penalty.

SECTION 3. Chapter fifty-six of the General Laws is hereby amended by inserting after section sixty-five, as so appearing, the following section: — *Section 65A.* Violation of section thirty-four B of chapter fifty-five shall be punished by a fine of not more than one hundred dollars.

Approved June 9, 1943.

AN ACT TO PROVIDE FOR FURNISHING WITHOUT CHARGE COPIES OF RECORDS RELATING TO CERTAIN SOLDIERS, SAILORS AND MARINES. *Chap.*484

Be it enacted, etc., as follows:

Chapter two hundred and sixty-two of the General Laws is hereby amended by striking out section forty-six A, inserted by chapter two hundred and thirty-two of the acts of nineteen hundred and thirty-eight, and inserting in place thereof the following section: — *Section 46A.* No fee for a copy of any record relating to the birth, death, marriage, adoption or change of name of any soldier, sailor or marine who served in the army, navy or marine corps of the United States in time of war or insurrection and received an honorable discharge therefrom or release from active duty therein, or who during a war or insurrection is serving therein or died while serving therein, shall be demanded or received by any officer of the commonwealth or of any county, city or town, who has charge of such record, from any such soldier, sailor or marine, or from his widow, dependents or legal representatives; provided, that such copy is for use in relation to a claim against the United States.

G. L. (Ter. Ed.), 262, § 46A, etc., amended.

Certain records to be furnished without fee.

The word "soldier", "sailor" or "marine", as used in this section, shall include a man or a woman.

Approved June 9, 1943.

AN ACT RELATIVE TO THE LIABILITY OF PERSONS PARTICIPATING IN THE USE OF MOTOR VEHICLES UNDER CAR OR RIDE SHARING PLANS, SO CALLED. *Chap.*485

Whereas, Because of the existing state of war and the shortage of rubber and gasoline it is necessary that owners and operators of motor vehicles share the use of such vehicles with other persons, and

Emergency preamble.

Whereas, The civil liability of such persons may be seriously affected thereby, and

Whereas, It is necessary for the successful prosecution of the war effort that persons engaged in such car or ride sharing plans shall have immediate protection of their civil rights and that their civil liabilities shall not be increased, therefore it is hereby declared to be an emergency law, necessary for the preservation of the public safety and convenience.

Be it enacted, etc, as follows:

SECTION 1. No occupant of a motor vehicle, as such term is defined in section one of chapter ninety of the General Laws, who shares the use of such vehicle with the owner or operator thereof under a car or ride sharing plan, so called, whether for compensation or otherwise, shall, by reason of participating in such plan, be deemed to be engaged in a joint enterprise with such owner or operator.

SECTION 2. This act shall cease to be operative upon the termination of the existing states of war between the United States and certain foreign countries.

Approved June 9, 1943.

Chap.486 AN ACT AUTHORIZING THE CITY OF HOLYOKE TO APPROPRIATE MONEY FOR THE PAYMENT OF, AND TO PAY, CERTAIN UNPAID BILLS.

Be it enacted, etc., as follows:

SECTION 1. The city of Holyoke is hereby authorized to appropriate money for the payment of, and after such appropriation the treasurer of said city is hereby authorized to pay, an unpaid bill, amounting to two thousand, five hundred and ninety-seven dollars and ninety-seven cents of the city of Holyoke gas and electric department for a balance due for the cost of street lighting in said city during the year nineteen hundred and forty-two, and an unpaid bill amounting to two hundred and sixty-nine dollars and sixty-five cents, of Reardon's garage, for repairs to the automobile known as the police cruiser during the year nineteen hundred and forty-two, both as set forth in a list on file in the office of the director of accounts in the department of corporations and taxation, said bills being legally unenforceable against said city, either by reason of their being incurred in excess of available appropriations or by reason of the failure of said city to comply with the provisions of its charter, said bills having been certified for payment by the heads of the departments wherein the bills were contracted; provided, that the money so appropriated to pay such bills shall be raised by taxation in said city in the current year.

SECTION 2. No bill shall be approved by the city auditor of said city for payment or paid by the treasurer thereof under authority of this act unless and until certificates have been signed and filed with said city auditor, stating under the penalties of perjury that the goods, materials or services for which bills have been submitted were ordered by an official or an employee of said city, and that such goods and materials were delivered and actually received by said city or that such services were rendered to said city, or both.

SECTION 3. Any person who knowingly files a certificate required by section two which is false and who thereby receives payment for goods, materials or services which were not received by or rendered to said city shall be punished by imprisonment for not more than one year or by a fine of not more than three hundred dollars, or both.

SECTION 4. This act shall take effect upon its passage.

Approved June 9, 1943.

AN ACT CHANGING THE MEMBERSHIP OF THE COMMISSION ON WAYS AND DRAINAGE IN THE CITY OF LYNN. *Chap.*487

Be it enacted, etc., as follows:

SECTION 1. Section twenty-two of chapter three hundred and forty of the Special Acts of nineteen hundred and seventeen, as amended, is hereby further amended by striking out the first sentence and inserting in place thereof the following sentence: — The mayor, city engineer, superintendent of streets, commissioner of water supply, superintendent of sewers, and the four members of the city council who are elected at large, shall constitute a commission on ways and drainage, of which the mayor shall be chairman.

SECTION 2. This act shall be submitted for acceptance to the registered voters of the city of Lynn at the biennial municipal election to be held in said city in the current year in the form of the following question which shall be placed on the official ballot to be used in said city at said election: "Shall an act of the General Court passed in the current year, entitled 'An Act changing the membership of the commission on ways and drainage in the city of Lynn', be accepted?" If a majority of the votes in answer to said question is in the affirmative, this act shall thereupon take full effect, but not otherwise. *Approved June 9, 1943.*

AN ACT RELATIVE TO THE DEFENCE OF RELATIONSHIP IN PROSECUTIONS FOR BEING AN ACCESSORY AFTER THE FACT. *Chap.*488

Be it enacted, etc., as follows:

G. L. (Ter. Ed.), 274, § 4, amended

SECTION 1. Chapter two hundred and seventy-four of the General Laws is hereby amended by striking out section four, as appearing in the Tercentenary Edition, and inserting in place thereof the following: — *Section 4.* Whoever, after the commission of a felony, harbors, conceals, maintains or assists the principal felon or accessory before the fact, or gives such offender any other aid, knowing that he has committed a felony or has been accessory thereto before the fact, with intent that he shall avoid or escape detention, arrest, trial or punishment, shall be an accessory after the fact, and, except as otherwise provided, be punished by imprisonment in the state prison for not more than seven years or in jail for not more than two and one half years or by a fine of not more than one thousand dollars. The fact that the defendant is the husband or wife, or by consanguinity, affinity or adoption, the parent or grandparent, child or grandchild, brother or sister of the offender, shall be a defence to a prosecution under this section. If such a defendant testifies solely as to the existence of such relationship, he shall not be subject to cross examination on any other subject matter, nor shall his

Accessory after the fact.

criminal record, if any, except for perjury or subornation of perjury, be admissible to impeach his credibility.

G. L. (Ter. Ed.), 277, § 79, form of pleading, amended.

SECTION 2. The paragraph entitled "Accessory after the fact" in the schedule of forms of pleadings at the end of chapter two hundred and seventy-seven of the General Laws, as appearing in the Tercentenary Edition, is hereby amended by striking out all after the word "punishment" in the fifth line.

Effective date.

SECTION 3. This act shall take effect on October first in the current year. *Approved June 9, 1943.*

---

*Chap.*489 AN ACT MAKING CERTAIN CHANGES IN THE OLD AGE ASSISTANCE LAW, SO CALLED.

Be it enacted, etc., as follows:

G. L. (Ter. Ed.), 118A, § 1, etc., amended.

SECTION 1. Chapter one hundred and eighteen A of the General Laws is hereby amended by striking out section one, as most recently amended by section one of chapter seven hundred and twenty-nine of the acts of nineteen hundred and forty-one, and inserting in place thereof the following section: — *Section 1.* Adequate assistance to deserving citizens in need of relief and support sixty-five years of age or over who shall have resided in the commonwealth not less than three years during the nine years immediately preceding the date of application for such assistance and who shall have resided in the commonwealth continuously for one year immediately preceding said date of application shall be granted under the supervision of the department of public welfare, in this chapter called the department. Financial assistance granted hereunder shall be given from the date of application therefor, but in no event before the applicant reaches the age of sixty-five, and in determining the amount of assistance to be given for any period preceding the date on which the application was favorably passed upon, consideration shall be given to the amount of welfare relief, if any, given to such applicant during said period under any other provision of law. Such assistance shall, wherever practicable, be given to the aged person in his own home or in lodgings or in a boarding home, which for the purposes hereof shall include any institution providing shelter, care and treatment for aged persons which is not supported in whole or in part by public funds; provided, that no inmate of such a boarding home or institution shall be eligible for assistance under this chapter while being cared for under a contract; and provided, further, that for the purposes of this chapter any person who, while such an inmate, has lost his settlement or who shall lose his settlement at the time of admission to such home or institution shall be deemed to have no settlement in the commonwealth. Such assistance shall be paid by check or in cash, which shall be delivered to the applicant at his residence, if he so requests, and shall

Old age assistance, qualifications for.

be paid semi-monthly unless the applicant prefers less frequent payments. Such assistance shall be on the basis of need, and the amount thereof shall be determined in accordance with budgetary standards established by the local board of public welfare. Budgetary standards shall be subject to the approval of the department, but, except as hereinafter provided, such assistance shall be at not less than the following rates: In the case of an individual living within a family group not less than thirty dollars monthly; in the case of an individual living outside a family group not less than forty dollars monthly; in the case of a husband and wife living together within a family group, both of whom are eligible for such assistance, not less than fifty dollars monthly for both; in the case of a husband and wife living together outside a family group, both of whom are so eligible, not less than sixty-five dollars monthly for both; in the case of a husband and wife living together within a family group, one of whom is eligible for assistance and the other not yet sixty-five but over sixty, and eligible for public welfare, not less than fifty dollars monthly for both, the difference between the amount paid to the eligible one and the amount which should be paid if both were eligible for old age assistance to come from public welfare funds; in the case of a husband and wife living together outside a family group, one of whom is eligible for assistance and the other not yet sixty-five but over sixty, and eligible for public welfare, not less than sixty-five dollars monthly for both, the difference between the amount paid to the eligible one and the amount which should be paid if both were eligible for old age assistance to come from public welfare funds; in the case of sisters or brothers or sisters and brothers living together within a family group, all of whom are so eligible, not less than fifty dollars monthly for two and not less than fifteen dollars monthly for each additional brother or sister so eligible; or in the case of sisters or brothers or sisters and brothers living together outside a family group, all of whom are so eligible, not less than sixty-five dollars monthly for two and not less than fifteen dollars monthly for each additional brother or sister so eligible. The determination as to what constitutes a family group under the provisions of this section shall be made in accordance with rules and regulations established by the department, authority to establish the same being hereby granted. In computing the aforesaid minima the local board of public welfare, or the department acting on cases appealed, as the case may be, shall, in accordance with rules and regulations made by the department, deduct therefrom the amount of income the person assisted or to be assisted may be receiving from any source whatsoever, and may so deduct therefrom such reasonable amount as may be deemed to represent the financial value of board, lodging or other assistance which is being furnished to such person from any source whatever, except where income is received from children living with the aged parent or parents in payment of board and lodging to the amount set forth in clause 6 of section two A.

G. L. (Ter. Ed.), 118A, § 2, etc., amended.

SECTION 2. Said chapter one hundred and eighteen A is hereby further amended by striking out section two, as most recently amended by section two of said chapter seven hundred and twenty-nine, and inserting in place thereof the following section: — *Section 2.* Each board of public welfare shall, for the purpose of granting adequate assistance and service to such aged persons, establish a division thereof to be designated as the bureau of old age assistance. Boards of public welfare and bureaus of old age assistance in performing the duties imposed upon them and in exercising the powers granted to them under this chapter shall be subject to the supervision of the department and shall comply with all rules and regulations adopted by the department pursuant to the provisions of this chapter, and no city or town shall receive reimbursement from the commonwealth under this chapter with respect to any case unless the department determines that the provisions of this chapter relative to the minima provided in section one have been complied with by such city or town with respect to such case. In addition, no city or town shall receive reimbursement from the commonwealth under this chapter, or be entitled to participate in money received from the federal government under the provisions of section seven unless the department has approved its current budgetary standards and determined that the rules and regulations of said department in connection therewith have been complied with. No printed or written words referring to boards or departments of public welfare shall appear on any envelope mailed or delivered to an applicant for, or recipient of, assistance under this chapter. Boards of public welfare and bureaus of old age assistance shall give to each aged person when his first application is acted upon, or when any subsequent revision is made, a copy of the appeal blank which shall set forth the method of appeal to the department. In addition, the department shall distribute to all aged recipients a pamphlet or pamphlets explaining this chapter. In determining the need for financial assistance, said bureaus shall give consideration to the resources of the aged person. Action under sections twenty to twenty-two, inclusive, of chapter two hundred and seventy-three shall be brought by a local board of public welfare in connection with the granting of assistance under this chapter only with the approval and upon the direction of the department. In any case where the department approves the bringing of such action it shall order that such action be commenced within a specified period of time thereafter and shall send a copy of such order, attested by its proper officer, to the local board by registered mail as soon as may be. If the local board neglects or refuses to bring such action within the time limited by such order the department shall thereupon bring such action in the name and on behalf of such local board, or may with-

Bureau of old age assistance.

hold from any city or town any reimbursement from the commonwealth under this chapter and any reimbursement from the federal government under the provisions of section seven unless the action has been commenced by said local board. Until the matter is completely adjudicated and the resource in question is actually available to the aged person or persons otherwise eligible, assistance to him or them shall not be refused or reduced by reason of such resource. Upon adjudication in favor of the local board, said board shall be reimbursed by the child or children for the assistance granted pending adjudication in such amount as the court may order. Not later than fourteen days from the initial payment to applicants, notice on a form prescribed by the department shall be forwarded to the department, stating in each case any and all deductions from the amounts of assistance prescribed herein and the reasons for all such deductions. If said deductions in a particular case are not approved by the department they shall not be made in subsequent payments in said case and the amount of deductions made in such initial payment shall be added to the amount of the next succeeding payment. Separate records of all such aged persons who are assisted shall be kept in the manner prescribed by section thirty-four of chapter forty-one and by section thirty-two of chapter one hundred and seventeen. The department shall make an annual report, and also such reports to the social security board established under the federal social security act, approved August fourteenth, nineteen hundred and thirty-five, as may be necessary to secure to the commonwealth the benefits of said act.

G. L. (Ter. Ed.), 118A, § 2A, etc., amended.

SECTION 3. Said chapter one hundred and eighteen A is hereby further amended by striking out section two A, inserted by section three of said chapter seven hundred and twenty-nine, and inserting in place thereof the following section: — *Section 2A.* In determining the resources of an aged person under section two the following schedule relative to the financial ability to support by a child of such person shall be followed: —

Determination of resources of aged person.

1. If such child is married and living with his or her spouse and one dependent son or daughter, but living apart from the aged person, such child shall not be required to contribute to the support of such aged person unless such child is in receipt of income in excess of twenty-three hundred dollars annually or in excess of the equivalent of twenty-three hundred dollars annually.

2. If such child is married and living with his or her spouse and two dependent sons or daughters, but living apart from the aged person, such child shall not be required to contribute to the support of such aged person unless such child is in receipt of income in excess of twenty-eight hundred and seventy-five dollars annually or in excess of the equivalent of twenty-eight hundred and seventy-five dollars annually.

3. If such child is married and living with his or her spouse and three dependent sons or daughters, but living

apart from the aged person, such child shall not be required to contribute to the support of such aged person unless such child is in receipt of income in excess of thirty-four hundred and fifty dollars annually or in excess of the equivalent of thirty-four hundred and fifty dollars annually.

4. If a child of such an aged person is in receipt of an annual income in excess of thirty-four hundred and fifty dollars, in money or its equivalent, whether or not such a child shall be required to contribute to the support of the aged person shall be determined in each instance upon the merits of that particular case.

5. No unmarried child of such an aged person, living apart from such aged person and in receipt of an annual income not in excess of one thousand one hundred and fifty dollars, in money or its equivalent, shall be required to contribute to the support of such aged person.

6. In the case of an employed single child living with his aged parent or parents, income up to fourteen dollars a week shall be considered exempt and available to said child for his personal needs and board and lodging. In no instance shall any part of said income be deducted by the local board of public welfare or the department acting on appeal as a resource of the parent or parents. Of the amounts of income in excess of fourteen dollars a week received by said child fifty per cent shall be considered as a resource of the parent or parents.

7. In any case any unusual circumstances within the immediate family shall be considered with a view to determining whether such circumstances justify an exemption from the general rule relative to persons coming within the above classes. *Approved June 9, 1943.*

---

*Chap.*490 AN ACT RELATIVE TO REIMBURSEMENT OF CITIES AND TOWNS IN CONNECTION WITH PAYMENTS MADE UNDER THE OLD AGE ASSISTANCE LAW.

Emergency preamble.

Whereas, The deferred operation of this act would prevent the immediate establishment of a method of state reimbursement of cities and towns for old age assistance, so called, which will be in conformity with established practice, therefore this act is hereby declared to be an emergency law, necessary for the immediate preservation of the public convenience.

Be it enacted, etc., as follows:

G. L. (Ter. Ed.), 118A, § 8, etc., amended.

Section eight of chapter one hundred and eighteen A of the General Laws, as most recently amended by section eight of chapter seven hundred and twenty-nine of the acts of nineteen hundred and forty-one, is hereby further amended by inserting after the third sentence the two following sentences: — The approval of accounts by the department under this chapter shall have the effect of a provisional pre-audit of such accounts, and reimbursements based thereon

Approval of accounts, effect of.

shall be subject to verification and adjustment by the department. Such adjustments shall be made by reducing or increasing any subsequent reimbursements under this chapter by the amount of such adjustment.

Approved June 9, 1943.

AN ACT RELATIVE TO REIMBURSEMENT OF CITIES AND TOWNS IN CONNECTION WITH PAYMENTS MADE UNDER THE AID TO DEPENDENT CHILDREN LAW. *Chap.*491

Whereas, The deferred operation of this act would prevent the immediate establishment of a method of state reimbursement of cities and towns for aid furnished to dependent children which will be in conformity with established practice, therefore this act is hereby declared to be an emergency law, necessary for the immediate preservation of the public convenience. Emergency preamble.

Be it enacted, etc., as follows:

Section six of chapter one hundred and eighteen of the General Laws, as most recently amended by chapter four hundred and five of the acts of nineteen hundred and forty-one, is hereby further amended by adding at the end the two following sentences: — The approval of accounts by the department under this chapter shall have the effect of a provisional pre-audit of such accounts, and reimbursements based thereon shall be subject to verification and adjustment by the department. Such adjustments shall be made by reducing or increasing any subsequent reimbursements under this chapter by the amount of such adjustment. G. L. (Ter. Ed.), 118, § 6, etc., amended. Approval of accounts, effect of.

Approved June 9, 1943.

AN ACT RELATIVE TO TRANSFERS OF CIVIL SERVICE EMPLOYEES DURING THE PRESENT EMERGENCY. *Chap.*492

Whereas, A marked reduction in the number of persons available for service in the administration of state and municipal affairs due to existing war conditions makes it necessary that this act take effect without delay, therefore it is hereby declared to be an emergency law, necessary for the immediate preservation of the public convenience. Emergency preamble.

Be it enacted, etc., as follows:

SECTION 1. Notwithstanding the provisions of chapter thirty-one of the General Laws, an employee in the classified civil service of the commonwealth may, upon the recommendation of the director of civil service and with the approval of the governor, temporarily be transferred from his office or employment to any other; provided, that no such transfer shall be made if the employee informs said director of civil service in writing that such transfer would require a change of the employee's domicile and that he objects thereto. Any employee so transferred shall retain rights acquired by him in the department from which he was transferred hereunder with respect to promotion, seniority and salary or other compensation. The position from which the employee was transferred shall not be filled.

SECTION 2. Any employee transferred under this act shall be returned to his original position at the termination of the present emergency or within six months thereafter and he shall be entitled to all rights and privileges of said chapter thirty-one and the rules and regulations made thereunder.

SECTION 2A. Persons shall be transferred from, and returned to, their positions under this act according to their seniority in the department, division of a department, district or institution so that the oldest employees in point of service shall be transferred last and returned to their original positions first.

SECTION 3. This act shall be operative during the existing states of war between the United States and certain foreign countries, and for a period of six months following the termination of all such existing states of war.

Approved June 9, 1943.

---

*Chap.*493 AN ACT PROVIDING FOR EXTENDED SCHOOL SERVICES FOR CHILDREN OF EMPLOYED MOTHERS.

Emergency preamble.

Whereas, The deferred operation of this act would tend in part to defeat its purpose, which is to provide immediate care for children of mothers employed in activities related to the prosecution of the war, therefore it is hereby declared to be an emergency law, necessary for the immediate preservation of the public convenience.

Be it enacted, etc., as follows:

SECTION 1. If the school committee of any city or town determines that sufficient need exists in such city or town for extended school services for children, between three and fourteen years of age, of employed mothers, said school committee may with the approval of the city council or selectmen establish and maintain such services.

SECTION 2. If said school committee, upon determination by it of sufficient need, votes that said services should be established by it in such city or town, said school committee shall submit in writing a plan of said services to the state department of education for its written approval; provided, that said extended school services proposed in said plan shall consist of such care as may be determined by standards established by said department and shall be operated by said school committee under the general supervision of said department; and provided, further, that said extended school services shall be available, when needed, to said children during the hours their mothers are employed, except that no child under eight shall be allowed to attend said extended school services before six o'clock in the morning or after seven o'clock in the evening; and provided, further, that said school committee shall establish as one of the rules of admission to the benefits of said extended school services that the parents of each such child shall pay toward the cost of said services such sum, not exceeding four dollars per week for each such child, as said school committee shall determine.

SECTION 3. The commonwealth and the school committee of any city or town are hereby authorized to accept funds from the federal government for the purposes of this act. The school committee of any city or town is hereby authorized to receive contributions in the form of money, material, quarters or services for the purposes of this act from organizations, employers and other individuals. Such contributions received in the form of money, together with fees from parents and any allotments received from the federal government for the purposes of this act, shall be deposited with the treasurer of such city or town and held as a separate account and expended by said school committee without appropriation, notwithstanding the provisions of section fifty-three of chapter forty-four of the General Laws.

If a city or town shall have a written contract with the federal government, whereby said government grants or offers such city or town a sum of money to be used with funds which may be provided in said city or town for the purposes of this act and said city or town shall be required primarily to pay that portion of the expense for which reimbursement is to be received from the grant, the treasurer of such city or town, with the approval of the mayor, or of the city manager, if any, or of the selectmen, as the case may be, in anticipation of the receipt of the proceeds of such grant, may incur debt, outside the debt limit, to an amount not exceeding the amount of the grant as shown by the agreement, and may issue notes therefor, payable in not exceeding one year from their dates. Any loan so issued for a shorter period than one year may be refunded by the issue of other notes maturing within the required period; provided, that the period from the date of issue of the original loan to the date of maturity of the refunding loan shall not be more than one year. The proceeds of the grant, so far as necessary, shall be applied to the discharge of the loan.

SECTION 4. The provisions of this act shall be in full force and effect relative to all such services which may have been established as a result of the receipt of federal funds directly by any city or town prior to the effective date of this act or as a result of application for such funds by cities and towns which are in process of completion on said effective date, as well as a result of such application submitted after said date.

SECTION 5. This act shall be in effect during the existing state of war between the United States and any foreign country and for six months after the termination thereof.

Approved June 10, 1943.

Chap.494 AN ACT RELATIVE TO THE MINIMUM SALARY RATE FOR PUBLIC SCHOOL TEACHERS IN DAY SCHOOLS.

Be it enacted, etc., as follows:

G. L. (Ter. Ed.), 71, § 40, etc., amended.

Section forty of chapter seventy-one of the General Laws, as amended by chapter five hundred and seven of the acts of nineteen hundred and forty-one, is hereby further amended by striking out, in the fourth and fifth lines, the words "eight hundred and fifty" and inserting in place thereof the words: — one thousand dollars in towns of less than two million five hundred thousand dollars valuation for the fiscal year preceding and in all other towns at a rate of not less than twelve hundred, — so as to read as follows: — *Section 40.* The compensation of every teacher employed in any public day school in the commonwealth, except persons in training and those employed as temporary substitutes, shall be at a rate of not less than one thousand dollars in towns of less than two million five hundred thousand dollars valuation for the fiscal year preceding and in all other towns at a rate of not less than twelve hundred dollars for the school year in that school.

Minimum compensation for teachers.

Approved June 10, 1943.

Chap.495 AN ACT FURTHER REGULATING THE POWERS AND DUTIES OF THE COMMISSIONER OF AGRICULTURE.

Be it enacted, etc., as follows:

G. L. (Ter. Ed.), 128, new § 8A, added.

Destruction and control of certain rodents.

Chapter one hundred and twenty-eight of the General Laws is hereby amended by inserting after section eight, as appearing in the Tercentenary Edition, the following section: — *Section 8A.* In order to protect the food supplies, agricultural produce, growing crops, live stock, manufactured goods and buildings, and to safeguard the public health, the commissioner may investigate the life and habits of, and may take necessary measures to destroy or to control, rats, mice, woodchucks, and such other rodents not protected by law, as may from time to time be determined by him to be detrimental to one or more of such purposes. In performing such duties he may, by himself or by his authorized agent, with the consent of the owner or tenant, enter upon private premises for any of such purposes at any reasonable time. In order to carry out this section, the commissioner may enter into co-operative arrangements with the United States or any agency thereof, with any department, board or commission of this commonwealth or any political subdivision thereof, or with any association, corporation or individual owning, occupying or possessing any property within the commonwealth. Section eighty-seven of chapter one hundred and thirty-one shall not apply to the destruction of rodents under this section.

Approved June 10, 1943.

AN ACT TEMPORARILY RESTORING CERTAIN MORTALITY TABLES AND RATES OF INTEREST FOR THE TEACHERS' RETIREMENT SYSTEM. *Chap.*496

Be it enacted, etc., as follows:

The mortality tables and the rates of interest used in connection therewith for the teachers' retirement system which were in effect immediately prior to July second, nineteen hundred and forty-two are hereby restored and shall remain in full force and effect until July first, nineteen hundred and forty-five; and the commissioner of insurance and the teachers' retirement board are hereby authorized and directed to use the tables and rates hereby restored in computing the retirement allowances of teachers to and including said July first, nineteen hundred and forty-five. Any teacher who has been retired under said retirement system since July first, nineteen hundred and forty-two and prior to the effective date of this act shall, beginning June first, nineteen hundred and forty-three, receive a retirement allowance equal to that which he would have received if said tables and rates as restored by this act had been in effect at the time of his retirement. *Approved June 10, 1943.*

THE COMMONWEALTH OF MASSACHUSETTS,
EXECUTIVE DEPARTMENT, STATE HOUSE,
BOSTON, June 30, 1943.

Honorable FREDERIC W. COOK, *Secretary of the Commonwealth, State House, Boston.*

SIR: — I, Leverett Saltonstall, by virtue of and in accordance with the provisions of the Forty-eighth Amendment to the Constitution, "The Referendum II, Emergency Measures", do declare that in my opinion, the immediate preservation of the public peace, health, safety or convenience requires that the law passed on the 10th day of June in the year nineteen hundred and forty-three entitled, "An Act Temporarily Restoring certain Mortality Tables and Rates of Interest for the Teachers' Retirement System" should take effect forthwith and that it is an emergency law and that the facts constituting the emergency are as follows:

Because the delayed operation will unnecessarily increase and make more difficult the problem of administration of the Act, and unduly delay payments to newly retired teachers and increased allowances to certain present retired teachers.

Very truly yours,
LEVERETT SALTONSTALL,
Governor of the Commonwealth.

OFFICE OF THE SECRETARY, BOSTON, July 1, 1943.

I hereby certify that the accompanying statement was filed in this office by His Excellency the Governor of the Commonwealth of Massachusetts at ten o'clock and eight minutes, A.M., on the above date, and in accordance with Article Forty-eight of the Amendments to the Constitution said chapter takes effect forthwith, being chapter four hundred and ninety-six of the acts of nineteen hundred and forty-three.

F. W. COOK,
Secretary of the Commonwealth.

---

*Chap.*497 AN ACT CONTINUING IN EFFECT THE EXISTING MORTALITY TABLES AND RATES OF INTEREST APPLICABLE TO CERTAIN RETIREMENT SYSTEMS OF THE COMMONWEALTH AND THE POLITICAL SUBDIVISIONS THEREOF.

Be it enacted, etc., as follows:

The mortality tables and the rates of interest used in connection therewith for the retirement systems of the commonwealth and the political subdivisions thereof, other than the teachers' retirement system, which were in effect on January first, nineteen hundred and forty-three, shall continue in full force and effect until June thirtieth, nineteen hundred and forty-five; and the commissioner of insurance and the retirement boards of said retirement systems are hereby authorized and directed to use the tables and rates hereby continued in effect in computing the retirement allowances of persons under said systems up to and including said June thirtieth, nineteen hundred and forty-five.

Approved June 10, 1943.

---

*Chap.*498 AN ACT RELATIVE TO THE PAYMENT OF ASSESSMENTS INTO THE TEACHERS' ANNUITY FUND AND TO CONTRIBUTIONS BY THE COMMONWEALTH TO SAID FUND.

Be it enacted, etc., as follows:

G. L. (Ter. Ed.), 32, § 9, etc., amended.

Paragraph (2) of section nine of chapter thirty-two of the General Laws, as most recently amended by section fourteen of chapter five hundred and eight of the acts of nineteen hundred and thirty-nine, is hereby further amended by striking out the sentence contained in the twenty-first to the twenty-fourth lines, as appearing in section one of chapter four hundred and thirty-eight of the acts of nineteen hundred and thirty-seven, — so as to read as follows: —

Annuity fund.

(2) The annuity fund shall consist of assessments paid by members and interest derived from investments of the annuity fund. Each member shall pay into the annuity fund, by deduction from his salary in the manner provided in section twelve (5), such assessments upon his salary as may be determined by the board. The rate of assessment shall be

established by the board on the first day of July of each year after a prior notice of at least three months, and shall at any given time be uniform for all members of the association, and shall not be less than three nor more than seven per cent of the member's salary; provided, that when the total sum of assessments on the salary of any member at the rate established by the board would amount to more than one hundred and thirty dollars or less than thirty-five dollars for a full school year, such member shall in lieu of assessments at the regular rate be assessed at the rate of one hundred and thirty dollars a year or thirty-five dollars a year, payable in equal instalments, to be assessed for the number of months during which the schools of the community in which such member is employed are commonly in session. A member, within thirty days prior to the date that his retirement takes effect under section ten, may pay in one sum into the annuity fund established by this paragraph any amount which he may elect, but not exceeding the amount which he may have to his credit at the time of his retirement, and the amount so contributed shall be considered as part of his regular assessments for all purposes except that it shall in no way affect the amount of his pension. The commonwealth shall in each odd-numbered year contribute such amount as is necessary to make good any deficiency in the annuity fund for active or retired members as of the preceding thirty-first day of December.

Approved June 10, 1943.

AN ACT AUTHORIZING CERTAIN PAYMENTS TO OFFICERS AND EMPLOYEES OF CERTAIN COUNTIES AND MUNICIPALITIES WHO RESIGN OR ARE GRANTED A LEAVE OF ABSENCE TO ENTER INTO THE ARMED FORCES OF THE UNITED STATES DURING THE PRESENT WAR. *Chap.*499

Be it enacted, etc., as follows:

Any person in the service of any county, city or town in which this section is accepted by the county commissioners, mayor and city council or selectmen, as the case may be, who resigns or is granted a leave of absence from said service to enter into the military or naval service of the United States during the present war between the United States and certain foreign countries, shall be paid an amount equal to the vacation pay which he would have received in the year of his entry into said military or naval service, if his said employment had not been interrupted by said service; and in such case the official head of the department, board or commission in which he was last employed shall enter such amount on the pay roll of such department, board or commission. *Approved June 10, 1943.*

Chap.500 AN ACT RELATIVE TO ADMISSIONS TO AND CHARGES FOR THE SUPPORT OF PATIENTS IN COUNTY TUBERCULOSIS HOSPITALS.

Be it enacted, etc., as follows:

G. L. (Ter. Ed.), 111, § 85, etc., amended.

SECTION 1. Chapter one hundred and eleven of the General Laws is hereby amended by striking out section eighty-five, as most recently amended by section one of chapter four hundred and fourteen of the acts of the current year, and inserting in place thereof the following section: — *Section 85.* The county shall provide for the maintenance, operation and repair of said hospital, which shall, for the purposes of this section and section eighty-five A, include the maintenance, operation and repair of any preventorium erected by said county in accordance with section eighty-five B and also the cost of its construction and original equipment except when the cost of its construction, original equipment, maintenance, operation or repair is provided under said section eighty-five B to be paid from appropriations, and shall for said purposes include the establishment and maintenance of out-patient departments and the furnishing of supplementary diagnostic service under section eighty-five C; provided, that the expenditure of money for the purposes of this section shall be limited to such amounts as may be authorized by the general court. Every town shall pay to the county the sum of ten dollars and fifty cents per week for each person admitted from such town to said hospital in accordance with section eighty-eight. The county commissioners shall annually in January apportion the balance of the cost of the maintenance, operation and repair of said hospital, including interest paid or due on temporary notes issued therefor, for the previous year to the towns situated in the district, so that sixty-five per cent of such balance shall be apportioned on the basis of valuation as used in assessing county taxes and thirty-five per cent thereof shall be apportioned to such towns only as have had patients in said hospital during said year and in such proportion as the number of patient days chargeable to any town bears to the total number of patient days of all patients in said hospital during said year; and shall issue their warrants against the towns for the amount for which they are severally assessed to pay for the maintenance, operation and repair of said hospital. The county may, thirty days after a written demand for payment, recover in contract against any town liable to pay any part of the cost of construction or of the maintenance, operation and repair of said hospital the amount for which it may be liable. County commissioners of counties whose patients are cared for by contract under section seventy-nine may raise and expend the sums necessary to carry out the provisions thereof, and may borrow the same on the credit of the county, and issue therefor notes of the county, payable, in not more than eighteen months from their respective dates of issue, from the

Apportionment of maintenance of hospitals and preventoria.

reimbursements received from said towns. They shall annually in January determine the total amount already expended by or due from the county under such contracts during the previous year, and shall apportion the same to and may collect the same from the several towns liable, in like manner as in counties having their own hospitals, and the same shall be applied to the payment of the temporary debt incurred by said counties.

SECTION 2. Said chapter one hundred and eleven is hereby further amended by striking out section eighty-eight, as appearing in the Tercentenary Edition, and inserting in place thereof the two following sections: — *Section 88.* Patients shall be admitted to said hospitals through application by the boards of health of the towns served by said hospitals, and all patients shall be admitted in the order of their application. Upon the request of any registered physician the board of health shall forward forthwith to the hospital an application for admission of any person found to be afflicted with pulmonary tuberculosis. Whenever accommodations are available, patients not residents of the hospital district may be admitted on terms approved by the trustees, but not at rates lower than the total approximate cost for patients resident within the district. Patients may be discharged only in accordance with rules and regulations established by the medical staff of the hospital and approved by the superintendent thereof.

G. L. (Ter Ed.), 111, § 88, amended.

Admission of patients. Payment by cities and towns, etc.

Section 88A. The charge for the support of a patient in any of said hospitals shall be paid by the town sending him to the hospital. If the patient has no known settlement in the commonwealth the charge shall be paid by it, upon the approval of the bills by the department of public welfare, in the manner provided by section one hundred and sixteen. Such charges may afterward be recovered by the town or by the state treasurer, as the case may be, from the patient, if he is able to pay, or from any person or kindred bound by law to maintain him, in the manner provided by section sixty-six for the recovery of unpaid charges for the support of inmates of the state sanatoria.

Liability for charges.

SECTION 3. This act shall take effect on January first, nineteen hundred and forty-four.

Effective date.

Approved June 10, 1943.

AN ACT AUTHORIZING THE TOWN OF HULL TO CONTRIBUTE TOWARD THE COST OF STEAMBOAT SERVICE BETWEEN SAID TOWN AND THE CITY OF BOSTON.

*Chap.*501

Be it enacted, etc., as follows:

SECTION 1. The town of Hull may, from time to time, for the purpose of avoiding a reduction or discontinuance of steamboat service between said town and the city of Boston, enter into an agreement with the Nantasket-Boston Steamboat Company, Inc., its successors or assigns, providing for the payment by said town of any part or all of any excess of the cost of the service on the line of said company operated between said town and said city above the amount of the receipts from said line arising from the rates and fares in effect thereon during the period covered in any such agreement, and providing that no dividend shall be paid by said steamship company unless and until it has reimbursed said town for all moneys paid by it to said company under authority of this act. The department of public utilities shall, upon application of said town, determine any question relating to the character or extent of service rendered or facilities furnished in pursuance of any such agreement, in the event of differences arising between said steamship company and said town in relation thereto. Said town may raise by taxation such amounts, not in excess of ten thousand dollars in any one year, as may be necessary to carry out the provisions of this act.

SECTION 2. This act shall take full effect upon its acceptance by vote of the inhabitants of said town at an annual or special town meeting, but no agreement made under authority of this act shall be effective after May first, nineteen hundred and forty-five. *Approved June 10, 1943.*

---

*Chap.*502 AN ACT RELATIVE TO THE COMPENSATION PAYABLE TO FORMER OFFICERS AND EMPLOYEES OF THE COMMONWEALTH OR OF ANY POLITICAL SUBDIVISION THEREOF TEMPORARILY RE-EMPLOYED DURING THE CONTINUANCE OF THE EXISTING STATE OF WAR BETWEEN THE UNITED STATES AND ANY FOREIGN COUNTRY.

Emergency preamble.

Whereas, The deferred operation of this act would tend to defeat its purpose, which is to regulate the salaries paid to former officers and employees of the commonwealth and its political subdivisions during the existing state of war, therefore it is hereby declared to be an emergency law, necessary for the immediate preservation of the public convenience.

Be it enacted, etc., as follows:

SECTION 1. Chapter sixteen of the acts of nineteen hundred and forty-two is hereby amended by striking out section one and inserting in place thereof the following section: — *Section 1.* Any former officer or employee of the commonwealth or of any political subdivision thereof who has been retired under any retirement or pension law, or who has been separated from the public service by reason of superannuation or disability without receiving a retirement allowance or pension, may be employed in the service of any department, board or commission of the commonwealth or of any political subdivision thereof. No such person shall be employed by any appointing officer of a county, city, town or district except with the written approval of the county commissioners, the mayor or, in the city of Cambridge, the city manager, the selectmen or the prudential committee or other governing body in districts, as the case may be; provided, that no such approval shall be necessary in the case of a person formerly employed by a school committee or board of trustees of a school conducted under sections one to thirty-seven, inclusive, of chapter seventy-four, and employed by a school committee or such a board of trustees under authority of this act. The written approval of the director of civil service shall also be required for each appointment to any position or employment subject to chapter thirty-one of the General Laws. Any person so employed shall receive full compensation for such service less any pension received by him under any contributory or non-contributory retirement or pension law; provided, that any such person employed by the city of Boston or by the county of Suffolk may be paid such compensation as may be determined by the department head with the written approval of the mayor of said city.

SECTION 2. This act shall take effect as of January thirty-first, nineteen hundred and forty-two.

Approved June 10, 1943.

AN ACT AUTHORIZING THE DEPARTMENT OF PUBLIC WORKS TO CONVEY TO THE CITY OF LOWELL CERTAIN INTERESTS IN LAND TAKEN BY EMINENT DOMAIN. *Chap.*503

Be it enacted, etc., as follows:

The department of public works, acting for and in behalf of the commonwealth, may, subject to the approval of the governor and council, convey to the city of Lowell any interest, less than fee, in lands taken from said city by the commonwealth, through the department of public works, acting under chapter seventy-nine of the General Laws, under two orders of taking dated June eighteenth, nineteen hundred and forty, and recorded in the Middlesex North District Registry of Deeds on June twenty-eighth, nineteen hundred and forty, in Book 947 at pages 213 and 219, and may abandon any such interest in the lands acquired as aforesaid; provided, that, in the opinion of said department, such interest is no longer needed for or inconsistent with the purposes for which the land was acquired.

Approved June 10, 1943.

AN ACT RELATIVE TO THE PAYMENT OF EXPENSES FOR THE SUPPORT OF CERTAIN NEGLECTED CHILDREN. *Chap.*504

Be it enacted, etc., as follows:

G. L. (Ter. Ed.), 119, new § 47A, added.

Chapter one hundred and nineteen of the General Laws is hereby amended by inserting after section forty-seven, as appearing in the Tercentenary Edition, the following section: — *Section 47A.* The court by which a child is committed to the department or placed in the care of a suitable

Support of certain neglected children.

person or charitable corporation under section forty-three, forty-four or forty-seven may make an order for the payment, by his parents, or by his guardian out of the ward's property, to the department or such person or charitable corporation at times to be stated in the order, of sums not exceeding the cost of his support; provided, that no order for the payment of money shall be entered until the person by whom payments are to be made shall have been summoned before the court and given an opportunity to be heard. The court may from time to time, upon petition by or notice to the person ordered to pay such sum of money, revise or alter such order or make a new order, as the circumstances may require. *Approved June 10, 1943.*

---

*Chap.*505 AN ACT RELATIVE TO THE CHARGE TO BE MADE FOR THE CARE OF INSANE PERSONS BOARDED OUT BY THE DEPARTMENT OF MENTAL HEALTH DURING THE PRESENT EMERGENCY.

Be it enacted, etc., as follows:

SECTION 1. Notwithstanding the provisions of section sixteen of chapter one hundred and twenty-three of the General Laws, the cost to the commonwealth of the board of patients supported at the public expense and placed at board by the department of mental health under the provisions of said section sixteen shall not exceed eight dollars a week for each patient.

SECTION 2. This act shall cease to be operative on July first, nineteen hundred and forty-five.

Approved June 10, 1943.

---

*Chap.*506 AN ACT RELATIVE TO THE PAYMENT OF EXPENSES FOR MEDICAL, HOSPITAL AND OTHER SERVICES RENDERED TO OLD AGE ASSISTANCE RECIPIENTS

Emergency preamble.

Whereas, The deferred operation of this act would result in delaying the proper payment of certain pending bills for services rendered under the old age assistance law, so called, therefore it is hereby declared to be an emergency law, necessary for the immediate preservation of the public convenience.

Be it enacted, etc., as follows:

G. L. (Ter. Ed.), 118A, § 1, etc., amended.

Section one of chapter one hundred and eighteen A of the General Laws, as most recently amended by section one of chapter four hundred and eighty-nine of the acts of the current year, is hereby further amended by inserting at the end the following paragraph: —

Expenses for medical, etc., services to certain aged persons.

Expenses for medical, hospital and other services rendered to an aged person which remain unpaid at the time of his commitment to an institution as an insane person, or expenses for similar services rendered to an aged person which remain unpaid at the time of his death, and also the expenses of his funeral, may be paid directly to the person furnishing such service. *Approved June 11, 1943.*

---

*Chap.*507

AN ACT AUTHORIZING THE TOWN OF SAUGUS TO ACQUIRE AND PRESERVE THE OLD IRON WORKS HOUSE, SO CALLED, LOCATED IN SAID TOWN, AND PROVIDING FOR THE FINANCING THEREOF BY SAID TOWN, THE COMMONWEALTH AND ASSOCIATIONS OR INDIVIDUALS.

Be it enacted, etc., as follows:

SECTION 1. The town of Saugus is hereby authorized to appropriate a sum of money, not exceeding four thousand dollars, for the purpose of acquiring by purchase the Old Iron Works House, so called, in said town to be preserved and maintained as a place of historic interest; provided, that there shall have been contributed and paid by associations or individuals into the town treasury of said town an equal sum for said purpose. For the purpose of providing co-operation by the commonwealth with said town for said purpose, there may be paid, subject to appropriation, from the state treasury to said town the sum of four thousand dollars which shall be added to the amount to be used by said town for said purpose. Said house shall be preserved and maintained as an ancient landmark, possessing historical and antiquarian interest, and shall not be used as a dwelling house or for any other purpose, except that it may be occupied by a caretaker and his assistants.

Upon the acquisition of said property, said town is hereby authorized to preserve and maintain the same, and for the purpose of defraying the expense thereof may appropriate and expend money from the general revenue of the town or from money donated for the purpose, or both.

SECTION 2. This act shall take effect upon its passage.

Approved June 11, 1943.

---

*Chap.*508

AN ACT FURTHER REGULATING THE MAINTENANCE AND OPERATION OF SLAUGHTER HOUSES, AND MAKING CERTAIN CHANGES IN THE LAWS RELATING TO THE SLAUGHTERING OF CERTAIN CALVES AND TO THE SALE OF THE VEAL THEREOF FOR FOOD.

Be it enacted, etc., as follows:

G. L. (Ter. Ed.), 94, § 124, amended.

SECTION 1. Chapter ninety-four of the General Laws is hereby amended by striking out section one hundred and twenty-four, as appearing in the Tercentenary Edition, and inserting in place thereof the following section: — *Section 124.* All slaughter houses shall be under the supervision of the department of public health and subject to inspection by district health officers in their respective districts. Said department of public health shall establish, and may from time to time amend, modify, repeal or suspend, rules and

Supervision of slaughter houses by department of public health.

regulations, including uniform minimum requirements, for the maintenance and operation of slaughter houses. If any slaughter house licensed under section one hundred and nineteen is deemed by the local board of public health or by the department of public health to be operated or maintained in an unsanitary manner, or in violation of any of said rules and regulations, or not properly constructed or equipped for said business of slaughtering, said board or said department shall close such slaughter house until such time as it has been put in proper condition, and said board or said department may also suspend the license if the required changes are not made within a reasonable time.

G. L. (Ter. Ed.), 94, § 138, amended.

SECTION 2. Section one hundred and thirty-eight of said chapter ninety-four, as so appearing, is hereby amended by striking out, in the seventh to the ninth lines, inclusive, the words "or the carcass, or any part or product thereof, of any calf weighing less than forty pounds when dressed, with head, feet, hide and entrails removed,", — so as to read as follows: — *Section 138.* Whoever sells, offers or exposes for sale or delivers or causes or authorizes to be sold, offered or exposed for sale or delivered for use as food the carcass, or any part or product thereof, of any animal which has come to its death in any manner or by any means other than by slaughter or killing while in a healthy condition, or which at the time of its death was unfit for use as food, by reason of disease, exhaustion, abuse, neglect or otherwise, shall be punished by a fine of not more than two hundred dollars or by imprisonment for not more than six months.

Sale, etc., of certain carcasses prohibited. Penalty.

G. L. (Ter. Ed.), 94, § 146, etc., amended.

SECTION 3. The first paragraph of section one hundred and forty-six of said chapter ninety-four, as amended by section six of chapter three hundred and forty of the acts of nineteen hundred and thirty-four, is hereby further amended by striking out, in the eighth line, the word "four" and inserting in place thereof the word: — two, — so as to read as follows: — Each local board of health by themselves, their officers or agents, may inspect the carcasses of all slaughtered animals and all meat, fish, vegetables, produce, fruit or provisions of any kind found in their town, and all veal found, offered or exposed for sale or kept with intent to sell therein, and for such purpose may enter any place where such carcasses or articles are stored, kept or exposed for sale. If, in its opinion, said veal is that of a calf less than two weeks old when killed, or if on inspection it is found that said carcasses or articles are tainted, diseased, corrupted, decayed, unwholesome or unfit for food from any cause, the said board shall seize and cause the same to be destroyed forthwith or disposed of otherwise than for food. All money received by said board for property disposed of as aforesaid, after deducting the expenses of said seizure and disposal, shall be paid to the owner of such property. If said board seizes or condemns any such carcass or meat because affected with a contagious disease, it shall immediately give notice to the director of livestock disease control stating the name of the

Inspection of food stuffs.

owner or person in whose possession it was found, the nature of the disease and the disposition made of said meat or carcass.

SECTION 4. Said chapter ninety-four is hereby further amended by striking out section one hundred and fifty-one, as appearing in the Tercentenary Edition, and inserting in place thereof the following section: — *Section 151.* Whoever kills or causes to be killed a calf when less than two weeks old, with intent to sell for food the veal thereof, or knowingly sells for food, offers or exposes for sale therefor, or has in his possession with intent to sell for food, the veal of a calf so killed shall be punished by a fine of not more than one hundred dollars or by imprisonment for not more than two months, or both.

G. L. (Ter. Ed.), 94, § 151, amended.

Sale, etc., of certain veal prohibited. Penalty.

SECTION 5. Clause Sixth of section one of chapter two hundred and seventy-six of the General Laws, as appearing in the Tercentenary Edition, is hereby amended by striking out, in the fourth line, the word "four" and inserting in place thereof the word: — two, — so as to read as follows: — Sixth, Diseased animals or carcasses thereof, or any tainted, diseased, corrupted, decayed or unwholesome meat, fish, vegetables, produce, fruit or provisions of any kind, or the meat of any calf killed when less than two weeks old or any product thereof, if kept or concealed with intent to kill, sell or offer the same for sale for food.

G. L. (Ter. Ed.), 276, § 1, amended.

Unwholesome meat or provisions.

Approved June 11, 1943.

Chap.509

AN ACT FURTHER PROVIDING FOR THE INVESTMENT OF CERTAIN FUNDS OF THE COMMONWEALTH IN UNITED STATES WAR BONDS.

Be it enacted, etc., as follows:

Chapter two hundred and thirteen of the acts of the current year is hereby amended by striking out section one and inserting in place thereof the following section: — *Section 1.* The state treasurer may invest in the current issue of United States war bonds, commonly called the Second War Loan Bonds, such amount of the cash in the treasury of the commonwealth, not exceeding six million dollars, as he may, with the approval of the governor, determine; and said state treasurer may also, during the continuance of the existing state of war between the United States and any foreign country, invest in any other United States war bonds such amount of the cash in said treasury as he may, with like approval determine. Bonds purchased under this section shall be held in a separate fund in his custody.

Approved June 11, 1943.

*Chap.*510 AN ACT TEMPORARILY PROVIDING FOR A THIRD ASSISTANT REGISTER OF PROBATE FOR THE COUNTY OF ESSEX.

Emergency preamble.

Whereas, The deferred operation of this act would tend to defeat its purpose, which is to make immediately available to the probate court for the county of Essex the services of a third assistant register, whose services are made necessary by reason of the restrictions upon travel caused by the shortage in gasoline; therefore it is hereby declared to be an emergency law necessary for the immediate preservation of the public convenience.

Be it enacted, etc., as follows:

The judges of probate for Essex county may appoint a third assistant register for said county, who shall be subject to the laws relative to assistant registers, except that, unless sooner removed by the judges, his term of office shall expire on June thirtieth, nineteen hundred and forty-five.

Approved June 11, 1943.

---

*Chap.*511 AN ACT RELATIVE TO INCOME TAX DEDUCTIONS FOR CERTAIN DEPENDENTS.

Be it enacted, etc., as follows:

G. L. (Ter. Ed.), 62, § 6, amended.

Section six of chapter sixty-two of the General Laws is hereby amended by striking out clause (*h*), as appearing in the Tercentenary Edition, and inserting in place thereof the following clause: —

Tax deductions for certain dependents.

(*h*) The sum of five hundred dollars for a husband or wife with whom the taxpayer lives and, if entirely dependent on the taxpayer for support, the sum of two hundred and fifty dollars for each parent, for each child under the age of eighteen and for each child eighteen years of age or over incapable of self-support because of physical or mental disability. The aforesaid deduction shall not be allowed to both husband and wife, but may be allowed to either as they shall mutually agree, or shall be prorated between them in proportion to the net income of each in excess of two thousand dollars.

Approved June 11, 1943.

---

*Chap.*512 AN ACT REQUIRING THE APPROVAL OF THE DEPARTMENT OF PUBLIC WELFARE IN CONNECTION WITH CERTAIN PROCEEDINGS ON BONDS AND MORTGAGES GIVEN TO SECURE OLD AGE ASSISTANCE, AND MAKING CERTAIN PERSONS ELIGIBLE FOR SUCH ASSISTANCE NOTWITHSTANDING THEIR OWNERSHIP OF REAL ESTATE UPON WHICH THEY DO NOT RESIDE.

Be it enacted, etc., as follows:

G. L. (Ter. Ed.), 118A, § 4, etc., amended.

Chapter one hundred and eighteen A of the General Laws is hereby amended by striking out section four, as most recently amended by section four of chapter seven hundred and twenty-nine of the acts of nineteen hundred and forty-one, and inserting in place thereof the following section: —

Section 4. The ownership by an applicant of an equity in vacant land from which no income is derived, or the ownership of an equity in real estate by an applicant who resides thereon or who, in the opinion of the board, is residing elsewhere than on such real estate because of physical or mental incapacity, shall not disqualify him from receiving assistance under this chapter; provided, that if such equity, computed on the basis of assessed valuation, exceeds an average of three thousand dollars during the five years immediately preceding his application, the board of public welfare of the town rendering such assistance, or the bureau of old age assistance established by such board, shall, through the appropriate town official, require such applicant to execute a bond in a penal sum equal to the amount of the equity in excess of three thousand dollars, running to the treasurer of the town, conditioned on repayment to such town of all amounts of such assistance, without interest, such bond to be secured by mortgage of the applicant's real estate. Proceedings to realize upon any such bond or mortgage shall be brought only with the written approval of the department, which shall be granted upon application, except in any case where such a proceeding would, in the opinion of the department, result in undue hardship or would be inconsistent with the purposes of this chapter. Every such bond and mortgage shall be forthwith entered for record in the proper registry of deeds or registry district of the land court, as the case may be, and the register of deeds or assistant recorder of the land court shall thereupon record or register such bond and mortgage without fee. The proceeds realized by the town from any such bond and mortgage shall be apportioned among the federal government, the commonwealth and the town furnishing the assistance in proportion to the amount of their respective contributions, but in no case for more than the amount contributed, without interest.

Ownership of property not to disqualify applicants.

Approved June 11, 1943.

Chap. 513

AN ACT IN ADDITION TO THE GENERAL APPROPRIATION ACT FOR THE PERIOD BEGINNING DECEMBER FIRST, NINETEEN HUNDRED AND FORTY-TWO AND ENDING JUNE THIRTIETH, NINETEEN HUNDRED AND FORTY-THREE, MAKING APPROPRIATIONS TO SUPPLEMENT CERTAIN ITEMS CONTAINED THEREIN, AND FOR CERTAIN NEW PROJECTS.

Be it enacted, etc., as follows:

SECTION 1. To provide for supplementing certain items in the general appropriation act for the period beginning December first, nineteen hundred and forty-two and ending June thirtieth, nineteen hundred and forty-three, and for certain new activities and projects, the sums set forth in section two, for the particular purposes and subject to the conditions stated therein, are hereby appropriated from the general fund or ordinary revenue of the commonwealth, unless some other source of revenue is expressed, subject to the provisions of law regulating the disbursement of public funds and the approval thereof, for said period or for such other period as may be specified.

SECTION 2. The amount appropriated under each of the following items is to be in addition, in each instance, to any amount heretofore appropriated for the same purpose, unless otherwise specified:

Service of the Legislative Department.

Item		
0101-03	For the compensation of representatives	$2,500 00
0101-04	For the compensation for travel of representatives	105 00
0101-05	For the salaries of the clerk of the senate and the clerk of the house of representatives	1,000 00
0101-06	For the salaries of the assistant clerk of the senate and the assistant clerk of the house of representatives	625 00
0101-17	For the salaries of the chaplains of the senate and house of representatives, including not more than two permanent positions	250 00
0101-18	For personal services of the counsel to the senate and assistants, including not more than four permanent positions	100 00
0101-19	For personal services of the counsel to the house of representatives and assistants, including not more than seven permanent positions	1,200 00
0102-01	For traveling and such other expenses of the committees of the present general court as may be authorized by order of either branch of the general court	4,750 00
0102-04	For expenses in connection with the publication of the bulletin of committee hearings and of the daily list, with the approval of the joint committee on rules, including not more than one permanent position	1,000 00
0102-07	(See Item 0101-18.)	
0102-23	For stenographic services and expenses of the joint committee on rules in connection with a certain hearing, as authorized by certain Joint Orders of the general court	2,421 82
	Total	$13,951 82

Service of the Judicial Department.

	Superior Court:	
0302-02	For traveling allowances and expenses	$5,000 00
	Administrative Committee of the District Courts:	
0304-01	For compensation and expenses of the administrative committee of district courts	1,000 00
	Probate and Insolvency Courts:	
0305-03	For expenses of judges of probate when acting for other judges of probate	50 00
0306-13	For clerical assistance to the Register of Worcester county, including not more than twelve permanent positions	350 00

Service of the Board of Probation.

0311-01	For personal services of the commissioner, clerks and stenographers, including not more than forty-three permanent positions	4,000 00
	Total	$10,400 00

Service of the Executive Department.

Item		
0401-03	For the salaries of the eight councillors . .	$4,000 00

Service of the State Surgeon.

0407-03	For the examination of recruits . . .	$1,700 00

Service of the Commission on Administration and Finance.

0415-02	For personal services of the bureau of the comptroller, including not more than eighty-six permanent positions	$3,200 00
0415-04	For other personal services of the commission, including not more than thirty-three permanent positions	6,500 00
0415-05	For other expenses incidental to the duties of the commission	2,000 00
	Telephone service:	
0415-10	For telephone service in the state house and expenses in connection therewith . . .	8,100 00
	Central Mailing Room:	
0415-12	For personal services of the central mailing room, including not more than eight permanent positions	610 00
	Total	$20,410 00

Service of the State Superintendent of Buildings.

0416-01	For personal services of the superintendent and office assistants, including not more than five permanent positions	$131 00
0416-02	For personal services of engineers, assistant engineers, firemen and helpers in the engineer's department, including not more than forty-four permanent positions	1,650 00
0416-04	For personal services of janitors, including not more than twenty-one permanent positions .	500 00
	Other Annual Expenses:	
0416-13	For services, supplies and equipment necessary to furnish heat, light and power . . .	11,000 00
	Total	$13,281 00

Service of the State Racing Commission.

	The following item shall be payable from fees collected under chapter one hundred and twenty-eight A of the General Laws, as amended:	
0418-02	For other administrative expenses, including rent of offices, travel, and office and incidental expenses	$780 00

Service of the State Planning Board.

0419-01	For personal services of secretary, chief engineer, and other assistants, including not more than fourteen permanent positions	$46 00
0419-02	For services other than personal, including rent of offices, travel, and office supplies and equipment	1,350 00
	Total	$1,396 00

Service of the Commissioner of State Aid and Pensions.

Item		
0440-02	For personal services of agents, clerks, stenographers and other assistants, including not more than nineteen permanent positions . .	$2,800 00
0440-03	For services other than personal, traveling expenses of the commissioner and his employees, and necessary office supplies and equipment .	1,600 00
	Total	$4,400 00

For Expenses on Account of Wars.

0441-02	For certain care of veterans of the civil war, their wives and widows, as authorized by section twenty-five of chapter one hundred and fifteen of the General Laws, as appearing in the Tercentenary Edition thereof	$1,200 00

For the Maintenance of Old State House.

0444-01	For the contribution of the commonwealth toward the maintenance of the old provincial state house	$125 00

Service of the Secretary of the Commonwealth.

0501-02	For the salaries of officers and employees holding positions established by law, and other personal services, including not more than sixty-six permanent positions	$4,600 00
	For printing laws, etc.:	
0503-03	For printing and binding public documents .	800 00
	For matters relating to elections:	
0504-03	For furnishing cities and towns with ballot boxes, and for repairs to the same; for the purchase of apparatus to be used at polling places in the canvass and counting of votes; and for providing certain registration facilities	334 00
	Total	$5,734 00

Service of the Treasurer and Receiver-General.

	Commissioners on Firemen's Relief:	
0602-01	For relief disbursed, with the approval of the commissioners on firemen's relief, subject to the provisions of law	$1,800 00
0602-02	For expenses of administration by the commissioners on firemen's relief	100 00
	State Board of Retirement:	
0604-01	For personal services in the administrative office of the state board of retirement, including not more than eleven permanent positions . .	450 00
0604-03	For requirements of annuity funds and pensions for employees retired from the state service under authority of law, to be in addition to the amounts appropriated in item 2970-01 . .	20,810 00
	Total	$23,160 00

Service of the Attorney General's Department.

0801-02	For the compensation of assistants in his office, and for such other legal and personal services as may be required, including not more than thirty-six permanent positions	$11,000 00

Item		
0801-03	For services other than personal, traveling expenses, office supplies and equipment . .	$1,900 00
0802-02	For the settlement of certain small claims, as authorized by section three A of chapter twelve of the General Laws	99 43
	Total	$12,999 43

Service of the Department of Agriculture.

0901-01	For the salary of the commissioner	$500 00
0901-21	For services and expenses of apiary inspection, including not more than one permanent position	300 00
	Division of Dairying and Animal Husbandry:	
0905-01	For personal services, including not more than five permanent positions	250 00
0905-03	For administering the law relative to the inspection of barns and dairies by the department of agriculture, including not more than eight permanent positions	4,250 00
	Milk Control Board:	
0906-03	For expenses in connection with certain activities conducted in co-operation with the federal government, as authorized by section twenty-three of chapter ninety-four A of the General Laws .	1,700 00
	Division of Livestock Disease Control:	
0907-02	For personal services of clerks and stenographers, including not more than eighteen permanent positions	300 00
0907-03	For services other than personal, traveling expenses of the director, office supplies and equipment, and rent	180 00
	State Reclamation Board:	
0910-01	For expenses of the board, including not more than five permanent positions	300 00
	Total	$7,780 00

Service of the Department of Conservation.

	Administration:	
1001-04	For clerical and other assistance to the commissioner, including not more than twelve permanent positions	$470 00
	Division of Forestry:	
1002-01	For personal services of office assistants, including not more than four permanent positions . .	200 00
1002-02	For services other than personal, traveling expenses, necessary office supplies and equipment, and rent	200 00
1002-14	For the expenses of forest fire patrol, as authorized by section twenty-eight A of chapter forty-eight of the General Laws	1,300 00
1002-16	For reimbursement of certain towns for part of the cost of certain forest fire patrol, as authorized by chapter six hundred and eighty-eight of the acts of nineteen hundred and forty-one . .	2,000 00
1002-21	For the development of state forests, including not more than twenty-one permanent positions, and including salaries and expenses of foresters and the cost of maintenance of such nurseries	

Item		
	as may be necessary for the growing of seedlings for the planting of state forests, as authorized by sections one, six, nine and thirty to thirty-six, inclusive, of chapter one hundred and thirty-two of the General Laws . .	$4,500 00
	Division of Fisheries and Game:	
1004-02	For personal services of office assistants, including not more than ten permanent positions .	400 00
	Enforcement of laws:	
1004-11	For personal services of conservation officers, including not more than thirty-seven permanent positions	2,300 00
	Propagation of game birds, etc.:	
1004-31	For personal services of employees at game farms and fish hatcheries, including not more than twenty-four permanent positions . . .	2,500 00
	Supervision of public fishing and hunting grounds:	
1004-42	For other expenses	450 00
1004-45	For expenses of providing for the establishment and maintenance of public fishing grounds .	6,450 00
1004-46	For the cost of construction and improvement of certain fishways	300 00
	Division of Marine Fisheries:	
1004-71	For personal services, including not more than six permanent positions; provided, that this appropriation shall not be used for the payment of salaries of food inspectors regulating the sale and cold storage of fresh food fish . . .	15 00
	Total	$21,085 00

Service of the Department of Banking and Insurance.

Item		
	Supervisor of Loan Agencies:	
1102-01	For personal services of supervisor and assistants, including not more than seven permanent positions	$216 00
	Division of Savings Bank Life Insurance:	
1105-01	For personal services of officers and employees, including not more than twenty-nine permanent positions	550 00
	Total	$766 00

Service of the Department of Corporations and Taxation.

Item		
	Corporations and Tax Divisions:	
1201-02	For the salaries of certain positions filled by the commissioner, with the approval of the governor and council, and for additional clerical and other assistance, including not more than one hundred and twenty-six permanent positions, partly chargeable to item 2970-03 . . .	$500 00
	Administration of cigarette taxes:	
1201-11	For personal services for the administration of certain laws levying the cigarette taxes, so called, including not more than thirty-six permanent positions	5,000 00

Item		
	Income Tax Division (the two following appropriations are to be made from the receipts from the income tax):	
1202-01	For personal services of the director, assistant director, assessors, deputy assessors, clerks, stenographers and other necessary assistants, including not more than two hundred and sixty-three permanent positions	$5,000 00
1202-02	For services other than personal, and for traveling expenses, office supplies and equipment, and rent	19,000 00
	Division of Accounts:	
1203-11	For services and expenses of auditing and installing systems of municipal accounts, the cost of which is to be assessed upon the municipalities for which the work is done	7,000 00
	Total	$36,500 00

Service of the Department of Education.

Item		
1301-02	For personal services of officers, agents, clerks, stenographers and other assistants, including not more than forty-six permanent positions, but not including those employed in university extension work	$1,780 00
1301-03	For traveling expenses of members of the advisory board and of agents and employees when required to travel in discharge of their duties .	130 00
1301-06	For printing school registers and other school blanks for cities and towns	220 00
1301-10	For the maintenance and operation of the state building on Newbury street, Boston, including not more than four permanent positions . .	450 00
	Division of Vocational Education:	
1301-31	For the training of teachers for vocational schools, to comply with the requirement of federal authorities under the provisions of the Smith-Hughes act, so called, including not more than twenty permanent positions	1,000 00
	Education of deaf and blind pupils:	
1301-41	For the education of deaf and blind pupils of the commonwealth, as provided by section twenty-six of chapter sixty-nine of the General Laws .	11,600 00
	English-speaking Classes for Adults:	
1301-64	For personal services of administration, including not more than four permanent positions . .	65 00
	Division of the Blind:	
1304-03	For the maintenance of local shops, including not more than nine permanent positions . .	4,900 00
1304-04	For maintenance of Woolson House industries, so called, to be expended under the authority of said division, including not more than four permanent positions	3,900 00
1304-05	For the maintenance of certain industries for men, to be expended under the authority of said division, including not more than six permanent positions	9,500 00
1304-10	For expenses of administering and operating the services of piano tuning and mattress renovating under section twenty-five of chapter sixty-nine of the General Laws	880 00

Item		
	Teachers' Retirement Board:	
1305-02	For services other than personal, traveling expenses, office supplies and equipment, and rent	$300 00
	Massachusetts Maritime Academy:	
1306-01	For personal services of the secretary and office assistants, including not more than two permanent positions	650 00
	For the maintenance of the state teachers' colleges, and the boarding halls attached thereto, with the approval of the commissioner of education, as follows:	
1308-21	State teachers' college at Fitchburg, boarding hall, including not more than nine permanent positions	8,500 00
1314-32	State teachers' college at Westfield, personal services and expenses of boarding hall for army signal corps trainees	4,575 00
	Massachusetts State College:	
1341-00	For maintenance and current expenses of the Massachusetts state college, with the approval of the trustees, including not more than four hundred and eighty-one permanent positions .	8,400 00
1341-79	For necessary expenditures in connection with the establishment and maintenance of the fighter command training school at the Massachusetts state college, the sum of thirty-seven thousand seven hundred dollars is hereby appropriated and made available for transfer to the amounts previously appropriated in Items 1341-00, 1341-77 and 1341-78 of chapter sixty-eight of the acts of the present year, with the approval of the commission on administration and finance, and any unexpended balance of this appropriation remaining on June thirtieth, nineteen hundred and forty-three, shall be available in the fiscal year nineteen hundred and forty-four	37,700 00
	Total	$94,550 00

Service of the Department of Civil Service and Registration

Item		
	Division of Registration:	
1403-01	For the salary of the director	$13 34
	Board of Dental Examiners:	
1405-02	For traveling expenses	100 00
	Board of Registration in Embalming and Funeral Directing:	
1409-02	For traveling expenses	100 00
	Board of Registration in Optometry:	
1410-02	For traveling expenses	40 00
	Board of Registration in Veterinary Medicine:	
1411-01	For personal services of members of the board, including not more than five permanent positions	350 00
1411-02	For other services, traveling expenses, office supplies and equipment	150 00
	Board of Registration of Professional Engineers and of Land Surveyors:	
1412-01	For personal services and other expenses, including travel	300 00

Item		
	Board of Registration of Architects:	
1413-01	For personal services and other expenses, including travel	$1,300 00
	Board of Registration of Barbers:	
1420-01	For personal services of members of the board and assistants, including not more than eight permanent positions	84 00
	Total	$2,437 34

Service of the Department of Industrial Accidents.

1501-01	For personal services of members of the board, including not more than seven permanent positions	$1,128 00
1501-02	For personal services of secretaries, inspectors, clerks and office assistants, including not more than eighty-seven permanent positions	6,030 00
1501-04	For other services, necessary office supplies and equipment	600 00
	Total	$7,758 00

Service of the Department of Labor and Industries.

1601-51	For personal services for the division on necessaries of life, including not more than five permanent positions	$157 00
1601-53	For personal services in administering sections two hundred and ninety-five A to two hundred and ninety-five O, inclusive, of chapter ninety-four of the General Laws, relating to the advertising and sale of motor fuel at retail, including not more than twelve permanent positions	680 00
1601-71	For personal services of investigators, clerks and stenographers for the minimum wage service, including not more than eighteen permanent positions	1,973 00
	Total	$2,810 00

Service of the Department of Mental Health.

1701-03	For transportation and medical examination of state charges under its charge	$450 00
1701-11	For the support of state charges in the Hospital Cottages for Children	3,000 00
	Division of Mental Hygiene:	
1702-21	For the cost of boarding certain feeble-minded persons in private homes	200 00
	For the maintenance of the following institutions under the control of the Department of Mental Health:	
1710-00	Boston psychopathic hospital, including not more than one hundred and fifty-six permanent positions	5,000 00
1719-00	Taunton state hospital, including not more than four hundred and seventy-two permanent positions	8,300 00
	Total	$16,950 00

Service of the Department of Correction.

Item		
	Division of Classification of Prisoners:	
1801–08	For expenses of the division hereby authorized, including not more than eight permanent positions; provided, that the persons employed hereunder shall not be subject to civil service laws or the rules and regulations made thereunder	$1,000 00

Service of the Department of Public Welfare.

Item		
	Administration:	
1901–03	For services other than personal, traveling expenses, including expenses of auxiliary visitors, office supplies and expenses	$350 00
	State Board of Housing:	
1902–01	For personal services, including not more than nine permanent positions	350 00
	Division of Child Guardianship:	
1906–01	For personal services of officers and employees, including not more than one hundred and thirty-six permanent positions	7,000 00
1906–03	For the care and maintenance of children, including not more than two permanent positions .	76,000 00
	The following items are for reimbursement of cities and towns:	
1907–05	For the payment of suitable aid to certain dependent children	900,000 00

The sum of twenty-five thousand five hundred dollars is hereby transferred from the appropriation made by Item 1907–09 of chapter sixty-eight of the acts of the present year to the appropriation made by Item 1907–07 of said chapter sixty-eight.

The sum of forty-two thousand dollars is hereby transferred from the appropriation made by Item 1907–09 of chapter sixty-eight of the acts of the present year to the appropriation made by Item 1907–08 of said chapter sixty-eight.

Item		
	Division of Juvenile Training, Trustees of Massachusetts Training Schools:	
1908–02	For services other than personal, traveling and other expenses of the members of the board and employees, office supplies and equipment .	150 00
	Boys' Parole:	
1908–12	For services other than personal, including traveling expenses of the agents and boys, and necessary office supplies and equipment	1,100 00
1908–13	For board, clothing, medical and other expenses incidental to the care of boys	1,800 00
	Girls' Parole:	
1908–31	For personal services of agents in the division for girls paroled from the industrial school for girls, including not more than eighteen permanent positions	900 00
1908–32	For traveling expenses of said agents for girls paroled, for board, medical and other care of girls, and for services other than personal, office supplies and equipment	2,000 00

Item		
	For the maintenance of the institutions under the control of the trustees of the Massachusetts training schools, with the approval of said trustees, as follows:	
1915–00	Industrial school for boys, including not more than one hundred permanent positions . .	$6,000 00
1916–00	Industrial school for girls, including not more than eighty-nine permanent positions . . .	6,000 00
1917–00	Lyman school for boys, including not more than one hundred and thirty-eight permanent positions	3,000 00
	Tewksbury State Hospital and Infirmary:	
1919–24	For the purchase and installation of certain coal burning equipment in the power plant at the Tewksbury State Hospital and Infirmary .	65,000 00
	Total	$1,069,650 00

Service of the Department of Public Health

Item		
	Administration:	
2001–02	For personal services of the health council and office assistants, including not more than twenty-three permanent positions . . .	$2,850 00
	Service of Adult Hygiene (cancer):	
2003–02	For other expenses of the division, including cancer clinics	6,500 00
	Service of Child and Maternal Hygiene:	
2004–02	For services other than personal, traveling expenses, office supplies and equipment . .	1,200 00
	Antitoxin and Vaccine Laboratories:	
2007–07	For personal services in the investigation and production of antitoxin and vaccine lymph and other specific material for protective inoculation and diagnosis of treatment, including not more than forty-seven permanent positions .	700 00
2007–08	For other services, supplies, materials and equipment necessary for the production of antitoxin and other materials as enumerated above, and for rent	3,500 00
	Inspection of Food and Drugs:	
2012–01	For personal services of the director, analysts, inspectors and other assistants, including not more than thirty permanent positions . .	700 00
2012–02	For other services, including traveling expenses, supplies, materials and equipment . . .	500 00
	Shellfish Enforcement Law:	
2013–01	For personal services for administering the law relative to shellfish, including not more than one permanent position	76 66
2013–02	For other expenses for administering the law relative to shellfish	50 00
	Total	$16,076 66

Service of the Department of Public Safety.

Item		
	Division of State Police:	
2102–02	For personal services of civilian employees, including not more than one hundred and six permanent positions	$7,100 00
2102–04	For expert assistance to the commissioner and for maintenance of laboratories, including not more than four permanent positions . . .	500 00

Item		
	Fire Prevention Service:	
2103-02	For personal services of fire and other inspectors, including not more than nineteen permanent positions	$2,950 00
2103-03	For other services, office rent and necessary office supplies and equipment	100 00
2103-04	For traveling expenses of fire and other inspectors	1,400 00
	Division of Inspection:	
2104-21	For the salaries of officers for the boiler inspection service, including not more than twenty-six permanent positions	51 00
2104-22	For traveling expenses of officers for the boiler inspection service	1,200 00
	State Boxing Commission:	
2105-02	For other expenses of the commission	500 00
	Total	$13,801 00

Service of the Department of Public Works.

	Functions of the department relating to waterways and public lands:	
2202-07	For the operation and maintenance of the New Bedford state pier, including not more than seven permanent positions	$3,700 00

Service of the Department of Public Utilities.

2301-01	For personal services of the commissioners, including not more than five permanent positions	$155 55
2301-05	For personal services of the telephone and telegraph division, including not more than seven permanent positions	34 00
2301-06	For traveling expenses of the commissioners and employees	1,000 00
2301-08	For stenographic reports of evidence at inquests held in cases of death by accident on or about railroads	68 00
	Investigation of Gas and Electric Light Meters:	
2302-01	For personal services of the division of inspection of gas and gas meters, including not more than twelve permanent positions	1,050 00
	Commercial Motor Vehicle Division:	
2304-01	For personal services of the director and assistants, including not more than thirty-two permanent positions	650 00
	Total	$2,957 55
	Bunker Hill Monument:	
2801-00	For the maintenance of Bunker Hill monument and the property adjacent, to be expended by the metropolitan district commission	$6,712 00

Unclassified Accounts and Claims.

2805-02	For payment of any claims, as authorized by section eighty-nine of chapter thirty-two of the General Laws, for allowances to the families of members of the department of public safety doing police duty killed or fatally injured in the discharge of their duties	$70 00

Item		
2811-02	For the compensation of veterans who may be retired by the governor under the provisions of sections fifty-six to fifty-nine, inclusive, of chapter thirty-two of the General Laws . .	$16,000 00
2811-03	For the compensation of certain prison officers and instructors formerly in the service of the commonwealth, now retired	1,200 00
2811-04	For the compensation of state police officers formerly in the service of the commonwealth, now retired	1,200 00
2820-06	For reimbursement of persons for funds previously deposited in the treasury of the commonwealth and escheated to the commonwealth . .	250 00
	Total	$18,720 00

DEFICIENCIES.

For deficiencies in certain appropriations of previous years, in certain items, as follows:

Service of the Legislative Department.

For printing, binding and paper ordered by the senate and house of representatives, or by concurrent order of the two branches, with the approval of the clerks of the respective branches . $138 99

Service of the Judicial Department.

Justices of District Courts:
For reimbursing certain counties for compensation of certain special justices for services in holding sessions of district courts in place of the justice, while sitting in the superior court . 774 93

Administrative Committee of District Courts:
For compensation and expenses of the administrative committee of district courts . . . 66 20

Administrative Committee of Probate Courts:
For expenses of the administrative committee of probate courts 32 00

Suffolk County Court House.

For reimbursing the city of Boston for thirty per cent of the cost of maintenance of the Suffolk County Court House, as provided by and subject to the conditions of section six of chapter four hundred and seventy-four of the acts of the year nineteen hundred and thirty-five; provided, that this appropriation shall not be construed as fixing the specific amount for which the commonwealth shall be liable on account of said maintenance 10,000 00

Service of the State Quartermaster.

For expense of maintaining and operating the Camp Curtis Guild rifle range . . . 94 89

Service of the Secretary of the Commonwealth.

Medical Examiners' Fees:
For medical examiners' fees, as provided by law . 46 20

Service of the Department of Corporations and Taxation.

Item

Corporations and Tax Divisions:	
For other services, necessary office supplies and equipment, travel, and for printing the annual report, other publications and valuation books	$203 47
For expenses of the department for legal services, evidence and other information relative to domicile cases	179 61

Service of the Department of Education.

Reimbursement and aid:	
For the reimbursement of certain towns for the payment of tuition of pupils attending high schools outside the towns in which they reside, as provided by law	1,369 60

Service of the Department of Civil Service and Registration.

Division of Registration:	
For services of the division other than personal, printing the annual reports, office supplies and equipment, except as otherwise provided	161 98

Service of the Attorney General's Department.

For services and expenses of the attorney general in preparing and furnishing information for use by the commission appointed to study and investigate the service of the New York, New Haven and Hartford Railroad Company	1,023 95

Service of the Department of Correction.

For traveling expenses of officers and employees of the department, when required to travel in the discharge of their duties	200 27
For the maintenance of the reformatory for women, including not more than one hundred and three permanent positions	2,872 01

Service of the Department of Public Welfare.

Division of Child Guardianship:	
For the care and maintenance of children, including not more than two permanent positions	343 70
Tuition of Children:	
For tuition in the public schools, including transportation to and from school, of children boarded by the department	2,426 30

Unclassified Accounts and Claims.

For the compensation of veterans who may be retired by the governor under the provisions of sections fifty-six to fifty-nine, inclusive, of chapter thirty-two of the General Laws	153 50

Service of the Department of Agriculture.

Division of Markets:	
For the cost of work of inspecting certain orchards within the commonwealth to provide for effective apple pest control	123 21

Item	*Service of the Department of Mental Health.*	
	For the maintenance of the Belchertown state school, including not more than two hundred and ninety-eight permanent positions . .	$43 90
	Total	$20,254 71

THE FOLLOWING APPROPRIATIONS ARE MADE FROM THE HIGHWAY FUND:

Service of the Department of Public Works.

	Public Works Building:	
2922-02	For the salaries of guards for the public works building, including expense of uniforms, and including not more than seventeen permanent positions	$725 00
2922-03	For other expenses for the maintenance and operation of the public works building . . .	1,100 00
	Total	$1,825 00

Metropolitan District Commission.

	The following items are to be paid with the approval of the metropolitan district commission:	
2931-00	For maintenance of boulevards and parkways, including installation of traffic lights . .	$500,000 00

DEFICIENCIES.

	For deficiencies in certain appropriations of previous years, in certain items, as follows:	
	For maintenance of boulevards and parkways, including installation of traffic lights, to be paid with the approval of the metropolitan district commission	$223 46

THE FOLLOWING APPROPRIATIONS ARE MADE FROM THE PORT OF BOSTON FUND:

Service of the Department of Public Works.

	Functions of the department relating to Port of Boston:	
3132-14	For personal services and other expenses of the cost of operating the Commonwealth Airport, so-called	$8,000 00

THE FOLLOWING APPROPRIATIONS ARE PAYABLE FROM THE PARKS AND SALISBURY BEACH RESERVATION FUND:

Division of Parks and Recreation.

4013	For the development of recreational opportunities in state forests, including personal services and other expenses	$4,300 00
4021	For the maintenance of the Standish monument reservation	210 00
	Salisbury Beach Reservation:	
4031	For the maintenance of Salisbury beach reservation, including not more than one permanent position	3,700 00
	Total	$8,210 00

THE FOLLOWING APPROPRIATIONS ARE PAYABLE FROM THE PRISON INDUSTRIES FUND:

Item		
	The following amounts appropriated in Items 4511 and 4711 include, in each instance, partial compensation of not more than seven additional permanent employees in industries at the State Prison:	
4511	For salaries of persons employed in industries at the Reformatory for Women, including not more than thirteen permanent positions .	$2,034 00
4711	For salaries of persons employed in industries at the State Prison Colony, including not more than sixteen permanent positions . . .	1,006 00
	Total	$3,040 00

Metropolitan District Commission Funds.

DEFICIENCIES.

For deficiencies in certain appropriations of previous years, in certain items, as follows:	
For maintenance of parks reservations, including the purchase of land and the retirement of veterans under the provisions of the General Laws	$19 44

General Fund	$1,457,045 51
Highway Fund	502,048 46
Port of Boston Fund	8,000 00
Special Assessment Funds	8,210 00
Prison Industries Fund	3,040 00
Metropolitan District Commission Funds . . .	19 44

SECTION 3. No payment shall be made or obligation incurred under authority of any special appropriation made by this act for construction of public buildings or other improvements at state institutions until plans and specifications have been approved by the governor, unless otherwise provided by such rules and regulations as the governor may make.

SECTION 4. This act shall take effect upon its passage.

Approved June 11, 1943.

---

*Chap.*514 AN ACT RELATIVE TO THE RETIREMENT ALLOWANCES OF CERTAIN WAR VETERANS IN THE PUBLIC SERVICE.

Be it enacted, etc., as follows:

G. L. (Ter. Ed.), 32, § 56, amended.

Retirement if incapacitated.

SECTION 1. Chapter thirty-two of the General Laws is hereby amended by striking out section fifty-six, as appearing in the Tercentenary Edition, and inserting in place thereof the following section: — *Section 56.* A person who has served in the army, navy or marine corps of the United States in the Spanish war or Philippine insurrection between April twenty-first, eighteen hundred and ninety-eight, and July fourth, nineteen hundred and two, or in the world war between April sixth, nineteen hundred and seventeen, and November eleventh, nineteen hundred and eighteen, and has been honorably discharged from such service or released from active duty therein, in sections fifty-six to sixty, inclusive, called a veteran, who is in the service of the commonwealth, or of any county, city, town or district thereof, shall be retired, with the consent of the retiring authority, if incapacitated for active service, at one half of the highest regular rate of compensation, including any allowance for maintenance, payable to him while he was holding the grade held by him at his retirement, and payable from the same source; provided, that he has been in the said service at least ten years, has reached the age of fifty, and has a total income from all sources, exclusive of such retirement allowance and of any sum received from the government of the United States as a pension for war service, not exceeding five hundred dollars.

G. L. (Ter. Ed.), 32, § 57, amended.

Retirement after ten years' service, etc.

SECTION 2. Said chapter thirty-two is hereby further amended by striking out section fifty-seven, as so appearing, and inserting in place thereof the following section: — *Section 57.* A veteran who has been in the service of the commonwealth, or of any county, city, town or district thereof, for a total period of ten years, may, upon petition to the retiring authority, be retired, in the discretion of said authority, from active service, at one half of the highest regular rate of compensation, including any allowance for maintenance, payable to him while he was holding the grade held by him at his retirement, and payable from the same source, if he is found by said authority to have become incapacitated for active service; provided, that he has a total income, from all sources, exclusive of such retirement allowance and of any sum received from the government of the United States as a pension for war service, not exceeding five hundred dollars.

G. L. (Ter. Ed.), 32, § 58, amended.

Retirement after thirty years' service.

SECTION 3. Said chapter thirty-two is hereby further amended by striking out section fifty-eight, as so appearing, and inserting in place thereof the following section: — *Section 58.* A veteran who has been in the service of the commonwealth, or of any county, city, town or district, for a total period of thirty years, shall, at his own request, with the approval of the retiring authority, be retired from active service at one half of the highest regular rate of compensation, including any maintenance allowance, payable to him while he was holding the grade held by him at his retirement, and payable from the same source.

Application of act.

SECTION 4. This act shall apply to the retirement allowances of veterans subject to any provisions of sections fifty-six to fifty-eight, inclusive, of chapter thirty-two of the General Laws, as amended by sections one to three, inclusive, of this act, retired since December thirty-first, nineteen hundred and twenty, and prior to the effective date of this act, as well as to those retired on or after said effective date.

Approved June 11, 1943.

Chap.515 AN ACT FURTHER AMENDING THE LAWS RELATIVE TO THE MAYOR OF THE CITY OF NORTHAMPTON, AND PROVIDING FOR A UNICAMERAL CITY COUNCIL IN SAID CITY.

Be it enacted, etc., as follows:

SECTION 1. The inhabitants of the city of Northampton, for all the purposes for which towns and cities are, by law, incorporated in this commonwealth, shall continue to be one body politic, in fact and in name, under the style and denomination of the city of Northampton, and as such shall have, exercise, and enjoy all the rights, immunities, powers and privileges, and shall be subject to all the duties and obligations, now incumbent upon and appertaining to said city as a municipal corporation.

SECTION 2. The administration of the fiscal, prudential and municipal affairs of said city, and the government thereof, shall be vested in an officer to be called the mayor, and a council of eleven to be called the city council, who shall be sworn to the faithful performance of their duties. A majority of said council shall constitute a quorum for the transaction of business. The city council may establish salaries for its members not exceeding two hundred and fifty dollars each per annum. The salaries of members of the city council shall not be increased or diminished during the term for which such members are elected.

SECTION 3. On the first Tuesday of November in the year nineteen hundred and forty-five and on the first Tuesday of November of each odd numbered year thereafter, the qualified voters in the several wards shall give their votes, by ballot, for mayor, city clerk, city treasurer, city councilors, superintendents of Smith's Agricultural School to hold office for the term of two years from the first Monday in January following and until their successors are elected and qualified; and an elector under the Oliver Smith will to hold office for the term of two years from the first Wednesday of May following and until his successor is elected and qualified; and members of the school committee if then to be elected, trustees under the will of Charles E. Forbes if then to be elected, secretary of the trustees of Forbes Library if then to be elected and treasurer of the trustees of Forbes Library if then to be elected for the term of four years from the first Monday of January following and until their successors are elected and qualified. All the votes so given shall be assorted, counted, declared and recorded in open ward meeting, by causing the names of the persons voted for and the number of votes given for each to be written in the ward record at length. The clerk of the ward, within twenty-four hours thereafter, shall deliver to the city clerk a copy of the record of such election, certified by the warden and clerk and a majority of the inspectors. The city council shall, within ten days thereafter, examine the copies of the records of the several wards, certified as aforesaid, and shall cause the person who shall have been elected mayor to be notified in writing of his election; but if no person is elected, or if the person elected shall refuse to accept the office, the city council shall issue warrants for a new election, and the same proceedings shall be had in all respects as are hereinbefore provided for the election of mayor, and from time to time shall be repeated until a mayor shall be elected and shall accept said office. Each city councilor shall be notified in writing of his election by the city clerk. The oath prescribed by this act shall be administered to the mayor by the city clerk or by any justice of the peace. The city council-elect shall meet on the first Monday of January of each even numbered year, at ten o'clock in the forenoon, when the oath required by this act shall be administered to the members present, by the mayor or city clerk, or by any justice of the peace; and, a certificate of such oath having been taken, shall be entered upon the journal of the city council by its clerk. After the oath has been administered as aforesaid, the city council shall be organized by the election of one of its own members as president, to hold office during that and the subsequent municipal year. In case of the absence of the mayor-elect on said first Monday of January, or if a mayor shall not then have been elected, the city council shall organize itself in the manner hereinbefore provided, and may proceed to business in the same manner as if the mayor were present; and the oath of office may at any time thereafter be administered to the mayor, and any member of the city council who may have been absent at the organization. The city council shall keep a record of its proceedings and shall judge of the elections of its members.

SECTION 4. Except as otherwise provided herein, any vacancy in the aforementioned offices may be filled by a majority vote of the city council and the person or persons so chosen shall hold office until the next succeeding municipal election.

SECTION 5. The mayor shall be the chief executive officer of the city. He shall cause the laws and regulations of the city to be enforced and keep a general supervision over the conduct of all subordinate officers; and he may, for a period not exceeding seven days, suspend and, with the consent of the city council, for cause remove any officer over whose appointment he, or his predecessor, has, in accordance with the provisions of this charter, exercised the power of nomination. He may call special meetings of the city council when in his opinion the interests of the city require it, by causing notice to be left at the usual place of residence of each member thereof. He may, from time to time, communicate to the city council such information, and recommend such measures, as the business and interests of the city may in his opinion require. He shall at all times have the control and direction of the police force, subject only to the ordinances of the city.

He shall receive such salary, not exceeding three thousand dollars per annum, as the city council shall from time to time by ordinance determine. The salary shall be payable at stated periods, but shall not be increased or diminished during the term, or during the unexpired balance of term, as the case may be, for which he is elected.

SECTION 6. The mayor, subject to confirmation by the city council, shall have full power to appoint a chief of police and all other police officers under the provisions of chapter thirty-one of the General Laws; and shall, subject to confirmation by the city council, appoint all constables and other subordinate officers whose election or appointment is not otherwise provided for. The compensation of the police and other subordinate officers shall be fixed by vote of the city council.

SECTION 7. There shall be a city solicitor of the city, who shall be appointed by the mayor, without confirmation by the city council, during the month of January following his election, or whenever a vacancy in the office of city solicitor shall occur and who may be removed at any time by the mayor in like manner. The city solicitor shall assume the duties of his office on the day following his appointment and shall serve until the day following the appointment of his successor.

SECTION 8. The city council shall consist of eleven members, four of whom shall be elected at large in the city and one by and from the qualified voters of each ward of said city, to serve for two years from the first Monday in January following their election and until their respective successors are qualified. They shall be called city councilors. Said city council shall be the sole judge of the election and qualification of its members; shall elect from its members, by vote of a majority of all the members, a president, who, when present, shall preside at the meetings; and shall from time to time establish rules for its proceedings. In the event of a tie vote in an election, affecting membership in the city council, the remaining members shall, by vote, determine which candidate for election to admit to their membership. The several city councilors shall be sworn to the faithful discharge of their duties. Any vacancy in the city council may be filled by a majority vote of the remaining members of the city council. The city councilor so chosen shall be an enrolled member of the same political or municipal party as his predecessor, and, if such predecessor was elected by and from the qualified voters of a ward, the city councilor chosen as aforesaid shall be a qualified voter and resident of that ward; otherwise, he shall be a qualified voter and resident of said city. Each city councilor elected or chosen as aforesaid shall, unless sooner removed, hold office until the qualification of his successor. All sessions of the city council shall be public.

SECTION 9. During the absence of the mayor, or his inability to perform the duties of his office, the president of the city council shall perform them, or, if the president of the city council is absent or unable from any cause to perform such duties, they shall be performed by such councilor as the city council may from time to time designate, until the mayor or the president of the city council is able to attend to said duties or until the vacancy is filled as hereinafter provided. The person upon whom such duties devolve shall be called "acting mayor", shall possess the powers of mayor only in matters not admitting of delay, and shall not make permanent appointments.

SECTION 10. If a vacancy occurs in the office of mayor, whether by death, resignation or otherwise, the city council shall by vote so declare, stating therein the cause of such vacancy. If, at the time such vacancy occurs, the term of said office will not expire for more than one year, the city council shall forthwith order an election, by the qualified voters of said city, of a mayor to serve during the balance of said unexpired term. If, at the time such vacancy occurs, the term of said office will expire within a shorter period, the president of the city council shall be the mayor of said city for the balance of such unexpired term. The person holding the office of mayor for the balance of such unexpired term shall have all the powers and privileges conferred, and be subject to all the duties and obligations imposed, by law upon the mayor of said city.

SECTION 11. The city council shall have the care and superintendence of the city buildings and the custody and management of all city property, with power to let what may be legally let, and to sell, purchase, or hire property, real or personal, in the name and for the use of the city, whenever the interests or convenience of the city may in their judgment require it; and they shall, as often as once a year, cause to be published for the use of the inhabitants, a particular account of receipts and expenditures, and a schedule of city property and of the city debt.

SECTION 12. The city council elected in accordance with this act, and their successors, shall thereafter have all the powers and privileges conferred, and be subject to all the duties and obligations imposed, by law upon the city council, board of aldermen and common council, or any of them, of said city, as existing immediately prior to the effective date of this act, except as herein otherwise provided.

SECTION 13. No member of the city council shall be eligible during the term for which he is elected, by appointment or election, to any office, the salary of which is payable out of the city treasury.

SECTION 14. The city council shall, as soon after its organization as may be convenient, elect by ballot a collector of taxes, a city physician and a city auditor, who shall be legal voters of said city and shall hold their respective offices for the terms of two years from the first Monday of March then next ensuing and until the election of their respective successors, provided, that any of such officers may be removed for cause at any time by the city council. Vacancies occurring in any of the above named offices may be filled by vote of the city council at any time. Compensation of the officers above referred to shall be fixed from time to time by vote of the city council.

SECTION 15. The city council shall elect by ballot all other officers whose appointment or election is not herein provided for.

SECTION 16. Every ordinance, order, resolution or vote of the city council involving expenditure of money, shall be presented to the mayor. If he approves thereof he shall signify his approval by signing the same, but if he does not approve thereof he shall return the ordinance, order, resolution or vote with his objections thereto in writing, to the city council, which shall enter the objections of the mayor at large on its records, and shall proceed to reconsider such ordinance, order, resolution or vote; and if after such reconsideration two thirds of the members present and voting agree to pass such ordinance, resolution or vote, notwithstanding such objections, it shall be in force but in all such cases the vote shall be determined by yeas and nays; and if such ordinance, order, resolution or vote is not returned by the mayor within ten days after presented to him, the same shall be in force; provided, that if any ordinance, order, resolution or vote embraces distinct subjects the mayor may approve the provisions relating to one or more of the subjects and not approve of the other provisions, and so much of the same as the mayor may not approve of shall be reconsidered as above provided.

SECTION 17. Until a redivision of the wards of said city, as provided by law, the territory of said city shall continue to be divided into seven wards, so that the wards will contain, as nearly as may be consistent with well-defined limits, an equal number of voters; and such wards shall be designated by numbers; but the number of wards shall never be less than seven.

SECTION 18. The city clerk shall be clerk of the city council and shall be sworn to the faithful performance of his duties as such. He shall perform such duties as shall be prescribed by the city council and in addition shall perform all the duties and exercise all the powers incumbent upon him by law. Upon the qualification of his successor in office he shall deliver to such successor all the records, journals, documents, papers and property held by him in his capacity as clerk of the city council. In case of the temporary absence or disability of the city clerk the mayor, with the advice and consent of the city council, shall appoint a clerk of the city council pro tempore.

SECTION 19. The fire department for said city shall consist of a chief engineer, and of as many assistant engineers, engine men, hose men, hook and ladder men, and assistants, as the said city council, by ordinance, shall from time to time prescribe; and the city council shall have authority to define their offices and duties, and in general to make such regulations concerning the pay, conduct, and government of such department, and the conduct of persons attending fires, as they may deem expedient, and may affix such penalties for any violation of such regulations as are provided for the breach of the ordinances of said city. The appointment of all the officers and members of such department shall be vested in the mayor and city council exclusively, who shall also have the authority to remove from office any officer or member, for cause at their discretion. The engineers so appointed shall be the fire-wards of the city, but the mayor and city council may appoint additional fire-wards. The compensation of the members of the fire department shall be fixed by vote of the city council.

SECTION 20. All acts and parts of acts affecting said city, so far as inconsistent with this act, are hereby repealed; all ordinances and parts of ordinances of said city, so far as inconsistent with this act, are hereby annulled; and all acts and parts of acts affecting said city, and all ordinances and parts of ordinances of said city, not inconsistent with this act, are continued in force.

SECTION 21. There is hereby established in said city a department to be known as the department of engineering. Said department shall be under the control of an officer to be known as the city engineer, who shall be a competent civil engineer, and whose office shall be subject to chapter thirty-one of the General Laws and the rules and regulations thereunder; provided, that the city engineer in office upon the effective date of this act shall continue to hold this position without passing any examination and shall be the first appointee hereunder. Said city engineer shall perform such duties for the city as may be required of him by the mayor and city council, and may employ such assistants as may be necessary, and may discharge them for cause.

SECTION 22. In the month of February following the acceptance of this act there shall be established in said city a board of water commissioners, a board of sewer commissioners, a board of cemetery commissioners, a board of health, a board of welfare commissioners, and a board of assessors. Each of said boards shall consist of three persons, registered voters of said city, who shall be appointed as follows: — The mayor shall appoint, subject to confirmation by the city council, to each of said boards one person to serve for the term of one year, one to serve for the term of two years and one to serve for the term of three years, from the first Monday of March next following their appointment; and thereafter, in the month of February of each year, the mayor shall appoint, subject to such confirmation, one person to each of said boards for the term of three years from the first Monday of March then next following. A vacancy in any such board may be filled at any time for the balance of the unexpired term by appointment of the mayor, subject to confirmation of the city council. No member of any such board shall be eligible to election or appointment to any paid position within the gift of the board during his term of office or for one year thereafter. One member of each such board shall be a member of one of the two leading political parties and one shall be a member of the other of such parties. The third member may be appointed from either of such parties.

SECTION 23. This act shall be submitted for acceptance to the qualified voters of the city of Northampton at the biennial municipal election in the current year in the form of the following question, which shall be placed upon the official ballot to be used in said city at said election: — "Shall an act of the General Court passed in the current year, entitled 'An Act further amending the laws relative to the mayor of the city of Northampton, and providing for a unicameral city council in said city', be accepted?" If a majority of the voters voting thereon vote in the affirmative in answer to said question, then this act shall take full effect for the nomination and election of municipal officers in said city in the year nineteen hundred and forty-five, and for all other purposes it shall take full effect upon the organization of the city government on the first week day following January first, nineteen hundred and forty-four.

Approved June 11, 1943.

---

*Chap.*516 AN ACT ENABLING CERTAIN OFFICIALS AND EMPLOYEES OF THE CITY OF BOSTON AND THE COUNTY OF SUFFOLK TO PARTICIPATE IN THE BENEFITS OF AN EMERGENCY COMPENSATION ALLOTMENT PLAN, SO CALLED.

Be it enacted, etc., as follows:

SECTION 1. During the fiscal year of the city of Boston beginning January first, nineteen hundred and forty-three, and ending December thirty-first, nineteen hundred and forty-three, an emergency compensation allotment of two hundred dollars per annum may be allowed and paid from the treasury of said city to any official or employee of the city of Boston or of the county of Suffolk whose salary is paid in whole or in part from the treasury of said city, notwithstanding any provisions of general or special law which determine or limit the salary of such official or employee.

SECTION 2. The mayor of said city may by executive order continue in full force and effect the provisions of section one for the fiscal year of the city of Boston beginning January first, nineteen hundred and forty-four and ending December thirty-first, nineteen hundred and forty-four; provided, that, if said mayor shall modify the amount of emergency compensation allotment paid during said last mentioned period to those officials and employees of the city of Boston or the county of Suffolk whose salaries are not determined or limited by any provision of general or special law, then an equal amount shall be allowed and paid to every official or employee of the city of Boston or the county of Suffolk described in section one.

SECTION 2A. The words "official or employee of the city of Boston or of the county of Suffolk" shall include every person whose salary is paid in whole or in part from the treasury of the city of Boston.

SECTION 3. This act shall take effect upon its passage.

Approved June 11, 1943.

AN ACT AUTHORIZING THE EMERGENCY PUBLIC WORKS COMMISSION TO PREPARE A POST-WAR PROGRAM OF PUBLIC WORKS, MAKING THE CHAIRMAN OF THE STATE PLANNING BOARD A MEMBER THEREOF, AND EXTENDING THE LIFE OF SAID COMMISSION. *Chap.*517

Emergency preamble.

Whereas, The deferred operation of this act would, in part, defeat its purpose, which is to prepare with the utmost expedition a program of post-war public works which may be undertaken by the commonwealth, therefore it is hereby declared to be an emergency law, necessary for the immediate preservation of the public convenience.

Be it enacted, etc., as follows:

SECTION 1. The emergency public works commission, established by section one of chapter three hundred and sixty-five of the acts of nineteen hundred and thirty-three, is hereby authorized and directed to prepare a program of post-war public works which may be undertaken by the commonwealth, and to submit such program to the governor. In the preparation of the program said commission shall give due consideration to war and post-war conditions, and the program shall include provisions deemed desirable for the preparation, during the continuance of the war, of plans, surveys and other information needed to permit prompt, effective and economical action in the period immediately following the termination of the existing states of war between the United States and certain foreign countries. Said commission shall prepare and maintain current progress information on the design of post-war projects by municipalities of the commonwealth, and maintain liaison with federal officials and agencies concerned with post-war planning.

SECTION 2. Said commission, with the approval of the governor, may accept on behalf of the commonwealth any federal funds or federal assistance, or both, for financing the cost of such plans and specifications as the commission may deem necessary in order to prepare a program of post-war projects which may readily be undertaken when funds are made available for the construction thereof, and for such plans and specifications may expend, under the provisions of said chapter three hundred and sixty-five, and acts in amendment thereof and in addition thereto, any unexpended balance of state or federal funds made available by or under the provisions of said act and amendments thereof or additions thereto. In carrying out the provisions of this act, said commission shall have all the powers and duties hitherto conferred and imposed upon it by said chapter three hundred and sixty-five, and acts in amendment thereof and in addition thereto. Said commission may request and shall receive from the several officers, departments, boards and commissions of the commonwealth such assistance as it may require for the adequate preparation of the aforesaid post-war program of public works. For the purposes of this act only, the commission shall also include in its membership the chairman of the state planning board, ex officio.

SECTION 3. The existence of said emergency public works commission, as heretofore extended, is hereby further extended to December thirty-first, nineteen hundred and forty-seven.

SECTION 4. If the chairman of the commission on administration and finance is unable by reason of absence or disability to perform his duties as a member, ex officio, of said emergency public works commission in carrying out the provisions of this act, the governor may designate a person who shall perform such duties in case of and during such absence or disability. *Approved June 11, 1943.*

---

*Chap.*518 AN ACT INCREASING THE PENALTY FOR LARCENY FROM THE PERSON.

Be it enacted, etc., as follows:

G. L. (Ter. Ed.), 266, § 25, amended.

SECTION 1. Section twenty-five of chapter two hundred and sixty-six of the General Laws, as appearing in the Tercentenary Edition, is hereby amended by inserting after the word "two" in the third line the words: — and one half, — so as to read as follows: — *Section 25.* Whoever commits larceny by stealing from the person of another shall be punished by imprisonment in the state prison for not more than five years or in jail for not more than two and one half years.

Larceny. Penalty.

Effective date.

SECTION 2. This act shall take effect on October first in the current year and shall apply in the case of crimes committed on or after said date; but the provisions of said section twenty-five, as in effect immediately preceding said date, shall continue to apply in the case of crimes committed prior thereto. *Approved June 11, 1943.*

---

*Chap.*519 AN ACT PROVIDING FOR THE EQUITABLE APPORTIONMENT IN CERTAIN CASES OF ESTATE TAXES AND THE COLLECTION AND PAYMENT THEREOF.

Be it enacted, etc., as follows:

G. L. (Ter. Ed.), 65A, § 5, amended, new §§ 5A and 5B, added.

Reimbursement, etc., to certain persons paying tax.

SECTION 1. Chapter sixty-five A of the General Laws is hereby amended by striking out section five, as appearing in the Tercentenary Edition, and inserting in place thereof the three following sections: — *Section 5.* Whenever it appears upon any accounting, or in any appropriate action or proceeding, that an executor, administrator, trustee or other person acting in a fiduciary capacity, has paid or may be required to pay an estate tax levied or assessed under the provisions of this chapter, or under the provisions of any estate tax law of the United States heretofore or hereafter enacted, upon or with respect to any property required to be included in the gross estate of a decedent under the provisions of any such law, the amount of the tax so paid or payable, except as otherwise directed or provided in the decedent's will, and, where all or part of a fund created by written instrument executed inter vivos is included in the gross estate, except as otherwise provided in such written instrument, or amendment thereof, shall be equitably apportioned and prorated among the persons interested in the estate. Such apportionment and proration shall be made in the proportion as near as may be that the value of the property, interest or benefit of each such person bears to the total value of the property, interests and benefits received by all such persons interested in the estate; provided, that it shall accord with applicable estate tax laws of the United States where such laws specify with respect to an apportionment. In making such apportionment and proration allowance shall be made for any exemptions granted by the act imposing the tax, and for any deductions allowed by such act for the purpose of arriving at the value of the net estate; and in cases where a trust is created or other provision made whereby any person is given an interest in income or an estate for years, or for life, or other temporary interest in any property or fund, the tax on both such temporary interest and on the remainder thereafter shall be charged against and be paid out of the corpus of such property or fund without apportionment between remainders and temporary estates. For the purposes of this section and sections five A and five B, the term "persons interested in the estate" shall, with respect to both state and federal taxes, include all persons who may be entitled to receive or who have received any property or interest which is so required to be included in the gross estate of a decedent, or any benefit whatsoever with respect to any such property or interest, whether under a will or intestacy, or by reason of any transfer, trust, estate, interest, right, power, relinquishment of power, or otherwise, taxable under any of the aforementioned laws but shall not include any bank, trust company or other banking institution in so far as it is the depository of any account standing in the joint names of the decedent and any other person.

Recovery of proportionate part of tax.

Section 5A. In all cases in which any property required to be included in the gross estate referred to in section five does not come into the possession of the executor or administrator as such, he shall, in the case of a trust involving temporary interests as described in section five, be entitled to recover from the fiduciary in possession of the corpus of such trust, and in all other cases from the persons interested in the estate the proportionate amount of such tax payable by such fiduciary or persons with which they are chargeable under the provisions of section five; provided, that no such tax or any part thereof shall be recovered from any company issuing (1) any policy of insurance, annuity or endowment contract on the life of or insuring the decedent, including accident and health policies, or (2) any such policy or contract insuring the decedent and one or more other persons jointly, or (3) any such policy or contract on the life of or insuring one or more persons other than the decedent in which the decedent owned any interest at the time of his death. Any person who shall have paid more than the proportionate amount of the tax apportionable to him under said section five on any property or interest passing to him, or in his possession, shall be entitled to a just and equitable contribution from those who shall not have paid the full amount of the tax apportionable to them respectively.

Jurisdiction of probate court.

Section 5B. The probate court having jurisdiction of the estate of a decedent, or of any trust or person affected by sections five and five A, and by this section, or any of them, shall have jurisdiction to hear and determine all questions arising under said sections, and to make apportionments and prorations, determine the amounts thereof and of reimbursements, contributions and other payments therein provided for, and by order or decree to direct the making of any such payments, and issue execution therefor, and to make such other determinations, orders and decrees as may be required under said sections, subject to appeal as in other cases.

Application of act limited.

SECTION 2. This act shall not apply to amounts paid as estate taxes nor to distributions made by an administrator, executor or trustee before the date on which the act becomes effective. *Approved June 11, 1943.*

---

*Chap.*520 AN ACT AUTHORIZING CERTAIN PROMOTIONS FROM THE LABOR SERVICE TO THE OFFICIAL SERVICE OF A DEPARTMENT, BOARD OR COMMISSION UNDER THE CIVIL SERVICE LAWS.

Be it enacted, etc., as follows:

G. L. (Ter. Ed.), 31, new § 15B, added.

Promotion of employees in labor service.

Chapter thirty-one of the General Laws is hereby amended by inserting before section sixteen, as appearing in the Tercentenary Edition, the following section: — *Section 15B.* An appointing official, with the approval of the director, may promote to the lowest grade in the official service of a department, board or commission employees in the labor service of the same department, board or commission who pass a competitive promotional examination open to all the employees in said labor service of said department, board or commission. *Approved June 11, 1943.*

AN ACT RELATIVE TO ABATEMENTS IN CONNECTION WITH CERTAIN EXCISES. *Chap.*521

Be it enacted, etc., as follows:

SECTION 1. Section twenty-seven of chapter fifty-eight of the General Laws, as appearing in the Tercentenary Edition, is hereby amended by striking out the first sentence and inserting in place thereof the following sentence: — If it shall appear that an income tax, a legacy and succession tax, or a tax or excise upon a corporation, foreign or domestic, or an excise upon the sale of gasoline, or an excise on alcoholic beverages or alcohol, or an excise upon charges for meals was in whole or in part illegally assessed or levied, or was excessive or unwarranted, the commissioner may, with the approval of the attorney general, issue a certificate that the party aggrieved by such tax or excise is entitled to an abatement, stating the amount thereof.

G. L. (Ter. Ed.), 58, § 27, amended.

Statement relative to abatement.

SECTION 2. Section six of chapter sixty-four B of the General Laws, inserted by section seventeen of chapter seven hundred and twenty-nine of the acts of nineteen hundred and forty-one, is hereby amended by adding at the end the following paragraph: —

G. L. (Ter. Ed.), 64B, § 6, etc., amended.

The commissioner may allow to the taxpayer an amount, which may be paid without any appropriation, in the form of abatement by reason of bad debts and such other causes as the commissioner may deem sufficient.

Abatement by reason of bad debts, etc.

Approved June 11, 1943.

AN ACT CHANGING THE TERM OF OFFICE OF THE SUPERINTENDENT OF STREETS IN THE CITY OF TAUNTON. *Chap.*522

Be it enacted, etc., as follows:

SECTION 1. In the year nineteen hundred and forty-six and in every third year thereafter, the municipal council of the city of Taunton shall, during the month of January, elect a superintendent of streets to serve for three years. Any vacancy in said office shall be filled by the municipal council for the unexpired term. The superintendent of streets elected on January fifth, nineteen hundred and forty-three, for the term of one year shall continue to serve until the qualification of his successor who shall be elected in the year nineteen hundred and forty-six as herein provided.

SECTION 2. So much of the provisions of chapter two hundred and eleven of the acts of eighteen hundred and eighty-two, and acts in amendment thereof and in addition thereto, as is inconsistent with this act, is hereby repealed.

SECTION 3. This act shall be submitted for acceptance to the qualified voters of the city of Taunton at the biennial municipal election in the current year in the form of the following question, which shall be placed upon the official ballot to be used in said city at said election: "Shall an act passed by the general court in the year nineteen hundred and forty-three, entitled 'An act changing the term of office of the superintendent of streets in the city of Taunton', be accepted?" If a majority of the votes cast on said question is in the affirmative, then this act shall take full effect on the first Monday of January in the year nineteen hundred and forty-four, but not otherwise. *Approved June 11, 1943.*

---

*Chap.*523 AN ACT REPEALING THE ACT RESTRICTING THE APPOINTMENT OF CERTAIN PERSONS FOR TEMPORARY EMPLOYMENT UNDER THE CIVIL SERVICE LAWS.

Be it enacted, etc., as follows:

G. L. (Ter. Ed.), 31, § 15A, etc., repealed.

Section fifteen A of chapter thirty-one of the General Laws, as amended, is hereby repealed.
Approved June 11, 1943.

---

*Chap.*524 AN ACT RELATIVE TO EXPENDITURES BY THE COMMITTEE ON POST-WAR READJUSTMENT.

Be it enacted, etc., as follows:

The committee on post-war readjustment is hereby authorized to expend for clerical and other services and expenses such sums, not exceeding, in the aggregate, fifty thousand dollars, as may hereafter be appropriated therefor, in addition to such other moneys as may be available for expenditure by said committee. *Approved June 11, 1943.*

---

*Chap.*525 AN ACT FURTHER REGULATING THE TERMS OF OFFICE OF THE MEMBERS OF THE SCHOOL COMMITTEE OF THE CITY OF EVERETT.

Be it enacted, etc., as follows:

SECTION 1. At the biennial municipal election to be held in the city of Everett in the current year a member of the school committee from ward four shall be elected to serve for the balance of the unexpired term of the member from said ward who was elected in the year nineteen hundred and forty-one and for an additional term of two years and until the qualification of his successor who shall be elected in the year nineteen hundred and forty-seven. At the biennial municipal election to be held in said city in the year nineteen hundred and forty-seven, and in each fourth year thereafter, a member of the school committee from ward four shall be elected to serve for a term of four years.

SECTION 2. So much of chapter three hundred and fifty-five of the acts of eighteen hundred and ninety-two, as affected by chapter three hundred and sixty-one of the acts of nineteen hundred and thirty, as is inconsistent with this act is hereby repealed. *Approved June 11, 1943.*

AN ACT RELATIVE TO THE AIDING OF BLIND PERSONS BY THE DIVISION OF THE BLIND. *Chap.*526

Be it enacted, etc., as follows:

Chapter sixty-nine of the General Laws is hereby amended by striking out section twenty-three, as appearing in the Tercentenary Edition, and inserting in place thereof the following section: — *Section 23.* The director may ameliorate the condition of the blind by devising means to facilitate the circulation of books, by promoting visits among the aged or helpless blind in their homes, by aiding individual blind persons with money or other assistance, or by any other method he may deem expedient; provided, that contributions by the division for aid to any blind person shall be based on the needs of the recipient, with a minimum of forty dollars per month, less whatever resources he may have.

G. L. (Ter. Ed.), 69, § 23, amended.

Helping blind by lending books, etc.

(This bill, returned by the governor to the House of Representatives, the branch in which it originated, with his objections thereto, was passed by the House of Representatives, June 10, 1943, and, in concurrence, by the Senate, June 11, 1943, the objections of the governor notwithstanding, in the manner prescribed by the constitution; and thereby has "the force of a law".)

AN ACT MAKING CERTAIN SUPPLEMENTAL APPROPRIATIONS FOR BRISTOL AND DUKES COUNTIES. *Chap.*527

Be it enacted, etc., as follows:

SECTION 1. The following sums are hereby appropriated for the county of Bristol for the years nineteen hundred and forty-three and nineteen hundred and forty-four, in addition to the sums already appropriated by section one of chapter four hundred and sixty-five of the acts of the current year:

Item		Appropriation Fiscal Year 1943.	Appropriation Fiscal Year 1944.
3	For salaries of county officers and assistants, a sum not exceeding . . .	$1,740 00	$3,570 00

SECTION 2. The following sums are hereby appropriated for the county of Dukes for the years nineteen hundred and forty-three and nineteen hundred and forty-four, in addition to the sums already appropriated by section one of chapter four hundred and sixty-five of the acts of the current year:

Item		Appropriation Fiscal Year 1943.	Appropriation Fiscal Year 1944.
3	For salaries of county officers and assistants, a sum not exceeding . . .	$1,035 00	$2,070 00

SECTION 3. The sums appropriated by sections one and two shall be added to the amounts to be levied as the county tax for the counties of Bristol and Dukes, respectively, for

the years nineteen hundred and forty-three and nineteen hundred and forty-four, as the case may be, as provided by section one of chapter four hundred and sixty-five of the acts of the current year.

SECTION 4. This act shall take effect upon its passage.

Approved June 12, 1943.

---

*Chap.*528 AN ACT PROVIDING FOR THE IMPROVEMENT, ENLARGEMENT, EXTENSION, DEVELOPMENT, CONSTRUCTION, ALTERATION AND OPERATION OF THE COMMONWEALTH AIRPORT — BOSTON, SO CALLED, AND PROVIDING FURTHER FOR EASEMENTS, ROADS, HIGHWAYS, APPROACHES AND MEANS OF ACCESS BY RAILROAD OR OTHERWISE IN CONNECTION THEREWITH.

Emergency preamble.

Whereas, The deferred operation of this act would tend to defeat its purpose, which is to prepare with the utmost expedition for national defense in the present emergency, therefore it is hereby declared to be an emergency law, necessary for the immediate preservation of the public safety and convenience.

Be it enacted, etc., as follows:

SECTION 1. The state department of public works, in this act called the department, is hereby authorized and directed to enlarge, extend, improve and develop the Commonwealth Airport — Boston, so called, and is authorized to dredge, fill, grade, construct sewers, drains, runways, dikes and bulkheads, and to make other improvements, and to provide for railroad and trolley tracks, roadways and appurtenances, and, for the purpose of providing railway facilities on the airport property and of providing connections with existing street railway tracks outside said property, the department may grant locations or alterations or extensions of locations for tracks, poles, wires, conduits and incidental railway structures in or upon said airport property and in or upon public lands and ways leading thereto; and to do any other work at or adjacent to the airport property which, in its opinion, is necessary to enlarge, extend, improve and develop said airport in accordance with plans prepared by or under the direction of the department; provided, that no work shall be done in accordance therewith unless a copy of such plans shall first have been submitted to the Massachusetts aeronautics commission and said commission shall have made to the department its recommendations relative thereto or thirty days have elapsed without any such recommendations.

For the purposes of this act, the department is hereby authorized to acquire by purchase, deed, gift or otherwise, or to take by eminent domain under chapter seventy-nine of the General Laws, lands other than public lands or rights therein as may be needed for the construction of necessary sewers or drains or their outlets or to provide railroad or railway tracks or roadways or appurtenances as means of access by railroad, railway or otherwise in connection with said airport or to provide for locations or alterations or extensions of locations for tracks, poles, wires, conduits and incidental railway structures in connection with said airport, and to acquire or take such air rights as may be necessary to provide unobstructed air space for the safe and convenient landing and taking off of aircraft utilizing the airport, and to acquire or take the right or easement, for a limited period of time or perpetually, to place and maintain such radio beacons and such suitable marks for the day time, and to place, operate and maintain such suitable lights for the night time, marking of buildings, or other structures or obstructions, as may be necessary for the safe and convenient operation of aircraft utilizing the airport. Before work shall commence or contracts be let final approval of plans, specifications and contracts shall be made by the governor and council.

SECTION 2. The work hereby authorized, or any part thereof, may be extended outside that portion of the harbor line established by chapter four hundred and eleven of the acts of nineteen hundred and thirty-nine and lying between the points designated in said act by the letters B–C–D–E–F–G–S–T–U and R–2.

SECTION 3. The department, acting in the name and behalf of the commonwealth, may lease or convey to the United States, with or without consideration, such property of the airport as may be necessary for the construction and maintenance of any aid to navigation, and may lease to the federal government such part of the said airport as may seem advisable. The department may enter into such agreements with the federal government relative to the construction, maintenance and operation of the airport or any part thereof and may receive and expend federal funds in addition to any moneys provided by section four.

SECTION 4. To meet the expenditures necessary in carrying out the provisions of this act the state treasurer shall upon request of the governor and council issue and sell at public or private sale bonds of the commonwealth, registered or with interest coupons attached, as he may deem best, to an amount to be specified by the governor and council from time to time, but not exceeding, in the aggregate, the sum of four million, seven hundred and fifty thousand dollars. All bonds issued by the commonwealth as aforesaid shall be designated on their face "COMMONWEALTH AIRPORT — BOSTON IMPROVEMENT LOAN" and shall be on the serial payment plan for such maximum term of years, not exceeding five years, as the governor may recommend to the general court pursuant to section 3 of Article LXII of the amendments to the Constitution of the Commonwealth, the maturities thereof to be so arranged that the amounts payable in the several years other than the final year shall be as nearly equal as in the opinion of the state treasurer it is practicable to make them. Said bonds shall bear interest semi-annually at such rate as the state treasurer, with the approval of the governor, shall fix, but such bonds shall be payable not earlier than July first, nineteen hundred and forty-five, nor later than July first, nineteen hundred and fifty.

SECTION 5. The commissioner of public works may temporarily employ such engineering, clerical and other assistants as he deems necessary for the purpose of carrying out the work authorized by this act. Such persons shall be employed subject to chapter thirty-one of the General Laws, except that their employment may continue until the completion of said work, any provision of said chapter thirty-one to the contrary notwithstanding.

SECTION 6. The department of public works may make such rules, regulations and charges for the use of said airport or part thereof as it may from time to time deem reasonable and expedient, subject to the approval of the governor and council.

SECTION 7. Nothing in this act shall be construed to authorize any expenditures from the Highway Fund.

SECTION 8. Said airport shall be known and designated as the General Edward Lawrence Logan Airport, and a suitable tablet or marker bearing said designation shall be erected at said airport by the department.

Approved June 12, 1943.

---

*Chap.*529 AN ACT REQUIRING EMPLOYERS TO PROVIDE COMPENSATION FOR EMPLOYEES RECEIVING INJURIES WHICH ARISE OUT OF AND IN THE COURSE OF THEIR EMPLOYMENT, AND PERMITTING CERTAIN EMPLOYERS TO PROVIDE FOR SUCH COMPENSATION BY SELF-INSURANCE.

Be it enacted, etc., as follows:

G. L. (Ter. Ed.), 152, § 1, etc., amended.

SECTION 1. Section one of chapter one hundred and fifty-two of the General Laws is hereby amended by striking out paragraph (1), as amended by section one of chapter three hundred and thirty-two of the acts of nineteen hundred and thirty-five, and inserting in place thereof the following paragraph: —

"Average weekly wages" defined.

(1) "Average weekly wages", the earnings of the injured employee during the period of twelve calendar months immediately preceding the date of injury, divided by fifty-two; but if the injured employee lost more than two weeks' time during such period, the earnings for the remainder of such twelve calendar months shall be divided by the number of weeks remaining after the time so lost has been deducted. Where, by reason of the shortness of the time during which the employee has been in the employment of his employer or the nature or terms of the employment, it is impracticable to compute the average weekly wages, as above defined, regard may be had to the average weekly amount which, during the twelve months previous to the injury, was being earned by a person in the same grade employed at the same work by the same employer, or, if there is no

person so employed, by a person in the same grade employed in the same class of employment and in the same district. In case the injured employee is employed in the concurrent service of more than one insured employer or self-insurer, his total earnings from the several insured employers and self-insurers shall be considered in determining his average weekly wages. Weeks in which the employee received less than five dollars in wages shall be considered time lost and shall be excluded in determining the average weekly wages; provided, however, that this exclusion shall not apply to employees whose normal working hours in the service of the employer are less than fifteen hours each week.

SECTION 1A. Said section one of said chapter one hundred and fifty-two, as amended, is hereby further amended by striking out paragraph (5), as appearing in the Tercentenary Edition, and inserting in place thereof the following paragraph: — G. L (Ter. Ed.), 152, § 1, etc., amended.

(5) "Employer", an individual, partnership, association, corporation or other legal entity, including the legal representatives of a deceased employer, or the receiver or trustee of an individual, partnership, association, or corporation or other legal entity, employing employees subject to this chapter. "Employer" defined.

SECTION 2. Said section one of said chapter one hundred and fifty-two is hereby further amended by adding at the end of paragraph (6), as appearing in the Tercentenary Edition, the words: — or is a self-insurer under subsection 2 (*a*) or 2 (*b*) of section twenty-five A, — so as to read as follows: — G. L (Ter. Ed.), 152, § 1, amended.

(6) "Insured" or "insured person", an employer who has provided by insurance for the payment to his employees by an insurer of the compensation provided for by this chapter, or is a self-insurer under subsection 2 (*a*) or 2 (*b*) of section twenty-five A. "Insured", etc., defined.

SECTION 3. Said section one of said chapter one hundred and fifty-two, as amended, is hereby further amended by striking out paragraph (4), as amended by chapter four hundred and six of the acts of nineteen hundred and thirty-five, and inserting in place thereof the following paragraph: — G. L (Ter. Ed.), 152, § 1, etc., amended.

(4) "Employee", every person in the service of another under any contract of hire, express or implied, oral or written, excepting masters of and seamen on vessels engaged in interstate or foreign commerce, persons employed by an express company, sleeping car company, or carrier subject to Part I or Part II of the Interstate Commerce Act, and persons employed by telephone companies subject to the federal communications act and excepting one whose employment is not in the usual course of the trade, business, profession or occupation of his employer, but not excepting a person conclusively presumed to be an employee under section twenty-six of this chapter. The provisions of this chapter shall remain elective as to employers of the following: —persons employing six or less, or persons employed as domestic servants and farm laborers, members of an employer's family dwelling in "Employee" defined.

his household, and persons other than laborers, workmen and mechanics employed by religious, charitable or educational institutions.

Any reference to an employee who has been injured shall, when the employee is dead, also include his legal representatives, dependents and other persons to whom compensation may be payable.

G. L. (Ter. Ed.), 152, § 21, amended.

SECTION 4. Section twenty-one of said chapter one hundred and fifty-two, as appearing in the Tercentenary Edition, is hereby amended by adding at the end the words: — or by self-insurance, as provided by this chapter, — so as to read as follows: — *Section 21.* Every insured person shall, as soon as he secures a policy, give written or printed notice to all persons under contract of hire with him that he has provided for payment to injured employees by the insurer, or by self-insurance, as provided by this chapter.

Notice to employees.

G. L. (Ter. Ed.), 152, § 23, amended.

SECTION 5. Said chapter one hundred and fifty-two is hereby further amended by striking out section twenty-three, as so appearing, and inserting in place thereof the following section: — *Section 23.* If an employee files any claim for, or accepts payment of, compensation on account of personal injury under this chapter, or makes any agreement, or submits to a hearing before a member of the department under section eight, such action shall constitute a release to the insured or self-insurer of all claims or demands at law, if any, arising from the injury.

Acceptance of payment, etc., by employee to release employer from liability.

G. L. (Ter. Ed.), 152, § 24, amended.

SECTION 6. Section twenty-four of said chapter one hundred and fifty-two, as so appearing, is hereby further amended by striking out, in the first line, the words "of an insured person", — by inserting after the word "person" in the seventh line the words: — or self-insurer, — and by striking out, in the eighth line, the words "notice of such insurance" and inserting in place thereof the words: — the time said employer became an insured person or a self-insurer, — so as to read as follows: — *Section 24.* An employee shall be held to have waived his right of action at common law or under the law of any other jurisdiction in respect to an injury therein occurring, to recover damages for personal injuries if he shall not have given his employer, at the time of his contract of hire, written notice that he claimed such right, or, if the contract of hire was made before the employer became an insured person or self-insurer, if the employee shall not have given the said notice within thirty days of the time said employer became an insured person or a self-insurer. An employee who has given notice to his employer that he claimed his right of action as aforesaid may waive such claim by a written notice, which shall take effect five days after it is delivered to the employer or his agent. The notices required by this section shall be given in such manner as the department may approve.

Notice by employee to retain common law rights.

G. L. (Ter. Ed.), 152, new §§ 25A-25D, added.

SECTION 7. Said chapter one hundred and fifty-two is hereby further amended by inserting after section twenty-five, as so appearing, under the caption COMPULSORY COMPEN-

SATION AND SELF-INSURANCE, the four following sections: — *Section 25A.* In order to promote the health, safety and welfare of employees, every employer shall provide for the payment to his employees of the compensation provided for by this chapter in the following manner: — New heading. Compulsory compensation and self-insurance.

(1) By insurance with an insurer, or

(2) Subject to the rules of the department, by obtaining from the department annually a license as a self-insurer by conforming to the provisions of one of the two following sub-paragraphs and also to the provisions of sub-paragraph (*c*), if required: —

(*a*) By keeping on deposit with the state treasurer in trust for the benefit and security of employees such amount of securities, not less in market value than ten thousand dollars, as may be required by the department, said securities to be in the form of cash, bonds, stocks or other evidences of indebtedness as the department may require, and to be used, liquidated and disbursed only upon the order of the department for the purposes of paying the benefits provided for by this chapter. The department shall, from time to time, determine the liabilities of a self-insurer both incurred or to be incurred because of personal injuries to employees under this chapter. The department may at any time require an additional deposit or further security or permit a decrease in the market value of said deposit provided the value of said deposit in no case shall be less than ten thousand dollars. The department may permit a substitution of securities in place of those deposited. Interest, dividends and other income from said deposit or deposits shall be payable to the employer who deposited them, unless and until the department shall direct otherwise. The deposit or deposits may be returned to the employer if the employer shall insure with an insurer under subsection (1) of this section, or qualify as a self-insurer under sub-paragraph (*b*) of this section, or if he shall cease to transact business in the commonwealth; provided, that in any case he satisfies the department that he is not under any obligation to pay compensation under this chapter, or, if the department so requires, he furnishes the department with a single premium non-cancellable policy, approved by the department, securing him against any liability that may have arisen under this chapter. No deposit so deposited shall be assignable or subject to attachment or be liable in any way for the debt of the self-insurer. Deposit with state treasurer.

(*b*) By furnishing annually to the state treasurer a bond with a corporate surety company authorized to do business in this commonwealth, in such form and in such an amount not less than ten thousand dollars as may be required by the department, said bond, however, to be upon the condition that if the license of the principal shall be revoked or if the department shall refuse to renew the license, the principal shall upon demand fully comply with sub-paragraph (*a*) of this section relative to the deposit of securities or a single premium non-cancellable policy. The department shall, from Surety company bond.

time to time, determine the liabilities of a self-insurer both incurred or to be incurred because of personal injuries to employees under this chapter. The department may at any time require an additional bond, similarly conditioned, or further security or permit a decrease in the amount of said bond provided the amount of the bond or the bonds in no case shall be less than ten thousand dollars. The liability of the surety shall not exceed in the aggregate the penal sum or sums stated in any such bond or bonds or in any endorsements giving effect to any such increase or reduction. The department may permit a substitution of a new bond or bonds for the bond or bonds which have been furnished.

Reinsurance against catastrophe. (c) As a further guarantee of a self-insurer's ability to pay the benefits provided for by this chapter to injured employees, the department may require that a self-insurer reinsure his compensation risk against catastrophe, and such reinsurance, when so required, shall be placed only with an insurance company admitted to do business in this commonwealth.

Rules and regulations, hearings, etc. (3) The department may make rules governing self-insurers, and may revoke or refuse to renew the license of a self-insurer because of the failure of such self-insurer promptly to make payments of compensation provided for by this chapter, or for any other reasonable cause. Any person aggrieved by the action of the department in refusing to grant a license or in revoking, or refusing to renew, a license of a self-insurer under this section or by the action of the department in requiring an additional deposit or further security under sub-paragraph (*a*) of this section, or in requiring a further bond or security for an additional sum under sub-paragraph (*b*) of this section may demand a hearing before the department, and if, after said hearing, the department denies his petition, he may within ten days after receipt of a notice stating reasons for such denial, file a petition in the superior court for Suffolk county for a review thereof; but the filing of such a petition shall not suspend the action of the department unless a stay thereof shall be allowed by the justice pending a final determination by the court. The court shall summarily hear the petition and may make any appropriate order or decree.

Expenses. (4) Such expenses as shall be determined by the department of administration and finance as necessary to carry out the provisions of this chapter relating to self-insurance shall be assessed against all self-insurers, including for this purpose employers who have ceased to exercise the privilege of self-insurance but whose securities are retained on deposit in accordance with the rules of the department. The basis of assessment shall be the proportion of such expense that the total securities deposited by each self-insurer or penal sum of bond or bonds furnished by each self-insurer at the close of each fiscal year bears to the total deposits and bonds of all self-insurers. All such assessments when collected shall be paid into the state treasury.

Section 25B. Section twenty-five A shall not apply to the commonwealth or the various counties, cities, towns and districts provided for in sections sixty-nine to seventy-five, inclusive. Any employer may bring an employee or employees for whom he is not required by this chapter to provide for the payment of compensation within the coverage of this chapter by providing for the payment of compensation to such employee or employees as provided by this chapter.

Section 25A not applicable to cities, towns, etc.

Section 25C. If an employer who is required to provide for the payment to his employees of the compensation provided for by this chapter fails to do so, he shall be punished by a fine of not more than five hundred dollars or by imprisonment for not more than one year, or both. Failure of an employer, after imposition of the foregoing penalty, to provide for the payment of compensation under this chapter after notice by the department to such employer so to do shall, as to each such notice, be deemed a further violation in respect thereof and the same penalty shall be imposed. If such employer is a corporation, the president or treasurer, or both, shall be liable for such penalty.

Failure to insure, etc. Penalty.

Section 25D. No self-insurer or attorney acting in its behalf shall engage a service company or like organization to investigate, adjust, or settle claims under this chapter or to represent it in any matter before the department. Any violation of this section shall constitute reasonable cause for revocation of the license of a self-insurer under section twenty-five A of this chapter.

Self-insurer, etc., not to engage service company, etc.

SECTION 8. Said chapter one hundred and fifty-two is hereby further amended by striking out section twenty-six, as most recently amended by chapter three hundred and two of the acts of the current year, and inserting in place thereof the following section: — *Section 26.* If an employee who has not given notice of his claim of common law rights of action under section twenty-four, or who has given such notice and has waived the same, receives a personal injury arising out of and in the course of his employment, or arising out of an ordinary risk of the street while actually engaged, with his employer's authorization, in the business affairs or undertakings of his employer, and whether within or without the commonwealth, he shall be paid compensation by the insurer or self-insurer, as hereinafter provided; provided, that as to an injury occurring without the commonwealth he has not given notice of his claim of rights of action under the laws of the jurisdiction wherein such injury occurs or has given such notice and has waived it. For the purposes of this section any person, while operating or using a motor or other vehicle, whether or not belonging to his employer, with his employer's general authorization or approval, in the performance of work in connection with the business affairs or undertakings of his employer, and whether within or without the commonwealth, and any person who, while engaged in the usual course of his trade, business, profession or occupation, is ordered by an em-

G. L. (Ter. Ed.), 152, § 26, etc., amended

Payments. Presumption of employment. Extraterritoriality.

ployer, or by a person exercising superintendence on behalf of such employer, to perform work which is not in the usual course of such work, trade, business, profession or occupation, and while so performing such work, receives a personal injury, shall be conclusively presumed to be an employee, and if an employee while acting in the course of his employment receives injury resulting from frost bite, heat exhaustion or sunstroke, without having voluntarily assumed increased peril not contemplated by his contract of employment, or is injured by reason of the physical activities of fellow employees in which he does not participate, whether or not such activities are associated with the employment, such injury shall be conclusively presumed to have arisen out of the employment.

G. L. (Ter. Ed.), 152, § 28, etc., amended.

SECTION 9. Said chapter one hundred and fifty-two is hereby further amended by striking out section twenty-eight, as amended by section two of chapter two hundred and ninety-two of the acts of nineteen hundred and thirty-four, and inserting in place thereof the following section: — *Section 28.* If the employee is injured by reason of the serious and wilful misconduct of an employer or of any person regularly intrusted with and exercising the powers of superintendence, the amounts of compensation hereinafter provided shall be doubled. In case the employer is insured, he shall repay to the insurer the extra compensation paid to the employee. If a claim is made under this section, and the employer is insured, the employer may appear and defend against such claim only. The employment of any minor, known to be such, in violation of any provision of sections sixty to seventy-four, inclusive, or of section one hundred and four of chapter one hundred and forty-nine shall constitute serious and wilful misconduct under this section.

Wilful misconduct by employer.

Double compensation

G. L. (Ter. Ed.), 152, § 66, amended.

SECTION 9A. Said chapter one hundred and fifty-two is hereby further amended by striking out section sixty-six, as appearing in the Tercentenary Edition, and inserting in place thereof the following section: — *Section 66.* In an action to recover damages for personal injury sustained by an employee in the course of his employment or for death resulting from personal injury so sustained, it shall not be a defense:

Certain defenses denied to employer.

1. That the employee was negligent;
2. That the injury was caused by the negligence of a fellow employee;
3. That the employee had assumed voluntarily or contractually the risk of the injury;
4. That the employee's injury did not result from negligence or other fault of the employer, if such injury arose out of and in the course of employment.

G. L. (Ter. Ed.), 152, § 67, amended.

SECTION 10. Said chapter one hundred and fifty-two is hereby further amended by striking out section sixty-seven, as so appearing, and inserting in place thereof the following section: — *Section 67.* Section sixty-six shall not apply to actions to recover damages for personal injuries sustained by domestic servants and farm laborers, nor to actions for such injuries received by employees of an insured person or a self-insurer.

Application of § 66, limited.

Paragraph 4 of said section sixty-six shall not apply to actions to recover damages for personal injuries sustained by any person, whose employer has a right of election as provided in paragraph 4 of section one.

G. L. (Ter Ed.), 152, § 68, amended.

SECTION 11. Said chapter one hundred and fifty-two is hereby further amended by striking out section sixty-eight, as so appearing, and inserting in place thereof the following section: — *Section 68.* Chapter one hundred and fifty-three and sections four and seven to ten, inclusive, of chapter two hundred and twenty-nine shall not apply to employees of an insured person or a self-insurer, nor to laborers, workmen or mechanics employed by the commonwealth or any county, city, town or district subject to sections sixty-nine to seventy-five, inclusive, who are entitled to the benefits provided by said sections, while this chapter is applicable thereto.

Application of certain other laws.

G. L. (Ter. Ed.), 152, § 76, etc., amended.

SECTION 12. Said chapter one hundred and fifty-two is hereby further amended by striking out section seventy-six, inserted by section one of chapter four hundred and sixty-five of the acts of nineteen hundred and thirty-nine, and inserting in place thereof the following section: — *Section 76.* The right to and liability for and the amounts of compensation payable for personal injuries arising out of and in the course of employment in the granite industries and resulting from silicosis or other occupational pulmonary dust disease shall be subject to and governed by sections seventy-seven to eighty-five, inclusive, anything in this chapter to the contrary notwithstanding. An employer, the compensation for whose employees is subject to and governed by said sections seventy-seven to eighty-five, inclusive, may, in lieu of becoming an insured person become a self-insurer; and said sections seventy-seven to eighty-five, inclusive, shall apply to an employer who is a self-insurer as well as to an employer who is an insured person.

Silicosis, etc.

G. L. (Ter. Ed.), 152, § 22, amended.

SECTION 13. Section twenty-two of said chapter one hundred and fifty-two, as appearing in the Tercentenary Edition, is hereby amended by adding the words: — or by means of self-insurance as provided in this chapter, — at the end of the first sentence, — and by inserting after the word "insured", in the fourth line, the words: — by an insurance company, — so as to read as follows: — *Section 22.* Every insured person shall give written or printed notice to every person with whom he is about to enter into a contract of hire that he has provided for payment to injured employees by the insurer or by means of self-insurance as provided in this chapter. An employer ceasing to be insured by an insurance company shall, on or before the day on which his policy expires, give written or printed notice thereof to all persons under contract with him. In case of the renewal of the policy no notice shall be required. He

Notice to employees.

shall file a copy of said notice with the department. The notices required by this and the preceding section may be given in the manner therein provided or in such other manner as may be approved by the department.

Effective date.

SECTION 14. This act shall take effect on November fifteenth in the year nineteen hundred and forty-three.

Approved June 12, 1943.

---

*Chap.*530 AN ACT AUTHORIZING THE APPOINTMENT TO THE REGULAR FIRE FORCE IN CITIES OF CERTAIN CALL MEMBERS THEREOF.

Be it enacted, etc., as follows:

G. L. (Ter. Ed.), 31, § 19A, etc., amended.

Section nineteen A of chapter thirty-one of the General Laws, as most recently amended by chapter thirty-eight of the acts of nineteen hundred and forty-one, is hereby further amended by adding at the end the following new sentence: — The provisions of this section shall not be deemed to prevent the appointment to the regular force of a city of a call fireman who has been a call member in such city for more than five years prior to June fifteenth, nineteen hundred and forty-three, — so as to read as follows: — *Section 19A.* In each city in which there has been established a reserve force of firemen in its fire department under the provisions of sections fifty-nine B to fifty-nine D, inclusive, of chapter forty-eight, appointments to the regular force shall be made by the appointing authority upon certification by the director from the list of members of the reserve force of firemen, in accordance with the rules of the commission, except that the basis of certification shall be the order of appointment to the reserve force, or, if not ascertainable, the order of the respective ratings of such members obtained in the examination upon which the list of eligibles for appointment to such reserve force was based. No person who has passed his fiftieth birthday shall be appointed from such a reserve force to such a regular force. The provisions of this section shall not be deemed to prevent the appointment to the regular force of a city of a call fireman who has been a call member in such city for more than five years prior to June fifteenth, nineteen hundred and forty-three.

Appointment to regular fire forces in certain cities.

Approved June 12, 1943.

---

*Chap.*531 AN ACT RELATIVE TO THE TAXATION OF LIFE INSURANCE COMPANIES.

Be it enacted, etc., as follows:

G. L. (Ter. Ed.), 63, § 20, etc., amended.

SECTION 1. Chapter sixty-three of the General Laws is hereby amended by striking out section twenty, as most recently amended by section five of chapter five hundred and nine of the acts of nineteen hundred and forty-one, and inserting in place thereof the following section: — *Section 20.*

Every life insurance company, as defined by section one hundred and eighteen of chapter one hundred and seventy-five, authorized to transact business in the commonwealth shall annually pay an excise, as determined by the commissioner, of two per cent upon all new and renewal premiums received during the preceding calendar year for all policies allocable to this commonwealth, as hereinafter provided. In the case of a foreign life insurance company, the policy shall be deemed to be allocable to this commonwealth if the insured is a resident of the commonwealth at the time of payment of the premium therefor. In the case of a domestic life insurance company, the policy shall be deemed to be allocable to this commonwealth unless the insured at the time of payment of the premium therefor is a resident of a state or country to which such company actually pays an insurance excise. Taxation of life insurance companies.

The word "premiums" as used in this section shall include all amounts received as consideration for life insurance policies without deduction for amounts paid to other companies for reinsurance and shall include dividends applied to purchase additional insurance or to shorten the premium paying period. In the case of domestic life insurance companies only, it shall include amounts received as consideration for annuity contracts which shall be deemed to be allocable in the same manner as policies of life insurance. In determining the amount of the excise payable hereunder there shall be deducted, to the extent that they are properly allocable to premiums taxable hereunder, (*a*) all premiums returned to policyholders during said preceding calendar year but not including cash surrender values, and (*b*) dividends which during said year have been paid or credited to policyholders or applied to purchase additional insurance or to shorten the premium paying period. "Premiums" defined.

All premiums received by any life insurance company for contingencies of any character insured against by such company under authority of clause sixth of section forty-seven of chapter one hundred and seventy-five shall be excluded, except as hereinafter provided, from taxation under this section and shall be taxable under sections twenty-two and twenty-three of this chapter. All premiums received by any such company for provisions for total and permanent disability or accidental death benefit incorporated in policies or contracts under section twenty-four of said chapter one hundred and seventy-five or any supplemental policies issued under said section twenty-four shall be taxable under this section. Exclusion of certain premiums.

Every life insurance company shall annually, on or before March first, make a return to the commissioner on oath of its president or secretary and its actuary, in such form and containing such information as the commissioner may deem necessary for the determination of the tax due under this section and under section twenty-one. Annual returns.

Excise on net value of policies rather than on premiums.

SECTION 2. Any life insurance company, authorized to transact business in the commonwealth on December thirty-first, nineteen hundred and forty-three, which would be required under section twenty of chapter sixty-three of the General Laws, as amended by section one of this act, to pay a premium excise greater than an excise upon the net value of its policies under said section twenty as effective on said date, in the year nineteen hundred and forty-four and in any subsequent consecutive year, in lieu of the two per cent premium excise as provided in said section twenty, as amended by section one of this act, shall, except as hereinafter provided, annually pay the excise upon the net value of policies imposed by said section twenty as effective on December thirty-first, nineteen hundred and forty-three. Said excise shall be paid for each year until the year for which the amount thereof equals or exceeds the amount of the premium excise imposed by said section twenty, as amended by section one of this act, and for that year and annually thereafter such company shall pay an excise on the premium basis. All the provisions of said chapter sixty-three as effective on December thirty-first, nineteen hundred and forty-three, applicable to the excise imposed by said section twenty as then effective, shall continue to apply to the excise payable under the authority of this section upon the basis of net value, and to any life insurance company liable to said excise.

Tax when premium excise less than excise on net value of policies.

SECTION 3. Any life insurance company, authorized to transact business in the commonwealth on December thirty-first, nineteen hundred and forty-three, which would be required under section twenty of chapter sixty-three of the General Laws, as amended by section one of this act, to pay a premium excise less than an excise upon the net value of its policies under said section twenty as effective on said date, in the year nineteen hundred and forty-four and in any subsequent consecutive year, in lieu of the two per cent premium excise as provided in said section twenty, as amended by section one of this act, shall, except as hereinafter provided, annually pay an excise of one quarter of one per cent computed upon said net value of all policies in force on December thirty-first, nineteen hundred and forty-three, issued or assumed by such company on the lives of residents of this commonwealth, or upon a lesser amount as determined by the commissioner of corporations and taxation if, by reason of the cessation of business, the net value of all policies in force on the lives of Massachusetts residents on any subsequent December thirty-first is less than the net value of such policies in force on December thirty-first, nineteen hundred and forty-three. Such excise shall be paid for each year until the year for which the amount of the premium excise imposed by section twenty, as amended by section one of this act, equals or exceeds such excise upon the basis of net value, and for that year and annually thereafter such company shall pay such premium excise. All the provisions of said chapter sixty-three as effective on December thirty-first, nineteen hundred and forty-three, applicable to the excise imposed by said section twenty as then effective, shall except as herein modified continue to apply to the excise payable under the authority of this section upon the basis of net value, and to any life insurance company liable to said excise.

G. L. (Ter. Ed.), 63, § 24, amended.

SECTION 4. Section twenty-four of said chapter sixty-three, as appearing in the Tercentenary Edition, is hereby amended by striking out, in the second line, the word "twenty-one,", — so as to read as follows: — *Section 24.* In determining the amount of the tax payable under sections twenty-two and twenty-three, there shall be deducted all premiums on policies written but not taken, or cancelled through default of payment, and all premiums returned or credited to policyholders during the year for which the tax is determined, provided that all such premiums have been included as premium receipts in a return made under the following section and a tax assessed thereon, and all premiums paid to authorized companies for reinsurance, provided that it is shown to the satisfaction of the commissioner that the tax on such premiums has been or will be paid in full by such reinsuring company.

Deductions.

G. L. (Ter. Ed.), 63, § 25, amended.

SECTION 5. Section twenty-five of said chapter sixty-three, as so appearing, is hereby amended by striking out, in the second line, the word "twenty-one,", — so as to read as follows: — *Section 25.* Every insurance company liable to taxation under section twenty-two or twenty-three shall annually in January make a return to the commissioner in such form as he shall prescribe, on oath of its secretary or other officer having knowledge of the facts, setting forth: if a domestic company, the total amount of gross premiums for all policies written or renewed, of all additional premiums charged and of all assessments made, during the preceding calendar year, and the amount of each class of deductions claimed under any provision of this chapter; if a foreign company, the total amount of gross premiums for all policies written or renewed, of all additional premiums charged and of all assessments made, during the preceding calendar year for insurance of property or interests in this commonwealth, or which are subjects of insurance by contracts issued through companies or agents therein, and the amount of each class of deductions claimed under any provision of this chapter, and in addition to the above any information which the commissioner may require in assessing an excise under any provision of law.

Returns of fire, marine and other insurance companies.

For cause, the commissioner may extend the time within which any such statement may be filed, but not to a date later than March first.

G. L. (Ter. Ed.), 63, § 28, etc., amended.

SECTION 6. Said chapter sixty-three is hereby further amended by striking out section twenty-eight, as most recently amended by section six of said chapter five hundred and nine, and inserting in place thereof the following sec-

Payment of, excise, etc.

tion: — *Section 28.* Every life insurance company liable to taxation under section twenty shall pay to the commissioner at the time fixed for filing its return by said section the amount of the excise thereby imposed and the amount of the retaliatory tax imposed by section twenty-one if such company is also liable to taxation thereunder. As soon as may be, the commissioner from the return required by section twenty and from such other evidence as he may obtain shall make assessment of such excise, giving to each such company notice of the correct amount thereof.

Assessment and notice.

The commissioner shall assess upon all insurance companies liable to taxation under sections twenty-two and twenty-three the excise thereby imposed, and shall forthwith upon making such assessment give to every such company notice of the amount thereof. Such excise shall become due and payable to the commissioner thirty days after the date of such notice but not later than June first.

Interest.

All taxes or any portion thereof not paid when due shall bear interest at the rate of six per cent per annum from the date payable until June first and, whether assessed before or after June first, shall bear interest at the rate of twelve per cent per annum from June first until they are paid.

Application for correction of excise.

Within sixty days after date of notice of assessment, any insurance company may apply to the commissioner for a correction of its excise, and in default of settlement may, upon application within thirty days of the date of notification of the commissioner's decision, be heard thereon by the appellate tax board. If abatement of an excise paid is granted, the overpayment with interest thereon at the rate of six per cent per annum from the date of payment shall be refunded to the company by the state treasurer without any appropriation therefor by the general court.

Effective date.

SECTION 7. This act shall take effect on January first, nineteen hundred and forty-four.

Approved June 12, 1943.

---

*Chap.*532 AN ACT RELATIVE TO GENERAL OR BLANKET POLICIES OF ACCIDENT OR HEALTH INSURANCE FOR THE BENEFIT OF MEMBERS OF TRADE UNIONS AND OTHERS.

Be it enacted, etc., as follows:

G. L. (Ter. Ed.), 175, § 110, etc., amended.

SECTION 1. Chapter one hundred and seventy-five of the General Laws is hereby amended by striking out section one hundred and ten, as most recently amended by section three of chapter four hundred and twenty-four of the acts of nineteen hundred and forty-three, and inserting in place thereof the following section: — *Section 110.* Nothing in sections one hundred and eight and one hundred and nine shall be construed to apply to or affect or prohibit the issue of any general or blanket policy of insurance to (*a*) any employer, whether an individual, association, copartnership, or cor-

Sections 108 and 109 not applicable to certain policies.

poration, or (*b*) any municipal corporation or any department thereof not referred to in (*c*), or (*c*) any police or fire department, or (*d*) any college, school or other institution of learning, or the head or principal thereof, or (*e*) any organization for health, recreational or military instruction or treatment, or (*f*) any underwriters' corps, salvage bureau or like organization, or (*g*) any trade union, under which the officers, members or employees, or classes or departments thereof, or the students or patients thereof, as the case may be, are insured against loss or damage from disease or specified accidental bodily injuries or death caused by such injuries, contracted or sustained while exposed to the hazards of the occupation, the course of instruction or treatment, or otherwise, for a premium intended to cover the risks of all persons insured under such policy. A policy on which the premiums are paid by the employer and the employees jointly, or by the employees, and the benefits of which are offered to all eligible employees, and insuring not less than seventy-five per cent of such employees, or the members of an association of such employees if the members so insured constitute not less than seventy-five per cent of all eligible employees, shall be deemed a general or blanket policy within the meaning of this section. When the premium is to be paid by the trade union and its members jointly, or by its members, and the benefits of the policy are offered to all members, not less than seventy-five per cent of such members may be so insured.

General or blanket policy.

(1) The employer, whether an individual, corporation, co-partnership or association, or a municipal corporation or department thereof including a police or fire department, in case of such a general or blanket policy issued by a domestic mutual life company to such employer, or (2) the college, school or other institution of learning, in case of such a policy so issued to such institution, or (3) the head or principal of the college, school or other institution of learning, in case of such a policy so issued to the head or principal of such institution, or (4) such person as the organization for health, recreation or military instruction or treatment, the underwriters' corps, salvage bureau or like organization or the trade union shall designate, in case of such a policy so issued to such organization or union, shall alone be a member of the company and entitled to one vote by virtue of such policy at the meetings of the company.

Nothing in sections one hundred and eight and one hundred and nine shall be construed to apply to or affect or prohibit the issue of any general or blanket policy of insurance to any association of state, county or municipal employees who are regularly and permanently employed by the commonwealth, a county or a municipality and, if employed by the commonwealth or the city of Boston are paid by a common paymaster, as defined in section one hundred and thirty-three, and are eligible for membership in the retirement association for the employees of the commonwealth or of the city of Boston, or to an association of employees of two or more municipalities within one county who are regularly and permanently employed by one or more such municipalities, insuring the members of the association against loss or damage from disease or specified accidental bodily injuries or death caused by such injuries, contracted or sustained while exposed to the hazards of their occupation, for a premium intended to cover the risks of all the persons insured under such policy. No person shall be eligible for coverage under such a policy as a member of more than one such association. A policy on which the premium is paid by the members of the association and the benefits of which are offered to all its members, and insuring not less than fifty members and seventy-five per cent of all persons eligible for membership in the association shall be deemed to be a general or blanket policy within the meaning of this section.

The provisions of section one hundred and thirty-eight A shall apply to deductions on pay-roll schedules from the salary of any state, county or municipal employee for the payment of premiums on a general or blanket policy issued to such an association of state, county or municipal employees.

Any blanket or general policy issued under this section to an employer or to an association of state, county or municipal employees may also insure the dependents of employees or members insured thereunder, in respect to medical, surgical and hospital expenses.

G. L. (Ter. Ed.), 175, § 94, etc., amended.

SECTION 2. The first paragraph of section ninety-four of said chapter one hundred and seventy-five, as most recently amended by section two of chapter two hundred and eighteen of the acts of nineteen hundred and thirty-eight, is hereby further amended by inserting after the word "and" in the thirteenth line the words: — , except as provided in section one hundred and ten, — so as to read as follows: — Except as provided in this section and in sections thirty-six and one hundred and thirty-seven, every person insured under a policy of life or endowment insurance issued by a domestic mutual life company shall be a member thereof and entitled to one vote, and one vote additional for each five thousand dollars of insurance in excess of the first five thousand dollars, every person holding an annuity or pure endowment contract issued by any such company shall be a member thereof and entitled to one vote and, in the case of an annuity contract, one vote additional for each one hundred and fifty dollars of annual annuity income in excess of the first one hundred and fifty dollars, and, except as provided in section one hundred and ten, every person insured under any policy of insurance issued by any such company under clause sixth of section forty-seven shall be a member thereof and entitled to one vote. Holders of such policies or contracts shall be notified of the annual meetings of the company by written notice, or by an imprint in the form prescribed by section seventy-six upon the filing back of its policies or contracts, or, in the case of policies upon which

Mutual life companies. Members. Proxies. Directors.

premiums are payable monthly or oftener, on some other prominent place on each policy, and also upon premium receipts or certificates of renewal. *Approved June 12, 1943.*

AN ACT RESTRICTING THE OPERATION OF A LAW PASSED IN THE CURRENT YEAR RELATIVE TO THE TAKING OF LOBSTERS AND EDIBLE CRABS FROM THE COASTAL WATERS OF ESSEX COUNTY. *Chap.* 533

Be it enacted, etc., as follows:

SECTION 1. Section thirty-seven of chapter one hundred and thirty of the General Laws, as most recently amended by chapter one hundred and forty-nine of the acts of the current year, is hereby further amended by striking out the paragraph amended by said chapter one hundred and forty-nine and inserting in place thereof the following paragraph: — G. L. (Ter. Ed.), 130, § 37, etc., amended.

In the waters of Dukes county, and of Marblehead and Swampscott in Essex county, no such pot, trap or other contrivance shall be buoyed otherwise than separately and plainly. Buoying of pots, traps, etc.

SECTION 2. This act shall take effect upon its passage. Effective date.

Approved June 12, 1943.

AN ACT MAKING CERTAIN CHANGES IN THE EMPLOYMENT SECURITY LAW. *Chap.* 534

Whereas, The deferred operation of this act would tend to defeat one of its principal purposes which is to make available immediately during the present emergency increased benefits under the employment security law, to be computed from April first of the current year, therefore this act is hereby declared to be an emergency law, necessary for the immediate preservation of the public convenience. Emergency preamble.

Be it enacted, etc., as follows:

SECTION 1. Section fourteen of chapter one hundred and fifty-one A of the General Laws, as appearing in section one of chapter six hundred and eighty-five of the acts of nineteen hundred and forty-one, is hereby amended by striking out subsection (*b*) (2) and inserting in place thereof the following subsection: — G. L. (Ter. Ed.), 151A, § 14, etc., amended.

(2) When, in any calendar year, beginning not earlier than nineteen hundred and thirty-nine, a worker is paid benefits for the first compensable week of unemployment with respect to the benefit year to which the claim applies, his wages from each employer during his base period shall be termed "worker's benefit wages" and shall be treated for the purposes of this subsection as if they had been paid in the year in which the first week of benefits is paid. "Worker's benefit wages" when used with respect to benefits paid for the first compensable week of unem- "Worker's benefit wages" defined.

ployment on claims originally arising in the year nineteen hundred and thirty-nine or in the years nineteen hundred and forty, nineteen hundred and forty-one, nineteen hundred and forty-two and prior to April first, nineteen hundred and forty-three, shall include the wages not in excess of one thousand dollars in those quarters upon which the benefits available to the claimant were computed, assignable to its respective year of nineteen hundred and thirty-nine to nineteen hundred and forty-three, inclusive, in accordance with this subsection. For the purposes of this subsection, and effective as of April first, nineteen hundred and forty-three, benefit wages charged against each employer shall include only that part of wages not in excess of twelve hundred dollars paid by him in a base period.

G. L. (Ter. Ed.), 151A, § 14, etc., amended.

SECTION 1A. Section fourteen of said chapter one hundred and fifty-one A is hereby amended by inserting after subsection fourteen (*b*) the following: —

Merger, consolidation, etc., of employing units.

14. (*c*) For the purposes of this section, when the employing enterprises of an employer or employers are continued solely and without interruption by an employing unit not previously subject to this chapter, the contribution record of the predecessors and the record of workers' benefit wages which were charged or would have been charged to the predecessor employer or employers, if no change in legal identity or form had occurred, shall cease to be the records of the predecessor employer and shall become part of the records of the successor employing unit in determining his benefit wage ratio in the following cases:

1. Where two or more employers are consolidated into a new employing unit.

2. Where a new employing unit consisting of one or more of the former partners or one or more of the former partners and one or more individuals so succeeds to the employing enterprises of the previous partnership.

3. Where a partnership of which the individual is a member so succeeds to the employing enterprises formerly carried on by that individual.

4. Where a receiver, trustee, executor, administrator or other officer under designation or approval of a court for the purposes of carrying on pending liquidation or reorganization as such, so succeeds to the employing enterprises carried on by his predecessor.

Provided, however, that in each instance, except item 4 above, the succeeding employing unit shall have guaranteed to the director payment of all contributions required of the predecessors; and provided, further, that for the balance of the calendar year in which any such change of identity or form occurs the contribution rate of the succeeding employing unit shall be the rate applicable to the predecessor or predecessors except under item 1 above when for the balance of such year the rate shall be 2.7%.

The provisions of this subsection shall apply in determining the contribution rates of employers for the year nineteen hundred and forty-two and for subsequent years provided that the successor employing unit has filed with the director a notice of such change in legal identity or form of the employer or employers, such notice to be filed in the form and manner prescribed by the director within three months after the date on which this act becomes effective, or within two months after the last day of the quarter in which said change occurred, whichever is later.

The provisions of this subsection shall not apply where an employer acquires the employing enterprises of another employing unit.

SECTION 1B. The designations of subsections (*c*) and (*d*) of said section fourteen are hereby changed to subsections (*d*) and (*e*), respectively. Designations of subsections (*c*) and (*d*), changed.

SECTION 2. Said chapter one hundred and fifty-one A is hereby further amended by striking out the period at the end of section eight, as so appearing, and inserting in place thereof the following: — ; or G. L. (Ter. Ed.), 151A, § 8, etc., amended.

(*g*) Has taken under designation of a court temporary or permanent control or custody of the organization, trade or business, or substantially all the assets, of an employer subject to this chapter and employs one or more individuals whose wages are paid from or are chargeable upon the assets or estate of said employer; or Employers, who are.

(*h*) Has taken under an assignment or agreement of parties temporary or permanent control or custody of the organization, trade or business, or substantially all the assets, of an employer subject to this chapter and employs one or more individuals whose wages are paid from or are chargeable upon the assets or estate of said employer.

SECTION 3. Section twenty-three of said chapter one hundred and fifty-one A, as so appearing, is hereby further amended by striking out subsection (*e*). G. L. (Ter. Ed.), 151A, § 23, etc., amended.

SECTION 4. Said chapter one hundred and fifty-one A is hereby further amended by striking out section thirty-three, as so appearing. G. L. (Ter. Ed.), 151A, § 33, etc., stricken out.

SECTION 5. Effective as of April first, nineteen hundred and forty-three, said chapter one hundred and fifty-one A is hereby further amended by striking out section twenty-nine (*a*), as so appearing, and inserting in place thereof the following: — *Section 29.* (*a*) An individual in total unemployment and otherwise eligible for benefits shall be paid for each week of unemployment an amount based on the highest quarterly wage of his base period as provided in the following table: — G. L. (Ter. Ed.), 151A, § 29 (*a*), etc., amended. Weekly benefit rates.

Total Wages earned in Highest Quarter.	Weekly Benefit Rate.
$119 99 or less	$6 00
120 00–$139 99	7 00
140 00– 159 99	8 00
160 00– 179 99	9 00
180 00– 199 99	10 00
200 00– 219 99	11 00
220 00– 239 99	12 00

Total Wages earned in Highest Quarter.	Weekly Benefit Rate.
$240 00–$259 99	$13 00
260 00– 279 99	14 00
280 00– 299 99	15 00
300 00– 319 99	16 00
320 00– 339 99	17 00
340 00 and over	18 00

G. L. (Ter. Ed.), 151A, § 42, etc., amended.

Review in district court. Petition, etc.

SECTION 6. Said chapter one hundred and fifty-one A is hereby further amended by striking out section forty-two, as so appearing, and inserting in place thereof the following section: — *Section 42.* The director or any interested person aggrieved by any decision in any proceeding before the board of review may obtain judicial review of such decision by filing, within twenty days of the date of mailing of such decision, a petition for review thereof in the district court within the judicial district whereof he lives, or is or was last employed, or has his usual place of business, and in such proceeding every other party to the proceeding before the board shall be made a party respondent. The petition for review need not be verified but shall state the grounds upon which such review is sought. The director shall be deemed to be a party to any such proceeding. It shall not be necessary as a condition precedent to the judicial review of any decision of the board of review to enter exceptions to the rulings of such board. Upon the filing of a petition for review by an aggrieved party other than the director a notice and copy of the petition shall be served upon the director by registered mail fourteen days at least before the return day, and at the same time there shall be delivered to the director as many copies of the notice and petition as there are parties respondent. With his answer or petition the director shall file with the court a certified copy of the decision of the board of review, including all documents and papers and a transcript of all testimony taken at the hearing before said board. Upon the filing of a petition for review by the director or upon the service of a petition on him, the director shall forthwith send by registered mail to each other party to the proceeding a copy of such notice and petition, and such mailing shall be deemed to be completed service upon all such parties. In any proceeding under this section the findings of the board of review as to the facts, if supported by any evidence, shall be conclusive, and the court shall render a decision or decree in accordance with such findings. Any proceeding under this section shall be heard in a summary manner and shall be given precedence over all other civil cases. An appeal may be taken from the decision of the district court to the supreme judicial court. Upon the final determination of such judicial proceeding the director shall enter an order in accordance with the terms of the decision or decree terminating such proceeding.

Approved June 12, 1943.

AN ACT TO MEET CERTAIN CONTINGENCIES ARISING IN CONNECTION WITH THE SERVICE OF PUBLIC OFFICERS AND EMPLOYEES AND CERTAIN OTHER PERSONS IN THE CLASSIFIED CIVIL SERVICE OF THE UNITED STATES AND THE COMMONWEALTH OF MASSACHUSETTS DURING THE EXISTING STATE OF WAR. *Chap.*535

Emergency preamble.

Whereas, The deferred operation of this act would tend to defeat its purpose, which in part is to protect the rights of certain persons in the classified civil service of the United States and the commonwealth of Massachusetts during the existing state of war, whose employment in the service of the division of employment security of this commonwealth was terminated by reason of executive order number 8990, December twenty-third, nineteen hundred and forty-one, of the President of the United States, and to facilitate their reinstatement in their former offices or positions in the official service of the commonwealth, therefore it is hereby declared to be an emergency law, necessary for the preservation of the public convenience.

Be it enacted, etc., as follows:

SECTION 1. (*a*) All employees, except as otherwise provided in this section, in the division of employment security who had been appointed on a permanent basis, including employees who had not completed their probationary period, and whose employment in the service of the commonwealth was terminated on December thirty-first, nineteen hundred and forty-one, by reason of executive order number 8990, issued by the President of the United States on December twenty-third, nineteen hundred and forty-one, and who, for the purpose of service during the existing state of war, were inducted into the United States employment service, shall be reinstated in the division of employment security or its successor providing the offices or positions formerly held by them are reestablished in the division of employment security or its successor. Such reinstatement shall be in accordance with the civil service laws and rules of the commonwealth and shall confer upon the employees the full promotional privileges and seniority rights which would have accrued to them under said laws and rules if they had remained in the employ of said division of employment security or its successor.

(*b*) In the event that the offices or positions formerly held by them in the division of employment security are not reestablished in said division or its successor, they may, upon request of the appointing authority and the approval of the director of civil service, be reemployed in similar positions in the division of employment security or its successor or in any other department of the commonwealth. If such appointments are made, their seniority shall be determined in accordance with the civil service laws and rules of the commonwealth.

(c) In the event that there are no offices or positions vacant in the division of employment security or its successor or in any other department, board or commission of the commonwealth at the time of the termination of their employment in the United States employment service or its successor, their names shall be placed on a special list in accordance with the provisions of the civil service laws and rules of the commonwealth.

(d) Paragraphs (a), (b) and (c) shall apply to employees who have served in the United States employment service or its successor continuously since their induction under said executive order number 8990, or whose services have been terminated without fault or delinquency on their part, or who have terminated their services with the United States employment service or its successor for the express purpose of accepting an offer of reinstatement or reemployment in the division of employment security, or who were ordered or transferred without their consent to some other position in the United States civil service from the United States employment service or its successor after they were inducted into the United States employment service by said executive order number 8990.

(e) All persons referred to in paragraphs (a), (b), (c) and (d) shall be entitled to all rights and privileges provided by chapter seven hundred and eight of the acts of nineteen hundred and forty-one, as amended; provided, that they would have been subject to the provisions of said chapter seven hundred and eight, as amended, had they remained in the service of the division of employment security or its successor; and provided, further, that the same or similar positions are reestablished in the division of employment security or its successor or exist in some other department, board or commission of the commonwealth.

(f) An employee, as referred to in paragraph (a), who is transferred with his consent to some other position in the United States civil service from the United States employment service or its successor after he was inducted into the United States employment service by said executive order number 8990 shall, at the time of termination of his employment in the United States civil service, have his name placed on a special list in accordance with the provisions of the civil service laws and rules of the commonwealth; provided, that such termination is without fault or delinquency on his part; and provided, further, that such employee makes application for the placement of his name on such special list within sixty days after the termination of his employment in such other position in the United States civil service.

(g) The director of civil service shall for the purpose of this section make all determinations as to whether an employee's services were terminated without fault or delinquency on his part or whether or not a transfer has been with his consent or without his consent.

SECTION 1A. Any person referred to in paragraphs (*a*), (*b*), (*c*) and (*d*) of section one who, during his employment in the United States employment service, or its successor, is promoted to a higher position, and said promotion is made in conformance with the provisions of the civil service laws and rules of the commonwealth, may, upon the request of the director of said division of employment security and with the approval of the director of civil service, be reemployed in the same or similar position in said division of employment security. The seniority of such persons shall be established in accordance with the civil service laws and rules of the commonwealth. The provisions of this section shall in no way affect any rights and privileges granted to persons under section one of this act.

SECTION 2. Whenever a person is certified for appointment to the United States employment service or its successor, in accordance with the civil service laws and rules of the commonwealth, for the duration of the war, and such person has served a probationary period, and his employment is terminated without fault or delinquency of his own, his name shall be placed upon a special list in accordance with the civil service laws and rules of the commonwealth. Such person, upon the request of the appointing authority and with the approval of the director of civil service, may be appointed to the same or similar position in the classified service. Any rights, if he is so appointed, that he would be entitled to under the civil service laws and rules of the commonwealth if he had been appointed in the first instance to said division of employment security rather than to the United States employment service, shall be credited or available to him from the date of his appointment to said United States employment service during the existing state of war. If he is appointed to any other department, his seniority shall be determined in accordance with the civil service laws and rules of the commonwealth.

SECTION 3. (*a*) Any person referred to in section one shall, when reinstated, appointed or reemployed in his former position or in a similar position, as provided by this act, be restored to full status under the contributory retirement system or any other pension or retirement law under which he had actual or inchoate rights at the time of the termination of his employment in the service of said division of employment security, and shall receive credit for his full service while he was a member of the federal and state retirement systems if his accumulated deductions in the state retirement system have not been withdrawn, or if he pays into the annuity savings fund of said state retirement system, as provided by chapter thirty-two of the General Laws, the full amount withdrawn by him upon the termination of his employment in the service of said division of employment security, and in either case an additional amount equal to the payments, with regular interest, which he would have contributed if he had remained a member of said state retirement system.

(b) Any person referred to in section two shall, when appointed to a state department, commission or board, receive credit for his full service while he was a member of the federal retirement system, if he pays into the annuity savings fund of the state retirement system, as provided by chapter thirty-two of the General Laws, an amount equal to the payments, with regular interest, which he would have contributed if he had been appointed in the first instance to the state service rather than to the United States employment service or its successor.

SECTION 4. Any person who returns or is restored to service in an office or position in the service of said division of employment security or its successor after having terminated his service with the United States employment service or its successor, shall be entitled to all seniority rights to which he would have been entitled if his service with said division of employment security had not been terminated, and any such person whose salary is fixed under a classified compensation plan shall be eligible to a salary rate which includes accrued step-rate increments to which he would have been eligible except for his absence from the service of said division of employment security.

SECTION 5. Service with the United States employment service or its successor, referred to in this act, shall, except as otherwise provided herein, mean such service occurring on and after January first, nineteen hundred and forty-two, and prior to the date on which said service of such individuals has terminated. *Approved June 12, 1943.*

---

*Chap.*536 AN ACT RELATIVE TO CONTRIBUTIONS BY THE TOWN OF HULL TOWARD THE COST OF STEAMBOAT SERVICE BETWEEN SAID TOWN AND THE CITY OF BOSTON.

Be it enacted, etc., as follows:

SECTION 1. The town of Hull may appropriate from available funds the sum of ten thousand dollars for the purpose of carrying out for the year nineteen hundred and forty-three the provisions of chapter five hundred and one of the acts of nineteen hundred and forty-three, anything to the contrary contained in said chapter notwithstanding.

SECTION 2. This act shall take full effect only if and when said chapter five hundred and one is accepted by vote of the inhabitants of said town, as provided by said chapter.

Approved June 12, 1943.

AN ACT RELATIVE TO STATE WIDE VERIFICATION OF VOTING LISTS. Chap.537

Be it enacted, etc., as follows:

SECTION 1. Chapter four hundred and fifty of the acts of nineteen hundred and thirty-nine is hereby amended by striking out section one and inserting in place thereof the following: — *Section 1.* The registrars of voters or officers under special laws performing like duties in each city and town, in this act called registrars, shall, between June first in the year nineteen hundred and forty-five and December thirty-first in the year nineteen hundred and forty-six, verify the voting lists and certify them as required by section three of this act, and for this purpose may appoint such temporary assistant registrars as may be necessary.

SECTION 2. Said chapter four hundred and fifty is hereby further amended by striking out section two and inserting in place thereof the following: — *Section 2.* The state secretary shall, on or after June first in the year nineteen hundred and forty-five, at the expense of the commonwealth, furnish to the registrars of each city and town such filing or other equipment and such number of registration forms or cards, hereinafter called cards, as may be necessary to carry out this act. Such cards shall be known as registration record cards and shall be of such size and form as the state secretary may determine, and shall have printed thereon the schedule as provided for the general register under section thirty-six of chapter fifty-one of the General Laws, together with the following:

Sex.

The city or town where last previously registered, if any.

Date of birth.

Height.

Such cards containing all facts required by the foregoing shall be signed by each voter whose name appears on any nineteen hundred and forty-seven voting list and by each applicant for registration on or after December first in the year nineteen hundred and forty-five. Such cards shall be used at polling places for the purpose of identification of voters after January first, nineteen hundred and forty-seven. The signature on such card of the applicant for registration or the voter shall be made, under the penalties of perjury, in the presence of a registrar, or assistant registrar, who shall affix his name thereto.

SECTION 3. Said chapter four hundred and fifty is hereby further amended by striking out section three and inserting in place thereof the following: — *Section 3.* Upon the completion of the verification of the voting list, but in no event later than December thirty-first in the year nineteen hundred and forty-six, the registrars shall file with the mayor in cities or the selectmen in towns, as the case may be, the following certificate: —

We, the registrars of voters or election commissioners of the city (or town) of do hereby certify that we have verified the list of registered voters in the city (or town), as required by chapter four hundred and fifty of the acts of nineteen hundred and thirty-nine, as amended, as of November first, nineteen hundred and forty-six.

SECTION 4. Section four of said chapter four hundred and fifty is hereby amended by striking out, in the second line, the word "forty-four" and inserting in place thereof the word: — forty-seven, — so as to read as follows: — *Section 4.* On January first, nineteen hundred and forty-seven, the registrars shall revise the general register and the annual register compiled under section thirty-seven of chapter fifty-one of the General Laws as affected by this act and strike therefrom the names of all persons who have not signed the registration record cards as provided in this act; provided, that there shall not be stricken from said registers the name of any person unless such person shall, not less than thirty days prior to such action, have been notified by the registrars by mail of his failure to sign the registration record card and informed of the procedure to be followed in order to have his name retained on said registers, nor unless such person shall have been given a reasonable opportunity to follow said procedure. *Approved June 12, 1943.*

---

*Chap.*538 AN ACT PROVIDING FOR THE REFINANCING OF CERTAIN INVESTMENTS IN THE PRESENT STATE SINKING FUND.

Be it enacted, etc., as follows:

SECTION 1. When the sinking fund of the commonwealth with its accumulations added, calculated on the basis on which funds therein are figured, contains, in the opinion of the state treasurer and the governor and council, less than an amount sufficient to extinguish at maturity any indebtedness for the extinguishment of which the fund was established, the governor and council may withdraw from such sinking fund securities which at that time cannot be sold or otherwise disposed of at par value and place such securities in the sinking fund established in the office of the state treasurer under section two.

SECTION 2. The state treasurer, with the approval of the governor and council, shall borrow from time to time, on the credit of the commonwealth, sums not exceeding, in the aggregate, the aggregate par value of the securities so withdrawn and may issue bonds of the commonwealth therefor. Such bonds shall be issued for such terms of years as the governor may recommend to the general court in accordance with section 3 of article LXII of the amendments to the constitution of the commonwealth, but shall be payable not earlier than the date when the securities so withdrawn are payable. Such bonds shall bear interest at such rates as shall be fixed by the state treasurer, with the approval of the governor and council. The provisions of section forty-nine of chapter twenty-nine of the General Laws shall not apply to the issue of bonds under this section. Any such bonds may be called, retired and cancelled by the commonwealth on any date upon which interest is payable thereon, after five years from their respective dates of issue, by payment by the commonwealth of the amount of the face of said bonds with any accumulated unpaid interest, if notice of the call is given to the holders thereof at least ninety days before the call date, and the bonds shall contain a statement to that effect. The proceeds of such bonds shall be used to pay at maturity any indebtedness for the extinguishment of which the sinking fund referred to in section one was established or shall be paid into said sinking fund. There shall be established in the office of the state treasurer a sinking fund for the purpose of extinguishing indebtedness incurred under this section, but such bonds shall nevertheless be general obligations of the commonwealth.

SECTION 3. The state treasurer, with the approval of the governor, if said state treasurer believes it to be in the best interests of the commonwealth, may dispose of any securities which under section one are placed in the sinking fund established by section two. The receipts therefrom shall be reinvested in securities maturing at a time not later than the maturity of the bonds issued under section two and such new securities shall be placed in said sinking fund.

SECTION 4. So much of the interest received on securities placed in the sinking fund established under section two as is necessary to pay any interest charges on the bonds issued under section two shall be used by the state treasurer to pay such interest; provided, that any excess interest received by him shall be added to said sinking fund and become a part thereof and that any deficit in interest requirements on bonds issued under section two shall be paid from the general fund. *Approved June 12, 1943.*

AN ACT PROVIDING FOR THE ESTABLISHMENT OF FOREST CUTTING PRACTICES. *Chap.539*

Be it enacted, etc., as follows:

G. L. (Ter. Ed.), 132, new §§ 40–45, added. New caption.

Chapter one hundred and thirty-two of the General Laws is hereby amended by inserting at the end, under the caption FOREST CUTTING PRACTICES, the six following sections: — *Section 40.* It is hereby declared that the public welfare requires the rehabilitation and protection of forest lands for the purpose of conserving water, preventing floods and soil erosion, improving the conditions for wildlife and recreation, and providing a continuing and increasing supply of forest products for farm use and for the woodusing industries of the commonwealth. Therefore, it is hereby declared to be the policy of the commonwealth that all lands devoted to forest growth shall be kept in such condition as shall not

Policy of commonwealth regarding forest lands.

jeopardize the public interests, and that the policy of the commonwealth shall further be one of co-operation with the land owners and other agencies interested in forestry practices for the profitable management of all forest lands in the interest of the owner, the public and the users of forest products.

State forestry committee. Appointment of members, etc.

Section 41. The governor, with the advice and consent of the council, shall appoint a state forestry committee, to consist of four members representing, respectively, (*a*) farm woodlot owners, (*b*) industrial woodland owners, (*c*) other woodland owners and (*d*) the general public. The director of the division of forestry shall be a member of the committee, ex-officio. In the initial appointments of said members, one shall be appointed for a one year term, one for a two year term, one for a three year term and one for a four year term. Thereafter, as the term of a member expires, his successor, with like qualifications as his predecessor, shall be appointed for a term of four years. Said committee shall select its own chairman. The members of said committee shall serve without pay, but shall be reimbursed for actual traveling expenses within the commonwealth, when approved by said director. Said committee shall prepare tentative practices for forest cutting. Among such practices, it shall be required that trees of desirable species and of suitable size shall be retained uncut so as to stand singly or in groups and be distributed in the manner and in the numbers best designed to secure restocking; except that provision shall be made for clear cutting in such individual cases as shall be approved by said director. Before adopting and promulgating any forest practices, said committee shall hold hearings, due notice being given, in at least four places conveniently located throughout the commonwealth. Said committee may thereafter adopt such practices or modifications thereof and submit them to the commissioner. Upon approval by the commissioner, he shall thereupon promulgate them and place them in effect, by posting in all city and town halls in the region affected and by publication in at least one daily newspaper in every county affected. Such approved practices may be amended at any time by said committee in the same manner, of its own motion or upon petition of not less than twenty-five forest owners or operators of the region. In order to suit the practices to local conditions, the commonwealth may be divided by said committee into not exceeding four regions with practices adapted to the particular forest conditions of each region.

Notice of intent to cut timber.

Section 42. Every owner or operator who proposes to cut on land devoted to forest purposes, except as provided in section forty-five, shall give written notice of his intention to begin any cutting operation to said director at least thirty days in advance of the date on which he proposes to begin the operation, but said director may waive the thirty day requirement in any emergency. Said director, or an employee of the division of forestry at the direction of said director, shall forthwith examine the forest to be cut and advise and assist the owner or operator to prepare and carry out a plan of operations that shall be best calculated to conform to the forest practices adopted for the region. The plan shall also be delivered to the owner or operator in writing. Where necessary to provide for reseeding, said director may also mark or otherwise designate a minimum number of seed trees to remain standing. Said director shall inspect the property during the operation, and upon its completion, to determine whether the operation has been executed in accordance with the plan and practices and shall report in writing to said committee the nature of the operation, its extent, the amount of product cut, and such other information as said committee may require.

Failure to give notice. Penalty.

Section 43. Whoever, not being exempt from sections forty-two and forty-three under the provisions of section forty-four, fails to give notice to said director as provided by said section forty-two shall be punished by a fine of not more than twenty-five dollars.

Sections 42 and 43 not to apply in certain cases.

Section 44. The provisions of sections forty-two and forty-three shall not apply to (1) cutting by any owner or tenant of any forest product for his own use; (2) clearing land for building or for purposes of cultivation; (3) cutting of such products for sale by any owner to an amount not exceeding forty thousand board feet and one hundred cords in any calendar year; (4) maintenance cutting in pastures; or (5) cutting for clearance or maintenance on rights of way pertaining to municipal lighting plants, electric companies, gas companies, railroads, electric street railway companies and companies incorporated for the transmission of oil or water, or of intelligence by electricity.

Co-operation with other agencies.

Section 45. For the purposes of sections forty to forty-four, inclusive, said director may co-operate with the Massachusetts State College and the United States Forest Service and may authorize their employees to perform the duties outlined in section forty-two. The members of said committee and said director and his agents may in the performance of their duties under said sections pass through or over private property. *Approved June 12, 1943.*

AN ACT EXTENDING THE SCOPE OF VOCATIONAL EDUCATION. *Chap.*540

Be it enacted, etc., as follows:

G. L. (Ter. Ed.), 74, § 14, amended.

Chapter seventy-four of the General Laws is hereby amended by striking out section fourteen, as appearing in the Tercentenary Edition, and inserting in place thereof the two following sections: — *Section 14.* Towns may, through school committees or trustees for vocational education, establish and maintain household and other practical art classes. Such classes shall be open to persons over sixteen years of age, and may be established and maintained as approved state aided practical art classes under sections one

Practical art classes.

to twenty-two, inclusive, so far as not inconsistent therewith, and for the following purposes:

(1) Providing opportunities for rehabilitation of disabled soldiers and disabled workers in industry and aiding them to become self-respecting and self-supporting.

(2) Providing additional opportunities for livelihood for inhabitants of certain of the smaller towns of the commonwealth.

(3) Providing further and greater opportunities for persons trained in war industries to participate in handicrafts.

May expend federal funds.

Section 14A. The commissioner, in the name and on behalf of the commonwealth, may apply for and receive, and thereafter expend for any or all of the purposes of section fourteen any funds received for any of such purposes from the federal government or any of its agencies.

Approved June 12, 1943.

---

*Chap.*541 AN ACT PROVIDING FOR THE ALLOTMENT BY THE GOVERNOR OF CERTAIN SUMS AVAILABLE FOR EXPENDITURE BY AGENCIES OF THE COMMONWEALTH.

Emergency preamble.

Whereas, The deferred operation of this act would unduly interfere with the operation of the allotment system of appropriations, so called, as provided by law, therefore this act is hereby declared to be an emergency law, necessary for the immediate preservation of the public convenience.

Be it enacted, etc., as follows:

Sums which were made available prior to December first, nineteen hundred and forty-one for expenditure by any agency of the commonwealth and remain so available on July first in the current year shall, on and after said July first, be subject to allotment under the provisions of section nine B of chapter twenty-nine of the General Laws, inserted by section one of chapter five hundred and sixty-four of the acts of nineteen hundred and forty-one.

Approved June 12, 1943.

---

*Chap.*542 AN ACT MAKING SUNDRY CHANGES IN THE LAWS RELATING TO ALCOHOLIC BEVERAGES.

Be it enacted, etc., as follows:

G. L. (Ter. Ed.), 138, § 2, etc., amended.

SECTION 1. Section two of chapter one hundred and thirty-eight of the General Laws is hereby amended by striking out the first sentence, as appearing in section one of chapter four hundred and seventy of the acts of nineteen hundred and thirty-nine, and inserting in place thereof the following sentence: — No person shall manufacture, with intent to sell, sell or expose or keep for sale, store, transport, import or export alcoholic beverages or alcohol, except as authorized by this chapter; but the provisions of this chapter shall not apply to sales, storage or transportation by a

Authority to sell, of receivers, etc.

person or public officer under a provision of law which requires him to sell personal property, or to sales, storage or transportation by executors, administrators, receivers and trustees duly authorized by proper judicial order or decree, except that any receiver or trustee in bankruptcy or otherwise appointed by any court, who is authorized by said court to conduct in whole or in part any business, authority to grant a license for which is given by this chapter, or who does conduct any such business in whole or in part, shall be subject to all provisions of the sections under which their licenses were issued and to all other provisions of this chapter applicable to such business the same as if it were conducted by an individual, partnership or corporation.

G. L. (Ter. Ed.), 138, § 10A, etc., amended.

SECTION 2. Said chapter one hundred and thirty-eight is hereby further amended by striking out section ten A, inserted by section two of chapter three hundred and seventy-six of the acts of nineteen hundred and thirty-three, and inserting in place thereof the following section: — *Section 10A.* The local licensing authorities shall file with the commission, on or before February fifteenth next following a license year in which the granting of licenses for the sale of any alcoholic beverage was authorized, a full report of their action during said license year, with the number of licenses of each class granted, and the revenue thereof, together with the established schedule of fees for all classes of licenses.

Annual statement by local licensing authorities.

G. L. (Ter. Ed.), 138, § 12, etc., amended.

SECTION 3. The first paragraph of section twelve of said chapter one hundred and thirty-eight, as most recently amended by chapter three hundred and thirty-one of the acts of nineteen hundred and thirty-seven, is hereby further amended by striking out the last sentence and inserting in place thereof the following sentence: — During such time as the sale of such alcoholic beverages is authorized in any city or town under this chapter, the authority to grant innholders' and common victuallers' licenses therein under chapter one hundred and forty shall be vested in the local licensing authorities; provided, that if a person applies for the renewal of both a common victualler's license or an innholder's license under said chapter one hundred and forty and a hotel or a restaurant license, as the case may be, under this section and the local licensing authorities refuse to grant said common victualler's or innholder's license or fail to act on the applications therefor within a period of thirty days, such applicant may appeal therefrom to the commission in the same manner as provided in section sixty-seven and all the provisions of said section relative to licenses authorized to be issued by local licensing authorities under this chapter shall apply in the case of such common victualler's license or innholder's license.

Innholders' and common victuallers' licenses.

G. L. (Ter. Ed.), 138, § 12, etc., amended.

SECTION 4. The second paragraph of said section twelve of said chapter one hundred and thirty-eight, as most recently amended by section two of chapter three hundred and sixty-eight of the acts of nineteen hundred and thirty-six, is hereby further amended by inserting before the word "counter" in the fifth line the words: — bar or, — so as to read as follows: —

Restriction on sales.

No alcoholic beverage shall on secular days be served to or drunk by a woman as patron, guest or member in a public room or area of a hotel, or in a restaurant or club, licensed under this section, except while seated at a table or seated at a bar or counter equipped with stools; and no such beverage shall on Sundays be served to or drunk by any patron, guest or member at a bar or counter in such a hotel, restaurant or club.

G. L. (Ter. Ed.), 138, § 15A, etc., amended.

SECTION 5. Section fifteen A of said chapter one hundred and thirty-eight, as most recently amended by chapter four hundred and fourteen of the acts of nineteen hundred and thirty-nine, is hereby further amended by striking out, in the twenty-eighth, fifty-fifth, fifty-eighth and sixty-fourth lines the word "revoke" and inserting in place thereof, in each instance, the word: — cancel, — by striking out, in the twenty-ninth and sixty-fifth lines, the word "revocation" and inserting in place thereof, in each instance, the word: — cancellation, — and by striking out, in the sixty-seventh line, the word "revoked" and inserting in place thereof the word: — cancelled, — so as to read as follows: — *Section 15A.* Notation of the date and hour of filing shall be made on every application for a license under section twelve, fifteen or thirty A. Within ten days after the receipt of any such application, the local licensing authorities shall cause a notice thereof to be published at the expense of the applicant. Such notice shall be published in a newspaper published in the city or town in which the premises whereon the license is intended to be exercised are situated, or if no newspaper is published in such city or town, then in some newspaper published in the county. The notice shall set forth the name of the applicant in full, the kind of license applied for, a particular description of the premises on which the license is intended to be exercised, designating the building or part of the building to be used and, if practicable, the street and number. No application shall be acted upon by the local licensing authorities until ten days after the publication of such notice. An affidavit of the person making such publication on behalf of such authorities, together with an attested copy of the notice published, shall be filed in the office of such authorities, and a certified copy of such affidavit shall be prima facie evidence that such notice has been published in accordance with this section. If any citizen of the city or town within which any such license is issued makes complaint in writing to the commission that such license was granted without such previous publication, and after due hearing it appears that such publication was not made as aforesaid, the commission shall cancel the license and give notice of such cancellation to the authorities issuing the license.

Notices of applications for licenses, etc.

Every applicant for an original license under section twelve, fifteen or thirty A, or for a transfer of such a license from one location to another, or some one in his behalf, shall, within three days after publication as hereinbefore provided, cause a copy of the published notice to be sent by registered mail to each of the persons appearing upon the assessors' most recent valuation list as the owners of the property abutting on the premises where the license is intended to be exercised and, if a school, which gives not less than the minimum instruction and training to children of compulsory school age required by chapter seventy-one, or a church or hospital, is located within a radius of five hundred feet from said premises, to such school, church or hospital. An affidavit of the applicant or of the person mailing such notice in his behalf, together with an attested copy of the notice mailed, shall be filed in the office of the local licensing authorities, and a certified copy of such affidavit shall be prima facie evidence that such notice has been mailed in accordance with this section. If any abutter or the authorities in charge of any such school, church or hospital shall make complaint in writing to the local licensing authorities that such license was granted or transferred hereunder without such notice having been mailed to him or them as required hereby, and after due hearing it appears that such notice was not mailed as aforesaid, the local licensing authorities may cancel the license. Any person who has filed a complaint with the local licensing authorities under this section who is aggrieved by the action of such authorities in refusing to cancel a license hereunder or by their failure to act upon such a complaint within a period of thirty days may appeal to the commission in writing within five days following receipt of written notice of such action or within five days following the expiration of the thirty day period, and the commission may, after hearing, cancel such a license and in such event, shall send notice of the cancellation to the local licensing authorities. Nothing herein contained shall be construed to prohibit a licensee whose license has been cancelled by the local licensing authorities under authority contained in this section from appealing to the commission as provided in section sixty-seven. Notice to abutters, churches, etc.

SECTION 6. Section sixteen B of said chapter one hundred and thirty-eight, as most recently amended by chapter ninety-two of the acts of nineteen hundred and thirty-nine, is hereby further amended by inserting after the word "authorities" in the sixth line the words: — , and applications for transfers of licenses issued by such local licensing authorities under section twenty-three, — and by striking out, in the sixteenth line, the word "three" and inserting in place thereof the word: — seven, — so as to read as follows: — G. L. (Ter. Ed.), 138, § 16B, etc., amended.

Section 16B. - Applications for licenses or permits authorized to be granted by the commission shall be granted or dismissed not later than thirty days after the filing of the Time within which licenses shall be granted.

same, and, except as provided in section sixteen A, applications for licenses authorized to be granted by the local licensing authorities, and applications for transfers of licenses issued by such local licensing authorities under section twenty-three, shall be acted upon within a like period and if favorably acted upon by the said authorities shall be submitted for approval by the commission not later than three days following such favorable action; provided, however, that local licensing authorities shall not be required to act prior to December fifteenth in any year on applications for the renewal of annual licenses filed in accordance with the provisions of section sixteen A or prior to April fifteenth in any year on applications for the renewal of seasonal licenses so filed. A license so approved shall be issued by said authorities not later than seven days following receipt of notice of approval by the commission. Any applicant for a license under this chapter who fails to comply with the requirements of section seventy within fourteen days after notice that a license has been authorized to be granted to him shall forfeit any right thereto, unless the licensing authorities to which application was made otherwise determine.

Applications for licenses limited.

The licensing authorities shall not receive more than one application for a license under section twelve or fifteen to be exercised on the same premises during the same license year, except in any case where they otherwise determine.

G. L. (Ter. Ed.), 138, § 18, etc., amended.

SECTION 7. Section eighteen of said chapter one hundred and thirty-eight, as most recently amended by section sixteen of chapter four hundred and forty of the acts of nineteen hundred and thirty-five, is hereby further amended by striking out the first sentence and inserting in place thereof the following sentence: — The commission may issue to any individual who is both a citizen and resident of the commonwealth and to partnerships composed solely of such individuals, and to corporations organized under the laws of the commonwealth whereof all the directors are citizens of the United States and a majority thereof residents of the commonwealth, licenses as wholesalers and importers (1) to sell for resale to other licensees under this chapter alcoholic beverages manufactured by any manufacturer licensed under the provisions of section nineteen and to import alcoholic beverages into the commonwealth from holders of certificates issued under section eighteen B whose licensed premises are located in other states and foreign countries for sale to such licensees, or (2) to sell for resale wines and malt beverages so manufactured to such licensees and to import as aforesaid wines and malt beverages for sale to such licensees.

Wholesalers' and importers' licenses.

G. L. (Ter. Ed.), 138, § 18, etc., amended.

SECTION 8. Said section eighteen of said chapter one hundred and thirty-eight, as so amended, is hereby further amended by adding at the end the following paragraph: —

Granting, etc., of licenses.

No vote in any city or town under section eleven shall

prevent the granting or renewal of a license under this section.

SECTION 9. Said chapter one hundred and thirty-eight is hereby further amended by inserting after section eighteen A, as amended by section seventeen of chapter four hundred and forty of the acts of nineteen hundred and thirty-five, the following section: — *Section 18B.* The commission shall issue a certificate of compliance to a licensee having a place of business located, and a license granted, outside the commonwealth and whose license authorizes the exportation or sale of alcoholic beverages to licensees in this commonwealth; provided, that such certificate shall be issued upon the condition that the holder shall furnish from time to time as the commission may require, but in no event more often than once each month, information concerning all shipments or sales of alcoholic beverages made by him to licensees in this commonwealth, and that he comply with the provisions of this chapter and any rules or regulations made under authority contained therein which pertain to a licensee of the same class, type or character, doing business in this commonwealth under a license issued by the commission. The commission may suspend, cancel or revoke any certificate issued hereunder for a violation of the terms or conditions thereof. All certificates shall be issued to expire December thirty-first of the year of issuance and the fee therefor shall not exceed ten dollars.

G. L. (Ter. Ed.), 138, new § 18B, added.

Certificate of compliance

SECTION 10. Said chapter one hundred and thirty-eight is hereby further amended by striking out section twenty, as most recently amended by sections six and seven of chapter three hundred and sixty-eight of the acts of nineteen hundred and thirty-six, and inserting in place thereof the following section: — *Section 20.* The commission may grant to any holder of a manufacturer's or wholesaler's and importer's license under this chapter a permit to store alcoholic beverages in any city or town; provided, that there shall not be granted to such manufacturer or wholesaler and importer, in the aggregate, more than three such permits in the commonwealth, nor more than one such permit in any city or town. A permit so granted to the holder of such a license shall authorize him to deliver such beverages from any place of storage for which he has such a permit upon orders, which need not be in writing, received by him at the premises covered by his manufacturer's or wholesaler's and importer's license and transmitted to the place of storage covered by the permit. The commission may establish annual fees therefor not exceeding five hundred dollars for any one permit.

G. L. (Ter. Ed.), 138, § 20, etc., amended.

Storage permits.

Special warehouse permits may be granted by the commission for the storage of alcoholic beverages in a duly licensed bonded warehouse. A special permit so granted shall authorize the holder thereof to transfer such beverages between any premises for which he has such special permit and any premises covered by his manufacturer's or wholesaler's and importer's license. The fee for such a special permit shall be not less than fifty nor more than two hundred dollars.

Special seasonal permits may be granted by the commission upon payment of a fee of twenty-five dollars for each such permit, which shall authorize any licensee under section eighteen or nineteen to store malt beverages in the same city or town in which their licensed premises are located; provided, that such storage shall be in a place properly equipped for the refrigeration of malt beverages and that such an authorization shall be effective only for the period between April first and October thirty-first in any year.

Nothing in this section shall be deemed to authorize the transportation of alcoholic beverages in any vehicle not covered by a permit issued under section twenty-two.

No vote in any city or town under section eleven shall prevent the renewal of any permit under this section.

The commission may make and enforce rules and regulations covering the storage of alcoholic beverages under permits granted under this section.

G. L. (Ter. Ed.), 138, § 21, etc., amended.

SECTION 11. The first paragraph of section twenty-one of said chapter one hundred and thirty-eight, as appearing in section one of chapter three hundred and sixty-seven of the acts of nineteen hundred and thirty-nine, is hereby amended by striking out, in the second line, the words "hereinafter defined" and inserting in place thereof the words: — defined in this chapter, — so as to read as follows: — Every licensed manufacturer of alcoholic beverages or alcohol as defined in this chapter and every holder of a wholesaler's and importer's license for the sale and importation thereof and every licensee under section seventy-six shall, in addition to the license fees elsewhere provided in this chapter, be liable for and pay to the commonwealth an excise, for the privilege enjoyed by him as such manufacturer, wholesaler and importer, or licensee under section seventy-six, to be levied on sales within the commonwealth of alcoholic beverages or alcohol, other than wines to be used for sacramental purposes only and other than malt beverages imported into the commonwealth, and to be levied on importations of malt beverages into the commonwealth, as follows:

Importation of malt beverages.

G. L. (Ter. Ed.), 138, § 23, etc., amended.

SECTION 12. Said chapter one hundred and thirty-eight is hereby further amended by striking out section twenty-three, as most recently amended by chapter five hundred and seventy-eight of the acts of nineteen hundred and forty-one, and inserting in place thereof the following section: — *Section 23.* The terms licenses and permits, wherever employed as substantives in this chapter, are used in their technical sense of a license or permit, transferable only as provided in this chapter, and revocable at pleasure and without any assignment of reasons therefor by the granting authority, the commonwealth, acting through the same offi-

Terms "licenses" and "permits" construed.

cers or agents and under the same delegated authority, as authorized the issue of such licenses or permits. The provisions for the issue of licenses and permits hereunder imply no intention to create rights generally for persons to engage or continue in the transaction of the business authorized by the licenses or permits respectively, but are enacted with a view only to meet the reasonable demand of the public for pure alcoholic beverages and, to that end, to provide, in the opinion of the licensing authorities, an adequate number of places at which the public may obtain, in the manner and for the kind of use indicated, the different sorts of beverages for the sale of which provision is made.

No holder of such a license or permit hereunder shall have any property right in any document or paper evidencing the granting of such license or permit and issued by the licensing authorities, and said authorities, upon the expiration, suspension, revocation, cancellation or forfeiture of such a license or permit shall be entitled upon demand to the immediate possession thereof. The superior court shall have jurisdiction in equity, on petition of the licensing authorities, to enforce this provision.

No license issued under section twelve, fourteen or fifteen, and no certificate of fitness issued under section thirty, shall authorize the sale of any alcoholic beverages other than those purchased from a licensee under section eighteen or nineteen or from a holder of a special permit to sell issued under section twenty-two A; provided, that the holder of a license under section twelve or fifteen may sell alcoholic beverages acquired as the result of the purchase of a warehouse receipt for such beverages if the said receipt was purchased from the holder of a license under section eighteen or nineteen, or from a broker registered under chapter one hundred and ten A who is authorized thereunder to deal in warehouse receipts for alcoholic beverages; and provided, further, that nothing contained in this section shall be construed to authorize a licensee under section twelve or fifteen to import alcoholic beverages into this commonwealth except through the holder of a license issued under section eighteen.

Suspension, revocation, etc., of licenses.

Whenever, in the opinion of the local licensing authorities, any applicant for a license under section twelve, fourteen, fifteen or thirty A fails to establish to their satisfaction his compliance with the requirements of this chapter, or any other reasonable requirements which they may from time to time make with respect to licenses under said sections respectively, or to the conduct of business by any licensee thereunder, said authorities may refuse to issue or reissue to such applicant any such license; and whenever in their opinion any holder of such a license fails to maintain such compliance or whenever it shall appear to them that the nature of the business, or of the equipment of and service of any hotel, restaurant, club or tavern no longer satisfies the definition thereof contained in this chapter, or that alcoholic beverages are being or have been sold, served or drunk therein in violation of any provision of this chapter, they may, after hearing or opportunity therefor modify, suspend, revoke or cancel such license.

Whenever, in the opinion of the commission, any holder of a license or permit originally issued by it fails to maintain compliance with the requirements of this chapter, or any other reasonable requirements which it may from time to time make with respect to any such license or permit or to the conduct of business by any such licensee or permittee, it may, after hearing or opportunity therefor, modify, suspend, revoke or cancel such license or permit.

In case of modification, suspension, revocation or cancellation of a license issued by the licensing authorities or of a permit issued by the commission, no abatement or refund of any part of the fee paid therefor shall be made.

Refund of fee, when permitted.

The licensing authorities empowered to issue any license or permit may order refunded the whole or any part of the fee for such a license or permit in case of an error in the kind of a license or permit issued, or may order the fee paid for such a license or permit refunded to the applicant if he has withdrawn his application prior to the issuance of the license or permit applied for, or to the licensee or permittee if he has surrendered the license or permit issued to him and such licensing authorities are satisfied that no right, power or privilege has been exercised thereunder. Any sums ordered refunded as aforesaid shall be paid from any available funds in the treasury of the commonwealth or municipality as the case may be.

Transfer of licenses from one location to another.

Any license issued under this chapter may, upon application by the holder thereof to the licensing authorities issuing the same, be transferred from one location to another, but no new license fee shall be required. A transfer of location of a license issued by the local licensing authorities shall be subject to the prior approval of the commission. The local licensing authorities may transfer a common victualler's or innholder's license issued under chapter one hundred and forty from one location to another if the applicant therefor is also the holder of a license for the sale of alcoholic beverages at the location from which the transfer is sought. If the local licensing authorities of any city or town refuse to grant or fail to act upon an application for a transfer of location of any license as authorized by this section, the applicant therefor may appeal to the commission under section sixty-seven in the same manner as though such authorities had refused to grant or failed to act upon an application for an original license under this chapter, and all the provisions of said section shall apply to such an appeal. Nothing herein contained shall be construed to limit or prevent the transfer from one location to another by local licensing authorities of common victuallers' or innholders' licenses issued under chapter one hundred and forty if the applicant for such a transfer is not the holder of a license for the sale of alcoholic beverages.

Any license under this chapter held by an individual, partnership or corporation may be transferred to any individual, partnership or corporation qualified to receive such a license in the first instance, if, in the opinion of the licensing authorities, such transfer is in the public interest. If the local licensing authorities determine that an individual, partnership or corporation is not entitled to a transfer as aforesaid of a license granted by them, the applicant for such transfer may appeal to the commission as if such authorities had refused to grant the license to such individual, partnership or corporation upon an original application therefor, and the decision of the commission upon such appeal shall be final. Transfer from one licensee to another.

In the case of the death of an individual holder of any license or permit under this chapter, such license or permit, unless earlier surrendered, revoked or cancelled, shall authorize the executor or administrator of the deceased licensee or permittee to exercise all authority conferred upon such licensee or permittee until the termination thereof. In case of the appointment of a receiver or trustee in bankruptcy or otherwise of a licensee under this chapter, such license, unless earlier surrendered, revoked or cancelled, shall authorize such receiver or trustee to exercise all authority conferred on such licensee until the termination thereof. License to continue upon death of licensee.

Every license and permit granted under the provisions of this chapter, unless otherwise provided in such provisions, shall expire on December thirty-first of the year of issue, subject, however, to revocation or cancellation within its term. Expiration of licenses.

SECTION 13. Said chapter one hundred and thirty-eight is hereby further amended by striking out section twenty-four, as most recently amended by chapter two hundred and thirty-two of the acts of nineteen hundred and thirty-four, and inserting in place thereof the following section: — *Section 24.* The commission shall, with the approval of the governor and council, make regulations not inconsistent with the provisions of this chapter for clarifying, carrying out, enforcing and preventing violation of, all and any of its provisions, for inspection of the premises and method of carrying on the business of any licensee, for insuring the purity, and penalizing the adulteration, or in any way changing the quality or content, of any alcoholic beverage, for the proper and orderly conduct of the licensed business, for establishing maximum prices chargeable by licensees under this chapter, and regulating all advertising of alcoholic beverages, and shall, with like approval, make regulations governing the labelling of packages of alcoholic beverages as to their ingredients and the respective quantities thereof. Every such regulation, when so approved, shall be printed in full in one issue of some newspaper of general circulation published on the same day in each of the cities of Boston, New Bedford, Lowell, Worcester, Springfield and Pittsfield and copies of such regulations shall be furnished to each licensee. Fourteen days from and after the date of such publication, any such regulation made and approved as aforesaid shall G. L. (Ter. Ed.), 138, § 24, etc., amended. Regulations, publication, etc. Copies to be furnished licensees.

have the force and effect of law unless and until amended or annulled by the commission with the approval of the governor and council.

The commission shall, at least annually on or before December thirty-first of each year, publish in a convenient pamphlet form all regulations then in force, and shall, upon request, furnish a copy of such pamphlets to any licensee authorized under the provisions of this chapter to sell alcoholic beverages.

G. L. (Ter. Ed.), 138, § 30, etc., amended.

SECTION 14. Section thirty of said chapter one hundred and thirty-eight, as most recently amended by section one of chapter eighty-three of the acts of nineteen hundred and thirty-five, is hereby further amended by striking out, in the tenth line, the word "and" and inserting in place thereof the word: — or, — so as to read as follows: — *Section 30.* The board of registration in pharmacy may, upon the payment of a fee of not more than five dollars by a registered pharmacist who desires to exercise the authority conferred by section twenty-nine, issue to him a certificate of fitness, which shall expire on the thirty-first day of December of the year for which or part of which the same was issued, stating that in the judgment of said board he is a proper person to be intrusted with such authority and that the public good will be promoted by the granting thereof. The board or the local licensing authorities may, after giving a hearing to the parties interested, revoke or suspend such certificate for any cause which they may deem proper, and such revocation or suspension shall revoke or suspend all authority conferred by section twenty-nine.

Certificate of fitness for registered pharmacist.

G. L. (Ter. Ed.), 138, § 34, etc., amended.

SECTION 15. Section thirty-four of said chapter one hundred and thirty-eight, as most recently amended by section five of chapter four hundred and twenty-four of the acts of nineteen hundred and thirty-seven, is hereby further amended by inserting after the word "twelve" in the eleventh line the words: — or fifteen, — and by inserting after the word "establishment" in the twelfth line the words: — if licensed under said section twelve, or in any area of such establishment if licensed under said section fifteen, — so as to read as follows: — *Section 34.* No person shall receive a license or permit under this chapter who is under twenty-one years of age. Whoever, being licensed under this chapter, employs any person under twenty-one years of age in the direct handling or selling of alcoholic beverages or alcohol or whoever makes a sale or delivery of any such beverages or alcohol to any person under twenty-one years of age, either for his own use or for the use of his parent or of any other person or whoever, being a patron of an establishment licensed under section twelve or fifteen, delivers or procures to be delivered in any public room or area of such establishment if licensed under said section twelve, or in any area of such establishment if licensed under said section fifteen, any such beverages or alcohol to or for the use of a person whom he knows or has reason to believe to be under twenty-one years of age, shall be punished by a fine of not more than

Employment of minors prohibited.

two hundred dollars or by imprisonment for not more than six months, or both.

SECTION 16. Said chapter one hundred and thirty-eight is hereby further amended by striking out section sixty-three A, as most recently amended by section forty-one of chapter four hundred and forty of the acts of nineteen hundred and thirty-five, and inserting in place thereof the following section: — *Section 63A.* Any person who hinders or delays any authorized investigator of the commission or any investigator, inspector or any other authorized agent of local licensing authorities in the performance of his duties, or who refuses to admit to or locks out any such investigator, inspector or agent from any place which such investigator, inspector or agent is authorized to inspect, or who refuses to give to such investigator, inspector or agent such information as may be required for the proper enforcement of this chapter, shall be punished by a fine of not less than fifty nor more than two hundred dollars or by imprisonment for not more than two months, or both.

G. L. (Ter. Ed.), 138, § 63A, etc., amended.

Penalty for interfering with inspector, etc.

SECTION 17. Said chapter one hundred and thirty-eight is hereby amended by striking out section sixty-five, inserted by section two of chapter three hundred and seventy-six of the acts of nineteen hundred and thirty-three, and inserting in place thereof the following section: — *Section 65.* Upon suspension, revocation, cancellation or forfeiture by the licensing authorities of a license or permit granted under this chapter, the holder thereof shall forthwith deliver the same to such authorities. Refusal so to deliver, or failure so to do for seven days following a request therefor by such authorities, shall be punished by a fine of not more than one hundred dollars or by imprisonment for not more than three months, or both.

G. L. (Ter. Ed.), 138, § 65, etc., amended.

Licensee to deliver license upon revocation.

Penalty.

SECTION 18. Section sixty-seven of said chapter one hundred and thirty-eight, as most recently amended by chapter four hundred of the acts of nineteen hundred and thirty-eight, is hereby further amended by inserting after the word "in" in the sixth line the word: — modifying, — so that the first paragraph of said section will read as follows: — Any applicant for a license who is aggrieved by the action of the local licensing authorities in refusing to grant the same or by their failure to act within the period of thirty days limited by section sixteen B, or any person who is aggrieved by the action of such authorities in modifying, suspending, cancelling, revoking or declaring forfeited the same, may appeal therefrom to the commission within five days following notice of such action or following the expiration of said period, upon petition in writing, setting forth all the material facts in the case. The commission may, after hearing, due notice whereof shall have been given, sustain the action of the local licensing authorities or may sustain the appeal, in which latter case it shall set forth in writing in its decision its reasons therefor, and the decision of the commission shall be final; but, pending a decision on the appeal, the action of

G. L. (Ter. Ed.), 138, § 67, etc., amended.

Appeals from local licensing authorities.

the local licensing authorities shall have the same force and effect as if the appeal had not been taken. Upon the petition of twenty-five persons who are taxpayers of the city or town in which a license has been granted by such authorities or who are registered voters in the voting precinct or district wherein the licensed premises are situated, or upon its own initiative, the commission may investigate the granting of such a license or the conduct of the business being done thereunder and may, after a hearing, modify, suspend, revoke or cancel such license if, in its opinion, circumstances warrant.

G. L. (Ter. Ed.), 138, § 77, etc., amended.

Termination of licenses in certain cases.

SECTION 19. Said chapter one hundred and thirty-eight is hereby further amended by striking out section seventy-seven, inserted by section two of chapter three hundred and seventy-six of the acts of nineteen hundred and thirty-three, and inserting in place thereof the following: — *Section 77.* The licensing authorities may, after hearing or reasonable opportunity therefor, cancel any license issued under this chapter if the licensee ceases to conduct the licensed business. If the local licensing authorities determine that a license should be cancelled as aforesaid the licensee may appeal to the commission as if such authorities had refused to grant the license upon an original application therefor, and the decision of the commission upon such appeal shall be final.

License to be held in reserve when federal authorities take over property.

SECTION 20. Any holder of a hotel or a club license under section twelve of chapter one hundred and thirty-eight of the General Laws who ceases to exercise such license by reason of the use of the hotel or club covered thereby by the military or naval authorities of the United States during the continuation of the existing state of war between the United States and any foreign country shall, upon surrender of his license, be entitled to have said license held in reserve by the authorities which issued the same. Any license surrendered and held in reserve hereunder shall, for the purposes of the quota restrictions under section seventeen of said chapter one hundred and thirty-eight, be counted as a license issued and outstanding, and any such license shall be restored to the former holder upon the termination of the use of the hotel or club covered thereby for military or naval purposes, if application for such restoration of the license is made within ninety days after the termination of said use of the hotel or club. No license shall be reserved hereunder unless the licensee who surrendered the same pays such annual fee, not exceeding ten per cent of the annual license fee last paid, as may be determined by the licensing authorities reserving the same.

License to be held in reserve if licensee enters armed forces.

SECTION 21. Any holder of a license under chapter one hundred and thirty-eight of the General Laws who is prevented from exercising such license by reason of service in the military or naval forces of the United States, or any of the allies thereof, or by reason of orders of the military authorities of the United States, during the continuation of the existing state of war between the United States and any foreign country shall, upon surrender of his license, be entitled to have said license held in reserve by the authorities which issued the same. Any license surrendered and held in reserve hereunder shall, for the purposes of the quota restrictions under section seventeen of said chapter one hundred and thirty-eight, be counted as a license issued and outstanding, and any such license shall be restored to the former holder upon application for such restoration of the license made within six months after his discharge or release from such service, or from such orders, as the case may be.

Approved June 12, 1943.

Chap. 543

AN ACT RELATIVE TO THE FURNISHING OF WATER TO TOWNS IN THE METROPOLITAN WATER DISTRICT AND CERTAIN OTHER TOWNS.

Be it enacted, etc., as follows:

G. L. (Ter. Ed.), 92, § 10, amended.

SECTION 1. Chapter ninety-two of the General Laws is hereby amended by striking out section ten, as appearing in the Tercentenary Edition, and inserting in place thereof the following section: — *Section 10.* The commission shall construct, maintain and operate a system of metropolitan water works and shall provide thereby a sufficient supply of pure water for the following named towns and the inhabitants thereof: — Arlington, Belmont, Boston, Brookline, Chelsea, Everett, Lexington, Malden, Milton, Medford, Melrose, Nahant, Newton, Quincy, Revere, Somerville, Stoneham, Swampscott, Watertown and Winthrop, which shall be members of and shall constitute the metropolitan water district; shall secure and protect the purity of said water; shall on application furnish water to any town aforesaid that at the time of application owns its water pipe system; shall on application admit to membership in said water district any other town any part of which is within ten miles of the state house, and any other town any part of which is within fifteen miles of the state house as to which the commission has certified, as prescribed by this section, that it can reasonably supply it with water, and shall furnish water to the same on the terms prescribed by this chapter for the towns aforesaid, upon payment of an entrance fee in the amount prescribed by this section; and shall, upon application, furnish water to any water company owning the water pipe system in any member town, upon the assumption in writing by such water company of the assessments, if any, of the town, and upon making such payment as the commission may determine. The commission shall furnish water to the member town or company, by delivering it into a main water pipe, reservoir or tank of the town or company, under sufficient pressure for use without local pumping, unless delivered in some other manner by mutual agreement between the parties interested; and shall have the direction and control of the connections between the metropolitan and local systems.

Construction and maintenance of water works.

Cities and towns in district.

Furnishing water in and beyond district.

The commission, on application of any non-member town, water company or water supply, water, fire or fire and water district, may, with the approval of the state department of public health, hereinafter, in this section, called said department, construct a suitable connection with its system of metropolitan water works and furnish water therefrom to any such non-member town, water company or district on payment of such sum, limited as prescribed by this section, as the commission may, after October first in the year nineteen hundred and forty-three, determine, and may continue to furnish the same notwithstanding any provision of section forty of chapter forty of the General Laws. Payment by each non-member town, water company or district so supplied for such water shall include its fair share, as determined by the commission, of the cost of connection which may, if and as so determined, be distributed over a period not exceeding ten years. Payment for water so supplied to a town eligible, as previously prescribed in this section, for membership in the metropolitan water district shall, in any case, be at a higher rate per million gallons than, in the opinion of the commission, such town would be assessed were it a member of said district.

The commission, subject to all the provisions relating to the construction, operation and maintenance by it of a water supply system set forth in this chapter, may sell and deliver water from any of the reservoirs or aqueducts of the metropolitan water system to any concentration camp established in the commonwealth by the United States, and lay and maintain pipe lines and other works necessary therefor, upon terms and conditions to be agreed upon by the duly authorized officer or representative of the United States government and the commission.

On or before October first, nineteen hundred and forty-three, the commission shall transmit to said department of public health a certified list of towns not members of the metropolitan water district located wholly or in part within fifteen miles of the state house which the district can reasonably supply with water under the same conditions as are prescribed by this section for delivery to member towns and which have by their proper officials in writing requested and been furnished directly, with a supply of water from the district, and of member towns which have not made application to the district for water; and the commission shall include in supplementary certified lists from time to time other towns within the fifteen-mile limit requesting water, as the district becomes able to so supply them. On or before February first in the year nineteen hundred and forty-two, said department shall determine, in the case of each town eligible to membership in the district and on or before November first in each year, commencing with the year nineteen hundred and forty-three, in the case of each town listed as hereinbefore prescribed in this section, the maximum continuous rate at which the water supply sources for said town may be safely depended upon to furnish a suitable supply of water during the next succeeding three years, not including water supplied from any other town, water company or district, or water diverted from the watershed of the Charles river in excess of amounts specifically permitted by legislative provisions, or water obtained under section forty of chapter forty of the General Laws, or from said metropolitan water district; provided, that the right of any town to make full use of any source of supply owned by it prior to said October first, nineteen hundred and forty-three, shall be recognized by said department in determining said maximum continuous rate of supply. Coincidentally with such determination, said department shall report to the commission the name of each of said towns which it finds cannot so supply continuously its own inhabitants, in addition to meeting obligations, if any, imposed upon it by law to supply other towns, with a quantity ten per cent in excess of its average consumption during the three previous years, and shall notify each of said towns of its finding with respect thereto. Each town shall have the right to have a hearing before said department prior to the department making any report. If a town after such hearing is not so reported, it still may request a connection with the metropolitan water system by a two thirds vote of its governing legislative body in a city or a town having a form of representative town meeting government, or, by a two thirds vote of a town meeting in any other town; and said commission may thereupon install said connection subject to such terms as may be agreed upon by such city or town and said commission.

The supreme judicial court, on application by any town so reported, received prior to January first next following such determination and report of said department, and after notice to such town so reported and to said department, and after a hearing, shall appoint three commissioners, hereinafter referred to as assessment commissioners. Such assessment commissioners shall, after due notice and hearing, and in such manner and to such extent as they shall deem just and equitable, review and, if necessary, modify the findings of said department as to such lack of an excess supply; determine whether any or all of such towns shall be provided with a water supply connection and be assessed as prescribed by this section, and report the results of their determinations to said court on or before March first next following or as soon thereafter as may be. When said report shall have been accepted by the court it shall be conclusive and binding upon said district and town or towns, which shall thereupon pay the compensation and expenses of the assessment commissioners in accordance with the order of the court, such portion as said district is required to pay being added by the state treasurer to the cost of maintenance and operation of the metropolitan water works, and such cost as any of said towns is required to pay being paid by the town to the commonwealth at the time required for payment of, and as part of, its state taxes. The court shall fix and determine the compensation of said assessment commissioners and shall allow such expenses incurred by them in carrying out the provisions of this section as it shall approve.

The metropolitan water district shall provide a connection to supply immediate needs to each town the inadequacy of the water supply of which has been so reported by said department and, in case of application to the supreme judicial court as hereinbefore provided, has been confirmed by the determination of said court, unless such town is already adequately connected either to the supply lines of said district or to those of an adjoining town, water company or district obtaining its water supply wholly or in part from the metropolitan water district. Each such town shall be assessed and pay, as prescribed by section twenty-six, its fair share of the cost of said connection as determined by the commission and certified to the state treasurer, which may, if and as determined by the commission, be distributed over a period not exceeding ten years. Each town so reported, upon the providing of such connection, and each town not so reported, except as hereinafter provided, which is given or continues to have a connection directly between its own mains and the supply mains of the metropolitan water district's distributing system, shall annually, until it becomes a member of said district, be assessed and pay, as prescribed by said section twenty-six, a premium equal, in the year nineteen hundred and forty-two, to three hundredths of one per cent, and in subsequent years to three two hundredths of one per cent, of its valuation; and any water company which is supplied by the metropolitan water district and which has a connection for supplying any town so reported by said department, shall annually, until such town becomes a member of said district, pay, as prescribed by said section twenty-six, a premium equal to three two hundredths of one per cent of the valuation of such town so supplied; provided, that the assessment of such premium shall cease upon the failure of said department to so report a town, either in the case of any town which does not have a direct connection with said system, or in the case of any town which breaks its connection within thirty days after it ceases to be so reported; and provided, further, that, subsequent to the year in which the aggregate amount of all such premiums paid by any town, commencing in nineteen hundred and forty-two, shall equal the amount of the limiting entrance fee prescribed by this section for admission of such town in that year, the premium of such non-member town shall be reduced to a sum equivalent to the assessment paid by a member town which has not yet made application to the district for water, so that such non-member town shall thereafter, in addition to payments for water purchased from the district, share with the member towns the total district assessment, there being included in the reckoning of its proportionate share only one fifth of its valuation and nothing for its consumption of water.

Until its premium has been so reduced, any town may pay annually a premium of more than three two hundredths of one per cent of its valuation; and such town may at any time pay the balance needed to so reduce the amount of premium, and, for the purpose of providing funds therefor, may borrow a sum not exceeding such balance and may issue bonds or notes therefor bearing on their face the words: "City (or town) of , Water Loan Act of 1943" and payable within thirty years from their dates or within such shorter time as may be fixed by the director of accounts in the department of corporations and taxation. Indebtedness so incurred shall be inside the statutory limits of indebtedness provided by section eight of chapter forty-four of the General Laws, and, except as provided herein, shall be subject to all provisions of said chapter forty-four.

Until such town upon its application is admitted to the metropolitan water district, it may purchase water in any quantity from the district at a cost per million gallons equal to fifty dollars plus the product of twenty-five dollars by the ratio of the town's valuation to the aggregate valuation of all members of the district and by the inverse ratio of the town's total water consumption to the aggregate consumption of all members in the preceding year. Each town which is a member of said district, and which is supplied wholly or in part from sources the inadequacy of which has been so reported by said department, and which report, in the case of application to the supreme judicial court, has been confirmed by it, shall, for the purpose of determining the method of its assessment under said section twenty-six, be considered as having reached the safe capacity of its present sources of supply or of the sources of supply of the water company by which it is supplied, as the case may be, and as having made application to the metropolitan water district for water. Authority is hereby granted to any water company or town adjoining any town so reported and obtaining its water supply wholly or in part from the metropolitan water district to provide a connection and a supply of water to such town so reported or found to have inadequate water supply. Any town or water company obtaining its water supply wholly or in part from the metropolitan water district shall promptly upon request furnish to the commission a certified statement and description of its connections for supplying water to any town specified in such request.

As used in this chapter, the word "valuation" means the taxable valuation last established by the general court as a basis of apportionment for state and county taxes, and the words "membership", "eligibility to membership" and words of like import refer only to the membership which is subject to the annual assessment by apportionment, as provided in said section twenty-six, following voluntary application by the town and admission by the commission, and not to towns subject to the assessment of premiums as prescribed in this section nor to towns purchasing water from the district.

Any town may be admitted to membership in the metropolitan water district without payment of any entrance fee, if it takes its entire water supply from the commission, and the entrance fee of any town which does not so take its entire water supply shall be that determined by the commission, but not more than such entering town's proportionate share, determined as hereinafter provided, of the aggregate total assessments that have been made, prior to the first assessment to be shared by such entering town, on account of the retirement of bonds issued in and after the year nineteen hundred and twenty-seven to finance the construction of the metropolitan water works, less the net water debt, if any, on December first immediately prior to said first assessment shared, on account of the cost of works constructed by the commission prior to the year nineteen hundred and twenty-seven. Such proportionate share of the net sum to be apportioned shall be determined by taking only one third of said net sum, apportioning this among all towns which are members of the metropolitan water district and all towns which are not members but eligible to membership, in proportion to their respective valuations, and deducting from such entering town's share a credit of the aggregate total of any annual premiums paid as prescribed by this section.

All payments made as aforesaid for admission of towns and for furnishing water to water companies and to towns, and for selling and delivering water to any concentration camp, shall be appropriated to the payment of the cost incurred by the district in connecting such town, water company or concentration camp with the metropolitan water system, and the balance after such cost is paid, as well as all other payments for furnishing water to a town or water company in case of fire or other emergency, or as otherwise authorized, except payments as annual assessments by towns or water companies, shall be applied by the state treasurer to the sinking fund established for the payment of bonds, or to the payment of serial bonds, issued on account of the metropolitan water district. All payments made as annual assessments, either by towns or by water companies, shall be applied as provided in section twenty-five.

May borrow funds for construction, etc.

SECTION 1A. In order to provide funds to construct any water supply connection provided under section ten of chapter ninety-two of the General Laws, as amended by section one of this act, in anticipation of the payment therefor by the town to be connected, the state treasurer, with the approval of the governor, may borrow from time to time, on the credit of the commonwealth, such amounts as may be certified by the metropolitan district commission to be necessary to provide such temporary funds, not exceeding two hundred and fifty thousand dollars in any year, and the state treasurer may issue notes of the commonwealth therefor, bearing interest payable at such times and at such rates as shall be fixed by him with the approval of the governor. Such notes shall be issued for such terms as the governor may recommend to the general court in accordance with section three of Article LXII of the amendments to the constitution of the commonwealth.

SECTION 2. Section twenty-six of said chapter ninety-two, as so appearing, is hereby amended by striking out the first paragraph and inserting in place thereof the following paragraph: — The state treasurer, for the purpose of making the apportionment to the towns in the metropolitan water district of the amount required in each year to pay the interest, sinking fund requirements and expenses of maintenance and operation of the metropolitan water system, shall, in each year, apportion such amount to the towns in said district, one third in proportion to their valuations, and the remaining two thirds in proportion to their consumption, in the preceding year, of water received from all sources of supply as determined by the commission and certified to said state treasurer; provided, that there shall be included in reckoning such proportion only one fifth of the total valuation, and nothing for consumption of water, for any town which has not reached the safe capacity of its present sources of supply or of the sources of supply of the water company by which it is supplied, as the case may be, determined as aforesaid, or which has not made application to said commission for water; and provided, further, that the assessment of any town assessed upon its full valuation, which obtains a part of its water supply from other than district sources, shall not exceed, by more than three two hundredths of one per cent of such valuation, the product of the total number of million gallons of water supplied to said town in the preceding year from the metropolitan water system by a cost per million gallons equal to forty dollars plus the product of twenty dollars by the ratio of the town's valuation to the aggregate valuation of all members of the district and by the inverse ratio of the town's total water consumption to the aggregate consumption of all members in the preceding year. If any town is admitted to the metropolitan water district too late in any year to share with the other members the total district assessment for that year, it shall be assessed and pay as a part of its assessment for the following year a sum equal to the product of the total number of million gallons of water furnished it by the district during the balance of the year of its admission by a cost per million gallons equal to forty dollars plus the product of twenty dollars by the ratio of the town's valuation to the aggregate valuation of all members of the district and by the inverse ratio of the town's total water consumption to the aggregate consumption of all members in the preceding year. The state treasurer shall annually notify each town assessed under the provisions of this section and of section ten, of the amount of its assessment, and the same

G. L. (Ter. Ed.), 92, § 26, amended.

Apportionment of expenses.

shall be paid by the town to the commonwealth at the time required for the payment of, and as a part of, its state tax. The commission shall annually notify the commissioner of corporations and taxation of the liability of any water company for the payment of a premium under the provisions of section ten hereof, and said commissioner shall assess such premium as a part of the franchise tax of such water company. Said commissioner shall collect such premium as a part of such franchise tax and the proceeds from all such payments shall be transferred to the state treasurer and used by him to meet the expenses of maintenance and operation of the metropolitan water works.

1941, ch. 727, repealed.

SECTION 3. Chapter seven hundred and twenty-seven of the acts of nineteen hundred and forty-one is hereby repealed. *Approved June 12, 1943.*

Chap.544 AN ACT ESTABLISHING WITHIN THE DEPARTMENT OF PUBLIC SAFETY A BOARD OF STANDARDS AND APPEALS, AND ESTABLISHING ITS POWERS AND DUTIES, AND MAKING CERTAIN CORRECTIVE CHANGES IN THE LAWS RELATIVE TO THE INSPECTION AND REGULATION OF, AND LICENSES FOR, BUILDINGS.

Be it enacted, etc., as follows:

G. L. (Ter. Ed.), 22, new § 13 added.

SECTION 1. Chapter twenty-two of the General Laws is hereby amended by inserting after section twelve, as appearing in the Tercentenary Edition, the following new section: — *Section 13.* There shall be in the department, but not under the control of the commissioner, a board to be known as the board of standards and appeals, which shall consist of five members, to be appointed by the governor, with the advice and consent of the council, for terms of five years each. One of such members shall, when appointed, be a registered architect, one a registered professional engineer, one a contractor, one a representative of the building trades unions, and one a safety engineer. Of the members of said board originally appointed the governor shall designate one member as chairman. Upon the termination of service on said board of such chairman, and thereafter, the member senior in service, and with the longest original term of office, if a member of the board originally appointed under this section, shall be the chairman.

Board of standards and appeals.

Appointment, qualifications, etc.

There shall also be five associate members of said board, to be appointed in the same manner and for the same terms as the members of said board. One of such associate members shall, when appointed, be a registered architect, one a registered professional engineer, one a contractor, one a representative of the building trades unions, and one a safety engineer. In the event of the absence, disability or disqualification of a member of such board, the chairman shall designate the associate member thereof, having like qualifications, to sit on the board during such absence, disability or disqualification.

No member or associate member shall act as a member of the board, or vote as such, in connection with any matter as to which his private right, distinct from the public interest, is immediately concerned.

A majority of said board, constituted as above provided, may transact business, but a lesser number may adjourn from time to time.

Each member of said board, and each associate member while sitting as a member of said board, shall be paid twenty dollars for each day while in the actual performance of his duties as such, but not exceeding one thousand dollars in any fiscal year, and shall also receive from the commonwealth all expenses necessarily incurred by him in connection with his official duties.

G. L. (Ter Ed.), 143, § 3, amended, and new §§ 3A–3H, added.

SECTION 2. Chapter one hundred and forty-three of the General Laws is hereby amended by striking out section three, as appearing in the Tercentenary Edition, and inserting in place thereof the following nine sections: — *Section 3.* Every city, subject to the provisions of any special law relative thereto, and every town may, for the prevention of fire, and the preservation of life, health and morals, by ordinances or by-laws consistent with law and applicable throughout the whole or any defined part of its territory, regulate the inspection, materials, construction, alteration, repair, height, area, location and use of buildings and other structures within its limits, except such as are owned or occupied by the United States, or owned or occupied by the commonwealth other than those used in whole or in part as a place of assembly, and except bridges, quays and wharves, and may prescribe penalties not exceeding one hundred dollars for every violation of such ordinances or by-laws.

Regulations by cities and towns

Certain municipal officials to be deemed agents, etc., of commissioner of public safety.

Section 3A. For the purposes of this chapter the administrative head of the fire department in each city or town, and the officer or board charged with the duty of inspecting or issuing permits or licenses for the construction, reconstruction, alteration, repair, demolition, removal, use and occupancy of any places of assembly therein, or, if there is no such administrative head, officer or board in any town, the board of selectmen thereof, shall be deemed to be authorized representatives of the commissioner of public safety, in this and the seven following sections called the commissioner, for the enforcement of all laws, rules and regulations, ordinances and by-laws relative to the protection of life and limb in all places of assembly in any city or town and may take any action necessary to insure compliance therewith.

Rules and regulations, approval of, etc.

Section 3B. The commissioner of public safety, herein and in the six following sections called the commissioner, subject to the approval of the board of standards and appeals shall, and said board of its own motion may, make rules and regulations relating to the construction, reconstruction, alteration, repair, demolition, removal, use and occupancy, and to the standards of materials to be used in such construction, reconstruction, alteration, repair, demolition, removal, use and occupancy of any building or portion thereof which, under section one, may be deemed to be a place of assembly; and such rules and regulations shall be in accord with the generally accepted standards of engineering practice and not inconsistent with law. The commissioner, within ten days after approval thereof by the board of standards and appeals, shall deposit with the state secretary a copy of the rules and regulations as so approved, and the same shall become effective when so deposited. One copy of each issue of such rules and regulations shall be forwarded by registered mail to the officer or board in each city or town charged with the duty of issuing permits or licenses for the construction, reconstruction, alteration, repair, demolition, removal, use and occupancy of such places of assembly; and registry return receipts shall be filed in the department. All provisions of this chapter and of the rules and regulations issued thereunder shall be binding, without further acceptance, upon each city and town and upon each such officer or board; or, if there is no such officer or board in any town, then upon the board of selectmen thereof; but this section shall not be construed as prohibiting any city, subject to the provisions of any special law relative thereto, or any town, by ordinance or by-law, from making further restrictions, in accordance with the generally accepted standards of engineering practice and not inconsistent with law, for the protection of life and limb in any of said places of assembly, except theatres.

Appeals, notice, etc.

Section 3C. Any person aggrieved by a decision of the officer or board of a city or town charged with the duty of inspecting or issuing permits or licenses for the construction, reconstruction, alteration, repair, demolition, removal, use and occupancy of places of assembly therein, or, if there is no such officer or board in any town, then the board of selectmen thereof, may, within ten days after having received written notice of such a decision, appeal therefrom to the commissioner, who, after fourteen days' notice to the appealing parties and to such other persons as he shall determine to be interested parties, shall give a hearing and shall, within thirty days thereafter, render his decision on said appeal and give written notice of his decision to all persons interested, as above provided. Any person or party interested aggrieved by a decision of the commissioner on such an appeal may, within thirty days after having received written notice of the commissioner's decision on such an appeal, appeal to the board of standards and appeals who, after fourteen days' notice to the appealing parties and to such other persons as it deems to be parties in interest, shall give a hearing and shall, within thirty days thereafter, confirm or modify the commissioner's decision or confirm the original decision of the officer or board above referred to, and shall forthwith give written notice of such decision to all parties in interest, as above determined.

Any person aggrieved by a decision of said board may, within thirty days after receiving written notice thereof, bring a petition in the supreme judicial or superior court for the county where the property in question lies for a writ of certiorari to correct errors of law in the proceedings, and the provisions of section four of chapter two hundred and forty-nine of the General Laws, so far as apt, shall apply to said petition.

Section 3D. The commissioner or his authorized representative may inspect at any time any place of assembly or any building, portion of a building or room in which such place of assembly is located, for the purpose of ascertaining whether or not there has been or is a violation of any law, rule, regulation, ordinance or by-law for the protection of life and limb in such place of assembly. **Inspection of places of assembly.**

The commissioner may require that any room, portion of a building or building which, by reason of use or occupancy, may be deemed to be a place of assembly, shall comply with all provisions of law, rules and regulations, ordinances and by-laws relative to the protection of life and limb in such places of assembly.

Section 3E. Every decision of the board of standards and appeals shall be in writing and shall be filed forthwith in the office of the commissioner. A certified copy of such decision shall be sent to the officer or board in the city or town charged with the duty of inspecting or issuing permits or licenses for the construction, reconstruction, alteration, repair, demolition, removal, use and occupancy of places of assembly therein, or, if there is no such officer or board in any town, then the board of selectmen thereof, and shall be kept on file in the office of such officer or board and open to public inspection. **Decisions of board to be in writing.**

Pending an appeal from any order or decision of the commissioner, on appeal from action of the local officer or board, the order or decision of the commissioner shall remain in full force and effect. If his order or decision is confirmed upon appeal it shall thereafter have full force and effect, but if it is modified or annulled upon appeal the commissioner shall issue an order in accordance therewith within a period of not exceeding ten days following the date of receipt by him of written notification of such modification or annulment.

Section 3F. When a decision upon appeal has been rendered by the board of standards and appeals no further petition relative to the same place of assembly shall be filed with the commissioner for the period of at least one year thereafter, unless in the opinion of the commissioner the new petition is substantially different in character from the one originally submitted or unless the conditions surrounding the original petition have so changed as to justify a **Effect of decision upon appeal.**

rehearing thereon; and in each instance the commissioner shall promptly inform in writing the petitioner as to his decision.

Maximum number of persons to be permitted in place of assembly.

Section 3G. The officer or board of a city or town charged with the duty of inspecting or issuing permits or licenses for the construction, reconstruction, alteration, repair, demolition, removal, use and occupancy of places of assembly therein, or, if there is no such officer or board in any town, then the board of selectmen thereof, shall determine the maximum number of persons to be permitted in any place of assembly at any one time, and shall order the owner, tenant or lessee of such place of assembly to post in such building or portion of the building within which the place of assembly is located as he deems necessary a placard, or placards, setting forth the maximum number of persons to be permitted to assemble therein and indicating the location of each exit or means of egress from such place of assembly. Every such placard shall be of such size and form as may be prescribed from time to time by the commissioner.

This section shall not apply to theatres, special halls and public halls.

Application of §§ 3–3G.

Section 3H. Sections three to three G, inclusive, shall apply to all municipal, county and state buildings which are used in whole or in part as places of assembly, as well as to all private buildings used for the same purposes.

G. L. (Ter. Ed.), 143, etc., amended.

SECTION 3. Said chapter one hundred and forty-three is hereby further amended in sections fifteen, sixteen, twenty-one, twenty-four to thirty-three, inclusive, forty-three, forty-five, forty-six, forty-nine and fifty-one, as so appearing or as amended, by striking out, in each instance, the phrase "Except in Boston" and any other word or phrase exempting said city from the provisions of said sections; and, in section fifty-two of said chapter one hundred and forty-three, by striking out in line four the words "or the mayor of Boston" and, in lines five and six, by striking out the words "or an inspector of the building department of Boston".

G. L. (Ter. Ed.), 143, § 34, amended.

SECTION 4. Said chapter one hundred and forty-three is hereby amended by striking out section thirty-four, as so appearing, and inserting in place thereof the following section: — *Section 34.* In sections thirty-four to thirty-eight, inclusive, the term "licensing officer" shall mean the commissioner of public safety. Said commissioner shall issue licenses for theatres, special halls and public halls. He may require such changes in the structural or other condition of any building before issuing any license as in his opinion the public safety requires, but no change shall be ordered in excess of the requirements for a new building of like character. In buildings existing on November first, nineteen hundred and thirteen, and in Boston in buildings in existence on October first, nineteen hundred and forty-three, an equivalent of the conditions required by law may be accepted by the licensing officer; provided, that such equivalents are set

Licenses for theatres, etc.

forth in detail in the license. The licenses provided for herein shall be conspicuously posted near the main entrance of the theatre, special hall or public hall. Licenses for theatres shall expire on September first, for special halls on August first, and for public halls on July first of each year.

Section 5. Said chapter one hundred and forty-three is hereby further amended by striking out section fifty-four, as so appearing, and inserting in place thereof the following section: — *Section 54.* Sections fifteen to fifty-two, inclusive, shall, except when otherwise specifically provided, be enforced by the commissioner of public safety, the chief of inspections of the department and the inspectors. The commissioner of public safety shall issue regulations necessary for their uniform enforcement.

G. L. (Ter. Ed.), 143, § 54, amended.

Enforcement of §§ 15–52.

Section 6. Said chapter one hundred and forty-three is hereby further amended by striking out section fifty-nine, as so appearing, and inserting in place thereof the following section: — *Section 59.* The supreme judicial or superior court may, upon the application of the commissioner of public safety or his authorized representative, enforce, by any suitable process or decree, any provision of sections fifteen to fifty-two, inclusive, and any order or requirement of any person made under authority thereof.

G. L. (Ter. Ed.), 143, § 59, amended.

Enforcement of orders.

Section 7. Before November first, nineteen hundred and forty-three, the governor, with the advice and consent of the council, shall appoint five members of the board of standards and appeals in the department of public safety, with the qualifications set forth in section thirteen of chapter twenty-two of the General Laws, of whom one shall be appointed for the term of one year, one for the term of two years, one for the term of three years, one for the term of four years, and one for the term of five years; five associate members of said board, with the qualifications set forth in said section thirteen, of whom one shall be appointed for the term of one year, one for the term of two years, one for the term of three years, one for the term of four years, and one for the term of five years. Salaries or compensation of the persons so appointed shall not exceed the maximum set forth for the respective offices by said section thirteen.

Appointment of members of board of standards and appeals.

Compensation.

Section 7A. During the continuance of the existing state of war between the United States and certain foreign countries, and for the period of six months following the termination of such existing states of war, non-compliance with any provision of chapter one hundred and forty-three of the General Laws or of any provision of law inserted or amended by any section of this act, which non-compliance is solely the result of federal law, rule or regulation preventing such compliance, shall not be deemed to be a violation of such provision.

Effect of act during existing war.

Section 7B. Section one of said chapter one hundred and forty-three, as amended, is hereby further amended by striking out, in lines seven to nine, inclusive, as appearing in the

G. L. (Ter. Ed.), 143, § 1, etc., amended.

Tercentenary Edition, the words "in sections thirty-four to thirty-eight, inclusive, 'inspector' shall include the inspectors of the building department of Boston and".

Effective date.

SECTION 8. So much of this act as provides for any action or decision which may be appealed from under section three C of chapter one hundred and forty-three of the General Laws, as inserted by section two of this act, shall not take effect until the effective date of the first issue of the rules and regulations provided for in section three B of said chapter one hundred and forty-three, as inserted by said section two. *Approved June 12, 1943.*

---

*Chap.*545 AN ACT RELATIVE TO THE RETIREMENT OF CERTAIN OFFICERS IN THE DIVISION OF STATE POLICE IN THE DEPARTMENT OF PUBLIC SAFETY.

Be it enacted, etc., as follows:

G. L. (Ter. Ed.), 32, § 68, amended.

Pensions for state police.

SECTION 1. Chapter thirty-two of the General Laws is hereby amended by striking out section sixty-eight, as appearing in the Tercentenary Edition, and inserting in place thereof the following: — *Section 68.* Any officer or inspector of the department of public safety, who began continuous service prior to July first, nineteen hundred and twenty-one, if in the judgment of the commissioner of public safety he is disabled for useful service in the department and a physician designated by said commissioner certifies that he is permanently incapacitated, either physically or mentally, for the further performance of his duty in the department, by injuries sustained through no fault of his own in the actual performance of his duty, or any such officer or inspector of said department who shall have attained the age of sixty-five, shall be retired, and shall annually receive a pension from the commonwealth equal to one half the compensation received by him at the time of his retirement. Said commissioner may in an emergency call upon any person so pensioned for such temporary service as a member of the department as he may be fitted to perform, and during such service there shall be paid to him the difference between the rate of full pay for such employment and the rate of pension received by him. Any former inspector of the district police transferred to the state board of labor and industries under authority of section eight of chapter seven hundred and twenty-six of the acts of nineteen hundred and twelve shall, for the purposes of this section, be deemed an inspector of the department of public safety.

G. L. (Ter. Ed.), 32, § 68C, etc., amended.

Length of service requirements.

SECTION 2. Said chapter thirty-two is hereby further amended by striking out section sixty-eight C, inserted by section three of chapter five hundred and three of the acts of nineteen hundred and thirty-nine, and inserting in place thereof the following: — *Section 68C.* (1) Any officer or inspector whose last appointment was under section six of chapter twenty-two, and who was so last appointed on or after September first, nineteen hundred and twenty-one, who has performed service in the division of state police or in the division of inspections in the department of public safety for not less than twenty years, shall be retired by the state board of retirement upon attaining age fifty-five or upon the expiration of such twenty years, whichever last occurs, unless the rating board certifies to the commissioner of public safety upon examination of the officer or inspector when he attains age fifty-five and annually thereafter, that the mental and physical condition of the officer or inspector is such that he should be continued in his employment, but in any event no such officer or inspector shall remain beyond his sixty-fifth birthday. An officer appointed under section nine A of said chapter who has performed service in the division of state police in said department for not less than twenty years shall be retired by said board upon attaining age fifty, or upon the expiration of said twenty years, whichever last occurs.

(2) An officer or inspector who has performed service in either of said divisions for not less than twenty years and has not attained age fifty-five, or age fifty in the case of an officer appointed under said section nine A, shall be retired by the state board of retirement in case the rating board, after an examination of such officer or inspector by a registered physician appointed by it, shall report in writing to the state board of retirement that he is physically or mentally incapacitated for the performance of duty, and that such incapacity is likely to be permanent.

Amount of Allowance.

(3) Upon retirement under paragraph (1) or paragraph (2) of this section, the officer or inspector shall receive a retirement allowance consisting of:

(*a*) A life annuity as provided in said section four G; and

(*b*) A pension of such amount as will, together with the life annuity set forth in paragraph (1) (*a*) of section four G, be equal to one half of his average annual rate of regular compensation during the five years immediately prior to the date of his retirement. *Approved June 12, 1943.*

AN ACT DEFINING "PLACE OF ASSEMBLY", AS USED IN CERTAIN BUILDING LAWS, AND FURTHER REGULATING THE MEANS OF INGRESS TO AND EGRESS FROM PLACES OF ASSEMBLY. *Chap.*546

Whereas, The recent terrible loss of life occurring in connection with a fire at one of the places of public assembly within the city of Boston has made apparent the urgent need of immediate change in the laws relative to means of ingress to and egress from such places and the deferred operation of this act would in part tend to defeat its purpose, which is to make immediately effective certain laws

Emergency preamble.

relative thereto, therefore it is hereby declared to be an emergency law, necessary for the immediate preservation of the public safety and convenience.

Be it enacted, etc., as follows:

G. L. (Ter. Ed.), 143, § 1, etc., amended.

SECTION 1. Section one of chapter one hundred and forty-three of the General Laws, as amended by chapter six hundred and ninety-four of the acts of nineteen hundred and forty-one, is hereby further amended by inserting after the paragraph contained in the twelfth to the fourteenth lines, inclusive, as appearing in the Tercentenary Edition, the following paragraph: —

"Place of assembly" defined.

"Place of assembly", any building, or any portion of a building, designed, constructed, reconstructed, remodeled, altered, used, or intended to be used, for fifty or more persons to assemble therein for any of the following: — Dance halls; cabarets; restaurants, including the type of restaurant commonly known as a night club; all places in which alcoholic beverages are sold or for sale to be consumed on the premises; any room or space used for public or private banquets, feasts, dances, socials, card parties, or weddings or religious services except in the case of funerals in private homes; lodge and meeting halls or rooms; skating rinks; gymnasiums; swimming pools; billiard, pool, bowling and table tennis rooms; halls or rooms used for public or private catering purposes; funeral parlors; recreation rooms; concert halls; theatres; broadcasting studios; school and college auditoriums; places of assemblage; and all other places of similar occupancy. Nothing in this paragraph shall apply to a single family or two-family dwelling, or to a place of incarceration or detention, a convent, a monastery, a church or a synagogue.

G. L. (Ter. Ed.), 143, § 21, amended.

Fire escapes, exits, signs, etc.

SECTION 2. Said chapter one hundred and forty-three is hereby further amended by striking out section twenty-one, as appearing in the Tercentenary Edition, and inserting in place thereof the following section: — *Section 21.* Any building in whole or in part used as a public building, and any building in which ten or more persons are employed in a factory, workshop, mercantile or other establishment, and an office building, dormitory, hotel, family hotel, apartment house, boarding house, lodging house or tenement house which has eight or more rooms, or in which ten or more persons are accommodated, lodge or reside above the second story, the owner, lessee or mortgagee in possession whereof is notified in writing by an inspector that sections fifteen to sixty, inclusive, apply thereto, shall be provided with proper egresses or other means of escape from fire sufficient for the use of all persons accommodated, assembled, employed, lodged or resident therein; but no owner, lessee or mortgagee in possession of such building shall be deemed to have violated this provision unless he has been notified in writing by an inspector as to what additional egresses or means of escape from fire are necessary, and for thirty days has neglected or refused to provide the same. The egresses and means of escape shall be kept unobstructed, in good repair and ready for use, and, if the inspector so directs in writing, every such egress shall be properly lighted and provided with a sign having on it the word "Exit" in letters not less than five inches in height, and so made and placed as plainly to indicate to persons within the building the situation of such egresses; stairways shall have suitable hand rails; women or children shall not be employed in a factory, workshop, mercantile or other establishment in a room above the second story from which there is only one egress. Portable seats shall not be allowed in the aisles or passageways of such buildings during any service or entertainment held therein. Stairways on the outside of the building shall have suitable railed landings at each story above the first, accessible at each story from doors or windows, and such landings, doors and windows shall be kept clear of ice, snow and other obstructions.

Nothing in this chapter shall be construed as prohibiting any city or town from enacting from time to time supplementary ordinances or by-laws imposing further restrictions as to egresses and means of escape, subject, however, in the case of a city to the provisions of any special law relative thereto, but no authority of any such city or town shall have power to minimize, avoid or repeal any provision of this chapter.

G. L. (Ter. Ed.), 143, new §§ 21A and 21B, added.

SECTION 3. Said chapter one hundred and forty-three is hereby further amended by inserting after said section twenty-one, as so amended, the two following sections: —

Safety devices for doorways and windows.

Section 21A. All doorways and windows which serve as exits or as means of egress from any building subject to section twenty-one or from a place of assembly, as defined in section one, shall open in the direction of egress and, where used as means of egress from a place of assembly, shall not be so equipped as to be locked, bolted or otherwise fastened so that they cannot be opened from the inside by the use of the ordinary door knob or by pressure on the door or window or on a panic release device, so called. Any place of assembly, as defined in section one, which is wholly or partly below the ground level shall have at least two means of egress directly to the ground or street level, such means of egress to be located at points as widely separated from one another as may be reasonably feasible.

Use of revolving doors in places of public assembly prohibited.

Penalty.

Section 21B. Whoever, after July first, nineteen hundred and forty-five, installs as a means of ingress to or egress from any place of assembly, as defined in section one, in any building or part thereof, a revolving door, so called, or after the expiration of sixty days from said July first, maintains or uses a revolving door as a means of ingress to or egress from any place of assembly, as so defined, in any building or part thereof, shall be punished by a fine of not more than five hundred dollars or by imprisonment for not more than one year, or by both such fine and imprisonment; and any revolving door, so called, which is installed, maintained or used in violation of the foregoing shall be deemed a common nuisance, without other proof thereof than proof of its installation, maintenance or use, as the case may be. The board or officer in charge of the enforcement of building laws in the municipality where such nuisance exists shall order the owner or occupant, being the party in control thereof, at his own expense to remove such nuisance within twenty-four hours, or within such other time as it or he considers reasonable, after notice.

Notice.

Such order shall be in writing and may be served personally on the owner or occupant, being the party in control, or his authorized agent by any person authorized to serve civil process; or a copy of the order may be left at the last and usual place of abode of the owner or occupant, being the party in control, or his agent, if he is known and within the commonwealth. If the premises are unoccupied and the residence of the owner or agent is unknown or is without the commonwealth, the board or officer may order the notice to be served by posting it on the premises and by advertising it in one or more newspapers.

If the owner or occupant, being the party in control, fails to comply with such order, the board or officer may cause the nuisance to be removed, and all expenses incurred thereby shall be paid by the person who caused or permitted the same.

G. L. (Ter. Ed.), 148, § 28, amended.

SECTION 4. Section twenty-eight of chapter one hundred and forty-eight of the General Laws, as appearing in the Tercentenary Edition, is hereby amended by striking out, in the forty-third line, the words "public assembly" and inserting in place thereof the words: — assembly, as such term is defined in section one of chapter one hundred and forty-three, — so that paragraph L will read as follows: —

Inflammable decorations.

L. Prohibiting or regulating inflammable decorations in stores, halls and places of assembly, as such term is defined in section one of chapter one hundred and forty-three.

Application of act limited.

SECTION 5. During the continuance of the existing state of war between the United States and certain foreign countries, and for the period of six months following the termination of such existing states of war, non-compliance with any provision of this act, which non-compliance is solely the result of federal law, rule or regulation preventing such compliance, shall not be deemed to be a violation of such provision.

Effective dates.

SECTION 6. So much of section three of this act as inserts in chapter one hundred and forty-three of the General Laws a new section to be known as section twenty-one A shall take effect on January first, nineteen hundred and forty-four. So much of said section three as inserts in said chapter one hundred and forty-three a new section to be known as twenty-one B shall take effect on July first, nineteen hundred and forty-five. *Approved June 12, 1943.*

AN ACT REQUIRING PERSONS OPERATING OR MAINTAINING EDUCATIONAL INSTITUTIONS TO FURNISH, UPON REQUEST, CERTAIN TRANSCRIPTS OF RECORDS. *Chap.* 547

Whereas, The deferred operation of this act would prevent certain persons in the armed forces of the United States from promptly obtaining benefits by presenting proof of their having certain educational attainments in the form of transcripts of records of educational institutions within the commonwealth; therefore it is hereby declared to be an emergency law, necessary for the immediate preservation of the public convenience. Emergency preamble.

Be it enacted, etc., as follows:

Chapter seventy-one of the General Laws is hereby amended by inserting after section thirty-four, as amended, the two following sections: — *Section 34A*. Any person operating or maintaining an educational institution within the commonwealth shall, upon request of any student or former student thereof, furnish to him a written transcript of his record as a student. There shall be no charge for any transcript originally furnished by any such person hereunder, but for any duplicate or additional transcript furnished hereunder a charge of not exceeding one dollar for each page, but not exceeding five dollars for an entire transcript, may be made by such person. G. L. (Ter. Ed.), 71, new §§ 34A and 34B, added. Certain transcripts of records to be furnished, etc.

Section 34B. In case any person subject to section thirty-four A shall refuse or neglect for thirty days after such request to furnish such a written transcript, the student or former student requesting the same or, if a minor, his guardian or next friend, may present to the superior court for the county within which such person so subject resides or such institution is located, or for the county of Suffolk, a petition addressed to said court and praying for such relief as it may deem proper in the circumstances; and thereupon such court shall have jurisdiction of such petition and may issue such orders relative thereto as it may deem proper, and any failure or refusal to obey any such order may be treated by the court as a contempt thereof. Upon any such petition the court may award costs and reasonable attorney's fees to the petitioner. *Approved June 12, 1943.* Failure to furnish written transcript upon request. Penalty.

AN ACT TO MEET CERTAIN CONTINGENCIES ARISING IN CONNECTION WITH THE SERVICE OF PUBLIC OFFICERS AND EMPLOYEES AND CERTAIN OTHER PERSONS IN THE MILITARY OR NAVAL FORCES OF THE UNITED STATES DURING THE PRESENT NATIONAL EMERGENCY. *Chap.* 548

Whereas, The deferred operation of this act would tend to defeat its purpose, which in part is to protect the rights of certain persons in the military or naval service of the United States and to facilitate the temporary appointment Emergency preamble.

of persons to perform their duties in their absence, therefore, it is hereby declared to be an emergency law, necessary for the preservation of the public convenience.

Be it enacted, etc., as follows:

SECTION 1. Chapter seven hundred and eight of the acts of nineteen hundred and forty-one is hereby amended by striking out section one, as amended by chapter one hundred and seventy-two of the acts of the current year, and inserting in place thereof the following section: — *Section 1.* Notwithstanding any contrary provisions of general or special law any person who, on or after January first, nineteen hundred and forty, shall have tendered his resignation from an office or position in the service of the commonwealth, or any political subdivision thereof, or otherwise terminated such service, for the purpose of serving in the military or naval forces of the United States and who does or did so serve or was or shall be rejected for such service, shall, except as hereinafter provided, be deemed to be or to have been on leave of absence; and no such person shall be deemed to have resigned from his office in the service of the commonwealth, or any political subdivision thereof, or to have terminated such service, until the expiration of one year from the termination of said military or naval service by him.

When a person holding an office or position in the service of the commonwealth, or any political subdivision thereof, enters the military or naval service of the United States and files a resignation in writing stating his reason for such resignation, the resignation shall be considered a final determination of the reason for leaving the service of the commonwealth, or a political subdivision thereof. If no written resignation is filed, entrance into the military or naval service of the United States by a person holding a position in the service of the commonwealth, or a political subdivision thereof, shall be prima facie evidence that his service to the commonwealth, or a political subdivision thereof, is terminated for the purpose of entering said military or naval service. The phrase "serving in the military or naval forces of the United States", the phrase "service in the military or naval forces of the United States" and the phrase "military or naval service", as used in this act, shall be taken to include service other than in a civilian capacity as a member of any corps or unit established under the laws of the United States for the purpose of enabling women to serve with, or as auxiliary to, the armed forces of the United States.

SECTION 2. Section three of said chapter seven hundred and eight is hereby amended by adding at the end the following paragraph: —

Any person who is in such military or naval service and who is certified in accordance with the civil service law and rules to a permanent office or position classified under chapter thirty-one of the General Laws may be permanently appointed to such office, or position and employed therein provided he makes request for employment in writing of the appointing authority within three months after termination of such military or naval service, and files with the division of civil service the certificate of a registered physician that he is not physically disabled or incapacitated for performing the duties of the office or position. Any such appointment shall be subject to a probationary period of six months to be served upon actual employment after return from the military or naval service. Any appointment, transfer or promotion to fill such office or position while he is so serving shall be temporary only and shall be filled by a military substitute who shall hold such office or position, subject to the same limitations and with the same rights as a military substitute appointed under section two.

SECTION 3. Said chapter seven hundred and eight is hereby further amended by inserting after section ten the following section: — *Section 10A.* In case an elected officer of a city, except in Boston, excluding the mayor but including members of the city council, is unable to perform the duties of his office by reason of said military or naval service, an acting officer who in his absence from the city shall possess all the rights and powers, perform all the duties, and be subject to all the obligations, of said office until the return of the absent officer to the duties of such office or until the expiration of the term thereof, whichever first occurs, shall be selected as follows: (1) If the said vacancy is in a board consisting of two or more members, the remaining members shall give written notice to the mayor of said vacancy, and said members and the mayor, acting as a special board, shall fill such vacancy by ballot by a majority vote, or in case of failure to fill such vacancy, in the manner hereby provided, within one week after the giving of such notice, such vacancy shall be filled by the mayor, except that in a city having a Plan E charter, so-called, such a vacancy shall be filled in accordance with the provisions of section one hundred and two of chapter forty-three of the General Laws, or

(2) If the said vacancy is in an office held by an individual not a member of a board, the mayor may appoint a person to fill the vacancy.

If the holder of an office, other than that of a member of a board, in a city other than Boston, which is filled by the city council, whether by appointment or election, is unable to perform the duties of his office by reason of said military or naval service, an acting officer who in his absence from the city shall possess all the rights and powers, perform all the duties, and be subject to all the obligations, of said office until the return of the absent officer to the duties of such office or until the expiration of the term thereof, whichever first occurs, may be appointed by the city council.

A person appointed under the provisions of this section to fill a vacancy in the office of an elected officer, as defined in section twelve, shall receive from the city one half of the salary or compensation fixed for the position, which shall be deducted from and charged against the appropriation voted for such salary or compensation, plus such additional amount, if any, as may be appropriated therefor. The salary or compensation paid to the elected officer, as defined in section twelve, on leave of absence shall be one half of the amount fixed for the office until the expiration of the term of office for which he was elected, or until his return to the duties of such office, whichever first occurs.

SECTION 4. Section eleven of said chapter seven hundred and eight is hereby amended by adding at the end of the first paragraph the following sentence: — In case of failure to fill such vacancy in the manner hereby provided within one week, such vacancy shall be filled by the selectmen, — and by striking out the second paragraph and inserting in place thereof the following paragraph: —

A person appointed under the provisions of this section shall receive from the town one half of the salary or compensation fixed for the position, which shall be deducted from and charged against the appropriation voted for such salary or compensation, plus such additional amount, if any, as may be voted by the town. The salary or compensation paid to the elected official on leave of absence shall be one half of the amount fixed for the office until the expiration of the term of office for which he was elected, or until his return to the duties of such office, whichever first occurs.

SECTION 5. Said chapter seven hundred and eight is hereby further amended by inserting after section eleven the four following sections: — *Section 11A.* In case any elected officer of a fire, water, light or improvement district is unable to perform the duties of his office by reason of service in the military or naval forces of the United States during the existing state of war between the United States and any foreign country, a majority of the members of a board established as hereinafter provided may in writing appoint an acting officer who in the absence of such absent officer shall possess all the rights and powers, perform all the duties and be subject to all the obligations of said office until the expiration of the term of the absent officer or until his return to the duties of such office, whichever first occurs. Said board shall consist of the prudential committee or body having like powers, or, in filling a vacancy in any other elective body of any such district, the members of such other body, and in addition in each case the district clerk and the district treasurer; provided, that any such officer shall not be a member of such board when his office is being filled. No member of any such board shall have more than one vote.

A person appointed under the provisions of this section shall receive from the district one half of the salary or compensation fixed for the position, which shall be deducted from and charged against the appropriation voted for such salary or compensation, plus such additional amount, if any, as may be voted by the district. The salary or compensation paid to the elected official on leave of absence shall be one half of the amount fixed for the office until the expiration of the term of office for which he was elected, or until his return to the duties of such office, whichever first occurs.

Section 11B. In case an elected county officer, other than the register of probate, is unable to perform the duties of his office by reason of said military or naval service, a board consisting of the county commissioners together with the clerk of court and the county treasurer, may in writing appoint an acting officer who in his absence shall possess all the rights and powers and perform all the duties of said office until the expiration of the term of office of the absent officer, or until his return to the duties of such office, whichever shall occur first. In case of failure to fill such vacancy in the manner hereby provided within one week, such vacancy shall be filled by the county commissioners.

A person appointed under the provisions of this section shall receive from the county one half of the salary or compensation fixed for the position, which shall be deducted from and charged against the appropriation voted for such salary or compensation, plus such further sum, if any, as may be provided from an appropriation voted or a transfer from the reserve fund set up in the budget. The salary or compensation paid to the elected official on leave of absence shall be one half of the amount fixed for the office until the expiration of the term of office for which he was elected, or until his return to the duties of such office, whichever first occurs.

Section 11C. In case a register or an assistant register of probate enters the military or naval service of the United States, the judge or judges of probate of any such county shall appoint a temporary register or assistant register to act until the return of the absent officer to the duties of his office or until the expiration of his term, whichever first occurs, who shall have all the rights and powers and perform all the duties and be subject to all the obligations of said office.

The compensation of a register or assistant register appointed under the provisions of this section shall be the same salary fixed for said position and shall be paid by the commonwealth.

Section 11D. The treasurer of any county, city, town or district, when so authorized by the absent officer, shall retain his compensation for the benefit of the county, city, town or district.

SECTION 6. Section six of chapter four of the acts of nineteen hundred and forty-two is hereby repealed.

SECTION 7. Said chapter seven hundred and eight is hereby further amended by striking out section twelve and inserting in place thereof the following section: — *Section 12.* The term "elected officer", as used in this act, shall mean an officer elected by and from all the voters of a county, city, town or district respectively, and shall include a member of a body, board or commission.

SECTION 8. Said chapter seven hundred and eight is hereby further amended by adding at the end the following section: — *Section 26.* Nothing in this act shall be construed as giving the benefits thereof to any person who is dishonorably discharged from such military or naval service.

SECTION 9. Section eighteen of said chapter seven hundred and eight is hereby amended by striking out the last sentence and inserting in place thereof the following sentence: — Each such officer shall specify in writing the date and shall add after his signature his rank and organization.

SECTION 10. Section twenty-five of said chapter seven hundred and eight is hereby amended by striking out, in the fifth line, the word "forty-four" and inserting in place thereof the word: — forty-six, — so as to read as follows: — *Section 25.* Service in the military or naval forces of the United States referred to in this act shall, except as otherwise provided thereby, mean such service occurring on or after July first, nineteen hundred and forty and prior to January first, nineteen hundred and forty-six.

SECTION 11. The provisions of sections two and eight shall take effect as of October twenty-ninth, nineteen hundred and forty-one. *Approved June 12, 1943.*

Chap. 549 AN ACT ESTABLISHING A BOARD OF COLLEGIATE AUTHORITY IN THE DEPARTMENT OF EDUCATION, AND FURTHER REGULATING CERTAIN EDUCATIONAL INSTITUTIONS.

Emergency preamble.

Whereas, The deferred operation of this act would in part tend to defeat its purpose, which is immediately to assist citizens of this commonwealth who are or hereafter shall be in the armed forces of the United States during the present war in obtaining higher rank in such forces based in part upon proof of having satisfactorily completed courses of instruction in certain educational institutions within the commonwealth, therefore this act is hereby declared to be an emergency law, necessary for the preservation of the public convenience.

Be it enacted, etc., as follows:

G. L. (Ter. Ed.), 15, new § 3A, added.

Board of collegiate authority.

SECTION 1. Chapter fifteen of the General Laws is hereby amended by inserting after section three the following new section: — *Section 3A.* There shall be in the department a board of collegiate authority, consisting of the commissioner, who shall be chairman, the members of the advisory board of education, and four citizens of the commonwealth to be appointed by the governor, with the advice and consent of the council. Of the members originally appointed hereunder, two shall be appointed for terms of three years each and two for terms of four years each, and thereafter as the term of an appointed member expires, his successor shall be appointed by the governor, with like advice and consent, for a term of five years. Any vacancy in the appointive membership of said board shall be filled by appointment by the

Appointment of members, etc.

governor, with like advice and consent, for the remainder of the unexpired term. Of the appointive members of said board, at least one shall represent colleges and universities, one shall represent junior colleges and one shall represent the secondary school system of the public schools of the commonwealth. The members of said board shall serve without compensation, but shall be reimbursed for their necessary expenses actually incurred in the performance of their official duties.

G. L. (Ter. Ed.), 3, §§ 6 and 6A, repealed.

SECTION 2. Sections six and six A of chapter three of the General Laws are hereby repealed.

G. L. (Ter. Ed.), 3, § 7, etc., amended.

SECTION 2A. Section seven of said chapter three, as most recently amended by section three of chapter three hundred and sixty-four of the acts of nineteen hundred and thirty-seven, is hereby further amended by striking out, in the sixth line, the words "or six", — so that the first sentence of said section three will read as follows: — Any petition to the general court for the establishment or revival, or for the amendment, alteration or extension of the charter or corporate powers or privileges, or for the change of name, of any corporation, except a petition subject to the provisions of section five, which is seasonably filed in the office of the clerk of either branch and is accompanied by a bill embodying in substance the legislation petitioned for, shall, with said accompanying bill, be transmitted as soon as may be by the clerk of the branch in which they were filed to the office of the commissioner of corporations and taxation.

Petitions for legislation affecting corporations not subject to section 5

G. L. (Ter. Ed.), 69, new §§ 30 and 31 added, new heading.

SECTION 3. Chapter sixty-nine of the General Laws is hereby amended by adding at the end, under the caption BOARD OF COLLEGIATE AUTHORITY, the two following new sections: — *Section 30.* The commissioner of corporations and taxation, before approving a certificate of organization in connection with the proposed incorporation of a college, junior college, university or other educational institution with power to grant degrees, or articles of amendment to the charter of an existing educational institution which will give it such power, or changing its name to a name which will include the term "college", "junior college" or "university", shall refer such certificate or articles to the board of collegiate authority established by section three A of chapter fifteen. Said board shall immediately make an investigation as to the applicants for incorporation of such an institution and as to the purposes thereof and any other material facts relative thereto. In the case of a proposed amendment to the charter of an existing educational institution which will give it power to grant degrees, or change its name as aforesaid, said board shall make an investigation of the institution, its faculty, equipment, courses of study, financial organization, leadership, and other material facts relative thereto. In acting upon any such certificate or articles referred to it hereunder, said board shall give a public hearing, notice of which shall, at the expense of the applicants, be published once a week for three successive weeks in two newspapers,

Investigation of applicants for incorporation of college, etc.

Publication, hearing, etc.

one of which is published in the county where the institution has or is to have its principal office or place of business, the last publication to be at least three days before the date set for the hearing. Said board after making its investigation hereunder and subject to the provisions of section thirty-one, shall make a determination approving or disapproving the certificate of organization or articles of amendment referred to it hereunder and shall forthwith report its findings to the commissioner of corporations and taxation. If it appears from the report so submitted to him that said board does not approve of such certificate or articles, he shall refuse to endorse his approval thereon, otherwise he shall endorse his approval thereon unless he finds that the provisions of law relative to the organization of the corporation or the amendment to its charter have not been complied with. If such certificate or articles are not approved hereunder, the applicant or applicants may appeal to the superior court, which shall hear the case and determine whether or not the certificate or articles shall be approved.

Incorporation of junior colleges, requirements for.

Section 31. Said board of collegiate authority, in acting upon the certificate of organization in connection with the proposed incorporation of a junior college, with power to grant degrees, or in acting upon articles of amendment to the charter of any existing educational institution which will give it power to grant junior college degrees, or changing its name to a name which will include the term "junior college", shall not approve such certificate or articles unless —

First, The institution is offering instruction on a level and to a degree of thoroughness distinctly above that of the secondary school and below that of advanced senior college specialization, and offering either (*a*) a two-year course of study on a collegiate level, equivalent in content, scope and thoroughness to that offered in the standard four-year colleges and universities, or (*b*) a two-year terminal course of study of a vocational or semi-professional training, or both.

Second, The institution is organized under the laws of the commonwealth as a non-profit educational institution, and shall have operated as such an institution for a period of not less than one year immediately prior to the filing of the petition for such privilege. The general character of the institution, its professional outlook, and the character and quality of its leadership and personnel shall be determining factors in the approval of the institution.

Third, The faculty of the institution consists of teachers with adequate preparation and successful experience in their respective training fields, and in academic courses, a high percentage of the instructors have satisfactorily completed one year of advanced study after having attained the baccalaureate degree, and in terminal, semi-professional courses, instructors are able to provide evidence of a high degree of proficiency in their special fields.

Fourth, The basis for admission to the institution is the

satisfactory completion of a secondary school program, or its equivalent.

Fifth, Requirements for graduation are based upon the satisfactory completion of a minimum of sixty semester hours of study, exclusive of physical training and exercise and institutions organized on other than the semester hour basis give evidence of the equivalence of the work provided. A semester hour, for the purposes of this clause, is hereby defined as a class, meeting for one hour weekly for at least fifteen weeks.

Sixth, The institution, if offering two-year courses of study on a collegiate level, undertakes to provide the equivalent of the general education of the first two years of the standard four-year college, and gives satisfactory evidence that its semi-professional curricula are designed to provide reasonably proper instruction to students taking courses of a vocational or semi-professional nature.

Seventh, The institution has an adequate library, adequately housed, properly catalogued, has an adequate supply of current periodicals, including scientific and research journals, if such journals are properly related to the courses of study offered, and has a satisfactory annual appropriation for its continued maintenance.

Eighth, Laboratories, when necessary in connection with the courses of study offered, are adequately equipped for instructional purposes with sufficient space and suitable apparatus and equipment to meet the educational objectives of the institution, whether they be cultural or semi-professional.

Ninth, The material equipment of the institution, including its lands, buildings, classrooms and dormitories, is sufficient to insure efficient operation, and its physical plant provides safe, sanitary and healthful conditions, as judged by modern standards.

Tenth, Teaching or classroom hours of teaching in the institution do not exceed eighteen hours weekly, and classes are ordinarily limited to thirty students and the ratio of students to instructors above the level of assistants is not unreasonably excessive.

Eleventh, The institution, if seeking to provide a program equivalent to the first two years of the standard college program, offers work in at least five separate departments: English, mathematics, foreign languages, natural sciences and social sciences.

Twelfth, If the institution intends to operate a junior college and a preparatory or secondary school under the same administration, provision is made for a separation between the two divisions of the institution, and, if the institution maintains housing quarters for its students, junior college students and secondary school students will be housed in separate quarters.

Thirteenth, In addition to satisfying the authorities that it meets the provisions of a tax-free non-profit educational institution, the institution submits evidence of sound financial structure and operation over a period of at least two years.

G. L. (Ter. Ed.), 155, § 10, etc., amended.

SECTION 4. Section ten of chapter one hundred and fifty-five of the General Laws, as amended by chapter eleven of the acts of nineteen hundred and thirty-three, is hereby further amended by striking out the third sentence and inserting in place thereof the following: — Such articles shall be submitted to the commissioner who shall examine them, and if he finds that they conform to the requirements of law, he shall, subject to section thirty of chapter sixty-nine if applicable to such articles, so certify and endorse his approval thereon.

Change of name.

G. L. (Ter. Ed.), 180, § 3, amended.

SECTION 5. Section three of chapter one hundred and eighty of the General Laws, as appearing in the Tercentenary Edition, is hereby amended by inserting after the word "to" in the second line the words: — section thirty of chapter sixty-nine, — so as to read as follows: — *Section 3.* The corporation shall be formed in the manner prescribed in and subject to section thirty of chapter sixty-nine, section nine of chapter one hundred and fifty-five and sections six and eight to twelve, inclusive, of chapter one hundred and fifty-six, except as follows:

Organization.

The capital stock, if any, shall not exceed five hundred thousand dollars.

The agreement of association of a corporation having no capital stock may omit the statement of the amount of the capital stock and the par value and number of its shares. The par value of its shares, if any, may be ten, twenty-five, fifty or one hundred dollars. The fee to be paid to the state secretary upon the filing of the certificate of organization shall be twenty-five dollars.

G. L. (Ter. Ed.), 180, § 10, etc., amended.

SECTION 6. Said chapter one hundred and eighty is hereby further amended by striking out section ten, as most recently amended by section one of chapter one hundred and fifty-one of the acts of nineteen hundred and thirty-seven, and inserting in place thereof the following: — *Section 10.* Any corporation heretofore or hereafter organized under general or special law for any of the purposes mentioned in this chapter may, at a meeting duly called for the purpose, by vote of two thirds of the capital stock outstanding and entitled to vote, or, in case such corporation has no capital stock, by vote of two thirds of the persons legally qualified to vote in meetings of the corporation, or by a larger vote if its agreement of association or by-laws shall so require, add to or change the purposes for which it was incorporated, if the additional or new purpose is authorized by section two. The presiding, financial and recording officers and a majority of its other officers having the powers of directors shall forthwith make, sign and swear to a certificate setting forth such addition to or change of purposes. Such certificate shall be submitted to the commissioner of corporations and taxation who shall examine it, and if he finds that it conforms to the

Change of purpose of corporation.

requirements of law, he shall, subject to section thirty of chapter sixty-nine if applicable to such certificate, so certify and endorse his approval thereon. The certificate shall thereupon be filed in the office of the state secretary.

Section 7. Chapter two hundred and sixty-six of the General Laws is hereby amended by striking out section eighty-nine, as appearing in the Tercentenary Edition, and inserting in place thereof the following: — *Section 89.* Whoever, in a book, pamphlet, circular, advertisement or advertising sign, or by a pretended written certificate or diploma, or otherwise in writing, knowingly and falsely pretends to have been an officer or teacher, or to be a graduate or to hold any degree, of a college or other educational institution of this commonwealth or elsewhere, which is authorized to confer degrees, or of a public school of this commonwealth, and whoever, without having lawful authority to confer degrees, offers or confers degrees as a school, college or as a private individual, alone or associated with others, shall be punished by a fine of not more than one thousand dollars or by imprisonment for not more than one year, or both. Any individual, school, association, corporation or institution of learning, not having lawful authority to confer degrees, using the designation of "university" or "college" shall be punished by a fine of one thousand dollars; but this shall not apply to any educational institution whose name on July ninth, nineteen hundred and nineteen, included the word "university" or "college". *Approved June 12, 1943.*

G. L. (Ter. Ed.), 266, § 89, amended.

Knowingly pretending to hold a degree, etc., or granting degrees without authority.

Use of word "college" or "university".

An Act authorizing Dean Academy to grant the degrees of associate in arts and of associate in science to graduates of its junior college division. *Chap.*550

Be it enacted, etc., as follows:

Dean Academy, a corporation incorporated by chapter one hundred and seven of the acts of eighteen hundred and sixty-five, is hereby authorized to grant the degree of Associate in Arts or of Associate in Science, or both of said degrees, to students properly accredited and recommended by the faculty of the junior college division of said academy, upon their graduation from said division.

Approved June 12, 1943.

An Act authorizing the board of regents of the New England School of Theology to grant the degree of bachelor of arts in theology. *Chap.*551

Be it enacted, etc., as follows:

The board of regents of The New England School of Theology, a corporation incorporated under general law on May twelfth, nineteen hundred and two, under the name of The Boston Bible School and Ransom Institute, which latter name was changed to The New England School of Theology on January thirtieth, nineteen hundred and eighteen, is hereby authorized to confer the degree of Bachelor of Arts in Theology. *Approved June 12, 1943.*

---

*Chap.*552 AN ACT AUTHORIZING LASELL JUNIOR COLLEGE TO GRANT THE DEGREES OF ASSOCIATE IN ARTS AND ASSOCIATE IN SCIENCE.

Be it enacted, etc., as follows:

Lasell Junior College, a corporation incorporated under general law, is hereby authorized and empowered to grant the degree of Associate in Arts or of Associate in Science, or both of said degrees, to students particularly accredited and recommended by the faculty of said junior college.

Approved June 12, 1943.

---

*Chap.*553 AN ACT AUTHORIZING THE TRUSTEES OF THE LESLEY SCHOOL TO GRANT THE DEGREE OF BACHELOR OF SCIENCE IN EDUCATION.

Be it enacted, etc., as follows:

The trustees of The Lesley School, a corporation organized under general law, are hereby authorized to confer the degree of Bachelor of Science in Education.

Approved June 12, 1943.

---

*Chap.*554 AN ACT CHANGING THE NAME OF ENDICOTT INCORPORATED TO ENDICOTT JUNIOR COLLEGE.

Be it enacted, etc., as follows:

The name of Endicott Incorporated, a corporation incorporated under general law, is hereby changed to Endicott Junior College; and said corporation may use the designation of "junior college" as aforesaid notwithstanding the provisions of section six A of chapter three of the General Laws, inserted by section two of chapter four hundred and twenty-four of the acts of nineteen hundred and thirty-nine, and of section eighty-nine of chapter two hundred and sixty-six of the General Laws. *Approved June 12, 1943.*

---

*Chap.*555 AN ACT CHANGING THE NAME OF BECKER SCHOOL OF BUSINESS ADMINISTRATION AND SECRETARIAL SCIENCE TO BECKER JUNIOR COLLEGE OF BUSINESS ADMINISTRATION AND SECRETARIAL SCIENCE, AND AUTHORIZING SAID JUNIOR COLLEGE TO CONFER THE DEGREE OF ASSOCIATE IN SCIENCE.

Be it enacted, etc., as follows:

SECTION 1. The name of Becker School of Business Administration and Secretarial Science, a corporation incorporated under the provisions of chapter one hundred and eighty of the General Laws on December fourth, nineteen hundred and forty, is hereby changed to Becker Junior College of Business Administration and Secretarial Science.

SECTION 2. Said corporation is hereby authorized and empowered to grant to students properly accredited and recommended by its faculty, upon completion of the two-year course in said junior college, the degree of Associate in Science. *Approved June 12, 1943.*

AN ACT AUTHORIZING CAMBRIDGE JUNIOR COLLEGE TO CONFER THE DEGREES OF ASSOCIATE IN ARTS AND ASSOCIATE IN SCIENCE. *Chap.*556

Be it enacted, etc., as follows:

Cambridge Junior College, a corporation incorporated under general law in the year nineteen hundred and thirty-six, and authorized to use its present name and the designation of "junior college" by chapter two hundred and fifty-four of the acts of nineteen hundred and forty-one, is hereby authorized to grant the degrees of Associate in Arts and Associate in Science to students properly accredited and recommended by its faculty, upon completion by such students of a two years' course of instruction in said junior college.

Approved June 12, 1943.

AN ACT AUTHORIZING BABSON INSTITUTE TO CONFER THE DEGREES OF BACHELOR OF SCIENCE AND MASTER OF BUSINESS ADMINISTRATION. *Chap.*557

Be it enacted, etc., as follows:

Babson Institute, a corporation organized under chapter one hundred and eighty of the General Laws, is hereby authorized to confer the degree of Bachelor of Science, with specification in Business Administration; provided, that said degree shall not be granted to any person until after such person shall have completed to the satisfaction of the president and faculty of said Institute at least one hundred and twenty semester hours of work; and to confer the degree of Master of Business Administration; provided, that said degree shall not be granted to any person unless such person shall have received a bachelor's degree, and, after having received such degree, shall have completed to the satisfaction of the president and faculty of said Institute at least forty semester hours in graduate study and research.

Approved June 12, 1943.

*Chap.*558 AN ACT ESTABLISHING IN THE SUPERIOR COURT AN APPELLATE DIVISION FOR THE REVIEW OF CERTAIN SENTENCES IN CRIMINAL CASES.

Be it enacted, etc., as follows:

G. L. (Ter. Ed.), 278, new §§ 28A–28D, added.

SECTION 1. Chapter two hundred and seventy-eight of the General Laws is hereby amended by inserting after section twenty-eight, as appearing in the Tercentenary Edition, the four following sections: — *Section 28A.* There shall be an appellate division of the superior court for the review of sentences to the state prison imposed by final judgments in criminal cases, except in any case in which a different sentence could not have been imposed. Said appellate division shall consist of three justices of the superior court to be designated from time to time by the chief justice of said court, and shall sit in Boston or at such other place as may be designated by the chief justice, and at such times as he shall determine. No justice shall sit or act on an appeal from a sentence imposed by him. Two justices shall constitute a quorum to decide all matters before the appellate division.

Appellate division of the superior court.

A designation by the chief justice of the members of the appellate division shall be recorded by the clerk for criminal business in Suffolk county who shall forthwith send copies thereof to the several clerks of the superior court.

Procedure before appellate division.

Section 28B. A person aggrieved by a sentence which may be reviewed may within three days after the date of the imposition thereof, notwithstanding any partial execution of such sentence, file with the clerk a request for leave of the justice who imposed the sentence to appeal to the appellate division for the review of such sentence. Upon the imposition of such a sentence to the state prison the clerk of the court shall notify the person sentenced of his right to request such leave. If such leave to appeal is not granted within ten days after such request, the person sentenced shall forthwith be notified by the clerk of his right to request said appellate division within ten days for leave to appeal for the review of such sentence. The justice imposing the sentence may grant such leave at any time before the request to the appellate division is considered. Whenever leave to appeal is granted the defendant shall be notified by the clerk, and the appeal shall be filed with the clerk for the county where the judgment was rendered within ten days after notice that leave is granted. Said division may for cause shown consider any late request for leave to appeal filed within one month from the imposition of sentence and may grant such leave. A request for leave to appeal or an appeal shall not stay the execution of a sentence. The clerk shall forthwith notify the chief justice, the justice who imposed the sentence appealed from and the appellate division of the filing of such an appeal. Such justice may transmit to the appellate division a statement of his reasons for imposing the sentence and shall make such a statement within seven days if requested to do so by the appellate division.

If leave to appeal is granted in accordance with this section, the appellate division shall have jurisdiction to consider the appeal with or without a hearing, review the judgment so far as it relates to the sentence imposed, and also any other sentence imposed when the sentence appealed from was imposed, notwithstanding the partial execution of any such sentence, and shall have jurisdiction to amend the judgment by ordering substituted therefor a different appropriate sentence or sentences or any other disposition of the case which could have been made at the time of the imposition of the sentence or sentences under review, but no sentence shall be increased without giving the defendant an opportunity to be heard. If the appellate division decides that the original sentence or sentences should stand, it shall dismiss the appeal. Its decision shall be final. The clerk shall forthwith notify the chief justice and the justice who imposed the sentence appealed from of the final action by the appellate division on the appeal. The appellate division may require the production of any records, documents, exhibits or other thing connected with the proceedings. The superior court shall by rule establish forms for requests for leave to appeal and for appeals hereunder and may by rule make such other regulations of procedure relative thereto, consistent with law, as justice may require.

Section 28C. If an appeal is dismissed, the clerk for the county where the judgment was rendered shall forthwith notify the appellant and the warden of the state prison. If the judgment is amended by an order substituting a different sentence or sentences, or disposition of the case, the court sitting in any convenient county shall resentence the defendant or make any other disposition of the case ordered by the appellate division. Time served on a sentence appealed from shall be deemed to have been served on a substituted sentence.

Dismissal of appeal.

Amendment of judgment

Section 28D. When an appeal is considered or heard in a county other than that in which the judgment was rendered, or when a defendant is brought before the court for resentence or other disposition in such a county, the clerk for such county or an assistant clerk shall act as clerk for the county in which the judgment was rendered and shall issue any process required, and shall transmit copies thereof with a statement of the proceedings to the last mentioned clerk.

Clerk of courts for one county to act as clerk for other county in certain cases.

SECTION 2. This act shall become operative November first, nineteen hundred and forty-three, and shall apply only to sentences imposed on or after said date.

Effective date.

Approved June 12, 1943.

Chap.559 An Act relative to the exemption of persons seventy years of age or over from the payment of poll taxes.

Be it enacted, etc., as follows:

G. L. (Ter. Ed.), 59, § 5, etc., amended.

Clause Seventeenth A of section five of chapter fifty-nine of the General Laws, inserted by section four of chapter one hundred and eighty-six of the acts of nineteen hundred and thirty-eight, is hereby amended by adding at the end the following sentence: — In case a male inhabitant of the commonwealth, who is seventy years of age or over, shall in any year request that he be exempt from payment of a poll tax, such request shall be deemed to continue in effect with respect to poll taxes assessed in subsequent years unless such inhabitant shall otherwise in writing direct.

Exemption from poll tax.

Approved June 12, 1943.

Chap.560 An Act relative to the pensioning of laborers, foremen, mechanics, craftsmen and chauffeurs in the employ of the city of Lowell.

Be it enacted, etc., as follows:

Section 1. Chapter two hundred and forty-three of the acts of the current year is hereby amended by inserting after section one the following new section: — *Section 1A.* This act shall apply to the retirement allowances of laborers, foremen, mechanics, craftsmen and chauffeurs of said city retired since January first, nineteen hundred and thirty-one and prior to the effective date of this act as well as to those retired after said effective date, subject, however, to section ten of chapter two hundred and eighty-five of the acts of nineteen hundred and thirty-four, as amended by section ten of chapter one hundred and two of the acts of nineteen hundred and thirty-seven.

Section 2. This act shall take effect as of the effective date of said chapter two hundred and forty-three of the acts of the current year. *Approved June 12, 1943.*

Chap.561 An Act to further regulate the filing of notice of intention of marriage and the issuance of certificates of such filing.

Emergency preamble.

Whereas, The deferred operation of this act would tend to defeat its purpose, which is in part to authorize immediately certain physicians and certain medical officers of the armed forces of the United States to issue medical certificates to persons filing notices of intention of marriage, therefore it is hereby declared to be an emergency law, necessary for the immediate preservation of the public convenience.

Be it enacted, etc., as follows:

SECTION 1. Chapter two hundred and seven of the General Laws is hereby amended by inserting after section twenty-eight, as amended, the following section: — *Section 28A.* Except as hereinafter provided, a certificate shall not be issued by the clerk or registrar under section twenty-eight until he has received from each party to the intended marriage a medical certificate signed by a qualified physician registered and practicing in the commonwealth, a physician registered or licensed to practice in any other state of the United States, or a commissioned medical officer on active service in the armed forces of the United States who has examined such party as hereinafter provided. Such examination shall be made only to ascertain the presence or absence of evidence of syphilis, and shall include a serological test for syphilis. Said test shall be made by a laboratory of the state department of public health or by a laboratory meeting standards approved by said department or, if not located within the commonwealth, approved by the United States Public Health Service. The examination by such physician and the laboratory test shall be made not more than thirty days before a certificate is issued under section twenty-eight. If such physician, in making such examination, discovers evidence of any such disease, he shall inform both parties to the intended marriage of the nature of such disease and of the possibilities of transmitting the same to his or her marital partner or to their children.

G. L. (Ter. Ed.), 207, new § 28A, added.

Notice of intention of marriage, physician's certificate.

Such medical certificate by a physician registered and practicing in the commonwealth shall read as follows: — I, (name and address of physician), a registered physician of (city or town) in the commonwealth of Massachusetts, declare that on (month, day, year) I examined (name and address of person) in accordance with section twenty-eight A of chapter two hundred and seven of the General Laws of the commonwealth. This certificate is made under the penalties of perjury.

Such medical certificate by a physician registered in any other state of the United States shall read as follows: — I, (name and address of physician), a physician registered or licensed to practise in (state, territory or District of Columbia), on oath declare that on (month, day, year) I examined (name and address of person) in accordance with section twenty-eight A of chapter two hundred and seven of the General Laws of the commonwealth of Massachusetts.

Such medical certificate by a commissioned medical officer on active service in the armed forces of the United States shall read as follows: — I, (name and address of physician), a (rank or title) serving in the (army) (navy) of the United States, on oath declare that on (month, day, year) I examined (name and home address of person) in accordance with section twenty-eight A of chapter two hundred and seven of the General Laws of the commonwealth of Massachusetts.

Blank forms of medical certificates required under this section shall be furnished to city and town clerks by the department of public health.

The clerk or registrar receiving such medical certificates in the case of an intended marriage shall endorse on the certificate to be issued by him under section twenty-eight in relation to the marriage a statement that such medical certificates have been received.

In emergency cases where the death of either party to the intended marriage is imminent or where the female is near the termination of her pregnancy, upon the authoritative request of a minister, clergyman, priest, rabbi or attending physician, the clerk or registrar may issue a certificate under section twenty-eight without having received the medical certificate, or having endorsed on his certificate a statement of such receipt, as provided by this section.

Penalty.

Whoever, being subject to the laws of the commonwealth fails to comply with any provision of this section shall be punished by a fine of not less than ten nor more than one hundred dollars.

G. L. (Ter. Ed.), 207, § 20B, etc., repealed.

SECTION 2. Section twenty B of said chapter two hundred and seven, as most recently amended by sections one and two of chapter six hundred and ninety-seven of the acts of nineteen hundred and forty-one, is hereby repealed.

G. L. (Ter. Ed.), 207, § 20, etc., amended.

Notice of intention of marriage.

SECTION 3. Section twenty of said chapter two hundred and seven, as amended by chapter one hundred and twenty-seven of the acts of nineteen hundred and thirty-three, is hereby further amended by inserting after the word "residence" in the eighteenth line the following sentence: — In case of persons, one or both of whom are in the armed forces, such notice may be given by either party, provided that one is domiciled within the commonwealth.

Approved June 12, 1943.

---

*Chap.*562 AN ACT EXEMPTING CERTAIN OFFICES AND POSITIONS FROM THE PROVISIONS OF THE ACT TEMPORARILY INCREASING THE SALARIES OF THE OFFICERS AND EMPLOYEES OF THE COMMONWEALTH.

Whereas, The deferred operation of this act would tend to defeat its purpose which is to exempt certain offices and positions in the service of the commonwealth from the operation of chapter one hundred and seventy of the acts of the current year which temporarily increases the salaries of officers and employees in the service of the commonwealth, therefore it is hereby declared to be an emergency law, necessary for the immediate preservation of the public convenience.

Be it enacted, etc., as follows:

Chapter one hundred and seventy of the acts of the current year is hereby amended by inserting after section two the following section: — *Section 2A.* Any person appointed to an office or position subject to any provision of this act may, before qualifying for such office or position, file with the state comptroller a waiver of the increase in compensation provided for such office or position by this act and, if he files such a waiver, shall not receive the additional compensation provided therefor hereby.

Approved June 12, 1943.

AN ACT AUTHORIZING THE STATE TREASURER TO EXEMPT HIMSELF AND ANY OTHER PUBLIC OFFICER FROM THE PROVISIONS OF THE ACT REQUIRING THAT EMPLOYERS PAYING WAGES BY CHECK SHALL PROVIDE REASONABLE FACILITIES FOR THE CASHING OF THE SAME. *Chap.* 563

Be it enacted, etc., as follows:

G. L. (Ter. Ed.), 149, § 148, amended.

The paragraph inserted in section one hundred and forty-eight of chapter one hundred and forty-nine of the General Laws by chapter three hundred and seventy-eight of the acts of the current year is hereby amended by inserting at the end the following sentence: — The state treasurer may in his discretion in writing exempt himself and any other public officer from the provisions of this paragraph. (Exemption.)

Approved June 12, 1943.

AN ACT MAKING CERTAIN CHANGES WITH RESPECT TO THE FORM OF TAX BILLS AND NOTICES. *Chap.* 564

Be it enacted, etc., as follows:

G. L. (Ter. Ed.), 60, § 3A, etc., amended.

SECTION 1. Chapter sixty of the General Laws is hereby amended by striking out section three A, as most recently amended by section three of chapter one hundred and sixty-six of the acts of nineteen hundred and forty-three, and inserting in place thereof the following section: — *Section 3A.* (Contents of tax bills, etc.) Every tax bill or notice, other than a bill or notice of a poll tax, shall state the assessed valuation of each parcel of land included in the assessment of the tax for which the bill or notice is sent and of each building or structure on each such parcel or affixed thereto and shall also state the total assessed valuation and the tax rate for the year to which the tax relates. Such bill or notice shall also contain a statement indicating the provisions of law governing the imposition of penalties, interest, charges and fees in case the tax for which the bill or notice is sent remains unpaid after the due date.

SECTION 2. This act shall not become effective until the termination of the existing states of war between the United States and certain foreign countries, and shall apply only to assessments made subsequent to such termination. (Effective date.)

Approved June 12, 1943.

*Chap.*565 AN ACT RELATIVE TO THE REGISTRATION OF HAIRDRESSERS AND THE REGULATION OF THE OCCUPATION OF HAIRDRESSING.

Be it enacted, etc., as follows:

G. L. (Ter. Ed.), 112, § 87T, etc., amended.

SECTION 1. Chapter one hundred and twelve of the General Laws is hereby amended by striking out section eighty-seven T, as amended by sections one and two of chapter six hundred and twenty-six of the acts of nineteen hundred and forty-one, and inserting in place thereof the following section: — *Section 87T.* The following words, as used in sections eighty-seven T to eighty-seven JJ, inclusive, shall have the following meanings: —

Definitions.

"Board", the board of registration of hairdressers established by section forty-two of chapter thirteen.

"Demonstrator", any person who engages in behalf of a manufacturer, wholesaler, retailer or distributor in demonstrating the use of any machine or other article pertaining to hairdressing without charge to the person who is subject to such demonstration.

"Hairdresser", any person who engages in hairdressing for compensation, except the following persons: —

1. A barber engaged in his usual occupation, or only in cutting the hair of any female, in any location not subject to said sections eighty-seven T to eighty-seven JJ, inclusive.

2. A person who engages in behalf of a manufacturer or distributor solely in demonstrating the use of any machine or other article for purposes of sale, without charge to the person who is the subject of such demonstration.

"Hairdressing", arranging, dressing, curling, waving, cleansing, cutting, singeing, bleaching, coloring, or similarly treating the hair of any female, or performing work as a cosmetologist as defined in section eight-seven F, or any combination of any of the foregoing, but not including the removal of superfluous hair or skin blemishes by direct application of an electric current or any treatment of the bust.

"Instructor", a person who teaches all branches of hairdressing and manicuring in a registered school.

"Operator", a person engaged in hairdressing or in any of its branches under the supervision of a registered hairdresser.

"Manicurist", any person who engages in manicuring for compensation.

"Manicuring", the cutting, trimming, polishing, tinting, coloring or cleansing the nails of any person.

"Manicuring shop", a shop licensed to do manicuring only on the nails of any person.

"School", except in section eighty-seven Z, a school or other institution privately owned, conducted for the purpose of teaching hairdressing or such of its branches as the board may require.

"Shop", a beauty shop to which customers come for hairdressing and cosmetology.

"Student", a person studying hairdressing or manicuring in a school.

G. L. (Ter. Ed.), 112, § 87V, etc., amended.

SECTION 2. Said chapter one hundred and twelve is hereby further amended by striking out section eighty-seven V, as most recently amended by section four of chapter six hundred and twenty-six of the acts of nineteen hundred and forty-one, and inserting in place thereof the following section: — *Section 87V.* Any registered student who has completed a course of at least six months, including at least one thousand hours of professional training, in a school approved by the board, if such registrant after application accompanied by an examination fee as provided in section eighty-seven CC for a first examination, together with two photographs of the applicant, or a fee as provided in said section eighty-seven CC for a second or subsequent examination, passes an examination satisfactory to the board, may be registered by the board as an operator, and as such may practice hairdressing for compensation under the supervision of a registered hairdresser during the period of such original registration, and thereafter, upon payment annually of a renewal fee as provided in said section eighty-seven CC. Any person making application for examination hereunder may be allowed to practice as an operator until the next examination by the board, and the board may grant, without charge, a permit authorizing him to practice as such operator until such next examination, and the board may extend such permit until a subsequent examination by the board.

Examination of operators.

G. L. (Ter. Ed.), 112, § 87W, etc., amended.

SECTION 3. Said chapter one hundred and twelve is hereby further amended by striking out section eighty-seven W, as most recently amended by section five of said chapter six hundred and twenty-six, and inserting in place thereof the following section: — *Section 87W.* Any operator who has had not less than six months' practical experience as such, and who, after application accompanied by an examination fee as provided in section eighty-seven CC for a first examination, together with two photographs of the applicant, or a fee as provided in said section eighty-seven CC for a second or subsequent examination, passes a practical examination satisfactory to the board, may be registered by the board as a hairdresser, and thereafter may practice hairdressing in a registered shop for compensation and may supervise operators, without additional payment for the period during which such person was originally registered as an operator, and thereafter upon payment annually of a hairdresser's renewal fee as provided in said section eighty-seven CC.

Registration of hairdressers.

Examination, fee, etc.

Any demonstrator who has had at least three months' practical experience as such, and who after application, accompanied by a notarized affidavit from each manufacturer or distributor for whom she is or was employed during such period and the fee as provided in said section eighty-seven CC, together with two pictures of the applicant, may be registered by the board as a demonstrator, and thereafter may practice as a demonstrator.

G. L. (Ter. Ed.), 112, § 87X, etc., amended.

Registration of manicurists.

Examination, fee, etc.

SECTION 4. Said chapter one hundred and twelve is hereby further amended by striking out section eighty-seven X, as amended by section six of said chapter six hundred and twenty-six, and inserting in place thereof the following section: — *Section 87X.* Any registered student who has completed a course of at least one month, including at least one hundred hours of professional training in manicuring, in a school approved by the board, if such registrant after application accompanied by an examination fee as provided in section eighty-seven CC for a first examination, together with two photographs of the applicant, or a fee as provided in said section eight-seven CC for a second or subsequent examination, passes an examination satisfactory to the board, may be registered by the board as a manicurist and may practice manicuring for compensation during the period of such original registration, and thereafter upon payment annually of a renewal fee as provided in said section eighty-seven CC.

G. L. (Ter. Ed.), 112, § 87Z, etc., amended.

Registration without examination.

SECTION 5. Said chapter one hundred and twelve is hereby further amended by striking out section eighty-seven Z, as amended by section five of chapter three hundred and eighty-five of the acts of nineteen hundred and thirty-seven, and inserting in place thereof the following section: — *Section 87Z.* The board may register, without examination, any hairdresser, operator or manicurist who has been registered as such under the laws of another state which, in the opinion of the board, maintains a standard substantially equivalent to that of this commonwealth, and in which hairdressers, operators and manicurists registered in this commonwealth are given like recognition, upon payment of the fee prescribed in section eighty-seven CC. Any person who has completed in another state, or in a school in this commonwealth supported by public funds, a course of professional training, substantially equivalent to that required by section eighty-seven V, and who, after application accompanied by an examination fee as prescribed in section eighty-seven CC for a first examination, or a fee as prescribed in said section eighty-seven CC for a second or subsequent examination, passes an examination satisfactory to the board, may be registered by the board as an operator.

G. L. (Ter. Ed.), 112, § 87AA, etc., amended.

Registered beauty, etc., shop.

SECTION 6. Said chapter one hundred and twelve is hereby further amended by striking out section eighty-seven AA, as amended by section seven of said chapter six hundred and twenty-six, and inserting in place thereof the following section: — *Section 87AA.* The board may authorize one or more registered hairdressers or manicurists, or any person employing one or more registered hairdressers or manicurists, upon payment to the board of a beauty shop or manicure shop registration fee as provided in section eighty-seven CC, to operate a registered beauty shop or manicure shop, and such person or persons may thereafter operate such beauty shop or manicure shop upon payment annually of a beauty shop or manicure shop registration renewal fee as provided in said section eighty-seven CC; provided, that, in the case of a beauty shop or manicure shop conducted solely by a hairdresser or manicurist owning the same, the beauty shop or manicure shop registration fee and beauty shop or manicure shop renewal fee shall each be as provided in said section eighty-seven CC.

The owner of such beauty shop or manicure shop shall not employ for hire or allow any hairdresser, operator, demonstrator or manicurist to work in such beauty shop or manicure shop unless registered in accordance with sections eighty-seven T to eighty-seven JJ, inclusive.

G. L. (Ter. Ed.), 112, § 87BB, etc., amended.

SECTION 7. Said chapter one hundred and twelve is hereby further amended by striking out section eighty-seven BB, as amended by section six of said chapter three hundred and eighty-five, and inserting in place thereof the following section: — *Section 87BB.* The board may register any school which it approves, upon payment of a school registration fee as provided in section eighty-seven CC, and such school may annually be registered upon payment of a renewal fee as provided in said section eighty-seven CC; provided, that standards of professional training satisfactory to the board are there maintained and a sufficient course is there given. Any registered hairdresser who has had not less than three years practical experience as such, and who, after application accompanied by an examination fee as provided in said section eighty-seven CC for a first examination, or a fee as provided in said section eighty-seven CC for a second or subsequent examination, passes an examination satisfactory to the board, may be registered by the board as an instructor, and thereafter may instruct in hairdressing in any registered school during the period of original registration, and thereafter, upon payment annually of a renewal fee as provided in said section eighty-seven CC.

Registered school.

No person not so registered may instruct in hairdressing in any registered school except as authorized by the board.

The board may make such reasonable rules and regulations as are necessary for the proper conduct of schools, qualifications of instructors, courses of study, and hours of study, and as to standards of professional training.

G. L. (Ter. Ed.), 112, § 87 CC, etc., amended.

SECTION 8. Said chapter one hundred and twelve is hereby further amended by striking out section eighty-seven CC, as amended by section eight of said chapter six hundred and twenty-six, and inserting in place thereof the following section: — *Section 87CC.* The board shall make such uniform and reasonable rules and regulations as are necessary for the proper conduct of its business, the establishment of proper standards of professional skill in relation to, and the proper supervision of, hairdressers, demonstrators, manicurists, operators, beauty shops, manicure shops, schools, students and

Rules and regulations concerning hairdressers, etc.

instructors, and especially may prescribe such sanitary rules, subject to the approval of the department of public health, as it may deem necessary to prevent the spreading of infectious or contagious diseases, or both, but nothing herein shall authorize the board to limit the number of hairdressers, demonstrators, manicurists, beauty shops, manicure shops, schools, operators, students or instructors in the commonwealth or in any given locality, or to regulate or fix compensation or prices, or to refuse to register a shop solely for the reason that such shop is to be conducted by a person in his own home on a full or part time basis, or to interfere in any way with the conduct of the business of hairdressing or manicuring, except so far as is necessary for the protection of the public health, safety or morals.

Before engaging in actual employment in the practice of hairdressing, manicuring or demonstrating, and at least once every twelve months thereafter, every registered hairdresser, operator, instructor, manicurist or demonstrator shall secure from a physician a certificate stating that such person is not afflicted with tuberculosis, venereal disease in a communicable form, or with any other communicable disease. Said certificate shall be on a form furnished by the board and shall be kept conspicuously posted with the license certificate.

The following fees shall be paid to the board by applicants before a certificate of registration shall be issued to them: —

APPLICANT.	Original.	Renewal.
School	$50 00	$25 00
Beauty shop (employing help)	10 00	5 00
Manicure shop (employing help)	10 00	5 00
Beauty shop (working alone)	2 00	2 00
Manicure shop (working alone)	2 00	2 00
Hairdressers	10 00	2 00
Hairdressers, re-examination	5 00	2 00
Hairdressers (nonresident)	20 00	2 00
Operators	5 00	2 00
Operators, re-examination	3 00	2 00
Operators (nonresident)	15 00	2 00
Manicurist	3 00	2 00
Manicurist, re-examination	2 00	2 00
Manicurist (nonresident)	5 00	2 00
Instructors	15 00	2 00
Instructors, re-examination	10 00	2 00
Demonstrators	5 00	2 00
Duplicate certificate of registration, $1.00.		

A booth in a beauty shop or manicure shop, which is operated independently thereof, shall be subject to regulations and registration fees the same as in an independent shop.

G. L. (Ter. Ed.), 112, § 87DD, etc., amended.

SECTION 9. Said chapter one hundred and twelve is hereby further amended by striking out section eighty-seven DD, as appearing in section two of chapter four hundred and twenty-eight of the acts of nineteen hundred and thirty-five, and inserting in place thereof the following section: — *Section 87DD.* Any member or agent of the board may enter and inspect any beauty shop, manicure shop or school in a proper manner at any time during business hours thereof. Whenever a complaint is made to the board that any person has suffered personal injury as a result of the practice of the occupation of hairdressing, or that any female person has been exposed to moral hazard, or that any contagious or infectious disease has been imparted, at any beauty shop, manicure shop, or school, or that any beauty shop, manicure shop, or school is kept in an unsanitary condition, or that any person has been engaged in hairdressing or manicuring for compensation in violation of any provision of sections eighty-seven T to eighty-seven JJ, inclusive, a member or agent of the board shall visit and inspect such beauty shop, manicure shop, school or place whereat such violation is alleged to have occurred, and enforce the provisions of said sections eighty-seven T to eighty-seven JJ, inclusive. The board and its members and agents may investigate the standard of professional training at any school, and the sufficiency of the course or courses there given.

Inspection of schools and shops.

SECTION 10. Said chapter one hundred and twelve is hereby further amended by striking out section eighty-seven GG, as most recently amended by section nine of said chapter six hundred and twenty-six, and inserting in place thereof the following section: — *Section 87GG.* Each registration granted under sections eighty-seven T to eighty-seven JJ, inclusive, shall expire on December thirty-first next succeeding its date, and shall be renewed upon the filing of an application therefor, and the payment of the prescribed renewal fee, on or before its expiration. No person registered under said sections as a hairdresser, manicurist, instructor, demonstrator or operator shall engage in the occupation covered by such registration until the prescribed renewal fee shall have been paid. No hairdresser, manicurist, instructor, demonstrator or operator whose registration has not been so renewed within three years following the date of expiration thereof shall be entitled to renewal of such registration but shall register anew under said sections eighty-seven T to eighty-seven JJ, inclusive.

G. L. (Ter. Ed.), 112, § 87GG, etc., amended.

Expiration of registrations.

SECTION 11. Said chapter one hundred and twelve is hereby further amended by striking out section eighty-seven II, as most recently amended by section ten of said chapter six hundred and twenty-six, and inserting in place thereof the following section: — *Section 87II.* Whoever engages in or follows, or attempts to engage in or follow, the occupation of an instructor or of hairdressing, demonstrating or manicuring, unless duly registered by the board or unless granted a permit by the board under section eighty-seven V, and whoever conducts, or attempts to conduct, a beauty shop, manicure shop, or school not so registered, and whoever violates any provision of sections eighty-seven T to

G. L. (Ter. Ed.), 112, § 87II, etc., amended.

Failure to register.

Penalty.

eighty-seven HH, inclusive, or any rule or regulation made under authority thereof, shall, in addition to any other penalty prescribed or authorized by said sections, be punished by a fine of not more than one hundred dollars.

G. L. (Ter. Ed.), 112, § 87JJ, etc., amended.

Limitation of certain sections.

SECTION 12. Said chapter one hundred and twelve is hereby further amended by striking out section eighty-seven JJ, as amended by section eleven of said chapter six hundred and twenty-six, and inserting in place thereof the following section: — *Section 87JJ.* Nothing in sections eighty-seven T to eighty-seven II, inclusive, shall be deemed to authorize a hairdresser, demonstrator, instructor or operator to engage in massage or other occupation requiring a license, unless duly licensed therefor, or to prohibit a person registered under said sections from practicing or teaching any such occupation, if duly licensed therefor.

Approved June 12, 1943.

---

*Chap.*566 AN ACT LIMITING THE TIME WITHIN WHICH PETITIONS FOUNDED UPON CLAIMS AGAINST THE COMMONWEALTH MAY BE BROUGHT.

Be it enacted, etc., as follows:

G. L. (Ter. Ed.), 260, new § 3A, added.

Limitation, petitions against commonwealth.

SECTION 1. Chapter two hundred and sixty of the General Laws is hereby amended by inserting after section three, as appearing in the Tercentenary Edition, the following section: — *Section 3A.* Petitions founded upon claims against the commonwealth prosecuted under chapter two hundred and fifty-eight shall be brought only within three years next after the cause of action accrues.

G. L. (Ter. Ed.), 258, § 5, repealed.

SECTION 2. Section five of chapter two hundred and fifty-eight of the General Laws, as so appearing, is hereby repealed. *Approved June 12, 1943.*

---

*Chap.*567 AN ACT RELATIVE TO THE TERMS OF CERTAIN BONDS AND NOTES TO BE ISSUED BY THE COMMONWEALTH.

Emergency preamble.

Whereas, The deferred operation of this act would tend to defeat one of its principal purposes, which is to prepare with the utmost expedition for national defence in the present emergency, therefore it is hereby declared to be an emergency law, necessary for the immediate preservation of the public safety and convenience.

Be it enacted, etc., as follows:

SECTION 1. Notwithstanding any provision of law to the contrary, the bonds which the state treasurer is authorized to issue under section four of chapter five hundred and twenty-eight of the acts of the current year, providing for the improvement, enlargement, extension, development, construction, alteration and operation of the Commonwealth Airport–Boston, so called, and providing further for easements, roads, highways, approaches and means of access by railroad or otherwise in connection therewith, shall be issued for terms not exceeding five years from their dates of issue; and such bonds shall be payable not earlier than July first, nineteen hundred and forty-five, nor later than July first, nineteen hundred and fifty, and the maturities thereof shall be so arranged that the amounts payable in the several years, other than the final year, shall be as nearly equal as in the opinion of the state treasurer it is practicable to make them, as recommended by the governor in his message to the general court, dated June eleventh, nineteen hundred and forty-three, in pursuance of section 3 of Article LXII of the amendments to the constitution of the commonwealth.

SECTION 2. Notwithstanding any provision of law to the contrary, the bonds which the state treasurer is authorized to issue under section two of chapter five hundred and thirty-eight of the acts of the current year, providing for the refinancing of certain investments in the present state sinking fund, shall be issued for terms which, in the opinion of the state treasurer with the approval of the governor and council, will permit said act to be carried out in accordance with its provisions, provided that bonds issued for the purpose of withdrawing any particular securities from said sinking fund shall be payable not earlier than the date when the securities so withdrawn are payable nor later than December thirty-first, nineteen hundred and seventy-five, substantially as recommended by the governor in his message to the general court dated June eleventh, nineteen hundred and forty-three, in pursuance of section 3 of Article LXII of the amendments to the constitution of the commonwealth.

SECTION 3. Notwithstanding any provision of law to the contrary, the notes which the state treasurer is authorized to issue under section one A of chapter five hundred and forty-three of the acts of the current year, relative to the furnishing of water to towns in the metropolitan water district and certain other towns, shall be issued for terms not exceeding five years from their dates of issue, as recommended by the governor in his message to the general court dated June twelfth, nineteen hundred and forty-three, in pursuance of section 3 of Article LXII of the amendments to the constitution of the commonwealth.

Approved June 12, 1943.

*Chap.*568 AN ACT TO APPORTION AND ASSESS FOR THE CURRENT YEAR A STATE TAX OF FIVE MILLION DOLLARS, FOR THE YEAR NINETEEN HUNDRED AND FORTY-FOUR A STATE TAX OF TWELVE MILLION ONE HUNDRED THOUSAND DOLLARS AND FOR THE SIX MONTHS' PERIOD COMMENCING JANUARY FIRST AND ENDING JUNE THIRTIETH IN THE YEAR NINETEEN HUNDRED AND FORTY-FIVE A STATE TAX OF SIX MILLION EIGHT HUNDRED THOUSAND DOLLARS.

Be it enacted, etc., as follows:

PART I.

SECTION 1. There shall be a state tax for the current year amounting in the aggregate to five million dollars. The cities and towns in the commonwealth shall be assessed and charged with, and shall pay, said tax in the proportions established for them, respectively, by chapter one hundred and forty-one of the acts of nineteen hundred and forty-one, as amended by chapter six hundred and thirty-three of the acts of said year. The comptroller shall, as soon as may be, prepare a schedule showing the sum with which each city and town is charged in accordance with this part and transmit the same to the commissioner of corporations and taxation, who shall verify the sums appearing in such schedule and as soon as may be thereafter shall certify it as so verified to the state treasurer. A copy of the schedule as so verified shall be kept in the office of said commissioner and shall be open to public inspection.

SECTION 2. Upon receipt by the state treasurer from said commissioner of said schedule as verified and certified by him, said treasurer shall forthwith send his warrants to the selectmen or assessors of each city and town taxed as aforesaid, requiring them respectively to assess in the manner provided in section twenty-one of chapter fifty-nine of the General Laws, as most recently amended by section two of chapter three hundred and seventy-six of the acts of nineteen hundred and thirty-six, the sum so charged, and any other taxes or charges which may be due and payable to the commonwealth as specifically provided by law or as certified to him by the proper state board, department or commission, and to add the amount of such taxes and charges to the amount of city, town and county taxes to be assessed by them respectively on each city and town.

SECTION 3. The state treasurer in his warrant shall require the selectmen or assessors to pay, or issue severally their warrant or warrants requiring the treasurers of their several cities and towns to pay, to the state treasurer, on or before November twentieth in the current year, the sums with which their respective cities and towns are charged as provided in section one; and the selectmen or assessors, respectively, shall return a certificate of the names of the treasurers of their several cities and towns, with the sum which each may be required to collect, to the state treasurer at some time before September first in the current year.

Section 4. If the amount due from any city or town, as provided in this part, is not paid to the state treasurer within the time specified, the state treasurer shall notify the treasurer of such delinquent city or town, who shall pay into the treasury of the commonwealth, in addition to the tax, such further sum as would be equal to one per cent per month during the delinquency from and after November twentieth of the current year; and if the same remains unpaid after December first of the current year, an information may be filed by the state treasurer in the supreme judicial court, or before any justice thereof, against such delinquent city or town; and upon notice to such city or town, and a summary hearing thereon, a warrant of distress may issue against such city or town to enforce the payment of said taxes under such penalties as the court, or the justice thereof before whom the hearing is had, shall order. The state treasurer may deduct at any time from any moneys which may be due from the commonwealth to any city or town the whole or any part of the tax in this part apportioned or any other tax or charge which may be due to the commonwealth from such city or town, with the interest accrued thereon.

Part II.

Section 5. There shall be a state tax for the year nineteen hundred and forty-four amounting in the aggregate to twelve million one hundred thousand dollars. The cities and towns in the commonwealth shall be assessed and charged with, and shall pay, said tax in the proportions established for them, respectively, by chapter two hundred and ninety-four of the acts of nineteen hundred and forty-three. The comptroller shall, as soon as may be, prepare a schedule showing the sum with which each city and town is charged in accordance with this part and transmit the same to the commissioner of corporations and taxation, who shall verify the sums appearing in such schedule and as soon as may be thereafter shall certify it as so verified to the state treasurer. A copy of the schedule as so verified shall be kept in the office of said commissioner and shall be open to public inspection.

Section 6. Upon receipt by the state treasurer from said commissioner of said schedule as verified and certified by him, said treasurer shall forthwith send his warrants to the selectmen or assessors of each city and town taxed as aforesaid, requiring them respectively to assess in the manner provided in section twenty-one of chapter fifty-nine of the General Laws, as most recently amended by section two of chapter three hundred and seventy-six of the acts of nineteen hundred and thirty-six, the sum so charged, and any other taxes or charges which may be due and payable to the commonwealth as specifically provided by law or as certified to him by the proper state board, department or commission, and to add the amount of such taxes and charges to the amount of city, town and county taxes to be assessed by them respectively on each city and town.

SECTION 7. The state treasurer in his warrant shall require the selectmen or assessors to pay, or issue severally their warrant or warrants requiring the treasurers of their several cities and towns to pay, to the state treasurer, in two equal instalments, on or before June twentieth and on or before November twentieth, in the year nineteen hundred and forty-four, the sums with which their respective cities and towns are charged as provided in section five; and the selectmen or assessors, respectively, shall return a certificate of the names of the treasurers of their several cities and towns, with the sum which each may be required to collect, to the state treasurer at some time before June first in the year nineteen hundred and forty-four.

SECTION 8. If the amount due from any city or town, as provided in this part, is not paid to the state treasurer within the time specified, the state treasurer shall notify the treasurer of such delinquent city or town, who shall pay into the treasury of the commonwealth, in addition to the tax, such further sum as would be equal to one per cent per month during the delinquency from and after June twentieth of the year nineteen hundred and forty-four in the case of such first instalment, and from and after November twentieth of the year nineteen hundred and forty-four in the case of such second instalment; and if such first instalment remains unpaid after July first in the year nineteen hundred and forty-four, or if such second instalment remains unpaid after December first in the year nineteen hundred and forty-four, an information may be filed by the state treasurer in the supreme judicial court, or before any justice thereof, against such delinquent city or town; and upon notice to such city or town, and a summary hearing thereon, a warrant of distress may issue against such city or town to enforce the payment of said taxes under such penalties as the court, or the justice thereof before whom the hearing is had, shall order. The state treasurer may deduct at any time from any moneys which may be due from the commonwealth to any city or town the whole or any part of the tax in this part apportioned or any other tax or charge which may be due to the commonwealth from such city or town, with the interest accrued thereon.

PART III.

SECTION 9. There shall be a state tax for the six months' period commencing January first and ending June thirtieth in the year nineteen hundred and forty-five amounting in the aggregate to six million eight hundred thousand dollars. The cities and towns in the commonwealth shall be assessed and charged with, and shall pay, said tax in the proportions established for them, respectively, by chapter two hundred and ninety-four of the acts of nineteen hundred and forty-three. The comptroller shall, as soon as may be, prepare a schedule showing the sum with which each city and town is charged in accordance with this part and transmit the same to the commissioner of corporations and taxation, who shall verify the sums appearing in such schedule and as soon as may be thereafter shall certify it as so verified to the state treasurer. A copy of the schedule as so verified shall be kept in the office of said commissioner and shall be open to public inspection.

SECTION 10. Upon receipt by the state treasurer from said commissioner of said schedule as verified and certified by him, said treasurer shall forthwith send his warrants to the selectmen or assessors of each city and town taxed as aforesaid, requiring them respectively to assess in the manner provided in section twenty-one of chapter fifty-nine of the General Laws, as most recently amended by section two of chapter three hundred and seventy-six of the acts of nineteen hundred and thirty-six, the sum so charged, and any other taxes or charges which may be due and payable to the commonwealth as specifically provided by law or as certified to him by the proper state board, department or commission, and to add the amount of such taxes and charges to the amount of city, town and county taxes to be assessed by them respectively on each city and town.

SECTION 11. The state treasurer in his warrant shall require the selectmen or assessors to pay, or issue severally their warrant or warrants requiring the treasurers of their several cities and towns to pay, to the state treasurer, on or before June twentieth in the year nineteen hundred and forty-five, the sums with which their respective cities and towns are charged as provided in section nine; and the selectmen or assessors, respectively, shall return a certificate of the names of the treasurers of their several cities and towns, with the sum which each may be required to collect, to the state treasurer at some time before June first in the year nineteen hundred and forty-five.

SECTION 12. If the amount due from any city or town, as provided in this part, is not paid to the state treasurer within the time specified, the state treasurer shall notify the treasurer of such delinquent city or town, who shall pay into the treasury of the commonwealth, in addition to the tax, such further sum as would be equal to one per cent per month during the delinquency from and after June twentieth of the year nineteen hundred and forty-five; and if the same remains unpaid after July first of the year nineteen hundred and forty-five, an information may be filed by the state treasurer in the supreme judicial court, or before any justice thereof, against such delinquent city or town; and upon notice to such city or town, and a summary hearing thereon, a warrant of distress may issue against such city or town to enforce the payment of said taxes under such penalties as the court or the justice thereof before whom the hearing is had, shall order. The state treasurer may deduct at any time from any moneys which may be due from the commonwealth to any city or town the whole or any part of the tax in this part apportioned or any other tax or charge which may be due to the commonwealth from such city or town, with the interest accrued thereon.

Approved June 12, 1943.

Chap.569 AN ACT PROVIDING FOR THE PAYMENT IN EACH OF THE YEARS NINETEEN HUNDRED AND FORTY-FOUR AND NINETEEN HUNDRED AND FORTY-FIVE BY THE COMMONWEALTH TO ITS MUNICIPALITIES OF A PORTION OF THE HIGHWAY FUND TO BE EXPENDED BY THEM FOR LOCAL HIGHWAY PURPOSES.

Be it enacted, etc., as follows:

SECTION 1. There shall be paid, without further appropriation, from the Highway Fund to the cities and towns of the commonwealth the sum of seven million one hundred thousand dollars as early as may be in the year nineteen hundred and forty-four, and the sum of six million eight hundred thousand dollars as early as may be in the year nineteen hundred and forty-five. The amounts to be paid the several cities and towns in the year nineteen hundred and forty-four and in the year nineteen hundred and forty-five shall be as shown in the following schedule: —

BARNSTABLE COUNTY.

	1944.	1945.
Barnstable	$34,888 83	$33,655 83
Bourne	12,862 17	12,406 17
Brewster	4,038 25	3,936 25
Chatham	8,444 34	8,114 34
Dennis	8,206 34	7,993 34
Eastham	3,528 82	3,459 82
Falmouth	28,231 98	27,181 98
Harwich	12,044 08	11,699 08
Mashpee	2,299 23	2,254 23
Orleans	5,736 45	5,529 45
Provincetown	5,935 42	5,668 42
Sandwich	6,047 68	5,912 68
Truro	3,058 66	2,980 66
Wellfleet	3,828 30	3,729 30
Yarmouth	9,034 90	8,737 90
Totals	$148,185 45	$143,259 45

BERKSHIRE COUNTY.

	1944.	1945.
Adams	$14,040 22	$13,470 22
Alford	1,199 74	1,184 74
Becket	3,779 33	3,740 33
Cheshire	3,289 02	3,232 02

BERKSHIRE COUNTY — CONCLUDED.

	1944.	1945.
Clarksburg	$1,539 28	$1,497 28
Dalton	8,544 08	8,199 08
Egremont	2,659 18	2,611 18
Florida	3,578 82	3,509 82
Great Barrington	12,192 53	11,757 53
Hancock	1,929 59	1,905 59
Hinsdale	2,699 23	2,654 23
Lanesborough	3,528 82	3,459 82
Lee	7,445 62	7,190 62
Lenox	7,025 98	6,791 98
Monterey	3,339 28	3,297 28
Mount Washington	1,179 85	1,170 85
New Ashford	669 90	663 90
New Marlborough	5,688 76	5,616 76
North Adams	25,371 51	24,294 51
Otis	2,709 43	2,676 43
Peru	2,149 74	2,134 74
Pittsfield	67,127 32	64,058 32
Richmond	2,419 38	2,383 38
Sandisfield	4,659 43	4,626 43
Savoy	3,029 85	3,020 85
Sheffield	5,568 61	5,487 61
Stockbridge	6,696 14	6,471 14
Tyringham	1,729 59	1,705 59
Washington	2,729 85	2,720 85
West Stockbridge	3,178 82	3,109 82
Williamstown	10,854 03	10,506 03
Windsor	3,729 59	3,705 59
Totals	$226,282 52	$218,854 52

BRISTOL COUNTY.

	1944.	1945.
Acushnet	$4,687 22	$4,525 22
Attleboro	32,186 52	30,818 52
Berkley	2,999 23	2,954 23
Dartmouth	20,219 80	19,625 80
Dighton	5,597 17	5,432 17
Easton	8,135 67	7,883 67
Fairhaven	13,270 58	12,721 58
Fall River	116,147 87	110,780 87
Freetown	3,728 82	3,659 82
Mansfield	10,743 31	10,353 31
New Bedford	122,673 85	117,072 85
North Attleborough	13,651 19	13,138 19
Norton	5,187 99	5,070 99
Raynham	4,048 46	3,958 46
Rehoboth	8,267 58	8,126 58
Seekonk	8,115 26	7,839 26
Somerset	14,658 82	14,007 82
Swansea	7,536 19	7,314 19
Taunton	42,230 08	40,487 08
Westport	11,455 31	11,182 31
Totals	$455,540 92	$436,952 92

COUNTY OF DUKES COUNTY.

	1944.	1945.
Chilmark	$1,419 38	$1,383 38
Edgartown	6,196 14	5,971 14
Gay Head	429 85	420 85
Gosnold	1,298 97	1,238 97
Oak Bluffs	6,596 14	6,371 14
Tisbury	6,245 37	5,975 37
West Tisbury	1,369 38	1,333 38
Totals	$23,555 23	$22,694 23

ESSEX COUNTY.

	1944.	1945.
Amesbury	$12,123 15	$11,724 15
Andover	23,334 55	22,434 55
Beverly	41,807 61	39,920 61
Boxford	3,789 02	3,732 02
Danvers	16,308 57	15,642 57
Essex	2,488 76	2,416 76
Georgetown	3,608 40	3,515 40
Gloucester	41,129 82	39,371 82
Groveland	2,998 71	2,923 71
Hamilton	7,125 47	6,861 47
Haverhill	54,928 95	52,537 95
Ipswich	10,223 92	9,869 92
Lawrence	97,461 26	92,874 26
Lynn	138,017 83	131,483 83
Lynnfield	6,395 62	6,140 62
Manchester	10,642 02	10,177 02
Marblehead	23,491 67	22,423 67
Merrimac	3,468 35	3,372 35
Methuen	25,122 80	24,120 80
Middleton	3,598 20	3,493 20
Nahant	6,245 37	5,975 37
Newbury	4,118 09	4,007 09
Newburyport	14,629 75	14,032 75
North Andover	11,903 00	11,495 00
Peabody	28,179 66	26,994 66
Rockport	6,735 16	6,453 16
Rowley	3,108 66	3,030 66
Salem	58,422 77	55,671 77
Salisbury	4,287 48	4,140 48
Saugus	16,917 23	16,173 23
Swampscott	24,650 33	23,504 33
Topsfield	4,707 63	4,569 63
Wenham	4,726 76	4,537 76
West Newbury	3,228 82	3,159 82
Totals	$719,925 39	$688,782 39

FRANKLIN COUNTY.

	1944.	1945.
Ashfield	$5,198 97	$5,138 97
Bernardston	2,899 23	2,854 23
Buckland	5,067 58	4,926 58

FRANKLIN COUNTY — CONCLUDED.

	1944.	1945.
Charlemont	$3,349 23	$3,304 23
Colrain	5,808 66	5,730 66
Conway	4,559 18	4,511 18
Deerfield	7,766 55	7,565 55
Erving	3,178 04	3,064 04
Gill	2,659 18	2,611 18
Greenfield	32,685 23	31,242 23
Hawley	2,689 79	2,677 79
Heath	3,009 69	2,991 69
Leverett	2,379 59	2,355 59
Leyden	2,249 74	2,234 74
Monroe	1,859 18	1,811 18
Montague	16,931 55	16,439 55
New Salem	3,649 74	3,634 74
Northfield	5,158 40	5,065 40
Orange	8,396 14	8,171 14
Rowe	2,659 43	2,626 43
Shelburne	5,687 22	5,525 22
Shutesbury	2,159 69	2,141 69
Sunderland	2,898 97	2,838 97
Warwick	3,159 69	3,141 69
Wendell	2,699 74	2,684 74
Whately	3,258 92	3,195 92
Totals	$142,019 33	$138,485 33

HAMPDEN COUNTY.

	1944.	1945.
Agawam	$11,922 12	$11,463 12
Blandford	4,539 28	4,497 28
Brimfield	4,019 12	3,968 12
Chester	4,718 87	4,652 87
Chicopee	44,445 86	42,456 86
East Longmeadow	6,666 03	6,435 03
Granville	5,508 40	5,415 40
Hampden	2,659 18	2,611 18
Holland	1,839 79	1,827 79
Holyoke	83,672 33	79,730 33
Longmeadow	18,855 73	18,024 73
Ludlow	12,223 15	11,824 15
Monson	8,607 12	8,439 12
Montgomery	1,699 74	1,684 74
Palmer	16,153 00	15,745 00
Russell	4,926 50	4,722 50
Southwick	4,538 25	4,436 25
Springfield	260,936 53	248,501 53
Tolland	2,419 64	2,398 64
Wales	1,609 69	1,591 69
West Springfield	29,108 47	27,854 47
Westfield	26,752 13	25,711 13
Wilbraham	5,317 32	5,161 32
Totals	$563,138 25	$539,153 25

HAMPSHIRE COUNTY.

	1944.	1945.
Amherst	$13,721 61	$13,232 61
Belchertown	6,608 66	6,530 66
Chesterfield	3,489 54	3,462 54
Cummington	2,989 54	2,962 54
Easthampton	13,260 88	12,729 88
Goshen	1,809 69	1,791 69
Granby	3,359 18	3,311 18
Hadley	5,657 63	5,519 63
Hatfield	5,107 63	4,969 63
Huntington	3,019 12	2,968 12
Middlefield	2,349 74	2,334 74
Northampton	33,316 88	31,969 88
Pelham	1,659 43	1,626 43
Plainfield	2,749 74	2,734 74
South Hadley	11,712 43	11,271 43
Southampton	3,939 02	3,882 02
Ware	10,224 44	9,900 44
Westhampton	2,659 69	2,641 69
Williamsburg	3,478 82	3,409 82
Worthington	4,119 38	4,083 38
Totals	$135,233 05	$131,333 05

MIDDLESEX COUNTY.

Acton	$6,906 60	$6,708 60
Arlington	57,523 03	54,787 03
Ashby	3,998 97	3,938 97
Ashland	4,597 68	4,462 68
Ayer	5,416 81	5,230 81
Bedford	4,557 63	4,419 63
Belmont	52,237 62	49,768 62
Billerica	12,642 53	12,207 53
Boxborough	1,509 69	1,491 69
Burlington	4,287 99	4,170 99
Cambridge	172,886 42	164,522 42
Carlisle	3,239 02	3,182 02
Chelmsford	13,993 56	13,618 56
Concord	15,009 85	14,418 85
Dracut	7,896 14	7,671 14
Dunstable	2,269 64	2,248 64
Everett	74,558 35	70,967 35
Framingham	39,350 75	37,646 75
Groton	8,146 14	7,921 14
Holliston	6,156 86	5,973 86
Hopkinton	6,647 17	6,482 17
Hudson	9,604 03	9,256 03
Lexington	25,290 64	24,162 64
Lincoln	6,086 45	5,879 45
Littleton	4,977 53	4,833 53
Lowell	103,247 96	98,468 96
Malden	73,420 36	69,946 36
Marlborough	19,496 82	18,728 82
Maynard	8,723 92	8,369 92
Medford	81,653 20	77,762 20

MIDDLESEX COUNTY — CONCLUDED.

	1944.	1945.
Melrose	$41,177 50	$39,284 50
Natick	23,963 11	22,979 11
Newton	164,826 82	157,068 82
North Reading	4,207 89	4,084 89
Pepperell	6,327 53	6,183 53
Reading	20,335 32	19,480 32
Sherborn	4,907 63	4,769 63
Shirley	4,578 04	4,464 04
Somerville	107,761 16	102,586 16
Stoneham	17,387 64	16,667 64
Stow	3,468 87	3,402 87
Sudbury	6,607 12	6,439 12
Tewksbury	7,486 19	7,264 19
Townsend	5,887 99	5,770 99
Tyngsborough	3,428 82	3,359 82
Wakefield	23,612 08	22,568 08
Waltham	56,894 73	54,257 73
Watertown	54,026 12	51,470 12
Wayland	7,915 26	7,639 26
Westford	8,616 29	8,400 29
Weston	12,890 99	12,365 99
Wilmington	6,546 40	6,336 40
Winchester	34,472 45	32,867 45
Woburn	24,192 18	23,154 18
Totals	$1,487,851 49	$1,422,112 49

NANTUCKET COUNTY.

Nantucket	$16,799 91	$16,211 91
Totals	$16,799 91	$16,211 91

NORFOLK COUNTY.

Avon	$2,758 40	$2,665 40
Bellingham	5,087 73	4,955 73
Braintree	29,547 24	28,221 24
Brookline	144,639 44	137,616 44
Canton	10,732 58	10,300 58
Cohasset	10,861 91	10,390 91
Dedham	27,718 68	26,476 68
Dover	6,785 42	6,518 42
Foxborough	8,515 00	8,224 00
Franklin	13,652 48	13,214 48
Holbrook	4,557 12	4,389 12
Medfield	4,867 58	4,726 58
Medway	5,427 27	5,268 27
Millis	5,097 43	4,947 43
Milton	40,997 14	39,083 14
Needham	27,798 52	26,547 52
Norfolk	3,598 71	3,523 71
Norwood	28,727 60	27,422 60

NORFOLK COUNTY — CONCLUDED.

	1944.	1945.
Plainville	$3,278 56	$3,194 56
Quincy	128,645 46	122,555 46
Randolph	8,584 13	8,242 13
Sharon	9,005 06	8,717 06
Stoughton	11,252 48	10,814 48
Walpole	19,715 68	18,881 68
Wellesley	44,814 47	42,744 47
Westwood	9,293 82	8,933 82
Weymouth	52,898 08	50,456 08
Wrentham	5,986 70	5,794 70
Totals	$674,844 69	$644,826 69

PLYMOUTH COUNTY.

Abington	$7,065 52	$6,804 52
Bridgewater	9,534 64	9,222 64
Brockton	75,411 44	72,000 44
Carver	5,947 68	5,812 68
Duxbury	10,643 82	10,283 82
East Bridgewater	7,075 98	6,841 98
Halifax	3,078 82	3,009 82
Hanover	6,376 24	6,157 24
Hanson	4,487 73	4,355 73
Hingham	19,306 25	18,505 25
Hull	17,547 07	16,794 07
Kingston	6,286 19	6,064 19
Lakeville	3,708 66	3,630 66
Marion	6,125 73	5,876 73
Marshfield	11,663 46	11,282 46
Mattapoisett	5,046 91	4,866 91
Middleborough	15,842 28	15,392 28
Norwell	4,687 99	4,570 99
Pembroke	5,137 73	5,005 73
Plymouth	29,860 79	28,741 79
Plympton	2,269 38	2,233 38
Rochester	3,938 76	3,866 76
Rockland	10,732 58	10,300 58
Scituate	15,729 49	15,117 49
Wareham	18,048 36	17,370 36
West Bridgewater	5,417 06	5,246 06
Whitman	9,773 15	9,374 15
Totals	$320,743 71	$308,728 71

SUFFOLK COUNTY.

Boston	$1,295,347 74	$1,232,308 74
Chelsea	44,403 74	42,291 74
Revere	39,268 33	37,423 33
Winthrop	24,590 12	23,432 12
Totals	$1,403,609 93	$1,335,455 93

WORCESTER COUNTY.

	1944.	1945.
Ashburnham	$5,488 51	$5,401 51
Athol	17,698 88	17,050 88
Auburn	10,134 13	9,792 13
Barre	8,317 58	8,176 58
Berlin	3,089 02	3,032 02
Blackstone	4,137 99	4,020 99
Bolton	3,729 07	3,675 07
Boylston	2,899 23	2,854 23
Brookfield	3,128 82	3,059 82
Charlton	7,538 25	7,436 25
Clinton	13,230 52	12,678 52
Douglas	5,837 99	5,720 99
Dudley	6,806 86	6,623 86
East Brookfield	1,969 12	1,918 12
Fitchburg	56,667 72	54,204 72
Gardner	25,291 41	24,208 41
Grafton	7,996 14	7,771 14
Hardwick	5,758 66	5,680 66
Harvard	5,137 99	5,020 99
Holden	7,506 86	7,323 86
Hopedale	7,494 34	7,164 34
Hubbardston	4,529 33	4,490 33
Lancaster	5,487 99	5,370 99
Leicester	6,597 17	6,432 17
Leominster	30,048 78	28,812 78
Lunenburg	5,637 99	5,520 99
Mendon	3,238 76	3,166 76
Milford	18,216 97	17,457 97
Millbury	8,524 70	8,215 70
Millville	1,809 18	1,761 18
New Braintree	3,049 49	3,019 49
North Brookfield	5,977 79	5,848 79
Northborough	4,508 15	4,400 15
Northbridge	12,391 25	11,881 25
Oakham	2,669 64	2,648 64
Oxford	6,477 27	6,318 27
Paxton	2,469 12	2,418 12
Petersham	4,718 87	4,652 87
Phillipston	2,409 69	2,391 69
Princeton	4,848 97	4,788 97
Royalston	4,069 38	4,033 38
Rutland	4,778 82	4,709 82
Shrewsbury	12,601 71	12,118 71
Southborough	5,597 17	5,432 17
Southbridge	18,587 13	17,837 13
Spencer	9,606 09	9,378 09
Sterling	5,638 25	5,536 25
Sturbridge	5,418 35	5,322 35
Sutton	6,238 25	6,136 25
Templeton	6,267 32	6,111 32
Upton	4,498 71	4,423 71
Uxbridge	12,333 36	11,946 36
Warren	5,817 84	5,691 84
Webster	12,940 47	12,385 47
West Boylston	4,477 79	4,348 79
West Brookfield	4,088 76	4,016 76
Westborough	7,536 19	7,314 19

WORCESTER COUNTY — CONCLUDED.

	1944.	1945.
Westminster	$5,758 40	$5,665 40
Winchendon	11,225 47	10,961 47
Worcester	291,320 47	277,367 47
Totals	$782,270 13	$753,149 13

RECAPITULATION.

	1944.	1945.
Barnstable	$148,185 45	$143,259 45
Berkshire	226,282 52	218,854 52
Bristol	455,540 92	436,952 92
Dukes	23,555 23	22,694 23
Essex	719,925 39	688,782 39
Franklin	142,019 33	138,485 33
Hampden	563,138 25	539,153 25
Hampshire	135,233 05	131,333 05
Middlesex	1,487,851 49	1,422,112 49
Nantucket	16,799 91	16,211 91
Norfolk	674,844 69	644,826 69
Plymouth	320,743 71	308,728 71
Suffolk	1,403,609 93	1,335,455 93
Worcester	782,270 13	753,149 13
Totals	$7,100,000 00	$6,800,000 00

SECTION 2. The sums received by each city or town hereunder shall be expended only for local highway purposes, including construction, reconstruction, maintenance and repair of local roads, streets and highways other than state highways, and surface drainage works, sidewalks, curbings and bridges, removal of snow, installation and maintenance of traffic lights, signs and signals and traffic policing. Cities and towns in the metropolitan parks district may apply, to the extent deemed necessary, sums received hereunder to the payment of their respective assessments in the year of receipt for the construction and maintenance of parkways and boulevards under the jurisdiction of the metropolitan district commission. Said sums received by each city or town hereunder shall, in the year of receipt, be included by the assessors thereof as an estimated receipt and deducted from the amount required to be raised by taxation to meet appropriations made in that year for highway purposes. Said sums may be expended by a city or town for the purposes aforesaid in addition to federal funds, if any, allocated to such city or town and available for such expenditure.

SECTION 3. If the state comptroller, prior to the making of payments to the several cities and towns under this act in the year nineteen hundred and forty-four or in the year nineteen hundred and forty-five certifies to the governor and council that the aggregate amount of the Highway Fund available for such payments in such year is less than the aggregate amount expressly provided to be paid in such year under section one, the governor and council shall determine the aggregate amount of such fund which will be available for such payments in such year. If the aggregate amount available for such payments in such year, as so determined, is less than the aggregate amount expressly provided to be paid in such year under section one, the aggregate amount as so determined shall be paid to such cities and towns in proportion to the respective amounts expressly provided to be paid under section one in such year, notwithstanding the provisions of section one. *Approved June 12, 1943.*

AN ACT RELATIVE TO THE TERMS OF CERTAIN NOTES TO BE ISSUED BY THE COMMONWEALTH. *Chap.*570

Whereas, The deferred operation of this act would tend to defeat one of its principal purposes, which is to provide immediately necessary municipal funds in the present emergency, therefore it is hereby declared to be an emergency law, necessary for the immediate preservation of the public convenience. Emergency preamble.

Be it enacted, etc., as follows:

Notwithstanding any provision of law to the contrary, the notes which the state treasurer is authorized to issue under section five of chapter forty-nine of the acts of nineteen hundred and thirty-three, as most recently amended by section two of chapter four hundred and thirteen of the acts of the current year, shall be issued for maximum terms of years to expire not later than November thirtieth, nineteen hundred and forty-nine, as recommended by the governor in a message to the general court dated June twelfth, nineteen hundred and forty-three, in pursuance of section 3 of Article LXII of the amendments to the constitution of the commonwealth. *Approved June 12, 1943.*

AN ACT AUTHORIZING THE TRUSTEES OF THE BOSTON SCHOOL OF PHARMACY TO GRANT THE DEGREE OF BACHELOR OF SCIENCE IN PHARMACY. *Chap.*571

Be it enacted, etc., as follows:

The trustees of The Boston School of Pharmacy, a corporation organized under chapter one hundred and eighty of the General Laws, are hereby authorized to confer the degree of Bachelor of Science in Pharmacy, if and when said school complies with the requirements of the board of collegiate authority established by chapter five hundred and forty-nine of the acts of nineteen hundred and forty-three.
Approved June 12, 1943.

*Chap.*572 AN ACT IN ADDITION TO THE GENERAL APPROPRIATION ACT MAKING APPROPRIATIONS TO SUPPLEMENT CERTAIN ITEMS CONTAINED THEREIN, AND FOR CERTAIN NEW ACTIVITIES AND PROJECTS.

Be it enacted, etc., as follows:

SECTION 1. To provide for supplementing certain items in the general appropriation act, and for certain new activities and projects, the sums set forth in section two, for the particular purposes and subject to the conditions stated therein, are hereby appropriated from the general fund or ordinary revenue of the commonwealth, unless some other source of revenue is expressed, subject to the provisions of law regulating the disbursement of public funds and the approval thereof, for the fiscal year ending June thirtieth, nineteen hundred and forty-four, and for the fiscal year ending June thirtieth, nineteen hundred and forty-five, or for such other period as may be specified.

SECTION 2.

Item		Appropriation Fiscal Year 1944.	Appropriation Fiscal Year 1945.
	Service of the Legislative Department.		
0101-01	For the compensation of senators, to be in addition to any amount heretofore appropriated for the purpose	$14,400 00	
0101-03	For the compensation of representatives, to be in addition to any amount heretofore appropriated for the purpose . . .	86,400 00	
0101-05	For the salaries of the clerk of the senate and the clerk of the house of representatives, to be in addition to any amount heretofore appropriated for the purpose .	2,000 00	$2,000 00
0101-06	For the salaries of the assistant clerk of the senate and the assistant clerk of the house of representatives, to be in addition to any amount heretofore appropriated for the purpose . . .	1,250 00	1,250 00
0101-07	For such additional clerical assistance to, and with the approval of, the clerk of the senate, as may be necessary for the proper despatch of public business, including not more than one permanent position, to be in addition to any amount heretofore appropriated for the purpose .	700 00	700 00
0101-08	For such additional clerical assistance to, and with the approval of, the clerk of the house of representatives, as may be necessary for the proper despatch of public business, including not more than three permanent positions, to be in addition to any amount here-		

Item		Appropriation Fiscal Year 1944.	Appropriation Fiscal Year 1945.
	tofore appropriated for the purpose	$500 00	$500 00
0101-21	For clerical and other assistance of the house committee on rules, including not more than four permanent positions in the year nineteen hundred and forty-four and three permanent positions in the year nineteen hundred and forty-five, to be in addition to any amount heretofore appropriated for the purpose . . .	1,760 00	1,760 00
0102-11	For contingent expenses of the senate and house of representatives, and necessary expenses in and about the state house, with the approval of the sergeant-at-arms, to be in addition to any amount heretofore appropriated for the purpose	250 00	
0102-17	For office and other expenses of the joint recess committee on ways and means, including travel .	500 00	500 00
0102-19	For expenses of the committees of the senate and house for the purpose of representing the senate and house in the Evacuation Day parade at South Boston in the year nineteen hundred and forty-four, as authorized by a joint order of the general court; provided, that not more than one hundred dollars shall be allowed for each of said committees .	200 00	
0102-20	For expenses of the committees of the senate and house for the purpose of representing the senate and house at the celebration to be held in Charlestown on June seventeenth, nineteen hundred and forty-four, as authorized by a joint order of the general court; provided, that not more than one hundred dollars shall be allowed for each of said committees .	200 00	
0102-22	For expenses of the committees of the senate and house for the purpose of representing the senate and house in the Dorchester Day parade at Dorchester on the first Saturday in June, nineteen hundred and forty-four, as authorized by a joint order of the general court; provided, that not more than one hundred dollars shall be allowed for each of said committees	200 00	

Service of the Judicial Department.

	Superior Court, as follows:		
0302-02	For traveling allowances and expenses, to be in addition to any		

Item		Appropriation Fiscal Year 1944.	Appropriation Fiscal Year 1945.
	amount heretofore appropriated for the purpose . . .	$2,000 00	$2,000 00
	For clerical assistance to Registers of the several counties, as follows:		
0306–13	Worcester, including not more than twelve permanent positions, to be in addition to any amount heretofore appropriated for the purpose	400 00	400 00
	Service of the Land Court.		
0308–02	For engineering, clerical and other personal services, including not more than twenty-four permanent positions, to be in addition to any amount heretofore appropriated for the purpose . . .	2,200 00	2,560 00
	Service of the State Quartermaster.		
0405–02	For the salaries of armorers and assistant armorers of armories of the first class, superintendent of armories, and other employees, including not more than eighty-two permanent positions, to be in addition to any amount heretofore appropriated for the purpose	600 00	600 00
0417–01	For personal services, including not more than forty-five permanent positions, to be in addition to any amount heretofore appropriated for the purpose . . .	240 00	400 00
	Service of the Treasurer and Receiver-General.		
	State Board of Retirement:		
0604–04	To meet deficits in the annuity reserve fund of the state employees' retirement system up to and including December thirty-first, nineteen hundred and forty-two, and to restore to the surplus interest account the amounts which the state board of retirement has previously been authorized and directed by the general court to transfer from said surplus interest account to meet deficits in said annuity fund	36,358 23	74,671 31
	Service of the Auditor of the Commonwealth.		
0701–02	For personal services of deputies and other assistants, including not more than twenty-five permanent positions, to be in addition to any amount heretofore appropriated for the purpose .	2,500 00	2,500 00
0701–03	For services other than personal, traveling expenses, office supplies		

Item		Appropriation Fiscal Year 1944.	Appropriation Fiscal Year 1945.
	and equipment, to be in addition to any amount heretofore appropriated for the purpose . .	$2,200 00	$2,200 00
	Service of the Attorney General's Department.		
0801-02	For the compensation of assistants in his office, and for such other legal and personal services as may be required, including not more than thirty-six permanent positions, to be in addition to any amount heretofore appropriated for the purpose	10,000 00	10,000 00
	Service of the Department of Agriculture.		
	Milk Control Board:		
0906-01	For personal services of members of the board and their employees, including not more than fifty-three permanent positions, to be in addition to any amount heretofore appropriated for the purpose	480 00	480 00
0906-03	For expenses in connection with certain activities conducted in co-operation with the federal government, as authorized by section twenty-three of chapter ninety-four A of the General Laws, to be in addition to any amount heretofore appropriated for the purpose	2,500 00	2,500 00
	Service of the Department of Conservation.		
	Supervision of public fishing and hunting grounds:		
1004-46	For the cost of construction and improvement of certain fishways, to be in addition to any amount heretofore appropriated for the purpose	1,500 00	1,500 00
	Division of Wild Life Research and Management:		
1004-51	For personal services, including not more than three permanent positions, to be in addition to any amount heretofore appropriated for the purpose . . .	2,000 00	2,000 00
	Service of the Department of Banking and Insurance.		
	Division of Insurance:		
1103-02	For other personal services of the division, including expenses of the board of appeal and certain other costs of supervising motor vehicle liability insurance, and including not more than one hundred and fifty-nine permanent positions, partly chargeable to item 2970-02, to be in addition to any amount		

Item		Appropriation Fiscal Year 1944.	Appropriation Fiscal Year 1945.
	heretofore appropriated for the purpose	$16,460 00	$16,460 00
1103-03	For other services, including printing the annual report, traveling expenses, necessary office supplies and equipment and rent of offices, to be in addition to any amount heretofore appropriated for the purpose	5,000 00	5,000 00
	The unexpended balance of the appropriations made by item 2970-08 of chapter seven hundred and thirty of the acts of nineteen hundred and forty-one is hereby reappropriated.		

Service of the Department of Education.

Item		Appropriation Fiscal Year 1944.	Appropriation Fiscal Year 1945.
	Teachers' Retirement Board:		
1305-07	To meet deficits in the annuity reserve fund of the teachers' retirement fund up to and including December thirty-first, nineteen hundred and forty-two, and to restore to the surplus interest account the amounts which the teachers' retirement board has heretofore been authorized and directed by the general court to transfer from said surplus interest account to meet deficits in said annuity fund, the sum of thirty-three thousand five hundred sixty-eight dollars and twenty-nine cents is appropriated for the year nineteen hundred and forty-four, and the sum of one hundred thousand dollars is appropriated for the year nineteen hundred and forty-five; and the sums of one hundred thousand dollars for the year nineteen hundred and forty-four and one hundred thousand dollars for the year nineteen hundred and forty-five are hereby transferred to this item from the appropriations made by item 1305-05 of chapter three hundred and seventy of the acts of the current year	33,568 29	100,000 00
1313-33	For the cost of repairs of certain ceilings at the state teachers' college at Salem	2,375 00	
	Textile Schools:		
1331-00	For the maintenance of the Bradford Durfee textile school of Fall River, with the approval of the commissioner of education and the trustees, including not more than twenty-one permanent positions, to be in addition to any amount heretofore appropriated for the purpose . . .	2,500 00	

Item		Appropriation Fiscal Year 1944	Appropriation Fiscal Year 1945.
	Service of the Department of Civil Service and Registration.		
	Division of Registration:		
1403–02	For clerical and certain other personal services of the division, including not more than thirty-eight permanent positions, to be in addition to any amount heretofore appropriated for the purpose .	$640 00	$480 00
	Service of the Department of Labor and Industries.		
1601–11	For personal services for the inspectional service, including not more than sixty-nine permanent positions, and for traveling expenses of the commissioner, assistant commissioner, associate commissioners and inspectors of labor, and for services other than personal, printing the annual report, rent of district offices, and office supplies and equipment for the inspectional service, to be in addition to any amount heretofore appropriated for the purpose .	920 00	1,100 00
	Service of the Department of Mental Health.		
	Division of Mental Hygiene:		
1702–00	For expenses, including not more than sixty-one permanent positions, of investigating the nature, causes and results of mental diseases and defects and the publication of the results thereof, and of what further preventive or other measures might be taken and what further expenditures for investigation might be made which would give promise of decreasing the number of persons afflicted with mental diseases or defects, to be in addition to any amount heretofore appropriated for the purpose . . .	12,620 00	10,620 00
	Service of the Department of Public Works.		
	Item 2202–11 of chapter three hundred and seventy of the acts of the present year is hereby amended by adding at the end thereof the following: — ", to be available until July first, nineteen hundred and forty-five."		
	The unexpended balance of the appropriation made by item 638 of section 2 of chapter two hundred and forty-five of the acts of nineteen hundred and thirty-one, as		

Item		Appropriation Fiscal Year 1944.	Appropriation Fiscal Year 1945.
	most recently reappropriated by chapter four hundred and nineteen of the acts of nineteen hundred and forty-one, for certain work in the Taunton river authorized by chapter four hundred and five of the acts of nineteen hundred and thirty, is hereby again reappropriated.		
	The appropriation made by item 624a of section 2 of chapter five hundred and eighteen of the acts of nineteen hundred and thirty-nine, as most recently reappropriated by chapter four hundred and nineteen of the acts of nineteen hundred and forty-one, for certain improvements in Menemsha Creek in the towns of Chilmark and Gay Head as authorized by and subject to the conditions of chapter seventy of the resolves of nineteen hundred and thirty-nine, is hereby again reappropriated.		

Service of the Department of Public Utilities.

Item		1944	1945
2301-06	For traveling expenses of the commissioners and employees, to be in addition to any amount heretofore appropriated for the purpose	$1,000 00	$1,000 00
2301-07	For other services, including printing the annual report and necessary office supplies and equipment, to be in addition to any amount heretofore appropriated for the purpose . . .	500 00	
	Commercial Motor Vehicle Division:		
2304-01	For personal services of the director and assistants, including not more than eighteen permanent positions, to be in addition to any amount heretofore appropriated for the purpose . . .	720 00	1,440 00
2304-02	For other services, necessary office supplies and equipment, and for rent, to be in addition to any amount heretofore appropriated for the purpose . . .	1,300 00	1,300 00

UNCLASSIFIED ACCOUNTS AND CLAIMS.

Item		1944	1945
2805-01	For the payment of certain annuities and pensions of soldiers and others under the provisions of certain acts and resolves . .	$525 00	$525 00

Item		Appropriation Fiscal Year 1944.	Appropriation Fiscal Year 1945.

DEFICIENCIES.

For deficiencies in certain appropriations of previous years, in certain items as follows: —

Service of the Department of Mental Health.

	For the installation of cables in conduits on the ceilings of tunnels at the Metropolitan state hospital .	$879 20	

Service of the Department of Public Works.

Item 2900–17 of chapter three hundred and seventy of the acts of the current year is hereby amended by adding at the end thereof the following: ", and the amount herein appropriated for the year nineteen hundred and forty-four is in addition to the unexpended balance of any amount previously appropriated for the same purpose."

Item 2900–18 of chapter three hundred and seventy of the acts of the current year is hereby amended by adding at the end thereof the following: ", and the amount herein appropriated for the year nineteen hundred and forty-four is in addition to the unexpended balance of any amount previously appropriated for the same purpose."

The unexpended balance of the appropriations made by item 3132–13 of chapter four hundred and nineteen of the acts of nineteen hundred and forty-one is hereby reappropriated, to be available until July first, nineteen hundred and forty-five.

Metropolitan District Commission Funds

The following appropriations are for the fiscal year ending November thirtieth, nineteen hundred and forty-three, and for the fiscal year ending November thirtieth, nineteen hundred and forty-four, or for such other period as may be specified, and are to be assessed upon the several districts in accordance with the methods fixed by law, unless otherwise provided, and to be expended under the direc-

Item		Appropriation Fiscal Year 1944.	Appropriation Fiscal Year 1945.
	tion and with the approval of the metropolitan district commission:		
8607-00	For maintenance of the Charles River basin, including retirement of veterans under the provisions of the General Laws, to be in addition to any amount heretofore appropriated for the purpose .	$400 00	$1,600 00
8607-22	For the cost of certain construction and repairs to the locks and gates on the Charles River dam, to be assessed as part of the cost of maintenance of the Charles River basin	15,000 00	
8802-00	For the maintenance and operation of a system of sewage disposal for the north metropolitan sewerage district, including retirement of veterans under the provisions of the General Laws, to be in addition to any amount heretofore appropriated for the purpose .	5,000 00	5,000 00
8802-24	For payment, with the approval of the attorney general, of a certain judgment in favor of Thomas A. Berrigan for compensation for services previously rendered, to be assessed as part of the cost of maintenance of the north metropolitan sewerage system, and to be in addition to the amount appropriated in item 8807-24 .	1,176 01	
8807-00	For the maintenance and operation of a system of sewage disposal for the south metropolitan sewerage district, including retirement of veterans under the provisions of the General Laws, to be in addition to any amount heretofore appropriated for the purpose .	5,000 00	5,000 00
8807-24	For payment, with the approval of the attorney general, of a certain judgment in favor of Thomas A. Berrigan for compensation for services previously rendered; to be assessed as part of the cost of maintenance of the south metropolitan sewerage system, and to be in addition to the amount appropriated in item 8802-24 .	1,176 01	
8902-00	For the maintenance and operation of the metropolitan water system, including retirement of veterans under the provisions of the General Laws, to be in addition to any amount heretofore appropriated for the purpose	17,155 00	35,100 00

Item		Appropriation Fiscal Year 1944.	Appropriation Fiscal Year 1945.
	MISCELLANEOUS.		
0401-56	For expenditure by the Committee on Post War Readjustment as authorized by chapter five hundred and twenty-four of the acts of the present year	$50,000 00	-
0230	For continuing the investigation and study relative to intergovernmental relations and the laws relating thereto, as authorized by chapter fifty-nine of the resolves of the present year, to be in addition to any amount heretofore appropriated for the purpose .	2,500 00	
0901-04	For services other than personal, printing the annual report, office supplies and equipment, and printing and furnishing trespass posters, to be in addition to any amount heretofore appropriated for the purpose	2,500 00	$2,500 00
1907-08	For expenses in connection with smallpox and other diseases dangerous to the public health, to be in addition to any amount heretofore appropriated for the purpose	-	10,000 00
1907-09	For the support of sick indigent persons who have no legal settlement, to be in addition to any amount heretofore appropriated for the purpose	-	50,000 00
1201-01	For the salary of the commissioner, to be in addition to any amount heretofore appropriated for the purpose	920 00	1,000 00
1101-01	For the salary of the commissioner, to be in addition to any amount heretofore appropriated for the purpose	1,500 00	1,500 00
1103-01	For the salary of the commissioner, to be in addition to any amount heretofore appropriated for the purpose	1,500 00	1,500 00
1601-01	For the salaries of the commissioner, assistant and associate commissioners, including not more than five permanent positions, to be in addition to any amount heretofore appropriated for the purpose	3,680 00	4,000 00
0305-05	For the salaries of assistant registers, including not more than twenty-four permanent positions, to be in addition to any amount heretofore appropriated for the purpose	5,220 00	5,520 00
0425-01	For compensation of the commissioners, including not more than three permanent positions, to be in addition to any amount heretofore appropriated for the purpose	1,500 00	1,500 00

Item		Appropriation Fiscal Year 1944.	Appropriation Fiscal Year 1945.
0425–02	For expenses, including travel, supplies and equipment, to be in addition to any amount heretofore appropriated for the purpose .	$750 00	$750 00
0401–03	For the salaries of the eight councillors, to be in addition to any amount heretofore appropriated for the purpose	8,000 00	8,000 00
0441–03	For expenses of the Grand Army of the Republic Department of Massachusetts, as authorized by chapter seventeen of the resolves of the present year, to be in addition to any amount heretofore appropriated for the purpose .	1,600 00	1,600 00
2970–09	It is hereby provided that from the aggregate of the appropriations made by items 0415–01, 0415–02, 0415–03, 0415–04, 0415–05, 0601–02, 0601–03, 0701–02 and 0701–03 of chapter three hundred and seventy of the acts of the present year, sums totalling not in excess of one hundred eleven thousand dollars shall be charged to the Highway Fund.		
2220–17	For certain improvements at the Gloucester fish pier, so called, as authorized by chapter three hundred and ninety-three of the acts of the present year	15,000 00	

Service of the Attorney General's Department.

Item		Appropriation Fiscal Year 1944.	Appropriation Fiscal Year 1945.
801–02	For the compensation of assistants in his office, and for such other legal and personal services as may be required, including not more than thirty-six permanent positions, to be in addition to any amount heretofore appropriated for the purpose	10,000 00	10,000 00
	Specials:		
0803–04	For expenses incidental to special litigation to recover certain bank deposits, as authorized by section forty-one of chapter one hundred and sixty-eight of the General Laws, to be in addition to any amount heretofore appropriated for the purpose	2,000 00	–
2931–00	For maintenance of boulevards and parkways, including installation of traffic lights, to be in addition to any amounts heretofore appropriated for the purpose . .	143,000 00	243,500 00
8611–00	For maintenance of the Nantasket Beach reservation, to be in addition to any amount heretofore appropriated for the purpose .	–	2,400 00

Item		Appropriation Fiscal Year 1944.	Appropriation Fiscal Year 1945.
2012-02	For other services, including traveling expenses, supplies, materials and equipment, to be in addition to any amount heretofore appropriated for the purpose . .	$500 00	$500 00
1304-08	For aiding the adult blind, subject to the conditions provided by law, to be in addition to any amount heretofore appropriated for the purpose	100,000 00	100,000 00
0441-12	For participation by the commonwealth in the purchase of a building in the town of Saugus known as The Old Iron Works, as authorized by chapter five hundred and seven of the acts of the current year	4,000 00	
0227	For continuing the investigation and study of the laws relating to primaries and elections, as authorized by chapter fifty-seven of the resolves of the current year	2,500 00	
0238	For an investigation and study relative to rapid transit in the metropolitan area, and other related matters, as authorized by chapter fifty-six of the resolves of the current year	40,000 00	
0239	For an investigation and study relative to the laws of the commonwealth relating to fraternal benefit societies, as authorized by chapter forty-four of the resolves of the current year	2,000 00	
0222	For an investigation relative to the retirement systems of the commonwealth and of the political subdivisions thereof, as authorized by chapter forty-nine of the resolves of the current year .	1,500 00	
0241	For an investigation and study relative to the matter of discrimination against persons in employment because of their race, color, religion, or nationality, as authorized by chapter thirty-nine of the resolves of the current year .	1,000 00	
0242	For an investigation and study relative to old age assistance and certain related matters, as authorized by chapter thirty-eight of the resolves of the current year .	2,000 00	–
2960-02	For reimbursement, in part, of the city of Boston for expenses incurred by said city in the operation and maintenance of the Sumner Tunnel therein, as authorized by chapter twenty-five of the resolves of nineteen hundred and forty-three	100,000 00	100,000 00

Item		Appropriation Fiscal Year 1944.	Appropriation Fiscal Year 1945.
0243	For an investigation and study relative to housing, for preparing a housing law and related matters, as authorized by chapter fifty of the resolves of the current year .	$1,500 00	
2932–05	For the payment of a certain claim, as authorized by chapter twenty-one of the resolves of the current year	36 40	
0204	For continuing the investigation relative to transportation facilities, as authorized by chapter thirty-five of the resolves of the current year	7,500 00	
2970–10	For an investigation and study of traffic congestion for the purpose of recommending a post-war program of highway construction projects throughout the commonwealth, and for other purposes, as authorized by chapter forty-six of the resolves of the current year, to be paid from the Highway Fund	30,000 00	
2820–08	For the payment of certain claims, as authorized by chapters twenty-four, twenty-eight, twenty-nine and fifty-two of the resolves of the present year and chapter three hundred and forty of the acts of the current year . .	4,759 41	
0217	For an investigation and study of the criminal laws of the commonwealth, as authorized by chapter sixty of the resolves of the current year	500 00	
8602–32	For the sanding of Malibu Beach, so-called, as authorized by chapter four hundred and forty-six of the acts of the current year .	8,000 00	
8602–33	For the erection of a fence on land bordering the Neponset River, as authorized by chapter four hundred and sixty-six of the acts of the current year	18,000 00	
0503–03	For printing and binding public documents, to be in addition to any amount heretofore appropriated for the purpose . . .	1,000 00	
0244	For expenses of the committee on taxation of the general court in attending the annual conference of the national tax association during the year nineteen hundred and forty-three, as authorized by a joint order of the general court; provided, that any expenditures shall be made with the approval and under the direction of the governor and council . .	2,000 00	
0245	For clerical and other necessary expenses of a joint special committee established for the purpose of		

Item		Appropriation Fiscal Year 1944	Appropriation Fiscal Year 1945
	making an investigation and study of the various aspects of the emergency relative to the production, rationing, transportation and distribution of food, fuel and other commodities and necessaries of life, and of business conditions with reference to small business, so-called, as authorized by a joint order of the general court . .	$20,000 00	–
0424-01	For expenses of the commission, to be in addition to any amount heretofore appropriated for the purpose	200 00	
2930-11	For the payment of certain claims, as authorized by chapter eighteen of the resolves of the current year	9,246 50	
1701-12	For expenditure by the department of mental health on account of the additional expense for boarding out of patients by the several institutions in said department, as authorized by chapter five hundred and five of the acts of the present year	36,000 00	$45,000 00
2820-09	For the payment of a certain claim, as authorized by chapter fifty-two of the resolves of the present year	1,000 00	
2805-01	For the payment of certain annuities and pensions under the provisions of certain acts and resolves of the present year, to be in addition to any amount heretofore appropriated for the purpose .	14,200 00	5,510 00
2820-06	For reimbursement of persons for funds previously deposited in the treasury of the commonwealth and escheated to the commonwealth, as authorized by chapter thirty-two of the resolves of the present year	1,986 71	
1501-21	For personal services and expenses of the department of industrial accidents in carrying out the provisions of chapter five hundred and twenty-nine of the acts of the present year, to be expended with the approval of the governor	50,000 00	90,000 00
0228	For continuing the investigation and study of the problems arising from the holding of property for public purposes, as authorized by chapter sixty-four of the resolves of the present year . .	1,500 00	
3170-01	For clerical and other expenses of the committee on harbors and public lands of the general court relating to the zoning of Boston harbor for maritime purposes, as authorized by a joint order of the general court	2,000 00	

Item		Appropriation Fiscal Year 1944	Appropriation Fiscal Year 1945
0251	For an investigation and study of the laws pertaining to the safety of persons in certain places of assembly, as authorized by chapter sixty-seven of the resolves of the present year	$5,000 00	
0240	For an investigation and study of the problem of drunkenness, as authorized by chapter sixty-two of the resolves of the present year	2,000 00	
1904–01	For personal services of officers and employees, including not more than one hundred and thirty-eight permanent positions, to be in addition to any amount heretofore appropriated for the purpose	8,280 00	$8,280 00
0247	For an investigation and study relative to the regulation and control of the agricultural and dairy industry in the commonwealth, as authorized by chapter sixty-nine of the resolves of the present year	1,000 00	
0101–24	For additional compensation to the sergeant-at-arms, the employees in his office and the document room, and the doorkeepers, assistant doorkeepers and general court officers, as authorized by a joint order of the general court . .	6,600 00	
1002–18	For personal services and expenses, including not more than two permanent positions, in connection with establishing forest cutting practices, as authorized by chapter five hundred and thirty-nine of the acts of the present year .	2,580 00	4,660 00
2104–11	For the salaries of officers and employees for the building inspection service, including not more than twenty-seven permanent positions, to be in addition to any amount heretofore appropriated for the purpose	12,900 00	13,860 00
2104–12	For traveling expenses of officers for the building inspection service, to be in addition to any amount heretofore appropriated for the purpose	2,000 00	2,000 00
2104–13	For personal services and expenses of the board of standards and appeals, including not more than ten permanent positions, as authorized by chapter five hundred and forty-four of the acts of the present year	6,000 00	4,000 00
2811–04	For the compensation of state police officers formerly employed in the service of the commonwealth, now retired, to be in addition to any amount heretofore appropriated for the purpose	31,650 00	31,650 00
1907–04	The unexpended balance of the appropriations made by item		

Item		Appropriation Fiscal Year 1944	Appropriation Fiscal Year 1945.
	1907–04 of chapter four hundred and nineteen of the acts of nineteen hundred and forty-one is hereby reappropriated, to be available until July first, nineteen hundred and forty-five.		
0101–14	For additional compensation of the pages of the senate and house of representatives, as authorized by a joint order of the general court, to be in addition to any amount heretofore appropriated for the purpose	$1,400 00	
2820–14	For payment of a certain claim as authorized by chapter seventy of the resolves of the current year .	272 50	
2410–00	For the payment of interest on the direct debt of the commonwealth, to be in addition to the amounts appropriated in item 2951–00, and to be in addition to any amount heretofore appropriated for the purpose	12,656 25	$38,337 50
2420–00	For sinking fund requirements and for certain serial bonds maturing during the years nineteen hundred and forty-four and nineteen hundred and forty-five, to be in addition to the amounts appropriated in item 2952–00, and to be in addition to any amount heretofore appropriated for the purpose	125,000 00	125,000 00
0906–03	For expenses in connection with certain activities conducted in co-operation with the federal government, as authorized by section twenty-three of chapter ninety-four A of the General Laws, to be in addition to any amount heretofore appropriated for the purpose	2,500 00	2,500 00
0250	For an investigation and study relative to adjustments of grievances of employees of the commonwealth and the maintenance of employees in the several institutions of the commonwealth and the laws, rules and regulations applicable thereto, as authorized by chapter seventy-three of the resolves of the present year .	5,000 00	
0246	For an investigation and study of Post War Problems of the Commonwealth relative to economic and other conditions, as authorized by chapter seventy-one of the resolves of the current year .	25,000 00	
0216	For continuing the investigation and study relative to the civil service laws and regulations of the commonwealth, as authorized by chapter seventy-two of the resolves of the current year	3,000 00	

SECTION 3. Notwithstanding any other provision of law, the state comptroller is hereby authorized to certify for payment from the Highway Fund liabilities incurred by the department of public works for the construction of additional highways; provided, that the construction is undertaken at the request of the federal government and the federal government has certified that it will reimburse the commonwealth for substantially all of the cost of each project; and, provided further, that each project shall have been approved by the commission on administration and finance and the governor before any liability with respect thereto is incurred.

SECTION 4. This act shall take effect upon its passage.

Approved June 12, 1943.

RESOLVES.

RESOLVE VALIDATING THE ACTS OF NELLIE F. MALONE OF WALTHAM AS A NOTARY PUBLIC. *Chap.* 1

Resolved, That the acts of Nellie F. Malone of Waltham as a notary public, between October thirty-first, nineteen hundred and thirty-six, and July seventeenth, nineteen hundred and forty-two, both dates inclusive, in so far as the same may have been invalid by reason of the fact that, upon the change of her name from Nellie F. Anderson, she failed to re-register under her new name and pay to the state secretary a fee of one dollar as required by section thirteen of chapter thirty of the General Laws, are hereby confirmed and made valid. *Approved February 2, 1943.*

RESOLVE VALIDATING THE ACTS OF CECILIA F. WELCH OF FALL RIVER AS A NOTARY PUBLIC. *Chap.* 2

Resolved, That the acts of Cecilia F. Welch of Fall River as a notary public between June fifteenth, nineteen hundred and forty and September fifteenth, nineteen hundred and forty-two, both dates inclusive, in so far as the same may have been invalid by reason of the fact that, upon the change of her name from Cecilia F. Newton, she failed to re-register under her new name and pay to the state secretary a fee of one dollar as required by section thirteen of chapter thirty of the General Laws, are hereby confirmed and made valid.
Approved February 2, 1943.

RESOLVE VALIDATING THE ACTS OF HARRY P. LEVOWICH OF BOSTON AS A NOTARY PUBLIC. *Chap.* 3

Resolved, That the acts of Harry P. Levowich of Boston as a notary public, between May twenty-second, nineteen hundred and forty-two, and January twenty-fifth, nineteen hundred and forty-three, both dates inclusive, are hereby confirmed and made valid to the same extent as if during said time he had been qualified to discharge the duties of said office. *Approved February 18, 1943.*

RESOLVE VALIDATING THE ACTS OF GERTRUDE E. MCMAHON, OF BOSTON, AS A NOTARY PUBLIC. *Chap.* 4

Resolved, That the acts of Gertrude E. McMahon of Boston as a notary public between June tenth, nineteen hundred and thirty-nine, and September twenty-eighth, nineteen hundred and forty-two, both dates inclusive, in so far as the same may have been invalid by reason of the fact that, upon the change of her name from Gertrude E. McCarthy, she failed to re-register under her new name and pay to the state secretary a fee of one dollar, as required by section thirteen of chapter thirty of the General Laws, are hereby confirmed and made valid. *Approved February 18, 1943.*

Chap. 5 RESOLVE PROVIDING FOR AN INVESTIGATION BY THE JUDICIAL COUNCIL RELATIVE TO THE GUARDIANSHIP OF INCOMPETENT VETERANS, AND OTHER INCOMPETENT AND MINOR BENEFICIARIES OF THE VETERANS ADMINISTRATION, AND RELATIVE TO THE COMMITMENT TO THE VETERANS ADMINISTRATION OR OTHER AGENCY OF THE UNITED STATES OF PERSONS ELIGIBLE FOR CARE OR TREATMENT AND TO MAKE UNIFORM THE LAW WITH REFERENCE THERETO.

Resolved, That the judicial council be requested to investigate the subject matter of current senate document numbered two hundred and eighty-three, relative to the guardianship of incompetent veterans, and other incompetent and minor beneficiaries of the veterans administration, and relative to the commitment to the veterans administration or other agency of the United States of persons eligible for care or treatment and to make uniform the law with reference thereto, and to include its conclusions and recommendations, if any, in relation thereto, with drafts of such legislation as may be necessary to give effect to the same, in its annual report for the year nineteen hundred and forty-four.
Approved March 10, 1943.

Chap. 6 RESOLVE PROVIDING FOR AN INVESTIGATION BY THE JUDICIAL COUNCIL RELATIVE TO THE FORECLOSURE OF MORTGAGES OF LAND, RELATIVE TO ACKNOWLEDGMENTS OF WRITTEN INSTRUMENTS AND MAKING UNIFORM THE LAW WITH RELATION THERETO, AND RELATIVE TO PERMITTING CHARITABLE CONTRIBUTIONS BY THE GUARDIANS OF INSANE PERSONS.

Resolved, That the judicial council be requested to investigate the subject matter of current senate document numbered one hundred and sixty-eight, relative to the foreclosure of mortgages of land, of current senate document numbered two hundred and thirty-one, relative to acknowledgments of written instruments and making uniform the law with relation thereto, and of current house document numbered six hundred and eighty-two, relative to permitting charitable contributions by the guardians of insane persons, and to include its conclusions and recommendations, if any, in relation thereto, with drafts of such legislation as may be necessary to give effect to the same, in its annual report for the year nineteen hundred and forty-four. *Approved March 31, 1943.*

RESOLVE VALIDATING THE ACTS OF KATHRYN F. HARDY OF PLYMOUTH AS A NOTARY PUBLIC. *Chap.* 7

Resolved, That the acts of Kathryn F. Hardy of Plymouth as a notary public between January first, nineteen hundred and thirty-seven, and December fourth, nineteen hundred and forty-two, both dates inclusive, in so far as the same may have been invalid by reason of the fact that, upon the change of her name from Kathryn M. Ferioli, she failed to re-register under her new name and pay to the state secretary a fee of one dollar as required by section thirteen of chapter thirty of the General Laws, are hereby confirmed and made valid. *Approved April 7, 1943.*

RESOLVE PROVIDING FOR AN INVESTIGATION BY THE JUDICIAL COUNCIL RELATIVE TO THE FORECLOSURE OF MORTGAGES, AND CERTAIN RELATED MATTERS. *Chap.* 8

Resolved, That the judicial council be requested to investigate the subject matter of current house document numbered fourteen hundred and seventeen, relative to the foreclosure of mortgages of real estate, actions brought for the purpose of recovering deficiency judgments on notes secured by such mortgages, and the admissibility of evidence in such actions as to the fair market value of the mortgaged property, to investigate relative to the time within which such actions should be brought, and to investigate in general the duty of mortgagees to mortgagors of real estate in regard to foreclosure sales, and to include its conclusions and recommendations in relation thereto, with drafts of such legislation as may be necessary to give effect to the same, in its annual report for the year nineteen hundred and forty-four. *Approved April 14, 1943.*

RESOLVE VALIDATING THE ACTS OF HYMAN F. GOLDMAN OF BOSTON AS A NOTARY PUBLIC. *Chap.* 9

Resolved, That the acts of Hyman F. Goldman of Boston as a notary public, between January twenty-second and March ninth, both dates inclusive, in the current year, are hereby confirmed and made valid to the same extent as if during said time he had been qualified to discharge the duties of said office. *Approved April 15, 1943.*

RESOLVE VALIDATING THE ACTS OF ISRAEL ISENBERG AS A NOTARY PUBLIC. *Chap.* 10

Resolved, That the acts of Israel Isenberg, sometimes known as Isadore Isenberg, as a notary public, between January twenty-ninth, nineteen hundred and thirty-six, and January twenty-ninth, nineteen hundred and forty-three, both dates inclusive, are hereby confirmed and made valid insofar as they may have been invalid by reason of having been performed by said Isenberg under the assumed name of Isadore Isenberg, in which name the commission was granted. *Approved April 16, 1943.*

Chap. 11 RESOLVE PROVIDING FOR AN INVESTIGATION BY THE JUDICIAL COUNCIL RELATIVE TO THE SCOPE OF COMPULSORY MOTOR VEHICLE LIABILITY INSURANCE AND THE FURTHER REGULATION OF THE OPERATION IN THE COMMONWEALTH OF MOTOR VEHICLES AND TRAILERS OWNED BY CERTAIN NON-RESIDENTS.

Resolved, That the judicial council be requested to investigate the subject matter of current house document numbered eleven hundred and sixteen, relative to the scope of compulsory motor vehicle liability insurance; and the subject matter of current house document numbered twelve hundred and seventy-five relative to further regulating the operation in this commonwealth of motor vehicles and trailers owned by certain non-residents, and to include its conclusions and recommendations, if any, in relation thereto, with drafts of such legislation as may be necessary to give effect to the same, in its annual report for the year nineteen hundred and forty-four. *Approved April 28, 1943.*

Chap. 12 RESOLVE VALIDATING THE ACTS OF DORA MILLER AS A NOTARY PUBLIC.

Resolved, That the acts of Dora Miller of Chelsea as a notary public between August third, nineteen hundred and thirty-three and March fourth, nineteen hundred and thirty-eight, both dates inclusive, in so far as the same may have been invalid by reason of the fact that, upon the change of her name from Dora Ginsburg, she failed to re-register under her new name and pay to the state secretary a fee of one dollar as required by section thirteen of chapter thirty of the General Laws, are hereby confirmed and made valid. *Approved May 5, 1943.*

Chap. 13 RESOLVE PROVIDING FOR AN INVESTIGATION BY THE JUDICIAL COUNCIL RELATIVE TO SALVAGE OPERATIONS OF TRUSTEES.

Resolved, That the judicial council be requested to investigate the subject matter of current senate document numbered four hundred and five, relative to salvage operations of trustees, and to include its conclusions and recommendations, if any, in relation thereto, with drafts of such legislation as may be necessary to give effect to the same, by filing the same with the clerk of the senate on or before the seventeenth day of May in the current year.

Approved May 5, 1943

RESOLVE PROVIDING FOR AN INVESTIGATION BY THE JUDICIAL COUNCIL RELATIVE TO PROVIDING A PENALTY FOR FRAUDULENT CLAIMS UNDER MOTOR VEHICLE LIABILITY INSURANCE POLICIES. *Chap.* 14

Resolved, That the judicial council be requested to investigate the subject matter of current house document numbered nine hundred and sixty-five, relative to providing a penalty for fraudulent claims under motor vehicle liability insurance policies, and to include its conclusions and recommendations, if any, in relation thereto, with drafts of such legislation as may be necessary to give effect to the same, in its annual report for the year nineteen hundred and forty-four. *Approved May 6, 1943.*

RESOLVE VALIDATING THE ACTS OF MAYBELLE E. O'BRIEN AS A NOTARY PUBLIC. *Chap.* 15

Resolved, That the acts of Maybelle E. O'Brien of Brookline, formerly of Boston, as a notary public between May twentieth, nineteen hundred and thirty-nine and April fifteenth, nineteen hundred and forty-three, both dates inclusive, in so far as the same may have been invalid by reason of the fact that, upon the change of her name from Maybelle E. Harte, she failed to re-register under her new name and pay to the state secretary a fee of one dollar as required by section thirteen of chapter thirty of the General Laws, are hereby confirmed and made valid.

Approved May 7, 1943.

RESOLVE AUTHORIZING AN INVESTIGATION AND STUDY BY THE METROPOLITAN DISTRICT WATER SUPPLY COMMISSION RELATIVE TO THE FLOW OF WATER FROM THE QUABBIN RESERVOIR WITH A VIEW TO IMPROVING THE CONDITIONS OF THE SWIFT AND WARE RIVERS. *Chap.* 16

Resolved, That the metropolitan district water supply commission is hereby authorized and directed to investigate and study the possibility and feasibility of dividing the flow of water from the Quabbin reservoir between the Swift and Ware rivers in such a manner as shall best serve to prevent the pollution of either river, and be of industrial use by maintaining a steady flow of water in both, and in such manner as shall best prevent the flow in either river from reaching the flood stage. Said commission shall report to the general court the results of its investigation and study, and its recommendations, if any, including drafts of legislation necessary to carry its recommendations into effect and estimates of any costs which may be necessary to the same purpose, by filing the same with the clerk of the house of representatives on or before the first Wednesday of November, nineteen hundred and forty-four. *Approved May 19, 1943.*

Chap. 17 RESOLVE IN AID OF THE GRAND ARMY OF THE REPUBLIC, DEPARTMENT OF MASSACHUSETTS.

Resolved, That, subject to appropriation, there be allowed and paid from the treasury of the commonwealth a sum not exceeding sixteen hundred dollars in each of the years nineteen hundred and forty-three and nineteen hundred and forty-four, in addition to any amount heretofore appropriated for the same purpose, to aid in defraying the expenses of the Grand Army of the Republic, Department of Massachusetts; and any unexpended balance of said sum remaining at the end of either of said years may be used in the succeeding year. Payments for such aid shall be made upon the presentation to the comptroller of vouchers therefor, approved by the assistant adjutant general and the commander of said department. *Approved May 20, 1943.*

Chap. 18 RESOLVE PROVIDING FOR PAYMENTS BY THE COMMONWEALTH OF CERTAIN SUMS OF MONEY AS FULL COMPENSATION FOR CERTAIN PROPERTY TAKEN BY THE COMMONWEALTH THROUGH ITS DEPARTMENT OF PUBLIC WORKS.

Resolved, That, for the purpose of discharging the moral obligation of the commonwealth, and subject to appropriation, there be paid out of the Highway Fund to the parties and in the amounts hereinafter specified, as full compensation for certain property taken by eminent domain under chapter seventy-nine of the General Laws by the commonwealth through its department of public works:

Names of Parties.	Amounts of Payments.
Heirs of Patrick Flanagan	$150 00
Estate of Arthur Michael	4,825 00
Everett S. Osterbanks	187 50
Edward J. McLaughlin	4,084 00

No payment shall be made hereunder to any party entitled thereto until such party shall have signed and filed with the comptroller an agreement that the amount, if any, paid or to be paid for legal services rendered on his behalf in connection with the passage of this resolve shall not exceed ten per cent of the sum so payable to such party.

Approved May 24, 1943.

Chap. 19 RESOLVE VALIDATING THE ACTS OF HELEN N. DEVLIN AS A NOTARY PUBLIC.

Resolved, That the acts of Helen N. Devlin of Boston as a notary public between June twenty-second, nineteen hundred and forty-one, and July tenth, nineteen hundred and forty-two, both dates inclusive, in so far as the same may have been invalid by reason of the fact that, upon the change of her name from Helen J. Niewoyno, she failed to re-register under her new name and pay to the state secretary a fee of one dollar as required by section thirteen of chapter thirty of the General Laws, are hereby confirmed and made valid. *Approved May 24, 1943.*

RESOLVE VALIDATING THE ACTS OF MOSES M. FRANKEL OF WAKEFIELD AS A NOTARY PUBLIC. *Chap.* 20

Resolved, That the acts of Moses M. Frankel of Wakefield as a notary public, between January first and April thirtieth, nineteen hundred and forty-three, both dates inclusive, are hereby confirmed and made valid to the same extent as if during said time he had been qualified to discharge the duties of said office. *Approved May 26, 1943.*

RESOLVE IN FAVOR OF THEODORE FREITAS. *Chap.* 21

Resolved, That, subject to appropriation, there shall be allowed and paid from the state treasury to Theodore Freitas, a former member of the police force of the metropolitan district commission who resigned in the year nineteen hundred and forty-one, the sum of thirty-six dollars and forty cents to compensate him for services rendered prior to his resignation on certain days on which he was entitled to be off duty. No payment shall be made hereunder to any party entitled thereto until such party shall have signed and filed with the comptroller an agreement that the amount, if any, paid or to be paid for legal services in connection with the passage of this resolve shall not exceed ten per cent of the sum so payable to such party. *Approved May 28, 1943.*

RESOLVE PROVIDING FOR AN INVESTIGATION AND STUDY RELATIVE TO OPPORTUNITIES FOR THE DEVELOPMENT AND UTILIZATION OF THE MUNICIPALLY-OWNED AIRPORT IN THE TOWN OF ORANGE. *Chap.* 22

Resolved, That the Massachusetts aeronautics commission is hereby authorized and directed to make an investigation and study relative to opportunities for the development and utilization of the municipally-owned airport in the town of Orange. Said commission shall confer with the appropriate authorities of the federal government, of commercial airlines and of airplane manufacturers with a view to the utilization of the facilities of said airport so that it may have the fullest possible development in the field of commercial aviation, both transcontinental and international, and in the field of airplane manufacture. Said commission shall, from time to time during the progress of its investigation and study hereunder, confer with the board of selectmen of said town and give to said board such information as to any of its findings then made as said commission may have available. Said commission shall also report to the general court the results of its investigation, and its recommendations, if any, together with drafts of such legislation as may be necessary to carry such recommendations into effect, by filing the same with the clerk of the house of representatives on or before the first Wednesday in November in the year nineteen hundred and forty-four.

Approved May 28, 1943.

Chap. 23 RESOLVE PROVIDING FOR AN INVESTIGATION BY THE DEPARTMENT OF PUBLIC WELFARE RELATIVE TO AMOUNTS PAYABLE BY THE COMMONWEALTH FOR THE EXPENSES OF THE FUNERAL OF CERTAIN POOR PERSONS.

Resolved, That the department of public welfare is hereby authorized and directed to investigate the subject matter of current house document numbered twelve hundred and fifteen, relative to amounts payable by the commonwealth for the expenses of the funeral of certain poor persons. Said department shall report to the general court the results of its investigation, and its recommendations, if any, together with drafts of legislation necessary to carry such recommendations into effect, by filing the same with the clerk of the house of representatives on or before the first Wednesday of November in the year nineteen hundred and forty-four.

Approved May 28, 1943.

Chap. 24 RESOLVE IN FAVOR OF THE TOWN OF BELCHERTOWN.

Resolved, That, subject to appropriation and subject to the approval of the commissioner of public welfare, there shall be paid from the state treasury to the town of Belchertown the sum of ten hundred and twenty-eight dollars, as reimbursement for welfare assistance granted to Marion Tribe and Stanley Tribe, Jr. No payment shall be made hereunder to any party entitled thereto until such party shall have signed and filed with the comptroller an agreement that the amount, if any, paid or to be paid for legal services rendered in connection with the passage of this resolve shall not exceed ten per cent of the sum so payable to such party. *Approved May 28, 1943.*

Chap. 25 RESOLVE PROVIDING FOR THE REIMBURSEMENT IN PART OF THE CITY OF BOSTON BY THE COMMONWEALTH FOR EXPENSES INCURRED BY SAID CITY IN THE OPERATION AND MAINTENANCE OF THE SUMNER TUNNEL THEREIN.

Resolved, That, subject to appropriation, there be allowed and paid by the commonwealth from the Highway Fund to the city of Boston the sum of two hundred thousand dollars, to reimburse said city in part for expenses incurred by it in the operation and maintenance of the vehicular tunnel between Boston proper and East Boston, known as the Sumner tunnel, one half of said sum to be paid as aforesaid on September first in the current year and one half on November first in the year nineteen hundred and forty-four.

Approved June 1, 1943.

Resolve providing for the compiling, printing and distribution of the laws of the commonwealth relating to veterans and their organizations. *Chap.* 26

Resolved, That the state secretary shall cause the laws of the commonwealth, including those enacted in the current year, relating to veterans, and to their organizations, to be compiled, indexed and annotated, and shall cause to be printed in pamphlet form an edition of not more than fifteen thousand copies of such compilation, and shall distribute them as follows: To such free public libraries of the commonwealth as the state secretary shall designate, to such other free public libraries as shall make written application therefor, to each post, camp or other organization of such veterans within the commonwealth, and to the national headquarters of such organizations, one copy each; to the headquarters of the Massachusetts Department of the Grand Army of the Republic, The American Legion, the United Spanish War Veterans and the Veterans of Foreign Wars of the United States and the Disabled American Veterans of the World War, not exceeding one hundred copies each. The remaining copies shall be distributed by the state secretary in the manner provided for the distribution of public documents. To carry out the provisions of this resolve, the state secretary may expend such amount, not exceeding one thousand dollars, as the general court may appropriate.

Approved June 1, 1943.

Resolve providing for a survey by the division of personnel and standardization with respect to rules and regulations applicable to certain employees of the commonwealth who are required to work on holidays. *Chap.* 27

Resolved, That the division of personnel and standardization is hereby directed to make a survey with respect to employees of the commonwealth, other than those employed by the day, who are required to work on holidays, with a view to the adoption, to take effect at the termination of the existing states of war between the United States and any foreign country, of rules and regulations providing for compensating such employees by the granting of days off or otherwise for such holiday work, having particularly in mind those departments in which certain employees regularly have holidays off duty and others by reason of the nature of their work or otherwise do not have holidays off duty. Said division in making its survey shall consider the subject-matter of current house documents five hundred and eighteen and five hundred and twenty-one. It shall report its recommendations hereunder to the commission on administration and finance. *Approved June 1, 1943.*

Chap. 28 RESOLVE IN FAVOR OF THE TOWN OF NATICK.

Resolved, That, subject to appropriation, there shall be allowed and paid out of the state treasury to the town of Natick the sum of four hundred and seventeen dollars and twenty cents, being the amount paid by said town to the commonwealth from the proceeds of a sum of money recovered by said town from the estate of Bessie Davis for old age assistance furnished to said Bessie Davis during her lifetime, which sum of money said town was later required, through court proceedings, to repay to said estate. No payment shall be made hereunder to any party entitled thereto until such party shall have signed and filed with the comptroller an agreement that the amount, if any, paid or to be paid for legal services in connection with the passage of this resolve shall not exceed ten per cent of the sum so payable to such party. *Approved June 2, 1943.*

Chap. 29 RESOLVE PROVIDING FOR THE PAYMENT BY THE COMMONWEALTH OF CERTAIN OBLIGATIONS INCURRED BY A CERTAIN UNIT OF THE MASSACHUSETTS NATIONAL GUARD.

Resolved, That, for the purpose of discharging a moral obligation of the commonwealth in the premises, and subject to appropriation, there shall be paid from the treasury of the commonwealth to the estate of Carleton H. Parsons and to the estate of Arthur E. Herrick, both formerly of Gloucester, the sum of one hundred and ninety dollars and twenty-four cents each, to the estate of Arthur B. Sewall, formerly of Rockport, the sum of one hundred and ninety dollars and twenty-five cents, and to Clarence Birdseye of Gloucester the sum of one thousand two hundred and twenty-nine dollars and twenty-seven cents, as reimbursement for obligations incurred by said persons in the payment of certain notes signed by Battery A, one hundred and second regiment, field artillery, Massachusetts national guard, as security for money loaned to said battery for expenses incurred for improvements to the state armory in Gloucester. No payment of any sum shall be made hereunder to any person entitled thereto until such person shall have signed and filed with the comptroller an agreement that the amount, if any, paid or to be paid by him for legal services rendered in connection with the passage of this resolve shall not exceed ten per cent of the sum payable to him hereunder.

Approved June 2, 1943.

RESOLVE AUTHORIZING THE ART COMMISSION TO PROVIDE CERTAIN TEMPORARY MEMORIALS IN THE STATE HOUSE. *Chap.* 30

Resolved, That the art commission be authorized to provide suitable temporary memorials to Colonel Thomas Cass and the officers and men of the Ninth Regiment of Infantry, Massachusetts Volunteers, and the members of the Massachusetts state guard who served in such state guard during the period between April fifteenth, nineteen hundred and seventeen and December twenty-first, nineteen hundred and nineteen. For said purpose the art commission may expend such sums as may hereafter be appropriated.

Approved June 3, 1943.

RESOLVE PROVIDING FOR AN INVESTIGATION BY THE JUDICIAL COUNCIL RELATIVE TO THE GIVING OF NOTICE OF ACCIDENTS CAUSED BY DEFECTS IN WAYS AND PREMISES. *Chap.* 31

Resolved, That the judicial council is hereby requested to consider the subject matter of current house document numbered seventy-two, relative to the giving of notice of accidents caused by defects in ways and premises, and to include its conclusions and its recommendations, if any, in relation thereto, with drafts of such legislation as may be necessary to give effect to the same, in its annual report for the year nineteen hundred and forty-four.

Approved June 3, 1943.

RESOLVE PROVIDING FOR THE PAYMENT FROM THE STATE TREASURY OF THE BALANCE OF THE ESTATE OF THE LATE NELLIE SULLIVAN, WHICH ESTATE ESCHEATED TO THE COMMONWEALTH. *Chap.* 32

Resolved, That, subject to appropriation, there be allowed and paid from the state treasury, under the direction of the attorney general, to the heirs at law or next of kin of Nellie Sullivan, who died in the city of Boston in May or June, nineteen hundred and twenty-eight, or to their lawful representatives, such sum, if any, as may be found by the attorney general to have been paid into said treasury as the balance of the assets belonging to the estate of said Nellie Sullivan, under section ten of chapter one hundred and ninety-four of the General Laws, or corresponding provision of earlier law, notwithstanding the expiration of the time limited under said section for the recovery of such sum. No payment shall be made hereunder until there shall have been filed with the comptroller an agreement signed by the heirs at law or next of kin of said Nellie Sullivan, or their respective lawful representatives, that the amount, if any, paid or to be paid for legal services rendered in connection with the passage of this resolve shall not exceed ten per cent of the sum payable to them.

Approved June 3, 1943.

Chap. 33 RESOLVE RELATIVE TO THE OBSERVANCE DURING THE YEAR NINETEEN HUNDRED AND FORTY-FOUR OF THE THREE HUNDREDTH ANNIVERSARY OF THE ESTABLISHMENT IN DEDHAM OF THE FIRST FREE PUBLIC SCHOOL IN AMERICA SUPPORTED WHOLLY BY PUBLIC TAXATION.

Whereas, During the year nineteen hundred and forty-four will occur the three hundredth anniversary of the establishment in Dedham of the first free public school in America supported wholly by public taxation; and

Whereas, A committee has been formed in said town to commemorate suitably said anniversary; and

Whereas, It is highly fitting that the commonwealth should participate in the celebration of that historical event; therefore be it

Resolved, That the governor is hereby requested to issue a proclamation commemorative of the establishment of said school, and to provide for the representation of the commonwealth at any celebration of said anniversary in said town. *Approved June 3, 1943.*

Chap. 34 RESOLVE IN FAVOR OF JAMES M. HAJJAR OF LAWRENCE.

Resolved, That, for the purpose of discharging a moral obligation of the commonwealth and of promoting the public good, and after an appropriation has been made therefor, there be allowed and paid out of the state treasury the sum of one thousand five hundred dollars to James M. Hajjar of Lawrence, as full compensation for injuries sustained by him on August twenty-ninth, nineteen hundred and forty-two, while in the performance of military duty with C company, twenty-fourth infantry, Massachusetts state guard. Said compensation shall be paid in twenty-five monthly installments of sixty dollars each, beginning July first in the current year. No payment shall be made hereunder until said Hajjar shall have signed and filed with the comptroller an agreement that the amount, if any, paid or to be paid for legal services rendered in connection with the passage of this resolve shall not exceed ten per cent of the sum so payable to him. *Approved June 5, 1943.*

Chap. 35 RESOLVE REVIVING AND CONTINUING THE SPECIAL COMMISSION TO INVESTIGATE RELATIVE TO RAILROAD TRANSPORTATION FACILITIES WITHIN THE COMMONWEALTH.

Resolved, That the unpaid special commission, established by chapter sixty-four of the resolves of nineteen hundred and thirty-nine, is hereby revived and continued for the purpose of continuing its investigation relative to transportation facilities within the commonwealth. Said commission shall, in the course of its investigation, confer and co-operate with such agencies of the commonwealth or any political subdivision thereof, and with such civic and other associations or organizations, as may be engaged in making an investigation and study of said railroad facilities for the purpose of co-ordinating the activities of said agencies, associations and organizations in carrying out said investigations and studies. The commission shall also study the subject matter of current house document number five hundred and eighty. Said commission may call upon the department of public utilities and other departments, boards, commissions and officers of the commonwealth for such information as it may desire in the course of its investigation. Said commission shall be provided with quarters in the state house or elsewhere, shall hold public hearings, shall have the power to summon witnesses and to require the production of books, records, contracts and papers and the giving of testimony under oath, and may expend for expert, clerical and other services and expenses such sums, not exceeding, in the aggregate, seventy-five hundred dollars as may hereafter be appropriated therefor. Said commission shall make a supplementary report to the general court of the results of its investigation and its recommendations, if any, together with drafts of legislation necessary to carry its recommendations into effect, by filing the same with the clerk of the house of representatives as soon as may be, but in any event, not later than the first Wednesday of November, nineteen hundred and forty-four.

Said commission shall, at the time of filing its supplementary report with the clerk of the house of representatives as aforesaid, file a copy thereof with the governor.

Approved June 5, 1943.

RESOLVE VALIDATING THE ACTS OF MARY CATENA LOVERME AS A NOTARY PUBLIC. *Chap.* 36

Resolved, That the acts of Mary Catena LoVerme of Medford, formerly of Boston, as a notary public, between August twenty-sixth, nineteen hundred and forty-two, and May twenty-sixth, nineteen hundred and forty-three, both dates inclusive, are hereby confirmed and made valid to the same extent as if during said time she had been qualified to discharge the duties of said office. *Approved June 7, 1943.*

RESOLVE IN FAVOR OF WILLIAM L. SEARLE OF CONCORD. *Chap.* 37

Resolved, That for the purpose of discharging a moral obligation of the commonwealth in the premises and after an appropriation has been made therefor there be allowed and paid out of the treasury of the commonwealth to William L. Searle of Concord, who served the commonwealth faithfully and is now permanently disabled for further performance of duty on account of injury sustained, while in the performance of duties as a guard at the Massachusetts reformatory, by reason of being assaulted by certain inmates of said reformatory, an annuity equal to three fourths the salary received by him during the last year of his active service. Said annuity shall be payable in equal monthly installments from and after the period covered by chapter fifty-six of the resolves of nineteen hundred and thirty-nine and shall cease upon the decease of said Searle. No payment shall be made hereunder until there shall have been filed with the comptroller an agreement signed by William L. Searle that the amount, if any, paid or to be paid for legal services rendered in connection with the passage of this resolve shall not exceed ten per cent of said sum. *Approved June 7, 1943.*

Chap. 38 RESOLVE PROVIDING FOR AN INVESTIGATION AND STUDY BY A SPECIAL COMMISSION RELATIVE TO THE OLD AGE ASSISTANCE LAW, SO CALLED, AND CERTAIN RELATED MATTERS.

Whereas, The laws relating to old age assistance, so called, its benefits and administration, federal, state and local, both jointly and separately, are of continuing interest and importance to the committee on pensions and the members of the general court; and

Whereas, It is the opinion of the committee on pensions that the main cause of complaints as to the inadequacy or inequality of assistance under the old age assistance law, so called, is the result of defects in administration of the law rather than legal defects; and

Whereas, There is considerable doubt as to whether or not aid to the blind should be handled by the state department of public welfare rather than the state department of education; and

Whereas, Certain changes are recommended in the old age assistance law, so called, and the results of such changes should be closely observed during the next two years; and

Whereas, It is the feeling that much of the administration weakness stems from lack of proper organization within the department with too much of a burden upon the commissioner of public welfare; therefore be it

Resolved, That an unpaid special commission, to consist of one member of the senate to be designated by the president thereof, three members of the house of representatives to be designated by the speaker thereof, and three persons to be appointed by the governor, is hereby established for the purpose of reviewing the operation of the old age assistance law, so called, with particular emphasis on recent changes, with a view to determining the advisability or necessity of revising or liberalizing said law, particularly with reference to eligibility requirements as to age, amount of payments, resources of applicants, support of aged persons by their children, separation of boards of public welfare from bureaus of old age assistance, benefits to the blind and to crippled and totally disabled persons, the financing of said law, and related matters. In addition, the commission shall study the desirability of a reorganization of the department of public welfare, the transfer of aid to the blind from the department of education to the department of public welfare, and whether or not there is a need for a deputy commissioner with full administrative authority over old age assistance, so called, and any and all matters pertaining to such assistance. Said commission may expend for clerical and other assistance and expenses such sums, not exceeding, in the aggregate, two thousand dollars, as may hereafter be appropriated therefor. Said commission shall be provided with quarters in the state house or elsewhere, may hold hearings, may require by summons the attendance and testimony of witnesses and the production of books and papers. The commission shall report to the general court the results of its investigations and its recommendations, if any, together with drafts of legislation necessary to carry its recommendations into effect, by filing one or more reports with the clerk of the house of representatives at such time or times as the commission may elect; provided, that the commission shall so file its final report not later than the first Wednesday of November in the year nineteen hundred and forty-four. *Approved June 8, 1943.*

RESOLVE PROVIDING FOR AN INVESTIGATION BY A SPECIAL COMMISSION RELATIVE TO THE MATTER OF DISCRIMINATION AGAINST PERSONS IN EMPLOYMENT BECAUSE OF THEIR RACE, COLOR, RELIGION OR NATIONALITY. *Chap.* 39

Resolved, That a special unpaid commission, to consist of one member of the senate to be designated by the president thereof, three members of the house of representatives to be designated by the speaker thereof, and three persons to be appointed by the governor, is hereby established to investigate the matter of discrimination against persons in employment because of their race, color, religion or nationality, and to make such studies within the spirit of this resolve as shall be helpful in abolishing such discrimination. In making said investigation, said commission shall consider the report of the Massachusetts commission on the employment problems of negroes referred to in current house document numbered two hundred and sixteen, and shall consider the subject matter of current senate documents numbered two hundred and twenty-two, two hundred and twenty-three, and current house documents numbered four hundred and forty-four, four hundred and forty-five, four hundred and forty-six and four hundred and forty-seven. Said commission shall hold hearings, shall be provided with quarters in the state house or elsewhere and shall have power to summon witnesses, require the production of books, records, contracts and papers, and require the giving of testimony under oath. Said commission may expend for expenses and legal, clerical and other assistance such sums, not exceeding, in the aggregate, one thousand dollars, as may hereafter be appropriated. Said commission shall report to the general court the results of its investigation and its recommendations, if any, together with drafts of legislation necessary to carry said recommendations into effect, by filing the same with the clerk of the house of representatives not later than the first Wednesday of November in the year nineteen hundred and forty-four.

Approved June 8, 1943.

Chap. 40 RESOLVE PROVIDING FOR A STUDY AND SURVEY BY THE METROPOLITAN DISTRICT COMMISSION AND THE DEPARTMENT OF PUBLIC HEALTH OF THE NEPONSET RIVER.

Resolved, That the metropolitan district commission and the department of public health, acting as a joint board, are hereby authorized and directed to make a complete survey and study of the Neponset river with a view to preparing plans and specifications for the improvement and beautification of both banks of said river, with special attention being given to the recreational potentialities of the improved area, and for eliminating and preventing the pollution of said river.

Said joint board shall report to the general court the results of its survey and study, and its recommendations, if any, together with estimates of cost and drafts of legislation necessary to carry such recommendations into effect, by filing the same with the clerk of the house of representatives on or before the first Wednesday of November in the year nineteen hundred and forty-four.

Approved June 8, 1943.

Chap. 41 RESOLVE PROVIDING FOR A SURVEY BY THE DIVISION OF PERSONNEL AND STANDARDIZATION WITH RESPECT TO THE CLASSIFICATION OF SOCIAL WORKERS.

Resolved, That the division of personnel and standardization is hereby directed to make a survey with respect to the classification of social workers with particular reference to the question of an intermediate classification between that of social worker and that of head social worker to cover those social workers who are not under the immediate supervision of a head social worker, but to whom special responsibilities are assigned. Said division, in making its survey, shall consider the subject matter of current senate document numbered four hundred and ninety-six. It shall report its recommendations hereunder to the commission on administration and finance. *Approved June 9, 1943.*

Chap. 42 RESOLVE IN FAVOR OF THE SISTER OF THE LATE JOHN Q. KNOWLES.

Resolved, That, for the purpose of promoting the public good, there be allowed and paid out of the state treasury to the sister of the late John Q. Knowles, who died while a member of the present house of representatives, the balance of the salary to which he would have been entitled for the current session had he lived and served until the end of said session. Said sum shall be paid from the amount appropriated by item 0101–03 of section two of chapter sixty-eight of the acts of the current year. *Approved June 9, 1943.*

RESOLVE IN FAVOR OF THE WIDOW OF THE LATE NELSON B. CROSBY. *Chap.* 43

Resolved, That, for the purpose of promoting the public good, there be allowed and paid out of the state treasury to the widow of the late Nelson B. Crosby, who died while a member of the present house of representatives, the balance of the salary to which he would have been entitled for the current session had he lived and served until the end of said session. Said sum shall be paid from the amount appropriated by item 0101–03 of section two of chapter sixty-eight of the acts of the current year. *Approved June 9, 1943.*

RESOLVE PROVIDING FOR A STUDY BY A SPECIAL COMMISSION RELATIVE TO THE LAWS OF THE COMMONWEALTH RELATING TO FRATERNAL BENEFIT SOCIETIES. *Chap.* 44

Whereas, Many difficulties have arisen with reference to fraternal benefit societies because of recent court decisions concerning practices followed by such organizations under existing laws for many years; and

Whereas, It has proved impossible to solve the problems relating to such societies in the limited time available because of their complicated nature and far reaching effect; and

Whereas, It is desirable to maintain the status quo until such time as a thorough study has been made with a view to promulgating remedial and protective legislation; therefore be it

Resolved, That a special unpaid commission, to consist of one member of the senate to be designated by the president thereof, three members of the house of representatives to be designated by the speaker thereof, the commissioner of insurance or a member of his department designated by him, and two persons to be appointed by the governor, with the advice and consent of the council, is hereby established for the purpose of making a study of the laws of the commonwealth relative to fraternal benefit societies, with a view to making such changes in said laws and additions thereto as may be necessary for the best interests of the public. In making its study hereunder, said commission shall consider the subject matter of current house documents numbered sixty-six, sixty-eight, two hundred and twenty, two hundred and twenty-one, eight hundred and eight, eight hundred and sixteen and eight hundred and seventeen. Said commission may expend for clerical and other services and expenses such sums, not exceeding, in the aggregate, two thousand dollars, as may hereafter be appropriated therefor. Said commission shall report to the general court the results of its study, and its recommendations, if any, together with drafts of legislation necessary to carry said recommendations into effect, by filing the same with the clerk of the house of representatives on or before the first Wednesday of November in the year nineteen hundred and forty-four.

Approved June 9, 1943.

Chap. 45 RESOLVE PROVIDING FOR AN INVESTIGATION AND STUDY BY A SPECIAL COMMISSION OF THE LAWS GOVERNING ASSESSMENT OF TAXES ON REAL ESTATE, THE ABATEMENT OF SUCH TAXES, AND RELATIVE TO THE FORM OF TAX BILLS AND NOTICES, AND TO CERTAIN RELATED MATTERS.

Whereas, The present war has already caused fundamental changes in our economic structure, and

Whereas, Already there is apparent the need for a broad reconsideration of revenue sources for public purposes, and

Whereas, Real estate taxation still continues to be the largest source of such revenue in Massachusetts, and

Whereas, Federal rent ceilings set a limit on income from real estate holdings, while no such limit is placed on taxes, and

Whereas, Rationing and price control are gradually taking millions of dollars out of our tax structure through the closing of manufacturing plants and wholesale and retail outlets considered non-essential to the war effort, and

Whereas, The real estate assessment process followed in Massachusetts has demonstrated inequalities in peace time and has shown even greater weaknesses under war conditions, making it evident that but a small percentage of property is assessed on "a fair cash value", therefore be it

Resolved, That an unpaid special commission, to consist of one member of the senate, to be designated by the president thereof, three members of the house of representatives, to be designated by the speaker thereof and three persons to be appointed by the governor, is hereby established for the purpose of making an investigation and study of the laws and practices governing real estate taxation, the possibility of establishing further provisions of law for review of valuations, the abatement of taxes and appeal from refusals of assessors to abate, the advisability of a form of tax limitation upon real estate, and to recommend such changes in the laws and city and town practices as may be necessary or desirable to place real estate assessment in the cities and towns on an equitable basis, and to give study to the matter of selecting assessors and requirements to be placed on cities and towns as to properly implementing the assessing practices of such cities and towns so that real estate will not bear an unfair and unreasonable share of the tax burden. Said commission in making its investigation and study hereunder may call upon officers of the commonwealth and its political subdivisions for such information as it may desire. In such investigation and study it shall consider the subject matter of current senate document numbered three hundred and seven, relative to legislation to make certain changes with respect to the form of tax bills and notices, current senate document numbered three hundred and twelve, relative to legislation to make certain corrective changes with respect to valuation of property for local taxes and with respect to abatements of such taxes, of current house document numbered seven hundred and six, relative to limitation of appropriations by cities, and of current senate document numbered four hundred and thirty-two, relative to providing for an investigation and study of the laws governing the assessment of real estate and the equality thereof. It shall be provided with quarters in the state house or elsewhere, shall have the power to summon witnesses and to require the production of books, records and papers, and the giving of testimony under oath, and it may hire technical assistance and may spend for clerical and other services and expense such sums, not exceeding, in the aggregate, twenty thousand dollars, as may hereafter be appropriated therefor, of which sum not more than one thousand dollars shall be expended for clerical services and expenses other than technical services. Said commission shall report to the general court the result of its investigation and study and its recommendations, if any, together with drafts of legislation necessary to carry into effect its recommendations in so far as they relate to changes in the laws of this commonwealth, by filing same with the clerk of the house of representatives as soon as may be, but not later than the first Wednesday of November in the year nineteen hundred and forty-four.

Approved June 9, 1943.

RESOLVE PROVIDING FOR A SPECIAL UNPAID COMMISSION TO CONSIDER AND RECOMMEND A POST-WAR PROGRAM OF HIGHWAY PROJECTS THROUGHOUT THE COMMONWEALTH. *Chap.* 46

Resolved, That an unpaid special commission, to be known as the Post-war Highway Commission and hereinafter referred to as the commission, consisting of two members of the senate to be designated by the president thereof, five members of the house of representatives to be designated by the speaker thereof, one person to be appointed by the governor, the commissioner of public works, the mayor of the city of Boston or a person appointed by him, and the chairman of the metropolitan district commission or a person appointed by him, is hereby established for the purpose of making a study of such highway projects throughout the commonwealth as may, in its opinion, be necessary or advisable to be carried out after the termination of the present war, with a view to recommending a post-war program of highway and traffic improvements. The commission, in carrying out its study hereunder, shall consider, with respect to each highway project which it may deem necessary or advisable for inclusion in such a program, as to whether public convenience requires the construction or carrying out thereof, and, if so, it shall determine as to said project (1) the probable cost; (2) how the cost of said improvement, and of land takings, if necessary, therefor, should be apportioned; (3) by whom said improvement should be made; and (4) by whom said improvement should be maintained upon its completion.

The commission, within thirty days after the appointment of the members thereof, shall transmit to the state department of public works a list of post-war projects designed to relieve or eliminate traffic congestion in the commonwealth, and may supplement such list at such later dates as it may determine. Said department, for the purpose of determining the projects to be planned under this paragraph, may, with the approval of the governor, omit or modify any of said projects or add thereto other post-war projects designed to relieve such traffic congestion; and said department shall, as promptly as possible, prepare plans, specifications, detail of location and amount of necessary land takings or acquisitions, detailed cost of estimates, and all other things necessary or proper as a prerequisite to the actual construction of the projects so determined. Said department shall report in detail to the commission, on or before October first, nineteen hundred and forty-four, the material so prepared and its recommendations in regard thereto.

For the purpose of carrying out the provisions of this resolve, there may be expended by the commission for expenses and clerical and other assistance such sums, not exceeding, in the aggregate, thirty thousand dollars, as may be appropriated therefor from the Highway Fund.

Notwithstanding any other provision of law, the state department of public works may, with the approval of the governor, accept on behalf of the commonwealth and expend any federal funds which may hereafter be made available for financing the cost of activities in connection with the preparation of a program of post-war highway construction. Authority to make application for such federal funds is hereby granted to said state department of public works or to such other agency of the commonwealth as the governor may designate.

The commission shall report to the general court its findings and its recommendations, if any, together with drafts of legislation necessary to carry such recommendations into effect, by filing the same with the clerk of the house of representatives on or before the first Wednesday of November in the year nineteen hundred and forty-four.

Approved June 10, 1943.

RESOLVE PROVIDING FOR AN INVESTIGATION BY THE COMMISSION ON ADMINISTRATION AND FINANCE RELATIVE TO CHANGING THE FISCAL YEAR OF THE METROPOLITAN DISTRICT COMMISSION. *Chap.* 47

Resolved, The commission on administration and finance is hereby authorized and directed to make an investigation relative to changing the fiscal year of the metropolitan district commission to conform to that of the commonwealth. In making its investigation, said commission shall consider so much of the message of the governor, printed as current house document numbered eighteen hundred and twenty-eight, as relates to the subject matter of this resolve. Said commission shall report to the general court the results of its investigation, and its recommendations, if any, together with drafts of legislation necessary to carry such recommendations into effect, by filing the same with the clerk of the house of representatives on or before the first Wednesday of November in the year nineteen hundred and forty-four.

Approved June 10, 1943.

RESOLVE IN FAVOR OF FRANK L. GRAY OF ASHFIELD. *Chap.* 48

Resolved, That, for the purpose of discharging a moral obligation of the commonwealth in the premises, and subject to appropriation, there be allowed and paid out of the state treasury to Frank L. Gray, of Ashfield, the sum of five thousand dollars on the effective date of this resolve and the further sum of twelve hundred dollars a year for life to reimburse him for the loss to him occasioned by reason of an error by a state employee in the office of the registrar of motor vehicles. Said reimbursement shall be exempted from all taxes imposed by the commonwealth, or by any other government in so far as this commonwealth may so provide. No payment shall be made hereunder until there shall have been filed with the comptroller an agreement, signed by said Frank L. Gray, that the amount, if any, paid or to be paid for legal services rendered in connection with the passage of this resolve shall not exceed ten per cent of the sums paid or payable hereunder. *Approved June 10, 1943.*

RESOLVE PROVIDING FOR A FURTHER INVESTIGATION BY A SPECIAL COMMISSION RELATIVE TO THE RETIREMENT SYSTEMS OF THE COMMONWEALTH AND OF THE POLITICAL SUBDIVISIONS THEREOF. *Chap.* 49

Resolved, That a special unpaid commission, consisting of one member of the senate to be designated by the president thereof, three members of the house of representatives to be designated by the speaker thereof, and three persons to be appointed by the governor, is hereby established for the purpose of making a further investigation of the retirement systems of the commonwealth and the political subdivisions thereof, with a view to co-ordinating said systems and making such other changes as may be found necessary or advisable. For such purpose said commission may expend, with the approval of the governor and council, for expenses and for expert, actuarial and other assistance such sums, not exceeding, in the aggregate, fifteen hundred dollars, as may hereafter be appropriated therefor. Said commission shall consider, among other matters, the subject matter of current house document numbered one hundred and forty-five and current house documents numbered fifteen hundred and thirty and sixteen hundred and forty-six. It shall also investigate and study the desirability of a change in the basis of contributory retirement systems maintained, in whole or in part, by public funds and the possibility or desirability of changing such basis from the money purchase plan, so called, to the unit purchase plan, so called. The commission shall also give special study to the present pension plan for justices of the courts, with a view to determining whether such pensions should or should not be put on a contributory basis. In carrying out its investigation and study hereunder the commission shall also consider the matter of retirement allowances and pensions for veterans of World War II, so called, and shall consider the subject matter of current senate documents numbered forty-six, seventy, seventy-two, two hundred and ninety-three and two hundred and forty-five, and of current house documents numbered one hundred and forty-five, four hundred and eighty-nine, four hundred and ninety-five and eight hundred and sixty. Said commission shall report to the general court its findings, and its recommendations, if any, together with drafts of legislation necessary to carry such recommendations into effect, by filing the same with the clerk of the house of representatives on or before the first Wednesday in November in the year nineteen hundred and forty-four. *Approved June 10, 1943.*

Chap. 50 RESOLVE ESTABLISHING A SPECIAL COMMISSION FOR THE PURPOSE OF MAKING AN INVESTIGATION AND STUDY OF THE LAWS OF THE COMMONWEALTH RELATING TO HOUSING AND OF DRAFTING A HOUSING LAW.

Resolved, That a special unpaid commission consisting of one member of the senate to be designated by the president thereof, three members of the house of representatives to be designated by the speaker thereof, five persons to be appointed by the governor, the chairman of the state board of housing, the commissioner of public safety, the chairman of the state planning board and the chief sanitary engineer of the state department of public health, is hereby established for the purpose of inquiring into the problem of housing, particularly with reference to the laws of the commonwealth relating to the construction, maintenance and use of places used for human habitation, with a view to revising and perfecting the same. Said commission may require from the several departments, boards, commissions and officers of the commonwealth such information as it may desire in the course of its investigations.

Said commission shall be provided with quarters in the state house or elsewhere, may hold hearings, may require by summons the attendance and testimony of witnesses and the production of books and papers; and may expend for necessary assistance and expenses such sums, not exceeding, in the aggregate, fifteen hundred dollars, as may hereafter be appropriated therefor. The commission shall report to the general court the results of its investigations and its recommendations, if any, together with drafts of legislation necessary to carry its recommendations into effect, by filing the same with the clerk of the house of representatives not later than the first Wednesday of November in the year nineteen hundred and forty-four.

Approved June 10, 1943.

RESOLVE IN FAVOR OF JOHN GANLEY OF LYNN. *Chap.* 51

Resolved, That, for the purpose of discharging the moral obligation of the commonwealth, and subject to appropriation, there be allowed and paid from the state treasury to John Ganley of Lynn, who was injured and permanently disabled on August twenty-third, nineteen hundred and twenty-five, while in the performance of duty as a patrolman in the uniformed division of the state police, the sum of five thousand dollars on the passage of this resolve, and the further sum of one thousand and eighty dollars a year for five years thereafter. Said reimbursement shall be exempted from all taxes imposed by the commonwealth, or by any other government in so far as this commonwealth may so provide. No payment shall be made hereunder until there shall have been filed with the comptroller an agreement signed by said John Ganley that the amount, if any, paid or to be paid for legal services rendered in connection with the passage of this resolve shall not exceed ten per cent of the amounts paid or payable hereunder. *Approved June 10, 1943.*

RESOLVE IN FAVOR OF THE HEIRS OF HOWARD MURPHY. *Chap.* 52

Resolved, That for the purpose of discharging a moral obligation of the commonwealth and after an appropriation has been made therefor, there be allowed and paid out of the state treasury under the direction of the attorney general to the heirs of Howard Murphy, late of Taunton, the sum of one thousand dollars, as full compensation for the death of said Murphy, a former guard at the State Farm who was killed January first, nineteen hundred and forty-two, by an inmate thereof. No payment shall be made hereunder until there shall have been filed with the comptroller an agreement signed by said heirs that the amount, if any, paid or to be paid for legal services rendered in connection with the passage of this resolve shall not exceed ten per cent of said sum. *Approved June 10, 1943.*

Chap. 53 RESOLVE PROVIDING FOR A SURVEY BY THE DIVISION OF PERSONNEL AND STANDARDIZATION WITH RESPECT TO THE CLASSIFICATION OF POSITIONS IN THE LABOR SERVICE OF THE METROPOLITAN DISTRICT COMMISSION.

Resolved, That the division of personnel and standardization is hereby directed to make a survey with respect to the classification of positions in the labor service of the metropolitan district commission. Said division, in making its survey, shall consider the subject matter of current senate document numbered three hundred and one. It shall report its recommendations hereunder to the commission on administration and finance. *Approved June 11, 1943.*

Chap. 54 RESOLVE PROVIDING FOR AN INVESTIGATION RELATIVE TO THE PAYMENT OF BENEFITS UNDER THE EMPLOYMENT SECURITY LAW TO EMPLOYEES WHO ARE ABSENT FROM WORK ON ACCOUNT OF SICKNESS.

Resolved, That the state advisory council in the division of employment security is hereby authorized and directed to make an investigation of the subject matter of current senate document numbered two hundred and twenty-nine, and of current house documents four hundred and fifty-eight, eleven hundred and twenty-four and eleven hundred and thirty-three, relative to the payment of benefits under the employment security law to employees absent from work on account of sickness. Said advisory council shall report to the general court its findings, and its recommendations, if any, together with drafts of legislation necessary to carry such recommendations into effect, by filing the same with the clerk of the senate on or before the first Wednesday in November in the year nineteen hundred and forty-four.

Approved June 11, 1943.

Chap. 55 RESOLVE PROVIDING FOR AN INVESTIGATION BY THE DEPARTMENT OF CONSERVATION RELATIVE TO THE ACQUISITION BY THE COMMONWEALTH OF CERTAIN PROPERTIES IN THE TOWNS OF OAK BLUFFS AND EDGARTOWN FOR PUBLIC BEACH PURPOSES.

Resolved, The department of conservation is hereby authorized and directed to investigate the subject matter of current house document numbered seventeen hundred and twenty-six, relative to the acquisition by the commonwealth of certain properties in the towns of Oak Bluffs and Edgartown for public beach purposes. Said department shall report to the general court the results of its investigation, and its recommendations, including estimates of cost and recommendations as to the allocation of such cost, together with drafts of legislation necessary to carry said recommendations into effect, by filing the same with the clerk of the house of representatives on or before the first Wednesday of November in the year nineteen hundred and forty-four.

Approved June 11, 1943.

RESOLVE PROVIDING FOR AN INVESTIGATION AND STUDY RELATIVE TO RAPID TRANSIT IN THE BOSTON METROPOLITAN AREA. *Chap.* 56

Resolved, That an unpaid special commission, to consist of one member of the senate to be designated by the president thereof, three members of the house of representatives to be designated by the speaker thereof, and the commissioners of the department of public utilities, is hereby established for the purpose of making an investigation and study of the subject of rapid transit in the Boston metropolitan area. For the purpose of such investigation and study said commission may employ necessary engineering, legal and other assistance, and shall prepare a comprehensive plan or plans showing the rapid transit routes which it recommends, the district which it recommends to be served, and such statistical information and data as it may deem to be of assistance to the general court in the consideration of any legislation recommended. Said commission may utilize the services of the department of public utilities, the Boston transit commission, the state planning board, the state department of public works and any engineering or other departments, suitably organized to prepare plans or other information, of any city or town within the district which it expects will be served by the proposed rapid transit system, and out of the sum which it is hereby authorized to expend may make funds available to said commission, board and departments, or any of them.

Said special commission shall make its report to the general court by filing the same with the clerk of the house of representatives on or before November first in the year nineteen hundred and forty-four, accompanied by such plans, statistics and drafts of legislation as it may deem necessary or appropriate.

For the purposes of this resolve, said commission may expend an amount not exceeding forty thousand dollars, which shall be apportioned equitably among the cities and towns benefited when a rapid transit system is established pursuant to said report, and shall be paid to the commonwealth according to the method of apportionment to be included in the recommendations of said commission.

Approved June 11, 1943.

Chap. 57 RESOLVE REVIVING AND CONTINUING THE SPECIAL COMMISSION TO INVESTIGATE THE LAWS RELATING TO PRIMARIES AND ELECTIONS.

Resolved, That the unpaid special commission, established by chapter seventy-four of the resolves of nineteen hundred and forty-one, is hereby revived and continued for the purpose of continuing its investigation relative to the laws relating to primaries and elections, with a view to completing revision and perfection of the same. The commission shall be provided with quarters in the state house, may hold hearings therein and elsewhere, and shall be entitled to receive the assistance of the state secretary and all other public officers. The commission may summon and examine witnesses and require by subpoena the production of books and papers, and may expend for clerical and other assistance such sums, not exceeding, in the aggregate, twenty-five hundred dollars, as may be appropriated therefor. The payment by said commission of compensation for services rendered to it in the preparation of changes in the primary and election laws shall not be subject to section twenty-one of chapter thirty of the General Laws. Said commission shall make a supplementary report to the general court of the results of its investigation and its recommendations, if any, together with drafts of legislation necessary to carry its recommendations into effect, by filing the same with the clerk of the house of representatives as soon as may be, but in no event later than the first Wednesday of November in the year nineteen hundred and forty-four. *Approved June 11, 1943.*

Chap. 58 RESOLVE PROVIDING FOR AN INVESTIGATION BY THE ARMORY COMMISSION RELATIVE TO THE ERECTION OF ARMORIES IN THE EAST BOSTON DISTRICT OF BOSTON, IN THE CITIES OF CHICOPEE AND GARDNER, AND IN OTHER CITIES AND TOWNS IN THE COMMONWEALTH.

Resolved, That the armory commission is hereby authorized and directed to investigate the subject matter of current senate document numbered one hundred and seventy-six, relative to the erection of a new armory in the East Boston district of Boston; the subject matter of current house document numbered one hundred and ninety-two, relative to the erection of a new armory in the city of Gardner; the subject matter of current house document numbered eleven hundred and sixty-four, relative to the erection of a new armory in the city of Chicopee; and to investigate relative to the erection of one or more new armories in any other city or town in the commonwealth; with a view to determining suitable locations for and the probable cost of said armories, including the cost of acquiring such land as may be necessary therefor. Said commission in making its investigation hereunder shall consider the number of military units now located or proposed to be located in said cities and towns. Said commission shall report to the emergency public works commission as soon as may be the results of its investigations hereunder, and its recommendations, if any, and said emergency public works commission shall, in preparing its program of post-war public works projects under authority of an act passed in the current year, consider such recommendations as may be contained in said report.

Approved June 11, 1943.

RESOLVE REVIVING AND CONTINUING THE SPECIAL COMMISSION APPOINTED TO INVESTIGATE AND STUDY INTERGOVERNMENTAL RELATIONS. *Chap.* 59

Resolved, That the unpaid special commission established by chapter eighty-four of the resolves of nineteen hundred and forty-one is hereby revived and continued for the purpose of continuing its investigation and study of the co-related functions and activities of the federal, state, county, city, town and district governments, the time within which such commission might report to the general court having been extended to February nineteenth in the current year. Said commission shall make a supplementary report to the general court of the results of its investigation and study hereunder, by filing the same with the clerk of the senate on or before the first Wednesday of November in the year nineteen hundred and forty-four, and may also so report from time to time to the general court on or before said date whenever it deems such action advisable. Reports made hereunder shall include drafts of legislation necessary to carry into effect any recommendations for legislation contained therein. For the purposes of this resolve, said commission may travel within and without the commonwealth and may expend, subject to appropriation, the sum of twenty-five hundred dollars in addition to the unexpended balance of the amount appropriated by item 0230 of section two of chapter seven hundred and thirty of the acts of nineteen hundred and forty-one, and said balance is hereby made available for the payment of expenses incurred by said commission. *Approved June 11, 1943.*

RESOLVE REVIVING AND CONTINUING THE SPECIAL COMMISSION APPOINTED TO INVESTIGATE AND STUDY THE CRIMINAL LAWS OF THE COMMONWEALTH, AND TO DRAFT A PENAL CODE. *Chap.* 60

Resolved, That the unpaid special commission, established by chapter forty-eight of the resolves of nineteen hundred and forty-one, is hereby revived and continued for the purpose of continuing its investigation and study relative to the criminal laws of the commonwealth and of drafting a penal code. Said commission shall also study the subject matter of current senate document numbered four hundred and sixty-two, relating to larceny. Said commission may hold hearings, shall be provided with quarters in the state house or elsewhere, and may expend for clerical and other assistance and expenses such sums, not exceeding, in the aggregate, five hundred dollars, as may hereafter be appropriated therefor. Said commission shall make a supplementary report to the general court of the results of its investigation and study, and the penal code drafted by it, by filing the same with the clerk of the senate on or before the first Wednesday of November in the year nineteen hundred and forty-four. *Approved June 11, 1943.*

Chap. 61 RESOLVE IN FAVOR OF THE WIDOW OF THE LATE WALTER R. McDONALD, A FORMER MEMBER OF THE DEPARTMENT OF PUBLIC SAFETY DOING POLICE DUTY.

Resolved, That, for the purpose of discharging a moral obligation of the commonwealth, and after an appropriation has been made therefor, there shall be allowed and paid out of the state treasury to Mary T. McDonald of Waltham, widow of Walter R. McDonald, former member of the department of public safety doing police duty, who, while on duty at the Wareham barracks on September nineteenth, nineteen hundred and forty, sustained fatal injuries, which resulted in his death on said September nineteenth, nineteen hundred and forty, an annuity of twelve hundred dollars, payable in equal monthly instalments, for a period of six years commencing the first day of June, nineteen hundred and forty-three. Said annuity shall be reduced to one thousand dollars when the minor daughter of said Mary T. McDonald reaches the age of eighteen years, and it shall cease upon the remarriage of said Mary T. McDonald, if it occurs prior to the expiration of said period of six years. No payment shall be made hereunder until there has been filed with the comptroller an agreement signed by said Mary T. McDonald that the amount, if any, paid or to be paid for legal services rendered in connection with the passage of this resolve shall not exceed ten per centum of the maximum amount payable hereunder.

(This resolve, returned by the governor to the House of Representatives, the branch in which it originated, with his objections thereto, was passed by the House of Representatives, June 9, 1943, and, in concurrence, by the Senate, June 11, 1943, the objections of the governor notwithstanding, in the manner prescribed by the constitution; and thereby has "the force of a law".)

RESOLVE PROVIDING FOR AN INVESTIGATION BY A SPECIAL COMMISSION RELATIVE TO THE PROBLEM OF DRUNKENNESS IN THIS COMMONWEALTH. *Chap.* 62

Resolved, That the chairman of the parole board, the commissioner of mental health and a justice of the municipal court of the city of Boston to be appointed by the governor, acting as a joint board, are hereby authorized and directed to make a study and investigation of all factors relating to the problem of drunkenness in Massachusetts to the end that, because of the high expense involved to the taxpayers and the fact that there is medical evidence that this problem is more medical than criminal, such change may be made in the laws of this commonwealth as may be necessary. Said joint board may expend for clerical and other expenses such sums, not exceeding, in the aggregate, two thousand dollars, as may hereafter be appropriated therefor. Said board shall report to the general court the result of its investigation and its recommendations, if any, together with such drafts of legislation as may be necessary to carry such recommendations into effect, by filing the same with the clerk of the house of representatives on or before the first Wednesday of November in the year nineteen hundred and forty-four. *Approved June 12, 1943.*

RESOLVE IN FAVOR OF WILLIAM W. DRUMMEY. *Chap.* 63

Resolved, That, for the purpose of discharging a moral obligation of the commonwealth and of promoting the public good, there be paid from the state treasury, out of the money appropriated by item one hundred and thirty-one a of section two of chapter five hundred and seven of the acts of nineteen hundred and thirty-eight, and made available for expenditure by section four of said chapter five hundred and seven to William W. Drummey of Boston, the sum of three hundred and fifty-seven dollars and thirty-four cents, being the amount determined to be due said Drummey under the terms of a certain authorization or of an agreement between the commonwealth and him for services rendered in connection with work performed on certain property of the commonwealth made necessary by the hurricane and floods of September, nineteen hundred and thirty-eight. No payment shall be made hereunder until said Drummey shall have signed and filed with the comptroller an agreement that the amount, if any, paid or to be paid for legal services rendered in connection with the passage of this resolve shall not exceed ten per cent of the sum payable hereunder, nor until said Drummey shall execute and file with the comptroller a release, satisfactory in form to the attorney general, in full satisfaction of all claims asserted by him for compensation for services under said authorization or agreement, whether or not legal proceedings therefor are pending upon the effective date of this resolve. *Approved June 12, 1943.*

Chap. 64 RESOLVE PROVIDING FOR THE CONTINUATION AND ENLARGEMENT OF THE WORK OF INVESTIGATION BY A SPECIAL COMMISSION RELATIVE TO CERTAIN PROBLEMS ARISING FROM THE HOLDING OF PROPERTY IN THE COMMONWEALTH FOR PUBLIC PURPOSES.

Resolved, That a special unpaid commission, to consist of one member of the senate to be designated by the president thereof, three members of the house of representatives to be designated by the speaker thereof, the senate and house chairmen of the committees on municipal finance and on taxation, the commissioner of corporations and taxation and the chairman of the commission on administration and finance, is hereby established for the purpose of continuing the investigation of the advisability of revising the laws of the commonwealth relative to the reimbursement of municipalities for loss of taxes by reason of lands therein owned by the commonwealth or a political subdivision thereof, or by any other governmental unit, or changing the established practice of aiding municipalities in which the commonwealth or any of its political subdivisions acquire property for any purpose. Said commission may, if it deems it desirable, broaden the scope of its inquiry to include consideration of any form of payment or compensation to any political subdivision of the commonwealth for or on account of property acquired or held in such political subdivision by the federal government, the commonwealth or any political subdivision of the commonwealth. Said commission, in carrying out its work, shall consider the subject matter of current senate document numbered four hundred, relative to the payments of moneys by the city of Fall River in lieu of taxes to the town of Westport on property owned by said city, and pertaining to its domestic water supply to the town of Westport, and of current senate document numbered four hundred and one, relative to the apportionment to the towns of Dartmouth and Westport of tax revenues received by the city of Fall River for furnishing water to certain persons and corporations, and shall also consider the subject matter of current house document numbered fourteen hundred and sixty-eight. For the purposes of this resolve, said commission may expend for clerical and other services and expenses such sums, not exceeding, in the aggregate, fifteen hundred dollars, as may hereafter be appropriated therefor. Said commission shall report to the general court the results of its investigation, and its recommendations, if any, together with drafts of legislation necessary to carry such recommendations into effect, by filing the same with the clerk of the house of representatives on or before November first in the year nineteen hundred and forty-four.

Approved June 12, 1943.

RESOLVE VALIDATING THE ACTS OF JOHN J. McLAUGHLIN OF WOBURN AS A NOTARY PUBLIC. *Chap.* 65

Resolved, That the acts of John J. McLaughlin of Woburn as a notary public between February twelfth and June tenth, nineteen hundred and forty-three, both dates inclusive, are hereby confirmed and made valid to the same extent as if during said time he had been qualified to discharge the duties of said office. *Approved June 12, 1943.*

RESOLVE INCREASING THE SCOPE OF THE INVESTIGATION AND STUDY BY THE SPECIAL COMMISSION ESTABLISHED TO CONSIDER AND RECOMMEND A POST-WAR PROGRAM OF HIGHWAY PROJECTS THROUGHOUT THE COMMONWEALTH. *Chap.* 66

Resolved, That the special unpaid commission established by chapter forty-six of the resolves of the current year, to consider and recommend a post-war program of highway projects throughout the commonwealth, shall, in carrying out its investigation and study under said resolve, consider the subject matter of current house document numbered one hundred and seven, relative to warning signs at grade crossings of railroads, and of current house document numbered one hundred and nine, relative to the speed of motor vehicles and the operation thereof on state highways. Said commission shall include its findings and its recommendations, if any, relative to the subject matter of said documents, together with drafts of legislation necessary to carry the same into effect, in its report to be filed as provided in said resolve. *Approved June 12, 1943.*

RESOLVE PROVIDING FOR AN INVESTIGATION AND STUDY BY A SPECIAL UNPAID COMMISSION RELATIVE TO THE LAWS PERTAINING TO THE SAFETY OF PERSONS IN CERTAIN PLACES OF ASSEMBLY. *Chap.* 67

Resolved, That an unpaid special commission, consisting of one member of the senate to be designated by the president thereof, three members of the house of representatives to be designated by the speaker thereof, and three persons to be appointed by the governor, is hereby authorized and directed to investigate the subject matter of safety in buildings, other than single or two-family dwellings, and particularly in places of assembly, including means of ingress to and egress from such buildings and places of assembly. In connection with such investigation said commission shall study the subject matter of current senate document numbered twenty-one, relating to the time during which owners of buildings, except in the city of Boston, shall comply with the orders of a building inspector relating to means of escape from fire and other related matters; current senate document numbered twenty-two, relating to the time during which owners of buildings in the city of Boston shall comply with the orders of a building inspector relating to means of escape from fire and other related matters; current senate document numbered twenty-three, relating to an investigation by the state fire marshal of the circumstances of the fire occurring at the Cocoanut Grove in Boston; current senate document numbered two hundred and eighty-nine, relating to the establishment and maintenance of local building inspection departments; current senate document numbered three hundred and fifty-five, relating to the appointment of an unpaid special commission to investigate and study the feasibility of requiring night clubs and similar places to furnish security for the civil liability on account of personal injuries sustained by patrons; current senate document numbered three hundred and ninety-nine, being the report of the committee on building codes and policies bearing upon "The Safety of Our Citizens in Places of Assembly"; current house document numbered eighty-seven, relating to the requiring approval of hospital buildings by the department of public safety; current house document numbered one hundred and sixty, relating to restricting the number of persons present in premises where alcoholic beverages are served; current house document numbered two hundred and five, relating to providing further for the protection of life and property against fire and other hazards in certain places of public resort in the city of Boston; current house document numbered two hundred and six, relating to requiring certain places of public resort to be equipped with automatic sprinklers; current house document numbered two hundred and sixty-three, relating to smoking or possessing of lighted pipes, cigars or cigarettes being prohibited in stores where inflammable goods are on display; current house document numbered three hundred and thirty, relating to fire prevention and the safety of life and property in theatres and public halls being made applicable to certain other places of public resort; current house document numbered four hundred and seventy-four, relating to seating accommodations in establishments wherein food and alcoholic beverages are sold to be consumed on the premises; current house document numbered four hundred and seventy-six, relating to prohibition of smoking or the possession of lighted cigars, cigarettes, pipes or matches in or upon docks and piers on the waterfront of the city of Boston; current house document numbered four hundred and eighty-three, relating to requiring that public buildings have posted therein plans of egress therefrom and for the projection on screens of plans showing egress and for fire drills in theatres; current house document numbered six hundred and ninety-three, relating to facilitating the inspection of wires in buildings in the city of Boston; current house document numbered six hundred and ninety-six, relating to requiring notices to inspectors of wires or certain other persons and to granting the right of entry to such inspectors and the examiners of electricians; current house document numbered seven hundred, relating to clarifying and amending existing provisions of law with respect to fire prevention; current house document numbered nine hundred and ninety-three, relating to investigating and studying general and special laws relating to public safety with special reference to laws dealing with licensing, inspection of buildings and fire prevention; current house document numbered nine hundred and ninety-eight, relating to more adequate fire inspection of certain places of public assembly; current house document numbered one thousand one hundred and sixty-five, relating to the installation of fire alarm systems by hotels and rooming houses; current house document numbered one thousand one hundred and sixty-six, relating to aldermen in cities and selectmen in towns providing for surveys of municipal regulations relating to the safety of certain institutions; and current house document numbered one thousand one hundred and sixty-nine, relating to making certain changes in the building laws of the city of Boston relative to fire extinguishing apparatus. Said commission may also examine all records of every city and town within the commonwealth relative to licensing and inspection of the construction, alteration, repair, use and occupancy of buildings therein and may require the attendance and assistance of all officers or boards of such cities and towns charged with the duties of licensing or inspecting any of said buildings.

Said commission shall be provided with quarters in the state house or elsewhere, may hold hearings, may require by summons the attendance and testimony of witnesses and the production of books and papers; may travel within and without the commonwealth; and may expend for necessary assistance and expenses such sums, not exceeding, in the aggregate, five thousand dollars, as may hereafter be appropriated therefor. The commission shall report to the general court the results of its investigations and its recommendations, if any, together with drafts of legislation necessary to carry its recommendations into effect, by filing the same with the clerk of the senate not later than the first Wednesday of November in the year nineteen hundred and forty-four. *Approved June 12, 1943.*

RESOLVE VALIDATING THE ACTS OF JAMES T. STOMBER OF GARDNER AS A NOTARY PUBLIC. *Chap.* 68

Resolved, That the acts of James T. Stomber, of Gardner, as a notary public between March fourth and June eleventh, nineteen hundred and forty-three, both dates inclusive, are hereby confirmed and made valid to the same extent as if during said time he had been qualified to discharge the duties of said office. *Approved June 12, 1943.*

Chap. 69 RESOLVE PROVIDING FOR AN INVESTIGATION AND STUDY RELATIVE TO THE REGULATION AND CONTROL OF THE AGRICULTURAL AND DAIRY INDUSTRY IN THIS COMMONWEALTH.

Resolved, That an unpaid special commission, to consist of one member of the senate to be designated by the president thereof, three members of the house of representatives to be designated by the speaker thereof and three persons to be appointed by the governor, with the advice and consent of the council, is hereby established for the purpose of making an investigation and study relative to license, inspection and other requirements imposed by existing law on the agricultural and dairy industry in this commonwealth, with a view to recommending such changes in said laws, or such additions thereto, as said commission may deem advisable. Said commission shall particularly consider the advisability of providing for a more centralized regulation and control of said industry in lieu of the multiplicity of agencies now provided for such regulation and control. Said commission may require of the department of agriculture, or any of the divisions thereof, the commission on administration and finance, the department of public health and such other departments, commissions and officers of the commonwealth as have or can obtain information in relation to the subject matter of this resolve, such assistance as may be helpful in the course of its investigation and study. Said commission may expend for clerical and other services and expenses such sums, not exceeding, in the aggregate, one thousand dollars, as may hereafter be appropriated therefor. Said commission shall report to the general court the results of its investigation and study, and its recommendations, if any, together with drafts of legislation necessary to carry such recommendations into effect, by filing the same with the clerk of the house of representatives on or before the first Wednesday of November in the year nineteen hundred and forty-four.

Approved June 12, 1943.

Chap. 70 RESOLVE IN FAVOR OF COURTNEY HARDWARE COMPANY.

Resolved, That, for the purpose of discharging a moral obligation of the commonwealth, there be paid out of the state treasury the sum of two hundred seventy-two dollars and fifty cents to the Courtney Hardware Company of three hundred and sixty-six Washington street, Dorchester, on account of materials furnished the commonwealth by said company. No payment shall be made hereunder until there shall have been filed with the state treasurer an agreement signed by said company that the amount, if any, paid or to be paid for services rendered in connection with the passage of this resolve shall not exceed ten per cent of said sum.

Approved June 12, 1943.

RESOLVE PROVIDING FOR A SURVEY AND STUDY BY AN UNPAID SPECIAL COMMISSION, TO BE KNOWN AS THE POST-WAR REHABILITATION COMMISSION, OF POST-WAR PROBLEMS OF THE COMMONWEALTH RELATIVE TO ECONOMIC AND OTHER CONDITIONS. *Chap.* 71

Resolved, That an unpaid special commission, to be known as the Post-War Rehabilitation Commission, consisting of five members of the senate to be designated by the president thereof, thirteen members of the house of representatives to be designated by the speaker thereof, and seven persons to be appointed by the governor, with the advice and consent of the council, is hereby established for the purpose of making a survey and study of such problems relative to economic and other conditions as, in the opinion of said commission, will have to be met by the commonwealth upon the termination of the present war. Said commission shall make a study of the economic resources within the confines of the commonwealth, including agriculture, industry, housing and urban redevelopment and man-power, with a view to providing for a minimum of unemployment and a maximum of opportunity for work for persons now in the armed forces of the United States who, at the time of their demobilization, will be seeking employment, as well as for persons now engaged in a civilian capacity in war work who may be unemployed at the time when industry will be converted from a wartime producing program to a peacetime producing program. Said commission shall also study measures for the assistance of veterans of the present world war and previous wars and military expeditions in which the United States has been engaged, and shall study post-war problems with reference to veterans' bonus and veterans' legislation. Said commission, in making its study hereunder, shall also consider the subject matter of so much of current senate document number one as refers on pages five and six thereof to the abovementioned matters, of current senate documents, numbers forty-one and one hundred and seventy-five, of current house documents, numbers one hundred and ninety-four, two hundred and sixty-five, four hundred and eighty-one, six hundred and ninety-nine, eight hundred and forty-four, eight hundred and forty-five, eight hundred and forty-six, eight hundred and forty-seven, eight hundred and forty-eight, eight hundred and forty-nine, eleven hundred and sixty-three, eleven hundred and sixty-seven, eleven hundred and seventy and eleven hundred and seventy-one. Said commission shall be provided with quarters in the state house or elsewhere, and may expend for necessary assistance and expenses such sums, not exceeding, in the aggregate, twenty-five thousand dollars, as may hereafter be appropriated therefor. The commission shall report to the general court the results of its survey and study and its recommendations, if any, together with drafts of legislation necessary to carry its recommendations into effect, by filing one or more reports with the clerk of the house of representatives at such time or times as the commission may elect; provided, that the commission shall file a report not later than the first Wednesday of November in the year nineteen hundred and forty-four. *Approved June 12, 1943.*

Chap. 72 RESOLVE REVIVING AND CONTINUING THE SPECIAL COMMISSION APPOINTED TO MAKE AN INVESTIGATION AND STUDY RELATIVE TO THE CIVIL SERVICE LAWS AND RULES AND REGULATIONS OF THE COMMONWEALTH, AND INCREASING THE MEMBERSHIP OF SAID COMMISSION.

Resolved, That the special unpaid commission established by chapter thirty-six of the resolves of nineteen hundred and forty-one is hereby revived and continued for the purpose of continuing its investigation and study of the civil service laws of the commonwealth and the rules and regulations made thereunder, with a view to making such changes therein and additions thereto as may be necessary for the best interests of the public. The membership of said commission is hereby increased by the addition of eight members, two of whom shall be members of the senate to be designated by the president thereof, four of whom shall be members of the house of representatives to be designated by the speaker thereof and two of whom shall be appointed by the governor. Said commission, in making its investigation and study hereunder, shall consider the proposed revision of the civil service laws of the commonwealth as set forth in current house document numbered seventeen hundred and eighty-six. The commission shall be provided with quarters in the state house or elsewhere, and may expend, with the approval of the governor and council, for clerical and other services and expenses such sums, not exceeding, in the aggregate, three thousand dollars, as may hereafter be appropriated therefor. Said commission shall make a supplementary report to the general court of the results of its investigation and study hereunder, by filing the same with the clerk of the house of representatives on or before the first Wednesday of November in the year nineteen hundred and forty-four. Reports made hereunder shall include drafts of legislation necessary to carry into effect any recommendations for legislation contained therein.

Approved June 12, 1943.

RESOLVE PROVIDING FOR AN INVESTIGATION AND STUDY BY A SPECIAL COMMISSION RELATIVE TO ADJUSTMENTS OF GRIEVANCES OF EMPLOYEES OF THE COMMONWEALTH AND TO THE MAINTENANCE OF EMPLOYEES IN THE SEVERAL INSTITUTIONS OF THE COMMONWEALTH AND THE LAWS, RULES AND REGULATIONS APPLICABLE THERETO. *Chap.* 73

Resolved, That a special commission to consist of one member of the senate to be designated by the president thereof, three members of the house of representatives to be designated by the speaker thereof, and three persons to be appointed by the governor, is hereby established for the purpose of making an investigation and study concerning the present methods by which grievances of employees of the commonwealth may be presented and adjusted, and the adequacy of present methods, including the subject matter of current senate document numbered thirty-one; and also concerning the laws and rules and regulations applicable to the maintenance of employees of the several institutions of the commonwealth, including requirements as to living in, the treatment of maintenance in determination of salary, both of those who live in and those who live out, the accommodations provided or available at the several institutions for employees who live in and the adequacy of these accommodations for housing those employees who in the interest of safety and efficiency or by reason of inadequacy of accommodations on private property in the vicinity should reside on the premises, including the subject matter of current senate document numbered two hundred and ninety-nine. The commission shall also consider the subject matter of current house document numbered seventeen hundred and seventy-seven, being a resolve providing for an investigation and study by a special commission relative to adjustments of grievances of employees of the commonwealth and the laws, rules and regulations applicable thereto. The commission shall be provided with quarters in the state house or elsewhere, and may expend with the approval of the governor and council for clerical and other services and expenses such sums not exceeding in the aggregate five thousand dollars as may hereafter be appropriated therefor. Said special commission shall report to the general court the results of its investigation and its recommendations, if any, together with drafts of legislation or rules or regulations necessary to carry said recommendations into effect, by filing the same with the clerk of the house of representatives on or before the first Wednesday of November in the year nineteen hundred and forty-four. *Approved June 12, 1943.*

The Commonwealth of Massachusetts

IN THE YEAR ONE THOUSAND NINE HUNDRED AND FORTY-ONE.

PROPOSAL FOR A LEGISLATIVE AMENDMENT OF THE CONSTITUTION TO PROVIDE THAT THE GENERAL COURT MAY PRESCRIBE THE TERMS AND CONDITIONS UNDER WHICH PARDONS OF OFFENCES WHICH ARE FELONIES MAY BE GRANTED.

Proposed amendment to the constitution to provide that the general court may prescribe the terms and conditions under which pardons of offences which are felonies may be granted.

A joint session of the Senate and House of Representatives hereby declares it to be expedient to alter the Constitution by the adoption of the following Article of Amendment, to the end that it may become a part of the Constitution, if similarly agreed to in a joint session of the next General Court and approved by the people at the state election next following:

ARTICLE OF AMENDMENT.

Article VIII of section I of chapter II of Part the Second of the Constitution of the Commonwealth is hereby annulled and the following is adopted in place thereof: —

Art. VIII. The power of pardoning offences, except such as persons may be convicted of before the senate by an impeachment of the house, shall be in the governor, by and with the advice of council, provided, that if the offence is a felony the general court shall have power to prescribe the terms and conditions upon which a pardon may be granted; but no charter of pardon, granted by the governor, with advice of the council before conviction, shall avail the party pleading the same, notwithstanding any general or particular expressions contained therein, descriptive of the offence or offences intended to be pardoned.

IN JOINT SESSION, July 8, 1941.

The foregoing legislative amendment of the Constitution is agreed to in joint session of the two houses of the General Court, the said amendment having received the affirmative votes of a majority of all the members elected; and it is referred to the next General Court in accordance with a provision of the Constitution.

IRVING N. HAYDEN,
Clerk of the Joint Session.

IN JOINT SESSION, May 12, 1943.

The foregoing legislative amendment is agreed to in joint session of the two houses, the said amendment having received the affirmative votes of a majority of all the members elected; and this fact is hereby certified to the Secretary of the Commonwealth, in accordance with a provision of the Constitution.

Certified to the secretary of the commonwealth for submission to the people at the next state election.

IRVING N. HAYDEN,
Clerk of the Joint Session.

The Commonwealth of Massachusetts

IN THE YEAR ONE THOUSAND NINE HUNDRED AND FORTY-ONE.

PROPOSAL FOR A LEGISLATIVE AMENDMENT OF THE CONSTITUTION TO PROVIDE FOR A FAIR, CONCISE SUMMARY, INSTEAD OF A DESCRIPTION, OF EACH PROPOSED AMENDMENT TO THE CONSTITUTION AND EACH LAW SUBMITTED TO THE PEOPLE, UNDER THE INITIATIVE AND THE REFERENDUM, AND CERTAIN CHANGES RELATIVE TO THE FILING OF INITIATIVE PETITIONS.

Proposed amendment to the constitution to provide for a fair, concise summary, instead of a description, of each proposed amendment to the constitution and each law submitted to the people, under the initiative and the referendum, and certain changes relative to the filing of initiative petitions.

A joint session of the Senate and House of Representatives hereby declares it to be expedient to alter the Constitution by the adoption of the following Article of Amendment, to the end that it may become a part of the Constitution, if similarly agreed to in a joint session of the next General Court and approved by the people at the state election next following:

ARTICLE OF AMENDMENT.

SECTION 1. Article XLVIII of the amendments to the constitution is hereby amended by striking out section three, under the heading "THE INITIATIVE. *II. Initiative Petitions.*", and inserting in place thereof the following: — *Section 3. Mode of Originating.* — Such petition shall first be signed by ten qualified voters of the commonwealth and shall be submitted to the attorney-general not later than the first Wednesday of the August before the assembling of the general court into which it is to be introduced, and if he shall certify that the measure and the title thereof are in proper form for submission to the people, and that the measure is not, either affirmatively or negatively, substantially the same as any measure which has been qualified for submission or submitted to the people at either of the two preceding biennial state elections, and that it contains only subjects not excluded from the popular initiative and which are related or which are mutually dependent, it may then be filed with the secretary of the commonwealth. The secretary of the commonwealth shall provide blanks for the use of subsequent signers, and shall print at the top of each blank a fair, concise summary, as determined by the attorney-general, of the proposed measure as such summary will appear on the ballot together with the names and residences of the first ten signers. All initiative petitions, with the first ten signatures attached, shall be filed with the secretary of the commonwealth not earlier than the first Wednesday of the September before the assembling of the general court into which they are to be introduced, and the remainder of the required signatures shall be filed not later than the first Wednesday of the following December.

SECTION 2. Section three of that part of said Article XLVIII, under the heading "THE REFERENDUM. *III. Referendum Petitions.*", is hereby amended by striking out the words "The secretary of the commonwealth shall provide blanks for the use of subsequent signers, and shall print at the top of each blank a description of the proposed law as such description will appear on the ballot together with the names and residences of the first ten signers.", and inserting in place thereof the words "The secretary of the commonwealth shall provide blanks for the use of subsequent signers, and shall print at the top of each blank a fair, concise summary of the proposed law as such summary will appear on the ballot together with the names and residences of the first ten signers."

SECTION 3. Section four of that part of said Article XLVIII, under the heading "THE REFERENDUM. *III. Referendum Petitions.*", is hereby amended by striking out the words "The secretary of the commonwealth shall provide blanks for the use of subsequent signers, and shall print at the top of each blank a description of the proposed law as such description will appear on the ballot together with the names and residences of the first ten signers.", and inserting in place thereof the words "The secretary of the commonwealth shall provide blanks for the use of subsequent signers, and shall print at the top of each blank a fair, concise summary of the proposed law as such summary will appear on the ballot together with the names and residences of the first ten signers."

SECTION 4. Said Article XLVIII is hereby further amended by striking out, under the heading "GENERAL PROVISIONS", all of subheading "*III. Form of Ballot.*" and all of subheading "*IV. Information for Voters.*", and inserting in place thereof the following: —

III. Form of Ballot.

A fair, concise summary, as determined by the attorney general, subject to such provision as may be made by law, of each proposed amendment to the constitution, and each law submitted to the people, shall be printed on the ballot, and the secretary of the commonwealth shall give each question a number and cause such question, except as otherwise authorized herein, to be printed on the ballot in the following form: —

In the case of an amendment to the constitution: Do you approve of the adoption of an amendment to the constitution summarized below, (here state, in distinctive type, whether approved or disapproved by the general court, and by what vote thereon)?

YES.	
NO.	

(Set forth summary here)

In the case of a law: Do you approve of a law summarized below, (here state, in distinctive type, whether approved or disapproved by the general court, and by what vote thereon)?

YES.	
NO.	

(Set forth summary here)

IV. Information for Voters.

The secretary of the commonwealth shall cause to be printed and sent to each registered voter in the commonwealth the full text of every measure to be submitted to the people, together with a copy of the legislative committee's majority and minority reports, if there be such, with the names of the majority and minority members thereon, a statement of the votes of the general court on the measure, and a fair, concise summary of the measure as such summary will appear on the ballot; and shall, in such manner as may be provided by law, cause to be prepared and sent to the voters other information and arguments for and against the measure.

IN JOINT SESSION, July 8, 1941.

The foregoing legislative amendment of the Constitution is agreed to in joint session of the two houses of the General Court, the said amendment having received the affirmative votes of a majority of all the members elected; and it is referred to the next General Court in accordance with a provision of the Constitution.

IRVING N. HAYDEN,
Clerk of the Joint Session.

IN JOINT SESSION, May 12, 1943.

Certified to the secretary of the commonwealth for submission to the people at the next state election.

The foregoing legislative amendment is agreed to in joint session of the two houses, the said amendment having received the affirmative votes of a majority of all the members elected; and this fact is hereby certified to the Secretary of the Commonwealth, in accordance with a provision of the Constitution.

IRVING N. HAYDEN,
Clerk of the Joint Session.

The Commonwealth of Massachusetts

IN THE YEAR ONE THOUSAND NINE HUNDRED AND FORTY-ONE.

PROPOSAL FOR A LEGISLATIVE AMENDMENT OF THE CONSTITUTION RESTORING ANNUAL SESSIONS OF THE GENERAL COURT AND AN ANNUAL BUDGET.

A joint session of the Senate and House of Representatives hereby declares it to be expedient to alter the Constitution by the adoption of the following Article of Amendment, to the end that it may become a part of the Constitution, if similarly agreed to in a joint session of the next General Court and approved by the people at the state election next following:

Proposed amendment to the constitution restoring annual sessions of the general court and an annual budget.

ARTICLE OF AMENDMENT.

Article LXXII of the amendments to the constitution providing for biennial sessions of the general court and a biennial budget is hereby annulled, and all provisions of this constitution and of the amendments thereto which were annulled or affected by said Article shall have the same force and effect as though said Article had not been adopted.

IN JOINT SESSION, July 8, 1941.

The foregoing legislative amendment of the Constitution is agreed to in joint session of the two houses of the General Court, the said amendment having received the affirmative votes of a majority of all the members elected; and it is referred to the next General Court in accordance with a provision of the Constitution.

IRVING N. HAYDEN,
Clerk of the Joint Session.

IN JOINT SESSION, May 12, 1943.

The foregoing legislative amendment is agreed to in joint session of the two houses, the said amendment having received the affirmative votes of a majority of all the members elected; and this fact is hereby certified to the Secretary of the Commonwealth, in accordance with a provision of the Constitution.

Certified to the secretary of the commonwealth for submission to the people at the next state election.

IRVING N. HAYDEN,
Clerk of the Joint Session.

The Commonwealth of Massachusetts

IN THE YEAR ONE THOUSAND NINE HUNDRED AND FORTY-ONE.

PROPOSAL FOR A LEGISLATIVE AMENDMENT OF THE CONSTITUTION PROVIDING FOR ABSENT VOTING BY QUALIFIED VOTERS WHO BY REASON OF PHYSICAL DISABILITY ARE UNABLE TO VOTE IN PERSON.

Proposed amendment to the constitution providing for absent voting by qualified voters who by reason of physical disability are unable to vote in person.

A joint session of the Senate and House of Representatives hereby declares it to be expedient to alter the Constitution by the adoption of the following Article of Amendment, to the end that it may become a part of the Constitution, if similarly agreed to in a joint session of the next General Court and approved by the people at the state election next following:

ARTICLE OF AMENDMENT.

Article XLV of the articles of amendment is hereby annulled and the following is adopted in place thereof: —

Article XLV. The general court shall have power to provide by law for voting, in the choice of any officer to be elected or upon any question submitted at an election, by qualified voters of the commonwealth who, at the time of such an election, are absent from the city or town of which they are inhabitants or are unable by reason of physical disability to cast their votes in person at the polling places.

IN JOINT SESSION, July 8, 1941.

The foregoing legislative amendment of the Constitution is agreed to in joint session of the two houses of the General Court, the said amendment having received the affirmative votes of a majority of all the members elected; and it is referred to the next General Court in accordance with a provision of the Constitution.

IRVING N. HAYDEN,
Clerk of the Joint Session.

IN JOINT SESSION, May 27, 1943.

Certified to the secretary of the commonwealth for submission to the people at the next state election.

The foregoing legislative amendment is agreed to in joint session of the two houses, the said amendment having received the affirmative votes of a majority of all the members elected; and this fact is hereby certified to the Secretary of the Commonwealth, in accordance with a provision of the Constitution.

IRVING N. HAYDEN,
Clerk of the Joint Session.

The Commonwealth of Massachusetts

IN THE YEAR ONE THOUSAND NINE HUNDRED AND FORTY-THREE.

PROPOSAL FOR A LEGISLATIVE AMENDMENT OF THE CONSTITUTION PROVIDING THAT THE GENERAL COURT MAY PRESCRIBE A RETIREMENT AGE FOR JUDGES.

A joint session of the Senate and House of Representatives hereby declares it to be expedient to alter the Constitution by the adoption of the following Article of Amendment, to the end that it may become a part of the Constitution, if similarly agreed to in a joint session of the next General Court and approved by the people at the state election next following:

Proposed amendment to the constitution providing that the general court may prescribe a retirement age for judges.

ARTICLE OF AMENDMENT.

SECTION 1. Article LVIII of the articles of amendment to the constitution is hereby annulled and the following is adopted in place thereof: —

Article LVIII. Article I of Chapter III of Part the Second of the constitution is hereby amended by the addition of the following words: — and provided also that the governor, with the consent of the council, may after due notice and hearing retire them because of advanced age or mental or physical disability and provided also that the legislature, by a vote, taken by the yeas and nays, of two-thirds of each house of the general court present and voting thereon, may prescribe a compulsory retirement age for all judicial officers. Any such retirement shall be subject to any provisions made by law as to pensions or allowances payable to such officers upon their voluntary retirement.

SECTION 2. This article shall apply to all judicial officers in office upon the date of its adoption.

IN JOINT SESSION, May 12, 1943.

The foregoing legislative amendment of the Constitution is agreed to in joint session of the two houses of the General Court, the said amendment having received the affirmative votes of a majority of all the members elected; and it is referred to the next General Court in accordance with a provision of the Constitution.

Certified to the secretary of the commonwealth and referred to the next general court.

IRVING N. HAYDEN,
Clerk of the Joint Session.

The Commonwealth of Massachusetts

OFFICE OF THE SECRETARY,
BOSTON, September 28, 1943.

Petition filed requesting referendum on chapter 267, Acts of 1943.

Pursuant to the provisions of Article XLVIII of the Amendments to the Constitution, "The Referendum. III. Referendum Petitions. Section 4", a petition was filed in this office June 14, 1943, by the required number of qualified voters, asking for a referendum on Chapter 267, Acts of 1943, entitled, "An Act repealing the provisions of law authorizing the licensing and conducting of the game commonly called beano", approved May 14, 1943, and requesting that said law be repealed.

Submission to people.

Said petition was completed by the filing in this office August 12, 1943, of more than a sufficient number (12,260) of subsequent signatures of qualified voters of the Commonwealth. Said law will be submitted to the people at the state election November 7, 1944, for their approval or disapproval.

FREDERIC W. COOK,
Secretary of the Commonwealth.

NUMBER OF ACTS AND RESOLVES APPROVED, AND LIST OF ACTS AND RESOLVES VETOED BY THE GOVERNOR AND PASSED OVER HIS VETO AND ACTS DECLARED EMERGENCY LAWS BY THE GOVERNOR UNDER AUTHORITY OF THE CONSTITUTION.

The general court, during its biennial session held in 1943, passed 570 Acts and 72 Resolves, which received executive approval.

The governor returned 22 Acts and 4 Resolves with his objections thereto in writing. Upon 20 Acts and 3 Resolves his objections were sustained.

Twenty (20) Acts entitled, respectively, "An Act authorizing the town of Bedford to vote at its current annual town meeting on the question of granting licenses for the sale in said town of alcoholic beverages in packages"; "An Act to authorize deductions from the wages or salaries of employees of counties, districts and municipalities of the commonwealth for the purpose of making certain payments to credit unions of such employees"; "An Act providing that applicants for examination for admission to the bar shall not be restricted as to the number of examinations which they may take"; "An Act further regulating the establishment of the salaries of court officers in attendance upon the superior court in Suffolk county"; "An Act establishing the compensation of special justices of district courts, other than the municipal court of the city of Boston, and of the Boston juvenile court"; "An Act authorizing the city of Boston to pay a sum of money to the father of Kenneth Baldassari"; "An Act partially exempting sales of shares and securities of certain co-operative corporations from the sale of securities law, so called"; "An Act authorizing the city of Somerville to pay an annuity to the widow of Patrick Brady, a former employee in the sanitary department of said city"; "An Act authorizing the city of Peabody to increase the pension of John F. Ward, a former employee in the electric light department of said city"; "An Act relative to the termination, upon their honorable discharge from the armed forces of the United States, of the sentences of certain persons entering such forces during the present war while on parole from certain state institutions"; "An Act authorizing the city of Boston to pay certain compensation to John A. Curley of Boston"; "An Act prohibiting the increasing of the original sentence of a surrendered person"; "An Act authorizing the county of Bristol to increase the retirement allowance of James W. Wilding'; "An Act relative to the enforcement of the laws concerning the manufacture and sale of meat sausages, to the sale of unwholesome food, and to prosecutions for violation of the food and drug law, so called"; "An Act placing under civil service certain employees at institutions under the control of the departments of mental health, public health and correction"; "An Act providing for the reimbursement by the commonwealth of the town of Norfolk for tuition and transportation furnished by said town to school children whose parents are state employees and reside on state property in said town"; "An Act relative to the time at which compensation shall begin to be paid under the workmen's compensation law to certain employees of the commonwealth and of certain cities, towns and districts thereof"; "An Act providing for the restoring of Ethel S. Greene to certain benefits of the state retirement system"; "An Act authorizing the town of Swampscott to increase the retirement allowance of Simeon J. Strong, formerly employed by said town as a school janitor"; "An Act temporarily increasing the salaries of the justices, special justices, clerks and assistant clerks of the district courts in the county of Suffolk, other than the municipal court of the city of Boston"; and three (3) Resolves entitled, respectively, "Resolve providing for an investigation by the department of public utilities relative to the advisability and feasibility of abolishing certain grade crossings in the city of Cambridge"; "Resolve in favor of Forest C. Rowell of Haverhill" and "Resolve providing for an investigation during the recess of the general court by the committee on public welfare relative to the re-opening of the nurses' training school at the Tewksbury state hospital and infirmary" were passed and laid before the governor for his approval; were returned by him with his objections thereto, to the branch in which they respectively originated; were reconsidered, and the vote being taken on their passage, the objections of the governor thereto notwithstanding, they were rejected, and said acts and resolves thereby became void.

Two (2) Acts entitled, respectively, "An Act relative to the handling, transportation and delivery of fish and perishable foodstuffs at wholesale on the Lord's day" (Chapter 473); "An Act relative to the aiding of blind persons by the division of the blind" (Chapter 526) and one (1) Resolve entitled "Resolve in favor of the widow of the late Walter R. McDonald, a former member of the department of public safety doing police duty" (Chapter 61) were returned by him with his objections thereto, to the branch in which they respectively originated; were reconsidered, agreeably to the provisions of the constitution, and the vote being taken on their passage, the objections of the governor thereto notwithstanding, they were passed, and said acts and resolve have thereby the force of law.

Three (3) Acts entitled, respectively, "An Act relative to

the furnishing of ballot boxes to cities and towns for election purposes" (Chapter 240); "An Act repealing the provisions of law authorizing the licensing and conducting of the game commonly called beano" (Chapter 267) and "An Act temporarily restoring certain mortality tables and rates of interest for the teachers' retirement system" (Chapter 496) were declared to be emergency laws by the governor in accordance with the provisions of the forty-eighth amendment to the Constitution "The Referendum. II. Emergency Measures". Said Chapter 240 thereby took effect at 12.02 P.M. on June 15, 1943; said Chapter 267 at 12.55 P.M. on June 15, 1943 and said Chapter 496 at 10.08 A.M. on July 1, 1943.

The general court was prorogued on Saturday, June 12, 1943, at midnight, the session having occupied 158 days.

RETURN OF VOTES ON QUESTION NO. 1, BEING AN INITIATIVE PETITION, SUBMITTED UNDER THE PROVISIONS OF ARTICLE XLVIII OF THE AMENDMENTS TO THE CONSTITUTION TO THE VOTERS OF THE COMMONWEALTH AT THE STATE ELECTION HELD NOVEMBER 3, 1942.

Question No. 1 — Law Proposed by Initiative Petition.

Shall the proposed measure which provides that the present statutes which make it a crime punishable by fine or imprisonment knowingly to advertise, print, publish, distribute or circulate any matter containing reference to any person from whom or place where any drug, instrument or means whatever, or any advice or information may be obtained, for the purpose of preventing pregnancy, or to sell, lend, give away, exhibit, offer or advertise any drug, medicine, instrument or other article for the prevention of conception, or to write or print information of any kind stating when, where, how, of whom, or by what means such article can be obtained, or to manufacture or make such article, shall not apply to treatment or prescription given to married persons for protection of life or health by or under the direction of registered physicians nor to teaching in chartered medical schools nor to publication or sale of medical treatises or journals, which was disapproved in the House of Representatives by a vote of 77 in the affirmative and 133 in the negative and in the Senate by a vote of 16 in the affirmative and 18 in the negative, *be approved?*

County of Barnstable.

Cities and Towns.	Yes.	No.	Blanks.	Total Ballots.
Barnstable	1,066	871	613	2,550
Bourne	473	372	332	1,177
Brewster	132	55	113	300
Chatham	301	214	279	794
Dennis	358	192	269	819
Eastham	70	39	82	191
Falmouth	732	698	420	1,850
Harwich	377	222	217	816
Mashpee	58	28	57	143
Orleans	271	111	159	541
Provincetown	289	419	112	820
Sandwich	213	205	161	579
Truro	91	86	48	225
Wellfleet	124	100	109	333
Yarmouth	382	243	228	853
Totals	4,937	3,855	3,199	11,991

County of Berkshire.

Cities and Towns.	Yes.	No.	Blanks.	Total Ballots.
Adams	1,047	2,174	1,123	4,344
Alford	25	12	14	51
Becket	73	50	44	167
Cheshire	203	204	115	522
Clarksburg	99	195	119	413
Dalton	998	595	304	1,897
Egremont	90	49	69	208
Florida	20	49	25	94
Great Barrington	881	800	684	2,365
Hancock	49	32	54	135
Hinsdale	184	136	102	422

County of Berkshire — Concluded.

Cities and Towns.	Yes.	No.	Blanks.	Total Ballots.
Lanesborough	272	126	113	511
Lee	503	639	319	1,461
Lenox	416	403	197	1,016
Monterey	76	34	51	161
Mount Washington	17	10	9	36
New Ashford	17	3	14	34
New Marlborough	123	64	71	258
NORTH ADAMS	1,544	3,911	1,459	6,914
Otis	56	31	40	127
Peru	20	8	12	40
PITTSFIELD	7,493	6,841	3,474	17,808
Richmond	121	41	34	196
Sandisfield	44	20	65	129
Savoy	25	34	52	111
Sheffield	251	122	150	523
Stockbridge	289	220	107	616
Tyringham	50	9	13	72
Washington	32	12	17	61
West Stockbridge	116	95	107	318
Williamstown	533	487	256	1,276
Windsor	40	22	33	95
Totals	15,707	17,428	9,246	42,381

County of Bristol.

Cities and Towns.	Yes.	No.	Blanks.	Total Ballots.
Acushnet	309	440	255	1,004
ATTLEBORO	2,211	3,029	1,482	6,722
Berkley	90	87	69	246
Dartmouth	912	746	515	2,173
Dighton	292	341	207	840
Easton	771	691	473	1,935
Fairhaven	1,159	1,127	579	2,865
FALL RIVER	8,259	20,095	6,691	35,045
Freetown	248	120	130	498
Mansfield	738	812	545	2,095
NEW BEDFORD	9,133	15,611	6,785	31,529
North Attleborough	1,262	1,891	774	3,927
Norton	393	341	209	943
Raynham	238	233	169	640
Rehoboth	313	233	198	744
Seekonk	462	400	331	1,193
Somerset	607	907	371	1,885
Swansea	542	644	274	1,460
TAUNTON	2,616	5,325	2,547	10,488
Westport	398	424	273	1,095
Totals	30,953	53,497	22,877	107,327

County of Dukes County.

Cities and Towns.	Yes.	No.	Blanks.	Total Ballots.
Chilmark	49	16	22	87
Edgartown	165	126	89	380
Gay Head	8	8	11	27
Gosnold	12	11	11	34
Oak Bluffs	162	188	134	484
Tisbury	215	133	113	461
West Tisbury	38	10	22	70
Totals	649	492	402	1,543

County of Essex.

Cities and Towns.	Yes.	No.	Blanks.	Total Ballots.
Amesbury	895	1,858	728	3,481
Andover	2,033	1,538	668	4,239
BEVERLY	3,851	3,629	1,881	9,361
Boxford	148	72	39	259
Danvers	1,460	1,491	670	3,621
Essex	203	120	112	435
Georgetown	352	232	209	793

County of Essex — Concluded.

Cities and Towns.	Yes.	No.	Blanks.	Total Ballots.
GLOUCESTER	1,917	1,911	1,520	5,348
Groveland	347	277	150	774
Hamilton	477	291	111	879
HAVERHILL	4,761	6,154	2,516	13,431
Ipswich	747	817	387	1,951
LAWRENCE	5,802	15,229	5,853	26,884
LYNN	11,267	16,132	5,499	32,898
Lynnfield	624	320	201	1,145
Manchester	451	365	201	1,017
Marblehead	2,703	1,518	606	4,827
Merrimac	398	266	256	920
Methuen	2,763	3,110	1,220	7,093
Middleton	233	174	120	527
Nahant	378	391	164	933
Newbury	240	173	147	560
NEWBURYPORT	1,619	2,157	1,781	5,557
North Andover	1,257	1,244	493	2,994
PEABODY	1,591	3,477	1,317	6,385
Rockport	629	342	276	1,247
Rowley	249	204	151	604
SALEM	3,845	10,027	2,501	16,373
Salisbury	289	235	261	785
Saugus	2,195	1,764	764	4,723
Swampscott	2,383	1,695	583	4,661
Topsfield	258	90	59	407
Wenham	368	157	86	611
West Newbury	216	115	99	429
Totals	56,949	77,575	31,628	166,152

County of Franklin.

Cities and Towns.	Yes.	No.	Blanks.	Total Ballots.
Ashfield	119	59	62	240
Bernardston	134	74	75	283
Buckland	228	230	148	606
Charlemont	104	84	80	268
Colrain	167	164	88	419
Conway	151	72	82	305
Deerfield	337	246	188	771
Erving	108	122	70	300
Gill	156	40	73	269
Greenfield	2,581	1,825	777	5,183
Hawley	15	20	12	47
Heath	29	35	15	79
Leverett	54	28	28	110
Leyden	24	25	34	83
Monroe	29	23	19	71
Montague	757	888	491	2,136
New Salem	50	33	36	119
Northfield	327	150	105	582
Orange	664	606	592	1,862
Rowe	26	12	19	57
Shelburne	351	178	146	675
Shutesbury	16	21	14	51
Sunderland	144	54	45	243
Warwick	61	38	37	136
Wendell	34	21	29	84
Whately	105	73	107	285
Totals	6,771	5,121	3,372	15,264

County of Hampden.

Cities and Towns.	Yes.	No.	Blanks.	Total Ballots.
Agawam	951	877	396	2,224
Blandford	105	45	31	181
Brimfield	150	96	68	314
Chester	146	108	102	356
CHICOPEE	3,290	7,420	3,045	13,755
East Longmeadow	642	438	222	1,302
Granville	80	44	58	182
Hampden	233	138	83	454
Holland	52	33	17	102

County of Hampden — Concluded.

Cities and Towns.	Yes.	No.	Blanks.	Total Ballots.
HOLYOKE	5,754	10,755	3,456	19,965
Longmeadow	1,685	632	249	2,566
Ludlow	754	950	341	2,045
Monson	425	467	306	1,198
Montgomery	13	19	9	41
Palmer	746	1,405	694	2,845
Russell	145	140	105	390
Southwick	183	97	110	390
SPRINGFIELD	20,546	22,775	8,064	51,385
Tolland	15	1	15	31
Wales	46	31	29	106
West Springfield	2,374	2,216	784	5,374
WESTFIELD	2,215	2,507	1,325	6,047
Wilbraham	491	384	152	1,027
Totals	41,041	51,578	19,661	112,280

County of Hampshire.

Cities and Towns.	Yes.	No.	Blanks.	Total Ballots.
Amherst	1,473	684	274	2,431
Belchertown	317	268	155	740
Chesterfield	77	23	27	127
Cummington	112	33	39	184
Easthampton	1,035	1,366	553	2,954
Goshen	60	18	31	109
Granby	144	131	69	344
Hadley	239	220	110	569
Hatfield	148	252	124	524
Huntington	121	168	87	376
Middlefield	22	15	9	46
NORTHAMPTON	3,160	3,211	1,104	7,475
Pelham	107	17	23	147
Plainfield	32	18	30	80
South Hadley	1,116	1,039	353	2,508
Southampton	185	96	69	350
Ware	554	1,157	739	2,450
Westhampton	65	28	18	111
Williamsburg	306	253	112	671
Worthington	75	22	26	123
Totals	9,348	9,019	3,952	22,319

County of Middlesex.

Cities and Towns.	Yes.	No.	Blanks.	Total Ballots.
Acton	510	331	211	1,052
Arlington	5,541	7,756	1,611	14,908
Ashby	186	47	51	284
Ashland	491	460	207	1,158
Ayer	366	390	167	923
Bedford	367	284	138	789
Belmont	4,942	4,953	1,024	10,919
Billerica	886	1,131	361	2,378
Boxborough	61	37	29	127
Burlington	287	283	173	743
CAMBRIDGE	11,042	19,004	4,719	34,765
Carlisle	133	55	50	238
Chelmsford	1,103	1,079	489	2,671
Concord	1,384	1,093	392	2,869
Dracut	459	1,100	329	1,888
Dunstable	62	31	17	110
EVERETT	4,467	7,110	2,512	14,089
Framingham	2,694	3,851	1,279	7,824
Groton	479	410	207	1,096
Holliston	465	446	196	1,107
Hopkinton	431	555	190	1,176
Hudson	708	1,395	511	2,614
Lexington	2,353	1,548	478	4,379
Lincoln	467	175	62	704
Littleton	278	154	112	544

County of Middlesex — Concluded.

Cities and Towns.	Yes.	No.	Blanks.	Total Ballots.
LOWELL	6,859	21,880	5,507	34,246
MALDEN	6,329	8,443	3,591	18,363
MARLBOROUGH	1,571	3,683	1,438	6,692
Maynard	790	1,099	493	2,382
MEDFORD	6,941	12,397	3,226	22,564
MELROSE	5,930	3,808	1,300	11,038
Natick	1,954	2,638	894	5,486
NEWTON	14,515	11,233	2,977	28,725
North Reading	391	425	237	1,053
Pepperell	345	348	190	883
Reading	2,301	1,564	580	4,445
Sherborn	187	100	52	339
Shirley	233	289	142	664
SOMERVILLE	8,920	18,318	5,405	32,643
Stoneham	1,619	1,611	591	3,821
Stow	202	123	90	415
Sudbury	396	196	104	696
Tewksbury	382	485	168	1,035
Townsend	333	179	177	689
Tyngsborough	185	184	81	450
Wakefield	2,513	2,647	1,075	6,235
WALTHAM	5,033	7,089	2,339	14,461
Watertown	4,101	6,579	1,674	12,354
Wayland	663	467	275	1,405
Westford	356	525	228	1,109
Weston	1,106	595	168	1,869
Wilmington	540	613	245	1,398
Winchester	3,026	2,130	614	5,770
WOBURN	1,585	3,776	973	6,334
Totals	119,468	167,102	50,349	336,919

County of Nantucket.

Nantucket	338	296	508	1,142

County of Norfolk.

Avon	267	346	160	773
Bellingham	200	626	272	1,098
Braintree	3,018	2,426	1,053	6,497
Brookline	10,871	6,641	2,664	20,176
Canton	824	1,010	329	2,163
Cohasset	624	459	178	1,261
Dedham	2,467	2,757	1,005	6,229
Dover	343	157	79	579
Foxborough	666	624	357	1,647
Franklin	654	1,074	579	2,307
Holbrook	586	541	292	1,419
Medfield	354	287	220	861
Medway	389	471	299	1,159
Millis	298	382	249	929
Milton	3,635	4,660	882	9,177
Needham	3,221	1,471	745	5,437
Norfolk	208	152	88	448
Norwood	1,684	2,657	723	5,064
Plainville	302	218	207	727
QUINCY	10,004	10,994	4,616	25,614
Randolph	864	1,252	465	2,581
Sharon	766	479	290	1,535
Stoughton	947	1,361	491	2,799
Walpole	1,171	1,053	520	2,744
Wellesley	3,967	1,709	628	6,304
Westwood	885	490	226	1,601
Weymouth	3,116	3,309	1,346	7,771
Wrentham	368	298	250	916
Totals	52,699	47,904	19,213	119,816

County of Plymouth.

Cities and Towns.	Yes.	No.	Blanks.	Total Ballots.
Abington	793	850	356	1,999
Bridgewater	733	597	414	1,744
BROCKTON	7,019	10,039	3,902	20,960
Carver	112	64	54	230
Duxbury	508	199	154	861
East Bridgewater	558	422	273	1,253
Halifax	125	78	44	247
Hanover	361	240	168	769
Hanson	279	193	146	618
Hingham	1,535	1,050	265	2,850
Hull	306	531	178	1,015
Kingston	349	274	190	813
Lakeville	182	129	118	429
Marion	328	190	173	691
Marshfield	503	241	178	922
Mattapoisett	214	173	144	531
Middleborough	1,069	1,022	671	2,762
Norwell	403	200	135	738
Pembroke	308	120	92	520
Plymouth	1,501	1,302	868	3,671
Plympton	76	37	29	142
Rochester	107	81	49	237
Rockland	740	1,340	415	2,495
Scituate	752	559	274	1,585
Wareham	641	650	443	1,734
West Bridgewater	416	324	207	947
Whitman	917	1,221	555	2,693
Totals	20,835	22,126	10,495	53,456

County of Suffolk.

Cities and Towns.	Yes.	No.	Blanks.	Total Ballots.
BOSTON	70,706	139,307	38,929	248,942
CHELSEA	3,461	4,686	2,649	10,796
REVERE	2,719	4,919	1,509	9,147
Winthrop	2,385	3,078	788	6,251
Totals	79,271	151,990	43,875	275,136

County of Worcester.

Cities and Towns.	Yes.	No.	Blanks.	Total Ballots.
Ashburnham	348	238	140	726
Athol	1,200	1,449	703	3,352
Auburn	1,082	914	448	2,444
Barre	423	402	237	1,062
Berlin	169	129	86	384
Blackstone	231	1,108	280	1,619
Bolton	121	75	69	265
Boylston	228	91	67	386
Brookfield	206	136	91	433
Charlton	263	263	186	712
Clinton	1,287	2,908	1,173	5,368
Douglas	308	458	116	882
Dudley	259	588	223	1,070
East Brookfield	88	128	38	254
FITCHBURG	4,835	7,329	2,332	14,496
GARDNER	2,278	2,697	1,313	6,288
Grafton	705	848	388	1,941
Hardwick	209	368	179	756
Harvard	206	111	67	384
Holden	1,073	463	232	1,768
Hopedale	476	523	244	1,243
Hubbardston	173	53	64	290
Lancaster	395	280	154	829
Leicester	528	792	208	1,528
LEOMINSTER	2,216	3,570	1,312	7,098
Lunenburg	448	233	151	832
Mendon	190	215	105	510
Milford	1,057	2,188	1,457	4,702
Millbury	666	941	313	1,920
Millville	60	323	120	503
New Braintree	27	60	25	112

County of Worcester — Concluded.

Cities and Towns.	Yes.	No.	Blanks.	Total Ballots.
North Brookfield	295	461	192	948
Northborough	424	366	127	917
Northbridge	1,061	1,903	557	3,521
Oakham	74	53	27	154
Oxford	432	581	249	1,262
Paxton	195	85	42	322
Petersham	167	67	76	310
Phillipston	54	24	27	105
Princeton	118	48	60	226
Royalston	102	55	51	208
Rutland	260	220	93	573
Shrewsbury	1,288	923	333	2,544
Southborough	350	310	118	778
Southbridge	947	2,616	773	4,336
Spencer	507	1,069	364	1,940
Sterling	370	160	116	646
Sturbridge	181	230	117	528
Sutton	264	370	131	765
Templeton	527	377	278	1,182
Upton	308	417	209	934
Uxbridge	575	1,169	440	2,184
Warren	353	504	348	1,205
Webster	943	2,620	819	4,382
West Boylston	374	166	113	653
West Brookfield	187	174	111	472
Westborough	799	793	316	1,908
Westminster	311	117	111	539
Winchendon	620	689	425	1,734
WORCESTER	23,157	28,628	9,776	61,561
Totals	56,998	75,076	28,920	160,994

Aggregate of Votes.

Counties.	Yes.	No.	Blanks.	Total Ballots.
BARNSTABLE	4,937	3,855	3,199	11,991
BERKSHIRE	15,707	17,428	9,246	42,381
BRISTOL	30,953	53,497	22,877	107,327
DUKES COUNTY	649	492	402	1,543
ESSEX	56,949	77,575	31,628	166,152
FRANKLIN	6,771	5,121	3,372	15,264
HAMPDEN	41,041	51,578	19,661	112,280
HAMPSHIRE	9,348	9,019	3,952	22,319
MIDDLESEX	119,468	167,102	50,349	336,919
NANTUCKET	338	296	508	1,142
NORFOLK	52,699	47,904	19,213	119,816
PLYMOUTH	20,835	22,126	10,495	53,456
SUFFOLK	79,271	151,990	43,875	275,136
WORCESTER	56,998	75,076	28,920	160,994
Totals	495,964	683,059	247,697	1,426,720

APPENDIX

The following table and indexes have been prepared by FERNALD HUTCHINS, Esq., and HENRY D. WIGGIN, Esq., counsel, respectively, to the Senate and House of Representatives, in accordance with section fifty-one of chapter three of the General Laws, as amended.

TABLE

SHOWING

TO WHAT EXTENT THE GENERAL LAWS OF THE COMMONWEALTH, AS APPEARING IN THE TERCENTENARY EDITION, HAVE BEEN AFFECTED BY LEGISLATION ENACTED BY THE GENERAL COURT SINCE JANUARY FIRST, NINETEEN HUNDRED AND THIRTY-TWO.* †

Chapter 1. — Jurisdiction of the Commonwealth and of the United States.

SECT. 3 revised, 1933, 278 § 1.

Chapter 2. — Arms, Great Seal and Other Emblems of the Commonwealth.

SECT. 8 added, 1941, 121 (designating the American elm as the state tree).

SECT. 9 added, 1941, 121 (designating the Chickadee as the state bird).

Chapter 3. — The General Court.

SECT. 5 amended, 1937, 364 § 1; 1939, 508 § 1.

SECT. 6 revised, 1937, 364 § 2; amended, 1939, 424 § 1; repealed, 1943, 549 § 2. (See 1939, 424 § 3.)

SECT. 6A added, 1939, 424 § 2 (imposing restrictions on the granting of authority to use the designation of junior college); repealed, 1943, 549 § 2. (See 1939, 424 § 3.)

SECT. 7 revised, 1937, 364 § 3; first sentence amended, 1943, 549 § 2A.

SECT. 9 revised, 1937, 236 § 1; 1941, 307 § 1; amended, 1941, 600 § 1. (See 1941, 307 § 2; 1941, 600 § 2.)

SECT. 11 repealed, 1937, 236 § 2.

SECT. 12 revised, 1937, 360 § 1; 1943, 260 § 1. (See 1937, 360 §§ 3–5; 1943, 260 § 3.)

SECT. 13 revised, 1937, 360 § 2; amended, 1941, 230; revised, 1943, 260 § 2. (See 1937, 360 §§ 3–5; 1943, 260 § 3.)

SECT. 18 amended, 1941, 433 § 1; 1943, 104. (See 1941, 433 § 4.)

SECT. 19 amended, 1935, 210.

---

* For table showing changes in legislation made during the years 1921 to 1931, inclusive, see Table of Changes contained in pages 485–597 of the Acts and Resolves of 1932.

† References in this table are to the Tercentenary Edition of the General Laws, as most recently amended, unless otherwise specified.

SECT. 20 revised, 1939, 508 § 2; amended, 1941, 433 § 2. (See 1941, 433 § 4.)
SECT. 20A added, 1937, 189 (relative to the purchase of uniforms for the sergeant-at-arms, doorkeepers, assistant doorkeepers, general court officers and pages of the general court).
SECT. 22 amended, 1939, 508 § 3.
SECT. 23 revised, 1941, 347.
SECT. 46 amended, 1939, 508 § 4.
SECT. 47 amended, 1939, 508 § 5.
SECT. 49 amended, 1939, 508 § 6.
SECT. 51 amended, 1939, 508 § 7.
SECT. 53 revised, 1939, 376 § 1. (See 1939, 376 § 2.)

Chapter 4. — Statutes.

SECT. 5 revised, 1935, 69.
SECT. 7, clause Ninth revised, 1941, 509 § 1; clause Eighteenth amended, 1934, 283; 1935, 26; 1936, 180; 1937, 38; 1938, 245; 1941, 91 § 1. (See 1941, 509 § 9.)
SECT. 10. Affected, 1942, 5.

Chapter 5. — Printing and Distribution of Laws and Public Documents.

As to the distribution of the Tercentenary Edition of the General Laws, see 1932, Resolve 53; 1933, Resolve 19; 1935, Resolve 18; 1937, Resolve 16; 1939, Resolve 19; 1941, Resolve 19.
SECT. 1, last paragraph revised, 1932, 254; two paragraphs added at end, 1937, 373; section revised, 1938, 419; amended, 1941, 428.
SECT. 2, paragraphs (4) and (6) revised, 1939, 508 § 8.
SECT. 3, paragraphs in twelfth to forty-second lines, amended, 1938, 196; 1941, 351 § 1.
SECT. 6 amended, 1939, 508 § 9; revised, 1943, 344 § 1.
SECT. 9 amended, 1933, 245 § 1.
SECT. 10 revised, 1939, 508 § 10.
SECT. 11, paragraph in thirteenth line revised, 1941, 329.
SECT. 18 amended, 1935, 226 § 1; revised, 1943, 313.

Chapter 6. — The Governor, Lieutenant Governor and Council, Certain Officers under the Governor and Council, and State Library.

For temporary legislation establishing an emergency finance board, and defining its powers and duties, see 1933, 49.
For temporary legislation establishing the emergency public works commission, and defining its powers and duties, see 1933, 365, as affected by 1933, 368; term extended, 1935, 380; 1937, 338; 1938, 20, 501 § 3; 1941, 720 § 16; 1943, 517 § 3.
SECT. 3 amended, 1943, 314 § 1. (See 1943, 314 § 2.)
SECT. 8 amended, 1941, 722 § 1; revised, 1943, 348 § 1.
SECT. 12B added, 1932, 14 (relative to the observance of the anniversary of the death of Brigadier General Casimir Pulaski).
SECT. 12C added, 1932, 153 (relative to the observance of the anniversary of the battle of Bunker Hill). (See 1941, 91.)

SECT. 12D added, 1932, 242 (relative to the observance of the anniversary of the Boston Massacre, etc.).

SECT. 12E added, 1934, 191 (relative to the observance of the anniversary of the death of Commodore John Barry).

SECT. 12F added, 1935, 23 (relative to the observance of the anniversary of the battle of New Orleans); amended, 1938, 49.

SECT. 12G added, 1935, 96 (providing for an annual proclamation by the governor relative to American Education Week).

SECT. 12H added, 1935, 148 (relative to the observance of the anniversary of the death of General Marquis de Lafayette).

SECT. 12I added, 1935, 184 (relative to the annual observance of Indian Day); revised, 1939, 56.

SECT. 12J added, 1938, 22 (relative to the annual observance of April nineteenth as Patriots' Day).

SECT. 12K added, 1938, 80 (relative to the annual observance of Evacuation Day, so called).

SECT. 12L added, 1941, 387 (relative to the annual observance of Veteran Firemen's Muster Day).

SECT. 16 amended, 1941, 490 § 1.

SECT. 17 amended, 1932, 305 § 1; 1933, 120 § 1, 336 § 1; 1934, 374 § 1; 1935, 475 § 1; revised, 1939, 393 § 1. (See 1933, 336 § 3.)

SECT. 18 and heading stricken out and new section inserted, under heading "ARMORY COMMISSION", 1937, 300 § 1; sentence added at end, 1941, 19. (See 1937, 300 § 2.)

SECT. 22 amended, 1936, 341 § 1; heading and section amended, 1943, 455 § 1. (See 1936, 341 § 2.)

SECT. 24 amended, 1941, 596 § 1; 1943, 455 § 2.

SECT. 28 amended, 1938, 18.

SECT. 28A amended, 1934, 208 § 1.

SECT. 28E added, 1934, 208 § 2 (relative to the dissemination of information concerning the public bequest fund).

SECT. 31 revised, 1943, 479.

SECT. 32, paragraph added at end, 1937, 227; same paragraph revised, 1938, 473 § 1; same paragraph revised, 1943, 43.

SECT. 42 added, under caption "MILK REGULATION BOARD", 1932, 305 § 2.

SECTS. 43–45 added, 1933, 120 § 2 (relative to the alcoholic beverages control commission).

SECT. 43 amended, 1933, 375 § 1.

SECT. 44, first paragraph revised, 1933, 376 § 1.

SECT. 45 revised, 1941, 596 § 2.

SECTS. 46 and 47 added, 1933, 336 § 2 (relative to the Greylock reservation commission). (See 1933, 336 § 3.)

SECT. 48 added, under caption "STATE RACING COMMISSION", 1934, 374 § 2; last paragraph revised, 1941, 596 § 3.

SECTS. 49–52 added, under caption "STATE PLANNING BOARD", 1935, 475 § 2.

SECT. 49 amended, 1936, 307; 1939, 451 § 1; revised, 1941, 466 § 5. (See 1941, 466 §§ 1–4, 7A, 8.)

SECT. 50A added, 1941, 466 § 7 (relative to the powers and duties of the state planning board formerly exercised by the metropolitan planning division). (See 1941, 466 §§ 1–4, 7A, 8.)

Chapter 7. — Commission on Administration and Finance.

SECT. 6A added, 1941, 433 § 3 (providing for the appointment of the postmaster and assistant postmaster of the central mailing room by the Commission on Administration and Finance). (See 1941, 433 § 4.)

SECT. 22, clause (17) revised, 1933, 353 § 1.

SECT. 23A added, 1933, 353 § 2 (providing a preference in the purchase of supplies and materials by contractors for certain state work in favor of domestic supplies and materials).

SECT. 25A added, 1943, 344 § 2 (authorizing the state purchasing agent to regulate purchases of supplies and transfers thereof from one state agency to another).

SECT. 26 amended, 1939, 451 § 2.

SECT. 33 revised, 1939, 499 § 1.

Chapter 8. — State Superintendent of Buildings, and State House.

SECTS. 1–12 affected, 1935, 327; 1941, 627 § 3.

SECT. 1 revised, 1938, 249 § 1. (See 1938, 249 § 6.)

SECT. 4 amended, 1935, 251; revised, 1937, 84 § 1; 1938, 249 § 2. (See 1937, 84 § 2; 1938, 249 § 6.)

SECT. 5 revised, 1935, 460 § 1; amended, 1938, 387 § 1. (See 1935, 460 § 2; 1938, 387 § 2.)

SECT. 9 amended, 1938, 249 § 3. (See 1938, 249 § 6.)

SECT. 10 amended, 1938, 249 § 4; 1943, 440 § 1. (See 1938, 249 § 6.)

SECT. 10A revised, 1933, 170; 1941, 267; amended, 1943, 440 § 2.

SECT. 12 revised, 1938, 249 § 5. (See 1938, 249 § 6.)

SECT. 17 amended, 1932, 188 § 1; 1933, 199 § 1.

SECT. 18 amended, 1932, 188 § 2; 1933, 199 § 2.

Chapter 9. — Department of the State Secretary.

SECT. 2 revised, 1935, 416; 1939, 283; 1941, 587.

SECT. 6 amended, 1934, 25 § 1.

SECT. 7 amended, 1934, 25 § 2; 1939, 342 § 1.

SECT. 9 amended, 1934, 127.

SECT. 15 amended, 1934, 19.

SECT. 17 amended, 1934, 37; revised, 1936, 31 § 1.

SECT. 20 added, 1935, 402 (regulating the publication and sale of the Massachusetts Reports and of the advance sheets of the opinions and decisions of the Supreme Judicial Court); revised, 1943, 426.

SECTS. 21–25 added, under the caption "COMMISSION ON INTERSTATE CO-OPERATION", 1937, 404 § 1 (establishing a commission on interstate co-operation as successor to the commission on interstate compacts affecting labor and industries and defining its powers and duties, and providing for a commission required to be established under an interstate compact on the minimum wage). (See 1937, 404 §§ 2, 3.)

SECT. 21 amended, 1941, 394 § 1.

SECT. 23 amended, 1941, 394 § 2.

SECT. 25 repealed, 1943, 255 § 2. (See 1943, 255 § 3.)

Chapter 10. — Department of the State Treasurer.

For temporary legislation establishing an emergency finance board, and defining its powers and duties, see 1933, 49.

For temporary legislation establishing the emergency public works commission, and defining its powers and duties, see 1933, 365, as affected by 1933, 368; 1939, 417, 418; term extended, 1935, 380; 1937, 338; 1938, 20, 501 § 3; 1941, 720 § 16; 1943, 517 § 3.

SECT. 5, first sentence revised, 1941, 596 § 4.

SECT. 8 amended, 1932, 180 § 1; revised, 1943, 427 § 1.

SECT. 11 revised, 1939, 499 § 2.

SECT. 17 amended, 1941, 194 § 1.

SECT. 17A added, 1943, 362 § 2 (providing for the receipt and disposal, by the state treasurer, of certain gifts made to the commonwealth for military purposes).

Chapter 11. — Department of the State Auditor.

SECT. 2, first sentence revised, 1941, 596 § 5.

Chapter 12. — Department of the Attorney General, and the District Attorneys.

SECT. 2 amended, 1934, 133 § 1; revised, 1941, 647 § 2. (See 1934, 133 § 2.)

SECT. 3, last sentence amended, 1932, 180 § 2; section amended, 1943, 83 § 1.

SECT. 3B amended, 1933, 318 § 1; 1934, 291 § 1; paragraph inserted after first paragraph, 1943, 409 § 3. (See 1933, 318 § 9; 1934, 291 § 6.)

SECT. 11 amended, 1939, 499 § 3.

SECT. 14, paragraph in lines 5 and 6 revised, 1935, 209; paragraph in lines 7 and 8 revised, 1935, 433 § 1; section revised, 1935, 458 § 1; next to last paragraph revised, 1941, 470 § 1.

SECT. 15 revised, 1935, 458 § 2; paragraph in line 8 revised, 1937, 279 § 1.

SECT. 16, paragraph in lines 9–11 revised, 1935, 433 § 2; section revised, 1935, 458 § 3; paragraph in lines 23 and 24 revised, 1937, 279 § 2; next to last paragraph revised, 1941, 470 § 2.

SECT. 25 amended, 1937, 64 § 1.

Chapter 13. — Department of Civil Service and Registration.

SECT. 1 revised, 1939, 238 § 1. (See 1939, 238 §§ 52–55.)

SECT. 2 revised, 1939, 238 § 2; paragraph inserted after second paragraph, 1941, 403. (See 1939, 238 §§ 52–55.)

SECT. 2A added, 1939, 238 § 3 (relative to the appointment and compensation of civil service commissioners); fourth sentence revised, 1941, 457. (See 1939, 238 §§ 52–55.)

SECT. 3 amended, 1932, 180 § 3; revised, 1939, 238 § 4. (See 1939, 238 §§ 52–55.)

SECT. 4 revised, 1939, 238 § 5.

SECT. 5 revised, 1939, 238 § 6.
SECT. 6 revised, 1939, 238 § 7.
SECT. 8 amended, 1934, 329.
SECT. 10 amended, 1932, 8; 1939, 36.
SECT. 11 amended, 1937, 379.
SECT. 12 repealed, 1937, 425 § 13. (See 1937, 425 § 15.)
SECTS. 12A–12C added, under the heading "BOARD OF REGISTRATION IN CHIROPODY (PODIATRY)", 1937, 425 § 1. (See 1937, 425 §§ 14, 15.)
SECTS. 13–15 and the heading before section 13 stricken out and new sections 13–15D added under heading "BOARD OF REGISTRATION IN NURSING", 1941, 620 § 2. (See 1941, 620 §§ 1, 4–12.)
SECT. 17 revised, 1934, 339 § 1.
SECT. 25 revised, 1941, 596 § 6.
SECT. 29 and its caption stricken out and new section inserted, under the caption "BOARD OF REGISTRATION IN EMBALMING AND FUNERAL DIRECTING", 1936, 407 § 1. (See 1936, 407 §§ 5–8.)
SECT. 31 revised, 1936, 407 § 2. (See 1936, 407 §§ 5–8.)
SECT. 32 revised, 1935, 420 § 1; amended, 1939, 238 § 8. (See 1935, 420 § 2.)
SECT. 36, second paragraph revised, 1941, 596 § 7.
SECT. 39 amended, 1941, 385 § 1. (See 1941, 385 § 2.)
SECT. 40 amended, 1933, 149 § 1; two sentences added at end, 1934, 299 § 1. (See 1934, 299 § 2.)
SECT. 41 amended, 1938, 337 § 1. (See 1938, 337 § 2.)
SECTS. 42–44 added, under caption "BOARD OF REGISTRATION OF HAIRDRESSERS", 1935, 428 § 1. (See 1935, 428 §§ 5, 7.)
SECT. 43 amended, 1937, 385 § 1.
SECTS. 44A–44D added, under caption "BOARD OF REGISTRATION OF ARCHITECTS", 1941, 696 § 1. (See 1941, 696 §§ 3, 4.)
SECTS. 45–47 added, under caption "BOARD OF REGISTRATION OF PROFESSIONAL ENGINEERS AND OF LAND SURVEYORS", 1941, 643 § 1. (See 1941, 643 §§ 3–5.)
SECT. 47 amended, 1941, 722 § 1A.

Chapter 14. — Department of Corporations and Taxation.

SECT. 2 amended, 1943, 316.
SECT. 4 revised, 1941, 596 § 8.

Chapter 15. — Department of Education.

SECT. 3 amended, 1941, 138.
SECT. 3A added, 1943, 549 § 1 (establishing a board of collegiate authority in the department of education).
SECT. 4 revised, 1939, 409 § 2. (See 1939, 409 §§ 1, 5.)
SECT. 5 revised, 1941, 596 § 9.
SECT. 6A amended, 1938, 446 § 13; revised, 1941, 531. (See 1938, 446 § 14.)
SECT. 6B added, 1941, 676 § 1 (relative to the supervisor of guidance and placement). (See 1941, 646.)
SECT. 12 revised, 1935, 367; 1939, 409 § 3. (See 1939, 409 §§ 1, 5.)
SECT. 19 amended, 1942, 1 § 2. (See 1942, 1 § 9.)

SECT. 22. Caption preceding section changed, 1942, 1 § 3; section amended 1942, 1 § 4. (See 1942, 1 § 9.)

Chapter 16. — Department of Public Works.

SECT. 5 revised, 1941, 596 § 10.
SECT. 5A added, 1938, 407 § 1 (establishing a division of waterways in the department of public works). (See 1941, 695 § 14.)
SECT. 6 amended, 1935, 418 § 1; 1939, 393 § 2. (See 1939, 393 § 5.)

Chapter 17. — Department of Public Health.

SECT. 3 revised, 1939, 233 § 1. (See 1939, 233 §§ 2, 3.)
SECT. 4 revised, 1941, 596 § 11; 725 § 1. (See 1941, 725 §§ 4–6.)
SECT. 6 revised, 1941, 725 § 2. (See 1941, 725 §§ 4–6.)
SECT. 7 revised, 1941, 725 § 3. (See 1941, 725 §§ 4–6.)

Chapter 18. — Department of Public Welfare.

SECT. 7 amended, 1935, 311 § 1; revised, 1941, 596 § 12.
SECT. 8 revised, 1941, 351 § 2.
SECT. 9 revised, 1941, 596 § 13.
SECTS. 17 and 18 added, under caption "STATE BOARD OF HOUSING", 1933, 364 § 1 (establishing within the department a state board of housing).
SECT. 17 amended, 1935, 449 § 1; 1938, 485 § 1. (See 1938, 485 § 2.)
SECT. 18 amended, 1935, 449 § 1A; first sentence revised, 1941, 596 § 14.

Chapter 19. — Department of Mental Health.

Name of department of mental diseases changed to department of mental health, 1938, 486 § 1. (See 1938, 486 §§ 21, 22.)
Title revised, 1941, 194 § 2.
SECT. 1 revised, 1938, 486 § 2; 1939, 511 § 1. (See 1938, 486 §§ 1, 21, 22; 1939, 511 § 3.)
SECT. 2 revised, 1938, 486 § 3; 1939, 511 § 2. (See 1938, 486 §§ 21, 22; 1939, 511 § 3.)
SECT. 3 repealed, 1938, 486 § 4.
SECT. 4 revised, 1938, 486 § 5. (See 1938, 486 §§ 21, 22.)
SECT. 4A amended, 1938, 486 § 6. (See 1938, 486 §§ 21, 22.)
SECT. 5 amended, 1935, 314 § 2, 421 § 3. (See 1935, 421 §§ 5, 6.)

Chapter 20. — Department of Agriculture.

SECT. 4 amended, 1933, 74 § 1; revised, 1934, 340 § 1; amended, 1941, 490 § 2; revised, 1941, 596 § 15; amended, 1943, 447. (See 1934, 340 § 18.)
SECT. 6 added, 1934, 340 § 2 (experts and assistants in division of livestock disease control). (See 1934, 340 § 18.)
SECTS. 7–9 added, under caption "DIVISION OF MILK CONTROL", 1941, 691 § 1. (See 1941, 691 §§ 3–6.)
(For prior temporary legislation, see 1934, 376; 1936, 300; 1938, 334; 1939, 413; 1941, 418 § 1; 631 § 1.)

Chapter 21. — Department of Conservation.

SECT. 1 amended, 1934, 340 § 3; revised, 1939, 491 § 1. (See 1934, 340 § 18; 1939, 491 § 12.)

SECT. 3 revised, 1933, 75 § 1; amended, 1934, 340 § 4; revised, 1939, 491 § 2. (See 1934, 340 § 18; 1939, 491 § 12.)

SECTS. 3A and 3B repealed, 1932, 180 § 4.

SECT. 4 revised, 1939, 491 § 3. (See 1939, 491 § 12.)

SECT. 6 revised, 1939, 491 § 4. (See 1939, 491 § 12.)

SECT. 6A inserted, 1941, 599 § 3 (establishing a bureau of law enforcement in the division of fisheries and game). (See 1941, 599 § 4A.)

SECT. 7 revised, 1933, 329 § 3; 1937, 413 § 1. (See 1937, 413 §§ 3, 4.)

SECT. 7A added, 1934, 173 § 1 (establishing the office of state ornithologist in the division of fisheries and game); revised, 1939, 491 § 5. (See 1934, 173 § 2; 1939, 491 § 12.)

SECTS. 7B and 7C added, 1939, 491 § 6 (relative to the division of wildlife research and management). (See 1939, 491 § 12.)

SECT. 8 repealed, 1939, 491 § 7. (See 1939, 491 § 12.)

SECT. 8A revised, 1933, 329 § 4. Section stricken out and new sections 8A-8C added, 1939, 491 § 8. (See 1939, 491 § 12.)

SECTS. 8B-8C stricken out and new sections 8B-8D inserted, 1941, 598 § 6. (See 1941, 598 §§ 8, 9.)

SECTS. 9 and 10 repealed, 1934, 340 § 5. (See 1934, 340 § 18.)

SECT. 11 revised, 1933, 75 § 2; section and its caption stricken out and new section inserted under the caption "DIVISION OF PARKS AND RECREATION", 1939, 491 § 9. (See 1939, 491 § 12.)

SECT. 12 revised, 1933, 75 § 3; amended, 1941, 490 § 3.

Chapter 22. — Department of Public Safety.

SECT. 9A, sentence added at end, 1939, 503 § 4; same sentence revised, 1943, 175. (See 1939, 503 § 5.)

SECT. 9B amended, 1939, 508 § 11.

SECT. 9C added, 1933, 239 (relative to the uniform of members of the state police).

SECT. 13 added, 1943, 544 § 1 (establishing within the department of public safety, a board of standards and appeals). (See 1943, 544, § 7.)

Chapter 23. — Department of Labor and Industries.

SECT. 2 revised, 1943, 321.

SECT. 3 amended, 1934, 331 § 1; two sentences revised, 1935, 479 § 1; section amended, 1941, 490 § 4. (See 1935, 479 § 7.)

SECT. 4 amended, 1934, 331 § 2; 1935, 479 § 2; first two sentences amended, 1939, 261 § 1; section amended, 1941, 490 § 5; first two sentences revised, 1941, 596 § 16; same two sentences revised, 1941, 707 § 1. (See 1939, 261 § 25.)

SECT. 5 amended, 1935, 479 § 3. (See 1935, 479 § 7.)

SECT. 8 amended, 1939, 261 § 2. (See 1939, 261 § 25.)

SECT. 9 revised, 1935, 60 § 1.

SECT. 9A revised, 1932, 99; repealed, 1933, 73.

SECT. 9B repealed, 1933, 73.
SECT. 9C revised, 1932, 187; repealed, 1933, 73.
SECT. 9D repealed, 1939, 261 § 3.
SECT. 9E amended, 1941, 490 § 6.
SECT. 9G amended, 1939, 459 § 2. (See 1939, 459 § 3.)
SECT. 9H revised, 1933, 362; 1939, 261 § 4.

SECTS. 9I–9N added, 1935, 479 § 4 (establishing the Unemployment Compensation Commission, and defining its powers and duties); same sections revised and the powers and duties of the commission conferred and imposed upon the director of the division of unemployment compensation, 1939, 20 § 1; name of said division changed to division of employment security, 1941, 685 § 4. (See 1935, 479 §§ 6, 7; 1939, 20 §§ 6, 7, 8, 9.)

SECT. 9I, paragraph (*a*) revised, 1941, 685 § 4; 709 § 4; paragraph (*b*) revised, 1941, 596 § 17. (See 1941, 685 § 6; 709 §§ 1–3.)

SECT. 9K, first sentence revised, 1941, 709 § 5. (See 1941, 709 §§ 1–3.)

SECT. 9L amended, 1941, 709 § 6.

SECT. 9N, paragraph (*b*) revised, 1941, 611 § 1; section revised, 1941, 685 § 5. (See 1941, 611 §§ 2, 3, 685 § 6.)

SECTS. 9O–9R added, under the caption "LABOR RELATIONS COMMISSION", 1938, 345 § 1 (incorporating the provisions of 1937, 436 relative to the labor relations commission as an addition to the general laws). (See 1938, 345 §§ 3, 4.)

SECT. 11A (and caption) added, 1934, 331 § 3 (division of occupational hygiene).

SECTS. 11B–11D added, under the caption "THE MASSACHUSETTS DEVELOPMENT AND INDUSTRIAL COMMISSION", 1937, 427 (establishing the Massachusetts development and industrial commission for the promotion and development of the industrial, agricultural and recreational resources of the commonwealth).

SECT. 11C revised, 1941, 596 § 17A.

SECTS. 11E–11L added, under the caption "DIVISION OF APPRENTICE TRAINING", 1941, 707 § 2. (For prior temporary legislation see 1938, 448; 1939, 471.)

Chapter 25. — Department of Public Utilities.

SECT. 4 revised, 1938, 221.

SECT. 8A added, 1939, 442 § 2 (authorizing the appointment of employees for the administration and enforcement of the sale of securities law).

SECT. 9A added, 1933, 76 § 2 (providing for certain employees serving directly under the commission of the department to perform its duties relative to smoke abatement in Boston and vicinity); repealed, 1934, 352 § 2.

SECT. 10 amended, 1933, 76 § 3; 1934, 352 § 3; 1939, 442 § 3.

SECT. 10A added, 1933, 76 § 4 (providing for the apportionment of expenses incurred by the department in the performance of its duties relative to smoke abatement in Boston and vicinity); repealed, 1934, 352 § 4.

SECTS. 11 and 12 repealed, 1935, 411 § 1. (See 1935, 411 § 2.)

SECT. 12A revised, 1938, 445 § 1; repealed, 1939, 442 § 1.

SECT. 12B revised, 1932, 290 § 2; repealed, 1939, 442 § 1.
SECTS. 12C–12F repealed, 1933, 76 § 1; new sections 12C–12E added, under caption "DIVISION OF SMOKE INSPECTION", 1934, 352 § 1.
SECT. 12C revised, 1941, 596 § 18.
SECT. 12F added, 1935, 405 § 1 (establishing in the department a commercial motor vehicle division, under the charge of a director thereof); phrase added at end, 1935, 477 § 2; section amended, 1939, 335 § 1; revised, 1941, 596 § 19; new sentence added at end, 1941, 653 § 1. (See 1939, 335 § 2.)
SECT. 12G added, 1936, 117 (authorizing the director of the commercial motor vehicle division in the department of public utilities to summon witnesses, administer oaths and take testimony).

Chapter 26. — Department of Banking and Insurance.

For temporary legislation providing for the liquidation of certain trust companies, see 1939, 515; 1941, 143; 1943, 122.
SECT. 2 amended, 1943, 315.
SECT. 3 revised, 1941, 596 § 20.
SECT. 4 revised, 1941, 596 § 21.
SECT. 6 amended, 1943, 317.
SECT. 8A revised, 1934, 2; amended, 1935, 419.
SECT. 10, sentence added at end, 1943, 346.

Chapter 27. — Department of Correction.

SECT. 2 revised, 1939, 90; 1941, 596 § 22.
SECT. 4 repealed, 1941, 690 § 7.
SECT. 5 revised, 1934, 350 § 1; 1937, 399 § 1. (See 1934, 350 §§ 2–4; 1937, 399 §§ 3–6.)
SECT. 5A added, 1941, 690 § 6 (relative to the employment of agents and employees of the parole board to perform duties in connection with the release of prisoners). (See 1941, 690 §§ 8, 10.)

Chapter 28. — Metropolitan District Commission.

SECT. 3 revised, 1936, 244 § 1; 1941, 596 § 23. (See 1936, 244 § 4.)
SECT. 4 amended, 1936, 244 § 2. (See 1936, 244 § 4.)
SECTS. 5 and 6 repealed, 1941, 466 § 6.

Chapter 29. — State Finance.

For temporary legislation as to emergency state financing, see 1933, 49, 104, 307, 341, 365, 367, 368; 1934, 41, 66, 313, 335; 1935, 221, 300, 380, 392, 456; 1936, 309; 1937, 338; 1938, 20, 57, 481, 501 § 3; 1939, 288, 417, 418, 496; 1941, 129; 1943, 413.
For legislation relative to the collection of certain taxes and other charges due the commonwealth, see 1935, 498 §§ 2, 3, 4; 1936, 440 §§ 2, 3, 4; 1937, 444 §§ 2, 3, 4; 1938, 503 §§ 2, 3, 4; 1939, 516 §§ 2, 3, 4, 6, 7, 8; 1941, 731 §§ 2, 3, 4, 6, 7, 8; 1943, 568 §§ 2, 3, 4, 6, 7, 8, 10, 11, 12.

For legislation providing for the establishment of a surplus commodity stamp trust fund, see 1942, 9, 17.

SECT. 1, paragraph added at end, 1939, 502 § 1; same paragraph revised, 1941, 509 § 2. (See 1941, 509 § 9.)

SECT. 3 revised, 1939, 502 § 2.

SECT. 4 amended, 1939, 502 § 3.

SECT. 5 revised, 1939, 502 § 4; 1941, 656 § 2. (See 1941, 656 § 17.)

SECT. 5A amended, 1939, 502 § 5.

SECT. 6 amended, 1937, 426 § 1; revised, 1939, 502 § 6; amended, 1941, 490 § 7; 656 § 3. (See 1937, 426 § 2; 1941, 656 § 17.)

SECT. 8A added, 1939, 427 (relative to competitive bidding on state contracts); revised, 1941, 547 § 1.

SECT. 9A revised, 1939, 502 § 7; amended, 1941, 656 § 4. (See 1941, 656 § 17.)

SECT. 9B added, 1941, 564 § 1 (providing for the allotment of certain appropriations by the governor). (See 1941, 564 § 2.)

SECT. 10 amended, 1936, 256; revised, 1939, 502 § 8; 1941, 656 § 5. (See 1941, 656 § 17.)

SECT. 11 amended, 1939, 502 § 9; 1941, 656 § 6. (See 1941, 656 § 17.)

SECT. 12 amended, 1939, 502 § 10.

SECT. 14 revised, 1939, 502 § 11.

SECT. 20A added, 1937, 407 (relative to public inspection of certain orders and claims, in advance of approval or rejection thereof, in connection with state contracts).

SECT. 25 amended, 1941, 656 § 7. (See 1941, 656 § 17.)

SECT. 26 revised, 1939, 502 § 12; amended, 1941, 656 § 8. (See 1941, 656 § 17.)

SECT. 27 amended, 1937, 359; revised, 1939, 502 § 13; amended, 1941, 656 § 9. (See 1941, 656 § 17.)

SECT. 29 amended, 1939, 502 § 14; 1943, 345.

SECT. 31, last sentence amended, 1932, 127 § 2; section amended, 1941, 508.

SECT. 34 amended, 1936, 333.

SECT. 38, subdivision (*h*) added, 1934, 356.

SECT. 48A added, 1937, 252 (authorizing the use of facsimile signatures of the governor on certain bonds and notes of the commonwealth).

SECT. 50 revised, 1939, 502 § 15; 1941, 656 § 10. (See 1941, 656 § 17.)

SECT. 62 repealed, 1943, 83 § 2.

SECT. 63 added, 1937, 157 (providing for taxpayers' petitions for enforcement of certain provisions of law relative to state finance).

Chapter 30. — General Provisions Relative to State Departments, Commissions, Officers and Employees.

For temporary act increasing the salaries of certain officers and employees in the service of the commonwealth, see 1942, 12; 1943, 170, 562.

Provisions relative to expenses incurred for certain meals by state employees, 1933, 174 § 8; 1934, 162 § 6; 1935, 249 § 7; 1936, 304 § 7; 1937, 234 § 6; 1938, 356 § 5; 1939, 309 § 4; 1941, 419 § 4; 1943, 68 § 4; 370 § 4.

Provisions relative to the purchase of passenger automobiles, 1939, 309 § 4; 1941, 419 § 4; 1943, 68 § 4; 370 § 4.

Provisions relative to expenses incurred by state employees in the operation of motor vehicles, 1939, 309 § 5; 1941, 419 § 5; 1943, 68 § 5; 370 § 5.

For legislation relative to commencement of terms of certain state officers, see 1939, 304.

SECT. 7 revised, 1937, 414 § 1; amended, 1941, 512.

SECT. 24 revised, 1937, 430.

SECT. 28 revised, 1941, 656 § 11. (See 1941, 656 § 17.)

SECT. 32 revised, 1939, 499 § 4.

SECT. 32A added, 1939, 499 § 4A (relative to the force and effect of rules and regulations included in annual reports).

SECT. 33 revised, 1939, 499 § 5.

SECT. 33A amended, 1939, 499 § 6.

SECT. 39 revised, 1934, 351; amended, 1935, 217 § 1; revised, 1935, 472 § 1.

SECT. 42 revised, 1936, 359; amended, 1941, 450 § 1.

SECT. 44B added, 1941, 678 § 1 (relative to pipe lines for conveying petroleum and its products and by-products).

SECT. 47, last sentence revised, 1941, 656 § 12. (See 1941, 656 § 17.)

Chapter 31. — Civil Service.

For temporary legislation protecting the civil service rights of certain persons in the military or naval service of the United States, see 1941, 708; 1943, 172, 338, 548.

For temporary legislation relative to transfers of civil service employees during the present emergency, see 1943, 492.

SECT. 1, definitions contained in fourth to eighth lines revised, 1939, 238 § 9. (See 1939, 238 §§ 52–55.)

SECT. 2 revised, 1939, 238 § 10. (See 1939, 238 §§ 52–55.)

SECT. 2A added, 1939, 238 § 11 (relative to the duties of the director of civil service); clause (*b*) revised, 1939, 506 § 1; clause (*e*) revised, 1941, 402 § 2; clause (*c*) amended, 1941, 721. (See 1939, 238 §§ 52–55.)

SECT. 3, clause (*g*) added, 1937, 223 (giving preference to blind persons in the employment of typists in certain cases by state departments, boards and commissions); section amended, 1939, 238 § 12; revised, 1939, 498 § 1; clause (*a*) revised, 1941, 190. (See 1939, 238 §§ 51–55.)

SECT. 4, fourth paragraph amended, 1938, 72; paragraph in line 19 stricken out and new paragraph inserted, 1941, 49; sixth paragraph revised, 1932, 282 § 1; section amended, 1939, 238 § 13; paragraph added at end, 1939, 256 § 1; paragraphs added at end by 1941, 625 § 1, 1941, 627 § 1 and 1941, 686 § 2, respectively; paragraphs added at end by 1943, 246 § 1 and 1943, 402 § 1, respectively. (See 1932, 282 § 4; 1943, 246 § 2; 402 § 2.)

SECT. 5 amended, 1935, 405 § 2; 1936, 244 § 3; 1939, 238 § 14; revised, 1941, 402 § 3.

SECT. 5A added, 1937, 414 § 2 (relative to the employment by certain municipal officers of persons to serve in a confidential capacity).

SECT. 6, sentence added at end, 1932, 260; section amended, 1939, 238 § 15.

SECT. 6A added, 1935, 228 (dispensing with educational requirements as a condition of taking certain civil service examinations).
SECT. 7 revised, 1939, 397.
SECT. 8 amended, 1939, 238 § 16; revised, 1939, 396.
SECT. 10 revised, 1939, 238 § 17; 1939, 498 § 2.
SECT. 12 amended, 1939, 238 § 18.
SECT. 13 amended, 1938, 174 § 2.
SECT. 13A amended, 1939, 238 § 19.
SECT. 14 amended, 1939, 238 § 20.
SECT. 15 revised, 1939, 238 § 21; 1939, 506 § 2; 1941, 491.
SECT. 15A added, 1933, 267 (restricting the appointment of persons for temporary employment under the civil service laws); amended, 1934, 105; repealed, 1943, 523.
SECT. 15B added, 1943, 520 (authorizing certain promotions from the labor service to the official service of a department, board or commission under the civil service laws).
SECT. 16A added, 1939, 506 § 3 (relative to transfers under the civil service laws).
SECT. 17 amended, 1934, 94; revised, 1939, 76; amended, 1939, 238 § 22.
SECT. 18 amended, 1939, 238 § 23.
SECT. 18A added, 1941, 627 § 4 (positions in the labor service of the department of public works to be classified by districts).
SECT. 19A added, 1932, 146 (relative to appointments to the regular fire forces in certain cities having reserve fire forces); amended, 1939, 238 § 24; revised, 1941, 38; amended, 1943, 530.
SECT. 20 amended, 1939, 238 § 25; revised, 1939, 419 § 3.
SECT. 20A amended, 1939, 238 § 26; revised, 1941, 39.
SECT. 20B added, 1937, 416 § 3 (providing for appointments to the regular police force of the metropolitan district commission from the list of members of the reserve police force); amended, 1939, 238 § 27; repealed, 1939, 441 § 2. (See 1937, 416 § 5; repealed, 1939, 441 § 3.)
SECT. 20C added, 1941, 621 (relative to appointments to the regular police force in certain cities and towns).
SECT. 21 amended, 1932, 89; revised, 1933, 137; amended, 1939, 238 § 28; 1943, 194, 469.
SECT. 22 amended, 1939, 238 § 29.
SECT. 23 amended, 1939, 238 § 30.
SECT. 24 amended, 1939, 238 § 31.
SECT. 25 amended, 1939, 238 § 32.
SECT. 29 amended, 1939, 238 § 33.
SECT. 30 amended, 1939, 238 § 34.
SECT. 31 amended, 1939, 238 § 35; revised, 1939, 422 § 1.
SECT. 31A added, 1939, 422 § 2 (relative to the making of reports by department heads pertaining to civil service employees).
SECT. 31B added, 1941, 165 § 1 (relative to the preparation and keeping of rosters of positions in the classified civil service and incumbents thereof in connection with the payment of salaries or compensation). (See 1941, 165 § 2.)
SECT. 32 amended, 1939, 238 § 36; revised, 1939, 420 § 1.
SECT. 32A added, 1939, 420 § 2 (providing that records and files relating to civil service employees be public records).

SECT. 33 amended, 1939, 238 § 37; revised, 1939, 420 § 3.
SECT. 34 amended, 1939, 238 § 38; revised, 1939, 420 § 4.
SECT. 35 repealed, 1941, 559.
SECT. 36 amended, 1939, 238 § 39.
SECT. 37 amended, 1939, 238 § 40.
SECT. 38 amended, 1939, 238 § 41; revised, 1939, 422 § 3.
SECT. 39 amended, 1939, 238 § 42.
SECT. 40 amended, 1939, 238 § 43.
SECT. 42 amended, 1939, 238 § 44.
SECT. 45 amended, 1934, 249 § 2.

SECT. 45A added, 1934, 190 (providing a method of avoiding multiplicity of petitions for judicial review to determine seniority rights in the classified labor service); amended, 1941, 166.

SECT. 45B added, 1941, 135 (requiring clerks of district courts to furnish certain information to the director of civil service).

SECT. 46 amended, 1932, 282 § 2; revised, 1934, 249 § 1; amended, 1941, 257.

SECT. 46B amended, 1939, 238 § 45.

SECTS. 46C and 46D added, 1933, 320 (providing for the reinstatement of certain municipal officers and employees).

SECT. 46C amended, 1934, 84; 1936, 66; revised, 1938, 297 § 1; amended, 1939, 238 § 46.

SECT. 46E added, 1934, 207 (providing that a leave of absence of less than six months shall not be deemed a separation from the classified civil service in certain cases); paragraph added at end, 1936, 297; same paragraph amended, 1939, 238 § 47; 1941, 136.

SECT. 46F added, 1935, 337 (providing for the reinstatement of members of the police force of the metropolitan district commission in certain cases); amended, 1939, 238 § 48.

SECT. 46G added, 1935, 408 (relative to seniority rights in respect to the suspension and re-employment of persons in the classified civil service in certain cases); revised, 1938, 297 § 2.

SECT. 46H added, 1936, 287 § 1 (providing for the reinstatement in the classified civil service of retired municipal officers and employees in certain cases of invalid retirement); amended, 1939, 238 § 49.

SECT. 47A added, 1941, 195 (providing that certain employees in the classified public service shall not be subject to a probationary period).

SECT. 47B added, 1941, 290 (relative to the classification and establishment of seniority of certain civil service employees).

SECTS. 47C and 47D added, 1941, 402 § 1 (establishing a merit system, substantially similar to the civil service system, for certain officers and employees of local boards of public welfare). (See 1941, 402 §§ 4–9.)

SECT. 47C amended, 1941, 588 § 1. (See 1941, 588 § 3.)

SECT. 49A added, 1939, 183 (authorizing cities and towns to place certain offices under the civil service laws by vote of the voters thereof); revised, 1941, 414.

Chapter 32. — Retirement Systems and Pensions.

For temporary legislation protecting the retirement rights of certain persons in the military or naval service of the United States, see 1941, 708; 1943, 172, 419, 548.

For legislation relative to the abolition of non-contributory pensions and retirement allowances for employees of counties, cities, towns and districts under special acts, see 1934, 285 § 10; 1937, 102 § 10.

For legislation relative to the temporary re-employment of former officers and employees of the commonwealth or of any political subdivision thereof during the continuance of the existing state of war between the United States and any foreign country, see 1942, 16; 1943, 502.

SECT. 1, new paragraph added, 1934, 360 § 1. (See 1934, 360 § 5; 1937, 271.)

SECT. 2, paragraphs (10) and (11) revised, 1935, 390.

SECT. 3, paragraph (4) revised, 1932, 268.

SECT. 4, sentence added at end of paragraph (*2*) *A* (*c*), 1934, 360 § 2; paragraph (3) amended, 1936, 370 § 1. (See 1934, 360 § 5; 1936, 370 § 2; 1937, 271.)

SECT. 5, paragraph added at end of paragraph (*2*) *C* (*c*), 1934, 360 § 3; paragraph H added at end, 1934, 360 § 4. (See 1934, 360 § 5; 1937, 271.)

Sects. 1–5, as amended, stricken out and sixteen new sections 1–5A inserted, 1938, 439 § 1. (See 1938, 439 §§ 6, 7; 1939, 16 §§ 1, 2.)

The following references to sections 1 to 5A apply to sections inserted by 1938, 439 § 1:

SECT. 1, definition of "Member" revised, 1941, 379 § 1.

SECT. 2, paragraph (5) amended, 1941, 194 § 3; paragraph (14) amended, 1939, 503 § 1; paragraph (15) stricken out and new paragraphs (14A) and (15) inserted, 1939, 503 § 2; paragraph (16) amended, 1939, 433. (See 1939, 503 § 5.)

SECT. 4, paragraph (1) (*a*) amended, 1941, 670 § 1.

SECT. 4F, paragraph (1) revised, 1941, 379 § 2, 722 § 2; paragraph (2) revised, 1941, 722 § 3; paragraph (4) revised, 1941, 379 § 3.

SECT. 4H, paragraph added at end, 1941, 379 § 4.

SECT. 5A, paragraph (3) (*a*) amended, 1939, 451 § 3; paragraph (8) revised, 1939, 508 § 12.

SECT. 6, definition of "Teacher" amended, 1937, 232 § 1; same definition revised, 1938, 444 § 1; paragraph defining "Salary" inserted, 1941, 671 § 1. (See 1941, 671 §§ 2, 3.)

SECT. 7, first sentence of paragraph (3) revised, 1937, 232 § 2; same paragraph amended, 1938, 385; paragraph (4) amended, 1932, 127 § 18; paragraph (5) added, 1937, 232 § 3; paragraph (6) added, 1938, 444 § 2. (See 1937, 232 § 4.)

SECT. 9, paragraph (1) amended, 1939, 508 § 13; paragraph (2) revised, 1937, 438 § 1; amended, 1939, 508 § 14; revised, 1943, 498; paragraph (5) added at end, 1937, 302; paragraph (6) added, 1938, 444 § 3. (See 1939, 508 § 17.)

SECT. 10, paragraph (2) revised, 1932, 255; paragraph (4) amended, 1937, 438 § 2; paragraph (8) amended, 1936, 386 § 1; paragraph (10) amended, 1936, 386 § 2, revised, 1937, 438 § 3; paragraphs (11) and

(12) stricken out, 1937, 438 § 4; paragraph (17) amended, 1938, 444 § 4; paragraph (19) revised, 1938, 444 § 5; paragraph (20) added, 1938, 444 § 6.

SECT. 11, paragraph (1) revised, 1943, 337 § 1; paragraph (2) stricken out, 1943, 337 § 2; paragraph (5) revised, 1936, 400 § 2. (See 1943, 337 § 3.)

SECT. 16, paragraph (2) revised, 1939, 508 § 15.

SECT. 19, second paragraph revised, 1939, 451 § 4.

SECT. 20,* paragraph added, 1934, 258 § 1.

SECT. 23,* paragraph (5) revised, 1934, 258 § 2.

SECT. 24,* paragraph *(2) A* amended, 1935, 243.

SECT. 25,* paragraph *(2) A (b)* revised, 1936, 301 § 1; paragraph *(2) B (b)* revised, 1936, 301 § 2; paragraph *(F)* added at end, 1936, 301 § 3.

SECTS. 20–25, as amended, and the heading before said section 20, stricken out and new sections 20–25I inserted, under heading "COUNTY AND CERTAIN HOSPITAL DISTRICT RETIREMENT SYSTEMS", 1936, 400 § 1 (providing for contributory retirement systems for counties and certain hospital districts). (See 1936, 400 § 5; 1937, 336 § 3.)

The following references to sections 20-25I apply to sections inserted by 1936, 400 § 1:

SECT. 20, definitions of "Employee" and of "Regular interest" revised, 1937, 336 § 1; definition of "Employee" revised, 1938, 217, 464 § 3; definition of "Member" revised, 1941, 379 § 5.

SECT. 21, paragraph (1) *(a)*, revised, 1939, 158 § 1; 1941, 670 § 2; paragraphs (1) *(b)*, (1) *(c)* and (1) *(d)* revised, 1937, 336 § 2; paragraph (1) *(e)* revised, 1941, 670 § 3; paragraph *(f)* added at end of subdivision (1), 1939, 158 § 2; stricken out, 1941, 670 § 3A; subdivision (2) revised, 1941, 335; subdivision (3) amended, 1941, 670 § 4. (See 1937, 336 § 3.)

SECT. 22, paragraph (5) amended, 1937, 336 § 4; 1941, 670 § 5.

SECT. 23, paragraph added at end of subdivision (1), 1937, 336 § 5.

SECT. 24, subdivision (1) amended, 1941, 670 § 6; subdivision (3) inserted after subdivision (2) *(c)*, 1943, 425 § 1.

SECT. 25, paragraph (1) amended, 1941, 670 § 7; first clause of paragraph (2) revised, 1937, 336 § 6.

SECT. 25B, revised, 1941, 379 § 6.

SECT. 25D, revised, 1941, 379 § 7.

SECT. 25F, paragraph (6) amended, 1937, 336 § 7.

SECT. 25G, paragraph (1) *(a)* amended, 1937, 336 § 8; paragraph (1) *(d)* amended, 1937, 336 § 9.

SECT. 25H, paragraph (1) revised, 1941, 113 § 2.

SECT. 25I, last paragraph revised, 1937, 336 § 10.

Sects. 26–31 stricken out and new sections 26–31I inserted, 1936, 318 § 1 (providing for contributory retirement systems for cities and towns that may be accepted by them). (See 1936, 318 §§ 5–7.)

The following references to sections 26 to 31I are to sections inserted by 1936, 318 § 1:

SECT. 26, definitions of "Employee" and of "Regular interest" revised, 1937, 336 § 11; definition of "Employee" revised, 1938, 464 § 4; 1941, 411 § 1; definition of "Member" revised, 1941, 379 § 8. (See 1941, 411 § 3.)

---

* See later amendments to sections 20 to 25, inclusive.

SECT. 27, paragraph (1) (*a*) revised, 1938, 360 § 1; 1941, 670 § 8; paragraph (1) (*b*) revised, 1937, 336 § 12; last sentence revised, 1938, 360 § 2; paragraph (1) (*c*) revised, 1937, 336 § 12; paragraph (1) (*d*) revised, 1937, 336 § 12; last sentence revised, 1938, 360 § 3; paragraph (1) (*e*) revised, 1938, 360 § 4; 1941, 670 § 9; paragraph (1) (*f*) added, 1938, 360 § 5; paragraph (1) (*g*) added, 1941, 670 § 10; paragraph (2) revised, 1939, 228; amended, 1941, 670 § 11; paragraph (3) amended, 1941, 670 § 12.

SECT. 28, paragraph (2) revised, 1941, 670 § 12A; paragraph (5) amended, 1937, 336 § 13; 1941, 670 § 13.

SECT. 29, subdivision (1) amended, 1941, 670 § 14; second paragraph of subdivision (1) stricken out and two paragraphs inserted, 1937, 336 § 14; second of said inserted paragraphs amended, 1941, 670 § 15; paragraph added after second of said inserted paragraphs, 1941, 670 § 16; paragraph (2) (*b*) revised, 1938, 360 § 6; paragraph (2) (*c*) amended, 1938, 270; paragraph (2) (*d*) amended, 1937, 336 § 15; second sentence revised, 1938, 360 § 7; paragraph (2) (*e*) revised, 1938, 360 § 8; paragraph (2) (*g*) added, 1941, 409 § 1.

SECT. 30, subdivision (1) amended, 1941, 670 § 17; subdivision (3) inserted after subdivision (2) (*c*), 1943, 425 § 2.

SECT. 31, subdivision (1) amended, 1941, 670 § 18; first paragraph of subdivision (2) revised, 1937, 336 § 16; paragraph added at end of subdivision (2), 1941, 670 § 19.

SECT. 31B revised, 1941, 379 § 9; sentence added at end, 1941, 670 § 20.

SECT. 31D revised, 1941, 379 § 10.

SECT. 31E, paragraph (4) added at end, 1941, 409 § 2.

SECT. 31F, paragraph (1) (*b*) amended, 1937, 57 § 1; paragraph 1A added, 1937, 57 § 2; paragraph (1) (*c*) revised, 1938, 284 § 1, 464 § 5; paragraph (2) revised, 1938, 464 § 6. (See 1937, 57 § 4; 1938, 284 § 2.)

SECT. 31G, paragraph (1) (*a*) revised, 1941, 411 § 2; paragraph (1) (*d*) amended, 1937, 336 § 17; paragraph (6) (*a*) revised, 1938, 360 § 9; paragraph (6) (*b*) amended, 1938, 360 § 10. (See 1941, 411 § 3.)

SECT. 31H, paragraph (1) revised, 1941, 113 § 1.

SECT. 31I, paragraph (3) amended, 1937, 57 § 3; paragraph (4) added, 1941, 377; paragraph (4) added, 1941, 386; paragraph last referred to stricken out and paragraph (5) substituted, 1941, 722 § 4; paragraph (4) (*b*) revised, 1943, 236 § 1. (See 1937, 57 § 4; 1943, 236 § 2.)

SECT. 31J inserted after the heading "GENERAL PROVISIONS" immediately before section 32, 1936, 400 § 3 (relative to the definition of certain words used in said General Provisions).

SECT. 33 amended, 1936, 301 § 4; 318 § 2; repealed, 1936, 400 § 4. (See 1936, 318 §§ 5–7; 400 §§ 2 and 5.)

SECT. 34, second paragraph revised, 1941, 584 § 1.

SECT. 34A added, 1941, 584 § 2 (relative to the expense incurred by the commissioner of insurance in examining the affairs of certain retirement systems).

SECT. 36 amended, 1937, 336 § 18.

SECTS. 37A–37D added, 1936, 318 § 3 (miscellaneous provisions relative to contributory retirement systems under G. L. chap. 32). (See 1936, 318 §§ 5–7.)

SECT. 37C, paragraph added at end, 1938, 360 § 10A; section revised, 1938, 439 § 2. (See 1938, 360 § 10B; 439 § 7.)

SECT. 37D, first paragraph revised, 1937, 336 § 19; first paragraph stricken out, and two paragraphs inserted, 1939, 449 § 1; paragraph added at end, 1938, 464 § 1. (See 1939, 449 § 2.)

SECT. 37E added, 1937, 336 § 20 (providing minimum retirement allowances for certain members of county, city or town contributory retirement systems); paragraph (1) revised, 1941, 184 § 1; paragraph (2) revised, 1938, 360 § 11; paragraph (3) added at end, 1938, 439 § 3; paragraph (4) added at end, 1941, 670 § 21; paragraph (5) added at end, 1943, 189. (See 1938, 439 § 7; 1941, 184 § 2.)

SECT. 37F added, 1938, 464 § 2 (permitting members of certain contributory retirement systems of governmental units to make contributions on account of prior service with other such units having no such systems); revised, 1939, 316; 1941, 670 § 22.

SECT. 37G added, 1941, 670 § 23 (relative to the rights of employees of two or more governmental units having retirement systems).

SECT. 38 amended, 1937, 336 § 21.

SECT. 38A added, 1938, 439 § 4 (relative to the definitions of certain terms or words used in sections thirty-two to thirty-eight, inclusive). (See 1938, 439 § 7.)

SECT. 44 revised, 1934, 135; paragraph added at end, 1934, 285 § 1; section amended, 1936, 223; last paragraph amended, 1937, 102 § 1. (See 1937, 202.)

SECT. 46 revised, 1941, 344 § 1.

SECT. 47 amended, 1941, 344 § 2.

SECT. 48 revised, 1938, 379.

SECT. 52 amended, 1932, 114 § 1.

SECT. 53 amended, 1932, 114 § 2.

SECT. 56 revised, 1943, 514 § 1. (See 1943, 514 § 4.)

SECT. 57 revised, 1943, 514 § 2. (See 1943, 514 § 4.)

SECT. 58 revised, 1943, 514 § 3. (See 1943, 514 § 4.)

SECT. 60, paragraph added at end, 1934, 285 § 2; same paragraph amended, 1937, 102 § 2; 1938, 452 § 1. (See 1938, 452 § 2.)

SECT. 60A, paragraph added at end, 1934, 285 § 3; amended, 1937, 102 § 3.

SECTS. 61–64 repealed, 1937, 409 § 2. (See 1937, 409 §§ 5–7.)

SECT. 65, last sentence stricken out, 1937, 336 § 22; section repealed, 1937, 409 § 2. (See 1937, 409 §§ 5–7.)

SECT. 65A added, 1937, 409 § 1 (relative to the retirement or resignation of members of the judiciary); amended, 1939, 451 § 5. (See 1937, 409 §§ 5–7.)

SECT. 65B added, 1941, 689 § 1 (providing pensions for special justices of district courts); revised, 1943, 398. (See 1941, 689 § 2.)

SECT. 66, paragraph added at end, 1934, 285 § 4; amended, 1937, 102 § 4.

SECT. 68 revised, 1943, 545 § 1.

SECTS. 68A–68C added, 1939, 503 § 3 (relative to the retirement of members of the state police). (See 1939, 503 § 5.)

SECT. 68C revised, 1943, 545 § 2.

SECT. 70, paragraph added at end, 1934, 285 § 5; amended, 1937, 102 § 5; section revised, 1937, 416 § 4; repealed, 1939, 441 § 4. (See 1937, 416 § 5; 1939, 441 §§ 3, 5.)

SECT. 75, paragraph added at end, 1934, 285 § 6; amended, 1937, 102 § 6; section revised, 1938, 323 § 1.
SECT. 76 revised, 1938, 323 § 2.
SECT. 77, paragraph (a) revised, 1936, 290 § 1; 1939, 243; paragraph (c) added at end, 1936, 290 § 2. (Affected, 1937, 102 § 7, 283.)
SECT. 78 revised, 1939, 361 § 1. (Affected, 1937, 102 § 7, 283; 1939, 361 § 2.)
SECT. 78A added, 1934, 285 § 7 (providing for the ultimate abolition of non-contributory pensions under certain provisions of general law for laborers); amended, 1937, 102 § 7; revised, 1937, 283 § 1. (See 1937, 283 § 2.)
SECT. 80, paragraph added at end, 1934, 285 § 8; section amended, 1936, 439 § 1; last paragraph amended, 1937, 102 § 8.
SECT. 81 amended, 1933, 103; 1938, 277 § 1. (See 1938, 277 § 3.)
SECT. 83 amended, 1936, 439 § 2; 1938, 277 § 2; last sentence of first paragraph revised, 1939, 264 § 1. (See 1938, 277 § 3; 1939, 264 § 2.)
SECT. 85 amended, 1936, 439 § 3.
SECT. 85A revised, 1935, 31 § 1. (See 1935, 31 § 2.)
SECT. 85B added, 1932, 253 (regulating the retirement and pensioning of certain members of the police forces of park boards of cities and towns).
SECT. 85C added, 1934, 285 § 9 (providing for the ultimate abolition of non-contributory pensions under certain provisions of general law for policemen and firemen); amended, 1937, 102 § 9.
SECT. 85D added, 1937, 220 (relative to the retirement of certain call members of fire departments in certain towns).
SECT. 89 revised, 1932, 276; amended, 1933, 340 § 1; 1934, 343; revised, 1935, 466; amended, 1936, 326; first paragraph amended, 1943, 366. (See 1933, 340 § 2.)
SECT. 90 revised, 1936, 439 § 4.
SECT. 90A added, 1943, 452 § 1 (authorizing certain cities and towns to increase the retirement allowances of certain former employees retired on account of accidental disability). (See 1943, 452 § 2.)
SECT. 91 revised, 1938, 439 § 5; amended, 1941, 670 § 24. (See 1938, 439 § 7; 1941, 670 § 26.)

Chapter 33. — Militia.

Act establishing a special military reservation commission, and authorizing the acquisition by the commonwealth for military purposes of certain properties in Sandwich, Bourne, Falmouth and Mashpee, 1935, 196; powers and duties of the commission defined, 1936, 344 §§ 1, 2; reservation enlarged, 1941, 5. (See 1938, 331.)

The following references are to chapter 33, as appearing in the Tercentenary Edition:

SECT. 6 revised, 1933, 254 § 1; 1938, 440 § 1A. (See 1933, 254 § 66; 1938, 440 § 23.)
SECT. 7 revised, 1938, 440 § 1. (See 1938, 440 § 23.)
SECT. 18 amended, 1932, 15.
SECT. 22, paragraph in third line revised, 1937, 192 § 1.
SECT. 25A added, 1935, 295 § 1 (further regulating the calling out of the militia as an aid to the civil power of the commonwealth).
SECT. 26 amended, 1935, 295 § 2.

SECT. 31 amended, 1935, 295 § 3.
SECT. 32 revised, 1935, 295 § 4.
SECT. 33 revised, 1935, 295 § 5.
SECT. 34 amended, 1935, 295 § 6.
SECT. 48, subsection (*a*) revised, 1932, 161; same subsection amended, 1933, 166.
SECT. 60 amended, 1933, 153 § 1; 1934, 120; 1939, 144 § 1.
SECT. 67 revised, 1935, 205.
SECT. 82, subsection (*e*) added, 1938, 433 (making the United States property and disbursing officer for Massachusetts the finance officer of the Massachusetts National Guard, defining his powers and duties and establishing his compensation).
SECT. 90, paragraph in lines 63–65 revised, 1934, 106; last sentence of paragraph (*k*) revised, 1933, 17; paragraph (*k*) revised, 1937, 192 § 2.
SECT. 98, sentence added at end, 1933, 6.

Chapter stricken out and new chapter 33 inserted, 1939, 425 § 1. (See 1939, 425 § 2.)

The following references are to the new chapter 33:

SECT. 1 revised, 1943, 35 § 1.
SECT. 6, paragraph (*a*) revised, 1943, 35 § 2.
SECT. 24 revised, 1943, 35 § 3.
SECT. 26A added, 1943, 348 § 2 (providing for the incurring by the governor of extraordinary expenses in aid of the civil power).
SECT. 47 revised, 1941, 318.
SECT. 49 amended, 1941, 217 § 1.
SECT. 55 revised, 1943, 35 § 4.
SECTS. 55A–55F added, 1943, 409 § 1 (providing for the acquiring of motor vehicles or for obtaining the use thereof by the military division of the executive department, and for the settlement of certain claims against the commonwealth arising out of the operation of such motor vehicles).
SECT. 56 revised, 1943, 35 § 5.
SECT. 65, paragraph (*a*) amended, 1941, 395.
SECT. 66 revised, 1943, 35 § 6.
SECT. 68A added, 1943, 35 § 7 (providing that the state guard shall consist of such organizations and units as the commander-in-chief shall prescribe or authorize to be formed and defining the composition thereof).
SECT. 69, subdivision (*c*) amended, 1941, 577 § 1. (See 1941, 577 § 2.)
SECT. 79 amended, 1941, 490 § 8.
SECT. 104A added, 1943, 362 § 1 (authorizing the adjutant general to accept on behalf of the commonwealth certain gifts of personal property for military purposes).
SECT. 114, paragraphs (*a*) and (*b*) revised, 1943, 394 § 1; paragraph (*d*) amended, 1943, 394 § 2.
SECT. 126, sentence added at end, 1943, 262 § 1. (See 1943, 262 § 3.)
SECTS. 126A and 126B added, 1943, 262 § 2 (further regulating allowances in the military division of the executive department). (See 1943, 262 § 3.)
SECT. 153 amended, 1941, 458.

Chapter 34. — Counties and County Commissioners.

SECT. 1 revised, 1933, 278 § 2.

SECT. 4 amended, 1935, 257 § 1; revised, 1939, 31 § 1. (See 1935, 257 § 12.)

SECT. 5, schedule revised, 1943, 102 § 1. (See 1943, 102 § 2).

SECT. 7 amended, 1935, 257 § 2; last sentence stricken out, 1939, 31 § 2. (See 1935, 257 § 12.)

SECT. 12 revised, 1935, 257 § 3. (See 1935, 257 § 12.)

SECT. 17 revised, 1932, 74; affected, 1939, 452 § 7.

SECT. 19 amended, 1935, 257 § 4. (See 1935, 257 § 12.)

SECT. 23 added, 1932, 297 (authorizing counties to receive certain gifts).

Chapter 35. — County Treasurers, State Supervision of County Accounts and County Finances.

For temporary legislation increasing the salaries of certain officers and employees in the service of certain counties, see 1942, 15; 1943, 224.

For emergency legislation incident to the National Industrial Recovery Act, the Emergency Relief Appropriation Act of 1935 and certain other federal acts, see 1933, 366; 1934, 21; 1935, 404; 1936, 64, 83, 414; 1938, 50; 1939, 423 §§ 1, 2; 1941, 639 § 1; 1943, 58.

For legislation relative to the issuance and renewal of certain temporary loans in anticipation of federal grants for public works projects, see 1938, 82; 1941, 639 §§ 2, 3.

Provisions relative to travel allowance of county employees using certain cars on official business, 1933, 322 § 4; 1939, 452 § 2; 1941, 528 § 3; 1943, 465 § 3.

Provisions relative to expenses incurred for meals by county employees, 1939, 452 § 3; 1941, 528 § 2; 1943, 465 § 2.

SECT. 3 revised, 1932, 56; sentence added at end, 1939, 109 § 2.

SECT. 11 amended, 1943, 65.

SECT. 21 amended, 1937, 64 § 2.

SECT. 25 amended, 1933, 175 § 1.

SECT. 27 amended, 1933, 175 § 2.

SECT. 28 amended, 1933, 318 § 2; 1934, 291 § 2; revised, 1939, 501 § 1. (See 1933, 318 § 9; 1934, 291 § 6.)

SECT. 28A added, 1943, 414 § 2 (establishing a budget system for county tuberculosis hospitals).

SECT. 29 revised, 1939, 501 § 2.

SECT. 30 revised, 1939, 501 § 3; sentence added at end, 1943, 39.

SECT. 34 revised, 1937, 36; amended, 1939, 501 § 4.

SECT. 36A amended, 1939, 501 § 5; revised, 1943, 80.

SECT. 37 amended, 1933, 28.

SECT. 37A amended, 1933, 29.

SECT. 40 amended, 1936, 23 § 1.

SECT. 43A revised, 1939, 214 § 1.

SECT. 43B added, 1939, 214 § 2 (relative to the effect of the filing of annual fidelity bonds by county officers and employees).

SECT. 49 amended, 1935, 182 § 1; 1938, 347 § 1; 1939, 165 § 1; 1941,

447 § 1; 1943, 136 § 1. (See 1935, 182 § 6; 1938, 347 § 3; 1939, 165 § 3; 1941, 447 §§ 4, 5; 1943, 136 § 3.)
SECT. 51 amended, 1938, 73 § 2.
SECT. 52, second paragraph revised, 1938, 73 § 1.

Chapter 36. — Registers of Deeds.

SECT. 3 revised, 1937, 219 § 1; 1939, 214 § 3.
SECT. 24A added, 1941, 89 (authorizing the recording of certified copies of petitions, decrees and orders filed or made pursuant to the federal bankruptcy laws and thereby giving effect to certain provisions of said laws).

Chapter 37. — Sheriffs.

SECT. 2 revised, 1937, 219 § 2.
SECT. 21 revised, 1943, 159 § 1. (See 1943, 159 § 2.)
SECT. 22 amended, 1932, 180 § 5.
SECT. 23 amended, 1936, 31 § 2; repealed, 1937, 148.

Chapter 38. — Medical Examiners.

SECT. 1, paragraph in lines 70–76 amended, 1939, 260; section amended, 1939, 451 § 6.
SECT. 2A added, 1943, 153 § 1 (authorizing associate medical examiners in Barnstable County to perform the duties of medical examiner thereof in certain cases). (See 1943, 153 § 2.)
SECT. 3 revised, 1939, 214 § 4.
SECT. 6 amended, 1939, 475.
SECT. 7 amended, 1941, 366.
SECT. 8 revised, 1932, 118 § 1; amended, 1939, 30 § 1. (See 1939, 30 § 2.)
SECT. 11 amended, 1941, 499.

Chapter 39. — Municipal Government.

SECT. 10 amended, 1935, 403 § 1; 1939, 182. (See 1935, 403 § 2.)
SECT. 14, first and second paragraphs revised, 1943, 453 §§ 1 and 2, respectively.
SECT. 19 repealed, 1934, 39 § 1.
SECT. 20 amended, 1934, 39 § 2.
SECT. 23 amended, 1934, 39 § 3.

Chapter 40. — Powers and Duties of Cities and Towns.

Temporary act relative to the care and disposal of land acquired by cities and towns through foreclosure of tax titles, 1938, 358; amended to include care and disposal of lands of low value acquired by cities and towns through purchase, 1939, 123; further amended and extended, 1941, 296.
SECT. 4, third paragraph revised, 1932, 271 § 6; section amended, 1941, 351 § 3. (See 1932, 271 § 7.)
SECT. 5, clause (1) amended, 1933, 318 § 3 (see 1933, 318 § 9); 1935, 106; revised, 1935, 179; amended, 1939, 19; clause (2) amended, 1936, 390; clause (5A) added, 1938, 172 § 1 (authorizing appropriations to

establish a water supply); clause (12) amended, 1932, 114 § 3; 1933, 153 § 2, 245 § 2; revised, 1936, 132 § 1, 163; amended, 1941, 217 § 2; 1943, 99; clause (28) revised, 1936, 211 § 5 (see 1936, 211 § 7); clause (37) revised, 1943, 177 § 1 (see 1943, 177 § 2); clause (38) added, 1934, 154 § 1 (authorizing appropriations for protection of interests in real estate held under tax title or taking); clause (39) added, 1935, 28 (authorizing appropriations for the purpose of co-operating with the federal government in certain unemployment relief and other projects); clause (40) added, 1937, 185 (authorizing appropriations for eyeglasses for needy school children); clause (41) added, 1938, 142 § 1 (authorizing cities and towns to appropriate money for stocking inland waters therein with fish and for liberating game therein); amended, 1941, 599 § 4. (See 1938, 142 § 2.)

SECT. 5A added, 1936, 40 (providing for the establishment of reserve funds for cities); amended, 1937, 34.

SECTS. 5, 6. Temporary acts, effective during 1935 to 1943, inclusive, authorizing appropriations for a general unemployment relief fund, 1935, 90; 1937, 4; 1939, 46 §§ 1, 2.

SECTS. 6C and 6D added, 1943, 225 (relative to the removal by cities and towns of snow and ice from private ways therein open to public use).

SECT. 9 amended, 1933, 245 § 3; 1935, 305; 1936, 271; paragraph added at end, 1937, 255.

SECT. 11 amended, 1941, 490 § 9.

SECT. 12A repealed, 1941, 598 § 5.

SECT. 13, paragraph added at end, 1941, 130.

SECT. 14 revised, 1933, 283 § 1.

SECT. 17 amended, 1933, 254 § 2. (See 1933, 254 § 66.)

SECT. 21, clause (16) added at end, 1941, 346 § 1.

SECTS. 25–33. For special zoning provisions for Boston, see 1924, 488 and amendments prior to 1932; 1932, 143; 1933, 204; 1934, 210; 1936, 240; 1941, 373.

SECTS. 25–30A stricken out, and new sections 25–30A (municipal zoning laws) inserted, 1933, 269 § 1. (See 1933, 269 § 4.)

SECT. 27 revised, 1941, 320.

SECT. 27A added, 1938, 133 § 1 (to prevent multiplicity of proposals for the same change in zoning ordinances or by-laws).

SECT. 28 revised, 1941, 176.

SECT. 30, paragraph in lines 54–60 (as appearing in 1933, 269 § 1) stricken out and two paragraphs added, 1941, 198 § 1; paragraph in lines 61–70 (as so appearing) amended, 1935, 388 § 1; clause (1) in lines 72–76 (as so appearing) revised, 1941, 198 § 2; paragraph in lines 80–90 (as so appearing) amended, 1935, 388 § 2. (See 1941, 198 § 3.)

SECT. 30A stricken out and reinserted as section 30B and new section 30A inserted, 1938, 133 § 2 (to prevent multiplicity of proposals for the same change in the application of zoning ordinances or by-laws).

SECT. 32 revised, 1933, 185 § 1; amended, 1941, 520 § 1. (See 1933, 185 § 2; 1941, 520 § 2.)

SECT. 38 revised, 1938, 172 § 2; paragraph added at end, 1941, 465 § 1.

SECTS. 39A–39G added, 1938, 172 § 3 (authorizing the establishment and maintenance of water supply and distributing systems).

SECT. 39A revised, 1941, 465 § 2.
SECT. 39H added, 1943, 125 (authorizing cities, towns and districts, through their water departments, and water companies, to aid similar municipal and other corporations relative to their water supply).
SECT. 40 revised, 1933, 314.
SECT. 42A revised, 1932, 197 § 2; amended, 1936, 42 § 1; revised, 1938, 415 § 1; amended, 1941, 380 § 1. (See 1932, 197 § 3; 1938, 415 § 7; 1941, 380 § 7.)
SECT. 42B amended, 1935, 56 § 1; revised, 1936, 42 § 2; 1938, 415 § 2; revised, 1941, 380 § 2. (See 1935, 56 § 2; 1938, 415 § 7; 1941, 380 § 7.)
SECT. 42C amended, 1935, 248 § 1; revised, 1938, 415 § 3; 1941, 380 § 3. (See 1938, 415 § 7; 1941, 380 § 7.)
SECT. 42D, last sentence revised, 1935, 248 § 2; section revised, 1938, 415 § 4; 1941, 380 § 4. (See 1938, 415 § 7; 1941, 380 § 7.)
SECT. 42E, last sentence amended, 1932, 180 § 6; same sentence revised, 1939, 451 § 7; section amended, 1941, 380 § 5. Affected, 1938, 415 § 7. (See 1941, 380 § 7.)
SECT. 42F affected, 1938, 415 § 7; 1941, 380 § 7.
SECT. 43A (relative to pipe lines for conveying petroleum and its products and by-products) added under the heading "PETROLEUM AND ITS PRODUCTS AND BY-PRODUCTS", 1941, 678 § 2.
SECT. 51 revised, 1937, 196.

Chapter 41. — Officers and Employees of Cities, Towns and Districts.

Provisions of G. L. chapter 41 authorizing or requiring the fixing of terms of office of members of any board, commission or body affected by 1938, 341 § 2.
SECT. 1, first paragraph revised, 1943, 453 § 3; paragraph in line 10 revised, 1934, 155 § 1; paragraph in lines 15, 16 revised, 1939, 129; paragraph in line 25 revised, 1939, 3; paragraph added at end, 1938, 341 § 2.
SECT. 5 amended, 1934, 39 § 4.
SECT. 11 amended, 1938, 341 § 3.
SECT. 13 amended, 1936, 18; 1937, 143 § 1.
SECT. 13A added, 1932, 289 § 5 (provisions relative to bonds of city clerks). [For prior legislation, see G. L. chapter 140 § 148, repealed by 1932, 289 § 6.]
SECT. 19, last sentence revised, 1938, 66.
SECT. 19A added, 1933, 70 § 1 (requiring the filing with the state secretary of certificates of appointment or election of clerks or assistant or temporary clerks of cities or towns, and granting authority to said secretary to authenticate attestations of any such officer). (See 1933, 70 § 2.)
SECT. 21, last paragraph revised, 1934, 155 § 2. (See 1934, 155 § 4.)
SECT. 24A repealed, 1937, 129 § 1.
SECT. 25 revised, 1937, 129 § 2.
SECT. 25A revised, 1937, 129 § 3.
SECT. 26 revised, 1937, 129 § 4.
SECT. 26A added, 1935, 149 (relative to employment of counsel by boards of assessors in certain cases).

SECT. 27 revised, 1936, 118 § 1. (See 1936, 118 § 3.)
SECT. 28 amended, 1939, 342 § 2.
SECT. 35 revised, 1937, 143 § 2; sentence added at end, 1939, 109 § 1.
SECT. 37 revised, 1933, 82 § 2; amended, 1934, 259 § 2.
SECT. 38A amended, 1936, 201; revised, 1941, 211.
SECT. 39A added, 1939, 89 (providing for the appointment of assistant treasurers of cities and towns).
SECT. 39B added, 1943, 284 (authorizing the suspension and removal of city and town collectors and the appointment of temporary collectors under certain circumstances).
SECT. 40 revised, 1937, 143 § 3.
SECT. 43A added, 1939, 88 (requiring municipalities to indemnify and protect collectors of taxes in the performance of their duties in certain cases); revised, 1941, 99.
SECT. 54A amended, 1936, 62.
SECT. 59 amended, 1936, 94.
SECT. 61A revised, 1937, 143 § 4.
SECT. 66 revised, 1934, 155 § 3.
SECTS. 69A and 69B added, 1938, 172 § 4 (relative to the establishment and powers and duties of boards of water commissioners in certain towns).
SECT. 70, paragraph added at end, 1936, 211 § 1. (See 1936, 211 § 7.)
SECT. 71 amended, 1943, 266.
SECT. 72 revised, 1936, 211 § 2. (See 1936, 211 § 7.)
SECT. 73, paragraph added at end, 1936, 211 § 3. (See 1936, 211 § 7.)
SECTS. 81A–81J added, under caption "IMPROVED METHOD OF MUNICIPAL PLANNING", 1936, 211 § 4. (See 1936, 211 § 7.)
SECT. 81A, last paragraph revised, 1938, 113.
SECT. 86 amended, 1939, 261 § 5.
SECT. 91B added, 1933, 128 (further regulating the appointment of constables).
SECT. 96A added, 1938, 342 (disqualifying felons from appointment to the police forces or departments of cities, towns and districts).
SECT. 99 amended, 1932, 124.
SECT. 100, sentence added at end, 1933, 324 § 3; section amended, 1938, 298.
SECT. 100A amended, 1933, 318 § 4; 1934, 291 § 3. (See 1933, 318 §§ 8, 9; 1934, 291 § 6.)
SECT. 105 amended, 1936, 132 § 2.
SECT. 111 revised, 1932, 109; amended, 1936, 242; revised, 1937, 15; 1941, 368; fourth sentence stricken out and two sentences inserted, 1943, 280.
SECT. 111A amended, 1934, 107.

Chapter 42. — Boundaries of Cities and Towns.

Boundary line between Saugus and Wakefield (portion) established, 1933, 298; between Woburn and Reading (portion) established, 1934, 177; between Oak Bluffs and Tisbury (portion) established, 1935, 145; between Brewster and Orleans (portion) established, 1935, 356; between Middleton and Topsfield established, 1936, 96; between Foxborough and Walpole established, 1937, 140; between Edgartown and Oak

Bluffs (portion) established, 1937, 265; between Arlington and Belmont (portion) established, 1938, 371; between Rochester and Wareham and between Marion and Wareham (portion) established, 1939, 279; between Fitchburg and Leominster (portion) established, 1941, 37, 698; between Bellingham and Franklin, 1941, 641.

SECT. 1 revised, 1933, 278 § 3.

Chapter 43. — City Charters.

SECT. 1, three paragraphs inserted after word "inclusive" in line 22, 1938, 378 § 1.

SECT. 5, paragraph added at end, 1938, 378 § 2.

SECT. 7 amended, 1939, 451 § 8.

SECT. 8, form of petition revised, 1938, 378 § 3.

SECT. 9 revised, 1941, 640 § 1. (See 1941, 640 § 7.)

SECT. 10, paragraph added at end, 1938, 378 § 4.

SECT. 11 revised, 1941, 640 § 2. (See 1941, 640 § 7.)

SECT. 15 amended, 1933, 313 § 7; last paragraph amended, 1938, 378 § 5; section revised, 1941, 640 § 3. (See 1941, 640 § 7.)

SECT. 17 revised, 1938, 378 § 6.

SECT. 18, paragraph numbered 4 inserted, 1938, 378 § 7.

SECT. 19 revised, 1938, 378 § 8.

SECT. 23 amended, 1935, 68 § 1.

SECT. 26, first paragraph revised, 1937, 224 § 1; amended, 1938, 378 § 9.

SECT. 29 revised, 1938, 378 § 10.

SECT. 30 revised, 1938, 378 § 11.

SECT. 31 amended, 1938, 378 § 12.

SECT. 36 revised, 1938, 378 § 13.

SECT. 42 amended, 1935, 68 § 2.

SECT. 44A amended, 1933, 313 § 8; last two sentences stricken out, and paragraph added at end, 1934, 30; first paragraph revised, 1938, 378 § 14; last sentence of first paragraph stricken out, 1941, 640 § 4. (See 1941, 640 § 7.)

SECT. 44C, first paragraph amended, 1937, 147; 1943, 229 § 1.

SECT. 44H amended, 1932, 180 § 7; 1941, 640 § 5. (See 1941, 640 § 7.)

SECT. 46 amended, 1939, 451 § 9.

SECT. 50A added, 1936, 135 (relative to the filling of vacancies in the city council in cities having a Plan A form of charter).

SECT. 56 amended, 1937, 224 § 2.

SECT. 59A added, 1937, 224 § 3 (relative to the filling of vacancies in the city council in cities having a Plan B form of charter).

SECTS. 93–116 added, under the heading "PLAN E. — GOVERNMENT BY A CITY COUNCIL INCLUDING A MAYOR ELECTED FROM ITS NUMBER, AND A CITY MANAGER, WITH ALL ELECTIVE BODIES ELECTED AT LARGE BY PROPORTIONAL REPRESENTATION", 1938, 378 § 15 (providing an additional optional standard form of city charter under which substantial control of the city government is vested in a city council elected at large by proportional representation, with a city manager appointed and removable at pleasure by the city council).

SECT. 100 amended, 1941, 722 § 5.

SECT. 102 amended, 1941, 722 § 6.

SECT. 110, form of petition amended, 1941, 722 § 7.

Chapter 43A. — Standard Form of Representative Town Meeting Government.

Act relative to Wellesley, 1932, 202; to Needham, 1932, 279; to Webster, 1933, 13; to South Hadley, 1933, 45: to Easthampton, 1933, 178; to Milford, 1933, 271; to Adams, 1935, 235; to Falmouth, 1935, 349; to Amherst, 1936, 10; to Amesbury, 1936, 39; to Braintree, 1936, 56; 1937, 17; to Natick, 1938, 2; to Palmer, 1939, 110; to Reading, 1943, 7.

SECT. 3, first paragraph amended, 1937, 267 § 2.

SECT. 4, first paragraph amended, 1936, 128.

SECT. 6 revised, 1943, 1 § 1; 1943, 453 § 4. (See 1943, 1 § 2.)

SECT. 8, first sentence revised, 1943, 453 § 5.

Chapter 44. — Municipal Finance.

For temporary legislation establishing an emergency finance board in the department of the state treasurer, and providing for the borrowing of money by cities and towns against certain tax titles, see 1933, 49, 104; 1935, 221, 300, 456; 1936, 281; 1938, 57; 1939, 288, 496; 1941, 129; 1943, 413.

For emergency legislation incident to the National Industrial Recovery Act, the Emergency Relief Appropriation Act of 1935 and certain other federal acts, see 1933, 366; 1934, 21; 1935, 404; 1936, 64, 83, 414; 1937, 159; 1938, 50; 1939, 423 §§ 1, 2; 1941, 639 § 1; 1943, 58.

For emergency legislation authorizing cities and towns to make certain appropriations during the existing state of war, see 1943, 75 §§ 1, 2, 4, 5. [For prior legislation, see 1941, 487; 1942, 4 § 5; 1943, 5 § 6.]

For legislation authorizing the renewal by cities and towns of certain temporary revenue loans, see 1935, 12; 1938, 25; 1939, 68; 1941, 134; 1943, 60.

For legislation relative to the collection of certain taxes and other charges due the commonwealth, see 1935, 498 §§ 2, 3, 4; 1936, 440 §§ 2, 3, 4; 1937, 444 §§ 2, 3, 4; 1938, 503 §§ 2, 3, 4; 1939, 516 §§ 2, 3, 4, 6, 7, 8; 1941, 731 §§ 2, 3, 4, 6, 7, 8; 1943, 568 §§ 2, 3, 4, 6, 7, 8, 10, 11, 12.

For temporary act authorizing cities and towns to borrow on account of public welfare and soldiers' benefits from the commonwealth and elsewhere, and authorizing the commonwealth to issue bonds or notes to provide funds therefor, see 1933, 307 (as changed by 1933, 344 §§ 3, 4; 1934, 335; and as affected by 1933, 367 § 1).

For legislation authorizing cities, towns and districts to borrow, in the years 1935 to 1944, inclusive, on account of public welfare and soldiers' benefits and their share of the cost of certain federal emergency unemployment relief projects, see 1935, 188; 1936, 80; 1937, 107; 1938, 58; 1939, 72, 453; 1941, 92; 1943, 44.

For legislation authorizing cities, towns and districts to borrow, in the years 1941 to 1944, inclusive, on account of the distribution of surplus commodities in co-operation with the federal government, see 1941, 92; 1943, 44.

For legislation authorizing temporary borrowings by cities, towns and districts in anticipation of receipts from federal grants for emergency public works, see 1935, 213, 404 § 8; renewal of such borrowings, 1936, 64; further provision for the issuance and renewal of such borrowings, 1938, 82; 1941, 639 §§ 2, 3.

For temporary legislation authorizing any city or town to expend money in co-operation with the federal government prior to the passage of its annual budget, see 1938, 180; 1941, 58.

For legislation regulating the use of receipts from the sale by cities and towns of federal surplus commodity stamps, 1941, 65.

SECT. 2 revised, 1936, 224 § 4. (See 1936, 224 §§ 11, 12.)

SECT. 4 amended, 1934, 11 § 1; affected, 1934, 11 §§ 2, 3; amended, 1936, 16.

SECT. 4A added, 1935, 68 § 3 (temporary loans by cities in anticipatiou of revenue exempted from charter provisions relative to publication and referendum).

SECT. 5 amended, 1939, 37.

SECT. 5A amended, 1935, 68 § 4.

SECT. 5B added, 1943, 61 § 1 (relative to borrowing for liabilities incurred by districts prior to the annual appropriations).

SECT. 7 amended, 1936, 224 § 5. (See 1936, 224 §§ 11, 12.)

SECT. 8, clause (3) revised, 1938, 172 § 5; clause (5) revised, 1941, 83; clause (9) amended, 1939, 457.

SECT. 8A added, 1939, 108 § 1 (providing for submitting to the voters of certain cities the question of approving or disapproving orders authorizing the issue of bonds, notes or certificates of indebtedness for certain purposes). (See 1939, 108, § 2.)

SECT. 9 amended, 1941, 376.

SECT. 10 amended, 1936, 224 § 6; 1939, 24 § 1. (See 1936, 224 §§ 11, 12.)

SECT. 11 amended, 1936, 224 § 7. (See 1936, 224 §§ 11, 12.)

SECT. 12 amended, 1936, 224 § 8. (See 1936, 224 §§ 11, 12.)

SECT. 13A added, 1943, 61 § 2 (relative to the incurring of liabilities by districts prior to the annual appropriations).

S c . 16, last sentence stricken out, 1936, 224 § 10. (See 1936, 224 §§ 11, 12.)

SECT. 22 amended, 1936, 224 § 9. (See 1936, 224 §§ 11, 12.)

SECT. 29. As to tax limit of Boston, see 1932, 125; 1933, 159; 1934, 201; 1935, 284; 1936, 224.

SECT. 31A added, 1941, 473 § 1 (relative to budgets in certain cities).

SECT. 32, paragraphs added at end, 1938, 175 § 1, 378 § 16; section revised, 1941, 473 § 2.

SECT. 33 revised, 1941, 473 § 3.

SECT. 33A stricken out and new sections 33A and 33B inserted, 1943, 62 (amending and clarifying the law relative to budgets in cities).

SECT. 34 revised, 1938, 170; paragraph added at end, 1941, 93.

SECT. 35 amended, 1941, 454.

SECT. 40 amended, 1939, 339.

SECT. 46A added, 1932, 155 (making permanent certain provisions of law relative to investigations of municipal accounts and financial transactions by the director of accounts). [For prior temporary legislation, see 1926, 210; 1929, 335.]

SECT. 51 amended, 1934, 355; repealed, 1938, 458.

SECT. 54 amended, 1933, 200.

SECT. 56A added, 1934, 229 § 1 (relative to the financial year of cities). (See 1934, 229 §§ 2, 3.)

SECT. 64 added, 1941, 179 (authorizing towns to appropriate money for the payment of certain unpaid bills of previous years).

Chapter 45. — Public Parks, Playgrounds and the Public Domain.

SECT. 2 amended, 1941, 10 § 1.

SECT. 17A added, 1938, 220 (authorizing cities and towns to use certain ways therein for playground purposes).

Chapter 46. — Return and Registry of Births, Marriages and Deaths.

SECT. 1, third sentence of second paragraph revised, 1933, 280 § 1; fourth paragraph amended, 1941, 51.

SECT. 1A added, 1939, 61 § 1 (further regulating the making and recording of certificates of birth of certain abandoned children and foundlings).

SECT. 2A added, 1933, 279 (regulating the impounding of birth records of children born out of wedlock); amended, 1937, 78 § 1; revised, 1939, 269 § 1.

SECT. 3, paragraph added at end, 1939, 326 § 1.

SECT. 4A added, 1941, 434 (providing for the verification of returns of births).

SECT. 6 revised, 1939, 61 § 2.

SECT. 9 amended, 1936, 100.

SECT. 12 amended, 1937, 78 § 2.

SECT. 13, paragraph in first to sixth lines amended, 1939, 61 § 3; second paragraph amended, 1933, 280 § 2; second paragraph stricken out and two new paragraphs inserted, 1938, 63; first paragraph so inserted revised, 1943, 72 § 2; paragraph in eighteenth and nineteenth lines, as appearing in Tercentenary Edition, amended, 1938, 97; fourth paragraph, as so appearing, amended, 1941, 50; paragraph added at end, 1939, 61 § 4.

SECT. 16 amended, 1941, 351 § 4.

SECT. 17 revised, 1932, 12; amended, 1939, 269 § 2.

SECT. 19 revised, 1943, 228 § 1. (See 1943, 228 § 2.)

SECT. 20 revised, 1941, 351 § 5.

SECT. 26 amended, 1939, 326 § 2.

Chapter 48. — Fires, Fire Departments and Fire Districts.

For emergency legislation incident to the National Industrial Recovery Act, the Emergency Relief Appropriation Act of 1935 and certain other federal acts, see 1933, 366; 1934, 21; 1935, 404; 1936, 64, 83, 414; 1938, 50; 1939, 423 §§ 1, 2; 1941, 639 § 1; 1943, 58.

For legislation authorizing cities, towns and districts to borrow, in the years 1935 to 1944, inclusive, on account of public welfare and soldiers' benefits and their share of the cost of certain federal emergency unemployment relief projects, see 1935, 188; 1936, 80; 1937, 107; 1938, 58; 1939, 72, 453; 1941, 92; 1943, 44.

For legislation authorizing cities, towns and districts to borrow, in the years 1941 to 1944, inclusive, on account of the distribution of surplus commodities in co-operation with the federal government, see 1941, 92; 1943, 44.

For legislation authorizing temporary borrowings by cities, towns and districts in anticipation of receipts from federal grants for emergency public works, see 1935, 213, 404 § 8; renewal of such borrowings, 1936, 64; further provision for the issuance and renewal of such loans, 1938, 82; 1941, 639 §§ 2, 3.

For legislation authorizing the renewal by certain districts of certain temporary revenue loans, see 1939, 68; 1941, 134; 1943, 60.

For emergency legislation authorizing certain districts to make certain appropriations during the existing state of war, see 1943, 75 §§ 1, 2, 4, 5. [For prior legislation, see 1941, 487; 1942, 4 § 5; 1943, 5 § 6.]

SECT. 8 amended, 1941, 490 § 10.

SECT. 13 amended, 1938, 204; revised, 1941, 581.

SECT. 15 amended, 1932, 180 § 8; 1941, 490 § 11.

SECT. 16 revised, 1943, 103 § 1.

SECT. 18 revised, 1943, 103 § 2.

SECT. 28A amended, 1941, 490 § 12.

SECT. 28B. See 1941, 688.

SECT. 58A added, 1941, 638 (further regulating the hours of duty of permanent members of fire departments in certain cities and towns).

SECT. 59E added, 1939, 419 § 1 (providing for the ultimate abolition of reserve fire forces in certain cities and towns).

Chapter 50. — General Provisions relative to Primaries, Caucuses and Elections.

SECT. 1, paragraph defining "Ballot labels" inserted, 1941, 511 § 1; paragraph in lines 19–21 revised, 1943, 453 § 6; paragraph in lines 54 and 55 revised, 1941, 511 § 2; paragraph in lines 56–62 amended, 1943, 318 § 5; paragraph in lines 91 and 92 revised, 1943, 453 § 7; paragraph inserted after paragraph in line 93, 1943, 453 § 8.

SECT. 2 amended, 1932, 141 § 1; sentence added at end, 1938, 341 § 4.

SECT. 8 amended, 1943, 453 § 9.

Chapter 51. — Voters.

For legislation providing for a state wide verification of voting lists, see 1938, 427; repealed and superseded by 1939, 450; amended, 1943, 537.

SECT. 1, first paragraph revised, 1943, 453 § 10; paragraph added at end, 1932, 206.

SECT. 2 amended, 1933, 254 § 3. (See 1933, 254 § 66.)

SECT. 3 amended, 1933, 254 § 4; revised, 1943, 453 § 11. (See 1933, 254 § 66.)

Heading before section 4 revised, 1943, 453 § 12.

SECT. 4 amended, 1933, 254 § 5; first paragraph revised, 1935, 345 § 1; amended, 1937, 1 § 1; revised, 1938, 186 § 1; section revised, 1938, 440 § 2; section amended, 1943, 453 § 13. (See 1933, 254 §§ 65, 66; 1937, 226; 1938, 186 § 5, 440 § 23.)

SECT. 5 revised, 1938, 440 § 3; 1939, 188 § 1. (See 1938, 440 § 23.)
SECT. 6 revised, 1938, 440 § 4; 1939, 188 § 2. (See 1938, 440 § 23.)
SECT. 7 amended, 1933, 254 § 6; revised, 1935, 345 § 2; amended, 1938, 440 § 5; revised, 1939, 188 § 3. (See 1933, 254 §§ 65, 66; 1938, 440 § 23.)
SECT. 8 amended, 1933, 254 § 7; 1937, 1 § 2; revised, 1938, 186 § 2, 440 § 6. (See 1933, 254 § 66; 1938, 186 § 5, 440 § 23.)
SECT. 9 amended, 1933, 254 § 8; revised, 1938, 440 § 7. (See 1933, 254 § 66; 1938, 440 § 23.)
SECT. 10 amended, 1938, 440 § 8; repealed, 1943, 453 § 14. (See 1938, 440 § 23.)
SECTS. 10A and 10B added, 1939, 369 § 1 (providing for the securing of information relative to persons residing at inns, lodging houses and public lodging houses); sections stricken out and new section 10A inserted, 1943, 320 § 1.
SECT. 11 revised, 1938, 440 § 9. (See 1938, 440 § 23.)
SECT. 12 revised, 1938, 440 § 10. (See 1938, 440 § 23.)
SECT. 13 repealed, 1943, 453 § 15.
SECT. 14A revised, 1938, 440 § 11. (See 1938, 440 § 23.)
SECT. 14B added, 1933, 254 § 9 (amending special acts relative to the listing of voters in certain municipalities so as to conform to the change in taxing date from April 1 to January 1); revised, 1938, 440 § 12; amended, 1943, 453 § 16. (See 1933, 254 §§ 65, 66; 1938, 440 § 23.)
SECT. 20 revised, 1943, 453 § 17.
SECT. 22 amended, 1938, 280; revised, 1943, 453 § 18.
SECT. 23 amended, 1943, 453 § 19.
SECT. 26 amended, 1932, 48 § 1; 1935, 37 § 1; 1938, 473 § 2; 1943, 453 § 20.
SECT. 27 revised, 1932, 48 § 2; amended, 1935, 37 § 2; 1938, 473 § 3; amended, 1943, 109 § 1; revised, 1943, 453 § 21.
SECT. 29A amended, 1943, 109 § 2.
SECT. 29B added, 1938, 179 (providing for sessions of registrars of voters in all the wards of every city prior to each biennial state election); amended, 1943, 453 § 22.
SECT. 30, first sentence amended, 1943, 453 § 23.
SECT. 32 amended, 1933, 254 § 10. (See 1933, 254 § 66.)
SECT. 34 amended, 1933, 254 § 11. (See 1933, 254 § 66.)
SECT. 35 revised, 1938, 440 § 13; amended, 1939, 451 § 10. (See 1938, 440 § 23.)
SECT. 36 amended, 1933, 254 § 12; paragraph added at end, 1943, 453 § 24. (See 1933, 254 § 66.)
SECT. 37 amended, 1933, 254 § 13; revised, 1938, 440 § 14; fourth sentence amended, 1939, 369 § 2; 1943, 320 § 2; last sentence stricken out, 1941, 328 § 2; section revised, 1943, 453 § 25. (See 1933, 254 § 66; 1938, 440 § 23.)
SECT. 38 revised, 1943, 453 § 26.
SECT. 39 amended, 1938, 440 § 15. (See 1938, 440 § 23.)
SECT. 41 revised, 1943, 453 § 27.
SECT. 41A added, 1941, 328 § 1 (ensuring that certain laws relative to registration of persons residing at inns and lodging houses are of general application); revised, 1943, 320 § 3.

SECT. 43 amended, 1933, 254 § 14; revised, 1938, 440 § 16. (See 1933, 254 § 66; 1938, 440 § 23.)
SECT. 44 amended, 1943, 453 § 28.
SECT. 45 revised, 1943, 108.
SECT. 50 amended, 1938, 440 § 17. (See 1938, 440 § 23.)
SECT. 55 amended, 1933, 254 § 15; sentence added at end, 1936, 2 § 1; same sentence revised, 1938, 473 § 4; section amended, 1943, 453 § 29. (See 1933, 254 § 66.)
SECT. 57 amended, 1943, 453 § 30.
SECT. 61 amended, 1937, 21 § 1.
SECT. 62 amended, 1943, 453 § 31.
SECT. 63 revised, 1943, 453 § 32.

Chapter 52. — Political Committees.

The following references are to chapter 52, as appearing in the Tercentenary Edition:
SECT. 1 amended, 1932, 310 § 1; revised, 1934, 288 § 1; 1936, 99. (See 1934, 288 § 5; 1937, 384, 435.)
SECT. 2 amended, 1932, 310 § 2; revised, 1934, 288 § 2; amended, 1936, 11 § 2. (See 1934, 288 § 5; 1936, 11 § 3; 1937, 384, 435.)
SECT. 4 amended, 1934, 288 § 3. (See 1934, 288 § 5.)
SECT. 7 amended, 1934, 118; first paragraph stricken out, 1934, 288 § 4. (See 1934, 288 § 5; 1937, 384, 435.)
SECT. 9 amended, 1932, 310 § 3; 1937, 24 § 1. (See 1937, 384, 435.)
Chapter stricken out and new chapter inserted, 1938, 346 § 1. (See 1938, 346 §§ 3, 4.)
The following reference is to the new chapter 52:
SECT. 9 revised, 1941, 337 § 1.

Chapter 53. — Nominations, Questions to be submitted to the Voters, Primaries and Caucuses.

SECT. 1 amended, 1939, 371.
SECT. 2 amended, 1932, 310 § 4; last sentence revised, 1934, 32 § 1; section revised, 1938, 473 § 5; 1941, 337 § 2. (See 1937, 384, 435.)
SECT. 3 revised, 1936, 116 § 1; amended, 1937, 45 § 1; revised, 1943, 334 § 1.
SECT. 6 amended, 1936, 101; revised, 1939, 191; 1941, 266; amended, 1943, 50; revised, 1943, 334 § 2.
SECT. 7 amended, 1933, 254 § 16; sentence inserted, 1936, 2 § 2; section revised, 1936, 4 § 1; amended, 1937, 25 § 1; 1938, 341 § 5; first and second sentences revised, 1943, 334 § 3. (See 1933, 254 § 66.)
SECT. 7A added, 1943, 229 § 2 (relative to the certification of nomination petitions for preliminary elections in cities).
SECT. 8, first paragraph amended, 1932, 135 § 4; section amended, 1933, 35 § 1; first sentence amended, 1938, 473 § 6; section revised, 1943, 334 § 4.
SECT. 10, first paragraph amended, 1934, 111; revised, 1937, 45 § 2; amended, 1938, 373 § 4; second paragraph revised, 1933, 313 § 2; 1941, 278; amended, 1941, 472 § 4; 1943, 229 § 3; third paragraph revised, 1937, 77 § 2; amended, 1943, 334 § 5.
SECT. 11, sentence added at end, 1933, 313 § 3; revised, 1937, 77 § 3; section revised, 1937, 212 § 1; amended, 1943, 334 § 6.

SECT. 12 revised, 1937, 212 § 2; first paragraph amended, 1943, 334 § 7; paragraph added at end, 1939, 166.
SECT. 12A added, 1933, 305 (to prevent certain fraudulent nominations).
SECT. 13, sentence added at end, 1933, 313 § 4; section amended, 1937, 26, 77 § 4.
SECT. 14, sentence inserted after third sentence, 1943, 334 § 8.
SECT. 15 amended, 1943, 334 § 9.
SECT. 17 amended, 1943, 334 § 10.
SECT. 17A added, under the heading "ENDORSEMENT FOR NOMINATION OF MEMBERS OF STATE POLITICAL COMMITTEES BY CONVENTIONS", 1938, 397.
SECT. 18 revised, 1934, 282.
SECT. 20 revised, 1943, 334 § 11.
SECT. 22A amended, 1932, 80; 1938, 192; 1943, 51.
SECT. 22B added, 1938, 191 (requiring persons circulating initiative and referendum petitions to attest the validity of signatures thereto under the penalties of perjury).
SECT. 24. See 1937, 275.
SECT. 26 amended, 1943, 334 § 12.
SECT. 28 amended, 1932, 310 § 5; revised, 1933, 313 § 5; amended, 1934, 32 § 2; revised, 1938, 473 § 7. (See 1937, 384, 435.)
SECT. 32 amended, 1932, 310 § 6; 1938, 473 § 8. (See 1937, 384, 435.)
SECT. 33, sentence added at end, 1941, 511 § 3.
SECT. 34 revised, 1932, 310 § 7; first paragraph revised, 1938, 436 § 1; fourth paragraph revised, 1937, 22; section revised, 1938, 473 § 9; second and third paragraphs revised, 1941, 337 § 3; fifth paragraph revised, 1941, 352; amended, 1943, 334 § 13. (See 1937, 384, 435.)
SECT. 35 amended, 1932, 310 § 8; 1938, 473 § 10; amended, 1941, 337 § 4. (See 1937, 384, 435.)
SECT. 35A added, 1943, 301 (relative to pasters or stickers for use at primaries).
SECT. 36 amended, 1941, 511 § 4.
SECT. 37 revised, 1943, 334 § 14.
SECT. 38 amended, 1938, 299; 1943, 334 § 15.
SECT. 40 revised, 1932, 30.
SECT. 40A added, 1943, 334 § 16 (requiring petitions for recounts at primaries of a political party to be signed by enrolled voters thereof).
SECT. 41 revised, 1932, 310 § 9; section and title preceding it stricken out and new section inserted under the heading "PROVISIONS APPLYING TO STATE PRIMARIES", 1938, 473 § 11; section revised, 1941, 337 § 5. (See 1937, 384, 435.)
SECT. 42 amended, 1932, 310 § 10; 1937, 24 § 2; revised, 1938, 373 § 1. (See 1937, 384, 435.)
SECT. 43 amended, 1932, 310 § 11; 1937, 201. (See 1937, 384, 435.)
SECT. 44 revised, 1932, 310 § 12; amended, 1935, 38; revised, 1938, 373 § 2, 473 § 12; amended, 1941, 337 § 6. (See 1937, 384, 435.)
SECT. 45 amended, 1932, 310 § 13; first paragraph amended, 1936, 22; 1938, 84; section revised, 1938, 473 § 13; amended, 1941, 337 § 7. (See 1937, 384, 435.)
SECT. 46 amended, 1936, 4 § 2; revised, 1937, 25 § 2; amended, 1941, 337 § 8.

SECT. 47 amended, 1932, 310 § 14; 1938, 473 § 14. (See 1937, 384, 435.)

SECT. 48 amended, 1932, 310 § 15; first paragraph revised, 1938, 373 § 3; paragraph added at end, 1938, 272; same paragraph amended, 1941, 563; paragraph added at end, 1941, 675; section amended, 1943, 53. (See 1937, 384, 435.)

SECT. 49 revised, 1932, 310 § 16; 1938, 473 § 15. (See 1937, 384, 435.)

SECT. 51 amended, 1932, 310 § 17; 1938, 473 § 16. (See 1937, 384, 435.)

SECT. 52 amended, 1932, 310 § 18; revised, 1938, 473 § 17; amended, 1941, 337 § 9. (See 1937, 384, 435.)

SECT. 53 revised, 1932, 310 § 19; 1938, 473 § 18; amended, 1941, 337 § 10. (See 1937, 384, 435.)

SECT. 53A amended, 1932, 310 § 20; revised, 1938, 473 § 19. (See 1937, 384, 435.)

SECT. 54 revised, 1932, 310 § 21; two sentences added, 1935, 482 § 1; section amended, 1936, 11 § 1; 1937, 24 § 3; section (and heading) revised, 1938, 346 § 2; section amended, 1941, 337 § 11. (See 1936, 11 §§ 2, 3; 1937, 384, 435; 1938, 346 §§ 3, 4.)

SECTS. 54A and 54B added, 1932, 310 § 22 (relative to proceedings at pre-primary conventions, to the form of certificates of nomination of candidates thereat, and to the acceptance of such nominations); repealed, 1938, 473 § 20. (See 1937, 384, 435.)

SECT. 55, paragraph added at end, 1936, 116 § 2.

SECT. 56, amended, 1943, 334 § 17.

SECT. 57 amended, 1937, 410.

SECT. 61 amended, 1936, 140; 1937, 411; 1941, 272.

SECTS. 65–70 (and caption) repealed, 1932, 310 § 23. (See 1937, 384, 435; 1938, 473 § 21.)

SECTS. 70A–70H added, under heading "PROVISIONS APPLYING TO PRESIDENTIAL PRIMARIES," 1938, 473 § 21.

SECT. 70B amended, 1941, 337 § 12.

SECT. 70F amended, 1939, 451 § 11.

SECT. 71. See 1937, 275.

SECT. 72A added, 1933, 313 § 6 (relative to caucuses before regular city elections in cities having absent voting); revised, 1937, 77 § 5.

SECT. 112 amended, 1935, 59 § 2.

SECT. 117 amended, 1932, 141 § 2.

SECT. 121 added, 1932, 141 § 3 (authorizing the nomination by caucuses other than those of political or municipal parties of two candidates for each town office); revised, 1936, 204.

Chapter 54. — Elections.

For temporary legislation relative to qualification of and absent voting by members of the armed forces during the present war, see 1943, 390.

SECT. 2 amended, 1943, 411 § 1.

SECT. 4 revised, 1935, 482 § 2; amended, 1936, 185; revised, 1937, 412.

SECT. 5 revised, 1943, 209 § 1.

SECT. 6 revised, 1943, 411 § 2.

SECT. 7 revised, 1943, 411 § 3.

SECT. 9A added, 1937, 267 § 1 (relative to the use of precincts in certain towns in the formation of representative districts).

SECT. 11 amended, 1932, 76 § 1; 1934, 158 § 1; 1937, 27; 1938, 341 § 6; revised, 1941, 432 § 1.

SECT. 11A added, 1932, 76 § 2 (dispensing with the appointment of deputy election officers in certain cities).

SECT. 11B added, 1941, 432 § 2 (relative to the appointment of election officers in certain cities); revised, 1943, 230.

SECT. 12 amended, 1934, 158 § 2.

SECT. 13 amended, 1934, 158 § 3; 1943, 411 § 4.

SECT. 14 amended, 1943, 411 § 5.

SECT. 16A added, 1943, 411 § 6 (relative to the temporary filling of vacancies in the offices of election officers).

SECT. 19 amended, 1934, 158 § 4.

SECT. 21 amended, 1934, 158 § 5.

SECT. 22 amended, 1943, 411 § 7.

SECT. 23 amended, 1943, 411 § 8.

SECT. 24, last sentence stricken out and two new sentences inserted, 1943, 209 § 2.

SECT. 25 revised, 1943, 411 § 9.

SECT. 26 amended, 1938, 281 § 1; 1943, 240.

SECT. 30 amended, 1943, 310 § 1.

SECT. 30A added, 1943, 310 § 2 (relative to election officers in places where voting machines are used).

SECT. 31, paragraph added at end, 1943, 310 § 3.

SECT. 33, last sentence stricken out, and paragraph inserted at end, 1935, 238 § 1.

SECTS. 33A-33D added, 1943, 310 § 4 (relative to the use of voting machines at primaries and elections).

SECT. 34 revised, 1936, 205 § 1; second paragraph stricken out, 1938, 281 § 2.

SECT. 35 revised, 1943, 310 § 5.

SECTS. 35A and 35B added, 1938, 281 § 3 (relative to voting by challenged voters at polling places where voting machines are used and to the counting of votes where such machines are used).

SECT. 35A, sentence added at end, 1941, 511 § 5.

SECT. 35B, second sentence of second paragraph revised, 1941, 511 § 6; second paragraph revised, 1943, 310 § 6; third paragraph amended, 1941, 511 § 7.

SECT. 38 revised, 1936, 205 § 2.

SECT. 41, third paragraph amended, 1933, 35 § 2; 1938, 190; second sentence of same paragraph revised, 1938, 436 § 2; last paragraph stricken out and three paragraphs inserted, 1943, 411 § 11.

SECT. 42 amended, 1932, 135 § 5; first paragraph amended, 1935, 238 § 2; same paragraph revised, 1941, 292; last paragraph amended, 1943, 411 § 12.

SECT. 43 revised, 1932, 135 § 1.

SECT. 44 amended, 1943, 411 § 13.

SECT. 45, first sentence revised, 1943, 281 § 1; paragraph added at end, 1943, 281 § 2.

SECT. 48 amended, 1943, 290.

SECT. 49 amended, 1943, 411 § 14.
SECT. 60, last sentence amended, 1938, 281 § 6.
SECT. 62 amended, 1935, 257 § 5. (See 1935, 257 § 12.)
SECT. 64, last paragraph amended, 1934, 39 § 5.
SECT. 65 revised, 1933, 289 § 1; amended, 1943, 411 § 15.
SECT. 70 revised, 1943, 411 § 16.
SECT. 71. See 1937, 275.
SECT. 71A added, 1943, 411 § 17 (requiring that election officers in cities and in certain towns be supervised by the city or town clerk).
SECT. 75 amended, 1943, 411 § 18.
SECT. 76 revised, 1943, 411 § 19.
SECT. 76A added, 1943, 411 § 20 (requiring a person applying to vote to write his name upon request of any election officer).
SECT. 78 revised, 1932, 135 § 2.
SECT. 79 amended, 1943, 411 § 21.
SECT. 85A added, 1937, 275 § 1 (relative to the challenging of voters at polling places at certain elections, primaries and caucuses). (See 1937, 275 § 2.)
SECT. 87, subsection (*b*) revised, 1936, 404 § 1; subsection (*c*) revised, 1936, 404 § 2; amended, 1937, 162 § 2; 1941, 279 § 2; subsection (*d*) revised, 1941, 333.
SECT. 89 revised, 1936, 404 § 3.
SECT. 92 revised, 1936, 404 § 4; amended, 1937, 162 § 1; 1941, 279 § 1.
SECT. 93 revised, 1936, 404 § 5; amended, 1941, 722 § 8.
SECT. 95 revised, 1936, 404 § 6.
SECT. 96 amended, 1936, 404 § 7.
SECT. 100 revised, 1936, 404 § 8.
SECT. 103A added, 1933, 313 § 1 (providing for absent voting at regular city elections); affected, 1936, 404 § 9; revised, 1937, 77 § 1; first paragraph amended, 1939, 152.
SECT. 104 amended, 1934, 39 § 6.
SECT. 105, fourth paragraph amended, 1938, 341 § 7.
SECT. 107 revised, 1943, 411 § 22.
SECT. 109 amended, 1943, 411 § 23.
SECT. 112 amended, 1935, 257 § 6; 1939, 31 § 3. (See 1935, 257 § 12.)
SECT. 122 amended, 1935, 257 § 7. (See 1935, 257 § 12.)
SECT. 132 amended, 1932, 33.
SECT. 133 amended, 1937, 21 § 2.
SECT. 134 amended, 1943, 411 § 24.
SECT. 135, first paragraph amended, 1933, 254 § 17; section revised, 1933, 270; first paragraph revised, 1935, 59 § 1; 1938, 250 § 1; 1941, 236; third paragraph revised, 1937, 303; same paragraph amended, 1941, 350; last paragraph revised, 1938, 250 § 2; paragraph inserted after first paragraph, 1938, 281 § 4; section revised, 1943, 417. (See 1933, 254 § 66.)
SECT. 135A added, 1938, 281 § 5 (relative to the recounting of votes where voting machines are used); amended, 1943, 411 § 25.
SECT. 137 amended, 1935, 55.
SECT. 138, last paragraph amended, 1937, 23 § 1.
SECT. 139 amended, 1943, 49.
SECT. 141 amended, 1939, 508 § 16.

SECT. 144 revised, 1935, 257 § 8; first paragraph amended, 1939, 31 § 4. (See 1935, 257 § 12.)

SECT. 146 amended, 1935, 257 § 9. (See 1935, 257 § 12.)

SECT. 148 amended, 1937, 23 § 2.

SECT. 151 amended, 1932, 135 § 3.

SECT. 158 amended, 1935, 257 § 10; first paragraph revised, 1939, 31 § 5. (See 1935, 257 § 12.)

SECT. 161 (except last paragraph) amended, 1934, 265. (See 1939, 467.)

Chapter 54A. — Election of City and Town Officers by Proportional Representation and Preferential Voting.

New chapter inserted, 1937, 345.

Chapter inserted by 1937, 345 stricken out and new chapter inserted, 1938, 341 § 1.

SECT. 1 amended, 1941, 345.

SECT. 2, paragraph added at end, 1938, 378 § 17; section revised, 1941, 640 § 6. (See 1941, 640 § 7.)

Chapter 55. — Corrupt Practices and Election Inquests.

SECT. 1 revised, 1943, 318 § 1.

SECT. 5 amended, 1943, 318 § 2.

SECT. 6 amended, 1943, 318 § 3.

SECT. 7 amended, 1938, 75; revised, 1943, 273 § 1.

SECT. 8 revised, 1939, 223.

SECT. 16, sentence added at end, 1941, 280 § 1.

SECT. 17 amended, 1941, 280 § 2.

SECT. 17A added, 1943, 273 § 2 (requiring the filing of statements of receipts and expenditures on account of activities of certain corporations when affected by initiative petitions).

SECT. 34B added, 1943, 483 § 1 (prohibiting interference with the delivery to voters of circulars and other printed matter or the unlawful removal thereof).

SECT. 36, paragraph inserted after paragraph contained in line 10, 1943, 483 § 2.

SECT. 37 revised, 1943, 318 § 4.

Chapter 56. — Violations of Election Laws.

SECT. 1 repealed, 1939, 342 § 3.

SECT. 2 revised, 1938, 440 § 18. (See 1938, 440 § 23.)

SECT. 4 amended, 1939, 451 § 12.

SECT. 5 revised, 1938, 440 § 19; sentence added at end, 1943, 320 § 4. (See 1938, 440 § 23.)

SECT. 6 revised, 1938, 440 § 20. (See 1938, 440 § 23.)

SECT. 7 amended, 1938, 440 § 21. (See 1938, 440 § 23.)

SECT. 8 revised, 1938, 440 § 22. (See 1938, 440 § 23.)

SECT. 22 revised, 1938, 341 § 8; amended, 1943, 411 § 26.

SECT. 28 amended, 1938, 341 § 9.

SECT. 33 amended, 1939, 299 § 1.

SECT. 35 amended, 1939, 299 § 2.
SECT. 39 revised, 1933, 289 § 2.
SECT. 40 amended, 1938, 341 § 10.
SECT. 44 amended, 1938, 341 § 11.
SECT. 45 amended, 1938, 341 § 12.
SECT. 48 amended, 1939, 451 § 13.
SECT. 65A added, 1943, 483 § 3 (penalizing interference with the delivery to voters of circulars and other printed matter or the unlawful removal thereof).
SECT. 68 amended, 1939, 299 § 3.

Chapter 57. — Congressional, Councillor and Senatorial Districts, and Apportionment of Representatives.

SECT. 1 revised, 1941, 556.
SECT. 2 revised, 1939, 507 § 1.
SECT. 3 revised, 1939, 507 § 2.
SECT. 4 revised, 1939, 467 § 1. (See 1939, 467 §§ 2, 3, 4.)
SECT. 5. See 1939, 467.

Chapter 58. — General Provisions relative to Taxation.

For legislation providing for temporary cigarette taxes, see 1939, 454 §§ 1–18; 1941, 417; 1943, 407. (See 1941, 715.)

For legislation relative to the collection of certain taxes and other charges due the commonwealth, see 1935, 498 §§ 2, 3, 4; 1936, 440 §§ 2, 3, 4; 1937, 444 §§ 2, 3, 4; 1938, 503 §§ 2, 3, 4; 1939, 516 §§ 2, 3, 4, 6, 7, 8; 1941, 731 §§ 2, 3, 4, 6, 7, 8; 1943, 568 §§ 2, 3, 4, 6, 7, 8, 10, 11, 12.

SECT. 1, first sentence revised, 1943, 428 § 2; fifth sentence amended, 1932, 180 § 9; same sentence revised, 1937, 108 § 2.
SECT. 2 amended, 1933, 254 § 18; paragraph added at end, 1941, 726 § 2. (See 1933, 254 § 66.)
SECT. 3 amended, 1933, 254 § 19. (See 1933, 254 § 66.)
SECT. 8 revised, 1935, 322 § 1.
SECT. 9 revised, 1939, 346; 1941, 112.
SECT. 10 amended, 1934, 323 § 9. (See 1934, 323 § 11.)
SECT. 11 amended, 1939, 451 § 14; repealed, 1941, 609 § 1.
SECT. 12 amended, 1941, 490 § 13; repealed, 1941, 609 § 1.
SECT. 13 amended, 1933, 254 § 20. (See 1933, 254 § 66.)
SECT. 14 amended, 1939, 451 § 15.
SECT. 15 amended, 1933, 254 § 21; revised, 1941, 490 § 14. (See 1933, 254 § 66.)
SECT. 17A amended, 1939, 451 § 26.
SECT. 18 revised, 1933, 350 § 7; amended, 1936, 405 § 1; 1939, 451 § 16; affected, 1933, 357 § 4; 1935, 438 § 2. (See 1933, 307 § 11, 350 § 9; 1936, 362 § 4.)
SECT. 20 revised, 1936, 362 § 3; amended, 1937, 108 § 1; 1941, 656 § 1. (See 1936, 362 §§ 4, 8; 1937, 108 § 3.)
SECT. 20A added, 1936, 376 § 3 (relative to the set-off of money due to the commonwealth from a city or town against sums due to the city or town from the commonwealth).

SECT. 21 amended, 1933, 254 § 22; repealed, 1934, 323 § 1. (See 1933, 254 § 66; 1934, 323 § 11.)
SECTS. 22 and 23 repealed, 1934, 323 § 1. (See 1934, 323 § 11.)
SECT. 24 amended, 1933, 254 § 23. (See 1933, 254 § 66.)
SECT. 24A revised, 1934, 323 § 2. (See 1934, 323 § 11.)
SECT. 25 revised, 1934, 323 § 3; amended, 1939, 451 § 17; first sentence revised, 1941, 729 § 11. (See 1934, 323 § 11; 1941, 729 § 15.)
SECT. 25A revised, 1934, 323 § 4. (See 1934, 323 § 11.)
SECT. 26 amended, 1933, 254 § 24; repealed, 1934, 323 § 1. (See 1933, 254 § 66; 1934, 323 § 11.)
SECT. 27, first sentence revised, 1943, 521 § 1.
SECT. 31 added, under heading "FORMS", 1937, 135 § 1 (relative to forms of application for abatement of taxes and certain other forms and the approval thereof by the commissioner of corporations and taxation).

Chapter 58A. — Appellate Tax Board (former title, Board of Tax Appeals).

Title revised, 1937, 400 § 2.
SECT. 1 revised, 1937, 400 § 3. (See 1937, 400 §§ 1, 2, 4, 5, 7.)
SECT. 5 revised, 1941, 381, 596 § 24.
SECT. 6 amended, 1932, 180 § 10; revised, 1933, 167 § 4; amended, 1934, 323 § 10; revised, 1938, 478 § 4; first sentence revised, 1941, 609 § 2; same sentence amended, 1941, 726 § 1. (See 1933, 167 § 5; 1934, 323 § 11; 1937, 400 § 1.)
SECT. 7 revised, 1933, 321 § 2; amended, 1939, 451 § 18. (See 1933, 321 § 9.)
SECT. 7A added, 1933, 321 § 3 (providing for the establishment of informal procedure before the appellate tax board); revised, 1935, 447; third sentence revised, 1938, 384; 1943, 282. (See 1933, 321 §§ 8, 9.)
SECT. 8 revised, 1933, 321 § 4. (See 1933, 321 § 9.)
SECT. 8A added, 1935, 276 § 1 (providing for adequate discovery in tax appeal cases).
SECT. 10 revised, 1933, 321 § 5. (See 1933, 321 § 9.)
SECT. 12 amended, 1933, 321 § 6. (See 1933, 321 § 9.)
SECT. 12A added, 1943, 430 (relative to taxation of costs by the appellate tax board in certain appeals as to the assessed value where it exceeds the value as recently determined by said board).
SECT. 13 revised, 1933, 321 § 7; one sentence revised, 1933, 350 § 8; same sentence amended, 1935, 218 § 1; 1939, 366 § 1. (See 1933, 321 § 9, 350 § 9.)

Chapter 59. — Assessment of Local Taxes.

For temporary legislation exempting persons in the military and naval service of the United States from the payment of poll taxes, see 1943, 406.

For temporary legislation exempting from taxation certain real property of residents of the commonwealth serving in the armed forces of the United States, and their spouses, see 1943, 412.

For legislation relative to the collection of certain taxes and other charges due the commonwealth, see 1935, 498 §§ 2, 3, 4; 1936, 440

§§ 2, 3, 4; 1937, 444 §§ 2, 3, 4; 1938, 503 §§ 2, 3, 4; 1939, 516 §§ 2, 3, 4, 6, 7, 8; 1941, 731 §§ 2, 3, 4, 6, 7, 8; 1943, 568 §§ 2, 3, 4, 6, 7, 8, 10, 11, 12.

Temporary act relative to the taking of appeals involving real estate in which closed banks have an interest, 1941, 145 § 2.

As to Boston taxes, see 1932, 125; 1933, 159; 1934, 201; 1935, 284; 1936, 224.

SECT. 1 amended, 1936, 202 § 1; revised, 1938, 186 § 3. (See 1936, 202 § 2; 1938, 186 § 5.)

SECT. 5, clause First revised, 1936, 81; 1938, 47; clause Third, subsection (*c*) amended, 1933, 198 § 1 (see 1933, 198 § 2); clause Eleventh revised, 1938, 317; clause Sixteenth revised, 1936, 362 § 1; 1941, 467 (see 1936, 362 §§ 4, 8); clause Seventeenth revised, 1935, 294; amended, 1939, 451 § 19; revised, 1941, 227 § 1; clause Seventeenth A added, 1938, 186 § 4; sentence added at end, 1943, 559 (see 1938, 186 § 5); clause Eighteenth revised, 1941, 227 § 2; clause Twentieth revised, 1937, 132; 1941, 482; clause Twenty-second amended, 1939, 451 § 20; clause Twenty-third amended, 1932, 114 § 4; clause Thirty-fifth revised, 1939, 24 § 2.

SECT. 5A added, 1941, 227 § 3 (relative to collection of taxes from estates of persons who were relieved therefrom for lack of ability to pay, or otherwise).

SECT. 6 amended, 1933, 254 § 25; 1936, 59 § 1; first paragraph amended, 1941, 440. (See 1933, 254 § 66; 1936, 59 § 3.)

SECTS. 6 and 7. See 1934, 307.

SECT. 7, first paragraph amended, 1936, 59 § 2; section amended, 1939, 451 § 21. (See 1936, 59 § 3.)

SECT. 8 amended, 1933, 80, 254 § 26; paragraph added at end, 1935, 119 § 1. (See 1933, 254 § 66; 1935, 119 § 2.)

SECT. 9 amended, 1933, 254 § 27; revised, 1939, 342 § 4. (See 1933, 254 § 66.)

SECT. 10 amended, 1933, 254 § 28. (See 1933, 254 § 66.)

SECT. 11 amended, 1933, 254 § 29; revised, 1936, 92; 1939, 175. (See 1933, 254 § 66.)

SECT. 16 amended, 1937, 114.

SECT. 18, opening paragraph and clauses First and Second amended, 1933, 254 § 30; clause Second revised, 1936, 362 § 2. (See 1933, 254 § 66; 1936, 362 § 8.)

SECT. 19 amended, 1933, 254 § 31. (See 1933, 254 § 66.)

SECT. 20 revised, 1933, 254 § 32; amended, 1936, 376 § 1. (See 1933, 254 § 66.)

SECT. 21 revised, 1933, 254 § 33; 1936, 376 § 2. (See 1933, 254 § 66.)

SECT. 23, paragraph added at end, 1938, 175 § 2.

SECT. 27 amended, 1936, 118 § 2. (See 1936, 118 § 3.)

SECT. 29, last three sentences revised, 1933, 254 § 34. (See 1933, 254 § 66.)

SECT. 33 amended, 1933, 254 § 35. (See 1933, 254 § 66.)

SECT. 39 amended, 1933, 254 § 36; 1939, 451 § 22. (See 1933, 254 § 66.)

SECT. 41 amended, 1933, 254 § 37. (See 1933, 254 § 66.)

SECT. 45 amended, 1933, 254 § 38; form appended to section amended, 1933, 254 § 39. (See 1933, 254 § 66.)

Sect. 47 amended, 1933, 254 § 40. (See 1933, 254 § 66.).
Sect. 49 amended, 1933, 254 § 41. (See 1933, 254 § 66.)
Sect. 57 amended, 1933, 151 § 1; revised, 1933, 254 § 42; 1935, 158 § 1; amended, 1937, 203 § 1; revised, 1938, 330 § 1; 1941, 258 § 1. (See 1933, 151 § 2, 254 § 66; 1935, 158 § 2; 1937, 203 § 2; 1938, 330 § 2.)
Sect. 59, sentence added at end, 1933, 165 § 1; section revised, 1933, 254 § 43, 266 § 1; 1934, 136 § 2; amended, 1935, 187 § 1; revised, 1939, 250 § 1; first sentence revised, 1943, 166 § 1. (See 1933, 254 § 66, 266 § 2; 1934, 136 § 3; 1935, 187 § 2.)
Sect. 60 revised, 1941, 209.
Sect. 61, last sentence revised, 1933, 165 § 2.
Sect. 61A added, 1935, 276 § 2 (providing for adequate discovery in proceedings for tax abatement).
Sect. 63 amended, 1943, 79.
Sect. 64, first paragraph amended, 1933, 130 § 1; second paragraph amended, 1935, 218 § 2; section revised, 1937, 400 § 6; 1938, 478 § 1; first sentence amended, 1939, 31 § 6; second paragraph amended, 1939, 366 § 2; 1943, 248. (See 1937, 400 §§ 1–5, 7.)
Sect. 65 amended, 1933, 130 § 2, 167 § 1; revised, 1938, 478 § 2; 1939, 31 § 7.
Sect. 65A added, 1932, 218 § 1 (providing that the sale or taking of real property for payment of unpaid taxes thereon shall not prejudice proceedings for the abatement of such taxes); revised, 1933, 325 § 18. (See 1932, 218 § 2; 1933, 325 § 19.)
Sect. 65B added, 1938, 478 § 3 (relative to appeals to the appellate tax board from the refusal of assessors to abate certain taxes on real estate).
Sect. 69 amended, 1935, 218 § 3; 1939, 366 § 3.
Sect. 73 amended, 1933, 254 § 44. (See 1933, 254 § 66.)
Sect. 74 amended, 1933, 254 § 45; 1939, 24 § 3. (See 1933, 254 § 66.)
Sect. 75 amended, 1934, 104.
Sect. 78 amended, 1941, 258 § 5.
Sect. 79 amended, 1938, 150 § 1.
Sect. 83 amended, 1933, 254 § 46; 1939, 24 § 4. (See 1933, 254 § 66.)
Sect. 84 amended, 1933, 254 § 47. (See 1933, 254 § 66.)
Sect. 85 amended, 1933, 254 § 48. (See 1933, 254 § 66.) Affected, 1941, 609.
Sect. 86 amended, 1933, 254 § 49. (See 1933, 254 § 66.)

Chapter 60. — Collection of Local Taxes.

Temporary act relative to the care and disposal of land acquired by cities and towns through foreclosure of tax titles, 1938, 358; amended to include care and disposal of lands of low value acquired by cities and towns through purchase, 1939, 123; further amended and extended, 1941, 296.
Sect. 1, third paragraph revised, 1933, 164 § 1; last two paragraphs amended, 1943, 37 § 1.
Sect. 3 revised, 1933, 254 § 50; amended, 1941, 258 § 2; 1943, 37 § 2; sentence inserted after third sentence, 1943, 166 § 2. (See 1933, 254 § 66.)

SECT. 3A added, 1934, 136 § 1 (requiring that certain information relative to abatement or exemptions be included in tax bills); amended, 1936, 156; revised, 1943, 166 § 3, 564 § 1. (See 1934, 136 § 3; 1943, 564 § 2.)

SECT. 3B added, 1935, 322 § 2 (relative to the suspension of payment of certain assessments payable by certain persons entitled to exemption from local taxes).

SECT. 4 revised, 1939, 342 § 5.

SECT. 5 revised, 1933, 168 § 2; amended, 1941, 258 § 3.

SECT. 13, sentence added at end, 1937, 143 § 5; section revised, 1939, 44; 1941, 308.

SECT. 15, first paragraph amended, 1934, 151 § 2; 1935, 252 § 1; section revised, 1943, 179.

SECT. 15A added, 1935, 252 § 2 (further regulating charges and fees for the collection of poll taxes).

SECT. 16 revised, 1933, 168 § 1; amended, 1933, 254 § 51. (See 1933, 168 § 4, 254 § 66.)

SECT. 18 repealed, 1932, 54 § 1.

SECT. 22 revised, 1933, 254 § 52; affected, 1933, 308. (See 1933, 254 § 66.)

SECT. 22A added, 1941, 573 § 1 (relative to bills for taxes on parcels of real estate and payments on account thereof). (See 1941, 573 § 2.)

SECT. 23 revised, 1932, 197 § 1; two sentences added at end, 1943, 478 § 3.

SECT. 35 revised, 1938, 150 § 2.

SECT. 37 amended, 1933, 254 § 53, 325 § 1; 1934, 131 § 2; revised, 1934, 169; amended, 1935, 269; 1936, 146; last sentence revised, 1941, 84 § 1; section revised, 1943, 478 § 1. (See 1933, 254 § 66; 1934, 131 § 3; 1941, 84 § 2.)

SECT. 37A added, 1943, 478 § 2 (relative to the continuance of local tax liens during the existence of legal impediments to sales or takings thereunder).

SECT. 38 amended, 1933, 254 § 54, 325 § 2. (See 1933, 254 § 66, 325 § 21.)

SECT. 39 amended, 1933, 325 § 3.

SECT. 42 revised, 1933, 164 § 2.

SECT. 43, last sentence revised, 1932, 54 § 2; section amended, 1935, 183, 236.

SECT. 45 amended, 1933, 325 § 4; 1937, 209; 1938, 339 § 1.

SECT. 46, paragraph added at end, 1934, 131 § 1.

SECT. 48 amended, 1933, 325 § 5. (See 1933, 325 § 20.)

SECT. 50 revised, 1933, 325 § 6; amended, 1935, 414 § 1; 1936, 93 § 2; amended, 1941, 319 § 1. (See 1935, 414 § 4; 1941, 319 §§ 3, 4.)

SECT. 50A added, 1934, 154 § 2 (providing for protection of interests in real estate held under tax sales or takings).

SECT. 51 amended, 1933, 254 § 55. (See 1933, 254 § 66.)

SECT. 52 revised, 1936, 392 § 1.

SECT. 53 revised, 1933, 164 § 3. (See 1933, 325 § 20.)

SECT. 54 amended, 1933, 325 § 7; 1938, 339 § 2.

SECT. 55 amended, 1933, 325 § 8.

SECT. 58 revised, 1932, 2; 1939, 250 § 2.

SECT. 59 amended, 1933, 254 § 56. (See 1933, 254 § 66.)

SECT. 61 revised, 1933, 325 § 9; amended, 1934, 48; 1936, 93 § 1. (See 1933, 325 § 20.)

SECT. 61A added, 1943, 188 (relative to taking for nonpayment of taxes lands subject to tax titles held by municipalities when the assessment unit is changed).

SECT. 62 revised, 1933, 325 § 10; first paragraph amended, 1934, 218; same paragraph revised, 1935, 414 § 2; second paragraph revised, 1935, 278; section revised, 1936, 392 § 2; second paragraph amended, 1941, 231; paragraph inserted after the second paragraph, 1938, 415 § 5. (See 1935, 414 § 4.)

SECT. 63 amended, 1933, 325 § 11; revised, 1936, 392 § 3.

SECT. 65 amended, 1933, 325 § 12; 1938, 305.

SECT. 66 amended, 1935, 224 § 1. (See 1935, 224 § 6.)

SECT. 67 amended, 1935, 224 § 2. (See 1935, 224 § 6.)

SECT. 68 amended, 1935, 224 § 3; paragraph added at end, 1935, 354 § 1; section amended, 1935, 414 § 3. (See 1935, 224 § 6, 354 § 3, 414 § 4.)

SECT. 69 amended, 1935, 224 § 4. (See 1935, 224 § 6.)

SECT. 70 amended, 1935, 224 § 5. (See 1935, 224 § 6.)

SECT. 71 amended, 1941, 319 § 2. (See 1941, 319 §§ 3, 4.)

SECT. 75 amended, 1936, 189 § 1.

SECT. 76 revised, 1935, 318 § 1; amended, 1936, 189 § 2. (See 1935, 318 §§ 2, 8.)

SECT. 76A added, 1935, 354 § 2 (providing for redemption in part from tax sales in certain cases); paragraph added at end, 1939, 181. (See 1935, 354 § 3.)

SECT. 76B added, 1938, 415 § 6 (relative to the effect of errors or irregularities in respect to water rates and charges included in a tax title account).

SECT. 77, paragraph added at end, 1938, 339 § 3.

SECT. 78 amended, 1933, 325 § 13; repealed, 1936, 194. (See 1933, 325 § 20.)

SECT. 79, second paragraph amended, 1933, 325 § 14; 1935, 173 § 1; section revised, 1941, 594 § 1.

SECT. 80 amended, 1933, 325 § 15; revised, 1935, 173 § 2; amended, 1941, 594 § 2. (See 1939, 123; 1941, 296.)

SECTS. 80A and 80B added, 1941, 594 § 3 (relative to the validity of title acquired at sales of lands of low value held by cities and towns under tax titles).

SECT. 84 revised, 1935, 260.

SECT. 84A revised, 1933, 325 § 16; 1935, 181 § 1. (See 1935, 181 § 2.)

SECT. 92 revised, 1933, 82 § 1; amended, 1934, 259 § 1.

SECT. 93 revised, 1943, 199.

SECT. 95 revised, 1933, 325 § 17; amended, 1934, 315 § 2; revised, 1935, 248 § 3; amended, 1939, 451 § 23; 1941, 380 § 6; sentence added at end, 1943, 107. (See 1934, 315 § 3.)

SECT. 97 revised, 1934, 151 § 1.

SECT. 104 revised, 1937, 43.

SECT. 105 revised, 1933, 168 § 3; 1941, 258 § 4.

Form 2 in schedule at end of chapter repealed, 1932, 54 § 1; schedule of forms at end of chapter stricken out, 1933, 168 § 3.

Chapter 60A. — Excise Tax on Registered Motor Vehicles in Lieu of Local Tax.

SECT. 1, first paragraph amended, 1936, 384 § 1; last paragraph amended, 1936, 384 § 2; paragraph added at end, 1938, 111; section revised, 1938, 480 § 1; fourth paragraph amended, 1941, 718 § 1. (See 1941, 718 § 2.)

SECT. 2 revised, 1936, 384 § 3; 1938, 480 § 2; ninth sentence amended, 1939, 366 § 4.

SECT. 2A added, 1938, 492 § 1 (providing for the suspension of certificates of registration in cases of nonpayment of the excise on registered motor vehicles); last sentence stricken out, 1943, 18.

SECT. 3 revised, 1936, 384 § 4; 1938, 480 § 3.

SECT. 4 revised, 1938, 480 § 4, 492 § 2.

SECT. 6 amended, 1936, 384 § 5; revised, 1938, 480 § 5.

Chapter 61. — Classification and Taxation of Forest Lands and Forest Products (former title Taxation of Forest Products and Classification and Taxation of Forest Lands).

SECT. 3 amended, 1933, 254 § 57. (See 1933, 254 § 66.)

SECT. 5 amended, 1941, 490 § 15.

Chapter stricken out, and new chapter 61 (with new title) inserted, 1941, 652 § 1. (See 1941, 652 § 2.)

SECT. 1, first paragraph stricken out and two paragraphs inserted, 1943, 461 § 1. (See 1943, 461 §§ 4 and 5.)

SECT. 2, second schedule and all preceding such schedule revised, 1943, 461 § 2. (See 1943, 461 §§ 4 and 5.)

SECT. 6 amended, 1943, 461 § 3. (See 1943, 461 §§ 4 and 5.)

Chapter 62. — Taxation of Incomes.

For legislation establishing an additional tax upon personal incomes to provide funds for old age assistance. See 1941, 729 §§ 9, 15; 1943, 482 § 3.

For temporary legislation relative to the taxation of dividends of certain corporations, see 1933, 307, 357; 1935, 489; 1936, 82 § 1; 1937, 395; 1938, 489 §§ 2-5; 1939, 373; 1941, 331; 1943, 285.

For temporary legislation providing for additional taxes upon personal incomes, see 1935, 480; 1936, 397; 1937, 422; 1938, 502; 1939, 454 § 19; 1941, 416 §§ 1, 3; 1943, 482 §§ 1, 3, 4.

SECT. 1, subsection (*c*), paragraph Third added, 1935, 489 § 6; subsection (*e*) amended, 1935, 489 § 7.

SECT. 3 revised, 1943, 45 § 1.

SECT. 5, paragraph (*b*) amended, 1935, 489 § 8; same paragraph revised, 1939, 486 § 1; paragraph (*c*) revised, 1934, 363 § 1; 1935, 481 § 1. (See 1934, 363 § 2; 1935, 481 § 2; 1939, 486 § 3.)

SECT. 6, clause (*g*) revised, 1935, 436 § 1; clause (*h*) revised, 1943, 511. (See 1935, 436 § 2.)

SECTS. 7A and 7B added, 1935, 438 § 1 (relative to income taxation of gains from certain transactions in real property).

SECT. 18. See Sect. 18 of Chapter 58 in this Table.

SECT. 21A added, under caption "PRESUMPTION AS TO INHABITANCY", 1936, 310 (providing that individuals under certain circumstances shall be presumed to be inhabitants of the Commonwealth for income tax purposes); repealed, 1938, 489 § 8.
SECT. 22 revised, 1939, 486 § 2. (See 1939, 486 § 3.)
SECT. 24 revised, 1943, 45 § 2.
SECT. 25A added, 1935, 438 § 3 (relative to returns of taxable gains from certain transactions in real property).
SECT. 30 amended, 1935, 152.
SECT. 31 revised, 1943, 45 § 3.
SECT. 33, first paragraph revised, 1943, 45 § 4; paragraph added, 1932, 186.
SECT. 36 amended, 1933, 167 § 2.
SECT. 37 revised, 1933, 350 § 1. (See 1933, 350 § 9.)
SECT. 37A added, 1933, 350 § 2 (providing for the payment of income taxes in two installments). (See 1933, 350 § 9.)
SECT. 39, first sentence revised, 1933, 350 § 3. (See 1933, 350 § 9.)
SECT. 41 revised, 1932, 152; 1933, 350 § 4. (See 1933, 350 § 9.)
SECT. 43 amended, 1933, 350 § 5; 1937, 135 § 2. (See 1933, 350 § 9.)
SECT. 45 amended, 1939, 451 § 24.
SECT. 46 revised, 1933, 350 § 6. (See 1933, 350 § 9.)
SECT. 56 revised, 1943, 45 § 5.

Chapter 63. — Taxation of Corporations.

SECT. 1, paragraph defining "Bank" revised, 1943, 472; paragraph defining "Net income" revised, 1933, 327 § 1. (See 1933, 327 § 7.)
SECT. 2 amended, 1933, 327 § 2; 1939, 451 § 25; 1941, 509 § 3. (See 1933, 327 § 7; 1941, 509 § 9.)
SECT. 3 amended, 1933, 254 § 58; 1934, 323 § 5. (See 1933, 254 § 66; 1934, 323 § 11.)
SECT. 4 amended, 1939, 368; 1941, 509 § 4. (See 1941, 509 § 9.)
SECT. 5 amended, 1933, 254 § 59; repealed, 1934, 323 § 1. (See 1933, 254 § 66; 1934, 323 § 11.)
SECT. 6 repealed, 1934, 323 § 1. (See 1934, 323 § 11.)
SECT. 12, paragraph (*c*) amended, 1937, 274 § 1; paragraph (*h*) added at end, 1934, 362.
SECT. 18 revised, 1939, 447 § 1. (See 1939, 447 § 3.)
SECT. 18A amended, 1939, 447 § 2. (See 1939, 447 § 3.)
SECT. 20 amended, 1941, 509 § 5; revised, 1943, 531 § 1. (See 1941, 509 § 9; 1943, 531 §§ 2, 3, 7.)
SECT. 24 amended, 1943, 531 § 4. (See 1943, 531 § 7.)
SECT. 25 amended, 1943, 531 § 5. (See 1943, 531 § 7.)
SECT. 28 amended, 1939, 451 § 27; 1941, 509 § 6; revised, 1943, 531 § 6. (See 1941, 509 § 9; 1943, 531 § 7.)
SECTS. 30–51. See 1934, 317 § 2.
SECTS. 30–60. For legislation establishing an additional tax under these sections to provide funds for old age assistance, see 1941, 729 §§ 9, 15; 1943, 482 § 3.
For temporary legislation providing for additional taxes levied under these sections, see 1935, 480; 1936, 397; 1937, 422; 1938, 502; 1939, 454 § 19; 1941, 416 §§ 1, 3; 1943, 482 §§ 1, 3, 4.

SECT. 30, paragraph 2 revised, 1943, 459 § 1; paragraph 3, subdivision (*a*) revised, 1939, 24 § 5; paragraph contained in lines 48–51 amended, 1933, 58 § 3, revised, 1943, 459 § 2; paragraph contained in lines 52–69 revised, 1934, 237 § 1; paragraph 4, subdivision (*a*) revised, 1939, 24 § 6; paragraph contained in lines 70–74 amended, 1933, 58 § 4, revised, 1934, 237 § 1, 1943, 459 § 3; paragraph 5 revised, 1933, 327 § 3. (See 1933, 58 § 5, 327 § 7; 1934, 237 § 2.)

SECT. 32 revised, 1933, 342 § 1; amended, 1936, 362 § 5; 1939, 363 § 1. (See 1933, 342 § 6; 1936, 362 § 8; 1939, 363 § 2.)

SECT. 32A amended, 1933, 342 § 2. (See 1933, 342 § 6.)

SECT. 33 revised, 1933, 303 § 1. (See 1933, 303 § 3.)

SECT. 34 amended, 1933, 327 § 4. (See 1933, 327 § 7.)

SECT. 35 revised, 1933, 58 § 1.

SECT. 36 revised, 1933, 327 § 5; amended, 1935, 473 § 2. (See 1933, 327 § 7; 1935, 473 § 7.)

SECT. 38, paragraph 10 added at end, 1933, 342 § 3. (See 1933, 342 § 6.)

SECT. 38B, last paragraph amended, 1935, 473 § 3. (See 1935, 473 § 7.) [For temporary legislation affecting taxation, during the years 1934 to 1946, inclusive, of corporations subject to this section, see 1934, 317 § 1; 1935, 489 § 4; 1937, 395 § 5; 1938, 489 § 6; 1939, 373 § 5; 1941, 331 § 5; 1943, 285 § 5.]

SECT. 38C revised, 1937, 383 § 1. (See 1937, 383 § 3.)

SECT. 39, subsection (1) revised, 1936, 362 § 6; last paragraph amended, 1933, 327 § 6; new paragraph added at end, 1933, 342 § 4. (See 1933, 327 § 7, 342 § 6; 1936, 362 § 8.)

SECT. 39A revised, 1933, 303 § 2; first paragraph amended, 1934, 134. (See 1933, 303 § 3.)

SECT. 40 revised, 1933, 58 § 2.

SECT. 42, last sentence amended, 1932, 180 § 11; section revised, 1933, 342 § 5. (See 1933, 342 § 6.)

SECT. 42B revised, 1937, 383 § 2. (See 1937, 383 § 3.)

SECT. 43. See 1933, 307 § 9A; 1935, 489 § 2; 1937, 395 § 2; 1938, 489 § 3; 1939, 373 § 2; 1941, 331 § 2; 1943, 285 § 2.

SECT. 44 amended, 1935, 473 § 4; 1936, 362 § 7. (See 1935, 473 § 7; 1936, 362 § 8.)

SECT. 45 amended, 1933, 195 § 1; revised, 1935, 473 § 5; amended, 1943, 395. (See 1933, 195 § 2; 1935, 473 § 7.)

SECT. 48 revised, 1935, 473 § 1. (See 1935, 473 § 7.)

SECT. 53, first paragraph amended, 1933, 254 § 60; 1941, 509 § 7; clause Fourth revised, 1934, 323 § 6. (See 1933, 254 § 66; 1934, 323 § 11; 1941, 509 § 9.)

SECT. 54, paragraph in lines 9–17 amended, 1933, 254 § 61; same paragraph revised, 1934, 323 § 7; last paragraph amended, 1934, 323 § 7A. (See 1933, 254 § 66; 1934, 323 § 11.)

SECT. 55, first paragraph amended, 1936, 134; section amended, 1939, 24 § 7.

SECT. 56A revised, 1934, 317 § 3. (See 1934, 317 § 4.)

SECT. 59 amended, 1934, 323 § 8. (See 1934, 323 § 11.)

SECT. 60 amended, 1939, 451 § 28; 1941, 509 § 8. (See 1941, 509 § 9.)

SECT. 68A amended, 1939, 24 § 8.

SECT. 70 revised, 1935, 473 § 6. (See 1935, 473 § 7.)

SECT. 71 amended, 1933, 167 § 3; 1939, 451 § 29.
SECT. 71A amended, 1935, 150; 1939, 451 § 30.
SECT. 71B added, 1937, 135 § 3 (providing that applications for abatement or correction of taxes, made pursuant to any provision of this chapter, shall be in writing upon forms approved by the commissioner).
SECT. 81 revised, 1939, 24 § 9.

Chapter 64. — Taxation of Stock Transfers.

SECT. 6 amended, 1939, 451 § 31.

Chapter 64A. — Taxation of Sales of Gasoline and Certain Other Motor Vehicle Fuel.

Chapter affected, 1932, 248; 1935, 336; 1936, 398; 1938, 431 § 2; 1939, 408; 1941, 330; 1943, 270.
SECT. 1, paragraph (*d*) revised, 1936, 357 § 1; paragraph (*g*) amended, 1941, 490 § 16. (See 1936, 357 § 3.)
SECT. 3, last sentence amended, 1943, 420 § 1.
SECT. 4 revised, 1938, 431 § 1.
SECT. 5 amended, 1936, 357 § 2; 1939, 451 § 32; revised, 1943, 420 § 2. (See 1936, 357 § 3.)
SECT. 7 revised, 1943, 420 § 3.
SECT. 10 amended, 1939, 451 § 33; revised, 1943, 420 § 4.
SECT. 12 revised, 1941, 490 § 17.

Chapter 64B. — Excise upon Charges for Meals served to the Public.

New chapter inserted, 1941, 729 § 17. (See 1941, 729 § 15.)
SECT. 6, paragraph added at end, 1943, 521 § 2.

Chapter 65. — Taxation of Legacies and Successions.

For legislation establishing an additional tax upon legacies and successions to provide funds for old age assistance, see 1941, 729 §§ 9A, 15; 1943, 482 § 3.
For temporary legislation providing for additional taxes upon legacies and successions, see 1935, 480; 1936, 397; 1937, 422; 1938, 502; 1939, 454 §§ 20, 22; 1941, 416 §§ 2, 3; 1943, 482 §§ 2, 3, 4.
SECT. 1, table revised, 1933, 293; 1941, 415 § 1; first sentence revised, 1941, 605 § 1. (See 1941, 415 § 2, 605 § 2.)
SECT. 3 amended, 1939, 380.
SECTS. 24A–24F added, 1933, 319 (providing reciprocal relations in respect to death taxes upon estates of non-resident decedents).
SECT. 25 amended, 1939, 451 § 34; revised, 1939, 494 § 1.
SECT. 26 amended, 1939, 451 § 35; revised, 1939, 494 § 2.
SECT. 32 amended, 1939, 451 § 36.

Chapter 65A. — Taxation of Transfers of Certain Estates.

SECT. 1, paragraph added at end, 1932, 284; second paragraph revised, 1933, 316 § 1; section amended, 1937, 420 § 1. (See 1933, 316 § 2; 1937, 420 § 4.)
SECT. 5 stricken out, and new sections 5–5B inserted, 1943, 519 § 1

(providing for the equitable apportionment in certain cases of estate taxes and the collection and payment thereof). (See 1943, 519 § 2.)

SECT. 6 amended, 1937, 420 § 2; last sentence revised, 1943, 471. (See 1937, 420 § 4.)

SECT. 7 repealed, 1937, 420 § 3. (See 1937, 420 § 4.)

Chapter 65B. — Settlement of Disputes respecting the Domicile of Decedents for Death Tax Purposes.

New chapter inserted, 1943, 428 § 1. (See 1943, 428 § 3.)

Chapter 66. — Public Records.

SECT. 3 revised, 1936, 305; 1941, 662 § 1.

SECTS. 5, 7 and 16 affected, 1941, 662 § 2.

SECT. 8, amended, 1943, 128.

SECT. 15 amended, 1939, 40.

SECT. 17A added, 1941, 630 § 1 (making records relating to old age assistance, aid to dependent children and aid to the blind confidential); revised, 1943, 169.

Chapter 68. — Donations and Conveyances for Pious and Charitable Uses.

SECT. 10, sentence added at end, 1934, 238.

Chapter 69. — Powers and Duties of the Department of Education.

SECT. 6 amended, 1932, 127 § 3.

SECT. 7 amended, 1935, 275; 1937, 213, 327; 1938, 315; revised, 1938, 424; amended, 1941, 351 § 6, 561; revised, 1943, 403.

SECT. 8 amended, 1932, 127 § 4.

SECT. 9 amended, 1938, 442 § 1.

SECT. 9A added, 1938, 442 § 2 (further regulating education in the use of English and certain other subjects adapted to fit persons for American citizenship).

SECT. 11 revised, 1939, 409 § 4. (See 1939, 409 §§ 1, 5.)

SECT. 19 amended, 1943, 89 § 1.

SECT. 19A added, 1943, 89 § 2 (requiring reports to the director of the division of the blind of results of examinations of blind persons).

SECT. 23 revised, 1943, 526.

SECT. 23A added, 1938, 28 (requiring the furnishing of information to the director of the division of the blind by certain banks and other depositories).

SECT. 25 revised, 1935, 397.

SECTS. 25A–25E added, 1938, 329 (regulating the raising of funds for the benefit of the blind).

SECT. 26, paragraph added at end, 1935, 286.

SECT. 26A added, 1941, 630 § 2, (relative to information concerning recipients of aid to the blind).

SECT. 29 added, 1938, 313 (relative to instruction in lip reading for certain school children whose hearing is defective).

SECTS. 30 and 31 added, 1943, 549 § 3, under caption "Board of Collegiate Authority" (relative to approval by said board of the organization of certain educational institutions and of certain amendments to their charters).

Chapter 70. — School Funds and Other State Aid for Public Schools.

SECT. 1A added, 1941, 524 (relative to reimbursement to cities and towns for certain school salaries).
SECT. 2 amended, 1932, 127 § 5; paragraph (3) revised, 1943, 12.
SECT. 4, last paragraph amended, 1934, 143.
SECT. 6 amended, 1932, 127 § 6.
SECT. 11, paragraph contained in lines 6–9 revised, 1943, 14; paragraph (3) revised, 1941, 532.
SECT. 18 amended, 1932, 127 § 7.

Chapter 71. — Public Schools.

SECT. 2 amended, 1938, 246 § 1.
SECT. 7 amended, 1941, 590.
SECT. 13A added, 1938, 241 (requiring the teaching of the Italian language in certain public high schools in certain cases).
SECT. 13B added, 1939, 311 (relative to the teaching of modern languages in certain public high schools).
SECT. 19 amended, 1939, 461 § 1.
SECT. 30A added, 1935, 370 § 1 (requiring that an oath or affirmation be taken and subscribed to by certain professors, instructors and teachers in the colleges, universities and schools of the commonwealth). (See 1935, 370 §§ 2, 2A, 3.)
SECT. 34 revised, 1939, 294.
SECTS. 34A and 34B added, 1943, 547 (requiring persons operating or maintaining educational institutions to furnish, upon request, certain transcripts of records).
SECTS. 38A–38F added, 1941, 676 § 2 (relative to occupational guidance and placement). (See 1941, 646.)
SECT. 40 amended, 1941, 507; 1943, 494.
SECT. 42 revised, 1934, 123.
SECT. 46 amended, 1941, 194 § 4.
SECT. 46A amended, 1932, 159.
SECT. 47 revised, 1935, 199.
SECT. 48A amended, 1935, 47.
SECT. 52 amended, 1932, 90.
SECT. 54 amended, 1938, 265 § 1.
SECT. 55 revised, 1938, 265 § 2.
SECT. 55A added, 1938, 265 § 3 (relative to the disposition of children showing signs of ill health or of being infected with a dangerous disease).
SECT. 56 revised, 1938, 265 § 4.
SECT. 57 revised, 1943, 384.
SECT. 58 amended, 1932, 127 § 8; revised, 1935, 287.
SECT. 66, paragraph added at end, 1937, 281.
SECT. 68 revised, 1934, 97 § 1. (See 1934, 97 § 2.)
SECT. 69 revised, 1935, 258.
SECT. 71 amended, 1935, 193.

Chapter 72. — School Registers and Returns.

SECT. 3, paragraph in lines 6–10 revised, 1939, 461 § 2.

Chapter 73. — State Teachers Colleges (former title, State Normal Schools).

Title changed, 1932, 127 § 9.
SECT. 1 amended, 1932, 127 § 10.
SECT. 2 amended, 1932, 127 § 11.
SECT. 2A added, 1938, 246 § 2 (making the constitutions of the United States and of this Commonwealth required subjects of instruction in State Teachers Colleges).
SECT. 3 amended, 1932, 127 § 12.
SECT. 4 amended, 1932, 127 § 13.
SECT. 4A amended, 1932, 127 § 14.
SECT. 5 amended, 1932, 127 § 15. (Temporarily affected, 1933, 233; 1934, 130; 1935, 277.)
SECT. 6 amended, 1932, 127 § 16.
SECT. 7 amended, 1932, 127 § 17; revised, 1935, 21.

Chapter 74. — Vocational Education.

SECT. 1 revised, 1938, 446 § 1; amended, 1941, 617 § 1. (See 1938, 446 § 14.)
SECT. 2 amended, 1938, 446 § 2. (See 1938, 446 § 14.)
SECT. 3 amended, 1938, 446 § 3. (See 1938, 446 § 14.)
SECT. 4 amended, 1938, 446 § 4. (See 1938, 446 § 14.)
SECT. 6 amended, 1938, 446 § 5 (See 1938, 446 § 14.)
SECT. 7 amended, 1938, 446 § 6. (See 1938, 446 § 14.)
SECT. 8A revised, 1937, 323; paragraph added at end, 1939, 308.
SECT. 9 amended, 1938, 446 § 7. (See 1938, 446 § 14.)
SECT. 11 amended, 1933, 102 § 2; 1941, 617 § 2. (See 1933, 102 § 4.)
SECT. 13 amended, 1938, 446 § 8. (See 1938, 446 § 14.)
SECT. 14 revised, 1943, 540.
SECT. 14A added, 1943, 540 (relative to federal funds for vocational education).
SECT. 19 revised, 1938, 446 § 9. (See 1938, 446 § 14.)
SECT. 21 amended, 1938, 446 § 10. (See 1938, 446 § 14.)
SECT. 22 amended, 1938, 446 § 11. (See 1938, 446 § 14.)
SECT. 22A amended, 1938, 446 § 12. (See 1938, 446 § 14.)
SECT. 28 revised, 1939, 501 § 6.
SECT. 30 amended, 1937, 41.
SECT. 31A added, 1934, 65 (authorizing the trustees of the Essex county agricultural school to pay transportation costs of certain pupils attending said school); amended, 1943, 42.
SECT. 47E, paragraph added at end, 1935, 22.
SECT. 49, caption preceding section changed, 1942, 1 § 3; section amended, 1942, 1 § 5. (See 1942, 1 § 9.)
SECT. 53 revised, 1942, 1 § 6. (See 1942, 1 § 9.)

Chapter 75. — Massachusetts State College.

SECT. 5 revised, 1935, 288.

SECT. 5A added, 1939, 329 (authorizing the trustees of Massachusetts State College to retain and manage in a revolving fund receipts from student activities).

SECT. 6 amended, 1935, 462 § 2. (See 1935, 462 § 1.)

Chapter 76. — School Attendance.

SECT. 1 revised, 1939, 461 § 3; amended, 1941, 423

SECTS. 7–10. See 1939, 454 § 21.

SECT. 15 revised, 1938, 265 § 5.

Chapter 77. — School Offenders and County Training Schools.

SECT. 1 revised, 1933, 295 § 1; amended, 1943, 82.

Chapter 78. — Libraries.

SECT. 4 revised, 1935, 202.

Chapter 79. — Eminent Domain.

SECT. 3, first paragraph amended, 1938, 172 § 6; two sentences added at end of first paragraph, 1943, 251 § 1. (See 1943, 251 § 4.)

SECT. 8 amended, 1936, 187 § 1; sentence inserted after second sentence, 1943, 251 § 2. (See 1943, 251 § 4.)

SECT. 9, last sentence amended, 1938, 172 § 7.

SECT. 15 repealed, 1936, 385 § 1. (See 1936, 385 § 2.)

SECT. 16 amended, 1936, 187 § 2; 1938, 185; revised, 1943, 95; paragraph added at end, 1943, 251 § 3. (See 1943, 251 § 4.)

SECT. 44A added, 1935, 189 (relative to certain tax liens upon real estate taken by right of eminent domain); amended, 1936, 137.

Chapter 80. — Betterments.

SECT. 1 amended, 1933, 254 § 62. (See 1933, 254 § 66.)

SECT. 4 revised, 1933, 63 § 1.

SECT. 5 amended, 1933, 157 § 2. (See 1933, 157 § 3.)

SECT. 10 revised, 1933, 147.

SECT. 10A added, 1933, 157 § 1 (providing that failure of a board of officers to take action upon a petition for abatement of a betterment assessment shall, for the purposes of appeal, be equivalent to refusal to abate the assessment). (See 1933, 157 § 3.)

SECT. 12 revised, 1943, 252 § 1, 478 § 4.

SECT. 13 amended, 1933, 63 § 2, 254 § 63; revised, 1934, 315 § 1; last sentence stricken out and new paragraph added, 1938, 489 § 1; first sentence of section amended, 1941, 595. (See 1933, 254 § 66; 1934, 315 § 3; 1941, 724.)

SECT. 13A added, 1943, 252 § 2 (relative to the time within which certain betterment and other assessments on unimproved land shall be paid.)

Chapter 81. — State Highways.

SECT. 5 revised, 1937, 218 § 1.

SECT. 7A added, 1937, 344 (granting certain powers to the department of public works with respect to certain ways connecting with state highways).

SECT. 7B added, 1941, 519 (giving the department of public works the power to take a slope easement, so called, in certain cases).

SECT. 7C added, 1943, 397 (relative to limited access ways).

SECT. 8 revised, 1936, 371; amended, 1937, 218 § 2.

SECT. 13A added, 1936, 342 (authorizing the department of public works to accept in behalf of the commonwealth gifts of certain easements for the purpose of landscaping along state highways, and to do such landscaping).

SECT. 19, last four sentences stricken out, 1933, 187 § 1. (See 1933, 187 § 2.)

SECT. 26 amended, 1934, 366.

SECT. 27 amended, 1939, 224.

SECT. 29A added, 1943, 416 (authorizing the department of public works to lay out and alter ways other than state highways and facilitating the securing of federal aid in connection therewith).

Chapter 82. — The Laying Out, Alteration, Relocation and Discontinuance of Public Ways, and Specific Repairs Thereon.

SECT. 7 amended, 1933, 283 § 2.

SECT. 32B added, 1933, 283 § 3 (authorizing the taking of easements of slope, so called, by county, city or town officers in connection with the laying out, widening, altering or relocating of public ways).

SECT. 34 amended, 1935, 309; 1941, 533.

Chapter 83. — Sewers, Drains and Sidewalks.

SECT. 19 revised, 1943, 252 § 4. (See 1943, 252 § 6.)

SECT. 27, last sentence revised, 1943, 252 § 5.

SECT. 29 added, 1943, 252 § 3 (relative to the continuance of liens created under special acts in connection with certain betterment and other assessments).

Chapter 84. — Repair of Ways and Bridges.

SECT. 18 revised, 1933, 114 § 1.

SECT. 19 amended, 1933, 114 § 2.

SECT. 20 revised, 1933, 114 § 3; amended, 1939, 147.

SECT. 25. Temporarily affected, 1934, 163.

Chapter 85. — Regulations and By-Laws relative to Ways and Bridges.

SECT. 2A added, 1941, 346 § 2 (authorizing the department of public works to remove vehicles from state highways when said vehicles interfere with the removal of snow and ice).

SECT. 11A added, 1941, 710 § 1 (relative to the registration and operation of certain bicycles).

Sects. 12–14 repealed, 1941, 710 § 2.

Sect. 14B added, 1938, 432 (requiring the use of certain signal lights at locations on unlighted ways where certain vehicles are disabled).

Sect. 17B added, 1933, 43 (prohibiting riding upon the rear or on the side of street railway cars or motor buses without the consent of the persons in charge thereof); revised, 1943, 322 § 2.

Sect. 30 amended, 1935, 30; 1938, 171 § 1.

Sect. 31 revised, 1938, 171 § 2.

Chapter 87. — Shade Trees.

Sect. 5 amended, 1941, 490 § 18.

Chapter 89. — Law of the Road.

Sect. 2 revised, 1933, 301.

Sect. 5 amended, 1936, 49. (See 1938, 149.)

Sect. 7B added, 1934, 382 (relative to the application of traffic laws and regulations to fire apparatus and other emergency vehicles).

Chapter 90. — Motor Vehicles and Aircraft.

Sect. 1, paragraph (defining "heavy duty platform trailer") added, 1939, 354 § 1; same paragraph amended, 1941, 30; paragraph (defining "motor vehicles") amended, 1932, 182; 1938, 36; paragraph in lines 41–45 (defining "register number") revised, 1935, 43; two paragraphs (defining "semi-trailer" and "semi-trailer unit") added, 1933, 332 § 1; paragraph (defining "school bus") added, 1932, 271 § 1; paragraph in lines 52–56 stricken out, and two paragraphs (defining "tractor" and "trailer") inserted, 1933, 332 § 2; paragraph (defining "trailer") amended, 1939, 354 § 2. (See 1932, 271 § 7; 1933, 332 § 5.)

Sect. 1A amended, 1933, 372 § 3; 1934, 264 § 2.

Sect. 2, fourth paragraph revised, 1932, 5; seventh paragraph revised, 1939, 436 § 1; last paragraph revised, 1933, 54.

Sect. 3, first sentence revised, 1933, 188; section revised, 1939, 325; paragraph added at end, 1941, 282.

Sect. 3C revised, 1937, 387.

Sect. 5A added, 1943, 409 § 2 (relative to the use of a general distinguishing mark or number on all motor vehicles under the control of the military forces).

Sect. 6, first sentence revised, 1939, 436 § 2.

Sect. 7 amended, 1932, 123 § 1; 1933, 51; second sentence amended, 1933, 109; sentence added after fourth sentence, 1939, 153; paragraph added at end of section, 1941, 443. (See 1932, 123 § 2.)

Sect. 7A revised, 1932, 41, 271 § 2. (See 1932, 271 § 7.)

Sect. 7B added, 1932, 271 § 3 (prerequisites to operation of school bus). (See 1932, 271 § 7.)

Sect. 8 amended, 1934, 103; 1937, 284.

Sect. 9 amended, 1934, 361; 1941, 283.

Sect. 9A revised, 1932, 168 § 1; 1935, 393 § 1. (See 1932, 168 §§ 2, 3; 1935, 393 § 2.)

Sect. 10 amended, 1935, 219.

Sect. 14 amended, 1938, 166.

SECT. 15 amended, 1932, 271 § 5; 1933, 26 § 1. (See 1932, 271 § 7.)

SECT. 17, sentence added at end, 1932, 271 § 4. (See 1932, 271 § 7.)

SECT. 19, last sentence revised, 1933, 332 § 3; 1935, 223 § 1; section revised, 1935, 326 (but see 1935, 465); amended, 1936, 388 § 1; revised, 1941, 314. (See 1933, 332 § 5; 1935, 223 § 2; 1936, 388 § 2.) Affected by 1941, 589.

SECT. 20A added, 1934, 368 § 1 (providing for the non-criminal disposition of charges for violation of motor vehicle parking rules, regulations, orders, ordinances and by-laws); revised, 1935, 176; first paragraph revised, 1938, 201. (See 1934, 368 § 2.)

SECT. 21 amended, 1936, 406.

SECT. 22, two paragraphs added at end, 1933, 191; first sentence (as appearing in 1933, 191) amended, 1941, 312.

SECT. 22A added, 1932, 304 § 1 (requiring the suspension of licenses to operate motor vehicles issued to persons who do not satisfy judgments in motor vehicle accident cases involving property damage). (See 1932, 304 § 2.)

SECT. 23, new paragraph added at end, 1933, 69.

SECT. 24 amended, 1932, 26 § 1; first sentence amended, 1936, 182 § 1; sentence contained in lines 65–97 amended, 1935, 360; paragraph added at end, 1936, 182 § 2; section revised, 1936, 434 § 1; paragraph (1) (*a*) amended, 1938, 145; paragraph (1) (*c*) revised, 1939, 82; paragraph (2) (*a*) amended, 1937, 230 § 1; paragraph (2) (*c*) amended, 1937, 117. (See 1937, 230 § 2.)

SECT. 29, last sentence amended, 1932, 26 § 2; section amended, 1935, 477 § 1; second sentence revised, 1936, 391; last two sentences revised, 1938, 146.

SECT. 32B repealed, 1934, 209 § 2. (See 1934, 209 § 3.)

SECTS. 32C–32F added, 1934, 209 § 1 (further regulating the business of leasing motor vehicles upon a mileage basis). (See 1934, 209 § 3.)

SECT. 33, first four paragraphs stricken out, and five new paragraphs inserted, 1932, 249 § 1; fourth paragraph (as appearing in 1932, 249 § 1) amended, 1933, 183 § 1; paragraph in lines 21–41 amended, 1932, 180 § 12; same paragraph stricken out, and two paragraphs inserted, 1933, 332 § 4; two paragraphs so inserted stricken out, and new paragraph inserted, 1935, 409 § 1; the paragraph so inserted amended, 1936, 380 § 1; subdivisions (2) and (3) of the paragraph so inserted revised, 1937, 377; subdivision (3) of said paragraph amended, 1938, 430; subdivision (4) of said paragraph amended, 1939, 354 § 3; subdivision (6) of said paragraph amended, 1939, 354 § 4; last paragraph amended, 1936, 401. (See 1932, 249 § 2; 1933, 183 § 2, 332 § 5; 1935, 409 § 2; 1936, 380 § 2.)

SECT. 34, four words stricken out, 1933, 197 § 3; first paragraph amended, 1934, 364 § 1; section revised, 1943, 427 § 2. (See 1934, 364 § 3.)

SECT. 34A, new paragraph (defining "guest occupant") added, 1935, 459 § 1; paragraphs defining "motor vehicle liability bond" and "motor vehicle liability policy" revised, 1935, 459 § 2. (See 1935, 459 § 5.)

SECT. 34B, second paragraph revised, 1933, 83 § 1; 1935, 302; fourth paragraph revised, 1933, 83 § 2. (See 1933, 83 § 3.)

SECT. 34C amended, 1932, 180 § 13.

SECT. 34D revised, 1935, 459 § 3. (See 1935, 459 § 5.)

Sect. 34H, first paragraph amended, 1933, 119 § 4; new paragraph inserted, 1933, 119 § 5. (See 1933, 119 § 6.)

Sect. 53, last sentence amended, 1932, 180 § 14.

Sects. 35-60 stricken out, and new sections 35-50 (uniform aeronautical code) inserted, 1935, 418 § 2. (See also below.)

Sect. 36 revised, 1938, 417 § 1.
Sect. 37 revised, 1938, 417 § 2.
Sect. 38 revised, 1938, 417 § 3.
Sect. 39 revised, 1938, 417 § 4.
Sect. 40 revised, 1938, 417 § 5.
Sect. 41 revised, 1938, 417 § 6.
Sect. 42 revised, 1938, 417 § 7.
Sect. 43 revised, 1938, 417 § 8.

Sect. 43A added, 1938, 417 § 9 (relative to the powers and duties of police and certain other officers as to aircraft accidents and violations of the laws, rules and regulations relative to aircraft).

Sect. 44 revised, 1938, 417 § 10.
Sect. 45 revised, 1938, 417 § 11.
Sect. 46 revised, 1938, 417 § 12.

Sects. 35-43 and 44-50, inc. (inserted by 1935, 418 § 2, as amended) and sect. 43A (inserted by 1938, 417 § 9) stricken out and new sections 35-52 inserted, 1939, 393 § 3 (further revising the laws relative to aviation). (See 1939, 393 §§ 4-6.)

Sect. 35, paragraph defining "Airport" amended, 1941, 537 § 1; paragraph inserted after said paragraph, 1941, 537 § 2; paragraph defining "Landing field" amended, 1941, 537 § 3; two paragraphs added at end, 1941, 537 § 4.

Sect. 39, first paragraph revised, 1941, 695 § 13.

Sects. 40A-40I inserted, 1941, 537 § 5 (relative to protecting the approaches to publicly owned airports).

Sect. 42 amended, 1941, 537 § 6.
Sect. 44 amended, 1941, 537 § 7.
Sect. 45 amended, 1941, 537 § 8.

Chapter 91. — Waterways.

Sect. 6. See 1941, 695 § 15.

Sect. 9A added, 1938, 407 § 2 (providing a method for the development of waterfront terminal facilities).

Sect. 12A added, 1939, 513 § 6 (licensing and otherwise regulating structures, filling and excavations in certain rivers and streams).

Sect. 27, paragraph added at end, 1937, 372 § 2.

Sect. 46A added, 1935, 362 § 1 (penalizing the unlicensed breaking up or altering of vessels, scows, lighters or certain other structures).

Sect. 49 revised, 1935, 362 § 2.

Chapter 92. — Metropolitan Sewers, Water and Parks.

For legislation including a certain portion of Lexington in the north metropolitan sewerage system, see 1934, 225.

Sect. 10 revised, 1943, 543 § 1. (See 1943, 543 §§ 1A, 3.)

Sect. 26, first paragraph revised, 1943, 543 § 2.

Sect. 48 amended, 1934, 266 § 1. (See 1934, 266 § 4.)

SECT. 56 revised, 1933, 197 § 1; sentence added at end, 1939, 429 § 1. (See 1939, 429 §§ 2, 4.)
SECT. 57 amended, 1933, 197 § 2.
SECT. 60 revised, 1939, 429 § 3. (See 1939, 429 § 4.)
SECT. 60A added, 1937, 352 § 1 (regulating the making and awarding of certain contracts by the metropolitan district commission and metropolitan district water supply commission); repealed, 1941, 547 § 2. (See 1937, 352 § 2; 1941, 547 § 1.)
SECT. 62 revised, 1938, 396; amended, 1941, 658 § 1. (See 1941, 658 § 2.)
SECT. 62A added, 1937, 416 § 1 (providing for a reserve police force for the metropolitan district commission); revised, 1939, 441 § 1. (See 1937, 416 § 5; 1939, 441 §§ 3, 5.)
SECT. 63 repealed, 1937, 416 § 2. (See 1937, 416 § 5; 1939, 441 § 3.)
SECT. 93 amended, 1934, 266 § 2. (See 1934, 266 § 4.)
SECT. 94 amended, 1934, 266 § 3. (See 1934, 266 § 4.)
SECT. 100 revised, 1939, 499 § 7.

Chapter 93. — Regulation of Trade and Certain Enterprises.

SECT. 8, sentence added at end, 1938, 410 § 2.
SECTS. 14A–14D added, under heading "FAIR TRADE", 1937, 398 (protecting trade mark owners, distributors and the public against injurious and uneconomic practices in the distribution of articles of standard quality under a trade mark, brand or name).
SECT. 14A amended, 1939, 231.
SECT. 14B amended, 1939, 313.
SECT. 14C revised, 1943, 40.
SECTS. 14E–14K added, under heading "UNFAIR SALES", 1938, 410 § 1 (defining and prohibiting unfair sales practices, with a view to preventing the advertising or offering for sale, or the selling below cost, of merchandise for the purpose of injuring competitors or destroying competition). (See 1941, 715.)
SECT. 14E paragraphs (*a*) and (*b*) amended, 1939, 189 § 1; paragraph (*h*) added at end, 1939, 189 § 2.
SECT. 14F revised, 1941, 494.
Caption immediately preceding section 21 amended, 1939, 343 § 3.
SECT. 21 amended, 1939, 343 § 1; 1941, 583 § 1.
SECTS. 21A–21D added, 1941, 583 § 2 (defining and further regulating private trade schools).
SECT. 22 amended, 1939, 343 § 2; 1941, 583 § 3.
SECTS. 28A–28D added, under heading "REGULATING CLOSING OUT SALES, SO CALLED, AND SIMILAR TYPES OF SALES", 1938, 165.
SECT. 28A revised, 1939, 207.
SECT. 34. For temporary act to enable savings banks and certain other banking institutions to co-operate in the distribution of United States defense savings bonds and defense postal savings stamps, see **1941, 221, 575.**

Chapter 94. — Inspection and Sale of Food, Drugs and Various Articles.

SECT. 1, paragraph in lines 128–132 (defining "pasteurized milk") revised, 1932, 158; section amended in part, 1933, 67 §§ 1–5; paragraph (defining "milk plant" and "manufactory") added, 1933, 338 § 1; paragraph in lines 30–36 (defining "butter" and "cheese") stricken out and new paragraph defining "butter" inserted, 1937, 335 § 1; paragraph in line 40 reading, "cheese", see "butter", stricken out and four new paragraphs inserted 1937, 335 § 2 (defining cheese and cream cheese); paragraph (defining "bakery") amended, 1937, 362 § 1; paragraphs in lines 148–164 (defining "agricultural seeds" or "agricultural seed", "noxious weed seeds" and "weed seeds") revised and definition of "vegetable seeds" added, 1938, 363 § 1; paragraph in lines 177–181 revised, 1939, 196 § 1. (See 1937, 362 § 7.)

SECT. 6 amended, 1937, 362 § 2. (See 1937, 362 § 7.)

SECT. 7 amended, 1941, 490 § 19.

SECT. 8 revised, 1937, 53.

SECT. 9 amended, 1939, 261 § 6.

SECTS. 9A–9M added, 1937, 362 § 3 (changing the position in the General Laws of certain provisions of law relative to bakeries). (For prior legislation, see G. L. chap. 111 §§ 34–43, 46–49, repealed by 1937, 362 § 6.) (See 1937, 362 §§ 6, 7.)

SECT. 10 amended, 1937, 362 § 4. (See 1937, 362 § 7.)

SECTS. 10A–10E stricken out, and new sections 10A–10G (regulating the manufacture, bottling and sale of certain non-alcoholic beverages) inserted, 1935, 441.

SECT. 10F amended, 1941, 119.

SECTS. 12–48A. For temporary legislation establishing within the department of agriculture a milk control board, and defining its powers and duties, see note to G. L. chapter 94A, inserted by 1941, 691 § 2.

SECTS. 13, 14, 14A and 15 stricken out, and new sections 13–13E (relative to the grading of milk) inserted, 1933, 263 § 1. (See 1933, 263 § 3.)

SECT. 16 stricken out and sections 16–16I (regulating the production, sale and distribution of milk) inserted, 1932, 305 § 3. (See 1932, 305 §§ 5, 6.)

SECT. 16C amended, 1941, 374.

SECT. 17A amended, 1933, 124.

SECT. 18 revised, 1933, 263 § 2. (See 1933, 263 § 3.)

SECT. 20 revised, 1939, 212.

SECT. 29A revised, 1933, 253.

SECT. 30 revised, 1933, 253.

SECT. 31 revised, 1933, 253.

SECT. 40 amended, 1941, 298.

SECT. 42A stricken out, and new sections 42A–42K (requiring dealers in milk or cream to be licensed and bonded) inserted, 1933, 338 § 2; affected, 1939, 421.

SECT. 42A amended, 1935, 126.

SECT. 42F revised, 1934, 180 § 1.

SECT. 42H, paragraph 2 revised, 1934, 180 § 2.

SECT. 43 revised, 1932, 305 § 4; amended, 1935, 88; first paragraph amended, 1936, 210. (See 1932, 305 §§ 5, 6.)

SECT. 45 revised, 1935, 317.

SECT. 48B added, 1935, 259 (requiring institutions supported wholly or in part by funds of the commonwealth to use milk, other than cream and certified milk, produced within the commonwealth).

SECT. 48C added, 1939, 317 (regulating the manufacture, sale and delivery of certain milk beverages, so called).

SECT. 50 amended, 1937, 335 § 3.

SECT. 60 revised, 1934, 373 § 2.

SECT. 61A added, 1937, 335 § 4 (relative to the manufacture and sale of certain cheese).

SECTS. 64, 64A, 65, 65A, 65B, 65E and 65F, and the caption of said section 64, stricken out, and sections 65G–65S inserted, under caption "FROZEN DESSERTS AND ICE CREAM MIX", 1934, 373 § 1. (See 1934, 373 § 8.)

SECT. 65J, second paragraph revised, 1937, 341 § 1.

SECT. 65L, subdivision (*c*) amended, 1937, 341 § 2.

SECT. 65P, paragraph (*f*) added at end, 1937, 341 § 3.

SECT. 74 revised, 1933, 329 § 5; repealed, 1941, 598 § 2.

SECT. 74A added, 1933, 329 § 6 (definition of "fish"); repealed, 1941, 598 § 2.

SECTS. 75 and 76 repealed, 1933, 329 § 7.

SECT. 77, first sentence stricken out, 1933, 329 § 8; repealed, 1941, 598 § 2.

SECT. 77A added, 1934, 216 (regulating the importation of fresh swordfish).

SECT. 78 revised, 1933, 329 § 9; repealed, 1941, 598 § 2.

SECT. 78A added, 1933, 329 § 10 (prohibiting certain misrepresentations in the sale of lobsters); repealed, 1941, 598 § 2.

SECT. 79 repealed, 1933, 329 § 7.

SECT. 80 repealed, 1941, 598 § 2.

SECT. 81 revised, 1933, 329 § 11; 1939, 491 § 10; repealed, 1941, 598 § 2. (See 1939, 491 § 12.)

SECT. 82 repealed, 1941, 598 § 2.

SECT. 83 revised, 1933, 329 § 12; repealed, 1941, 598 § 2.

SECT. 85 amended, 1939, 261 § 7.

SECT. 88A revised, 1933, 329 § 13; repealed, 1941, 598 § 2.

SECT. 88B added, 1936, 176 (requiring that shucked scallops and quahaugs in the shell be sold only by weight).

SECT. 90A added, 1935, 369 (relative to the sale and distribution of eggs).

SECT. 90B added, 1938, 404 (establishing standard sizes in connection with the sale and distribution of eggs).

SECT. 92B added, under caption "MEATS AND POULTRY", 1935, 97 (requiring the retail sale of meats and poultry to be by weight).

SECT. 98 amended, 1939, 261 § 8.

SECT. 99A amended, 1939, 261 § 9.

SECT. 118 amended, 1943, 332 § 1.

SECT. 119 amended, 1943, 332 § 2.

SECT. 120 amended, 1943, 332 § 3.

SECT. 120A amended, 1943, 332 § 4.

SECT. 123 amended, 1932, 180 § 15; 1943, 332 § 5.

SECT. 124 revised, 1943, 508 § 1.

SECT. 131 revised, 1943, 332 § 6.

SECT. 133 amended, 1943, 332 § 7.
SECT. 135 amended, 1943, 332 § 8.
SECT. 138 amended, 1943, 508 § 2.
SECT. 146, first paragraph amended, 1934, 340 § 6; 1943, 508 § 3. (See 1934, 340 § 18.)
SECT. 148, second paragraph amended, 1934, 340 § 6A. (See 1934, 340 § 18.)
SECT. 151 revised, 1943, 508 § 4.
SECTS. 152A–152C added, 1934, 296 (relative to the sale and transportation of poultry).
SECT. 152A amended, 1935, 157 § 1.
SECT. 152B revised, 1935, 157 § 2.
SECT. 153A added, 1933, 116 (relative to the sale of meat and meat products containing certain preservatives); revised, 1933, 311.
SECT. 172 revised, 1939, 122.
SECT. 181 amended, 1939, 261 § 10.
SECT. 182 amended, 1939, 261 § 11.
SECT. 184 amended, 1939, 261 § 12.
SECT. 185A repealed, 1937, 341 § 4.
SECT. 197, paragraph in lines 10–15 revised, 1935, 412 § 1; amended, 1943, 305 § 1; fourth paragraph revised, 1943, 305 § 2.
SECT. 198 amended, 1935, 412 § 2.
SECTS. 198A and 198B added, 1935, 412 § 3 (relative to the licensing of certain dealings in narcotic drugs).
SECT. 201 amended, 1935, 412 § 4.
SECT. 203 amended, 1935, 412 § 5.
SECT. 206 amended, 1935, 412 § 6.
SECT. 211 amended, 1935, 412 § 7; revised, 1938, 321 § 1.
SECT. 212 amended, 1938, 321 § 2.
SECT. 212A added, 1938, 321 § 3 (providing for the arrest without a warrant and punishment of a person present where a narcotic drug is unlawfully kept or deposited).
SECT. 214 amended, 1935, 412 § 8; 1943, 357.
SECT. 215 amended, 1935, 412 § 9.
SECT. 217 amended, 1935, 412 § 10.
SECT. 225, paragraph added at end, 1939, 69.
SECT. 239A amended, 1939, 261 § 13.
SECT. 244 amended, 1941, 155 § 1.
SECT. 245 revised, 1933, 94 § 2; amended, 1939, 261 § 13A; revised, 1941, 155 § 2.
SECT. 246 revised, 1941, 155 § 4.
SECT. 248 amended, 1934, 184; 1939, 261 § 14; revised, 1943, 241 § 1.
SECT. 249A amended, 1939, 261 § 15.
SECT. 249B amended, 1939, 261 § 16.
SECT. 249E revised, 1943, 241 § 2.
SECT. 249E½ added, 1943, 241 § 3 (relative to the allowable amount of non-combustible residue of coal and coke).
SECT. 249F amended, 1939, 261 § 17; 1943, 241 § 4.
SECT. 249G added, under caption "MATERIAL FOR ROAD CONSTRUCTION", 1933, 94 § 1 (authorizing certain officers to direct the weighing of material for road construction); amended, 1939, 261 § 17A; repealed, 1941, 155 § 3.
SECT. 250 revised, 1933, 67 § 6.

SECT. 252 amended, 1933, 67 § 7.
SECT. 254 amended, 1933, 67 § 8.
SECT. 255 amended, 1933, 67 § 9.
SECT. 256 revised, 1933, 67 § 10.
SECT. 257 revised, 1933, 67 § 11.
SECT. 258 revised, 1933, 67 § 12.
SECT. 261A amended, 1938, 363 § 2.
SECT. 261B amended, 1938, 363 § 3.
SECT. 261C revised, 1938, 363 § 4.
SECT. 261D revised, 1938, 363 § 5.
SECT. 261E, paragraph added at end, 1938, 363 § 6.

SECTS. 261H–261L stricken out, and new sections 261H–261L inserted, 1937, 288 § 1. (See 1937, 288 § 2.)

SECT. 261H, paragraph added at end, 1938, 363 § 7.
SECT. 261K amended, 1938, 363 § 8.
SECT. 261L revised, 1938, 363 § 9.
SECT. 270, paragraph added at end, 1937, 176.

SECTS. 270A and 270B added, 1935, 439 (providing for the sterilization of feathers, down and second-hand material intended for use in the manufacture of any article of bedding or of upholstered furniture).

SECT. 270C added, 1939, 196 § 2 (relative to the marking of certain articles of bedding and upholstered furniture consisting in whole or in part of second-hand metal).

SECT. 270D added, 1939, 351 (further regulating the sale within the commonwealth of articles of bedding and upholstered furniture); repealed, 1941, 57.

SECT. 276 amended, 1939, 196 § 3.

SECT. 277A added, 1941, 422 (requiring the marking or labelling of furs, imitation furs and articles made therefrom, and prohibiting misrepresentation in such marks or labels).

SECT. 283 amended, 1939, 261 § 17B.

SECT. 295A added, under heading "PETROLEUM PRODUCTS", 1933, 228 (relative to prevention of fraud and misrepresentation in the sale of gasoline, lubricating oils and other motor fuels, and to prevention of the adulteration thereof).

SECTS. 295B and 295C added, 1938, 411 (prohibiting and penalizing the use of misleading signs relating to the price of gasoline and other motor fuel).

SECT. 295C revised, 1939, 218.

SECTS. 295A–295C stricken out, and new sections 295A–295O inserted, 1939, 459 § 1 (further regulating the advertising and sale of motor fuel at retail). (See 1939, 459 § 3.)

SECT. 295G revised, 1941, 311.
SECT. 298 amended, 1934, 109 § 1.
SECT. 299 amended, 1934, 109 § 2.

SECTS. 303A–303E added, under caption "METHYL OR WOOD ALCOHOL", 1934, 372 § 3 (relative to such alcohol and to certain preparations containing such alcohol).

SECT. 303A amended, 1935, 342; 1936, 53.
SECT. 303B amended, 1937, 177 § 1.
SECT. 303C revised, 1937, 177 § 2.

SECT. 303F added, under caption "FUEL OILS", 1935, 95 (regulating the sale of fuel oils).
SECT. 305A amended, 1937, 362 § 5. (See 1937, 362 § 7.)

Chapter 94A. — Milk Control.

New chapter inserted, 1941, 691 § 2. (See 1941, 691 §§ 3–6.)
(For prior temporary legislation establishing within the department of agriculture a milk control board, and defining its powers and duties, see 1934, 376; term of office of said board extended, 1936, 300; 1938, 334; 1939, 413; 1941, 418 § 1; 631 § 1; legislation amended, 1937, 428; 1938, 279; 1939, 302.)
SECT. 12A added, 1943, 445 (defining the powers and duties of the milk control board in case of a failure to pay the official minimum price for the sale or delivery of milk).
SECT. 22 revised, 1943, 164.
SECT. 22A added, 1943, 147 (in aid of the construction and enforcement of the state milk control law, so called).

Chapter 95. — Measuring of Leather.

SECT. 1 amended, 1939, 261 § 18.

Chapter 97. — Surveying of Land.

SECTS. 8–13 added, 1941, 47 (defining and authorizing the use of a system of plane co-ordinates for designating and stating positions of points on the surface of the earth within the commonwealth).

Chapter 98. — Weights and Measures.

SECT. 1 amended, 1939, 261 § 19.
SECT. 14A amended, 1936, 73.
SECT. 20 amended, 1934, 373 § 3.
SECT. 21 amended, 1934, 373 § 4.
SECT. 22 amended, 1939, 261 § 19A; revised, 1941, 59.
SECT. 30 repealed, 1935, 60 § 2.
SECT. 32 amended, 1935, 60 § 3.
SECT. 37 amended, 1936, 72.
SECT. 41 amended, 1941, 462.
SECT. 56, paragraph (b½) added, 1934, 98 (establishing fees for sealing certain liquid-measuring meters); section revised, 1937, 74; paragraph (b½) added, 1937, 305 § 1. (See 1937, 305 § 2.)
SECT. 56A added, 1941, 60 (relative to the location of scales and other weighing devices used in weighing food sold at retail by weight).

Chapter 99. — The Metric System of Weights and Measures.

SECT. 1 amended, 1939, 261 § 20.
SECT. 3 amended, 1939, 261 § 21.
SECT. 4 amended, 1939, 261 § 22.

Chapter 100. — Auctioneers.

SECT. 1, paragraph added at end, 1936, 209 § 1.
SECT. 2 revised, 1941, 81.
SECT. 5 amended, 1932, 156 § 1.
SECT. 14 revised, 1932, 156 § 2.
SECT. 16 revised, 1932, 156 § 3.
SECTS. 18–21 added, 1936, 209 § 2 (relative to bankruptcy auctions and other auctions of similar type and relative to certain fraudulent practices at auctions).

Chapter 101. — Transient Vendors, Hawkers and Pedlers.

SECT. 1, second paragraph revised, 1936, 218; section amended, 1941, 490 § 21.
SECT. 3 amended, 1939, 261 § 23; 1941, 490 § 22.
SECT. 5 amended, 1933, 254 § 64. (See 1933, 254 § 66.)
SECT. 6A added, 1938, 85 (providing that applications for transient vendors' licenses shall contain irrevocable power of attorney for service of process, and providing for service of process under authority thereof).
SECT. 15 amended, 1937, 214; revised, 1937, 333.
SECT. 16 revised, 1935, 42; amended, 1937, 130.
SECT. 19 amended, 1934, 114; 1937, 73.
SECT. 24 amended, 1936, 74.
SECT. 27 amended, 1941, 490 § 23.
SECT. 30 amended, 1934, 77.
SECT. 32 amended, 1941, 490 § 24.

Chapter 102. — Shipping and Seamen, Harbors and Harbor Masters.

SECT. 15 revised, 1932, 232 § 1.
SECT. 15A added, 1932, 232 § 2 (penalty for improper operation of motor and other boats).
SECT. 17 revised, 1932, 57.

Chapter 105. — Public Warehouses.

SECT. 1 amended, 1935, 310 § 1.
SECTS. 2A and 2B added, 1935, 122 § 1 (relative to the termination of liability of sureties on bonds furnished by public warehousemen). (See 1935, 122 § 3.)
SECT. 6 revised, 1935, 122 § 2. (See 1935, 122 § 3.)
SECT. 9, clause (*h*) revised, 1935, 310 § 2.

Chapter 107. — Money and Negotiable Instruments.

SECT. 31 amended, 1941, 215.

Chapter 108A. — Partnerships.

SECT. 34, first paragraph amended, 1932, 180 § 16.

Chapter 110. — Labels, Trade Marks, Names and Registration Thereof.

SECT. 21 amended, 1934, 373 § 5.

Chapter 110A. — Promotion and Sale of Securities.

Chapter stricken out and new chapter inserted, 1932, 290 § 1. (See 1932, 290 §§ 3, 4.)

The following references are to the new chapter 110A:

SECT. 2, paragraph (*a*) revised, 1939, 442 § 4; paragraph (*c*) amended, 1936, 316; 1938, 445 § 2; paragraph (*f*) revised, 1938, 445 § 3.

SECT. 4, paragraph (*g*) revised, 1938, 445 § 4; paragraph (*j*) added, 1938, 445 § 5.

SECT. 5, paragraph inserted before the last paragraph, 1938, 445 § 6.

SECT. 9, last sentence stricken out, 1938, 445 § 7.

SECT. 10, fourth sentence stricken out and two new sentences inserted, 1938, 445 § 8.

SECT. 11A added, 1938, 445 § 9 (regulating the sale by a corporation of its securities to employees). [For prior legislation, see General Laws, chapter 155 § 23A, repealed by 1938, 445 § 13.]

SECT. 12 revised, 1938, 445 § 10; last paragraph amended, 1939, 442 § 5.

SECT. 12A added, 1938, 445 § 11 (relative to the modifying or annulling by the commission of orders or findings made by the director of the securities division and to review of such action); repealed, 1939, 442 § 6.

SECT. 13 amended, 1936, 68.

SECT. 18 revised, 1938, 445 § 12.

Chapter 111. — Public Health.

SECT. 1, paragraph added at end, 1938, 265 § 6.

SECT. 5, paragraph added at end, 1941, 388.

SECT. 5A added, 1941, 612 (relative to the preparation and distribution by the department of public health of products applicable to the prevention or cure of diseases of man).

SECT. 6 revised, 1938, 265 § 7.

SECT. 11 revised, 1934, 328 § 1.

SECT. 12 revised, 1943, 331 § 1.

SECT. 13, last sentence revised, 1943, 331 § 2.

SECT. 15 amended, 1934, 340 § 7. (See 1934, 340 § 18.)

SECT. 16 amended, 1934, 340 § 8. (See 1934, 340 § 18.)

SECT. 17 amended, 1937, 340.

SECT. 24 amended, 1937, 365; revised, 1939, 234.

SECT. 27A revised, 1932, 209.

SECT. 31 amended, 1937, 285.

SECT. 31A stricken out, and new sections 31A and 31B inserted, 1937, 282.

SECTS. 34–43 and 46–49, and the caption preceding section 34, repealed, 1937, 362 § 6. (See 1937, 362 §§ 1–5, 7.)

SECT. 51 revised, 1943, 16 § 1.

SECT. 53 amended, 1943, 16 § 2.

SECT. 54 amended, 1943, 16 § 3.

SECT. 57A added, 1943, 436 § 1 (permitting the department of public health to establish and maintain cancer clinics). (See 1943, 436 § 2.)
SECT. 65A amended, 1936, 346 § 1; 1941, 506. (See 1936, 346 § 2.)
SECT. 66 amended, 1934, 219. (See 1936, 346 § 2.)
SECT. 66A added, 1937, 392 (permitting the admission to state sanatoria and county tuberculosis hospitals, for purposes of diagnosis and observation, of certain patients with diseases of the lungs other than recognizable tuberculosis).
SECTS. 67A–67D added, under caption "CARE OF CERTAIN INFANTS PREMATURELY BORN", 1937, 332.
SECT. 67A revised, 1939, 246 § 1.
SECT. 67C revised, 1939, 246 § 2.
SECT. 69A amended, 1936, 337 § 1.
SECT. 69C amended, 1936, 337 § 2.
SECT. 70 amended, 1941, 194 § 5, 389 § 1.
SECTS. 71–73 stricken out, and sections 71–72A and 73 inserted, 1941, 661 § 1. (See 1941, 661 § 2.)
SECT. 74 amended, 1941, 72.
SECTS. 78–90 affected (as to district of Chelsea, Revere and Winthrop), 1934, 78.
SECT. 78. See 1935, 52.
SECT. 79 revised, 1936, 343.
SECT. 83A added, 1933, 318 § 6 (relative to the indemnification or protection of officers and employees of tuberculosis hospital districts in connection with actions for personal injuries arising out of the operation of vehicles owned by such districts); amended, 1934, 291 § 5. (See 1933, 318 § 9; 1934, 291 § 6.)
SECT. 85, first sentence revised, 1943, 414 § 1; section revised, 1943, 500 § 1. (See 1943, 500 § 3.)
SECT. 85A revised, 1932, 65.
SECT. 88 revised, 1943, 500 § 2. (See 1943, 500 § 3.)
SECT. 88A added, 1943, 500 § 2 (relative to charges for the support of patients in county tuberculosis hospitals). (See 1943, 500 § 3.)
SECT. 96 revised, 1938, 265 § 8.
SECT. 96A added, 1938, 265 § 9 (regulating the transportation to another town of a person infected with a disease dangerous to public health).
SECT. 97 revised, 1938, 265 § 10.
SECT. 104 revised, 1938, 265 § 11.
SECT. 107 revised, 1938, 265 § 12.
SECT. 109 revised, 1938, 265 § 13.
SECT. 109A added, 1936, 115 (relative to the treatment of infants' eyes at time of birth); amended, 1943, 46.
SECT. 110, second sentence amended, 1932, 180 § 17.
SECT. 111 revised, 1938, 265 § 14.
SECT. 112 amended, 1938, 265 § 15.
SECT. 113 revised, 1938, 265 § 16.
SECT. 116, sentence in lines 24–32 amended, 1943, 275 § 1.
SECT. 116A added, under caption "CHRONIC RHEUMATISM", 1937, 393 (providing for the hospitalization of patients with chronic rheumatism).
SECT. 117 revised, 1935, 155; 1937, 391.
SECT. 118 amended, 1933, 44.

SECT. 121A added, 1939, 407 (requiring a serological test for syphilis of pregnant women).
SECT. 127 revised, 1937, 339.
SECT. 128, two paragraphs added at end, 1943, 468.
SECT. 141 revised, 1937, 278.
SECT. 143 revised, 1933, 269 § 2.
SECT. 151 amended, 1943, 332 § 9.
SECT. 154 amended, 1934, 340 § 9. (See 1934, 340 § 18.)
SECT. 173A added, 1938, 293 (extending the jurisdiction of certain police officers employed to protect public sources of water supply from pollution).
SECT. 173B added, 1943, 84 (authorizing water commissioners and others to enter premises within the watersheds of certain sources of supply).
SECT. 175 revised, 1941, 353.
SECTS. 176–180 repealed, 1938, 265 § 17.
SECT. 184A added, 1939, 344 (authorizing the state department of public health to issue certificates of approval relative to bacteriological laboratories).

Chapter 112. — Registration of Certain Professions and Occupations.

SECT. 2, second sentence revised, 1933, 171 § 1, 1936, 247 § 1; three paragraphs added at end of section, 1936, 247 § 2; section amended, 1938, 210; paragraph added at end, 1939, 415 § 1; section revised, 1939, 451 § 37; amended, 1941, 722 § 9. Affected, 1938, 259. (See 1933, 171 § 2; 1936, 247 §§ 3–6; 1939, 415 §§ 3, 4.)
SECT. 5 revised, 1937, 425 § 12. (See 1937, 425 § 15.)
SECT. 9 revised, 1933, 152.
SECT. 12A amended, 1943, 41.
SECT. 13 amended, 1937, 425 § 2. (See 1937, 425 § 15.)
SECT. 14 amended, 1937, 425 § 3. (See 1937, 425 § 15.)
SECT. 15 amended, 1937, 425 § 4. (See 1937, 425 § 15.)
SECT. 16 revised, 1937, 425 § 5. (See 1937, 425 § 15.)
SECT. 17 revised, 1937, 425 § 6. (See 1937, 425 § 15.)
SECT. 17A added, 1937, 425 § 7 [defining certain duties of the board of registration in chiropody (podiatry)]. (See 1937, 425 § 15.)
SECT. 18 amended, 1937, 425 § 8. (See 1937, 425 § 15.)
SECT. 19 amended, 1937, 425 § 9. (See 1937, 425 § 15.)
SECT. 20 amended, 1937, 425 § 10. (See 1937, 425 § 15.)
SECT. 21 amended, 1937, 425 § 11. (See 1937, 425 § 15.)
SECT. 23 repealed, 1937, 425 § 13. (See 1937, 425 § 15.)
SECT. 24 amended, 1932, 227; 1933, 126; 1937, 343 § 1; revised, 1941, 52 § 1. (See 1941, 52 § 2; 1943, 165.)
SECT. 27 revised, 1934, 328 § 2; amended, 1937, 343 § 2.
SECT. 30 amended, 1937, 343 § 3.
SECT. 32 amended, 1934, 328 § 3.
SECT. 34 amended, 1934, 328 § 4.
SECT. 35 amended, 1934, 328 § 5; 1935, 306; 1937, 343 § 4.
SECT. 36 revised, 1934, 328 § 6.
SECT. 38 revised, 1934, 236.
SECT. 39 amended, 1939, 138.

Sect. 40 amended, 1934, 328 § 6A; 1937, 343 § 5.
Sect. 42A added, 1937, 343 § 6 (relative to the retail drug business and pharmacy).
Sect. 45, second sentence amended, 1932, 180 § 18; paragraph added at end, 1939, 415 § 2. (See 1939, 415 § 3.)
Sect. 46, clause Third amended, 1934, 108.
Sect. 50 amended, 1935, 344.
Sects. 52A and 52B added, 1934, 281 (relative to methods and practices of dentists and dental hygienists).
Sect. 52A revised, 1937, 253.
S c . 55 amended, 1937, 66; revised, 1939, 251 § 1. (See 1939, 251 §§ 2, 3, 4.)
Sects. 60A–60J added under caption "REGISTRATION OF ARCHITECTS", 1941, 696 § 2. (See 1941, 696 §§ 3, 4.)
Sect. 60C, clause (*c*) revised, 1943, 167.
Sects. 66–73 stricken out, and new sections 66–73 inserted, 1934, 339 § 2.
Sect. 72 amended, 1938, 434 § 1. (See 1938, 434 § 4.)
Sect. 73 amended, 1938, 434 § 2. (See 1938, 434 § 4.)
Sect. 73A added, 1937, 287 § 1 (regulating advertising in connection with the sale of eyeglasses, lenses or eyeglass frames). (See 1937, 287 § 2.)
Sect. 73B added, 1938, 434 § 3 (further regulating optometrists with respect to premises where practice may be carried on and to the sharing of their fees). (See 1938, 434 § 4.)
Sects. 74–81 stricken out, and new sections 74–81C added, 1941, 620 § 3. (See 1941, 620 §§ 1, 4–12.)
Sects. 81A–81Q inserted under caption "REGISTRATION OF PROFESSIONAL ENGINEERS AND OF LAND SURVEYORS", 1941, 643 § 2. (See 1941, 643 §§ 3–5.)
Sect. 81A, as so inserted, amended and renumbered 81D, 1941, 722 § 9A.
Sect. 81L amended, 1941, 722 § 9B.
Sects. 81B–81Q, inclusive, inserted by 1941, 643 § 2, renumbered 81E–81T, inclusive, 1941, 722 § 9C.
Sects. 82–87, and caption before said section 82, stricken out, and new sections 82–87 inserted, under caption "REGISTRATION OF EMBALMERS AND FUNERAL DIRECTORS", 1936, 407 § 3. (See 1936, 407 §§ 5–8.)
Sect. 82, definition of "Funeral directing", revised, 1939, 160 § 1.
Sect. 83, third paragraph amended, 1939, 160 § 4.
Sect. 85 amended, 1941, 232.
Sect. 87 amended, 1937, 13; 1939, 160 § 2.
Sects. 87F–87S. See 1937, 184.
Sect. 87F, paragraph contained in lines 4–9 revised, 1934, 260 § 1.
Sect. 87H, four sentences added at end, 1934, 260 § 2; section amended, 1936, 314 § 1; second paragraph amended, 1937, 94; same paragraph revised, 1941, 619 § 1. (See 1941, 619 § 2.)
Sect. 87I amended, 1936, 314 § 2.
Sect. 87K, paragraph added at end, 1936, 314 § 3.
Sect. 87M amended, 1936, 314 § 4.
Sect. 87O amended, 1933, 149 § 2. (See 1933, 149 § 3.)

SECT. 87P amended, 1934, 260 § 3.

SECT. 87R amended, 1936, 314 § 5.

SECTS. 87T–87JJ added, under caption "REGISTRATION OF HAIRDRESSERS", 1935, 428 § 2. (See 1935, 428 §§ 6, 7.)

SECT. 87T, definition of "Apprentice" stricken out and definition of "Instructor" added, 1941, 626 § 1; definition of "shop" revised, 1941, 626 § 2; section revised, 1943, 565 § 1.

SECT. 87U amended, 1937, 385 § 2; revised, 1941, 626 § 3.

SECT. 87V amended, 1937, 385 § 3; revised, 1941, 626 § 4; 1943, 565 § 2.

SECT. 87W amended, 1937, 385 § 4; revised, 1941, 626 § 5; 1943, 565 § 3.

SECT. 87X revised, 1941, 626 § 6; 1943, 565 § 4.

SECT. 87Z amended, 1937, 385 § 5; revised, 1943, 565 § 5.

SECT. 87AA revised, 1941, 626 § 7; 1943, 565 § 6.

SECT. 87BB amended, 1937, 385 § 6; revised, 1943, 565 § 7.

SECT. 87CC revised, 1941, 626 § 8; 1943, 565 § 8.

SECT. 87DD revised, 1943, 565 § 9.

SECT. 87EE revised, 1937, 385 § 7.

SECT. 87GG revised, 1941, 626 § 9; 1943, 565 § 10.

SECT. 87II amended, 1937, 385 § 8; revised, 1941, 626 § 10; 1943, 565 § 11.

SECT. 87JJ revised, 1941, 626 § 11; 1943, 565 § 12.

SECT. 88, clause (3) amended, 1941, 626 § 13.

Chapter 113. — Promotion of Anatomical Science.

SECT. 1 amended, 1941, 351 § 7.

Chapter 114. — Cemeteries and Burials.

SECT. 1 amended, 1936, 319 § 1. (See 1936, 319 § 7.)

SECT. 6 amended, 1936, 319 § 2. (See 1936, 319 § 7.)

SECT. 7 revised, 1936, 319 § 3. (See 1936, 319 § 7.)

SECT. 8 revised, 1936, 319 § 4. (See 1936, 319 § 7.)

SECT. 9 amended, 1936, 319 § 5. (See 1936, 319 § 7.)

SECT. 25 amended, 1934, 85 § 1. (See 1934, 85 § 2.)

SECTS. 43A–43N added, under caption "MISCELLANEOUS PROVISIONS", 1936, 319 § 6 (relative to the ownership, maintenance and operation of cemeteries and crematories and to the disposal of dead human bodies). (See 1936, 319 § 7.)

SECT. 49 revised, 1936, 407 § 4; last paragraph amended, 1939, 160 § 3. (See 1936, 407 §§ 5–8.)

Chapter 115. — State and Military Aid, Soldiers' Relief, etc.

For legislation providing for payments for the benefit of soldiers and sailors serving in the present war, see 1942, 11; 1943, 211.

SECT. 1, paragraph in third line revised, 1943, 455 § 3.

SECT. 2A added, 1932, 113 (requiring the furnishing of information to the commissioner of state aid and pensions by certain banks and other depositories relative to certain deposits therein); paragraph added at end, 1943, 455 § 4.

SECT. 6, fourth paragraph amended, 1943, 455 § 5; sixth paragraph amended, 1943, 455 § 6; sixteenth paragraph amended, 1943, 455 § 7.
SECT. 7 amended, 1937, 273 § 1; revised, 1938, 316 § 1.
SECT. 9 amended, 1943, 455 § 8.
SECT. 10, second paragraph amended, 1943, 455 § 9.
SECT. 12A added, 1933, 363 (making certain Massachusetts veterans receiving hospital treatment outside the commonwealth eligible to receive military aid).
SECT. 15 amended, 1932, 106.
SECT. 17, first paragraph amended, 1936, 77; 1939, 295; paragraph added, 1932, 63.
SECT. 18, sentence added at end of first paragraph, 1933, 323; paragraph added at end, 1932, 270.
SECT. 19 amended, 1932, 250; 1934, 336 § 1; 1937, 273 § 2; revised, 1938, 316 § 2; amended, 1943, 455 § 10.
SECT. 20 amended, 1932, 251; 1934, 336 § 2; revised, 1943, 455 § 11.
SECT. 21 amended, 1943, 455 § 12.

Chapter 116. — Settlement.

SECT. 1, clause Fifth amended, 1943, 455 § 13.
SECT. 2 revised, 1933, 213; amended, 1943, 379.
SECT. 5 amended, 1943, 455 § 14.

Chapter 117. — Support by Cities and Towns.

SECT. 1 amended, 1934, 124.
SECT. 2A added, 1933, 181 (authorizing local boards of public welfare to aid needy persons in the cultivation of vegetable gardens).
SECT. 3A added, 1937, 277 (protecting needy persons from the public view while applying for public relief and support).
SECT. 3B added, 1939, 127 (prohibiting local boards of public welfare from making the institution of ejectment proceedings a prerequisite to the payment by them of rent owed for dwellings by certain persons on welfare relief).
SECT. 5 amended, 1937, 125.
SECT. 6 revised, 1936, 108.
SECT. 6A added, 1938, 211 (preventing discrimination against certain persons with respect to the payment of welfare relief).
SECT. 13, new sentence added at end, 1941, 608.
SECT. 14 revised, 1937, 113; amended, 1938, 275; 1939, 39 § 1. (See 1939, 39 § 2.)
SECT. 16 repealed, 1936, 328.
SECT. 17 amended, 1939, 370; 1941, 351 § 8. (See 1939, 454 § 21.)
SECT. 18 amended, 1934, 45; 1938, 425; revised, 1941, 351 § 9. (See 1939, 454 § 21.)
SECT. 18A added, 1938, 465 (relative to the payment by cities and towns of the expense of the funeral and burial of certain poor and indigent persons).
SECT. 19, paragraph added at end, 1937, 86.
SECT. 21 amended, 1941, 196.
SECT. 24 revised, 1935, 164; sentence added at end, 1943, 481.

SECT. 35 amended, 1932, 180 § 19.

SECTS. 44–46 added, 1938, 476 (authorizing the establishment of public welfare districts in cities and towns).

Chapter 118. — Aid to Dependent Children (former title, Aid to Mothers with Dependent Children).

The following reference is to chapter 118, as appearing in the Tercentenary Edition:

SECT. 1 revised, 1935, 494 § 2. (See 1935, 494 § 1.)

Chapter stricken out and new chapter (with new title) inserted, 1936, 413 § 1. (See 1936, 413 § 2.)

The following references are to chapter 118, as inserted by 1936, 413 § 1:

SECT. 1 amended, 1939, 487.

SECT. 2 amended, 1941, 593 § 1; 1943, 97.

SECT. 4A added, 1943, 117 (permitting recipients of aid to dependent children, so-called, to leave the commonwealth without suspension of such aid).

SECT. 5 revised, 1941, 593 § 2.

SECT. 6 revised, 1941, 405; two sentences added at end, 1943, 491. (See 1939, 454 § 21.)

SECT. 8 revised, 1939, 248.

Chapter 118A. — Adequate Assistance to Certain Aged Citizens.

The following references are to chapter 118A, as appearing in the Tercentenary Edition:

SECT. 1 amended, 1933, 219; revised, 1933, 328; amended, 1935, 494 § 3. (See 1934, 374 § 3 subsection 15; 1935, 494 § 1.)

SECT. 2A added, 1933, 285 (providing for appeals by persons aggrieved by failure of cities and towns to render old age assistance).

SECT. 3 revised, 1932, 259 § 3.

Chapter stricken out and new chapter 118A inserted, 1936, 436 § 1. (See 1936, 436 § 4.)

The following references are to chapter 118A, as inserted by 1936, 436 § 1:

SECT. 1 amended, 1937, 440 § 1; last sentence amended, 1938, 274; section revised, 1941, 729 § 1; 1943, 489 § 1; paragraph added at end, 1943, 506. (See 1941, 729 § 15.)

SECT. 2 revised, 1937, 440 § 2; amended, 1941, 597 § 1; revised, 1941, 729 § 2; 1943, 489 § 2. (See 1941, 729 § 15.)

SECT. 2A added, 1941, 729 § 3 (relative to the liability of children to contribute to the support of aged parents); revised, 1943, 489 § 3. (See 1941, 729 § 15.)

SECT. 3 revised, 1937, 440 § 3; last sentence revised, 1938, 285; section revised, 1939, 481.

SECT. 4 amended, 1938, 467; amended, 1941, 729 § 4; revised, 1943, 512. (See 1941, 729 §§ 14, 15.)

SECT. 4A added, 1941, 729 § 5 (making a recipient of old age assistance liable to repay the same in certain cases). (See 1941, 729 § 15.)

SECT. 5 revised, 1938, 408; amended, 1941, 729 § 6. (See 1941, 729 § 15.)

SECT. 6A added, 1937, 165 (permitting recipients of old age assistance, so called, to leave the commonwealth without suspension of such assistance); amended, 1941, 729 § 7; revised, 1943, 470. (See 1941, 729 § 15.)

SECT. 8 amended, 1941, 729 § 8; two sentences inserted after third sentence, 1943, 490. (See 1939, 454 § 21; 1941, 729 § 15.)
SECT. 10 revised, 1941, 597 § 2.
SECT. 11 added, 1941, 729 § 10 (establishing the old age assistance fund). (See 1941, 729 §§ 9, 9A, 15.)

Chapter 119. — Protection and Care of Children, and Proceedings against Them.

SECT. 1 revised, 1941, 629 § 1.
SECT. 2 revised, 1941, 629 § 2.
SECT. 6 revised, 1941, 629 § 3.
SECT. 9 amended, 1941, 629 § 4.
SECT. 10 amended, 1941, 629 § 5.
SECT. 12 revised, 1932, 180 § 20.
SECT. 14 revised, 1941, 629 § 6.
SECT. 22 amended, 1941, 351 § 10.
SECT. 28 amended, 1941, 629 § 7.
SECT. 29 amended, 1941, 629 § 8.
SECT. 47A added, 1943, 504 (relative to the payment of expenses for the support of certain neglected children).
SECT. 56 revised, 1943, 244 § 1.
SECT. 58, paragraph inserted after third paragraph, 1941, 264 § 1.
SECT. 58A amended, 1941, 194 § 6; revised, 1941, 327.
SECT. 59, second paragraph stricken out, 1941, 648 § 1.
SECT. 60 stricken out and new sections 60 and 60A inserted, 1938, 174 § 1 (relative to the use of information and records in cases of waywardness or delinquency).
SECT. 63 revised, 1932, 95 § 1.
SECT. 65 amended, 1932, 95 § 2.
SECT. 66 revised, 1941, 648 § 2; 1943, 244 § 2.
SECT. 67 amended, 1941, 648 § 3; revised, 1943, 244 § 2.
SECT. 68 revised, 1943, 244 § 2.
SECT. 69 revised, 1943, 244 § 2.
SECT. 74 amended, 1933, 196 § 1.
SECT. 75 amended, 1933, 196 § 2.

Chapter 120. — Massachusetts Training Schools.

SECT. 21, first sentence amended, 1932, 180 § 21.

Chapter 121. — Powers and Duties of the Department of Public Welfare, and the Massachusetts Hospital School.

For legislation relative to the Federal Surplus Commodity Stamp Plan, so called, see 1941, 65, 92, 634; 1942, 9, 17.
SECT. 4A added, 1941, 630 § 3 (relative to information concerning recipients of old age assistance and aid to dependent children).
SECT. 6 amended, 1941, 351 § 11.
SECT. 7 amended, 1941, 351 § 12; revised, 1941, 404.
SECT. 8A added, 1935, 311 § 2 (relative to funds received by the director of the division of aid and relief for the benefit of persons under the care and supervision of the department); revised, 1941, 523.
SECT. 8B added, 1941, 618 (relative to the disposition of certain un-

claimed moneys held by the division of child guardianship for the benefit of certain wards thereof).

SECT. 9 amended, 1941, 351 § 13.

SECT. 9A added, 1934, 167 (relative to the interstate transportation of poor and indigent persons).

SECT. 12 amended, 1941, 351 § 14.

SECT. 13 amended, 1941, 351 § 15.

SECT. 15 amended, 1941, 351 § 16.

SECT. 23 (and caption) amended, 1933, 364 § 2; section amended, 1935, 449 § 2; revised, 1935, 475 § 3. (See 1933, 364 § 8.)

SECT. 24 amended, 1933, 364 § 3. (See 1933, 364 § 8.)

SECT. 24A added, 1935, 449 § 2A (authorizing the acceptance and use by the state board of housing of grants of federal funds).

SECT. 24B added, 1935, 485 § 1 (authorizing the state board of housing to take land by eminent domain in order to aid or co-operate with the United States with respect to federal housing projects).

SECT. 25 revised, 1933, 364 § 4. (See 1933, 364 § 8.)

SECT. 26 amended, 1933, 364 § 5; revised, 1935, 475 § 4; amended, 1936, 211 § 6. (See 1933, 364 § 8; 1936, 211 § 7.)

SECTS. 26A–26H added, 1933, 364 § 6 (relative to the powers and duties of the state board of housing, and to limited dividend corporations under its control.) (See 1933, 364 § 8.)

SECT. 26H revised, 1935, 449 § 3.

SECTS. 26I–26BB, under caption "HOUSING AUTHORITIES", added, 1935, 449 § 5 (relative to the establishment, powers and duties, and discontinuance, of local housing authorities).

SECT. 26Q, subsection (*c*) added, 1935, 485 § 2 (authorizing local housing authorities to take land by eminent domain in order to aid or co-operate with the United States with respect to federal housing projects).

SECTS. 26I–26BB stricken out and new sections 26I–26II inserted, 1938, 484 § 1 (to relate the Massachusetts Housing Authority Law to the United States Housing Act of 1937). (See 1938, 484 § 2; 1941, 269 § 2; 1941, 317.)

SECT. 26W amended, 1943, 148.

SECT. 26AA, clause (*d*) stricken out and new clauses (*d*) and (*e*) inserted, 1941, 269 § 1.

SECT. 26BB, amended, 1941, 291.

SECT. 26DD revised, 1939, 26.

SECT. 27 repealed, 1933, 364 § 7.

SECT. 39 amended, 1941, 351 § 17.

SECT. 40 amended, 1941, 656 § 13. (See 1941, 656 § 17.)

SECT. 42 amended, 1932, 180 § 22; 1941, 406.

Chapter 122. — Tewksbury State Hospital and Infirmary (former title, State Infirmary).

Title revised, 1941, 351 § 18.

Name of State Infirmary changed to Tewksbury State Hospital and Infirmary, 1939, 272 § 1.

SECT. 1 amended, 1941, 351 § 19; revised, 1941, 596 § 25.

SECT. 2 amended, 1941, 351 § 20.

SECT. 2A amended, 1941, 351 § 21.

SECTS. 2B–2E added, 1936, 295 (relative to Patients' Funds at the state infirmary and the disposition of unclaimed property and moneys represented by bank books belonging to former patients).
SECT. 2B amended, 1941, 351 § 22.
SECT. 2C amended, 1941, 351 § 23.
SECT. 2D revised, 1941, 351 § 24.
SECT. 2E revised, 1941, 351 § 25.
SECT. 3 amended, 1941, 351 § 26.
SECT. 4 amended, 1941, 351 § 27.
SECT. 5 amended, 1941, 351 § 28.
SECT. 6 amended, 1933, 345; 1941, 351 § 29.
SECT. 8 amended, 1941, 351 § 30.
SECT. 10 amended, 1941, 351 § 31.
SECT. 13 amended, 1941, 351 § 32.
SECT. 14 amended, 1941, 351 § 33.
SECT. 15 amended, 1936, 325; 1941, 351 § 34.
SECT. 16 amended, 1941, 351 § 35.
SECT. 17 amended, 1941, 351 § 36.
SECT. 18 amended, 1936, 378; 1941, 351 § 37; revised, 1941, 412; first sentence amended, 1943, 275 § 2; fourth sentence stricken out and two sentences inserted, 1943, 476. (See 1939, 454 § 21.)
SECT. 20 amended, 1941, 351 § 38.
SECT. 20A added, 1941, 201 (penalizing the unlawful possession, handling or consumption of certain things by inmates of said hospital and infirmary).
SECT. 23 amended, 1941, 351 § 39.
SECT. 24 revised, 1941, 191.

Chapter 123. — Commitment and Care of the Insane and Other Mental Defectives.

For legislation relative to the establishment of the Norfolk state hospital for the care of the criminal insane, see 1935, 421; 1939, 485; 1941, 194 §§ 20, 21, 722 §§ 12, 13.
SECT. 1, definition of "commissioner" and "department" revised, 1938, 486 § 7. (See 1938, 486 §§ 1, 21, 22.)
SECT. 4 revised, 1938, 486 § 8. (See 1938, 486 §§ 21, 22.)
SECT. 8A added, 1935, 301 (providing for co-operation between the departments of mental diseases and public works relative to roads at state hospitals).
SECT. 10 amended, 1941, 490 § 25.
SECT. 13 revised, 1936, 286.
SECT. 15 amended, 1941, 656 § 14. (See 1941, 656 § 17.)
SECT. 16 revised, 1938, 486 § 9; amended, 1939, 500 § 1. (See 1938, 486 §§ 21, 22; 1943, 505.)
SECT. 16A amended, 1938, 486 § 10. (See 1938, 486 §§ 21, 22.)
SECT. 19 repealed, 1935, 163.
SECT. 22 revised, 1941, 351 § 40, 706.
SECT. 22A amended, 1941, 194 § 7.
SECT. 25 amended, 1935, 314 § 3, 421 § 4. (See 1935, 421 § 6.)
SECT. 26 repealed, 1938, 486 § 11.
SECT. 28 revised, 1938, 486 § 12. (See 1938, 486 §§ 20–22.)

SECT. 29 revised, 1938, 486 § 13. (See 1938, 486 §§ 21, 22.)
SECT. 30 revised, 1938, 486 § 14. (See 1938, 486 §§ 21, 22.)
SECT. 31 revised, 1938, 486 § 15. (See 1938, 486 §§ 21, 22.)
SECT. 32 revised, 1933, 115; 1938, 486 § 16. (See 1938, 486 §§ 21, 22.)
SECT. 36 revised, 1939, 500 § 12.
SECT. 39, sentence added at end, 1936, 291 § 1.
SECT. 39A amended, 1936, 291 § 2.
SECT. 39B added, 1932, 204 (relative to the disposition of unclaimed belongings at certain state hospitals, known as "patients' valuables"); revised, 1936, 291 § 3.
SECT. 39C added, 1933, 256 (relative to the disposition of moneys represented by certain bank books belonging to former patients of certain state hospitals); revised, 1936, 291 § 4.
SECT. 40 amended, 1939, 500 § 13.
SECT. 43 repealed, 1939, 500 § 2.
SECT. 45 amended, 1938, 486 § 17. (See 1938, 486 §§ 21, 22.)
SECT. 46 amended, 1938, 486 § 18. (See 1938, 486 §§ 21, 22.)
SECT. 47 revised, 1938, 486 § 19. (See 1938, 486 §§ 21, 22.)
SECT. 50 revised, 1935, 314 § 4.
SECT. 52 amended, 1932, 85.
SECT. 53 revised, 1941, 645 § 1.
SECT. 56 repealed, 1939, 500 § 4.
SECT. 62 amended, 1941, 655 § 1.
SECT. 66, paragraph added at end, 1939, 500 § 6.
SECT. 66A amended, 1941, 194 § 8.
SECT. 77, first sentence amended, 1935, 314 § 5; section revised, 1939, 500 § 5.
SECT. 78, first sentence revised, 1935, 314 § 6.
SECT. 79, first sentence revised, 1935, 314 § 7; section revised, 1939, 500 § 7; amended, 1941, 216 § 1; revised, 1941, 645 § 2.
SECT. 80 amended, 1939, 500 § 8.
SECT. 82 amended, 1939, 500 § 9.
SECT. 84 revised, 1941, 481; amended, 1941, 490 § 26; revised, 1941, 722 § 10.
SECT. 86 amended, 1935, 314 § 8; revised, 1939, 500 § 10.
SECT. 87 amended, 1939, 500 § 11.
SECT. 89 revised, 1941, 216 § 3.
SECT. 89A amended, 1941, 194 § 9.
SECT. 89B amended, 1938, 254 § 1; 1941, 194 § 10.
SECT. 90, first sentence amended, 1932, 180 § 23.
SECT. 96 amended, 1941, 351 § 41; third paragraph revised, 1941, 398.
SECT. 100A amended, 1941, 194 § 11.
SECT. 102 revised, 1934, 15; paragraph added at end, 1938, 226; section amended, 1941, 344 § 3.
SECT. 105 revised, 1936, 130; last paragraph amended, 1939, 54; 1941, 216 § 2.
SECT. 110 amended, 1937, 136.
SECT. 113 amended, 1941, 194 § 12; revised, 1943, 185 § 1.
SECT. 114 revised, 1943, 185 § 2.
SECT. 115 revised, 1943, 185 § 3.
SECT. 116 revised, 1943, 185 § 4.

SECT. 117 amended, 1941, 655 § 2.
SECT. 117A added, 1936, 32 (providing in certain cases for the return to penal institutions of prisoners removed therefrom to departments for defective delinquents); revised, 1943, 185 § 5.
SECT. 118 revised, 1938, 254 § 2; 1943, 185 § 6.
SECT. 119 revised, 1938, 254 § 3.

Chapter 124. — Powers and Duties of the Department of Correction.

SECT. 1 amended, 1939, 451 § 38; 1941, 344 § 4.
SECT. 5 amended, 1941, 344 § 5.
SECT. 6 amended, 1936, 23 § 2; 1939, 451 § 39.
SECT. 7 amended, 1939, 451 § 40.
SECT. 8 amended, 1935, 48 § 1. (See 1935, 48 § 2.)

Chapter 125. — Penal and Reformatory Institutions of the Commonwealth.

SECT. 2 amended, 1941, 344 § 6.
SECT. 3 amended, 1941, 344 § 7.
SECT. 4 amended, 1932, 282 § 3; 1941, 344 § 8.
SECT. 4A added, 1939, 360 § 1 (changing the minimum age requirement for appointment of correction officers at certain state penal and reformatory institutions). (See 1939, 238 § 50.)
SECT. 10 revised, 1937, 20 § 1. (See 1937, 20 § 2.)
SECT. 11 amended, 1935, 437 § 1. (See 1935, 437 § 8.)
SECT. 13 amended, 1936, 276; 1939, 360 § 2.
SECT. 30 amended, 1932, 180 § 24.
SECTS. 39–41 (and heading before said section 39) repealed, 1941, 344 § 9.
SECT. 46 repealed, 1941, 596 § 26
SECT. 49 revised, 1936, 125.

Chapter 126. — Jails, Houses of Correction and Reformation, and County Industrial Farms.

SECT. 16 revised, 1937, 219 § 6.
SECT. 37 amended, 1936, 228.

Chapter 127. — Officers and Inmates of Penal and Reformatory Institutions, Paroles and Pardons.

For legislation providing for the disposition of certain prisoners confined in the prison camp and hospital prior to its discontinuance, see 1935, 111.
SECT. 1 revised, 1941, 490 § 27.
SECT. 2 amended, 1941, 344 § 10.
SECT. 10 amended, 1936, 23 § 3; 1941, 656 § 15. (See 1941, 656 § 17.)
SECT. 11 revised, 1941, 344 § 11.
SECT. 12 amended, 1941, 344 § 12.
SECT. 14 amended, 1939, 200.
SECT. 16, last sentence stricken out, 1933, 77 § 1; section amended, 1941, 344 § 13.
SECT. 17 revised, 1933, 77 § 2.

Sect. 18 amended, 1933, 77 § 3.
Sect. 23 amended, 1941, 69.
Sect. 35 amended, 1941, 344 § 14.
Sect. 36 revised, 1941, 237 § 1.
Sect. 37 revised, 1941, 237 § 2.
Sect. 50 revised, 1941, 344 § 15.
Sect. 51 amended, 1941, 344 § 16.
Sect. 67A added, 1932, 252 § 1 (regulating the sale of prison made goods). (See 1932, 252 § 2.)
Sect. 71 revised, 1941, 344 § 17.
Sect. 72 amended, 1941, 344 § 18; revised, 1941, 436 § 1. (See 1941, 436 § 2.)
Sect. 78 and sections 79–82 (and heading preceding said section 79) repealed, 1941, 344 § 19.
Sect. 84 amended, 1941, 490 § 28.
Sect. 87 amended, 1941, 344 § 20.
Sect. 90A revised, 1938, 65.
Sect. 96 amended, 1941, 351 § 42.
Sects. 96A and 96B added, 1936, 383 (providing for the disposition of unclaimed money and property of former prisoners).
Sect. 97 revised, 1943, 113.
Sect. 109 repealed, 1941, 344 § 21.
Sect. 109B added, 1935, 113 § 1 (relative to the transfer of certain prisoners from the Massachusetts Reformatory to the State Prison). (See 1935, 113 § 2.)
Sect. 111A added, 1933, 169 (relative to transfers of defective delinquents and drug addicts from one institution to another under the department of correction).
Sect. 117 revised, 1941, 510 § 1; 1943, 120.
Sect. 118 revised, 1938, 456; amended, 1941, 351 § 43; revised, 1941, 510 § 2.
Sect. 123 amended, 1941, 510 § 3.
Sect. 127 amended, 1938, 71; 1941, 70; 1941, 690 § 5A. (See 1941, 690 §§ 8–10.)
Sect. 128 amended, 1939, 451 § 41; revised, 1941, 690 § 1. (See 1941, 690 §§ 8–10.)
Sect. 129 revised, 1937, 399 § 2. (See 1937, 399 §§ 3–6.)
Sects. 129–139 stricken out and new sections 129–136 and 136A inserted, 1941, 690 § 2. (See 1941, 690 §§ 8–10.)
Sect. 130 revised, 1938, 264 § 1; amended, 1941, 277. (See 1938, 264 § 2.)
Sect. 131 amended, 1939, 451 § 42.
Sect. 132 amended, 1939, 451 § 43.
Sect. 133 revised, 1933, 134 § 1; amended, 1939, 451 § 44. (See 1933, 134 § 2.)
Sect. 135 amended, 1939, 451 § 45.
Sect. 136 amended, 1939, 451 § 46.
Sect. 137 amended, 1939, 451 § 47; repealed, 1941, 344 § 22.
Sect. 137A amended, 1939, 451 § 48.
Sect. 138 amended, 1939, 451 § 49.
Sect. 139 amended, 1939, 451 § 50; revised, 1941, 344 § 23.
Sect. 141 amended, 1941, 174 § 1.

SECT. 146 revised, 1932, 221 § 1.

SECT. 149 amended, 1939, 451 § 51; revised, 1941, 174 § 2; amended, 1941, 690 § 3. (See 1941, 690 §§ 8–10.)

SECT. 151, last sentence amended, 1932, 180 § 25.

SECTS. 151A–151G added, under the heading "INTERSTATE SUPERVISION OF PROBATIONERS AND PAROLEES", 1937, 307 § 1 (providing for the entry of this commonwealth into compacts with any of the United States for mutual helpfulness in relation to persons convicted of crimes or offences who are on probation or parole). (See 1937, 307 § 2.)

SECT. 152 revised, 1939, 479; fourth paragraph amended, 1941, 297.

SECT. 154 amended, 1939, 451 § 52; revised, 1941, 690 § 4. (See 1941, 690 §§ 8–10.)

SECT. 154A added, 1935, 225 (requiring consideration by the advisory board of pardons of the cases of certain life prisoners on the question of extending clemency); amended, 1939, 451 § 53.

SECT. 158 revised, 1941, 344 § 24.

SECT. 160 revised, 1941, 344 § 25; 1943, 433.

SECTS. 166–169 added, 1939, 484 (regulating the payment or receipt of money or other rewards or gratuities for the purpose of obtaining the granting of any pardon, parole, or commutation of or respite from sentence).

SECTS. 166 and 167 revised, 1941, 690 § 5. (See 1941, 690 §§ 8–10.)

Chapter 128. — Agriculture.

SECT. 1 amended, 1941, 490 § 29.

SECT. 2, paragraph (*a*) revised, 1941, 490 § 30; paragraph (*f*) amended, 1937, 415 § 1; 1938, 230; paragraph (*g*) added, 1933, 291 § 1; same paragraph repealed, 1941, 598 § 3.

SECT. 6 amended, 1933, 291 § 2; 1941, 598 § 4.

SECT. 8A added, 1943, 495 (relative to the control or destruction of certain rodents by the commissioner of agriculture).

SECT. 10 amended, 1934, 340 § 10. (See 1934, 340 § 18.)

SECT. 13 amended, 1934, 340 § 11. (See 1934, 340 § 18.)

SECTS. 16–31A affected, 1939, 405.

SECT. 16 amended, 1941, 490 § 32.

SECT. 22 amended, 1941, 490 § 33.

SECT. 23 amended, 1941, 490 § 34.

SECT. 24A added, 1939, 136 (providing for the control of the dutch elm disease).

SECT. 27 revised, 1938, 309.

SECT. 31A revised, 1943, 144.

SECT. 39 repealed, 1933, 74 § 2.

SECT. 42 revised, 1932, 166.

Chapter 128A. — Horse and Dog Racing Meetings.

New chapter inserted, 1934, 374 § 3.

SECT. 3, first paragraph revised, 1935, 454 § 2; 1943, 269; clause (*c*) amended, 1941, 382; clause (*e*) revised, 1939, 505 § 1; clause (*f*) amended, 1935, 454 § 3; clause (*h*) amended, 1935, 454 § 4; clause (*i*) revised, 1939, 505 § 2; clause (*n*) added, 1935, 239 (forbidding the licensed racing of horses and dogs under the pari-mutuel system of betting, on publicly owned premises); clause (*n*) added, 1935, 471 § 1 (forbidding the licensed racing of dogs under such system, in certain residential neighborhoods); designation of the clause added by 1935, 471 § 1 changed from (*n*) to (*o*), 1936, 405 § 3. (See 1935, 471 § 2; 1939, 505 § 3.)

SECT. 4, last paragraph revised, 1939, 356.

SECT. 5, first paragraph revised, 1935, 454 § 1; second and third paragraphs revised, 1936, 351; third paragraph revised, 1939, 473; last paragraph amended, 1939, 497.

SECT. 9, last paragraph revised, 1935, 454 § 5.

SECT. 9A added, 1935, 454 § 6 (relative to rules, regulations and conditions to be prescribed by the state racing commission).

SECT. 10 revised, 1936, 268.

SECT. 13 amended, 1935, 454 § 7.

SECT. 13A added, 1935, 454 § 8 (relative to the application of certain laws as to betting and certain local requirements as to race tracks and public amusements, in the case of racing meetings under this chapter); revised, 1939, 159; amended, 1941, 295. (See 1935, 471 § 2.)

SECT. 13B added, 1937, 322 (prohibiting and penalizing the use of drugs for the purpose of affecting the speed of horses at horse racing meetings).

SECT. 14 revised, 1935, 279 § 2; 1936, 253 § 2; amended, 1938, 282. (See 1935, 279 § 3; 1936, 253 § 1.)

SECT. 14A added, 1935, 279 § 1 (providing for the resubmission to the voters of the several counties of the question of licensing dog races at which the pari-mutuel system of betting shall be permitted); repealed, 1936, 253 § 1. (See 1935, 279 § 3; 1936, 253 § 1.)

SECT. 15 revised, 1936, 436 § 2; 1941, 729 § 12. (See 1936, 436 § 4; 1941, 729 § 15.)

Chapter 129. — Livestock Disease Control (former title, Animal Industry).

Title of chapter changed, 1941, 490 § 35.

SECT. 1 revised, 1934, 340 § 12; paragraph (defining "Domestic animals") added, 1935, 70. (See 1934, 340 § 18.)

SECT. 8A added, 1941, 375 (establishing a scale of fees for the inoculation of swine against hog cholera).

SECT. 9 amended, 1943, 332 § 10.

SECT. 10 amended, 1934, 340 § 13. (See 1934, 340 § 18.)

SECT. 15 revised, 1941, 162.

SECT. 26A revised, 1938, 168; amended, 1941, 173.

SECT. 29 amended, 1938, 308.

SECT. 32 amended, 1939, 451 § 54.

SECT. 33 amended, 1934, 272.

SECT. 33B revised, 1934, 96.

SECT. 36A added, 1935, 426 (providing for the licensing of certain dealers in bovine animals); repealed, 1941, 607 § 2.

SECT. 36B added, 1938, 314 (providing for the vaccination of certain cattle to curtail the spread of Bang's disease, so called); revised, 1943, 56.

SECT. 36C added, 1938, 386 (regulating the transportation of neat cattle); repealed, 1941, 607 § 2.

SECT. 38 revised, 1934, 340 § 14. (See 1934, 340 § 18.)

SECTS. 39–43 added, 1941, 607 § 1 (to further regulate the dealing in and transportation of bovine animals and to prevent the spread of disease among such animals).

Chapter 129A. — Marine Fish and Fisheries, Inland Fish and Fisheries, Birds and Mammals, General Provisions.

New chapter inserted, 1933, 329 § 1.

SECT. 1, definition of "Warden" revised, 1937, 413 § 2; definitions of "Coastal Warden", "Deputy Coastal Warden" and "Supervisor", revised, 1939, 491 § 11. (See 1937, 413 §§ 3, 4; 1939, 491 § 12.)

SECT. 10, sentence added at end, 1941, 171.

Chapter 129A repealed in part, 1941, 598 § 7; entirely repealed, 1941, 599 § 1. (See 1941, 598 § 9, 599 § 7.)

Chapter 130. — Marine Fish and Fisheries (former title, Marine Fish and Fisheries, including Crustacea and Shellfish).

The following reference is to chapter 130, as appearing in the Tercentenary Edition:

SECT. 48A added, 1933, 118 (prohibiting the taking of certain herring or alewives from the waters of Plymouth harbor, Kingston bay, Duxbury bay and certain waters of Plymouth bay).

Chapter stricken out, and new chapter 130 (with new title) inserted, 1933, 329 § 2.

The following references are to chapter 130 as so inserted:

SECT. 3A added, 1935, 324 (providing for state aid to coastal cities and towns in conserving and increasing the supply of shellfish and in exterminating the enemies thereof).

SECT. 6B added, 1934, 115 § 1 (providing for the filing with the supervisor of marine fisheries of copies of rules and regulations made by cities and towns under the marine fisheries laws, and for notifying him of permits and licenses issued under said laws). (See 1934, 115 § 2.)

SECT. 11A added, 1941, 172 (penalizing the taking of certain herring or alewives from the waters of Plymouth Harbor, Kingston Bay, Duxbury Bay and certain waters of Plymouth Bay).

SECT. 23 amended, 1937, 168.

SECTS. 27A and 27B added, 1939, 385 § 1 (relative to the establishment and maintenance of a plant for the propagation of lobsters). (See 1939, 385 § 2.)

SECT. 41A added, 1937, 121 (prohibiting, during certain months of the year, the taking of edible crabs from the waters of the commonwealth).

SECT. 48, first paragraph amended, 1935, 110.

SECT. 73 amended, 1935, 117.

SECTS. 77, 78, 79 revised, 1937, 246.

SECT. 84A added, 1934, 129 (regulating the disposition of starfish caught in or taken from the coastal waters of the commonwealth).

Chapter stricken out, and new chapter 130 (with new title) inserted, 1941, 598 § 1. (See 1941, 598 § 9.)

SECT. 37, paragraph contained in lines 10 and 11 amended, 1943, 149; same paragraph revised, 1943, 533 § 1. (See 1943, 533 § 2.)

Chapter 131[*] — Powers and Duties of the Division of Fisheries and Game (former title, Game and Inland Fisheries).

The following references are to chapter 131, as appearing in the Tercentenary Edition:

Title amended, 1933, 329 § 14.

SECTS. 1–4 repealed, 1933, 329 § 20.

SECT. 5 amended, 1932, 272 § 1; 1933, 214 § 1; 1937, 191 § 1.

SECT. 6 revised, 1932, 272 § 2.

SECT. 7 revised, 1932, 272 § 3.

SECT. 8 revised, 1932, 272 § 4; new paragraph added (summer three-day fishing license), 1934, 156; same paragraph revised, 1938, 121 § 1. (See 1938, 121 § 2.)

SECT. 8A added, 1933, 214 § 2 (establishing special fox hunting licenses for non-resident members and guests of clubs or associations conducting fox hunts).

SECT. 8B added, 1937, 191 § 2 (authorizing the issuance to certain officials of certain other states of complimentary certificates entitling them to hunt and fish in this commonwealth).

SECTS. 9–11 repealed, 1933, 329 § 20.

SECT. 12 amended, 1932, 272 § 5; revised, 1933, 214 § 3.

SECT. 13 revised, 1933, 329 § 15.

SECT. 13A added, 1941, 159 § 1 (imposing a penalty for carrying firearms, while intoxicated, in places where hunting is permitted). (See 1941, 159 § 2.)

SECTS. 14–24 repealed, 1933, 329 § 20.

SECT. 24A added, 1932, 78 (relative to the establishment in certain brooks and streams of breeding areas for fish).

SECT. 25, paragraph added at end, 1934, 33.

SECTS. 27–34 repealed, 1933, 329 § 20.

SECT. 42 repealed, 1933, 329 § 20.

SECT. 43A added, 1936, 294 (relative to fishing in ponds situated partly in the commonwealth and partly in another state).

SECT. 44 revised, 1933, 329 § 16.

SECT. 45, sentence added at end, 1932, 77.

SECT. 48 revised, 1936, 69.

SECT. 49 amended, 1933, 329 § 17.

SECT. 49A added, 1937, 123 (establishing a close season for fish with respect to which no close season is otherwise established by law).

SECTS. 52–55 repealed, 1933, 329 § 20.

SECT. 56 amended, 1934, 51.

SECT. 57 amended, 1934, 149; 1936, 425 § 1; 1937, 116.

SECT. 59 revised, 1936, 425 § 2; 1937, 269.

SECT. 61A added, 1933, 329 § 18 (regulating the taking of smelt in great ponds).

SECT. 66 amended, 1934, 40.

SECT. 68 revised, 1935, 120.

SECT. 73A added, 1935, 98 (authorizing the use of certain traps for the purpose of catching fish bait in the inland waters of the commonwealth).

SECT. 74 revised, 1932, 272 § 6.

SECT. 77 revised, 1933, 154.

SECT. 83 revised, 1935, 107.
SECT. 85 amended, 1932, 28; 1935, 13; 1937, 167.
SECT. 86A added, 1932, 60 (authorizing the director of fisheries and game to suspend or modify the open season or bag limit as to ruffed grouse and quail).
SECT. 87A added, 1933, 122 (relative to the taking or killing of waterfowl and other migratory birds in certain cases).
SECT. 92 amended, 1932, 52.
SECT. 94 amended, 1934, 183; 1937, 172; revised, 1937, 316.
SECT. 97 revised, 1934, 70; amended, 1936, 13.
SECT. 99 amended, 1932, 180 § 26.
SECT. 100A added, 1932, 82 (prohibiting the hunting of beavers).
SECT. 103 revised, 1938, 301.
SECT. 104 revised, 1933, 192 § 1; 1937, 324; amended, 1941, 175.
SECT. 104A added, 1939, 462 (restricting the carrying of certain firearms in motor vehicles in areas used for hunting).
SECT. 105A revised, 1933, 203; repealed, 1934, 275 § 2.
SECTS. 105B and 105C added, 1934, 275 § 1 (regulating the use of traps and other devices for the capture of fur-bearing animals and providing for local option thereon). (See 1934, 275 § 4.)
SECT. 109 revised, 1932, 264; 1933, 192 § 2; amended, 1935, 5 § 1; 1936, 21 § 1, 138 § 1; 1937, 89 § 1, 243 § 1.
SECT. 112 revised, 1933, 192 § 3; amended, 1935, 5 § 2; 1936, 21 § 2, 138 § 2; 1937, 243 § 2.
SECT. 114 revised, 1937, 89 § 2; last paragraph amended, 1937, 372 § 1.
SECT. 114A added, 1934, 275 § 3 (authorizing the commissioner of conservation to temporarily suspend, within certain specified territory, the provisions of section 105B).
SECT. 124 amended, 1937, 229.
SECT. 135 revised, 1932, 81, 272 § 7.
SECT. 137 added, 1933, 329 § 19 (relative to the protection of salmon fry in the Merrimack river).
Chapter stricken out, and new chapter 131 (with new title) inserted, 1941, 599 § 2. (See 1941, 599 §§ 5-7.)
The following references are to chapter 131 as so inserted:
SECT. 1, definition of "Birds" revised, 1941, 663 § 1; definition of "Mammals" revised, 1941, 663 § 2. (See 1941, 663 § 3.)
SECT. 8, last paragraph of clause (1) revised, 1943, 265.
SECT. 14, paragraph contained in lines 65–73 amended, 1943, 216 § 1; paragraph contained in lines 74–86 amended, 1943, 216 § 2.
SECT. 68 amended, 1943, 90.
SECT. 97A added, 1943, 463 (relative to the disposition by counties of revenue received from the federal government by reason of federal wildlife refuges situated therein).
SECT. 101 revised, 1943, 100.

Chapter 132. — Forestry.

SECT. 1 amended, 1937, 415 § 2; 1941, 490 § 36.
SECT. 5 repealed, 1932, 180 § 27.
SECT. 6 revised, 1941, 455.
SECT. 11 revised, 1937, 415 § 3.

SECT. 12 amended, 1937, 415 § 4.
SECT. 13 revised, 1935, 87; amended, 1937, 415 § 5.
SECT. 14 revised, 1937, 415 § 6.
SECT. 17 amended, 1937, 415 § 6A.
SECT. 18 amended, 1937, 415 § 6B.
SECT. 22 amended, 1937, 415 § 7.
SECT. 25 revised, 1937, 415 § 8.
SECT. 26 amended, 1937, 415 § 9.
SECT. 27 amended, 1937, 415 § 10.
SECT. 28 amended, 1937, 415 § 11.
SECT. 33 amended, 1935, 373; 1936, 415 § 1. (See 1936, 415 § 3.)
SECT. 34, new paragraph added at end, 1935, 233.
SECT. 36 revised, 1936, 415 § 2. (See 1936, 415 § 3.)
SECTS. 40–45 added, under caption "Forest Cutting Practices", 1943, 539.

Chapter 132A. — State Parks and Reservations Outside of the Metropolitan Parks District.

SECT. 2 amended, 1941, 490 § 37.
SECT. 7 revised, 1941, 722 § 11.
SECT. 9 amended, 1933, 75 § 4.

Chapter 135. — Unclaimed and Abandoned Property.

SECT. 8 amended, 1938, 98 § 1.
SECT. 9 amended, 1938, 98 § 3.
SECT. 11 amended, 1938, 98 § 2.

Chapter 136. — Observance of the Lord's Day.

SECT. 2 amended, 1933, 150 § 1; 1934, 63; 1935, 78.
SECT. 4A added, 1933, 150 § 2 (relative to the licensing of certain enterprises to be held on the Lord's day at amusement parks and beach resorts); revised, 1933, 309 § 1. (See 1933, 309 § 2.)
SECT. 6, second and third paragraphs amended, 1934, 328 § 7; fourth paragraph amended, 1932, 96; 1934, 354; paragraph added at end, 1933, 150 § 3; section revised, 1934, 373 § 6; third paragraph amended, 1936, 129; 1937, 286; fourth paragraph amended, 1938, 143; same paragraph revised, 1943, 473.
SECT. 7 amended, 1934, 328 § 8; revised, 1934, 373 § 7.
SECT. 8 amended, 1937, 124.
SECT. 13 amended, 1932, 105.
SECT. 17, sentence added at end, 1933, 150 § 4; section amended, 1934, 55; revised, 1938, 60.
SECT. 21 revised, 1935, 104, 169.
SECT. 22. See 1933, 136; 1935, 49.

Chapter 138. — Alcoholic Liquors (Old Title, Intoxicating Liquors and Certain Non-Intoxicating Beverages).

Beer bill, so called, 1933, 120 (amended by 1933, 216, 234, 346). (See also 1933, Res. 47.)
Act providing for a convention to act upon a proposed amendment

to the constitution of the United States relative to the repeal of the eighteenth amendment, 1933, 132.

The following references are to chapter 138, as appearing in the Tercentenary Edition:

SECT. 1, paragraph in lines 4–7 amended, 1933, 97 § 1. (See 1933, 97 § 3, 346 § 9.)

SECT. 2 affected, 1933, 120 § 53.

SECT. 3 amended, 1933, 97 § 2. (See 1933, 97 § 3, 346 § 9.)

Chapter stricken out, and new chapter 138 inserted, 1933, 376 § 2.

The following references are to the new chapter 138:

SECT. 1, new paragraph (definition of "Alcohol") added, 1935, 440 § 1; definition of "Restaurant" amended, 1936, 368 § 1; eighth paragraph (definition of "Club"), revised, 1934, 385 § 1; definition of "Tavern" amended, 1934, 121 § 1; 1935, 253 § 1; definition of "Wines" revised, 1941, 637 § 1. (See 1941, 637 § 3.)

SECT. 2 revised, 1934, 305, 372 § 4; 1935, 440 § 2; first sentence revised, 1939, 470 § 1; 1943, 542 § 1.

SECT. 3 amended, 1935, 440 § 3.

SECT. 4 amended, 1934, 385 § 2.

SECT. 7 amended, 1935, 440 § 4.

SECT. 10 amended, 1935, 440 § 5.

SECT. 10A revised, 1943, 542 § 2.

SECT. 10B added, 1934, 370 § 11 (authorizing the alcoholic beverages control commission to remove a member of a local licensing board under certain conditions).

SECT. 11 revised, 1936, 207 § 1. (See 1935, 281.)

SECT. 11A, first paragraph amended, 1934, 142 § 1; paragraph inserted, 1934, 142 § 2; paragraph added at end, 1934, 142 § 3; section revised, 1934, 211 § 1; last paragraph stricken out, 1935, 440 § 6. (See 1934, 142 § 4, 211 § 2.)

SECT. 12, first paragraph amended, 1934, 121 § 2; last sentence of first paragraph revised, 1934, 370 § 1; second paragraph amended, 1934, 121 § 2; sentence contained in lines 42–53 revised, 1934, 370 § 2; section revised, 1934, 385 § 3; first paragraph amended, 1935, 253 § 2; revised, 1935, 440 § 7; new paragraph inserted after first paragraph, 1935, 253 § 3; proviso contained in lines 46–48 stricken out, 1935, 253 § 4; third paragraph revised, 1935, 440 § 8; next to last paragraph stricken out, 1935, 440 § 9; section revised, 1935, 468 § 1; first paragraph amended, 1936, 207 § 2; last sentence of first paragraph revised, 1937, 331; 1943, 542 § 3; second paragraph revised, 1936, 368 § 2; amended, 1943, 542 § 4; paragraph added at end, 1937, 264. (See 1943, 542 § 20.)

SECT. 13, last two sentences stricken out, 1934, 385 § 4; section revised, 1935, 440 § 10.

SECT. 14 amended, 1934, 370 § 3; paragraph added at end, 1935, 440 § 11.

SECT. 15, first paragraph amended, 1934, 385 § 5; revised, 1935, 440 § 12; last paragraph revised, 1934, 370 § 4; last sentence revised, 1936, 225 § 1; second paragraph revised, 1938, 353.

SECT. 15A added, 1934, 370 § 5 (relative to the publication of applications for original licenses); revised, 1935, 440 § 13; 1939, 414; amended, 1943, 542 § 5.

SECT. 16 revised, 1936, 368 § 3.

SECT. 16A revised, 1934, 385 § 6; 1937, 424 § 1.

SECT. 16B revised, 1935, 440 § 14; paragraph added at end, 1937, 291; section revised, 1937, 424 § 2; second paragraph revised, 1939, 92; section amended, 1943, 542 § 6.

SECT. 17, second proviso of first paragraph amended, 1934, 385 § 7; first paragraph amended, 1935, 81; last paragraph revised, 1934, 83; section revised, 1935, 440 § 15; first paragraph amended, 1936, 136, 245; 1937, 14 § 1; second paragraph revised, 1936, 199; paragraph added after the second paragraph, 1936, 368 § 4; section revised, 1937, 424 § 3; paragraph in lines 106–118 revised, 1939, 263; paragraph in lines 119–122 revised, 1941, 522. (See 1937, 14 § 2.)

SECT. 18, first paragraph revised, 1935, 440 § 16; first sentence revised, 1943, 542 § 7; two paragraphs added, 1934, 385 § 8; paragraph added at end, 1943, 542 § 8.

SECT. 18A added, under caption "SELLING AGENTS OF FOREIGN IMPORTERS AND MANUFACTURERS", 1934, 312; first paragraph revised, 1935, 440 § 17.

SECT. 18B added, 1943, 542 § 9 (relative to the issuance of certificates of compliance to persons licensed outside the commonwealth to export and sell alcoholic beverages to licensees under this chapter).

SECT. 19, first paragraph revised, 1935, 440 § 18; second paragraph amended, 1934, 385 § 9; last paragraph amended, 1934, 385 § 10; 1935, 440 § 19; paragraph added at end, 1936, 368 § 5.

SECT. 19A added, 1934, 385 § 11 (relative to the licensing of salesmen for manufacturers and for wholesalers and importers); revised, 1935, 440 § 20.

SECT. 20 revised, 1934, 385 § 12; first paragraph amended, 1936, 368 § 6; paragraph inserted, 1936, 368 § 7; section revised, 1943, 542 § 10.

SECT. 20A added, 1937, 424 § 4 (relative to granting permits to public warehousemen to store and warehouse alcoholic beverages).

SECT. 21 revised, 1934, 385 § 13; first paragraph amended, 1935, 440 § 21; first six paragraphs revised, 1936, 411 § 1; 1939, 367 § 1; first paragraph (as appearing in 1939, 367 § 1) amended, 1943, 542 § 11; third paragraph (as so appearing) stricken out and two new paragraphs inserted, 1941, 637 § 2; sixth paragraph (as so appearing) revised, 1943, 36; next to the last paragraph (as appearing in 1934, 385 § 13) amended, 1936, 368 § 8; last paragraph (as so appearing) revised, 1939, 451 § 55; paragraph added at end, 1939, 394. [Temporary additional excise, 1939, 434; 1941, 339; 1943, 423.] (See 1936, 411 § 2; 1939, 367 § 2; 1941, 637 § 3.)

SECT. 22 revised, 1934, 385 § 14; 1935, 440 § 22; fourth and fifth paragraphs stricken out and new paragraph inserted, 1937, 418.

SECT. 22A added, 1934, 385 § 15 (providing for the granting by the alcoholic beverages control commission in certain cases of permits to sell alcoholic beverages).

SECT. 23, sentence added at end of fourth paragraph, 1934, 370 § 6; last paragraph amended, 1934, 245; section revised, 1934, 385 § 16; fifth paragraph amended, 1935, 253 § 5; last four paragraphs stricken out, and five new paragraphs inserted, 1935, 440 § 23; second of the paragraphs so inserted revised, 1941, 578; fourth paragraph revised, 1938, 238; sentence added at end of next to last paragraph, 1939, 470 § 2; section revised, 1943, 542 § 12.

SECT. 24, first sentence amended, 1934, 232; section revised, 1943, 542 § 13.

SECT. 26, first paragraph amended, 1935, 440 § 24.
SECT. 27 revised, 1934, 301 § 1; amended, 1934, 385 § 23; revised, 1935, 442; amended, 1936, 436 § 3; revised, 1936, 438; 1941, 729 § 13. (See 1936, 436 § 4; 1941, 729 § 15.)
SECT. 28 amended, 1934, 112.
SECT. 29 revised, 1935, 440 § 25.
SECT. 30 amended, 1935, 83 § 1; 1943, 542 § 14. (See 1935, 83 § 2.)
SECT. 30A revised, 1934, 370 § 7; 1935, 440 § 26.
SECT. 30B amended, 1935, 440 § 27; paragraph added at end, 1936, 368 § 9.
SECT. 30D amended, 1935, 440 § 28.
SECT. 30E, first paragraph amended, 1935, 440 § 29.
SECT. 30F revised, 1935, 440 § 30.
SECT. 30G amended, 1935, 440 § 31.
SECT. 30H added, 1935, 440 § 32 (possession or transportation of alcoholic beverages or alcohol under certain circumstances deemed prima facie evidence of violation of law).
SECT. 31 amended, 1935, 440 § 33; revised, 1936, 368 § 10.
SECT. 32 amended, 1934, 370 § 8.
SECT. 33 revised, 1934, 370 § 9; amended, 1935, 468 § 2; last sentence revised, 1936, 225 § 2; section amended, 1937, 268; 1941, 356.
SECT. 34 amended, 1935, 440 § 34; revised, 1936, 171; 1937, 424 § 5; amended, 1943, 542 § 15.
SECT. 34A added, 1935, 146 (relative to procuring by false representation sales or delivery of alcoholic beverages to minors); revised, 1935, 440 § 35.
SECT. 36 amended, 1934, 385 § 17.
SECT. 37 revised, 1934, 385 § 18.
SECT. 38 amended, 1941, 199.
SECTS. 42–55 affected, 1935, 440 § 36.
SECT. 42, paragraph added at end, 1935, 440 § 36.
SECT. 46 amended, 1934, 370 § 10; 1935, 440 § 37.
SECT. 56 revised, 1935, 440 § 38; 1936, 368 § 11.
SECT. 57 revised, 1936, 368 § 12.
SECT. 62 amended, 1935, 440 § 39.
SECT. 63, first sentence revised, 1934, 385 § 19; section revised, 1935, 440 § 40; 1936, 368 § 13.
SECT. 63A revised, 1935, 440 § 41; 1943, 542 § 16.
SECT. 64 revised, 1934, 385 § 20.
SECT. 65 revised, 1943, 542 § 17.
SECT. 67 amended, 1934, 385 § 21; revised, 1935, 440 § 42; amended, 1938, 400; first paragraph amended, 1943, 542 § 18.
SECT. 70 revised, 1934, 301 § 2.
SECTS. 72–75 repealed, 1934, 372 § 1.
SECT. 76 revised, 1934, 372 § 2; next to last sentence revised, 1934, 385 § 22; section revised, 1935, 440 § 43.
SECT. 77 revised, 1943, 542 § 19.

Chapter 139. — Common Nuisances.

SECT. 14, caption amended, 1934, 328 § 9; section amended, 1934, 328 § 10.
SECT. 16 amended, 1934, 328 § 11.

SECT. 16A amended, 1934, 328 § 12.
SECT. 17 repealed, 1934, 328 § 13.
SECT. 19 amended, 1934, 328 § 14.
SECT. 20 amended, 1934, 328 § 15.

Chapter 140. — Licenses.

For legislation providing for the temporary licensing of distributors and dealers in cigarettes and cigarette vending machines, see 1941, 417; 1943, 407.

SECT. 4 amended, 1934, 171 § 1.

SECT. 6 amended, 1937, 424 § 6; revised, 1941, 439 § 1.

SECT. 6A added, 1937, 424 § 7 (providing for the granting of common victuallers' licenses and licenses to sell alcoholic beverages upon condition that licensed premises are equipped and furnished according to plans and estimates approved in advance); repealed, 1941, 439 § 2.

SECT. 8 amended, 1936, 368 § 14; revised, 1943, 328.

SECT. 9A added, 1939, 431 (relative to the keeping of the premises of common victuallers open for business).

SECT. 10 amended, 1935, 167.

SECT. 12 revised, 1932, 86; 1933, 92; 1943, 31.

SECTS. 21E and 21F added, under caption "ORGANIZATIONS DISPENSING FOOD OR BEVERAGES TO MEMBERS AND GUESTS", 1933, 284 (providing for the regulation of such organizations).

SECT. 21E, last sentence revised, 1934, 328 § 16; affected, 1934, 328 § 17.

SECTS. 32A–32E added, 1939, 416 (requiring the licensing of recreational camps, overnight camps or cabins and trailer camps).

SECT. 32B amended, 1941, 396.

SECT. 48 repealed, 1937, 342 § 2.

SECT. 51 amended, 1932, 275; 1935, 428 § 3; 1936, 55 § 1; revised, 1941, 626 § 12. (See 1935, 428 §§ 6, 7; 1936, 55 § 2.)

SECT. 52 amended, 1935, 428 § 4. (See 1935, 428 § 7.)

SECT. 55 amended, 1938, 59.

SECT. 59 amended, 1934, 254 § 1; 1938, 96. (See 1934, 254 § 2.)

SECT. 71 revised, 1943, 154.

SECT. 90, three sentences added at end, 1934, 179 § 1.

SECT. 96, sentence added at end, 1934, 179 § 2; section amended, 1941, 158 § 1. (See 1941, 158 §§ 2, 3.)

SECT. 121 amended, 1934, 359 § 1.

SECT. 131 revised, 1936, 302.

SECT. 131C added, 1934, 246 (prohibiting persons licensed to carry pistols and revolvers from carrying the same in vehicles unless said weapons are under their control therein).

SECT. 133 amended, 1939, 451 § 56.

SECT. 136A, under caption "DOGS", added, 1934, 320 § 1 (definitions of certain words and phrases in sections 137–175); amended, 1943, 111 § 1. (See 1934, 320 § 34.)

SECT. 137 amended, 1932, 289 § 1; revised (and caption stricken out) 1934, 320 § 2; revised, 1943, 111 § 2. (See 1934, 320 § 34.)

SECTS. 137A–137C added, 1934, 320 § 3 (relative to kennel licenses and regulating holders of such licenses). (See 1934, 320 § 34.)

SECT. 137A, paragraph added at end, 1937, 95; first paragraph stricken out and three paragraphs inserted, 1943, 111 § 3.
SECT. 137C revised, 1939, 206.
SECT. 138 revised, 1934, 320 § 4; 1938, 92; 1943, 111 § 4. (See 1934, 320 § 34.)
SECT. 139 amended, 1934, 320 § 5; sentence added at end, 1939, 23; sentence added at end, 1941, 132. (See 1934, 320 § 34.)
SECT. 140 repealed, 1934, 320 § 6. (See 1934, 320 § 34.)
SECT. 141 revised, 1934, 320 § 7. (See 1934, 320 § 34.)
SECTS. 142–144 repealed, 1934, 320 § 8. (See 1934, 320 § 34.)
SECT. 145 amended, 1932, 289 § 2.
SECT. 145A added, 1932, 289 § 3 (relative to the furnishing of anti-rabic vaccine); revised, 1934, 320 § 9; 1937, 375; last sentence revised, 1939, 42. (See 1934, 320 § 34.)
SECT. 146 revised, 1934, 320 § 10; 1941, 133 § 1. (See 1934, 320 § 34.)
SECT. 147 revised, 1932, 289 § 4; 1934, 320 § 11; amended, 1941, 133 § 2. (See 1934, 320 § 34.)
SECT. 148 repealed, 1932, 289 § 6. (See G. L. chapter 41 § 13A, inserted by 1932, 289 § 5.)
SECT. 150 revised, 1934, 320 § 12. (See 1934, 320 § 34.)
SECT. 151 revised, 1934, 320 § 13. (See 1934, 320 § 34.)
SECT. 151A added, 1934, 320 § 14 (powers and duties of dog officers under annual warrants from mayors or selectmen). (See 1934, 320 § 34.)
SECT. 152 revised, 1934, 320 § 15. (See 1934, 320 § 34.)
SECT. 153 revised, 1934, 320 § 16. (See 1934, 320 § 34.)
SECT. 154 repealed, 1934, 320 § 17. (See 1934, 320 § 34.)
SECT. 155 revised, 1934, 320 § 18. (See 1934, 320 § 34.)
SECT. 156 revised, 1934, 320 § 19. (See 1934, 320 § 34.)
SECT. 157 revised, 1934, 320 § 20. (See 1934, 320 § 34.)
SECT. 158 revised, 1934, 320 § 21. (See 1934, 320 § 34.)
SECT. 159 revised, 1934, 320 § 22. (See 1934, 320 § 34.)
SECT. 160 revised, 1934, 320 § 23. (See 1934, 320 § 34.)
SECT. 161, first two sentences amended, 1932, 289 § 7; section amended, 1934, 320 § 24. (See 1934, 320 § 34.)
SECT. 161A added, 1934, 320 § 25 (reimbursement for damages by dogs regulated). (See 1934, 320 § 34.)
SECT. 162 revised, 1934, 320 § 26. (See 1934, 320 § 34.)
SECT. 163 amended, 1934, 320 § 27. (See 1934, 320 § 34.)
SECT. 164 amended, 1934, 320 § 28. (See 1934, 320 § 34.)
SECT. 165 revised, 1934, 320 § 29. (See 1934, 320 § 34.)
SECT. 166 amended, 1934, 320 § 30. (See 1934, 320 § 34.)
SECT. 170 amended, 1934, 320 § 31. (See 1934, 320 § 34.)
SECT. 171 revised, 1934, 320 § 32. (See 1934, 320 § 34.)
SECT. 172 revised, 1932, 289 § 8.
SECT. 175 revised, 1932, 289 § 9; 1934, 320 § 33; 1943, 93. (See 1934, 320 § 34.)
SECTS. 180A–180D added, under caption "THEATRICAL BOOKING AGENTS, PERSONAL AGENTS AND MANAGERS", 1935, 378 (providing for the licensing and bonding of certain theatrical booking agents, personal agents and managers).
SECT. 181. Affected by 1935, 454 § 8.

Sect. 183A amended, 1935, 102 § 1; 1936, 71 § 1. (See 1935, 102 § 2.)
Sect. 183B repealed, 1936, 71 § 2.
Sect. 184 amended, 1934, 328 § 18.
Sect. 185A amended, 1936, 279; paragraph added at end, 1941, 247.
Sect. 185H added, 1939, 253 (relative to the licensing and supervision of dancing schools, so called).
Sect. 186 amended, 1936, 169 § 1.
Sect. 187 amended, 1936, 169 § 2.
Sect. 202 revised, 1936, 169 § 3.

Chapter 141. — Supervision of Electricians.

Sect. 1, first paragraph amended, 1943, 308.
Sect. 3, clause (4) amended, 1934, 347 § 1.

Chapter 142. — Supervision of Plumbing.

Sect. 6 revised, 1934, 347 § 2.
Sect. 13 amended, 1934, 284.
Sect. 17 revised, 1936, 234; 1941, 518 § 1.
Sect. 18 revised, 1941, 518 § 2.
Sect. 19 revised, 1941, 518 § 3.
Sect. 21 added, 1938, 302 (providing for regulation of plumbing in buildings owned and used by the commonwealth).
Sect. 22 added, 1941, 518 § 4 (providing for the enforcement of certain laws relative to the marking, construction and installation of hot water tanks).

Chapter 143. — Inspection and Regulation of, and Licenses for, Buildings, Elevators and Cinematographs.

Sect. 1, definition of "Inspector" amended, 1943, 544 § 7B; definition of "Place of assembly" inserted after paragraph in lines 12–14, 1943, 546 § 1; definition of "Special hall" revised, 1941, 694.
Sect. 3 revised, 1943, 544 § 2.
Sects. 3A–3H added, 1943, 544 § 2 (providing for rules and regulations for protecting life and limb in places of assembly and for the enforcement of laws, rules and regulations, ordinances and by-laws for protecting the same therein). (See 1943, 544 §§ 7A and 8.)
Sects. 15 and 16 amended, 1943, 544 § 3. (See 1943, 544 § 7A.)
Sect. 21 amended, 1943, 544 § 3; revised, 1943, 546 § 2. (See 1943, 544 § 7A, 546 § 5.)
Sects. 21A and 21B added, 1943, 546 § 3 (further regulating the means of ingress to and egress from places of assembly and certain other places). (See 1943, 546 §§ 5 and 6.)
Sects. 24–33 amended, 1943, 544 § 3. (See 1943, 544 § 7A.)
Sect. 34 revised, 1943, 544 § 4. (See 1943, 544 § 7A.)
Sect. 43 amended, 1943, 544 § 3. (See 1943, 544 § 7A.)
Sects. 45 and 46 amended, 1943, 544 § 3. (See 1943, 544 § 7A.)
Sect. 49 amended, 1943, 544 § 3. (See 1943, 544 § 7A.)
Sects. 51 and 52 amended, 1943, 544 § 3. (See 1943, 544 § 7A.)
Sect. 54 revised, 1943, 544 § 5. (See 1943, 544 § 7A.)
Sect. 59 revised, 1943, 544 § 6. (See 1943, 544 § 7A.)

SECT. 74 revised, 1941, 553 § 1. (See 1941, 553 § 9.)
SECT. 75 revised, 1941, 553 § 2. (See 1941, 553 § 9.)
SECT. 76 revised, 1941, 553 § 3. (See 1941, 553 § 9.)
SECTS. 77 and 78 repealed, 1941, 553 § 4. (See 1941, 553 § 9.)
SECT. 79 revised, 1941, 553 § 5. (See 1941, 553 § 9.)
SECT. 80 repealed, 1941, 553 § 4. (See 1941, 553 § 9.)
SECT. 82 amended, 1941, 553 § 6. (See 1941, 553 § 9.)
SECT. 85 amended, 1941, 553 § 7. (See 1941, 553 § 9.)
SECT. 86 amended, 1941, 553 § 8. (See 1941, 553 § 9.)

Chapter 145. — Tenement Houses in Towns.

SECT. 17A added, 1934, 168 (relative to the erection of garages in the yards of certain tenement houses).

Chapter 146. — Inspection of Boilers, Air Tanks, etc., Licenses of Engineers, Firemen, and Operators of Hoisting Machinery.

SECT. 2 amended, 1941, 459.
SECT. 16 revised, 1932, 180 § 28.
SECT. 34 revised, 1938, 319 § 1.
SECT. 35 amended, 1938, 319 § 2.
SECT. 50 amended, 1935, 67.
SECT. 67 revised, 1941, 525 § 1. (See 1941, 525 § 2.)

Chapter 147. — State and Other Police, and Certain Powers and Duties of the Department of Public Safety.

SECT. 4B added, 1939, 116 (providing that local police authorities and district attorneys be furnished with information relative to certain persons charged with or convicted of sex crimes, so called, upon their release or discharge from certain institutions).

SECT. 8A added, 1938, 296 (authorizing the carrying of certain weapons by sheriffs, deputy sheriffs and special sheriffs, and certain officers in the department of correction); revised, 1939, 174.

SECT. 10 amended, 1934, 23.

SECTS. 13B and 13C added, 1939, 419 § 2 (providing for the ultimate abolition of reserve police forces in certain cities and towns).

SECT. 16A added, 1937, 85 § 1 (providing for one day off in every seven days for police officers in certain cities and towns); revised, 1938, 426 § 1.

SECT. 16B added, 1938, 426 § 2 (providing for one day off in every six days for police officers of certain cities and towns).

SECT. 17 amended, 1937, 85 § 2; 1938, 426 § 3.

SECT. 19, sentence added after the first sentence, 1939, 256 § 2. (See 1939, 256 § 3.)

SECTS. 25A–25C added, 1937, 437 § 1 (relative to promoting peaceful industrial relations by regulating certain forms of private police and detective activity in labor disputes and related matters).

SECT. 26 amended, 1937, 437 § 2.
SECT. 30 revised, 1937, 437 § 3.
SECT. 32 revised, 1935, 262 § 1.
SECT. 33 amended, 1935, 262 § 2.
SECT. 35 revised, 1934, 69.
SECT. 36 revised, 1932, 79.

Chapter 148. — Fire Prevention.

SECT. 1, definition of "local licensing authority" amended, 1932, 102.

SECT 10A added, 1932, 75 (relative to the granting of certain permits and the making of certain inspections by municipal officers designated by the state fire marshal).

SECT. 13, first paragraph amended, 1932, 22 § 1; section amended, 1935, 123 § 1; revised, 1936, 394 § 1; third paragraph amended, 1939, 333; last paragraph amended, 1938, 99. (See 1932, 22 § 2; 1936, 394 §§ 2, 3.)

SECT. 14 amended, 1938, 103.

SECT. 16 amended, 1941, 288.

SECT. 18 repealed, 1934, 182 § 2.

SECT. 23 amended, 1935, 123 § 2.

SECT. 27A added, 1932, 283 (relative to the protection of life and property from fire hazards incident to the present industrial emergency).

SECT. 28, paragraph L amended, 1943, 546 § 4. (See 1943, 546 § 5.)

SECT. 29 amended, 1939, 205.

SECT. 38A added, 1938, 95 (prohibiting the removal of certain gasoline tanks without a permit).

SECT. 39 revised, 1943, 291 § 1.

SECT. 39A added, 1943, 291 § 2 (authorizing the making of rules and regulations for the granting of permits for supervised displays of fireworks).

SECT. 49A added, 1934, 182 § 1 (relative to the inspection of kerosene or any product thereof kept for sale for illuminating, heating or cooking purposes).

SECT. 50 amended, 1943, 291 § 3.

SECT. 53 repealed, 1943, 291 § 4.

Chapter 149. — Labor and Industries.

For temporary legislation authorizing the commissioner of labor and industries to suspend certain laws, rules and regulations relative to the employment of women and minors when necessary to provide relief from conditions resulting from the present shortage of man power, see 1943, 382.

For legislation relative to interstate compacts affecting labor and industry, see 1933, Res. 44; 1934, 383, Res. 25; 1935, 315 §§ 1–3; 1936, Res. 68; 1937, 404; 1943, 255.

SECT. 1, paragraph defining "co-operative courses" amended, 1939, 461 § 4; paragraph defining "discrimination" inserted, 1937, 367 § 1; paragraph defining "employment permit", "permit for employment" or "employment certificate" inserted, 1939, 461 § 4A; paragraph defining "mercantile establishments" amended, 1936, 78.

SECT. 6 amended, 1934, 132 § 1; 1937, 249. (See 1934, 132 § 2.)

SECT. 8 amended, 1943, 441.

SECT. 11 amended, 1935, 328.

SECT. 20A added, 1933, 351 § 1 (relative to the judicial enforcement of certain contracts relative to membership in labor or employers' organizations). (See 1933, 351 § 2.)

SECTS. 20B and 20C added, 1935, 407 § 1 (regulating the liability of labor unions and others involved in labor disputes, and defining labor disputes and other terms used in connection therewith). (See 1935, 407 § 6.)

SECT. 20C. See 1937, 436 § 10; G. L. 150A § 6 (*h*) inserted by 1938, 345 § 2.

SECT. 23 amended, 1935, 114.

SECT. 23A added, 1934, 233 (regulating the employment of armed guards in connection with strikes, lockouts and other labor troubles).

SECT. 24 amended, 1933, 272.

SECTS. 24A–24J added, under the caption "DISCRIMINATION AGAINST CERTAIN PERSONS IN EMPLOYMENT ON ACCOUNT OF AGE", 1937, 367 § 2.

SECTS. 26 and 27 stricken out, and new sections 26–27D added, 1935, 461 (relative to preference and minimum wages of veterans and others in certain employments on certain public works).

SECT. 26, paragraph added at end, 1937, 346; same paragraph revised, 1938, 413.

SECT. 27E added, 1938, 67 (establishing residential requirements to be observed in the employment of certain persons by the department of public works).

SECT. 29 amended, 1935, 217 § 2; revised, 1935, 472 § 2; 1938, 361.

SECT. 30 revised, 1936, 367 § 1.

SECT. 34 amended, 1936, 367 § 2.

SECT. 34A added, 1938, 438 (requiring contractors on public buildings and other public works to provide and continue in force, during the full term of the contract, insurance under the Workmen's Compensation Law, so called).

SECT. 34B added, 1939, 252 (regulating the rate of compensation paid to reserve police officers by contractors on certain public works).

SECT. 36 amended, 1942, 1 § 7. (See 1942, 1 § 9.)

SECT. 39 revised, 1935, 444 § 1. (See 1935, 444 § 2.)

SECTS. 44A–44D added, 1939, 480 (requiring fair competition for bidders on the construction, reconstruction, alteration, remodelling or repair of certain public works by the commonwealth or any political subdivision thereof).

SECT. 44A revised, 1941, 699 § 1.

SECT. 44C, subsection (B) revised, 1941, 699 § 2; subsection (D) amended, 1941, 699 § 3; first paragraph of subsection (E) revised, 1941, 699 § 4; sentence added at end of subsection (E), 1941, 699 § 5; last paragraph of "Draft of Proposal Form" amended, 1941, 699 § 6; paragraph contained in lines 14–18 of the "Proposal Form (Sub-Bidder)" amended, 1941, 699 § 7.

SECT. 48 revised, 1935, 185, 423 § 3; amended, 1938, 320; revised, 1939, 235 § 1.

SECT. 49 amended, 1937, 221; revised, 1938, 295.

SECT. 50 revised, 1933, 225; amended, 1935, 423 § 1.

SECT. 50A added, 1935, 423 § 2 (making one day's rest in seven law applicable to watchmen and employees maintaining fires in certain establishments).

SECT. 51 revised, 1939, 235 § 2.

SECT. 56 amended, 1932, 110 § 1; revised, 1935, 200; first sentence stricken out and two sentences inserted, 1939, 377; section amended, 1941, 574, 610 § 1. (See 1941, 610 §§ 2, 3.)

SECT. 57 amended, 1932, 110 § 2.

SECT. 59 amended, 1933, 193 § 1; 1936, 170 § 1. (For temporary act, authorizing the commissioner of labor and industries to suspend certain provisions relative to the hours of employment of women in the textile and leather industries, see 1933, 347; time for suspension as to the textile industry extended, 1935, 429; 1936, 154; 1937, 153; 1938, 68; 1939, 96; 1941, 154; 1943, 306.)

SECT. 60 revised, 1935, 203; paragraph added at end, 1939, 193 § 1; section revised, 1939, 273, 461 § 5. (See 1939, 461 § 13.)

SECT. 62, clause (13) amended, 1934, 328 § 19.

SECT. 65 amended, 1939, 352; revised, 1939, 461 § 6.

SECT. 66 amended, 1933, 193 § 2; 1936, 170 § 2; 1939, 255.

SECT. 67 revised, 1939, 348.

SECTS. 69–73. See 1934, 114.

SECT. 69 amended, 1939, 461 § 7.

SECT. 70, sentence added at end, 1939, 94.

SECT. 73 revised, 1939, 461 § 8.

SECT. 78 amended, 1934, 292 § 1.

SECT. 84 amended, 1932, 180 § 29.

SECT. 86 revised, 1939, 461 § 9.

SECT. 87 revised, 1939, 461 § 10.

SECT. 94 revised, 1939, 461 § 11.

SECT. 100 amended, 1939, 280.

SECT. 101 revised, 1938, 335.

SECT. 104 amended, 1932, 27; 1939, 193 § 2.

SECT. 113 revised, 1934, 255.

SECT. 117 revised, 1935, 208.

SECT. 135 amended, 1933, 64.

SECTS. 142A–142F added, under caption "BENZOL AND MIXTURES CONTAINING BENZOL", 1933, 304 (regulating the sale, distribution, storage and use of benzol and its compounds).

SECT. 142A amended, 1935, 463 § 1.

SECT. 142B revised, 1935, 463 § 2.

SECTS. 143–147A, and the heading above section 143, stricken out, and new sections 143–147H inserted, under the heading "INDUSTRIAL HOMEWORK", 1937, 429.

SECT. 147 amended, 1941, 539.

SECT. 147A added, 1932, 234 (requiring the furnishing of certain information to the department of labor and industries with respect to the performance of certain industrial work in tenements and dwelling houses); section stricken out and new section inserted, 1937, 429; amended, 1939, 461 § 12.

SECT. 148, last sentence amended, 1932, 101 § 1; section revised, 1935, 350; 1936, 160; paragraph inserted after first paragraph, 1943, 467; paragraph inserted after third paragraph, 1943, 378; same paragraph amended, 1943, 563.

SECT. 150, sentence added at end, 1932, 101 § 2.

SECT. 150A added, 1938, 403 (requiring employers to furnish certain information to employees relative to deductions from wages for social security and unemployment compensation benefits).

SECT. 150B added, 1943, 385 (prohibiting labor unions from requiring payment of certain fees as a condition of securing or continuing employment).

SECT. 156 amended, 1935, 363 § 1; 1941, 164. (See 1935, 363 § 2.)

SECT. 157A added, 1933, 268 (insuring to piece or job workers in factories and workshops information relative to their compensation).

SECT. 159A added, 1937, 342 § 1 (to prevent the misleading of patrons of certain places as to the beneficiaries of tips given to hat-check and cigarette girls and the like).

SECT. 178A added, 1932, 175 (authorizing the payment of small amounts of wages or salary of intestate employees to certain next of kin without administration).

SECT. 179B added, 1941, 642 (requiring the giving of notice to the Commissioner of Labor and Industries of the commencement or a change of location of operations by industries in this commonwealth).

Chapter 150. — Conciliation and Arbitration of Industrial Disputes.

SECT. 3 amended, 1938, 364 § 1; 1939, 111.

SECT. 5 revised, 1938, 364 § 2.

Chapter 150A. — Labor Relations.

New chapter inserted, 1938, 345 § 2 (incorporating the provisions of 1937, 436, relative to labor relations as an addition to the General Laws). (See 1938, 345 §§ 3, 4.)

SECT. 5, subsection (*b*) amended, 1939, 318.

SECT. 6, subsection (*h*) amended, 1941, 261.

Chapter 151. — Minimum Fair Wages for Women and Minors (former title, The Minimum Wage).

The following references are to chapter 151, as appearing in the Tercentenary Edition:

SECT. 8 amended, 1933, 110.

SECTS. 11A–11D added, 1933, 220 § 1 (relative to the more effective enforcement of decrees of the minimum wage commission). (See 1933, 220 § 2.)

Chapter stricken out, and new chapter 151 inserted, 1934, 308 § 1. (See 1934, 308 §§ 2, 3; 1935, 267. See also 1933, Res. 44; 1934, 383, Res. 25).

The following references are to chapter 151, as inserted by 1934, 308 § 1:

SECT. 1 revised, 1936, 430 § 1. (See 1936, 430 §§ 18–22.)

SECT. 2 revised, 1936, 430 § 2. (See 1936, 430 §§ 18–22.)

SECT. 3 amended, 1936, 430 § 3. (See 1936, 430 §§ 18–22.)

SECT. 4 revised, 1936, 430 § 4. (See 1936, 430 §§ 18–22.)

SECT. 7 revised, 1936, 430 § 5. (See 1936, 430 §§ 18–22.)

SECT. 10 revised, 1936, 430 § 6. (See 1936, 430 §§ 18–22.)

SECT. 12 revised, 1936, 430 § 7. (See 1936, 430 §§ 18–22.)

SECT. 13 amended, 1936, 175; revised, 1936, 430 § 8. (See 1936, 430 §§ 18–22.)

SECT. 14 revised, 1936, 430 § 9. (See 1936, 430 §§ 18–22.)

SECT. 15 revised, 1936, 430 § 10. (See 1936, 430 §§ 18–22.)

SECT. 16 amended, 1936, 430 § 11. (See 1936, 430 §§ 18–22.)

SECT. 17 amended, 1936, 430 § 12. (See 1936, 430 §§ 18–22.)

SECT. 20 amended, 1936, 430 § 13. (See 1936, 430 §§ 18–22.)

SECT. 21 revised, 1936, 430 § 14. (See 1936, 430 §§ 18–22.)

SECT. 22 revised, 1936, 430 § 15. (See 1936, 430 §§ 18–22.)

SECT. 23 amended, 1936, 430 § 16. (See 1936, 430 §§ 18–22.)
SECT. 24 revised, 1936, 430 § 17. (See 1936, 430 §§ 18–22.)
Chapter stricken out, and new chapter 151 (with new title) inserted, 1937, 401 § 1. (See 1937, 401 §§ 2, 3.)
The following references are to chapter 151, as inserted by 1937, 401 § 1:
SECT. 19, paragraph added at end, 1938, 237.
SECT. 20A added, 1939, 275 (relative to evidence of the establishment of minimum fair wage rates).

Chapter 151A. — Employment Security (former title, Unemployment Compensation).

For legislation providing for the payment of unemployment compensation benefits to persons upon termination of service in the military or naval forces of the United States during the present national emergency, see 1941, 701; 1943, 319.
New chapter inserted, 1935, 479 § 5. (See 1935, 479 §§ 6, 7; 1936, 12 § 3, 249 § 16.)
The following references are to chapter 151A, as inserted by 1935, 479 § 5:
SECT. 1, clauses (1) to (9), inclusive, of paragraph (*a*) revised, 1936, 249 § 1; paragraph (*b*) amended, 1936, 249 § 2; paragraph (*k*) amended, 1936, 249 § 3; paragraph (*m*) amended, 1936, 249 § 4; paragraph (*n*) revised, 1936, 249 § 5.
SECT. 3 revised, 1936, 249 § 6.
SECT. 4 revised, 1936, 249 § 7.
SECT. 7, paragraph added at end, 1936, 249 § 8.
SECT. 7A added, 1936, 249 § 9 (relative to refunding of over-payments or collection of under-payments of contributions).
SECT. 10 amended, 1936, 249 § 10.
SECT. 12 amended, 1936, 12 § 1.
SECT. 17, paragraph (*a*) amended, 1936, 249 § 11.
SECT. 18, paragraph (*a*) amended, 1936, 249 § 12.
SECT. 19, paragraph defining "suitable employment" amended, 1936, 12 § 2.
SECT. 20 amended, 1936, 249 § 13.
SECT. 24, second paragraph stricken out, 1936, 249 § 14.
SECT. 48 amended, 1936, 249 § 15.
Chapter stricken out, and new chapter 151A (with same title) inserted, 1937, 421 § 1. (See 1937, 421 §§ 2-4.)
The following references are to chapter 151A, as inserted by 1937, 421 § 1:
SECT. 1, paragraphs (1) and (2) inserted after subsection (*a*), 1939, 490 § 1; subsection (*b*) revised, 1939, 20 § 2; subsection (*f*) clause (5) amended, 1939, 319 § 1; subsection (*f*) clause (8) added, 1939, 374 § 1 (see 1939, 374 § 6); subsection (*f*) revised, 1939, 490 § 2; subsection (*k*) revised, 1938, 469 § 1; amended, 1939, 490 § 3; subsection (*l*) revised, 1938, 469 § 2; amended, 1939, 490 § 4; subsection (*n*) amended, 1939, 490 § 19. (See 1938, 469 § 20; 1939, 20 §§ 6–9; 1939, 319 §§ 10, 11.)
SECT. 1A, subsections (1) and (2) revised, 1938, 469 § 3; subsection (6) added, 1938, 469 § 4. (See 1938, 469 § 20.)
SECT. 3 revised, 1939, 319 § 2; amended, 1939, 490 § 17; revised, 1939, 490 § 23. (See 1939, 319 §§ 10, 11.)
SECT. 4, first paragraph revised, 1938, 469 § 5; fifth paragraph stricken out, 1938, 469 § 6; paragraph inserted before the last paragraph, 1938, 469 § 7; last paragraph revised, 1938, 470 § 2; section

revised, 1939, 319 § 3. (See 1938, 469 § 20, 470 §§ 1 and 3; 1939, 319 §§ 10, 11.)

SECT. 8, last paragraph stricken out, 1939, 319 § 4. (See 1939, 319 §§ 10, 11.)

SECT. 9 amended, 1939, 319 § 5. (See 1939, 319 §§ 10, 11.)

SECT. 10 amended, 1939, 319 § 6. (See 1939, 319 §§ 10, 11.)

SECT. 11, subsection (*a*) revised, 1938, 469 § 8. (See 1938, 469 § 20.)

SECT. 12, last sentence stricken out, 1939, 319 § 7. (See 1939, 319 §§ 10, 11.)

SECT. 14, subsection (*a*) revised, 1938, 469 § 9; 1939, 490 §§ 5, 6; subsection (*c*) revised, 1938, 469 § 10; subsection (*d*) added, 1938, 469 § 11. (See 1938, 469 § 20.)

SECT. 15, subsection (*a*) revised, 1938, 469 § 12; 1939, 490 § 7. (See 1938, 469 § 20.)

SECT. 16, subsection (*c*) revised, 1939, 490 § 8; first paragraph of subsection (*d*) revised, 1938, 469 § 13; subsection (*e*) revised, 1939, 490 § 9; subsection (*f*) added, 1938, 469 § 14; subsections (*g*), (*h*) added, 1939, 374 § 2. (See 1938, 469 § 20; 1939, 374 § 6.)

SECT. 17 revised, 1938, 469 § 15; 1939, 490 § 10. (See 1938, 469 § 20.)

SECT. 18, subsection (*a*) revised, 1938, 469 § 16; amended and revised, 1939, 490 § 11; subsection (*b*) stricken out, 1939, 490 § 13; subsection (*c*) stricken out, 1939, 490 § 13; subsection (*d*) revised, 1938, 469 § 17; 1939, 490 § 12; stricken out, 1939, 490 § 13. (See 1938, 469 § 20.)

SECT. 19 revised, 1939, 490 § 14.

SECT. 22A revised, 1939, 319 § 8. (See 1939, 319 §§ 10, 11.)

SECT. 26 amended, 1938, 469 § 18. (See 1938, 469 § 20.)

SECTS. 26–33, stricken out and new sections 26–31 inserted, 1939, 20 § 3.

SECTS. 26, 27, 28 (as appearing in 1939, 20 § 3) revised, 1939, 490 § 15.

SECT. 30 (as appearing in 1939, 20 § 3) amended, 1939, 490 § 16.

SECT. 35 amended, 1939, 490 § 21.

SECT. 36 amended, 1939, 490 § 18.

SECT. 41, second sentence revised, 1939, 20 § 4.

SECT. 42 amended, 1939, 319 § 9. (See 1939, 319 §§ 10, 11.)

SECT. 43 revised, 1939, 374 § 3. (See 1939, 374 § 6.)

SECT. 45 revised, 1939, 20 § 5.

SECT. 47 revised, 1938, 163.

SECT. 47A added, 1939, 374 § 4 (authorizing the director of the division of unemployment compensation to co-operate with certain federal agencies charged with the administration of laws relative to unemployment). (See 1939, 374 § 6.)

SECT. 48, paragraph added at end, 1939, 374 § 5. (See 1939, 374 § 6.)

SECT. 52 added, 1938, 469 § 19 (powers of the unemployment compensation commission when employer fails or refuses to make any required report or return). (See 1938, 469 § 20.)

SECT. 53 added, 1938, 469 § 19 (authorizing the payment without administration of unemployment compensation benefits due a deceased person in certain cases); revised, 1939, 490 § 20. (See 1938, 469 § 20.)

NOTE — SEE SECT. 53, INFRA.

SECT. 53 added, 1939, 490 § 22 (relative to the preparation, use as evidence and disposition of certain records, reports, claims and other papers). NOTE — SEE SECT. 53, SUPRA.

SECT. 54 added, 1938, 469 § 19 (relative to the effect to be given any ruling or decision of the unemployment compensation commission). (See 1938, 469 § 20.)

Chapter stricken out, and new chapter 151A (with new title) inserted, 1941, 685 § 1. (See 1941, 685 §§ 7-11; 1941, 686.)

The following references are to chapter 151A, as so inserted:

SECT. 8, subsections (*g*) and (*h*) added at end, 1943, 534 § 2.

SECT. 11 revised, 1941, 685 § 2.

SECT. 14, subsection (*b*) (2) revised, 1943, 534 § 1; subsection (*c*) added, 1943, 534 § 1A; designations of subsections (*c*) and (*d*) changed to (*d*) and (*e*), respectively, 1943, 534 § 1B.

SECT. 15, subsection (*c*) revised, 1943, 373.

SECT. 23, subsection (*a*) revised, 1941, 685 § 3; subsection (*e*) stricken out, 1943, 534 § 3.

SECT. 29, subsection (*a*) revised, 1943, 534 § 5.

SECT. 33 repealed, 1943, 534 § 4.

SECT. 42 revised, 1943, 534 § 6.

Chapter 152. — Workmen's Compensation.

For legislation requiring manufacturers to insure under the workmen's compensation act where employees work on machinery, see 1936, 426.

SECT. 1, two sentences added at end of paragraph (1), 1935, 332 § 1; paragraph (1) revised, 1943, 529 § 1; paragraph (4) revised, 1935, 406; 1943, 529 § 3; paragraph (5) revised, 1943, 529 § 1A; paragraph (6) amended, 1943, 529 § 2; paragraph (7A) added, 1941, 437. (See 1943, 529 § 14.)

SECT. 4 revised, 1939, 83.

SECT. 5, paragraph added at end, 1943, 359.

SECT. 9A revised, 1938, 381.

SECT. 9B added, 1935, 424 (providing for the reference of certain cases under the workmen's compensation law to industrial disease referees); revised, 1938, 462.

SECT. 11 amended, 1932, 129 § 1; paragraph added at end, 1935, 484; paragraph added at end, 1939, 213 § 1. (See 1939, 213 § 2.)

SECT. 12, last paragraph amended, 1932, 117 § 1. (See 1932, 117 § 2; 1935, 351.)

SECT. 13, sentence added at end, 1933, 68.

SECT. 15 revised, 1939, 401; 1943, 432.

SECT. 15A amended, 1934, 252.

SECT. 18, sentence added at end, 1938, 102; section amended, 1939, 93.

SECT. 19, paragraph in lines 17 and 18 revised, 1935, 339; same paragraph revised, 1939, 245; paragraph added at end, 1941, 379 § 11.

SECT. 19A added, 1935, 359 (requiring certain notices from employers not insured under the workmen's compensation law).

SECT. 19B added, 1941, 410 (requiring the posting of notices by certain employers not covering their employees by workmen's compensation insurance).

SECT. 20 revised, 1935, 340.
SECT. 21 amended, 1943, 529 § 4. (See 1943, 529 § 14.)
SECT. 22 amended, 1943, 529 § 13. (See 1943, 529 § 14.)
SECT. 23 revised, 1943, 529 § 5. (See 1943, 529 § 14.)
SECT. 24 amended, 1943, 529 § 6. (See 1943, 529 § 14.)
SECTS. 25A–25D added, 1943, 529 § 7, under caption "Compulsory Compensation and Self-Insurance." (See 1943, 529 § 14.)
SECT. 26 amended, 1937, 370 § 1; revised, 1943, 302; 529 § 8. (See 1943, 529 § 14.)
SECT. 26A added, 1937, 370 § 2 (providing for payment of workmen's compensation in certain cases of suicide).
SECT. 27 revised, 1935, 331.
SECT. 28 amended, 1934, 292 § 2; revised, 1943, 529 § 9. (See 1943, 529 § 14.)
SECT. 29 revised, 1935, 372; 1937, 382.
SECT. 30 revised, 1936, 164; 1943, 181.
SECT. 31, first paragraph amended, 1934, 250; paragraph contained in the seventh to the forty-fourth lines revised, 1937, 325; same paragraph amended, 1943, 368; last paragraph revised, 1943, 400.
SECT. 32, new paragraph added, 1935, 361 (relative to payments under the workmen's compensation law to dependents of deceased minor employees).
SECT. 33 revised, 1939, 81; 1941, 495.
SECT. 34 revised, 1935, 332 § 2; 1941, 624.
SECT. 34A added, 1935, 364 (providing for payments for total and permanent disability under the workmen's compensation law, and establishing methods of determining the same); amended, 1943, 276.
SECT. 35 amended, 1943, 299.
SECT. 36, paragraph (*j*) revised, 1933, 257; section revised, 1935, 333.
SECT. 37 amended, 1937, 321.
SECT. 39 amended, 1937, 317.
SECT. 46 amended, 1941, 378.
SECT. 52A added, 1939, 465 § 2 (relative to insuring against silicosis and other occupational pulmonary dust diseases). (See 1939, 465 § 4.)
SECT. 54A added, 1935, 425 (relative to safeguarding and extending the workmen's compensation law by making void certain contracts or agreements in the nature of insurance which do not insure the payment of the compensation provided for by said law).
SECT. 55, second paragraph revised, 1934, 137 § 1.
SECT. 65 amended, 1935, 395; 1936, 162; 1937, 394; revised, 1939, 465 § 3; amended, 1943, 367. (See 1939, 465 § 4.)
SECTS. 65A–65M added, 1939, 489 (providing for the equitable distribution of rejected risks among insurers of workmen's compensation, and the pooling of losses in connection with such risks).
SECT. 66 revised, 1943, 529 § 9A. (See 1943, 529 § 14.)
SECT. 67 revised, 1943, 529 § 10. (See 1943, 529 § 14.)
SECT. 68 revised, 1943, 529 § 11. (See 1943, 529 § 14.)
SECT. 69 revised, 1933, 318 § 7; 1936, 260; amended, 1936, 403; revised, 1939, 435; last sentence revised, 1939, 468; section amended, 1941, 614.
SECT. 69A added, 1933, 315 (regulating workmen's compensation payments by the commonwealth).

SECT. 69B added, 1936, 427 (further regulating workmen's compensation payments by the commonwealth).
SECT. 73, first sentence amended, 1936, 318 § 4; 1937, 336 § 23; 1941, 379 § 12.
SECT. 73A added, 1941, 649 (to provide for the employment of partially disabled public employees and temporary filling of their original positions).
SECT. 74 amended, 1939, 451 § 57; 1941, 344 § 26.
SECT. 75 revised, 1932, 19.
SECTS. 76–85 added, 1939, 465 § 1 (providing workmen's compensation benefits for employees in the granite industry contracting silicosis and other occupational pulmonary dust diseases). (See 1939, 465 § 4.)
SECT. 76 revised, 1943, 529 § 12. (See 1943, 529 § 14.)

Chapter 153. — Liability of Employers to Employees for Injuries not resulting in Death.

SECT. 6 amended, 1935, 387.

Chapter 154. — Assignment of Wages.

SECT. 8 added, 1933, 96 (exempting orders for payment of labor or trade union or craft dues or obligations from the operation of the laws regulating assignments of wages); amended, 1939, 125.

Chapter 155. — General Provisions relative to Corporations.

SECT. 1 revised, 1935, 297 § 1. (See 1935, 297 § 3.)
SECT. 9 amended, 1938, 327 § 1; revised, 1943, 295. (See 1938, 327 § 2.)
SECT. 10 amended, 1933, 11; third sentence revised, 1943, 549 § 4.
SECT. 12A added, 1938, 164 § 1 (making permanent certain provisions of law authorizing domestic corporations to contribute to certain funds for the benefit of social and economic conditions). (See 1938, 164 § 2.)
SECT. 15 revised, 1939, 14.
SECT. 23A added, 1935, 297 § 2 (regulating sales of stocks, bonds and other securities of corporations to their employees); repealed, 1938, 445 § 13. (See 1935, 297 § 3; G. L. chapter 110A § 11A, inserted by 1938, 445 § 9.)
SECT. 50 amended, 1933, 66.
SECT. 50A added, 1939, 456 § 1 (relative to the dissolution of domestic corporations); amended, 1943, 383.
SECT. 56, first sentence revised, 1939, 456 § 2.

Chapter 156. — Business Corporations.

SECT. 5 amended, 1939, 301 § 1.
SECT. 6, clause (*e*) amended, 1939, 15 § 1.
SECT. 12, form of certificate revised, 1932, 67.
SECT. 30 amended, 1937, 52.
SECT. 36 revised, 1941, 514 § 1.
SECT. 41 revised, 1932, 136.

SECT. 42 amended, 1943, 38 § 1.
SECT. 46, sentence added at end, 1943, 38 § 2.
SECTS. 46A-46E added, under the heading "MERGER AND CONSOLIDATION", 1941, 514 § 2.
SECT. 46B, paragraph contained in lines 102-108 revised, 1943, 405 § 1.
SECT. 46D, paragraph contained in lines 64-73 revised, 1943, 405 § 2.
SECT. 49 revised, 1941, 276.
SECT. 54 amended, 1932, 180 § 30.

Chapter 157. — Co-operative Corporations.

SECT. 16, last sentence amended, 1932, 180 § 31.

Chapter 159. — Common Carriers.

SECT. 14A added, 1941, 713 (authorizing the department of public utilities to regulate rates for the transportation of persons or property within the commonwealth by common carriers by aircraft).
SECT. 15, paragraph added at end, 1937, 247; same paragraph stricken out, 1938, 155 § 2.
SECT. 16A added, 1938, 243 (relative to the discontinuance of service by railroads).
SECT. 20 amended, 1939, 18.
SECT. 59 revised, 1933, 326 § 1.
SECT. 60 amended, 1933, 326 § 2; 1941, 233.
SECT. 61 amended, 1933, 326 § 3.
SECT. 62 amended, 1933, 326 § 4.
SECT. 65 amended, 1937, 270.
SECT. 70 revised, 1934, 357 § 1.
SECT. 80 amended, 1934, 357 § 2.
SECT. 89 revised, 1936, 363 § 1.
SECT. 90 revised, 1936, 363 § 2.
SECT. 91 revised, 1936, 363 § 3.
SECT. 92 amended, 1936, 363 § 4.
SECT. 93 amended, 1936, 363 § 5.
SECT. 94 amended, 1936, 363 § 6.
SECT. 103 amended, 1933, 10; 1941, 54; 1943, 322 § 1.

Chapter 159A. — Common Carriers of Passengers by Motor Vehicle.

[Title amended, and headings, "PART I", "CARRIERS OF PASSENGERS BY MOTOR VEHICLE", inserted before section 1, 1933, 372 § 1.]
[SECTS. 17-30 added, under headings, "PART II", "CARRIERS OF PROPERTY BY MOTOR VEHICLE", 1933, 372 § 2 (regulating carriers of property by motor vehicle).]
NOTE — 1933, 372 repealed by 1934, 264 § 5.
SECT. 11A added, 1939, 404 § 1 (placing special and chartered buses, so called, under the supervision of the department of public utilities); amended, 1941, 480. (See 1939, 404 § 2.)

Chapter 159B. — Carriers of Property by Motor Vehicle.

New chapter inserted, 1934, 264 § 1.

The following references are to chapter 159B, as inserted by 1934, 264 § 1:

SECT. 2 revised, 1936, 345 § 1.

SECT. 6 revised, 1936, 345 § 2.

SECT. 7 revised, 1936, 345 § 3; amended, 1938, 332.

SECT. 8 affected, 1935, 24.

SECT. 9 revised, 1936, 345 § 4.

SECT. 10 revised, 1936, 345 § 5; 1937, 381.

SECT. 10A added, 1936, 345 § 6 (prohibiting rebates, discrimination and evasion of regulation in the carrying of property by motor vehicle).

SECT. 13 amended, 1937, 122.

Chapter stricken out and new chapter 159B (with same title) inserted, 1938, 483 § 1. (See 1938, 483 §§ 2-5.)

The following references are to chapter 159B, as inserted by 1938, 483 § 1:

SECT. 2, definition of "Irregular route common carrier" revised, 1941, 653 § 2; definition of "Regular route common carrier" revised and paragraph defining "Regular routes" added, 1941, 653 § 3; definition of "Agricultural carrier by motor vehicle" inserted, 1941, 704 § 1; definitions of "Contract carrier by motor vehicle", "Motor carrier" and "Permit" revised, 1941, 704 § 2. (See 1941, 704 § 4.)

SECT. 3, paragraph (*b*) revised, 1941, 592 § 1.

SECT. 4, third paragraph revised, 1941, 592 § 2.

SECT. 7, paragraph (*a*) revised, 1939, 171.

SECT. 9 amended, 1941, 483 § 1.

SECT. 10, paragraph added at end, 1939, 306; amended, 1941, 483 § 2.

SECT. 10A added, 1939, 322 (relative to replacing lost or mutilated plates and lost or destroyed certificates, permits and licenses issued to carriers of property by motor vehicle).

SECT. 11 amended, 1941, 483 § 3.

SECT. 12, first paragraph revised, 1941, 653 § 4.

SECT. 13 amended, 1941, 692.

SECT. 14 amended, 1941, 653 § 5.

SECT. 15A added, 1941, 704 § 3 (relative to agricultural carriers of property by motor vehicles). (See 1941, 704 § 4.)

SECT. 16A added, 1939, 307 (giving the department of public utilities authority to obtain certain information of persons engaged in leasing motor vehicles for the transportation of property for hire).

Chapter 160. — Railroads.

SECT. 68 revised, 1943, 33.

SECT. 70 amended, 1932, 238.

SECT. 70A revised, 1932, 236; amended, 1934, 264 § 3.

SECT. 85 amended, 1941, 53.

SECT. 102 amended, 1941, 496 § 1

SECT. 104 revised, 1933, 176.

SECT. 134 amended, 1941, 273 § 1.

SECT. 138 amended, 1941, 273 § 2.

SECT. 142 amended, 1938, 29.

SECT. 167 amended, 1941, 273 § 3.

SECT. 185A added, 1943, 333 (providing that railroad and terminal corporations shall provide reasonable lavatory and sanitary facilities for their employees).

SECT. 198A. See 1936, 267.

SECT. 198B added, 1936, 267 (prohibiting the scalping, so called, of tickets issued by railroad corporations).

SECT. 235 amended, 1941, 490 § 38.

SECT. 245 amended, 1941, 273 § 4, 496 § 2.

Chapter 161. — Street Railways.

Name of Metropolitan Transit District changed to Boston Metropolitan District, and authority to issue notes and bonds defined, 1932, 147.

Temporary act, extending to January 15, 1939, the period of public control and management of the Eastern Massachusetts Street Railway Company, 1933, 108; further extension of five years, 1938, 173; further extension of five years, 1943, 98.

Temporary acts relative to the purchase of bonds of the Boston Elevated Railway Company by the Boston Metropolitan District, 1933, 235; 1934, 334; 1935, 451; 1936, 308; 1937, 357; 1941, 567.

SECT. 20A amended, 1939, 28.

SECT. 35 amended, 1943, 342.

SECT. 42, third sentence amended, 1934, 328 § 20.

SECT. 44 amended, 1934, 264 § 4.

SECT. 77 revised, 1934, 310 § 1.

SECT. 86 revised, 1934, 310 § 2.

SECT. 91A added, 1935, 101 (relative to the number of guards on passenger trains operated by street railway companies).

Chapter 163. — Trackless Trolley Companies.

SECT. 12 added, 1932, 185 (requiring trackless trolley companies to furnish security for civil liability on account of personal injuries or property damage caused by their vehicles).

SECT. 13 added, 1943, 141 (providing a penalty for the improper operation of trackless trolley vehicles, so called).

Chapter 164. — Manufacture and Sale of Gas and Electricity.

For legislation authorizing compacts relative to the interstate transmission of electricity and gas, see 1933, 294.

SECT. 4 amended, 1938, 44.

SECT. 14 amended, 1935, 222.

SECT. 17A added, 1932, 132 (regulating the lending of money by gas and electric companies).

SECT. 31 amended, 1939, 301 § 2.

SECT. 33 amended, 1932, 180 § 32.

SECT. 34 amended, 1937, 235 § 1. (See 1937, 235 § 2.)

SECT. 76A added, 1935, 335 § 1 (giving to the department of public utilities supervision over certain affiliates of gas and electric companies).

SECT. 84A added, 1934, 202 § 1 (requiring gas and electric companies to make additional annual returns).

SECT. 85, second paragraph amended, 1935, 335 § 2.

SECT. 85A added, 1933, 202 § 1 (requiring the filing with the department of public utilities of certain contracts of gas and electric companies with affiliated companies).

SECT. 94, paragraph in lines 29–37 amended, 1939, 178 § 1. (See 1939, 178 § 2.)

SECT. 94A amended, 1941, 400 § 1.

SECT. 94B amended, 1941, 400 § 2.

SECT. 94C added, 1935, 227 (relative to payments, charges, contracts, purchases, sales or obligations or other arrangement between gas or electric companies and affiliated companies, and the burden of proving the reasonableness thereof).

SECT. 94D added, 1936, 243 (prohibiting gas and electric companies from collecting penalty charges for delinquency in the payment of bills for gas or electricity used for domestic purposes).

SECT. 94E added, 1941, 400 § 3 (relative to notice of the termination of certain contracts of gas and electric companies).

SECT. 96 revised, 1939, 229 § 1.

SECT. 97 amended, 1943, 55.

SECT. 102 revised, 1939, 229 § 2.

SECT. 105A added, 1932, 119 (regulating the storage, transportation and distribution of gas).

SECT. 115A added, 1936, 259 § 1 (requiring the periodic replacement of meters for measuring gas); amended, 1937, 40 § 1. (See 1936, 259 §§ 2, 3; 1937, 40 §§ 2, 3.)

SECT. 119 revised, 1934, 365.

SECT. 119A added, 1936, 76 § 1 (requiring bills for gas or electricity used for domestic purposes to be itemized); revised, 1939, 145 § 1. (See 1936, 76 § 2; 1939, 145 § 2.)

SECT. 124 amended, 1935, 237, 376 § 2.

SECT. 124A added, 1935, 376 § 1 (relative to the shutting off of gas or electric service in homes where there is serious illness).

Chapter 165. — Water and Aqueduct Companies.

SECT. 4A added, 1933, 202 § 2 (requiring the filing with the department of public utilities of certain contracts of water companies with affiliated companies).

SECT. 19 repealed, 1941, 275 § 1.

SECT. 28 added, under caption "GENERAL PROVISIONS", 1941, 275 § 2 (further regulating the acquisition and holding of real estate by water and aqueduct companies).

Chapter 166. — Telephone and Telegraph Companies, and Lines for the Transmission of Electricity.

SECT. 12A added, 1934, 202 § 2 (requiring telephone and telegraph companies to make additional annual returns).

SECT. 15A added, 1935, 242 (regulating charges by telephone companies for the use of hand sets, so called).

SECT. 15B added, 1939, 162 (authorizing the sale and transfer of property and the transfer of locations by domestic telephone and telegraph companies to domestic or foreign telephone and telegraph companies and validating certain locations so transferred).
SECT. 21 amended, 1939, 161.
SECT. 22, second paragraph amended, 1932, 36.
SECT. 22A added, 1932, 266 (relative to the placing underground of certain wires); revised, 1933, 251.

Chapter 167. — Banks and Banking.

For temporary act, authorizing the commissioner of banks to borrow within two years from March 30th, 1932, funds for the payment of dividends in liquidation of certain closed banks, see 1932, 122; time increased to four years, 1934, 304; time further increased to six years, 1936, 263; act amended, 1937, 371; time further increased to eight years, 1938, 261; time further increased to nine years, 1939, 292; time further increased to eleven years, 1941, 145 § 1.
For temporary act, providing for the establishment of a fund for the insurance of deposits in certain savings banks, see 1934, 43; amended, 1936, 149 §§ 2–4; 1938, 125 §§ 1, 2; 1939, 149 §§ 2, 3; 1941, 78 § 2.
For temporary act, providing for the establishment of a fund for the insurance of shares in co-operative banks, see 1934, 73; amended, 1935, 76, 80; 1936, 155; 1938, 244 §§ 2–5; 1939, 227 §§ 2–5.
For temporary act, authorizing banking institutions, during a three-year period, to make loans insured under the provisions of the National Housing Act, see 1935, 162; amended and extended to July 1, 1939, 1937, 240; further extended to July 1, 1941, 1939, 241; further extended to July 1, 1943, 1941, 260; amended and extended to July 1, 1945, 1943, 126. (See also 1943, 339.)
For temporary act, modifying requirements for investments in real estate mortgages, see 1936, 191; amended, 1936, 405 § 2; extended, 1939, 98; 1941, 40.
For temporary act providing for the liquidation of certain trust companies, see 1939, 515; 1941, 143; 1943, 122
For temporary act to enable certain banking institutions to co-operate in the distribution of United States defense savings bonds and defense postal savings stamps, see 1941, 221, 575.
SECT. 1 amended, 1935, 452 § 1.
SECT. 2 revised, 1934, 251; first paragraph amended, 1935, 452 § 2.
SECT. 2A added, 1933, 310 (improving the method of examination of banks).
SECT. 4 amended, 1934, 270 § 1:
SECT. 5 revised, 1933, 337.
SECT. 9 revised, 1939, 499 § 8.
SECT. 11 revised, 1934, 270 § 2.
SECT. 11A added, 1938, 266 § 1 (placing all corporations conducted on the Morris plan under the supervision of the commissioner of banks and further regulating the business of banking companies).
SECT. 12 revised, 1935, 452 § 3.
SECT. 14 revised, 1933, 334 § 1.
SECT. 17 repealed, 1933, 334 § 2.

SECT. 18 amended, 1943, 110 § 1.
SECT. 20 amended, 1933, 190; 1943, 22.
SECT. 20A added, 1933, 292 (permitting certain public officers to participate in certain bank reorganizations).
SECTS. 22–36. See 1934, 43 § 11.
SECT. 22, second paragraph amended, 1943, 121. (See 1933, 59 § 5, 112 § 9.)
SECT. 23. See 1933, 112 § 6.
SECT. 24 amended, 1932, 294; 1933, 41 § 4.
SECT. 31A added, 1933, 277 (authorizing payment of dividends on small deposits in closed banks to certain minors and to the next of kin of certain deceased persons without probate proceedings); revised, 1937, 170.
SECT. 35. See 1936, 428.
SECT. 35A added, 1933, 302 (authorizing the destruction of certain books, records and papers relating to closed banks).
SECT. 35B added, 1934, 241 (providing for semi-annual reports by the commissioner of banks as to progress of liquidation of certain banks).
SECT. 36 amended, 1939, 451 § 58.
SECT. 46 amended, 1943, 110 § 2.
SECT. 47 amended, 1943, 110 § 3.
SECT. 48 added, 1939, 244 § 6 (relative to payments of moneys on deposit in the name of a minor).
SECT. 49 added, 1941, 444 (relative to adverse claims to certain bank deposits and to certain securities held by banks for the account of others).

Chapter 168. — Savings Banks.

For temporary act, establishing the Mutual Savings Central Fund, Inc., for the term of five years, see 1932, 44; term extended to ten years, 1936, 149 § 1; term extended to twenty-five years, 1939, 149 § 1; act amended, 1941, 78 § 1.

For temporary act, providing for the establishment of a fund for the insurance of deposits in certain savings banks, see 1934, 43; amended, 1936, 149 §§ 2–4; 1938, 125 §§ 1, 2; 1939, 149 §§ 2, 3; 1941, 78 § 2.

For temporary act, authorizing banking institutions, during a three-year period, to make loans insured under the provisions of the National Housing Act, see 1935, 162; amended and extended to July 1, 1939, 1937, 240; further extended to July 1, 1941, 1939, 241; further extended to July 1, 1943, 1941, 260; amended and extended to July 1, 1945, 1943, 126. (See also 1943, 339.)

For temporary act, modifying requirements for investments in real estate mortgages, see 1936, 191; amended, 1936, 405 § 2; extended, 1939, 98; 1941, 40.

For temporary act modifying the requirements for making certain railroad bonds legal investments for savings banks, institutions for savings and trust companies in their savings departments, see 1939, 87; 1941, 115; temporary act repealed, 1941, 413 § 11.

For temporary act to enable certain banking institutions to co-operate in the distribution of United States Defense Savings Bonds and Defense Postal Savings Stamps, see 1941, 221, 575.

SECT. 1, two paragraphs (defining "deposit book [etc.]" and "savings bank") added at end, 1933, 334 § 3.
SECT. 2 revised, 1933, 334 § 4.
SECT. 2A added, 1933, 46 § 1 (authorizing savings banks to become members of the Federal Home Loan Bank established for the district of New England).
SECT. 5. See 1936, 143 § 2.
SECT. 11 amended, 1933, 334 § 5.
SECT. 13 amended, 1933, 334 § 6. (See 1933, 41 § 1.)
SECT. 17 revised, 1933, 334 § 7.
SECT. 25 revised, 1933, 334 § 8.
SECT. 25A added, 1933, 334 § 8 (authorizing the collection of savings from school children through principals, teachers, etc.).
SECT. 26 revised, 1933, 334 § 9; 1943, 21 § 1.
SECT. 27 amended, 1933, 334 § 10.
SECT. 28 revised, 1933, 334 § 11. (See 1943, 30.)
SECT. 29 amended, 1933, 334 § 12.
SECT. 33A revised, 1933, 334 § 13.
SECT. 33B added, 1941, 103 (relative to the sale of checks by savings banks).
SECT. 34 revised, 1933, 334 § 14.
SECT. 35 revised, 1933, 334 § 15.
SECT. 44 amended, 1941, 186.
SECT. 45 amended, 1933, 334 § 16.
SECT. 47 revised, 1933, 334 § 17.
SECT. 49 amended, 1933, 334 § 18; 1941, 105.
SECT. 50 revised, 1933, 334 § 19.
SECT. 51 revised, 1932, 245 § 1.
SECT. 51A revised, 1933, 334 § 20; amended, 1943, 27 § 1.
SECT. 53 revised, 1933, 334 § 21.
SECT. 54, clause First, first two paragraphs revised, 1933, 334 § 22; same clause revised, 1937, 180; subdivision (*d*) revised, 1943, 94 § 1; subdivision (*e*) revised, 1943, 94 § 2; clause Second, subdivisions (*a*), (*e*) and (*f*) revised, 1933, 334 § 23; subdivision (*h*) added, 1933, 334 § 24 (forbidding investment of funds in bonds or notes of county, etc., in default, and defining term "in default"); subdivisions (*a*), (*b*), (*c*) and (*d*) affected, 1939, 112 § 2; clause Second revised, 1941, 413 § 1; subdivisions (*h*), (*i*), (*j*) stricken out and subdivisions (*h*) and (*i*) added, 1943, 215 § 1 (see 1943, 215 § 12); clause Third affected, 1933, 111; 1934, 79; 1935, 72 §§ 1, 2; 1936, 84; 1937, 56; 1939, 87; 1941, 115, 413 § 11; subdivision (*p*) of clause Third revised, 1936, 79; clause Third revised, 1941, 413 § 2; subdivision (3) revised, 1943, 215 § 2; first paragraph of subdivision (6) amended, 1943, 215 § 5; paragraph (*d*) of the definitions at the end of clause Third revised, 1943, 215 § 3; clause Third A added, 1943, 215 § 4 (relative to the investments of deposits and the income derived therefrom of savings banks in obligations of certain reorganized railroad corporations); clause Fourth amended, 1932, 112; stricken out, 1941, 413 § 3; clause Fifth revised, 1941, 413 § 4; clauses Fifth A–Fifth D added, 1941, 413 § 5; clause Sixth A, first paragraph amended, 1937, 96; clause Sixth A revised, 1941, 413 § 6; clause Seventh, first paragraph amended, 1937, 87; second paragraph revised, 1932, 220; clause Seventh revised, 1941, 413 § 7; 1943, 215 § 6; clause Ninth, subdivision (*c*) (2) stricken out, 1933, 334 § 25; subdivision (*d*) stricken out,

1941, 413 § 8; subdivision (*e*) (2) revised, 1933, 334 § 26; amended, 1943, 110 § 4; revised, 1943, 215 § 7; subdivision (*e*) (3) revised, 1933, 334 § 26; 1943, 215 § 8; subdivision (*e*) (4) stricken out, 1943, 110 § 5; subdivision (*e*) (5) revised, 1933, 334 § 26; amended, 1943, 110 § 6; subdivision (*e*) (6) amended, 1939, 244 § 5; 1941, 234; clause Tenth A added, 1941, 106; clause Twelfth amended, 1937, 274 § 2; revised, 1943, 215 § 9; clause Thirteenth A added, 1941, 107; clause Fifteenth revised, 1941, 413 § 9; subdivision (*a*) revised, 1943, 215 § 10; clause Sixteenth affected, 1933, 111; 1934, 79; 1935, 72 §§ 1, 2; 1936, 84; 1937, 56; 1939, 87; 1941, 115, 413 § 11; clause Sixteenth stricken out, 1941, 413 § 10; clause Seventeenth revised, 1943, 215 § 11. (See 1943, 215 § 12.)

SECT. 55, paragraph added at end, 1933, 334 § 27 (authorizing the continuing of the offices of a merged savings bank as branch offices of the continuing bank).

SECT. 56 added, 1933, 41 § 1 (authorizing savings banks to purchase, loan upon or participate in loans upon the assets of certain closed and other banks).

SECT. 57 added, 1933, 334 § 28 (authorizing savings banks to become members of savings bank associations).

SECTS. 58–60 added, 1943, 249 (providing for the establishment of a contributory savings bank employees retirement association).

Chapter 170. — Co-operative Banks.

For temporary act, establishing the Co-operative Central Bank for the term of five years, see 1932, 45; term extended to ten years, 1935, 82; amount which a member bank may borrow without collateral further regulated, 1935, 136; 1941, 86; term further extended to twenty-five years, 1938, 244 § 1; refunds to member banks regulated, 1939, 227 § 1; act further amended, 1943, 219.

For temporary act, providing for the establishment of a fund for the insurance of shares in co-operative banks, see 1934, 73; amended, 1935, 76, 80; 1936, 155; 1938, 244 §§ 2–5; 1939, 227 §§ 2–5.

For temporary act, authorizing banking institutions, during a three-year period, to make loans insured under the provisions of the National Housing Act, see 1935, 162; amended and extended to July 1, 1939, 1937, 240; further extended to July 1, 1941, 1939, 241; further extended to July 1, 1943, 1941, 260; amended and extended to July 1, 1945, 1943, 126. (See also 1943, 339.)

For temporary act, modifying requirements for investments in real estate mortgages, see 1936, 191; amended, 1936, 405 § 2; extended, 1939, 98; 1941, 40.

For temporary act, authorizing co-operative banks to borrow from any source to make real estate loans, see 1936, 195; duration of act extended, 1938, 81; further extended, 1939, 104.

For temporary act to enable certain banking institutions to co-operate in the distribution of United States Defense Savings Bonds and Defense Postal Savings Stamps, see 1941, 221, 575.

The following references are to chapter 170, as appearing in the Tercentenary Edition:

SECT. 16 revised, 1932, 292 § 1.

SECT. 19 amended, 1932, 292 § 2.

SECT. 20A added, 1932, 292 § 3 (authorizing payment to spouse or next of kin without administration in case value of shares does not exceed two hundred dollars).

SECT. 36A added, 1932, 292 § 4 (authorizing and regulating borrowings to meet withdrawals and to loan against shares).

SECT. 40, paragraph added at end, 1932, 233 § 1.

SECT. 41 amended, 1932, 233 § 2.

SECT. 42 amended, 1932, 233 § 3.

SECT. 45A added, 1933, 46 § 2 (authorizing co-operative banks to become members of the Federal Home Loan Bank established for the district of New England).

SECT. 50 added, 1932, 201 (authorizing co-operative banks to become members of certain leagues).

Chapter stricken out and new chapter inserted, 1933, 144.
The following references are to the new chapter 170:

SECT. 7 amended, 1938, 162 § 1.

SECT. 12 amended, 1936, 196 § 1; 1938, 159; 1941, 73.

SECT. 16, second paragraph revised, 1936, 196 § 2; 1938, 244 § 7.

SECT. 17A added, 1941, 116 (providing for the temporary suspension of payments on certain shares of co-operative banks owned by persons engaged in the military or naval service of the United States, or by their dependents); revised, 1943, 142.

SECT. 23 revised, 1941, 76.

SECT. 25, sentence added at end, 1935, 174.

SECT. 32A added, under heading "OTHER AUTHORIZED PAYMENTS", 1938, 197 (permitting acceptance of certain payments by co-operative banks).

SECT. 33 amended, 1935, 190.

SECT. 34 amended, 1934, 203 § 1.

SECT. 35, last paragraph stricken out, 1934, 203 § 2.

SECTS. 36A–36D added under caption "DIRECT-REDUCTION LOANS" (changing and making permanent the law authorizing co-operative banks to make direct-reduction loans on real estate and providing for the suspension of payments thereon by persons in the military or naval service and others), 1941, 293 § 1. For prior temporary legislation (repealed by 1941, 293 § 2) see 1935, 191; 1936, 203; 1937, 233; 1938, 199.

SECT. 39 amended, 1941, 77.

SECT. 40 revised, 1941, 75.

SECT. 43A added, 1943, 77 (authorizing the sale of checks by co-operative banks).

SECT. 44, second paragraph revised, 1936, 159.

SECT. 46 revised, 1943, 81.

SECT. 47 revised, 1935, 75; 1936, 133.

SECT. 50, first paragraph amended, 1935, 54; 1937, 174.

SECT. 50A added, under caption "CONVERSION", 1935, 215 (establishing the procedure to be followed by a co-operative bank in converting into a federal savings and loan association); first paragraph amended, 1938, 162 § 2; 1943, 235 § 1; second and third paragraphs revised, 1938, 244 § 6. (See 1943, 235 § 2.)

SECT. 54 revised, 1943, 191.

Chapter 171. — Credit Unions.

For temporary act, establishing the Central Credit Union Fund, Inc., for the term of five years, see 1932, 216; amended, 1934, 221; 1939, 112 § 2. Term extended to ten years, 1936, 70. Term extended to twenty years, 1941, 177.

For temporary act, authorizing banking institutions, during a three-year period, to make loans insured under the provisions of the National Housing Act, see 1935, 162; amended and extended to July 1, 1939, 1937, 240; further extended to July 1, 1941, 1939, 241; further extended to July 1, 1943, 1941, 260; amended and extended to July 1, 1945, 1943, 126. (See also 1943, 339.)

For temporary act, modifying requirements for investments in real estate mortgages, see 1936, 191; amended, 1936, 405 § 2; extended, 1939, 98; 1941, 40.

For temporary act to enable certain banking institutions to co-operate in the distribution of United States Defense Savings Bonds and Defense Postal Savings Stamps, see 1941, 221, 575.

SECT. 3, second paragraph revised, 1936, 323.

SECT. 5 amended, 1939, 112 § 1.

SECT. 15, last sentence stricken out, and paragraph added at end, 1933, 163 § 1; new paragraph added, 1935, 272; paragraph added by 1935, 272 revised, 1936, 329.

SECT. 17. See 1943, 30.

SECT. 19A added, 1938, 239 (relative to the liability of certain endorsers upon notes held by credit unions and authorizing the establishment of contingent funds by credit unions); revised, 1941, 79.

SECT. 20A added, 1936, 119 (relative to the impairment of the capital of credit unions).

SECT. 21 amended, 1933, 163 § 2; 1937, 228; revised, 1943, 118.

SECT. 24, paragraph added at end of subdivision (A), 1933, 163 § 3; first four paragraphs and subdivision (A) revised, 1941, 102.

SECT. 29, first paragraph revised, 1936, 139.

Chapter 172. — Trust Companies.

For temporary act, authorizing banking institutions, during a three-year period, to make loans insured under the provisions of the National Housing Act, see 1935, 162; amended and extended to July 1, 1939, 1937, 240; further extended to July 1, 1941, 1939, 241; further extended to July 1, 1943, 1941, 260; amended and extended to July 1, 1945, 1943, 126. (See also 1943, 339.)

For temporary act, modifying requirements for investments in real estate mortgages, see 1936, 191; amended, 1936, 405 § 2; extended, 1939, 98; 1941, 40.

For temporary act providing for the liquidation of certain trust companies, see 1939, 515; 1941, 143; 1943, 122.

SECT. 1 revised, 1934, 349 § 1.

SECT. 7, clause Fourth revised, 1934, 349 § 2.

SECT. 9, fifth sentence amended, 1934, 349 § 3.

SECT. 10, first paragraph amended, 1934, 349 § 4.

SECT. 11 revised, 1934, 349 § 5.

SECT. 12 revised, 1934, 349 § 6.
SECT. 13 revised, 1934, 349 § 7.
SECT. 14 revised, 1934, 349 § 8; 1935, 40; amended, 1936, 143 § 1.
SECT. 14A added, 1934, 349 § 9 (relative to the submission of a monthly report by the treasurer of a trust company to its board of directors); subparagraph 3 stricken out and subparagraphs 3 and 3A inserted, 1939, 244 § 1.
SECT. 15 revised, 1934, 349 § 10.
SECT. 16, paragraph added at end, 1934, 349 § 11.
SECT. 18 revised, 1934, 349 § 12; amended, 1935, 18; second paragraph revised, 1943, 110 § 8.
SECT. 19 amended, 1934, 349 § 13.
SECT. 19A added, 1943, 237 (providing for notice to the commissioner of banks of certain transfers of stock of trust companies).
SECT. 24 revised, 1934, 349 § 14; two paragraphs added at end, 1937, 248.
SECT. 25 amended, 1934, 349 § 15.
SECT. 26 amended, 1934, 349 § 16; revised, 1943, 21 § 2.
SECT. 30A, sentence added at end, 1934, 349 § 17.
SECT. 31 revised, 1934, 349 § 18; last sentence amended, 1939, 124.
SECT. 33 revised, 1941, 484 § 1. (See 1941, 484 §§ 4, 5.)
SECT. 34 revised, 1934, 349 § 19; 1939, 244 § 2.
SECT. 40 revised, 1941, 484 § 2. (See 1941, 484 §§ 4, 5.)
SECT. 40A added, 1943, 261 (clarifying the limits on the total liabilities of any one borrower to a trust company in its commercial and savings departments).
SECT. 43 revised, 1934, 349 § 20; 1941, 484 § 3. (See 1941, 484 §§ 4, 5.)
SECT. 44 revised, 1939, 187.
SECT. 44A added, 1933, 41 § 2 (authorizing trust companies to purchase, loan upon or participate in loans upon the assets of certain closed and other banks).
SECT. 45 revised, 1934, 349 § 21; amended, 1939, 244 § 3. (See 1943, 192.)
SECT. 46 revised, 1934, 349 § 22; amended, 1939, 244 § 4. (See 1943, 192.)
SECT. 48 revised, 1934, 349 § 23; paragraph (*c*) added at end, 1937, 276.
SECT. 54 amended, 1934, 349 § 24; 1935, 172 § 1.
SECT. 54A added, 1935, 172 § 2 (authorizing trust companies under certain conditions to deposit in their commercial departments certain funds held in their trust departments).
SECT. 57 revised, 1934, 349 § 25.
SECT. 60 amended, 1934, 349 § 26.
SECT. 61 amended, 1933, 41 § 3.
SECT. 62 amended, 1934, 349 § 27; revised, 1941, 104.
SECT. 66 revised, 1932, 245 § 2.
SECT. 66A revised, 1943, 27 § 2.
SECT. 67, paragraph added at end, 1933, 334 § 29 (regulating the declaration and payment of interest on deposits in savings departments of trust companies).
SECT. 69 amended, 1943, 110 § 7.
SECT. 70. See 1943, 30.

SECT. 74 amended, 1934, 349 § 28.
SECT. 75 revised, 1934, 349 § 29; last sentence revised, 1943, 193.
SECT. 76 amended, 1934, 349 § 30.
SECT. 80 revised, 1934, 349 § 31 (but see 1934, 349 § 32.)
SECT. 82 added, under caption "SET-OFF OR RECOUPMENT OF DEPOSITS", 1932, 295 § 1. (See 1932, 295 § 2.)
SECTS. 83–89 added, under caption "CONSERVATORSHIP", 1933, 87 § 1.
SECTS. 83, 88. See 1933, 112 §§ 6, 9.
SECT. 90 added, 1933, 273 (relative to the enforcement of conservatorship proceedings in respect to trust companies).

Chapter 172A. — Banking Companies.

New chapter inserted, 1935, 452, § 4.

For temporary act to enable certain banking institutions to co-operate in the distribution of United States Defense Savings Bonds and Defense Postal Savings Stamps, see 1941, 221, 575.

SECT. 1 revised, 1938, 266 § 2; amended, 1941, 391 § 1. (See 1941, 391 §§ 2, 3.)

SECT. 1A added, 1938, 266 § 3 (authorizing certain existing corporations to vote to carry on the business of a banking company on certain conditions).

SECT. 2 amended, 1938, 266 § 4.
SECT. 3 revised, 1938, 266 § 5.
SECT. 4 amended, 1938, 266 § 6.
SECT. 5, first paragraph revised, 1938, 266 § 7.
SECT. 6 revised, 1938, 266 § 9.
SECT. 7, clause Second revised, 1943, 208.

SECT. 7A added, 1938, 266 § 8 (relative to the carrying and disposition by certain existing corporations of certain assets not authorized as investments after they become subject to this chapter).

SECT. 15 added, 1941, 438 (authorizing banking companies to sell certain negotiable checks).

Chapter 175. — Insurance.

For temporary act, authorizing insurance companies, during a three-year period, to make loans insured under the provisions of the National Housing Act, see 1935, 162; amended and extended to July 1, 1939, 1937, 240; further extended to July 1, 1941; 1939, 241; affected, 1939, 359; further extended to July 1, 1943, 1941, 260; amended and extended to July 1, 1945, 1943, 126. (See also 1943, 339.)

For temporary act, modifying the requirements for investments in real estate mortgages, see 1936, 191; amended, 1936, 405 § 2; extended, 1939, 98; 1941, 40.

SECT. 1, paragraph added (after definition of "Foreign company") defining "Industrial life insurance policy" or "policy of industrial life insurance", 1943, 227 § 11; paragraph added after word "law" in the fifty-second line, 1938, 306 (defining "resident" with respect to the incorporators, officers and directors of insurance companies). (See 1943, 227 §§ 13, 14.)

SECT. 4, first paragraph revised, 1938, 357 § 1; fourth paragraph amended, 1939, 472 § 4; revised, 1941, 324.

SECT. 5 amended, 1933, 107 § 2.

SECT. 6, first paragraph amended, 1933, 107 § 3; section amended, 1939, 472 § 1; first paragraph amended, 1939, 488 § 2. (See 1939, 488 § 9.)

SECT. 9, clause Second revised, 1941, 326 § 1; clause Fourth revised, 1941, 326 § 2; section revised, 1943, 227 § 1. (See 1943, 227 §§ 13, 14.)

SECT. 11, first paragraph amended, 1934, 92 § 1; revised, 1943, 207 § 3; third paragraph amended, 1933, 5. (See 1943, 207 § 4.)

SECT. 12 amended, 1943, 183 § 1. (See 1943, 183 § 2.)

SECT. 12A added, 1943, 183 § 2 (relating to the computation of reserves required of certain domestic liability insurance companies with respect to certain policies of liability insurance).

SECT. 14 amended, 1939, 395 § 2; revised, 1941, 635 § 3, 693; paragraph inserted after paragraph contained in line 14, 1943, 54 § 1; paragraph contained in lines 22–26 revised, 1943, 288; seventeenth paragraph revised, 1943, 54 § 2, 227 § 2.

SECT. 16, second paragraph amended, 1939, 395 § 3.

SECT. 19A amended, 1934, 137 § 2; revised, 1941, 364 § 1.

SECT. 19B added, 1939, 375 (authorizing domestic insurance companies to merge or consolidate with foreign insurance companies in certain cases); revised, 1941, 364 § 2.

SECT. 19C added, 1941, 364 § 3 (relative to rights of stockholders of merging or consolidating corporations).

SECT. 20, new paragraph inserted after fifth paragraph, 1941, 343.

SECT. 22A revised, 1935, 234; last paragraph amended, 1938, 181.

SECT. 25, last paragraph of Form A stricken out, 1934, 12; last paragraph of section amended, 1934, 92 § 2.

SECT. 29 revised, 1939, 167.

SECT. 32 revised, 1938, 357 § 2; amended, 1941, 342 § 1.

SECT. 36, second paragraph revised, 1935, 140; 1936, 61; two paragraphs added at end, 1938, 218 § 1.

SECT. 47, clause First revised, 1938, 176; clause Fourth revised, 1938, 307; clause Sixth amended, 1941, 243; clause Seventh amended, 1937, 261; clause Twelfth revised, 1935, 204.

SECT. 49, paragraph inserted after second paragraph, 1939, 15 § 2; paragraph contained in the twenty-second to the twenty-eighth lines revised, 1941, 342 § 2; last paragraph stricken out, 1941, 342 § 3.

SECT. 50, third sentence amended, 1932, 180 § 33.

SECT. 54, clause (*e*) revised, 1939, 488 § 3. (See 1939, 488 § 9.)

SECT. 54A added, 1932, 165 (permitting certain insurance companies to make outside the commonwealth contracts insuring personal property against all risks or hazards); amended, 1938, 198.

SECT. 64, second paragraph amended, 1936, 213; third paragraph revised, 1943, 207 § 2; paragraph added at end, 1941, 548. (See 1943, 207 § 4.)

SECT. 66A added, 1943, 207 § 1 (relative to the construction, operation and maintenance of low rental housing projects by domestic life insurance companies). (See 1943, 207 § 4.)

SECT. 72 amended, 1936, 212.

SECT. 73, first paragraph revised, 1939, 300 § 1.

SECT. 77 amended, 1941, 365 § 1. (See 1941, 365 § 2.)

SECT. 79 revised, 1933, 23 § 1.
SECT. 80, paragraph inserted after the word "classified" in the twenty-third line, 1936, 315.
SECT. 83, paragraph added at end, 1941, 716 § 5. (See 1941, 723.)
SECT. 85A added, 1941, 716 § 1 (providing that the commissioner of insurance may authorize certain domestic mutual insurance companies to issue non-assessable policies); sentence added at end, 1943, 247 § 1. (See 1941, 723; 1943, 247 § 4.)
SECT. 87 repealed, 1934, 22.
SECT. 90, first paragraph amended, 1941, 716 § 2. (See 1941, 723.)
SECT. 90A amended, 1939, 300 § 2.
SECT. 90B revised, 1933, 23 § 2.
SECT. 93, first paragraph revised, 1939, 488 § 1; 1941, 654 § 1. (See 1939, 488 § 9.)
SECT. 93B revised, 1939, 488 § 4. (See 1939, 488 § 9.)
SECT. 93C revised, 1939, 488 § 5. (See 1939, 488 § 9.)
SECT. 93D revised, 1939, 488 § 6. (See 1939, 488 § 9.)
SECT. 93F added, 1941, 716 § 3 (permitting certain domestic mutual insurance companies to issue non-assessable policies); sentence added at end, 1943, 247 § 2. (See 1941, 723; 1943, 247 § 4.)
SECT. 94, first two paragraphs stricken out, and two new paragraphs inserted, 1933, 81; first paragraph amended, 1938, 218 § 2; 1943, 532 § 2.
SECT. 97 amended, 1933, 31.
SECT. 99, clause Ninth revised, 1934, 95; paragraph of the standard form appearing in lines 14–23 revised, 1943, 462.
SECT. 102 amended, 1932, 174 § 1; revised, 1934, 110 § 1. (See 1932, 174 § 2; 1934, 110 § 2.)
SECT. 106 revised, 1932, 150 § 1; amended, 1939, 400 § 1. (See 1932, 150 § 4.)
SECT. 110, sentence added at end, 1939, 133; section amended, 1941, 118; revised, 1943, 424 § 3, 532 § 1.
SECT. 110A added, 1938, 401 (relative to exemption of the benefits of disability insurance from attachment and execution).
SECT. 110B added, 1939, 209 (relative to the termination or lapsing of certain accident and health policies for non-payment of premiums).
SECT. 111C added, 1943, 375 § 1 (providing for the inclusion of accident benefits in certain liability insurance policies).
SECT. 113A, provision (2) amended, 1933, 119 § 1, revised, 1933, 145 § 1; provision (2A) added, 1933, 145 § 2, amended, 1935, 296 § 1; provision (6) revised, 1936, 272. (See 1933, 145 § 3; 1935, 296 § 2.)
SECT. 113B, paragraph inserted after first paragraph, 1935, 459 § 4. (See 1935, 459 § 5.)
SECT. 113D, first paragraph revised, 1933, 119 § 2; fourth paragraph revised, 1933, 146 § 1; sixth paragraph revised, 1933, 146 § 2, amended, 1934, 46; first sentence of sixth paragraph amended, 1938, 311; paragraph added at end, 1933, 119 § 3; paragraph added at end, 1934, 379. (See 1933, 119 § 6, 146 § 3.)
SECT. 113E added, 1934, 61 (prohibiting certain discrimination in the issuance or execution of motor vehicle liability policies or bonds); amended, 1941, 401.
SECT. 113F added, 1937, 390 (relative to the renewal of motor vehicle

liability policies or bonds, so called, in certain cases); first paragraph amended, 1938, 351.

SECT. 113G added, 1939, 406 § 1 (relative to the relations of officers, directors and employees of certain domestic insurance companies with certain insurance agencies and finance companies). (See 1939, 406 § 2.)

SECT. 114 amended, 1932, 180 § 34; 1939, 225.

SECT. 116A amended, 1932, 180 § 35.

SECT. 117A, first paragraph amended, 1938, 216 § 1; heading before section 117A stricken out and "MARINE AND AUTOMOBILE AND SPRINKLER LEAKAGE INSURANCE" inserted, 1938, 216 § 2.

SECT. 123 revised, 1943, 186.

SECT. 125. See 1933, 42.

SECT. 126 amended, 1943, 227 § 5. (See 1933, 42 §§ 13, 14; 1943, 227.)

SECT. 132, first paragraph revised, 1933, 101 § 1; first paragraph amended, 1943, 227 § 6; provisions numbered 6, 7, 8, 9, revised, 1943, 227 § 7. (See 1943, 227 §§ 13, 14.)

SECT. 133, clause (*b*) amended, 1938, 362 § 2; clause (*b*) amended, 1943, 424 § 1; clause (*c*) added, 1938, 362 § 1; clause (*d*) added, 1943, 424 § 2.

SECT. 134, sentence added at end of provision numbered 4, 1938, 362 § 3; said provision revised, 1939, 170; 1941, 456; last paragraph stricken out and three new paragraphs inserted, 1938, 362 § 4.

SECT. 138A added, 1943, 424 § 4 (relative to deductions from salaries of state, county and municipal employees for payment of premiums on certain group life insurance policies).

SECT. 140, second paragraph revised, 1943, 227 § 12; third paragraph amended, 1933, 101 § 2. (See 1943, 227 §§ 13, 14.)

SECT. 142 revised, 1943, 227 § 8. (See 1943, 227 §§ 13, 14.)

SECT. 143 revised, 1943, 227 § 9. (See 1943, 227 §§ 13, 14.)

SECT. 144, last paragraph revised, 1933, 101 § 3; first three paragraphs stricken out and four new paragraphs inserted, 1938, 209 § 1; section revised, 1943, 227 § 3. (See 1938, 209 § 3; 1943, 227 §§ 13, 14.)

SECT. 146 revised, 1943, 227 § 4. (See 1943, 227 §§ 13, 14.)

SECT. 147 amended, 1938, 209 § 2; repealed, 1943, 227 § 10. (See 1943, 227 §§ 13, 14.)

SECT. 147A repealed, 1943, 227 § 10. (See 1943, 227 §§ 13, 14.)

SECT. 147B added, 1935, 232 (requiring foreign life insurance companies to provide for paid-up and extended term insurance and cash surrender values on policies of industrial life insurance issued in the commonwealth); repealed, 1943, 227 § 10. (See 1943, 227 §§ 13, 14.)

SECT. 151, clause Second amended, 1933, 107 § 1; clause Second, subdivision (3) (*c*) revised, 1939, 488 § 7; clause Second, subdivision (3) (*f*) revised, 1939, 488 § 8. (See 1939, 488 § 9.)

SECT. 152A added, 1941, 716 § 4 (relative to the issue by certain foreign mutual insurance companies of non-assessable policies); sentence added at end, 1943, 247 § 3. (See 1941, 723; 1943, 247 § 4.)

SECT. 155, clause First revised, 1932, 150 § 2, amended, 1939, 400 § 2. (See 1932, 150 § 4.)

SECT. 156A amended, 1933, 30.

SECT. 157, paragraph added at end, 1939, 315; section revised, 1941, 451.

SECT. 160A added, 1933, 25 § 1 (prohibiting the printing or publication of certain advertisements for or on behalf of unlicensed insurance companies).

SECT. 160B added, 1934, 14 § 1 (authorizing the commissioner of insurance to publish certain information relative to unlicensed foreign insurance companies or societies).

SECT. 162, third paragraph revised, 1941, 286.

SECT. 163, paragraph added at end, 1941, 502; same paragraph revised, 1943, 85.

SECT. 164A added, 1938, 225 (providing that no insurance agent shall be charged with a decrease or deduction from his commission or salary on account of industrial life insurance policies lapsed or surrendered after being paid on for three years); revised, 1943, 226.

SECT. 167A amended, 1934, 137 § 3; 1937, 260.

SECT. 172, last sentence revised, 1941, 703.

SECT. 174C added, 1941, 493 (relative to the qualifications and licensing of insurance agents, insurance brokers and special insurance brokers).

SECTS. 177A–177D added, 1939, 395 § 1 (defining and providing for the licensing of insurance advisers).

SECT. 177B, second and third paragraphs stricken out, and new paragraph inserted, 1941, 635 § 1; paragraph added at end, 1941, 635 § 2.

SECT. 178 amended, 1941, 450 § 2.

SECT. 179, sentence added at end, 1939, 472 § 2; section revised, 1941, 452.

SECT. 180A stricken out, and new sections 180A–180L inserted, 1939, 472 § 3 (relative to the rehabilitation, conservation and liquidation of certain domestic and foreign insurers).

SECT. 181 revised, 1934, 160; amended, 1939, 395 § 4.

SECT. 184 amended, 1937, 103.

SECT. 185, first paragraph amended, 1939, 400 § 3; second paragraph revised, 1932, 150 § 3; first and second paragraphs revised, 1941, 654 § 2; section revised, 1943, 238 § 2.

SECT. 187C, first paragraph amended, 1934, 34; 1936, 215 § 1. (See 1936, 215 § 2.)

SECT. 192, sentence added at end, 1943, 375 § 2.

SECT. 193B added, 1937, 314 (authorizing the payment of motor vehicle insurance premiums in instalments).

Chapter 176. — Fraternal Benefit Societies.

SECT. 3 amended, 1941, 336 § 1.

SECT. 4 amended, 1939, 139.

SECT. 5 amended, 1933, 25 § 2; 1934, 14 § 2; 1943, 238 § 3.

SECT. 11 amended, 1943, 309 § 1.

SECT. 12, first paragraph revised, 1941, 310.

SECT. 16 amended, 1938, 93.

SECT. 18 revised, 1941, 336 § 2.

SECT. 19A added, 1939, 236 § 1 (relating to the granting of annuities by certain fraternal benefit societies).

SECT. 21 amended, 1934, 170; revised, 1937, 79; amended, 1939, 236 § 2.

SECT. 22 amended, 1941, 336 § 3.
SECT. 23 amended, 1932, 46; 1938, 94.
SECT. 24 amended, 1941, 322.
SECT. 25 revised, 1938, 157.
SECT. 30 amended, 1941, 336 § 4.
SECT. 32 revised, 1943, 309 § 2.
SECT. 32A added, 1943, 74 (providing a penalty for the alteration, defacement, mutilation, destruction or concealment of any record of a fraternal benefit society).
SECT. 36, first paragraph amended, 1941, 336 § 5.
SECT. 40, first two sentences amended, 1932, 180 § 36.
SECT. 41 amended, 1939, 168.
SECT. 42A added, 1943, 238 § 1 (further regulating the admission of certain foreign fraternal benefit societies to transact business within the commonwealth).
SECT. 45, second sentence amended, 1939, 254 § 1; paragraph added after first paragraph, 1943, 309 § 3; second paragraph amended, 1932, 104.
SECT. 46, fifth paragraph amended, 1939, 254 § 2; paragraph inserted after third paragraph, 1941, 274; three sentences added at end of paragraph so inserted, 1943, 86.
SECT. 46B added, 1932, 47 § 1 (authorizing certain fraternal benefit societies to acquire, hold, manage and dispose of real property, and confirming title to such property heretofore acquired by certain of such societies).
SECT. 46C added, 1941, 397 (permitting certain fraternal benefit societies to contract with insurance companies for the payment of benefits).

Chapter 176A. — Non-Profit Hospital Service Corporations.

New chapter inserted, 1936, 409.
SECT. 2, second sentence amended, 1939, 312 § 7.
SECT. 3 amended, 1939, 312 § 1.
SECT. 4 amended, 1939, 312 § 2.
SECT. 5 revised, 1939, 312 § 3.
SECT. 7 amended, 1939, 312 § 4.
SECT. 9 revised, 1939, 312 § 5.
SECT. 11 added, 1939, 312 § 6 (relative to the payment of salaries, compensation or emoluments by certain non-profit hospital service corporations).
SECT. 12 added, 1943, 424 § 5 (relative to deductions from salaries of state, county and municipal employees of amounts payable under contracts issued by non-profit hospital service corporations).

Chapter 176B. — Medical Service Corporations.

New chapter inserted, 1941, 306.
SECT. 16A added, 1943, 424 § 6 (relative to deductions from salaries of state, county and municipal employees of amounts payable under certificates issued by certain medical service corporations).

Chapter 176C. — Non-Profit Medical Service Plans.

New chapter inserted, 1941, 334.

SECT. 16A added, 1943, 424 § 7 (relative to deductions from salaries of state, county and municipal employees of amounts payable under contracts issued by certain medical service corporations).

Chapter 178. — Savings Bank Life Insurance.

For legislation relative to the computation of the reserve liability with respect to life insurance policies issued by savings and insurance banks and to the non-forfeiture benefits under such policies, see 1943, 227.

SECT. 10 amended, 1935, 330 § 1.

SECT. 11 amended, 1935, 330 § 2.

SECT. 11A added, 1935, 330 § 3 (relative to non-payment of premiums on annuity and certain other contracts).

SECT. 15 amended, 1935, 330 § 4; 1936, 285 § 1.

SECT. 17 revised, 1935, 330 § 5; 1939, 391 § 1. (See 1939, 391 § 2.)

SECT. 18 amended, 1943, 210 § 1.

SECT. 18A added, 1943, 210 § 2 (relative to payments to the general insurance guaranty fund).

SECT. 19 amended, 1935, 330 § 6.

SECT. 21 revised, 1935, 330 § 7; amended, 1936, 285 § 2.

SECT. 26 revised, 1932, 103.

SECT. 29 amended, 1936, 285 § 3; revised, 1941, 108 § 1.

SECT. 30 amended, 1936, 285 § 4.

SECT. 31 revised, 1941, 108 § 2.

Chapter 179. — Proprietors of Wharves, Real Estate lying in Common, and General Fields.

SECT. 3 revised, 1943, 130 § 1. (See 1943, 130 § 2.)

Chapter 180. — Corporations for Charitable and Certain Other Purposes.

SECT. 3 amended, 1943, 549 § 5.

SECT. 5 amended, 1934, 328 § 21.

SECT. 10 amended, 1932, 180 § 37; revised, 1937, 151 § 1; 1943, 549 § 6.

SECT. 11 revised, 1937, 151 § 2.

SECT. 12A amended, 1935, 246.

SECT. 26A added, 1933, 236 § 1 (requiring the filing of annual returns by certain incorporated clubs and other corporations). (See 1933, 236 § 2.)

SECT. 27 amended, 1934, 328 § 22.

Chapter 181. — Foreign Corporations.

SECT. 3 revised, 1943, 459 § 4.

Chapter 183. — Alienation of Land.

SECT. 4 revised, 1941, 85.

SECT. 43 amended, 1937, 101 § 1.

SECT. 44 amended, 1937, 101 § 2.

Chapter 184. — General Provisions relative to Real Property.

SECT. 13 amended, 1937, 112; revised, 1937, 245 § 1; first paragraph amended, 1943, 52 § 1. (See 1937, 245 § 2; 1943, 52 § 2.)
SECT. 15 amended, 1941, 88 § 1. (See 1941, 88 § 2.)
SECT. 17A added, 1939, 270 (relative to the effect of agreements for the purchase and sale of real estate).

Chapter 185. — The Land Court and Registration of Title to Land.

SECT. 1, clause (*b*) revised, 1935, 318 § 3; clause (*c*) revised, 1935, 318 § 4; clause (*j*½) added, 1934, 263 § 1 (granting to land court exclusive original jurisdiction to determine by declaratory judgment the validity and extent of municipal zoning ordinances, by-laws and regulations); clause (*k*) revised, 1934, 67 § 1; clauses (*l*) and (*m*) added, 1935, 318 § 5 (granting to said court original jurisdiction concurrent with supreme judicial and superior courts of certain suits in equity); paragraph in lines 44–50, inclusive, revised, 1937, 183 § 1. (See 1934, 67 § 2; 1935, 318 § 8; 1937, 183 § 2.)
SECT. 2 amended, 1937, 409 § 3. (See 1937, 409 § 7.)
SECT. 2A repealed, 1937, 409 § 4. (See 1937, 409 § 7.)
SECT. 12, sentence added at end, 1941, 27; section revised, 1943, 29.
SECT. 25A added, 1933, 55 (relative to the power of the land court to enforce its orders and decrees, and relative to service of its processes).
SECT. 40 amended, 1937, 118.
SECT. 78 amended, 1937, 144 § 1. (See 1937, 144 § 2.)

Chapter 188. — Homesteads.

SECT. 1 amended, 1939, 32 § 1. (See 1939, 32 § 5.)
SECT. 9 amended, 1939, 32 § 2. (See 1939, 32 § 5.)

Chapter 189. — Dower and Curtesy.

SECT. 3 revised, 1936, 91 § 1. (See 1936, 91 § 2.)

Chapter 190. — Descent and Distribution of Real and Personal Property.

SECT. 7 amended, 1943, 72 § 1.

Chapter 190A. — Effect of Apparently Simultaneous Deaths upon Devolution and Disposition of Property, including Proceeds of Insurance.

New chapter inserted, 1941, 549 § 1. (See 1941, 549 § 2.)

Chapter 192. — Probate of Wills and Appointment of Executors.

SECT. 1A added, 1934, 113 (requiring that the attorney general be made a party in certain proceedings relative to the probate of wills).
SECT. 7. See 1937, 408 § 3.

Chapter 193. — Appointment of Administrators.

SECT. 3 amended, 1938, 328.

Chapter 194. — Public Administrators.

SECT. 7 revised, 1933, 100.

SECT. 9, last sentence amended, 1932, 180 § 38; section affected, 1932, 180 § 45.

SECT. 10. See 1936, 428.

Chapter 195. — General Provisions relative to Executors and Administrators.

SECTS. 1–4 repealed, 1933, 221 § 1. (See 1933, 221 § 8.)

SECT. 8 amended, 1933, 221 § 2. (See 1933, 221 § 8.)

Chapter 196. — Allowances to Widows and Children, and Advancements.

SECT. 2 amended, 1933, 36; revised, 1936, 214.

Chapter 197. — Payment of Debts, Legacies and Distributive Shares.

SECT. 2 amended, 1933, 221 § 3. (See 1933, 221 § 8.)

SECT. 2A added, 1939, 298 (establishing limitations applicable to suits against, and regulating the payments of debts by, administrators de bonis non).

SECT. 9 amended, 1933, 221 § 4. (See 1933, 221 § 8.)

Chapter 200. — Settlement of Estates of Absentees.

SECT. 12 revised, 1941, 399 § 1.

SECTS. 13 and 14 stricken out and new section 13 inserted, 1941, 399 § 2.

Chapter 201. — Guardians and Conservators.

SECT. 6 amended, 1941, 194 § 13.

SECT. 7 amended, 1941, 194 § 14.

SECT. 13, sentence added at end, 1934, 204 § 1; section amended, 1941, 194 § 15.

SECT. 13A added, 1941, 325 (providing for the removal of a permanent guardian of an insane person).

SECT. 14 amended, 1941, 194 § 16.

SECT. 18, new sentence added at end, 1934, 204 § 2.

SECT. 30 amended, 1939, 57.

SECT. 39A added, 1936, 270 (authorizing payments from estates of minors under guardianship for expenses for the funerals of the parents in certain cases).

SECT. 47A added, 1937, 312 § 1 (permitting guardians and conservators to invest funds in certain insurance policies and annuity contracts).

SECT. 48A revised, 1941, 241.

Chapter 202. — Sales, Mortgages and Leases of Real Estate by Executors, Administrators, Guardians and Conservators.

SECT. 4A added, 1933, 129 (relative to the use and management of real estate of a decedent by his executor or administrator for the purpose of the payment of debts from the rents thereof).

SECT. 12 amended, 1941, 194 § 17.
SECT. 14 amended, 1934, 157 § 1.
SECT. 19 amended, 1941, 341 § 1. (See 1941, 341 § 2.)
SECT. 20 revised, 1933, 221 § 5. (See 1933, 221 § 8.)

Chapter 203. — Trusts.

SECT. 13 revised, 1943, 201 § 1. (See 1943, 201 § 3.)
SECT. 16 amended, 1934, 157 § 2.
SECT. 17A added, 1932, 50 (relative to the sale of real estate by foreign testamentary trustees).
SECT. 22 amended, 1936, 184 § 1. (See 1936, 184 § 2.)
SECTS. 24A and 24B added, under caption "SALVAGE OPERATIONS OF TRUSTEES", 1943, 389 § 1. (See 1943, 389 § 2.)
SECT. 25A added, under the heading "PURCHASE OF INSURANCE POLICIES OR ANNUITY CONTRACTS", 1937, 312 § 2 (permitting trustees to invest funds in certain insurance policies and annuity contracts).

Chapter 203A. — Collective Investment of Small Trust Funds.

New chapter inserted, 1941, 474.

Chapter 204. — General Provisions relative to Sales, Mortgages, Releases, Compromises, etc., by Executors, etc.

SECT. 26 amended, 1933, 221 § 6. (See 1933, 221 § 8.)
SECTS. 27–36 added, 1943, 152 (authorizing releases and disclaimers of powers of appointment and providing for the methods of releasing and disclaiming the same).
SECT. 37 added, 1943, 201 § 2 (authorizing the resignation of fiduciaries by their guardians, conservators or committees, or other like officers, acting in their behalf).

Chapter 205. — Bonds of Executors, Administrators, Guardians, Conservators, Trustees and Receivers.

SECT. 4 amended, 1941, 45 § 1.
SECT. 5 amended, 1941, 45 § 2.

Chapter 206. — Accounts and Settlements of Executors, Administrators, Guardians, Conservators, Trustees and Receivers.

SECT. 7 amended, 1941, 194 § 18.
SECT. 16 amended, 1941, 36.
SECT. 17 amended, 1936, 208.
SECT. 19 repealed, 1938, 154 § 2.
SECT. 23 repealed, 1938, 154 § 2.
SECT. 24 revised, 1938, 154 § 1.

Chapter 207. — Marriage.

SECT. 5 amended, 1941, 194 § 18A.
SECT. 7 revised, 1941, 270 § 1.
SECT. 20 amended, 1933, 127; sentence inserted after the word "residence" in line 18, 1943, 561 § 3.

Sect. 20A added, 1939, 269 § 3 (relative to the duties of city and town clerks in the case of the filing of notices of intention of marriage of pregnant females).

Sect. 20B added, 1941, 601 § 1 (requiring pre-marital physical examination); first paragraph amended, 1941, 697 § 1; second paragraph stricken out and three paragraphs inserted, 1941, 697 § 2; repealed, 1943, 561 § 2. (See 1941, 697 § 3.)

Sect. 21, paragraph added at end, 1943, 168 § 2.

Sect. 28 amended, 1941, 601 § 2. (See 1941, 601 § 4.)

Sect. 28A added, 1943, 561 § 1 (further regulating pre-marital examinations).

Sect. 30 amended, 1937, 11 § 1. (See 1937, 11 § 2.)

Sect. 33 amended, 1941, 270 § 2.

Sect. 38 revised, 1932, 162.

Sect. 47A added, under heading "breach of contract to marry not actionable", 1938, 350 § 1 (abolishing causes of action for breach of contract to marry). (See 1938, 350 § 3.)

Sect. 52 revised, 1943, 312 § 1. (See 1943, 312 § 2.)

Sect. 57 amended, 1941, 601 § 3. (See 1941, 601 § 4.)

Chapter 208. — Divorce.

Sect. 2 revised, 1937, 76 § 1. (See 1937, 76 § 2.)

Sects. 9–11 revised, 1943, 196 § 1. (See 1943, 196 § 2.)

Sect. 19 revised, 1932, 3.

Sect. 21, sentence added at end, 1934, 181 § 1. (See 1934, 181 § 2.)

Sect. 24 amended, 1943, 168 § 1.

Sect. 33 revised, 1936, 221 § 1. (See 1936, 221 § 2.)

Sect. 38 revised, 1933, 288.

Chapter 209. — Husband and Wife.

Sect. 21 amended, 1939, 32 § 3. (See 1939, 32 § 5.)

Sect. 32, sentence added at end, 1938, 136.

Sect. 33 revised, 1933, 360.

Chapter 210. — Adoption of Children and Change of Names.

Sect. 1 amended, 1941, 44.

Sect. 3 amended, 1941, 61.

Sect. 6, paragraph added at end, 1943, 155 § 1.

Sect. 13, paragraph added at end, 1943, 155 § 2.

Chapter 211. — The Supreme Judicial Court.

Sect. 11 revised, 1933, 300 § 1. (See 1933, 300 § 4.)

Sect. 19 revised, 1938, 115 § 1.

Chapter 212. — The Superior Court.

For act further extending to December 31, 1945, the operation of certain provisions of law (1923, 469, as amended) relative to the more prompt disposition of criminal cases in the superior court, see 1943, 140.

For act relative to sittings and sessions of the superior court, see 1932, 144. (For prior temporary legislation, see 1927, 306; 1928, 228.)
SECT. 14 revised, 1932, 144 § 1. (For prior temporary legislation, see 1927, 306; 1928, 228.)
SECT. 14A added, 1932, 144 § 2 (regulating the establishing of sessions and sittings of the superior court). (For prior temporary legislation, see 1927, 306; 1928, 228.)
SECTS. 15–18 repealed, 1932, 144 § 3.
SECT. 22 amended, 1934, 287; 1943, 145 § 1; sentence added at end, 1943, 244 § 3. (See 1943, 145 § 2.)
SECT. 24 amended, 1943, 244 § 4.
SECT. 25 amended, 1932, 144 § 4.
SECT. 26A added, 1935, 229 § 1 (providing for the transfer from the superior court to the land court of certain actions at law and suits in equity where any right, title or interest in land is involved). (See 1935, 229 § 2.)

Chapter 213. — Provisions Common to the Supreme Judicial and Superior Courts.

SECTS. 1A and 1B added, 1939, 257 § 1 (granting to the superior court jurisdiction of certain extraordinary writs and certain other matters, concurrently with the supreme judicial court). (See 1939, 257 § 2.)
SECT. 1A amended, 1941, 28, 180.
SECTS. 1C and 1D added, 1943, 374 § 4 (providing for changing a petition for certiorari into a petition for mandamus and vice versa and providing for appeals from judgments upon such petitions).
SECT. 3, clause Tenth B added, 1943, 374 § 3 (providing for the presentation at hearings upon petitions for certiorari of evidence at proceedings complained of in such petitions).
SECT. 6 amended, 1932, 144 § 5.

Chapter 214. — Equity Jurisdiction and Procedure in the Supreme Judicial and Superior Courts.

SECT. 1 amended, 1935, 407 § 2. (See 1935, 407 § 6; 1937, 436 § 10; G. L. 150A § 6 (*h*) inserted by 1938, 345 § 2.)
SECT. 2. Affected, 1939, 257 § 2.
SECT. 3, clause (12) added at end, 1939, 194 § 1.
SECT. 9 amended, 1934, 381; 1935, 407 § 3. (See 1935, 407 § 6; 1937, 436 § 10; G. L. 150A § 6 (*h*) inserted by 1938, 345 § 2.)
SECT. 9A added, 1935, 407 § 4 (limiting authority of courts to grant injunctive relief in cases involving or growing out of labor disputes). (See 1935, 407 § 6; 1937, 436 § 10; G. L. 150A § 6 (*h*) inserted by 1938, 345 § 2.)

Chapter 215. — Probate Courts.

SECT. 6 amended, 1933, 237 § 1; revised, 1937, 257; amended, 1939, 194 § 2.
SECT. 6B added, 1935, 247 § 1 (providing for interpretative judgments in the probate courts as to the meaning of written instruments). (See 1935, 247 § 2.)
SECT. 30A amended, 1934, 330.

Sect. 44, last sentence revised, 1941, 323 § 1; section amended, 1943, 91. (See 1941, 323 § 2.)
Sect. 61 repealed, 1939, 65 § 1. (See 1939, 65 § 2.)
Sect. 62, paragraph in lines 17–20 revised, 1932, 107; 1936, 241; paragraph in lines 29–33 revised, 1934, 24; paragraph in lines 34–37 amended, 1934, 54; same paragraph revised, 1934, 175 § 1; paragraph in lines 45–51 revised, 1935, 132; paragraph in lines 56 and 57 revised, 1933, 274. (See 1934, 175 § 2.)

Chapter 217. — Judges and Registers of Probate and Insolvency.

For legislation relative to abolition of office of special judge of probate and insolvency on the death, resignation or removal of the incumbent, see 1937, 408 § 8.
Sect. 1 amended, 1935, 434 § 1.
Sect. 2 amended, 1934, 290; 1935, 434 § 2.
Sects. 5 and 6 stricken out and new sections 5, 5A, 6, 6A inserted, 1937, 408 § 3. (See 1937, 408 § 9.)
Sect. 7, sentence added at end, 1937, 408 § 4. (See 1937, 408 §§ 3, 9.)
Sect. 8 revised, 1937, 408 § 5. (See 1937, 408 § 9.)
Sect. 24 amended, 1943, 464 § 1. (See 1943, 464 § 2.)
Sect. 24A revised, 1939, 392.
Sect. 30 revised, 1935, 143 § 1;* 1935, 313 § 1; 1936, 252 § 1; 1941, 226 § 1. (See 1935, 313 § 3; 1936, 252 § 2; 1941, 226 § 2.)
Sect. 31A added,* 1935, 313 § 2 (providing for the appointment of a messenger for the probate court of Essex county). (See 1935, 313 § 3.)
Sect. 34 revised, 1937, 408 § 1. (See 1937, 408 § 9.)
Sect. 38 repealed, 1937, 408 § 2.
Sect. 40 revised, 1937, 408 § 6. (See 1937, 408 § 9.)
Sect. 41 amended, 1937, 408 § 7; 1941, 503. (See 1937, 408 §§ 8, 9.)

Chapter 218. — District Courts.

For act further extending to December 31, 1945, the operation of certain provisions of law (1923, 469, as amended) authorizing certain justices of district courts to sit in criminal cases in the superior court, see 1943, 140.
For legislation limiting the number of special justices of certain district courts, see 1941, 664.
Sect. 1, first paragraph under caption "*Franklin*" revised, 1932, 87 § 1; section amended, 1939, 451 § 59.
Sect. 6, first paragraph revised, 1941, 664 § 1. (See 1941, 664 §§ 2, 3.)
Sect. 8 revised, 1936, 282 § 1. (See 1936, 282 § 3.)
Sect. 9, sentence added at end, 1934, 217 § 1.
Sect. 10 amended, 1932, 160 § 1; 1937, 297 § 1; 1938, 193 § 1; last paragraph revised, 1938, 222 § 1; paragraph added at end, 1941, 309 § 1. (See 1937, 297 § 2; 1938, 193 § 2, 222 § 2.)
Sect. 13 revised, 1937, 59; first paragraph stricken out, 1939, 157 § 1. (See 1939, 157 § 4.)
Sect. 15 revised, 1939, 230 § 1, 347 § 1. (See 1939, 230 § 2.)

* Void for non-acceptance.

SECT. 16 revised, 1937, 219 § 3; 1939, 214 § 5.
SECT. 19 amended, 1934, 387 § 1; 1943, 296 § 1. (See 1934, 387 § 5; 1943, 296 § 6, 437.)
SECT. 22 amended, 1937, 310.
SECT. 26 revised, 1937, 301 § 1; 1938, 365 § 1. (See 1937, 301 § 2; 1938, 365 § 2.)
SECT. 29 amended, 1932, 55.
SECT. 30 amended, 1941, 194 § 19.
SECT. 35A added, 1943, 349 § 1 (providing that certain persons against whom complaints are made in district courts may be given an opportunity to be heard before issuance of process). (See 1943, 349 § 2.)
SECT. 38, second sentence revised, 1939, 347 § 2.
SECT. 43 amended, 1939, 347 § 3.
SECT. 43A, first paragraph amended, 1938, 324; section revised, 1941, 682 § 1; first paragraph amended, 1943, 101. (See 1941, 682 §§ 1A, 2.)
SECT. 53, paragraph added after the first paragraph, 1936, 230.
SECT. 58 revised, 1936, 282 § 2. (See 1936, 282 § 3.)
SECT. 62 amended,* 1932, 235 § 1; revised,* 1932, 247 § 1; amended, 1935, 71 § 1; 1937, 298; revised, 1939, 305; amended, 1941, 309 § 3, 348. (See 1935, 71 § 2.)
SECT. 63 revised, 1935, 341.
SECT. 76 amended, 1932, 269 § 1; 1935, 366 § 1; 1937, 378 § 1; revised, 1939, 451 § 60. (See 1935, 366 § 3.)
SECT. 77 revised, 1937, 294.
SECT. 79 amended, 1941, 309 § 2; revised, 1941, 447 § 2; amended, 1943, 136 § 2. (See 1941, 447 §§ 4, 5; 1943, 136 § 3.)
SECT. 80, sentence added at end, 1935, 366 § 2; section amended, 1936, 229 § 1; 1937, 378 § 2; revised, 1941, 447 § 3. (See 1935, 366 § 3; 1936, 229 § 2; 1941, 447 §§ 4, 5.)
SECT. 81 revised, 1939, 296 § 1. (See 1939, 296 § 3.)

Chapter 219. — Trial Justices.

SECT. 28 amended, 1934, 328 § 23.

Chapter 220. — Courts and Naturalization.

SECTS. 13A and 13B added, 1935, 407 § 5 (regulating procedure in trials for contempt arising out of disobedience to decrees or process of courts in labor dispute cases). (See 1935, 407 § 6; 1937, 436 § 10; G. L. 150A § 6 (*h*) inserted by 1938, 345 § 2.)
SECT. 14A added, 1936, 206 § 1 (relative to the time within which certain justices shall render their decisions). (See 1936, 206 § 2.)
SECTS. 16 and 17 repealed, 1932, 144 § 3.
SECT. 19 repealed, 1932, 16.

Chapter 221. — Clerks, Attorneys and Other Officers of Judicial Courts.

SECT. 4 amended, 1935, 89 § 1; 1937, 158 § 1; 1943, 336 § 1. (See 1935, 89 § 2; 1937, 158 § 2; 1943, 336 § 3.)
SECT. 5 amended, 1932, 51; 1943, 336 § 2. (See 1943, 336 § 3.)

---

* Void for non-acceptance.

SECT. 12 revised, 1937, 219 § 4; 1939, 214 § 6.
SECT. 24 revised, 1936, 31 § 3.
SECT. 27 revised, 1939, 157 § 2. (See 1939, 157 § 4.)
SECT. 27A added, 1939, 157 § 3 (relative to the disposal of certain obsolete and useless papers of courts). (See 1939, 157 § 4.)
SECT. 43 revised, 1939, 197 § 1.
SECTS. 44A and 44B added, 1939, 197 § 2 (prohibiting employees and other persons connected with hospitals from furnishing certain information about certain personal injury cases to attorneys at law).
SECT. 44A amended, 1943, 293.
SECT. 46 revised, 1935, 346 § 1.
SECTS. 46A and 46B added, 1935, 346 § 2 (prohibiting individuals not members of the bar from practising law or attempting so to do and providing a means of restraining unauthorized practice of law).
SECT. 47 repealed, 1935, 346 § 3.
SECT. 49 repealed, 1935, 346 § 3.
SECT. 53 amended, 1939, 151.
SECT. 58 amended, 1932, 40 § 1.
SECT. 60 repealed, 1932, 40 § 2.
SECT. 63 amended, 1939, 6 § 1. (See 1939, 6 §§ 2, 3.)
SECT. 73 revised, 1935, 182 § 2; 1938, 347 § 2; 1941, 448 § 1. (See 1935, 182 §§ 5, 6; 1938, 347 § 3; 1941, 448 § 3.)
SECT. 73A added, 1938, 347 § 2; amended, 1941, 448 § 2. (See 1938, 347 § 3; 1941, 448 § 3.)
SECT. 76 revised, 1935, 182 § 3; first sentence stricken out and two new sentences added, 1939, 258 § 1; second and third sentences revised, 1939, 165 § 2. (See 1935, 182 §§ 5, 6; 1939, 165 § 3, 258 § 2.)
SECT. 80 amended, 1935, 182 § 4. (See 1935, 182 § 6.)
SECT. 94, first sentence amended, 1932, 180 § 39.

Chapter 223. — Commencement of Actions, Service of Process.

SECT. 2 revised, 1934, 387 § 2; last sentence of first paragraph revised, 1943, 296 § 2. (See 1934, 387 § 5; 1943, 296 § 6, 437.)
SECT. 2A added, 1935, 483 § 1 (providing for trial together of two or more actions arising out of the same motor vehicle accident pending in district courts). (See 1935, 483 §§ 2, 3.) Section stricken out and new sections 2A–2C inserted, 1943, 369 § 1 (relative to the trial and disposition of certain actions and proceedings pending in different courts). (See 1943, 369 § 2.)
SECT. 24 amended, 1938, 115 § 2.
SECT. 38 amended, 1939, 451 § 61.
SECT. 42 amended, 1937, 295 § 1.
SECT. 42A added, 1943, 234 § 1 (relative to the amount for which attachments may be made on liquidated claims). (See 1943, 234 § 3.)
SECT. 44A added, 1937, 295 § 2 (further regulating the attachment of motor vehicles on mesne process in actions of contract)
SECT. 48 revised, 1937, 308; amended, 1938, 348 § 1. (See 1938, 348 § 2.)
SECT. 74 revised, 1943, 298 § 1. (See 1943, 298 § 10.)
SECT. 75 revised, 1943, 298 § 2. (See 1943, 298 § 10.)
SECT. 76 revised, 1943, 298 § 3. (See 1943, 298 § 10.)

SECT. 78 revised, 1943, 298 § 4. (See 1943, 298 § 10.)
SECT. 79 revised, 1943, 298 § 5. (See 1943, 298 § 10.)
SECT. 80 revised, 1943, 298 § 6. (See 1943, 298 § 10.)
SECT. 81 revised, 1943, 298 § 7. (See 1943, 298 § 10.)
SECT. 82 revised, 1943, 298 § 8. (See 1943, 298 § 10.)
SECT. 83A added, 1943, 298 § 9 (providing that sections 74-83 shall not apply to conditional sales, notices of which are recordable under G. L. 184 § 13). (See 1943, 298 § 10.)
SECT. 114 amended, 1938, 325 § 1; revised, 1943, 234 § 2 (See 1938, 325 § 2; 1943, 234 § 3.)

Chapter 224. — Arrest on Mesne Process and Supplementary Proceedings in Civil Actions.

SECT. 16 amended, 1943, 292 § 1. (See 1943, 292 § 2.)

Chapter 228. — Survival of Actions and Death and Disabilities of Parties.

SECT. 1 revised, 1934, 300 § 1. (See 1934, 300 § 2.)
SECT. 5 amended, 1933, 221 § 7; revised, 1937, 406 § 1. Affected, 1938, 16. (See 1933, 221 § 8.)

Chapter 229. — Actions for Death and Injuries Resulting in Death.

SECT. 1 revised, 1943, 444 § 1.
SECT. 2 amended, 1941, 460 § 1, 504 § 1.
SECT. 3, first sentence revised, 1941, 460 § 2; section amended, 1941, 504 § 2.
SECT. 5 amended, 1937, 406 § 3; 1941, 504 § 3.
SECT. 5A added, 1938, 278 § 1 (to permit recovery in certain death cases notwithstanding that the death of the tortfeasor occurred before that of the person whose death he caused). (See 1938, 278 § 2.)
SECT. 6 amended, 1939, 451 § 62.
SECTS. 6A and 6B added, 1943, 444 § 2 (relative to the disposition of money recovered in certain actions for death).
SECT. 9 amended, 1941, 504 § 4.

Chapter 230. — Actions By and Against Executors and Administrators.

SECT. 5 amended, 1934, 116.

Chapter 231. — Pleading and Practice.

SECT. 4A added, 1943, 350 § 1 (providing for the joinder of parties in one action in certain cases). (See 1943, 350 §§ 3, 4.)
SECT. 6A added, 1939, 372 § 1 (relative to the recovery of certain medical expenses by the husband of a married woman or the parent or guardian of a minor, in actions to recover for personal injuries by married women and minors). (See 1939, 372 § 2.)
SECT. 7, clause Sixth revised, 1939, 67 § 1. (See 1939, 67 § 2.)
SECT. 55 amended, 1935, 318 § 6. (See 1935, 318 § 8.)
SECT. 59C added, under caption "SPEEDY TRIAL OF CERTAIN ACTIONS FOR MALPRACTICE, ERROR OR MISTAKE", 1935, 118 § 1 (relative to the

advancement for speedy trial in the superior court of actions against physicians and others for malpractice, error or mistake). (See 1935, 118 § 2.)

SECT. 63 amended, 1932, 84 § 1.

SECT. 69 amended, 1932, 177 § 1. (See 1932, 177 § 2.)

SECT. 73 repealed, 1932, 180 § 40.

SECT. 78 repealed, 1932, 180 § 40.

SECT. 84A added, 1933, 247 § 1 (relative to the joint trial in the superior court of actions involving the same subject matter). (See 1933, 247 § 2.)

SECTS. 85B and 85C added, 1937, 439 § 1 (relative to procedure in certain actions to recover damages arising out of motor vehicle accidents and in suits by judgment creditors in actions to reach and apply the proceeds of motor vehicle liability policies and in actions to recover on motor vehicle liability bonds). (See 1937, 439 § 2.)

SECT. 91 revised, 1943, 365 § 1. (See 1943, 365 § 2.)

SECT. 93 revised, 1943, 360.

SECT. 94 amended, 1943, 361.

SECT. 102A added, 1934, 387 § 3 (relative to the removal to the superior court of an action of tort arising out of the operation of a motor vehicle); amended, 1937, 133 § 1; revised, 1938, 338 § 1; first paragraph amended, 1941, 203 § 1; second paragraph amended, 1941, 203 § 2; section repealed, 1943, 296 § 3. (See 1934, 387 § 5; 1937, 133 § 2; 1938, 338 § 2; 1941, 203 § 3; 1943, 296 § 6.)

SECT. 107 revised, 1943, 296 § 4. (See 1943, 296 § 6.)

SECT. 108, second paragraph revised, 1939, 382; second sentence of third paragraph revised, 1933, 255 § 1. (See 1933, 255 § 2.)

SECT. 115 amended, 1939, 451 § 63.

SECT. 133 amended, 1933, 300 § 2. (See 1933, 300 § 4.)

SECT. 135, two paragraphs inserted after first paragraph, 1941, 187 § 1. (See 1941, 187 § 2.)

SECT. 140A added, 1932, 130 § 1 (relative to the effect of a settlement by agreement of an action of tort growing out of a motor vehicle accident upon the right of a defendant in such action to maintain a cross action).

SECT. 141 amended, 1932, 130 § 2; 1933, 300 § 3; 1934, 387 § 4; 1943, 296 § 5, 350 § 2. (See 1933, 300 § 4; 1934, 387 § 5; 1943, 296 § 6, 350 §§ 3, 4.)

SECT. 142 amended, 1935, 318 § 7. (See 1935, 318 § 8.)

SECT. 145 amended, 1939, 451 § 64.

SECT. 147, Form 8 repealed, 1938, 350 § 2.

Chapter 233. — Witnesses and Evidence.

SECT. 3A added, 1933, 262 (authorizing the commissioner of banks to respond to summonses or subpoenas by an employee or other assistant in his department).

SECT. 8 amended, 1933, 269 § 3, 376 § 3.

SECTS. 13A–13D added, 1937, 210 § 1 (making uniform the law securing the attendance of witnesses from without a state in criminal proceedings). (See 1937, 210 § 2.)

SECT. 22 amended, 1932, 97 § 1.

SECT. 26 amended, 1932, 71 § 1.

SECT. 29 amended, 1932, 71 § 2.
SECT. 30 amended, 1932, 71 § 3.
SECT. 32 amended, 1932, 71 § 4.
SECT. 33 amended, 1932, 71 § 5.
SECT. 34 amended, 1932, 71 § 6.
SECT. 45 amended, 1932, 71 § 7.
SECT. 46 amended, 1932, 71 § 8.
SECT. 47 amended, 1932, 71 § 9.
SECT. 48 amended, 1932, 71 § 10.
SECT. 49 amended, 1932, 71 § 11.

SECT. 65 amended, 1941, 363 § 1; 1943, 105 § 1; revised, 1943, 232 § 1. (See 1941, 363 § 2; 1943, 105 § 2, 232 § 2.)

SECT. 75, sentence added at end, 1943, 190 § 1. (See 1943, 190 § 2.)

SECT. 76A added, 1938, 213 § 1 (relative to the use of authenticated copies of certain papers and documents filed with the federal securities and exchange commission). (See 1938, 213 § 2.)

SECT. 79 revised, 1941, 389 § 2; amended, 1943, 233 § 1. (See 1943, 233 § 2.)

SECT. 79A added, 1941, 662 § 2 (relative to the use in evidence of photographic and microphotographic records and copies).

Chapter 234. — Juries.

SECT. 1 amended, 1935, 257 § 11; 1936, 25. (See 1935, 257 § 12.)
SECT. 11 amended, 1934, 150.
SECT. 15 repealed, 1936, 161 § 1. (See 1936, 161 § 3.)
SECT. 24 amended, 1941, 90.

Chapter 236. — Levy of Executions on Land.

SECT. 18 revised, 1939, 32 § 4. (See 1939, 32 § 5.)

Chapter 239. — Summary Process for Possession of Land.

SECT. 1 amended, 1941, 242 § 1.

SECT. 6A added, 1941, 242 § 2 (relative to conditions of bonds in actions of summary process for recovery of possession of land after tax title foreclosures).

SECTS. 9-13 affected, 1941, 700.

Chapter 240. — Proceedings for Settlement of Title to Land.

SECT. 14A added, 1934, 263 § 2 (providing for determination by the land court by declaratory judgment as to the validity and extent of municipal zoning ordinances, by-laws and regulations).

Chapter 244. — Foreclosure and Redemption of Mortgages.

For legislation concerning judicial determination of rights to foreclose real estate mortgages in which soldiers or sailors may be interested, see 1941, 25; 1943, 57.

Chapter 246. — Trustee Process.

SECT. 1 revised, 1938, 303 § 1; amended, 1943, 17 § 1. (See 1938, 303 § 2; 1943, 17 § 2.)

SECT. 28 revised, 1935, 410 § 1; 1941, 338 § 1. (See 1935, 410 §§ 2, 3; 1941, 338 § 2.)

SECT. 32, paragraph added at end, 1938, 343.

Chapter 249. — Audita Querela, Certiorari, Mandamus and Quo Warranto.

SECT. 4 amended, 1943, 374 § 1. (See 1939, 257; 1941, 28, 180; 1943, 374 §§ 3, 4.)

SECT. 5 amended, 1938, 202; 1943, 374 § 2. (See 1939, 257; 1941, 28, 180; 1943, 374 § 4.)

Chapter 250. — Writs of Error, Vacating Judgment, Writs of Review.

SECT. 16 amended, 1933, 244 § 1. (See 1933, 244 § 2.)

Chapter 255. — Mortgages, Conditional Sales and Pledges of Personal Property, and Liens thereon.

SECT. 1. See 1933, 142 (recording of federal crop loans to farmers). See also 1936, 264 subsection 20 (relative to trust receipt and pledge transactions).

SECT. 3 amended, 1935, 86 § 2.

SECTS. 7A–7E added, 1935, 86 § 1 (relative to the mortgaging of crops and certain other classes of personal property).

SECT. 11 revised, 1939, 509 § 1.

SECT. 12 revised, 1939, 509 § 1; 1943, 410 § 1. (See 1943, 410 § 2.)

SECT. 13 revised, 1939, 509 § 1; amended, 1941, 285.

SECT. 13A added, 1935, 348 § 1 (regulating conditional sales of motor vehicles); revised, 1939, 509 § 1. (See 1935, 348 § 2.)

SECT. 13B added, 1935, 396 (relative to certain contracts of conditional sale of household or personal effects).

SECTS. 13C and 13D added, 1937, 315 (relative to contracts of conditional sale of household furniture or other household or personal effects except jewelry).

SECT. 13C revised, 1938, 367.

SECTS. 13C and 13D stricken out, and new sections 13C–13G inserted, 1939, 509 § 2.

SECT. 13H added, 1941, 468 (relative to conditional sales of textile and other machinery, seats for theatres and other places of public assembly, and parts, accessories, appliances and equipment therefor).

SECT. 35 amended, 1938, 83 § 1. (See 1938, 83 § 2.)

Chapter 255A. — Trust Receipts and Pledges without Possession in the Pledgee.

New chapter inserted, 1936, 264.

Chapter 258. — Claims against the Commonwealth.

SECT. 3 revised, 1932, 180 § 41.

SECT. 5 repealed, 1943, 566 § 2.

Chapter 260. — Limitation of Actions.

SECT. 3A added, 1943, 566 § 1 (limiting the time within which petitions founded upon claims against the commonwealth may be brought).
SECT. 4 amended, 1933, 318 § 5; 1934, 291 § 4; 1937, 385 § 9; paragraph added at end, 1943, 409 § 4. (See 1933, 318 § 9; 1934, 291 § 6; 1937, 385 § 10.)
SECT. 10, sentence added at end, 1937, 406 § 2.

Chapter 261. — Costs in Civil Actions.

SECT. 4 amended, 1937, 44 § 1. (See 1937, 44 § 2; 1943, 296 §§ 3, 6.)

Chapter 262. — Fees of Certain Officers.

SECT. 2 revised, 1939, 345 § 1. (See 1939, 345 § 3.)
SECT. 4, seventh paragraph amended, 1937, 188; seventh to tenth paragraphs stricken out, 1939, 345 § 2. (See 1939, 345 § 3.)
SECT. 5 amended, 1933, 201.
SECT. 25 amended, 1933, 162; 1934, 141.
SECT. 32 revised, 1935, 280.
SECT. 34 amended, 1933, 21.
SECT. 34A added, 1938, 380 (authorizing the charging of certain fees by city and town clerks or registrars for the expense of the examination or copying by them of records of births, marriages and deaths).
SECT. 38, second paragraph amended, 1937, 97.
SECT. 39, paragraph added at end, 1939, 13.
SECT. 40 revised, 1934, 324 § 1. (See 1934, 324 § 2.)
SECT. 46A added, 1938, 232 (to provide for furnishing without charge copies of records relating to soldiers, sailors and marines in certain cases); revised, 1943, 484.
SECT. 53 amended, 1936, 251.

Chapter 263. — Rights of Persons Accused of Crime.

SECT. 4A added, 1934, 358 (expediting the arraignment of persons charged with crimes not punishable by death by permitting them to waive indictment proceedings).
SECT. 6 amended, 1933, 246 § 1. (See 1933, 246 § 2.)

Chapter 264. — Crimes against Governments.

SECT. 5 revised, 1932, 298; amended, 1933, 153 § 3; 1934, 56; revised, 1941, 117 § 1. (See 1941, 117 § 2.)
SECT. 10A revised, 1933, 276.

Chapter 265. — Crimes against the Person.

SECT. 13A added, 1943, 259 § 1 (providing a penalty for the crimes of assault and assault and battery). (See 1943, 259 § 2.)
SECT. 17 revised, 1943, 250 § 1. (See 1943, 250 § 2.)
SECT. 25 revised, 1932, 211.
SECT. 26 amended, 1934, 1.

Chapter 266. — Crimes against Property.

SECT. 1 revised, 1932, 192 § 1.
SECT. 2 revised, 1932, 192 § 2.
SECTS. 3 and 4 repealed, 1932, 192 § 3.
SECT. 5 revised, 1932, 192 § 4.
SECT. 5A added, 1932, 192 § 5 (defining and providing penalties for attempts to commit arson).
SECT. 6 repealed, 1932, 192 § 3.
SECT. 8 revised, 1932, 192 § 6.
SECT. 10 revised, 1932, 192 § 7.
SECT. 16 revised, 1943, 343 § 1. (See 1943, 343 § 2.)
SECT. 22 amended, 1935, 365.
SECT. 25 amended, 1943, 518 § 1. (See 1943, 518 § 2.)
SECT. 37 revised, 1937, 99.
SECT. 52 amended, 1934, 270 § 3.
SECT. 54. See 1933, 59 § 3.
SECT. 70 amended, 1933, 245 § 4; 1939, 144 § 2; 1941, 217 § 3.
SECTS. 75A and 75B added, 1932, 11 (penalizing the fraudulent operation of slot machines, coin-box telephones and other coin receptacles, and the manufacture and sale of devices intended to be used in such operation).
SECT. 89 revised, 1943, 549 § 7.
SECT. 94 amended, 1939, 451 § 65.
SECT. 116A added, 1935, 116 (providing for the protection of wild azaleas, wild orchids and cardinal flowers).
SECT. 123 revised, 1941, 344 § 27.

Chapter 268. — Crimes against Public Justice.

SECT. 14A added, 1936, 168 (imposing a penalty for depriving employees of their employment because of jury service).
SECT. 16 revised, 1934, 344; last sentence stricken out, 1941, 344 § 28; section amended, 1943, 19 § 1.
SECT. 16A added, 1943, 19 § 2 (relative to the penalty for escapes or attempted escapes from the reformatory for women).
SECT. 26 amended, 1934, 328 § 24.
SECT. 27 amended, 1934, 328 § 25.
SECT. 29 amended, 1934, 328 § 26.
SECT. 33 amended, 1935, 440 § 44; 1941, 71.

Chapter 269. — Crimes against Public Peace.

SECT. 10 amended, 1935, 290; 1936, 227 § 1; 1937, 250 § 1. (See 1936, 227 § 2; 1937, 250 § 2.)
SECT. 10B added, 1934, 359 § 2 (further regulating the sale, rental and leasing of rifles and shotguns).
SECTS. 11A–11D added, under caption "TAMPERING WITH IDENTIFYING NUMBERS OF CERTAIN FIREARMS", 1937, 199 (relative to certain firearms, the serial or identification numbers of which have been removed, defaced, altered, obliterated or mutilated).

Chapter 270. — Crimes against Public Health.

SECT. 5 amended, 1934, 328 § 27.

Chapter 271. — Crimes against Public Policy.

SECT. 6A added, 1938, 144 (making certain endless chain transactions subject to the laws relative to lotteries).

SECT. 22A revised, 1934, 371; paragraphs added at end, 1936, 222, 283; section revised, 1943, 267.

SECT. 23 amended, 1934, 235 § 3, 303 § 1.

SECTS. 31, 33, 34 affected by 1935, 454 § 8, 471 § 2.

SECT. 43 added, 1941, 630 § 4 (imposing a penalty for the misuse of information relative to recipients of general public assistance, old age assistance, aid to dependent children and aid to the blind).

Chapter 272. — Crimes against Chastity, Morality, Decency and Good Order.

SECT. 25 revised, 1933, 376 § 4.

SECT. 26 amended, 1939, 451 § 66.

SECT. 28 amended, 1934, 231; 1943, 239.

SECT. 53 revised, 1943, 377.

SECT. 66 amended, 1939, 451 § 67.

SECTS. 79A and 79B added, 1934, 234 § 1 (relative to the cutting of the muscles or tendons of horses' tails and to the showing or exhibiting of horses whose tails have been so cut or have been docked). (See 1934, 234 § 2.)

SECT. 80 repealed, 1934, 234 § 1. (See 1934, 234 § 2.)

SECT. 92A added, 1933, 117 (preventing advertisements tending to discriminate against persons of any religious sect, creed, class, denomination or nationality by places of public accommodation, resort or amusement).

SECT. 97A added, 1934, 164 (prohibiting the use of documents drawn to imitate judicial process).

SECT. 98 amended, 1934, 138.

SECT. 98A added, 1938, 155 § 1 (entitling blind persons accompanied by "seeing eye" dogs, so called, to certain accommodations, advantages, etc.).

SECT. 98B added, 1941, 170 (to prevent discrimination in employment on public works and projects and in the dispensing of public welfare because of race, color, religion or nationality).

SECT. 98C added, 1943, 223 (penalizing the libel of groups of persons because of race, color or religion).

SECT. 103 added, 1936, 417 (prohibiting marathon dances, other marathons or walkathons, so called).

Chapter 273. — Desertion, Non-support and Illegitimacy.

SECT. 1 amended, 1939, 177 § 1. (See 1939, 177 § 2.)

SECT. 2 amended, 1933, 224; revised, 1943, 87 § 1. (See 1943, 87 § 2.)

SECT. 9 repealed, 1938, 219 § 1.

SECT. 10 revised, 1938, 219 § 2.

SECT. 14, sentence added at end, 1943, 13.

SECTS. 20–22. See 1937, 440 § 2; 1941, 597 § 1, 729 § 2; 1943, 489 § 2.

Chapter 274. — Felonies, Accessories and Attempts to Commit Crimes.

Sect. 4 revised, 1943, 488 § 1. (See 1943, 488 §§ 2, 3.)

Chapter 275. — Proceedings to prevent Crimes.

Sect. 15 repealed, 1932, 180 § 42.

Chapter 276. — Search Warrants, Rewards, Fugitives from Justice, Arrest, Examination, Commitment and Bail. Probation Officers and Board of Probation.

Sect. 1, first paragraph amended, 1934, 303 § 2; clause Sixth amended, 1943, 508 § 5; clause Eleventh amended, 1934, 235 § 1.

Sect. 3 amended, 1934, 340 § 15. (See 1934, 340 § 18.)

Sect. 3A added, 1934, 247 (concerning the service of search warrants).

Sect. 7 amended, 1934, 235 § 2.

Sects. 10A–10D added, under caption "extra-territorial arrest on fresh pursuit", 1937, 208 § 1 (making uniform the law as to extra-territorial arrest on fresh pursuit and authorizing this commonwealth to co-operate with other states in connection therewith). (See 1937, 208 § 2.)

Sects. 11–20 and caption "fugitives from justice" stricken out and new sections 11–20R inserted, under caption "procedure on interstate rendition", 1937, 304 § 1. (See 1937, 304 §§ 2, 3.)

Sect. 37A added, 1932, 180 § 43 (relative to the assignment of counsel to appear, on behalf of a person accused of a capital crime, at his preliminary examination). [For prior legislation, see G. L. chapter 277 §§ 48, 49, repealed by 1932, 180 § 44.]

Sect. 52A added, 1943, 131 (providing that persons held in jail for trial may be removed in certain cases to a jail in another county).

Sect. 57, sentence added at end of second paragraph, 1943, 330; paragraph added at end, 1939, 299 § 4.

Sect. 83 revised, 1936, 360; amended, 1937, 186.

Sect. 83A added, 1941, 677 § 1 (providing that certain district courts may join in the appointment of probation officers to act exclusively in juvenile cases therein).

Sect. 84 revised, 1937, 219 § 5; 1939, 214 § 7.

Sect. 87 amended, 1941, 264 § 2.

Sect. 89, sentence added at end, 1934, 217 § 2; paragraph added at end, 1941, 477 § 1.

Sect. 90 amended, 1938, 174 § 3.

Sect. 94 amended, 1939, 155; revised, 1939, 296 § 2. (See 1939, 296 § 3.)

Sect. 97 revised, 1941, 677 § 2.

Sect. 98 amended, 1932, 145.

Sect. 100 amended, 1943, 64.

Sect. 101 amended, 1936, 30 § 1. (See 1936, 30 § 2.)

Chapter 277. — Indictments and Proceedings before Trial.

SECT. 2 amended, 1932, 144 § 6.

SECTS. 48 and 49 repealed, 1932, 180 § 44. (See G. L. chapter 276 § 37A, inserted by 1932, 180 § 43.)

SECT. 50 repealed, 1936, 161 § 1. (See 1936, 161 § 3.)

SECT. 58A added, 1943, 311 § 1 (relative to the venue of the crime of buying, receiving or aiding in the concealment of stolen or embezzled property). (See 1943, 311 § 2.)

SECT. 65 amended, 1936, 161 § 2. (See 1936, 161 § 3.)

SCHEDULE OF FORMS OF PLEADINGS at end of chapter amended, 1934, 328 § 29.

Paragraph entitled "Accessory after the fact" amended by striking out all after word "punishment" in line 5, 1943, 488 § 2. (See 1943, 488 § 3.)

Chapter 278. — Trials and Proceedings before Judgment.

SECT. 25 amended, 1937, 311.

SECTS. 28A–28D added, 1943, 558 § 1 (establishing in the superior court an appellate division for the review of certain sentences in criminal cases). (See 1943, 558 § 2.)

SECT. 29 revised, 1939, 271 § 1. (See 1939, 271 § 2.)

SECT. 33 amended, 1933, 265.

SECT. 33E amended, 1939, 341.

Chapter 279. — Judgment and Execution.

SECT. 1 amended, 1934, 205 § 1; 1935, 358 § 1; first paragraph amended, 1938, 354; second paragraph amended, 1936, 434 § 2; 1939, 299 § 5. (See 1934, 205 § 3; 1935, 358 § 2.)

SECT. 1A amended, 1934, 205 § 2. (See 1934, 205 § 3.)

SECT. 3A amended, 1935, 50 § 2, 437 § 2. (See 1935, 50 § 6, 437 § 8.)

SECT. 4 revised, 1935, 50 § 3, 437 § 3. (See 1935, 50 § 6, 437 § 8.)

SECT. 9 amended, 1932, 221 § 2.

SECT. 11 amended, 1934, 328 § 28.

SECT. 43 revised, 1935, 50 § 4, 437 § 4. (See 1935, 50 § 6, 437 § 8.)

SECT. 44 revised, 1935, 50 § 5, 437 § 5. (See 1935, 50 § 6, 437 § 8.)

SECT. 45 revised, 1935, 437 § 6. (See 1935, 437 § 8.)

Chapter 280. — Fines and Forfeitures.

SECT. 2, last sentence stricken out, 1934, 364 § 2; sentence added at end, 1935, 303 § 1. (See 1934, 364 § 3; 1935, 303 § 2.)

SECT. 6 revised, 1937, 251 § 1. (See 1937, 251 § 2.)

The Commonwealth of Massachusetts

Office of the Secretary, Boston, November 30, 1943.

I certify that the acts and resolves contained in this volume are true copies of the originals on file in this department.

I further certify that the table of changes in general laws has been prepared, and is printed as an appendix to this edition of the laws, by direction of the Joint Committee on Rules of the General Court, in accordance with the provisions of General Laws, Tercentenary Edition, chapter 3, section 51, as amended by Acts of 1939, chapter 508, section 7.

FREDERIC W. COOK,
Secretary of the Commonwealth.

INDEX.

A.

B.

C.

D.

E.

INDEX.

G.

H.

J.

M.

N.

P.

Q.

R.

S.

T.

U.

V.

W.

Z.

Lightning Source UK Ltd.
Milton Keynes UK
UKHW012353210119
335965UK00006B/109/P

9 780332 295190